THE PENGUIN
ROGET'S THESAURUS
OF ENGLISH WORDS AND PHRASES

Susan M. Lloyd (née Emmerson) was born at Keynsham, near Bristol, England, and educated in Bristol and Surrey. Work in public libraries and as a civil servant in Cheltenham was followed by a B.A. Honours Degree in French and Latin at Bristol University.

Susan Lloyd worked as a teacher in Birmingham and in Uganda before settling in East Anglia with her husband, who is head teacher of a comprehensive school. She gained an M. Phil. degree at the University of East Anglia with research on Edmond Rostand's play *Cyrano de Bergerac*. She edited the first revision for twenty years of *Roget's Thesaurus*, published by Longman in 1982, which has been specially adapted for this paperback edition. She has contributed talks on word origins to the B.B.C. External Service's Speaking of English series. She enjoys reading, local history and gardening.

THE PENGUIN
ROGET'S THESAURUS

OF ENGLISH WORDS AND PHRASES

NEW EDITION COMPLETELY
REVISED, UPDATED AND ABRIDGED
BY SUSAN M. LLOYD

PENGUIN BOOKS

Penguin Books Ltd, Harmondsworth, Middlesex, England
Viking Penguin Inc., 40 West 23rd Street, New York, New York 10010, U.S.A.
Penguin Books Australia Ltd, Ringwood, Victoria, Australia
Penguin Books Canada Limited, 2801 John Street, Markham, Ontario, Canada L3R 1B4
Penguin Books (N.Z.) Ltd, 182–190 Wairau Road, Auckland 10, New Zealand

—

First published 1852
Published in Penguin Books 1953
Reprinted twelve times
New edition first published by Longman 1962
Published in Penguin Books 1966
Reprinted 1968, 1969, 1970, 1971, 1972 (twice), 1973 (twice), 1974 (three times),
1975 (three times), 1976, 1977 (twice), 1978 (twice), 1979 (twice),
1980 (twice), 1981 (twice), 1982, 1983
This new and revised edition published by Longman 1982
Abridged and published in Penguin Books 1984
Reprinted 1984 (twice), 1985 (twice), 1986 (twice), 1987

—

Copyright © Longman Green & Co. Ltd, 1962, 1966, 1982
All rights reserved

—

Photoset by Rowland Phototypesetting Ltd
Bury St Edmunds, Suffolk
Printed and bound in Great Britain by
Cox & Wyman Ltd, Reading
Set in Linotron Times

PREFACE TO THE FIRST EDITION, 1852

IT IS now nearly fifty years since I first projected a system of verbal classification similar to that on which the present Work is founded. Conceiving that such a compilation might help to supply my own deficiencies, I had, in the year 1805, completed a classed catalogue of words on a small scale, but on the same principle, and nearly in the same form, as the *Thesaurus* now published. I had often during that long interval found this little collection, scanty and imperfect as it was, of much use to me in literary composition, and often contemplated its extension and improvement; but a sense of the magnitude of the task, amidst a multitude of other avocations, deterred me from the attempt. Since my retirement from the duties of Secretary of the Royal Society, however, finding myself possessed of more leisure, and believing that a repertory of which I had myself experienced the advantage might, when amplified, prove useful to others, I resolved to embark in an undertaking which, for the last three or four years, has given me incessant occupation, and has, indeed, imposed upon me an amount of labour very much greater than I had anticipated. Notwithstanding all the pains I have bestowed on its execution, I am fully aware of its numerous deficiencies and imperfections, and of its falling far short of the degree of excellence that might be attained. But, in a Work of this nature, where perfection is placed at so great a distance, I have thought it best to limit my ambition to that moderate share of merit which it may claim in its present form; trusting to the indulgence of those for whose benefit it is intended, and to the candour of critics who, while they find it easy to detect faults, can at the same time duly appreciate difficulties.

29 April 1852   P. M. Roget

PREFACE TO THIS EDITION

IT IS over one hundred and thirty years since Dr Peter Mark Roget first published his *Thesaurus of English Words and Phrases*, but it continues to be rediscovered by each new generation as a valued reference book and treasured companion. 'Thesaurus' means treasury or storehouse, and *Roget's Thesaurus* is a storehouse of the English language, collecting together words and phrases of every kind and register, from the formal to the colloquial, from poetic and archaic to modern slang; it includes, too, illustrations from art, literature, history and modern life. All these expressions are sorted into groups of related meanings under such headings as Circularity, Hopefulness, Receptacle and Freedom, and the groups themselves are arranged into a logical sequence.

This arrangement is what makes a thesaurus complementary to a dictionary. A dictionary gives the meaning of a particular word, while a thesaurus offers a variety of words in which to express a given meaning. You cannot find a word you have forgotten or do not know in a dictionary, as without knowing how it is spelt you have no means of looking it up. But find a word of similar meaning in a thesaurus, and you will discover a variety of expressions which should include the one at the back of your mind, or perhaps an unfamiliar word which, when checked in the dictionary, proves even more appropriate. The cross-references to related groups offer an even wider choice.

It is the range and diversity of its vocabulary which constitute one of the advantages of the *Thesaurus*, enabling you to choose the most accurate, the most apt or the most telling term for your purpose. This is not only helpful in writing well: the very act of selection encourages you to be quite clear in your own mind about what it is you are trying to say. And, in this age of propaganda and doubletalk, such awareness is valuable in assessing what others say, too. Seeing euphemisms listed next to the unpleasant truths they seek to hide can be revealing. But the *Thesaurus* is more than a useful tool for writing (and reading). As a treasury of English words and phrases it can give great pleasure to word-lovers, who enjoy browsing through its pages, savouring the richness of our multifaceted language. And, of course, it can be a great help in solving crossword puzzles.

Crossword puzzles had not been thought of as a popular pastime when Roget published his *Thesaurus*. He saw it mainly as a practical aid to self-expression, and had developed it from a collection of words and phrases he had begun to compile as a young man. Finding it invaluable in writing and lecturing, he resolved to offer it, in a fuller and improved form, to the general public. It was so well received that new editions followed one another in quick succession. After Roget's death in 1869, first his son and then his grandson took on the work of revision. In 1952 the copyright passed to the original publishers, now known as Longman. The first Penguin edition appeared in 1953; the second, in 1966, was based by the editor, Robert A. Dutch, on his completely new edition for Longman four years earlier. The present Penguin version is an abridgement of my own edition of 1982, which was an updating and revision of Dutch's.

The main task of the 1982 edition was to bring the *Thesaurus* up to date, in particular by adding the many new words and phrases which had come into circulation over the intervening twenty years as a result of rapid technological change, and the corresponding changes in our lifestyle. In addition, expressions no longer useful or current were deleted and headings which had become incomprehensible or ambiguous were replaced. The aim throughout was to mirror the language and attitudes of our present society. This included taking into account the increasing tendency to counter the sexism present in our language by inventing new neutral terms. These, and female equivalents such as 'spokeswoman', have been added to their male counterparts. To ensure accuracy, all cross-references were checked by computer, and the index was compiled from a complete computer listing of the text.

This new paperback version is about the same size as its Penguin predecessors. This was made possible by cutting back all peripheral material, removing wordy phrases and paraphrases, and generally keeping much more closely to the particular topic being dealt with. Unusual words were given fewer entries, and modern expressions were preferred to old-fashioned ones. Conjugate forms, especially adverbs, were omitted where they could be easily deduced by the reader from forms already listed. Some paragraphs were deleted entirely, with essential items transferred to another paragraph. In the index, priority was given to words and phrases in common use, and to general terms rather than specific ones. Less relevant references were omitted: this should simplify selection of the most appropriate one.

The aim overall has been to produce a concise, practical edition which retains all the improvements made to the main edition.

S. M. L.

HOW TO USE THIS BOOK

The Text

The *Thesaurus* consists of two parts, the text and an alphabetical index. It is possible to rely totally on the index to find the place you want in the text, but to get full value from the work it is best to become familiar with Roget's classification system. This organizes the vocabulary in the text into six Classes, which are subdivided into Sections. The Sections themselves are further subdivided into the numbered Heads to which references are given in the index. Roget's framework follows a logical pattern. The first three Classes cover the external world: Class One, *Abstract Relations*, deals with such ideas as number, order and time; Class Two, *Space*, is concerned with movement, shapes and sizes, while Class Three, *Matter*, covers the physical world and humankind's perception of it by means of the five senses. The last three Classes deal with the internal world of human beings: the human mind (Class Four, *Intellect*), the human will (Class Five, *Volition*), and the human heart and soul (Class Six, *Emotion, Religion and Morality*). There is a progression from abstract concepts, through the material universe, to mankind itself, culminating in what Roget saw as humanity's highest achievements: morality and religion.

To see at a glance how Roget's system works, see the *Plan of Classification*. This shows the six Classes, further subdivided into *Sections*. Each Section deals with a particular aspect of the Class within which it is found. So under Class One, *Abstract Relations*, we find Sections for *Quantity*, *Order*, *Time* and so on. The Sections themselves are further subdivided into *Heads*. Within Class One Section Six, *Time*, for instance, there are thirty-five Heads dealing with, among others, the ideas of *Present Time*, *Past Time*, *Transience* and *Age*. Each Head is numbered. There are 990 in the present edition, a slight reduction from Roget's original 1,000. It is the Heads which form the basic units of the book, and they follow each other in a logical progression. It is a sign of Roget's skill in compiling the *Thesaurus* that this basic framework has remained virtually intact through edition after edition.

The Heads themselves are divided into paragraphs, grouped together according to their part of speech. Head 852, *Hope*, for example, has three paragraphs of nouns (marked N.), two of adjectives (Adj.), two of verbs (Vb.) and one of interjections (Int.). Each paragraph begins with a word in italics known as the *keyword*. This is both a clue to the kind of words found in that paragraph, and also itself part of the vocabulary. It is called the *keyword* because it is both the 'key' to the rest of the paragraph, and the 'open sesame' to the whole book, being used to identify the position of other words in the index and cross-references.

Within the paragraphs, words are grouped according to their meaning or register (formal, colloquial and so on). Cross-references, consisting of Head numbers and *keywords*, lead you to groups of similar words elsewhere in the *Thesaurus*. Most Heads are in pairs, representing the positive and negative aspects of an idea, as in Heads 824 and 825, Joy and Suffering. Sometimes several consecutive Heads deal with variations on the same idea: Heads 534 to 539, for instance, are concerned with education.

A few conventions should be explained. These have mainly been designed to avoid repetition and save space. Conjugate forms are often indicated by the use of 'etc.'. For instance, 'be content, etc. adj.' suggests that readers can form further verbs for themselves on the same pattern. Where consecutive expressions use the same word, two means are used to avoid repeating it. The phrases may be linked by '*or*', as in 'drop a brick *or* a clanger', 'countryman *or* -woman'. Alternatively, the repeated word is simply indicated by its first letter, followed by a full stop: 'weasel word, loan w., nonce w.,' and so on. 'Tdmk' in brackets following a noun indicates a registered trade mark. An 'e' in brackets added to the end of a word means that it is of French origin and requires a final 'e' if applied to a woman. '**See** . . .' is used to refer the reader to another paragraph within the same Head, where the idea under consideration is dealt with more thoroughly.

The Index

The index is intended as a guide to the most appropriate part of the text in which to begin your search for the right word. It is not a complete list of every item in the text, and the word you look up may not be present at every reference given for it, as it is acting as a signpost to the ideas which it represents. For the same reason, it does not matter whether you look up a noun, a verb, or an adjective: any will lead you to a suitable Head, and as references to one part of speech are not always repeated under another, it is best to check all three.

These references consist of: a Head number; a *keyword* in italics, and a part of speech label (n. for nouns, adj. for adjectives, vb. for verbs, adv. for adverbs, and int. for interjections). The *keyword* is given to identify the correct paragraph; and gives an indication of the ideas it contains. To use the index, look up a word of similar meaning to the one you want to find, turn to the Head number given in your chosen reference, and under the relevant part of speech you will find a paragraph beginning with the *keyword* given in the index. Here you should begin your search.

Some points to note about the index

1. Items are listed in alphabetical order, regardless of breaks between words. The only exceptions are 'a', 'the' and 'be', which are not taken into account, and verbal phrases and idioms, which are listed directly after their verb, which is represented by a dash.

2. Objects and names of things should be looked up under a general rather than a specific term: 'ship' rather than 'clipper', for instance.

3. (s) after a word means the references may apply either to the single or the plural form.

4. Spelling is uniform with Penguin house style. Accepted alternatives are given after the main form; 'ise' for 'ize' and 'eable' for 'able' are so well-known and occur so frequently that they are simply noted here.

PLAN OF CLASSIFICATION

THESAURUS
OF ENGLISH WORDS AND PHRASES

Class One

ABSTRACT RELATIONS

Section 1: Existence

1. Existence – N. *existence*, being, entity; aseity, self-existence; monad, a being, an entity, ens; Platonic idea, universal; subsistence 360 *life*; survival, eternity 115 *perpetuity*; preexistence 119 *priority*; this life 121 *present time*; prevalence 189 *presence*; entelechy, realization, becoming 147 *conversion*; creation 164 *production*; potentiality 469 *possibility*; ontology, metaphysics; realism, idealism, existentialism 449 *philosophy*.

reality, realness, actuality, Dasein; material existence 319 *materiality*; thatness 80 *speciality*; positiveness; historicity, factuality 494 *truth*; fact, fact of life, matter of f., fait accompli 154 *event*; real thing, not a dream, no joke; realities, basics, fundamentals, bedrock, brass tacks 638 *important matter*.

essence, nature, quiddity 3 *substance*; sum and substance 5 *essential part*; soul, heart, core 224 *interiority*.

Adj. *existing*, existent, in esse, ontic; existential; essential 5 *intrinsic*; absolute, given, self-existent, uncreated; being, in existence, under the sun, living 360 *alive*; eternal, enduring 115 *perpetual*; extant, standing, surviving 113 *lasting*; rife, prevalent 189 *ubiquitous*; ontological, metaphysical.

real, essential, substantive 3 *substantial*; actual, positive, factual, historical, well-grounded 494 *true*; natural, physical, flesh and blood 319 *material*; concrete, solid, tangible 324 *dense*.

Vb. *be*, exist, have being; be the case 494 *be true*; consist in, inhere in, reside in 5 *be intrinsic*; subsist, abide, continue 146 *go on*; endure 113 *last*; vegetate; be alive, breathe 360 *live*; be found, be met with 189 *be present*; be rife 189 *pervade*; occur 154 *happen*; represent, stand for 13 *be identical*.

become, come to be, come into existence, take flesh, be born; arise 68 *begin*; unfold, develop, grow, take shape, evolve, turn out, change into 147 *be turned to*.

Adv. *actually*, really; ipso facto; in fact, in point of f.

2. Nonexistence – N. *nonexistence*, non-being, non-entity, nothingness, nullity; nonexistence in time 109 *neverness*; nonexistence in space 190 *absence*; blank, vacuum 190 *emptiness*; nothing 103 *zero*; a nothing 4 *insubstantial thing*; no such thing 190 *nobody*; nihilism, negativeness.

extinction, oblivion, nirvana; no life 361 *death*; obsolescence 51 *decay*; annihilation 165 *destruction*; amnesty 506 *oblivion*; cancellation 550 *obliteration*.

Adj. *nonexistent*, inexistent, unexisting, without being; null, minus; nowhere, missing 190 *absent*; null and void 752 *abrogated*.

unreal, without reality, baseless, groundless, unfounded 495 *erroneous*; fictitious, fabulous, visionary 513 *imaginary*, 4 *insubstantial*; unrealized, potential, in posse 469 *possible*, 512 *suppositional*.

unborn, uncreated, unmade; unbegotten, unconceived; undiscovered, uninvented, unimagined; yet to come, in the womb of time 124 *future*.

extinct, died out, no more, defunct 361 *dead*; obsolescent 361 *dying*; obsolete, finished, over and done with 125 *past*.

Vb. *not be*, have no existence, exist only in the imagination; fail to materialize, not come off 728 *miscarry*.

pass away, die out, vanish from the face of the earth 361 *die*; sink into oblivion 506 *be forgotten*; go, vanish, leave no trace; dematerialize, melt into thin air, evaporate 446 *disappear*.

nullify, annihilate, extinguish, snuff out; render null and void 752 *abrogate*; neutralize 533 *negate*; cancel 550 *obliterate*; abolish, wipe out 165 *destroy*.

3. Substantiality – N. *substantiality*, essentiality 1 *reality*; personality; substantivity, objectivity; corporeity; tangibility, solidity 319 *materiality*; ponderability 322 *gravity*; pithiness, meatiness; stuff, material 319 *matter*; totality of existence, world of nature 321 *universe*.

substance, hypostasis; entity, thing, something, somebody 319 *object*; body, flesh and blood 360 *life*; solid, concretion 324 *solid body*; pith, marrow, meat.

Adj. *substantial*, hypostatic, personal 5 *intrinsic*; real, objective, corporeal, phenomenal, physical 319 *material*; concrete, solid, tangible, palpable 324 *dense*; bulky 195 *large*, 322 *weighty*; pithy, meaty.

4. Insubstantiality – N. *insubstantiality*, unsubstantiality 2 *nonexistence*; naught, nothing, not a scrap 103 *zero*; abstraction, incorporeity 320 *immateriality*; imponderability 323 *lightness*; tenuity 206 *thinness*; sparseness 325 *rarity*; superficiality 212 *shallowness*; intangibility; vacuity, vacancy, void, hollowness 190 *emptiness*; hallucination, fantasy 513 *ideality*; maya, unreality.

insubstantial thing, token, symbol 547 *indication*; mind, soul 447 *spirit*; abstraction, shadow, ghost, phantom, vision, dream, mirage 440 *visual fallacy*; air, thin a., wind, breath, vapour, mist; bubble,

snowflake 163 *weak thing*; wisp, straw 639 *trifle*; vain thing, bauble; vanity, fool's paradise, pipedream 513 *fantasy*; cock and bull story; gossip, rumour 515 *empty talk*; tall talk 546 *exaggeration*; cry of 'wolf' 665 *false alarm*; mockery, pretence; chimera, figment; nine days' wonder, flash in the pan; cipher, figurehead, man of straw 639 *nonentity*.

Adj. *insubstantial*, abstract, metaphysical, ideal, noumenal; nonphysical 320 *immaterial*; bodiless, bloodless, incorporeal; airy, ethereal 323 *light*; thin, tenuous, gauzy, gossamer 422 *transparent*; pale, colourless; vaporous, misty; fragile, delicate 163 *flimsy*; ghostly, spectral 970 *spooky*; fleeting, shadowy, vague; vacuous, hollow, void 190 *empty*; vain, inane; nominal, paper, fictitious, mythical; symbolic, token 547 *indicating*; groundless, unfounded, visionary, dreamy, chimerical 513 *imaginary*; blank, characterless, featureless; superficial 212 *shallow*.

5. Intrinsicality – N. *intrinsicality*, inherence, immanence; potentiality 160 *ability*; introversion, autism; subjectivity; ego, personality 80 *self*.

essential part, sine qua non; prime constituent 1 *essence*; principle, property, attribute 89 *concomitant*; virtue, capacity; quintessence, distillation, inscape; stuff, quiddity 3 *substance*; sap, lifeblood 360 *life*; heart, backbone, marrow, fibre; core 225 *centre*; gist, nub 638 *chief thing*.

character, nature, quality; make-up, type, breed 77 *sort*; constitution, characteristics, ethos; cast, colour, hue, complexion; aspects, features.

temperament, temper, humour, disposition, mood, spirit 817 *affections*; grain, vein, streak, strain, trait 179 *tendency*; idiosyncrasy, habit, peculiarity 80 *speciality*.

heredity, endowment; chromosome, gene; original sin; ancestry 169 *genealogy*; telegony, atavism; heritability; Galton's law, Mendel's law, genetics 358 *biology*.

Adj. *intrinsic*, immanent, deep-seated, deep-rooted, ingrained; inherent, integral

58 *component*; indwelling 224 *interior*; inwrought, implicit, part and parcel of, built-in 78 *included*; autistic, subjective, introversive, reflexive, introverted; characteristic, personal; indigenous, native; natural, instinctive; basic, radical, organic 156 *fundamental*; original, elemental, cardinal; essential, constitutional; potential.

genetic, inherited, hereditary, atavistic, heritable; native, inborn, innate, congenital; inbred, bred in the bone.

characteristic 80 *special*; characterizing, qualitative; diagnostic, idiomorphic, proper; constant 153 *established*.

Vb. *be intrinsic*, inhere, indwell, belong; inherit, take after, run in the blood; be marked with, be characterized by.

Adv. *intrinsically*, at bottom, essentially, virtually; per se, as such.

6. Extrinsicality – N. *extrinsicality*, objectiveness, objectivity; transcendence; otherness, the other, non-ego 59 *extraneousness*; externality, outwardness 223 *exteriority*; objectification, externalization; projection, extrapolation; extroversion, extrovert; accident, contingency 159 *chance*; acquired characteristic 40 *adjunct*.

Adj. *extrinsic*, alien 59 *extraneous*; transcendent; outward, external 223 *exterior*; outward-looking, extroverted; derived, acquired; inbred, instilled, inculcated; accessory 38 *additional*; incidental, contingent 159 *casual*; nonessential, inessential; subsidiary.

Vb. *be extrinsic*, lie without, not belong; transcend; supervene 38 *accrue*.

make extrinsic, objectify, project 223 *externalize*; body forth 551 *represent*.

7. State: absolute condition – N. *state*, modal existence, state of being, condition; estate, lot, walk of life; case, way, plight 8 *circumstance*; position, status, footing, standing, rank; habitude, disposition 5 *temperament*; attitude, frame of mind, mood 817 *affections*; state of mind, spirits, morale; trim, fettle, fig.

modality, mode, manner, fashion, style; stamp, mould 243 *form*; shape, frame 331 *structure*; aspect, phase, light, complexion, character, guise 445 *appearance*; tenor, tone 179 *tendency*.

Adj. *such*; modal, conditional, formal 243 *formative*; organic 331 *structural*; in a state of; in condition, in form.

Vb. *be in a state of*, be such, be so; stand, lie, labour under; do, fare.

8. Circumstance: relative condition – N. *circumstance*, situation, circumstances, conditions, factors; the times; environment, milieu 230 *surroundings*; context 9 *relation*; state of affairs, regime, set-up 7 *state*; posture, attitude; aspect 445 *appearance*; lie of the land 186 *situation*; sphere, background, standing, status 73 *serial place*, 9 *relativeness*; awkward situation, corner 700 *predicament*.

juncture, stage, point 154 *event*; contingency, eventuality; cross-roads, turning point; moment, hour, opportunity 137 *occasion*; emergency 137 *crisis*.

Adj. *circumstantial*, given, modal 7 *such*; environmental, situational, contextual 230 *circumjacent*; limiting, circumscribed; modifying 468 *qualifying*; provisional, relative, contingent; critical, crucial; appropriate, convenient 642 *advisable*.

Adv. *if*, in the event of, in case; provisionally 7 *conditionally*.

Section 2: Relation

9. Relation – N. *relation*, relatedness, connectedness, rapport, reference, respect, regard; bearing, direction; concern, interest 638 *importance*; import, intention 514 *meaning*; involvement, implication 5 *intrinsicality*; relationship, affinity; kinship 11 *consanguinity*; classification, classifiability 62 *arrangement*; alliance 706 *association*; relations, intimacy 880 *friendship*; connection, link, tie-up 47 *bond*; something in common, common reference, common denominator; interdependence, ecology; context, milieu, environment 8 *circumstance*.

relativeness, relativity; mutual relation 12 *correlation*; homology, correspondence 13 *identity*, 28 *equality*; analogy 18 *similarity*; comparability 462 *comparison*; approximation 200 *nearness*; proportionality, perspective, proportion, ratio, scale; cause and effect 156 *causation*; dependence 157 *effect*; logical relation (**see** *relevance*); relative position 27 *degree*; serial order 65 *sequence*.

relevance, logicality 475 *reasoning*; chain of reasoning 475 *argumentation*; point, application, applicability, appositeness, pertinence, comparability 24 *fitness*; case in point, good example 83 *example*.

referral, reference, cross-r.; allusion, mention; citation, quotation; frame of reference, referent; referee.

Adj. *relative*, not absolute 8 *circumstantial*; relational, referential, respective; relativistic; referable; related, connected, en rapport; bearing upon, concerning, appertaining, appurtenant 78 *included*; in common, mutual, reciprocal 12 *correlative*; classifiable 62 *arranged*; serial, consecutive 65 *sequential*; cognate, kindred 11 *akin*; homologous, analogous 18 *similar*; comparable 462 *compared*; approximative 200 *near*; collateral 219 *parallel*; proportional, proportionate, in ratio, to scale; proportionable, commensurate 245 *symmetrical*; perspectival, in perspective; contextual, environmental, ecological.

relevant, logical, in context; apposite, pertinent, applicable; pointed, to the point, to the purpose, well-directed; proper, appropriate 24 *apt*.

Vb. *be related*, have reference to, refer to, regard, respect, have to do with; bear upon, be a factor 178 *influence*; touch, concern, deal with, interest, affect; belong, pertain, appertain; answer to, correspond, reciprocate 12 *correlate*; have a connection, tie in with; be proportionate, vary as; be relevant, have some point.

relate, bring into relation, put in perspective, get into proportion; connect with, gear to; apply, bring to bear upon; link, connect, bracket together 45 *tie*; put in context, provide a background; compare 18 *liken*; proportion, balance 28 *equalize*;

draw a parallel 475 *reason*; refer to, touch on, allude to, mention; index 547 *indicate*.

Adv. *relatively*, not absolutely, in a context, conditionally; in some degree, comparatively; proportionally, in ratio, to scale, in perspective.

concerning, touching, regarding; as to, as regards, with respect to; relative to, vis-à-vis, with reference to, about, re; in connection with; bearing on; speaking of, apropos, by the way, by the bye, on the subject of; in the matter of.

10. Unrelatedness: absence of relation

N. *unrelatedness*, absoluteness; noninvolvement, independence; arbitrariness; unilaterality; insularity; isolation 46 *separation*; individuality 80 *speciality*; rootlessness, homelessness; lack of connection, no context; unclassifiability; randomness 61 *disorder*; inconsequence (**see** irrelevance); disconnectedness; disproportion, asymmetry 246 *distortion*; incommensurability 29 *inequality*; diversity 17 *nonuniformity*, 82 *multiformity*; intrusion, no concern of, no business of; square peg in a round hole 25 *misfit*; alien element 59 *extraneousness*.

irrelevance, illogicality 477 *sophism*; pointlessness, inapplicability; inconsequence, non sequitur; parenthesis 231 *interjection*; diversion, red herring, episode 154 *event*; nonessential 639 *unimportance*.

Adj. *unrelated*, irrelative, absolute, self-existent; independent 744 *unconfined*; owing nothing to 21 *original*; irrespective, regardless; unilateral, arbitrary; unclassified, unclassifiable, rootless, homeless; adrift 282 *deviating*; kinless, isolated 88 *alone*; unconcerned, uninvolved 860 *indifferent*; detached, unconnected 46 *disunited*; digressive, parenthetic; episodic 72 *discontinuous*; separate, individual 80 *special*; of no concern, nothing to do with; inessential 6 *extrinsic*; exotic, foreign 59 *extraneous*; intrusive; inappropriate 25 *disagreeing*; disparate 29 *unequal*; disproportionate 246 *distorted*; irreconcilable 14 *contrary*.

irrelevant, illogical; inapposite, inapplicable, pointless 25 *unapt*; misplaced, misdirected 495 *erroneous*; wandering 570 *diffuse*; adrift, beside the point, off the point, neither here nor there; inessential 639 *unimportant*; inconsequent, inconsequential; incidental 159 *casual*; far-fetched, forced, strained; academic, impractical, immaterial.

Vb. *be unrelated*, have nothing to do with, have no bearing on; owe nothing to; not be one's business, not concern, be irrelevant, draw a red herring; drag in by the heels; lose the thread 570 *be diffuse*.

11. Consanguinity: relations of kindred
N. *consanguinity*, kinship, blood 169 *parentage*; filiation, relationship affinity; agnation, cognation, ancestry, lineage 169 *genealogy*; connection, alliance, family; nepotism; atavism 5 *heredity*.

kinsman, kinswoman, kin, kindred, kith and kin, kinsfolk, relations; relative, next of kin; blood relation, one of the family; father, mother 169 *parentage*; children, offspring, one's flesh and blood 170 *posterity*; agnate, cognate, collateral; twin; sibling, sib; sister, brother; cousin, cousin german, uncle, aunt, nephew, niece; clansman, tribesman, compatriot.

family, matriarchy, patriarchy; motherhood, fatherhood, brotherhood, sisterhood, fraternity, sorority; foster child, godchild, stepchild, adopted child; in-laws; one's people, one's folks; family circle 882 *sociality*; old folks at home, household 192 *home*; nuclear family, extended f.

race, stock, breed, strain, line, side, spear s., distaff s.; house, tribe, clan, phratry, sept; ethnic group; nation, people.

Adj. *akin*, sib, kindred, kin, consanguineous; matrilinear, out of; patrilinear, by; maternal, paternal 169 *parental*; sibling, fraternal, brotherly, sisterly, cousinly; avuncular; novercal; family, familial, collateral, allied, affined; connatural, congeneric; agnate, cognate, german, uterine; related; once removed, twice r.; next-of-kin; step-.

ethnic, racial, tribal, clannish 371 *national*; interracial, intertribal; inter-

bred 43 *mixed*; Caucasian, Mongolian, Negroid.

Vb. *be akin*, share the blood of; marry into 894 *wed*; sire 167 *generate*; affiliate, adopt, foster, bring into the family.

12. Correlation: double or reciprocal relation – N. *correlation*, correlativity, functionality 9 *relation*; proportion 245 *symmetry*; pattern 62 *arrangement*; grid 222 *network*; correspondence, opposite number; mutuality, interrelation, interconnection; interdependence, mutualism; interaction, interplay; alternation, turn and turn about; reciprocity, reciprocation 151 *interchange*; each, each other, one another; give and take 770 *compromise*; exchange, tit for tat.

Adj. *correlative*, reciprocal, functional 9 *relative*; corresponding, answering to, analogous; proportional, proportionate 245 *symmetrical*; complementary, complemental, interdependent; mutual, requited; reciprocating, reacting, alternating, seesaw 317 *oscillating*; balancing 28 *equivalent*; interlocking, geared, interacting; patterned, woven; interchangeable, exchangeable 151 *interchanged*; inter-, two-way, bilateral.

Vb. *correlate*, interrelate, interconnect, interplay, interact; interdepend; vary as, be a function of; proportion, symmetrize; correspond, answer to, react 280 *recoil*; alternate, reciprocate, exchange, counterchange, swap; balance, set off 31 *compensate*.

Adv. *correlatively*, as . . . so . . . ; mutually, each other, one another; alternately, turn and turn about; vice versa.

13. Identity – N. *identity*, identicalness, sameness, oneness 88 *unity*; the same, no other 494 *authenticity*; the real thing, absolutely it 21 *no imitation*; the very words, ipsissima verba; other self, alter ego, double; oneness with, identification, interchangeability, equivalence, no difference, indistinguishability; homogeneity 16 *uniformity*; no change, invariability, constant 153 *fixture*; duplicate 22 *copy*; twin 18 *analogue*.

Adj. *identical*, same, selfsame; one and the same 88 *one*; identified with, indistinguishable, interchangeable, unisex; equivalent, synonymous; unchanging 153 *unchangeable*; homogeneous 16 *uniform*; tautologous 106 *repeated*.

Vb. *be identical*, coincide, coalesce, merge, be one with, sink one's identity.

identify, treat as one, not distinguish 464 *not discriminate*; equate 28 *equalize*; assimilate 18 *liken*.

14. Contrariety – **N.** *contrariety*, nonidentity 15 *difference*; mutual exclusiveness, irreconcilability; contrariness, antagonism 704 *opposition*; antidote 182 *counteraction*; clash 279 *collision*; discord 25 *disagreement*; contrast, relief, variation, counterpoint 15 *differentiation*; contraindication 467 *counterevidence*; antonym, antinomy, antilogy; inconsistency, contradiction 17 *nonuniformity*; paradox, ambivalence; antithesis, direct opposite, antipodes, antipole 240 *contraposition*; extreme, quite the reverse; reverse, inverse 221 *inversion*; converse; headwind, undertow 182 *counteraction*.

polarity, contraries, *opposites*; positive and negative; day and night; fire and water; black and white; yin and yang, male and female 19 *dissimilarity*.

Adj. *contrary*, nonidentical, as different as chalk from cheese, anything but 15 *different*; contrasting, incompatible, clashing, discordant 25 *disagreeing*; inconsistent 17 *nonuniform*; ambivalent, bittersweet, love-hate, sweet and sour; contradictory, antithetic; diametrically opposite, poles asunder, antipodal, antipodean 240 *opposite*; reverse, converse, inverse; adverse, untoward 704 *opposing*; counteractive, antidotal 182 *counteracting*; counter-, contra-, anti-.

Vb. *be contrary*, have nothing in common 10 *be unrelated*, 15 *differ*; contrast, stand out 25 *disagree*; clash, conflict with; run counter to 240 *be opposite*; contravene, disobey, fly in the face of 704 *oppose*; exclude, deny, contradict 533 *negate*; cancel out 182 *counteract*; turn the tables.

Adv. *contrarily*, per contra, contrariwise; vice versa, on the contrary; otherwise.

15. Difference – **N.** *difference*, unlikeness 19 *dissimilarity*; disparity 29 *inequality*; margin, differential; heterogeneity, diverseness 17 *nonuniformity*; divergence 282 *deviation*; otherness, distinctness 10 *unrelatedness*, 21 *originality*; discrepancy, incongruity 25 *disagreement*; discord, variance; contrast 14 *contrariety*; opposite, antithesis 240 *contraposition*; variation, modification, alteration 143 *change*, 147 *conversion*.

differentiation 463 *discrimination*; specification 80 *speciality*; contradistinction, distinction, nice d., nuance, nicety, shade of difference 514 *meaning*; distinction without a difference 13 *identity*.

variant, different thing, something else; this, that or the other; quite another matter, different kettle of fish; horse of another colour; special case 80 *speciality*; freak, sport 84 *nonconformist*.

Adj. *different*, differing, unlike 19 *dissimilar*; original 126 *new*; various, diverse 17 *nonuniform*; multifarious 82 *multiform*; assorted 43 *mixed*; distinct 46 *separate*; divergent 282 *deviating*; odd 84 *unusual*; discordant, clashing 25 *disagreeing*; disparate 29 *unequal*; contrasting, contrasted; far from it, wide apart 14 *contrary*; other, another; peculiar 80 *special*; changed, altered 147 *converted*.

distinctive 5 *characteristic*; differentiating, comparative.

Vb. *differ*, vary from 282 *deviate*; contrast, disagree; modify, vary.

differentiate, distinguish 463 *discriminate*; shade, refine, particularize 80 *specify*.

16. Uniformity – **N.** *uniformity*, uniformness, consistency 153 *stability*; regularity 71 *continuity*, 146 *continuance*, 60 *order*; homogeneity, homology 18 *similarity*; monolithic quality; unity, unison 24 *agreement*; evenness 258 *smoothness*; sameness 13 *identity*; invariability, monotony, even tenor; mixture as before; even pace, rhythm; routine 610 *habit*; monotone, drone, monologue; monolith; assimilation, standardization, mass production 83 *conformity*.

Adj. *uniform*, all of a piece, solid, monolithic; homogeneous 18 *similar*; same, consistent, self-c., constant, steady 153 *fixed*; undeviating, unchanging, unvarying, invariable; measured, even-paced; undiversified, undifferentiated, unrelieved, unbroken; without contrast, lacking variety; uniformed, liveried; characterless, featureless, faceless, blank; monotonous, monotone; monochrome, grey; standard, normal 83 *typical*; patterned, standardized, stereotyped, mass-produced, unisex; orderly, regular 245 *symmetrical*; straight, even, flush, level 216 *flat*.

Vb. *make uniform*, homogenize; stamp, run through 547 *mark*; level up *or* down, abolish differentials 28 *equalize*; assimilate 18 *liken*; size, assort, grade; drill, align; regiment, institutionalize; standardize, stereotype, pattern; mass-produce; normalize, regularize 83 *make conform*.

17. Nonuniformity – N. *nonuniformity*, variability, patchiness 72 *discontinuity*; unpredictability 152 *changeableness*; inconsistency, irregularity 61 *disorder*; asymmetry 244 *amorphism*; raggedness, unevenness, jerkiness 259 *roughness*; heterogeneity, heteromorphism 15 *difference*; contrast 14 *contrariety*, 19 *dissimilarity*; diversity, variety 82 *multiformity*; all sorts and conditions, all shapes and sizes, mixed bag 43 *medley*; patchwork 437 *variegation*; abnormality, exception 84 *nonconformity*; odd man out, uniqueness, individuality 80 *speciality*.

Adj. *nonuniform*, variable, unpredictable 152 *changeful*; spasmodic 142 *fitful*; inconsistent, patchy 29 *unequal*; irregular, unsystematic; asymmetrical; out of order; uneven, bumpy, lumpy, jerky 259 *rough*; erratic, out of step, out of time; heterogeneous, various, diverse 15 *different*, 19 *dissimilar*; multifarious, miscellaneous 82 *multiform*; divergent 282 *deviating*, 25 *disagreeing*; atypical, exceptional 84 *abnor-*mal*; unique 80 *special*; individual, handmade.

Adv. *nonuniformly*, irregularly, erratically, unsystematically; all anyhow, here, there and everywhere.

18. Similarity – N. *similarity*, resemblance, likeness, similitude; semblance 445 *appearance*; fashion 243 *form*; affinity, kinship 9 *relation*; connaturality; comparability, analogousness, analogy, correspondence, correlation; equivalence, parity; no difference 13 *identity*; family likeness; striking 1. 551 *representation*, 494 *accuracy*; approximation, adumbration, suggestion, hint; fair comparison, about the size of it.

assimilation, likening 462 *comparison*; identification 13 *identity*; simulation 20 *imitation*; parable, allegory; portrayal 590 *description*.

analogue, congener, the like, suchlike; type 83 *example*; simile, parallel, metaphor; equivalent 150 *substitute*; brother, sister, twin; match, fellow, mate, companion, pendant; complement, counterpart; alter ego, other self, double, ringer, lookalike; likeness, reflection; the picture of 551 *image*; spitting image, chip off the old block; pair 90 *duality*; two of a kind, birds of a feather; clone 22 *duplicate*.

Adj. *similar*, resembling, like, alike, twin, matching, like as two peas, tarred with the same brush; much of a muchness, nothing to choose between 13 *identical*; of a piece 16 *uniform*; analogous, parallel 28 *equivalent*; homogeneous 11 *akin*; close, approximate 200 *near*; in the style of, à la; such as, quasi; rhyming 106 *repeated*; punning 518 *equivocal*.

lifelike, realistic, photographic, exact, faithful, natural, typical; good of one, true to life.

simulating 20 *imitative*; seeming 542 *deceiving*; mock, pseudo.

Vb. *resemble*, pass for, mirror, reflect 20 *imitate*; seem, look like, take after, put one in mind of, savour of, approximate to 289 *approach*; match 24 *accord*; typify 551 *represent*.

liken, assimilate to 462 *compare*; reduce

to 13 *identify*; pair, bracket with 28 *equalize*; allegorize; portray 20 *imitate*.

Adv. *similarly*, as, like, quasi, so to speak; allegorically 519 *metaphorically*; likewise, so, by the same token.

19. Dissimilarity – N. *dissimilarity*, dissimilitude, unlikeness; incomparability 10 *unrelatedness*; disparity 29 *inequality*; divergence 15 *difference*; variation 17 *nonuniformity*, 82 *multiformity*; contrast 14 *contrariety*; nothing in common 25 *disagreement*; uniqueness 21 *originality*; dissemblance, dissimilation 525 *concealment*, 527 *disguise*; bad likeness 552 *misrepresentation*; odd man out 25 *misfit*.

Adj. *dissimilar*, unlike, distinct, diverse 15 *different*; various 82 *multiform*; disparate 29 *unequal*; unalike, not comparable 10 *unrelated*; unmatched 17 *nonuniform*; unique 21 *inimitable*; untypical 84 *unconformable*; novel 126 *new*; a far cry from 199 *distant*; not true to life, unrealistic.

Vb. *be unlike*, bear no resemblance, have nothing in common 15 *differ*.

make unlike, distinguish 15 *differentiate*; modify, change 147 *convert*; caricature 552 *misrepresent*, 246 *distort*; disguise 525 *conceal*.

20. Imitation – N. *imitation*, emulation 716 *contention*; conventionality 83 *conformity*; want of originality, slavishness; imitativeness (see *mimicry*); mimesis 551 *representation*; reflection, mirror, echo; borrowing 788 *stealing*; forgery 541 *falsehood*; transcription 22 *copy*; duplication 166 *reproduction*.

mimicry 551 *representation*; onomatopoeia; mime, pantomime 594 *dramaturgy*; sign language 547 *gesture*; ventriloquism 579 *speech*; portrayal, caricature 851 *satire*; travesty 552 *misrepresentation*; imitativeness, apishness, parrotry 106 *repetition*, 850 *affectation*; simulation, disguise, protective colouring, camouflage, dissimulation 18 *similarity*, 19 *dissimilarity*; pretence, mockery 542 *sham*.

imitator, copycat, ape, sedulous a., monkey; mockingbird, parrot, echo; sheep 83 *conformist*, 284 *follower*; poseur

850 *affecter*; yes-man 925 *flatterer*; mocker, parodist 839 *humorist*, 926 *detractor*; actor, mime, ventriloquist, mimic, impersonator, drag artiste 594 *entertainer*; realist, naturalist 556 *artist*; shammer 545 *impostor*; borrower, plagiarist; duplicator, copier, photocopier.

Adj. *imitative*, mimetic; onomatopoeic, echoic; apish, parrot-like; echoing, flattering; disguised, camouflaged; mock, mimic; simulating 541 *hypocritical*; sham, imitation, synthetic, counterfeit 541 *false*; unoriginal, uninventive 610 *usual*; unimaginative, derivative 106 *repeated*; conventional 83 *conformable*; modelled on, moulded on; copied, slavish, literal; caricatured, etc. vb; imitable.

Vb. *imitate*, ape, parrot, flatter, echo 18 *resemble*; pose 850 *be affected*; pretend, make-believe, mimic, mime, portray, paint 551 *represent*; parody, take off 851 *ridicule*; sham, simulate, put on 541 *dissemble*; disguise, camouflage 525 *conceal*.

copy, draw, trace; reprint 587 *print*; duplicate, cyclostyle, photocopy; multiply 166 *reproduce*; copy out, transcribe; crib, plagiarize, borrow 788 *steal*; counterfeit 541 *fake*.

do likewise, mould or pattern oneself on; take a leaf out of another's book; follow, follow suit, follow my leader 83 *conform*; echo, ditto 106 *repeat*; emulate, rival.

Adv. *imitatively*, parrot-fashion; literally, word for word, verbatim.

21. Originality – N. *originality*, creativeness, inventiveness 513 *imagination*; creation, invention 10 *unrelatedness*; uniqueness 88 *unity*; independence, line of one's own; precedent 23 *prototype*; new departure 68 *beginning*; innovation, freshness 126 *newness*; eccentricity, individuality 84 *nonconformity*; unlikeness 19 *dissimilarity*.

no imitation, genuineness 494 *authenticity*; real thing 13 *identity*; autograph.

Adj. *original*, creative, inventive 513 *imaginative*; unimitated, underived; prototypal, archetypal; primordial 119 *prior*; fresh, novel 126 *new*; individual, personal

80 *special*; independent, eccentric 84 *unconformable*.

inimitable, incomparable 34 *superior*; not imitated 15 *different*; unique, one and only 88 *one*; authentic 494 *genuine*.

22. Copy – N. *copy*, exact c.; clone 166 *reproduction*; replica, facsimile, tracing; fair copy, transcript 18 *analogue*; cast, death mask; stamp, seal, impress, imprint; print 587 *letterpress*, 555 *engraving*; photocopy, Xerox (tdmk), photograph, photostat 551 *photography*; microfilm 548 *record*; dummy, forgery 542 *sham*; crib 20 *imitation*; a likeness 18 *similarity*, 553 *picture*; image 551 *representation*; model, effigy; faithful copy, mirror 106 *repetition*, 417 *reflection*; apology for, caricature, parody 851 *ridicule*; first copy, draft; paraphrase 520 *translation*.

duplicate, carbon copy; transfer, rubbing; reprint 589 *edition*; specimen 83 *example*.

23. Prototype – N. *prototype*, archetype, antitype; type, biotype, norm 30 *average*; protoplasm 358 *organism*; original 68 *origin*; precedent, test case 119 *priority*; guide, rule 693 *precept*; standard, criterion, touchstone 9 *referral*; ideal 646 *perfection*; cynosure 646 *paragon*; tuning fork 465 *gauge*; module, unit; specimen 83 *example*; model, subject; exemplar, pattern, paradigm; copybook, copy, manuscript; blueprint 623 *plan*; outline, draft, sketch.

mould, matrix, mint; plate, shell; stencil, template; frame 243 *form*; last; die, stamp, punch, seal 555 *printing*.

Adj. *prototypal*, paradigmatic, exemplary, model, standard, classic, copybook.

Vb. *be an example*, serve as e.

24. Agreement – N. *agreement* 181 *concurrence*; accord, accordance, unison 16 *uniformity*; harmony 410 *melody*; consonance, concordance; concert, entente 710 *concord*; unanimity 488 *consensus*.

conformance 83 *conformity*; congruence, coincidence 13 *identity*; congruity 16 *uniformity*; coherence 475 *reasoning*; correspondence 18 *similarity*.

fitness, aptness, qualification 694 *aptitude*; suitability, propriety 642 *good policy*; the right person in the right place, the very thing; relevancy, pertinence, admissibility 9 *relevance*; commensurability, proportion; timeliness 137 *occasion*.

adaptation, conformation, harmonization, synchronization, matching, reconcilement, accommodation 770 *compromise*; attunement, adjustment 62 *arrangement*; compatibility, congeniality, naturalness; good fit, perfect f.

Adj. *agreeing*, right, accordant, in accord, in accordance with, in keeping; correspondent, answering; proportionate, commensurate, according to 12 *correlative*; coincident, congruent, congruous 28 *equal*; conforming 83 *conformable*; in step, in phase, in tune, synchronized, of a piece with, consistent 16 *uniform*; consonant, concordant, harmonious; suiting, matching 18 *similar*; becoming 846 *tasteful*; natural, congenial, sympathetic; reconcilable, compatible; agreeable, acquiescent 488 *assenting*; concurrent, at one, unanimous; united, like-minded 706 *cooperative*.

apt, applicable, admissible, germane, appropriate 9 *relevant*; to the purpose, bearing upon; pat, apropos; right, happy, felicitous, idiomatic 575 *elegant*; at home, in one's element; seasonable, opportune 137 *timely*.

fit, fitting, befitting, seemly, decorous; suited, well-adapted; capable, qualified, cut out for 694 *skilful*; suitable, up one's street 642 *advisable*; meet, proper 913 *right*.

adjusted 60 *orderly*, 494 *accurate*; focused, tuned, fine-t. 412 *musical*; trimmed, balanced 28 *equal*; well-cut, well-fitting, tight; tailor-made, snug, comfortable.

Vb. *accord*, agree, concur 488 *assent*; coincide, square with, dovetail 45 *join*; fit like a glove, fit to a T; tally, correspond, match 18 *resemble*; go with, comport with, tone in w., harmonize; come naturally to; take to like a duck to water; fit in, belong, feel at home; answer, do, meet, suit, suit down to the ground 642 *be expedient*; fall pat, come apropos, beseem, befit; pull together 706 *cooperate*; be consistent, hang together 475 *be reasonable*; negotiate 766 *make terms*; get on with, hit it off 880 *befriend*.

adjust, make adjustments 654 *rectify*; fit, suit, adapt, accommodate, conform; tune up, harmonize; modulate, tune in; proportion 12 *correlate*; dress, align 62 *arrange*; cut, tailor, trim 31 *compensate*; focus, synchronize.

25. Disagreement – N. *disagreement*, disaccord; nonagreement 489 *dissent*; disunion, disunity 709 *dissension*; jar, clash 279 *collision*; variance, divergence, discrepancy 15 *difference*; two voices, ambivalence 518 *equivocalness*; inconsistency, credibility gap; opposition, contradiction, conflict 14 *contrariety*; discordance, inharmoniousness 411 *discord*; noncoincidence, incongruence 10 *unrelatedness*; disparity 29 *inequality*.

inaptitude, unfitness 695 *unskilfulness*; unfittingness, unsuitability, indecorousness, impropriety 643 *inexpedience*, 847 *bad taste*; inapplicability 10 *irrelevance*; incompatibility 84 *nonconformity*.

misfit, maladjustment, bad fit, bad match; incongruity, false note 411 *discord*; fish out of water, square peg in a round hole; outsider 59 *intruder*; joker, odd man out 84 *nonconformist*; eccentric, oddity, mutton dressed up as lamb.

Adj. *disagreeing* 489 *dissenting*; at odds, at cross purposes, at variance 709 *quarrelling*; hostile, antagonistic 881 *inimical*; uncongenial, antipathetic 861 *disliked*; conflicting, contradictory 14 *contrary*; unnatural, against one's nature; inconsistent 17 *nonuniform*; inconsonant, unadaptable 84 *unconformable*; odd, foreign 59 *extraneous*; incommensurable 10 *unrelated*; out of proportion 246 *distorted*; inharmonious, grating 411 *discordant*; mismatched, misallied; ill-assorted, discrepant 15 *different*; incongruous.

unapt, unfitted, unsuited; maladjusted; wrong, unfitting, unsuitable,

unbecoming, improper, undue, inappropriate 643 *inexpedient*; impracticable 470 *impossible*; unfit for, ineligible; unseasonable 138 *inopportune*; malapropos, inadmissible 10 *irrelevant*; unidiomatic 576 *inelegant*; out of character, out of keeping; misplaced, out of place, out of joint, out of step.

Vb. *disagree* 489 *dissent*; differ, fall out 709 *quarrel*; clash, conflict, collide 14 *be contrary*; diverge 15 *differ*; not play, noncooperate 702 *be obstructive*; have nothing to do with 10 *be unrelated*; be incongruous, stick out like a sore thumb, strike a false note, jar.

Section 3: Quantity

26. Quantity – N. *quantity*, amount; sum 38 *addition*; total 52 *whole*; magnitude, extent 465 *measurement*; mass, bulk 195 *size*; dimensions, longitude 203 *length*; width, thickness 205 *breadth*; altitude 209 *height*; deepness 211 *depth*; area, volume 183 *space*; weight 322 *gravity*, 323 *lightness*; force, flow 160 *energy*; numbers 104 *multitude*; fraction, multiple 85 *number*, 86 *mathematics*, 101 *plurality*, 102 *fraction*, 103 *zero*, 107 *infinity*; mean 30 *average*.

finite quantity, matter of; ceiling 236 *limit*; quantum, quota, quorum; measure, dose 465 *measurement*; avoirdupois 322 *weighing*; ration 783 *portion*; spoonful, thimbleful, sackful; lot, batch; lorryload 193 *contents*; lock, stock and barrel 52 *whole*; masses, heaps 32 *great quantity*; bit 33 *small quantity*; more, majority 36 *increase*, 104 *greater number*; less 37 *decrease*, 105 *fewness*; stint 682 *labour*.

Adj. *quantitative*, some, certain, any; so many, so much.

Vb. *quantify*, allot, ration 783 *apportion*.

27. Degree: relative quantity – N. *degree*, relative quantity, proportion 9 *relativeness*, 462 *comparison*; extent, intensity, frequency 26 *quantity*; level, pitch; reach, scope 183 *range*; rate, speed 265 *motion*;

gradation, calibration, differential 15 *differentiation*; grade, remove, stepping-stone; step, rung 308 *ascent*; point, stage, milestone 8 *juncture*; mark, peg, notch, score 547 *indicator*; value 465 *measurement*; ranking 77 *classification*; standard, grade 73 *serial place*; hierarchy 733 *authority*.

Adj. *gradational*, hierarchical, graded, scaled; gradual.

comparative, proportional, in scale 9 *relative*; within the bounds of 236 *limited*.

Vb. *graduate*, rate, class, rank; grade; scale, calibrate; compare, measure.

shade off, taper, die away, dissolve, fade out; whittle down 204 *shorten*.

Adv. *by degrees*, gradually, little by little, step by step, drop by drop, bit by bit, by slow degrees; just a bit.

28. Equality: sameness of quantity or degree – **N.** *equality*, parity, coincidence 24 *agreement*; symmetry, balance, poise; level 258 *smoothness*, 216 *horizontality*; monotony 16 *uniformity*.

equivalence, likeness 18 *similarity*; sameness 13 *identity*, 219 *parallelism*; equation; interchangeability 151 *interchange*; fair exchange 791 *barter*; par, quits; equivalent, value 809 *price*; not a pin to choose, six of one and half a dozen of the other; level bet, even money.

equilibrium, equipoise, balance, poise; even keel, steadiness; balance of forces; deadlock, status quo; equilibration, homoeostasis; sea legs, seat 153 *stability*; tightrope walker, acrobat.

equalization, equation; balancing 322 *weighing*; adjustment 31 *compensation*; going halves 92 *bisection*, 775 *participation*; reciprocity 12 *correlation*; equalizer, counterpoise 31 *offset*; standardizer, bed of Procrustes.

draw, drawn game, tie, dead heat; stalemate; photo finish; love all, deuce.

compeer, peer, equal, match, fellow 18 *analogue*; equivalent, parallel, opposite number, counterpart, shadow; rival 716 *contender*.

Adj. *equal*, equi-, iso-, co-; same 13 *identical*; like 18 *similar*; coequal, coor-dinate, coextensive 24 *agreeing*; equidistant; isotropic; balanced, poised, in equilibrium; homoeostatic, stable 153 *fixed*; even, level, flush 258 *smooth*; equilateral, regular 16 *uniform*, 245 *symmetrical*; equable, unvarying 153 *unchangeable*; competitive, rival, dingdong, Greek meeting Greek, matched, drawn, tied; parallel, level-pegging, neck-and-neck; sharing, cosharing; half-and-half, fifty-fifty; impartial, equitable; on equal terms, on a par; par, quits, upsides with.

equivalent, comparable, parallel, interchangeable, synonymous, virtual; corresponding, reciprocal 12 *correlative*; tantamount, much the same, all one, as broad as it is long, pot calling the kettle black 18 *similar*; worth, valued at.

Vb. *be equal*, equal, balance; compensate 31 *set off*; come to the same thing, coincide 24 *accord*; make the grade 635 *suffice*; hold one's own, keep up with, keep pace w., parallel; match, twin 18 *resemble*; tie, draw; break even; go halves.

equalize, equate; bracket, match; parallel 462 *compare*; balance, strike a b., poise; trim, dress, square, level 258 *smooth*, 16 *make uniform*; accommodate 24 *adjust*; counterpoise, even up 31 *set off*; redress the balance, handicap 31 *compensate*; set on an even keel, equilibrate 153 *stabilize*; right oneself, keep one's balance.

Adv. *equally*, pari passu, ceteris paribus; on equal terms.

29. Inequality: difference of quantity or degree – **N.** *inequality* 34 *superiority*, 35 *inferiority*; irregularity 17 *nonuniformity*; unevenness 259 *roughness*; disproportion 25 *disagreement*; bias, skewness, lopsidedness 246 *distortion*; disparity 19 *dissimilarity*; disequilibrium, imbalance, dizziness, preponderance, overweight 322 *gravity*; short weight 323 *lightness*, 636 *insufficiency*; odds 15 *difference*; makeweight 31 *offset*.

Adj. *unequal*, disparate, incongruent 15 *different*, 25 *disagreeing*, 19 *dissimilar*; unique, unequalled, at an advantage 34

11

superior, 644 *excellent*; at a disadvantage, below par 35 *inferior*; lopsided 246 *distorted*; irregular, scalene 17 *nonuniform*; askew, awry, odd, uneven; unequable, variable, patchy 437 *variegated*; inadequate 636 *insufficient*; unbalanced, swaying, rocking 152 *unstable*; top-heavy, listing 220 *oblique*; off balance, toppling; unequitable, partial 481 *biased*.

Vb. *be unequal*, not balance, fall short 35 *be inferior*; preponderate 34 *be superior*; be deficient 636 *not suffice*; overcompensate, tip the scales 322 *weigh*; unbalance, throw off balance; list, lean 220 *be oblique*; rock, sway.

30. Mean – N. *average*, medium, mean, median 86 *statistics*; intermedium; balance, happy medium 177 *moderation*; standard product 79 *generality*; norm, par 732 *averageness*.

middle point, midpoint 70 *middle*; middle years 131 *middle age*; middle course 625 *middle way*; neutrality 606 *no choice*.

common man 869 *commoner*; man *or* woman in the street 79 *everyman*.

Adj. *median*, mean, average, medial 70 *middle*; intermediate, normal, standard, par, ordinary, commonplace, run-of-the-mill, mediocre 732 *middling*; moderate, middle-of-the-road 625 *neutral*; middle class, middlebrow.

Vb. *average out*, average, take the mean; split the difference 770 *compromise*; strike a balance 28 *equalize*.

31. Compensation – N. *compensation*, weighting 28 *equalization*; reaction 182 *counteraction*; redemption, recoupment; redress 787 *restitution*; amends 941 *atonement*; recompense, measure for measure 12 *correlation*.

offset, allowance, makeweight, balance, weighting, counterweight, counterpoise, counterbalance, ballast 28 *equalization*; indemnity, reparations, compensation, costs, damages 787 *restitution*; refund, one's money back; quid pro quo 150 *substitute*; swings and roundabouts 151 *interchange*; concession 770 *compromise*.

Adj. *compensatory*, balancing 28 *equivalent*; self-correcting, self-cancelling; in the opposite scale, weighed against 462 *compared*.

Vb. *compensate*, make amends, indemnify, restore 787 *restitute*; make good, make up 150 *substitute*; add a makeweight, ballast; repay, reimburse, redeem, outweigh; overcompensate, lean over backwards.

set off, offset, allow for; countervail, balance 28 *equalize*; neutralize, cancel 182 *counteract*; cover, hedge, concede 770 *compromise*.

recoup, recover, retrieve; make up leeway, take up the slack; get back 786 *take*.

32. Greatness – N. *greatness*, bigness 195 *size*; large scale, generous proportions, vastness 195 *hugeness*; abundance 635 *plenty*; amplitude, fullness 54 *completeness*, *plenitude*; superabundance 637 *redundance*; boundlessness 107 *infinity*; numerousness 104 *multitude*; dimensions, magnitude 26 *quantity*, 27 *degree*; spaciousness, roominess 183 *room*; mightiness, strength, intensity 160 *power*, 178 *influence*; intensification, magnification, multiplication 197 *expansion*; aggrandizement 36 *increase*; significance 638 *importance*; eminence 34 *superiority*; grandeur 868 *nobility*, 871 *pride*; majesty 733 *authority*.

great quantity, muchness, galore 635 *plenty*; crop, harvest, profusion, abundance, productivity 171 *productiveness*; shower, torrent 637 *redundance*; expanse, sheet, lake; sight of, world of, mort of, power of; much, lot, deal, mint, mine 632 *store*; mountain 74 *accumulation*; quantities, lots, lashings, oodles, scads, wads, pots, bags; heaps, loads, masses, stacks; oceans, seas, floods, streams; volumes, reams, numbers, crowds, masses, hosts, swarms 104 *multitude*; all, entirety 52 *whole*.

main part, almost all 52 *chief part*; greater part, majority 104 *greater number*; body, bulk, mass, substance 1 *essence*.

Adj. *great*, main, most 34 *superior*;

maximum 34 *supreme*; grand, big, mickle 195 *large*; substantial, considerable, respectable; sizable, full-size; bulky, massive 322 *weighty*; puffed up, swollen 197 *expanded*; ample, generous, voluminous, capacious 183 *spacious*; profound 211 *deep*; tall, lofty 209 *high*; Herculean 162 *strong*; mighty 160 *powerful*, 178 *influential*; intense 174 *vigorous*; noisy 400 *loud*; soaring 308 *ascending*; culminating, at the maximum, at the peak, at its height 213 *topmost*; abundant, overflowing 635 *plenteous*; superabundant 637 *redundant*; many, swarming, teeming 104 *multitudinous*; imperial, august 644 *valuable*, 868 *noble*; sublime, exalted 821 *impressive*; glorious, famous 866 *renowned*, *worshipful*; grave, solemn, serious 638 *important*; excelling, excellent 306 *surpassing*, 644 *best*; eminent 638 *notable*.

extensive, wide-ranging, far-flung, far-reaching 183 *spacious*; widespread, prevalent, epidemic; worldwide, universal, cosmic; mass, indiscriminate, wholesale, whole-hogging, full-scale, all-embracing, sweeping, comprehensive 78 *inclusive*.

enormous, immense, colossal, giant, gigantic, monumental 195 *huge*; towering, sky-high 209 *high*; record, record-breaking 306 *surpassing*.

prodigious, marvellous, astonishing 864 *wonderful*; fantastic, fabulous, incredible, unbelievable, passing belief 486 *unbelieved*, 472 *improbable*, 470 *impossible*; stupendous, tremendous, terrific; frightful 854 *frightening*; breathtaking, out of this world 821 *impressive*; remarkable, outstanding 84 *unusual*.

whopping, walloping, whacking, spanking, thumping, thundering, socking, rattling, howling, father and mother of; hefty, husky, hulking, strapping, overgrown, clumsy 195 *unwieldy*.

exorbitant, extortionate 735 *oppressive*; excessive, extreme, utmost; monstrous, outrageous, swingeing, unconscionable; inordinate, preposterous, extravagant, astronomical 546 *exaggerated*.

consummate 54 *complete*; flawless 646 *perfect*; thoroughgoing; utter, total, out and out, dyed in the wool, double-dyed;

absolute, sheer; pure, stark, regular, downright, unmitigated.

Vb. *be great*, bulk, loom; stretch 183 *extend*; tower, soar 308 *ascend*; transcend 34 *be superior*; know no bounds 306 *overstep*; enlarge 36 *augment*, 197 *expand*; swamp 54 *fill*.

Adv. *greatly*, much, well; very, right, so; mighty, ever so; utterly, without reservation 54 *completely*; widely, extensively, universally; largely, mainly, mostly; considerably, fairly, pretty well; a sight, a deal, materially, substantially; dearly, deeply; on a large scale, in a big way; hugely, enormously; heavily, strongly; actively, strenuously, vigorously, heartily, intensely; closely, intensively, hotly, bitterly, fiercely; acutely, sharply, shrewdly, exquisitely; enough, abundantly, prodigiously; generously, richly, magnificently; supremely, preeminently, superlatively; wonderfully, strangely; immeasurably, infinitely.

extremely, ultra-, to extremes, to the limit, to the nth degree; no end of; beyond measure, beyond compare; overly, unduly, to a fault; out of all proportion; bitterly, harshly, with a vengeance; immoderately, uncontrollably, desperately, madly, frantically, furiously 176 *violently*; exceedingly, inordinately; foully, abominably, horribly; confoundedly, deucedly, devilishly, damnably; tremendously, terribly, fearfully, dreadfully, awfully, frightfully; unforgivably, mortally.

remarkably, noticeably, markedly, pointedly; notably, strikingly, conspicuously, signally, glaringly, flagrantly, blatantly; preeminently 34 *eminently*; outstandingly, unco; singularly, unusually; surprisingly, wonderfully.

painfully, unsparingly, till it hurts; badly, bitterly, hard; seriously, sorely, grievously; sadly, miserably, wretchedly; pitiably, woefully, lamentably; cruelly; savagely; unbearably, intolerably; exquisitely, excruciatingly, terrifyingly.

33. Smallness – N. *smallness*, diminutiveness 196 *littleness*; brevity 204 *shortness*;

meagreness 206 *thinness*; paucity 105 *fewness*; 140 *infrequency*; inadequacy 636 *insufficiency*, 307 *shortfall*; exiguity, scantiness; moderation; intermediate technology, applied t.; pettiness, insignificance 639 *unimportance*, 35 *inferiority*; mediocrity 732 *averageness*; no depth 212 *shallowness*; compression 198 *contraction*; diminution 37 *decrease*.

small quantity, fraction, modicum, minimum; minutiae, trivia; peanuts 639 *trifle*; detail; nutshell 592 *compendium*; drop in the bucket *or* the ocean; homoeopathic dose, trifling amount; thimbleful, mouthful; trickle, dribble, sprinkling, dash, splash, squirt, squeeze; tinge, tincture, trace, spice, smack, lick, smell, breath, whisper, suspicion, vestige, soupçon, suggestion, nuance, shade, shadow, touch, cast; vein, strain, streak; spark, scintilla, gleam, flash, flicker, ray; pinch, snatch, handful; snack, sip, bite, mite, scrap, morsel, sop; dole, pittance, fragment 53 *piece*; whit, bit, mite, iota, jot, tittle; ounce 322 *weighing*; inch 200 *short distance*; nanosecond 116 *instant*; next to nothing, hardly anything; the shadow of a shade 4 *insubstantial thing*.

small thing 196 *miniature*; particle, atom; dot, point, pinpoint; dab, spot, fleck, speck, mote, smut; grain, crumb 332 *powder*; drop, droplet, driblet; thread, wisp, shred, rag, fragment 53 *piece*; smithereens, confetti; flake, snippet, gobbet, finger; splinter, chip, shaving; sliver, slip; pinprick, snick, prick, nick.

Adj. *small*, exiguous, not much, moderate, modest, homoeopathic, minimal, infinitesimal; microscopic, tiny, minute, diminutive 196 *little*; smaller 35 *lesser*; least, minimum; small-sized 196 *dwarfish*; slim, slender, meagre 206 *narrow*; slight, feeble 163 *weak*; delicate, dainty, minikin 330 *brittle*; flimsy 323 *light*; fine, subtle, rarefied 325 *rare*; low, faint 401 *muted*; squat 210 *low*; brief, skimpy 204 *short*; compact, thumbnail 198 *contracted*; scanty 307 *deficient*; 636 *insufficient*; reduced, declining, at a low ebb, less 37 *decreasing*.

inconsiderable, minor, lightweight, trifling, trivial, petty, paltry, insignificant 639 *unimportant*; not many 105 *few*; imperceptible, shadowy, tenuous; marginal, negligible, remote, slight; superficial, cursory 4 *insubstantial*; skin-deep 212 *shallow*; average, so-so 30 *median*; modest, humble, passable 732 *middling*; not much of a, no great shakes, second-rate 35 *inferior*; no more than, just, only, mere, bare.

Adv. *slightly*, little; lightly, softly, faintly, feebly; superficially, gradually, imperceptibly, insensibly, on a small scale, in a small way; fairly, tolerably, quite; comparatively, relatively; enough, well e.; indifferently, poorly, hardly, scarcely, barely, only just; narrowly, by the skin of one's teeth; hardly at all, no more than; only, at least, at the very least.

partially, to a certain extent; after a fashion, sort of, in a manner of speaking; somewhat, a little, just a bit.

almost, all but, on the brink of, within sight of 200 *near*; near upon 200 *nearly*; virtually.

in no way, by no means, in no respect, not at all, not in the least; not a bit, not in the slightest; not a whit, not a jot, not by a long chalk.

34. Superiority – N. *superiority*, loftiness 209 *height*; transcendence 32 *greatness*, 306 *overstepping*; top 213 *summit*; quality, excellence 644 *goodness*; ne plus ultra 646 *perfection*; preferability 605 *choice*; primacy, pride of place, seniority 64 *precedence*; preeminence 866 *prestige,* 868 *nobility,* 689 *management*; overlordship, paramountcy, supremacy 733 *authority*; ascendancy, domination, hegemony 178 *influence*; prominence 638 *importance*; one-upmanship 727 *success*; zenith, maximum, peak, pinnacle, crest, high 213 *summit*.

advantage, privilege, prerogative, favour 615 *benefit*; head start, lead, pole position, inside track; odds, pull, edge; command, upper hand, whip h.; trump card, ace up one's sleeve, ace in the hole; majority 104 *greater number*; vantage ground.

superior, superman, wonderwoman 644 *exceller*; first choice 890 *favourite*; select few 644 *elite*; one's betters, top people 638 *bigwig*; overlord, lord, sovereign 741 *master*; commander 690 *leader*; boss 690 *director*; model 646 *paragon*; star, virtuoso 696 *proficient person*; specialist 696 *expert*; mastermind 500 *sage*; world-beater, record-breaker; champion 727 *victor*; first-born, elder, senior; Triton among the minnows, big fish in a small pool.

Adj. *superior*, more so; comparative, superlative; major, greater 32 *great*; upper, higher, senior, over-, super-, supra-, hyper-; above average, in a different class 15 *different*; better, a cut above, head and shoulders above 644 *excellent*; more than a match for; one up, streets ahead 64 *preceding*; preferable 605 *chosen*; record, exceeding, overtopping, outclassing 306 *surpassing*; on top, winning 727 *successful*; outstanding, distinguished 866 *noteworthy*; top-level, high-l., high-powered 689 *directing*, 638 *important*.

supreme, arch-, greatest 32 *great*; highest, uppermost 213 *topmost*; first, chief, foremost 64 *preceding*; main, principal, leading, overruling, overriding, cardinal, capital 638 *important*; excellent, superlative, first-class, front-rank, world-beating 644 *best*; top of the class, nulli secundus, second to none, none such; dominant, paramount, preeminent, incomparable, unrivalled, matchless, peerless, unequalled, unsurpassable 21 *inimitable*; transcendent, unsurpassed, ultimate, the last word in 306 *surpassing*; without comparison 646 *perfect*.

Vb. *be superior*, transcend, rise above 209 *be high*; go beyond 306 *overstep*; take the cake *or* the biscuit; carry off the laurels, bear the palm, wear the crown; pass, surpass, beat the record, reach a new high; improve on, go one better, cap, trump, overtrump; shine, excel 644 *be good*; steal the show, outshine, eclipse, overshadow; put one's nose out of joint, score off, have the laugh on; best, outrival, outclass, outrank 306 *outdo*; outplay, outwit 542 *befool*; overtake 277 *outstrip*; get the better of, worst, beat hollow, knock into a cocked hat, beat all comers 727 *defeat*; rise to the occasion.

predominate, overweigh, tip the scale 29 *be unequal*; override 178 *prevail*; have the advantage, have the upper hand, have the edge on; hold all the aces; lead, be one up.

culminate, come to a head; crown all 213 *crown*; reach a new high 725 *climax*.

Adv. *beyond*, more, over; above the mark, above par; upwards of, over and above; on the crest, at its height.

eminently, preeminently, outstandingly, surpassingly, supremely; above all, of all things; to crown it all, to cap it all; par excellence; a fortiori, even more, far and away, by far 32 *extremely*.

35. Inferiority – N. *inferiority*, minority 105 *fewness*; littleness 33 *smallness*; subordinacy, dependence 745 *subjection*; secondariness, supporting role, second fiddle 639 *unimportance*; lowliness, humbleness 872 *humility*; back seat, obscurity, commonness 869 *commonalty*; disadvantage, handicap 702 *hindrance*; defect 647 *imperfection*; deficiency, inadequateness 307 *shortfall*, 636 *insufficiency*; failure 728 *defeat*; poor quality, second best 645 *badness*; decline 655 *deterioration*; record low, minimum, nadir, rock bottom 214 *base*; mediocrity 732 *averageness*.

inferior, subordinate, underling; subsidiary 707 *auxiliary*; pawn 628 *instrument*; follower 742 *dependant*; menial, hireling 742 *servant*; poor relation, small fry 639 *nonentity*; subject, underdog 742 *slave*; back-bencher, private, other ranks, lower classes 869 *commonalty*; second, runner-up; second best, second string, second fiddle, second-rater; poor second, also-ran; failure, reject, dregs; junior, minor.

Adj. *lesser*, less, minor, small-time, one-horse 639 *unimportant*; small 33 *inconsiderable*; diminished 37 *decreasing*; reduced 198 *contracted*; least, smallest, minimal, minimum; lowest, bottommost 214 *undermost*; minus 307 *deficient*.

inferior, lower, junior, under-, sub-;

subordinate 742 *serving*; dependent 745 *subject*; secondary, tributary, ancillary, subsidiary 703 *aiding*, 639 *unimportant*; second, second-best, second-class, second-rate, mediocre; third-rate 922 *contemptible*; humble, lowly, menial; substandard, low-grade, not up to snuff 607 *rejected*; below average, below par 307 *deficient*; spoilt, marred 655 *deteriorated*; unsound, defective 647 *imperfect*; shoddy 645 *bad*, 812 *cheap*; low, common, low-caste 869 *plebeian*; scratch, makeshift 670 *unprepared*; feeble 163 *weak*; outclassed, outshone, worsted, beaten 728 *defeated*; unworthy, not fit to hold a candle to, not a patch on; nothing special, nothing to shout about, nothing to write home about.

Vb. *be inferior*, come short of 307 *fall short*; lag, trail, fall behind; want, lack 636 *not suffice*; not make the grade 728 *fail*; bow to 739 *obey*; hand it to, knuckle under 721 *submit*; play second fiddle 742 *serve*; take a back seat, sink into obscurity; get worse 655 *deteriorate*; slump, sink, touch rock bottom 309 *descend*.

36. Increase – N. *increase*, augmentation, crescendo; growth, growth area, boom town; buildup, development 164 *production*; growing pains 68 *beginning*; extension 203 *lengthening*; spread, escalation, inflation 197 *expansion*; proliferation 171 *productiveness*; multiplication 86 *numerical operation*; adding 38 *addition*; enlargement, magnification, aggrandizement 32 *greatness*; overenlargement, excess 546 *exaggeration*; enhancement, appreciation; concentration, intensification, stepping up; acceleration 277 *spurt*; excitation 174 *stimulation*; exacerbation 832 *aggravation*; boost 654 *improvement*; rise, spiral, upward trend, upswing 308 *ascent*; flood, tide, rising t., swell, surge, cumulativeness, snowball 74 *accumulation*.

increment, accretion; bulge 38 *addition*; supplement, pay rise 40 *extra*; padding, stuffing 303 *insertion*; commission, interest, profit 771 *gain*.

Adj. *increasing*, progressive, escalating 32 *great*; growing, waxing, on the increase; supplementary 38 *additional*; ever-increasing, snowballing, cumulative 71 *continuous*; intensive; productive, fruitful 171 *prolific*; stretched.

Vb. *grow*, increase, gain, develop, escalate; swell, bulge, wax 197 *expand*; fill out, fatten, thicken 205 *be broad*; sprout, bud, burgeon, flower, blossom 167 *reproduce itself*; breed, spread, mushroom, multiply 104 *be many*, 171 *be fruitful*; grow up 669 *mature*; spring up, shoot up, flare up 209 *be high*; spiral, climb, mount, rise, rocket, skyrocket, take off 308 *ascend*; gain strength 162 *be strong*; flourish, thrive, prosper; gain ground, advance, snowball, accumulate 285 *progress*; earn interest, appreciate 771 *be profitable*; boom, surge 637 *superabound*, 32 *be great*; rise to a maximum 34 *culminate*.

augment, increase, bump up, double, triple; multiply, grow, breed 369 *breed stock*, 370 *cultivate*, 699 *mature*; enlarge, magnify, blow up 197 *expand*; amplify, develop, build up, fill out, pad out 54 *make complete*; condense, concentrate; supplement, enrich, superadd, repay with interest 38 *add*; extend, stretch 203 *lengthen*; broaden, widen, thicken, deepen; heighten, enhance, send up; raise, exalt 310 *elevate*; advance, aggrandize 285 *promote*; accelerate, intensify, redouble, step up, stimulate 174 *invigorate*; recruit, reinforce, boost 685 *refresh*, 656 *restore*, 162 *strengthen*; glorify 546 *exaggerate*, 482 *overrate*; stoke, add fuel to the flames, exacerbate 832 *aggravate*; maximize, bring to a head 725 *climax*.

37. Decrease: no increase – N. *decrease*, getting less, lessening, dwindling, falling off; waning, fading 198 *contraction*; shrinking 206 *narrowing*; ebb, reflux, neap tide; subsidence, sinking, decline, declension, downward curve, fall, drop 309 *descent*; deflation, depreciation, recession, slump 655 *deterioration*; weakening, enfeeblement 163 *weakness*; impoverishment, shortage 636 *scarcity*; diminishing returns, exhaustion; shrinkage, evaporation, erosion, attrition 655 *dilapidation*; spoilage, leakage, wastage, damage, loss, wear and tear 42 *decrement*; no increase, underproduction 175 *inertness*.

diminution, making less; deduction 39 *subtraction*; abatement, reduction, restriction; deceleration 278 *slowness*; retrenchment, cut, economization, pruning, curtailment, abridgement, abbreviation 204 *shortening*; compression, squeeze 198 *contraction*; abrasion, erosion 333 *friction*; scattering 75 *dispersion*; weeding out, elimination 62 *sorting*; extenuation, alleviation, minimization 177 *moderation*; belittlement, undervaluation 483 *underestimation*, 926 *detraction*; demotion, degradation 872 *humiliation*.

Adj. *decreasing*, dwindling; waning, fading; abated, decreased; declining, sinking, ebbing etc. vb.

Vb. *abate*, make less, diminish, decrease, lessen, minify; take away 39 *subtract*; reduce, attenuate, scale down, whittle d., pare 206 *make thin*; slash 46 *cut*; shrink, abridge 204 *shorten*; squeeze, compress, contract 198 *make smaller*; limit, curtail 747 *restrain*; cut down, cut back, retrench 814 *economize*; decelerate 278 *retard*; send down 311 *lower*; tone down, minimize 177 *moderate*; ease, allay, alleviate 831 *relieve*; deflate, puncture; disparage, decry, belittle 483 *underestimate*, 926 *detract*; dwarf, overshadow, put in the shade 34 *be superior*; degrade, demote 872 *humiliate*; remit 909 *forgive*; unload 701 *disencumber*, 323 *lighten*; run down, drain 300 *empty*; consume, fritter away 634 *waste*; melt down 337 *liquefy*; grind, crumble 332 *pulverize*; rub away, abrade; gnaw, nibble at, eat away; erode 655 *impair*; strip 229 *uncover*; plunder, dispossess 786 *deprive*; emasculate 161 *disable*; dilute, water down 163 *weaken*; thin out 105 *render few*; eliminate 300 *eject*; decimate 165 *destroy*; annihilate 2 *nullify*; damp down, cool; quell, subdue.

decrease, grow less, lessen, abate, slacken, ease, moderate, subside, die down; dwindle, shrink, shrivel up, contract 198 *become small*; wane, waste, wear away, wither away 655 *deteriorate*; fade, die away; retreat, ebb 290 *recede*; run low,

run down, ebb away, drain away, dry up, fail 636 *not suffice*; tail off, taper off, peter out; subside, sink, decline, fall, drop, spiral, slump, collapse 309 *descend*; level off 278 *decelerate*; melt away 466 *disappear*; evaporate; thin, become scarce 75 *disperse*; die out, become extinct 2 *pass away*; shed, rid oneself of 772 *lose*.

Adv. *diminuendo*, decrescendo, decreasingly; less and less; in decline, on the wane, at low ebb.

38. Addition – N. *addition*, annexation, agglutination 45 *union*; prefixion 64 *precedence*; suffixion, affixture 65 *sequence*; supplementation, suppletion 725 *completion*; contribution 703 *aid*; superaddition, imposition 702 *encumbrance*; accession, accretion, accrual; reinforcement 36 *increase*; increment, addendum 40 *adjunct*; total 86 *numeration*.

Adj. *additional*, additive; adventitious, supervenient, adscititious 59 *extraneous*, 6 *extrinsic*; supplementary 725 *completive*; conjunctive 45 *joined*; subsidiary, auxiliary, contributory; another, further, more; extra, spare 637 *superfluous*.

Vb. *add*, add up, sum, total 86 *do sums*; append, subjoin, attach, pin to, clip to, tag on, tack on, stick on 45 *join, tie*; preface, prefix, affix, suffix, infix; introduce 231 *put between*; engraft 303 *insert*; bring to, contribute to, make one's contribution 36 *augment*; swell 197 *enlarge*; supplement 54 *make complete*; impose, saddle with 187 *stow*, 702 *hinder*; superadd, superimpose, pile on, heap on 74 *bring together*; ornament, embellish 844 *decorate*, 266 *overlay*; mix with 43 *mix*; annex 786 *take*; include 299 *admit*.

accrue, be added 78 *be included*; supervene; adhere 50 *combine*; reinforce 162 *strengthen*; swell the ranks, fill the gap.

Adv. *in addition*, additionally, more, plus, extra; with interest, with a vengeance; with knobs on; and, too, also, furthermore, further; to boot; et cetera; and so on, moreover, into the bargain, over and above, with, as well as, not to mention, let alone, not forgetting; together with; for all that.

39. Subtraction – N. *subtraction*, deduction 86 *numerical operation*; diminution 37 *decrease*; abstraction, removal, withdrawal 786 *taking*; elimination 300 *ejection*; abrasion, erosion 333 *friction*; retrenchment, curtailment 204 *shortening*; amputation, excision 46 *scission*; expurgation, deletion 550 *obliteration*; minuend 85 *numerical element*; discount 42 *decrement*.

Adj. *subtracted*, subtractive, deducted; minus, without 307 *deficient*.

Vb. *subtract*, take away, deduct; detract from, diminish, decrease 37 *abate*; cut 810 *discount*; take off, knock o., allow 31 *set off*; except, take out, leave o. 57 *exclude*; abstract, withdraw, remove 786 *take*; shift 272 *transfer*; draw off 300 *empty*; file down 333 *rub*; eradicate, pull out 304 *extract*; pick 605 *select*; cross out, delete 550 *obliterate*; amputate, excise; shear, clip 46 *cut*; retrench, cut back, cut down, prune, curtail 204 *shorten*; castrate 161 *unman*; divest, denude 229 *uncover*.

40. Adjunct: thing added – N. *adjunct*, something added 38 *addition*; addendum, supplement, annex; attachment, fixture; inflexion, affix, suffix, prefix, infix 564 *part of speech*; tab, tag 547 *label*; appendage, tail 67 *sequel*; wake, trail 65 *sequence*; appendix, postscript 69 *extremity*; codicil, rider, marginalia, footnotes; corollary, complement; appurtenance, accessory 89 *concomitant*; extension, annexe 164 *edifice*; offshoot, branch; arm, accretion 59 *extraneousness*; increment 36 *increase*; patch 656 *repair*; padding, stuffing 303 *insertion*; gusset, gore, flap, lappet, lapel; admixture 58 *component*; fringe, border 234 *edge*; embroidery 844 *ornamentation*; garnish 389 *sauce*; frills, trimmings, trappings; equipment, furnishing 633 *provision*.

extra, additive, by-product; interest; bonus, tip, perk 962 *reward*; free gift, gratuity, windfall, find, lucky f.; allowance 31 *offset*; oddment, item; supernumerary, extra; reserves, spares; reinforcements 707 *auxiliary*; surplus 637 *superfluity*.

41. Remainder: thing remaining – N. *remainder*, residue, residuum; residual, result, resultant 157 *effect*, 164 *product*; margin 15 *difference*; balance 31 *offset*; surplus, carry-over 36 *increment*; excess 637 *superfluity*; relic, rest, remnant 105 *fewness*; rump, stump, stub, butt end 69 *extremity*; torso, trunk 53 *piece*; fossil, bones 363 *corpse*; husk, shell; wreckage, debris 165 *ruin*; ashes 332 *powder*; track, fingerprint 548 *record*, *trace*; wake, afterglow 67 *sequel*; vestige, remains.

leavings, leftovers; precipitate, deposit, sediment; drift, detritus 272 *thing transferred*; grounds, lees, heeltaps, dregs; scum, dross, scoria, slag, sludge; bilge, dottle; scrapings, shavings, crumbs 332 *powder*; husks, chaff, stubble; peel, peelings; skin, slough; remnants; scraps, odds and ends, lumber 641 *rubbish*; rejects 779 *derelict*; waste, sewage 302 *excrement*; refuse, litter 649 *dirt*.

survivor, finisher; successor 776 *beneficiary*; widower, widow 896 *widowhood*; orphan 779 *derelict*; descendant 170 *posterity*.

Adj. *remaining*, surviving, left, vestigial, resting, resultant; residual, residuary; left behind, deposited, precipitated 187 *located*; abandoned, discarded 779 *not retained*; on the shelf 860 *unwanted*; over, left over, odd; net, surplus; unspent, unexpended, unexpired, unconsumed; outstanding, carried over; spare, to s., superfluous 637 *redundant*; cast-off, outcast 607 *rejected*; orphaned, widowed.

42. Decrement: thing deducted – N. *decrement*, deduction, depreciation, cut 37 *diminution*; allowance; remission; rebate 810 *discount*; refund, loss, forfeit 963 *penalty*; leakage 298 *outflow*; shrinkage 204 *shortening*; spoilage, wastage, consumption 634 *waste*; rakeoff 786 *taking*; toll 809 *tax*.

43. Mixture – N. *mixture*, mingling, mixing, stirring; blending, harmonization 45 *union*; admixture 38 *addition*; immixture 303 *insertion*; interlarding 231 *inter-*

jacency; interweaving, interlacing 222 *crossing*; amalgamation, integration 50 *combination*; merger 706 *association*; syncretism, eclecticism; fusion, infusion, suffusion, instillation, impregnation 341 *moistening*; adulteration 655 *impairment*; infiltration, permeation 297 *ingress*; interbreeding, miscegenation, intermarriage; cross-fertilization, hybridism, hybridization, mongrelism; miscibility 337 *liquefaction*; crucible, melting pot; mixer 315 *rotator*.

tincture, admixture; ingredient 58 *component*; strain, streak; sprinkling, infusion; drop, dash 33 *small quantity*; smack, hint, flavour, taste; seasoning, spice 389 *condiment*; stain, dye 425 *hue*.

a mixture, mélange; blend, harmony 710 *concord*; composition 331 *structure*; amalgam, alloy, compound, concoction 50 *combination*; stew, hash, ragout, olla podrida, salmagundi 301 *dish*; cocktail, brew, witches' b.

medley, heterogeneity, complexity, variety 17 *nonuniformity*, 82 *multiformity*; motley, patchwork, mosaic 437 *variegation*; assortment, miscellany, miscellanea, mixed bag, job lot, ragbag, lucky dip; farrago, gallimaufry, hotchpotch, mishmash, potpourri; jumble, conglomeration 74 *accumulation*; 61 *confusion*; phantasmagoria, kaleidoscope; omnium gatherum, motley crew; all sorts, odds and ends, bits and pieces, paraphernalia, oddments.

hybrid, cross, cross-breed, mongrel; half-blood, half-breed, half-caste; mestizo; quadroon, octaroon.

Adj. *mixed*, in the melting pot, stirred; well-integrated, blended, harmonized; alloyed 50 *combined*; tempered, qualified; adulterated, watered down 163 *weakened*; amalgamated 45 *joined*; composite, half-and-half, fifty-fifty; complex, involved, intricate; tangled, confused, jumbled; unsorted, out of order 61 *orderless*; heterogeneous 17 *nonuniform*; kaleidoscopic, phantasmagoric 82 *multiform*; patchy, dappled, motley 437 *variegated*; miscellaneous, random 464 *indiscriminate*; miscible, soluble 337 *liquefied*; pervasive, spreading 653 *infectious*; hy-

brid, mongrel; cross-bred, crossed; half-blooded, half-caste; interbred; intermixed, multiracial.

Vb. *mix*, make a mixture, mix up, stir, shake; shuffle, scramble 63 *jumble*; knead, pound 332 *pulverize*; brew, compound 56 *compose*; fuse, alloy, merge, amalgamate 45 *join*; interfuse, blend 50 *combine*; mingle, intermingle, commingle, intersperse 437 *variegate*; immix, intermix, interlard, interleave 303 *insert*; intertwine 222 *weave*; tinge, dye 425 *colour*; imbue, instil, impregnate 303 *infuse*; besprinkle 341 *moisten*; adulterate 163 *weaken*; temper, doctor, tamper with 143 *modify*; season, spice, fortify, lace, spike; hybridize, mongrelize, cross, cross-fertilize, cross-breed 167 *generate*.

be mixed, be entangled with, be involved, be mixed up in; pervade, permeate, run through 297 *infiltrate*; infect, contaminate; stain 425 *colour*; intermarry, interbreed.

44. Simpleness: freedom from mixture – N. *simpleness*, homogeneity 16 *uniformity*; purity 648 *cleanness*; oneness 88 *unity*; absoluteness, sheerness 1 *essence*; indivisibility, insolubility, asexuality; lack of complication, simplicity, plainness, freedom from mixture, not a trace of, not a hint of 190 *absence*; simplification, elimination.

Adj. *simple*, homogeneous, monolithic, all of a piece 16 *uniform*; sheer, mere, utter, nothing but; undifferentiated, asexual; single, unified 88 *one*; elemental, indivisible, entire 52 *whole*; primary, irreducible 5 *intrinsic*; elementary, uncomplicated, unravelled, disentangled, simplified; direct, plain.

unmixed, pure and simple, without alloy; clear, pure, unpolluted, clarified, purified 648 *clean*; purebred, thoroughbred; free from, exempt f.; unblemished, untarnished 646 *perfect*; unmingled, unalloyed, uncompounded, uncombined; undiluted, unadulterated, neat 162 *strong*; unqualified, unmodified; unfortified; unflavoured, untinged with.

Vb. *simplify*, render simple 16 *make*

uniform; narrow down, break d., factorize, reduce 51 *decompose*; disentangle, unscramble 62 *unravel*; unify, make one.

eliminate, sift 62 *class*; winnow, sieve, pan; purge 648 *purify*; clear, clarify, cleanse, distil; get rid of, weed out 57 *exclude*; expel 300 *eject*.

45. Union – **N.** *union*, junction, coming together, conjunction 293 *convergence*; clash 279 *collision*; contact 202 *contiguity*; concourse 74 *assembly*; confluence 76 *focus*; concrescence, coalescence, fusion, merger 43 *mixture*; unification 50 *combination*; agglutination 48 *coherence*; concretion, coagulation 324 *condensation*; coalition 706 *association*; connection, linkage, tieup, hookup, linkup 47 *bond*; syngamy, wedlock 894 *marriage*; interconnection, cross-connection 222 *crossing*; intercommunication, intercourse 882 *sociability*; go-between 231 *intermediary*.

coition, coitus, copulation, sexual intercourse, sex, intimacy, carnal knowledge; mating, coupling 167 *propagation*; union 894 *marriage*; enjoyment, consummation; violation 951 *rape*.

joint, joining, juncture, commissure; crease 261 *fold*; suture, seam, stitching 47 *bond*; weld, splice, mitre, dovetail, dovetail and mortise joint; ball and socket j.; hasp, latch, catch, hinge; ginglymus 247 *angularity*; node; junction, intersection, crossroads 222 *crossing*.

Adj. *joined*, united etc. vb.; conjoint 775 *sharing*; conjunct, joint; incorporated, merged 706 *cooperative*, 708 *corporate*; wedded 894 *married*; hand in hand, arm in arm; coalescent 48 *cohesive*; composite 50 *combined*; put together 74 *assembled*; articulated, jointed 331 *structural*; stitched up.

conjunctive, copulative, adhesive 48 *cohesive*; coincident 181 *concurrent*; copulatory, coital, venereal.

firm, close, fast, secure 153 *fixed*; solid, set 324 *dense*; cemented 48 *cohesive*; close-set, crowded, tight, wedged, jammed, stuck; inextricable, inseparable, immovable, unshakable; packed, jam-p. 54 *full*.

Vb. *join*, conjoin, couple, yoke, hyphenate, harness together; pair, match 18 *liken*, 462 *compare*, 894 *marry*; bracket 28 *equalize*; assemble, unite 50 *combine*; collect, gather 74 *bring together*; add to 38 *add*; ally, twin (town); merge 43 *mix*; incorporate, unify; include 78 *comprise*; grip, grapple 778 *retain*; hinge, articulate, dovetail, mortise, mitre, rabbet; interlock, engage; wedge, jam 303 *insert*; solder, fuse 48 *agglutinate*; draw together, lace, knit, sew, stitch; pin, buckle; infibulate; do up, fasten 264 *close*; close a gap, seal up; mend, heal over 656 *repair*.

connect, attach, annex (**see** *affix*); staple, clip, pin together; thread t., string t., rope t., link t., chain t., catenate; contact 378 *touch*; make contact, plug in, earth, interconnect, inosculate, open into; link, bridge, span, straddle, bestride 305 *pass*; communicate, intercommunicate; put through to, hook up with, tie up w. 9 *relate*.

affix, attach, fix, fasten 38 *add*; leash, bridle; pin on, hang on, hook on, stick on 48 *agglutinate*; implant 303 *insert*; impact, drive in 279 *strike*; wedge, jam; screw, nail, rivet, bolt, clamp, clinch.

tie, knot, hitch, lash, belay; knit, sew, stitch, tack, baste; twine, twist, lace 222 *weave*; truss, rope, strap; tether, picket, moor; shackle 747 *fetter*; bind, splice, gird, bandage, swathe, swaddle, wrap; enfold, grip 235 *enclose*, 778 *retain*.

unite with, join, meet 293 *converge*; hold tight, stick to 48 *cohere*; mesh, interlock, engage; grapple, clinch; embrace, entwine; associate with, league together 708 *join a party*; marry, get hitched 894 *wed*; live with, cohabit; go to bed with, lie w., sleep w., make love, have sex with; have intercourse; consummate a marriage; know, enjoy, possess, have, do; tumble; knock off, have it off *or* away with; take by force 951 *debauch*; copulate, couple, mate, pair 167 *generate*; mount, tup, cover, serve; cross with, breed w.

46. Disunion – **N.** *disunion*, disjunction, being separated; disconnection, disconnectedness, incoherence, break 72 *discontinuity*; separability 49 *non-coherence*; diffusion 75 *dispersion*; breakup, disintegration, dissolution, decay 51 *decomposition*; dissociation, disengagement 621 *relinquishment*; surrender 779 *nonretention*; moving apart 294 *divergence*; split, schism (**see** *separation*); detachment, isolation, quarantine 883 *seclusion*; zone, compartment; insularity 620 *avoidance*; lack of unity 709 *dissension*; immiscibility, separateness; isolationism, separatism 80 *particularism*; no connection 10 *unrelatedness*; distance apart 199 *farness*; dichotomy 15 *difference*; interval, space, opening; cleavage, slit 201 *gap*.

separation, severance, parting 896 *divorce*; unravelling, laddering; loosing, freeing 746 *liberation*; segregation, apartheid 57 *exclusion*; expulsion 300 *ejection*; selection 605 *choice*; expropriation 786 *taking*; detachment, withdrawal, removal, transfer 188 *displacement*; dispersal 75 *dispersion*; dissolution 51 *decomposition*; dissection, analysis, breakdown; fragmentation 165 *destruction*; fission 160 *nucleonics*; rupture, fracture 330 *brittleness*; dividing line, caesura 231 *partition*.

scission, section, cleavage, cutting, tearing; division 92 *bisection*; subdivision, segmentation; partition 783 *apportionment*; abscission, cutting off 204 *shortening*, 37 *diminution*; cutting away, resection, circumcision; cutting open, incision 658 *surgery*; dissection; rending, clawing, laceration; tearing off, avulsion.

Adj. *disunited*, disjoined, divorced; separated, disconnected, interrupted 72 *discontinuous*; divided, subdivided, partitioned, bipartite, multi-partite; in pieces, quartered, dismembered; severed, cut; torn, rent, riven, cleft, cloven; digitate 201 *spaced*; radiating, divergent 282 *deviating*; scattered, dispersed, fugitive 75 *unassembled*; untied, loosened, loose 746 *liberated*.

separate, apart, asunder; adrift, unfastened, unattached; distinct, discrete, differentiated, separable, distinguishable 15 *different*; excepted 57 *excluded*; hived off, abstracted 304 *extracted*; unassimilable 49 *nonadhesive*; alien 59 *extraneous*; external 6 *extrinsic*; insular, self-sufficient, isolated 88 *alone*, 883 *friendless*; shunned, boycotted 620 *avoiding*; cast-off 607 *rejected*; set apart 605 *chosen*; antipathetic 14 *contrary*; disjunctive, separative; dichotomous.

severable, separable, detachable; partible, divisible, fissionable, fissile, scissile; dissoluble, dissolvable; biodegradable 51 *decomposable*.

Vb. *separate*, stand apart, not mix 620 *avoid*; go 296 *depart*; go different ways, radiate 294 *diverge*; part, part company, cut adrift, cut loose, divorce; get loose 667 *escape*; break away 746 *achieve liberty*; cast off, let go 779 *not retain*; leave, quit, 621 *relinquish*; scatter, break up 75 *disperse*; spring apart 280 *recoil*; come apart, fall a., break, come to bits, disintegrate 51 *decompose*; come undone, unravel, ladder, run; fall off 49 *come unstuck*; split, crack 263 *open*.

disunite, disjoin, dissociate, divorce; part, separate, sunder, sever, dissever; uncouple, unhitch, disconnect, unplug; disengage, dislocate; detach, unseat, dismount 49 *unstick*; remove 39 *subtract*, 272 *transfer*; peel 229 *uncover*; unfasten, undo, unbutton, unhook, unzip, unclasp 263 *open*; untie, cut the knot 62 *unravel*; unstitch, unpick; loosen, unbind, unloose, loose 746 *liberate*; expel 300 *eject*; dispel, scatter, break up, disband, demobilize 75 *disperse*; disintegrate, break down 51 *decompose*, 332 *pulverize*.

set apart, put aside 666 *preserve*; mark out, distinguish 15 *differentiate*; single out 605 *select*; leave out 57 *exclude*; black, blacklist 757 *prohibit*; insulate, isolate, cut off 235 *enclose*; compartmentalize 232 *circumscribe*; segregate, sequester, quarantine, maroon 883 *seclude*; keep apart, drive a wedge between, estrange, alienate, set against 881 *make enemies*.

sunder (**see** *disunite*); divide, keep apart; subdivide, fragment, fractionate, segment, sectionalize, fractionalize, reduce, factorize, analyse; dissect, anatomize 51 *decompose*; halve 92 *bisect*;

divide up, split, partition 783 *apportion*;
dismember, quarter (see *cut*); behead, decapitate, amputate, take apart, take to
pieces, cannibalize, dismantle, break up;
force apart, wedge a. 263 *open*; cleave,
slit, split, rive.

cut, hew, hack, slash, gash 655 *wound*;
prick, stab, knife 263 *pierce*; cut through,
cleave, saw, chop; cut open, slit 263 *open*;
cut into, incise, engrave; cut to the bone,
carve, slice; pare, whittle, chisel, chip,
trim, bevel, skive; clip, snick, snip; shave
204 *shorten*; cut down, fell, scythe, mow;
cut off, lop, prune, dock, curtail (see *sunder*); cut up, chop up, dice, shred, mince,
make mincemeat of; bite, scratch, scarify,
score 262 *groove*; nick 260 *notch*.

rend, rive (see *sunder*); tear, scratch,
claw; gnaw, fret, fray, make ragged; rip,
slash, slit (see *cut*); lacerate, dismember;
tear limb from limb, tear to pieces, tear to
shreds 165 *destroy*; pluck to pieces;
mince, grind, crunch, scrunch 301 *chew*,
332 *pulverize*; burst, explode, blow up,
blow to pieces.

break, fracture, rupture, bust; split,
burst, explode; smash, shatter, splinter
165 *demolish*; fragment, crumble 332
pulverize; disintegrate, cave in 51 *decompose*; break up, dismantle (see *sunder*);
chip, crack, damage 655 *impair*; buckle,
warp 246 *distort*; snap, knap; cleave, force
apart 263 *open*.

Adv. *separately*, severally, piecemeal;
discontinuously, unconnectedly.

apart, asunder, adrift; limb from limb.

47. Bond: connecting medium – N. *bond*,
connecting medium, coupling, chain,
shackle, fetter, tie, band, hoop, yoke;
nexus, connection, link, liaison 9 *relation*;
junction, hinge 45 *joint*; connective, copula; hyphen 547 *punctuation*; cement (see
adhesive); bondstone, binder; tie-beam
218 *beam*; interconnection 624 *access*;
span, arch 624 *bridge*; lifeline; umbilical
cord.

cable, line, guy, hawser, painter, moor-
ings; towline, towrope, rope, cord, whipcord 208 *fibre*; chain, wire.

tackling, tackle, cordage; rig, rigging,
shroud, ratline; sheets, guy, stay; halyard,
bowline, lanyard; harness.

ligature, ligament, tendon, muscle; tendril, withy, osier, bast, bass, raffia 208
fibre; lashing, binding; string, cord,
thread, tape, band, ribbon; bandage 228
belt, 198 *compressor*; drawstring, thong,
lace, tie, braid, plait 222 *network*; knot,
hitch, bend; slip knot, granny k., reef k.;
half hitch, clove h.; sheepshank, Turk's
head; true-love knot, Gordian k.

fastening 45 *joining together*; fastener,
snap f., press-stud, popper, zip fastener,
zip; drawstring, ripcord; stitch, basting;
button, buttonhole, eyelet, loop, frog;
hook and eye; stud, cufflink; suspender,
braces; tiepin, brooch 844 *jewellery*; hairpin, hatpin; drawing pin, safety p.; peg,
dowel, nail, tack, tintack 256 *sharp point*;
staple, clamp, brace 778 *nippers*; nut,
bolt, screw, rivet; buckle, clasp, hasp,
hinge 45 *joint*; catch, latch, bolt; lock 264
closure; padlock, handcuffs 748 *fetter*;
cleat; bollard.

halter, collar, noose; tether, lead, leash,
jess, reins; lasso, lariat.

adhesive, glue, lime, birdlime, gum;
fixative, lacquer; solder; paste, size,
cement, putty, mortar 226 *facing*; wafer,
sealing wax; sticker, stamp, adhesive tape
48 *coherence*.

48. Coherence – N. *coherence*, cohesion,
cohesiveness; tenaciousness 778 *retention*;
adhesion, adhesiveness; stickiness 354
viscidity; cementation, agglutination, con-
glutination 45 *union*; compaction, conglomeration, set 324 *condensation*; inseparability 88 *unity*; phalanx, serried
ranks, unbroken front; monolith, ag-
glomerate 324 *solid body*; leech, limpet;
gum, toffee 47 *adhesive*.

Adj. *cohesive*, coherent, adhesive,
adherent; clinging, tenacious; indigestible
329 *tough*; sticky, tacky 354 *viscid*; compact, well-knit, solid 324 *dense*; shoulder
to shoulder, phalanxed, serried; monolithic 16 *uniform*; united, infrangible, indivisible, inseparable, inextricable; close,
tight, skin-tight, figure-hugging, clinging.

Vb. *cohere*, grow together 50 *combine*;

hold, stick close, hold fast; bunch, close the ranks, stand shoulder to shoulder, rally 74 *congregate*; grip, take hold of 778 *retain*; hug, clasp, embrace, twine round; close with, clinch; fit, mould, adhere, cling, stick; cleave to, come off on, rub off on; cling like a shadow, cling like ivy; solidify, freeze 324 *be dense*.

agglutinate, glue, gum, paste, cement, weld, braze 45 *join*; stick to, affix 38 *add*.

49. Noncoherence – N. *noncoherence*, noncombination 51 *decomposition*: scattering 75 *dispersion*; separability, immiscibility; looseness, bagginess; loosening, nonadhesion 46 *separation*; runniness 335 *fluidity*; frangibility, friability, rope of sand 330 *brittleness*.

Adj. *nonadhesive*, nonadhering, not sticky, dry; detached 46 *separate*; noncohesive, incoherent; slippery, loose, like grains of sand; unconfined, free, slack, baggy, loose-fitting, floppy, flapping, flying, streaming; liquid, runny 335 *fluid*; pendulous, dangling 217 *hanging*; uncombined 51 *decomposed*; immiscible, unassimilated 59 *extraneous*.

Vb. *unstick*, peel off; detach, unpin, unfasten; free, loosen, slacken 46 *disunite*; shake off, shed, slough 229 *doff*.

come unstuck, peel off, melt, thaw, run; totter, slip 309 *tumble*; dangle, flap 217 *hang*; rattle, shake.

50. Combination – N. *combination*, composition 45 *joining together*; coalescence 45 *union*; fusion, blending, conflation, synthesis 43 *mixture*; amalgamation, assimilation 299 *reception*; unification, integration, centralization 88 *unity*; incorporation, embodiment; synchronization 706 *cooperation*; coagency 181 *concurrence*; marriage, union, alliance 706 *association*; chorus 24 *agreement*; harmony, orchestration 710 *concord*; aggregation 74 *assemblage*; synopsis 592 *compendium*.

compound, blend, composite 43 *a mixture*; mosaic, jigsaw, collage 56 *composition*.

Adj. *combined* 88 *one*; integrated, centralized; incorporate, embodied; inbred 5 *intrinsic*; fused, impregnated 43 *mixed*; blended, harmonized 24 *adjusted*; connected 45 *joined*; congregated 74 *assembled*; coalescent, coagent 181 *concurrent*.

Vb. *combine*, put together, fit t.; make up 56 *compose*; intertwine 222 *weave*; harmonize 24 *accord*; bind, tie 45 *join*; unite, unify, centralize; incorporate, embody, integrate, absorb, assimilate; merge, amalgamate, pool; blend, fuse 43 *mix*; impregnate 303 *infuse*; lump together 38 *add*; group, regroup, rally 74 *bring together*; band together, league with 706 *cooperate*; coalesce, grow together, run t.; have an affinity, combine with.

51. Decomposition – N. *decomposition* 46 *disunion*; division, partition, compartmentation 46 *separation*; dissection, dismemberment; anatomization, analysis, breakdown; factorization, simplification; resolution, electrolysis; atomization; dissolution 337 *liquefaction*; fission 160 *nucleonics*; decentralization, devolution, delegation; regionalism; collapse, breakup, disintegration, entropy 165 *destruction*; chaos 17 *nonuniformity*.

decay 655 *dilapidation*; erosion, wear and tear 37 *diminution*; disintegration 361 *death*; corruption, mouldering, rotting putrefaction, mortification, necrosis, gangrene, caries 649 *uncleanness*; rot, rust, mould 659 *blight*; carrion 363 *corpse*.

Adj. *decomposed* resolved, reduced, disintegrated, chaotic 46 *disunited*; corrupted, mouldering 655 *dilapidated*; putrid, gangrenous, rotten, bad, off.

decomposable, disposable, biodegradable, compostable, recyclable 656 *restored*.

Vb. *decompose*, unscramble; resolve, reduce, factorize 44 *simplify*; separate out, parse, dissect; break down, analyse, take to pieces 46 *sunder*; electrolyse, catalyse; split, fission 46 *disunite*; break up, atomize 165 *demolish*; decentralize, regionalize, dissolve, melt 337 *liquefy*; erode 37 *abate*; rot, rust, moulder, decay, crumble, perish 655 *deteriorate*; corrupt, putrefy 649 *be unclean*; disintegrate, go to pieces 165 *be destroyed*.

52. Whole. Principal part – N. *whole*, wholeness, fullness 54 *completeness*; integrity 88 *unity*; integer, entity 88 *unit*; entirety, ensemble, corpus, complex, four corners of; totality, sum; holism, universalization 79 *generality*; comprehensiveness, inclusiveness; collectivity, system, world, cosmos 321 *universe*; panorama, synopsis.

all, one and all, the quick and the dead, everyone 79 *everyman*; all the world 74 *crowd*; the whole, total, aggregate, gross amount, sum, sum total; length and breadth, rough with the smooth; lock, stock and barrel; unit, family, set; ensemble, outfit, pack; lot, whole 1., the whole kit and caboodle, the whole bang shoot, the works.

chief part, best part, principal p. 638 *chief thing*; ninety-nine per cent, bulk, mass, substance 32 *great quantity*; tissue, staple, stuff; lion's share, biggest slice of the cake; gist, sum and substance, the long and the short of it; almost all, everything but the kitchen sink; majority 104 *greater number*.

Adj. *whole*, total, universal, holistic; integral 44 *unmixed*; entire, sound 646 *perfect*; gross, full 54 *complete*; integrated 88 *one*; in one piece, seamless.

intact, untouched, unspoiled, virgin 126 *new*; undivided, undiminished, unbroken, unimpaired, without a scratch 646 *undamaged*; uncut, unabridged.

indivisible, impartible, indissoluble; indiscerptible 45 *joined*; monolithic 16 *uniform*.

comprehensive, omnibus, all-embracing, all-encompassing, full-length 78 *inclusive*; wholesale, sweeping 32 *extensive*; wide-spread, epidemic 79 *general*; international, world-wide, cosmic 79 *universal*, 189 *ubiquitous*.

Adv. *wholly*; body and soul, as a whole; entirely, in toto 54 *completely*; one hundred per cent.

on the whole, by and large, altogether, all in all, all things considered, in the long run; substantially, virtually, to all intents and purposes, in effect; as good as; in the main 32 *greatly*.

53. Part – N. *part*, portion; proportion, majority 32 *main part*, 104 *greater number*; minority 105 *fewness*, 33 *small quantity*; fraction, half, moiety, percentage; balance 41 *remainder*; quota, contingent; dividend, share 783 *portion*; item, detail, ingredient, element 58 *component*; leg, lap, round; excerpt, extract 605 *choice*; segment, sector, section 46 *scission*; instalment, advance 804 *payment*; sample 83 *example*; fragment (**see** *piece*); limb, member, organ, appendage 40 *adjunct*.

subdivision, segment, sector, section 46 *scission*; division, compartment; subgroup 74 *group*; classification 62 *arrangement*; ward 184 *district*; issue, instalment 589 *reading matter*.

branch, ramification, offshoot 40 *adjunct*; bough, limb, spur, shoot, scion, sucker, sprig 366 *foliage*.

piece, stump 41 *remainder*; limb, section (**see** *part*); patch, insertion, strip, swatch; fragment 55 *incompleteness*; bit, scrap, shred 33 *small thing*; morsel, crust, crumb 33 *small quantity*; splinter, sliver, chip, snip, snippet; cut, wedge, finger, slice, rasher; hunk, chunk, wad, wodge, slab 195 *bulk*; clod, divot 344 *soil*; shard, potsherd 207 *lamina*; dollop 783 *portion*; bits and pieces, flotsam and jetsam 43 *medley*; rubble, debris 41 *leavings*, 641 *rubbish*; rags, tatters 801 *poverty*; piece of land, parcel, plot.

Adj. *fragmentary*, broken, brashy, crumbly 330 *brittle*; in bits, in pieces 46 *disunited*; not whole 647 *imperfect*; partial, bitty, scrappy 636 *insufficient*; half-finished 55 *unfinished*; segmental, divided, multifid; departmentalized, compartmentalized 46 *separate*; shredded, wispy 33 *small*.

Adv. *piecemeal*, limb from limb; by instalments, by snatches, by inches, in dribs and drabs; bit by bit, inch by inch, foot by foot, drop by drop, a little at a time, by degrees; in detail, in lots.

54. Completeness – N. *completeness*, nothing lacking, nothing to add 52 *whole*; solidarity, integrality 88 *unity*; self-sufficiency 635 *sufficiency*; entirety, totality 52 *all*; universality, comprehensiveness 79 *generality*; the ideal 646 *perfection*; ne plus ultra 236 *limit*; peak, culmination, crown 213 *summit*; finish 69 *end*; last touch 725 *completion*; fulfilment, consummation 69 *finality*; whole hog; nothing less than, the utmost.

plenitude, fullness, amplitude, capacity, maximum, one's fill, saturation 635 *sufficiency*; saturation point 863 *satiety*; completion, filling, replenishment, refill; brimming, swamping, drowning 637 *redundance*; full house, full complement, full measure, brimmer, bumper; bellyful, skinful, repletion; full size, full length; complement, supplement 31 *compensation*.

Adj. *complete*, plenary, full; utter, total; integral 52 *whole*; entire, with all its parts, with nothing missing 52 *intact*, 646 *perfect*; full-blown, full-grown, full-fledged 669 *matured*; unbroken, undivided; self-contained, fully furnished 635 *sufficient*; comprehensive, full-scale 78 *inclusive*; exhaustive, detailed 570 *diffuse*; absolute, extreme, radical; thorough, thoroughgoing, whole-hogging, sweeping, wholesale 32 *consummate*; unmitigated, downright, plumb, plain 44 *unmixed*; crowning, completing, culminating, complementary 725 *completive*, 38 *additional*; unqualified 744 *unconditional*.

full, replete; replenished, topped up; well-filled, well-lined, bulging; brimful, level with, flush; overfull, overflowing, running over, slopping, saturated, oozing, leaking 637 *redundant*; coming out at the ears, bursting at the seams; crop-full, gorged, fit to burst, full to bursting 863 *sated*; chock-a-block, not an inch to spare; crammed, stuffed, jam-packed, packed like sardines 45 *firm*; laden, heavy-1., fraught, full to the hatches; standing room only; overrun, crawling with, lousy w., stiff w.; full of, rolling in; dripping with; inexhaustible 146 *unceasing*.

Vb. *be complete*, make a whole; touch perfection, have everything; culminate, come to a head 725 *climax*; come to a close 69 *end*; want nothing; reach maturity 669 *mature*; be filled, fill, brim, hold no more, run over, slop o., overflow 637 *superabound*; gorge 947 *gluttonize*.

make complete, complete, complement, integrate 45 *join*; make whole 656 *restore*; build up, piece together 56 *compose*; eke out, supplement, supply, fill a gap 38 *add*; make good 31 *compensate*; do thoroughly, leave nothing to add 725 *carry through*; overfulfil 637 *be superfluous*; put the finishing touch, round off 69 *terminate*.

fill, charge, fill up; saturate, overfill, swamp, drown, top up, replenish 633 *provide*; satisfy 635 *suffice*, 863 *sate*; fill to capacity, cram, pack, stuff; pack in, pile in, squeeze in, ram in, jam in 303 *insert*; load, ram down 187 *stow*; occupy 226 *cover*; extend to 183 *extend*; overrun 189 *pervade*; fit tight; fill in 38 *add*.

Adv. *completely*, fully, wholly, totally, entirely, utterly 32 *greatly*; all told, in all 52 *on the whole*; on all counts, in all respects, in every way; quite, altogether; outright, downright; to the heart, to the core, through and through; thoroughly, clean, stark, hollow; to the top of one's bent, to the full; out and out, heart and soul, up to the hilt, hook, line and sinker; root and branch; the last man, to the last breath; every whit, every inch; in full; as . . . as can be; to capacity.

throughout, from first to last, from beginning to end, the length and breadth of, from Land's End to John o' Groats 183 *widely*; from north and south and east and west; from top to bottom, from head to foot, to the bitter end.

55. Incompleteness – **N.** *incompleteness*, defectiveness 647 *imperfection*; unreadiness 670 *nonpreparation*; underdevelopment, immaturity 670 *undevelopment*; sketch, rough draft 623 *plan*; half measures 726 *noncompletion*; perfunctoriness, superficiality 4 *insubstantiality*, 458 *negligence*; nonfulfilment, deficiency 307 *shortfall*, 636 *insufficiency*; mutilation, impairment 655 *deterioration*; omission, break, gap 72 *discontinuity*; semi-, half, quarter 53 *piece*; instalment 53 *part*.

deficit, part wanting, screw loose 647

defect; shortfall, want, lack 627 *require-ment*.

Adj. *incomplete*, inadequate, defective 307 *deficient*; scant, unsatisfactory 636 *insufficient*; like Hamlet without the Prince 641 *useless*; lacking, short of 627 *demanding*; maimed, lame, marred, mutilated 163 *crippled*; without, -less; shortened 204 *short*; flawed 647 *imperfect*; half, semi-, partial 53 *fragmentary*; left unfinished, neglected 726 *uncompleted*; not ready 670 *unprepared*; undeveloped, underdeveloped 670 *immature*; raw, crude, roughhewn 244 *amorphous*; sketchy, scrappy, bitty, thin 4 *insubstantial*; half-hearted, half-done, undone 458 *neglected*; left in the air, left hanging; omitted, missing, lost 190 *absent*; interrupted 72 *discontinuous*.

unfinished, in progress, in hand, going on; in embryo, begun 68 *beginning*; in preparation, on the stocks.

56. Composition – N. *composition*, constitution, make-up; make, formation, build 331 *structure*; organization 62 *arrangement*; character, syndrome 5 *temperament*; embodiment, incorporation 78 *inclusion*; compound 43 *mixture*, 50 *combination*; artistic composition 412 *music*; 551 *art*; 553 *painting*; 554 *sculpture*; architecture 164 *edifice*; authorship 586 *writing*, 593 *poetry*; dramatic art 594 *drama*; setting-up, printing 587 *print*; compilation 74 *assemblage*; work, construction 164 *production*; choreography 594 *ballet*; orchestration 412 *musical piece*; pattern, design 12 *correlation*.

Vb. *constitute*, compose, form, make; make up, build up to; belong to, go to the making of, enter into.

compose, compound 43 *mix*, 50 *combine*; set in order 62 *arrange*; synthesize, put together 45 *join*; compile, assemble 74 *bring together*; compose, set up 587 *print*; draft, draw up 586 *write*; orchestrate, score 413 *compose music*; draw 553 *paint*; construct, make, fabricate 164 *produce*; pattern, design.

57. Exclusion – N. *exclusion*, exclusiveness, monopoly, closed shop, noninclu-sion, exception; leaving out, omission 607 *rejection*; non-admission, no entry; closed door, lockout; picket line; embargo, bar 757 *prohibition*; ostracism, boycott 620 *avoidance*; segregation, quarantine, caste system, colour bar, apartheid 883 *seclusion*, 481 *prejudice*; expulsion, eviction; dismissal, suspension, excommunication; deportation, exile, expatriation 188 *displacement*; dam, coffer d., barricade, Iron Curtain 235 *barrier*, 713 *defence*; ghetto, outer darkness 223 *exteriority*.

Adj. *excluding*, exclusive, exemptive; restrictive, cliquish 708 *sectional*; interdictory, prohibitive 757 *prohibiting*; preclusive, preemptive.

excluded, etc. vb.; not included, not admitted; peripheral; included out, counted o.; not allowed, banned 757 *prohibited*; disbarred, struck off 550 *obliterated*; shut out 607 *rejected*; inadmissible, beyond the pale 470 *impossible*, 59 *extraneous*.

Vb. *exclude*, preclude; preempt, forestall 64 *come before*; keep out, warn off 747 *restrain*; blackball, deny entry, shut out, debar, shut the door on 607 *reject*; bar, ban, taboo, black, disallow 757 *prohibit*; ostracize, cold-shoulder, boycott, send to Coventry 620 *avoid*, 883 *make unwelcome*; not include, leave out, count o.; exempt, except, make an exception; omit, miss out, pass over, disregard 458 *neglect*; put aside, relegate 46 *set apart*; strike out, disbar, strike off, remove, disqualify 188 *displace*, 963 *punish*; rule out, draw the line; wall off, curtain off, quarantine; excommunicate, segregate 883 *seclude*; extradite, exile, outlaw 300 *eject*; weed, sort out 44 *eliminate*; censor 648 *purify*; deny 760 *refuse*; abandon 779 *not retain*.

Adv. *exclusive of*, excepting, barring, bar, not counting, except, save; apart from.

58. Component – N. *component*, integral part, feature, element, item; unit, module; piece, bit, segment; constituent, part and parcel 53 *part*; factor, leaven 178 *influence*; one of, member 686 *personnel*; ingredient 193 *contents*, 43 *tincture*; works

224 *interiority*; nuts and bolts 630 *machine*; spare part 40 *extra*; set, outfit 88 *unit*.

Adj. *component*, constituent, composing; belonging, proper, inherent 5 *intrinsic*; built-in, appurtenant 45 *joined*; admitted, part of, one of, on the staff; involved 43 *mixed*.

59. Extraneousness – N. *extraneousness*, foreignness 6 *extrinsicality*, 223 *exteriority*; foreign parts 199 *farness*; foreign body, accretion 38 *addition*; alien element 84 *nonconformity*; exotica.

foreigner 268 *traveller*; alien, stranger, unco, emmet, Southerner, Northerner, Easterner, Westerner; Martian, Venusian, little green men; Celtic fringe; Sassenach, pommie, limey; Yank, Yankee, Aussie, Kiwi; gringo, paleface; colonial, Creole 191 *settler*; resident alien, expatriate; migrant, emigrant, émigré, exile; immigrant, declarant 297 *incomer*; refugee 268 *wanderer*.

intruder, interloper, trespasser, cuckoo in the nest, squatter; uninvited guest, gatecrasher, stowaway; outsider 126 *upstart*; not one of us, stranger in our midst; new face 297 *incomer*; invader 712 *attacker*.

Adj. *extraneous*, ulterior, outside 223 *exterior*, 6 *extrinsic*; ultramundane, extragalactic 199 *distant*; not indigenous, imported, foreign, alien, outlandish, barbarian; overseas, ultramarine, transatlantic, continental; unearthly, extraterrestrial; exotic, hothouse; nomad, wandering 267 *travelling*; unassimilated, unintegrated 46 *separate*; immigrant 297 *incoming*; intrusive, interloping, trespassing; infringing 712 *attacking*; exceptional 84 *unusual*; un-British, un-American 15 *different*; not of this world, supernatural 983 *magical*; inadmissible 57 *excluded*.

Adv. *abroad*, in foreign parts *or* lands; overseas; from outer space.

Section 4: Order

60. Order – N. *order*, state of order, orderliness, tidiness, neatness; propor-

tion, harmony 245 *symmetry*; economy, system, method, methodicalness, methodology, systematization; fixed order, pattern, rule 81 *regularity*, 16 *uniformity*; routine 610 *habit*; strict order, discipline, due order, hierarchy, gradation, subordination, position 73 *serial place*; course, even tenor, progression, series 71 *continuity*; logical order, serial o., alphabetical o. 65 *sequence*, 12 *correlation*; organization, putting in order, disposition, array 62 *arrangement*, 56 *composition*; a place for everything.

Adj. *orderly*, harmonious 710 *concordant*, 245 *symmetrical*; well-behaved, decorous 848 *well-bred*; well-drilled, disciplined 739 *obedient*; well-regulated, under control 81 *regular*; ordered, classified, schematic 62 *arranged*; methodical, systematic, businesslike; strict, invariable 16 *uniform*; routine, steady 610 *habitual*; correct, shipshape, Bristol fashion, trim, neat, tidy 648 *clean*; in good trim, well-kept, uncluttered, in apple-pie order, in its proper place 62 *arranged*; unruffled, unrumpled 258 *smooth*; direct 249 *straight*; clear, lucid 516 *intelligible*.

Vb. *be in order*, harmonize, synchronize 24 *accord*; fall in, range oneself, draw up, line up; take one's place, station oneself, take up one's position; keep one's place; follow routine 610 *be wont*.

Adv. *in order*, strictly, just so, by the book, to rule; in turn, seriatim; in orderly fashion, methodically, systematically, schematically; all correct, OK.

61. Disorder – N. *disorder*, nonarrangement, nonclassification; incoordination, muddle, no system (**see** *confusion*); chaos, mayhem 734 *anarchy*; irregularity, anomalousness 17 *nonuniformity*; disharmony, disaccord 25 *disagreement*; disorderliness, unruliness, no discipline 738 *disobedience*; violent behaviour (**see** *turmoil*); untidiness, sluttishness, slovenliness 649 *uncleanness*; disarray, dishevelment 63 *derangement*; dissolution, scattering 75 *dispersion*, 51 *decomposition*; upheaval, convulsion 149 *revolution*, 165 *havoc*.

confusion, welter, jumble, shambles, mix-up, embroilment, imbroglio 43 *mixture*; wilderness, jungle; chaos, fortuitous concourse of atoms; swarm, seething mass, scramble 74 *crowd*; muddle, litter, clutter 641 *rubbish*; farrago, mess, mish-mash, hash, hotchpotch 43 *medley*; Babel, bedlam (see *turmoil*).

complexity, complication, snarl-up 700 *difficulty*; implication, involvement, intricacy 251 *convolution*; maze, labyrinth, warren 222 *network*; coil, tangle, twist, snarl, ravel; knot, Gordian k. 47 *ligature*; wheels within wheels; puzzle 517 *unintelligibility*, 700 *predicament*.

turmoil, tumult, frenzy, ferment, storm, convulsion 176 *violence*; pandemonium, inferno; hullabaloo, hubbub, racket, row, riot, uproar 400 *loudness*; affray, fracas, dustup, mêlée 716 *fight*; hurly-burly, to-do, rumpus, ructions, shemozzle, trouble, disturbance 318 *commotion*; whirlwind, tornado, hurricane 352 *gale*; beargarden, shambles, madhouse, bedlam; Saturnalia, Bacchanalia; shindy, breach of the peace; roughhouse, rough and tumble, free for all, all hell broken loose, bull in a china shop; street fighting 709 *quarrel*; fat in the fire, devil to pay.

Adj. *orderless*, in disorder, in disarray, disordered, disarranged; disorganized, jumbled, shuffled; unclassified, ungraded, unsorted, out of order; out of joint, out of gear, dislocated, out of place 188 *displaced*; askew, awry, snafu; topsy-turvy, upside down; straggling, dispersed 75 *unassembled*; random, uncoordinated, unschematic, planless 244 *amorphous*; incoherent, rambling; irregular 17 *nonuniform*; unsystematic, unmethodical, desultory, aimless, casual; confused, muddled, chaotic, messy, all anyhow, haywire; unkempt, uncombed, dishevelled, tumbled, windswept, windblown, tousled, pulled through a hedge backwards; untidy, bedraggled 649 *dirty*; sloppy, slipshod, slack, careless 456 *inattentive*.

complex, intricate, involved, elaborate, sophisticated, complicated, over-involved 517 *puzzling*; mazy, winding, inextricable 251 *labyrinthine*; entangled, balled up, snarled, knotted.

disorderly, undisciplined, unruly; out of step, out of line; tumultuous, rumbustious 738 *riotous*; frantic 503 *frenzied*; orgiastic, saturnalian, bacchic, Dionysiac 949 *drunken*; rough, tempestuous, turbulent 176 *violent*, 318 *agitated*; anarchical, lawless 954 *lawbreaking*; wild, tomboyish, boisterous; scatterbrained 456 *lightminded*.

Vb. *rampage*, storm 176 *be violent*; rush, mob, roister, riot 738 *revolt*; romp 837 *amuse oneself*; give a riotous welcome 876 *celebrate*.

Adv. *confusedly*, in confusion, in disorder, anyhow, all a., all over the place; without rhyme or reason; by fits and starts; chaotically, pell-mell, higgledy-piggledy, helter-skelter, harum-scarum; in turmoil, in a ferment; on the rampage; topsy-turvy, upside down 221 *inversely*.

62. Arrangement: reduction to order – N. *arrangement*, ordering, disposal, disposition, marshalling 187 *location*; collocation, grouping 74 *assemblage*; distribution, allocation 783 *apportionment*; method, systematization, organization, rationalization; streamlining 654 *improvement*; centralization, decentralization; administration 689 *management*; planning 669 *preparation*; taxonomy, categorization, classification 561 *nomenclature*; analysis 51 *decomposition*; codification; gradation 71 *series*; timing, synchronization; formulation, construction 56 *composition*; array, system 60 *order*; layout, pattern 331 *structure*; collection, assortment 74 *accumulation*; register, file 548 *record*; inventory, catalogue, table 87 *list*; code, digest 592 *compendium*; scheme 623 *plan*; class, group 77 *classification*.

sorting, grading, seeding; reference system, cross-reference 12 *correlation*; filing system, card index, pigeonhole, slot.

Adj. *arranged*, etc. vb.; schematic, tabular; methodical, systematic, organizational; precise, definite, cut and dried; analysed, classified; unravelled, disentangled, unscrambled, straightened out;

regulated 81 *regular*; unconfused 60 *orderly*; sorted, graded, streamed.

Vb. *arrange*, set, dispose, set out, lay out; formulate, put into shape 56 *compose*; range, rank, align, line up, form up; position 187 *place*; marshal, array; rally 74 *bring together*; place *or* put *or* set in order; grade, size, group; collocate 45 *connect*; settle, allocate, assign 783 *apportion*; rearrange, trim, neaten tidy up (**see** *unravel*).

regularize, reduce to order; straighten out, put to rights 654 *rectify*, 24 *adjust*; regulate, coordinate, phase; organize, systematize, methodize, schematize; standardize 16 *make uniform*.

class, classify, subsume, group; specify 561 *name*; process, analyse, anatomize, divide; dissect 51 *decompose*; rate, rank, grade, evaluate 480 *estimate*; sort, sift, seed; sift out 44 *eliminate*; docket, label 547 *mark*; file, pigeonhole; index, cross-reference; tabulate, alphabetize; catalogue 87 *list*; register 548 *record*; codify, program, digest.

unravel, untangle, disentangle, comb out, unsnarl 316 *evolve*; uncrease, iron out 258 *smooth*; unscramble; straighten out, neaten 648 *clean*.

63. Derangement – N. *derangement*, shuffling 151 *interchange*, 272 *transference*; sabotage 702 *hindrance*; disarrangement, disorganization, discomposure, dishevelment; dislocation 46 *separation*; disturbance 138 *untimeliness*; timeslip 108 *time*; creasing, corrugation 261 *fold*; upsetting 221 *inversion*; convulsion 176 *violence*, 318 *agitation*, 61 *disorder*.

Vb. *derange*, disarrange, disorder; disturb, touch 265 *move*; meddle, interfere 702 *hinder*; mislay 188 *misplace*; disorganize, muddle, confound, confuse, convulse, make havoc, scramble; tamper with, spoil, sabotage 655 *impair*; strain, bend, twist 176 *force*; unhinge, dislocate, sprain, rick, dislodge, derail 188 *displace*; unbalance, upset, overturn 221 *invert*, 149 *revolutionize*; shake 318 *agitate*; trouble, perturb, unsettle, discompose, disconcert, ruffle, rattle, flurry, fluster 456 *distract*; interrupt 138 *mistime*; misdirect, disorientate 495 *mislead*; unhinge 503 *make mad*, 891 *enrage*.

jumble, shuffle, get out of order 151 *interchange*, 272 *transpose*; mix up 43 *mix*; tumble, agitate; ruffle, dishevel, tousle, fluff up; rumple, crumple, crease 261 *fold*; untidy, muck up; muddle, mess up, litter, clutter; scatter, fling about 75 *disperse*; play havoc with, play merry hell with 702 *hinder*.

bedevil, confuse, confound, complicate, perplex, involve, entangle, tangle, embroil; turn upside down, send haywire.

64. Precedence – N. *precedence*, antecedence 283 *preceding*; anteriority 119 *priority*; anteposition, prefixion; pride of place 34 *superiority*, 605 *choice*; preeminence 638 *importance*; the lead, the pas; 237 *front*; precedent 66 *precursor*.

Adj. *preceding*, precedent, antecedent, foregoing, outgoing; anterior 119 *prior*; before-mentioned, aforesaid; precursory, anticipatory; leading, guiding, pioneering, avant-garde; premonitory, prodromal; preliminary, proemial, prefatory, preparatory, introductory; prepositive, prosthetic, prefixed, prepositional; first come, first served.

Vb. *come before*, be first to arrive 283 *precede*; go first, lead, guide, conduct 547 *indicate*; pioneer, clear the way, blaze the trail 484 *discover*; head, take the lead 237 *be in front*; have precedence, take p., outrank 34 *be superior*; lead the dance, set the fashion 178 *influence*; open, lead off, kick off 68 *begin*; usher in 68 *auspicate*; have the start, get ahead 119 *be before*; antedate 125 *be past*.

put in front, lead with; advance, send ahead; prefix 38 *add*; front, face, tip, top 237 *be in front*; presuppose 512 *suppose*; preface, prelude 68 *initiate*.

Adv. *before*, in advance 283 *ahead*; earlier 119 *before* (in time); above 237 *in front*.

65. Sequence – N. *sequence*, coming after 120 *posteriority*; going after 284 *following*; inference 475 *reasoning*; postposition 38 *addition*; succession, Elijah's mantle 780 *transfer*; rota, Buggins's turn; series 71 *continuity*; successiveness, alternation, serialization; continuation 146 *continuance*; second place 35 *inferiority*; last place 238 *rear*; consequence 67 *sequel*, 157 *effect*.

Adj. *sequential*, sequent, following, succeeding, successional; incoming, ensuing; next 200 *near*; later 120 *subsequent*; another, second 38 *additional*; successive 71 *continuous*; alternate, every other; postpositional 238 *back*; consequent 157 *caused*.

Vb. *come after*, have one's turn, come next 284 *follow*; follow close, tread on the heels; succeed, inherit, step into the shoes of 150 *substitute*; alternate, take turn and turn about 141 *be periodic*; relieve, take over.

place after, suffix, append 38 *add*.

Adv. *after*, following; afterwards 120 *subsequently*, 238 *rearward*; in relays, in waves, successively; in the end 69 *finally*; next, later; infra, below.

66. Precursor – N. *precursor*, predecessor, ancestor, forebears 169 *parentage*; Adam and Eve, early man 371 *humankind*; the ancients, Deucalion and Pyrrha 125 *antiquity*; eldest, firstborn; protomartyr; discoverer, inventor 461 *experimenter*; pioneer, pathfinder, explorer 268 *traveller*; guide 690 *leader*; scout, skirmisher; vanguard, avant-garde, innovator, trail-blazer; trend-setter; forerunner, herald, harbinger 529 *messenger*; dawn, prefiguration, foretaste, preview, forewarning 664 *warning*, 511 *omen*; prodrome, trailer; precedent 83 *example*; antecedent, prefix 40 *adjunct*; eve 119 *priority*.

prelude, preliminary, prolusion, preamble, preface, prologue, foreword, avantpropos; proem, opening, exordium, prolegomena, introduction 68 *beginning*; heading 237 *front*; groundwork, foundation 669 *preparation*; aperitif, appetizer; overture.

Adj. *precursory*, preliminary, exploratory 669 *preparatory*; prelusory, proemial,

introductory, prefatory 68 *beginning*; precedent 64 *preceding*.

67. Sequel – N. *sequel*, result, aftermath, spin-off 157 *effect*; conclusion 69 *end*; sequela, aftereffect; hangover, morning after 949 *crapulence*; aftertaste; afterglow, fallout; afterbirth, placenta, legacy 777 *dower*; afterclap 508 *lack of expectation*; afterthought, second thoughts; afterword, postlude, epilogue, postscript; peroration, envoi, last words; followthrough, follow-up 725 *completion*; continuation, sequel; tag, tailpiece, coda 238 *rear*; appendage, supplement 40 *adjunct*; afters, dessert 301 *dish*; survival, afterlife, afterworld, hereafter 124 *future state*.

retinue 284 *follower*; queue 71 *series*; suite, train 71 *procession*; tailback, wake 89 *concomitant*.

successor, the unborn 170 *posterity*; heir, inheritor 776 *beneficiary*; next man in; replacement 150 *substitute*; fresh blood, newcomer 297 *incomer*.

68. Beginning – N. *beginning*, birth, rise (see *origin*); infancy, early days, dawn 130 *youth*, 126 *newness*; primitiveness 127 *oldness*; commencement; onset 295 *arrival*; emergence 445 *appearance*; inception, institution, foundation, establishment 156 *causation*; invention 484 *discovery*; innovation 21 *originality*; initiative, démarche; introduction, curtain-raiser 66 *prelude*; van 237 *front*; teething troubles, growing pains; first blush, first sight; rudiments, elements, first principles, outbreak, onset; preliminaries 669 *preparation*.

debut, initiation, launching; inauguration, opening, unveiling; premiere, first appearance, first step, move, gambit; maiden voyage, maiden speech; baptism of fire; debutante, starter 538 *beginner*.

start, outset; starting point, D-day; send-off, countdown 296 *departure*; kickoff; house-warming, honeymoon; fresh start, new beginning; threshold, gateway; new departure, thin end of the wedge, precedent.

origin, derivation, conception, genesis,

birth, nativity; provenance 169 *parentage*; fount, rise 156 *source*; bug, germ, seed, egg; primordial soup; cradle 192 *home*.

Adj. *beginning*, initiatory, inceptive; introductory 66 *precursory*; inaugural, foundational; elemental 156 *fundamental*; primeval, primordial 127 *primal*; rudimentary, elementary 670 *immature*; embryonic, nascent, budding, incipient 726 *uncompleted*; early, infant 126 *new*.

first, initial, primary, maiden, starting, natal; pioneering 21 *original*; unprecedented 126 *new*; foremost 237 *frontal*; chief 34 *supreme*.

Vb. *begin*, commence; set in, open, dawn, break out, burst forth, spring up, crop up; arise, emerge, appear; sprout, germinate; come into existence, be born; make one's debut, come out; start, enter upon, embark on 296 *start out*; kick off, clock in; roll up one's sleeves 669 *prepare*; run in; begin at the beginning, start from scratch; go back to square one, make a fresh start 148 *revert*; resume, recommence, put one's hand to the plough, set to, set about; attack, wade into 672 *undertake*.

initiate, found, launch; originate, invent, think of 484 *discover*; call into being, introduce; start up, switch on, ring up the curtain; prompt, promote, set in motion, get under way; take the initiative, lead the way, pioneer, open up, break new ground 64 *come before*; broach, open, break the ice, set the ball rolling; take the plunge, cross the Rubicon, burn one's boats; trigger off, spark off, set off.

auspicate, inaugurate, open; institute, install, induct 751 *commission*; found, set up, establish 156 *cause*; be a founder member, be in on the ground floor; baptize, christen, launch 561 *name*; initiate, blood, flesh; lay the foundations 669 *prepare*.

Adv. *initially*, originally, at the beginning, in the bud, in embryo, from the word go; first, in the first place, primarily, first of all, first and foremost; as a start, for starters, from scratch.

69. End – N. *end*, close, conclusion 725 *completion*; result 157 *effect*; expiration, lapse; termination, closure; finishing stroke, coup de grâce; knockout, finisher, clincher; catastrophe, denouement; ending, finish, finale, curtain; term, period, stop 145 *cessation*; beginning of the end 129 *evening*; swansong, coda 67 *sequel*; last lap, home stretch; last gasp, extremities 361 *decease*. See *finality*.

extremity, extreme, pole, ne plus ultra; world's end 199 *farness*; brink 234 *edge*; frontier 236 *limit*; terminus 295 *goal*, 617 *objective*; dregs, last d.; foot, bottom 214 *base*; tip, peak 213 *summit*; tail end 67 *sequel*; end, butt end, fag e. 238 *rear*; epilogue, postscript 40 *adjunct*.

finality, bitter end; time up, deadline; curtains, conclusion, end of the matter 54 *completeness*; break-up, wind-up 145 *cessation*; dissolution 165 *destruction*; eschatology, last things, last trump, crack of doom, end of the world 124 *future state*.

Adj. *ending*, final, terminal, last, ultimate, supreme, closing; extreme, polar; definitive, conclusive 725 *completive*; at an end; settled, finalized, over and done with; off, all off; played out, finished; eschatological; penultimate, antepenultimate, hindmost, caudal 238 *back*.

Vb. *end*, come to an end, expire, run out 111 *elapse*; close, finish, conclude, be all over; become extinct 2 *pass away*; come to a close, draw to a c., fade away, peter out, tail off; stop, clock out, go home 145 *cease*.

terminate, conclude, close, determine, decide, settle; apply the closure, bring to an end, put an end to, put a stop to, put paid to; discontinue, drop, finish, play out, act o., see it o. 725 *carry through*; ring down the curtain, shut up shop, wind up, close down, call it a day; stop 145 *halt*.

Adv. *finally*, in conclusion, in fine; at last, once for all, for good; never again, nevermore; to the bitter end; in the end, in the long run.

70. Middle – N. *middle*, midst, midpoint; mean 30 *average*; medium, middle term;

thick of things; heart, hub 225 *centre*; midweek, midwinter, half tide; midstream 625 *middle way*; midline 231 *partition*; middle distance, equidistance, halfway house.

Adj. *middle*, medial, mezzo, mid 30 *median*; midmost 225 *central*; intermediate, betwixt and between 231 *interjacent*; equidistant; equatorial.

Adv. *midway*, in the middle, in medias res; at the midpoint, halfway; mid-ships.

71. Continuity: uninterrupted sequence –
N. *continuity*, continuousness, uninterruptedness, unbrokenness 16 *uniformity*; continuation, overlap; consecutiveness, succession; line, descent; one thing after another 65 *sequence*; natural sequence, sere; continuum 115 *perpetuity*; assembly line, conveyor belt 146 *continuance*; rotation, cycle 106 *repetition*, 141 *periodicity*; cumulativeness, snowball 36 *increase*; course, flow, trend 179 *tendency*, 285 *progression*; circuit 314 *circuition*; daily round, routine 610 *habit*; concatenation, catena, chain; chain reaction, knock-on effect, domino theory; Möbius strip, circle, vicious c. 250 *circularity*.

series, succession, run, rally, break; progression, ascending order, descending o.; pedigree 169 *genealogy*; chain, line, string, thread; rank, file, echelon 62 *arrangement*; row, range, colonnade; ladder, steps 308 *ascent*; tier, storey 207 *layer*; set, suite, suit; assortment 77 *classification*; spectrum, rainbow; gamut, scale; stepping stones 624 *bridge*; hierarchy, pyramid.

procession 267 *marching*; crocodile, queue, traffic jam; tail, train, suite 67 *retinue*; caravan, file, single f., Indian f.; cortège 364 *obsequies*; cavalcade 875 *pageant*.

Adj. *continuous*, continued, run-on 45 *joined*; consecutive, running 65 *sequential*; serial, serialized; catenary; progressive, gradual; overlapping, unbroken, solid, smooth, uninterrupted, circular; direct, immediate, unmediated; continuing, ongoing; unremitting, nonstop 115 *perpetual*; rhythmic 110 *periodic*; recurrent 106 *repeated*, 16 *uniform*; linear 249 *straight*.

Vb. *run on*, continue; line up, fall in, join the queue; succeed, overlap 65 *come after*; file, defile; circle 626 *circuit*.

continue, run on 203 *lengthen*; serialize, concatenate, thread, string 45 *connect*.

Adv. *continuously*, consecutively; serially, seriatim; successively, in turn; at a stretch, together, running; without stopping, on the trot; around the clock, progressively; gradually 27 *by degrees*; in single file, in line ahead, nose to tail.

72. Discontinuity: interrupted sequence –
N. *discontinuity*, lack of continuity, intermittence; discontinuation 145 *cessation*; hiatus, time lag 145 *lull*; disconnectedness 61 *disorder*; unevenness 17 *nonuniformity*; dotted line; broken ranks; interruption, parenthesis; break 46 *separation*, 201 *gap*; missing link, lost connection; broken thread, non sequitur; purple patch 25 *misfit*; alternation 141 *periodicity*; irregularity 142 *fitfulness*.

Adj. *discontinuous*, interrupted, broken, stopping; disconnected 46 *disunited*; few and far between 140 *infrequent*; patchy, bitty 437 *variegated*; desultory, irregular, intermittent 142 *fitful*; alternating, stop-go, on-off; spasmodic, snatchy 17 *nonuniform*; jerky, uneven; incoherent, anacoluthic 477 *illogical*; parenthetic, episodic.

Vb. *be discontinuous*, halt 145 *pause*; alternate, intermit.

discontinue, suspend, break off; interrupt, chip in, interfere; interpose, punctuate 231 *put between*; break the connection 46 *disunite*.

Adv. *discontinuously*, at intervals, in jerks and snatches, in fits and starts; desultorily; passim.

73. Term: serial position – **N.** *serial place*, term 27 *degree*; rank, ranking, grade; station, place, position, slot; status, standing, footing; point, mark, pitch, level, storey, stage, milestone, climacteric.

74. Assemblage – N. *assemblage*, bringing together, collection 50 *combination*, 62 *arrangement*; collocation, juxtaposition 202 *contiguity*; compilation, anthology 56 *composition*; gathering, ingathering, reaping 771 *acquisition*; concentration, focusing; mobilization, muster; review, parade; march, demonstration, rally; roundup, lineup; collectivization; caucus 708 *party*.

assembly, getting together, forgathering, congregation, concourse 293 *convergence*; gathering, meeting, mass m.; meet, coven; conventicle, synod; convention 692 *council*; eisteddfod, festival 876 *celebration*; reunion, get-together 882 *social gathering*; company, party 882 *sociality*; encounter group 658 *therapy*; symposium 584 *conference*.

group, constellation, galaxy, cluster; pride (lions), troop, bevy, swarm, flock, herd; drove, team; pack, kennel; stable, string; brood, hatch, litter, kindle (kittens); gaggle, flight, skein, covey, wing (plovers), charm (goldfinches), exaltation (larks); shoal, school; unit, brigade; batch, lot, clutch; brace, pair 90 *duality*; leash; set, class 77 *sort*; tribe, clan 11 *family*; guild, union 706 *association*; club 708 *society*; sphere, quarter, circle, coterie 644 *elite*; social group, the classes 868 *nobility*, 869 *commonalty*; in-group, out-group; age group, year g.

band, company, troupe; cast 594 *actor*; brass band 413 *orchestra*; team, string, knot, bunch; set, coterie, clique, ring; gang, squad, party, crew 686 *personnel*; following 67 *retinue*; unit, regiment, corps; squad, posse; force, body 722 *armed force*, 104 *multitude*; brothers, sisters 880 *friendship*; committee, panel.

crowd, throng 104 *multitude*; huddle, cluster, knot, bunch; mass, mob 869 *rabble*; sea of faces, full house, houseful 54 *completeness*; congestion, press, squash, squeeze, jam, scrum, rush, crush; rush hour; volley, shower, hail 32 *great quantity*; populousness, infestation; herd instinct, crowd psychology, mass hysteria.

bunch, assortment, lot 43 *medley*; clump, tuft, wisp, handful; pencil (of rays), fan; bag, hand (tobacco), bundle, packet, wad; batch, pack, package, parcel; bale, roll; faggot; shock, sheaf, stook, truss, heap; bouquet, nosegay, posy, spray; skein, hank.

accumulation, heaping up; agglomeration, conglomeration, aggregation; amassment; concentration; pileup 279 *collision*; mass, pile, pyramid 164 *edifice*, 209 *high structure*; heap, drift, snowdrift; snowball 36 *increment*; debris 41 *leavings*; dump 641 *rubbish*; store, storage 633 *provision*, 799 *treasury*; magazine 723 *arsenal*; set, lot 71 *series*, 43 *medley*; kit, stock; range, selection, assortment 522 *exhibit*; museum 632 *collection*; menagerie 369 *zoo*; miscellany, compilation 56 *composition*; collector, squirrel, miser.

Adj. *assembled*, met, convened, etc. vb.; banded 62 *arranged*; crowded, packed, huddled, serried, high-density 324 *dense*; overcrowded, humming with 54 *full*; populous, teeming, swarming 104 *multitudinous*; seething, milling; in formation, in order 62 *arranged*.

Vb. *congregate*, meet, forgather, rendezvous; assemble, associate, come together, flock t., gather, collect, rally, roll up, swell the ranks; resort to, make for 293 *converge*; band together, gang up; mass, concentrate, mobilize; conglomerate, huddle, cluster, bunch, crowd; throng, swarm, seethe, mill around.

bring together, assemble, put together 45 *join*; draw, pack them in 291 *attract*; gather, collect, rally, muster, call up, mobilize; concentrate, consolidate; lump together, group, unite; compile 56 *compose*; convene, convoke, summon, hold a meeting; herd, shepherd, get in, whip in, call in, round up 235 *enclose*; mass, aggregate, accumulate, conglomerate, heap, amass; rake in, net 771 *acquire*; scrape together 632 *store*; truss, bundle, parcel; bunch 45 *tie*; pack 54 *fill*; pile up, stack 310 *elevate*.

Adv. *together*, as one; collectively, all together, en masse, in a body.

75. Nonassembly. Dispersion – N. *dispersion*, scattering, distribution; breakup 46 *separation*; spread, scatter, sprawl 294 *divergence*; delegation, decentralization; disintegration 51 *decomposition*; circulation, diffusion; dissemination, broadcasting; spraying, sprinkling; dispersal, disbandment, demobilization; Diaspora.

Adj. *unassembled*, dispersed, etc. vb.; scattered, dotted about, strung out 140 *infrequent*; broadcast, diffused; widespread, far-flung 183 *spacious*; in open order 46 *separate*; trailing, sprawling 61 *orderless*; decentralized; radiating 294 *divergent*; straggling, wandering 267 *travelling*.

Vb. *be dispersed*, disperse, scatter, spread, spread out, fan o. 325 *rarefy*; radiate 294 *diverge*; break ranks, fall out 46 *separate*; break away 49 *come unstuck*; drift away 267 *wander*; straggle, trail, fall behind 282 *stray*; sprawl over, litter 226 *overlie*; burst, fly apart 176 *be violent*; evaporate, melt, disintegrate 51 *decompose*.

disperse, scatter, diffract; spread out 294 *diverge*; separate 46 *sunder*; thin out, string o.; disseminate, diffuse, broadcast, sow, strew, spread; dissipate, dispel 51 *decompose*; dispense, deal out 783 *apportion*; decentralize; break up, disband, dismiss 46 *disunite*; draft off, detach; sprinkle, splash, spray, spatter 341 *moisten*; throw into confusion 63 *derange*; rout 727 *defeat*.

Adv. *sporadically*, here and there, sparsely, in twos and threes; passim, everywhere, in all quarters.

76. Focus: place of meeting – **N.** *focus*, focal point 293 *convergence*, 225 *centre*; nerve centre, hub, nub 70 *middle*; community centre, village green; campus, quad; market place 796 *market*; resort, haunt, stamping ground; club, pub, local 192 *tavern*; headquarters, depot; rallying point, standard; venue, rendezvous 192 *meeting place*; fireside, home; centre of attraction, honeypot 291 *attraction*; place of pilgrimage, Mecca, Rome, Zion, promised land 295 *goal*, 617 *objective*.

Vb. *focus*, centre on 293 *converge*; centralize, concentrate, focus upon.

77. Class – **N.** *classification*, categorization 62 *arrangement*; taxonomy; diagnosis, specification, designation; category, class, bracket; set, subset; head, heading, subhead, section, subsection 53 *subdivision*; division, branch, department, faculty; pigeonhole 194 *compartment*; rank, caste 27 *degree*; sex, gender; band, stream 74 *group*.

sort, order, type, version, variety, kind, species; manner, genre, style; nature, grade, calibre 5 *character*; mark, brand 547 *label*; ilk, stripe, kidney, feather, colour; stamp, shape, make 243 *form*.

breed, strain, blood, family, tribe, line 11 *race*, 169 *genealogy*; class, order, genus, species, subspecies; genotype, monotype.

Adj. *generic*, typical; sexual, masculine, feminine, neuter.

classificatory, classificational, taxonomic.

78. Inclusion – **N.** *inclusion*, comprising; incorporation, assimilation, comprehension, admission, integration 299 *reception*; admissibility, eligibility; membership 775 *participation*; inclusiveness, coverage 79 *generality*; comprehensiveness, no exception, nothing omitted; complement, package, package deal 52 *whole*; constitution 56 *composition*; capacity, volume; accommodation 183 *room*.

Adj. *inclusive*, including, comprising, consisting of; fully-furnished, all-inclusive, all-in; nonexclusive, nondiscriminatory, overall 52 *comprehensive*; wholesale, en bloc, blanket 32 *extensive*; without exception, total, global, universal; expansive 79 *general*.

included, admitted, counted; admissible, eligible; integrated, unsegregated; constituent, composing; inherent 58 *component*; belonging 9 *relative*; classified with, congeneric 18 *similar*; merged 45 *joined*.

Vb. *be included*, make one of; enlist, enrol oneself 708 *join a party*; come under, fall u.; merge in 43 *be mixed*; appertain to

9 *be related*; come in 297 *enter*; constitute 56 *compose*; belong 5 *be intrinsic*.

comprise, include, consist of, hold, have, count, boast; take, measure; take in 299 *admit*; accommodate, find room for; comprehend, encapsulate, cover; embody, incorporate; encompass 235 *enclose*, 54 *be complete*.

number with, count w., reckon among, enumerate with; place under, arrange in 62 *class*; not omit, take into account.

Adv. *including*, inclusively; from A to Z; et cetera.

79. Generality – N. *generality*, universality, catholicity, ecumenicity; generalization, universal; macrocosm 321 *universe*; globalization, world-view; panorama, conspectus 52 *whole*; comprehensivity, something for everybody 78 *inclusion*; currency, prevalence, ubiquity 189 *presence*; pandemic, epidemic; broadness, looseness, imprecision 495 *inexactness*, 464 *indiscrimination*; commonness, ruck, run, run of the mill 732 *averageness*; internationalism, cosmopolitanism; impersonality.

everyman, everywoman; man *or* woman in the street, man on the Clapham omnibus, little man; everybody, one and all, the long and the short and the tall, all and sundry, every mother's son, every man Jack, all hands 52 *all*; Tom, Dick and Harry, the masses 869 *commonalty*; anyone, whosoever 562 *no name*.

Adj. *general*, generic, typical, representative, standard; encyclopedic, broad-based; collective, pan-, blanket, across-the-board 52 *comprehensive*; broad, sweeping, panoramic, synoptic; current, prevalent 189 *ubiquitous*; normal, unexceptional 610 *usual*; vague, loose, indefinite 495 *inexact*; unspecified, impersonal 10 *unrelated*; common, ordinary, average 30 *median*; commonplace 83 *typical*; popular, mass 869 *plebeian*; multipurpose.

universal, catholic, ecumenical; national, international, cosmopolitan, global, worldwide, nationwide, widespread 32 *extensive*; pervasive, penetrating, besetting,

rampant, prevalent, epidemic, pandemic 189 *ubiquitous*; every, each, any, all 52 *whole*.

Vb. *be general*, cover all cases 78 *comprise*; prevail, obtain, be the rule 189 *pervade*.

generalize, broaden, widen, universalize, globalize; spread 75 *disperse*.

80. Speciality – N. *speciality*, specific quality, specificity, personality, uniqueness; singularity 88 *unity*; originality, individuality, particularity; personality, make-up 5 *character*; characteristic, personal c., one's middle name; idiosyncrasy, eccentricity, peculiarity, trademark, mannerism, quirk, foible; trait, mark, feature, attribute; sine qua non 89 *accompaniment*; distinction 15 *difference*; idiom, idiolect; exception, special case 84 *nonconformity*; specialty, specialization 694 *skill*.

particulars, details, minutiae, items, special points, specification; circumstances; the ins and outs of.

particularism, chosen race, chosen few, the elect; exclusiveness, class consciousness, caste; chauvinism, nationalism, individualism.

self, ego, id, identity, selfhood, personality; atman, psyche, soul 447 *spirit*; I, myself, number one; us, in-group; individual, being 371 *person*.

Adj. *special*, specific, respective, particular; sui generis, peculiar, singular, unique 88 *one*; individual, idiosyncratic, characteristic, idiomatic, original 21 *inimitable*; native, proper, personal, private; typical 5 *characteristic*; distinctive, uncommon 84 *unusual*.

definite, definitive, defining; determinate, quantified, specified; distinct, express, explicit, clear-cut, cut and dried; certain, exact, precise 494 *accurate*; itemized, detailed, circumstantial; made to order, made to measure, personalized.

Vb. *specify*, be specific; enumerate, particularize, itemize, detail 87 *list*; cite 561 *name*; spell out, come to the point; define, determine 236 *limit*, 463 *discriminate*; pinpoint, locate 187 *place*; denote

514 *mean*; designate 547 *indicate*; individualize, personalize 15 *differentiate*; specialize.

Adv. *specially*, especially, in particular; personally, for one's own part; specifically, ad hoc, to order.

namely, that is to say, videlicet, viz., to wit, i.e., e.g.

81. Rule – N. *rule*, norm, formula, canon, code; maxim, principle 693 *precept*; law, law of nature, hard and fast rule; law of the Medes and Persians; statute, by-law 953 *law*; regulation, order, standing o.; guide, precedent 23 *prototype*; standard, keynote 83 *example*.

regularity, consistency 16 *uniformity*; natural order 60 *order*; normality, normalcy; form, routine, fixed ways, custom 610 *habit*; methodicalness, method 62 *arrangement*; convention 83 *conformity*.

Adj. *regular*, constant, steady 141 *periodical*; even 245 *symmetrical*; standardized 16 *uniform*; regulated, according to rule, methodical, systematic 60 *orderly*; regulative, normative; legal, technical; normal 83 *typical*; customary 610 *usual*; conforming, conventional 83 *conformable*.

82. Multiformity – N. *multiformity*, multiplicity; heterogeneity, variety, diversity 17 *nonuniformity*; multifariousness, manysidedness, polymorphism; variability 152 *changeableness*; all-rounder; Proteus.

Adj. *multiform*, multifarious, polymorphous; multiple, manifold, many-headed, many-sided, hydra-headed, omnigenous, omnifarious; metamorphic; protean, versatile, all-round; variform, heterogeneous 17 *nonuniform*; motley 43 *mixed*; epicene; indiscriminate, irregular 437 *variegated*; divers, sundry; all manner of, of every description 15 *different*; variable 152 *changeful*.

83. Conformity – N. *conformity*, conformation, conformance 768 *observance*; accommodation, adjustment 24 *agreement*, *adaptation*; pliancy, malleability, acquiescence 721 *submission*; assimila-

tion, acclimatization, naturalization 147 *conversion*; conventionality, bourgeois ethic, traditionalism 976 *orthodoxy*; formalism, convention, form 848 *etiquette*, 610 *practice*; emulation 20 *imitation*; ordinariness 79 *generality*.

example, exemplar, type, pattern, model, precedent 23 *prototype*; exemplification, stock example, locus classicus; case, case in point, instance; illustration, object lesson; sample, specimen, crosssection; representative, representative selection; trailer 66 *precursor*.

conformist, conventionalist, traditionalist; philistine, Babbitt; organization man; formalist; copycat, yes-man 20 *imitator*, 925 *flatterer*; follower, loyalist.

Adj. *conformable*, adaptable, adjustable, malleable, pliant 327 *flexible*; complaisant, accommodating 24 *agreeing*; conforming, faithful, loyal 768 *observant*; conventional, traditional 976 *orthodox*; slavish, servile 20 *imitative*; acclimatized 610 *habituated*; assimilated, naturalized 78 *included*.

typical, normal, natural, everyday, ordinary, common or garden 79 *general*; average 732 *middling*; true to type; commonplace, prosaic; conventional; heterosexual, straight; habitual 610 *usual*; representative, stock, standard; normative; exemplary, illustrative; according to rule 60 *orderly*.

Vb. *conform*, adapt oneself, accommodate o. 24 *accord*; fit in, know one's place; bend, yield 327 *soften*; fall into line, toe the l., fall in with 721 *submit*; comply with 768 *observe*; rubberstamp, echo 106 *repeat*; stick to the rules, follow precedent 739 *obey*; keep in step, follow the crowd, do as others do, do as the Romans do; jump on the bandwagon, keep up with the Joneses 848 *be in fashion*; follow suit 20 *imitate*, *copy*; have no will of one's own, go with the stream 601 *be irresolute*; stick in a rut 610 *be wont*.

make conform, assimilate, naturalize 18 *liken*; acclimatize 610 *habituate*; systematize 62 *regularize*; normalize, conventionalize, standardize; drill 16 *make uniform*; shape, press 243 *form*; bend, twist

740 *compel*; accommodate, fit, fit in, square, rub off the corners 24 *adjust*.

exemplify, illustrate, cite, quote, instance.

84. Nonconformity – N. *nonconformity*, nonconformance, unconformity 25 *disagreement*; contrast, oasis 14 *contrariety*; strangeness 59 *extraneousness*; unorthodoxy 977 *heterodoxy*; disconformity, dissidence 489 *dissent*, 769 *nonobservance*; deviationism 744 *independence*; anomalousness, eccentricity, irregularity 282 *deviation*; informality, unconventionality, bizarrerie, freakishness, oddity; infringement; breach of practice, wonder, miracle 864 *prodigy*; special case, anomaly, exception 57 *exclusion*; individuality, idiosyncrasy 80 *speciality*; quirk, kink, peculiarity, singularity, mannerism; uniqueness 21 *originality*.

abnormality, aberration 282 *deviation*; mutation 15 *variant*; abortion, monstrosity, monster; bisexuality; sexual inversion, homosexuality, lesbianism; necrophilia, sadism, masochism, transvestism; hermaphroditism.

nonconformist, dissident, deviationist, dissenter, maverick 489 *dissentient*, 978 *sectarian*; blackleg, scab; unconventionalist, Bohemian, hippy, dropout, weirdie; rebel, recalcitrant, punk 738 *revolter*; fanatic 504 *crank*; outsider, outlaw 883 *outcast*; hermit, loner 883 *solitary*; gipsy, tramp 268 *wanderer*; joker, ugly duckling 25 *misfit*; deviant, albino, sport, freak; oddity, original, character, card, caution, odd customer, oddball 504 *crank*; queer fish 851 *laughingstock*; curiosity, rarity, one in a million; neither fish, flesh, fowl nor good red herring, neither one thing nor the other; transsexual, hermaphrodite, gynander, androgyne 161 *eunuch*; invert, homosexual, lesbian, gay; pansy, fairy, nancy, poof, queen, queer; transvestite; pervert, sadist, masochist.

rara avis, mythical beast, unicorn, phoenix, griffin, simurg, roc; sphinx, hippogriff, manticore, chimera, dragon, wyvern, firedrake, cockatrice, basilisk, salamander, hydra; leviathan, kraken, Loch Ness monster; mermaid, siren, gorgon, cyclops 970 *mythical being*.

Adj. *unconformable*, inadjustable 25 *unapt*; antipathetic 14 *contrary*; unmalleable, stiff 602 *obstinate*; recalcitrant 711 *defiant*; prickly, awkward, eccentric 604 *capricious*, 893 *sullen*; arbitrary, a law unto oneself 744 *independent*; freakish, outlandish; original, unique 80 *special*; solitary 883 *unsociable*; blacklegging 603 *trimming*; nonconformist, dissident 489 *dissenting*, 978 *sectarian*; unorthodox, heretical 977 *heterodox*; nonpractising 769 *nonobservant*; unconventional, offbeat, Bohemian, informal, unfashionable; irregular, against the rules, not done 924 *disapproved*; lawless 954 *illegal*; astray, off the rails 282 *deviating*; out of place, out of order 188 *displaced*, 61 *orderless*; incongruous, out of step, out of line, out of keeping 25 *disagreeing*; alien, exotic 59 *extraneous*; unclassifiable, hard to place; ambiguous 518 *equivocal*.

unusual, uncustomary 611 *unwonted*; unfamilar, out of the way 491 *unknown*; newfangled, exotic 59 *extraneous*; out of the ordinary, extraordinary, way-out; phenomenal, supernormal; unparalleled, unexampled; singular, rare 80 *special*, 140 *infrequent*; strange, bizarre, curious, odd, queer, rum, unco; funny, peculiar, fantastic, grotesque 849 *ridiculous*; noteworthy, remarkable, surprising, astonishing; miraculous, mysterious 864 *wonderful*; incredible 472 *improbable*; monstrous, miscreated; unnatural, preternatural, supernatural; outsize 32 *enormous*; outré 546 *exaggerated*; indescribable.

abnormal, unnatural (**see** *unusual*); aberrant, freakish; uncharacteristic, untypical, atypical, unrepresentative, exceptional; anomalous 17 *nonuniform*; morbid, kinky, deviant; homosexual, lesbian, gay, bent, queer; bisexual, AC/DC; epicene, androgynous, gynandrous; irregular, nonstandard; substandard, subnormal; deformed 246 *distorted*.

Vb. *be unconformable*, unconventional etc. adj.; not fit in, be the exception that proves the rule; infringe usage, break with custom, violate c.; drop out, freak o., do one's own thing 744 *be free*; be ahead of one's time 135 *be early*.

Section 5: Number

85. Number – N. *number*, round n., integer; numeral, cipher, digit, figure, character; Arabic numerals, Roman n., algorism; quantity, X, symbol, constant; function, variable; vector, matrix; surd; expression, quadratics; formula, series.

numerical element, subtrahend; multiplier; coefficient, multiple, dividend, divisor; aliquot; quotient, factor, submultiple, fraction; numerator, denominator; decimal, recurring d., repetend; reciprocal, complement; parameter; power, root; exponent, index, logarithm, antilogarithm; modulus, differential, derivative, integral, fluxion.

ratio, proportion; progression, arithmetical p., geometrical p., harmonic p.; sine, tangent, secant; cosine, cotangent, cosecant; pi; percentage, per cent.

numerical result, answer, product, equation; sum, total, aggregate 52 *whole*; difference, residual 41 *remainder*; score, tally 38 *addition*.

Adj. *numerical*, numerary, numeral, digital; arithmetical; cardinal, ordinal; even, odd; prime; figurate; positive, negative, surd, radical; divisible, aliquot; multiple, reciprocal, complementary; fractional, decimal; proportional; exponential, logarithmic, differential, fluxional, integral; algebraic.

86. Numeration – N. *numeration*, numbering, enumeration, census, counting, figuring, reckoning; sum, tally, score; count, recount, countdown; summation, calculation, computation 465 *measurement*; pagination; accountancy 808 *accounts*; counting heads, poll, headcount; numeracy.

numerical operation, figure-work, notation; addition, subtraction, multiplication, division, proportion, rule of three, practice, equations, analysis, extraction of roots; differentiation, integration, permutation.

mathematics, arithmetic, algebra; set theory, modern maths; differential calculus, fluxions; topology; geometry, trigonometry; graphs, logarithms; algorithm; systems analysis (**see** *data processing*); operational research, critical path analysis, linear programming 623 *policy*; axiomatics 475 *reasoning*.

statistics, figures, tables, averages; mode, mean 30 *average*; significance, deviation; distribution curve, skew; correlation; roll call, muster 87 *list*; demography, birth rate, death r.; vital statistics; bar graph, histogram, pie chart, flow c. 623 *plan*; cartogram 551 *map*.

data processing, computing; computer technology, cybernetics 630 *mechanics*; software, program, computer p.; input, output, throughput, feedback; machine code, computer language, BASIC; hardware (**see** *counting instrument*); data, bit, byte; floppy disk; word processor; data bank, memory; hard copy, printout; viewdata 524 *information*.

counting instrument, abacus; ready reckoner, multiplication table; tape measure, yardstick 465 *gauge*; slide rule; tallies, counters; comptometer (tdmk); calculator; cash register, totalizator, tote; computer, microcomputer, microprocessor 196 *microelectronics*.

enumerator, census-taker; calculator; counter, teller, pollster; mathematician, wrangler; arithmetician, geometrician, algebraist; programmer, computer p.; systems analyst 623 *planner*; statistician, actuary, bookkeeper 808 *accountant*.

Adj. *numerable*, numberable, countable; calculable, computable, measurable, mensurable 465 *metrical*.

statistical, digital, figured out; mathematical, arithmetical, algebraical; geometrical, trigonometrical; in ratio, in proportion, percentile, quartile.

computerized, automatic; programmable, processable; analogue, digital, binary, alphanumeric.

Vb. *number*, cast, count, tell; score, notch up; tick off, count down; foliate, paginate; enumerate, poll; muster, call over; take stock 87 *list*; check, balance 808 *account*.

do sums, count up, tot up; take away, multiply, divide; square, cube, extract roots; compute, calculate; reckon up 465 *measure*.

computerize, automate 160 *empower*; program, process; debug; compute 173 *operate*.

87. List – N. *list*, enumeration, items; inventory, stock list; table, catalogue, listing; portfolio 767 *security*; statement, schedule, manifest, bill of lading; checklist; invoice; tariff, bill, account 809 *price*; registry, cartulary; cadastre, terrier, Domesday Book; file, register 548 *record*; ledger, books 808 *account book*; table of contents, index; bill of fare, menu; playbill, programme, prospectus 592 *compendium*; roll, electoral r., voting list 605 *electorate*; muster roll, payroll; Army List, Navy L., active l., retired l. 686 *personnel*; sick list, waiting list, short l.; statistical list, census 86 *numeration*; bibliography, catalogue raisonnée, discography, filmography; rota, roster, panel; dramatis personae; pedigree 169 *genealogy*; scroll, roll of honour; blacklist, questionnaire; alphabetical list 60 *order*; thesaurus 559 *dictionary*.

directory, gazetteer, atlas; almanac, calendar, timetable 117 *chronology*; ABC 524 *guidebook*; Crockford, Debrett, Who's Who 589 *reference book*.

Vb. *list*, enumerate; itemize, inventory, catalogue, index, tabulate; enter 548 *register*; enlist, enrol, empanel, inscribe; keep the score, keep count 86 *number*.

88. Unity – N. *unity*, oneness 44 *simpleness*; integration, wholeness 52 *whole*; uniqueness, singularity 80 *speciality*; singleness 895 *celibacy*; isolation 883 *seclusion*; isolability 46 *separation*; indivisibility, solidarity 48 *coherence*; unification 50 *combination*.

unit, integer, one, ace, item, piece; individual, atom, monad, entity 371 *person*; monolith; singleton, nonce word; isolated instance, exception; solo, monologue; single person 895 *celibate*; single parent 896 *divorce*, *widowhood*; set, package 78 *inclusion*.

Adj. *one*, singular, sole, single, solitary; unique, only, lone, one and only; one and the same 13 *identical*; unrepeated, only-begotten; once only, one-off; individual 80 *special*; unitary; unilateral, mono-; all of a piece, monolithic 16 *uniform*; rolled into one 45 *joined*; indivisible, indissoluble.

alone, lonely, orphaned, deserted, forsaken 883 *friendless*; lonesome, solitary 883 *unsociable*; isolable, isolated, insular 199 *distant*; single-handed, on one's own; by oneself, on one's tod; unaccompanied, unescorted; unpaired, celibate 895 *unwedded*.

Adv. *singly*, one by one, one at a time; once only, just this once, never again, only, solely, simply; alone, on one's own, by oneself; in the singular.

89. Accompaniment – N. *accompaniment*, inseparability, concomitance 71 *continuity*, 45 *union*, 5 *intrinsicality*; society 882 *sociability*; companionship, togetherness 880 *friendship*; partnership 706 *association*; coexistence, coagency 181 *concurrence*; coincidence 123 *synchronism*; attendance, company.

concomitant, attribute, sine qua non 5 *essential part*; complement 54 *completeness*; accessory, appurtenance 40 *adjunct*; by-product, corollary; epiphenomenon, symptom 547 *indication*; coincidence 159 *chance*; context, circumstance 7 *state*; background, noises off; accompaniment, obbligato; entourage, court 742 *retainer*; attendant, following, suite 67 *retinue*; convoy, escort; chaperon, bodyguard 660 *protector*, 749 *keeper*; suitor 887 *lover*; tracker 619 *hunter*; inseparable, shadow, Mary's little lamb 284 *follower*; consort 894 *spouse*; companion 880 *friend*; stable companion, co-worker, accomplice, partner 707 *colleague*; twin, fellow 18 *analogue*; satellite, parasite, hanger-on.

Adj. *accompanying*, with, concomitant, attendant, background; inseparable 45

39

joined; hand-in-glove; belonging 58 *component*; parallel, collateral; incidental, coincidental 159 *casual*; coexistent, contemporaneous.

Vb. *accompany*, be found with, coexist; cohabit, live with, keep company w., consort w., string along with; attend, wait on 284 *follow*; squire, chaperon 660 *safeguard*; convoy, escort, conduct, usher 64 *come before*; track, dog, shadow 619 *pursue*; associate with, partner 706 *cooperate*; gang up with 880 *befriend*; coincide 181 *concur*; imply 5 *be intrinsic*; bring in its train 156 *cause*; be inseparable, go hand in hand with, follow as night follows day 157 *depend*; belong, go together 9 *be related*.

Adv. *with*, together with, along w. 38 *in addition*; in convoy, hand in hand, arm in arm; cheek by jowl; all together, in a body, collectively.

90. Duality – **N.** *duality*, dualism; dyad, two, deuce, duo, twain, couple, brace, pair; doublets, twins, Castor and Pollux, Gemini, Siamese twins, identical t., Tweedledum and Tweedledee 18 *analogue*; yoke, span; couplet, distich; double harness, twosome, two hander; duel; duet; tandem; biped; bivalve; Janus, Jekyll and Hyde.

Adj. *dual*, dualistic; dyadic, binary, bipartisan, bilateral, bicameral; twin, double-barrelled 91 *double*; paired, coupled etc. vb.; two by two; in twos, both; tête-à-tête; double-sided; biform, two-faced; di-, bi-.

Vb. *pair*, couple, match, bracket, yoke; mate, pair off.

91. Duplication – **N.** *duplication*, doubling 261 *fold*; gemination, reduplication 106 *repetition*; copy 22 *duplicate*; living image 18 *analogue*.

Adj. *double*, doubled, twice; duplex 90 *dual*; twofold, two-sided, two-edged; amphibious, ambidextrous; dual-purpose, two-way; bisexual, hermaphrodite; twin, duplicate, geminate; second.

Vb. *double*, redouble, square; geminate 106 *repeat*; duplicate 20 *copy*.

Adv. *twice*, once more 106 *again*; twofold; twice over; doubly.

92. Bisection – **N.** *bisection*, bipartition, dichotomy; halving etc. vb.; half, moiety 53 *part*; hemistich; hemisphere.

bifurcation, forking, branching 294 *divergence;* swallowtail, fork, prong.

dividing line, diameter, diagonal, equator; parting, seam; date line; party wall 231 *partition*.

Adj. *bisected*, etc. vb.; dimidiate, bifid, bipartite; bicuspid, bifurcate, forked; dichotomous; semi-, demi-, hemi-; cloven, cleft 46 *disunited*.

Vb. *bisect*, transect; divide, split 46 *sunder*; halve, dimidiate, dichotomize; share, go halves, go fifty-fifty 783 *apportion*.

bifurcate, fork 294 *diverge*.

93. Triality – **N.** *triality*, trinity, trimurti; triunity; trimorphism; triplicity 94 *triplication*.

three, triad, trine; Fates, Furies, Graces; Faith, Hope and Charity; threesome, triumvirate, leash; troika; triplet, trey, trio, tern, trigon; trimester, triennium; trefoil, triangle, trident, tripod, trivet, triskelion; three-wheeler, tricycle; three-decker, three-hander; three-headed monster, Cerberus; triphthong, triptych, trilogy, triolet, trimeter; third power, cube; third person, gooseberry; tertium quid.

Adj. *three*, triadic, triform, trinomial; three in one, triune, tripartite; triphibious; tricolour; three-dimensional; three-sided, triangular, deltoid, trigonal, trilateral; tricorn, tricuspid, tridentate; trimestrial, quarterly; tri-.

Adv. *in threes*, three times, thrice.

94. Triplication – **N.** *triplication*, triplicity; trebleness; hat trick; tercentenary.

Adj. *treble*, triple; trine, ternary; triplex, triplicate, threefold, three-ply; third, tertiary; trihedral; trilateral.

Vb. *treble*, triple, triplicate, cube.

Adv. *trebly*, triply, threefold; thrice; thirdly.

95. Trisection – N. *trisection*, tripartition, trichotomy; third, tierce.

Adj. *trifid*, trisected; tripartite, trichotomous, trifurcate, trifoliate.

Vb. *trisect*, trifurcate.

96. Quaternity – N. *quaternity*, four, tetrad, tetrarchy; square, tetragon, quadrilateral, quadrangle; tetrahedron; quadrature, quarter; fylfot, swastika 222 *cross*; tetrameter, quatrain; tetragram, Tetragrammaton; quaternion, quartet, foursome; four winds, four gospel-writers; four-in-hand, quadriga; quatrefoil; quadruplet, quad; quadruped, tetrapod; quadrennium.

Adj. *four*, quaternary, quadratic; quadrate, square, quadrilateral, tetrahedral, four-square; four-footed, quadrupedal; quadrennial; quadri-, tetra-.

97. Quadruplication – N. *quadruplication*, quadruplicity; squaring; quatercentenary.

Adj. *fourfold*, quadruple, quadruplicate, squared.

Vb. *quadruple*, quadruplicate, square, quadrate.

98. Quadrisection – N. *quadrisection*, quadripartition; quartering, fourth, quarterly; quart, quarter; farthing, quarto.

Adj. *quartered*; quadrifid, quadripartite.

Vb. *quadrisect*, quarter.

99. Five and over – N. *five*, cinque, quint, quintuplet, quin; quintet; lustrum; pentad; quincunx; pentagon, pentacle, pentagram, pentahedron; pentameter; Pentateuch; pentarchy; pentathlon; cinquefoil, quinquereme; five senses, Five Towns.

over five, six, half-a-dozen, sextet, hexad, sixer; hexagon, hexagram; Hexateuch; hexameter; seven, heptad, week, sabbatical year; septennium; septenary, septet; Pleiad; Heptateuch; Seven Deadly Sins, Seven Wonders of the World; eight, octave, octet, octad; octagon; nine, ennead, nonary; novena; nine Muses; ten, tenner, decade; decagon, decahedron; decemvirate; Decalogue, Ten Commandments; eleven, hendecasyllable; twelve, dozen; dodecahedron; twelve apostles, twelve tribes; thirteen, baker's dozen, long d.; double figures, teens.

twenty and over, twenty, a score; icosahedron; four and twenty, two dozen; twenty-five, pony; forty, two score; fifty, half a hundred, jubilee; sixty, three score; sexagenarian; seventy, three score and ten, septuagenarian; eighty, four score, octogenarian; ninety, nonagenarian.

hundred, century, centenary; hundredweight; centurion; centenarian; centipede; treble figures.

over one hundred, a gross; thousand, chiliad, grand; millennium; ten thousand, myriad; hundred thousand, lakh; million; ten million, crore; thousand million, milliard; billion; million million; trillion, quadrillion, centillion, multimillion; zillion; millionaire, billionaire, milliardaire.

Adj. *fifth and over*, fifth; quinquennial, quinary, quintuple, fivefold; sixfold etc. n.; senary, sextuple; sixth; septuple; seventh; octuple; eighth; nonary; ninth; tenfold, decimal, denary, decuple, tenth; eleventh; twelfth; duodenary, duodecimal; thirteenth etc. n.; vigesimal, twentieth; vicennial; centesimal, centuple, centuplicate, centennial, centenary; secular, hundredth; sesquicentenary, bicentenary, quincentenary; thousandth; millenary; bimillenary; millionth, billionth.

100. Multisection – N. *multisection*, decimation.

Adj. *multifid*, multifoil, multipartite, quinquepartite; octifid; decimal, tenth, tithe; duodecimal, twelfth; sexagesimal, sexagenary; hundredth, centesimal, millesimal.

Vb. *multisect*, decimate, decimalize.

101. Plurality – N. *plurality*, multiplicity 104 *multitude*; polygon, polyhedron; a number, some, two or three; a few, several; majority 104 *greater number*.

Adj. *plural*, not singular; composite, multiple; polydactyl, polypod; multiparous; polymorphic, multiform; many-sided; multilateral, multipurpose, multi-role, multi-, poly-; upwards of, more, in the majority 104 *many*.

102. Fraction: less than one – N. *fraction*, decimal 85 *numerical element*; fractional part, fragment 53 *part*, shred 33 *small quantity*.

Adj. *fractional*, partial 53 *fragmentary*, 33 *small*.

103. Zero – N. *zero*, nil, zilch, nothing, next to nothing, infinitely little; naught, nought, nix; no score, love, duck; blank; cipher; nullity, nothingness 2 *non-existence*, 4 *insubstantiality*; none, no-body, not a soul 190 *absence*; zero level, nadir.

Adj. *not one*, not any, zero; invisible, null 4 *insubstantial*, 2 *nonexistent*.

104. Multitude – N. *multitude*, numerous-ness, multiplicity; a quantity, lots, loads, heaps 32 *great quantity*; numbers, scores, myriads, millions, trillions, zillions 99 *over one hundred*; sea; forest, thicket; host, array 722 *army*; throng, mob, high turn-out, all the world and his wife 74 *crowd*; tribe, horde 74 *group*.

greater number, weight of numbers, majority, mass, bulk, mainstream 32 *main part*; multiplication, multiple 101 *plurality*.

Adj. *many*, myriad, several, sundry, div-ers, various, a thousand and one; quite a few; considerable, numerous, very many, a good many; many more, no end of, umpteen, n; untold, uncounted 107 *infinite*; multifarious, manifold 82 *multiform*; much, ample, multiple, multiplied 106 *re-peated*; in profusion, abundant, galore 635 *plenteous*, 32 *great*.

multitudinous, massed, crowded, thronged, studded with 54 *full*; populous, peopled 324 *dense*; teeming, crawling, humming, alive with 171 *prolific*; thick, thick on the ground, thick as flies; coming thick and fast 139 *frequent*; innumerable, countless 107 *infinite*.

Vb. *be many*, – various etc. adj.; swarm with, crawl w., hum w., bristle w., teem w. 54 *fill*; pullulate, multiply 171 *be fruitful*; clutter, crowd, throng, flock, troop 74 *congregate*; flood, snow under, swamp 637 *superabound*; infest, overrun 297 *burst in*; swell the ranks 36 *augment*; outnumber 32 *be great*.

105. Fewness – N. *fewness*, paucity, under-population; exiguity, sparsity, sparseness, rarity 140 *infrequency*; scantiness 636 *scarcity*; a few, a handful; wisps, tuft; trickle, mere t. 33 *small quantity*; limited number, minority, two or three, remnant 41 *remainder*.

Adj. *few*, precious few, scanty 636 *scarce*; thin, thin on the ground, sparse, rare, scattered, low-density, few and far between 140 *infrequent*; not many, hardly any; soon counted, to be counted on one's fingers; fewer 37 *decreasing*; too few, in a minority, without a quorum.

Vb. *render few*, reduce 198 *make smaller*; decimate, weed, thin, sort out 300 *eject*; defect, desert; underman, under-staff.

106. Repetition – N. *repetition*, iteration, reiteration; ditto, reduplication 20 *imita-tion*, 91 *duplication*; recapitulation; re-hearsal; renewal, resumption, reprise 68 *beginning*; harping, tautology 570 *diffuse-ness*; repeat, repeat performance, encore; playback, replay; chorus, refrain 412 *vocal music*; echo 404 *resonance*; cliché, hardy annual (see *recurrence*); chestnut 838 *tedium*; parrot-cry, gramophone record; reprint 589 *edition*; rifacimento, remake, rehash 656 *restoration*; repeater, cuckoo, parrot; creature of habit.

recurrence, repetitiveness 139 *fre-quency*; cycle, round 141 *regular return*; succession, run, serial 71 *series*; throw-back, atavism 5 *heredity*; reappearance, return; rhythm 141 *periodicity*; allitera-tion, assonance 18 *assimilation*; mono-tony 16 *uniformity*, 838 *tedium*; mixture as before, busman's holiday, routine 610 *habit*.

Adj. *repeated*, repetitional; recurrent 141 *periodical*; tautological, repetitive, repetitious, harping, iterative; stale, cliché-ridden 572 *feeble*; echoing, rhyming, chiming, alliterative, assonant 18 *similar*; monotonous, sing-song, dingdong 16 *uniform*, 838 *tedious*; rhythmical, incessant, habitual 139 *frequent*; retold, twice-told; above-mentioned, aforesaid, plagiarized 20 *imitative*.

Vb. *repeat*, do again, iterate, reiterate; duplicate, reduplicate 91 *double*; multiply 166 *reproduce*; recapitulate, go over, ring the changes on; retell, restate, reword, rephrase; recite, say after; echo, ditto, parrot 20 *copy*, 925 *flatter*; quote, cite 505 *remember*; practise, rehearse; play back, rerun, replay; recycle, reprocess; restart, resume 68 *begin*; reprint, reissue, rehash, remake 656 *restore*.

repeat oneself, give an encore; reecho 404 *resound*; chant, chorus; tautologize 570 *be diffuse*; stutter 580 *stammer*; trot out, plug, labour, harp on; din into, go on at, hammer at; revert to 505 *remember*; stick in a groove, be a creature of habit 610 *be wont*.

reoccur, recur, return; reappear, never hear the last of; turn up like a bad penny; haunt, obsess 505 *be remembered*.

Adv. *repeatedly* 139 *often*; by rote, parrot fashion; again and again, over and over, time after time; year in year out; morning, noon and night; ad nauseam.

again, afresh, anew, over again, once more; ditto; encore; bis; re-.

107. Infinity – N. *infinity*, infinitude, boundlessness, illimitability 183 *space*; eternity 115 *perpetuity*.

Adj. *infinite*, indefinite; immense, measureless; eternal 115 *perpetual*; numberless, countless, innumerable, immeasurable, illimitable, interminable; incalculable, unfathomable, incomprehensible, inexhaustible, without end, limitless, endless, boundless; untold, unnumbered 104 *many*; unbounded, unlimited.

Adv. *infinitely*, to infinity, ad infinitum; without end, indefinitely 32 *greatly*.

Section 6: Time

108. Time – N. *time*, tide; duration, extent 113 *long duration*; season, term, spell, stint, span, space 110 *period*; a bit, a while; lifetime; eternity 115 *perpetuity*; passage of time 111 *course of time*; years, days; Time, Father Time, Time's scythe, Time's hourglass, sands of time, whirligig of t.; fourth dimension, space-time; time-slip, timewarp.

date, day, age, reign 110 *era*; vintage, year 117 *chronology*; birthday 141 *anniversary*; day of the week, calends, ides, nones; time of day 117 *clock time*; moment 116 *instant*; target date, zero hour, D-Day; term, quarter day.

Adj. *dated*, calendared; temporal 141 *periodical*.

Vb. *pass time*, vegetate, subsist 360 *live*; age 131 *grow old*; spend time 678 *be busy*; while away time, kill t.; summer, winter, weekend 681 *have leisure*; waste time, fritter away t.; mark time 136 *wait*; enjoy a spell of, have one's day.

Adv. *while*, whilst, during, pending; in the course of, so long as; for the time being, meantime, meanwhile; between whiles, in the meantime; hourly 139 *often*; for a time, for a season; till, until, up to, yet; always, all the time; all along.

when, one day, once upon a time, one fine morning; in the days of, in the time of, in the year of; anno domini, AD; BC.

109. Neverness – N. *neverness*, Greek Calends; month of Sundays, blue moon; jam tomorrow, mañana; dies non; datelessness, eternity 115 *perpetuity*.

Adv. *never*, not ever, at no time, not in donkey's years; nevermore, never again; over one's dead body; never in one's born days; without date, sine die; out of time.

110. Period – N. *period*, matter of time; long run 113 *long duration*; short run 114 *transience*; season, close season 145 *lull*; time of day, time of year 128 *morning*, 129 *evening*; one's time, term; notice 766 *conditions*; time up 69 *finality*; spell, tour, stint, shift, span, stretch, sentence; innings, turn; round, bout, lap; vigil, watch, night-watch, dogwatch; second, minute, hour; pause, interval; day, weekday, working day; week, octave, novena; fortnight, month, calendar m., lunar m., moon, lunation; quarter, trimester; semester; twelvemonth, year, leap y.; Olympiad, lustrum, quinquennium; decade, decennium, Gay Nineties, Hungry Thirties, Swinging Sixties; jubilee 141 *anniversary*; century, millennium; annus mirabilis; one's born days; lifetime.

era, time, period, generation, age, days; epoch; aeon; cycle, Sothic c., Metonic c.; Platonic year, Great Year, Yuga, Kalpa; geological period, Ice Age; Stone A., Iron A. 125 *antiquity*; Renaissance, Age of Enlightenment, A. of Reason, belle époque, fin de siècle; Golden Age, A. of Aquarius.

Adj. *periodic*, annual 141 *seasonal*; hourly, horary; centennial; period 127 *olden*.

secular, epochal, millennial; Pre-Cambrian, Palaeozoic, Mesozoic, Cainozoic, Quaternary; Pleistocene, Holocene; neolithic 127 *primal*.

111. Course: indefinite duration – N. *course of time*, matter of t., lapse of t., flow of t., stream of t., march of t., flight of t.; duration 108 *time*, 146 *continuance*.

Vb. *elapse*, pass, lapse, flow, run, roll, proceed, advance 285 *progress*; wear on, drag on, crawl 278 *move slowly*; flit, fly, glide 277 *move fast*; run its course 69 *end*; go by, slip by 125 *be past*; spend time 108 *pass time*.

Adv. *in time*, in due time, in due season; in the course of time, in the process of t., in the fullness of t., with the years.

112. Contingent Duration – Adv. *provisionally*, by favour; at the pleasure of; for the present; as *or* so long as.

113. Long Duration – N. *long duration*, length of time, a long t., unconscionable t.; a month of Sundays, years, donkey's years, years on end, yonks; a lifetime, life

sentence; generations, a century, an age, ages, aeons 115 *perpetuity*; length of days, longevity 131 *old age*; antiquity 125 *past time*.

durability, endurance, stamina, staying power 162 *strength*; survival, long run, long innings 146 *continuance*; permanence 153 *stability*; inveteracy 127 *oldness*.

protraction, prolongation, extension 203 *lengthening*; dragging out, spinning o.; long wait, long haul 136 *delay*, 278 *slowness*; extra time 38 *addition*.

Adj. *lasting*, abiding 146 *unceasing*; secular, agelong, lifelong, livelong; long-time, longstanding, inveterate; long-term, long-service, marathon 203 *long*; too long, unconscionable; durable, perdurable, enduring 162 *strong*; longeval, long-lived 127 *immemorial*; unfading, eternal 115 *perpetual*; persistent, chronic; nonbiodegradable, permanent 153 *unchangeable*; protracted, interminable.

Vb. *last*, endure, stand, remain, abide, continue 146 *go on*; defy time 115 *be eternal*; wear well 162 *be strong*.

outlast, outlive, outstay, survive; remain, live to fight another day; have nine lives.

spin out, draw o., drag o.; protract, prolong 203 *lengthen*; temporize, gain time 136 *put off*; talk out 702 *obstruct*.

drag on, be interminable, never end; inch, creep 278 *move slowly*; tarry, delay 136 *be late*.

Adv. *for a long time*, long, for ages, for years, many a long day; for good, for better for worse; all one's life, from the cradle to the grave; till blue in the face; till the cows come home.

all along, all day long, the livelong day, as the day is long; all the year round, round the clock, day in day out.

at last, at long last, in the long run, not before it was time.

114. Transience – N. *transience*, transientness 4 *insubstantiality*; ephemerality, impermanence; evanescence 446 *disappearance*; volatility; fugacity; fragility 330 *brittleness*; mortality 361 *death*; frailty 163 *weakness*; mutability 152 *change-*

ableness; suddenness 116 *instantaneity*; temporariness, temporary arrangement, makeshift interim.

brief span, short space of time, short while 204 *shortness*; flash in the pan, nine days' wonder; ephemera, snows of yesteryear; April shower 4 *insubstantial thing*; ship that passes in the night; brief encounter; short run 110 *period*, 277 *spurt*; moment 116 *instant*.

Adj. *transient*, time-bound, temporal, impermanent, transitory, passing 4 *insubstantial*; fair-weather, summer; cursory, flying, fleeting, flitting, fugitive, fugacious 277 *speedy*; precarious, volatile, written in water; evanescent 446 *disappearing*; flickering, mutable 152 *changeful*.

ephemeral, of a day, short-lived, nondurable; throwaway, disposable, biodegradable; perishable, mortal 361 *dying*; annual, deciduous, frail 163 *weak*, 330 *brittle*; impermanent, temporary, acting, provisional, for the time being; doomed, under sentence.

brief, short-term 204 *short*; summary, short and sweet 569 *concise*; quick, fleet, brisk 277 *speedy*; momentary, meteoric 116 *instantaneous*; hurried 680 *hasty*.

Vb. *be transient*, – transitory etc. adj.; not stay, not last; flit, fleet 277 *move fast*; fade, flicker, vanish 446 *disappear*; fade like a dream, burst like a bubble, have no roots 2 *pass away*.

Adv. *transiently*, momentarily; awhile, in passing; temporarily, for the moment, for the time being, not for long; easy come, easy go; here today and gone tomorrow.

115. Perpetuity: endless duration – N. *perpetuity*, endless time 107 *infinity*; sempiternity, eternity, timelessness; interminability 113 *long duration*; endurance 144 *permanence*; immortality, deathlessness 146 *continuance*; perpetuation, immortalization; lasting monument 505 *reminder*.

Adj. *perpetual*, perennial, longlasting, enduring 113 *lasting*; constant, continual, ceaseless 146 *unceasing*; flowing, ever-flowing 71 *continuous*; dateless, ageless, unchanging, immutable 144 *permanent*;

evergreen, unfading, amaranthine, everlasting, incorruptible; imperishable, undying, deathless, immortal; unending, never-ending; endless, without end, timeless, eternal.

Vb. *perpetuate*, immortalize, eternalize.

be eternal, – perpetual etc. adj.; last for ever, endure, have no end, never cease.

Adv. *for ever*, in perpetuity; ever and always, evermore, for ever and ever 107 *infinitely*; world without end; for keeps, for good and all; to the end of time, to the crack of doom; from age to age, from generation to generation.

116. Instantaneity: point of time – N. *instantaneity*, immediacy; simultaneity 121 *present time*; suddenness, abruptness; precise time 135 *punctuality*; momentariness 114 *transience*.

instant, moment, point of time; second, split s., tick, trice, jiffy, breath; burst, crack; stroke; flash, twinkle, twinkling; the very moment, the stroke of.

Adj. *instantaneous*, simultaneous, immediate, instant, sudden, abrupt, snap; flickering, flashing; quick as thought, quick as lightning, like a flash 277 *speedy*; on time, punctual 135 *early*.

Adv. *instantaneously*, instantly, at once, immediately, directly; without delay, forthwith; in no time at all, in less than no time; promptly, presto, pronto; without warning, out of hand, abruptly; all at once, suddenly; plump, slap, slap-bang, at a stroke, at one fell swoop; in a trice, in a moment, in a wink, in the twinkling of an eye; in two ticks, in a brace of shakes; at the drop of a hat, on the spot, on the dot; extempore, impromptu, on the spur of the moment, off the cuff; before you could say Jack Robinson, before you could say knife; like a flash, like greased lightning 277 *swiftly*; no sooner said than done.

117. Chronometry – N. *chronometry*, horology; calendar-making, timetabling; timing, dating; timekeeping 108 *time*.

clock time, right time, sidereal t.,

Greenwich Mean Time, GMT, British Standard Time, BST, local time, date, date line; the hour, time of day, summer time, daylight saving.

timekeeper, chronometer, timepiece, clock, dial, face; hand; bob, pendulum, grandfather clock, carriage c., cuckoo c., alarm c.; Big Ben; water-clock, clepsydra; watch, ticker; turnip, fob-watch, hunter, repeater; wrist-watch, digital watch, dial w.; sundial, gnomon; hourglass, sandglass, egg timer; chronograph, chronoscope; time signal, pip, siren, hooter; gong, bell, minute-gun, time-ball; timeclock, timer, stopwatch; parking meter; time fuse, time switch, time bomb; metronome; watchmaker, clockmaker, horologist; chronologist, chronologer.

chronology, dendrochronology; radiocarbon dating, thermoluminescence; dating, chronogram; date, age, style 110 *era*; almanac, calendar; ephemeris; chronicle, annals, diary, journal, logbook 548 *record*; tidetable, timetable 87 *directory*.

Adj. *chronological*, horological, timekeeping; chronographic; annalistic 548 *recording*; calendrical, chronogrammatic, datal, temporal.

Vb. *time*, clock; timetable; match times 123 *synchronize*, 24 *adjust*; put the clock forward *or* back 135 *be early*, 136 *be late*; set the alarm 669 *make ready*; calendar, chronologize 548 *record*; date, be dated, measure time, mark t., beat t., keep t.; count the minutes, watch the clock; clock in *or* out 68 *begin*.

118. Anachronism – N. *anachronism*, parachronism, prochronism; mistiming, previousness, prolepsis 135 *anticipation*; unpunctuality 136 *lateness*; wrong moment 138 *untimeliness*.

Adj. *anachronistic*, misdated, undated; antedated, too early 135 *early*; parachronistic, post-dated 136 *late*; slow, losing; fast, gaining; out of date, behind the times 127 *antiquated*.

Vb. *misdate*, antedate 135 *be early*; postdate 136 *be late*; be fast, gain; be slow, lose.

119. Priority – N. *priority*, antecedence, anteriority, previousness, preexistence; primogeniture, birthright; eldest, firstborn, flying start 64 *precedence*; the past 125 *past time*; eve, day before; precedent, antecedent; foretaste, preview, prerelease; premonition, presentiment 510 *foresight*; herald 66 *precursor*.

Adj. *prior*, pre-, fore-; earliest, first, first in the field 64 *preceding*; previous, earlier, anterior, antecedent; antediluvian, prehistoric; prewar; preexistent; elder, eldest, firstborn; former, ci-devant, onetime, erstwhile, sometime, ex-; foregoing, aforesaid, prefatory 66 *precursory*; presupposed 512 *supposed*.

Vb. *be before* 135 *be early*; come before 283 *precede*; forerun, foreshadow, preexist.

Adv. *before*, pre-, prior to, beforehand, by; earlier, previously, formerly; already.

120. Posteriority – N. *posteriority*, subsequence, ultimogeniture, succession 65 *sequence*, 284 *following*; days to come 124 *futurity*; line, descent, successor, descendant 170 *posterity*; cadet; latecomer, new arrival; aftermath 67 *sequel*.

Adj. *subsequent*, post-, posterior, following, next, after, later; junior, cadet, younger, youngest; succeeding, designate, to be 124 *future*; posthumous, postobit; postindustrial, postwar; after Christ, AD; postprandial, after-dinner 65 *sequential*.

Vb. *ensue*, supervene, follow after 65 *come after*, 157 *result*; go after 284 *follow*; succeed, step into the shoes of 771 *inherit*.

Adv. *subsequently*, later, afterwards; at a later date; next; since, from that moment; after a while, soon after.

121. The Present Time – N. *present time*, contemporaneity, topicality 126 *modernism*; the present, present day; juncture, crisis 137 *occasion*; ongoing situation 146 *continuance*; the times, modern t., these days, this day and age; today, twentieth century, nowadays; present generation, one's contemporaries 123 *contemporary*.

Adj. *present*, actual, instant, current,

extant 1 *existing*; topical, contemporary, contemporaneous; present-day, latter-day, latest 126 *modern*.

Adv. *at present*, now, right now, at this moment; live; today, nowadays; even now, already; for the time being, for the nonce; on the spot 116 *instantaneously*; now or never.

122. Different time – **N.** *different time* 124 *futurity*, 125 *past time*; another time, some other t., not now, any time but this; jam yesterday, and jam tomorrow, but never jam today 109 *neverness*; parachronism 118 *anachronism*.

Adv. *not now*, ago, earlier, later, then; once; one of these days; someday, sometime, soon.

123. Synchronism – **N.** *synchronism*, synchrony; coexistence, coincidence, concurrence 89 *accompaniment*; simultaneousness, same time 116 *instantaneity*; contemporaneity 121 *present time*; coevality, twin birth; level-pegging, dead heat 28 *draw*; synchronization, sync, phasing, isochronism.

contemporary, coeval, twin 28 *compeer*; one's contemporaries, one's own generation; age group, peer g. 74 *group*.

Adj. *synchronous*, synchronic; contemporary, contemporaneous 121 *present*, 126 *modern*; simultaneous, coinstantaneous, coincident, coexistent, coeternal, conterminous 24 *agreeing*, 89 *accompanying*; level, neck and neck 28 *equal*; coeval, coetaneous, twin; of the same year, of the same vintage; synchronized, timed, phased, isochronous.

Vb. *synchronize*, sync, contemporize; concur, coincide, coexist 89 *accompany*; keep time, harmonize; tune, phase 24 *adjust*; pace, keep in step with.

Adv. *synchronously*, concurrently, at the same time, pari passu; in time, on the beat, simultaneously; in concert, in chorus, with one voice.

124. Futurity: prospective time – **N.** *futurity*, womb of time, time to come, morrow 120 *posteriority*; future, prospect, outlook 507 *expectation*; coming events, fate 154 *event*, 155 *destiny*; near future, tomorrow, mañana; advent 289 *approach*; long run, distant future, after ages; future generations 170 *posterity*; successorship, shadow cabinet.

future state 155 *destiny*; latter days, postindustrial age; doomsday 69 *finality*; afterlife, life to come, hereafter 971 *heaven*; good time coming, millennium 730 *prosperity*.

Adj. *future*, to be, to come 289 *approaching*; nigh, close at hand 200 *near*; on the horizon, in the wind; due, threatening, imminent 155 *impending*; in the future, ahead, yet to come; in embryo 669 *preparatory*; prospective, designate, earmarked 605 *chosen*; promised, looked for 507 *expected*; predicted, foreseeable 473 *certain*; ready to, getting on for; potential, promising; later 120 *subsequent*.

Vb. *be to come*, lie ahead; threaten, overhang 155 *impend*; near 289 *approach*; be imminent, be just round the corner, stare one in the face 200 *be near*.

Adv. *prospectively*, eventually, ultimately, in the fullness of time, in due course, in the long run, by and by; sooner or later 122 *not now*; hereafter; on the point of, about to; in the wings, in the offing.

henceforth, in future, from now on.

125. Past time: retrospective time – **N.** *past time*, past tense; retrospection, looking back 505 *remembrance*; preterite, perfect, pluperfect; the past, recent p., only yesterday 126 *newness*; distant past, history, antiquity; old story, ancient history 127 *oldness*; past times, good old days; auld lang syne, yesterday, yesteryear, former times; ancien régime; Victorian Age 110 *era*.

antiquity, eld; creation, when time began, time immemorial; prehistory, protohistory, ancient world; Stone Age, Dark Ages, Middle A. 110 *era*; the ancients; antiquities, relics 41 *remainder*; ruin, ancient monument, megalith, Stonehenge 548 *monument*, 253 *earthwork*; excavation, dig 484 *discovery*; museum 632 *collection*; fossil.

palaeology, palaeontology, palaeography; palaeoanthropology 371 *humankind*; archaeology, industrial a.; antiquarianism.

antiquarian, palaeontologist, archaeologist; antiquary 492 *scholar*; historian, medievalist 549 *chronicler*; archaist, Pre-Raphaelite.

Adj. *past*, historical; ancient, prehistoric 127 *olden*; early, primitive, proto-127 *primal*; gone, lost, irrecoverable, dead and buried 506 *forgotten*; no more, died out, dead as the dodo 2 *extinct*, 361 *dead*; passé, has-been, obsolete 674 *disused*, 127 *antiquated*; over, blown o., done, over and done with, behind one; lapsed, expired, run out 69 *ending*.

former, quondam, ex- 119 *prior*; foregoing, last 64 *preceding*; retired, outgoing 753 *resigning*; ancestral, ancient, prehistoric 127 *immemorial*; not within living memory.

retrospective, backward-looking; archaizing 505 *remembering*; diachronic, historical; retroactive, going back; with hindsight.

Vb. *be past*, have elapsed, have expired; have run its course, have had its day; pass, elapse, blow over, be o. 69 *end*; be a dead letter.

Adv. *formerly*, of old, of yore; time was, ago, long ago; once upon a time; yesterday.

retrospectively, retroactively; hitherto; no longer; from time immemorial, time out of mind; ex post facto.

126. Newness – N. *newness*, recency, recentness; recent date 121 *present time*; innovation 560 *neology*, 21 *originality*; novelty, freshness, dewiness 648 *cleanness*; greenness, rawness 130 *youth*; renovation, renewal 656 *revival*; new leaf, new broom.

modernism, modernity, modernness, modernization; up-to-dateness, topicality, contemporaneity 121 *present time*; the latest, latest fashion; the last word, dernier cri; new look 848 *fashion*.

modernist, neologist, neologian, futurist; avant-garde; bright young thing, trendy 848 *beau monde*; modern generation, younger g.

upstart, novus homo, parvenu, nouveau riche 847 *vulgarian*; Johnny-come-lately 297 *incomer*.

Adj. *new*, newish, recent, overnight; upstart, mushroom; novel, unprecedented, unheard of 21 *original*; brand-new, spick and span, like new, in mint condition 648 *clean*; green, evergreen, dewy 128 *vernal*; fresh as a daisy, fresh as paint; maiden, virgin, virginal; newborn 130 *young*; raw 670 *immature*; just out, hot from the press; new-made, new-laid; factory-fresh; unused, first-hand; untried, untrodden, unexplored 491 *unknown*; untested 461 *experimental*; budding, fledgling 68 *beginning*.

modern, late, latterday; contemporary, topical 121 *present*; up-to-the-minute, up-to-date, with it; trendy 848 *fashionable*; ultra-modern, modernistic, advanced, avant-garde, futuristic, untraditional, non-traditional, revolutionary; innovating, neoteric, newfangled, new-fashioned.

modernized, renewed, renovated, rejuvenated 656 *restored*; given a new look, brought up to date, revised; looking like new, freshened up 648 *clean*.

Vb. *modernize*, do up; update, bring up to date; have the new look, go modern, go contemporary, get with it; move with the times 285 *progress*.

Adv. *newly*, freshly, afresh, anew, like new; recently, overnight, not long ago, a short time a.; lately.

127. Oldness – N. *oldness*, primitiveness 68 *beginning*; olden times 110 *era*; age, dust of ages, ruins 125 *antiquity*; maturity 129 *autumn*; rust 51 *decay*; senility 131 *old age*.

archaism, antiquities 125 *antiquity*; ancien régime; thing of the past, relic of the p.; listed building; museum piece, antique, heirloom, bygone, Victoriana; dodo, dinosaur, fossil; oldie, golden o.; old fogey, fuddy-duddy; archaist, square, old-timer, has-been, back number.

tradition, lore, folklore, mythology; inveteracy, custom 610 *habit*; word of mouth 579 *speech*.

Adj. *olden*, old, ancient, antique, antiquarian, of historical interest; veteran, vintage; venerable, patriarchal; archaic, ancient; time-worn, ruined; prehistoric, mythological, heroic, classic, feudal, medieval, historical 125 *past*.

primal, prime, primitive, primeval, aboriginal 68 *beginning*; geological, fossil, palaeozoic 110 *secular*; palaeolithic, neolithic; early, proto-, dawn-, eo-; antediluvian.

immemorial, ancestral, traditional, time-honoured 610 *habitual*; venerable 866 *worshipful*; inveterate, established, long-standing 153 *fixed*; Ogygian, old as the hills, old as time, age-old 113 *lasting*.

antiquated, of other times, archaic; old-world, oldtime; olde worlde, ye olde; pre-war, interwar 119 *prior*; anachronistic, archaistic 125 *retrospective*; fossilized, ossified 144 *permanent*; behind the times, out of date, out of fashion, dated, Victorian, antediluvian, out of the ark, horse-and-buggy, silent-screen; old-school, square, not with it; outworn, outdated, outmoded; old fashioned, passé, démodé, vieux jeu, old hat; gone by 125 *past*; decayed 655 *dilapidated*; rusty, moth-eaten, crumbling; mildewed, moss-grown, mouldering 51 *decomposed*; fusty, stale, secondhand; obsolete, obsolescent; superannuated 674 *disused*.

128. Morning. Spring. Summer – N. *morning*, morn, forenoon, a.m.; small hours 135 *earliness*; matins, prime; dawn, dawning, cockcrow, dawn chorus 66 *precursor*; sunrise, sun-up, daybreak, dayspring 417 *light*; peep of day, break of d.; daylight, daytime; full day, prime of the morning; Aurora, Eos, rosy-fingered Dawn.

noon, high noon, meridian, midday, noonday, noontide; eight bells, twelve o'clock.

spring, springtime, springtide, Eastertide, seed-time, blossom-time, maying; first cuckoo; vernal equinox.

summer 379 *heat*; summertime, summer-tide, Whitsuntide; midsummer, summer solstice, Midsummer's Day, high summer, dog days; haymaking; aestivation; Indian summer, St Luke's s., St Martin's s.

Adj. *matinal*, matutinal, morning; diurnal, daytime; auroral, dawning, fresh, dewy 135 *early*; antemeridian.

vernal, equinoctial, spring; springlike, sappy, juicy, florescent 130 *young*.

summery, summer, aestival 379 *warm*.

Adv. *at sunrise*, at first light, at crack of dawn; with the lark; past midnight, in the small hours; a.m.

129. Evening. Autumn. Winter – N. *evening*, eventide, even, eve; evensong, vespers; afternoon, p.m.; matinée; dogwatches; sunset, sundown, evening star, Hesperus, Vesper; dusk, twilight, gloaming 419 *half-light*; cockshut, dewfall; moonrise, moonset; close of day, nightfall, dark, nighttime 418 *darkness*; bedtime 679 *sleep*; curfew, last post.

midnight, dead of night, witching time; nightwatch, small hours.

autumn, back-end, fall, fall of the leaf; harvest, harvest-time; harvest moon, hunter's m.; Michaelmas; Indian summer; autumnal equinox.

winter 380 *wintriness*; wintertime, wintertide; yuletide, Christmas; midwinter, winter solstice; hibernation.

Adj. *vespertine*, afternoon, postmeridian; vesperal, evening; dusky, crepuscular 418 *dark*, 419 *dim*; nocturnal, noctivagant; benighted, late; bedtime.

autumnal, equinoctial.

wintry, winter, brumal, brumous, snowbound 380 *cold*; leafless, stark, bleak.

130. Youth – N. *youth*, freshness, juiciness, sappiness 126 *newness*, 174 *vigorousness*; young blood, youthfulness, juvenility, juniority; babyhood, infancy, childhood, tender age 68 *beginning*; puppyhood, puppy fat; boyhood, girlhood; one's teens, adolescence, pubescence, puberty; boyishness, girlishness; awkward age, growing pains; younger generation, rising g., young idea 132 *youngster*; growing boy *or* girl, minor, ward; Peter Pan.

nonage, tender age, immaturity, minority, pupillage, wardship, leading strings; cradle, nursery, kindergarten.

salad days, heyday, prime of life, bloom.

Adj. *young*, youthful, boyish, girlish; virginal, maidenly, sweet-sixteen; adolescent, pubescent; teenage, subteenage, juvenile; maturing, developing, growing; budding, burgeoning, blooming, flowering 128 *vernal*; beardless, unripe, green, callow, raw, unfledged 670 *immature*; school-age, under-age, minor, infant, pre-school; younger, minor, junior, puisné, cadet; youngest; childish 132 *infantine*; juvenescent; young at heart, ever-young, evergreen, ageless.

131. Age – **N.** *age*, one's age, time of life, years, lifespan 113 *long duration*.

middle age, middle years, riper years, years of discretion 134 *adultness*; maturity, prime of life; a certain age, climacteric, change of life, menopause, male m., mid-life crisis.

old age, anno domini; pensionable age, retirement age; advanced years, grey hairs, white hairs 133 *old person*; senescence, declining years, vale of years, evening of one's days, winter of life 163 *weakness*; second childhood, dotage, anecdotage, anility, senility 655 *deterioration*; longevity, ripe old age.

seniority 64 *precedence*; primogeniture 119 *priority*; doyen 34 *superiority*; eldership; gerontocracy, senate 692 *council*.

gerontology, geriatrics, care of the aged 658 *therapy*.

Adj. *ageing*, aged, old, elderly, matronly; middle-aged, mature 669 *matured*; overblown, run to seed; not so young as one was, no chicken; past one's prime, getting on, getting old, greying; white-haired, hoary-headed, long in the tooth; senescent, moribund 361 *dying*; wrinkled, lined, rheumy-eyed, toothless, shrivelled, wizened, decrepit, rickety 655 *deteriorated*; drivelling, doddering, gaga 499

foolish; senile, anile; advanced in years, living on borrowed time, with one foot in the grave; longeval, old as Methuselah, old as Adam; well-preserved; venerable, patriarchal 920 *respected*; so many years old, turned, rising; too old, past it; retired; superannuated, passé(e) 127 *antiquated*; geriatric.

older, major; elder, senior 34 *superior*; eldest, primogenital 119 *prior*.

Vb. *grow old*, age; show one's years, have seen better days; go grey, turn white; pass three-score years and ten.

132. Young person. Young animal. Young plant – **N.** *child*, children, small fry; babe, baby, bundle of joy; infant, nursling, suckling; bairn, little one, tot, mite, moppet, toddler; brat, kid, kiddie; papoose, bambino; little monkey, little imp, cherub, young innocent; changeling. **See** *young creature*.

youngster, juvenile, young person, young adult, young hopeful, young'un; young people 130 *youth*; boy, schoolboy, stripling, adolescent; youth, young man, lad, laddie, sonny; urchin, nipper, cub, young shaver, whippersnapper; hobbledehoy, yob, yoblet; Ted, mod, rocker, punk, skinhead; girl, young woman; schoolgirl, lass, lassie, missie, wench, maid, maiden; chit, slip, puss, miss; teenager, teenybopper, groupie; tomboy, hoyden; little minx, baggage; colleen, damsel, nymph, nymphet. **See** *young creature*.

young creature, yearling, lamb, kid, calf, heifer; pigling, piglet; fawn, colt, foal, filly; kitten; puppy, pup, whelp, cub; chick, chicken, pullet; duckling, gosling, cygnet 365 *animal*, *bird*; fledgeling, nestling, eyas, squab; fry, litter, farrow, clutch, spawn, brood; larva, pupa, nymph; caterpillar, grub; chrysalis, cocoon; tadpole; embryo, foetus 156 *source*.

young plant, seedling, set; sucker, shoot, sprout, slip; twig, sprig, scion, sapling 366 *plant*.

Adj. *infantine*, baby, infantile, babyish, childish, childlike; juvenile, boyish, girlish 130 *young*; kittenish, coltish, hoydenish; newborn, new-fledged 126 *new*; in the cradle, in arms, at the breast; small, knee-high, half-grown 196 *little*.

133. Old person – N. *old person*, retired p., pensioner, senior citizen; old dear, old body; sexagenarian, septuagenarian, octogenarian, nonagenarian, centenarian; Methuselah.

old man, old gentleman, elderly g., patriarch 500 *sage*; grandsire, grandfather, grandad 169 *paternity*; veteran, old stager, oldtimer 696 *expert*; oldster, old'un, old boy, gaffer, greybeard; old geezer, o. codger, o. buffer, dotard.

old woman, old lady, elderly l., dowager; grandmother, granny; old girl, old trout; old dutch 894 *spouse*; no chicken; gammer, crone, hag, beldam, witch.

old couple, Darby and Joan, Philemon and Baucis, the old folks.

134. Adultness – N. *adultness*, adulthood, maturation 669 *preparedness*; riper years, years of discretion, matureness; legal age, voting a., majority, man's *or* woman's estate; manhood, womanhood, virility, nubility 372 *male*, 373 *female*; key of the door; maturity, prime, prime of life 131 *middle age*; bloom, florescence; floruit.

adult, grown-up; man 372 *male*; woman 373 *female*.

Adj. *grown-up*, adult, post-pubescent, out of one's teens; major, of age, responsible; mature, fully-developed, full-grown 669 *matured*; nubile, virile, marriageable; manly 372 *male*; womanly 373 *female*; blooming, florescent, full-blown, in full bloom, full-fledged; in one's prime.

Vb. *come of age*, grow up, mature, reach man's *or* woman's estate, attain one's majority; leave home, fly the nest.

135. Earliness – N. *earliness*, early hour 128 *morning*; early stage 68 *beginning*; early riser, early bird 66 *precursor*; aborigine 191 *native*.

punctuality, timeliness 137 *occasion*; dispatch, promptitude; immediacy 116 *instantaneity*.

anticipation, prevenience, a stitch in time 510 *foresight*, 669 *preparation*; prematurity, precocity; forestalling 64 *precedence*.

Adj. *early*, bright and e., in the small hours; prevenient, previous 119 *prior*; timely, in time, on t., in good t., punctual, prompt; forward, in advance; advanced, precocious, ahead of its time 126 *new*; sudden 116 *instantaneous*, 508 *unexpected*; forthcoming, ready 669 *prepared*; impending, imminent 200 *near*; too early, premature 670 *immature*.

Vb. *be early*, – premature etc. adj.; anticipate, nip in the bud; forestall, get there first 64 *come before*; corner the market, steal a march on 306 *outdo*; engage, book, preempt, reserve, secure, bespeak; expedite 277 *accelerate*; lose no time 680 *hasten*; start too soon, jump the gun.

Adv. *betimes*, early, soon, anon; first thing, with time to spare; punctually, to the minute; in good time.

136. Lateness – N. *lateness*, late hour, small hours 129 *midnight*; high time, eleventh hour, last minute; unreadiness, backwardness 670 *nonpreparation*; tardiness 278 *slowness*; afterthought, delayed reaction, esprit de l'escalier; latecomer, last arrival; late developer, slow starter; late riser, laggard 679 *idler*.

delay, cunctation, Fabian policy 858 *caution*; delaying tactics, gaining time, filibustering 113 *protraction*, 702 *hindrance*; holdup, check 278 *slowness*; postponement, adjournment, cooling-off period; pause, time lag, jet lag 145 *lull*; deferment, moratorium, respite, days of grace; suspension, stay of execution; procrastination, dilatoriness 679 *sluggishness*; red tape; shelving, cold storage 679 *inactivity*.

Adj. *late*, late in the day, eleventh-hour, last-minute, deathbed; too late, time up; overdue, delayed, belated, benighted; held up, bogged down; behind-hand, lagging; sluggish, tardy; backward 278 *slow*; unready, unpunctual; procrastinating, dilatory 679 *inactive*; delayed-action; deferred etc. vb.; posthumous 120 *subsequent*.

Vb. *be late*, sit up late, burn the midnight oil; lag behind 284 *follow*; stay, tarry, take one's time, be long about it, linger, dawdle 278 *move slowly*; hang back 679 *be inactive*; dally, dilly-dally; miss a chance, let the moment pass, oversleep 138 *lose a chance*; be behind-hand, have leeway to make up; put the clock back, not move with the times, look back.

wait, stay, bide one's time, hold one's horses, wait and see 145 *pause*; sleep on it, consult one's pillow 677 *not act*; hang on, hold on, stand about; be kept waiting, cool one's heels.

put off, defer, postpone, adjourn; keep, reserve, hold over; file, pigeonhole; shelve, keep on ice; suspend, hold in abeyance; procrastinate, delay, retard, set back, hold up, gain time 113 *spin out*; stall, keep one waiting 760 *refuse*.

Adv. *late*, after time, behind t.; late in the day, at the eleventh hour, last thing; at length, at last, ultimately; till all hours; too late, too late for.

137. Occasion: timeliness – N. *occasion*, happy chance, juncture 154 *event*; timeliness, opportuneness 24 *fitness*, readiness, ripeness 642 *good policy*; right time, auspicious hour, moment, well-chosen m.; nick of time 136 *lateness*.

opportunity, golden o. 469 *possibility*; break, lucky moment 159 *chance*; best chance 605 *choice*; opening, look-in, room 744 *scope*; liberty 744 *freedom*; convenience, spare time 681 *leisure*; no obstacle, clear field; handle, lever 630 *tool*, 629 *means*; stepping-stone 624 *bridge*.

crisis, critical time, key moment; turning point, psychological moment, crucial m.; emergency, extremity; pinch, push 700 *predicament*; eleventh hour, last minute.

Adj. *timely*, in time, on time, punctual 135 *early*; seasonable, welcome, well-timed; just in time, not before time, in the nick of t., at the eleventh hour.

opportune, favourable, providential, heaven-sent, auspicious, propitious; fortunate, lucky, happy 730 *prosperous*; for

the occasion, occasional, fitting 24 *apt*, 642 *advisable*.

crucial, critical, key, momentous, decisive 638 *important*.

Vb. *profit by*, improve the occasion; seize the chance, take the opportunity, make an opening; carpe diem, strike while the iron is hot, make hay while the sun shines; cash in on, capitalize, exploit, turn to good account 673 *use*.

Adv. *opportunely*, in due time, in due course, in the fullness of time; all in good time; in the nick of time, just in time, now or never.

138. Untimeliness – N. *untimeliness*, wrong time, inopportuneness 643 *inexpedience*; mishap, contretemps; evil hour 731 *misfortune*; off day; interruption, disturbance 72 *discontinuity*.

Adj. *ill-timed*, mistimed, misjudged, ill-judged; out of turn, untimely, untoward; interrupting, intrusive; malapropos, inconvenient, unsuited 25 *unapt*, 643 *inexpedient*; unseasonable, unpunctual 136 *late*; premature 135 *early*.

inopportune, untoward, inauspicious, unpropitious, unfavourable, ill-omened, ill-starred, unlucky, unhappy 731 *adverse*.

Vb. *mistime*, time it badly 481 *misjudge*; intrude, disturb, break in upon, find engaged.

lose a chance, waste time, miss the bus *or* the boat *or* the train 728 *fail*; drop a sitter, bungle 695 *be unskilful*; let the opportunity slip, let the occasion pass 136 *be late*; be otherwise engaged 678 *be busy*; let slip through one's fingers 458 *neglect*; stand in one's own light, shut the stable door after the horse has bolted 695 *act foolishly*.

Adv. *inopportunely*, amiss; as ill luck would have it, in an evil hour; a day after the fair.

139. Frequency – N. *frequency*, rapid succession, rapid fire 71 *continuity*; oftenness, regularity 141 *periodicity*, 106 *repetition*.

Adj. *frequent*, recurrent 106 *repeated*; common 104 *many*; thick on the ground 104 *multitudinous*; incessant, perpetual, continual, constant 146 *unceasing*; regular, hourly 141 *periodical*; assiduous 610 *habitual*.

Vb. *recur* 106 *reoccur*; keep on 146 *go on*, 106 *repeat oneself*; frequent, haunt 882 *visit*; obsess; plague, pester 827 *trouble*.

Adv. *often*, time and time again, times out of number; frequently, again and again 106 *repeatedly*; in quick succession, thick and fast; regularly, daily, hourly, ad libitum.

perpetually, continually, constantly, incessantly 71 *continuously*; night and day, day after day, morning, noon and night.

sometimes, occasionally, every so often, once in a while; now and then, from time to time, more often than not.

140. Infrequency – N. *infrequency*, rareness, rarity 105 *fewness*; intermittence 72 *discontinuity*; phoenix 84 *rara avis*.

Adj. *infrequent*, uncommon, sporadic, occasional; intermittent, few and far between 72 *discontinuous*; scarce, rare 105 *few*; almost unheard of, unprecedented 84 *unusual*.

Adv. *seldom*, little, once in a way; rarely, scarcely, hardly; not often, infrequently; scarcely ever, once in a blue moon.

141. Periodicity: regularity of recurrence – N. *periodicity*, regularity 16 *uniformity*; timing, phasing, serialization 71 *continuity*; alternation, turn and turn about; tide, ebb and flow, alternating current 317 *fluctuation*; to-and-fro movement, shuttle service; pulsation, pulse, tick, beat, throb, rhythm, swing 317 *oscillation*; chorus, refrain 106 *recurrence*; drumbeat 403 *roll*; frequency, wave f.; turn, round, circuit, lap; shift, relay 110 *period*.

regular return, rota, cycle, circuit, revolution, life cycle 314 *circuition*, 315 *rotation*; biorhythm; menstrual cycle, menses; yearly cycle, seasons 128 *morning*, 129 *evening*, 110 *period*; routine, daily round 60 *order*, 610 *habit*; days of the week, months of the year.

anniversary, birthday, jubilee, silver wedding, ruby w., golden w. 876 *special day*; centenary, bicentenary, tercentenary, quatercentenary, quincentenary.

Adj. *periodical*, periodic, cyclic, circling, revolving 315 *rotary*; tidal, fluctuating 317 *oscillating*; measured, rhythmical, even, like clockwork 81 *regular*; breathing, pulsating, pulsatory; throbbing, beating 318 *agitated*; recurrent, intermittent, remittent 106 *repeated*; reciprocal, alternating 12 *correlative*; serial, successive 71 *continuous*.

seasonal, anniversary; at fixed intervals, hourly, daily, nightly, diurnal, quotidian, tertian, biweekly, weekly, hebdomadal, fortnightly, monthly; menstrual; yearly, annual, biennial, triennial, quadrennial, quinquennial, decennial; bissextile, centennial, secular.

Vb. *be periodic*, recur 106 *reoccur*; serialize; revolve, return, come round again; alternate; reciprocate 12 *correlate*; fluctuate, undulate 317 *oscillate*; beat, pulse, pulsate, throb 318 *be agitated*; heave, pant 352 *breathe*; swing, sway 217 *hang*; ply, commute 610 *be wont*.

Adv. *periodically*, etc. adj.; regularly, punctually, at regular intervals; daily, weekly; per annum; at intervals, intermittently, every so often.

by turns, in turn, in rotation, turn and turn about, off and on.

142. Fitfulness: irregularity of recurrence – N. *fitfulness*, irregularity 61 *disorder*; jerkiness, fits and starts 17 *nonuniformity*, 318 *spasm*; remission 72 *discontinuity*; variability 114 *transience*, 152 *changeableness*; unpredictability, eccentricity; wobbling 317 *oscillation*.

Adj. *fitful*, periodic, intermittent, on-off, stop-go 72 *discontinuous*; irregular, uneven 29 *unequal*; occasional 140 *infrequent*; unrhythmical, unsteady, fluttering 17 *nonuniform*; inconstant, uncertain, unpunctual; variable, veering 152 *changeful*; spasmodic, jerky 318 *agitated*; wobbling, halting, wavering; desultory, unsystematic 61 *orderless*; erratic, eccentric 604 *capricious*.

Adv. *fitfully*, irregularly; unevenly, now and then 72 *discontinuously*.

Section 7: Change

143. Change: difference at different times – N. *change*, alteration, variation 15 *difference*; mutation, permutation, modulation, mutability, variability 152 *changeableness*; modification, adjustment, process, treatment 468 *qualification*; total change 147 *conversion*; sudden change 149 *revolution*; break with the past, innovation 126 *newness*; winds of change; change for the better 654 *improvement*; change for the worse 655 *deterioration*; change of direction, shift 282 *deviation*, 286 *regression*; transition 305 *passage*; transposition 151 *interchange*; alternation 141 *periodicity*; catalysis, leavening; change of mind 603 *change of allegiance*.

transformation, transfiguration, transfigurement; unrecognizability, transmogrification; metamorphosis; transmutation, transubstantiation 147 *conversion*; metempsychosis, transmigration, reincarnation, avatar.

alterer, alterant, activator, converter, transformer; catalyst, enzyme, ferment, leaven; adapter, reviser, bowdlerizer; alchemist, chemist; magician 983 *sorcerer*; improver, new broom 654 *reformer*.

Adj. *changeable*, variable, mutable; fickle 152 *changeful*; transitional, provisional, alternative, transmutative; kaleidoscopic 437 *variegated*.

modify, alter, vary, modulate; diversify, shift 437 *variegate*; superimpose 38 *add*; innovate 126 *modernize*; turn upside down 149 *revolutionize*, 221 *invert*; reverse 148 *revert*; rearrange 62 *arrange*; adapt 24 *adjust*; conform 83 *make conform*; recast, remould, reshape 243 *form*; process, treat; revise 654 *rectify*; reform 654 *make better*; revamp 656 *restore*; tamper with, mar, spoil 655 *impair*; bend, twist 246 *distort*; adulterate, doctor, qualify 43 *mix*, 163 *weaken*; disguise 525 *conceal*; change, ring the changes 151 *interchange*; 272 *transpose*; effect a change 156 *cause*; affect 178 *influence*; transform, transmute 147 *convert*.

144. Permanence: absence of change – N. *permanence*, no change, status quo; unchangeability 153 *stability*; persistence 600 *perseverance*; endurance, duration 113 *durability*, 115 *perpetuity*; fixity, immovableness 602 *obstinacy*; solidity 324 *density*; maintenance, conservation 666 *preservation*, 146 *continuance*; law, rule 153 *fixture*; long standing, inveteracy 127 *oldness*; tradition, custom 610 *habit*; fixed attitude, conservatism; routine 60 *order*; unprogressiveness 266 *quiescence*; traditionalist, conservative, true blue, stick-in-the-mud, die-hard 602 *obstinate person*.

Adj. *permanent*, enduring, durable 113 *lasting*; persistent, continuing, unfailing, sustained, maintained 146 *unceasing*, 115 *perpetual*; long-standing 127 *immemorial*; well-established, entrenched, unchangeable, immutable 153 *established*; intact, unchanged; living 666 *preserved*; unchanging, conservative, reactionary, dyed in the wool, diehard 602 *obstinate*; unprogressive, stationary, static 266 *quiescent*; unaltered, unaffected, still the same.

Vb. *stay*, come to stay, set in; abide, endure, survive 113 *last*; persist, hold good; hold on, maintain, sustain, keep up, keep on 146 *go on*; rest, remain, tarry; stand fast 600 *persevere*; stand one's ground; hold one's ground, keep one's footing 599 *stand firm*; stand still 266 *be quiescent*; allow to stand, let be, let alone, live and let live, let sleeping dogs lie 756 *permit*.

Adv. *as before*, in statu quo; at a standstill; permanently, for good.

145. Cessation: change from action to rest – N. *cessation*, ceasing; discontinuation 72 *discontinuity*; arrest 747 *restraint*; withdrawal 753 *resignation*.

stop, halt, dead stop; standstill, deadlock, stalemate 28 *draw*; checkmate 728 *defeat*; breakdown 728 *failure*; discontinuance, stoppage, stall; shutdown, nonresumption 69 *end*; hitch, check 702 *hindrance*; stasis, blockage 264 *closure*; interruption 72 *discontinuity*; closure of debate, guillotine 399 *silence*.

strike, stopping work 679 *inactivity*, 715

resistance; slowdown, work to rule; stoppage, walkout; unofficial strike, wildcat s., mutiny 738 *disobedience*; lockout 57 *exclusion*.

lull, interval, pause, remission, letup; break, breather, rest 685 *refreshment*; holiday, time off 681 *leisure*; interlude, breathing space; abeyance, suspension; close season, respite, moratorium, truce, cease-fire, standstill 136 *delay*.

stopping place, port of call, port, harbour; stop, halt, pull-up, whistle-stop, station; terminus, terminal; dead end, blind alley, cul-de-sac; destination 295 *goal*.

Vb. *cease*, stay, desist, refrain, hold; stop, halt, pull up, draw up; stand, rest, rest on one's oars 683 *repose*; have done with, see the last of, end, finish 69 *terminate*; interrupt, leave off, knock o.; break o., let up 72 *discontinue*; ring off, hang up 578 *be mute*; down tools, strike, come out; come to an end, dry up, peter out; run down, slacken off; fade out, fade away 446 *disappear*; come off, fold, collapse 728 *fail*; die away, blow over, clear up 125 *be past*; stand down, leave, retire 753 *resign*; give up, give over 621 *relinquish*; shut up, shut down, close; wind up; switch off; call it a day 266 *be quiescent*.

halt, stop, put a stop to; arrest, check, stem 702 *obstruct*; hold up, call off; pull up, cut short 747 *restrain*; bring to a standstill, freeze; checkmate 702 *hinder*; check oneself, stop short, stop dead; grind to a halt, seize up, stall, jam, stick, catch; put on the brake 278 *retard*.

pause, halt for a moment, stop for breath; hold back, hang fire 278 *move slowly*; stay one's hand, hold one's horses, hesitate 679 *be inactive*; suspend, adjourn, remit 136 *wait*; rest 683 *repose*.

Int. halt! stop! whoa! leave off! shut up! give over! cut it out! knock it off!

146. Continuance in action – N. *continuance*, continuation, flow 71 *continuity*, 144 *permanence*; maintenance, perpetuation 115 *perpetuity*; persistence 600 *perseverance*; progress 285 *progression*; break, run, rally 71 *series*; recurrence 106 *repetition*.

Adj. *unceasing*, etc. vb.; continual, steady, sustained; nonstop, unremitting, incessant 71 *continuous*; unrevoked, unvaried 153 *fixed*; undying 115 *perpetual*; unfailing, inexhaustible 635 *plenteous*; invariable 153 *unchangeable*; not out, in play 113 *lasting*; unstoppable, persistent 600 *persevering*; haunting, obsessive, recurrent 106 *repeated*.

Vb. *go on*, wag; continue, keep going, march on, proceed 285 *progress*; run on, never end 115 *be eternal*; – and – (e.g. rain and rain); roll on, take its course, trend 179 *tend*; endure, stick, hold, abide, rest, remain, linger 144 *stay*; obsess, haunt, frequent 139 *recur*; keep at it, persist, hold on, carry on, jog on, plod on 600 *persevere*; see the end of, hang on 725 *carry through*.

sustain, maintain, uphold 218 *support*; follow through 71 *continue*; keep up, keep alive 666 *preserve*; keep on, harp on 106 *repeat*; keep it up 113 *spin out*, 115 *perpetuate*; keep the pot boiling, keep the ball rolling; let things take their course 744 *give scope*.

Int. carry on! drive on! never say die! not out!

147. Conversion: change to something different – N. *conversion*, turning into, processing 164 *production*; reduction, resolution, crystallization; fermentation; chemistry, alchemy; mutation, transmutation, transfiguration 143 *transformation*; progress 285 *progression*; development 36 *increase*; evolution 358 *biology*; degeneration 655 *deterioration*; regeneration 654 *improvement*; assimilation, naturalization 78 *inclusion*; brainwashing, proselytization 178 *influence*; convertibility 469 *possibility*; transition, shift 143 *change*; crucible, melting pot.

changed person, new man *or* woman; convert 538 *learner*; renegade 603 *turncoat*.

Adj. *converted*, turned into etc. vb.; assimilated, naturalized; reborn, regenerate 656 *restored*; proselytized, brainwashed; becoming, transitional; evolving, developing, growing into; transformed, transfigured, bewitched, unrecognizable 15 *different*; convertible, impressionable 143 *changeable*.

Vb. *be turned to*, become, get; turn to, develop into, ripen i. 316 *evolve*; pass into, slide i., shift i.; melt into, merge i. 43 *be mixed*; settle into, sink i.; mellow 669 *mature*; wax 36 *grow*; degenerate 655 *deteriorate*; take the shape *or* the nature of, assume the character of; be transformed, not know oneself; suffer a sea change, turn over a new leaf, change; enter a phase.

convert, process, ferment, leaven; make into, reduce to, resolve into, turn i.; conjure i., enchant 983 *bewitch*; transmute, alchemize; render, make, mould, shape 243 *form*; brainwash 178 *influence*; proselytize, evangelize 534 *teach*; win over 485 *convince*; regenerate 656 *revive*; paganize 655 *pervert*.

transform, transfigure; disguise 525 *conceal*; deform 246 *distort*; change the face of 149 *revolutionize*; metamorphose 143 *modify*; reform, make something of 654 *make better*; remodel, reorganize; assimilate, naturalize, Americanize, Anglicize, Europeanize, Africanize, westernize, orientalize; internationalize; detribalize, denaturalize, alienize 916 *disentitle*, 57 *exclude*.

148. Reversion – N. *reversion*, reverting, return, retrogression 286 *regression*; tracing back, derivation 156 *source*; harking back 127 *archaism*; atavism, throwback 5 *heredity*; retrospection 505 *remembrance*; reaction, backlash 280 *recoil*; revulsion, disenchantment; counter-revolution, reversal · 149 *revolution*; retraction 603 *change of allegiance;* volte face, about-turn, U-t.; backsliding, recidivism 657 *relapse*; reconversion 656 *restoration*; retortion 248 *curvature*, 246 *distortion*; replacement, reinstatement 787 *restitution*; recovery, retrieval, escheat 771 *acquisition*; turn, turning point, turn of the tide, calm before the storm 137 *crisis*; swing 141 *periodicity*; round trip, there and back; back where one started, status quo; resumption, recommencement.

Adj. *reverted*, reversed, reversionary, retrograde, retrogressive, recessive, reflexive 286 *regressive*; recoiling; reactionary, atavistic 5 *genetic*; recycled, returned; recovered, disenchanted 656 *restored*; as you were.

Vb. *revert*, go back, return, retrace 286 *regress*; reverse, face about; slip back, slide b., backslide 657 *relapse*; back down, retract 603 *recant*; hark back, archaize; restart, go back to the beginning, undo, unmake 68 *begin*; restore the status quo, revive 656 *restore*; derestrict, decontrol; reconvert, disenchant 613 *dissuade*; resume, recover 656 *retrieve*; reinstate, replace 787 *restitute*.

149. Revolution: sudden or violent change – N. *revolution*, full circle, radical change; clean sweep 550 *obliteration*; catastrophe, coup d'état 508 *lack of expectation*; leap, plunge, throe 318 *spasm*; shift, swing, switch, landslide; bouleversement, upset, overthrow; convulsion, shake-up, upheaval 176 *outbreak*; avalanche, crash, debacle 165 *havoc*; revulsion, rebellion, counter-revolution 148 *reversion*, 738 *revolt*; abolition, nullification 752 *abrogation*.

revolutionist, radical, revolutionary, Marxist, Red 738 *revolter*; anarchist 654 *reformer*.

Adj. *revolutionary* 126 *new*; radical, thoroughgoing, root and branch 54 *complete*; cataclysmic, catastrophic, worldshaking 176 *violent*; seditious, subversive, Marxist 738 *disobedient*; anarchistic.

Vb. *revolutionize*, overturn 221 *invert*; uproot, eradicate, make a clean sweep 550 *obliterate*, 165 *demolish*; break with the past, remodel, refashion 126 *modernize*; change beyond recognition 147 *transform*.

150. Substitution: change of one thing for another – N. *substitution*, commutation, exchange, switch 151 *interchange*; supersession, replacement, transfer 272 *transference*; vicariousness; compensation 941 *atonement*.

substitute, sub; proxy, agent, representative 755 *deputy*; understudy, stand-in

594 *actor*; ghost 589 *author*; locum 658 *doctor*; reserve, reservist 707 *auxiliary*; supply, replacement, remount; relief 67 *successor*; double, changeling 545 *impostor*; mother figure, father f., foster parent; synonym, doublet; metaphor, symbol 551 *representation*; prosthesis, artificial limb, pacemaker; transplant; alternative, second best, pis aller, ersatz 35 *inferiority*; whipping boy, scapegoat, guilt-offering, sacrifice; makeshift, stopgap; sticking plaster 177 *moderator*; expedient, modus vivendi 770 *compromise*.

q̄uid pro quo, equivalent; consideration; value, worth 809 *price*; redemption, compensation; new lamps for old, replacement.

Adj. *substituted*, substitutive, substitutional; vicarious; substitutable, interchangeable 28 *equivalent*; dummy, imitation, ersatz, counterfeit 542 *spurious*; makeshift, stopgap, provisional, acting 114 *ephemeral*.

Vb. *substitute*, change for, commute; exchange, switch 151 *interchange*; take *or* offer in exchange 770 *compromise*; palm off with, fob off w. 542 *deceive*; make do with, put up w., make shift w.; put in the place of, replace with; count as, treat as, regard as; succeed 65 *come after*; supersede, supplant, displace; replace, take the place of, do duty for, stand in f., understudy f. 755 *deputize*; ghost for; shoulder the blame, take the rap for, cover up f.; rob Peter to pay Paul.

Adv. *instead*, in place, in lieu; in favour of; in loco parentis; by proxy; alternatively; in default of, for want of better.

151. Interchange: double or mutual change – N. *interchange*, interchangeability, reciprocality; swap, exchange 791 *barter*; permutation, anagram; transposal, transposition, mutual transfer; all change, general post; castling (chess), shuffle, shuffling 272 *transference*; interplay, two-way traffic, reciprocation 12 *correlation*; quid pro quo; rally (tennis), give and take; repartee 460 *rejoinder*; tit for tat 714 *retaliation*; logrolling 706 *cooperation*.

Adj. *interchanged*, exchanged etc. vb.;

in exchange, mutual, two-way 12 *correlative*; reciprocal 714 *retaliatory*; inter-, interchangeable, substitutable, convertible, commutable.

Vb. *interchange*, exchange, counterchange; change money, convert; swap, barter 791 *trade*; permute, commute; switch, shuffle 272 *transpose*; give and take 770 *compromise*; reciprocate, requite; give as good as one gets 714 *retaliate*; bandy words 460 *answer*; take in each other's washing, scratch each other's back 706 *cooperate*.

Adv. *in exchange*, vice versa, mutatis mutandis; to and fro, turn and turn about; each in turn; in kind; interchangeably, conversely.

152. Changeableness – N. *changeableness*, changeability, mutability, modifiability, changefulness 143 *change*; variability 17 *nonuniformity*, 437 *variegation*; inconsistency, irregularity; instability, unsteadiness; plasticity, pliancy 327 *softness*; fluidness 335 *fluidity*; mobility, restlessness 318 *agitation*; fluctuation, alternation 317 *oscillation*; chopping and changing 142 *fitfulness*; impermanence, flicker, flash 114 *transience*; vacillation, wavering 601 *irresolution*; fickleness, capriciousness 604 *caprice*.

changeable thing, variable; moon, Proteus, chameleon; changing scene, kaleidoscope; shifting sands; wax, clay; mercury, quicksilver; wind, weathercock, mobile 265 *motion*; fortune, wheel of Fortune 159 *chance*; grasshopper mind 456 *inattention*; floating voter 603 *turncoat*.

Adj. *changeful*, changing, mutable, alterable, phased 143 *changeable*; shifting, vicissitudinous; varying, variable 17 *nonuniform*; kaleidoscopic 437 *iridescent*; protean 82 *multiform*; quick-change, versatile 694 *skilful*; uncertain, unreliable, vacillating 601 *irresolute*; unpredictable, unaccountable 508 *unexpected*; never the same, volatile, mercurial 15 *different*; wayward, fickle 604 *capricious*; inconstant 603 *trimming*.

unstable, unsteady, unsound; wavering,

wobbling, rocky, tottering 317 *oscillating*; mobile, unquiet, restless, fidgety 318 *agitated*; spasmodic, flickering 142 *fitful*, 114 *transient*; shifting, veering, chopping and changing, unsettled, unattached; erratic, mercurial; rootless, homeless vagrant 59 *extraneous*; fluctuating 141 *periodical*; impressionable, malleable, plastic 327 *soft*; flowing 335 *fluid*.

Vb. *vary*, ring the changes 437 *variegate*; have as many phases as the moon; change, chop and change, change and change about; flitter 265 *be in motion*; leap, flicker, gutter 417 *shine*; flutter, flap 217 *hang*; wobble, rock, sway 317 *oscillate*; alternate, ebb and flow, wax and wane; veer, whiffle 352 *blow*; vacillate, waver 601 *be irresolute*; blow hot and cold, be inconstant 604 *be capricious*.

153. Stability – N. *stability*, immutability, unchangeableness; invariability 16 *uniformity*; firmness, fixity 144 *permanence*; immobility, immovability 266 *quiescence*; stableness, stabilization, steadiness, stable equilibrium, homoeostasis 28 *equality*; nerve, aplomb 599 *resolution*; stiffness, inflexibility 326 *hardness*, 602 *obstinacy*; solidarity 324 *density*; stabilizer, fin, keel.

fixture, establishment, firm foundation; foundations, rock, bedrock; pillar, tower; invariant, constant; leopard's spots; law of the Medes and Persians 953 *legality*.

Adj. *unchangeable*, stiff, inflexible 602 *obstinate*; unwavering 599 *resolute*; predictable, reliable 473 *certain*; immutable, incommutable; unalterable, inconvertible; irreducible, indissoluble; changeless, unchanging, inalterable; unshrinkable, shrinkproof; unvarying, invariable, constant 16 *uniform*; steady, undeviating 81 *regular*; durable 144 *permanent*, 115 *perpetual*; imperishable, indestructible 660 *invulnerable*. **See** fixed.

established, well-e., entrenched, vested, settled; inveterate, prescriptive 113 *lasting*; irrevocable, irreversible; incontrovertible, indefeasible, of right; confirmed, ratified 473 *undisputed*.

fixed, steadfast, firm, secure, immovable, irremovable; unassailable, unshakable, steady as a rock; steady, stable; fast, ingrained, indelible; engraved; ineradicable, rooted, deep-r.; deep-seated, foursquare, well-founded; stuck fast, stranded, grounded, high and dry; pinned down, transfixed; immobile, frozen 266 *still*.

Vb. *stabilize*, root, entrench, establish; erect, set up 218 *support*; fix, set; validate 488 *endorse*; bind, make fast; keep steady, balance 28 *equalize*.

154. Present Events – N. *event*, phenomenon; fact, matter of f. 1 *reality*; case, circumstance, occurrence, eventuality, incidence, realization, happening, turn of events; incident, episode, adventure, occasion; milestone 8 *juncture*; coincidence, accident, contingency 159 *chance*; misadventure, mishap 731 *misfortune*; emergency 137 *crisis*; encounter; issue, outcome 157 *effect*; catastrophe, peripeteia.

affairs, matters, doings, transactions 676 *deed*; agenda, order of the day; involvement, concerns, interests, irons in the fire, axes to grind 622 *business*; world, life, situation 8 *circumstance*; current affairs, state of affairs; course of events, run of affairs, chapter of accidents, vicissitudes 730 *prosperity*, 731 *adversity*.

Adj. *happening*, incidental, accidental, occasional; doing, current, on foot, afloat, in the wind, on the agenda; circumstantial, contingent.

eventful, stirring, bustling, busy 678 *active*; momentous, critical 638 *important*.

Vb. *happen*, become, come into existence; materialize, be realized, come off 727 *succeed*; take place, occur, come about, come to pass; befall, betide 159 *chance*; turn up, crop up, arise 295 *arrive*; present itself, announce i.; supervene 284 *follow*; eventuate, issue, transpire 157 *result*; turn out, fall o., pan o.; take its course, continue 146 *go on*; go off, pass o.; fall to one's lot, be so, prove.

meet with, incur, encounter 295 *meet*; realize, find 484 *discover*; experience, pass through, go t.; endure, undergo 825 *suffer*.

155. Destiny: future events – N. *destiny*, what's to come, one's stars 596 *fate*; horoscope, forecast 511 *prediction*; prospect, outlook 507 *expectation*; coming events 124 *futurity*; trouble in store 900 *threat*; imminence 289 *approach*; future existence 124 *future state*; world to come 971 *heaven*; foredoom, predestination 596 *necessity*.

Adj. *impending*, hanging over, louring, hovering, imminent 900 *threatening*; brewing, cooking 669 *preparatory*; destined, predestined, in the stars, in the lap of the gods 596 *fated*; predicted, forthcoming, forecast; inescapable, inevitable, due 473 *certain*; in the wind, on the cards 471 *probable*; in prospect, in the offing, on the horizon 443 *visible*; in the future, to come, in the womb of time 124 *future*; at hand, close; about to be, on the point of; pregnant with, heavy w. 511 *presageful*; in store 669 *prepared*; in embryo 68 *beginning*.

Vb. *impend* 124 *be to come*; hang over, hover, loom 900 *threaten*; draw nigh 289 *approach*; face, stare one in the f.; breathe down one's neck 200 *be near*; ripen 669 *mature*.

predestine, destine, doom, foredoom, preordain, foreordain 596 *necessitate*; foreshadow, adumbrate, presage 511 *predict*; have in store 669 *make ready*; plan, intend 608 *predetermine*.

Section 8: Causation

156. Cause: constant antecedent – N. *causation*, causality, cause and effect, ground and consequent; aetiology 158 *attribution*; authorship; origination, creation 21 *originality*; invention 484 *discovery*; inspiration 178 *influence*; generation, evocation, provocation, production; stimulation, fomentation, encouragement, motivation 612 *motive*.

cause, first c., final c.; prime mover, creator 164 *producer*; father 169 *parentage*; author, inventor, originator, founder; agent; spark, stimulus 174 *stimulant*; contributor, factor, decisive f., moment, determinant; inspirer, mainspring 612 *motivator*; fomenter, abettor; hidden hand, undercurrents 178 *influence*; fate 596 *necessity*; force 740 *compulsion*.

source, fountain, fount, fons et origo 68 *origin*; headwaters, spring, wellhead, fountainhead, wellspring; mine, quarry 632 *store*; birthplace, roots 192 *home*; genesis, ancestry 169 *parentage*; ancestor, progenitor; loins 167 *genitalia*; rudiment, element, principle, first p.; nucleus, germ, seed, sperm, spore; egg; chrysalis, cocoon 132 *young creature*; stock, rootstock; taproot 366 *plant*; foundation, bedrock 214 *base*; groundwork, spadework 68 *beginning*; raw material, ore 631 *materials*.

seedbed, hotbed; cradle, nursery 68 *origin*; fertile soil, breeding ground, hothouse, incubator, womb 167 *propagation*.

reason why, reason, cause; explanation, key 460 *answer*; excuse 614 *pretext*; ground, basis, rationale, motive, raison d'être.

Adj. *causal*, causative, formative, effective, effectual; pivotal, determinant, decisive; seminal, germinal 164 *productive*; suggestive, inspiring 178 *influential*; impelling 740 *compelling*; answerable, responsible; at the bottom of; creative, inventive 21 *inimitable*.

fundamental, primary, elemental, ultimate; foundational, radical, basic 5 *intrinsic*; crucial, central 638 *important*; original, primordial 127 *primal*.

Vb. *cause*, originate, create, make 164 *produce*; beget 167 *generate*; invent 484 *discover*; be the reason 158 *account for*; underlie, be at the bottom *or* the root of; sow the seeds of, be answerable, be responsible, have a hand in, be to blame; institute, found, lay the foundations 68 *auspicate*; launch, initiate, set up, set going, trigger off, spark off, touch o. 68 *begin*; sow, cultivate; contrive, effect, effectuate, bring about, procure, stage-manage, engineer 623 *plan*; bring on, induce, precipitate 680 *hasten*; bring out, evoke, elicit 291 *attract*; provoke, arouse, awaken, excite; stimulate 174 *invigorate*; kindle, inspire, incite; occasion 612 *motivate*; have an effect 178 *influence*; determine, decide, turn the scale 178 *prevail*, 34 *predominate*.

conduce, tend to 179 *tend*; lead to, contribute to, operate to 628 *be instrumental*; involve, imply; have the effect, entail, draw down, give rise to, open the door to 68 *initiate*; promote, advance, encourage, foster, foment, abet 703 *aid*.

157. Effect: constant sequel – N. *effect*, consequent, consequence, corollary 65 *sequence*; result, upshot, outcome, issue, denouement; development 154 *event*, 725 *completion*; visible effect, mark 548 *trace*; by-product, side effect, spin-off; aftermath, legacy, backwash, repercussion 67 *sequel*; response 460 *answer*; reaction, backlash 182 *counteraction*; offspring 170 *posterity*; handiwork 164 *product*; moral effect 178 *influence*.

Adj. *caused*, owing to, due to; consequential, resulting from, consequent upon 65 *sequential*; contingent, depending, dependent on; resultant, derivative, descended; hereditary 5 *genetic*; unoriginal, secondary 20 *imitative*; arising, emanating, developed from, born of, out of, by; effected, done.

Vb. *result*, be the r., come of; accrue, follow; be owing to, be due to; owe everything to, borrow from 9 *be related*; derive from, descend f., originate in; issue, proceed, emanate, emerge; grow from, spring f., arise f., flow f.; develop, unfold; bud, sprout, germinate; bear the stamp of; turn out 154 *happen*; result in 164 *produce*.

depend, hang upon, hinge on, pivot on, turn on 12 *correlate*.

Adv. *consequently,* in consequence; of course, necessarily; it follows that 158 *hence*.

158. Attribution: assignment of cause – N. *attribution*, imputation; theory, hypothesis, assumption, conjecture 512 *supposition*; explanation 520 *interpretation*; finding reasons, accounting for; aetiology 459 *inquiry*; rationale 156 *reason why*; affiliation, parentage; derivation 156 *source*; credit, acknowledgement.

Adj. *attributed*, assigned etc. vb.; attributable, assignable, imputable, referable 9 *relative*; credited, imputed, putative 512 *supposed*; inferred, inferable, derivable, traceable; owing to, explained by 157 *caused*.

Vb. *attribute*, ascribe, impute; predicate 532 *affirm*; grant, allow; put down to, set down to; assign to, point to, trace to, connect with, derive from 9 *relate*; lay at the door of, father upon; charge with, saddle on; found upon, ground u.; make responsible, scapegoat, blame for 928 *accuse*; credit with, acknowledge.

account for, explain 520 *interpret*; theorize, hypothesize, assume, infer 512 *suppose*.

Adv. *hence*, thence, therefore; whence; for, since, on account of, because, owing to, thanks to; ergo, thus, so; that's why.

159. Chance: no assignable cause – N. *chance*, blind c., fortuity, indeterminacy; randomness; fortuitousness; unpredictability 474 *uncertainty*; unaccountability 517 *unintelligibility*; wheel of Fortune 596 *fate*; potluck, luck of the draw; luck 730 *prosperity*; bad luck 731 *misfortune*; hap, hazard, accident, coincidence, chapter of accidents 154 *event*; fluke 618 *nondesign*; chance in a million 140 *infrequency*; chance discovery, serendipity 484 *discovery*.

equal chance, even c., fifty-fifty; toss-up, heads or tails, lucky dip, random sample; lottery 618 *gambling*.

fair chance, sporting c., fighting c. 469 *possibility*; half a chance 472 *improbability*; long odds, odds on 34 *advantage*; safe bet 471 *probability*.

calculation of chance, theory of probabilities; risk-taking, insurance, underwriting; bookmaking 618 *gambling*.

Adj. *casual*, fortuitous, aleatory, chance, haphazard, random, stray, out of a hat 618 *designless*; adventitious, accidental, incidental, contingent; coincidental 10 *unrelated*; chancy, fluky, dicey, incalculable, stochastic 474 *uncertain*.

causeless, unforeseeable, unpredictable; unmotivated, unintended, unplanned 618 *unintentional*; unaccountable, inexplicable 517 *puzzling*.

Vb. *chance*, hap, so happen 154 *happen*; chance upon, light u., hit u., stumble u., blunder u. 154 *meet with*, 484 *discover*; chance it 618 *gamble*.

Adv. *by chance*, by accident; accidentally, unintentionally, fortuitously, at random; luckily, unluckily; unpredictably, unaccountably.

160. Power – N. *power*, potency, mightiness 32 *greatness*; predominance 34 *superiority*; omnipotence 733 *authority*; control, sway 733 *governance*; ascendancy 178 *influence*; charisma, mana; witchcraft 983 *sorcery*; staying power, endurance 153 *stability*; driving force 612 *motive*; physical power, might, muscle 162 *strength*; might and main, effort 682 *exertion*; force 740 *compulsion*; stress, strain, shear; weight 322 *gravity*; weight of numbers 104 *greater number*; manpower 686 *personnel*; position of power 34 *advantage*; extra power, overdrive.

ability, capability, potentiality 469 *possibility*; competence, efficacy 694 *skill*; capacity, faculty, virtue, property 5 *intrinsicality*; qualification 24 *fitness*; attribute 89 *concomitant*; endowment, gift 694 *aptitude*; compass, reach, grasp 183 *range*; susceptibility 180 *liability*; empowering, enablement.

energy, vigour, drive 174 *vigorousness*; work; mechanical energy, pedal power, engine power, horsepower; inertia, vis inertiae 175 *inertness*; resistance 333 *friction*; force, field of f. 162 *science of forces*; force of gravity 322 *gravity*; buoyancy 323 *lightness*; compression, spring 328 *elasticity*; pressure, head, charge, steam; steam up; tension, high t.; motive power, pulling p. 288 *traction*; pushing power, thrust, jet, jet propulsion 287 *propulsion*; momentum, impetus 279 *impulse*; magnetic field 291 *attraction*; potential function, potential; erg, joule; newton; calorie.

sources of energy, coal, gas, oil 385 *fuel*; nuclear power (**see** *nucleonics*); renewable energy sources, wind power, wave p., geothermal p., solar energy, hydroelectricity; powerhouse, power station; tidal barrage; solar panel, heat exchanger 383 *heater*; generator, turbine, motor 630 *machine*.

electricity, thermoelectricity, photoelectricity, piezoelectricity; static electricity; lightning; electrodynamics, electrostatics, electromagnetism; induction, capacitance; resistance, conduction; pulsation, frequency; electric charge, pulse, shock; electric current, direct c., alternating c.; circuit, short c., closed c.; electrode; conductor, insulator; earth 662 *safeguard*; electrification, live wire.

electronics, electron physics 417 *optics*; lasers 417 *radiation*; computer electronics 196 *microelectronics*, 86 *data processing*; telegraph 531 *telecommunication*; electrical engineering; power line, pylon, national grid; magneto, dynamo; transformer, power pack; cell, battery, storage b.; accumulator; valve, transistor; voltage, volt, watt; ohm; ampere, amp.

nucleonics, nuclear physics; fission, fusion, thermonuclear reaction; atom-smasher, particle accelerator, linear a., cyclotron, synchrotron; nuclear reactor, fast breeder r., waste-reprocessing plant; Magnox reactor, AGR, LWR, PWR, SGHWR; radioactivity, fallout 417 *radiation*; atomic bomb 723 *bomb*.

Adj. *powerful*, potent 162 *strong*; puissant, mighty 32 *great*; rising, in the ascendant 36 *increasing*; prevailing, predominant 178 *influential*; almighty, omnipotent, irresistible 34 *supreme*; empowered, plenipotentiary 733 *authoritative*; competent, capable, able, equal to 635 *sufficient*; with resources 800 *rich*; efficacious, effective 727 *successful*; operative, workable, having teeth; in force, valid 153 *established*; cogent, compulsive 740 *compelling*; forcible 176 *violent*.

dynamic, energetic 174 *vigorous*; high-potential, high-tension, supercharged, souped-up; magnetic 291 *attracting*; tractive 288 *drawing*; propelling 287 *propulsive*, 279 *impelling*; locomotive, kinetic 265 *moving*; powered, engined, driven;

automated 630 *mechanical*; electric, electrical, electromagnetic, electronic; solid-state; live, charged; on stream; atomic, nuclear, thermonuclear; hydroelectric, geothermal.

Vb. *be able*, – powerful etc. adj.; can, have it in one's power, have it in one; be capable of, have the virtue, have the property; compass, manage 676 *do*; measure up to 635 *suffice*; have power, control 733 *dominate*; force 740 *compel*; gain power, come to p. 178 *prevail*.

empower, enable, endow, authorize; invest with power; put teeth into, arm 162 *strengthen*; electrify, charge, magnetize; transistorize, automate; power, drive.

161. Impotence – N. *impotence*, lack of power, no authority; invalidity, impuissance 163 *weakness*; inability, incapacity; incapability 728 *failure*; decrepitude 131 *age*; invalidation, disqualification 752 *abrogation*; sterility, sterilization 172 *unproductiveness*; demobilization 75 *dispersion*.

helplessness, defencelessness 661 *vulnerability*; powerlessness 745 *subjection*, 747 *restraint*; prostration, exhaustion 684 *fatigue*; collapse, unconsciousness 375 *insensibility*; stroke, paralysis, paraplegia 651 *disease*; atrophy 655 *deterioration*; ataxia; incontinence; senility, imbecility 503 *insanity*; legal incapacity 130 *nonage*; babyhood 163 *weakling*.

eunuch, castrato; gelding, capon, bullock, steer, neuter; freemartin, hermaphrodite.

ineffectuality, ineffectiveness, futility, uselessness 641 *inutility*; flash in the pan 114 *transience*; dead letter, scrap of paper; man of straw, broken reed 4 *insubstantial thing*; bluster 515 *empty talk*.

Adj. *powerless*, impotent, not able, unable; unempowered, without authority; nominal, figurehead, constitutional 4 *insubstantial*; invalid, null and void 954 *illegal*; without a leg to stand on 163 *weak*; inoperative, suspended 752 *abrogated*; obsolete; disqualified, deposed; kaput, dud, good for nothing 641 *useless*; in-

adequate 636 *insufficient*; ineffective, inefficacious, ineffectual, feeble 728 *unsuccessful*; incapable, unqualified 695 *unskilful*; unequipped 670 *unprepared*.

defenceless, helpless, without resource; bereaved 772 *losing*; orphan 883 *friendless*; weak, harmless; weaponless, unarmed 670 *unequipped*; unfortified, exposed, indefensible, untenable, pregnable 661 *vulnerable*.

impotent, powerless, feeble 163 *weak*; emasculated, etc. vb.; unsexed, unmanned, sterilized 172 *unproductive*; sexless, neuter; exhausted, effete; senile 131 *ageing*; arthritic, stiff; unconscious, drugged 375 *insensible*; incapacitated, disabled, paralysed 163 *crippled*; incontinent; done up, dead-beat, prostrated 684 *fatigued*; nerveless, spineless, boneless 601 *irresolute*; shattered, unhinged, unnerved, shell-shocked 854 *nervous*; baffled, thwarted, helpless, on one's beam ends 728 *grounded*.

Vb. *be impotent*, – defenceless etc. adj.; be unable, cannot, not work, not do, not alter things 641 *be useless*, 728 *fail*; have no power 745 *be subject*; go by the board; cut no ice 639 *be unimportant*; wring one's hands, gnash one's teeth 830 *regret*; look on, stand by; not have a leg to stand on; faint, pass out 375 *be insensible*; drop, collapse 163 *be weak*.

disable, incapacitate; disqualify 916 *disentitle*; invalidate 752 *abrogate*; disarm, demilitarize 163 *weaken*; neutralize 182 *counteract*; undermine, sap; wind, prostrate, knock out 279 *strike*; paralyse 679 *make inactive*; sprain, rick, wrench, twist, dislocate; cripple, lame, maim, hobble, nobble, hamstring 702 *hinder*, 655 *impair*; stifle, throttle, suffocate, strangle 362 *kill*; muzzle, deaden 399 *silence*; sabotage, spike the guns, draw the teeth, clip the wings; tie one's hands, cramp one's style; deflate, take the wind out of one's sails; unhinge, unstring; put out of action 674 *stop using*.

unman, unnerve, enervate, paralyse 854 *frighten*; devitalize 163 *weaken*; emasculate, castrate, neuter, spay, geld, caponize, effeminize.

162. Strength – N. *strength*, might, potency 160 *power*; energy 174 *vigorousness*; force, physical f., main f. 735 *brute force*; resilience 328 *elasticity*; tone, tonicity, temper; load-bearing capacity, tensile strength; iron, steel 326 *hardness*; oak, heart of oak 329 *toughness*; endurance, grit 600 *stamina*.

vitality, healthiness 650 *health*; vim, vigour, liveliness 360 *life*; animal spirits 833 *cheerfulness*; virility, red-bloodedness, guts, nerve 599 *resolution*; aggressiveness 718 *bellicosity*; physique, muscularity, muscle, biceps, sinews; beefiness, brawn 195 *size*; grip, iron g. 778 *retention*; titanic strength, strength of Hercules.

athletics 837 *sport*, 716 *contest*; athleticism, gymnastics, acrobatics, callisthenics 682 *exercise*; stadium, gymnasium 724 *arena*.

athlete, gymnast, tumbler, acrobat, funambulist, contortionist, trapeze artist, circus rider, bareback r., stunt man 594 *entertainer*; Blue, all-rounder 716 *contender*; wrestler 716 *wrestling*; heavyweight 722 *pugilist*; weight-lifter, strong man, muscle man; champion 644 *exceller*; strongarm man, bruiser, tough guy; amazon, virago; matador, picador, toreador; Tarzan, Hercules; Samson, Goliath, Atlas 195 *giant*.

strengthening, fortifying etc. vb.; reinforcement 703 *aid*; toughening, tempering 326 *hardening*; invigoration 174 *stimulation*; reanimation 685 *refreshment*; revival 656 *restoration*.

science of forces, dynamics, statics, hydrodynamics, electrodynamics, thermodynamics; triangle of forces.

Adj. *strong*, lusty, vigorous, virile, red-blooded, 130 *young*; mighty, high-powered, potent, armed 160 *powerful*; all-powerful, sovereign; overpowering, overwhelming 34 *superior*; irresistible, more than a match for; in full swing, undiminished 32 *great*; in high feather, in fine fettle, fit as a fiddle, sound as a bell 650 *healthy*; heavy 322 *weighty*; forceful, compulsive 740 *compelling*; tempered, steely 326 *hard*; reinforced 329 *tough*; solid, substantial 153 *fixed*; thick-ribbed, well-built, stout; strong as a horse *or* an ox; heady 949 *intoxicating*; undiluted, neat; strengthened, fortified, double-strength; entrenched, unassailable 660 *invulnerable*.

unyielding, staunch 599 *resolute*; stubborn 602 *obstinate*; persistent 600 *persevering*; inelastic 326 *rigid*; shatterproof, unbreakable, solid 324 *dense*; impregnable 660 *invulnerable*; indomitable, invincible 727 *unbeaten*; inextinguishable, unquenchable 146 *unceasing*; unflagging, tireless; indestructible, non-biodegradable 113 *lasting*; proof, sound; waterproof, weatherproof, impermeable 264 *sealed off*; bulletproof, bombproof.

stalwart, stout, sturdy, hardy, rugged, robust, doughty 174 *vigorous*; able-bodied, muscular, brawny; sinewy, wiry; strapping, well set-up, broad-shouldered, barrel-chested, thickset, stocky, mesomorphic, burly, beefy, husky, hefty, Herculean 195 *large*.

athletic, gymnastic, acrobatic; fit, fighting f., in training, in condition 650 *healthy*; amazonian.

Vb. *be strong*, – mighty etc. adj.; have what it takes; pack a punch; come in force; overpower 727 *overmaster*; rally, revive 656 *be restored*, 685 *be refreshed*.

strengthen, confirm, lend force to 36 *augment*; underline, stress 532 *emphasize*; reinforce, fortify, entrench; stuff, pad; buttress, prop 218 *support*; nerve, brace, steel 855 *give courage*; stiffen, toughen 326 *harden*; energize, put beef into 174 *invigorate*; beef up, build up, tone up 821 *excite*; reinvigorate 685 *refresh*; set on one's legs 656 *cure*.

163. Weakness – N. *weakness*, lack of strength, feebleness, helplessness 161 *impotence*; slightness, flimsiness, delicacy, fragility, frailness 330 *brittleness*; effeminacy, womanishness; unsteadiness, shakiness, ineffectiveness 161 *ineffectuality*; moral weakness, frailty, feet of clay; weakliness, debility, infirmity, caducity 131 *old age*; invalidism, delicate health 651 *ill health*; atony, no tone, flaccidity, flabbiness 327 *softness*; asthenia, cachexia; anaemia; enervation, inanition, faintness; exhaustion, prostration 684 *fatigue*; decline 655 *deterioration*; watering, dilution 43 *mixture*; enfeeblement, debilitation, devitalization 655 *impairment*; emasculation, evisceration; fault, flaw 845 *blemish*; strain, sprain; weak point, Achilles' heel 647 *defect*.

weakling, effeminate, pansy; cissy, milksop, mollycoddle, namby-pamby; invalid, hypochondriac 651 *sick person*; babe-in-arms, kitten 132 *young creature*; baby, crybaby 856 *coward*; mother's darling, teacher's pet 890 *favourite*; drip, weed, wet; doormat 825 *sufferer*.

weak thing, reed, thread, rope of sand; sandcastle, house of cards; cobweb, gossamer 4 *insubstantial thing*; matchwood, eggshell 330 *brittleness*; water, milk and water.

Adj. *weak*, powerless, strengthless 161 *impotent*; without force, invalid 161 *powerless*; understrength, underproof; unfortified, unstrengthened, unaided, helpless 161 *defenceless*; harmless 935 *innocent*; namby-pamby, babyish 132 *infantine*; effeminate, limp-wristed, poor, feeble; slight, puny 33 *small*; slightly built 323 *light*; feeble-minded 499 *foolish*; sheepish, gutless, weak-willed 601 *irresolute*; nerveless, unnerved 854 *nervous*; spineless, weak-kneed, submissive 721 *submitting*; untempered, unhardened, limp, flaccid, flabby, floppy 327 *soft*; drooping, sagging 217 *hanging*; untaut, unstrung, slack, loose; watery, wishy-washy, milk-and-water, insipid 387 *tasteless*; faint 401 *muted*; doddering, tottering, decrepit, old 131 *ageing*; past it, weak as a child, weak as a kitten; wavering, shaky 152 *unstable*; infant 130 *young*. See flimsy.

weakened, debilitated 37 *decreasing*; spent, effete, used up, burnt out 673 *used*; misused, abused; sapped, undermined, disarmed, disabled 161 *defenceless*; stripped, exposed, bare; flagging, failing, exhausted 684 *fatigued*; strained 246 *distorted*; weatherbeaten, worn, crumbling, tumbledown 655 *dilapidated*; the worse for wear, not what it was, on its last legs; rotten, rusting, decaying 51 *decomposed*;

deactivated, neutralized 175 *inert*; diluted, adulterated, watered down. **See** crippled.

weakly, infirm, asthenic, delicate, sickly 651 *unhealthy*; groggy, rocky; run down, seedy, poorly; anaemic, underweight, skinny 206 *lean*; languid, languishing, listless; faint, fainting; sallow, wan, lacklustre 426 *colourless*.

crippled, disabled; halt, lame, game, limping, hobbling; hamstrung, hobbled 161 *impotent*; arthritic, rheumatic, gouty; legless, armless.

flimsy, gossamer, wispy, tenuous 4 *insubstantial*; delicate, dainty, lacy; frail, fragile 330 *brittle*; gimcrack, jerry-built, shoddy 641 *useless*; rickety, ramshackle, wobbly, wonky 655 *dilapidated*.

Vb. *be weak*, weaken; sicken 651 *be ill*; faint, fail, flag 684 *be fatigued*; dwindle 37 *decrease*; decline 655 *deteriorate*; droop, wilt, fade; wear thin, split, yield; give way, sag 327 *soften*; totter, teeter, sway, reel 317 *oscillate*; tremble, shake 318 *be agitated*; limp, go lame 278 *move slowly*; have one foot in the grave.

weaken, enfeeble, debilitate, enervate; unnerve 854 *frighten*; slacken, unbrace, loosen, shake; strain, sprain, cripple, lame 161 *disable*; hurt, injure 655 *wound*; unman, disarm; take the edge off, cushion 257 *blunt*; impoverish, deprive; extenuate, lessen 37 *abate*; thin, dilute, water down; denature, devitalize, eviscerate; deactivate, neutralize; decimate 105 *render few*; muffle 401 *mute*; invalidate 752 *abrogate*; damage, sap, undermine 655 *impair*.

164. Production – N. *production*, creation; origination, invention; creative urge, productivity 171 *productiveness*; effort, endeavour; composition, authorship 551 *art*, 586 *writing*, 413 *musical skill*; performance, output, throughput, turnout 676 *action*; execution, achievement 725 *effectuation*; workmanship, craftsmanship; planning, design 623 *plan*; tectonics, engineering, civil e., building, architecture; construction, establishment, erection 310 *elevation*; making, fabrication, manufacture, industry 622 *business*; processing, process 147 *conversion*; machining, assembly; assembly line, production 1. 71 *continuity*, 630 *machine*; factory 687 *workshop*; technology, intermediate t.; industrialization, mass production, automation; development, growth 36 *increase*, 171 *abundance*; limits to growth 636 *scarcity*; farming, factory f. 370 *agriculture*; breeding 369 *animal husbandry*; procreation 167 *propagation*.

product, creature, creation, result 157 *effect*; output, turnout; printout; end product, by-p.; waste, slag 41 *leavings*; extract, essence; confection, concoction, compound 43 *a mixture*; handiwork, artefact; manufacture, article, finished a. 319 *object*; goods, wares 795 *merchandise*; goods and services, gross national product, GNP; earthenware, stoneware, hardware, ironware; cloth 222 *textile*; production, work, opus, oeuvre, piece 56 *composition*; chef d'oeuvre 694 *masterpiece*; fruit, flower, blossom, berry; produce, yield, return, harvest, crop; brainchild 451 *idea*; offspring 132 *young creature*.

edifice, building, structure, erection, pile, dome, tower 209 *high structure*; pyramid 548 *monument*; church 990 *temple*; mausoleum 364 *tomb*; mansion 192 *house*; bricks and mortar 631 *building material*.

producer, creator, maker, Nature; originator, inventor; founding father, founder, establisher 156 *cause*; writer 589 *author*; composer 413 *musician*; painter, sculptor 556 *artist*; designer 623 *planner*; developer, constructor, builder, architect, engineer; manufacturer, industrialist 686 *agent*; executive 676 *doer*; labourer 686 *worker*; artificer, craftsman *or* -woman 686 *artisan*; grower, gardener, agriculturalist 370 *farmer*; stock farmer 369 *breeder*.

Adj. *productive*, creative, inventive 513 *imaginative*; shaping, constructive, architectonic 331 *structural*; manufacturing, industrial; developed, industrialized; mechanized, automated; paying 640 *profitable*; fruitful 171 *prolific*; life-giving 167 *generative*.

produced, made, made up, cobbled together; artificial, man-made, synthetic, cultivated; manufactured, processed; handmade, homemade, homespun; architect-designed, craftsman-built; ready-made 243 *formed*; machine-made, mass-produced; bred, hatched 360 *born*; sown, grown; thought of, invented.

Vb. *produce*, create, originate, make; invent 484 *discover*; think up, conceive 513 *imagine*; write, design 56 *compose*; operate 676 *do*; frame, fashion, shape 243 *form*, 222 *weave*; sew, run up 45 *tie*; forge, chisel, carve; coin 797 *mint*; manufacture, fabricate, prefabricate, process, turn out, mill, machine; mass-produce, churn out 166 *reproduce*; construct, build, erect 310 *elevate*; make up, assemble, cobble together 45 *join*; blend 50 *combine*; establish, found 68 *initiate*; organize, get up 62 *arrange*; develop, exploit; industrialize, mechanize, automate; engineer, contrive 623 *plan*; perform, execute 725 *carry out*; bring about, yield results 156 *cause*; breed, hatch, rear 369 *breed stock*; sow, grow 370 *cultivate*; bear young 167 *reproduce itself*.

165. Destruction – N. *destruction*, unmaking, undoing, obliteration; annihilation, nullification 2 *extinction*; abolition, suppression; suffocation, stifling, silencing; subversion 221 *overturning*, 149 *revolution*; precipitation, overthrow 311 *lowering*; levelling, razing, dissolution 51 *decomposition*; breaking up, tearing down, demolition 655 *dilapidation*, 46 *disunion*; disruption 46 *separation*; crushing, grinding, pulverization; incineration; liquidation, elimination, extermination; extirpation, eradication 300 *ejection*; wiping out, mopping up 725 *completion*; decimation, massacre 362 *slaughter*; hatchet job; destructiveness, wanton d., mischief, vandalism, iconoclasm 176 *violence*; sabotage 702 *hindrance*; fire-raising, arson.

havoc, scene of destruction, disaster area, chaos 61 *confusion*, turmoil; desolation, wilderness, scorched earth 172 *desert*; carnage, shambles 362 *slaughterhouse*; upheaval, cataclysm 176 *outbreak*;

devastation, laying waste, ravages; depredation, raid 788 *spoliation*; blitz, explosion, nuclear blast 712 *bombardment*; holocaust, hecatomb 981 *oblation*.

ruin, downfall, ruination, perdition, one's undoing; crushing blow 731 *adversity*; castastrophe, disaster, act of God 731 *misfortune*; collapse, debacle, landslide 149 *revolution*; breakdown, meltdown, break-up, crack-up 728 *failure*; crash, smash 279 *collision*; wreck, shipwreck, wreckage, wrack; loss, total l.; Waterloo 728 *defeat*; knockout blow, KO 279 *knock*; beginning of the end, slippery slope, road to ruin 655 *deterioration*; coup de grace 725 *completion*; apocalypse, doom, crack of doom, knell, end 69 *finality*.

Adj. *destructive*, internecine, annihilating etc. vb.; consuming, ruinous 634 *wasteful*; apocalyptic, cataclysmic, overwhelming 176 *violent*; raging 176 *furious*; merciless 906 *pitiless*; mortal, suicidal 362 *deadly*; subversive, subversionary 149 *revolutionary*; incendiary, mischievous, pernicious 645 *harmful*.

destroyed, undone, ruined, fallen; wiped out etc. vb.; crushed, ground; pulped, broken up; lost, foundered, torpedoed, sunk, sunk without trace; dished, done for, had it, kaput; falling, crumbling, in ruins 655 *dilapidated*; in the breaker's hands, on the scrapheap 69 *ending*.

Vb. *destroy*, undo, unmake; destruct, self-d.; abolish, annihilate, liquidate, exterminate 2 *nullify*; devour, consume 634 *waste*; swallow up, engulf 299 *absorb*; swamp, overwhelm, drown 341 *drench*; incinerate, burn up, gut 381 *burn*; wreck, shipwreck, sink (**see** *suppress*); put an end to 69 *terminate*; do for, put down, do away with, make away w., get rid of 362 *kill*; decimate 105 *render few*; exterminate 362 *slaughter*; extirpate, eradicate 300 *eject*; wipe out, wipe off the map, expunge, efface, blot out 550 *obliterate*; revoke, tear up 752 *abrogate*; knock out, flatten out; put the skids under, make short work of, mop up; spifflicate, trounce 726 *defeat*; dish, cook one's goose, sabotage 702 *obstruct*; ruin 634 *waste*.

demolish, dismantle, break down, knock d., pull d., tear d. 46 *disunite*; level, raze, raze to the ground 216 *flatten*; throw down, steamroller, bulldoze 311 *fell*; cut down, mow d. 362 *slaughter*; overthrow 221 *invert*; sap, mine, dynamite, explode, blow up, blow sky-high; bomb, blitz, blow to bits 712 *fire at*; wreck, break up, smash up; smash, shatter 46 *break*; pulp, crush 332 *pulverize*; atomize, grind to bits, make mincemeat of; rend, tear up, tear to bits, pull to pieces 46 *sunder*; beat down, batter 279 *strike*; gut, strip bare 229 *uncover*.

suppress, quench, snuff o. 382 *extinguish*; nip in the bud, cut short, abort 72 *discontinue*; quell, put down, stamp out; trample under foot, stamp on, sit on 735 *oppress*; squelch, squash, flatten; quash 752 *abrogate*; blanket, stifle, smother, suffocate, strangle 161 *disable*; keep down, repress; drown, sink, scupper, torpedo 313 *plunge*.

lay waste, devastate 300 *empty*; despoil, ransack 788 *rob*; damage, ruin 655 *impair*; ravage, deal destruction 176 *be violent*; lay in ashes 381 *burn*; deforest, defoliate 634 *waste*; make a wilderness and call it peace.

consume, devour, swallow up, engulf 299 *absorb*; squander 634 *waste*.

be destroyed, go under, go down 361 *perish*; have had it, be all over with; fall, bite the dust 309 *tumble*; go on the rocks, break up, go to pieces, crumple up; go to rack and ruin, crumble 655 *deteriorate*; go to the wall, go to pot, go to the dogs, go to blazes.

Adv. *destructively*, crushingly, with crushing effect, with a sledge hammer.

166. Reproduction – **N.** *reproduction*, procreation 167 *propagation*; remaking, refashioning, reconstruction 164 *production*; reduplication 171 *productiveness*; multiplication, duplication 106 *repetition*; printing 587 *print*; renovation 656 *restoration*; resurrection, reappearance 106 *recurrence*; reincarnation, palingenesis; copy 22 *duplicate*; phoenix.

Adj. *reproduced*, renewed; reproductive 167 *generative*; renascent, resurgent, reappearing; hydra-headed, phoenix-like.

Vb. *reproduce*, remake, refashion, reconstruct; rebuild, refound, reestablish, rediscover; duplicate, clone 20 *copy*; take after, inherit 18 *resemble*; renovate, renew 656 *restore*; regenerate, resurrect 656 *revive*; reappear 106 *reoccur*; massproduce, multiply; print off, reel o. 587 *print*; breed 167 *reproduce itself*, 104 *be many*.

167. Propagation – N. *propagation* 166 *reproduction*; fertility, fecundity 171 *productiveness*; proliferation, multiplication 36 *increase*; incubation 369 *animal husbandry*; eugenics 358 *biology*; sex, facts of life, the birds and the bees; copulation 45 *coition*; generation, procreation 156 *source*; parthenogenesis, virgin birth; spontaneous generation; fertilization, pollination, fecundation; impregnation, insemination, artificial i., AID; test-tube baby; fertility drug 171 *fertilizer*; conception, pregnancy, germination, gestation (**see** *obstetrics*); birth, nativity, happy event 68 *origin*; stillbirth 728 *failure*; birth rate, natality; fruition 669 *maturation*; puberty 134 *adultness*: parenthood 169 *parentage*; procreator, begetter; inseminator, donor; fertilizer, pollinator; propagator, cultivator 370 *gardener*.

obstetrics, midwifery; parturition, birth, childbirth, childbed, confinement, lying in, accouchement; labour, labour pains, contractions; birth-throes, birth pangs; delivery, breech d., forceps d., caesarean section; bag of waters, caul, umbilical cord; placenta, afterbirth; gynaecologist, obstetrician, midwife 658 *nurse*; stork, gooseberry bush.

genitalia, loins, womb 156 *source*; genitals, reproductive organs; pudenda, private parts; male member, penis; testicles, scrotum; vulva, clitoris, vagina, uterus, ovary, Fallopian tubes; ovum, egg; semen, sperm; seed, pollen.

Adj. *generative*, potent, virile; fertile, productive, reproductive, procreative, philoprogenitive 171 *prolific*; life-giving, originative, germinal, seminal; spermatic,

genetic; sexual, bisexual, unisexual; genital, vulvar, clitoral, vaginal, penile; phallic.

fertilized, fecundated, impregnated; breeding, broody, pregnant, gravid; in an interesting *or* delicate condition; heavy with, big with; expecting, carrying, with child, in the family way; up the spout, in the club, fallen, preggers; parturient, brought to bed of, in labour; obstetric 658 *medical*; puerperal, childbed, maternity; antenatal, perinatal, postnatal; viviparous, oviparous.

Vb. *reproduce itself*, yield, give increase 171 *be fruitful*; hatch, breed, spawn, multiply, breed like rabbits 104 *be many*; germinate, sprout 36 *grow*; flower, fruit, bear fruit 669 *mature*; seed, seed itself; conceive, get pregnant; carry, bear; bring forth, give birth, have a baby; lay (eggs), drop, farrow, lamb, foal, calve, cub, pup, whelp, kitten, litter; have one's birth.

generate, evolve, produce; bring into existence, bring into the world; give life to, call into being; beget, get, engender, spawn, father, sire; copulate 45 *unite with*; fecundate, impregnate, inseminate, pollinate; procreate, propagate; breed, hatch, rear 369 *breed stock*; raise from seed 370 *cultivate*.

168. Destroyer – N. *destroyer*, demolisher, leveller; Luddite, iconoclast, nihilist, anarchist; wrecker, vandal, arsonist, pyromaniac; spoiler, despoiler, ravager, raider 712 *attacker*, 789 *robber*; saboteur 702 *hinderer*; hatchet man, killer, assassin 362 *murderer*; barbarian, Vandal, Hun; Time's scythe, angel of death 361 *death*; locust, moth, woodworm 51 *decay*; corrosive, acid, blight, poison 659 *bane*; earthquake, fire, flood 165 *havoc;* sword 723 *weapon*, 718 *war*; dynamite 723 *explosive*; blockbuster 723 *bomb*; juggernaut, bulldozer 216 *flattener*; Four Horsemen of the Apocalypse, Exterminating Angel.

169. Parentage – N. *parentage*, paternity, maternity; parenthood, fatherhood, motherhood; loins, womb 156 *source*; kinship 11 *family*; adoption, fostering 660 *protection*; Adam and Eve 371 *humankind*; parent, single p. 896 *divorce, widowhood*; godparent, guardian.

genealogy, family tree, lineage, kin 11 *consanguinity*; pedigree, heredity; line, blood, strain; blue blood 868 *nobility*; stock, stem, clan 11 *race*; descent, extraction, birth, ancestry 68 *origin*.

paternity, fatherhood; father, dad, daddy, pop, papa, pater, governor, the old man; head of the family, paterfamilias; procreator, begetter; grandfather, grandpa 133 *old man*; ancestor, progenitor, forefather, forebear, patriarch 66 *precursor*; father figure; foster-f., stepfather, father-in-law; fatherland.

maternity, motherhood; maternal instinct; expectant mother, mother-to-be 167 *propagation*; mother, dam; mamma, mummy, mum, mater; grandmother 133 *old woman*; materfamilias, matron, matriarch; ancestress, progenitrix; mother substitute, foster-mother, stepmother, mother-in-law; Mother Church, mother country.

Adj. *parental*, paternal; maternal, matronly; fatherly, fatherlike; motherly, stepmotherly; family, lineal, patrilinear, matrilinear; ancestral; hereditary 5 *genetic*; patriarchal 127 *immemorial*; racial, phyletic 11 *ethnic*.

170. Posterity – N. *posterity*, progeny, issue, seed, offspring, young, little ones 132 *child*; breed 11 *race*; brood, litter 132 *young creature*; children, grandchildren 11 *family*; succession, heirs, inheritance, heritage 120 *posteriority*; rising generation 130 *youth*.

descendant, son, daughter; chip off the old block, infant 132 *child*; scion, shoot, sprout 132 *young plant*; heir, heiress 776 *beneficiary*; love child 954 *bastardy*; branch, ramification, daughter-nation, colony; graft, offshoot, offset.

sonship, filiation, line, direct l., lineage, descent 11 *consanguinity*; indirect descent, collaterality; irregular descent, illegitimacy 954 *bastardy*; succession, heredity, heirship; primogeniture 119 *priority*.

Adj. *filial*, daughterly; descended, lineal; collateral; primogenital 119 *prior*; adopted, adoptive; step-; hereditary, inherited, Mendelian 5 *genetic*.

171. Productiveness – N. *productiveness*, productivity, mass production 164 *production*; boom 730 *prosperity*; overproductivity, superabundance, glut 637 *redundance*; fecundity, fertility, luxuriance, lushness, exuberance, richness, Green Revolution 635 *plenty*; high birthrate, baby boom, population explosion; productive capacity, biotic potential; procreation 167 *propagation*; fructification 669 *maturation*; inventiveness, resourcefulness 513 *imagination*.

fertilizer, manure, compost, bonemeal; phosphates, nitrates, potash, lime; topdressing, mulch 370 *agriculture*; fertility drug 167 *propagation*; fertility cult, f. rite, f. symbol, phallic s., phallus; lingam, yoni; Earth Mother, Ceres, Demeter.

abundance, wealth, riot, profusion, harvest 32 *great quantity*; teeming womb, mother earth, nursery 156 *seedbed*; cornucopia, horn of plenty, land flowing with milk and honey; milch cow; second crop, aftergrowth; rabbit warren, ant heap 104 *multitude*.

Adj. *prolific*, fertile, fecund; multiparous 167 *generative*; fruitful, fruit-bearing, fructiferous; pregnant, heavy with; exuberant, lush, leafy, verdant, luxuriant, rich, fat 635 *plenteous*; copious, streaming, pouring; paying 640 *profitable*; creative, inventive, resourceful.

Vb. *make fruitful*, make productive etc. adj.; make the desert bloom; plant, fertilize, water, irrigate 370 *cultivate*; impregnate, fecundate, inseminate 167 *generate*.

be fruitful, – prolific etc. adj.; fructify, flourish; burgeon, bloom, blossom; germinate; conceive, bear 167 *reproduce itself*; teem, proliferate, pullulate, swarm, multiply, mushroom 104 *be many*; send up the birthrate 36 *augment*; populate.

172. Unproductiveness – N. *unproductiveness*, unproductivity, dearth 636 *scarcity*;

sterility, barrenness, infertility 161 *impotence*; overfishing, overgrazing; deforestation, erosion; defoliation; scorched earth policy, desertification; dying race, zero population growth 37 *decrease*; contraception, birth control, planned parenthood, family planning; contraceptive, the pill; sterilization, vasectomy; change of life, menopause; poor return, unprofitability, fruitlessness 641 *inutility*; stagnation, slump; idleness 679 *inactivity*.

desert, aridity 342 *dryness*; desolation, waste, wastelands, lunar landscape; wild, wilderness, howling w.; desert sands, Sahara; dustbowl 634 *waste*.

Adj. *unproductive*, dried up, exhausted; waste, desert, desolate; treeless, bleak, gaunt, bare 190 *empty*; poor, stony, shallow, eroded; barren, infertile, sour, sterile; withered, shrivelled, blasted; unprolific, unfruitful; arid, unwatered, unirrigated 342 *dry*; fallow, stagnating 674 *disused*; unsown, uncultivated; impotent, sterilized, on the pill; childless, issueless; otiose 679 *inactive*; fruitless, unprofitable 641 *profitless*; ineffective; abortive 728 *unsuccessful*, 161 *impotent*.

Vb. *make sterile*, make unproductive 634 *waste*; sterilize, vasectomize, castrate, geld 161 *unman*; deforest, overgraze 165 *lay waste*; addle 51 *decompose*; pasteurize, disinfect 648 *purify*.

173. Agency – **N.** *agency*, operation, work 676 *action*; exercise 673 *use*; force, play 160 *power*; interaction 178 *influence*; procuration 689 *management*; service 628 *instrumentality*; effectiveness, efficiency 156 *causation*; co-agency 706 *cooperation*; implementation, execution 725 *effectuation*; process, processing, treatment, handling.

Adj. *operative*, effectual, efficacious 727 *successful*; executive, operational, functional; acting, working, in action, in operation, in force, in play, at work 676 *doing*, 673 *used*; up and doing 678 *active*; live, potent 160 *dynamic*, 174 *vigorous*; practical, workable, applicable 642 *advisable*; serviceable 640 *useful*.

Vb. *operate*, be in action, be in play; act,

work, go, run 676 *do*; serve, execute, perform 622 *function*; do its job, take effect 156 *cause*; act upon, play u. 178 *influence*; take action, strike 678 *be active*; crew, man; bring into play, wind up, turn on, switch on, flick the switch, press the button; actuate, power, drive 265 *move*; process, treat; manipulate, handle, wield 673 *use*.

174. Vigour: physical energy – **N.** *vigorousness*, lustiness, energy, vigour, life 678 *activity*; dynamism, force, impetus 160 *energy*; intensity, high pressure 162 *strength*; exertion, effort 682 *labour*; dash, élan, fervour, enthusiasm, zeal; gusto, relish, zest 824 *joy*; liveliness, spirit, vim, zip, éclat; fire, mettle 855 *courage*; ginger, fizz, verve, snap, pep, drive, go, get up and go; enterprise, initiative; vehemence 176 *violence*; aggressiveness, oomph, thrust, push, kick, punch 712 *attack*; grip, bite, teeth; backbone, spunk 599 *resolution*; guts, grit 600 *stamina*; virility 162 *vitality*; live wire, spark, dynamo, dynamite, quicksilver; rocket 277 *spurt*.

stimulation, activation, tonic effect; intensification, boost 36 *increase*; excitement 821 *excitation*; stir, perturbation 318 *agitation*; ferment, fermentation, ebullience, effervescence.

keenness, mordancy, causticity, virulence 388 *pungency*; point, edge 256 *sharpness*.

stimulant, energizer, activator, booster; yeast, leaven, catalyst; stimulus, fillip, shot, shot in the arm; spur, goad 612 *incentive*; restorative, pep pill 658 *tonic*; bracer, pick-me-up, aperitif, appetizer; seasoning, spice 389 *sauce*; liquor 301 *alcoholic drink*; aphrodisiac, philtre, love p.; pep talk 821 *excitant*.

Adj. *vigorous*, energetic 678 *active*; forcible, forceful, vehement 176 *violent*; dynamic, high-pressure, intense, strenuous 678 *industrious*; enterprising, go-getting; aggressive, pushful, thrustful 712 *attacking*; keen, alacritous 597 *willing*; double-distilled, potent; hearty, virile, full-blooded 162 *strong*; full of beans, zestful, lusty, mettlesome 819 *lively*; blooming, bouncing 650 *healthy*; brisk, nippy, snappy; fizzy, heady, racy; tonic, bracing, invigorating, stimulating 821 *exciting*; drastic, stringent 735 *severe*; intensified, stepped up; gingered up, souped up 160 *powerful*.

keen, acute, sharp, incisive, trenchant 571 *forceful*; mordant, biting, poignant 388 *pungent*; virulent, corrosive, caustic, acid.

Vb. *invigorate*, energize, activate; galvanize, electrify, intensify, double, redouble; step up, bump up, pep up, ginger up, boost 162 *strengthen*; rouse, kindle, inflame, stimulate 821 *excite*; hearten, animate 833 *cheer*; freshen, revive 685 *refresh*; give an edge to 256 *sharpen*.

Adv. *vigorously*, forcibly, hard, straight from the shoulder, with telling effect; zestfully, lustily, con brio, with a will; at full tilt, full steam ahead.

175. Inertness – N. *inertness*, inertia, accidie 677 *inaction*; lifelessness, languor, paralysis, torpor 375 *insensibility*; vegetation, stagnation, stasis, passivity 266 *quiescence*; dormancy 523 *latency*; apathy, dullness 679 *sluggishness*; immobility 602 *obstinacy*; impassiveness, stolidity 823 *inexcitability*; gutlessness 601 *irresolution*; vegetable, cabbage.

Adj. *inert*, unactivated, unaroused, passive, dead 677 *nonactive*; lifeless, languid, torpid 375 *insensible*; heavy, lumpish, sluggish 278 *slow*, 679 *inactive*; hibernating, vegetating, stagnant 266 *quiescent*; fallow; slack, low-pressure; limp, flaccid 163 *weak*; apathetic 820 *impassive*; unaggressive 823 *inexcitable*; uninfluential 161 *powerless*; deactivated 752 *abrogated*; smouldering, dormant 523 *latent*.

Vb. *be inert*, be inactive etc. adj.; slumber 679 *sleep*; hang fire, not catch; smoulder 523 *lurk*; stagnate, vegetate 266 *be quiescent*; just sit there 677 *not act*.

176. Violence – N. *violence*, vehemence, frenzy, impetuosity 174 *vigorousness*; destructiveness 165 *destruction*; boisterousness, turbulence 318 *commotion*; bluster, uproar, riot, row, roughhouse 61 *turmoil*;

roughness, rough handling 735 *severity*; force, hammer blows, high hand, strong-arm tactics, thuggery, terrorism 735 *brute force*; atrocity, outrage, torture 898 *cruel act*; barbarity, brutality, savagery, blood lust 898 *inhumanity*; fierceness, ferocity 906 *pitilessness*; rage, hysterics 822 *excitable state*; fit, throes, paroxysm, spasm; shock, clash 279 *collision*.

outbreak, outburst, ebullition 318 *agitation*; flood, cataclysm, convulsion, earthquake, tremor 149 *revolution*; eruption, explosion, burst, blast 165 *destruction*; detonation; rush, onrush 712 *attack*; gush, spurt, jet, torrent.

storm, turmoil, turbulence, war of the elements; weather, dirty w., rough w.; squall, tempest, typhoon, hurricane, cyclone 352 *gale*; thunder, thunder and lightning, fulguration; rainstorm, cloudburst 350 *rain*; blizzard 380 *wintriness*.

violent creature, brute, beast, wild b.; dragon, tiger, wolf, mad ' dog; demon, hellhound 938 *monster*; savage 168 *destroyer*; he-man, cave m. 372 *male*; butcher 362 *murderer*; berserker, homicidal maniac; tough, rowdy, thug, mugger 904 *ruffian*; hooligan, bully 735 *tyrant*; thunderer, fire-eater 877 *boaster*; firebrand 738 *agitator*; revolutionary, terrorist; hotspur, madcap 857 *desperado*; virago, termagant; spitfire, fury 892 *shrew*.

Adj. *violent*, vehement, forcible 162 *strong*; acute 256 *sharp*; unmitigated; excessive 32 *exorbitant*; rude, ungentle, extreme, severe, heavy-handed 735 *oppressive*; savage, brutal, bloody 898 *cruel*; hot-blooded 892 *irascible*; aggressive, bellicose 718 *warlike*; struggling, kicking, thrashing about 61 *disorderly*; rough, wild, furious, raging, blustery, tempestuous, stormy, uproarious, obstreperous 400 *loud*; rowdy, turbulent, tumultuous, boisterous 738 *riotous*; intemperate, immoderate, unbridled, unrestrained; ungovernable, unruly, uncontrollable 738 *disobedient*; irrepressible, inextinguishable 174 *vigorous*; ebullient, inflamed, fiery 381 *heated*; explosive, eruptive, cataclysmic, volcanic, seismic 165 *destruc-*

tive; convulsive 318 *agitated*; disturbed, troublous 61 *orderless*.

furious, fuming, boiling, towering; infuriated, mad, maddened 891 *angry*; rampant, roaring, howling; impetuous, headstrong 680 *hasty*; desperate, savage, tameless, wild; blustering, threatening 899 *cursing*; vicious, fierce, ferocious 898 *cruel*; bloodthirsty, ravening, rabid, berserk 362 *murderous*; frantic, hysterical, in hysterics 503 *frenzied*.

Vb. *be violent*, break bounds, run wild, run riot, run amok 165 *lay waste*; tear, rush, dash, hurtle, hurl oneself 277 *move fast*; crash in 297 *burst in*; surge forward, stampede, mob 712 *charge*; riot, roughhouse, kick up a shindy, raise the dust, go on the rampage 61 *rampage*; resort to violence 718 *go to war*, 738 *revolt*; see red, go berserk 891 *be angry*; storm, rage, roar, bluster 352 *blow*; ferment, foam, fume, boil over, effervesce; explode, go off, blow up, detonate, burst, flash, flare; let fly, fulminate; erupt, break out, fly o., burst o.; struggle, scratch, bite, kick, lash out; savage, maul 655 *wound*; tyrannize, out-Herod Herod 735 *oppress*.

force, use f., smash 46 *break*; tear 46 *sunder*; crush 332 *pulverize*; blow up 165 *demolish*; strain, wrench, twist 246 *distort*; force open, blow open, prize o. 263 *open*; shake 318 *agitate*; do violence to 675 *misuse*; violate, ravish, rape; torture 645 *illtreat*.

make violent, stir 821 *excite*; goad, lash, whip 612 *incite*; inflame, add fuel to the flames 381 *heat*; foment, exacerbate 832 *aggravate*; whet 256 *sharpen*; irritate, infuriate, madden 891 *enrage*.

Adv. *violently*, forcibly, by storm, by force, with might and main; tooth and nail, hammer and tongs; at the point of a sword, at the end of a gun; bodily, neck and crop; at one fell swoop; with a vengeance, like mad; precipitately, headlong, slap bang, wham; head first; like a bull at a gate, like Gadarene swine.

177. Moderation – N. *moderation*, nonviolence; mildness, gentleness 736 *leniency*; moderateness, reasonableness, measure;

golden mean, temperateness, restraint, self-control 942 *temperance*; soberness 823 *inexcitability*; mitigation 831 *relief*; relaxation, easing, alleviation; mollification, appeasement 719 *pacification*; tranquillization, sedation; control 747 *restraint*.

moderator, palliative; lenitive, alleviative 658 *balm*; syrup, milk, oil on troubled waters; calmative, sedative, tranquillizer; lullaby, nightcap 679 *soporific*; anodyne, opiate 375 *anaesthetic*; dummy 264 *stopper*; wet blanket, damper 613 *dissuasion*; brake, neutralizer; anaphrodisiac 658 *antidote*; cushion, shock absorber 327 *softness*; third force 720 *mediator*; controller, restraining hand, rein.

Adj. *moderate*, unextreme, nonviolent, reasonable, judicious; tame, gentle, harmless, mild, mild as milk 736 *lenient*; innocuous 163 *weak*; measured, limited, low-key 747 *restrained*; chastened, subdued, self-controlled, tempered, temperate, sober; cool, calm, composed 823 *inexcitable*; quiet, untroubled 266 *tranquil*; peaceable 717 *peaceful*; nonextreme, middle-of-the-road 625 *neutral*.

lenitive, unirritating, nonirritant 658 *remedial*; alleviative, pain-killing, anodyne, calmative, sedative 679 *soporific*; smooth, soothing, bland, demulcent; emollient.

Vb. *be moderate*, – gentle etc. adj.; go easy, keep within reason 942 *be temperate*; sober down, settle 266 *be quiescent*; disarm, keep the peace 717 *be at peace*; remit, relent 905 *show mercy*; not press 736 *be lenient*; not resist, go quietly.

moderate, mitigate, temper; tame, curb, control 747 *restrain*; lessen, slacken 37 *abate*; palliate, extenuate, qualify 163 *weaken*; obtund, take the edge off 257 *blunt*; break the fall, cushion 218 *support*; play down, soft-pedal; tone down, blue-pencil; sober down, dampen, cool, chill, throw cold water on 613 *dissuade*; bank down, subdue, quell 382 *extinguish*.

assuage, ease, pour balm, mollify 327 *soften*; alleviate, lighten 831 *relieve*; slake, deactivate, neutralize, take the sting out 182 *counteract*; allay, dull, deaden 375 *render insensible*; soothe, calm, tranquillize, comfort, still, quiet, hush, lull, rock, cradle 266 *bring to rest*; dulcify 392 *sweeten*; disarm, appease, smooth over, pour oil on troubled waters 719 *pacify*.

Adv. *moderately*, in moderation, within bounds, within limits, within compass, within reason; at half speed, gingerly, half-heartedly, nervously, softly softly 278 *gradatim*.

178. Influence – **N.** *influence*, capability, power 160 *ability*; prevalence, predominance 34 *superiority*; mightiness 638 *importance*; upper hand, whip h., casting vote; vantage ground, footing, hold, grip; leverage, play 744 *scope*; purchase 218 *pivot*; clout, weight, pressure; pull 291 *attraction*; counterattraction; thrust, drive, impact; leaven, contagion, infection; atmosphere, climate 8 *circumstance*; magic, spell 983 *sorcery*; stars, destiny 596 *fate*; fascination, hypnotism, mesmerism; curse 659 *bane*; impulse 817 *affections*; suasion, impulsion 612 *motive*; charisma, leadership 866 *prestige*; hegemony, ascendancy, domination 733 *authority*; sway, control, dominance, sphere of influence, orbit; factor, vital role, leading part 156 *cause*; indirect influence, patronage, interest, favour, pull, friend at court 703 *aid*; strings, lever 630 *tool*; secret influence, hidden hand, hand that rocks the cradle, power behind the throne, Grey Eminence 523 *latency*; force, lobby, pressure group 612 *inducement*; uncrowned king *or* queen, a host in oneself 638 *bigwig*; multinational, superpower; powers that be, the Establishment 733 *government*.

Adj. *influential*, dominant, predominant, prevalent 34 *supreme*; in power, ruling, listened to, obeyed 733 *authoritative*; rising, in the ascendant; strong, potent, mighty 32 *great*, 160 *powerful*; leading, guiding 689 *directing*; inspiring, encouraging; contributing, effective 156 *causal*; weighty, key, momentous, decisive 638 *important*; telling, moving 821 *impressive*; appealing, fascinating, charismatic; irresistible, hypnotic 740 *compelling*; persuasive 612 *inducing*;

catching 653 *infectious*; pervasive 189 *ubiquitous*.

Vb. *influence*, have i., carry weight, cut ice 638 *be important*; be well-connected, know the right people; have a hold on, have in one's power; have the ear of, be listened to; dominate, tower over; lead by the nose, have under one's thumb, wind round one's little finger; wear the trousers 34 *be superior*; make oneself felt, assert oneself; throw one's weight into the scale, weigh in; put pressure on, lobby, pull strings 612 *motivate*; make one's voice heard 455 *attract notice*; have a voice, have a say in; affect, tell, turn the scale; bear upon, work u., tell u. 821 *impress*; soften up 925 *flatter*; persuade, prevail upon 612 *induce*; sway, tyrannize; predispose, brainwash, prejudice 481 *bias*; fascinate, hypnotize, mesmerize 291 *attract*; be the making of, make or mar 147 *transform*; infect, contaminate; play a part, play a leading p., guide 689 *direct*; set the fashion.

prevail, outweigh, override, turn the scale 34 *predominate*; overcome, subdue; hold the whip hand, gain the upper hand, master 727 *overmaster*; control, rule, monopolize 733 *dominate*; take a hold on, gain a footing, take root; permeate 189 *pervade*; catch on, spread, rage, be rife, spread like wildfire.

179. Tendency – **N.** *tendency*, trend, tenor; set, drift 281 *direction*; mainstream, Zeitgeist, spirit of the times 178 *influence*; gravitation, affinity 291 *attraction*; gift, instinct for; proneness, proclivity, propensity, predisposition, readiness, inclination, penchant, predilection, liking, leaning, bias, prejudice; weakness 180 *liability*; cast, bent, turn, grain; vein, humour, mood; quality, nature, characteristic 5 *temperament*.

Adj. *tending*, trending, conducive, leading to, pointing to; working towards, in a fair way to, calculated to 471 *probable*; apt to, prone to; ready to, about to.

Vb. *tend*, trend, verge, lean, incline; set towards, gravitate t.; affect, dispose, carry, bias, bend to; point to, lead to

156 *conduce*; bid fair to, be calculated to 471 *be likely*; redound to, contribute to 285 *promote*.

180. Liability – N. *liability*, liableness, weakness, vulnerability; susceptibility, susceptivity; potentiality 469 *possibility*; likelihood 471 *probability*.

Adj. *liable*, apt to 179 *tending*; subject to, prey to, at the mercy of 745 *subject*; open to, exposed to, in danger of 661 *vulnerable*; dependent on, contingent; on the cards 469 *possible*; incurring, unexempt from; susceptible 819 *impressible*.

Vb. *be liable*, – subject to etc. adj.; incur, lay oneself open to, run the chance of; stand to; run the risk of 661 *be in danger*; lie under 745 *be subject*; open a door to 156 *conduce*.

181. Concurrence: combination of causes – N. *concurrence*, combined operation, joint effort, collaboration, coagency 706 *cooperation*; coincidence; concord 24 *agreement*; compliance, consensus; acquiescence 721 *submission*; concert, collusion, conspiracy; league, alliance 706 *association*; conjunction, liaison 45 *union*.

Adj. *concurrent*, coactive 706 *cooperative*; coincident, concomitant, parallel 89 *accompanying*; in alliance 708 *corporate*; of one mind, joint, combined; comforting 24 *agreeing*; colluding, conniving 703 *aiding*.

Vb. *concur*, collude, connive, conspire 623 *plot*; agree 24 *accord*; pull together

706 *cooperate*; contribute, help, abet, promote, subserve 156 *conduce*; go along with, run parallel to 89 *accompany*.

182. Counteraction – N. *counteraction*, opposing causes, action and reaction; polarity 240 *contraposition*; antagonism, clash, conflict 14 *contrariety*; reaction, repercussion, backlash 280 *recoil*; resistance 704 *opposition*; friction, drag 702 *hindrance*; interference, repression; neutralization 177 *moderation*; cancellation 165 *destruction*; cross-current, headwind 702 *obstacle*; counterspell, counterirritant, neutralizer 658 *antidote*; counterbalance 31 *offset*; counterblast, countermove 688 *tactics*; deterrent, preventive, preventative.

Adj. *counteracting*, counter, counteractive; conflicting 14 *contrary*; antagonistic, hostile 881 *inimical*; resistant 715 *resisting*; reactionary, reactive 280 *recoiling*; frictional 747 *restraining*; preventive; contraceptive; antidotal, corrective, compensatory 658 *remedial*.

Vb. *counteract*, counter, run c., cross, work against, go a., militate a.; not conduce to 702 *hinder*; react 280 *recoil*; resist 704 *oppose*; conflict with 14 *be contrary*; clash 279 *collide*; interfere 678 *meddle*; countervail, cancel out; repress 165 *suppress*; undo, cancel; neutralize, deactivate, demagnetize, degauss; cure 658 *remedy*; prevent, inhibit 757 *prohibit*.

Adv. *although*, in spite of, despite, notwithstanding; against, contrary to 704 *in opposition*.

Class Two

SPACE

Section 1:
Space in general

183. Space: indefinite space – N. *space*, expanse, extension, extent, surface, area; volume, cubic content; continuum, space-time; empty space, abyss 190 *emptiness*; unlimited space, infinite s. 107 *infinity*; sky, outer space 321 *heavens*; world, wide w.; vastness, immensity, vastitude; open space, open country; wide horizons, wide open spaces 348 *plain*; upland, moorland, prairie 348 *grassland*; wilderness, waste 172 *desert*; everywhere, ubiquity 189 *presence*.

measure, proportions, dimension 203 *length*, 205 *breadth*, 209 *height*, 211 *depth*; area, surface a.; square measure, acreage, acres; hectare, hide; volume 195 *size*.

range, reach, carry, compass, coverage; stretch, grasp, span; radius, latitude, amplitude; sweep, spread; play, swing 744 *scope*; sphere, field, arena 184 *region*; purview, prospect 438 *view*; perspective, focal distance 199 *distance*.

room, space, accommodation; capacity, stowage, storage space 632 *storage*; seating; standing room; margin, clearance, windage; room to spare, r. to manoeuvre, elbowroom, legroom; headroom, headway; sea room, seaway, leeway; opening, way 263 *open space*; living space, Lebensraum.

Adj. *spatial*, spatio-temporal, space-time, fourth-dimensional; volumetric, cubic, three-dimensional; flat, two-dimensional.

spacious 32 *extensive*; expansive, roomy, commodious; ample, vast, vasty, cavernous, capacious, broad, deep, wide; voluminous, baggy 195 *large*; far-flung, widespread, worldwide; boundless, shoreless, spaceless 107 *infinite*.

Vb. *extend*, spread, spread out, range, cover; span 226 *overlie*; extend to, reach to 202 *be contiguous*; branch, ramify.

Adv. *widely*, extensively, everywhere, far and wide, all over, the whole world over; from end to end, from pole to pole 54 *throughout*; here, there and everywhere, high and low, inside and out.

184. Region: definite space – N. *region*, locality, parts 185 *place*; sphere, hemisphere; zone, belt; latitude; clime, climate; tract, terrain, country 344 *land*; continent, landmass; global village 321 *world*; Old World, New W.; East and West, North and South; Third World 733 *political organization*; bounds, shore 236 *limit*; enclave, salient 235 *enclosure*; area, field, theatre 724 *arena*. **See** *territory*.

territory, sphere, zone; catchment area; beat, pitch, ground; lot, holding, claim 235 *enclosure*; grounds, park 777 *estate*; domain, territorial waters, airspace, defensible space; possession, colony, settlement; homeland 192 *home*; kingdom, realm, empire 733 *political organization*; debatable territory, no-man's-land, Tom Tiddler's ground.

district, purlieus, quarter 187 *locality*; state, province, county, shire, bailiwick, wapentake, hundred; tithing; diocese, bishopric; parish, ward, constituency; borough, township, municipality; county, district, metropolitan area; hamlet, village, town 192 *housing*; garden city, new town; suburb, dormitory, stockbroker belt; green belt; Home Counties, golden circle; north of Potters Bar, provinces, the sticks; Marches, Borders; Highlands, Lowlands, Wild West; outback, backwoods, bush; countryside 344 *land*; hinterland, heartland.

city, metropolis, megalopolis, conurbation; the Big City, the big smoke, the great wen, Cockaigne; Gotham, the Big Apple; uptown, downtown.

Adj. *regional*, territorial, continental, insular; national, state; subdivisional, local, municipal, parochial 192 *provincial*; suburban, urban; rural, up-country.

185. Place: limited space – N. *place*, site, location 186 *situation*; billet, socket, groove; centre 76 *focus*; quarter 187 *locality*; premises 192 *house*; spot, plot; point, dot, pinpoint; niche, nook, corner, pocket 194 *compartment*; confines 236 *limit*; precinct, bailey, compound 235 *enclosure*; quadrangle, square; yard, backyard, courtyard, court.

Adv. *somewhere*, here and there; locally 200 *near*.

186. Situation – N. *situation*, position, setting; scene, locale; time and place, when and where; location, address, whereabouts; point, stage 27 *degree*; site, seat, emplacement, base 185 *place*; habitat, biotype; post, station; standpoint, ground 7 *state*; side, aspect, attitude, posture; frontage, orientation; bearings, compass direction, latitude and longitude; geography, topography, chorography 321 *earth sciences*.

Adj. *situated*, situate, located at, to be found at; settled, set; occupying 187 *located*; local; topographical, geographical.

Vb. *be situated*, be found at 189 *be present*; be, lie, stand; live at 192 *dwell*.

187. Location – N. *location*, placing, placement, collocation, disposition 62 *arrangement*; posting, stationing; locating, pinpointing; localization, domestication, naturalization; settling, colonization; settlement, resettlement, establishment, fixation; installation 303 *insertion*; stowage.

locality, quarters, environs, environment, surroundings, milieu, neighbourhood, parts, neck of the woods 184 *district*; vicinity 200 *near place*; address, place of residence, habitat 192 *abode*; site 185

place; venue, haunt 76 *focus*; genius loci, spirit of place.

station, seat, site, emplacement, position 186 *situation*; depot, base; colony, settlement; anchorage, mooring; cantonment, lines; camp, encampment, bivouac 192 *abode*.

Adj. *located*, placed 186 *situated*; nestled, settled 153 *fixed*; camping, lodged, residing.

Vb. *place*, collocate, deploy 62 *arrange*; situate, position, site, locate; base, centre, localize; pinpoint, put one's finger on; aim well, hit; put, lay, set, stand, station, post, park; install, establish, bed down 153 *stabilize*; plant, slot in 303 *insert*; accommodate, find room for, lodge, house, quarter, billet; impose, saddle on; moor, anchor 45 *tie*; dock, berth 266 *bring to rest*; deposit, lay down, put d., set d.

replace, put back, sheathe; reinstate 272 *transpose*; replant, reset.

stow, put away, put by; pocket, pack, bale, store, lade, freight 193 *load*; squeeze in, cram in 54 *fill*.

place oneself, stand, take one's place; anchor, drop a. 266 *come to rest*; settle, strike root, take r.; entrench oneself, dig in 144 *stay*; perch, alight, sit on, sit, squat, park; pitch one's tent, encamp, camp, bivouac; stop at, lodge, put up; ensconce oneself, establish o., move in, put down roots; settle, colonize, populate, people 192 *dwell*.

188. Displacement – N. *displacement*, dislocation, derailment 63 *derangement*; misplacement, wrong place; shift, move 265 *motion*; red shift, Doppler effect; parallax; aberration 282 *deviation*; transfer 272 *transference*; mutual transfer 151 *interchange*; replacement 150 *substitution*; removal 304 *extraction*; unloading, unpacking, unshipping; expulsion 300 *ejection*; exile, banishment 883 *seclusion*; refugee 268 *wanderer*; fish out of water 25 *misfit*.

Adj. *displaced*, disturbed etc. vb.; transported 272 *transferable*; aberrant 282 *deviating*; unplaced, unhoused; rootless, unsettled, déraciné(e); roofless, houseless, homeless; out in the cold 57 *excluded*.

misplaced, ectopic; out of one's element, like a fish out of water; out of place, inappropriate 10 *irrelevant*; mislaid, lost 190 *absent*.

Vb. *displace*, disturb, disorientate, derail, dislocate; dislodge, unfix 46 *disunite*; scatter, send flying 75 *disperse*; shift, remove 265 *move*; transport 272 *transfer*; change round, transpose 151 *interchange*; relegate, banish, exile 300 *dismiss*; set aside, supersede 150 *substitute*, 752 *depose*; turn out, evict, unhouse 300 *eject*; discharge, off-load, tranship; clear away, sweep up, take away, cart a.; lift, raise; draw out, pull o. 304 *extract*.

misplace, mislay, lose, lose track of.

189. Presence – N. *presence*, existence; whereabouts 186 *situation*; ubiety; ubiquity, ubiquitousness, omnipresence; permeation, pervasion, diffusion; physical presence, attendance; residence, occupancy, occupation, sit-in 773 *possession*; visit, stay; person on the spot; spectator, bystander 441 *onlookers*.

Adj. *on the spot*, present, existent; in occupation; resident, domiciled; attendant, waiting, ready, on tap, available; at home, at hand, within reach, on call; looking on, standing by.

ubiquitous, omnipresent, permeating, pervading, pervasive 79 *universal*.

Vb. *be present*, exist, be; take up space, occupy; inhabit 192 *dwell*; stand, lie 186 *be situated*; look on, stand by, witness; stay, sojourn 882 *visit*; attend, assist at, take part, grace the occasion, honour with one's presence; show up, present oneself 295 *arrive*; show one's face, put in an appearance.

pervade, permeate, fill 54 *make complete*; be diffused through, imbue, impregnate, soak, run through; swarm over, spread, meet one at every turn 297 *infiltrate*; make one's presence felt.

Adv. *here*, there, where, everywhere, all over the place; in situ, in place; on location; on board, at home; on the spot; in the presence of, before, under the eyes *or* the nose of; personally, in person, in propria persona.

190. Absence – N. *absence*, nonpresence 446 *disappearance*; lack 636 *scarcity*; deprivation 772 *loss*; being nowhere, Utopia 513 *fantasy*; inexistence 2 *nonexistence*; being elsewhere, alibi; nonresidence, living out; leave of absence, furlough; nonattendance, nonappearance, truancy, absenteeism, French leave 620 *avoidance*; absentee, truant 620 *avoider*; absentee landlord, backwoodsman.

emptiness, bareness, empty space, void, vacuity, vacancy; blank 201 *gap*; hollowness, shell; vacuum, air pocket; virgin territory, no-man's-land; waste, desolation 172 *desert*; vacant lot, bomb site 183 *room*.

nobody, no one, not a soul, not a living thing.

Adj. *absent*, not present, unrepresented; away, out, not at home; gone, flown 446 *disappearing*; lacking, wanting, missing, wanted; absent without leave, AWOL; unavailable 636 *unprovided*; lost, mislaid, nowhere to be found; inexistent 2 *nonexistent*; on leave; omitted, left out 57 *excluded*.

empty, vacant, vacuous; void, devoid, bare; blank, clean; characterless, featureless; hollow; vacant, unoccupied, uninhabited, untenanted; depopulated; deserted 621 *relinquished*; unpeopled, godforsaken, lonely; bleak, desolate 172 *unproductive*; uninhabitable.

Vb. *be absent*, take no part in; absent oneself, not show up, stay away, keep away, cut, skip, play truant 620 *avoid*; be missed, leave a gap, be conspicuous by one's absence; leave empty, evacuate 300 *empty*.

go away, withdraw, leave 296 *depart*; slip away 296 *decamp*, 667 *escape*; vanish 446 *disappear*; move over, make room, vacate.

Adv. *not here*, neither here nor there; elsewhere, somewhere else; nowhere; in one's absence, behind one's back, in absentia.

191. Inhabitant – N. *dweller*, inhabitant, habitant, denizen, indweller; sojourner, transient, visitant; migrant, expatriate 59 *foreigner*; mainlander, continental; insular, islander; boat-dweller, water gipsy; hill-dweller, highlander, lowlander; frontiersman *or* -woman, borderer; city-dweller, town-d., suburbanite, commuter; metropolitan, provincial; country-dweller, ruralist, villager; peasant 370 *farmer*; desert-dweller, tent-d., bedouin; cave-dweller, troglodyte; slum-dweller 801 *poor person*. See *native*.

resident, householder, ratepayer; cottager, crofter; addressee, occupier, occupant, incumbent 776 *possessor*; tenant, sitting t., protected t., renter, lessee, lease-holder; inmate, in-patient; garrison, crew 686 *personnel*; lodger, boarder, au pair, paying guest; guest, visitor, inquiline, commensal; uninvited guest, cuckoo, squatter 59 *intruder*; parasite 659 *bane*.

native, aboriginal, aborigines, autochthones, earliest inhabitants, first-comers 66 *precursor*; people, tribe 371 *nation*; local, local inhabitant; parishioner, villager; townsperson, townee, city person, urbanite, city slicker, cockney, suburbanite, weekender; yokel, rustic 869 *country-dweller*; fellow countryman *or* -woman, fellow citizen; national, patrial, citizen, burgher, burgess, voter; John Bull, Uncle Sam; earth-dweller, terrestrial, tellurian; space-dweller, Martian 59 *foreigner*.

settler, pioneer, Pilgrim Fathers 66 *precursor*; immigrant, colonist, colonial, Creole; planter 370 *farmer*; resident alien 59 *foreigner*.

inhabitants, population, townspeople, country folk; populace, people, citizenry, tenantry, yeomanry; houseful 192 *housing*; household, ménage 11 *family*; settlement, colony, commune, community.

Adj. *native*, vernacular, popular, national, ethnic; indigenous, autochthonous, aboriginal, enchorial; earthbound, terrestrial, tellurian; home, domestic, domiciliary, domesticated; settled, domiciled, naturalized; resident.

192. Abode: place of habitation or resort –
N. *abode*, habitat, haunt 186 *situation*; place of residence 187 *locality*; habitation, address, domicile, residence; headquarters, base, seat 76 *focus*; temporary abode, hangout, pad, pied-à-terre; week-end cottage, country seat, holiday home, seaside resort, watering place, hill station 837 *pleasure ground*; spa, sanatorium 658 *hospital*; camp, refugee c.; campsite 187 *station*.

quarters, living q., married q., accommodation, lodging, billet, berth, squat; barracks; lodgings, rooms, chambers, digs; guest house, boarding h., lodging h., pension; boarding school, hostel, dormitory; hall of residence.

dwelling, roof over one's head 226 *roof*; tower, keep; cave, hut, kraal, igloo; wigwam, tepee, tent; lair, den, hole, burrow, warren, earth, sett 662 *shelter*.

nest, drey; eyrie, perch, roost; covert; rookery, swannery, aviary, apiary, hive; antheap, anthill.

home, home-sweet-home, hearth, fireside, paternal roof, ancestral halls; homestead, toft, household; cradle, birthplace 68 *origin*; native land, motherland, fatherland, homeland; home ground, home town, own backyard; haunt, stamping ground; familiar territory, second home; lares and penates.

house, building 164 *edifice*; home, residence, dwelling, dwelling house, messuage; country house, town h.; villa, semi, terraced house; council house, prefab; ranch house, chalet, bungalow, chalet-b.; seat, place, mansion, hall, stately home; palace, château, castle; manor house, dower h., manor, grange, lodge, priory, abbey; vicarage 986 *parsonage*; farmhouse, farmstead, croft 370 *farm*; official residence, residency; embassy, consulate.

small house, bijou residence; two-up two-down, back-to-back; chalet, lodge, cottage, cruck c., thatched c., cot, but and ben; cabin, log c., hut, Nissen h., shanty, bothy; hovel, dump, hole, box, hunting-box *or* -lodge; shed, shack, lean-to, out-house, outbuilding; kiosk, booth, stall, shieling; houseboat; mobile home, caravan. See *flat*.

housing, high-density h.; bricks and mortar 631 *building material*; built-up area, urban sprawl; urban blight; urbanization, conurbation; town, satellite t., burgh, suburb 184 *city*; housing estate, overspill e., residential area 184 *district*; villadom, suburbia, subtopia; crescent, close, terrace, circus, square, avenue, street 624 *road*; block, court, row, mansions, villas, buildings; houses, tenements; inner city, ghetto, slum, condemned building; shanty town, hutments, bustee, barrio; hamlet, village, thorp.

flat, flatlet, granny flat, furnished f.; service f., mews f., penthouse; apartment, suite, chambers; bedsitting room, bedsitter 194 *chamber*; maisonette, duplex, walkup; block of flats, apartment block, tower b.; mews, tenements.

stable, byre, cowshed, shippen; kennel, dog-house; sty, pigpen, sheepfold 235 *enclosure*; dovecote, pigeon loft; stall, cage, coop, hutch, battery; stabling, mews, coach-house, garage, carport, hangar; boathouse; marina, dock, dry d.; basin, wharf, roads, roadstead 662 *shelter*.

inn, hotel, hostelry, roadhouse, motel, bed and breakfast (**see** *quarters*); dosshouse, kip; hospice, night shelter; hostel; caravanserai, khan.

tavern, alehouse, pothouse, beerhouse, boozer; public house, pub, local; gin palace, saloon; speak-easy, dive, joint, honky-tonk; shebeen; wine cellar, wine bar, bodega; beer cellar, beer hall, beer garden; bar, taproom.

café, restaurant, self-service, cafeteria; eating-house, steakhouse, diner, brasserie, bistro, grill room, rotisserie; coffee shop, milk bar, ice-cream parlour, soda fountain; lunch counter, snack bar, sandwich bar; teahouse, teashop, tearoom; refreshment room, buffet, canteen, Naafi; fish and chip shop, chippy, take-away; coffee stall, pull-in, transport café.

meeting place, meeting house 990 *church*; day centre, community c., village hall *or* green; assembly rooms, pump r.; club, clubhouse 76 *focus*; sports centre 837 *place of amusement*; shopping centre 796 *market*; park 837 *pleasure ground*.

retreat, sanctuary 662 *refuge*; priesthole 527 *hiding-place*; den, snuggery, sanctum

194 *chamber*; cell, hermitage 883 *seclusion*; cloister 986 *monastery*; ashram; almshouse, grace and favour house; workhouse, poorhouse; orphanage, home, rest h., hospice; halfway house, sheltered housing.

Adj. *urban*, towny, metropolitan, cosmopolitan, inner-city, suburban; residential, built-up, citified, urbanized, suburbanized; bungaloid.

provincial, parochial, local, domestic, vernacular; up-country, countrified, rural, rustic 184 *regional*.

architectural, architectonic, edificial; designed, architect-d. 243 *formed*; Gothic, classical, neoclassical, Palladian, Tudor; timber-framed, half-timbered; thatched, tiled; modest, substantial, palatial, grand; detached, semi-d.; back-to-back; jerry-built; single-storey, multistorey, high-rise; double-fronted.

Vb. *dwell*, dwell in, inhabit, populate 189 *be present*; settle, take up residence, hang up one's hat, move in; reside, remain, abide, sojourn, live; put up at, stay, lodge; live in, board out, be in digs; hang out at; tenant, occupy, squat 773 *possess*; perch, roost, nest; doss down, make one's quarters 187 *place oneself*; berth, dock 266 *come to rest*.

urbanize, citify, suburbanize, develop, build up.

193. Contents: things contained – N. *contents*, ingredients, items, components, constituents, parts 58 *component*; inventory 87 *list*; furnishings, equipment 633 *provision*; load, payload, cargo, lading, freight, shipment 272 *thing transferred*; enclosure 224 *insides*; stuffing, filling 227 *lining*; handful, cupful.

Vb. *load*, charge, burden 187 *stow*; palletize, containerize; take in, take on board, ship; pack, pack in 303 *insert*; pack tight, squeeze in 54 *fill*.

194. Receptacle – N. *receptacle*, container, holder; frame 218 *prop*; cage 748 *prison*; folder, wrapper, envelope, cover, file 235 *enclosure*; net 222 *network*; sheath, cocoon; packaging 226 *wrapping*; capsule, ampoule; pod, calyx, boll; mould 243 *form*; socket, slot 255 *cavity*; groove, slot 262 *furrow*; hole 263 *opening*; bosom, lap 261 *fold*; catch-all, trap; well, repository 632 *store*; sump 649 *sink*.

bladder, airbladder, inflatable; inner tube; football; balloon, gasbag; sac, cyst, vesicle, blister 253 *swelling*; udder 253 *bosom*.

maw, stomach, tummy, breadbasket, little Mary; abdomen, belly, corporation, pot belly, paunch 253 *swelling*; gizzard, gullet, crop, craw, jaws, mouth 263 *orifice*.

compartment, cell, cellule, follicle, ventricle; tray, in t., out t.; cage, cubicle, carrel, booth, stall; box, sentry box; pew, choirstall; niche, nook, cranny, recess, bay, oriel; pigeonhole, cubbyhole; drawer, locker; shelving, rack 218 *shelf*; storey, deck 207 *layer*.

cabinet, closet, commode, wardrobe, press, chest of drawers, chiffonier, tallboy; cupboard, unit; whatnot, dresser, Welsh d.; buffet, sideboard 218 *stand*; freezer 384 *refrigerator*; cocktail cabinet, dumbwaiter; secretaire, escritoire, davenport, bureau, desk, writing d.; console; bookcase.

basket, creel; hamper, picnic basket; pannier, trug, punnet, pottle, frail; crib, cradle, bassinet; clothesbasket, workbasket, workbox; wickerwork, basketwork; crate 218 *frame*.

box, chest, ark; coffer, locker; case, canteen; safe, till, moneybox 799 *treasury*; coffin, sarcophagus 364 *tomb*; packing case, tea chest, tuckbox, attaché case, dispatch box; suitcase, trunk, valise, portmanteau; sea chest, ditty-box; bandbox, hat box; canister, caisson 723 *ammunition*; luggage, baggage, impedimenta; boot, luggage van.

small box, pill b., snuff b., cigar b., pencil b., matchbox; cardboard box, carton, packet; plastic box, airtight container; metal box, can, tin, caddie, tea caddie, canister; casket; castor; nest of boxes.

bag, sack, poke; handbag, vanity case, reticule, clutch bag, Dorothy b., shoulder b., tote b.; shopping bag, carrier b., paper

b.; cornet, twist, sachet; Gladstone bag, carpet b., travelling bag, overnight b., flight b., sponge b.; sleeping bag, survival bag; bedding-roll; holdall, grip; haversack, knapsack, rucksack, backpack; kitbag, ditty bag, duffle b.; pouch, sling; pannier, saddlebag, nosebag; school bag, satchel; bundle, swag.

case, étui, housewife; wallet, pocket book, notecase; spectacle case, cigarette c., compact; briefcase, portfolio; file, box f.; scabbard, sheath; holster; quiver.

pocket, fob, pouch; purse, sporran.

vat, butt, cask, barrel, tun, tub, keg, breaker; drum 252 *cylinder*; puncheon, hogshead, firkin, kilderkin 465 *metrology*; hopper, cistern, tank 632 *store*.

vessel, vase, urn, jar, amphora, ampulla, cruse, crock, pot, water p.; pipkin, pitcher, ewer, jug, toby jug; gourd, calabash; carafe, decanter, bottle; leather bottle, blackjack, wineskin; wine bottle, demijohn, magnum, jeroboam; flask, hip f., flagon, vial, phial; honeypot, jamjar; gallipot, carboy, crucible, retort; chamber pot, bedpan; pail, bucket, piggin; churn, can, watering c.; flowerpot, jardinière; bin, litter b., dustbin 649 *sink*; scuttle, coal s., hod; skip, kibble; bath, tub.

cauldron 383 *heater*; boiler, copper, kettle, skillet, pan, saucepan, stewpan, steamer, double-boiler; frying pan, grill p., girdle; casserole, Dutch oven, bain-marie; mess tin, dixie, billycan; tea urn, teapot, samovar, coffeepot, percolator; vacuum flask, thermos (tdmk); hot-water bottle, warming pan.

cup, eggcup, coffee cup, teacup, breakfast cup; chalice, goblet, beaker; drinking cup, loving c., quaich; horn; tankard, stoup, can, cannikin, pannikin, mug, stein, toby, noggin, rummer, schooner, tassie; tumbler, glass, liqueur g., wineglass, brandy balloon, pony.

bowl, basin, pudding basin, mixing bowl, punch bowl, jorum; porringer, ramekin; manger, trough; colander, tureen, terrine; rose bowl, vase 844 *ornamentation*.

plate, salver, tray, paten; platter,

trencher, charger, dish; palette; saucer; pan, scale; pallet; mortarboard, hod.

ladle, skimmer, dipper, baler, scoop, spoon, tablespoon, dessertspoon, tea-spoon;spade,trowel,spatula,slice,shovel.

chamber, room, apartment 192 *flat*; cockpit, cubicle, cab; cabin, stateroom; presence chamber, throne room; cabinet, closet, study, den, adytum 192 *retreat*; library, studio, atelier, workroom, office 687 *workshop*; playroom, nursery; reception room, drawing room, sitting r., living r., lounge, parlour, salon, boudoir; bedroom, dormitory; dressing room; bathroom, washroom; dining room, breakfast r.; messroom, mess, hall, refectory, canteen 192 *café*; gunroom, wardroom; smoking room, billiard r.; bar, snug 192 *tavern*; cookhouse, galley, kitchen; scullery, pantry, larder, stillroom; dairy, laundry, utility room, offices, outhouse; coachhouse, garage 192 *stable*; storeroom, box room, lumber r., glory hole 632 *storage*; cloakroom, smallest room 649 *latrine*. **See** *compartment*.

lobby, vestibule, foyer, anteroom, waiting room; corridor, passage, hall; gallery, verandah, patio, piazza, loggia, balcony, portico, porch; extension, lean-to.

cellar, cellarage, vault, crypt, basement; coalhole, bunker 632 *storage*; hold, dungeon 748 *prison*.

attic, loft, hayloft; penthouse, garret 213 *summit*.

arbour, alcove, bower, grotto, grot, summerhouse, gazebo, folly, pergola, pavilion; sun lounge, conservatory 370 *garden*.

Adj. *cellular*, multicellular, honeycombed 255 *concave*; compartmentalized; locular; marsupial, polygastric, ventricular; abdominal, gastral, ventral 253 *convex*.

capsular, sacculate, cystic; vascular, vesicular.

Section 2: Dimensions

195. Size – **N.** *size*, magnitude, order of m.; proportions, dimensions 183 *measure*; extent 183 *space*; extension 203 *length*, 209 *height*, 211 *depth*; width 205 *breadth*; girth, circumference 233 *outline*; bulk, mass 322 *gravity*; volume, capacity, tonnage; scantling, calibre 465 *measurement*; full size, life size, king size, magnum; maximum; hypertrophy.

hugeness, largeness, bigness, grandiosity 32 *greatness*; enormity, enormousness, immensity, vastness; towering proportions, monstrosity, gigantism 209 *height*.

bulk, mass, weight, avoirdupois 322 *gravity*; lump, block 324 *solid body*; hunk, chunk 53 *piece*; mountain 209 *high structure*; massiveness, bulkiness; obesity, corpulence, stoutness, chubbiness, plumpness, embonpoint; double chin, spare tyre, corporation 253 *swelling*; muscle man 162 *athlete*; fat person, tub, dumpling, mound of flesh, tub of lard, lard-lump, hulk; Bunter, Falstaff.

giant, giantess, colossus 209 *tall creature*; ogre, monster, King Kong; leviathan, behemoth, whale; elephant, jumbo; mammoth; Titan, Goliath.

whopper, spanker, walloper, whacker, humdinger; mountain of a, father and mother of a, a . . . and a half.

Adj. *large*, big 32 *great*; economy size, king s., jumbo; fair-sized, considerable, sizable; bulky, massive, massy 322 *weighty*; ample, capacious, voluminous, baggy; amplitudinous 205 *broad*; vast, extensive 183 *spacious*; monumental, towering, mountainous 209 *tall*; fine, magnificent; whacking 32 *whopping*; man-size, life-s.; well-grown, large-limbed, elephantine; macroscopic, large-scale, megalithic.

huge, immense, enormous, vast, mighty, grandiose, stupendous, monstrous, record, colossal, mammoth, gigantic, gigantesque, giant, mountainous; Brobdingnagian, titanic, Herculean, gargantuan; outsize, oversize 32 *exorbitant*; limitless 107 *infinite*.

fleshy, meaty, fat, stout, obese, overweight; well-covered, well-upholstered, Falstaffian; plump, ample, plumpish, chubby, podgy, pudgy 205 *thick*; squat, dumpy, chunky, stocky 205 *broad*; tubby, portly, corpulent, paunchy, pot-bellied 253 *convex*; puffy, pursy, bloated, bosomy 197 *expanded*; round, rotund, roly-poly; dimpled, dimply, buxom, on the plump side; strapping, lusty, burly, beefy, brawny 162 *stalwart*.

unwieldy, cumbersome, hulking, lumbering, gangling; lumpish, lubberly; elephantine, overweight; muscle-bound 695 *clumsy*.

Vb. *be large*, – big etc. adj.; become large 197 *expand*; bulk 183 *extend*; tower, soar 209 *be high*.

196. Littleness – N. *littleness*, daintiness etc. adj.; small size, diminutiveness 33 *smallness*; lack of height 204 *shortness*; dwarfishness, stuntedness; paucity, exiguity; meagreness 206 *thinness*; -kin, -let.

minuteness, point, pinpoint, pinhead; atom, molecule, particle, electron, neutron, proton, quark; nucleus, cell; drop, droplet, grain, g. of sand; seed, mustard s. 33 *small thing*; button, molehill 639 *trifle*.

miniature 553 *picture*; microdot, microfilm, microfiche 551 *photography*; pocket edition, Elzevir e., duo-decimo; thumbnail sketch 592 *compendium*; model, microcosm.

dwarf, midget, minikin, pigmy, lilliputian, halfling, hobbit; little people 970 *elf*; chit, slip, titch; mite, tot, tiddler 132 *child*; dapperling, dandiprat, cocksparrow, bantam; pipsqueak, squit, squirt 639 *nonentity*; manikin, doll, puppet; Tom Thumb, Hop-o'-my-thumb, homunculus; shrimp, runt, miserable specimen.

microorganism, protozoan, plankton, microfauna, animalcule, amoeba; bacillus, bacteria, microbe, germ, virus, bug; algae 366 *plant*.

microscopy, micrography, microphotography; microscope, electron m., microspectroscope, micrometer, vernier scale.

microelectronics, microminiaturization 160 *electronics*; integrated circuit, microcircuit; microchip, chip, silicon c.; microprocessor 86 *data processing*.

Adj. *little* 33 *small*; petite, dainty, dinky, dolly, elfin; diminutive, pigmy, Lilliputian; no bigger than; wee, titchy,

tiny, teeny, teeny-weeny; toy, baby, pocket, pocket-size, pocket-handkerchief, pint-size, mini-; miniature, model; portable, handy, compact, bijou; snug, cosy, poky, cramped, no room to swing a cat 206 *narrow*; runty, puny 163 *weak*; petty 33 *inconsiderable*; one-horse 639 *unimportant*.

dwarfish, dwarf, dwarfed, pigmy, under-sized, stunted, weazen, wizened, shrunk 198 *contracted*; squat, dumpy 204 *short*; knee-high, knee-high to a grasshopper.

exiguous, minimal, slight, scant 33 *small*; thin 206 *lean*; embryonic 68 *beginning*; bitty 53 *fragmentary*.

minute, micro-, microscopic, infinitesimal; atomic, molecular; granular 332 *powdery*; inappreciable, imperceptible, impalpable 444 *invisible*.

Adv. *in small compass*, in a nutshell; on a small scale, in miniature.

197. Expansion – N. *expansion*, enlargement, aggrandizement 36 *increase*; amplification 38 *addition*; giantism, gigantism; stretching, extension, spread, deployment, fanning out; ribbon development, urban sprawl; increment, accretion; upgrowth, overgrowth, development, growth; extensibility, expansibility, dilatability 328 *elasticity*.

dilation, dilatation, distension, diastole; inflation, reflation 352 *blowing*; swelling up, turgescence, turgidity, tumescence, tumefaction; puffiness 253 *swelling*.

Adj. *expanded*, blown up etc. vb.; larger, bigger; expanding 36 *increasing*; stuffed, padded; spreading, expansive 183 *spacious*; fan-shaped, flabellate, flared 205 *broad*; patulous, gaping 263 *open*; tumescent, budding, bursting; full-blown, fully-formed, out 669 *matured*; overblown, overgrown; obese, puffy, bloated 195 *fleshy*; swollen, turgescent; distended, stretched, tight; dropsical, varicose, bulbous 253 *convex*; ampullaceous, pouchy.

Vb. *expand*, wax, increase 36 *grow*; widen, broaden 205 *be broad*; spread, extend, sprawl 75 *be dispersed*; spread over, spread like wildfire, overrun 226 *cover*;

rise, prove (dough); gather, swell, distend, dilate, fill out; mushroom, balloon, belly 253 *be convex*; get fat, put on weight; burst at the seams; bud, burgeon, shoot, sprout, open, put forth, burst f., blossom, blow 171 *be fruitful*.

enlarge, expand; bore, ream; widen, broaden, open, let out; stretch, extend 203 *lengthen*; heighten, deepen, draw out; amplify 38 *add*; double, redouble; develop, build up 36 *augment*; distend, inflate, reflate, pump up, blow up, puff up 310 *elevate*; bulk, thicken; stuff, pad 227 *line*; feed up, fatten, plump up 54 *fill*; blow up, magnify 546 *exaggerate*.

198. Contraction – N. *contraction*, reduction, deflation 37 *diminution*; decrease, shrinkage 42 *decrement*; curtailment, abbreviation, elision 204 *shortening*; consolidation 324 *condensation*; pulling together, drawing t. 45 *joining together*, 264 *closure*; contracting, systole; contractions 167 *obstetrics*; attenuation, emaciation; bottleneck, hourglass, wasp-waist 206 *narrowness*.

compression, pressure, compressure, compaction, squeeze; strangulation, constriction, astringency; contractility, contractibility, compressibility.

compressor, squeezer, tightener, constrictor, astringent; bandage, binder, tourniquet 658 *surgical dressing*; belt, garter; corset; straitjacket; thumbscrew 964 *instrument of torture*; bear, python, boa constrictor.

Adj. *contracted*, shrunk, shrunken, smaller 33 *small*; waning 37 *decreasing*; constricted, strangled, strangulated; unexpanded, deflated, condensed 324 *dense*; compact, compacted, compressed; pinched, nipped, drawn tight 206 *narrow*, 264 *closed*; compressible, contractile, systaltic; stunted, shrivelled, wizened 196 *dwarfish*; astringent.

Vb. *become small*, dwindle, wane 37 *decrease*; shrivel, wither, waste away 51 *decompose*; lose weight; contract, shrink, narrow, taper, taper off, draw in; condense 324 *be dense*; draw together, close up 264 *close*; pucker, purse 261 *fold*.

make smaller, lessen, reduce 37 *abate*; contract, shrink, abridge, take in, cut down, dwarf, stunt 204 *shorten*; diet, slim 323 *lighten*; taper, narrow, thin, emaciate 206 *make thin*; puncture, deflate; boil down, evaporate, dehydrate; cramp, constrict, pinch, nip, squeeze, bind, corset; draw in, draw tight, tauten, tighten; draw together, clench 264 *close*; crush, strangle, strangulate; compress, compact, condense 324 *be dense*; huddle, crowd together; squeeze in, pack tight, cram, jam 54 *fill*; squash 216 *flatten*; cramp, restrict 747 *restrain*; chip away, whittle away, clip, trim, prune, pollard 46 *cut*; file, grind 332 *pulverize*; fold up, crumple 261 *fold*; press, flatten 258 *smooth*.

199. Distance – N. *distance*, astronomical d., light years 183 *space*; measured distance, mileage, footage 203 *length*; focal distance; elongation, aphelion, apogee; horizon, skyline, offing; background 238 *rear*; periphery, circumference; drift, dispersion 282 *deviation*; reach, grasp, span, stride, giant's s. 183 *range*; far cry, fair way, tidy step; marathon.

farness, far distance, remoteness; removal 46 *separation*; antipodes, pole 240 *contraposition*; world's end, ultima Thule, Pillars of Hercules; ne plus ultra, back of beyond; foreign parts 59 *extraneousness*; outpost 883 *seclusion*; purlieus, outskirts 223 *exteriority*; outer edge 236 *limit*.

Adj. *distant*, distal, peripheral, terminal; far, farther; ulterior; ultimate, farthest, furthest, furthermost; long-distance, long-range; outlying, peripheral; off-shore, on the horizon; remote, aloof, far-flung, godforsaken; hyperborean, antipodean; out of range, telescopic; lost to view, out of sight 444 *invisible*.

removed, separated, inaccessible, unapproachable, unget-at-able, out of the way; beyond, over the horizon; overseas, transmarine, transpontine, transoceanic, transatlantic, trans-Pacific, transalpine, ultramontane; ultramundane, out of this world.

Vb. *be distant*, stretch to, reach to, extend to, spread to, stretch away to 183 *extend*; carry, range; outdistance, outrange, outreach 306 *outdo*; keep one's distance, remain at a d., keep off, hold off, stand off, lie off; keep clear of, stand aloof, keep a safe distance, give a wide berth 620 *avoid*.

Adv. *afar*, away, far, far away, far off, way o.; yonder, in the distance, on the horizon, as far as the eye can see; at a distance, a great way off, a far cry from; out of sight; to the ends of the earth, east of the sun and west of the moon; far and wide 183 *widely*; asunder, apart, far a., abroad, afield; at arm's length.

beyond, further, farther; further on, ahead, in front; clear of, wide of; below the horizon, hull down.

too far, out of reach, out of range, out of sight, out of hearing.

200. Nearness – N. *nearness*, proximity, propinquity, closeness; near distance, foreground 237 *front*; vicinity, neighbourhood 230 *surroundings*; brink, verge 234 *edge*; adjacency 202 *contiguity*; approximation 289 *approach*; localization 187 *location*.

short distance, no d.; beeline, short cut; step, walk; walking distance, striking d., close quarters, close range, earshot, gunshot, bowshot, stone's throw, spitting distance; short span, hair's breadth 201 *gap*; close-up; perigee, perihelion.

near place, vicinage, vicinity, neighbourhood, environs 187 *locality*; approaches, marches, borderlands; ringside seat 202 *contiguity*.

Adj. *near*, proximate, proximal; very near, approximate; approximating 289 *approaching*; about to meet 293 *convergent*; nearby 289 *accessible*; not far, hard by, inshore; near at hand, handy 189 *on the spot*; home, local, vicinal; close to, next to, neighbouring, limitrophe, bordering on, verging on 202 *contiguous*; fronting, facing; close, at close quarters; close-run, neck-and-neck.

Vb. *be near*, be around, hang around 189 *be present*; approximate 289 *approach*; meet 293 *converge*; neighbour, abut, adjoin, border, verge upon 202 *be contiguous*; trench upon 306 *encroach*; hug the shore; skirt, graze, shave, brush, skim; jostle 702 *obstruct*; sit on one's tail, follow close, shadow 284 *follow*; hug 889 *caress*; huddle, crowd 74 *congregate*.

bring near, approach, approximate 202 *juxtapose*.

Adv. *near*, not far, locally; hard by, close to; at close range, at close quarters; close behind, right b.; within hearing, within earshot; only a step, not far from; next door, on one's doorstep, in one's own backyard; at one's side, under one's nose, at one's fingertips, within reach, close at hand; face to face, eyeball to eyeball; side by side, cheek by jowl, beside, alongside; on the skirts of, at the threshold; on the brink of, on the verge of.

nearly, practically, almost, all but; more or less, near enough, roughly, around; in the region of; about, approximately, thereabouts, circa; hard on, close on; well-nigh, as good as, within an ace of.

201. Interval – N. *interval*, space; hairspace 200 *short distance*; interspace, daylight; head, length; clearance, margin, freeboard 183 *room*; timelag, interim; pause, break 145 *lull*; hiatus 72 *discontinuity*; interruption; jump, leap.

gap, interstice, mesh 222 *network*; lacuna, hole 263 *orifice*; pass 305 *passage*; firebreak 662 *safeguard*; trench 351 *drain*; ha-ha 231 *partition*; ravine, gorge, gully, couloir 255 *valley*; chimney, crevasse, cleft, crevice, chink, crack, rift; cut, gash, tear, rent, slit 46 *scission*; flaw, fault, breach, break, split, fracture, fissure 46 *separation*; slot, groove 262 *furrow*; indentation 260 *notch*; seam, join 45 *joint*; leak 298 *outlet*; chasm 211 *depth*; void 190 *emptiness*; inlet, creek, gulch 345 *gulf*.

Adj. *spaced*, spaced out, intervallic; gappy, gapped; split, cloven, cleft, cracked, rimose 46 *disunited*; gaping 263 *open*; latticed, meshed, reticulated.

Vb. *space*, interval, space out 46 *set apart*; split, gape 263 *open*; clear, show daylight between; lattice, mesh, reticulate.

202. Contiguity – N. *contiguity*, juxtaposition, apposition, proximity, close p. 200 *nearness*, no interval 71 *continuity*; contact, tangency; abuttal, abutment; intercommunication, osculation; meeting, encounter, interface 293 *convergence*; conjunction (astronomy) 45 *union*; close contact, adhesion, cohesion 48 *coherence*; coexistence, coincidence, concomitance 89 *accompaniment*; grazing contact, tangent; border 234 *edge*; borderland, frontier 236 *limit*; buffer state 231 *interjacency*.

Adj. *contiguous*, touching, in contact; osculatory, intercommunicating; tangential, grazing, brushing, abutting, end to end, bumper-to-bumper; conterminous, adjacent 71 *continuous*; adjoining, close to, jostling, rubbing shoulders 200 *near*.

Vb. *be contiguous*, overlap 378 *touch*; make contact, brush, rub, skim, scrape, graze, kiss; join, meet 293 *converge*; adhere 48 *cohere*; abut on, adjoin, reach to 183 *extend*; rub shoulders with, jostle 200 *be near*; border with, march w. 234 *hem*; coexist, coincide 89 *accompany*; osculate, intercommunicate 45 *connect*.

juxtapose, set side by side, range together, bring into contact.

Adv. *contiguously*, tangentially; in contact, in close c.; next, close; end to end; cheek by jowl; hand in hand, arm in arm.

203. Length – N. *length*, longitude; extent, extension; reach, long arm; stretch, span, mileage, footage 199 *distance*; perspective 211 *depth*.

lengthening, extending etc. vb.; prolongation, extension 113 *protraction*; stretching, tension.

line, bar, rule, strip, stripe, streak; spoke, radius; single file, line ahead, crocodile, queue 65 *sequence*; straight line 249 *straightness*.

long measure, linear m. 465 *measurement*; micrometry; unit of length, finger, hand, palm, span, cubit; fathom; head, length; pace, step; inch, foot, yard; rod, pole, perch; chain, furlong; mile, knot, league; millimetre, centimetre, metre, kilometre; degree of latitude or longitude;

micro-inch, micron, wavelength; light year, parsec.

Adj. *long*, lengthy, extensive; long-drawn out, lengthened, elongated, outstretched, extended, strung out 75 *unassembled*; shoulder-length, ankle-length, down to . . . ; lank 206 *lean*; lanky, long-legged 209 *tall*; as long as my arm; long as a wet week, interminable, no end to 838 *tedious*, 570 *diffuse*; unabridged, full-length 54 *complete*.

longitudinal, oblong, linear; one-dimensional.

Vb. *be long*, – lengthy etc. adj.; stretch, outstretch, stretch out; make a long arm; reach, stretch to 183 *extend*; drag, trail 113 *drag on*.

lengthen, stretch, elongate, draw out, wiredraw 206 *make thin*; pull out, stretch o., spreadeagle 197 *expand*; sprawl, spread out, string o. 75 *disperse*; extend, pay out, let out, uncoil, unroll 316 *evolve*; produce, continue; prolong, protract 113 *spin out*.

Adv. *longwise*, longways, lengthwise; along, longitudinally, radially, in line ahead, in single file; in tandem; end to end, overall; fore and aft; head to tail, stem to stern, top to toe.

204. Shortness – N. *shortness*, squatness etc. adj.; brevity, briefness, concision 569 *conciseness*; low stature 196 *littleness*; no height 210 *lowness*; shrinkage 42 *decrement*; scantiness, exiguity; scarceness 636 *insufficiency*.

shortening, abridgement, abbreviation; précis 592 *compendium*; curtailment, cutback, cut, reduction 37 *diminution*; contraction 198 *compression*; aphaeresis, apocope, syncope.

Adj. *short*, brief 114 *transient*; dwarfish, stunted 196 *little*; squat, dumpy, stumpy, stocky 195 *fleshy*, 205 *thick*; not high 210 *low*; pug-nosed, snub-n.; snub, retroussé, blunt 257 *unsharpened*; skimpy, scanty 636 *insufficient*; foreshortened 246 *distorted*; shortened, sawn-off; cut, curtailed, docked; shaven, shorn, mown; terse 569 *concise*; compact 592 *compendious*; compressed 198 *contracted*.

Vb. *shorten*, abridge, abbreviate 592

abstract; contract, telescope 198 *make smaller*; foreshorten 246 *distort*; take up, turn up, tuck up, kilt; behead, axe 46 *sunder*; cut short, dock, curtail, truncate; cut back, cut down, lop, prune; shear, shave, trim, crop, clip 46 *cut*; stunt, check.

205. Breadth. Thickness – N. *breadth*,
width, latitude; span, wingspan, wingspread; diameter, radius; gauge, bore, calibre; broadness, expanse 183 *range*; wideness, fullness, amplitude, bagginess.

thickness, stoutness, corpulence 195 *bulk*.

Adj. *broad*, wide 183 *spacious*; widecut, full, flared, ample, baggy; fan-like, flabelliform, umbelliferous; outspread, outstretched, splayed out 197 *expanded*; bell-bottomed, broad-based; callipygian, wide-hipped; broad in the beam, beamy; wide-bodied; broad-brimmed, wide-awake (hat); wide-angle (lens); broad-shouldered, broad-chested 162 *stalwart*.

thick, stout, dumpy, squat 204 *short*; thick-set, tubby, stubby 195 *fleshy*; thick-lipped, blubber-l., full-l.; thick-necked, bull-n.; thick-skinned, pachydermatous; barrel-chested, stout-timbered 162 *strong*; thick as a rope; pyknic, endomorphic; solidly built 324 *dense*; to be cut with a knife 354 *viscid*.

Vb. *be broad*, – thick etc. adj.; broaden, widen, fatten, thicken; flare, splay 197 *expand*; straddle, bestride, span 226 *overlie*.

Adv. *broadways*, broadwise, widthways, widthwise; broadways on 239 *sideways*.

206. Narrowness. Thinness – N. *narrowness*,
tightness etc. adj.; tight squeeze, crack, chink 200 *short distance*; line, strip, stripe, streak 208 *filament*; knife-edge, razor's edge, tightrope, wire; narrow gauge; bottleneck; narrows, strait; ridge, col, saddle; ravine, gully 255 *valley*; pass, defile 305 *passage*; neck, isthmus, landbridge 624 *bridge*.

thinness, tenuity, fineness 325 *rarity*; slenderness, gracility; emaciation, consumption; scrag, skin and bone, skeleton; scarecrow, rake, beanpole, shadow, spindle-shanks, barebones; haggardness, lantern jaws, hatchet face, sunken cheeks; thread, paper, tissue 422 *transparency*; slip, wisp 208 *filament*.

narrowing, compression 198 *contraction*; tapering 293 *convergence*; neck, isthmus; stricture, constriction; waist, wasp-w., hourglass.

Adj. *narrow*, strait, tight, close; compressed, pinched 198 *contracted*; fine, thin, wafer-thin 422 *transparent*; attenuated, spun, fine-s. 203 *long*; thread-like 208 *fibrous*; tapering 293 *convergent*; slight, slightly-built, wispy, delicate 163 *weak*; gracile, attenuate, slender, slim, svelte, slinky, sylph-like; willowy, rangy; long-legged, leggy, lanky, gangling; narrow-waisted, wasp-w.; isthmian.

lean, thin, ectomorphic, spare, wiry; meagre, skinny, bony; cadaverous, flesh-less, skin-and-bone, skeletal, raw-boned, haggard, gaunt, drawn, lantern-jawed, hatchet-faced; twiggy, spindly, spindle-shanked, spidery; undersized, weedy, scrawny, scraggy; consumptive, emaciated, wasted, shrivelled, pinched, peaky 651 *sick*; wraith-like, worn to a shadow, thin as a rake, thin as a lath, without an ounce of flesh to spare.

Vb. *make thin*, contract, compress, pinch, nip 198 *make smaller*; starve, underfeed, reduce, lose weight; slenderize, slim; draw, spin 203 *lengthen*; attenuate 325 *rarefy*.

207. Layer – N. *layer*, stratum, underlay 214 *base*; bed, course, string c.; zone, vein, seam, lode; thickness, ply; storey, tier, floor, mezzanine f., entresol, landing; stage, planking, platform 218 *frame*; deck, orlop d., quarterdeck 275 *ship*; film, bloom, dross, scum; patina, coating, veneer 226 *covering*; scale, pellicle 226 *skin*; level, water table 216 *horizontality*.

lamina, sheet, slab, foil, strip; plate glass, tinplate, latten, plank, board, fascia; laminate, plywood; slat, lath, leaf; tablet, plaque, panel, pane; slab, flag, flagstone, slate; shingle, tile; lamella, slide, wafer, shaving, flake, slice; card 631 *paper*; platter, disc 250 *circle*.

stratification, stratigraphy; bedding, layering, lamination; laminability, flakiness, scaliness; overlapping, overlap; nest of boxes, Chinese b., Russian doll; onion skin; sandwich.

Adj. *layered*, lamellar, lamelliform, lamellate; laminated; laminable, flaky; micaceous, slaty, shaly; foliated, foliate, leaflike; bedded, stratified, stratiform; overlapping, clinker-built; tabular, decked, storeyed, scaly, squamous; membranous 226 *covered*.

Vb. *laminate*, layer, overlap 226 *overlay*; zone, stratify, sandwich; plate, veneer 226 *coat*; exfoliate, delaminate, split; flake off, skive, pare, peel, strip 229 *uncover*; shave, slice.

208. Filament – N. *filament*, flagellum, cilium; lash, down 259 *hair*; barb, harl 259 *plumage*; flock, lock, shred of wool, lock of hair, wisp, curl; fringe 234 *edging*; fibril, tendril 366 *plant*; whisker 378 *feeler*; gossamer, cobweb 222 *network*; wire, element, wick.

fibre, hair; Angora, mohair, cashmere; alpaca, vicuna; wool, botany w., merino; mungo, shoddy; silk, wild silk, tussore; floss; cotton, cotton wool, kapok; linen, flax; manila, hemp; jute, sisal, coir; tow, oakum; bast, raffia; worsted, yarn; thread, twine, twist, strand, line, rope 47 *cable*; artificial fibre, man-made f., acrylic f., rayon, nylon 222 *textile*; staple, denier 331 *texture*.

strip, fascia, band, bandage; braid, tape, strap, ribbon, ribband, fillet; lath, slat, batten 207 *lamina*; shaving, wafer; shred 53 *piece*; streak 203 *line*.

Adj. *fibrous*, fibrillose, fibrillar, fibrilliform; woolly, cottony, silky; filamentous, filiform; whiskery 259 *hairy*; wiry, threadlike; capillary, capillaceous; fine-spun, wire-drawn 206 *narrow*; stringy, ropy 205 *thick*; flagelliform, lashlike; ligulate, strap-shaped.

209. Height – N. *height*, altitude, elevation; loftiness, dizzy height; tallness, stature; eminence, sublimity 213 *summit*.

high land, highlands, heights, uplands, wold, moorland, downs; rise, bank, brae, slope, climb; hill, ben, eminence, mount, mountain; fell, scar, tor, alp; mountain range, chain, sierra, cordillera, massif; Alps, Himalayas; Andes, Rockies; ridge, hog's back, col, saddle, spur, headland, foothill 254 *projection*; hilltop 213 *summit*; precipice, cliff, crag, scar, bluff, escarpment; canyon 255 *valley*; mesa; plateau, tableland 216 *horizontality*.

small hill, knoll, hillock, hummock, hump, dune, sand d.; mound, cairn 253 *earthwork*; anthill, molehill, tussock.

high structure, column, pillar, obelisk, turret, tower; pile, noble p., skyscraper 164 *edifice*; steeple, spire, minaret; dome; pyramid, pagoda; mast, topmast, flagstaff, pike-staff; pole, maypole; pylon, radio mast; watchtower, lookout, crow's nest 438 *view*.

tall creature, giraffe; lamppost, beanpole, six-footer, grenadier, colossus 195 *giant*.

altimetry, altimeter, height-finder, hypsometer, barograph.

Adj. *high*, high-up, sky-high; uplifted, exalted, lofty, sublime 310 *elevated*; highest 213 *topmost*; aerial, midair, air-borne, flying; soaring, aspiring 308 *ascending*; spiry, towering, cloud-capp'd; steep, dizzy, vertiginous; knee-high, shoulder-h.; altitudinal.

tall, lanky, rangy, slab-sided 206 *narrow*; long-legged, long-necked, giraffelike; statuesque, Junoesque; colossal, gigantic, monumental 195 *huge*.

alpine, subalpine, Himalayan; mountainous, hilly, moorland, upland, highland; rolling, hillocky, hummocky; orogenetic, orological.

Vb. *be high*, – tall etc. adj.; tower, soar; surmount, clear, overtop, overlook, dominate 34 *be superior*; overhang; overshadow 226 *cover*; beetle, hang over 254 *jut*; rise 308 *ascend*; raise 310 *elevate*.

Adv. *aloft*, up, on high, high up, in the clouds; on top, above, overhead, upwards, skyward, heavenward; on tiptoe, on stilts.

210. Lowness – N. *lowness*, sea level, flatness 216 *horizontality*; flats, levels 347 *marsh*; steppe 348 *plain*; low elevation, lowlands; molehill, pimple; foothill; bottom, hollow, depression 255 *valley*; depths, cellar 211 *depth*; floor, foot 214 *base*; underside, undersurface, underbelly; low water, low tide, ebb t., neap t.; low ball, daisy-cutter.

Adj. *low*, squat 204 *short*; unerect, crouched, stooping 220 *oblique*; recumbent, prostrate 216 *supine*; low-lying 216 *flat*; low-level, single-storey; subjacent, lower, under, nether; sunken 255 *concave*; underground 211 *deep*; underfoot.

Vb. *be low*, lie low 216 *be horizontal*; crouch 311 *stoop*; crawl, grovel; depress 311 *lower*.

Adv. *under*, beneath, underneath; below, at the foot of; downwards, down; underfoot, underground, downstairs.

211. Depth – N. *depth*, drop, fall; deepness, profundity; lowest point, nadir; deeps 343 *ocean*; pit, mine, well 255 *cavity*; abyss, abysm, chasm 201 *gap*; dungeon 194 *cellar*; cave, bowels of the earth 210 *lowness*; pot-holing; underworld, bottomless pit; fathoming, soundings; submarine, frogman 313 *diver*; draught, displacement, sinkage; bathometer 465 *measurement*.

Adj. *deep*, steep, plunging, profound; abysmal, yawning, cavernous; deep-seated, deep-rooted 153 *fixed*; unplumbed, bottomless, fathomless; unsounded, unfathomed, subterranean, underground, hypogeal; underwater, undersea, subaqueous, submarine; buried, immersed, submerged, sunk 311 *lowered*; navigable; knee-deep, ankle-d.; bathypelagic, benthic; bathymetric.

Vb. *be deep*, be profound; gape, yawn; deepen 255 *make concave*; fathom, sound, drop, plumb the depths, touch bottom; sink, plunge 313 *founder*.

212. Shallowness – N. *shallowness*, no depth, superficiality 223 *exteriority*; veneer, thin coat 226 *skin*; scratch, pinprick, graze 639 *trifle*; shoals, shallows; ford; puddle; ripple, catspaw.

Adj. *shallow*, slight, superficial; surface, skin-deep; ankle-deep; shoaly, unnavigable; light, thin, thinly spread.

213. Summit – N. *summit*, sky, heaven; pole; top, peak, crest, apex, pinnacle, crown; maximum height, pitch; zenith, meridian, high noon, culmination, apogee; acme, ne plus ultra 646 *perfection*; crest of the wave, top of the tree, climax, highwater mark 236 *limit*; divide, water-shed 231 *partition*; coping, capstone, keystone; lintel, pediment; capital, cornice; battlements, parapet.

vertex, apex, crown, cap, brow, head; tip, cusp, spike, nib, end 69 *extremity*; spire, finial; hilltop, mountaintop 209 *high land*; treetop, housetop, rooftop; gable; ceiling 226 *roof*; garret 194 *attic*; top storey; topside; upper deck, quarter-deck, bridge 275 *ship*; masthead, crow's nest 209 *high structure*.

head, headpiece, pate, poll; noddle, nob, nut, noggin, coco, conk, bonce, crumpet, bean, block, chump; upper storey, belfry; brow, dome, temple, forehead; loaf, brain 498 *intelligence*; scalp, crown, double c.; skull, cranium, brainpan; occiput, sinciput; fontanelle; craniology, craniometry; phrenology.

Adj. *topmost*, top, highest 209 *high*; uppermost 34 *supreme*; polar, apical, crowning; capital, head; cranial, cephalic, dolicocephalic, brachycephalic; culminating, zenithal.

Vb. *crown*, cap, head, top, tip, surmount, crest, overtop 209 *be high*; culminate 725 *climax*; top out 54 *make complete*.

214. Base – N. *base*, foot, toe, skirt 210 *lowness*; bottom, fundus, root; lowest point, rock bottom, nadir, low water; footing, foundation 218 *basis*; groundwork, substructure, infrastructure 218 *frame*; substratum, floor, underlayer, bed, bedrock; ground, earth, foundations; footing, sill; damp course; basement, ground floor 194 *cellar*; flooring 226 *paving*; skirting board, wainscot, plinth, dado; keel, hold, bilge, sump.

foot, feet, pedal extremities; beetle-crusher; forefoot, hindfoot; sole, heel, instep, arch; toe; trotter, hoof; paw, pad; claw 778 *nippers*; ankle, fetlock, pastern.

Adj. *undermost*, lowermost, nethermost, bottom, rock-b. 210 *low*; basic, basal, fundamental; grounded; underlying 218 *supporting*.

footed, pedal; plantigrade, digitigrade; hoofed, cloven-h., ungulate; web-footed; soled, heeled, shod; toed, five-t.; clubfooted 845 *blemished*.

215. Verticality – N. *verticality*, the vertical, erectness, uprightness, upright carriage; steepness, sheerness, precipitousness 209 *height*; perpendicularity, right angle; elevation; plumb-line, plummet; upright, pole, stalagmite 218 *pillar*; sheer face, precipice, cliff, scarp, drop 209 *high land*.

Adj. *vertical*, upright, erect, standing; perpendicular; sheer, abrupt, steep, precipitous 209 *high*; straight, plumb; upstanding, standing up, on one's feet; bolt upright, stiff as a ramrod, unbowed; rampant, rearing; on end.

Vb. *be vertical*, stick up, cock up, bristle, stand on end; rise, stand; ramp, rear.

make vertical, erect, rear, raise 310 *elevate*; up-end; stand, set up.

Adv. *vertically*, etc. adj.; palewise (heraldry); upright, head-up; on end, endwise, up; standing; at right angles.

216. Horizontality – N. *horizontality*, horizontalness; horizontal, azimuth; ruled line; flatness 258 *smoothness*; level, plane, dead level; stratum; slab 207 *layer*; steppe 348 *plain*; flats 347 *marsh*; platform, ledge; terrace; tableland; platter; plate; spirit level, T-square; horizon 236 *limit*.

recumbency, supination; prostration; proneness, supineness.

flattener, iron, flatiron, press; rolling pin, roller 258 *smoother*; bulldozer, juggernaut 168 *destroyer*.

Adj. *flat*, horizontal, two-dimensional, level, plane, even, flush 258 *smooth*; trodden, beaten flat; flat as a pancake, unwrinkled, smooth, calm as a millpond.

supine, flat on one's back; prone, face down, prostrate; recumbent, procumbent; lying down, couchant; laid out; stretched out, sprawling, lolling.

Vb. *be horizontal*, lie, lie down, lie flat; measure one's length, recline, couch, sprawl, loll 311 *sit down*; straighten out, level out.

flatten, lay out, roll o., lay down, spread; tread flat, stamp down, trample d., squash; make flush, align, level, even, grade, plane 28 *equalize*; iron out, roll out, smooth; pat down, plaster d.; prostrate, floor 311 *fell*.

Adv. *horizontally*, flat, on one's back; fesse-wise.

217. Pendency – N. *pendency*, pensility; suspension, hanging; set, hang, drape.

hanging object, pendant, dangler, drop, earring 844 *jewellery*; tassel, tag 844 *trimming*; hangings, draperies, drapes, curtains 226 *covering*; train, skirt, coat-tails; flap, lappet, tippet; tail, pigtail; dewlap, lobe; pendulum, bob; swing, hammock 317 *oscillation*; chandelier 420 *lamp*; icicle, stalactite.

hanger, runner, rack; hook, peg, knob, nail 218 *prop*; suspender, braces; clotheshorse, airer; davit, crane gallows, gibbet.

Adj. *hanging*, pendent, pendulous, pensile; hanging from, suspended, penduline, dangling; nodding, drooping; overhanging, beetling; loose 46 *disunited*; baggy, flowing, floating, streaming; tailed, caudate; lop-eared.

Vb. *hang*, drape, set; hang down, draggle, trail, flow; swing from; swing, sway, dangle, bob; nod, loll, droop, sag, swag; stream, wave, float, ripple, flap; hang over, hover; overhang; suspend, hang up, sling, hook up, hitch, append 45 *join*.

218. Support – N. *support*, underpinning 703 *aid*; leg to stand on, point d'appui, footing, ground, terra firma; hold, foothold, handhold, toehold 778 *retention*; lifebelt 662 *safeguard*.

prop, support, mounting, bearing; carriage, carrier, underframe, chassis; buttress, flying b.; abutment, bulwark; embankment, wall, retaining w.; shore, jack; stanchion, rod, bar, transom, brace, strut; stay, mainstay 47 *tackling*; sprit, boom, spar, yardarm, crosstree 254 *projection*; trunk, stem, stalk, pedicel 366 *plant*; arch 248 *curve*; headstone, cornerstone, springer; cantilever; pier (**see** *pillar*); bandage, jockstrap, truss, splint; whalebone, corset 228 *underwear*; yoke 217 *hanger*; rest, headrest, backrest, footrest, stirrup; skid, chock, wedge; staff, stick, shooting s., walking s., alpenstock, crutch, crook; irons; bracket (**see** *shelf*); trivet (**see** *stand*); shoulder; broad shoulders; worldbearer, Atlas.

handle, holder 194 *receptacle*; hold, grip, hilt, pommel, haft; knob, doorhandle; lug, ear, loop; railing, handrail, rail, banisters, balustrade; shaft, loom; handlebar, tiller, winder, crank; lever, trigger 630 *tool*.

basis, foundation, footings, deck; raft, pallet, sleeper; substratum 207 *layer*; ground, floor, bed 214 *base*; flooring 226 *paving*; perch, footing, foothold.

stand, tripod, trivet, hob; table mat, coaster; anvil, block, bench; trolley, table, board; sideboard, dresser 194 *cabinet*; desk, counter; pedestal, plinth, socle; stylobate, podium; footplate, platform, staddle, gantry; dais 539 *rostrum*; step, tread, rung 308 *ascent*; stilt 310 *lifter*.

seat, throne; bank, bench, form, settle; bucket seat, box s., dicky; pew 990 *church interior*; stall 594 *theatre*; chair, armchair, easy chair, wing c., rocking c., basket c., Windsor c., high c., deck c., lounger; chaise longue; sofa, settee, divan, couch, ottoman, chesterfield, sociable; tabouret, pouffe, stool, footstool, faldstool, priedieu; saddle, side s., pillion, pad, howdah; lap, knees.

bed, cot, crib, cradle, bassinet; bunk; daybed, couch; tester, four-poster; bedstead, divan; charpoy, truckle bed, camp b., pallet, airbed, bedroll, shakedown;

hammock; litter, hurdle, stretcher; bier.

cushion, pillow; bolster, Dutch wife; mattress, palliasse; squab, hassock, kneeler.

beam, balk, joist, girder, box g., rafter, purlin, tie beam, truss; summer, bressummer; wall-plate; crossbeam, transom, crossbar; architrave, lintel.

pillar, shaft, pier, pile, pole, stake, stud, cruck 331 *structure*; post, king p., queen p., crown p.; jamb, doorpost; stanchion, puncheon; newelpost, banister, baluster; mullion; pilaster, column, caryatid; spinal column, spine, backbone, vertebrae; neck, cervix.

pivot, fulcrum, lever, purchase; hinge 45 *joint*; pole, axis; axle, swivel, spindle, pintle 315 *rotator*; bearing, gudgeon, trunnion; rowlock, tholepin.

shelf, ledge 254 *projection*; corbel, bracket, console; retable, niche 194 *compartment*; windowsill, mantelpiece, mantelshelf; rack, dresser 194 *cabinet*; plank, board, table, leaf, slab 207 *lamina*.

frame, bony f., skeleton, ribs; framework, staging, scaffolding 331 *structure*; trellis, espalier; chassis, fuselage, body, undercarriage; trestle, easel; housing 235 *enclosure*; picture frame, window f., sash 233 *outline*.

Adj. *supporting*, sustaining; fundamental, basal; columnar; cervical, spinal; structural, skeletal.

Vb. *support*, sustain, bear, carry, hold, shoulder; uphold, hold up, bear up, buoy up; prop, shore up, underprop, underpin, jack up 310 *elevate*; buttress, bolster, cushion; reinforce, underset 162 *strengthen*; bandage, brace, truss, steady, stay; cradle, pillow, cup; give support 703 *aid*; frame, set, mount 235 *enclose*; bottom, ground, found, base, embed 153 *stabilize*; take the strain 635 *suffice*.

be supported, stand on, repose on, rest on; bear on, press; lean on, rely on.

219. Parallelism – N. *parallelism*, nonconvergence, nondivergence, equidistance, collimation, concentricity; parallel, correspondence; tramlines, railway lines; parallel bars; parallelogram.

Adj. *parallel*, collateral, concurrent, concentric; equidistant 28 *equal*; corresponding 18 *similar*.

220. Obliquity – N. *obliquity*, obliqueness, skewness; transversal, diagonal; rhomboid 247 *angular figure*; oblique angle, inclination; indirectness, squint; camber, bend 248 *curve*; crookedness, zigzag, chevron; divagation, digression, stagger 282 *deviation*; splay, bias, warp 246 *distortion*; leaning, list, tip, cant; slope, slant, tilt, pitch, rake, rakish angle; sloping face, batter; sloping edge, bevel, bezel; inclined plane, ramp, chute, slide.

incline, rise, ascent; ramp, acclivity, gradient; hill, rising ground 209 *small hill*; hillside, versant; declivity, fall, dip, downhill 309 *descent*; gentle slope, dip s.; scarp s., escarpment 215 *verticality*; scarp 713 *fortification*; talus, bank, scree, landslip.

Adj. *oblique*, inclined, bevel; tipsy, tilted, rakish; biased, askew, skew, slant, aslant, out of true; out of the perpendicular, at an angle, battered, leaning; stooping; catercornered, rhomboidal 247 *angular*; wry, awry, skew-whiff, crooked, squinting, cock-eyed, knock-kneed 246 *distorted*; diagonal, transverse; athwart 222 *crossed*; indirect, zigzag, herringbone; bent 248 *curved*; stepped, in echelon; divergent 282 *deviating*.

sloping, acclivitous, uphill, rising 308 *ascending*; downhill, falling, dipping 309 *descending*; anticlinal, synclinal; declivitous, steep, vertiginous, breakneck 215 *vertical*; easy, gentle, shelving.

Vb. *be oblique*, – tilted etc. adj.; incline, lean, tilt; pitch, slope, slant, shelve, dip, decline 309 *descend*; rise, climb 308 *ascend*; cut across, transect 222 *cross*; lean, list, tip, lean over, bank, heel, careen, cant; bend, sag, give; bend over 311 *stoop*; walk sideways, edge, sidle, sidestep; squint; zigzag, jink, dodge, swerve; diverge, converge.

make oblique, incline, lean, slant, slope, cant, tilt, tip, rake; splay 282 *deviate*; bend, crook, twist, warp, skew, bias 246 *distort*; chamfer, bevel; divert 282 *deflect*; camber 248 *make curved*.

Adv. *obliquely*, diagonally, crosswise, across; catercorner, cornerwise; on the cross, on the bias; askew, aslant, on the slant; askance; edgewise, crabwise, sidelong, sideways.

221. Inversion – N. *inversion*, turning back to front, palindrome, hysteron proteron; turning inside out, eversion, evagination; turning backwards, retroversion, reversal 148 *reversion*; turning inward, introversion, invagination; inverted order, chiasmus, anastrophe, hyperbaton 519 *trope*.

overturning, capsizal, upset, spill; somersault, cartwheel, handspring; subversion, undermining 149 *revolution*; pronation 216 *recumbency*.

Adj. *inverted*, etc. vb.; inverse, back-to-front; upside down, inside out, wrong side out; capsized; topsy-turvy, head over heels, on one's head; prone 216 *supine*; reversed 14 *contrary*; chiastic, palindromic.

Vb. *be inverted*, turn round 286 *turn back*; turn over, heel o., keel o., capsize, turn turtle; tilt over, topple o. 309 *tumble*; stand on one's head; loop the loop; reverse 286 *regress*.

invert, transpose, put the cart before the horse; reverse, turn the tables; turn back or down 261 *fold*; introvert, invaginate; turn inside out, evaginate; upend, upturn, overturn, tip over, spill, upset, overset, capsize; turn topsy-turvy.

Adv. *inversely*, vice versa; contrariwise, other way round; back to front, upside down; arsy-versy, topsy-turvy, head over heels; face down, bottom side up.

222. Crossing: intertexture – N. *crossing*, weaving; crisscross, transection, intersection; decussation, X-shape; quincunx; interlacement, interdigitation, intertwinement, interweaving, arabesque 844 *pattern*; anastomosis, inosculation; braid, wreath, plait 251 *convolution*; entanglement, skein, cat's cradle 61 *complexity*; crossroads, intersection 624 *road*.

cross, crucifix; pectoral, ankh, ansate

cross, tau c., Latin c., c. of Lorraine, Greek c., Maltese c., Celtic c., St Andrew's C.; saltire, crosslet 547 *heraldry*; gammadion, swastika, fylfot; crossbones, skull and c.; scissors, nutcrackers.

network, reticulation, meshwork, netting, chicken wire; webbing, matting, wickerwork, basketwork, trellis, wattle; honeycomb, lattice, grating, grid, grille, gridiron; craquelure; tracery, filigree 844 *ornamental art*; lace, crochet, knitting, tatting, macramé 844 *needlework*; web, cobweb; net, fishnet, seine, purse-s., drag-net, trawl, beam t. 235 *enclosure*; plexus, mesh, reticle.

textile, weave, web, loom; woven stuff, piece goods, dry g.; bolt, roll, length, piece, cloth, stuff, material; broadcloth, fabric, tissue, suiting; batik 844 *ornamental art*; jute, hessian, gunny, sacking, hopsack, canvas, sailcloth, duck; ticking, crash, huckaback, towelling, terry t., candlewick; chintz, cretonne, damask, brocade, brocatelle, grosgrain, rep, chenille, tapestry 226 *covering*; mohair, cashmere 208 *fibre*; wool, worsted, grosgram; frieze, felt, baize; homespun, duffle, kersey, tweed, serge, shalloon, bombazine, gabardine, doeskin; flannel, swanskin, swansdown; paisley, jacquard 844 *pattern*; stockinette, jersey, tricot, nainsook, flannelette, winceyette; velvet, velveteen, velours; corduroy, needlecord; cotton, denim, drill, nankeen, cavalry twill, khaki; fustian, moleskin, sharkskin; poplin, calico, dimity, gingham, madras, seersucker, piqué; batiste, organdie, organza; cheesecloth, muslin, voile, percale; cambric, lawn, toile, holland, linen; silk, foulard, georgette, crêpe de chine, chiffon, mousseline; satin, sateen, taffeta, moiré; tussore, shantung, pongee; tulle, net, gauze; lace, guipure; rayon, nylon, crimplene (tdmk), polyester, fibreglass 208 *fibre*.

weaving, texture; web, warp, weft, woof, selvedge; nap, pile 259 *hair*; frame, loom, shuttle; weaver, knitter; knitting machine, sewing m.; spinning wheel, distaff, whorl; spinner, spider, weaverbird; Arachne, Penelope.

Adj. *crossed*, crossing, cross, crisscross; quadrivial; diagonal, transverse 220 *oblique*; decussate, X-shaped, quincunxial; cross-legged; cruciform, cruciate 247 *angular*; plexiform; knotted, matted 61 *complex*; plaited, etc. vb.; woven, hand-woven, tweedy; twill, herringbone; trellised, latticed, honeycombed, mullioned, barred 437 *variegated*.

reticular, reticulated, retiform, webby, lacy; netted, meshed, micromesh.

Vb. *cross*, cross over 305 *pass*; intersect, cut 220 *be oblique*; splice, dovetail; reticulate, mesh, net, knot.

weave, loom; pleach, plash, plait, braid; felt, twill, knit, crochet; spin, slub.

enlace, interlace, interlink, interlock, interdigitate, intertwine, intertwist, interweave, enmesh; twine, entwine, twist, raddle, wreathe; mat, ravel, snarl, tangle, entangle 63 *derange*.

Adv. *across*, athwart, transversely; cross-wise, saltire-wise.

223. Exteriority – N. *exteriority*, the external; outwardness, externality 230 *surroundings*; periphery, circumference, sidelines 233 *outline*; exterior, outward appearance 445 *appearance*; surface, superficies, superstratum, crust, shell 226 *skin*; face, facet, façade 237 *front*; outside, out of doors, open air; extraterritoriality 57 *exclusion*; outsider 84 *nonconformist*.

Adj. *exterior*, exoteric, outward, extra-; external 10 *unrelated*; outer, outermost, outlying, extraterrestrial 199 *distant*; outside, outboard; outdoor; extramural; foreign 59 *extraneous*; extrovert; centrifugal 620 *avoiding*; exogenous; surface, superficial, skin-deep 212 *shallow*.

Vb. *externalize*, body forth, objectify 6 *make extrinsic*; project, extrapolate; expel 300 *eject*.

Adv. *externally*, outwardly, outwards, superficially, on the surface; on the face of it; outside, extra muros; out, out of doors, in the open, alfresco.

224. Interiority – N. *interiority*, interior, inside, indoors; inner surface, undersurface; endoderm 226 *skin*; sapwood, heart-wood; inmost being, heart's blood, soul; heart, centre 225 *centrality*; inland, Midlands, heartland, hinterland, up-country; pith, marrow 3 *substance*; subsoil, substratum 214 *base*; penetralia, recesses 211 *depth*; inmate, indweller.

insides 193 *contents*; inner man *or* woman; viscera, vitals; heart, ticker; lungs, lights; liver, kidneys, spleen; bowels, entrails, innards, guts, pluck, tripe; intestines, colon, rectum; abdomen, belly; womb, uterus; stomach 194 *maw*; chest, solar plexus; gland; cell 358 *organism*.

Adj. *interior*, internal, inward 5 *intrinsic*; inside, inner, innermost 225 *central*; inland, up-country; intimate, domestic, home, vernacular; indoor; intramural; shut, in, enclosed; inboard, built-in; endemic, deep-seated; intestinal, visceral; intravenous, subcutaneous; interstitial 231 *interjacent*; introvert 5 *intrinsic*; endo-, endogenous.

Vb. *be inside*, lie within, lie beneath, be at the bottom of.

Adv. *inside*, within, in, deep down; inly, inwardly, intimately; deeply, profoundly, at heart; indoors, at home.

225. Centrality – N. *centrality*, centricity, centralness; concentricity; centralization, focalization, concentration.

centre, dead c.; centre of gravity; metacentre; nerve centre, ganglion; epicentre 76 *focus*; storm centre, hotbed; heart, core, kernel 5 *essential part*; omphalos, nub, hub; nucleus, nucleolus; navel, umbilicus; midriff 231 *partition*; spine, backbone, chine, midrib; marrow, pith 224 *interiority*; pole, axis 218 *pivot*; centre point 70 *middle*; eye, pupil; bull's-eye, target.

Adj. *central*, centro-, centric; nuclear, nucleolar; centremost, midmost 70 *middle*; axial, focal, pivotal; umbilical; homocentric, concentric; geocentric; heliocentric; spinal, vertebral; centripetal.

Vb. *centralize*, centre, focus, bring to a f., centre upon; concentrate, nucleate.

226. Covering – N. *covering*, capping etc. vb.; superposition, superimposition, overlaying; overlap, imbrication; coating, stratification 207 *layer*; topping, icing, frosting; cover, lid; gravestone, ledger; hatch, trap-door; flap, shutter, operculum; cap, top, plug 264 *stopper*; plaster 658 *surgical dressing*; shell, carapace; mail, plate, armour p. 713 *armour*; shield, cowl, cowling, bonnet, hood (of a car); ferrule, sheath, involucre, envelope 194 *receptacle*; soft furnishings, loose covers 217 *hanging object*; wallpaper 227 *lining*; mask 527 *disguise*.

roof, cupola 253 *dome*; mansard roof, hipped r., gable r.; housetop, rooftop, rooftree 213 *vertex*; leads, slates, tiles, tiling, pantile, thatch 631 *building material*; eaves 234 *edge*; ceiling, vaulting; rafters 218 *beam*.

canopy, baldachin; tilt, awning, sunblind 421 *screen*; marquee, pavilion, big top; tent, bell t., ridge t., frame t., tepee 192 *dwelling*; canvas, tarpaulin, fly sheet; mosquito net.

shade, hood, eyelid; blind, venetian b., roller blind, jalousie, persiennes, shutters, slats; curtain, veil; umbrella, gamp, brolly; parasol, sunshade; sun hat 228 *headgear*; peak, visor, eye shade 421 *screen*.

wrapping, wrapper; packaging, blister pack 194 *receptacle*; bandage, plaster cast 658 *surgical dressing*; dust jacket *or* cover; coat 228 *jacket*; mantle 228 *cloak*; scarf 228 *neckwear*; lagging 227 *lining*; cocoon, chrysalis; shroud, winding sheet.

skin, epithelium; outer skin, scarf s., epidermis, cuticle; true skin, cutis, dermis, derma, corium; tegument 223 *exteriority*; integument, peel, bark, crust, rind, coat, cortex; pericarp, husk, hull, shell, pod, jacket; pellicle, membrane, film; scalp 213 *head*; scale 207 *lamina*; pelt, fleece, fell, fur; leather, hide, rawhide; shagreen; patent leather; pigskin, morocco, calf, kid, suede, buff; rabbitskin, moleskin, sealskin; sheepskin, lamb, Persian l., astrakhan; mink, sable, ermine, vair, miniver, cony; chinchilla 208 *fibre*; feathers, coverts 259 *plumage*.

paving, flooring, floor, parquet, quarry tiles; deck, floorboards, duckboards; pavement, flags, paving stone, crazy paving; tarmac 624 *road*.

coverlet, bedspread, counterpane, bedding, bedclothes, bed linen; sheet, quilt, eiderdown, duvet; blanket, rug; caparison, housings, trappings; saddlecloth, horse-cloth; pall.

floor-cover, carpeting, carpet, fitted c., pile c., Persian c.; mat, doormat; rug, hearth r.; drugget; linoleum, lino, vinyl, tiles; matting.

facing, revetment, cladding 162 *strengthening*; veneer, coating, varnish, japan, lacquer, enamel, glaze; incrustation, roughcast, pebbledash; ashlar, weatherboarding 631 *building material*; stucco, compo, plaster, rendering; wash, whitewash, distemper, emulsion, paint; stain, polish, coat of paint.

Adj. *covered*, roofed, vaulted, etc. vb.; under cover, under canvas; cloaked, veiled, hooded 525 *concealed*; loricate, armour-plated, iron-clad; metalled, paved.

dermal, cutaneous, cortical, cuticular; scaly, squamous; epidermic, epidermal.

Vb. *cover*, superpose, superimpose; roof, roof in, cap, tip; ice, frost, spread, overlay, smother; lag 227 *line*; envelop 235 *enclose*; blanket, shroud, mantle, muffle; hood, veil 525 *conceal*; case, bind; box, pack, vacuum-pack; wrap, shrink-w.; bandage, swathe 658 *doctor*; encapsulate 303 *insert*; keep under cover, garage.

overlie, overarch, overhang, overlap; straddle, bestraddle 205 *be broad*; flood, inundate; skin over, crust, scab.

overlay, pave, floor; roof, vault, overarch, deck; tile, thatch; paper, wallpaper 227 *line*; topdress, mulch; spread, smear, besmear; butter, anoint; powder, dust; tarmac, metal.

coat, revet, face, do over; grout, roughcast, encrust; plaster, render 844 *decorate*; varnish, lacquer, japan, enamel, glaze, size; paint, whitewash, colourwash 425 *colour*; creosote, tar, pitch, pay; daub, bedaub, scumble, overpaint, lay it on thick; gild, plate, silver, besilver; electro-

plate, silverplate; waterproof, fireproof 660 *safeguard*.

227. Lining – N. *lining*, liner, interlining 231 *interjacency*; coating, inner c.; stuffing, wadding, padding, batting, quilting; kapok, foam 631 *materials*; lagging, insulation, double-glazing, sound-proofing; backing, facing; upholstery; wallpaper; panelling, wainscot, skirting board; brake lining; packing, dunnage; packaging 226 *wrapping*; filling, stopping (dentistry); washer, shim; bush.

Vb. *line*, encrust 226 *coat*; insulate 226 *cover*; interlard, inlay; back, face, paper, wallpaper; upholster, cushion; stuff, pad, wad; fill, pack 303 *insert*.

228. Dressing – N. *dressing*, investment, investiture; clothing, covering, toilet, toilette; vesture, dress, garb, attire, rig; panoply, array; garniture, trim, accoutrements, caparison, harness, housing, trappings; traps, paraphernalia, accessories; rig-out, turn-out; tailoring, dressmaking, millinery; haute couture; the rag trade 848 *fashion*.

clothing, wear, apparel, raiment, linen; clothes, garments, vestments, habiliments; togs, gear, kit, clobber; outfit, wardrobe, trousseau; maternity wear; layette, baby clothes; duds, reach-me-downs; cast-offs, rags; working clothes, slops; leisure wear, casual clothes; Sunday best, Sunday go-to-meeting, best bib and tucker; party dress, glad rags; pearlies, ostrich feathers 844 *finery*; fancy dress, masquerade; motley; silks, colours; costume, national c.

garment, article of clothing; collar (see *neckwear*); top, bodice, bosom; corsage, bib, stomacher; shirtfront, dicky; waistline (see *belt*); peplum, bustle, train; crutch, codpiece; arms, sleeve; flaps, coat tails 217 *hanging object*; placket, fly 263 *opening*, 194 *pocket*; gusset, gore, pleat, kick pleat; lapel, turn-up 261 *fold*; cuff, hemline 234 *edging*.

formal dress, correct d., court d., full d. 875 *formality*; grande toilette, evening dress, tails, white tie and tails; morning dress; academic dress, cap and gown, sub-fusc; mourning, black, widow's weeds.

uniform, regimentals 547 *livery*; dress uniform, mess kit; battledress, fatigues, khaki; school uniform; robes, vestments 989 *canonicals*.

informal dress, undress, mufti, civvies; casuals, slacks, jeans; déshabillé, dis-habille; dressing gown, peignoir, bath-robe, wrapper, housecoat; smoking jacket, slippers.

robe, gown, robes, drapery; sari; kim-ono, caftan; chiton, toga; cassock 989 *canonicals*.

dress, frock, gown; creation, number, cocktail dress; sheath d., cheongsam, chemise, shift, sack; shirtwaister, coat-dress, overdress, pinafore dress, gymslip; sundress.

suit, outfit, ensemble; coordinates, separates; lounge suit, zoot s., drape s., pinstripe s.; costume, tweeds, trouser suit; jumpsuit, catsuit, leotard, body stocking; overalls, boiler suit, siren s., tracksuit, wetsuit; G-suit, spacesuit.

jacket, coat, tail c., dinner jacket, tux-edo; monkey jacket, mess j., pea j., Eton j.; blazer, reefer, sports jacket, Norfolk j., hacking j., riding habit, hunting pink; donkey jacket, lumber j. (see *overcoat*); parka, windcheater, anorak, kagoule; bomber jacket, blouson; jerkin, doublet, tunic, tabard, surcoat, waistcoat, spencer; bolero, coatee, matinée jacket.

jersey, pullover, woolly, homeknit, jumper, sweater, sweatshirt, sloppy joe, guernsey, Fair Isle, cardigan, twin set.

trousers, trews, breeks; cords, flannels, pin-stripes; hipsters, drainpipes, bell-bottoms; slacks, bags, Oxford b., plus fours; galligaskins, breeches, jodhpurs, knickerbockers, pedal-pushers; chaps, dungarees, denims, jeans, blue j., Levis (tdmk); shorts, Bermuda s.; lederhosen; bloomers, pantaloons, rompers.

skirt, maxi s., midi s., miniskirt; dirndl, kilt, kirtle, filibeg; sarong; slit skirt, hobble s.; divided s., culottes; ballet skirt, tutu; crinoline, farthingale.

loincloth, lungi, dhoti, sarong; fig leaf, G-string; nappy *or* diaper.

apron, bib, pinafore, pinny, overall.

shirt, smock; dashiki, caftan; polo neck, T-shirt; blouse, choli, camisole, top, sun top.

underwear, underclothes, undies, linen; lingerie, smalls, unmentionables; under-pants, pants, Y-fronts, boxer shorts; briefs, panties, French knickers, cami-knickers, knickers, bloomers, drawers; combinations, long johns, thermal under-wear; singlet, vest, string v.; chemise, slip, half-slip, petticoat; foundation garment, corset; stays, girdle, pantie-g., roll-on; brassière, bra; suspender belt, braces.

nightwear, nightclothes, sleeping suit; nightgown, nightdress, nightie, negligée; nightshirt, pyjamas; bedsocks, bed jacket, nightcap.

beachwear, sunsuit, bikini, monokini; swimming costume, swimsuit, bathing suit, trunks.

overcoat, coat (see *jacket*); fur coat, mink c. 226 *skin*; topcoat, greatcoat, frock coat; redingote, raglan, ulster; car coat, duffle c.; waterproof, oilskins; mac, mackintosh, raincoat, gabardine; trench coat.

cloak, mantle; cape, cycling c.; pelisse, pelerine, dolman; domino 527 *disguise*; djellaba, burnous (see *robe*); shawl, plaid, poncho, afghan.

neckwear, scarf, fichu; stole, boa, tip-pet; comforter, muffler; neckerchief, stock, jabot, cravat, tie, bow t.; necklace 844 *jewellery*; ruff, collar, dog c. 989 *ca-nonicals*.

headgear, millinery; hat, cap, lid, titfer; headdress, mantilla; ribbons 844 *finery*; coronet, tiara 743 *regalia*; fillet, snood; juliet cap, skull c., coif; headscarf, ker-chief, bandanna, headband, sweatband; turban, puggaree; hood, cowl, wimple; veil, yashmak 421 *screen*; fez, tarboosh; shako, kepi, busby, bearskin, helmet 713 *armour*; tin hat, hard h., crash helmet, skidlid 662 *safeguard*; woolly hat, bobble h.; rainhat, sou'wester; cap, cloth c., beret, tam-o'shanter; glengarry, deer-stalker; Homburg, trilby, porkpie hat, billycock, fedora, beaver, bowler, derby; slouch hat, stetson, ten-gallon hat, sombrero, shovel hat, picture h., Dolly Varden, straw hat, boater, panama, coolie hat, bush h., sunhat, pith helmet, topee 226 *shade*; bonnet, poke b., mob cap, toque, cloche, pillbox; top hat, topper, silk hat, stovepipe h.; cocked h., tricorne, mortarboard; biretta 989 *canonicals*; witch's hat, dunce's cap.

belt, girdle, waistband; cummerbund, sash, obi; armlet, armband; bandolier, baldric.

glove, gauntlet; mitten, mitt, muff.

legwear, hosiery; stockings, nylons, tights, fleshings; trunks, hose; half-hose, socks, ankle s., bootees; leggings, gaiters, spats, puttees; greaves 713 *armour*; garter, suspender 47 *fastening*.

footwear, footgear, buskin, cothurnus, sock; slipper, mule; patten, clog, sabot; flip-flops, sandals, Jesus boots, chappals; rope-soled shoes, espadrilles; creepers, sneakers, plimsolls, gym shoes, tennis s.; pumps, ballet shoes; moccasins, slip-ons, casuals; brothel creepers, winklepickers, beetle-crushers, clodhoppers; shoe, court s., high heels, stiletto h., platform h., Cuban h., wedge h.; square-toed shoes, peep-toed s., slingbacks, lace-ups, buckled shoes; Oxfords, brogues; boots, thigh b., waders, wellingtons, wellies, gumboots; skates 274 *sledge*; running shoes, spikes.

clothier, outfitter, costumier; tailor, couturier, couturière; fashion designer 848 *fashion*; dressmaker, needlewoman, seamstress, modiste; shoemaker, bootmaker; cobbler, cordwainer; hosier, hatter, milliner, draper, haberdasher; Savile Row, Carnaby Street; boutique; valet 742 *domestic*; dresser 594 *stagehand*.

Adj. *dressed*, clothed, clad, dight; attired etc. adj.; rigged out, turned o.; uniformed, liveried; shod, gloved, hatted; well-dressed, soigné(e).

tailored, tailor-made, bespoke, made-to-measure; ready-to-wear, off-the-peg; unisex; classic, princess-line, Empire-line, A-line; step-in, pull-on, button-through, zip-up; skintight, slinky 24 *adjusted*; gathered, bloused, bouffant 205 *broad*; sartorial.

Vb. *dress*, clothe, array, apparel, garb, attire; robe, enrobe, drape, sheet, mantle; invest, accoutre, uniform, rig out, fit o., caparison; dress up, deck, prink 843 *primp*; envelop, wrap up, roll up in, swaddle, swathe, sheathe 226 *cover*.

wear, put on, don, slip on, slip into; clothe oneself, get dressed; button up, zip up, lace up 45 *tie*; get changed; have on, dress in, carry, sport; dress up 875 *be ostentatious*.

229. Uncovering – N.

uncovering, divestment, undressing; exposure 526 *disclosure*; nudism, naturism; striptease 594 *stage show*; undress, dishabille 228 *informal dress*; moulting, shedding; decortication, exfoliation, excoriation, peeling, desquamation; depilation, shaving; denudation.

bareness, décolleté, décolletage, bare neck, low n., plunging neckline; nudity, nakedness, state of nature, birthday suit, the altogether, the buff, the raw; baldness, hairlessness; tonsure; baldpate, baldhead.

stripper, ecdysiast, striptease artiste; flasher, streaker; nudist, naturist; nude; skinner, furrier; hair-remover, depilatory.

Adj. *uncovered*, bared; exposed, unveiled, showing 522 *manifest*; divested, debagged; stripped, peeled; unclad, unclothed, undressed; décolleté(e), off-the-shoulder, topless; barearmed, barelegged; barefoot, unshod; hatless, bareheaded; en déshabillé, in one's shirt-sleeves; miniskirted, bikini-clad; underclothed, underdressed, indecently dressed; bare, naked, nude, raw; in a state of nature, mother naked, in the buff, with nothing on, without a stitch on; stark naked, starkers; moulting, unfeathered, unfledged.

hairless, bald, baldheaded, smooth, beardless, shaved, shaven, clean-s., tonsured; bald as a coot; napless, threadbare; mangy; thin, thin on top.

Vb. *uncover*, unveil, undrape, unrobe, uncloak, undress, unclothe; divest; strip, skin, scalp, flay, tear off; pluck, peel;

decorticate, excoriate; hull, pod, shell; bone, fillet 300 *empty*; denude 165 *lay waste*; expose, bare 526 *disclose*; unsheathe, draw (a sword) 304 *extract*; unwrap, unfold, unpack 263 *open*; scrape off 333 *rub*.

doff, uncap, uncover, raise one's hat; take off, strip off, peel off, slip off, slip out of, step out of, divest oneself of; change; shed, cast; moult, slough, exuviate; flake off, scale; undress, disrobe, peel, strip; undo, untie 46 *disunite*.

230. Surroundings – N. *surroundings* 223 *exteriority*; circumambience, circumjacence; ambience, atmosphere, aura; medium, matrix; encompassment 235 *enclosure*; circumference, periphery, perimeter 233 *outline*; milieu, environment, background, setting, scene 186 *situation*; neighbourhood, vicinity 200 *near place*; outskirts, environs, suburbs, green belt; purlieus, precincts 192 *housing*; outpost 236 *limit*.

Adj. *circumjacent*, circumambient, circumfluent, ambient, atmospheric; surrounding, framing, circumferential, peripheral.

Vb. *surround*, encompass, environ, lap; encircle, girdle 235 *enclose*; wreathe around, twine a., embrace; contain 232 *circumscribe*; beset, blockade 712 *besiege*.

Adv. *around*, about, on every side, round about, all round.

231. Interjacency – N. *interjacency*, intermediacy; permeation, infiltration 189 *presence*; dovetailing 45 *union*.

partition, curtain 421 *screen*; wall, party w., bulkhead 235 *fence*; divide, watershed; division, interface; field boundary, hedge, ditch 236 *limit*.

intermediary, medium, intermedium; go-between, usual channels 720 *mediator*; marriage broker, matchmaker; agent 755 *deputy*; middleman; intercessor; buffer, bumper, fender; air lock, buffer state 70 *middle*.

interjection, interposition, sandwiching; interpolation, intercalation, interlineation 303 *insertion*; interruption,

intrusion 72 *discontinuity*; parenthesis, obiter dictum 40 *adjunct*; infix, insert.

Adj. *interjacent*, interposed, sandwiched; parenthetical, in brackets; intermediary, intervening; intercessory 720 *mediatory*; intercalary 303 *inserted*; inter-, interstitial, intermural; intermediate, median 70 *middle*.

Vb. *put between*, sandwich; cushion 227 *line*; interpose, interject; spatchcock, interpolate, intercalate, interline; interleave, interlard, intersperse; interdigitate 222 *enlace*; put between brackets, parenthesize.

Adv. *between*, betwixt and between; among, amongst, amid, amidst, in the middle of; parenthetically.

232. Circumscription – N. *circumscription*, enclosing 235 *enclosure*; circle, balloon; surrounding, framing, girdling, cincture; encirclement, containment 747 *restriction*; ring 235 *fence*.

Vb. *circumscribe*, ring round, encircle, encompass; close in, cut off, cordon off; hem in, corral; hedge in, fence in 235 *enclose*; frame 230 *surround*; edge, border 236 *limit*.

233. Outline – N. *outline*, circumference, perimeter, periphery; surround, frame, rim 234 *edge*; ambit, compass, circuit 250 *circle*; delineation, lines 445 *feature*; profile, relief 239 *laterality*; silhouette, sketch; figure, diagram, tracing; skeleton, framework 331 *structure*; contour, shape 243 *form*; coastline, bounds 236 *limit*; ring, cordon 235 *barrier*.

Adj. *outlined*, etc. vb.; in outline, etched; peripheral, perimetric, circumferential.

Vb. *outline*, describe a circle 232 *circumscribe*; frame 230 *surround*; delineate, draw, trace 551 *represent*; etch 555 *engrave*; map, block out, sketch o.; diagrammatize, not fill in.

234. Edge – N. *edge*, verge, brim; fly, hoist (of a flag); tip, brink, skirt, fringe, margin 69 *extremity*; confines, bounds, boundary, frontier, border 236 *limit*; littoral, coast, coastline, beach, strand, seaside, sea-shore, waterline, waterside, water's edge, front, waterfront 344 *shore*; wharf, quay 192 *stable*; sideline, side, kerb, bank 239 *laterality*; lip, ledge, eaves, cornice, rim, welt, flange, gunwale 254 *projection*; raised edge, coaming; horizon, skyline 199 *farness*.

edging, frame 233 *outline*; thrum, list, selvedge; hem, hemline, border; purfling, binding, piping; fringe, frill, ruffle 844 *trimming*; crenation, milling 260 *notch*; deckle edge, wavy edge, scallop, picot, purl 251 *coil*.

Adj. *marginal*, border, skirting, marginated; riverine, riparian, coastal; riverside, roadside, wayside; edged, trimmed, bordered.

Vb. *hem*, edge, border, trim, fringe, purl; mill, crenellate 260 *notch*; bound, confine 236 *limit*.

235. Enclosure – N. *enclosure*, case 194 *receptacle*; wrapper 226 *wrapping*; girdle, ring 233 *outline*; surround, frame; enceinte, precinct, close; cloister, courtyard; holding, claim 184 *territory*; fold, pen 369 *cattle pen*; garth, park; compound, yard, pound, paddock, field; corral, stockade 713 *defences*; net 542 *trap*; cell, box, cage 748 *prison*.

fence, chain-link f. 222 *network*; hurdle, wooden fence, picket f.; sunk f., hedge, hedgerow, rails, paling, railing; pale, wall, boundary w.; ha-ha, moat, dike, ditch, trench 713 *defences*.

barrier, wall 231 *partition*; sound-proofing, double-glazing 660 *protection*; barricade, cordon; balustrade, parapet; turnstile 702 *obstacle*; palisade, stockade; portcullis, gate 264 *closure*.

Vb. *enclose*, fence in, cordon, cordon off, surround, wall; pen, hem, ring 232 *circumscribe*; cloister, immure, cage 747 *imprison*; wrap, lap, enwrap, enfold 261 *fold*; hug, embrace 889 *caress*; frame, set, mount, box.

236. Limit – N. *limit*, limitation 747 *restriction*; delimitation, demarcation; upper limit, ceiling, high-water mark 213 *sum-mit*; lower limit, threshold, low-water mark 214 *base*; legal limit, Plimsoll line; saturation point 54 *completeness*; uttermost ends of the earth, ne plus ultra 69 *extremity*; terminus 69 *end*; turning point, point of no return; limit of endurance, end of one's tether; tidemark, landmark, boundary stone; metes and bounds, bourne, boundary; frontier, border, marches 234 *edge*; line, demarcation l. 231 *partition*; horizon, equator, terminator; deadline; speed limit; sound barrier.

Adj. *limited*, definite, conterminous; limitable, finite; limitative, limitary, terminal; frontier, border, borderline, boundary.

Vb. *limit*, bound, border, edge; top 213 *crown*; define, confine, restrict; encompass 232 *circumscribe*; draw the line, delimit, demarcate, stake out; mark out.

237. Front – N. *front*, fore, forefront; forepart; frontispiece; forecourt, anteroom, entrance 263 *doorway*; foreground 200 *nearness*; front rank, front line, forward line; avant-garde, vanguard, van; spearhead, bridgehead.

face, frontage, façade, fascia; face of a coin, obverse, head; right side, outer s., recto; front view, front elevation; brow, forehead 213 *head*; physiognomy, features, visage, countenance; phiz, phizog, mug, mush, kisser, dial, clock 445 *feature*; nose, chin 254 *protuberance*.

prow, nose, beak, rostrum, figurehead; bows; bowsprit; jib, foremast, forecastle, fo'c'sle.

Adj. *frontal*, fore, forward, front, obverse; head-on, facing 240 *opposite*; anterior, prefixed.

Vb. *be in front*, front, confront, face 240 *be opposite*; breast, stem, brave; come to the front, come to the fore, forge ahead; head 283 *precede*.

Adv. *in front*, ahead, in the foreground.

238. Rear – N. *rear*, rearward, afterpart, back end, tail end, stern 69 *extremity*; tailpiece, colophon; tail, brush, scut; wake, train 67 *sequel*; back seat; rear-guard; background, backdrop; hinter-

land, depths 199 *distance*; behind, backstage, back side; reverse side, wrong s., verso; reverse, other side, flip side; back, dorsum, chine; backbone, spine 218 *prop*; nape, scruff, short hairs.

buttocks, backside, behind, derrière, posterior; bottom, seat, sit-me-down; bum, arse; rear, stern, tail; hindquarters, croup, crupper; hips, haunches, hams, hunkers; rump, loin; dorsal region, lumbar r., small of the back, lower back, coccyx; fundament, anus.

poop, stern, quarter; rearmast, mizzenmast 275 *ship*.

Adj. *back*, rear, postern; posterior, after, hind, hinder, hindermost, rearmost, tail-end; bent back, backswept 253 *convex*; reverse 240 *opposite*; spinal, vertebral, retral, dorsal, lumbar; anal; caudal, caudate.

Vb. *be behind*, stand b.; back on, back; bring up the rear, lag, trail; tail, shadow 284 *follow*.

Adv. *rearward*, behind, in the rear, in the ruck; at the back, in the background; behind one's back; after, aftermost, sternmost; aft, abaft, astern, aback; at the back of, close behind; in tandem; back to back.

239. Laterality – N. *laterality*, sidedness; side movement 317 *oscillation*; sidestep 282 *deviation*; sideline, side, bank 234 *edge*; coast 344 *shore*; siding, side door; gable, gable-end; broadside; beam; flank, ribs; wing, fin, hand; cheek, jowl, chops, chaps, gills; temples, side-face, half-face; profile, side elevation; lee, lee side; weatherside; orientation, east, Orient, Levant; west, Occident; off side, on s., near s. 241 *dextrality*, 242 *sinistrality*.

Adj. *lateral*, laparo-; side 234 *marginal*; sidelong, glancing; buccal; costal; winglike, aliform; flanked, sided; manysided, multilateral, bilateral, trilateral, quadrilateral; collateral 219 *parallel*; eastern, western 281 *directed*.

Vb. *flank*, side, edge, skirt, border 234 *hem*; coast; passage, sidle; sideslip, sidestep; deploy, outflank.

Adv. *sideways*, crabwise, laterally; askance, sidelong 220 *obliquely*; half-face, in

profile; broadside on; abreast, abeam, alongside; aside, beside; side by side, cheek by jowl.

240. Contraposition – N. *contraposition*, opposition, antipodes 14 *contrariety*; frontage 281 *direction*; opposite side, other s.; opposite poles, North and South; crosscurrent, headwind.

Adj. *opposite*, contrapositive 14 *contrary*; facing, fronting, confronting, oncoming 237 *frontal*; diametrically opposite, antipodal, antipodean; polar; antarctic, arctic, northern, septentrional, southern, austral 281 *directed*.

Vb. *be opposite*, – facing etc. adj.; stand opposite, lie o.; subtend; face 237 *be in front*; oppose, contrapose.

Adv. *against*, over against; poles asunder; facing, vis-à-vis; back to back.

241. Dextrality – N. *dextrality*, right hand, right-handedness; ambidexterity, ambidextrousness; right, offside, starboard; right-hand page, recto; right wing, right-winger; dextral.

Adj. *dextral*, dexter, dextro-; right-hand, starboard, offside; right-handed, dextrous, ambidextral, ambidextrous 694 *skilful*; dextrorse, dextrorotatory; right-wing.

242. Sinistrality – N. *sinistrality*, left hand, left-handedness; left, near side, on s.; larboard, port; verso; left wing, left-winger; sinistral, south-paw.

Adj. *sinistral*, sinister, left, left-handed; onside, nearside, sinistrorse; laevorotatory.

Section 3: Form

243. Form – N. *form*, Gestalt, essence, inscape 5 *character*; shape, turn, lines, architecture; formation, conformation, configuration, fashion, style, design 331 *structure*; contour, silhouette, relief, profile, frame, outline; figure, cut, set, trim, build, physiognomy 445 *feature*; look, expression, appearance, mien; posture, attitude, stance; get-up, turnout, rig; type, kind, pattern, stamp, cast, mould 23 *prototype*; morphology, isomorphism.

Adj. *formed*, etc. vb.; plastic, fictile; shaped, fashioned, fully f., styled, stylized; ready-made; isomorphous.

formative, giving form, formal; plastic, glyptic, architectural 331 *structural*.

Vb. *form*, create, make 164 *produce*; formalize, shape, fashion, figure, pattern; throw (pots), blow (glass); turn, round, square; cut, tailor; cut out, silhouette 233 *outline*; sketch, draw 551 *represent*; model 554 *sculpt*; hew, rough-h. 46 *cut*; mould, cast; stamp, coin, mint; hammer out, block o.; carpenter, mason; forge, smith; knead, work, work up into; construct, build, frame 310 *elevate*; express, formulate, put into shape, pull into s., lick into s., knock into s.

244. Amorphism: absence of form – N.
amorphism, absence of form; confusion, chaos 61 *disorder*; amorphousness, lack of shape, shapelessness; lack of definition, vagueness, fuzziness; rawness 670 *undevelopment*; raw material 631 *materials*; disfigurement, deformation 246 *distortion*.

Adj. *amorphous*, formless, unformed, inchoate; liquid 335 *fluid*; shapeless, featureless, characterless; messy, chaotic 61 *orderless*; undefined, ill-defined, indistinct, fuzzy, blurred 419 *shadowy*; unfashioned, unformed; embryonic, raw 68 *beginning*; unhewn, in the rough 55 *incomplete*; rude, uncouth 699 *artless*; malformed, misshapen 246 *deformed*.

245. Symmetry: regularity of form – N.
symmetry, correspondence, proportion 12 *correlation*; balance 28 *equilibrium*; regularity, evenness 16 *uniformity*; arborescence, ramification 219 *parallelism*; shapeliness, regular features, classic f. 841 *beauty*; harmony, congruity 24 *agreement*.

Adj. *symmetrical*, balanced 28 *equal*; proportioned, well-p. 12 *correlative*; eurhythmic, harmonious, congruous 24 *agreeing*; corresponding 219 *parallel*; isosceles, equilateral; crystalline; arborescent, dendriform, branching, ramose;

formal, classic 841 *shapely*; undeformed, undistorted 249 *straight*.

246. Distortion: irregularity of form – N.
distortion, asymmetry, disproportion, disproportionateness; imbalance 29 *inequality*; lopsidedness, skewness 220 *obliquity*; anamorphosis; contortion, twisting; strain, shear; bias, warp; buckle, bend, twist 251 *convolution*; grimace 547 *gesture*.

deformity, malformation; monstrosity, teratogeny 84 *abnormality*; rickets 845 *blemish*; ugliness 842 *eyesore*; teratology.

Adj. *distorted*, contorted etc. vb.; irregular, asymmetric, scalene, unsymmetrical, disproportionate 17 *nonuniform*; not true, not straight; anamorphous, grotesque; out of shape, warped 244 *amorphous*; buckled, twisted, gnarled 251 *convoluted*; wry, awry, askew, crazy, crooked, on one side 220 *oblique*.

deformed, ugly 842 *unsightly*; misproportioned, ill-proportioned; defective, ill-made, misshapen; hunchbacked, humpbacked, crook-backed; bandy, bandy-legged, bow-legged, knock-kneed; pigeon-toed, club-footed; round-shouldered, pigeon-chested; snub-nosed, hare-lipped 845 *blemished*; stunted 204 *short*; haggard, gaunt 206 *lean*; bloated 195 *fleshy*.

Vb. *distort*, disproportion, weight, bias; contort, screw, twist 251 *twine*; bend, warp 251 *crinkle*; spring, buckle, crumple; strain, sprain, skew, wrest 63 *derange*; misshape, botch, deform; mangle, batter, knock out of shape 655 *impair*; grimace, make faces 547 *gesticulate*.

247. Angularity – N. *angularity*, angulation; crotchet, bracket, crook, hook; bend, angle; scythe, sickle, scimitar 248 *curvature*; chevron, zigzag 220 *obliquity*; V-shape, elbow, knee, knuckle, ankle 45 *joint*; crutch, crotch, fluke 222 *cross*; fork, bifurcation; quoin, corner; Roman nose, hook n.; wedge, arrowhead 256 *sharp point*; indentation 260 *notch*.

angular measure, goniometry, trigonometry, altimetry; second, degree, minute; radian; goniometer, altimeter; clinometer, level, theodolite; sextant, quadrant; protractor, set square.

angular figure, triangle, trigon; parallelogram, rectangle, square, quadrangle, quadrature; quadrilateral, lozenge, diamond; rhomb, rhombus, rhomboid; trapezium, trapezoid; tetragon, polygon, pentagon, hexagon, heptagon, octagon, decagon, dodecahedron, icosahedron; cube, pyramid, wedge; prism, parallelepiped; Platonic bodies.

Adj. *angular*, hooked, uncinate, hook-nosed, aquiline; unciform, falciform 248 *curved*; angled, cornered; staggered, crooked, zigzag 220 *oblique*; jagged, serrated 260 *notched*; jointed, elbowed; akimbo; knock-kneed; crotched, forked, bifurcate, furcate, V-shaped.

angulated, triangular, trigonal, trilateral; wedge-shaped, cuneate, cuneiform, fusiform; rectangular, right-angled, orthogonal; square, square-shaped, foursquare, quadrangular, quadrilateral, four-sided, squared; trapezoidal; multilateral, polygonal, decahedral, polyhedral; cubical, rhomboidal, pyramidal.

Vb. *make angular*, angle, corner; hook, crook, bend 248 *make curved*; zigzag 220 *be oblique*; fork, bifurcate 294 *diverge*.

248. Curvature – N. *curvature*, curvation, 255 *concavity*, 253 *convexity*; flexure, flexion 261 *fold*; bending, stooping 311 *obeisance*; recurvature 221 *inversion*; curling, sinuosity 251 *convolution*.

curve, camber; elbow 247 *angularity*; turn, bend, sharp b., hairpin b., U-turn; horseshoe, oxbow; bay 345 *gulf*; figure of eight 250 *loop*; ogee, S-shape; tracery, curl 251 *convolution*; festoon, swag 844 *pattern*; bow, Cupid's b., rainbow 250 *arc*; arch, ogee a., vault 253 *dome*; sickle, scimitar, crescent, lunula, half-moon; meniscus, lens; trajectory, catenary, parabola, hyperbola; swan neck.

Adj. *curved*, etc. vb.; flexed, bent 220 *oblique*; bowed, stooping; bowlike, curvilineal; rounded, curvaceous, curvy, wavy, billowy 251 *undulatory*; aquiline 247 *angular*; beaked, beaklike, bill-shaped; recur-

vate, retroflex; retroussé, turned-up, tip-tilted 221 *inverted*; ogival, vaulted 253 *arched*; bowlegged 246 *deformed*; hooked, falcate; semicircular 250 *round*; crescent, lunate, lunar, semilunar, horned; reniform; cordiform, cordate, heart-shaped, bell-s., pear-s.

Vb. *be curved*, – bent etc. adj.; curve, swerve, bend, loop, camber, arch, sweep, sag, swag 217 *hang*; recurve.

make curved, bend, crook 247 *make angular*; turn, round; incurvate, inflect; recurve, retroflect; bow, incline 311 *stoop*; arch, arch over; coil 251 *twine*; loop, curl 251 *crinkle*.

249. Straightness – N. *straightness*, directness, rectilinearity; perpendicularity; inflexibility, rigidity; chord, radius 203 *line*; straight line, direct l., beeline; Roman road; straight, reach; short cut.

Adj. *straight*, direct, even, right, true; in a line, linear; straight-lined, rectilineal; perpendicular 215 *vertical*; unbent, unwarped, undistorted; stiff, inflexible 326 *rigid*; uncurled, straightened, dekinked; dead straight, undeviating, unswerving, on the beam, straight as an arrow.

Vb. *straighten*, make straight, align; iron out 216 *flatten*; unbend (a bow); uncross (legs); dekink, uncurl 258 *smooth*; stretch tight; uncoil, unroll 316 *evolve*.

Adv. *straight on*, directly, as the crow flies 281 *towards*; straight, plumb.

250. Circularity: simple circularity – N. *circularity*, orbicularity, roundness, rondure 252 *rotundity*.

circle, circumference 233 *outline*; great circle, equator; plate, saucer; round, disc, discus; coin, button, sequin; washer, hoop, ring, quoit; eye, iris; eyelet 263 *orifice*; fairy ring; smoke ring; wheel, castor 315 *rotator*.

loop, figure of eight 251 *convolution*; bow, knot; ringlet, curl 259 *hair*; circlet, bracelet, armlet, torque; crown, coronet; corona, aureole, halo; wreath, garland, necklace; collar, band, girdle 228 *belt*.

arc, semicircle, half-circle, hemicycle, lunette; half-moon, crescent, rainbow 248 *curve*; sector, quadrant, sextant; ellipse, oval; ellipsoid, cycloid.

Adj. *round*, rounded, circular, cyclic, discoid; orbicular, ringlike, ringed, annular, annulate; semicircular, hemicyclic; oval, ovate, elliptic, ovoid, egg-shaped, crescent-s., pear-s. 248 *curved*; spherical 252 *rotund*.

251. Convolution: complex circularity – N. *convolution*, involution, circumvolution; intricacy; flexuosity, anfractuosity, sinuosity, sinuousness; tortuousness, torsion; ripple, wrinkle, corrugation 261 *fold*; waviness, undulation, ogee 248 *curve*.

coil, roll, twist; turban, Turk's head; spiral, helix; screw, worm, corkscrew; spring; whorl, snailshell, ammonite; whirlpool, eddy 315 *vortex*; verticil, tendril 366 *plant*; scollop, scallop 234 *edging*; kink, curl; ringlet, lovelock 259 *hair*; scroll, volute, fiddlehead, flourish, twirl, curlicue, squiggle 844 *ornamentation*.

meandering, meander, winding course, crankiness; windings and turnings, twists and turns, circumbendibus 282 *deviation*; labyrinth, maze 61 *complexity*; switchback, zigzag 220 *obliquity*.

Adj. *convoluted*, twisted, contorted 246 *distorted*; tortile, cranky, ambagious; winding, looping, twining, anfractuous, sinuous, tortuous, flexuous; indented 260 *notched*; crumpled, buckled 261 *folded*.

labyrinthine, mazy, Daedalian, meandering, serpentine; twisting, turning 314 *circuitous*.

snaky, serpentine, anguine, eel-like, anguilliform, wormlike, vermiform, vermicular; squiggly, squirming, wriggling, peristaltic; S-shaped, sigmoid.

undulatory, undulating, rolling, heaving; up-and-down, switchback; crinkle-crankle (wall), wavy, curly, frizzy, kinky, crinkly; crimped, curled; scolloped, wrinkled, corrugated, indented, ragged 260 *notched*; Flamboyant, Decorated.

coiled, spiral, helical, cochlear; convolute, involute, turbinate, whorled; scroll-like, verticillate; wound up, coiling, spiralling.

Vb. *twine*, twist, twirl, roll, coil, corkscrew, convolute, spiral 315 *rotate*; wreathe, entwine 222 *enlace*; be convoluted, – twisted etc. adj.; turn and twist, bend 248 *be curved*.

crinkle, crimp, frizz, crisp, curl; wave, undulate, ripple, popple; wrinkle, corrugate 261 *fold*; indent, scallop, scollop 260 *notch*; crumple 246 *distort*.

meander, loop, snake, crankle, twist and turn, zigzag, corkscrew.

wriggle, writhe, squirm, shimmy, shake; move sinuously, worm.

252. Rotundity – N. *rotundity*, roundness, orbicularity 250 *circularity*; sphericity, spheroidicity; globularity, globosity; cylindricality; gibbosity 253 *convexity*.

sphere, globe, orb, spheroid, ellipsoid, globoid; hollow sphere, bladder; balloon, bubble, ball, marble, ally, taw; cannonball, bullet, shot, pellet; bead, pill, pea, boll, puffball; spherule, globule; drop, droplet; onion, knob, pommel 253 *swelling*; mushroom 253 *dome*; round head, bullet h., turnip h.

cylinder, roll, rolypoly; roller, rolling pin; round, rung, rundle; round tower, column; bole, trunk, stalk; pipe, drainpipe 263 *tube*; funnel, chimneypot; hat box, pillbox; drum, barrel.

cone, conoid; shadow cone, penumbra; sugarloaf 253 *dome*; cornet, horn 194 *cup*; top, peg t.; pear shape, bell s., egg s.

Adj. *rotund*, orbicular 250 *round*; spherical, sphery, spherular; globular, global, globose, globoid; round-headed, bullet-headed, brachycephalic; beady, beadlike, moniliform; hemispherical; spheroidal, ovoid, oviform, egg-shaped; cylindrical, columnar, tubular; cigar-shaped 256 *tapering*; conic, conical, conoid; bell-shaped, campanulate, napiform, turnip-shaped; pyriform, pear-shaped; humped, gibbous; bulbous 253 *convex*; pot-bellied 195 *fleshy*.

Vb. *round*, make spherical; sphere, globe, ball, bead; balloon 253 *be convex*; coil up, roll up.

253. Convexity – N. *convexity*, convexness; camber, arch 248 *curve*; sphericity

252 *rotundity*; gibbosity, bulginess, humpiness, bulge, bump; protrusion, protuberance 254 *prominence*; excrescency, swelling 197 *dilation*; double convexity, lens.

swelling, bump, lump, bulge, growth, excrescence, gall, knot, nodosity, node, nodule, knuckle; oedema, emphysema; sarcoma, tumour; bubo, goitre; Adam's apple; bunion, corn, blain, wart, wen, verruca; boil, carbuncle, furuncle, sty, pimple, papula, blister, vesicle; polyp, adenoids, haemorrhoids, piles; proud flesh, weal, welt; bubble, drop 252 *sphere*; boss, torus, knob, nub, nubble; bulb, button, bud; belly, potbelly, paunch 195 *bulk*; billow, swell 350 *wave*.

bosom, bust, breast, breasts; boobs, tits; mamma, mamilla, papilla, nipple, pap, dug, teat, udder; thorax, chest; cuirass, breastplate.

dome, cupola, vault 226 *roof*; beehive, skep; brow, forehead 237 *face*; skull, cranium 213 *head*; hemisphere, arch of heaven; anticline, hog's back, mound; hump, hummock, hillock, mamelon, sugarloaf 209 *small hill*; molehill, mushroom, umbrella.

earthwork, tumulus; tell 548 *monument*; barrow, round b., long b.; hill fort 713 *defences*; cursus, embankment, levee.

Adj. *convex*, protruding 254 *projecting*; hemispherical, domelike 252 *rotund*; lentiform, lenticular; biconvex, gibbous, humpy, lumpy; curvaceous, bosomy, billowy 248 *curved*; billowing, bulging, bellying, ballooning, bouffant; swelling 197 *expanded*; barrel-chested 195 *fleshy*; turgid, tumid, tumescent; tuberous, nubbly 259 *rough*; warty, pimply, vesicular.

arched, arcuate, cambered, bowed 248 *curved*; rounded; hillocky, hummocky, anticlinal; mammiform.

Vb. *be convex*, camber, arch, bow; swell, belly, bulge, bag, balloon; make convex, emboss, chase.

254. Prominence – N. *prominence*, eminence 209 *high land*; conspicuousness 443 *visibility*; relief, high r. 554 *sculpture*.

projection, salient; bowsprit, cathead, outrigger; tongue of land, spit, point, mull, promontory, foreland, headland, naze, ness 344 *land*; peninsula; spur, foothill; jetty, mole, breakwater, groyne, pier 662 *shelter*; outwork 713 *fortification*; pilaster, buttress 218 *prop*; shelf, sill, ledge, soffit, balcony; eaves 226 *roof*; overhang, rake 220 *obliquity*; flange, lip 234 *edge*; nozzle, spout; tang, tongue; tenon 45 *joint*; snag, stump, outcrop; landmark 209 *high structure*.

protuberance, bump 253 *swelling*; nose, snout, schnozzle, conk; bill, beak; muzzle, proboscis, trunk; antenna 378 *feeler*; chin, jaw, brow, beetle brows 237 *face*; figurehead 237 *prow*; horn, antler 256 *sharp point*.

Adj. *projecting*, jutting, prominent, salient, bold; protuberant, protruding, bulging, etc. vb.; bug-eyed, goggle-e., pop-e.; toothy; beetle-browed, overhung; underhung, undershot; repoussé, raised, embossed, in relief; ridged, nobbly 259 *rough*.

Vb. *jut*, project, protrude, pout, pop, pop out, start o.; stand out, stick o., poke o., hang o. 443 *be visible*; bristle up, prick up, cock up 259 *roughen*; overhang, hang over, beetle over, impend 217 *hang*.

255. Concavity – N. *concavity*, concaveness, incurvation 248 *curvature*; hollow, depression, dint, dent, fossa; impression, stamp, imprint 548 *trace*; intaglio 555 *engraving*; indentation 260 *notch*.

cavity, hollow, niche, nook, cranny, recess; hole, den, burrow, warren; chasm 211 *depth*; cave, cavern, antre; grot, grotto, alcove 194 *arbour*; bowl, cup, saucer, basin, sink, trough 194 *vessel*; cell, follicle, alveolus, pore 263 *orifice*; dimple, pockmark; saltcellar, armpit; honeycomb, sponge 263 *porosity*; funnel, tunnel 263 *tube*; groove, socket, pocket 262 *furrow*; ditch, moat 351 *conduit*; dip, depression, pothole, swallowhole, punchbowl, crater, pit.

valley, vale, dale, dell, dingle, combe, corrie, strath, glen, dip, depression; ravine, chine, gill, clough, gorge, canyon, gully 201 *gap*.

excavation, dugout; grave, gravepit; opencast mining; shaft, borehole, well, mine, pit, quarry 632 *store*; adit, sap, trench, burrow, warren; underground railway, tube 263 *tunnel*; archaeological excavation, dig; cutting, cut.

excavator, miner, coal-m., quarrier; archaeologist, digger; dredger, drag-line; sapper, burrower, tunneller; ditcher, gravedigger.

Adj. *concave*, hollow, cavernous; vaulted, arched 248 *curved*; hollowed out, scooped o., dug o.; caved in, stove in; depressed, sunk, sunken; biconcave; saucer-shaped, cupped; capsular, funnel-shaped, infundibular; bell-shaped, campanulate; cellular, socketed, alveolate, dented, dimpled, pockmarked; full of holes, honeycombed; spongy, porous 263 *perforated*.

Vb. *make concave*, depress, press in, punch in, stamp, impress; buckle, dent, dint, stave in; beat in; excavate, hollow, dig, spade, delve, scrape, scratch, scrabble, trench, canalize 262 *groove*; mine, sap, undermine, burrow, tunnel, bore; honeycomb, perforate 263 *pierce*; scoop out, hollow o., dig o., gouge o., scratch o.; hole, pit, pockmark; indent 260 *notch*; sink a shaft; cut and cover.

256. Sharpness – N. *sharpness*, acuity, acuteness, pointedness; serration, saw-edge 260 *notch*; spinosity, thorniness, prickliness.

sharp point, sting, prick, point, cusp 213 *vertex*; nail, tack 47 *fastening*; nib, tag, pin, needle, stylus, bodkin, skewer, spit, broach, brochette; fleam, awl, gimlet 263 *perforator*; arrow, shaft, arrowhead; barb, fluke, swordpoint, rapier 723 *spear*; fishing spear, gaff, harpoon; dagger, stiletto 723 *side arms*; spike, caltrop, chevaux-de-frise, barbed wire 713 *defences*; spur, rowel, goad, ankus 612 *incentive*; fork, prong, tine, pick, horn, antler; claw, talon, nails 778 *nippers*; spire, flèche, steeple; peak, crag, arete 213 *summit*.

prickle, thorn, briar, bramble, thistle, nettle, cactus; bristle 259 *hair*; beard, awn, spica, spicule; porcupine, hedgehog; spine, needle, quill.

tooth, tusk, tush, fang; first teeth, milk tooth; canine tooth, eyetooth, incisor, grinder, molar, premolar teeth, wisdom t.; pearls, ivories; dentition, front teeth, back t., cheek t.; denture, false teeth, gold t., plate, bridge; comb, saw; cog, ratchet, sprocket, denticle, denticulation 260 *notch*.

sharp edge, cutting e., edge tool; jagged edge, broken glass; cutlery, steel, razor; blade, razor blade; ploughshare 370 *farm tool*; spade, mattock, trowel, shovel; scythe, sickle, hook, billhook; cutter, grass c., lawn mower; scissors, barber's s., pinking s.; shears, clippers, secateurs; surgical knife, scalpel, bistoury; chisel, plane, spokeshave, scraper, draw-knife 258 *smoother*; knife, bread-k., carver, carving knife, fish k., slicer, skiver; penknife, sheath k., clasp k., jack k., bowie k.; machete, kris, parang, panga; chopper, cleaver, wedge; hatchet, adze; battle-axe 723 *axe*; sword 723 *side arms*.

sharpener, knife s., pencil s., oilstone, whetstone, grindstone; hone, steel, file, strop; emery paper.

Adj. *sharp*, stinging, keen, acute; edged, cutting; pointed, unblunted; sharp-pointed, cusped, cuspidate, mucronate; barbed, spurred; sagittal, arrowy; spiked, spiky, spiny, spinous, thorny; brambly, thistly; needlelike; prickly, bristly, bristling, awned, bearded 259 *hairy*; hastate, spear-like; jagged 259 *rough*; comblike, pectinate 260 *notched*; sharp-edged, razor-e.; sharp-set, razor-sharp.

toothed, odontoid; toothy; tusky; fanged; dental, denticulate, dentiform; cogged, serrated 260 *notched*.

tapering, acuminate, fastigiate, conical, pyramidal 293 *convergent*; spired, spiry; horned, cornuted, corniculate; star-shaped, stellate, stellular; spindle-shaped, fusiform, lance-shaped, lanceolate.

Vb. *be sharp*, – stinging etc. adj.; have a point, prick, sting; bristle with; have an edge, bite 46 *cut*; taper, come to a point.

sharpen, edge, put an edge on, whet, hone, grind, file, strop; barb, spur, point, acuminate.

257. Bluntness – N. *bluntness*, flatness, bluffness; curves 258 *smoothness*; rustiness, dullness; toothlessness, lack of bite; blunt instrument, foil; blunt edge, blade, flat.

Adj. *unsharpened*, unwhetted; blunt, blunted, unpointed, obtuse; rusty, dull, dull-edged; edgeless, pointless; toothless, edentate; blunt-nosed, stubby, snub, square; round, rounded, curving 248 *curved*; flat, flattened, bluff.

Vb. *blunt*, make blunt, turn the edge; take off the point, bate (a foil); dull, rust; draw the teeth 161 *disable*.

258. Smoothness – N. *smoothness*, evenness, sleekness, silkiness; silk, satin, velvet, velours; fleeciness, down, swansdown 327 *softness*; smooth surface, mahogany, marble, glass, ice; dance floor, ice rink; flatness, levelness, lawn, bowling green, billiard table 216 *horizontality*; polish, varnish, gloss, glaze, shine, finish; slipperiness, slipway, slide; lubricity 334 *lubrication*; smooth water, dead w., calm, dead c.

smoother, roller, steamroller; bulldozer; rolling pin 216 *flattener*; iron, flat-iron; mangle, wringer; press, trouser p.; plane 256 *sharp edge*; rake, harrow; comb, brush; sandpaper, file, nail f.; burnisher, polish, French p. 226 *facing*; lubricator 334 *lubricant*.

Adj. *smooth*, nonfrictional, frictionless, nonadhesive, streamlined; without lumps 16 *uniform*; slithery, slippery, skiddy; lubricious, oily, greasy, buttery, soapy; greased, oiled, etc. vb.; polished, shiny; soft, suave, soothing 177 *lenitive*; smooth-textured, silky, silken, satiny, velvety; downy, fleecy; marble, glassy; bald, glabrous, clean-shaven 229 *hairless*; sleek, slick, well-brushed, unruffled; combed, carded, raked, harrowed; unwrinkled, uncrumpled; even, unbroken, level, flush 216 *flat*; glassy, quiet, calm, c. as a mill-pond 266 *still*; blunt, rounded, waterworn 248 *curved*, 257 *unsharpened*; smooth-skinned.

Vb. *smooth*, streamline; oil 334 *lubricate*; plane, even, level; rake, comb; file 333 *rub*; roll, calender, press, iron 216 *flatten*; mow, shave; smooth over, smooth down, smarm d., slick d.; iron out 62 *unravel*; starch 648 *clean*; shine, burnish 417 *make bright*; buff, polish, glaze 226 *coat*.

go smoothly, glide, float, roll, bowl along, run on rails; slip, slide, skid; skate, ski; coast, freewheel.

259. Roughness – N. *roughness*, asperity, harshness; salebrosity, broken ground; rough water, choppiness 350 *wave*; rough air, turbulence 352 *wind*; jaggedness 256 *sharp edge*; serration 260 *notch*; ruggedness, cragginess 209 *high land*; rough going, dirt road; unevenness, joltiness, bumpiness 17 *nonuniformity*; corrugation, rugosity 261 *fold*; rut 262 *furrow*; coarseness, coarse grain, knobbliness, nodosity 253 *convexity*; rough surface, grater, file; rough texture, sackcloth, tweed, homespun 222 *textile*; creeping flesh, gooseflesh, horripilation; rough skin, chap, crack; hispidity, scabrousness, bristliness, shagginess, hairiness; stubble, burr, bristle 256 *prickle*.

hair 208 *filament*; head of h., shock of h., matted h., thatch, fuzz, wool; crop, mop, mane, fleece, shag; bristle, stubble, five o'clock shadow; locks, tresses, curls, ringlet, kiss curl; strand, plait, braid; pigtail, ponytail, rat's tails; topknot, forelock, elflock, lovelock, scalplock, dreadlocks; fringe, cowlick, quiff, widow's peak; roll, French pleat, bun, chignon 843 *hairdressing*; false hair, hairpiece, switch, wig; beard, beaver, goatee, imperial, Vandyke; whiskers, face fungus, sideboards, sideburns, muttonchops, dundrearies; moustache, handlebars; eyebrows, eyelashes, cilia; woolliness, fleeciness, downiness, fluffiness, flocculence; down, pubescence, pappus, wool, fur 226 *skin*; wisp, tuft, flock, floccule; mohair 208 *fibre*; pile, nap; velvet, velours, plush 327 *softness*; floss, fluff, fuzz, thistledown 323 *lightness*; horsehair.

plumage, pinion 271 *wing*; quill, rachis, barb, web; feathers, coverts; hackle, ruff, frill, plume, panache, crest.

Adj. *rough*, uneven, broken; rippling, choppy, storm-tossed; rutty, rutted, pitted, potholed, trampled, poached; bumpy, jolting, bone-breaking; chunky, crisp, roughcast; lumpy, stony, nodular, knobbly, studded, roughened, frosted; muricate, nubbly, slubbed, bouclé; crinkled 251 *undulatory*; knotted, gnarled, knurled, cross-grained, coarse-g., coarse; cracked, chapped 845 *blemished*; lined, wrinkled, corrugated, ridged 262 *furrowed*; rough-edged, deckle-e. 260 *notched*; craggy, cragged, jagged; scabrous, scabby, scaly, blistered, blebby; ruffled, unkempt.

hairy, pilose; napped, brushed; woolly, fleecy, furry; hirsute, shaggy, tufty, matted, shock-headed; hispid, bristly 256 *sharp*; setaceous; wispy, filamentous, fimbriated, ciliated, fringed, befringed; bewhiskered, bearded, moustached; unshaven, unshorn; unplucked; curly, frizzy, fuzzy, tight-curled, woolly.

downy, pubescent, peachy, velvety, mossy 258 *smooth*; feathery, plumose; fleecy, woolly, fluffy, flocculent.

Vb. *be rough*, – hairy etc. adj.; bristle, bristle up 254 *jut*; creep (of flesh), horripilate; scratch, catch; jolt, bump, jerk 278 *move slowly*.

roughen, roughcast; mill, crenate, ser-rate 260 *notch*; stud, boss; crisp, corrugate, wrinkle 251 *crinkle*; disorder, ruffle, tousle 63 *derange*; rumple, crumple 261 *fold*; rub up the wrong way, set on edge.

260. Notch – N. *notch*, serration, serrulation, saw edge, ragged e. 256 *sharpness*; indentation, deckle edge; machicolation, crenellation; nick, snip, cut, gash; crenation, indent, dent 255 *concavity*; picot edge, scollop, scallop, dogtooth 844 *pattern*; sprocket, cog, ratchet; saw, hacksaw 256 *tooth*; battlement, embrasure.

Adj. *notched*, indented, jagged, jaggy 256 *sharp*; crenate, crenellated; toothed,

saw-t., dentate, serrated; emarginate; serrulate; palmate.

Vb. *notch*, serrate, tooth, cog; nick, blaze, score, scratch 46 *cut*; crenellate, machicolate; indent, scallop; jag, pink, slash; dent, mill, knurl 259 *roughen*; pinch, snip, crimp 261 *fold*.

261. Fold – N. *fold*, plication, flexure, flexion, doubling; facing, revers, hem; lapel, cuff, turnup, dog-ear; pleat, tuck, gather, pucker, ruche, ruffle; flounce, frill; crumple, rumple, crease; wrinkle, ruck; frown, lines, wrinkles, crow's feet; crinkle, crankle; joint, elbow 247 *angularity*; syncline, anticline.

Adj. *folded*, doubled; gathered etc. vb.; plicate, pleated; wrinkly, puckery; dog-eared; creased, crumpled.

Vb. *fold*, double, turn over, bend over, roll; crease, pleat; rumple, crumple 63 *derange*; pucker, purse 251 *crinkle*; ruffle, cockle, gather, frill, ruck, shirr, smock; tuck up, kilt; hem, cuff; turn up *or* down *or* under, double down; enfold, enwrap 235 *enclose*; fold up, roll up, furl, reef.

262. Furrow – N. *furrow*, groove, sulcus, chase, slot, slit, rabbet, mortise; crack, chink, cranny 201 *gap*; trough, hollow 255 *cavity*; glyph, triglyph; flute, fluting, goffering, rifling; chamfer, bezel, incision, gash, slash 46 *scission*; striation 437 *stripe*; wake, wheelmark, rut 548 *trace*; gutter, trench, dugout, moat, fosse 351 *conduit*; ravine 255 *valley*; corrugation; ripple 350 *wave*.

Adj. *furrowed*, etc. vb.; fluted, rifled, goffered; striated, sulcate; gullied, channelled, rutty; wrinkled, lined 261 *folded*; rippling, wavy 350 *flowing*.

Vb. *groove*, slot, flute, chamfer, rifle; chase; gash, score, incise 46 *cut*; striate, streak 437 *variegate*; grave, carve, enchase, etch 555 *engrave*; furrow, plough; rut, wrinkle, corrugate, goffer 261 *fold*.

263. Opening – N. *opening*, unstopping, uncorking 229 *uncovering*; dehiscence, bursting open, splitting; gaping; yawn; hiatus, lacuna 201 *gap*; aperture, split, crack, leak 46 *disunion*; hole, hollow 255 *cavity*; placket 194 *pocket*.

perforation, piercing, impalement, puncture; acupuncture, vene-puncture; boring, borehole, bore; pinhole, eyelet.

porosity, porousness, sponge; sieve, sifter, riddle, screen 62 *sorting*; strainer, colander; grater, holeyness, honeycomb.

orifice, aperture, slot; mouth, gob, trap; jaws, muzzle; throat 194 *maw*; sucker; mouthpiece 353 *air pipe*; nozzle, spout 298 *outlet*; blowhole, air-hole, spiracle; nostril, nosehole; inlet, outlet; rivermouth, embouchure; ostiole; foramen, pore; stomata; hole, crater, pothole 255 *cavity*; manhole, armhole, keyhole, buttonhole, punch hole, pin h.; pigeonhole 194 *compartment*; eye, eyelet; deadeye; grummet, ring 250 *circle*.

window, fenestration; embrasure, loophole; lattice, grille; oeil de boeuf; oriel, dormer; light, fanlight, skylight, sunshine roof; companion, port, porthole; peephole, keyhole; hagioscope, squint; windscreen, windshield; window frame, casement, sash; mullion, transom; window pane 422 *transparency*.

doorway, archway; doorstep, threshold 297 *way in*; exit, way out 624 *access*; gate, lychgate; portal, porch, propylaeum; door, swing doors, revolving d.; back door, postern; wicket; cat-flap; scuttle, hatch, hatchway; trapdoor, companionway; stairwell; door jamb, gatepost, lintel.

open space 183 *space*; yard, court; opening, clearing, glade; panorama, vista 438 *view*; landscape, open country 348 *plain*; alley, aisle, gangway, thoroughfare 305 *passage*.

tunnel, boring; subway, underpass, underground railway, tube; Channel Tunnel, Chunnel; mine, shaft, pit, gallery, adit 255 *excavation*; cave 255 *cavity*; bolthole, rabbit hole, fox h., mouse h. 192 *dwelling*; funnel 252 *cone*; sewer 351 *drain*.

tube, pipe, duct 351 *conduit*; tubing, piping, pipeline, hose; artery, vein, capillary; colon, gut 224 *insides*; funnel, fistula.

chimney, smokestack, funnel; smoke-duct, flue; volcano, fumarole 383 *furnace*.

opener, key, master k., skeleton k., passepartout; corkscrew, tin opener; aperient, purgative; password, open sesame; passport, safe conduct; pass, ticket 756 *permit*.

perforator, piercer, borer, corer; gimlet, wimble, corkscrew; auger, drill, pneumatic d.; burr, bit, brace and b.; reamer; probe, lancet, stylet; bodkin, needle, hypodermic n.; awl, bradawl 256 *sharp point*; pin, nail 47 *fastening*; spit, stiletto 723 *weapon*; punch, puncheon, stapler; dibble; digging stick; pickaxe, pick.

Adj. *open*, patent, exposed to view 522 *manifest*; unclosed, unstopped, unshut, ajar; unbolted, unbarred; yawning, wide-open, agape, gaping; dehiscent; open-mouthed, slack-jawed; blooming, out.

perforated, etc. vb.; honeycombed, riddled; peppered, shot through; cribriform; holey, full of holes; windowed.

porous, permeable, pervious, spongy, percolating, leachy, leaky, leaking.

tubular, piped; cylindrical 252 *rotund*; funnel-shaped, infundibular; fistular; vascular, capillary.

Vb. *open*, unclose, unfold, unwrap, unpack, undo; unlock, unlatch, unbolt; pull out (a drawer); uncover, unplug, uncork; lay open, throw o. 522 *show*; force open, steam o., cut open, rip o., tear o., crack o. 46 *disunite*; enlarge a hole, ream; dehisce, fly open, split, gape, yawn; burst, explode; crack at the seams, start, leak; space out 201 *space*; open out, fan o., deploy; unclench; bloom, be out.

pierce, transpierce, transfix, impale; gore, run through, stick, pink, lance, bayonet, spear 655 *wound*; spike, skewer, spit; prick, puncture, tattoo; probe, stab, poke; inject; punch, perforate, hole, riddle, pepper, honeycomb; scuttle, stave in; tap, drain 304 *extract*; bore, drill, trephine, trepan; tunnel 255 *make concave*; penetrate 297 *enter*.

264. Closure – N. *closure*, closing, shutting; occlusion, stoppage; contraction, strangulation 198 *compression*; sealing off

232 *circumscription*; embolism, obstruction, obturation; dead end, cul-de-sac, impasse; blind gut, caecum; imperviousness, impermeability.

stopper, stopple, cork, plug, bung, peg, spigot; ramrod, rammer, piston, valve; wedge, wad, dossil, pledget, tampon; stuffing, stopping 227 *lining*; dummy, gag, muzzle 748 *fetter*; tourniquet 198 *compressor*; damper, choke; tap, faucet, stopcock, bibcock; top, lid, cap, cover, seal 226 *covering*; lock, key, bolt, bar 47 *fastening*; door, gate 263 *doorway*.

doorkeeper, doorman, gatekeeper, porter, janitor, ostiary; commissionaire, concierge; night watchman 660 *protector*; warden, guard 749 *keeper*; Cerberus, Argus 749 *gaoler*.

Adj. *closed*, unopened, unopenable; shut etc. vb.; shuttered, bolted, barred; imperforate, unholed; nonporous, impervious, impermeable; impenetrable, impassable, unpassable; dead-end, blank; clogged up, stuffed up; strangulated 198 *contracted*; drawn together 45 *joined*.

sealed off, cloistered, claustral; close, unventilated, stuffy, muggy, fuggy, fusty 653 *insalubrious*; staunch, tight, airtight, watertight, proof 660 *invulnerable*.

Vb. *close*, shut, occlude, seal; put the lid on 226 *cover*; clap to, slam, bang (a door); lock, fasten; plug, caulk, bung, cork, stopper, obturate; button, zip up, do up 45 *join*; clench (fist); block, dam, staunch, choke, throttle, strangle; blockade, enclose, surround, shut in, seal off 232 *circumscribe*; bolt, bar; shut down, clamp d., batten d.; draw the curtains, put up the shutters.

Section 4: Motion

265. Motion: successive change of place –
N. *motion*, change of position 143 *change*; movement, going, move, march; speed, air s., ground s.; pace, tempo; locomotion, motility, mobility, movableness; kinetic energy, motive power, motivity; forward motion 285 *progression*; backward motion 286 *regression*, 290 *recession*; motion towards 289 *approach*, 293 *convergence*; shift 294 *divergence*, 282 *deviation*; rising 308 *ascent*; sinking 309 *descent*, 313 *plunge*; motion round 314 *circuition*; axial motion 315 *rotation*; fluctuation 317 *oscillation*; stir, bustle, unrest, restlessness 318 *agitation* 678 *activity*; rapid motion 277 *velocity*; slow motion 278 *slowness*; rhythm 141 *periodicity*; conduction 272 *transference*; current, flow, flux, drift; course, career; transit 305 *passage*; transportation 272 *transport*; travel 267 *land travel*, 269 *water travel*, 271 *air travel*; manoeuvre, footwork; exercise 162 *athletics*; gesticulation 547 *gesture*; laws of motion, kinematics, kinetics, dynamics.

gait, rolling g.; walk, port, carriage; tread, tramp, footfall, stamp; pace, step, stride; run, lope, jog; jog trot, dog t.; hop, skip, jump 312 *leap*; skid, slide; waddle, shuffle; swagger, march, stalk, strut, goosestep 875 *formality*; trot, piaffer, amble, canter, gallop, hand-g. 267 *equitation*.

Adj. *moving*, etc. vb.; in motion, under way; motive, motor; motile, movable, mobile; progressive, regressive; locomotive, automotive; shifting, mercurial 152 *changeful*; unquiet, restless 678 *active*; nomadic 267 *travelling*; drifting, erratic 282 *deviating*; kinematic, kinetic.

Vb. *be in motion*, move, go, hie, gang, wend; gather way 269 *navigate*; budge, stir; flutter, wave, flap 217 *hang*; march, tramp 267 *walk*; tread, trip, dance 312 *leap*; shuffle, waddle 278 *move slowly*; toddle, patter; run 277 *move fast*; roll, taxi; roll on 350 *flow*; skitter, slide, slither, glide 258 *go smoothly*; fly, flit, flitter, dart, hover; climb 308 *ascend*; sink 309 *descend*; cruise, steam, chug 146 *go on*; make one's way, pick one's w., elbow one's w. 305 *pass*; make a move, shift, dodge, duck, manoeuvre 282 *deviate*; twist 251 *wriggle*; creep, crawl, go on all fours; change places 151 *interchange*; move over, make room 190 *go away*; travel, stray 267 *wander*.

move, set going, actuate, switch on 173 *operate*; stir, jerk, pluck, twitch 318 *agitate*; budge, shift, manhandle, trundle, roll, wheel 188 *displace*; push, shove 279 *impel*; tug, pull 288 *draw*; fling, throw 287 *propel*; convey, transport, dispatch 272 *send*; scatter 75 *disperse*; raise 310 *elevate*; drop 311 *let fall*; motion, gesture 547 *gesticulate*.

Adv. *on the move*, under way, on one's w., on the go, on the hop, on the run; in transit; on the march, on the wing.

266. Quiescence – N. *quiescence*, motionlessness; dying down, running down, subsidence; rest, stillness; deathliness, deadness; stagnation 679 *inactivity*; pause, standstill 145 *lull*; stand, stoppage, halt 145 *stop*; fix, deadlock, lock; embargo, freeze; immobility, fixity; steadiness 153 *stability*; trance 375 *insensibility*.

quietude, quiet, quietness, stillness, hush 399 *silence*; tranquillity, peacefulness, rest 683 *repose*; slumber 679 *sleep*; calm, dead c., flat c. 258 *smoothness*; windlessness, not a breath of air; dead quiet, not a mouse stirring; armchair travel, staying at home; passivity, quietism; quietist 717 *pacifist*.

Adj. *quiescent*, quiet, still; asleep 679 *sleepy*; resting, at rest, becalmed; at anchor, at a standstill, stopped; idle 679 *inactive*; dormant; standing, stagnant; static, stationary 175 *inert*; sedentary, chair-borne; disabled, housebound 747 *restrained*; settled, stay-at-home, home-loving; untravelled.

tranquil, undisturbed, sequestered 883 *secluded*; peaceful, restful; uneventful; calm, windless, airless; sunny, halcyon 730 *palmy*; easeful, comfortable, relaxed 683 *reposeful*; sedated, under sedation; unruffled, serene 823 *inexcitable*.

still, unmoving; not fizzy, flat 387 *tasteless*; immobile, motionless, expressionless 820 *impassive*; steady, unwinking, unblinking 153 *unchangeable*; rooted to the ground 153 *fixed*; transfixed, spellbound; immovable, stuck; stiff, frozen 326 *rigid*; petrified, paralysed 375 *insensible*; quiet, soundless; stock-still.

Vb. *be quiescent*, subside, die down 37 *decrease*; stand still, lie s., keep quiet; stagnate, vegetate 175 *be inert*; stand,

mark time; stay put, sit tight, not stir, not budge; stand to, lie to, ride at anchor; tarry 145 *pause*; rest, take breath 683 *repose*; go to bed, doss down 679 *sleep*; ground, stick fast; catch, jam, lodge; be at a standstill 145 *cease*.

come to rest, stop, freeze 145 *halt*; pull up, draw up 278 *decelerate*; cast anchor.

bring to rest, quieten, quell 399 *silence*; bring to a standstill, bring to, lay to, heave to; brake 278 *retard*; immobilize 679 *make inactive*.

Int. stop! stay! halt! whoa! hold! hold on! hold it! don't move!

267. Land travel – N. *land travel*, travel, travelling, wayfaring; seeing the world, globe-trotting, tourism; walking, riding, driving, motoring, cycling, biking; journey, voyage, peregrination, odyssey; course, passage, sweep; pilgrimage, hadj; quest, expedition, safari, trek, field trip; reconnaissance, exploration, orienteering, youth hostelling; visit, trip, tour, grand t.; circuit, patrol, commuting; round trip 314 *circuition*; jaunt, hop, spin; ride, bike r., joy r., drive, excursion, outing, airing; promenade. See *pedestrianism*.

wandering, etc. vb; wanderlust, nomadism; vagrancy, vagabondage, no fixed address; walkabout, waltzing Matilda; itchy feet; migration, Völkerwanderung.

pedestrianism, walking, going on foot, Shanks's pony; foot-slogging, stumping, tramping, back-packing; ambulation, perambulation; walk, promenade, constitutional; stroll, saunter, amble, ramble; hike, tramp, march, walking tour; run, cross-country run, jog 265 *gait*; paddle, paddling, wading; marathon 716 *racing*; stalking 619 *chase*; sleepwalking, somnambulism.

marching, campaigning, campaign; manoeuvres, advance, retreat; march, forced m., route m., quick march, slow m.; march past, parade 875 *formality*; column, file, cortège, train, caravan.

equitation, equestrianism, horsemanship, manège, dressage 694 *skill*; show jumping, steeplechasing 716 *contest*;

horse racing; riding, bareback r.; caracole, piaffer, curvet 265 *gait*.

leg, limb, foreleg, hindleg; shank, shin, calf; thigh, ham, hamstrings; knee, kneecap; legs, pegs, pins 218 *prop*; stumps, stilts; wooden leg, artificial l.; bandy legs 845 *blemish*; thick legs, piano l.; long legs, spindle shanks.

itinerary, route 624 *way*; march, course 281 *direction*; route map, road m. 551 *map*; guide, timetable 524 *guidebook*; fingerpost 547 *signpost*; stopover 145 *stopping place*.

Adj. *travelling*, journeying, itinerant, vagrant, wayfaring, on the road; travel-stained, dusty 649 *dirty*; travelled, much-t.; touring, globe-trotting, rubbernecking; migratory, visiting; nomadic, nomad, floating, unsettled, restless; of no fixed address, homeless, rootless, déraciné(e) 59 *extraneous*; footloose, errant, roving, roaming, wandering 282 *deviating*; ambulant, strolling, peripatetic; tramping, vagabond; pedestrian, ambulatory, perambulatory; marching, foot-slogging, etc. vb.

legged, bow-l., bandy-l. 845 *blemished*; well-calved, well-hocked; long-legged, leggy 209 *tall*; spindly 206 *lean*.

Vb. *travel*, fare, journey, peregrinate; tour, see the world, visit, explore 484 *discover*; get around, knock about, go places; go on a pilgrimage; go on safari, trek, hike, backpack; be always on the move, live out of a suitcase; set out 296 *depart*; migrate 187 *place oneself*; shuttle, commute; go to, hie to, repair to, resort to, betake oneself to 295 *arrive*; go 265 *be in motion*; wend one's way, stir one's stumps, bend one's steps, shape one's course, make one's way, thread one's w., plough through; jog on, trudge on, shuffle on, pad on, plod on, tramp on, march on, chug on 146 *sustain*; course, race, post 277 *move fast*; proceed, advance 285 *progress*; roll along, bowl a., fly a. 258 *go smoothly*.

wander, migrate; rove, roam, bum around; ramble, amble, stroll, saunter, mosey along, potter, dawdle, walk about, trail around; gad, traipse, gallivant, gad about; dart a. 265 *be in motion*; prowl, skulk 523 *lurk*; straggle, trail 75 *be dispersed*; lose the way 282 *stray*.

walk, step, tread, pace, stride; stride out 277 *move fast*; strut, stalk, prance, mince 871 *be proud*; tread lightly, tiptoe, trip, skip, dance 312 *leap*; lumber, clump, stamp, tramp, goosestep; toddle, patter, pad; totter, stagger 317 *oscillate*; shuffle, dawdle 278 *move slowly*; paddle, wade; foot it, hoof it, hike, footslog, wear out shoe leather; plod, stump, trudge, jog; go for a walk, ambulate, perambulate, circumambulate, pace up and down; go for a run, take the air, take one's constitutional; march, troop; file, file past, defile 65 *ride after*.

ride, mount, hack; trot, amble, tittup, canter, gallop; prance, caper, curvet, piaffe, caracole, passage; cycle, bicycle, bike, motorcycle; freewheel; drive, motor; thumb a lift, hitch-hike.

Adv. *on foot*, on the beat; on hoof, on horseback, on Shanks's pony; en route 272 *in transit*; by road, by rail, awheel.

268. Traveller – N. *traveller*, itinerant, wayfarer; explorer, adventurer; voyager 270 *mariner*, 271 *aeronaut*; pioneer, pathfinder 66 *precursor*; mountaineer 308 *climber*; pilgrim, palmer, hadji; walker, hiker, rambler, trekker; backpacker, camper, caravanner, youth hosteller; globe-trotter, tourist, sightseer 441 *spectator*; tripper, excursionist; sunseeker, holidaymaker, visitor; roundsman, pedlar; commercial traveller 793 *seller*; messenger 529 *courier*; commuter, straphanger; Ulysses, Gulliver, Marco Polo.

wanderer, migrant, bird of passage, visitant 365 *bird*; floating population, nomad, bedouin; gipsy, didikoi, Romany, Bohemian, tzigane; rover, ranger, rambler, promenader, stroller; strolling player, wandering minstrel, touring company 594 *entertainer*; rolling stone, drifter, vagrant, vagabond, tramp, knight of the road; swagman, sundowner, hobo, bum; emigrant 59 *foreigner*; runaway, fugitive; refugee, déraciné(e); waif, stray; Flying Dutchman.

pedestrian, foot passenger, walker, tramper; jogger, sprinter 716 *contender*; toddler; skater, skier; hiker, hitch-h., foot-slogger; marcher 722 *infantry*; somnambulist, sleepwalker; prowler, loiterer; footpad 789 *robber*.

rider, horse-rider, camel-r., cameleer; elephant-rider, mahout; horseman, horsewoman, equestrian, equestrienne; postilion 529 *courier*; mounted police, Mounties; cavalier, knight 722 *cavalry*; hunt 619 *hunter*; jockey, show jumper 716 *contender*; trainer, breaker 369 *breeder*; roughrider, bareback r., broncobuster, cowboy, cowgirl, cowpuncher, gaucho; cyclist, bicyclist, pedal-pusher, roughstuffer; motorcyclist, moped rider, scooterist; back-seat driver, passenger, pillion p.

driver, drover, teamster, muleteer; charioteer, coachman, whip; carter, wagoner, drayman; car driver, chauffeur, motorist; roadhog; Jehu 277 *speeder*; taxi driver, cab d., cabby; bus driver, coach d.; lorry d., truck d., van d., trucker, routier, teamster; tractor d.; motorman, train driver, engine d.; stoker, footplateman, fireman; guard, conductor, ticket collector; pilot 271 *aeronaut*.

269. Water travel – N. *water travel*, river t., canal t., inland navigation; seafaring, navigation; sailing, cruising; coasting, longshore sailing; boating (**see** *aquatics*); voyage, navigation, cruise, sail; run, passage, crossing; circumnavigation 314 *circuition*; way, headway, steerage way, sternway, seaway 265 *motion*; leeway, driftway 282 *deviation*; wake, track, wash; ocean lane, steamer route 624 *route*; boat, sailing ship 275 *ship*; sailor 270 *mariner*.

navigation, pilotage 689 *directorship*; astronavigation; plane sailing, plain s., great-circle s.; compass reading, dead reckoning 465 *measurement*; seamanship 694 *skill*; weather eye, sea legs.

aquatics, boating, sailing, yachting, cruising; rowing, sculling, canoeing; water skiing, surf riding, surfing, wind s., watersports 837 *sport*; natation, swimming; breast stroke, back s., crawl, dog

paddle; diving 313 *plunge*; wading, paddling.

sailing aid, sextant, quadrant 247 *angular measure*; chronometer 117 *timekeeper*; log, line; lead, plummet 211 *depth*; anchor; compass, needle, card, compass c.; binnacle; gyrocompass 689 *directorship*; radar 484 *detector*; helm, wheel, tiller, rudder; sea mark, buoy, lighthouse 547 *signpost*; chart, Admiralty c., portolano; nautical almanac, ephemeris 524 *guidebook*.

Adj. *seafaring*, sea, salty, deep-sea, longshore; sailorly, seamanlike; nautical, naval 275 *marine*; navigational; sea-going, ocean-g.; at sea, on the high seas, afloat, waterborne, seaborne, on board; pitching, tossing, etc. vb.; close-hauled 281 *towards*; seaworthy, tight, snug.

swimming, natatory, floating; launched, afloat, buoyant; natatorial, aquatic, like a fish; amphibian.

Vb. *go to sea*, join the navy; get one's sea legs; sail before the mast; go sailing, boat, yacht; voyage, sail, take ship, book a passage, work one's p.; put to sea 296 *start out*; disembark, land 295 *arrive*; navigate, steam, ply, run, tramp, ferry; coast, hug the shore; roll, pitch, toss, wallow 317 *oscillate*.

navigate, man a ship, work a s., crew; put to sea, set sail; launch, push off, boom off; unmoor, cast off, weigh anchor; raise steam, get up s.; hoist sail, spread canvas; get under way, gather w. 265 *be in motion*; set a course, make for; pilot, steer, captain 689 *direct*; stroke, cox, coxswain; trim the sails; change course, veer, gybe, yaw; put about, wear ship; run before the wind, scud 277 *move fast*; tack, weather; circumnavigate 314 *circle*; careen, list, turn turtle, capsize 221 *invert*; ride out the storm; run for port; lie to, heave to 266 *bring to rest*; take soundings, heave the lead 465 *measure*; tow, haul, warp, kedge, clubhaul 288 *draw*; ground, run aground; sight land, make a landfall 289 *approach*; cast anchor, drop a.; moor, tie up, dock, disembark 295 *land*; surface, break water 298 *emerge*; flood the tanks, dive 313 *plunge*.

row, ply the oar, pull, stroke, scull; feather; catch a crab; ship oars; punt; paddle, canoe; boat; shoot the rapids.

swim, float, sail, ride; scud, skim, skitter; surf-ride, surf, water-ski, aquaplane; strike out; tread water; dive 313 *plunge*; bathe, dip, duck; wade, paddle, splash about 341 *be wet*.

Adv. *under way*, afloat, under sail, under canvas, under steam; before the mast; on deck; at the helm, at the wheel.

Int. ship ahoy! avast! belay there! all aboard! man overboard! yo-heave-ho! hard aport! hard astarboard! steady as she goes! land ahoy!

270. Mariner – N. *mariner*, sailor, sailorman, seaman, seafarer; old salt, seadog, shellback; tar, Jack Tar, limey, matelot; fairweather sailor, landlubber; skipper, master mariner, master; mate, boatswain, bosun; coxswain; able seaman, AB; deckhand; ship's steward, cabin boy 742 *servant*; shipmates, hearties; crew, men, watch 686 *personnel*; trawler, whaler, deep-sea fisherman; sea rover, Viking, pirate, privateer, buccaneer 789 *robber*; sea scout, sea cadet; argonaut, Jason; Ancient Mariner, Flying Dutchman, Sinbad the Sailor.

navigator, pilot, helmsman, steersman, quartermaster; man *or* woman at the wheel; cox 690 *leader*; lookout; foretopman, reefer; boatswain, bosun's mate.

boatman, waterman; galley slave; oar, oarsman, sculler, rower, punter; paddler, canoeist; yachtsman *or* -woman; gondolier, ferryman, Charon; wherryman, bargeman, bargee, lighterman; stevedore, docker, longshoreman; lock keeper, harbour master.

271. Aeronautics – N. *aeronautics*, aerodynamics, aerostatics; ballooning; aerospace, astronautics; aeroballistics, rocketry 276 *rocket*; flight, supersonic f. 277 *velocity*; stratospheric flight, space f.; aviation, flying, blind f.; gliding, hang-g.; parachuting, skydiving, free fall; flypast, formation flying, stunt f., aerobatics; skywriting, vapour trail; planing, volplaning,

looping the loop; spin, roll, side-slip; volplane, nose dive, pull-out; crash dive 309 *descent*; landing, crash l., forced l.; talkdown, touchdown 295 *arrival*; take-off, vertical t. 296 *departure*.

air travel, air transport, airlift 272 *transport*; air service, airline; scheduled flight, charter f.; airlane, flight path, glide p.; air space 184 *territory*; landing field, airbase; airstrip, runway, airfield, aerodrome, airport; heliport, helipad; fear of flying, aerophobia; jetlag.

space travel, space flight, manned s.f. 276 *spaceship*; lift-off, blast-off; orbit, flyby; docking, space walk; reentry, splash-down, soft landing; cosmodrome, space-port; launching pad.

aeronaut, aerostat, balloonist; glider, hang g., sky diver, parachutist; paratrooper 722 *soldier*; aviator, aviatrix, airman *or* -woman, birdman; astronaut, cosmonaut, spaceman, spacewoman, space traveller; air traveller, jet set 268 *traveller*; flyer, pilot, test p., jet p., copilot; automatic pilot, autopilot; navigator, air crew; pilot officer, flying o. 741 *air officer*; aircraft-man 722 *air force*; air personnel, ground crew; Icarus, Daedalus; Pegasus.

wing, pinion, feathers, wing spread 259 *plumage*; swept-back wing, delta w., aerofoil, aileron, flaps.

Adj. *flying*, on the wing; fluttering, flitting, hovering 265 *moving*; winged; aerial 340 *airy*; airworthy, airborne; air-to-air; soaring 308 *ascending*; in-flight; airsick; losing height 309 *descending*; grounded; aeronautical 276 *aviational*; aerobatic.

Vb. *fly*, wing, aviate; wing one's way, take one's flight, be wafted, soar 308 *ascend*; hover, overfly, hang over 217 *hang*; flutter, flit 265 *be in motion*; taxi, take off 296 *depart*; glide, plane 258 *go smoothly*; float, drift 323 *be light*; stunt, spin, roll, side-slip, loop the loop, volplane; hedgehop, skim, buzz 200 *be near*; stall, dive, power-dive, nose-d., spiral 313 *plunge*; crash, crash-land, pancake, ditch; pull out, flatten o.; touch down 295 *land*; bale out, parachute, eject; blast off, lift o., take o.; orbit, go into o. 314 *circle*.

272. Transference – N. *transference*, translocation, transplantation, transhipment, transfer, bussing; shift, drift, longshore d., continental d.; posting 751 *mandate*; transposition 151 *interchange*; removal, relegation, deportation, expulsion 300 *ejection*; unloading, air-drop 188 *displacement*; exportation 791 *trade*; importation 299 *reception*; distribution 633 *provision*; transmittal, forwarding, sending, remittance, dispatch; delivery; conveyance 780 *transfer*; committal, trust 751 *commission*; ferry, ferriage 305 *passage*; transmission, throughput; conduction, convection; transfusion; decantation; contagion, contamination 178 *influence*.

transport, transportation; conveyance, carriage, shipping, shipment; portage, porterage, haulage, draught 288 *traction*; carting, cartage, wagonage, freightage, air freight, airlift; means of transport 274 *vehicle*, 275 *ship*; pipeline, conveyor belt.

thing transferred, flotsam, jetsam, driftwood, drift, sea-d.; alluvium, detritus, scree, moraine, sediment, deposit; pledge, hostage 767 *security*; legacy 781 *gift*; cargo, load, payload, freight; import, export; consignment, shipment 193 *contents*; goods, mails; luggage, baggage, impedimenta; container, lorryload, trainload; passenger, commuter 268 *traveller*.

transferrer, conveyancer 781 *giver*; sender, remitter, dispatcher, dispatch clerk, consignor, addresser; shipper, shipping agent, transporter; exporter, importer 794 *merchant*; removal man, conveyor 273 *carrier*; post office, post 531 *postal communications*; communicator, transmitter, diffuser; vector, carrier (of a disease).

Adj. *transferable*, negotiable; transportable, movable, portable; roadworthy, airworthy, seaworthy; portative, transmissive, conductive; transmissible, communicable; contagious 653 *infectious*.

Vb. *transfer*, hand over, deliver 780 *assign*; commit, entrust 751 *commission*; transmit, hand down, hand on, pass on; make over, turn over to; pass the buck; export, transport, convey, ship, airlift, fly, ferry 273 *carry*; infect, contaminate 178 *influence*; conduct, convect.

transpose, shift, move, tranship 188 *displace*; draft, transfer, switch, shunt 151 *interchange*; deport, expel 300 *eject*; pull 288 *draw*; push 279 *impel*; containerize 193 *load*; transfuse, decant, siphon off 300 *empty*; unload, remove.

send, remit, transmit, dispatch; direct, consign, address; post, mail; redirect, readdress, post on, forward; send away, detach, detail.

Adv. *in transit*, en route, on the way; in the post; in the pipeline; by hand; from hand to hand, from pillar to post.

273. Carrier – N. *carrier*, haulier, carter, wagoner; shipper, transporter 272 *transferrer*; ferryman 270 *boatman*; lorry driver, bus d. 268 *driver*; delivery van, goods train 274 *vehicle*; freighter, tramp 275 *ship*; pallet, container; carrier bag 194 *bag*.

bearer, litter b., stretcher b.; caddy, golf c.; porter, coolie, stevedore; carrier pigeon, messenger 529 *courier*.

beast of burden, packhorse, pack train, sumpter-mule; ass, donkey, moke, Neddy, cuddy, burro; oxen, draught animals 365 *cattle*; sledge dog, husky; llama, camel, dromedary, ship of the desert.

horse, horseflesh; dobbin, nag; mount, steed; stallion, gelding, mare, colt, filly, foal; stud horse, brood mare; circus horse, liberty h.; roan, strawberry r., grey, dapple g., bay, chestnut, sorrel, piebald, skewbald, pinto, dun, palomino; winged horse, Pegasus; Black Bess; Houyhnhnm.

thoroughbred, purebred, bloodstock; Arab, Barbary horse; pacer, stepper, high-s., trotter; courser, racehorse, racer, sprinter 277 *speeder*; steeplechaser, hurdler, fencer, jumper, hunter, foxhunter.

draught horse, cart-h., dray h.; shafthorse, trace-h.; plough-h., shire h., Clydesdale, punch, Suffolk p., percheron; pit pony.

warhorse, cavalry h., remount; charger, destrier, courser, steed 722 *cavalry*; Bucephalus, Copenhagen, Marengo.

saddle horse, riding h.; mount, hack,

roadster; jade, screw, nag; pad, ambler; mustang, bronco; palfrey, jennet; pony, cob.

Vb. *carry*, bear 218 *support*; hump, heave, tote; caddie; stoop one's back to, shoulder; fetch and carry; transport, cart, truck, ship; lift, fly 272 *transfer*; carry over *or* across, ferry; convey, conduct, convoy 89 *accompany*; be saddled with, be loaded with.

274. Vehicle – N. *vehicle*, conveyance, public c.; public service vehicle, transport, public t.; vehicular traffic, motorized t., wheeled t.; pedal power, horse p.; sedan chair, palanquin; litter, horse l.; brancard, stretcher, hurdle; ambulance, fire engine; Black Maria, paddy wagon; tumbril, hearse; snowplough, snowmobile, weasel; tractor, caterpillar t., tracked vehicle; bulldozer; tank; amphibian, moon buggy; rollercoaster, switchback, dodgem car; time machine, magic carpet.

sledge, sled, sleigh, bobsleigh, bobsled, toboggan, luge, coaster; ice yacht; sand y., surfboard; skate, ice s., roller s., skateboard; snowshoes, skis, runner, skids, ski-bob.

bicycle, cycle, pedal c., bike, push b.; wheel, gridiron, crate; velocipede, hobbyhorse, boneshaker, penny-farthing, safety, sit-up-and-beg; racer, tourist, roadster; small-wheeler; tandem, randem; unicycle, tricycle, trike, quadricycle; motorized bicycle, moped; scooter, motor s., motorcycle, motorbike, trail bike, scrambler; sidecar; invalid carriage; pedicab, cycle-rickshaw, trishaw.

pushcart, perambulator, pram, baby buggy, pushchair; bath chair, wheelchair; wheelbarrow, handcart; go cart; trolley, truck, float.

cart, dray; farm cart, wain, wagon; caravan, trailer, horse-box, loose-b. **See** *lorry*.

carriage, equipage, turnout, rig; chariot, coach, coach and four; barouche, landau, berlin, victoria, brougham, phaeton, clarence; surrey, buckboard, buggy, wagonette; travelling carriage, chaise, shay, calash, britzka, droshky; troika; racing chariot, quadriga; four-in-

hand, drag, brake, charabanc; two-wheeler, cabriolet, curricle, tilbury, whisky, jaunting car; trap, gig, ponycart, dogcart, governess cart; carriole, sulky; shandrydan, rattle-trap.

stagecoach, stage, mail coach; diligence, post chaise. **See** *bus*.

cab, hackney carriage, hansom, fly; fiacre, droshky; gharry, tonga; taxicab, taxi, minicab; rickshaw.

bus, horsebus, motorbus; omnibus, doubledecker, single-d.; articulated bus, bendibus; trolleybus, coach, postbus, minibus.

tram, tramcar, streetcar, cablecar.

automobile, horseless carriage, car, motor car, motor; limousine, gas guzzler; saloon, tourer, roadster, runabout, buggy; hard-top, soft-t., convertible; coupé, sports car; racing car, stock c., dragster, hot-rod; hatchback, estate car, station wagon, brake, jeep; police car, patrol c.; veteran car, vintage car, model T; tin Lizzie, banger, bus, jalopy, old crock, rattletrap; bubble car, minicar; invalid car, three-wheeler; minibus, camper.

lorry, truck, pickup t., dump t.; refuse lorry, dustcart; container lorry, articulated l., roadliner, juggernaut; tanker, bowser; car transporter, low-loader; van, delivery v., removal v., pantechnicon; electric van, float.

train, railway t., boat t., motorail; express train, through t., intercity t., high speed t., HST; goods train, freight t., freightliner; milk train, mail t., night mail; rolling stock, multiple unit; coach, carriage, compartment; Pullman, wagon-lit, sleeping car, sleeper; restaurant car, dining c., buffet c., observation c.; guard's van, luggage v., brake v., caboose; truck, wagon, tank w., hopper w., trolley; bogie; live rail, pantograph 624 *railway*; Flying Scotsman, Golden Arrow, Orient Express.

locomotive, iron horse; diesel, steam engine, pony e., tank e., shunter, cab, tender; puffer, chuffer; traction engine, steam roller.

Adj. *vehicular*, wheeled, on wheels; on rails, on runners; horse-drawn, pedal-driven, motorized, electrified; automobile, automotive, locomotive.

275. Ship – N. *ship*, vessel, boat, craft; barque; cockleshell; bottom, keel, sail; hooker, tub, hull; hulk, prisonship; steamer, steamship, steamboat, motor vessel; paddle steamer, paddleboat, sternwheeler, riverboat, showboat; passenger ship; liner; channel steamer, ferry; hovercraft, hydrofoil; rotor ship; mailboat, packet, steam p.; dredger, hopper, icebreaker; transport, storeship, tender, escort vessel; tug, launch; lightship, weather ship; submarine 722 *warship*.

galley, galliot; privateer, corsair; longship; bireme, trireme, quadrireme, quinquereme.

merchant ship, merchantman, trader; galleon, argosy, dromond, carrack, polacre; caravel, galliot, Indiaman; banana boat, tea clipper; slaver; cargo boat, freighter, tramp; coaster, lugger, hoy; collier, tanker, supertanker; container ship.

fishing boat, inshore f. boat; fishing smack, dogger, hooker, buss, coble; drifter, trawler, purse-seiner; factory ship; whaler.

sailing ship, sailing boat, sailer; windjammer, clipper, tall ship; square-rigged ship; four-masted ship, threemaster; barque, barquentine; two-masted ship, brig, hermaphrodite b., brigantine, schooner, pinnace; frigate, corvette 722 *warship*; cutter, sloop, ketch, yawl; wherry; yacht, sailing dinghy, smack; xebec, felucca, caïque, dhow, junk, sampan.

sail, sailcloth, canvas; square sail, lugsail, lug, lateen sail, fore-and-aft s., leg-of-mutton s., spanker; course, mainsail, foresail, topsail, topgallant sail, royal, skysail; jib, staysail, spinnaker, balloon sail, studding s.; rigging 47 *tackling*; mast, foremast, mainmast, mizzenmast.

boat, skiff, foldboat, cockboat; lifeboat; ship's boat, tender, dinghy, pram; long-boat, jolly boat; whaleboat, dory; pinnace, cutter, gig; bumboat, surf boat; barge, lighter, pontoon; ferry, ferryboat, canalboat, narrowboat; houseboat; tug-boat, tug; powerboat, motorboat, motor launch; pleasure-boat, cabin cruiser; speedboat.

rowing boat, galley; eight, racing e.; sculler, shell, randan; skiff, dinghy, coracle, currach; punt, gondola; canoe, outrigger, dugout; piragua, proa, kayak, umiak.

raft, liferaft, balsa, catamaran, trimaran; float, pontoon.

shipping, craft, forest of masts; argosy, fleet, flotilla, squadron 722 *navy*; marine, mercantile marine, merchant navy, shipping line; flag of convenience 547 *flag*.

Adj. *marine*, maritime, naval, nautical, sea-going, ocean-g. 269 *seafaring*; seaworthy, water-w., weatherly; snug, tight, ship-shape; rigged, square-r.; clinkerbuilt, carvel-b.; flush-decked.

276. Aircraft – N. *aircraft* 271 *aeronautics*; aerodyne, flying machine; aeroplane, airplane, crate; plane, monoplane, biplane, triplane; amphibian; hydroplane, seaplane, flying boat; airliner, airbus, transport, freighter; warplane, fighter, bomber 722 *air force*; stratocruiser, jet, jumbo j., jump j., supersonic j., turbojet, turboprop; VTOL; helicopter, whirlybird, chopper, copter; hovercraft 275 *ship*; glider, sailplane; flying instruments, controls, joystick, rudder; aerofoil, fin, tail; flaps, aileron; prop; propeller; cockpit, flight deck; undercarriage, landing gear; parachute, ejector seat; test bed, wind tunnel; flight simulator; aerodrome 271 *air travel*.

airship, aerostat, balloon, hot-air b.; barrage balloon, blimp; dirigible, Zeppelin; kite; parachute, chute; hang glider; balloon-basket, nacelle, car, gondola.

rocket, rocketry; step rocket, multi-stage r.; booster; nose cone, warhead 723 *missile weapon*.

spaceship, spacecraft, space probe, space capsule, space shuttle; lunar module; space station, sputnik 321 *satellite*; flying saucer, UFO, unidentified flying object.

Adj. *aviational*, aeronautical, aerospace; aerodynamic, aerostatic; astronautical, space-travelling; airworthy 271 *flying*; heavier-than-air, lighter-than-air; supersonic; vertical take-off.

277. Velocity – N. *velocity*, celerity, rapidity, speed, swiftness, fleetness, quickness, alacrity; instantaneousness 116 *instantaneity*; promptness, expedition, dispatch; speed, tempo, rate, pace 265 *motion*; miles per hour, knots; Mach number; great speed, lightning s.; maximum speed, full steam; press of sail; precipitation 680 *haste*; streak, blue s., streak of lightning, flash; flight, jet f., supersonic f.; gale, hurricane; wind gauge; log, logline; speed trap; tachometer, speedometer.

spurt, acceleration, speed-up, overtaking; burst of speed; thrust, impetus 279 *impulse*; bound, pounce 312 *leap*; whiz, swoop, swoosh, zip, uprush, zoom; dive, power d.; flying start; rush, dash, scamper, run, sprint, gallop.

speeding, driving, hard d., scorching, racing, burn-up; bowling along, rattling a., batting a.; course, race, career, full c.; full speed, full lick; rate, pace, smart p., fair clip; quick march, double 680 *haste*; clean pair of heels; race course, speed track 716 *racing*.

speeder, hustler, speed merchant, speed maniac, scorcher 268 *driver*; runner, harrier; racer, sprinter; galloper; courser, racehorse 273 *thoroughbred*; greyhound, cheetah, hare, deer, ostrich; arrow 287 *missile*; jet, rocket; speedboat, clipper; express train; Ariel, Mercury 529 *courier*; seven-league boots.

Adj. *speedy*, swift, fast, quick, rapid, nimble, volant; darting, dashing, lively, brisk, smart, snappy, nifty, zippy 174 *vigorous*; expeditious, hustling 680 *hasty*; double-quick, rapid-fire; prompt 135 *early*; immediate 116 *instantaneous*; high-geared, high-speed, streamlined, souped-up; speeding, racing, ton-up; running, charging, runaway; flying, whizzing, hurtling, pelting; whirling, tempestuous; breakneck, headlong, precipitate 857 *rash*; fleet, wing-footed, light-f.; darting, flashing; swift-moving, agile, nimble; mercurial, like quicksilver 152 *changeful*; winged, arrowy; like a flash,

like greased lightning, like the wind, quick as lightning, quick as thought, like a bat out of hell; meteoric, transonic, supersonic, hypersonic, jet-propelled.

Vb. *move fast*, move, shift, travel, speed; drive, pelt, streak, flash, shoot; scorch, burn up the miles, scour the plain, tear up the road; scud, careen; skim, nip, cut; bowl along 258 *go smoothly*; sweep along, tear a., rattle a.; rip, zip, rush, dash; fly, wing, whiz, skirr; hurtle, zoom, dive; plunge, lunge, swoop; hare, run, trot, lope, spank, gallop; bolt, cut and run, hotfoot it, leg it, scoot, skedaddle, scamper, scurry, scuttle; start, dart; frisk, whisk; spring, pounce; put one's best foot forward, get a move on; hurry, post, haste 680 *hasten*; chase, charge, stampede, career, go full pelt, go all out.

accelerate, speed up, raise the tempo; gather momentum, spurt, sprint, put on speed, pick up s., step on it, put one's foot down, open up, let it rip; crowd on sail; quicken one's speed, mend one's pace; quicken, step up, drive, spur; lend wings to, expedite 680 *hasten*.

outstrip, overtake, overhaul, catch up; lap, outpace, outrun 306 *outdo*; gain on, distance, outdistance, leave behind; lose, shake off; make the running, have the legs of, romp home 34 *be superior*.

Adv. *swiftly*, rapidly etc. adj.; apace, posthaste, at full speed, at full tilt; all out, flat out; helter-skelter, head-long, lickety-split, hell for leather; presto, pronto, smartish, p.d.q.; like a shot, like the clappers, in a flash 116 *instantaneously*; under press of sail; under full steam, full speed ahead; nineteen to the dozen, hand over fist; at a rate of knots, at the double, in double-quick time, as fast as one's legs would carry one; by leaps and bounds, like wildfire.

278. Slowness – N. *slowness*, slackness, languor 679 *sluggishness*; deliberation, hesitation 858 *caution*; reluctance 598 *unwillingness*; go-slow, working to rule 145 *strike*; slow-down, deceleration, retardation 113 *protraction*; drag, brake, curb 747 *restraint*; no hurry, time to spare, easy stages 681 *leisure*; slow motion, low gear; slow march, dead m.; slow time, andante; foot pace, snail's p., crawl, creep, dawdle, amble 265 *gait*; limping, hobbling; lag, time lag 136 *delay*.

slowcoach, snail, tortoise; stopping train; funeral procession, cortège; dawdler, loiterer, lingerer; laggard 679 *idler*.

Adj. *slow*, painfully s.; slow-motion, time-lapse; trickling, dripping; creeping, crawling; tardigrade, slow-moving 695 *clumsy*; limping, halting; taking one's time, dilatory 136 *late*; long about it, unhurried 681 *leisurely*; sedate 875 *formal*; deliberate, painstaking 457 *careful*; groping, tentative 858 *cautious*; languid, sluggish 679 *lazy*; gradual, stealthy, imperceptible.

Vb. *move slowly*, go slow, amble, crawl, creep, inch along, ease a.; ooze, drip, trickle, dribble 350 *flow*; drift 282 *deviate*; shamble, slouch, mooch, shuffle, scuff; toddle, mince; plod, trudge; toil, labour, chug; limp, hobble, drag one's steps, flag, falter 684 *be fatigued*; trail, lag, fall behind; hang fire, drag one's feet; tarry, be long about it, take one's time 136 *be late*; linger, stroll, saunter, dawdle 267 *walk*; grope, feel one's way 461 *be tentative*; drawl 580 *stammer*.

decelerate, slow down, slow up, ease up, let up, lose momentum; reduce speed, slacken one's pace; smell the ground (of ships).

retard, rein in, throttle down; reef, shorten sail 269 *navigate*; brake 747 *restrain*; backpedal 286 *regress*; clip the wings 702 *hinder*.

Adv. *slowly*, deliberately etc. adj.; leisurely, lazily, sluggishly; at half speed, in low gear; at a foot's pace, at a snail's p.; with leaden step; gingerly; in one's own good time; adagio, largo, larghetto, lento, andante.

gradatim, gradually etc. adj.; by degrees, by inches, little by little, bit by bit, inch by inch, step by step, one at a time, by easy stages.

279. Impulse – N. *impulse*, impulsion, pressure; impetus, momentum; boost 174

stimulant; thrust, push, shove, heave; stroke; throw 287 *propulsion*; lunge, kick; percussion, drumming; beat 403 *roll*; ramming, butting, butt (**see** *collision*); concussion, shock, impact; slam, bang; flick, clip, tap 378 *touch*; shake, rattle, jolt, jerk, wrench 318 *agitation*; pulse 318 *spasm*; mechanics, dynamics.

knock, rap, tap, clap; dab, pat, flip, flick; nudge, dig 547 *gesture*; smack, slap; cuff, clout, clump, buffet, box on the ears; blow, four-penny one; lash, stroke, hit, crack; cut, drive (cricket); thwack, thump, biff, bang; punch, rabbit p., straight left, uppercut, jab, hook; body blow, wild b., haymaker, swipe; knock-out blow; stamp, kick; whop, swat; spanking, trouncing, dusting, pasting, licking, leathering, thrashing, rain of blows; hiding 963 *corporal punishment*; assault, assault and battery 712 *attack*; exchange of blows, fisticuffs 61 *turmoil*.

collision, clash, encounter, meeting; head-on collision; bird strike; graze, scrape 333 *friction*; cannon, carom; impact, bump, shock, crash, smash, smashup; brunt, charge, force 712 *attack*; collision course 293 *convergence*; multiple collision, pileup.

hammer, sledge h.; hammerhead, peen; punch, puncher; beetle, maul, mallet; flail; racket, bat, hockey stick, golf club; tapper, knocker, door k.; cosh, cudgel, 723 *club*; pestle, anvil.

ram, battering r., bulldozer; pile driver, monkey; ramrod; rammer, tamper; cue, billiard c., pusher 287 *propellant*.

Adj. *impelling*, pushing etc. vb.; impellent; dynamic, dynamical, thrusting; impelled etc. vb.

Vb. *impel*, fling, heave, throw 287 *propel*; give an impetus, impart momentum; slam, bang 264 *close*; press, push, thrust, shove; ram down, tamp; pole, punt; hustle, prod, spur 277 *accelerate*; fillip, flip, flick; jerk, shake, rattle, jog, jolt, jostle 318 *agitate*; shoulder, elbow 282 *deflect*; expel 300 *eject*; frogmarch; goad 612 *incite*.

collide, make impact 378 *touch*; impinge; come into collision, meet, encounter, clash; cross swords 712 *strike at*; ram, butt, bunt, batter, dint, dent; batter at, bulldoze; cannon into, bump into; graze 333 *rub*; crash into, smash i., run i., run over, clash with, collide w., fall foul of; run against, dash a. 712 *charge*; clash against, bark one's shins, stub one's toe; trip over 309 *tumble*.

strike, smite, hit, land a blow, plant a b.; hit out at; lunge at, poke at, strike at; lash out at, let fly; swing, flail, beat the air; slam, bang, knock; knock for six, knock into the middle of next week, send flying; knock down, floor 311 *fell*; pat, flip, fillip, tap, rap, clap; slap, smack; clump, clout, clobber; box, spar 716 *fight*; buffet, punch, thump, thwack, whack, wham, rain blows, pummel, trounce, belabour, beat up, sock it to, let one have it; give one a black eye *or* a bloody nose, make one see stars; pound, batter, bludgeon 332 *pulverize*; biff, bash, dash, slosh, sock, slog, slug, cosh, cudgel, club, mug, spifflicate; blackjack, sandbag, hit over the head, crown; concuss, stun, knock out; spank, wallop, thrash, lash, lam, lambaste, beat, cane, leather, strap, belt 963 *flog*; thresh, flail; hammer, drum; squash, swat 216 *flatten*; maul 655 *wound*; bayonet 263 *pierce*; throw stones at, stone, pelt 712 *lapidate*; head (a football); bat, swipe, drive, smash 287 *propel*.

kick, spurn, boot, knee, put the boot in; trample, tread on, stamp on; ride over, ride roughshod; spur, dig in one's heels; heel, dribble, shoot (a football).

280. Recoil – N. *recoil*, revulsion, reaction, retroaction, reflux 148 *reversion*; repercussion, reverberation, echo 404 *resonance*; reflex 417 *reflection*; kick, kickback, backlash; ricochet, cannon, carom; rebound, bounce, spring, springboard, trampoline 328 *elasticity*; ducks and drakes; swing-back 317 *oscillation*; volley, boomerang; rebuff, repulse.

Adj. *recoiling* rebounding etc. vb.; reactive, repercussive, refluent.

Vb. *recoil*, react 182 *counteract*; shrink, wince, flinch, jib, shy; kick back, hit b.; ricochet, cannon off; uncoil, spring back,

bound b., rebound, bounce; return, swing back 148 *revert*; have repercussions; reverberate, echo; boomerang.

281. Direction – N. *direction*, bearing, compass reading, lie of the land 186 *situation*; orientation, collimation, alignment; set, drift 350 *current*; course, beam; beeline, line of sight; course, tack; line, line of march, way 624 *route*; steering, aim, target 295 *goal*; compass 269 *sailing aid*; sights 442 *optical device*; fingerpost 547 *signpost*; direction finder; orienteering, cross-country race, point-to-point.

compass point, cardinal points, half points, quarter points; quarter, north, east, south, west; magnetic north; rhumb, azimuth.

Adj. *directed*, orientated, etc. vb.; aimed, well-a., well-directed 187 *located*; bound for 617 *intending*; axial, diagonal 220 *oblique*; facing 240 *opposite*; direct, undeviating, unswerving 249 *straight*; northbound, southbound; northern, northerly, southerly, meridional; western, occidental; eastern, oriental.

Vb. *orientate*, orientate oneself, take one's bearings, shoot the sun 269 *navigate*; see how the land lies; have a direction, bear; signpost, direct, show the way, put on the right track 547 *indicate*; pinpoint, locate 187 *place*; face, front 240 *be opposite*.

aim, level, point; take aim, aim at; train one's sights, draw a bead on, level at; cover, have one covered; collimate, set one's sights.

Adv. *towards*, versus, facing; through, via, by way of; straight, direct, in a direct line, in a line with; directly, as the crow flies; before the wind, close to the w.; against the w., in the wind's eye, close-hauled; seaward, landward, homeward; cross-country; hither, thither.

282. Deviation – N. *deviation*, disorientation, misdirection, wrong course, wrong turning; aberration, deflection, refraction; diversion, digression; shift 220 *obliquity*; flexion, swerve 248 *curvature*; branching off 294 *divergence*; deviousness, detour, bypath, circumbendibus, long way round 626 *circuit*; vagrancy 267 *wandering*; drift, leeway; oblique motion, crab-walk, sidestep; break, googly (cricket); knight's move (chess); yaw, tack; zigzag, slalom course.

Adj. *deviating*, digressing; off-centre; out of orbit; errant, wandering, rambling, roving, footloose 267 *travelling*; undirected, unguided, random, erratic 495 *inexact*; disorientated, off-course, off-beam, lost, astray; misdirected, misaimed, off-target, wide; devious, winding, roundabout 314 *circuitous*; indirect, crooked 220 *oblique*; branching 294 *divergent*.

Vb. *deviate*, digress, make a detour; branch 294 *diverge*; turn, filter, turn aside, swerve, slew; alter course, change direction, yaw, tack; veer, back (wind); bend, curve; zigzag, twist 251 *meander*; wobble 317 *oscillate*; steer clear of, sheer off; sidle, passage; slide, skid, sideslip; glance, fly off at a tangent 220 *be oblique*; shy, jib, sidestep 620 *avoid*.

stray, err, ramble, rove, drift, divagate, straggle 267 *wander*; go astray, go adrift, lose the way, get lost, lose one's bearings, lose one's sense of direction.

deflect, bend, warp 220 *make oblique*; skew; put off the scent, misdirect 495 *mislead*; avert 713 *parry*; divert, sidetrack, draw aside; bias, slice, pull, hook.

283. Preceding: going before – N. *preceding* 119 *priority*, 64 *precedence*; going before, leading, heading, flying start; preemption, queue-jumping; pride of place, lead 34 *superiority*; van, vanguard, avant-garde 237 *front*.

Adj. *foremost*, first; leading etc. vb.

Vb. *precede*, go before, forerun, herald; usher in, introduce; head, spearhead, lead, go in front, lead the way 689 *direct*; take the lead, steal a march on, preempt; get in front, jump the queue; get ahead of, lap 277 *outstrip*; be beforehand 135 *be early*; take precedence over 64 *come before*.

Adv. *ahead*, before, in advance, in the van, in front.

284. Following: going after – N. *following* 65 *sequence*; run, suit 71 *series*; subsequence 120 *posteriority*; pursuit 619 *chase*; last place 238 *rear.*

follower, attendant, hanger-on, camp follower, groupie 742 *dependant*; train, tail, wake, cortège, suite, followers 67 *retinue*; following, party, adherent 703 *aider*; satellite, moon; trailer, tender.

Adj. *following*, subsequent 65 *sequential*.

Vb. *follow*, come behind, follow on, follow after, sit on one's tail, tread on the heels of, come to heel 65 *come after*; attend, wait on 742 *serve*; tag along 89 *accompany*; dog, shadow, tail 619 *pursue*; drop behind 238 *be behind*.

Adv. *behind*, in the rear 238 *rearward*; on the heels of; in the train of, in the wake of, in tow 65 *after*; one after another.

285. Progression: motion forwards – N. *progression*, going forward; march, way, course, career; progress, steady p., forward march; stride, leap, jump, leaps and bounds 277 *spurt*; irresistible progress, flood, tide 350 *current*; gain, advance, headway 654 *improvement*; development, evolution 71 *continuity*; furtherance, advancement; progressiveness 654 *reformism*; achievement 727 *success*.

Adj. *progressive*, progressing, advancing etc. vb.; flowing on 265 *moving*.

Vb. *progress*, proceed 265 *be in motion*; advance, go forward; develop, evolve; show promise 654 *get better*; march on, flow on, jog on, slog on 146 *go on*; move with the times 126 *modernize*; maintain progress, hold one's lead; press on, push on, drive on, push forward, press f. 680 *hasten*; make a good start, gain, gain ground, make headway, make strides, cover the ground 277 *move fast*; get ahead, shoot a., forge a.; gain on, leave behind 277 *outstrip*; make up leeway, recover lost ground 31 *recoup*.

promote, further, contribute to, advance 703 *aid*; move up, raise; bring on, bring forward, push, force, develop; step up, speed up 277 *accelerate*; put ahead 64 *put in front*.

Adv. *forward*, onward, forth, on, ahead; progressively, by leaps and bounds; on the road to 272 *in transit*; in progress, in mid p., in sight of.

286. Regression: motion backwards – N. *regression*, regress; reverse direction, retroflexion, retrocession, retrogression, retrogradation, retroaction, backward step 148 *reversion*; motion from, retreat, withdrawal, retirement, disengagement 290 *recession*; sternway, reversing, backing; falling away, decline 655 *deterioration*.

return, remigration, homecoming 295 *arrival*; reentry 297 *ingress*; turn of the tide, reflux, refluence, ebb, regurgitation 350 *current*; veering, backing; U-turn, about-turn 148 *reversion*; countermarch, counter-movement 182 *counteraction*; turn, turning point 137 *crisis*; reflex 280 *recoil*.

Adj. *regressive*, receding, declining, ebbing; refluent, reflex; retrogressive, retrograde, backward; backward-looking, reactionary 125 *retrospective*; retroactive 280 *recoiling*; backing, anticlockwise, counterclockwise; remigrating, returning, homing, homeward bound.

Vb. *regress*, recede, retrogress, retrograde, retrocede; retreat, beat a r.; retire, withdraw, fall back, draw b.; turn away, turn tail 620 *run away*; disengage, back out, back down; backtrack, backpedal; give way, give ground; fall behind, fall astern 278 *move slowly*; reverse, back, back water, go backwards; run back, flow back, slip back; ebb, decline 309 *descend*; bounce back 280 *recoil*.

turn back, retrace one's steps; remigrate, go home, return 148 *revert*; look back, hark back 505 *retrospect*; turn one's back, turn on one's heel; veer round, wheel r., aboutface; double, double back, countermarch; come back, come back to where one started.

Adv. *backwards*, back, astern, in reverse; to the right about.

287. Propulsion – N. *propulsion*, jet p., drive; impulsion, push 279 *impulse*; pro-jection, throwing, hurling, etc. vb.; precipitation; cast, throw, chuck, toss, fling, sling, shy, cock-shy; pot shot, pot, shot; discharge, volley 712 *bombardment*; bowling, pitching, throw-in, full toss, yorker, lob (cricket); kick, punt, dribble (football); stroke, drive, swipe 279 *knock*; pull, slice (golf); rally, volley, smash (tennis); ballistics, musketry, archery, toxophily.

missile, projectile, shell, rocket 723 *missile weapon*; bullet, shot; brickbat, stone; arrow, dart; ball, football; bowl, wood, jack, puck; quoit, discus; javelin; hammer, caber.

propellant, thrust, driving force, jet, steam 160 *energy*; spray, aerosol; thruster, pusher, shover; tail wind, following w.; lever, treadle, pedal; oar, sweep, paddle; screw, blade, paddlewheel, propeller; coal, petrol, oil 385 *fuel*; dynamite 723 *explosive*; shotgun / 723 *firearm*; airgun, pop gun, water pistol; blowpipe, pea-shooter; catapult, sling, bow.

shooter, gunman, rifleman, musketeer, gunner, artilleryman 722 *soldiery*; archer, bowman *or* -woman, toxophilite; marks-man, markswoman, sharpshooter, sniper, shot, crack s. 696 *proficient person*.

thrower, hurler, etc. vb.; knife-thrower, javelin-t., discus-t., stone-t., slinger; bowler, pitcher, curler.

Adj. *propulsive*, propellant, propelling etc. vb.; expulsive, explosive, propelled etc. vb.; projectile, missile; ballistic.

Vb. *propel*, launch, project; flight, throw, cast, deliver, heave, pitch, toss, cant, chuck, shy, bung; bowl, lob, york; hurl, fling, sling, catapult; dart, flick; pelt, stone 712 *lapidate*; precipitate, send flying; expel, pitchfork 300 *eject*; blow up, explode; serve, return, volley, smash, kill (tennis); bat, slam, slog; sky, loft; drive, cut, pull, hook, glance (cricket); slice 279 *strike*; kick, dribble, punt (football); putt, push, shove, shoulder 279 *impel*; wheel, pedal, roll, bowl, trundle 315 *rotate*; move on, drive, hustle 265 *move*; sweep before one, put to flight.

shoot, fire, open fire, fire off; volley, fire a v.; discharge, explode, let off, set off;

draw a bead on, pull the trigger; cannonade, bombard 712 *fire at*; snipe, pot, pot
at, loose off at; pepper 263 *pierce*.

288. Traction – N. *traction*, drawing etc.
vb.; pulling back, retraction; retractility,
retractability; magnetism 291 *attraction*;
towage, haulage; draught, pull, haul; tug,
tow; towline, towrope; trawl, dragnet;
drawer, puller, retractor; windlass 310
lifter; tug, tugboat 275 *ship*; tractor, traction engine 274 *locomotive*; loadstone 291
magnet; strain, tug of war 716 *contest*.

Adj. *drawing*, pulling etc. vb.; trac-
tional, tractive; pulling back, retractive,
retractile, retractable; magnetic 291
attracting; tractile, ductile; drawn,
horse-d.

Vb. *draw*, pull, haul, heave, hale; trice,
warp, kedge 269 *navigate*; tug, tow, take
in tow; lug, drag, draggle, trail, trawl;
rake, harrow; winch, reel in, wind in 310
elevate; suck in 299 *absorb*; pluck, pull out
304 *extract*; wrench 246 *distort*; yank, jerk,
tweak, pluck at, snatch at 318 *agitate*; pull
towards 291 *attract*; pull back, draw b.,
pull in, draw in, retract, sheathe (claws).

289. Approach: motion towards – N.
approach, coming towards, advance 285
progression; approximation 200 *nearness*;
confluence 293 *convergence*; onset, advent, coming 295 *arrival*; advances, overture; means of approach, accessibility,
approaches 624 *access*.

Adj. *approaching*, nearing, getting
warm etc. vb.; close, approximate 200
near; meeting 293 *convergent*; confluent,
affluent, tributary; closing in, imminent
155 *impending*; advancing, coming,
oncoming, on the way 295 *arriving*.

accessible, approachable, get-at-able;
within reach, attainable 469 *possible*;
available, obtainable 189 *on the spot*;
wayside, roadside, nearby 200 *near*; welcoming, inviting 291 *attracting*.

Vb. *approach*, draw near 200 *be near*;
approximate 200 *bring near*; come within
range 295 *arrive*; come into view 443 *be
visible*; feel the attraction of, be drawn;
come closer 293 *converge*; near, draw n.;

step up to, sidle up to; roll up 74 *congregate*; waylay, buttonhole; accost 884 *greet*;
lean towards, incline, trend 179 *tend*;
move towards, make t., drift t. 265 *be in
motion*; advance 285 *progress*; advance
upon, bear down on 712 *attack*; close,
close in 232 *circumscribe*; hover 155 *impend*; gain upon, catch up with 277 *outstrip*; follow hard, narrow the gap, breathe
down one's neck, tread on one's heels, run
one close; be in sight of, hug the shore;
make a landfall 269 *navigate*.

290. Recession: motion from – N. *recession*, retirement, withdrawal, retreat 286
regression; leak 298 *outflow*; emigration,
evacuation 296 *departure*; flight 667
escape; revulsion 280 *recoil*.

Adj. *receding*, ebbing etc. vb.; retreat-
ing 286 *regressive*.

Vb. *recede*, retire, withdraw, fall back,
draw b., retreat 286 *regress*; ebb, subside,
shrink 37 *decrease*; fade from view 446
disappear; go, go away 296 *depart*; leak,
leak out 298 *flow out*; move away, move
off, move further, stand off, put space
between 199 *be distant*; stand aside, make
way, veer away, sheer off 282 *deviate*; drift
away 282 *stray*; back away, shrink a. 620
avoid; flee 620 *run away*; go back 286 *turn
back*; jump back 280 *recoil*.

291. Attraction – N. *attraction*, pull, drag,
draw, tug; drawing to, pulling towards;
magnetization, magnetism, magnetic
field; gravity, force of g.; itch for 859
desire; affinity, sympathy; attractiveness,
allure, appeal; lure, bait, decoy 612 *inducement*; charmer 612 *motivator*; centre
of attraction, cynosure 890 *favourite*.

magnet, bar m.; coil magnet, solenoid;
magnetite, magnetized iron, loadstone;
lodestar 520 *guide*; magnetizer.┗

Adj. *attracting*, drawing etc. vb.; adduc-
tive; magnetic, magnetized; attractive 612
inducing; centripetal.

Vb. *attract*, magnetize, pull, drag, tug
288 *draw*; adduct, exercise a pull; draw
towards, pull t., drag t., tug t.; lure, allure,
bait 612 *tempt*; decoy 542 *ensnare*.

292. Repulsion – N. *repulsion*, repellence; repulsive force, centrifugal f.; repulsiveness 842 *ugliness*; reflection 280 *recoil*; repulse, rebuff 607 *rejection*; brush-off 300 *ejection*.

Adj. *repellent*, repelling etc. vb.; repulsive, off-putting, antipathetic 861 *disliked*; centrifugal.

Vb. *repel*, put off 861 *cause dislike*; push away 279 *impel*; drive away, repulse, fend off 713 *parry*; dispel 75 *disperse*; head off, turn away, reflect 282 *deflect*; rebuff, snub, brush off 607 *reject*; cold-shoulder, keep at arm's length 883 *make unwelcome*; show the door to, send off with a flea in his *or* her ear, send packing, send about his *or* her business, give his *or* her marching orders; boot out, sack 300 *dismiss*.

Int. be off! away with you! scram! hop it! get lost!

293. Convergence – N. *convergence*, mutual approach 289 *approach*; narrowing gap; collision course 279 *collision*; confluence, conflux, meeting 45 *union*; concurrence, concentration 74 *assemblage*; closing in, pincer movement 232 *circumscription*; centring, focalization 76 *focus*; narrowing, tapering 206 *narrowness*; converging line, asymptote, tangent; perspective, vanishing point.

Adj. *convergent*, converging etc. vb.; focusing, focused; centripetal, centring; confluent, concurrent 45 *conjunctive*; tangential; pointed, conical 256 *tapering*.

Vb. *converge*, come closer, draw in, close in; narrow the gap; come together 295 *meet*; unite, gather together 74 *congregate*; roll in, pour in 297 *enter*; close with, intercept, head off; pinch, nip 198 *make smaller*; concentrate, focus, bring into f.; toe in; centre, centre on 225 *centralize*; taper, come to a point, narrow down.

294. Divergence – N. *divergence*, going apart, divarication; moving apart, parting 46 *separation*; aberration, declination 282 *deviation*; spread, fanning out, deployment 75 *dispersion*; parting of the ways,

fork, bifurcation, crossroads, points 222 *crossing*; radiation, ramification, branching out; Y-shape 247 *angularity*; star, rays, spokes.

Adj. *divergent*, diverging etc. vb.; divaricate, separated; radiating, radial, palmate, stellate; centrifugal, centrifuge 282 *deviating*.

Vb. *diverge*, radiate; divaricate, ramify, branch off, split off, fork, bifurcate; part, part ways 46 *separate*; glance off, fly off at a tangent 282 *deviate*; deploy, fan out, spread, scatter 75 *be dispersed*; straddle, spread-eagle; splay.

295. Arrival – N. *arrival*, advent, coming, accession, appearance 289 *approach*, 189 *presence*; onset 68 *beginning*; landfall, landing, touchdown, docking; debarkation, disembarkation 298 *egress*; meeting, greeting; homecoming 286 *return*; reception, welcome; guest, visitor, visitant 297 *incomer*; last lap, home stretch.

goal 617 *objective*; journey's end, terminus 69 *extremity*; stopover, stage, halt 145 *stopping place*; billet, resting place; landing stage, pier; port, harbour 662 *shelter*; dock, berth 192 *stable*; airport 271 *air travel*; rendezvous.

Adj. *arriving*, landing etc. vb.; homing, homeward-bound; terminal; nearing 289 *approaching*, 155 *impending*.

Vb. *arrive*, come, reach, fetch up at, get there 189 *be present*; make land, sight, raise; make port, dock, berth, tie up 266 *come to rest* (**see** *land*); unharness, unhitch, outspan; draw up, pull up, park; home, come h. 286 *regress*; hit, make, win to, gain, attain 725 *carry through*; make an entrance 297 *enter*; appear, show up, turn up, roll up, drop in, blow in 882 *visit*; put in, pull in, stop at, stop off, break one's journey 145 *pause*; clock in; be delivered, come to hand.

land, beach, ground, run aground, touch down, make a landing; go ashore, disembark 298 *emerge*; detrain, debus; get down, alight, dismount 309 *descend*.

meet, join, rejoin; receive, greet, welcome 882 *be sociable*; go to meet, keep a date, rendezvous; come upon, encounter, run into; bump into, collide with 279 *collide*; gather, assemble 74 *congregate*.

Int. welcome! welcome home! greetings! hullo! hi! pleased to meet you! aloha! shalom! salaam!

296. Departure – N. *departure*, leaving, parting, removal, going away; walk-out, exit 298 *egress*; pulling out, emigration 290 *recession*; remigration, going back 286 *return*; migration, exodus, hegira; hop, flight, flit, moonlight f., decampment, elopement, getaway 667 *escape*; embarkation, setting out 68 *start*; takeoff, blastoff 308 *ascent*; zero hour, point of departure; starting point, starting post, stakeboat.

valediction, valedictory; last post 364 *obsequies*; leave-taking, congé, dismissal; goodbyes, goodnights, farewells, adieus 884 *courteous act*; sendoff; last words, parting shot, Parthian s.; stirrup cup, one for the road.

Adj. *departing*, going etc. vb.; valedictory, farewell; parting, leaving, taking leave; outward bound; emigratory.

Vb. *depart*, quit, leave, abandon 621 *relinquish*; retire, withdraw 286 *turn back*; remove, move house; leave home, emigrate; leave the nest, take wing 190 *go away*; take one's leave, be going, be getting along; bid farewell, say goodbye, make one's adieus, tear oneself away, part, part company; get one's marching orders; quit the scene, leave the stage, bow out, make one's exit.

decamp, up sticks, strike tents, break camp, break up; march out, pack up, clear off; clear out, pull out, evacuate; make tracks, be off, beetle o., buzz o., slink o., slope o., swan o., push o., shove o., make oneself scarce; vamoose, skedaddle, beat it, hop it, scram, bolt 277 *move fast*; flee, take flight, make a break for it 620 *run away*; elope, abscond 667 *escape*.

start out, be off, get going, set out 68 *begin*; sally forth, strike out, light out 298 *emerge*; take ship, embark; hoist the Blue Peter, cast off, push off, get under way 269 *navigate*; mount, harness, saddle 267 *ride*; pile in, hop on; emplane, entrain; drive

off, take off, be on one's way; see off, wave goodbye, speed the parting guest.

Int. goodbye! farewell! adieu! au revoir! auf Wiedersehen! arrivederci! be seeing you! cheerio! ciao! bye-bye! ta-ta! so long! pleasant journey! bon voyage! God be with you!

297. Ingress: motion into – N. *ingress*, incoming, entry, entrance; reentry 286 *return*; inflow, influx; inpouring, inrush; intrusion, invasion, incursion 712 *attack*; immersion, diffusion, penetration, infiltration, insinuation 231 *interjacency*, 303 *insertion*; immigration, intake 299 *reception*; importation 272 *transference*; admittance, access, entrée 756 *permission*; open-door policy 791 *trade* 744 *scope*; foot in the door 263 *opener*.

incomer, newcomer, Johnny-come-lately; new arrival, new face; new boy 538 *beginner*; visitant, visitor 882 *sociable person*; immigrant, colonist, settler 59 *foreigner*; stowaway 59 *intruder*; invader, raider 712 *attacker*; house-breaker 789 *thief*.

Adj. *incoming*, ingoing, inward, homing; intrusive, trespassing; invasive 712 *attacking*; penetrating, flooding; allowed in, imported.

Vb. *enter*, turn into, go in, come in, breeze in, venture in, sidle in, step in, walk in, file in; set foot in, cross the threshold, darken the doors; let oneself in 263 *open*; gain admittance, be invited; call 882 *visit*; get in, hop in, jump in, pile in; squeeze into, jam oneself i.; creep in, slip in, edge in, sneak in, steal in; work one's way into, insinuate oneself, worm into; bore i. 263 *pierce*; bite into, cut i. 260 *notch*; tread in, fall into 309 *tumble*; sink into, dive i. 313 *plunge*; immigrate, settle in 187 *place oneself*.

infiltrate, percolate, seep, soak through; sink in, penetrate, permeate, interpenetrate 43 *mix*; taint, infect 655 *impair*; filter in, wriggle into, worm one's way i., find one's way in.

burst in, irrupt, rush in, charge in, crash in, break in, storm in 176 *force*; flow in, pour in, flood in 350 *flow*; crowd in, throng in, roll in, swarm in 74 *congregate*; invade, raid, board, storm, escalade 712 *attack*.

intrude, trespass, gatecrash; horn in, barge in, push in, muscle in, break in upon 63 *derange*; burgle 788 *steal*.

298. Egress: motion out of – N. *egress*, going out; exit, walkoff; walkout, exodus, evacuation 296 *departure*; emigration, expatriation, exile 883 *seclusion*; emergence, emerging, debouchment; emersion, surfacing; emanation (see *outflow*); eruption, outburst, outbreak; sortie, breakout 667 *escape*; exportation 272 *transference*; emigrant 59 *foreigner*; expatriate, colonist 191 *settler*; expellee, exile.

outflow, effluence, efflux, effusion; emission 300 *ejection*; issue, outpouring, gushing, streaming; exudation, oozing, dribbling, weeping; bleeding 302 *haemorrhage*; transudation, perspiration, sweat; percolation, filtration; leak, escape, leakage, seepage 634 *waste*; drain 772 *loss*; outfall, discharge, effluent, drainage 300 *voidance*; overflow, spill 350 *waterfall*; jet, fountain, spring; gush 350 *stream*; gusher, geyser.

outlet, vent, chute; nozzle, tap; pore 263 *orifice*; sluice, floodgate 351 *conduit*; exhaust, adjutage; spout, drainpipe, gargoyle; exit 263 *doorway*; loophole 667 *means of escape*.

Adj. *outgoing*, outward bound; emergent, issuing, emanating; oozy, runny, leaky; erupting, eruptive, explosive, expulsive, volcanic.

Vb. *emerge*, project 254 *jut*; pop out, peep out, peer out 443 *be visible*; surface, break water 308 *ascend*; emanate, transpire 526 *be disclosed*; egress, issue, debouch, sally, make a sortie; go out, come o.; jump out, bale o. 312 *leap*; clear out, evacuate 296 *decamp*; emigrate 267 *travel*; exit 296 *depart*; erupt, break out 667 *escape*.

flow out, flood o., pour o., stream o. 350 *flow*; gush, spirt, spout, jet 300 *emit*; drain out, run, drip, dribble, trickle, ooze; surge, well up, well over, boil o.; overflow, spill over, slop o.; run off, escape,

leak, vent itself, discharge i.; bleed, weep, effuse, extravasate.

exude, transude, perspire, sweat, steam 379 *be hot*; ooze, seep, percolate, filtrate, distil; run, dribble, drivel, drool, slaver, slobber, salivate 341 *be wet*; transpire, exhale 352 *breathe*.

299. Reception – N. *reception*, admission, admittance, entrée, access 297 *ingress*; receptivity, acceptance; open arms, welcome 876 *celebration*; naturalization 78 *inclusion*; initiation, baptism 68 *debut*; asylum, sanctuary, shelter 660 *protection*; introduction; importation 272 *transference*; radio receiver 531 *telecommunication*; indraught; inbreathing, inhalation 352 *respiration*; sucking, suction; assimilation, digestion, absorption, resorption; engulfment, swallowing, ingurgitation; ingestion (of food) 301 *eating*; imbibition, fluid intake 301 *drinking*; intake, consumption 634 *waste*; infusion 303 *insertion*; admissibility.

Adj. *admitting*, receptive; inviting, welcoming 289 *accessible*; receivable, admissible, acceptable; absorptive, absorbent, hygroscopic; ingestive; digestive, assimilative; introductory, initiatory.

Vb. *admit*, readmit; receive, accept, take in; naturalize; grant asylum 660 *safeguard*; welcome, fling wide the gates; invite, call in 759 *offer*; enlist, enrol, take on; give entrance *or* admittance to, allow in 263 *open*; bring in, import, land 272 *transfer*; let in, show in, usher in, introduce; initiate, baptize.

absorb, incorporate, assimilate, digest; suck, suck in; soak up, sponge, mop up, blot; resorb, reabsorb; internalize, take in, ingest, ingurgitate, imbibe; lap up, swallow, swallow up, ingulf; engorge, gulp, gobble 301 *eat*, *drink*; inhale 352 *breathe*; sniff, snuff up 394 *smell*.

300. Ejection – N. *ejection*, ejaculation, extrusion, expulsion; precipitation 287 *propulsion*; excommunication 57 *exclusion*; throwing out, chucking o., bum's rush; drumming out, marching orders; dismissal, discharge, sack, boot, push 607 *rejection*; repatriation, resettlement; deportation, extradition; relegation, exile, banishment 883 *seclusion*; eviction, dislodgment 188 *displacement*; dispossession 786 *expropriation*; jettison 779 *nonretention*; clean sweep, elimination 165 *destruction*; emission, effusion 298 *outflow*; emissivity 417 *radiation*; expellee, deportee, refugee 883 *outcast*.

ejector, evicter, dispossessor, bailiff; displacer, supplanter, superseder 150 *substitute*; expeller, chucker-out, bouncer; expellant, emetic, aperient 658 *purgative*; propellant 723 *explosive*; volcano 383 *furnace*; emitter, transmitter 531 *telecommunication*; ejector seat 276 *aircraft*.

voidance, clearance, clearage, drainage, curettage, aspiration; eruption 176 *outbreak*; egestion, regurgitation, disgorgement; vomiting, nausea, vomit, puke; eructation, gas, wind, burp, belch, fart; elimination, evacuation 302 *excretion*.

Adj. *expulsive*, expellent, extrusive, explosive, eruptive; radiating, emitting, emissive; sialogogue; vomitory, emetic; cathartic 302 *excretory*.

vomiting, sick, sickened, nauseated, green, g. around the gills; seasick, airsick, carsick; sick as a dog.

Vb. *eject*, expel, send down 963 *punish*; strike off, disbar, excommunicate 57 *exclude*; export, send away 272 *transfer*; deport, expatriate, repatriate, resettle; exile, banish, transport 883 *seclude*; extrude, throw up, cast up; spit out, spew o.; put out, push o., turf o., throw o., chuck o., fling o. 287 *propel*; kick out, boot o., bundle out, hustle o., drum out; precipitate 287 *propel*; pull out 304 *extract*; root out 165 *destroy*; exorcize, get rid of, rid oneself, get shot of; dispossess, expropriate 786 *deprive*; oust, evict, dislodge, unhouse, turn out, turn adrift 188 *displace*; hunt out, smoke o. 619 *hunt*; jettison, discard 779 *not retain*; blackball 607 *reject*; send to Coventry, give the cold shoulder 883 *make unwelcome*; supplant 150 *substitute*.

dismiss, discharge, lay off, make redundant, drop 674 *stop using*; axe, sack, fire,

give the sack *or* the boot, give the push 779 *not retain*; turn away, send packing 292 *repel*; see off, shoo away, show the door; exorcize.

empty, drain, void; evacuate, eliminate 302 *excrete*; vent, disgorge, discharge; pour out, decant 272 *transpose*; drink up, drain off, strain off; ladle out, bail o.; pump o., suck o., aspirate; run off, siphon o., open the sluices 263 *open*; draw off, tap, broach 263 *pierce*; milk, bleed 304 *extract*; clear, sweep away, make a clean sweep of; clean out, clear out, curette; unload, unpack 188 *displace*; disembowel, eviscerate, gut, clean, bone, fillet 229 *uncover*; disinfest 648 *purify*; depopulate, dispeople 105 *render few*.

emit, let out, give vent to; send out 272 *send*, 417 *radiate*; give off, exhale, breathe out, perfume, scent 394 *smell*; smoke, steam, puff 338 *vaporize*; spit, spatter, sputter, splutter; pour, spill, shed, sprinkle, spray; spurt, squirt, jet, gush 341 *moisten*; drip, drop, ooze 298 *exude*; sweat, perspire, secrete 302 *excrete*.

vomit, be sick, bring up, throw up, disgorge, retch, keck, gag; spew, puke, cat, honk, chunder, ralph; be seasick, feed the fishes; feel nausea, heave.

eruct, eructate, belch, burp, gurk; break wind, blow off, fart; hiccup, cough, hawk, clear the throat, expectorate, spit, gob.

301. Food: eating and drinking – N. *eating*, munching etc. vb.; ingestion; feeding, drip-f., force-f.; consumption, devouring; swallowing, downing; manducation, biting, chewing, mastication; rumination, digestion; chewing the cud; table, diet; dining, etc. vb.; communal feeding, messing; dining out 192 *café*; tasting, nibbling, pecking; lack of appetite, anorexia; ingurgitation, guzzling, overindulgence 944 *sensualism*, 947 *gluttony*; appetite 859 *hunger*; eating habits, table manners; omnivorousness; flesh-eating, carnivorousness, creophagy, ichthyophagy; anthropophagy, man-eating, cannibalism; herbivorousness, vegetarianism, veganism; food chain.

feasting, eating and drinking, gormandizing, guzzling, swilling; banqueting, regalement; orgy, Lucullan banquet, feast; beanfeast, beano, bunfight; blowout, spread (**see** *meal*); loaded table, festal cheer, groaning board; fleshpots 635 *plenty*; refectory 192 *café*.

dieting, dietetics 658 *therapy*; weight-watching, slimming, reducing, losing weight 946 *fasting*; diet, balanced d., crash d., macrobiotic d.; nouvelle cuisine, cuisine minceur; regimen, regime, course, dietary, diet sheet; malnutrition 651 *disease*; calories; dietitian, nutritionist.

gastronomy, gastrology, palate-tickling, epicurism 944 *sensualism*; gourmandise, good cheer 947 *gluttony*; refined palate 463 *discrimination*.

cookery, cooking, baking, cuisine, haute c.; domestic science, home economics, catering 633 *provision*; food processing (**see** *provisions*); baker, cook, chef, cuisinier, cordon bleu 633 *caterer*; bakery, rotisserie, restaurant 192 *café*; kitchen, cookhouse, galley; oven 383 *furnace*; recipe, cookery book, cookbook.

eater, feeder, consumer, partaker, etc. vb.; boarder, messmate; diner, banqueter, feaster, picnicker; gourmet, epicure; gourmand, good trencherman *or* -woman, bon vivant, Lucullus, belly-worshipper 947 *glutton*; flesh-eater, meat-e., carnivore; man-eater, cannibal, anthropophagite; vegetarian, vegan, herbivore; omnivore, hearty eater; mouth, belly 194 *maw*.

provisions, stores; provender, foodstuff, groceries; tinned *or* canned food, frozen f., convenience f., junk f.; keep, board 633 *provision*; self-sufficiency; commons, rations, iron r.; helping 783 *portion*; larder, cellar 632 *storage*.

provender, fodder, feed, pasture, pasturage, forage; corn, oats, barley, grain, hay, grass, clover, lucerne, silage; chickenfeed, pigswill, cattle cake; saltlick.

food, meat, bread, staff of life; aliment, nutriment; alimentation, nutrition; nurture, sustenance, nourishment, food and drink, pabulum, pap; manna; nectar and ambrosia; daily bread, staple food; food-stuffs, comestibles, edibles, eatables, eats, victuals, provender; grub, tuck, tucker, nosh, scoff, chow; tack, hard t., biscuit, pemmican; stodge 391 *unsavouriness*; wholefood, health food; delicatessen, delicacies; dainties, titbits 637 *superfluity*; garnish, flavouring 389 *condiment*; vitamins; calories, roughage, bulk, fibre; protein, amino acid; cholesterol, saturated fats, polyunsaturates; carbohydrates, starch; sugar; additive, preservative.

mouthful, bite, nibble, morsel 33 *small quantity*; sop, sip, swallow, bolus; gobbet, slice, titbit, bonne bouche; sandwich, snack, crust.

meal, refreshment, fare, cheer; light meal, snack, bite to eat; butty, sandwich, open s., hamburger, hot dog; packed lunch, ploughman's l.; square meal, sit-down meal, repast, collation, regalement, refection, spread, feed (**see** *feasting*); junket 837 *festivity*; picnic, fête champêtre, barbecue; austerity lunch, love-feast; potluck; breakfast, elevenses, luncheon, lunch, brunch, tiffin; tea, five o'clock, high tea; dinner, supper, fork s., buffet s.; table d'hôte, à la carte; menu, bill of fare; cover, table, place; helping, serving 783 *portion*.

dish, course; main dish, entrée; salad, entremets; dessert, savoury; plat du jour; meat and two veg (**see** *meat*); casserole, stew, Irish s., hotpot, ragout 43 *a mixture*; goulash, curry; pilaff, paella, risotto; chop suey, chow mein; pasta, ravioli, lasagne, macaroni, spaghetti, noodles; pizza, taco; pasty, pie, flan, quiche; fricassee, fritters, croquettes, fry-up, mixed grill, kebabs; fondue, soufflé, omelette; Welsh rarebit, scrambled eggs; réchauffé, rehash, leftovers.

hors-d'oeuvres, antipasto, smorgasbord; starter, appetizer, canapé; soup, broth, potage, consommé; stock, bouillon, julienne, bisque, chowder; mulligatawny, minestrone, borsch, gazpacho, bouillabaisse; cold meats, cooked m.; salami, pâté, terrine, galantine; salad, coleslaw, macedoine; mayonnaise 389 *sauce*.

fish food, fish and chips, fish cakes, fish fingers, quenelles, kedgeree; white fish, oily f., smoked f.; trout, salmon, eel; cod, coley, rock salmon, whiting, plaice, sole, skate, hake, halibut, haddock, turbot, mullet, mackerel, herring, brisling, whitebait, sprats; sardine, pilchard, anchovies, tuna *or* tunny; kippers, bloaters, Bombay duck; seafood, shellfish, oyster, lobster, crayfish, crab, shrimp, prawn, scampi; scallop, cockle, winkle, mussel, whelk, jellied eel; roe, soft r., hard r., caviar.

meat, flesh; human flesh, long pig; red meat, white m.; beef, mutton, lamb, veal, pork, venison, game; pheasant, chicken 365 *table bird*, *poultry*; Sunday joint, roast beef and Yorkshire pudding; boiled beef and carrots; haggis, black pudding; shepherd's pie, cottage p.; mince, meatballs, rissoles; sausage, banger, chipolata, frankfurter; toad in the hole, Cornish pasty, steak and kidney pudding; cut, joint, leg; baron of beef, sirloin; shoulder, hand of pork, skirt, scrag end, breast, brisket; shin, loin, flank, ribs, topside, silverside; cutlet, chop, escalope; steak, fillet s., rump s., porterhouse s.; pork pie, ham, bacon, boiled b., gammon; tongue, knuckle, Bath chap, brawn, oxtail, cowheel, pig's trotters, sweetbreads, tripe, chitterlings, pig's fry; offal, kidney, liver 224 *insides*; suet, dripping, crackling; forcemeat, stuffing.

dessert, pudding, sweet; milk pudding, rice p., semolina, tapioca, bread-and-butter pudding; steamed p., suet p., Christmas p., summer p., rolypoly, spotted dick; jam tart, mince pies (see *pastries*); crumble, charlotte, compote, fool; fresh fruit, fruit salad; ice cream, sorbet, mousse, soufflé, sundae, trifle, blancmange, jelly, custard 392 *sweet thing*; cheese board (see *milk*).

sweets, boiled s., confectionery; candy, chocolate, caramel, toffee, Turkish delight, marshmallows, mints, liquorice; acid drops, barley sugar, humbugs, butterscotch, nougat; chewing gum, lollipop 392 *sweet thing*; sweetmeat, comfit, bonbon; toffee apple, candyfloss.

fruit, soft fruit, berry, gooseberry, strawberry, raspberry, loganberry, blackberry, bilberry, mulberry; currant, redcurrant, blackcurrant; stone fruit, apricot, peach, nectarine, plum, greengage, damson, cherry; apple, crab a., pippin, russet, pear; citrus fruit, orange, grapefruit, lemon, citron, lime, tangerine, clementine, mandarin; banana, pineapple, grape; rhubarb; date, fig; dried fruit, currant, raisin, sultana, prune; pomegranate, passion fruit, guava, lychee; mango, avocado; melon, water m., cantaloupe, honeydew; pawpaw, breadfruit; nut, coconut, Brazil nut, cashew n., pecan, peanut *or* groundnut *or* monkey nut; almond, walnut, chestnut, hazel nut, cob n., filbert.

vegetable, greens 366 *plant*; root, tuber, turnip, swede, parsnip, carrot, Jerusalem artichoke; spud, potato, sweet p., yam; French fries, chips; cabbage, savoy, cauliflower, broccoli, calabrese, kale, curly k., seakale; sprouts, Brussel s., spring greens; peas, beans, French b., broad b., runner b.; okra, sorrel, spinach, chard, asparagus, globe artichoke; leek, onion, shallots, garlic (see *potherb*); marrow, courgette, pumpkin, squash; aubergine *or* eggplant, pepper, chilli; sweetcorn; salads, lettuce, cos l., chicory, endive; spring onion, radish, celery, beetroot; tomato, love-apple; cucumber, beansprouts, bamboo shoots; cress, mustard and cress; pulses, lentils, split peas, chick p.; haricot beans, butter b., kidney b., soya b.; mushroom, boletus, truffle; laver, laverbread, samphire; pease pudding, baked beans, bubble and squeak.

potherb, herb, bouquet garni; marjoram, rosemary, sage, mint, parsley, chervil, chives, thyme, basil, savory, tarragon, bayleaf, dill, fennel; coriander, caraway; caper, gherkins; horseradish 389 *condiment*; hops.

cereals, grains, wheat, maize, corn; rice, millet, sorghum; cornflakes, muesli, oatmeal, porridge, gruel; flour, meal, wholemeal, wheat germ, bran; batter, dough; bread, crust, crumb; toast, rusk, croutons; loaf, roll, bridge r., bap, bun (see *pastries*); crumpet, muffin, scone, teacake, oatcake, bannock; pancake, popadum, chapatti, tortilla; waffle, wafer, crispbread, cracker.

pastries, confectionery; patty, pasty, turnover, dumpling; tart, flan, puff, pie, pie-crust; pastry, patisserie, gateau, cake; meringue, éclair, macaroon; bun, currant b., Chelsea b., Bath b., doughnut, gingerbread, shortbread, cookies, biscuits.

drinking, imbibing, imbibition; potation; wine-tasting; swilling, soaking 949 *drunkenness*; libation 981 *oblation*; drinker, bibber, swiller, quaffer; toper 949 *drunkard*.

draught, drink, beverage, dram, bevvy; gulp, sip, sup; cuppa, pinta; glassful, bumper 194 *cup*; swig, nip, noggin, jigger, tot, slug; peg, double peg, snorter, snifter, chaser; long drink, thirst-quencher; short, snort; sundowner, nightcap; loving cup, stirrup c., doch-an-doris, one for the road; health, toast; cocktail 43 *mixture*; potion 658 *medicine*.

soft drink, nonalcoholic beverage; water, soda water, soda; table water, mineral w., tonic w., barley w., squash; iced drink, frappé; ginger beer, ginger ale; fizz, pop, lemonade, orangeade; tea, herb t., tisane 658 *tonic*; coffee, Irish c., Turkish c., espresso; cocoa (see *milk*).

alcoholic drink, strong d., booze, bevvy, wallop, tipple, poison; brew, fermented liquor (see *wine*); alcohol, malt liquor, John Barleycorn; beer, draught beer, keg b.; stingo; ale, real ale; barley wine; stout, lager, bitter, porter, mild, home brew; shandy; cider, perry, mead; palm wine, rice beer, toddy, sake; mescal, tequila; distilled liquor, spirituous l., spirits, aqua vitae, firewater, hooch, moonshine, mountain dew, rotgut, hard stuff; brandy, cognac, eau-de-vie; gin, schnapps, blue ruin; whisky, usquebaugh, Scotch whisky, Scotch; rye, bourbon; Irish whiskey, poteen; vodka, aquavit, ouzo, raki, arrack; rum, grog, hot g., punch, rum p.; egg flip, egg nog; cordial, spiced wine, mulled w., negus, posset, hippocras; cup, claret c.; pink gin, highball, brandy and soda; mint julep; cocktail; aperitif, liqueur.

wine, the grape; red wine, white w., rosé; vermouth; spumante, sparkling wine; sweet w., dry w., vintage w.; vin ordinaire, vino, plonk; table wine, dessert w.; fortified w., sack, sherry, port, Madeira; champagne, fizz, bubbly; claret, hock, riesling; retsina, Chianti.

milk, cream; beestings; koumiss; mother's milk, breast m.; buttermilk, skimmed m.; milk shake, malted milk, cocoa, chocolate; whey, curds, junket; dairy product, yoghurt, cheese.

Adj. *feeding*, eating, grazing etc. vb.; flesh-eating, meat-e.; carnivorous, creophagous, cannibalistic; insectivorous; herbivorous, graminivorous, frugivorous; vegetarian, vegan; omnivorous; greedy, wolfish 947 *gluttonous*; teetotal 942 *temperate*; tippling 949 *drunken*; well-fed, well-nourished; nursed, breast-fed; full up 863 *sated*.

edible, eatable; ritually pure, kosher; esculent, comestible; digestible, predigested; potable, drinkable; milky, lactic; palatable, succulent 386 *tasty*, 390 *savoury*; cereal, wheaten; fermented, distilled, spirituous, alcoholic, hard 949 *intoxicating*; nonalcoholic, soft.

nourishing, feeding, sustaining, nutritious, nutritive, nutritional; alimental, alimentary; dietary, dietetic; fattening, rich, calorific, high in calories; bodybuilding; wholesome 652 *salubrious*.

culinary, dressed, oven-ready, ready-to-serve; cooked, done to a turn, well-done; al dente; underdone, red, rare, raw; over-cooked, burnt to a cinder; roasted etc. vb. (see *cook*); gastronomic, epicurean; prandial, post-p., after-dinner; meal-time.

Vb. *eat*, feed, fare, board, mess; partake 386 *taste*; break bread; breakfast, lunch, have tea, dine, sup; dine out, feast, banquet, carouse 837 *revel*; eat well, have a good appetite, do justice to; water at the mouth, drool, raven 859 *be hungry*; fall to, set to, tuck in; fork in, spoon in, shovel in; stuff oneself 863 *sate*; guzzle, gormandize 947 *gluttonize*; put on weight 197 *expand*; swallow, gulp down, snap up, devour, dispatch, bolt, wolf, make short work of; feed on, live on, fatten on, batten on, prey on; nibble, peck, lick; play with one's food, nibble at, peck at; ingest, digest 299 *absorb*.

chew, masticate, manducate, champ, chomp, munch, crunch, scrunch; worry, gnaw 332 *pulverize*; bite, tear, chew up 46 *cut*.

graze, browse, pasture, crop, feed; ruminate, chew the cud.

drink, imbibe, suck 299 *absorb*; quaff, drink up, drink like a fish, slake one's thirst, lap, sip; wet one's lips *or* one's whistle; draw the cork, crack a bottle; lap up, soak up, wash down; swill, tipple 949 *get drunk*; toss off one's glass, drain one's g., knock it back; raise one's glass, pledge 876 *toast*; give to drink, wine, water.

feed, nourish, nurture, sustain, board; victual, cater, purvey 633 *provide*; nurse, breast-feed, give suck; pasture, graze, put out to grass; fatten, fatten up 197 *enlarge*; dine, wine and dine, feast, banquet, regale with 882 *be hospitable*.

cook, bake, brown; roast, spit-roast, pot-r., braise; broil, grill, barbecue, spatchcock, griddle, devil, curry; sauté, fry; scramble, poach; boil, parboil; coddle, seethe, simmer, steam; casserole, stew; baste, lard, bard; whip, whisk, beat, blend, liquidize, stir; stuff, dress, garnish; dice, shred, mince, grate; sauce, flavour, spice 388 *season*.

Int. bon appétit! here's health! here's mud in your eye! bottoms up! down the hatch! slà inte! prosit! skol! cheers!

302. Excretion – N. *excretion*, secretion, discharge 300 *ejection*; effusion, extravasation; emanation 298 *egress*; exhalation 352 *respiration*; exudation, perspiration 298 *outflow*; suppuration 651 *infection*; catarrh, hay fever; salivation, expectoration, spitting; coughing, cough; urination, micturition; waterworks; enuresis, incontinence.

haemorrhage, bleeding, extravasation, haemophilia 335 *blood*; menses, catamenia, period, the curse; dysmenorrhoea; leucorrhoea.

defecation, evacuation, elimination, clearance 300 *voidance*; bowel movement,

motion; one's natural functions; diarrhoea, constipation 651 *digestive disorders*.

excrement, waste matter; faeces, stool, excreta, ordure, night soil; coprolite; dung, cowpat, manure, muck; droppings, guano; pee, piss, urine, water; sweat, beads of s., lather; spittle, spit, sputum; saliva, slaver, slobber; phlegm, catarrh, mucus, snot; matter, pus; afterbirth, lochia; slough, cast, exuviae, pellet 649 *dirt*.

Adj. *excretory*, secretory; purgative, laxative, aperient; excretive, diuretic; menstrual; diaphoretic, sudorific; perspiratory; faecal, anal, urinary; rheumy, watery; mucous, phlegmy; castoff, exuvial.

Vb. *excrete*, secrete; pass, move; move one's bowels, defecate; be taken short, have the runs; relieve oneself, ease o., answer the call of nature, go to the lavatory; urinate, micturate, piddle, pee, piss; make water, spend a penny; sweat, perspire, steam, glow 379 *be hot*; salivate, slobber, snivel; cough, spit 300 *eruct*; weep 298 *exude*; foam at the mouth; cast, slough, shed one's skin 229 *doff*.

303. Insertion – N. *insertion*, introduction, insinuation 297 *ingress*; infixation, impaction; submersion 313 *plunge*; inoculation, injection 263 *perforation*; infusion, enema; insert, inset; stuffing 227 *lining*; parenthesis 231 *interjection*.

Adj. *inserted*, introduced etc. vb.; added 38 *additional*; intermediate 231 *interjacent*.

Vb. *insert*, introduce; weave into 222 *enlace*; put into, thrust i., intrude; poke into, stick i. 263 *pierce*; ram into, jam i., stuff i., push i., shove i., tuck i., press i., pop i. 193 *load*; pocket 187 *stow*; ease in, slide in; knock in 279 *impel*; inlay, inset 227 *line*; mount, frame 232 *circumscribe*; interpose 231 *put between*; drop in, put in 311 *let fall*; putt, hole out; pot, hole; bury 364 *inter*; sheathe, encase 226 *cover*; immerse, dip 311 *lower*.

infuse, drop in, instil, pour in 43 *mix*; imbue, impregnate 297 *infiltrate*; transfuse

272 *transpose*; squirt in, inject 263 *pierce*.

implant, plant, transplant; graft, engraft, bud; inoculate, vaccinate; embed, bury; wedge in, impact 45 *join*.

304. Extraction – N. *extraction*, withdrawal, removal 188 *displacement*; elimination, eradication 300 *ejection*; extirpation 165 *destruction*; extrication, disengagement, liberation 668 *deliverance*; evulsion, tearing out, ripping o.; cutting out, excision; Caesarian birth, forceps delivery; expression, squeezing out; suction, sucking out, aspiration; vacuuming, pumping; drawing out, pull, tug, wrench 288 *traction*; digging out 255 *excavation*; mining, quarrying; distillation 338 *vaporization*; drawing off, tapping, milking; thing extracted, essence, extract.

extractor, gouger; miner, quarrier; forceps, tweezers 778 *nippers*; mangle 342 *drier*; corkscrew, screwdriver 263 *opener*; lever 218 *pivot*; scoop, spoon, shovel; pick, pickaxe; toothpick; vacuum cleaner; excavator, dredge, dredger, dragline; syringe, siphon; aspirator, suction pump; Archimedes' screw, irrigator.

Adj. *extracted*, removed etc. vb.; extractive.

Vb. *extract*, remove, pull 288 *draw*; draw out, elicit, educe; pull out, take o., get o., pluck; withdraw, excise, cut out, rip o., tear o., whip o.; excavate, mine, quarry, dig out, unearth; dredge, dredge up; expel, lever out, winkle o., smoke o. 300 *eject*; extort, wring from; express, press out, squeeze o., gouge o.; force out, wring o., wrench o., drag o.; draw off, milk, tap; siphon off, aspirate, suck, void, pump; pull up, dig up, grub up, rake up; eliminate, weed out, root up, uproot, pluck up by the roots, eradicate, deracinate, extirpate 165 *destroy*; distil 338 *vaporize*; extricate, unravel, free 746 *liberate*; eviscerate, gut 300 *empty*; unwrap 229 *uncover*; pick out 605 *select*.

305. Passage: motion through – N. *passage*, transmission 272 *transference*; transportation 272 *transport*; passing through, traversing; transit, traverse, crossing, journey, patrol 267 *land travel*; penetration, infiltration; right of way 624 *access*; track, route, orbit 624 *path*; intersection, interchange 222 *crossing*; waterway, channel 351 *conduit*.

passing along, passage, thoroughfare; traffic, traffic movement, circulation; traffic load, traffic density; traffic jam, procession, queue; road user 268 *pedestrian, driver*; passerby.

traffic control, traffic engineering; traffic rules, highway code, Green Cross C. 693 *precept*; traffic lane, bus l., cycle l., dual carriageway, clearway 624 *road*; diversion 282 *deviation*; white lines, yellow l., cat's-eyes, sleeping policemen; street furniture, traffic lights, lampposts; roundabout; pedestrian crossing, zebra c., pelican c.; Belisha beacon, bollard, refuge, island; car park, parking meter, lay-by; point duty, road patrol, speed trap; traffic warden, lollipop man *or* lady.

Vb. *pass*, pass by, leave on one side, skirt, coast 200 *be near*; flash by 277 *move fast*, 114 *be transient*; go past 146 *go on*, 265 *be in motion*; pass along, circulate, weave; pass through 298 *emerge*; transit, traverse; shoot through 269 *navigate*; percolate, permeate 189 *pervade*; pass and repass, patrol, work over, beat, scour, go over the ground; pass into, penetrate 297 *enter*; bore 263 *pierce*; thread 45 *connect*; enfilade, rake; open a way, force a passage 297 *burst in*; squeeze through 285 *progress*; cross, go across, cross over, make a crossing; wade across, ford; get through, get past, negotiate; pass beyond 306 *overstep*; repass 286 *turn back*; pass in front 702 *obstruct*; transmit 272 *send*.

Adv. *en passant*, by the way; on the way, in transit.

306. Overstepping: motion beyond – N. *overstepping*, going beyond 305 *passage*; transcendence 34 *superiority*; excursion, digression 282 *deviation*; trespass 936 *guilty act*; encroachment, infringement; expansionism; overextension, ribbon development 197 *expansion*; overfulfilment 637 *redundance*.

Adj. *surpassing*, transcending etc. vb.; one up on 34 *superior*; overextended, overlong, overhigh; excessive 32 *exorbitant*; out of bounds, out of reach.

Vb. *overstep*, overpass; pass, leave behind; go beyond, go too far, throw out the baby with the bathwater; exceed, overrun, override, overshoot, overshoot the mark, aim too high; overlap 226 *overlie*; surmount, step over, cross 305 *pass*; cross the Rubicon, pass the point of no return; overgrow 637 *superabound*; overdo 546 *exaggerate*.

encroach, invade, make inroads on; infringe, trespass 954 *be illegal*; poach 788 *steal*; squat, usurp 786 *appropriate*; overlap, impinge, trench on; entrench upon; infest, overrun 297 *burst in*; overflow, flood.

outdo, exceed, surpass, outclass; transcend, rise above, soar a., outrange, outrival 34 *be superior*; go one better, overcall, overbid, outbid; overreach, outmanoeuvre, outflank, steal a march on; outpace 277 *move fast*; outwalk, outmarch, outrun, outride, outjump, outsail, outdistance, distance; overhaul, gain upon, overtake, shoot ahead; lap, leave standing 277 *outstrip*; leave behind, race.

307. Shortfall – N. *shortfall,* falling short etc. vb.; inadequacy 636 *insufficiency*; minus, deficit, short measure, shortage, loss 42 *decrement*; unfinished state 55 *incompleteness*; nonfulfilment, default 726 *noncompletion*; half measures 641 *lost labour*; no go 728 *failure*; fault, defect, shortcoming 647 *imperfection*; something missing, want, lack, need 627 *requirement*.

Adj. *deficient*, short, short of, minus, wanting, lacking, missing; catalectic; underpowered, substandard; undermanned, understaffed, below establishment; half-done, perfunctory 55 *incomplete*; out of one's depth, not up to scratch, inadequate 636 *insufficient*; failing, running short 636 *scarce*; below par 647 *imperfect*; unattained, unreached.

Vb. *fall short*, come s., run s. 636 *not suffice*; not stretch, not reach to; lack, want, be without 627 *require*; underachieve, not make the grade, not come up to scratch; miss, miss the mark; stop short, fall by the way, not stay the course; break down, get bogged down; fall behind, lose ground, slip back 286 *regress*; fall through, fizzle out 728 *miscarry*; labour in vain 641 *waste effort*; not come up to expectations 509 *disappoint*.

Adv. *behindhand*, in arrears; not enough; below the mark, far from it; to no purpose, in vain.

308. Ascent: motion upwards – N. *ascent*, ascension, lift, upward motion, gaining height; levitation; takeoff, lift-off 296 *departure*; flying up, soaring, spiral; zoom 271 *aeronautics*; culmination 213 *summit*; surfacing, breaking surface; going up, rising; rise, upgrowth, upturn; uprush, upsurge 36 *increase*; updraught, thermal; sunrise 128 *morning*; hill-climbing, mountaineering, alpinism; escalade 712 *attack*; jump, vault, pole v. 312 *leap*; bounce 280 *recoil*; rising ground 209 *high land*; gradient, slope, ramp 220 *incline*; stairs, steps, stile, flight of stairs, staircase; ladder, step-l., accommodation l., companionway; rope ladder, ratlines; stair, step, tread, rung; lift, ski l., escalator 310 *lifter*.

climber, mountaineer, alpinist, cragsman *or* -woman, fell walker; steeplejack; rocket, lark, skylark; gusher, geyser, fountain 350 *stream*.

Adj. *ascending*, rising etc. vb.; climbing, scansorial; rearing, rampant; buoyant, floating 323 *light*; supernatant; airborne, gaining height; anabatic, in the ascendant; uphill 215 *vertical*; ladderlike, scalariform; scalable, climbable.

Vb. *ascend*, rise, rise up, go up, leave the ground; defy gravity, levitate; take off, become airborne 271 *fly*; gain height, mount, soar, spiral, zoom, climb; reach the zenith, culminate; float up, bob up, surface, break water; jump up, spring, vault 312 *leap*; bounce 280 *recoil*; push up, shoot up 36 *grow*; tower, aspire, spire 209 *be high*; gush, spout, jet, play 298 *flow out*; get up, stand up, rear up, ramp 215 *be* *vertical*; rise to one's feet, get up; wind upwards 220 *be oblique*.

climb, walk up, struggle up; mount, make *or* work one's way up; go climbing, mountaineer; clamber, scramble, swarm up, shin up, go up hand over fist; surmount, top, breast, scale 209 *be high*; go over the top, escalade 712 *attack*.

Adv. *up*, uphill, upstairs; upwards 209 *aloft*; excelsior, ever higher; per ardua ad astra.

309. Descent – N. *descent*, declination 282 *deviation*; falling, dropping; cadence; landing; downward trend, spiral, decline, drop, slump 37 *decrease*; sunset, moonset; comedown, demotion 286 *regression*; downfall, debacle, collapse 165 *ruin*; trip, stumble; lurch, capsize 221 *overturning*; tumble, crash, spill, fall; cropper, purler; downrush, swoop, stoop, pounce; dive, header, bellyflop 313 *plunge*; nosedive, power-dive; landing, splashdown 295 *arrival*; sliding down, glissade; subsidence, landslide, avalanche; downdraught 352 *wind*; downpour, shower 350 *rain*; cascade 350 *waterfall*; tilt, dip 220 *incline*; chute, slide, helter-skelter; precipice, sheer drop 215 *verticality*; submergence, sinkage, slippage 311 *lowering*; speleology, pot-holing, caving; plunger 313 *diver*; miner, sapper 255 *excavator*; parachutist, paratrooper; speleologist, pot-holer, caver.

Adj. *descending*, dropping etc. vb.; descendent, declining, declivitous 220 *sloping*; swooping, stooping; tumbledown, falling, tottering; tilting, sinking, foundering; drooping 311 *lowered*; submersible, sinkable.

Vb. *descend*, come down, go d., dip d.; decline, abate, ebb 37 *decrease*; slump, fall, drop, sink; soak in, seep down 297 *infiltrate*; reach the depths, touch bottom 210 *be low*; gravitate, precipitate, settle; fall down, fall in, cave in, collapse; sink in, subside, slip, give way; hang down, droop, sag, swag 217 *hang*; submerge 313 *plunge*; go underground, dig down, tunnel, mine 255 *make concave*; swoop, stoop, pounce; fly down, flutter d., float d.; lose height,

drop down, swing low; touch down, alight, light, perch 295 *land*; lower oneself, abseil; get down, climb d., step d., get off, fall o., dismount; coast down, slide down, glissade, toboggan; shower, cascade 350 *rain*; come down a peg 286 *regress*; duck 311 *stoop*; flop, plop, splash down.

tumble, fall; topple, topple over, overbalance 221 *be inverted*; miss one's footing, slip, slip up, trip, stumble; lose one's balance, titubate, stagger, totter, lurch, tilt, droop 220 *be oblique*; rise and fall, pitch, toss, roll; take a header, dive 313 *plunge*; precipitate oneself 312 *leap*; take a fall, come a cropper, crash to the ground, fall flat on one's face, bite the dust, measure one's length; plop, plump, plump down, slump, sprawl; nosedive, crash.

Adv. *down*, downwards; downhill, downstairs, downstream.

310. Elevation – N. *elevation*, raising etc. vb.; erection, uplift, upheaval; lift, hoist, boost; leg-up 703 *aid*; exaltation, Assumption; uptrend, upswing 308 *ascent*; eminence 209 *high land*, 254 *prominence*; height above sea level 209 *height*.

lifter, erector, builder; raising agent, yeast 323 *leaven*; lever, jack 218 *pivot*; dredger 304 *extractor*; crane, derrick, hoist, windlass; winch, capstan; rope and pulley, block and tackle; forklift, elevator, dumb waiter, escalator, lift, ski l.; cable railway; hot air, hydrogen, helium; spring, springboard, trampoline; stilts; scaffolding, platform 218 *stand*.

Adj. *elevated*, raised etc. vb.; exalted, uplifted; erectile, erective; erected, set up; upright, erect 215 *vertical*; mounted, on high; towering over, head and shoulders above 209 *high*.

Vb. *elevate*, heighten, make higher; puff up, blow up, swell, leaven 197 *enlarge*; raise, erect, set up, put up, run up, rear up, build; lift, lift up, raise up, heave up; uplift, upraise; jack up, prop 218 *support*; stand on end 215 *make vertical*; hold up, bear up; buoy up; raise aloft, hold a.; hoist, haul up, pick up, take up; pull up, wind up; weigh, trip (anchor); fish up, drag up 304 *extract*; chair, shoulder, exalt, put on a pedestal 866 *honour*; put on top, mount 213 *crown*; give a leg-up; throw up, toss up; sky, loft; lob 287 *propel*; perk up (one's head), prick up (one's ears); bristle 215 *be vertical*.

Adv. *on*, on stilts, on tiptoe; on one's hind legs.

311. Lowering – N. *lowering*, depression, pushing down 279 *impulse*; ducking, sousing 313 *plunge*; overthrow, upset 221 *overturning*; keeping under, suppression; dent, dip 255 *cavity*; low pressure 340 *weather*.

Adj. *lowered*, depressed etc. vb.; at a low ebb 210 *low*; prostrate 216 *supine*; sedentary, sitting, sit-down; depressive, depressing; submersible.

Vb. *lower*, depress, push down, thrust d. 279 *impel*; shut down (a lid) 264 *close*; hold down, keep d., hold under 165 *suppress*; lower, let down, take d.; lower a flag, dip, half-mast, haul down, strike; deflate, puncture, flatten 198 *make smaller*; sink, scuttle, send to the bottom; duck, dip 313 *plunge*; weigh on, press on 322 *weigh*; capsize, roll over, tip, tilt 221 *invert*; crush, stave in, dent 255 *make concave*.

let fall, drop, shed; let go 779 *not retain*; let slip *or* slide through one's fingers; pour, decant 300 *empty*; spill, slop 341 *moisten*; sprinkle, shower, scatter, dust, dredge; sow, broadcast 75 *disperse*; lay down, put d., set d., throw down, fling d. (see *fell*); pitch *or* chuck overboard.

fell, trip, topple, tumble; prostrate, spread-eagle, lay low 216 *flatten*; knock down, bowl over, skittle, floor, overthrow; drop, down 279 *impel*; pull down, tear d., dash d., raze, level, pull about one's ears 165 *demolish*; hew down, cut d., axe 46 *cut*; blow down 352 *blow*; bring down, undermine; shoot down, wing 287 *shoot*.

sit down, sit, be seated, squat; subside, sink, lower oneself; kneel, recline, stretch oneself out 216 *be horizontal*; roost, nest 683 *repose*; take a seat, seat oneself, park oneself, perch.

stoop, bend, bend down, lean over; cringe, crouch, cower 721 *knuckle under*; slouch 248 *make curved*; bow, curtsy 884 *pay one's respects*; nod, incline one's head show respect.

312. Leap – N. *leap*, saltation, skipping, capering, leap-frogging; jump, hop, skip; spring, bound, vault; high jump, long j., running j.; triple j., hop, skip and a jump; caper, gambol, frolic; kick, high k.; prance, curvet, caracole, capriole, gambade; springy step, light tread 265 *gait*; dance step; dance, reel, jig 837 *dancing*.

jumper, high-j., pole-vaulter, hurdler, steeplechaser; skipper, hopper, leapfrogger; caperer, prancer; dancer, jiver; twister, rock 'n' roller 837 *dance*; tap dancer, clog d., morris d.; dancing girl 594 *entertainer*; kangaroo, goat, chamois, jerboa, frog, grasshopper, froghopper, flea; bucking bronco; jumping bean; jumping jack, Jack-in-the-box 837 *plaything*.

Adj. *leaping*, jumping etc. vb.; saltatory, saltatorial; skittish, frisky 819 *lively*; skipping, hopping; dancing, jiving; bobbing, bucking, bouncing; tossing 318 *agitated*.

Vb. *leap*, jump, take a running j.; spring, bound, vault, pole-v., hurdle, steeplechase, take one's fences; skip, hop, leapfrog, bob, bounce, rebound, buck, bob up and down 317 *oscillate*; trip, foot it, tread a measure 837 *dance*; caper, cut capers, gambol, frisk, romp; prance, paw the ground, ramp, rear, plunge; cavort, curvet, caracole; start, give a jump; jump on, pounce; leap up, spring up 308 *ascend*; jump over, clear; flounce, jerk 318 *be agitated*; writhe 251 *wriggle*.

313. Plunge – N. *plunge*, swoop, pounce, stoop 309 *descent*; nosedive 271 *aeronautics*; dive, header, bellyflop; swallow dive, duck d.; dip, ducking; immersion, submergence; drowning, sinking.

diver, skin d., scuba d., deepsea d., frogman *or* -woman, underwater swimmer, aquanaut; diving bird, dipper 365 *bird*; submariner; submarine, bathysphere, diving-bell; plunger, sinker, lead, plummet; fathometer 465 *meter*.

Vb. *plunge*, dip, duck 341 *be wet*; walk the plank, fall in, jump in, plump, plop; dive, take a header, go headfirst; welter, wallow, pitch and toss; souse, douse, immerse, drown; submerge, flood the tanks 309 *descend*; sink, scuttle, send to the bottom 311 *lower*; sound, fathom, plumb the depths 465 *measure*.

founder, go down 309 *descend*; drown, go to the bottom 211 *be deep*; plummet, sink, sink like a stone.

314. Circuition: curvilinear motion – N.
circuition, circulation, circumambulation, circumnavigation, circling, wheeling, gyre, spiral 315 *rotation*; turning, cornering, turn, U-turn; orbit; lap; circuit, tour, round trip, full circle; figure of eight 250 *circle*; helix 251 *coil*; unwinding 316 *evolution*; circuitousness 626 *circuit*.

circler, circumambulator; circumnavigator 270 *mariner*; roundsman *or* -woman 794 *tradespeople*; patrol, patrolman *or* -woman; moon, satellite 321 *planet*.

Adj. *circuitous*, turning etc. vb.; orbital, ecliptic; geostationary; circumnavigable; devious, roundabout.

Vb. *circle*, circulate, go the rounds; compass, circuit, make a c., lap; tour, do the round trip; go round, skirt; circumambulate, circumnavigate, circumaviate; turn, round, double a point; round a corner, corner, turn a c.; revolve, orbit; wheel, come full circle 315 *rotate*; put about, wheel a., face a., turn on one's heel 286 *turn back*; describe a circle 232 *circumscribe*; curve, wind one's way 251 *meander*; make a detour 626 *circuit*.

315. Rotation: motion in a continued circle
– N. *rotation*, orbital motion; revolution, full circle; gyration, circling, spiralling; circulation, circumfluence; spin, circumvolution; volution, spiral, roll, spin; turn, twirl, pirouette, waltz 837 *dance*; whirl, whirr; dizzy round, rat race 678 *overactivity*; dizziness, vertigo; gyrostatics.

vortex, whirl; whirlwind, tornado, cyc-

lone 352 *gale*; waterspout, whirlpool, swirl, eddy; maelstrom, Charybdis.

rotator, rotor, spinner; whirligig, teetotum, top, spinning t.; roundabout, merry-go-round; churn, whisk; potter's wheel, lathe, circular saw; wheel, spinning w.; girandole, catherine wheel; flywheel, prayer w., wheel of Fortune; gyroscope, turntable; record, disc; windmill, fan, sail; propeller, prop, screw; turbine; winder, capstan 310 *lifter*; swivel, hinge; spit, jack; spindle, shaft 218 *pivot*; spool, reel, roller 252 *cylinder*; rolling stone, planet, satellite 268 *wanderer*; whirling dervish; dancer, figure skater; Ixion.

Adj. *rotary*, rotating, spinning etc. vb.; rotatory, circumrotatory; gyratory, gyroscopic; circling, cyclic; vortical, vorticose; cyclonic; vertiginous, dizzy.

Vb. *rotate*, revolve, orbit 314 *circle*; turn right round, chase one's own tail; spin, twirl, pirouette; corkscrew 251 *twine*; gyre, gyrate, waltz, wheel, whirl; swirl, eddy 350 *flow*; bowl, trundle; roll, roll along; twirl, twiddle; churn, whisk 43 *mix*; turn, crank, wind, reel, spool, spin; slew round, swing round, swivel r.; roll up, furl 261 *fold*; roll itself up, curl up, scroll.

316. Evolution: motion in a reverse circle –
N. *evolution*, unrolling, unfolding, unfurling; eversion 221 *inversion*; development 157 *growth*.

Adj. *evolving*, unwinding etc. vb., evolved etc. vb.; evolutional.

Vb. *evolve*, unfold, unfurl, unroll, unwind, uncoil, uncurl, untwist, untwine, explicate, disentangle 62 *unravel*; evolute, develop, grow into 147 *be turned to*; roll back 263 *open*.

317. Oscillation: reciprocating motion – N.
oscillation, harmonic motion, swing of the pendulum; libration, nutation; vibration, tremor; vibrancy, resonance 141 *periodicity*; pulsation, rhythm; pulse, beat, throb; pitter-patter, flutter, palpitation 318 *agitation*; breathing 352 *respiration*; undulation, wave motion, frequency, wavelength 417 *radiation*; sound wave, radio w.; tidal

w. 350 *wave*; earthquake, tremor 176 *violence*; seismology, seismograph; oscillator, vibrator; pendulum, bob, yoyo 217 *hanging object*.

fluctuation, alternation, reciprocation 12 *correlation*; to and fro movement, coming and going, shuttle service; ups and downs, boom and bust, ebb and flow, flux and reflux, systole and diastole; night and day 14 *contrariety*; roll, pitch, lurch, stagger, reel; shake, nod, wag, dance; springboard 328 *elasticity*; swing, seesaw; rocker, rocking chair, rocking horse; shuttlecock, shuttle.

Adj. *oscillating*, undulating etc. vb.; oscillatory, undulatory; swaying, libratory; pulsatory, palpitating; vibrant, vibratory, vibratile; earth-shaking, seismic; pendulous, dangling; reeling, staggery, groggy; rhythmic, rhythmical 141 *periodical*.

Vb. *oscillate*, librate, nutate; emit waves 417 *radiate*; wave, undulate; vibrate, pulsate, pulse, beat, drum; tick, throb, palpitate; pant, heave 352 *breathe*; play, sway, nod; swing, dangle 217 *hang*; seesaw, rock; hunt (trains), lurch, reel, stagger, totter, wobble, wiggle, waggle, wag; bob, bounce, bob up and down, dance 312 *leap*; toss, roll, pitch, tumble, wallow; rattle, chatter, shake; flutter, quiver, shiver 318 *be agitated*; flicker 417 *shine*; echo 404 *resound*; fluctuate, ebb and flow; shuttle; slosh about, slop a.

brandish, wave, wag, waggle, shake, flourish; shake up and down, pump 318 *agitate*.

Adv. *to and fro*, backwards and forwards, back and forth; zigzag, seesaw, like a yoyo; shuttlewise.

318. Agitation: irregular motion – **N.** *agitation*, irregular motion, jerkiness, fits and starts 152 *changeableness*; joltiness, bumpiness, broken water, choppiness 259 *roughness*; flicker, twinkle 417 *flash*; start, jump 508 *lack of expectation*; hop 312 *leap*; shake, jig, jiggle; shock, jar, jolt, jerk, judder, jounce, bounce, bump 279 *impulse*; nudge, dig, jog 547 *gesture*; vibration, thrill, throb, pulse, pit-a-pat,

palpitation, flutter 317 *oscillation*; shudder, shiver, frisson; quiver, quaver, tremor; tremulousness, trembling (**see** *spasm*); restlessness, feverishness, fever; tossing, turning; jiving, rock 'n' roll 678 *activity*, 837 *dancing*; itch 378 *formication*; twitch, grimace; perturbation, disquiet 825 *worry*; trepidation, jumpiness, twitter, flap, butterflies 854 *nervousness*; the shakes, shivers, jumps, jitters, fidgets; aspen leaf.

spasm, ague, shivering, chattering; twitch, tic, nervous t.; chorea, St Vitus's dance; lockjaw, tetanus; cramp, throe 377 *pang*; convulsion, paroxysm, access, orgasm 503 *frenzy*; fit 651 *nervous disorders*; pulse, throb 317 *oscillation*; attack, seizure, stroke.

commotion, turbulence, tumult 61 *turmoil*; hurly-burly, hubbub, brouhaha; fever, flurry, rush, bustle 680 *haste*; furore 503 *frenzy*; fuss, bother, kerfuffle 678 *restlessness*; racket, din 400 *loudness*; stir, ferment 821 *excitation*; effervescence 355 *bubble*; ground swell, heavy sea; squall, tempest 176 *storm*; whirlpool 315 *vortex*; disturbance, atmospherics.

Adj. *agitated*, shaken, fluttering, waving, brandished; shaking etc. vb.; troubled, unquiet 678 *active*; feverish, fevered, restless; scratchy, jittery, jumpy, twitchy, flustered, in a flap, in a flutter 854 *nervous*; hopping, leaping, like a cat on hot bricks; breathless, panting; twitching, itchy; convulsive, spasmodic, spastic; saltatory; skittish 819 *lively*; doddering, shaky, wavery, tremulous; thrilling, vibrating 317 *oscillating*.

Vb. *be agitated*, ripple, popple, boil 355 *bubble*; shake, tremble, quiver, quaver, shiver; throw a fit; writhe, squirm, twitch 251 *wriggle*; toss, turn, toss about, thresh a.; plunge, rear 176 *be violent*; flounder, flop; sway, reel, fluctuate; pulse, beat, thrill, vibrate, judder, shudder; dodder, teeter, dither 317 *oscillate*; whirr, whirl 315 *rotate*; jig around, jump about, hop, bob, bounce, dance 312 *leap*; flicker, twinkle, gutter, sputter 417 *shine*; effervesce, froth, foam 355 *bubble*; flap, flutter, twitter, start, jump; throb, pant, palpitate, go pit-a-pat 821 *be excited*; bustle, mill around 61 *rampage*; ramp, roar 891 *be angry*.

agitate, disturb, rumple, ruffle 63 *derange*; discompose, perturb 827 *trouble*;

ripple, puddle, muddy; stir, stir up 43 *mix*; whisk, whip 315 *rotate*; shake; wag, waggle, wave, flourish 317 *brandish*; jog, joggle, jiggle, jolt, jounce, nudge, dig; jerk, pluck, twitch.

Class Three

MATTER

Section 1: Matter in general

319. Materiality – N. *materiality*, material-ness, empirical world, world of experience; corporeity, corporeality; material existence, world of nature 3 *substantiality*; physical being 1 *existence*; concreteness, solidity 324 *density*; weight 322 *gravity*; personality 80 *speciality*; embodiment, incarnation, reincarnation, metempsychosis; realization, materialization; positivism, materialism, dialectical m.; materialist, realist, positivist.

matter, brute m., stuff; plenum; hyle, prime matter; mass, material, fabric, body, frame 331 *structure*; substance, solid s., corpus; organic matter, flesh, flesh and blood, protoplasm 358 *organism*; real world, world of nature, Nature.

object, tangible o.; inanimate object, still life; physical presence, body 371 *person*; thing, gadget, something, commodity, article, item; stocks and stones 359 *mineral*.

element, elementary unit, sense datum; principle, first p. 68 *origin*; earth, air, fire, water; unit of being, monad; factor, ingredient 58 *component*; isotope; atom, molecule; elementary particle, electron, neutron, meson, proton, quark 196 *minuteness*; nucleus, nucleon; photon; quantum; ion.

physics, physical science, natural s.; chemistry, organic c., inorganic c., physical c.; mechanics, Newtonian m., quantum m., theory of relativity; thermodynamics; electromagnetism; atomic physics, nuclear physics 160 *nucleonics*; applied physics, technology 694 *skill*; natural philosophy, experimental p. 490 *science*; chemist, physicist, scientist.

Adj. *material*, hylic; real, natural; massy, solid, concrete, palpable, tangible, ponderable, sensible, weighty; physical, spatiotemporal; hypostatic 3 *substantial*; incarnate, embodied; corporal, somatic, corporeal, bodily, fleshly, of flesh and blood, carnal; reincarnated, realized, materialized; materialistic, worldly 944 *sensual*.

Vb. *materialize*, substantialize, hypostatize, corporealize, reify; objectify 223 *externalize*; realize, make real, body forth; embody, incarnate, personify.

320. Immateriality – N. *immateriality*, unreality 4 *insubstantiality*; incorporeity, incorporeality, dematerialization, disembodiment, imponderability, intangibility, ghostliness, shadowiness; immaterialism, idealism, Platonism; spirituality, otherworldliness; animism; spiritualism 984 *occultism*; other world, world of spirits; animist, spiritualist 984 *occultist*; idealist.

subjectivity, personality, selfhood, myself, me, yours truly 80 *self*; ego, id, superego; Conscious, Unconscious; psyche.

Adj. *immaterial*, without mass; incorporeal; abstract 447 *mental*; airy, aery, ghostly, shadowy 4 *insubstantial*; imponderable, intangible; bodiless, unembodied, discarnate, disembodied; supernal, extramundane, unearthly, transcendent; supersensory, psychic 984 *psychical*; spiritual, otherworldly 973 *religious*; personal, subjective; illusory 513 *imaginary*.

Vb. *disembody*, spiritualize, dematerialize, disincarnate.

321. Universe – N. *universe*, omneity 52 *whole*; world, creation; sum of things, plenum, matter and antimatter 319 *matter*; cosmos, macrocosm, microcosm; space-time continuum; expanding universe, metagalaxy; outer space, deep s., intergalactic s.; void; cosmogony, nebular hypothesis, planetesimal h.; big bang theory, steady state t.

world, wide w., four corners of the earth; sublunary sphere; earth, mother e., Gaia; middle earth, planet e., spaceship e.; globe, sphere, terrestrial s., terraqueous globe, geoid; geosphere, biosphere; crust; subcrust, moho; plate tectonics, continental drift 344 *land*; waters of the earth 343 *ocean*; atlas 551 *map*; Old World, New World 184 *region*; geocentric system, Ptolemaic s.; personal world 8 *circumstance*.

heavens, sky, welkin, empyrean, ether, ethereal sphere, celestial s.; firmament, vault of heaven; primum mobile, music of the spheres; night sky; aurora borealis 417 *glow*.

star, heavenly body 420 *luminary*; sidereal sphere, starry host; asterism, constellation, starlight, starshine; double star, binary; variable, cepheid; giant, supergiant, red giant; dwarf, red d., white d.; X-ray star, radio s. 417 *radiation*; quasi-stellar object, quasar, pulsar, neutron star, black hole; nova, supernova; pole star, Polaris; Milky Way; star cluster; galaxy, island universe; nebula, protogalaxy, protostar; cosmic dust, interstellar matter.

zodiac, signs of the z., Aries (the Ram), Taurus (the Bull), Gemini (the Twins), Cancer (the Crab), Leo (the Lion), Virgo (the Virgin), Libra (the Balance), Scorpio (the Scorpion), Sagittarius (the Archer), Capricorn (the Goat), Aquarius (the Watercarrier), Pisces (the Fishes); ecliptic; house, mansion, lunar m.

planet, major p., minor p., inferior p., superior p.; asteroid, planetoid; Mercury; Venus, morning star, evening s., Lucifer; Mars, red planet; Earth, Jupiter, Saturn, Uranus, Neptune, Pluto; comet.

meteor, falling star, shooting s., fireball, bolide; meteorite, aerolite, siderite, chondrite; meteoroid; meteor shower; radiant point.

sun, day-star, orb of day, eye of heaven; midnight sun; parhelion, mock sun; sunlight, photosphere, chromosphere; sun spot, solar flare, corona; solar wind; solar system, heliocentric s., Copernican s.

moon, new moon, crescent m., horned m., gibbous m., full m., harvest m., hunter's m.; paraselene, mock moon; moonscape, crater, mare, rill; man in the moon; parish lantern; moonlight, moonshine.

satellite, moon; earth satellite, orbiter, sputnik, weather satellite, communications s., comsat; space station, skylab 276 *spaceship*.

astronomy, star lore, stargazing; satellite tracking; radioastronomy; astrophysics; exobiology; selenography, selenology; uranometry, astrology 511 *divination*; observatory, planetarium; tracking station; altazimuth, transit instrument; radio telescope, parabolic reflector, dish 442 *telescope*; spectrohelioscope; orrery, celestial globe, astrolabe; planisphere; astronomer, radio a., astrophysicist; stargazer, star-watcher.

cosmography, cosmology, cosmogony, cosmogonist, cosmographer.

earth sciences, geography, orography, oceanography, physiography, geomorphology; geology, geodesy; geographer, geodesist, geologist; hydrology, hydrography.

Adj. *cosmic*, universal, cosmological, cosmogonic, cosmographical; interstellar, interplanetary, intermundane; galactic, intragalactic; extragalactic, ultramundane 59 *extraneous*; metagalactic.

celestial, heavenly, ethereal, empyreal; starry, star-spangled; sidereal, astral, stellar; solar, heliacal, zodiacal; lunar, lunate; lunisolar; nebular, nebulous; heliocentric, geocentric; cometary, meteoric; meteoritic; equinoctial, solstitial.

planetary, planetoidal, asteroidal, satellitic; Mercurian, Venusian, Martian, Jovian, Saturnian, Neptunian, Plutonian.

telluric, tellurian, terrestrial, terrene, terraqueous; sublunary, subastral; Old-World, New-World; polar, circumpolar, equatorial; worldwide, world, global, universal; worldly, earthly.

astronomic, astronomical, astrophysical, stargazing, star-watching; astrological, telescopic, spectroscopic.

geographic, geographical, oceanographic, orographical; geological, geomorphic; geodesic, geodetic, physiographic; hydrographic, hydrological.

322. Gravity – **N.** *gravity*, gravitation, force of gravity, gravitational pull; gravity feed; weight, weightiness, heaviness 195 *bulk*; specific gravity; pressure, displacement, sinkage, draught; encumbrance, load, burden; ballast, makeweight 31 *offset*; mass, lump 324 *solid body*; weight, bob, sinker, lead 313 *diver*; statics.

weighing, ponderation; balancing, equipoise 28 *equalization*; weights, avoirdupois weight, troy w., apothecaries' w.; grain, carat, scruple, pennyweight, drachm; quarter, quintal, hundredweight, ton; gram, kilogram, kilo; megaton, kiloton; axle load, laden weight.

scales, weighing machine; steelyard, weighbeam; balance, spring b.; pan, scale, weight; platform scale, weighbridge.

Adj. *weighty*, heavy, massive, ponderous, leaden; cumbersome, cumbrous, lumpish; pressing, oppressive; ponderable, having weight; weighted, loaded, laden; overloaded, top-heavy; gravitational.

Vb. *weigh*, have weight; balance 28 *be equal*; counterpoise 31 *compensate*; outweigh, overweigh, tip the scales; gravitate, settle 309 *descend*; weigh heavy, lie h.; press, weigh on, weigh one down 311 *lower*; load, cumber; take the weight of; weigh oneself 465 *measure*.

make heavy, weight, hang weights on; change, burden, overweight, overburden, overload 193 *load*; gain weight, put on w. 195 *be large*.

323. Lightness – **N.** *lightness*, portability; thinness, air, ether 325 *rarity*; buoyancy; volatility 338 *vaporization*; weightlessness, imponderability; defiance of gravity, levitation 308 *ascent*; feather, thistledown, fluff 4 *insubstantial thing*; cork, balloon, bubble; helium 310 *lifter*.

leaven, raising agent; ferment, enzyme, barm, yeast, baking powder.

Adj. *light*, underweight 307 *deficient*; lightweight, featherweight, portable; lightsome, light-footed; light on one's feet; light-handed, having a light touch; weightless, without weight, lighter than air; imponderable, unweighable; airy, volatile 325 *rare*; barmy, yeasty, fermenting, zymotic, enzymic; aerated, frothy, foamy, whipped; floating, buoyed up, buoyant, unsinkable; feathery, gossamery; light as air, light as a feather; lightening, raising, self-raising, leavening.

Vb. *be light*, buoyant, etc. adj.; defy gravity, levitate, surface, float, swim; drift, waft 271 *fly*; soar 308 *ascend*.

lighten, make light, make lighter 701 *disencumber*; reduce weight, lose w.; throw overboard, jettison 300 *empty*; volatilize, gasify, vaporize; leaven, work.

Section 2: Inorganic matter

324. Density – **N.** *density*, solidity, consistency; compactness, solidness, concreteness, thickness, concentration; incompressibility 326 *hardness*; impenetrability, impermeability; indissolubility; coalescence, cohesion 48 *coherence*; relative density, specific gravity; hydrometer, aerometer.

condensation, consolidation, concentration; concretion, nucleation; solidification; coagulation, congealment 354 *thickening*; crystallization 326 *hardening*; sedimentation, precipitation.

solid body, solid; block, mass 319 *matter*; knot, nugget, lump, burl; nucleus, hard core; aggregate, conglomerate, concretion; concrete, cement; stone, crystal 344 *rock*; precipitate, deposit, sediment; cake, clod, clump; bone, gristle 329 *toughness*; coagulum, curd, clot; phalanx, wall 702 *obstacle*.

Adj. *dense*, thick, crass; close, heavy, stuffy (air); lumpy, ropy, grumous, clotted, curdled; caked, matted 48 *cohesive*; monolithic, firm, close-textured; substantial, massy 322 *weighty*; concrete, solid, frozen; solidified etc. vb.; crystallized, condensed, nucleated; compact, close-packed, thickset; serried, massed; incompressible 326 *rigid*; impenetrable, impermeable, impervious; indissoluble, insoluble, undissolved; solidifying, congealing; styptic, haemostatic.

Vb. *be dense*, – solid etc. adj.; become solid, solidify, consolidate; conglomerate 48 *cohere*; condense, nucleate; thicken, inspissate; precipitate, deposit; freeze, set, gelatinize, jell; congeal, coagulate, clot, curdle; cake, crust; crystallize 326 *harden*; compact, compress, firm down 198 *make smaller*; pack, cram 193 *load*.

325. Rarity – N. *rarity*, low pressure, vacuum 190 *emptiness*; compressibility, sponginess 327 *softness*; tenuity 206 *thinness*; incorporeality 4 *insubstantiality*, 323 *lightness*; airiness 336 *gaseousness*, 340 *air*; rarefaction, expansion, attenuation.

Adj. *rare*, tenuous, thin, fine, subtle; flimsy, slight 4 *insubstantial*; low-pressure; compressible, spongy 328 *elastic*; rarefied 336 *gaseous*; ethereal, airy 323 *light*; wispy, straggly 75 *unassembled*.

Vb. *rarefy*, reduce the pressure, expand; make a vacuum, pump out 300 *empty*; subtilize, attenuate, refine, thin; dilute 163 *weaken*; volatilize 338 *vaporize*.

326. Hardness – N. *hardness*, resistance 329 *toughness*; starchiness, stiffness, rigidity, inflexibility, inelasticity; firmness, temper; callosity, callousness; stone, diamond, flint, granite 344 *rock*; steel, iron; cement, concrete; heartwood, hardwood; bone, gristle, cartilage; callus, corn; horn, ivory; crust, shell; hard core, hard centre, jaw-breaker; stiffener 218 *prop*.

hardening, induration; toughening, stiffening, backing; starching; steeling, tempering; vulcanization; petrifaction, lapidification, fossilization; crystallization, vitrification, glaciation; ossification; sclerosis.

Adj. *hard*, adamantine; unbreakable, armour-plated 162 *strong*; steeled, proof; iron, cast-i.; steel, steely; rock-hard; sun-

baked; stony, rocky, flinty, gritty; lithic, granitic; crystalline, vitreous, glassy; horny, corneous; callous, calloused 329 *tough*; bony, osseous, ossific; hardened, indurated, tempered, case-hardened; vitrified, fossilized, etc. vb.; icy, frozen.

rigid, stubborn, resistant, unmalleable, unadaptable; firm, inflexible, unbending 162 *unyielding*; incompressible, inelastic, unsprung; starched, boned, reinforced; muscle-bound 695 *clumsy*; braced, tense, taut, tight, set, solid; crisp 330 *brittle*; stiff, stark.

Vb. *harden*, indurate, temper, vulcanize, toughen 162 *strengthen*; crisp, bake 381 *heat*; petrify, fossilize, ossify; calcify, vitrify, crystallize 324 *be dense*; freeze 382 *refrigerate*; stiffen, back, bone, starch, wax (a moustache), tauten.

327. Softness – N. *softness*, tenderness; pliableness etc. adj.; pliancy, pliability, flexibility, plasticity, ductility, tractability; malleability, adaptability; suppleness, litheness; springiness 328 *elasticity*; impressibility, doughiness 356 *pulpiness*; sponginess, flaccidity, flabbiness, floppiness; laxity, looseness 354 *semiliquidity*; sogginess, squelchiness; flocculence, downiness; velvetiness; butter, wax, putty, clay, dough, soap; padding, cushion 376 *euphoria*; velvet, down, fleece 259 *hair*; snowflake 323 *lightness*.

Adj. *soft*, not tough, tender 301 *edible*; melting 335 *fluid*; giving, yielding, compressible; springy 328 *elastic*; cushiony, pillowed, padded; impressible, waxy, doughy, argilaceous; spongy, soggy, mushy, squelchy, squashy 356 *pulpy*; fleecy 259 *downy*; mossy, grassy; velvety, silky 258 *smooth*; unstiffened, unstarched; limp, flaccid, flabby, floppy; unstrung, relaxed, slack, loose; emollient 177 *lenitive*.

flexible, whippy, bendable 328 *elastic*; pliant, pliable; ductile, malleable, tractable, mouldable, plastic, thermoplastic; lithe, lithesome, willowy, supple, lissom, limber, loose-limbed, double-jointed; acrobatic.

Vb. *soften*, tenderize; mellow 669 *mature*; knead, mash, pulp; macerate 341 *drench*; melt 337 *liquefy*; cushion, pillow; yield, give, unbend.

328. Elasticity – N. *elasticity*, give, stretch; spring, springiness; suspension; stretchability, tensility, extensibility; resilience, bounce 280 *recoil*; buoyancy; rubber, elastomer; elastic; gum, chewing g.

Adj. *elastic*, stretchy, stretchable, tensile, extensile, extensible; rubbery, springy, bouncy 280 *recoiling*; buoyant; sprung, well-s.; ductile 327 *soft*.

Vb. *be elastic*, tensile etc. adj.; bounce, spring back 280 *recoil*; stretch, give.

329. Toughness – N. *toughness*, durability, infrangibility 162 *strength*; cohesion 48 *coherence*; leatheriness, inedibility, indigestibility; leather, gristle 326 *hardness*.

Adj. *tough*, durable, resisting; closewoven 162 *strong*; tenacious 48 *cohesive*; infrangible, unbreakable, shockproof; shatter-proof; vulcanized, toughened; tanned, weather-beaten; hardboiled, overdone; stringy, sinewy, woody, fibrous; gristly, cartilaginous; rubbery, leathery, coriaceous, tough as old boots *or* shoe leather; indigestible, inedible; inelastic 326 *rigid*.

Vb. *be tough*, – durable, etc. adj.; resist, be unbreakable; toughen, tan, caseharden; mercerize, vulcanize, temper, anneal 162 *strengthen*.

330. Brittleness – N. *brittleness*, crispness etc. adj.; frangibility; friability, crumbliness 332 *powderiness*; fissility 46 *scission*; laminability, flakiness 207 *lamina*; flimsiness, fragility, eggshell, pie crust, matchwood, glass, porcelain 163 *weak thing*.

Adj. *brittle*, breakable, frangible; inelastic 326 *rigid*; fragile, papery, like parchment; shattery, shivery, splintery; friable, crumbly 332 *powdery*; crisp, short, flaky, laminable; fissile 46 *severable*; frail, delicate, flimsy, eggshell 163 *weak*; gimcrack, jerry-built 4 *insubstantial*; tumbledown 655 *dilapidated*; ready to break, ready to burst, explosive.

Vb. *be brittle*, – fragile etc. adj.; fracture 46 *break*; crack, snap; star, craze; chip,

split, shatter, shiver, fragment; splinter, break off, snap off; burst, explode; fall to pieces 655 *deteriorate*; wear thin; crumble 332 *pulverize*.

331. Structure. Texture – N. *structure*, organization, pattern, plan; complex 52 *whole*; mould, shape, build 243 *form*; constitution, set-up, content, substance 56 *composition*; construction, workings; architecture, tectonics, architectonics; fabric, brickwork, stonework, timberwork 631 *materials*; substructure, superstructure 164 *edifice*; skeleton, framework, bodywork, shell 218 *frame*; lamination, cleavage 207 *stratification*; carcass, physique, anatomy 358 *organism*; science of structure, organology, physiology, histology 358 *biology*.

texture, contexture 222 *crossing*; tissue, fabric, stuff 222 *textile*; staple, denier 208 *fibre*; weave 222 *weaving*; granulation, grain, grit; fineness 258 *smoothness*; coarseness 259 *roughness*; surface 223 *exteriority*; feel 378 *touch*.

Adj. *structural*, organic; skeletal; anatomical; organismal, organological; organizational, constructional; tectonic, architectural.

textural, textile, woven 222 *crossed*; ribbed, twilled; grained, granular; satiny 258 *smooth*; gritty 259 *rough*; fine, fine-spun, delicate, gossamery, filmy; coarse, homespun, tweedy 259 *hairy*.

332. Powderiness – N. *powderiness*, crumbliness 330 *brittleness*; dustiness, sandiness, grittiness; granulation; pulverization, levigation, trituration; detrition, erosion 51 *decomposition*; abrasion 333 *friction*; fragmentation, comminution 46 *disunion*; dusting, powdering, frosting.

powder, talc, chalk; pollen, spore, sporule; dust, soot, ash 649 *dirt*; flour, farina; meal, bran; sawdust, filings; efflorescence, flowers; scurf, dandruff; detritus 41 *leavings*; sand, grit, gravel, shingle; grain, crumb, granule, flake, snowflake; smut.

pulverizer, miller, grinder; roller, crusher, masher, atomizer; mill, millstone, quern; pestle and mortar; grater, grindstone, file, abrasive; sledgehammer, bulldozer.

Adj. *powdery*, pulverulent; chalky, dusty, sooty 649 *dirty*; sandy, arenaceous 342 *dry*; farinaceous, branny, floury, mealy; granulated, granular; gritty, gravelly; flaky, furfuraceous; milled, ground, sifted, sieved; crumbling, crumbly, friable 330 *brittle*.

Vb. *pulverize*, powder; triturate, levigate, granulate; crush, kibble, mash, smash, comminute 46 *break*; grind, mill, mince, pound, bray; crumble, crumb, rub in (pastry); crunch, scrunch 301 *chew*; chip, flake, grate 333 *rub*; erode 51 *decompose*.

333. Friction – N. *friction*, frictional force, drag 278 *slowness*; attrition, rubbing etc. vb.; rubbing out 550 *obliteration*; abrasion, erosion 165 *destruction*; scrape, graze, brush, rub; polish, levigation, elbow grease; massage; pumice stone; eraser, rubber; whetstone 256 *sharpener*.

Adj. *rubbing*, frictional, abrasive; fricative.

Vb. *rub*, strike (a match); gnash, grind; fret, fray, chafe, gall; graze, scratch, bark 655 *wound*; rub off, abrade; scuff, scrape, scrub, scour, burnish; brush, rub down, towel, currycomb 648 *clean*; polish, buff, levigate 258 *smooth*; erase 550 *obliterate*; gnaw, erode, wear away; rasp, file, grind 332 *pulverize*; knead, massage; grate, catch, stick, snag; stroke 889 *caress*.

334. Lubrication – N. *lubrication*, greasing etc. vb.; anointment 357 *unctuousness*; nonfriction 258 *smoothness*.

lubricant, graphite, plumbago, black lead; glycerine, wax, grease 357 *oil*; soap 648 *cleanser*; saliva, spit; salve 658 *balm*; ointment 357 *unguent*; lubricator, oil-can, grease-gun.

Adj. *lubricated*, greased etc. vb.; nonfrictional, smooth-running, well-oiled.

Vb. *lubricate*, oil, grease, wax, soap, lather; butter 357 *grease*; anoint, pour balm.

335. Fluidity – N. *fluidity*, liquidity, wateriness 339 *water*; nonviscosity; liquescence 337 *liquefaction*; viscosity 354 *semiliquidity*; hydrology, hydrometry, hydrostatics, hydrodynamics; hydraulics, hydrokinetics; fluid mechanics.

fluid, nonelastic fluid, liquid 339 *water*; drink 301 *draught*; milk, juice, sap, latex; humour, chyle, rheum, mucus, saliva 302 *excrement*; serum, lymph, plasma; ichor, sanies; gore (**see** *blood*).

blood, claret; lifeblood 360 *life*; bloodstream, circulation; red blood 162 *vitality*; blue blood 868 *nobility*; blood of the gods, ichor; gore, cruor, grume; clot, blood c.; corpuscle, haemoglobin, blood group, Rhesus factor; blood count; haematology.

Adj. *fluid*, fluidic; liquid, not solid, not gaseous; in suspension; uncongealed, unclotted, clear, clarified; liquescent 337 *liquefied*; viscous 354 *viscid*; runny 350 *flowing*; rheumy, phlegmy 339 *watery*; juicy, sappy; serous, sanious, ichorous; suppurating 653 *toxic*.

sanguineous, haematic, haemal; lymphatic, plasmatic; bloody, sanguinary 431 *bloodstained*; gory, bleeding; haemophilic, haemolytic.

336. Gaseousness – N. *gaseousness*, vaporousness etc. adj.; windiness, flatulence; aeration, gasification; volatility 338 *vaporization*; aerostatics 340 *pneumatics*.

gas, vapour, elastic fluid; ether 340 *air*; effluvium, exhalation, miasma, flatus; fumes, reek, smoke; steam 355 *cloud*; methane 385 *fuel*; choke damp, fire d. 659 *poison*; gasworks; gasholder, gasometer.

Adj. *gaseous*, gasiform; volatile 338 *vaporific*; aerial, aeriform, ethereal 340 *airy*; carbonated, effervescent 355 *bubbly*; gassy, windy, flatulent; miasmic 659 *baneful*; aerostatic, aerodynamic.

Vb. *gasify*, vapour 338 *vaporize*; blow off steam 300 *emit*; carbonate, oxygenate 340 *aerate*.

337. Liquefaction – N. *liquefaction*, liquidization; fluidization; solubility, deliquescence 335 *fluidity*; thaw 381 *heating*; solvent, dissolvent, flux, diluent, menstruum, alkahest; liquefier, liquefacient; liquidizer; anticoagulant 658 *antidote*.

solution, decoction, infusion; aqua; suspension; flux, lixivium, lye.

Adj. *liquefied*, molten; runny, liquescent, uncongealed, deliquescent; liquefacient, solvent; soluble, dissoluble, liquefiable 335 *fluid*; in suspension.

Vb. *liquefy*, liquidize, clarify 350 *make flow*; liquate, dissolve, deliquesce, run 350 *flow*; thaw, melt 381 *heat*; render, clarify; leach, lixiviate; fluidize.

338. Vaporization – N. *vaporization*, gasification; exhalation 355 *cloud*; evaporation, volatilization, distillation, sublimation; fumigation; vapourability, volatility; atomization.

vaporizer, evaporator; atomizer, spray, aerosol; retort, still, distillery.

Adj. *vaporific*, volatilized etc. vb.; reeking, steaming etc. vb.; vaporous, vapoury, vapourish; steamy, gassy, smoky; evaporable, vaporable, vaporizable, volatile.

Vb. *vaporize*, evaporate; aerify, gasify; volatilize, distil, sublimate; exhale, transpire, blow off steam; smoke, fume, reek, steam; fumigate, spray; atomize.

339. Water – N. *water*, H_2O; heavy water D_2O; drinking water, tap w., Adam's ale; mineral w. 301 *soft drink*; water vapour 355 *cloud*; rain water 350 *rain*; running water, fresh w. 350 *stream*; weeping, tears 836 *lamentation*; saliva 335 *fluid*; standing water 346 *lake*; salt water 343 *ocean*; bath, shower 648 *ablutions*; lotion, lavender water 843 *cosmetic*; watering 341 *moistening*; tap 351 *conduit*; water supply, waterworks; well, borehole 632 *store*; hydrometry, hygrometry.

Adj. *watery*, aqueous, aquatic, lymphatic 335 *fluid*; hydro-, hydrated, hydrous; hydrological, hydrographic 321 *geographic*; diluted 163 *weak*; wet 341 *humid*.

Vb. *add water*, water, water down, dilute 163 *weaken*; steep, soak; irrigate 341 *moisten*; hydrate; slake.

340. Air – N. *air* 336 *gas*; thin air, ether 325 *rarity*; air pocket 190 *emptiness*; blast 352 *wind*; oxygen, nitrogen, argon; open air 183 *space*; sea air, ozone; fresh air, smokeless zone; airing 342 *desiccation*; aeration 338 *vaporization*; air-conditioning 352 *ventilation*; air-filter 648 *cleanser*; humidifier 341 *moisture*.

atmosphere, troposphere, stratosphere, ionosphere; mesosphere, exosphere; aerosphere; radiation layer, Van Allen belt; aeronomy, aerospace; greenhouse effect 381 *heating*.

weather, the elements; fair weather, fine w., halcyon days; dry spell, heat wave 379 *heat*; windless weather, doldrums; anticyclone, high pressure; cyclone, depression, low pressure; rough weather 176 *storm*, 352 *gale*; bad weather, foul w. 350 *rain*, 380 *wintriness*; meteorology, micrometeorology; weather forecast 511 *prediction*; isobar, millibar; glass, mercury, barometer; weathervane, weathercock; hygrometer, weather station, rain gauge; meteorologist; weatherman *or* -woman, clime, climate, microclimate; climatology, climatography; climatologist.

pneumatics, aerodynamics, aerology; barometry, aerometer, barometer, aneroid b., barograph.

Adj. *airy*, ethereal; skyey, aerial, aeriform; pneumatic; aerated, oxygenated; breezy 352 *windy*; well-ventilated, fresh, air-conditioned; meteorological, weatherwise; atmospheric, barometric; cyclonic, anticyclonic; high-pressure 324 *dense*; low-pressure 325 *rare*; climatic, climatological.

Vb. *aerate*, oxygenate; air, expose 342 *dry*; ventilate, freshen 648 *clean*; fan 352 *blow*.

Adv. *alfresco*, out of doors, in the open air, in the open, under the open sky.

341. Moisture – N. *moisture*, humidity, sap, juice 335 *fluid*; dampness, wetness, moistness, dewiness; dew point; dankness, condensation, rising damp; sogginess, saturation, saturation point; leakiness 298 *outflow*; raininess 350 *rain*; damp, wet; spray, spindrift 355 *bubble*; mist 355 *cloud*; Scotch mist, drizzle, drip, dew; drop, raindrop, dewdrop, teardrop, tears; saliva, slobber 302 *excrement*; ooze, slime 347 *marsh*.

moistening, humidification; damping, wetting, etc. vb.; saturation; spargefaction, sprinkling, aspersion; ducking, submersion, immersion; flood, inundation 350 *waterfall*; wash 648 *ablutions*; baptism 988 *Christian rite*; infiltration, percolation, leaching; irrigation, watering.

Adj. *humid*, wet 339 *watery*; pluvious, pluvial; drizzling 350 *rainy*; damp, moist, dripping; dank, muggy, foggy, misty; steaming, reeking; slimy, squelchy, splashy, plashy 347 *marshy*; dewy, fresh, bedewed; juicy, sappy 335 *fluid*; dribbling, seeping, percolating; sprinkled, dabbled, etc. vb.; gory 335 *sanguineous*.

drenched, saturated; watered, irrigated; soaking, sopping, streaming, soggy, sodden, soaked, deluged; wet through, wet to the skin, wringing wet, dripping w., sopping w.; wallowing, waterlogged, awash, swamped, drowned.

Vb. *be wet*, – moist etc. adj.; be soggy, squelch, suck; slobber, salivate, sweat 298 *exude*; steam, reek 300 *emit*; weep, bleed, stream; ooze, drip, leak 298 *flow out*; trickle, drizzle 350 *rain*; get wet, not have a dry stitch; duck, dive, bathe, wash; wallow; paddle.

moisten, humidify, wet, dampen; irrigate, water; hydrate 339 *add water*; lick, lap, wash; plash, splosh, splash, splatter; spill, slop; spray, shower, spatter, bespatter, sprinkle, besprinkle, sparge, syringe; bedew, bedabble, dabble; baste.

drench, saturate, imbrue, imbue; soak, deluge, wet through; wash, lave, bathe; hose down, sluice 648 *clean*; dip, submerge, drown 313 *plunge*; swamp, flood, inundate, waterlog; dunk, douse, souse, steep; macerate, marinade 666 *preserve*.

342. Dryness – N. *dryness*, aridity; drought, drouth, low rainfall; desert conditions 172 *desert*; dry climate, dry season; sun, sunniness 379 *heat*.

desiccation, drying, drying up; airing, evaporation; drainage; dehydration, insolation, sunning 381 *heating*.

drier, desiccator, evaporator; siccative, sand, blotting paper; absorbent, mop, swab, sponge, towel; spin drier, tumble d.

Adj. *dry*, unirrigated; arid, rainless, waterless, riverless; sandy, dusty 332 *powdery*; bare, grassless; desert, Saharan; anhydrous, dehydrated, desiccated; withered, sear; dried up, sapless, juiceless, mummified, parchment-like; sun-dried, wind-d., bleached; baked, parched 379 *hot*; sunny, fine, cloudless, fair; dried out, drained, evaporated; waterproof, showerproof, dampproof; watertight, proof; greaseproof; dry-shod; high and dry; dry, bone-dry; xerophilous; nongreasy, nonskid, skidproof.

Vb. *be dry*, – thirsty etc. adj.; keep dry, hold off the wet, dry up, evaporate 338 *vaporize*; become dry, dry off, dry out.

dry, dehumidify, desiccate, freeze-dry; dehydrate; drain 300 *empty*; wring out, spin-dry, tumble-d., drip-d.; hang out, peg o., air; insolate, sun-dry; smoke, kipper, cure; parch, bake 381 *heat*; sear, shrivel, bleach; mummify 666 *preserve*; dry up 350 *staunch*; blot, blot up, mop up, soak up 299 *absorb*; swab, wipe.

343. Ocean – N. *ocean*, sea, brine, briny; waters 350 *wave*; Davy Jones's locker; main, deep; high seas, great waters; trackless deep, watery waste; herring pond, drink; sea lane, shipping lane; ocean floor, sea bed, sea bottom, ooze, benthos; the seven seas; Neptune, Poseidon, Triton; sea nymph, mermaid 970 *mythical being*.

oceanography, hydrography, bathymetry; Admiralty chart; bathysphere, bathyscaphe; oceanographer, hydrographer.

Adj. *oceanic*, thalassic, pelagic, pelagian; sea, marine, maritime; ocean-going, sea-g., seaworthy 269 *seafaring*; submarine, subaqueous, subaquatic, subaqua, undersea, underwater; benthic;

abyssal 211 *deep*; hydrographic, bathymetric.

344. Land – N. *land*, dry l., terra firma; earth, crust, earth's c. 321 *world*; continent, mainland; heartland, hinterland; inland, interior 224 *interiority*; peninsula, delta, promontory 254 *projection*; isthmus, neck of land, landbridge; terrain, heights 209 *high land*; lowlands 210 *lowness*; reclaimed land, polder; steppe 348 *plain*; wilderness 172 *desert*; oasis; isle 349 *island*; zone, clime; country, district 184 *region*; territory 777 *lands*; physical features, landscape, scenery; topography, geography, stratigraphy, geology 321 *earth sciences*; landsman *or* -woman, landlubber 191 *dweller*.

shore, coastline 233 *outline*; coast, rocky c., ironbound c. 234 *edge*; continental shelf; strand, beach, sands, shingle; seaboard, seashore, seaside; sea cliff, sea wall; plage, lido, riviera; bank, river b., water meadow.

soil, farmland 370 *farm*; pasture 348 *grassland*; deposit, moraine, loess, geest, silt, alluvium; topsoil, subsoil; mould, humus; loam, clay, bole, marl; fuller's earth; argil, potter's clay, china c., kaolin 381 *pottery*; gravel; stone, pebble, flint; turf, sod, clod 53 *piece*.

rock, cliff, scar, crag; stone, boulder; reef; stack, skerry; dike, sill, batholith; igneous rock, plutonic r., volcanic r.; magma, lava, tuff; sedimentary rock, conglomerate; metamorphic rock; massive rock, bedded r.; ore 359 *mineralogy*; precious stone 844 *gem*.

Adj. *territorial*, agricultural 370 *agrarian*; terrigenous 321 *telluric*; earthy, alluvial, sandy, loamy; clayey, marly; chalky; flinty, pebbly, gravelly, stony, rocky; slaty, shaly; geological, morphological, orographical, topographical.

coastal, littoral, riparian, riverine, riverside, seaside; shore, onshore.

inland, continental, midland, mainland, interior, landlocked.

345. Gulf: inlet – N. *gulf*, bay, bight, cove, creek, reach, lagoon; road, roadstead; inlet, outlet; arm of the sea, fjord, ria; mouth, estuary; firth, frith, kyle; sound, strait, belt, gut, channel.

346. Lake. – N. *lake*, lagoon; loch, lough, llyn; inland sea, Dead Sea; oxbow lake, mortlake; broad; sheet of water, standing w.; mud flat, wash 347 *marsh*; pool, tarn, mere, pond, dewpond; fishpond, stew; millpond, millpool; dam, reservoir 632 *storage*; basin, tank, cistern; waterhole, puddle, splash, wallow.

Adj. *lacustrine*, lake-dwelling.

347. Marsh – N. *marsh*, morass; marshland, slobland, wetlands; washlands, flats, mud f., salt f., salt marsh; fen, carr, moor; moss, bog, quag, quagmire, quicksand; salina, saltpan; mudhole, wallow, slough, mire, mud, ooze; swamp, everglade, sudd.

Adj. *marshy*, paludal; swampy, boggy, fenny; oozy, quaggy, poached, trampled; squashy, squelchy, spongy 327 *soft*; slushy 354 *semiliquid*; muddy, miry 649 *dirty*; undrained, waterlogged.

348. Plain – N. *plain*, peneplain; dene, dale, flood plain, levels 216 *horizontality*; river basin, lowlands 255 *valley*; flats 347 *marsh*; delta, alluvial plain; waste 172 *desert*; tundra; ice field 380 *ice*; grasslands, steppe, prairie, pampas, savanna; heath, common, wold, downland, downs, moor, moorland, fell; plateau 209 *high land*; bush, veld, range, open country, rolling c. 183 *space*; champaign, campagna; fields, green belt, parkland, national park 263 *open space*.

grassland, pasturage 369 *animal husbandry*; sheeprun, sheepwalk; field, meadow, water m., mead, lea; chase, park, grounds; green, greensward, sward, lawn, turf.

Adj. *campestral*, rural; flat, open, steppelike, rolling.

349. Island – N. *island*, isle, islet, skerry; eyot, ait, holm; atoll, reef, coral r.; cay, key; sandbank, bar; floating island, iceberg; all-but island, peninsula; island continent; archipelago; insularity 883 *seclusion*; islander, islesman *or* -woman.

Adj. *insular*, sea-girt; islanded, isolated, marooned, isleted, archipelagic.

350. Stream: water in motion – N. *stream*, running water, watercourse, river, waterway; tributary, branch, feeder, distributary; streamlet, rivulet, brook, brooklet, bourne, burn, rill, beck, gill, runnel, runlet; freshet, torrent, force; spring, fountain, headwaters 156 *source*; jet, spout, gush; geyser, hot spring, well.

current, flow, flux, confluence 293 *convergence*; inflow, outflow, reflux, undercurrent, undertow, crosscurrent, rip tide; tide, spring t., neap t.; ebb and flow 317 *fluctuation*; tideway, race, millrace, millstream 351 *conduit*; bloodstream, circulation 314 *circuition*; eddy, whirlpool 315 *vortex*; surge, flush; wash, backwash.

waterfall, falls, cataract, Niagara; cascade, force, rapids, shoot, weir; chute, spillway, sluice; overflow, spill; fresh, freshet; flood, flash f., spate, inundation, deluge 298 *outflow*.

wave, bow w.; wash, swash, backwash; ripple, cat's-paw; swell, ground s.; billow, roller, comber, breaker; surf, spume, white horses, whitecap; tidal wave, tsunami; bore, eagre; rip, overfall; broken water, choppiness 259 *roughness*; sea, heavy s.; waviness, undulation.

rain, rainfall 341 *moisture*; precipitation; drizzle, mizzle, Scotch mist; sleet, hail 380 *wintriness*; shower, downpour, deluge, cloudburst, thunderstorm 176 *storm*; flurry 352 *gale*; pouring rain, teeming r., driving r., torrential r.; raininess, wet spell, foul weather; rainy season, the rains, monsoon; lovely weather for ducks; plash, patter; dripping etc. vb.; rainmaking, cloud-seeding; rain gauge; hyetograph.

Adj. *flowing*, falling etc. vb.; runny 335 *fluid*; riverine, fluvial, fluviatile, tidal; streaming, in flood, in spate; flooding, inundatory; rippling, purling, eddying; popply, choppy 259 *rough*; winding,

meandering 251 *labyrinthine*; oozy, sluggish 278 *slow*; pouring, sheeting, lashing, driving, dripping, dropping; gushing, spirting, spouting 298 *outgoing*.

rainy, showery, drizzly, spitting, spotting; wet 341 *humid*.

Vb. *flow*, run, course, pour; ebb, regurgitate 286 *regress*; swirl, eddy 315 *rotate*; surge, dash, ripple, popple; roll, swell; gush, rush, spurt, spout, spew, jet, play, squirt, splutter; well up, bubble up 298 *emerge*; pour, stream; trickle, dribble 298 *exude*; drip, drop 309 *descend*; plash, lap, wash, swash, slosh, splash 341 *moisten*; purl, trill, murmur, babble, bubble, burble, gurgle, guggle; glide, slide; overflow, cascade, flood, inundate, deluge 341 *drench*; flow into 297 *enter*; run off 298 *flow out*; leak, ooze, percolate 305 *pass*; wind 251 *meander*.

rain, shower, stream, pour, pelt; snow, sleet, hail; fall, come down, bucket d., rain hard, pour with rain, rain in torrents, rain cats and dogs; sheet; patter, drizzle, mizzle, drip, drop; set in.

make flow, send out a stream 300 *emit*; make *or* pass water 302 *excrete*; broach, tap 263 *open*; pour, decant 311 *let fall*; drain out 300 *empty*; water, irrigate; melt 337 *liquefy*.

staunch, stop the flow 342 *dry*; apply a tourniquet; stop a leak, plug 264 *close*; stem, dam 702 *obstruct*.

351. Conduit – N. *conduit*, water channel, tideway, riverbed; arroyo, wadi; trough, basin 255 *valley*; inland waterway, canal, channel, watercourse; ditch, dike, gully; trench, moat, runnel; Irish bridge; gutter, leat, mill race; duct, aqueduct; plumbing, pipe, water pipe, main; hosepipe, hose; standpipe, hydrant, siphon, tap, spout 263 *tube*; valve, sluice, weir, lock, floodgate, watergate, spillway; chute 350 *waterfall*; pipeline 272 *transferrer*; blood vessel, vein, artery.

drain, gully, gutter, gargoyle, waterspout; scupper, overflow, wastepipe, drainpipe 298 *outlet*; culvert; ditch, sewer 649 *sink*; intestine, colon, alimentary canal; catheter 300 *voidance*.

352. Wind: air in motion – N. *wind* 340 *air*; draught, downdraught, updraught, thermal; windiness etc. adj.; blast, blow (**see** *breeze, gale*); air stream, jet s.; current, air c., crosswind, headwind; tailwind, following wind; air flow, slip stream; seasonal wind, monsoon, Etesian winds; prevailing wind, trade w., antitrades, Roaring Forties; cave of Aeolus.

anemometry, aerodynamics 340 *pneumatics*; Beaufort scale; anemometer, wind gauge.

breeze, zephyr; breath of air, waft, whiff, puff, gust, capful of wind; light breeze, fresh b., stiff b.

gale, high wind; blow, blast, gust, flurry, flaw, squall; nor'wester, sou'wester, hurricane, whirlwind, cyclone, tornado, twister, typhoon 315 *vortex*; thunderstorm, dust devil, blizzard 176 *storm*; dirty weather, ugly w., gale force.

blowing, insufflation; inflation 197 *dilation*; blowing up, pumping up; pump, bellows, windbag, bagpipe; woodwind, brass; blowpipe.

ventilation, airing 340 *air*; crossventilation, draught; fanning, cooling; ventilator 353 *air pipe*; blower, fan, air-conditioner 384 *refrigerator*.

respiration, breathing, inhalation, exhalation; flatus, windiness, flatulence; belch 300 *voidance*; gills, lungs; respirator, iron lung, oxygen tent; windpipe 353 *air pipe*; sneezing, coughing; sigh, sob, gulp, hiccup, yawn; hard breathing, panting; wheeze, rattle, death r.

Adj. *windy*, airy, exposed, draughty, breezy, blowy; ventilated, fresh; gusty, squally; blustery, dirty, foul, stormy, boisterous 176 *violent*; windswept, windblown; stormtossed; fizzy, gassy 336 *gaseous*; aeolian, boreal, zephyrous; cyclonic; gale-force, hurricane-f.

puffing, huffing; snorting, wheezing; wheezy, asthmatic, stertorous; panting, breathless 318 *agitated*; sniffling, snuffly, sneezy; pulmonary, pulmonic; coughing, chesty.

Vb. *blow*, puff, blast; freshen, blow up, get up, blow hard, blow great guns 176 *be violent*; wail, howl, roar 409 *ululate*;

screech, scream, whistle, pipe 407 *shrill*; hum, moan, mutter, sough, sigh 401 *sound faint*; stream in the air, wave, flutter 318 *agitate*; draw, make a draught, ventilate, fan 382 *refrigerate*; blow along, waft 287 *propel*; veer, back 282 *deviate*; die down, drop, abate.

breathe, respire, breathe in, inhale; fill one's lungs; breathe out, exhale; aspirate, puff, huff, whiff, whiffle; sniff, sniffle, snuffle, snort; gasp, pant, heave; wheeze, sneeze, cough 407 *rasp*; sigh, sob, gulp, catch one's breath; hiccup, yawn; belch, burp 300 *eruct*.

blow up, pump up, inflate 197 *enlarge*; pump out, exhaust 300 *empty*.

353. Air pipe – N. *air pipe*, airway, air-passage, air shaft, wind tunnel; blowpipe, peashooter; windpipe, trachea, larynx; bronchia; throat, gullet; nose, nostril, spiracle, blowhole, nozzle, vent, mouthpiece 263 *orifice*; flue pipe 414 *organ*; pipe 388 *tobacco*; funnel, flue, exhaust pipe 263 *chimney*; air duct, ventilator, grating, louvre 263 *window*.

354. Semiliquidity – N. *semiliquidity*, mucosity, viscidity; semiliquid, colloid, emulsion; mucilage, phlegm; pus, matter; juice, sap 335 *fluidity*; soup, slop, curds 356 *pulpiness*; oil slick; slush, sludge, slime 347 *marsh*.

thickening, inspissation, curding, clotting 324 *condensation*; emulsification; thickener, starch, pectin.

viscidity, viscosity, glutinousness, glueyness, treacliness 48 *coherence*; glue, gluten, gum 47 *adhesive*; emulsion, colloid; glair, size, paste, glaze, slip; gel, jelly; treacle, syrup, honey, goo; wax 357 *resin*.

Adj. *semiliquid*, semifluid; stodgy, starchy, thick, lumpy, ropy 324 *dense*; curdled, clotted, coagulated, jellied, gelatinous, pulpy, juicy, sappy, milky, creamy, lactescent, lacteal; emulsive; colloidal; thawing, half-frozen, half-melted, mushy, slushy, sloppy, squishy, squidgy 347 *marshy*.

viscid, viscous, glutinous, gummy,

gooey 48 *cohesive*; slimy, clammy, sticky, tacky; treacly, syrupy, gluey; glairy, glaireous; mucilaginous, mucous.

Vb. *thicken*, inspissate 324 *be dense*; coagulate 48 *cohere*; emulsify; gelatinize, jelly; curdle, clot; whip up, beat up; mash, pulp 332 *pulverize*; muddy, puddle.

355. Bubble. Cloud: air and water mixed – **N.** *bubble*, bubbles, suds, soapsuds, lather, foam, froth; head, top; spume, surf, spray 341 *moisture*; mousse, soufflé, meringue, candyfloss; scum 649 *dirt*; bubbling, boiling, ebullition, effervescence; fermentation, yeastiness, fizziness, fizz.

cloud, cloudlet, scud, rack; cloudbank, cloudscape; wool-pack, cumulus, cirrus, stratus, nimbus; mackerel sky, mare's tail; vapour, steam 338 *vaporization*; brume, haze, mist, fog, smog, pea-souper; cloudiness, film 419 *dimness*; nebulosity.

Adj. *bubbly*, bubbling etc. vb.; effervescent, fizzy, sparkling 336 *gaseous*; mousseux, foaming, foamy; spumy, spumous; frothy, soapy, lathery; yeasty, aerated 323 *light*; scummy 649 *dirty*.

cloudy, clouded, overcast, overclouded; nebulous, foggy, hazy, misty, brumous 419 *dim*; vaporous, steamy 338 *vaporific*.

Vb. *bubble*, spume, foam, froth, cream, form a head; mantle, scum; work, ferment, fizz, sparkle, effervesce.

cloud, cloud over, overcast, overcloud; becloud, befog, fog over, mist up 419 *be dim*.

356. Pulpiness – N. *pulpiness*, doughiness, sponginess; fleshiness 327 *softness*; poultice, pulp, pith, pap, puree; mush, mash; jam 354 *viscidity*; mousse 355 *bubble*; ooze, slush 354 *semiliquidity*; papier mâché; pulping, mastication.

Adj. *pulpy*, pulped, mashed, crushed, pureed 354 *semiliquid*; mushy, pappy, squashy, overripe 327 *soft*; flabby 195 *fleshy*; doughy, pasty; soggy, spongy 347 *marshy*.

357. Unctuousness – N. *unctuousness*, unctuosity, oiliness, greasiness, lubricity,

soapiness 334 *lubrication*; fattiness, pinguidity; saponification; anointment, unction.

oil, cod-liver o.; olive o., castor o., palm o.; mineral oil, crude o., petroleum; refined oil, fuel oil, petrol 385 *fuel*; lubricating oil 334 *lubricant*.

fat, animal f., grease, adipocere; blubber, tallow, spermaceti; sebum, wax, beeswax, ceresin; suet, lard, dripping 301 *cookery*; glycerine; margarine, butter, ghee; cream, buttermilk; soap, soft s. 648 *cleanser*.

unguent, salve, unction, ointment; liniment, embrocation, lanolin; spikenard, nard; cream, cold c. 843 *cosmetic*.

resin, rosin, colophony, gum, gum arabic, tragacanth; amber, ambergris; pitch, tar, bitumen, asphalt; varnish, mastic, shellac, lac, lacquer, japan; synthetic resin, epoxy r., polyurethane, plastics.

Adj. *fatty*, pinguid, fat, adipose, blubbery 195 *fleshy*; sebaceous, waxy, waxen; saponaceous, soapy; buttery, creamy, rich 390 *savoury*.

unctuous, greasy, oily, oleaginous; anointed, basted; slippery, greased, oiled 334 *lubricated*.

resinous, resiny, resiniferous; bituminous, gummy 354 *viscid*.

Vb. *grease*, oil, anoint 334 *lubricate*; baste; butter; saponify; resinify, resin, rosin.

Section 3: Organic matter

358. Organisms: living matter – N. *organism*, organic matter, animate m.; living beings 360 *life*; animal and vegetable kingdom, flora and fauna, biota; ecosystem; biotype 77 *breed*; microscopic life 196 *microorganism*; cell, protoplasm, cytoplasm; nucleus, nucleolus; nucleic acid, RNA, DNA; germ plasm; chromosome, gene 5 *heredity*; albumen, protein; enzyme, globulin; organic remains, fossil.

biology, microbiology; biotechnology; natural history, nature study; biochemistry, biophysics, developmental biology, molecular b., cell b., cytology; histology; morphology, embryology; anatomy, physiology 331 *structure*; zoography 367 *zoology*; phytography 368 *botany*; ecology, bionomics; ethology, biogeography; marine biology; genetics, biogenetics, eugenics, genetic engineering; sociobiology; ontogeny, phylogeny; evolution, natural selection, survival of the fittest; Darwinism, Lamarckism, neo-Darwinism; biogenesis; vitalism; mechanism; naturalist, biologist, zoologist, ecologist; evolutionist, Darwinist.

Adj. *organic*, organized; biogenic; cellular, unicellular, multicellular; plasmic, protoplasmic, cytoplasmic.

biological, physiological, zoological, palaeontological; biogenetic; vitalistic; evolutionistic, evolutionary, Darwinian.

359. Mineral: inorganic matter – N. *mineral*, mineral world, mineral kingdom; inorganic matter, unorganized m.; inanimate m.; earth's crust 344 *rock*; ore, metal, noble m., precious m., base m.; alloy 43 *a mixture*; deposit, coal measures 632 *store*.

mineralogy, geology, lithology, petrography, petrology; metallurgy, metallography; speleology, glaciology 321 *earth sciences*.

Adj. *inorganic*, unorganized; inanimate, azoic; mineral, nonanimal, nonvegetable; mineralogical, petrological; metallurgical, metallic.

360. Life – N. *life*, living, being alive 1 *existence*; the living, living being; plant life 366 *vegetable life*; animal life 365 *animality*; human life 371 *humankind*; birth 68 *origin*; vivification, vitalization, animation; vitality, vital force, élan vital; soul 477 *spirit*; hold on life, survival; liveliness, animation 819 *moral sensibility*; vital spark, breath of life; pulse, heartbeat; heart, lifeblood, staff of life 301 *food*; biological function 167 *propagation*; living matter, protoplasm, bioplasm, tissue, macromolecule, bioplast; cell 358 *organism*; symbiosis 706 *association*; lifetime, one's born days; life expectancy, life span, life cycle; viability 469 *possibility*.

Adj. *alive*, living, quick, live; breathing, alive and kicking; animated 819 *lively*; incarnate, in the flesh; in the land of the living, above ground, on this side of the grave; long-lived 113 *lasting*; capable of life, viable; vital, vivifying, Promethean; vivified 656 *restored*; biotic, symbiotic, biological; protoplasmic, protoplastic, bioplasmic.

born, born alive; begotten, fathered, sired; mothered, dammed; foaled, dropped; out of, by 11 *akin*; spawned, littered; laid, new-l., hatched.

Vb. *live*, be alive, have life; respire, draw breath 352 *breathe*; exist 1 *be*; be born, come into the world; come to life, quicken, revive 656 *be restored*; not die, be spared, survive; cheat death, have nine lives; live in 192 *dwell*.

vitalize, give birth to, conceive 167 *generate*; vivify, breathe life into 174 *invigorate*; revitalize 656 *revive*; support life, provide a living; provide for, keep body and soul together 301 *feed*.

361. Death – N. *death*, no life 2 *extinction*; deathliness, dying (**see** *decease*); Dance of Death, mortality 114 *transience*; sentence of death, doom, death knell; execution, martyrdom; deathblow, quietus 362 *killing*; mortification, autolysis 51 *decay*; the beyond, the great divide; eternal rest, big sleep 266 *quietude*; Abraham's bosom 971 *heaven*; the grave 364 *tomb*; jaws of death, shadow of d.; Grim Reaper, Great Leveller; Lord of the Underworld, Pluto; post mortem, autopsy; mortuary 364 *cemetery*.

decease, clinical death, brain d.; extinction, exit, demise, curtains 69 *end*; departure, passing; natural death, quiet end; release, happy r., welcome end; loss of life, fatality; sudden death, violent d., untimely end; watery grave; mortal illness 651 *disease*; dying day, last hour; deathbed, deathwatch, death scene; last agony, last gasp, dying breath; swan song, death rattle, rigor mortis 69 *finality*.

the dead, forefathers 66 *precursor*;

loved ones, dear departed 968 *saint*; the shades 970 *ghost*; dead body 363 *corpse*; underworld, Sheol 972 *mythic hell*; Elysian fields 971 *mythic heaven*.

death roll, mortality, fatality, death toll, death rate; casualty list; necrology; martyrology; obituary; the dead, the fallen.

Adj. *dying*, expiring etc. vb.; mortal 114 *transient*; moribund, half-dead, with one foot in the grave, deathlike, deathly; given up, despaired of, all over with, not long for this world; done for, had it; sinking, on one's death bed, at death's door; in extremis; one's hour having come, one's number being up; life hanging by a thread, at the last gasp, at the point of death; under sentence of death, fey, doomed.

dead, deceased, demised, no more; passed away, departed, gone before; dead and gone, dead and buried 364 *buried*; born dead, still-born; lifeless, breathless; extinct, inanimate, exanimate; stone dead, cold, stiff; dead as mutton, dead as a doornail; kaput, done for, gone for a burton; off the hook, out of one's misery; gathered to one's fathers, asleep in Jesus, numbered with the dead; defunct, late, late-lamented, of sainted memory.

Vb. *die* (see *perish*); be dead, lie in the grave, be no more 2 *pass away*; die young, not make old bones; die a natural death, die in bed; end one's life, decease, predecease; expire, give up the ghost, breathe one's last; fall asleep, pass over, be taken; depart this life 296 *depart*; end one's earthly career, pay the debt of nature, go the way of all flesh; meet one's Maker, go to glory; awake to life immortal; croak, peg out, snuff it; cop it, have bought it, have had one's chips; pop one's clogs, hop the twig, kick the bucket, bite the dust, turn up one's toes, push up the daisies.

perish, die out, become extinct 2 *pass away*; go to the wall 165 *be destroyed*; turn to dust 51 *decompose*; meet one's end, die in harness, die with one's boots on; die hard, die fighting; get killed, fall in action, lose one's life; lay down one's l., make the supreme sacrifice; die untimely, catch

one's death, drop down dead; meet a sticky end; break one's neck; drown 313 *founder*; be put to death, die the death, walk the plank; commit suicide 362 *kill oneself*.

362. Killing: destruction of life – N. *killing*, slaying 165 *destruction*; blood sports 619 *chase*; bloodshed, blood-letting; vivisection; selective killing, cull; mercy killing, euthanasia; murder (**see** *homicide*); poisoning, drowning, suffocation, strangulation, hanging; ritual killing, immolation, sacrifice; martyrdom; execution 963 *capital punishment*; dispatch, deathblow, coup de grâce, quietus; violent death, fatal accident.

homicide, manslaughter; murder, capital m.; assassination; thuggery; crime passionel 911 *jealousy*; regicide, tyrannicide, parricide, matricide, fratricide; infanticide, exposure of infants; genocide (**see** *slaughter*).

suicide, self-slaughter, self-destruction, felo de se; self-immolation, suttee, hara-kiri; mass suicide, Gadarene swine, lemmings.

slaughter, bloodshed, butchery, carnage; bloodbath, massacre, noyade, fusillade, holocaust; pogrom, purge, liquidation, decimation, extermination, annihilation 165 *destruction*; genocide, Final Solution; war 718 *warfare*; Roman holiday 716 *duel*.

slaughterhouse, abattoir, knacker's yard, shambles; bullring 724 *arena*; field of battle 724 *battleground*; gas chamber, Auschwitz, Belsen.

killer, slayer; mercy killer; soldier 722 *combatant*; slaughterer, butcher, knacker; trapper 619 *hunter*; rat catcher, rodent officer, pest exterminator; toreador, picador, matador; executioner, hangman 963 *punisher*; homicide (**see** *murderer*); lynch mob; homicidal maniac, psychopath; head-hunter, cannibal; beast of prey, man-eater; pesticide, poison 659 *bane*.

murderer, homicide, killer, Cain; assassin, terrorist; poisoner, strangler, garrotter, thug; hatchet man, gangster, gunman; bravo, desperado, cutthroat 904 *ruffian*;

parricide, regicide, tyrannicide; suicide, kamikaze.

Adj. *deadly*, killing, lethal; fell, mortal, fatal, deathly; capital; malignant 653 *toxic*; inoperable, incurable.

murderous, slaughterous, homicidal, genocidal; suicidal, self-destructive; internecine; death-dealing, trigger-happy; sanguinary, bloody, red-handed; bloodthirsty 898 *cruel*; man-eating, cannibalistic.

Vb. *kill*, slay, take life; do in, do for 165 *destroy*; put down, put to sleep; put to death, send to the scaffold 963 *execute*; stone 712 *lapidate*; string up, lynch; make away with, do away w., dispatch, get rid of, send to his *or* her account, launch into eternity; deal a deathblow, give the coup de grace, put out of his *or* her misery, knife, stab, run through 263 *pierce*; shoot down, pick off, blow out the brains of 287 *shoot*; strangle, wring the neck of, garrotte, choke, suffocate, smother, stifle, drown; wall up, bury alive; brain, poleaxe 279 *strike*; send to the stake 381 *burn*; immolate, sacrifice; martyr, martyrize; sign one's death warrant, ring one's knell 961 *condemn*.

slaughter, butcher; massacre, put to the sword; decimate, scupper, wipe out; cut to ribbons, cut down, shoot d., mow d.; give no quarter 906 *be pitiless*; annihilate, exterminate, liquidate 165 *destroy*.

murder, commit m.; assassinate, finish off, do in, do for, fix, settle, bump off, rub out; strangle, poison, gas. **See** *kill*.

kill oneself, do oneself in, do away with oneself, commit suicide, put an end to one's life; commit hara-kiri, commit suttee; hang oneself, shoot o., blow out one's brains, cut one's throat, slash one's wrists; fall on one's sword, die Roman fashion; put one's head in the oven, gas oneself; take poison, take an overdose; drown oneself 361 *perish*.

363. Corpse – **N.** *corpse*, corse, dead body, body, stiff; defunct, goner; cadaver, carcass, skeleton, bones, dry b.; skull, death's-head, memento mori; mummy; reliquiae, mortal remains, relics, ashes;

clay, dust; carrion 301 *meat*; zombie 970 *ghost*.

Adj. *cadaverous*, corpselike; stiff, deathlike, deathly.

364. Interment – **N.** *interment*, burial, sepulture, entombment; inhumation, cremation, incineration, embalming, mummification; coffin, shell, casket, Canopic jar, urn, funeral u.; sarcophagus, mummy-case; pyre, funeral pile, burning-ghat, crematorium; mortuary, morgue, charnel house; bone-urn, ossuary; funeral parlour; sexton, gravedigger; undertaker, funeral director; mortician; embalmer.

obsequies, exequies; mourning, wake 836 *lamentation*; lying-in-state; last rites, burial service, funeral; cortège; knell, passing bell; dead march, muffled drum, last post, taps; memorial service, requiem, Dies irae; elegy, dirge 836 *lament*; epitaph, obituary, tombstone, gravestone, headstone, ledger; cross, war memorial, cenotaph 548 *monument*; mourner, weeper, keener.

grave clothes, cerements, cerecloth, shroud, winding sheet.

cemetery, burial place, boneyard, golgotha; churchyard, graveyard, God's Acre; catacombs, columbarium, cinerarium; tower of silence; necropolis, city of the dead; garden of remembrance.

tomb, vault, crypt; burial chamber; pyramid, mastaba; mausoleum, sepulchre; pantheon; grave, mass g., plague pit; grave pit, cist; barrow 548 *monument*.

inquest, inquiry; necropsy, autopsy, post-mortem; exhumation, disinterment.

Adj. *buried*, interred, etc. vb.; laid to rest, in the grave, below ground, six feet under 361 *dead*.

funereal, funerary, funebrial; sombre 428 *black*; mourning; elegiac, mortuary, cinerary, crematory, sepulchral; obsequial, obituary; necrological; dirgelike 836 *lamenting*.

Vb. *inter*, inhume, bury; lay out, close one's eyes; embalm, mummify; coffin, urn, entomb; lay to rest, put to bed with a shovel; cremate, incinerate 381 *burn*;

pay one's last respects, mourn 836 *lament*.

exhume, disinter, unbury; disentomb; unearth, dig up.

Adv. *in memoriam*, postmortem; hic jacet, RIP.

365. Animality. Animal – N. *animality*, animal life, wild life; animal kingdom, fauna, brute creation; flesh and blood; animalization, zoo-morphism, Pan; animalism 944 *sensualism*.

animal, created being, living thing; birds, beasts and fishes; creature, brute, beast, dumb animal, creeping thing; protozoan, metazoan; zoophyte 196 *microorganism*; mammal, amphibian, fish, bird, reptile; worm, mollusc, arthropod; crustacean, insect, arachnid; invertebrate, vertebrate; biped, quadruped; carnivore, herbivore, insectivore, omnivore, ruminant, maneater; wild animal, game, big game; prey, beast of prey; pack, flock, herd 74 *group*; stock, livestock 369 *stock farm*; tame animal, domestic a.; household pet, goldfish, cagebird, hamster, guinea pig, tortoise; young animal 132 *young creature*; draught animal 273 *horse*, *beast of burden*; extinct animal, dodo, dinosaur, mammoth, mastodon; fabulous beast, unicorn 84 *rara avis*.

mammal, man 371 *humankind*; primate, ape, gorilla, orang-outang, chimpanzee, gibbon, baboon, mandrill, monkey; marmoset, lemur; marsupial, kangaroo, wallaby, wombat, koala bear, opossum; rodent, rat, mouse, dormouse, shrew, vole, porcupine, mongoose, chipmunk, skunk, polecat, squirrel; insectivorous mammal, aardvark, anteater, mole; nocturnal mammal, bat, bush baby, raccoon, badger, hedgehog; stoat, weasel, ferret; fox, vixen, Reynard; jackal, hyena, lion (see *cat*); hare, rabbit, bunny; otter, beaver, water rat *or* vole; walrus, seal, sea lion; cetacean, dolphin, porpoise, whale; pachyderm, elephant, tusker, rhinoceros, hippopotamus; bear, polar b., grizzly b., bruin; giant panda; ungulate, giraffe, zebra (see *cattle*); deer, stag, hart, buck, doe; red deer, fallow d.,

roe d., muntjac; reindeer, caribou; elk, moose; gazelle, antelope, chamois, springbok, eland, hartebeest, wildebeest, gnu; horse, donkey, camel 273 *beast of burden*.

bird, winged thing, fowls of the air; fledgeling 132 *young creature*; avifauna, birdlife; cagebird, canary, budgerigar; parrot, polly, macaw, mynah bird; songbird, songster, warbler, nightingale, philomel, bulbul, lark, thrush, throstle, mavis, blackbird, linnet; curlew, plover, lapwing, peewit; dove, pigeon; woodpecker, yaffle, jay, magpie, pie; jackdaw, rook, raven, crow; finch, goldfinch, greenfinch, chaffinch; tit, wren, robin, sparrow, yellowhammer, wagtail, pied w.; exotic bird, humming b., sunbird, weaver b., bird of paradise, lyrebird; hoopoe, golden oriole; bird of passage, migrant, cuckoo, swallow, swift; redwing, fieldfare; flightless bird, emu, ostrich, rhea, cassowary, kiwi, penguin; nightbird, owl, nightjar; scavenging bird, vulture, marabou, carrion crow; bird of prey, raptor, eagle, golden e., bird of Jove, King of birds; kite, kestrel, harrier, osprey, buzzard, hawk, sparrowhawk, falcon, peregrine f., hobby, merlin, shrike; fishing bird, pelican, kingfisher, gannet, cormorant, shag; gull, herring g., kittiwake, tern, puffin, guillemot; ocean bird, albatross, shearwater, petrel, stormy p., Mother Carey's chickens; marsh bird, wader, stork, crane, avocet, heron, bittern; spoonbill, ibis, flamingo; waterfowl, swan, cob, pen; duck, drake; goose, gander, merganser, teal, mallard, widgeon; moorhen, coot, lily-trotter, diver, dipper, grebe, dabchick.

table bird, game b., woodcock, wood pigeon, squab; peafowl, peacock, peahen; grouse, ptarmigan, capercaillie, pheasant, partridge, quail; goose, duck, snipe; turkey, gobbler; guinea fowl.

poultry, fowl, hen, biddy; cock, cockerel, rooster, Chanticleer; chicken, pullet; spring chicken, boiler, broiler, roaster, capon; leghorn, bantam.

cattle, kine, livestock 369 *stock farm*; bull, cow, calf, heifer, fatling, yearling;

bullock, steer; beef cattle, dairy cattle, milch cow; zebu; ox, oxen; buffalo, bison; yak, musk ox; goat, billy g., nanny g.

sheep, ram, tup, wether, bell w., ewe, lamb, lambkin; teg; merino; mouflon.

pig, swine, boar, tusker, warthog; hog, sow, piglet, pigling, sucking pig, shoat, porker.

dog, canine, bow-wow, man's best friend; bitch, whelp, pup, puppy; cur, hound, tike, pooch, mutt; mongrel, pariah dog, pye-d.; guide dog, house d., watch d., bandog, bloodhound, mastiff; sheepdog, collie; bull terrier, bulldog, boxer; wolfhound, borzoi, Afghan hound, Alsatian, Dalmatian; Great Dane; St Bernard; greyhound, courser, whippet; foxhound, beagle; basset, dachshund; gun dog, retriever, pointer, setter; terrier, spaniel; show dog, toy d., chihuahua, chow; lap dog, pekinese, peke, pug; poodle, corgi; husky; wild dog, dingo; wolf, coyote.

cat, feline; grimalkin, moggie, pussy, kitty, kitten; tom, queen; mouser; tortoiseshell, tabby; big cat, lion, lioness, King of Beasts; tiger, leopard, cheetah, panther, puma, jaguar, cougar, ocelot; wildcat, bobocat, lynx.

amphibian, frog, toad, natterjack; newt, eft; salamander, axolotl.

reptile, ophidian, serpent, sea s.; snake, grass s., smooth s.; viper, adder, asp; cobra, hamadryad; puff adder, mamba, rattlesnake; anaconda, boa constrictor; python; crocodile, alligator, cayman; lizard, legless l., slow-worm, blindworm; chameleon, iguana, monitor, gecko; turtle, tortoise, terrapin.

marine life, denizens of the deep; nekton, benthos; cetacean (see *mammal*); sea urchin, sea horse, sea anemone, coral, jellyfish, starfish; shellfish, mollusc, bivalve, clam, oyster, mussel, cockle; whelk, winkle, limpet; cephalopod, cuttlefish, squid, octopus; crustacean, crab, lobster, crayfish, shrimp; barnacle.

fish, flying f., swordfish, angelfish, dogfish, moray eel, shark; piranha, barracuda; electric ray; marlin, tunny fish, turbot, bass, conger eel 301 *fish food*; coelacanth; blenny, goby, wrasse; pike, roach, perch, dace, bream, carp; trout, grayling; salmon, grilse; eel, elver, lamprey; minnow, stickleback.

insect, larva, pupa, imago; fly, house f., horse f., gadfly, bluebottle; mayfly, caddis fly; gnat, midge, tsetse fly, mosquito; greenfly, blackfly, aphid; ladybird, lacewing, hoverfly; firefly, glow-worm; dragonfly, crane fly, daddy longlegs; butterfly, moth, hawk m., clothes m.; bee, bumble bee, honey b., queen b., worker b., drone; wasp, hornet; beetle, cockroach; pests, vermin, parasites; bug, bed bug, flea, louse, nit, mite, tick, jigger; woodworm, weevil, borer, cockchafer 659 *blight*; ant, termite; stick insect, praying mantis; locust, grass-hopper, cicada, cricket.

creepy-crawly, grub, maggot, caterpillar, looper, inchworm; worm, earthworm, lugworm, wireworm, roundworm, flatworm, tapeworm, fluke; myriapod, centipede, millipede; slug, snail; earwig, woodlouse; spider, money s.; tarantula, scorpion 904 *noxious animal*.

Adj. *animal*, animalcular; brutish, beastly, bestial, subhuman; feral, domestic; therianthropic, theriomorphic, zoomorphic; zoological; vertebrate, invertebrate; mammalian, warm-blooded; primatial, anthropoid, simian; equine, asinine, mulish; cervine; bovine, taurine, ruminant; ovine, sheepish; goatish; porcine, piggy; bearish, ursine; elephantine; canine, doggy; lupine, wolfish; feline, catlike, cattish, tigerish, leonine; vulpine, foxy; avian, birdlike; aquiline, vulturine; passerine; owlish; gallinaceous, anserine; cold-blooded, fishy, piscine, molluscan; amphibian, amphibious, salientian; reptilian, saurian, ophidian, snaky, serpentine, viperish; vermicular, wormy, weevilly; verminous; lepidopterous, entomological.

366. Vegetable life – N. *vegetable life*, vegetable kingdom; flora, vegetation; biomass; flowering, blooming, florescence; lushness, rankness 171 *abundance*; Flora, Pan; faun, dryad 967 *nymph*.

wood, timber, lumber, softwood, hardwood, heartwood, sapwood; forest, virgin f., rain f., jungle; taiga; bush, scrub, maquis, chapparal; greenwood, woodland, copse, coppice, spinney; thicket, brake, covert; hurst, holt; plantation, arboretum, pinetum, pinery; orchard 370 *garden*; grove, clump; clearing, glade; brushwood, underwood, undergrowth; shrubbery, windbreak, hedge, hedgerow.

forestry, dendrology, silviculture; afforestation, conservation; woodman, forester, verderer; woodcutter, lumberjack; dendrologist 370 *gardener*.

tree, shrub, bush, sapling, scion, stock; pollard; bonsai; shoot, sucker, trunk, bole; limb, branch, bough, twig; conifer, evergreen; deciduous tree; fruit tree, nut t., timber t.; mahogany, ebony, teak, walnut, oak, elm, ash, beech, sycamore, maple, plane, lime, linden; cedar, larch, fir, spruce, pine, Scots p.; poplar, aspen, alder, sallow, willow; birch, silver b., rowan, mountain ash; crab apple, chestnut, hazel, elder, spindle, hawthorn, may, blackthorn, sloe; privet, yew, holly, ivy, box, bay, laurel; magnolia, laburnum, lilac; acacia, jacaranda; palm, baobab, banyan, mangrove; gum tree, eucalyptus.

foliage, foliation, frondescence; greenery, verdure; leafiness, leafage; herbage; umbrage; limb, branch, bough, twig, shoot; spray, sprig; leaf, frond, blade; leaflet, foliole; pine needle; cotyledon; petiole, stipule, node, stalk, stem; tendril, prickle, thorn.

plant, herb, wort, weed; root, tuber, rhizome, bulb, corm 156 *source*; stolon, cutting 132 *young plant*; culinary herb 301 *potherb*; medicinal herb 658 *remedy*; food plant, fodder 301 *vegetable*, *fruit*, *provender*; rose, leek, daffodil, thistle, shamrock; pansy, carnation, lily; lavender, honeysuckle 396 *fragrance*; daisy, dandelion, buttercup; cactus, succulent; bramble, gorse; creeper, climber, twiner, vine, bine; parasite, mistletoe; horsetail, fern, bracken; moss, sphagnum; liverwort; lichen, fungus, mushroom, toadstool; mould, penicillin; seaweed, wrack, kelp; algae 196 *microorganism*.

flower, floweret, floret, blossom, bloom, bud, burgeon; petal, sepal; corolla, calyx; fruit, berry, nut, drupe; seed vessel, pod, capsule, cone; pip, spore, seed 156 *source*; annual, biennial, perennial; house plant, pot p.; hothouse p., exotic 370 *garden*.

grass, mowing g., hay; pasture, herbage 348 *grassland*; verdure, turf, sod, lawn; bent, fescue; sedge, rush, reed; bamboo, sugar cane; grain plant, oats, barley, rice 301 *cereals*; stubble, straw.

Adj. *vegetal*, vegetative, vegetable, botanical; evergreen; deciduous; hardy, half-hardy; floricultural 370 *horticultural*; floral, flowery, blooming; rank, lush, overgrown; weedy; leafy, verdant, verdurous 434 *green*; grassy, mossy; turfy; gramineous, herbaceous, herbal; fungous, fungoid, fungiform; dicotyledonous, monocotyledonous.

arboreal, arboreous, dendriform, arborescent, treelike; forested, timbered; woodland, woody, wooded, sylvan, arboraceous; grovy, bosky; jungly, scrubby; bushy, shrubby; afforested, planted; dendrological.

wooden, woody, ligneous, ligniform; hard-grained, soft-grained.

Vb. *vegetate*, germinate 36 *grow*; plant 370 *cultivate*; forest, afforest, reforest, replant.

367. Zoology; the science of animals – N.

zoology, zoography, zootomy; zoogeography; physiology, morphology 331 *structure*; embryology 358 *biology*; anatomy; ethology; anthropography 371 *anthropology*; ornithology, bird watching; ichthyology, herpetology, ophiology, mammalogy, malacology, helminthology, entomology, conchology; palaeontology; taxidermy.

zoologist, ornithologist, etc. n.; entomologist, lepidopterist; anatomist.

368. Botany: the science of plants – N.

botany, phytography, phytotomy; taxonomy; plant physiology, plant pathology; plant ecology; dendrology 366 *forestry*; agrostology; mycology, fungology, bryology, algology; palaeobotany; botanical garden 370 *garden*; hortus siccus, herbarium, herbal; botanist, herbalist, taxonomist etc. n.

369. Animal husbandry – N. *animal husbandry*, animal management; training, manège; domestication; veterinary science; horse-breeding, cattle-raising; dairy farming, beef f. 365 *cattle*; sheep farming, pig-keeping, goat-k., bee-k., poultry farming; stirpiculture, pisciculture, aviculture, apiculture, sericulture; veterinary surgeon, vet, horse doctor 658 *doctor*; ostler, groom, stable lad *or* girl 742 *servant*; farrier, blacksmith; gamekeeper, gillie; game warden.

stock farm, stud f.; dairy farm, cattle f., ranch; fish farm, hatchery; piggery; beehive, hive, apiary; pasture, grazing 348 *grassland*; chicken run, free range; broiler house, battery, deep litter; factory farm.

cattle pen, byre 192 *stable*; sheepfold 235 *enclosure*; hutch, coop, henhouse; cowshed, pigsty; swannery; bird cage, aviary.

zoo, zoological gardens, menagerie, circus; Noah's Ark; aviary, vivarium, terrarium, aquarium; wildlife park, safari p.; game reserve.

breeder, stock b.; trainer, lion-tamer; cattle farmer, sheep f., pig-keeper, bee-k., apiarist; bird-fancier, pigeon-f.

herdsman, cowherd; stockman, cattleman; cowboy, cowgirl, cowpuncher; broncobuster, gaucho; shepherd, shepherdess; goatherd; goosegirl; milkmaid, dairymaid; kennel maid.

Vb. *break in*, tame, domesticate 610 *habituate*; train 534 *teach*; back, mount 267 *ride*; yoke, harness; round up, herd, corral 235 *enclose*.

breed stock, breed, rear, raise, grow, hatch, culture, incubate, nurture, fatten; ranch, farm 370 *cultivate*.

groom, currycomb, rub down, stable, bed down; tend, herd, shepherd; shear, fleece; milk; water, fodder 301 *feed*.

370. Agriculture – N. *agriculture*, agronomics, rural economy; agribusiness 622 *business*; cultivation, ploughing, sowing, reaping; harvest, crop, vintage 632 *store*; cash crop, catch c., fodder c.; husbandry, farming, mixed f., contract f., factory f., intensive f., organic f., monoculture; cattle farming 369 *animal husbandry*; cereal farming, arable f.; hydroponics, tray agriculture, tank farming; irrigation 341 *moistening*; geoponics; tillage, tilth, spadework; green fingers; floriculture, flower-growing; horticulture, gardening, market g.; viticulture, viniculture, wine-growing, vine-dressing; arboriculture 366 *forestry*; manure 171 *fertilizer*; silage, ensilage 632 *storage*.

farm, home f., grange; arable farm; dairy f. 369 *stock farm*; ranch, hacienda; farmstead, farmhouse; farmyard 235 *enclosure*; collective farm, kolkhoz, kibbutz; farmland, arable land, ploughed land, fallow; paddy, paddyfield; pasturage 348 *grassland*; demesne, manor farm, holding, smallholding, croft 777 *lands*; market garden, nursery, garden centre; vineyard; fruit farm, orchard; tea estate, coffee e., sugar plantation, rubber p.

garden, rose g., knot g., herb g., rock g., winter g.; cabbage patch, kitchen garden, allotment; orchard; arboretum 366 *wood*; patch, plot; greensward, lawn; park 235 *enclosure*; shrubbery, border, flowerbed 844 *ornamental art*; seedbed, cold frame, propagator; cloche, conservatory, hothouse, greenhouse, glasshouse, orangery.

farmer, husbandman, farm manager, bailiff; cultivator, planter, tea p.; agronomist, agriculturalist; peasant, serf; share-cropper, tenant farmer; gentleman farmer, yeoman; smallholder, crofter; fruit grower, wine-grower; farm hand, farm labourer, agricultural worker; land girl; ploughman, tractor driver, sower, reaper, harvester, gleaner; thresher; picker, hop p., fruit p., vintager; agricultural folk, farming community 869 *country-dweller*.

gardener, horticulturist, flower grower; topiarist, landscape gardener; seedsman, nurseryman *or* -woman; market gardener;

hop-grower, fruit-g., vine-grower, vine-dresser; arborist, arboriculturalist, silviculturist 366 *forestry*; planter, digger, delver, Adam.

farm tool, plough, ploughshare, coulter; harrow, ʾake; spade, fork, hoe; trowel; dibble, digging stick; drill; hayfork, pitchfork; scythe, sickle 256 *sharp edge*; flail; winepress, ciderpress; mowing machine, reaper, thresher, binder, baler, combine harvester, pea viner; tractor; hay wain, haystack; barn, hayloft, silo 632 *storage*.

Adj. *agrarian*, peasant, farming; agrestic, georgic, bucolic, pastoral, rural, rustic; agricultural, agronomic, geoponic; arable, cultivable; ploughed, dug, planted etc. vb.

horticultural, garden, gardening, topiary; silvicultural; herbal; cultured, forced, hothouse, exotic.

Vb. *cultivate*, bring under cultivation 171 *make fruitful*; farm, ranch, garden, grow; till the soil, dig, double-dig, delve, spade, dibble; seed, sow, broadcast; set, plant, prick out, transplant, plant out, bed o.; plough, harrow, rake, hoe; weed, prune, top and lop 204 *shorten*; graft, engraft 303 *implant*; layer, take cuttings; force, fertilize, topdress, mulch, manure 174 *invigorate*; grass over, rotate the crop; leave fallow; harvest, gather in 632 *store*; glean, reap, mow, cut, scythe; bind, bale, stook; flail, thresh, winnow; crop, pluck, pick, gather; ensile, ensilage; fence in 235 *enclose*; ditch, drain, reclaim; irrigate.

371. Humankind – N. *humankind*, mankind, womankind; humanity, human nature; flesh, mortality; the world, everybody, the living, ourselves; human race, hominid, homo sapiens, man; tellurian, earthling; human being, Adam, Eve, lords of creation; political animal 654 *civilization*; early humanity, Stone-Age h., Cro-Magnon, Neanderthal, cavemen and -women, troglodytes; cyborg; android; ethnic type 11 *race*.

anthropology, anthropography; craniometry, craniology; anthropogenesis, somatology; ethnology, ethnography, folklore, mythology; social anthropology, demography; social science 901 *sociology*; anthropologist, ethnographer, demographer, folklorist, humanist.

person, individual, human being; creature, fellow c., mortal, body, bod; being, soul, living s.; God's image; one, someone, so-and-so; party, customer, character, type, element; chap, fellow 372 *male*; girl, female 373 *woman*; personage, figure 638 *bigwig*; dramatis personae 686 *personnel*; unit, head, hand, nose.

social group, society, community 74 *group*; kinship group, tribalism 11 *family*; comity of nations 706 *cooperation*; community at large, people, persons, folk; public, you and me 79 *everyman*; population, populace, citizenry 191 *inhabitants*; the masses 869 *commonalty*; social classes 869 *lower classes*, middle c., 868 *upper class*, aristocracy.

nation, nationality, statehood, nationalism, national consciousness, race c.; Pan-Africanism, Negritude; ultranationalism, chauvinism, jingoism, expansionism, imperialism, colonialism; civil society, body politic, people, demos; state, nation s., multiracial s. 733 *political organization*.

Adj. *human*, creaturely, mortal, fleshly; earthborn, tellurian; anthropoid, hominoid; subhuman 35 *inferior*; anthropological, ethnographical 11 *ethnic*; anthropocentric, anthropomorphic; personal, individual.

national, state, civic, civil, public, general, communal, tribal, social, societal; cosmopolitan, international.

372. Male – N. *male*, male sex, man, he, him; Adam; manliness, masculinity, manhood; virility, machismo; male chauvinism; mannishness, virilism; gentleman, sir, esquire, master; lord, my l., his lordship; Mr, mister; squire, guvnor, guv; buster, Mac, Jock; buddy 880 *chum*; goodman, wight, swain; gaffer, buffer 133 *old man*; fellow, guy, scout, bloke, chap, chappie, johnny, gent; codger, card, cove, joker; blade 952 *libertine*; he-man, caveman, macho; male chauvinist pig, MCP; sissy 163 *weakling*; homosexual 84 *nonconformist*; eunuch, castrato; escort, beau, boy friend; bachelor, widower; bridegroom, married man, husband, house h. 894 *spouse*; family man, paterfamilias, patriarch; father 169 *paternity*; uncle, brother, nephew; lad, boy 132 *youngster*; son 170 *sonship*; spear side; stag party, menfolk.

male animal, jack, cock, drake, gander; buck, stag, hart; horse, stallion; bull, bullock, steer; ram, tup; he-goat, billy g.; dog, dog fox, tom cat; gelding, capon 161 *eunuch*.

Adj. *male*, masculine, manly, gentlemanly, chivalrous; virile, macho; mannish, manlike, butch, unfeminine, unwomanly.

373. Female – N. *female*, feminine gender, she, her; femineity, feminality, muliebrity; femininity, the eternal feminine; womanhood 134 *adultness*; womanliness, girlishness; feminism, women's rights, Women's Lib *or* Liberation; womanishness, effeminacy 163 *weakness*; gynaecology, gyniatrics.

womankind, second sex, female s., fair s., gentle s., weaker s.; distaff side, womenfolk; hen party; women's quarters, purdah, seraglio, harem.

woman, Eve, she; girl 132 *youngster*; virgin, maiden, maid; unmarried woman, old maid 895 *spinster*; bachelor girl, career woman; feminist, sister, women's libber; suffragette; bride, married woman, wife, widow, matron 894 *spouse*; dowager 133 *old woman*; mother, grandmother 169 *maternity*; unmarried mother, working wife *or* mother, housewife; aunt, niece; sister, daughter; wench, lass, nymph; colleen, damsel; petticoat, skirt, doll, chick, bird; honey, hinny, baby; brunette, blonde, platinum b., redhead; girl friend, sweetheart 887 *loved one*; crumpet, bit of fluff; broad, courtesan 952 *loose woman*; lesbian 84 *nonconformist*; virago, Amazon.

lady, gentlewoman; dame; milady, her ladyship; madam, ma'am, marm, mistress, Mrs, missus, Ms, miss; goody, goodwife.

female animal, hen, pen, bitch; mare, filly; cow, heifer; sow, gilt; ewe; nanny goat; hind, doe; vixen, tigress.

Adj. *female*, feminine, girlish, womanly, ladylike, maidenly, matronly; childbearing 167 *generative*; feminist, feministic; viraginous, amazonian; lesbian; womanish, effeminate, unmanly; feminized, androgynous.

374. Physical sensibility – N. *sensibility*, sensitivity; sensitiveness, soreness, tenderness; exposed nerve, unhealed wound; perceptivity, awareness, consciousness 819 *moral sensibility*; physical sensibility, susceptivity, susceptibility; hyperaesthesia, allergy; funny bone; sensuousness, aestheticism, aesthetics.

sense, sense-perception; sense organ, nervous system; five senses; touch, hearing, taste, smell, sight; sensation, impression 818 *feeling*; response, reaction, reflex, synaesthesia; sixth sense 984 *psychics*.

Adj. *sentient*, perceptive, sensitive, sensitized; sensible, susceptible, passible; sensory, perceptual; sensuous, aesthetic 818 *feeling*; percipient, aware, conscious 490 *knowing*; acute 377 *painful*; ticklish, itchy; tender, raw, sore, exposed; allergic, hypersensitive 819 *impressible*.

Vb. *have feeling*, sense, perceive 490 *know*; react, tingle; hear, see, touch, taste, smell; be alert, have one's wits about one; sensitize.

375. Physical insensibility – N. *insensibility*, impassibility, insensitiveness; imperceptiveness 499 *unintelligence*; impassivity 820 *moral insensibility*; insentience, anaesthesia; hypnosis, autohypnosis; suspended animation; paralysis; numbness; catalepsy, coma, trance, freak-out; faint, swoon, blackout, syncope, unconsciousness, senselessness; narcosis, drugged sleep 679 *sleep*.

anaesthetic, local a., general a. 658 *drug*; ether, morphine, chloral; gas, narcotic, knockout drops 679 *soporific*;

opium, laudanum; painkiller, analgesic 177 *moderator*; acupuncture.

Adj. *insensible*, insentient, insensate; imperceptive 499 *unintelligent*; unaware, oblivious; unhearing 416 *deaf*; unseeing 439 *blind*; senseless, unconscious; inert 679 *inactive*; inanimate, out cold 266 *quiescent*; numb, benumbed, frozen; paralysed, paralytic; doped, drugged; freaked out, spaced o.; stoned 949 *dead drunk*; anaesthetized, hypnotized; punch-drunk, dazed, stupefied; semiconscious, in a trance; cataleptic, comatose; anaesthetic, analgesic; hypnotic 679 *soporific*.

Vb. *be insensible*, become insensible, lose consciousness, pass out, black o., faint, swoon; go into a coma.

render insensible, blunt, deaden; paralyse, benumb; put to sleep, hypnotize, mesmerize 679 *make inactive*; anaesthetize, narcotize, drug, dope; dull, stupefy; stun, concuss, knock out.

376. Physical pleasure – N. *pleasure*, physical p.; thrill 821 *excitation*; enjoyment, gratification, sensuousness, sensuality; self-indulgence, animal gratification 944 *sensualism*; round of pleasure 943 *intemperance*; rest 685 *refreshment*; entertainment 837 *amusement*; feast 301 *feasting*; keen appreciation, delight 824 *joy*.

euphoria, well-being, contentment 828 *content*, 824 *happiness*; physical well-being 650 *health*; gracious living; ease, comfort, creature comforts; lap of luxury 800 *wealth*; feather bed, bed of roses 327 *softness*; peace, quiet 683 *repose*.

Adj. *pleasant*, pleasure-giving 826 *pleasurable*; pleasing, tickling, titillating; delightful, delightsome; welcome, grateful, gratifying, satisfying 685 *refreshing*; genial, congenial, cordial, heart-warming; nice, agreeable, enjoyable 837 *amusing*; palatable, delicious 386 *tasty*; perfumed 396 *fragrant*; tuneful 410 *melodious*; lovely 841 *beautiful*.

comfortable, comfy, homely, snug, cosy, warm, comforting, restful 683 *reposeful*; painless, peaceful 266 *tranquil*; convenient, easy; easeful, downy 327 *soft*;

luxurious, de luxe; euphoric, at one's ease, slippered; pampered, featherbedded; gratified 828 *content*.

sensuous, of the senses, bodily, physical 319 *material*; voluptuous, epicurean, hedonistic 944 *sensual*.

Vb. *enjoy*, relish, like; take pleasure in 824 *be pleased*; thrill to 821 *be excited*; luxuriate in, revel in, bask in, wallow in; gloat over, get a kick out of; lick one's lips, smack one's l. 386 *taste*; live off the fat of the land 730 *prosper*.

377. Physical pain – N. *pain*, physical p., bodily p.; discomfort, malaise; distress, thin time 731 *adversity*; exhaustion, weariness, strain 684 *fatigue*; hurt, bruise, sprain; cut, gash 655 *wound*; aching, smarting; anguish, agony 825 *suffering*; torment, torture; vivisection; rack 964 *instrument of torture*; painfulness, soreness, tenderness; hangover 949 *crapulence*.

pang, thrill, throes; stab, twinge, nip, pinch; pins and needles 378 *formication*; stitch, crick, cramp, convulsion 318 *spasm*; smart, sting, pain, shooting p.; ache, headache, splitting head, migraine; toothache, earache; stomachache 651 *digestive disorders*; neuritis, neuralgia, angina 651 *ill health*.

Adj. *painful*, paining, aching, agonizing, excruciating, exquisite; harrowing, racking, tormenting; poignant 827 *distressing*; burning, biting, stabbing, shooting, tingling, smarting, throbbing; sore, raw, tender; bitter 393 *sour*; disagreeable 827 *unpleasant*.

Vb. *give pain*, ache, hurt, pain, sting; inflict pain, torment 963 *torture*; flog, crucify 963 *punish*; vivisect 46 *cut*; touch the quick; prick, stab 263 *pierce*; gripe, nip, pinch, tweak, twinge; bite, gnaw; grind, grate, jar, set on edge; chafe, gall 333 *rub*; irritate 832 *aggravate*; put on the rack, break on the wheel; kill by inches, prolong the agony; distress 827 *trouble*.

feel pain 825 *suffer*; agonize, ache, smart, chafe; wince, flinch, writhe, squirm 318 *be agitated*; go through it 731 *have trouble*; shriek, scream 408 *cry*; lick one's wounds.

378. Touch: sensation of touch – N. *touch*, tactility, palpability; handling, feeling, palpation, manipulation; massage, kneading 333 *friction*; graze, contact 202 *contiguity*; stroke, pat, caress; flick, tap 279 *knock*.

formication, titillation, tickling sensation; creeps, gooseflesh; tingle, tingling, pins-and-needles; scratchiness, itchiness, itch, urtication; nettlerash, hives; rash, prickly heat 651 *skin disease*; pediculosis 649 *uncleanness*.

feeler, organ of touch, palp, antenna, whisker, tentacle; proboscis, tongue; digit (see *finger*); hand, paw, palm, flipper, mitt.

finger, forefinger, index, middle finger, ring f., little f., pinkie; thumb, pollex; toe 214 *foot*; bunch of fives, fist; 'pickers and stealers' 778 *nippers*; fingernail, talon, claw.

Adj. *tactual*, tactile; palpal, tentacular; prehensile 778 *retentive*; touching, licking, grazing etc. vb.; touchable, tangible, palpable; light of touch, light-handed, heavy-h. 695 *clumsy*.

handed, right-handed 241 *dextral*; left-handed 242 *sinistral*; thumbed, fingered, polydactyl; digitate, digital, manual.

Vb. *touch*, make contact, graze, scrape, shave, brush, glance, kiss 202 *be contiguous*; impinge, overlap; hit, meet 279 *collide*; feel, palpate; finger, thumb, pinch, nip; massage 333 *rub*; palm, stroke 258 *smooth*; wipe 648 *clean*; tap, pat, dab, flick, flip, tickle, scratch; lip, lap, lick, tongue; nuzzle, paw, fondle 889 *caress*; handle, twiddle, fiddle with; manipulate 173 *operate*; bruise, crush 377 *give pain*; fumble, grope, grabble, scrabble; put out a feeler 461 *be tentative*.

itch, tickle, tingle, creep, crawl; prick, prickle, titillate; thrill, excite, irritate.

379. Heat – N. *heat*, caloric; phlogiston; incandescence, flame, glow, flush, blush; warmth, tepidity, lukewarmness; blood heat, body h.; sweat, swelter; fever heat, pyrexia, fever 651 *disease*; high temperature, white heat; ebullition, boiling point, flash p., melting p.; tropical heat, flaming June 128 *summer*; heat wave, scorcher; hot springs, geyser, steam; tropics, torrid zone; sun, sunshine, solar heat 381 *heating*.

fire, flames; bonfire, beacon 417 *glow*; hellfire; pyre 364 *obsequies*; Greek fire 723 *bomb*; deflagration, conflagration, holocaust; heath fire, forest f.; fireball, blaze, flame, tongue of f., sheet of f.; spark, arc 417 *flash*; flare 420 *torch*; eruption, volcano 383 *furnace*; arson 381 *incendiarism*; salamander, phoenix.

thermometry, heat measurement; degree, kelvin, Kelvin scale; thermometer, Fahrenheit t., centigrade *or* Celsius t., Réaumur t.; thermostat, air-conditioner; pyrometer, calorimeter; British Thermal Unit, BTU, therm, calorie; thermodynamics.

Adj. *hot*, heated, superheated, overheated; inflamed, flaming, glowing, red-hot, white-h.; like an oven, hot as hell; piping hot, smoking h.; feverish, febrile, fevered; sweltering, sudorific; steaming, smoking; boiling, scalding; tropical, torrid, scorching, blistering, etc. vb.; scorched 381 *heated*; thirsty, parched 342 *dry*.

fiery, ardent, burning, blazing, flaming; unquenched, unextinguished; smoking, smouldering; ablaze, afire, on fire, in flames; candescent, incandescent, molten, glowing 431 *red*; ignited, lit, alight; volcanic.

warm, tepid, lukewarm; temperate, mild, genial, balmy; fair, sunny, sunshiny; summery, aestival; tropical, equatorial; torrid, sultry; stuffy, close, muggy; overheated, unventilated; oppressive, suffocating, stifling 653 *insalubrious*; warm as toast; snug 376 *comfortable*; at room temperature, at blood heat; caloric, calorific; thermic, thermal, isothermal.

Vb. *be hot*, be warm; burn, kindle, catch fire, draw; blaze, flare, flame; glow, flush; smoke, smoulder, steam 300 *emit*; boil, seethe; toast, grill, roast, sizzle, crackle, frizzle, fry, bake 381 *burn*; bask, sun oneself, sunbathe; sweat, perspire; melt, thaw; thirst, parch; run a temperature; keep warm, wrap up.

380. Cold – N. *coldness*, low temperature; cool, coolness, freshness; cold, freezing c., zero, freezing point; frigidity, gelidity; iciness, frostiness; chilliness, algidity; hypothermia; shivering, shivers, goose pimples, frostbite, chilblains; chill, catching cold; cold climate, Siberia, North Pole.

wintriness, winter; nip in the air, cold snap; inclemency, cold weather, cold front; arctic conditions, degrees of frost; snowstorm, hailstorm, blizzard; frost, Jack Frost, rime, hoarfrost; sleet, hail, black ice, freeze.

snow, snowfall, snowflake, snow crystal; avalanche, snowdrift, snowstorm, snow flurry; winter sports 837 *sport*.

ice, dry i., ice cube; hailstone, icicle; ice cap, ice sheet, ice floe, iceberg, glacier, icefall, serac; pack ice, icebreaker, ice yacht; icebox 384 *refrigerator*; glaciation 382 *refrigeration*; glaciology.

Adj. *cold*, impervious to heat, adiathermanous; cool, temperate; shady, chill, chilly, parky, nippy; unheated; fresh, raw, keen, bitter, nipping, biting, piercing; inclement, freezing, gelid, ice-cold, below zero; frigid, brumal 129 *wintry*; winterbound, frosty, snowy, snow-covered; slushy, sleety, icy; glacial, ice-capped, glaciated; boreal, polar, arctic, Siberian.

chilly, shivering, chattering, shivery, algid, aguish; blue with cold; perishing, chilled, frozen, frostbitten; like ice, cold as marble, stone-cold.

Vb. *be cold*, etc. adj.; lose heat, feel cold, chatter, shiver; freeze, starve, catch cold, get a chill; chill 382 *refrigerate*.

381. Heating – N. *heating*, calefaction, torrefaction; diathermancy; transcalency; space heating, central h., district heating system 383 *heater*; insolation 342 *desiccation*; melting, smelting, boiling; baking 301 *cookery*.

burning, combustion; inflammation, kindling, ignition; reheat; incineration 379 *fire*; cremation 364 *interment*; holocaust 981 *oblation*; cauterization, branding; scorching, singeing, charring, carbonization; inflammability, combustibility;

burner 383 *furnace*; cauterizer, branding iron; match 385 *lighter*; burn, brand, singe, scald, sunburn, tan.

incendiarism, arson, fire-raising, pyromania; incendiary, arsonist, fire-raiser.

ash, ashes; lava, tuff; carbon, soot, smut, smoke; clinker, charcoal, ember, cinder, coke, slag.

pottery, ceramics; earthenware, stoneware; majolica, faience, chinaware; porcelain; crockery, china, bone c.; delf, willow pattern; terracotta, tile, brick, adobe; pot 194 *vessel*.

Adj. *heated*, superheated 379 *hot*; lit, kindled, fired; incinerated, burnt, gutted; toasted etc. vb.; réchauffé, warmed up; melted, fused, molten; steamy, smoky; scorched, charred, singed, branded; bronzed, tanned, sun-t., sunburnt.

heating, warming etc. vb.; calefactive, calorific; caustic, burning; solid-fuel, coal-burning, oil-fired; incendiary, inflammatory; inflammable 385 *combustible*.

Vb. *heat*, warm, take the chill off; hot up, warm up, stoke up; thaw out; inflame, foment; overheat, stew, stifle, suffocate; insolate 342 *dry*; torrefy, toast, bake, roast 301 *cook*; melt, defrost, deice 337 *liquefy*; smelt, fuse, weld, vulcanize.

kindle, ignite, light; set fire to, fire; rekindle, relume; fuel, stoke, feed the flames.

burn, fire, set fire to, set on fire; cremate, incinerate; carbonize, oxidize; char, singe, scorch, tan; cauterize, brand; scald.

382. Refrigeration – N. *refrigeration*, cooling etc. vb.; freezing, glaciation, gelation, congelation 380 *ice*; exposure; ventilation, air-conditioning; cold storage 384 *refrigerator*; cryonic suspension.

extinguisher, fire e.; sprinkler, hydrant; fire engine, fire brigade, fire station; fireman *or* -woman, fire-fighter.

Adj. *cooled*, chilled etc. vb.; ventilated, air-conditioned; iced up; frozen, deep-frozen, freeze-dried; glaciated; frosted, iced, glacé, frappé, on the rocks 380 *cold*; frigorific, refrigeratory.

incombustible, unburnable; nonflammable; fire-resistant, fireproof, flame-proof; asbestive; damped, wetted 341 *drenched*.

Vb. *refrigerate*, cool, fan, air-condition 685 *refresh*; ventilate 340 *aerate*; shade, shadow 421 *screen*; frost, freeze, congeal, glaciate; deep-freeze, freeze-dry, lyophilize; ice; chill, benumb, starve, nip, pinch, pierce; frost-bite.

extinguish, quench, snuff, put out; stifle, smother; damp, damp down, bank d.; rake out, stamp o., stub o.; go out, burn o., die down.

383. Furnace – N. *furnace*, the stake; volcano, fumarole; forge, blast furnace; kiln; oasthouse; incinerator, destructor; crematory, crematorium; brazier, stove, primus s.; oven, cooker, range; gas ring, burner, bunsen b.; blowlamp, oxyacetylene lamp; fire, open f.; brand 385 *lighter*; fireplace, grate, hearth; flue 263 *chimney*.

heater, space h., radiator, solar panel; hot-air duct, hypocaust; immersion heater, geyser, boiler, back b., copper, kettle 194 *cauldron*; hotplate; warming pan, hot-water bottle; electric blanket, foot-warmer; still, retort, alembic 461 *testing agent*; blowpipe, bellows, damper; Turkish bath, sauna 648 *ablutions*; hothouse 370 *garden*; sun trap, solarium; grill, toaster; soldering iron, curling tongs; flame, sunlight 381 *heating*; solar energy 160 *sources of energy*; wood, coal 385 *fuel*.

384. Refrigerator – N. *refrigerator*, cooler; ventilator, fan, air-conditioner; fridge, chiller, cooler, ice bucket; coolant, ice, ice-cubes; icehouse, icebox, ice pack, cold p., icebag; cold storage, freezer, deep-freeze 382 *refrigeration*.

385. Fuel – N. *fuel*, inflammable material; firing, kindling; wood, brushwood, firewood, faggot, log, Yule l.; biomass 366 *vegetable life*; turf, peat; dung; lignite, charcoal; fossil fuel, coal, natural gas, petroleum 357 *oil*, 336 *gas*; nuclear fuel, uranium, plutonium 160 *nucleonics*; petrol, juice, gasoline; diesel oil, derv; paraffin,

kerosene; alcohol, methylated spirit; propane, butane, methane, biogas.

coal, black diamond, sea coal; anthracite, coke, smokeless fuel; coal dust, culm, slack; coal seam, coal measure 632 *store*; cinders, embers 381 *ash*.

lighter, igniter, light, pilot l.; taper, spill 420 *torch*; ember, brand; fire ship, incendiary bomb 723 *bomb*; wick, fuse, touchpaper, match; cap, detonator; flint, steel, tinder, touchwood, punk, spunk, amadou; tinderbox, matchbox.

Adj. *combustible*, burnable, inflammable, flammable, incendiary, explosive; carboniferous, coal-bearing, coaly.

386. Taste – N. *taste*, sapor, sapidity, savour; flavour, flavouring; smack, tang, twang, aftertaste; relish, zest; tasting, gustation; palate, tongue, tastebuds; tooth, sweet t.

Adj. *tasty*, sapid, saporous, palatable, flavourful, mouth-watering 390 *savoury*; well-seasoned, tangy 388 *pungent*; flavoured, spiced; strong, full-flavoured, full-bodied, fruity, hoppy, mellow, vintage; gustatory, gustative.

Vb. *taste*, smack one's lips, savour, sample, try; sip, nibble 301 *eat*; taste of, savour of, smack of; taste good, tickle the palate 390 *make appetizing*.

387. Insipidity – N. *insipidity*, vapidity, jejuneness, tastelessness etc. adj.; milk and water, pap, slops, catlap.

Adj. *tasteless*, devoid of taste; jejune, vapid, insipid, watery, milk-and-water; mild, underproof; diluted, adulterated 163 *weakened*; wishy-washy, sloppy; unappetizing 391 *unsavoury*; flat, stale; savourless, zestless, flavourless, unspiced, unseasoned.

388. Pungency – N. *pungency*, piquancy, sting, kick, bite, edge; spiciness; acridity, sharpness 393 *sourness*; roughness, harshness 391 *unsavouriness*; tang, twang, raciness; salt, pepper, pickle 389 *condiment*; pick-me-up, bracer 174 *stimulant*; tot 301 *draught*.

tobacco, nicotine; the weed, filthy w.; snuff, rappee, maccaboy; plug of tobacco, quid, fid, twist; flake, shag; cigar, cheroot; smoke, cigarette, coffin-nail; reefer, joint 949 *drug-taking*; tobacco pipe, churchwarden, briar; meerschaum; hubble-bubble, hookah, narghile; pipe of peace, calumet; smoker, pipe s., cigarette s., chain s.; tobacconist; snuff box, cigarette case, cigar c., humidor; smokeroom; smoking compartment.

Adj. *pungent*, penetrating, strong; mordant 256 *sharp*; caustic, burning, smoky; harsh 259 *rough*; bitter, acrid, tart 393 *sour*; heady, overproof; full-flavoured, nutty 386 *tasty*; strong-flavoured, high, gamy; highly-seasoned, spicy, spiced, curried; hot, gingery, peppery; zesty, tangy, minty, piquant 390 *savoury*.

salty, salt, brackish, briny, saline, pickled.

Vb. *be pungent*, sting, bite the tongue, set the teeth on edge, make the eyes water.

season, salt, brine, marinade, souse, pickle; flavour, sauce; spice, pepper, devil, curry; smoke, kipper 666 *preserve*.

smoke, indulge, draw, inhale; take a drag; puff, blow smoke rings; chainsmoke, smoke like a chimney; chew a quid; snuff, take snuff.

389. Condiment – N. *condiment*, seasoning, flavouring, dressing, relish, garnish; salt, mustard, pepper, cayenne, paprika, chilli, caper; peppercorn; curry powder, turmeric; onion, garlic 301 *potherb*; spicery, spices, spice, allspice, mace, cinnamon, ginger, nutmeg, clove.

sauce, roux; gravy, stock; tomato sauce, ketchup; chilli sauce, soy s., Worcester s.; chutney; pickles; salad dressing, mayonnaise.

390. Savouriness – N. *savouriness*, tastiness, palatability; raciness, fine flavour, full f., richness; body, bouquet; savoury, relish, appetizer; delicacy, dainty 301 *mouthful*; ambrosia, nectar; epicure's delight.

Adj. *savoury*, nice, good to eat; seasoned, spicy 386 *tasty*; done to a turn; tempting, appetizing, zestful 388 *pungent*; to one's taste, palatable, toothsome, sweet; dainty, delicate; delectable, delicious, exquisite, choice, epicurean; ambrosial, nectareous, fit for the gods; scrumptious, yummy, moreish; luscious, juicy, succulent; creamy, rich, velvety; gamy, racy, high; vintage.

Vb. *make appetizing*, spice, ginger, pep up 388 *season*; be savoury, tempt the appetite, tickle the palate; smell good, taste good; like, relish, savour, lap up, smack one's lips, roll on one's tongue, lick one's fingers, water at the mouth.

391. Unsavouriness – N. *unsavouriness*, unpalatability; rottenness, unwholesomeness; acerbity, acridity 393 *sourness*; austerity, bread and water; emetic, sickener 659 *poison*.

Adj. *unsavoury*, flat 387 *tasteless*; unpalatable, unappetizing, uninviting; raw, uncooked; overdone, burnt; uneatable, inedible; stale, hard, leathery 329 *tough*; soggy 327 *soft*; sugarless, unsweetened; acrid 388 *pungent*; bitter 393 *sour*; undrinkable, corked; rank, rancid, putrid, rotten, gone off, high 397 *fetid*; revolting 827 *unpleasant*; sickly, cloying; sickening, emetic; poisonous 653 *toxic*.

Vb. *be unpalatable*, etc. adj.; taste horrid; disgust, sicken, nauseate, turn the stomach 861 *cause dislike*; poison; lose its savour, pall.

392. Sweetness – N. *sweetness*, sweetening; sugariness, saccharinity; sweet tooth; saccharimeter.

sweet thing, sweetening, honey; saccharin, sugar; molasses, syrup, treacle; julep, nectar, hydromel, mead; conserve, preserve; jam, marmalade; marzipan; fudge, sugar candy 301 *sweets*; jujube, cachou, lozenge, pastille; confectionery, confection, cake 301 *pastries*, *dessert*.

Adj. *sweet*, sweetened, honeyed, candied, crystallized; iced, sugared; sugary, saccharine; delicious 390 *savoury*.

Vb. *sweeten*, sugar, candy; sugar the pill.

393. Sourness – N. *sourness*, acidity, acerbity; tartness, bitterness, sharpness 388 *pungency*; lemon, vinegar; gall, wormwood, absinth.

Adj. *sour*, sourish, acid, acidulous, acetous, acetic; acerbic, tart, bitter; sharp, astringent 388 *pungent*; vinegary 391 *unsavoury*; unripe, green; unsweetened, dry.

Vb. *be sour*, – acid etc. adj.; sour, turn; acidify, acidulate; ferment; set one's teeth on edge.

394. Odour – N. *odour*, smell, aroma, bouquet, nose; sweet smell 396 *fragrance*; bad smell 397 *stench*; exhalation, effluvium, emanation; smoke, fume, reek; breath, whiff, waft; odorousness, redolence; tang, scent, trail 548 *trace*; olfaction, sense of smell; olfactories, nostril, nose 254 *protuberance*; good nose, keen-scentedness.

Adj. *odorous*, odoriferous, smelling; scented 396 *fragrant*; strong, heady 388 *pungent*; smelly, redolent, reeking; malodorous 397 *fetid*; olfactory; keen-scented, sharp-nosed.

Vb. *smell*, smell of, breathe of, reek of; exhale; smell a mile off; smell out, scent, nose, wind 484 *detect*; get a whiff of; snuff, snuff up, sniff, breathe in, inhale 352 *breathe*.

395. Inodorousness – N. *inodorousness*, odourlessness, scentlessness; absence of smell; inability to smell, anosmia; deodorant, deodorizer; deodorization, ventilation 648 *cleansing*.

Adj. *odourless*, inodorous, scentless; unscented, unperfumed; deodorized.

Vb. *have no smell*, not smell; deodorize, ventilate, clear the air 648 *purify*; lose the scent.

396. Fragrance – N. *fragrance*, sweet smell; aroma, bouquet 394 *odour*; violet, roses 370 *garden*; buttonhole, nosegay; thurification; perfumery, perfumer.

scent, perfume; balm, incense; spicery 389 *condiment*; breath-sweetener, cloves, cachou; musk, civet, ambergris, camphor; sandalwood, patchouli; essential oil, otto,

attar; lavender, thyme, honeysuckle; toilet water, lavender w., eau-de-cologne 843 *cosmetic*; mothball, lavender bag, sachet; pomander, potpourri; joss stick, censer, thurible.

Adj. *fragrant*, redolent, odorous, odoriferous, aromatic, scented, perfumed 376 *pleasant*; incense-breathing, balmy, ambrosial; sweet-scented, sweetly-perfumed; thuriferous, perfumatory; musky, spicy, fruity; rose-scented, laid up in lavender.

Vb. *be fragrant*, smell sweet, have a perfume; scent, perfume, thurify, cense.

397. Stench – N. *stench*, fetor, fetidness, offensiveness; bad smell, bad odour, malodour; body odour, BO; foul breath, halitosis; stink, pong, reek; noxious stench, mephitis; fumes, miasma 336 *gas*; smell of death 51 *decay*; foulness 649 *dirt*; mustiness, fustiness, staleness; frowst, fug; stinkhorn, garlic, asafoetida; skunk, polecat; stinkard, stinker, stinkpot, stink bomb, bad egg; sewer 649 *sink*.

Adj. *fetid*, strong-smelling, reeking; malodorous, not of roses; smelly, whiffy, niffy, pongy, humming; stinking, rank, hircine, foxy; gamy, high; bad, gone b., tainted, rancid 51 *decomposed*; stale, airless, musty, fusty, frowsty, frowzy, fuggy, smoky, stuffy, suffocating; foul, noisome, noxious, sulphurous, mephitic, miasmic 653 *toxic*; acrid, burning 388 *pungent*; offensive 827 *unpleasant*.

Vb. *stink*, smell, reek, pong, niff, hum; make a smell, fart; have a bad smell, smell bad 51 *decompose*; make one hold one's nose; stink out.

398. Sound – N. *sound*, auditory effect; distinctness, audibility, reception 415 *hearing*; sounding, sonancy; audio, mono, monophonic sound, binaural s., stereophonic s., stereo, quadraphonic sound; sound waves, vibrations 417 *radiation*; sound effect, sound track, voiceover; sonority 404 *resonance*; noise 400 *loudness*; softness 401 *faintness*; tone, pitch, level, cadence; accent, intonation, timbre 577 *voice*; tune 410 *melody*, 412 *music*; types of sound 402 *bang*, 403 *roll*, 404 *resonance*, 405 *nonresonance*, 406 *sibilation*, 407 *stridor*, 408 *cry*, 409 *ululation*, 411 *discord*; transmission of sound 531 *telecommunication*; recorded sound, high fidelity 414 *gramophone*; loudspeaker 415 *hearing aid*; unit of sound, decibel, phon, sone; sonic barrier, sound b.

acoustics, phonics; phonology, phonography; phonetics; acoustician, sound engineer; phonetician, phoneticist, phonographer; audiometer; sonometer.

speech sound, simple s., phone, syllable, disyllable, polysyllable; consonant, fricative, affricate, plosive, implosive, spirant, liquid, sibilant; dental, alveolar, labial, bilabial, labiodental, nasal, palatal, guttural, velar, labiovelar; aspiration, inspiration, expiration; stop, glottal s.; click; sonant, sonorant, mute, aspirate, surd; semi-vowel; vowel; diphthong, triphthong 577 *voice*; vocable 559 *word*; sound symbol, phonogram 558 *letter*.

Adj. *sounding*, soniferous, sonant; sonic; plain, audible, distinct, heard; sonorous 404 *resonant*; stentorian 400 *loud*; auditory, acoustic; electrophonic, radiophonic; monaural, monophonic, mono; binaural, stereophonic, stereo, high fidelity, hi-fi; audio, audiovisual; phonic, phonetic; voiced 577 *vocal*; consonantal; vocalic, vowelled; surd, unvoiced, voiceless.

399. Silence – N. *silence*, soundlessness, inaudibility, not a sound; stillness, quiet 266 *quiescence*; muteness 578 *voicelessness*; deathly hush.

Adj. *silent*, still, stilly, hushed; quiet 266 *quiescent*; faint 401 *muted*; noiseless, soundless, inaudible; soundproof; speechless 578 *voiceless*; unsounded, unuttered, unspoken; deathlike, silent as the grave.

Vb. *silence*, still, hush, quiet, quieten; stifle, muffle, gag 578 *make mute*; drown the noise.

Int. hush! sh! silence! quiet! peace! soft! hold your tongue! keep your mouth shut! shut up! keep your trap shut! dry up! cut the cackle! stow it! mum's the word!

400. Loudness – N. *loudness*, audibility 398 *sound*; noise, ear-splitting n.; high volume; sonic boom, thunderclap 402 *bang*; siren 665 *danger signal*; reverberation 403 *roll*; gunfire, artillery 712 *bombardment*; stridency, shrillness 407 *stridor*; trumpet blast 547 *call*; sonority, clangour 404 *resonance*; peal 412 *campanology*; diapason, swell, crescendo, fortissimo, tutti, full blast; vociferation, clamour, outcry 408 *cry*; stertorousness 352 *respiration*; noisiness, din, row, racket, crash, clash, clatter, hubbub, hullabaloo 61 *turmoil*.

megaphone, amplifier 415 *hearing aid*; public address system, loudhailer, loudspeaker, speaker, microphone, mike; siren, hooter, horn, klaxon, gong; rattle, bullroarer; buzzer, bell, alarm; trumpet, brass; stentorian voice, lungs of brass, iron throat; Stentor, town crier.

Adj. *loud*, distinct, audible, heard; turned right up, at full volume; noisy, rackety 61 *disorderly*; multisonous, many-tongued 411 *discordant*; yelling, whooping, screaming, bellowing 408 *crying*; loud-mouthed; sonorous, booming, deep, full, powerful; lusty, full-throated, stentorian, brazen-mouthed, trumpet-tongued; ringing, carrying; deafening, dinning; piercing, ear-splitting; thundering, thunderous; crashing, pealing, clangorous; shrill 407 *strident*; blaring, brassy; resounding 404 *resonant*; swelling, crescendo; fortissimo, enough to waken the dead.

Vb. *be loud*, etc. adj.; give tongue, raise one's voice; call, catcall, caterwaul 407 *shrill*; vociferate, shout, scream 408 *cry*; clap, stamp; roar, bellow 409 *ululate*; din, sound, boom 404 *resound*; thunder, fulminate, storm, clash; ring, peal, clang, crash; bray, blare; slam 402 *bang*; hammer, drill; deafen, stun; split one's ears, ring in the ear; swell, fill the air; rend the skies, make the welkin ring, awake the echoes, waken the dead 61 *rampage*.

Adv. *loudly*, etc. adj.; aloud, at the top of one's voice; in full cry, full blast; fortissimo, crescendo.

401. Faintness – N. *faintness*, softness, indistinctness, inaudibility; low volume; sound-proofing, noise abatement; thump, bump 405 *nonresonance*; whisper, susurration; bated breath, muffled tones 578 *voicelessness*; undertone, murmur 403 *roll*; sigh, sough, moan; scratch, squeak, creak, pop; tick, click; tinkle, clink, chink; purr, purl, plash; swish; rustle, frou-frou; patter, pitter-patter; pad; soft voice, quiet tone.

silencer, mute, damper, muffler, soft pedal, sordine; cork, double-glazing; rubber soles; oil 334 *lubricant*; ear plugs.

Adj. *muted*, distant, faint, inaudible, barely audible; weak, unemphatic, soft, low, gentle; piano, subdued, hushed, stealthy, whispered; dull, dead 405 *nonresonant*; muffled, stifled 407 *hoarse*.

Vb. *sound faint*, drop one's voice, whisper, breathe, murmur, mutter; sing low, hum, croom, purr; babble, ripple, lap 350 *flow*; tinkle, chime; moan, sigh, sough; rustle, swish; steal on the air, die on the ear, fade away, sink into silence; thud 405 *sound dead*.

mute, soften, dull, deaden, dampen, soft-pedal; hush, muffle 399 *silence*.

Adv. *faintly*, in a whisper, with bated breath, under one's breath; sotto voce, aside, in an undertone; piano, pianissimo; inaudibly, distantly, out of earshot.

402. Bang: sudden and violent noise – N. *bang*, report, explosion, detonation, blast, blowout, backfire, sonic boom; peal, thunderclap, crash 400 *loudness*; crepitation, crackling, crackle; smack, crack, snap; slap, clap, tap, rap, rat-tat; knock, slam; pop, plop, plunk; burst, volley, salvo; pistol-shot; cracker, banger, squib; bomb, grenade 723 *firearm*.

Vb. *crackle*, crepitate; sizzle, fizzle, spit; click, rattle; crack, snap, clap, rap, tap, slap, smack; plop, plonk, plunk.

bang, slam, wham, clash, crash, boom; explode, blast; pop, go p.; backfire; burst 400 *be loud*.

403. Roll: repeated and protracted sounds – N. *roll*, rumbling, grumbling; mutter,

murmur; din, racket, clack, clatter, chatter; rattle, booming, clang, ping, reverberation 404 *resonance*; chugging; knocking, drumming, tattoo, devil's t., rat-a-tat, pit-a-pat; peal, carillon; quaver; trill, tremolo, vibrato, hum, whirr, buzz, drone, bombination; ringing, singing; drumfire, machine gun.

Vb. *roll*, drum, tattoo, beat a t.; tap, thrum; chug, rev up; boom, roar; grumble, rumble, drone, hum, whirr, bombinate; trill, chime, peal, toll; tremble, vibrate 317 *oscillate*; rattle, chatter, clatter, clack; reverberate 404 *resound*.

404. Resonance – N. *resonance*, sonorousness; reverberation, vibration 317 *oscillation*; echo 106 *recurrence*; twang, ringing, ringing in the ear, tinnitus; tintinnabulation 412 *campanology*; peal; sonority, boom; clang, clangour, plangency 400 *loudness*; peal, blare, bray; tinkle, jingle; chink, clink; ping, ring, chime; low note, bass n. 410 *musical note*; low voice, bass, baritone, bass b., contralto.

Adj. *resonant*, vibrant, reverberant, reverberative; fruity, carrying 400 *loud*; resounding etc. vb.; booming, echoing, lingering; sonorous, reboant, plangent; deep-toned, booming, hollow, sepulchral.

Vb. *resound*, vibrate, reverberate, echo, reecho 403 *roll*; whirr, buzz; hum, sing; ping, ring, ding; jingle, jangle, chink, clink, clank, clunk; ting, tinkle; twang, thrum; gong, chime, tintinnabulate; tootle, toot, trumpet, blare, bray 400 *be loud*.

405. Nonresonance – N. *nonresonance*, nonvibration, dead sound, dull s.; thud, thump, bump; plump, plop, plonk, plunk 401 *faintness*; mute, damper 401 *silencer*.

Adj. *nonresonant*, muffled, damped 401 *muted*; dead, dull, heavy; cracked 407 *hoarse*; soundproof 399 *silent*.

Vb. *sound dead*, not vibrate, fall dead on the ear; tink, click, flap; thump, thud, bump, pound; soft-pedal, muffle, soften, deaden 401 *mute*.

406. Sibilation: hissing sound – N. *sibilation*, sibilance, hissing, hiss; assibilation, sigma, sibilant; sputter, splutter; splash, plash; squelch; rustle; swish, swoosh; goose, serpent.

Adj. *sibilant*, hissing etc. vb.; wheezy, asthmatic.

Vb. *hiss*, sibilate, assibilate; snort, wheeze, snuffle, whistle; buzz, fizz, fizzle, sizzle, sputter, splutter, spit; splash, plash, effervesce; swish, swoosh, whiz; squelch, suck; rustle 407 *rasp*.

407. Stridor: harsh sound – N. *stridor*, stridency, cacophony 411 *discord*; raucousness, hoarseness, huskiness, gruffness; aspirate, guttural; squeakiness, scrape, scratch, creak, squeak; stridulation, screechiness; shriek, screech, squawk; shrillness, piping, whistling; bleep; soprano, treble, falsetto, tenor, countertenor; nasality, twang, drone; skirl, brassiness, blare 400 *loudness*; pipe, fife 414 *flute*.

Adj. *strident*, stridulous, stridulatory; grating, rusty, creaky, creaking, jarring (see *hoarse*); harsh, brassy, brazen, metallic; high, high-pitched, acute, shrill, piping; penetrating, piercing, tinny, ear-splitting 400 *loud*; blaring, braying; dry, reedy, squeaky, squawky, screechy, scratchy; cracked 405 *nonresonant*; sharp, flat 411 *discordant*.

hoarse, husky, throaty, guttural, raucous, rough, gruff; rasping, scraping, creaking; hollow, deep, sepulchral; snoring, stertorous.

Vb. *rasp*, stridulate, grate, crunch, scrunch, grind, saw, scrape, scratch, squeak; snore, snort; cough, hawk, choke, bray, screech 409 *ululate*; grunt, burr, gutturalize; crack, break (of the voice); jar, set the teeth on edge 411 *discord*.

shrill, bleep; drone, skirl; trumpet, blare 400 *be loud*; pipe, flute 413 *play music*; whistle, caterwaul 408 *cry*; scream, squeal, yelp, screech, squawk; whine 409 *ululate*; go right through one.

408. Human cry – N. *cry*, exclamation, ejaculation 577 *voice*; vociferation, vociferousness, clamorousness, shouting,

outcry, clamour 400 *loudness*; yodel, chant 412 *vocal music*; shout, yell, whoop, bawl; howl, scream, shriek 407 *stridor*; halloo, hail 547 *call*; hue and cry 619 *chase*; cheer, hurrah, huzza 835 *rejoicing*; hoot, boo 924 *disapprobation*; sob, sigh 836 *lamentation*; squeal, wail, whine; grunt, gasp 352 *respiration*.

Adj. *crying*, bawling, clamant, clamorous; loud, vocal, vociferous; stentorian, full-throated, lusty; sobbing 836 *lamenting*.

Vb. *cry*, cry out, exclaim, ejaculate 579 *speak*; call, call out, hail, whoop; hoot, boo, whistle 924 *disapprove*; cheer, hurrah (see *vociferate*); scream, screech, yowl, howl, groan; snigger 835 *laugh*; caterwaul, squall, boohoo, whine, whimper, wail, fret, mewl, pule 836 *weep*; yammer, moan, sob, sigh; mutter, grumble 401 *sound faint*; gasp, grunt, snort, snore 352 *breathe*; squeak, squawk 409 *ululate*.

vociferate, clamour, shout, bawl, yell, holler; chant 413 *sing*; exult 835 *rejoice*; cheer for, root for; hiss, hoot, boo, bawl out, shout down 924 *disapprove*; roar, bellow 409 *ululate*; yell, cry out, sing o.; raise one's voice, give v., strain one's lungs, make oneself hoarse, shout at the top of one's voice 400 *be loud*.

409. Ululation: animal sounds – N. *ululation*, animal noise, howling, barking, baying; buzzing, bombination, drone; warble, call, cry, note, woodnote, birdsong; squeak, cheep, twitter; buzz, hum; hee-haw; cock-a-doodle-doo, cuckoo, tu-whit tu-whoo. See *ululate*.

Adj. *ululant*, reboant; deep-mouthed, full-m.; full-throated 400 *loud*; roaring, lowing, cackling etc. vb.

Vb. *ululate*, cry, call, give tongue; squawk, screech, yawp; caterwaul, yowl, howl, wail; roar, bellow, bell; hum, drone, buzz, bombinate; spit 406 *hiss*; woof, bark, bay; yelp, yap; snap, snarl, growl, whine; trumpet, bell; bray, neigh, whinny, whicker; bleat, baa; low, moo; miaow, mew, mewl, purr; quack, cackle, gaggle; gobble, gabble, cluck; grunt, snort, squeal; pipe, pule; chatter, sing, chirp, chirrup, cheep, peep, tweet, twitter, churr, whirr, coo; caw, croak; hoot, honk, boom; squeak 407 *rasp*; warble, carol, whistle 413 *sing*.

410. Melody: concord – N. *melody*, musicality 412 *music*; musicalness, melodiousness, tonality, euphony; harmoniousness, harmony, concord, concert 24 *agreement*; consonance, assonance, attunement; unison, homophony; resolution (of a discord), cadence; harmonics, harmonization, counterpoint, polyphony; thorough bass, ground b., continuo; part, second, chorus; orchestration, instrumentation; tone, tone colour; phrasing 413 *musical skill*; phrase, passage, theme, leitmotiv; movement 412 *musical piece*.

musical note, note, keys, keyboard, manual, pedal point; black notes, white n., sharp, flat, accidental, natural, tone, semitone; keynote, tonic, dominant, diatesseron, diapason; octave, gamut, scale (**see** *key*); chord, triad, tetrachord, arpeggio; grace note, grace, appoggiatura, acciaccatura, mordent, shake, trill, tremolo, vibrato, cadenza; tone, tonality, register, pitch, concert p.; high note 407 *stridor*; low note 404 *resonance*; undertone, overtone, harmonic; monotone, drone.

notation, musical n., tonic sol-fa, solmization; sheet music, score; signature, clef; bar, stave, staff; line, space, brace; rest, pause, interval; breve, semibreve, minim, crotchet, quaver, semiquaver.

tempo, time, beat; rhythm 593 *prosody*; measure, timing; syncopation; upbeat, downbeat; suspension; prolongation; tempo rubato; rallentando, andante 412 *adagio*.

key, signature, clef, modulation, transposition; scale, diatonic s., chromatic s., twelve-tone s.; series, tone row; mode.

Adj. *melodious*, melodic, musical; lilting, tuneful, singable, catchy; tinkling, sweet, dulcet, velvet, mellifluous, Orphean; silvery, clear, clear as a bell, ringing, chiming; euphonious, euphonic, true, well-pitched; harmonious, concordant; homophonic.

harmonic, enharmonic, diatonic, chromatic; tonal, atonal, sharp, flat, twelvetoned; keyed, modal, minor, major.

411. Discord – N. *discord*, conflict of sounds, discordance, dissonance, disharmony 25 *disagreement*; atonality, twelvetone scale; harshness, cacophony 407 *stridor*; Babel, cat's concert, caterwauling 400 *loudness*; atmospherics, wow, flutter.

Adj. *discordant*, dissonant, jangling; jarring, grating, harsh, raucous, cacophonous 407 *strident*; inharmonious, unharmonized; unmelodious, unmusical, untuneful; untuned, cracked; off pitch, off key, out of tune, sharp, flat; atonal, toneless, tuneless.

Vb. *discord*, lack harmony 25 *disagree*; jangle, jar, grate, clash, crash; saw, scrape 407 *rasp*; thrum, drone, whine.

412. Music – N. *music*, harmony 410 *melody*; musicianship 413 *musical skill*; minstrelsy, music-making, playing; strumming, thrumming, vamping; improvisation; composition; counterpoint; classical music, chamber m.; light music, popular m., pop; programme music.; electronic m., musique concrète; canned music, piped m., musical wallpaper, muzak; disco music, dance m., waltztime; hot music, syncopation, jazz, blue note, blues, mainstream jazz, traditional j., trad, Dixieland, ragtime, swing, bebop, bop, stride piano, boogie-woogie; jive, rock 'n' roll, rock music, hard rock, heavy metal, new wave, punk; ska, reggae; soul m.; rhythm 'n' blues, country and western, blue grass, folk; written music, score; performance, recital, concert, promenade c., prom; jam session, gig; singsong; music festival, eisteddfod; school of music, conservatoire; Tin Pan Alley.

campanology, bell ringing, hand r.; ringing, chiming; carillon, chime, peal; touch; method-ringing, change-r., hunt, dodge; round; changes; method, Grandsire, Plain Bob, Treble Bob; set of bells, doubles, triples, caters, cinques; minor, major, royal; maximus; bell 414 *gong*; bell ringer, campanologist.

tune, melody, strain; theme song, signature tune; descant; reprise, refrain; melodic line; air, aria, solo; peal, chime; flourish, sennet, tucket; phrase, passage, measure; siren strains.

musical piece, piece, composition, opus, work; tape, recording 414 *gramophone*; orchestration, instrumentation; arrangement, adaptation, setting, transcription; accompaniment, obbligato; voluntary, prelude, overture, intermezzo; finale; incidental music, background m.; romance, rhapsody, extravaganza, impromptu, fantasia, caprice, capriccio, humoresque, divertissement, divertimento, variations, raga; medley; étude, study; suite, fugue, canon, toccata; sonata, sonatina, concerto, symphony, sinfonietta; symphonic poem, tone p.; pastorale, scherzo, rondo; minuet, mazurka 837 *dance*; march, wedding m., dead m., dirge, pibroch; nocturne, serenade, berceuse; anacrusis; statement, exposition, development, recapitulation, variation; theme, motive, leitmotiv; movement; passage, phrase; chord 410 *musical note*; cadenza, coda.

vocal music, singing, vocalism, lyricism; vocalization; scat singing; opera, operetta, light opera, comic o., opera bouffe, musical 594 *stage play*; choir-singing, oratorio, cantata, chorale; psalmody, hymnology; descant, chant, Gregorian c., Ambrosian c., plain chant, plainsong; cantus, cantillation, recitative; bel canto, coloratura, bravura; anthem, canticle, psalm 981 *hymn*; song, lay, roundelay, carol, lyric, lilt; lieder, ballad; folk song, popular *or* pop s., top twenty, hit parade; ditty, shanty, calypso; spiritual, blues; part song, glee, madrigal, round, catch, canon; chorus, refrain, burden; choral hymn, antiphony, dithyramb; boat song, barcarole; lullaby, cradle song, berceuse; serenade, aubade; song, birdsong, dawn chorus; requiem 836 *lament*; recitative; libretto.

duet, duo, trio, quartet, quintet, sextet, septet, octet; concerto, concerto grosso; solo, monody; ensemble, tutti.

Adj. *musical*, melodious; philharmonic,

symphonic, melodic, arioso, cantabile; vocal, singable; operatic, recitative; lyric, melic; choral, dithyrambic; hymnal, psalmodic; contrapuntal; orchestrated, scored; set, arranged; instrumental, orchestral; blue, cool; hot, jazzy, syncopated, swinging, swung.

Adv. *adagio*, lento, largo, larghetto, andante, andantino, maestoso, moderato, allegro, allegretto; spiritoso, vivace, accelerando, presto, prestissimo; piano, pianissimo, forte, fortissimo, sforzando, con brio, capriccioso, scherzando; glissando, legato, sostenuto; staccato; crescendo, diminuendo, rallentando; affettuoso, cantabile, parlante; tremolo, pizzicato, vibrato; rubato; da capo.

413. Musician – N. *musician*, artiste, virtuoso, soloist 696 *proficient person*; player, executant, performer, concert artist; ripieno 40 *extra*; bard, ministrel, troubadour, minnesinger; street musician, busker; composer, symphonist, contrapuntist; scorer, arranger, harmonist; syncopator, swinger, cat; librettist, song writer, lyricist; hymnwriter, hymnographer, psalmist; the Muses, Apollo, Orpheus; music lover, concertgoer 504 *enthusiast*.

instrumentalist, player, pianist, accompanist; organist, accordionist; violinist, fiddler; cellist; harpist, lutanist, sitarist, guitarist; strummer, thrummer; piper, fifer, flautist, flutist, clarinettist, oboist, bassoonist; saxophonist, horn player, trumpeter, bugler; cornet; drummer, drum major; percussionist, timpanist; organ-grinder.

orchestra, symphony o., chamber o., sinfonietta, quartet, quintet; ensemble, wind e.; strings, brass, woodwind, percussion, drums; band, string b., jazz b., ragtime b.; brass b., military b., pipe b.; steel band; rock group, punk g., pop g.; conductor, maestro, bandmaster; leader, first violin; orchestral player, bandsman.

vocalist, singer, songster, warbler, caroller, chanter; songstress, siren; melodist, troubadour, minstrel; ballad singer, folk s., pop s.; serenader, crooner, jazz singer, scat s.; opera singer, prima donna, diva; cantatrice, coloratura; castrato, treble, soprano, mezzo-s., contralto, alto, tenor, countertenor, baritone, bass b., bass, basso profondo; songbird 365 *bird*.

choir, chorus, waits, wassailers, carol singers, glee club, barbershop quartet; chorister, choirboy; precentor, cantor, choirmaster, choirleader.

musical skill, musicianship; performance, execution, fingering, touch, phrasing, expression; virtuosity, bravura 694 *skill*.

Vb. *compose music*, compose, set to music, score, arrange, transpose, orchestrate, harmonize, melodize, improvise, extemporize.

play music, play, perform, execute, render, interpret; pick out a tune; conduct, beat time; syncopate; accompany; pedal, vamp, strum; tickle the ivories; pluck, strike, thrum, twang; fiddle, bow, scrape, saw; squeeze the box; wind the horn, blow, bugle, sound, trumpet, toot, tootle; pipe, flute, whistle; drum, tattoo, beat, ruffle 403 *roll*; ring, toll, knell; tune, string; improvise, extemporize; strike up.

sing, vocalize, chant, hymn; intone, cantillate, descant; warble, carol, lilt, trill, croon, hum, whistle, yodel; harmonize; chorus, choir; serenade; chirp, pipe 409 *ululate*.

414. Musical instruments – N. *musical instrument*, strings, brass, wind, woodwind, percussion 413 *orchestra*; sounding board, diaphragm, sound box; synthesizer.

harp, lyre, lute, sitar; cithara, guitar, electric g., mandolin, ukulele, banjo, balalaika, zither; psaltery, vina; plectrum, fret.

viol, violin, fiddle, kit, rebec; viola, cello, double bass; bow, fiddlestick; string, catgut.

piano, pianoforte, grand piano, cottage p.; virginals, dulcimer, harpsichord, spinet, clavichord, celesta; player piano, pianola (tdmk); clavier, keyboard, manual, keys, ivories; pedal, damper.

organ, harmonium, melodeon; mouth

organ, harmonica; kazoo, comb; jew's-harp; accordion, concertina; barrel organ, hurdy-gurdy; organ pipe, flue p., stop.

flute, fife, piccolo, flageolet, recorder; woodwind, reed instrument, clarinet, basset horn; saxophone, sax, tenor s.; shawm, oboe, cor Anglais; bassoon; ocarina; pipe, reed, straw; bagpipes, musette; pan pipes, syrinx; nose flute; whistle; pitch-pipe; mouthpiece, embouchure.

horn, brass; bugle, trumpet, clarion; alpenhorn, French horn, flugelhorn, sousaphone; euphonium, ophicleide, serpent; cornet, trombone, sackbut, tuba; conch.

gong, bell, tintinnabulum; tocsin 665 *danger signal*; peal, carillon, chimes, bells; bones, rattle, clappers, castanets, maracas; cymbals; xylophone, marimba; vibraphone, vibes; musical glasses, harmonica; glockenspiel; triangle; tuning fork.

drum, big d., side d., snare d., kettle d., timpani; tomtom; tabor, tambourine; tabla.

gramophone, record player, phonograph, radiogram; deck, turntable; tape recorder, cassette r., hi-fi, stereo, music centre; playback; recording, tape r., tape, cassette; talking book; gramophone record, disc; album, single, track; musical box, jukebox.

415. Hearing – N. *hearing*, audition 398 *acoustics*; sense of hearing, good ear; audibility, reception, good r.; earshot; something to hear, earful.

listening, hearkening 455 *attention*; auscultation, aural examination 459 *inquiry*; listening-in, tuning-in; lip-reading 520 *interpretation*; eavesdropping, overhearing, wire-tapping, bugging; audition, voice test 461 *experiment*; interview, audience, hearing 584 *conference*.

listener, hearer, audience, auditorium 441 *spectator*; radio listener, radio ham; hi-fi enthusiast, audiophile; monitor, auditor 459 *questioner*; eavesdropper, little pitcher 453 *inquisitive person*.

ear, auditory apparatus, acoustic organ; lug, lobe, auricle, pinna, earhole, lughole;

cochlea, eardrum, tympanum; auditory canal; otology; otologist.

hearing aid, deaf-aid, ear trumpet; stethoscope, otoscope; loudspeaker, loudhailer 528 *publication*; microphone 400 *megaphone*; speaking tube; telephone, phone, blower; receiver, earpiece, headphones, earphones; walkie-talkie 531 *telecommunication*; sound recorder 549 *recording instrument*.

Adj. *auditory*, hearing, auricular, aural; audiovisual 398 *sounding*; otological; auditive, acoustic, audile, listening, tuned in; prick-eared, all ears 455 *attentive*; within earshot, audible, heard 398 *sounding*.

Vb. *hear*, catch; list, listen; auscultate, put one's ear to; lip-read 520 *interpret*; listen in, switch on, tune in; overhear, eavesdrop, keep one's ears open; intercept, bug, tap the wires; hearken, give ear, lend an e.; give audience, interview 459 *interrogate*; be all ears, lap up 455 *be attentive*; strain one's ears, prick up one's e.; be told, come to one's ears.

be heard, become audible, fall on the ear, sound 400 *be loud*; gain a hearing, have an audience; go out on the air.

416. Deafness – N. *deafness*, defective hearing, imperfect h.; hardness of hearing; deaf-mutism; deaf-and-dumb speech, dactylology; deaf-mute, the deaf and dumb.

Adj. *deaf*, hard of hearing, stone-deaf, deaf and dumb, deaf-mute; deafened, stunned, unable to hear; deaf to, unhearing, not listening 456 *inattentive*; tone-deaf, unmusical.

Vb. *be deaf*, not hear, fail to catch; not listen, stop one's ears, turn a deaf ear to 458 *disregard*; lip-read 520 *translate*; talk with one's fingers.

deafen, make deaf, split one's eardrum, drown one's voice 400 *be loud*.

417. Light – N. *light*, daylight, light of day, noon, broad day; sunbeam, sunlight, sun 420 *luminary*; starlight, moonlight, moonshine, earthshine; half-light, twilight 419 *dimness*; artificial light, candlelight, firelight 420 *lighting*; illumination, irradiation, splendour, resplendence, efful-

gence, refulgence, intensity, brightness, vividness, brilliance; luminousness, luminosity, luminance, candle power, magnitude; radiance (**see** *glow*); lustre (**see** *reflection*); blaze, glare, dazzle, dazzlement; flare, flame 379 *fire*; halo, nimbus, glory, gloriole, aureole, corona; variegated light, spectrum 437 *variegation*; coloration 425 *colour*.

flash, fulguration, coruscation; lightning, lightning flash; streak; beam, stream, shaft, bar, ray, pencil; scintillation, sparkle, spark; glint, glitter, play, play of light; blink, twinkle, flicker, glimmer, gleam, shimmer; spangle, tinsel; strobe light 420 *lamp*; firefly 420 *glow-worm*.

glow, flush; alpenglow, dawn, sunset, afterglow; lambency, soft light; aurora, aurora borealis, aurora australis; northern lights; zodiacal light 321 *heavens*; radiance, incandescence 379 *heat*; luminescence, fluorescence, phosphorescence; St Elmo's fire 420 *glow-worm*.

radiation, visible r., invisible r.; background r.; actinism, emission, absorption; radioactivity, irradiation 160 *nucleonics*; radioisotope; particle counter, Geiger c.; fallout, mushroom cloud 659 *poison*; radiation belt 340 *atmosphere*; radio wave, frequency w. 398 *sound*, 317 *oscillation*; wavelength, waveband; high frequency, VHF, UHF; interference, static 160 *electricity*; electromagnetic radiation, microwave; infrared radiation, ultraviolet r.; X-ray, gamma r., alpha r., beta r., cosmic radiation, cosmic noise; magnetic storm; photon; photoelectric cell; curie, millicurie, roentgen, rem; half-life.

reflection, refraction; diffraction, dispersion, scattering, interference, polarization; albedo, polish, gloss, sheen, shine, lustre; glare, dazzle, blink, ice b.; reflecting surface 442 *mirror*; mirror image, hologram 551 *image*.

light contrast, tonality, chiaroscuro; value; light and shade, black and white, half-tone, mezzotint; highlights.

optics, electro-optics, fibre optics; photics, photometry, actinometry; dioptrics, catoptrics, spectroscopy 442 *opti-*

cal device; holography 551 *photography*; radioscopy, radiometry, radiology; magnification 197 *expansion*.

Adj. *luminous*, luminiferous, lucid, lucent; light, lit, well-lit, floodlit; bright, gay, shining, fulgent, resplendent, splendent, splendid, brilliant, flamboyant, vivid; colourful 425 *coloured*; radiant, effulgent, refulgent; dazzling, blinding, glaring, lurid, garish; incandescent, flaring, flaming, aflame, aglow, ablaze 379 *fiery*; glowing, blushing 431 *red*; luminescent, fluorescent, phosphorescent; soft, lambent; beaming, glittery, flashing, glinting etc. vb.; scintillant, scintillating, sparkling; lustrous, shiny, sheeny, glossy; reflecting, catoptric; refractive, dioptric; optical, photometric; photosensitive.

undimmed, clear, bright, fair, set f.; cloudless, shadowless, unclouded, unshaded; sunny, sunshiny; moonlit, starlit, starry; burnished, polished, glassy, gleaming; pellucid 422 *transparent*.

radiating, radiant; cosmic, cosmogenic; radioactive, irradiated, hot; reflective, reflecting.

Vb. *shine*, be bright, burn, blaze 379 *be hot*; glow, incandesce, phosphoresce; glare, dazzle, bedazzle, blind; play, dance; flash, fulgurate, coruscate; glisten, glister, blink; glimmer, flicker, twinkle; glitter, shimmer, glance; scintillate, sparkle; reflect; gleam, glint.

radiate, beam, shoot 300 *emit*; reflect, refract; be radioactive, bombard; X-ray.

make bright, lighten, dawn; clear, clear up, lift, brighten; light 381 *kindle*; light up, switch on; shed lustre, throw light on; shine upon, irradiate, illuminate, illume; transilluminate; polish, burnish 648 *clean*.

418. Darkness – N. *darkness*, dark; black 428 *blackness*; night, nightfall; dead of night 129 *midnight*; obscurity, murk, gloom, dusk; shadiness, shadows 419 *dimness*; shade, shadow, umbra, penumbra; silhouette, shadowgraph 551 *photography*; darkroom.

obscuration, darkening 419 *dimness*; occultation, eclipse 446 *disappearance*; blackout, lights out; sunset 129 *evening*;

blackening, shading, hatching, cross-h.; dimmer, dip switch, off s.

Adj. *dark*, subfusc, sombre, dark-coloured 428 *black*; obscure, pitch-dark, pitchy, sooty, inky; cavernous, Stygian; murky; funereal, gloomy, dismal, darksome, sombre; louring, lurid 419 *dim*; tenebrous, shady 419 *shadowy*; darkened 421 *screened*; darkling, benighted.

unlit, unlighted, unilluminated; lightless, sunless, moonless, starless; eclipsed, overshadowed 421 *screened*; clouded 423 *opaque*; dipped, dimmed, blacked out; extinguished.

Vb. *darken*, black, brown; black out, dim o.; lower *or* dim the light; occult, eclipse, veil 421 *screen*; obscure 419 *bedim*; overshadow, adumbrate, cast a shadow; shade, hatch, cross-h., fill in 428 *blacken*.

snuff out, extinguish, quench, put out the light, blow out, switch off, dip, douse.

419. Dimness – N. *dimness*, indistinctness, vagueness, fuzziness, blur, soft focus; loom; fadeout, fade; faintness, paleness 426 *achromatism*; dullness, lacklustre, lack of sparkle, matt finish; leaden skies; poor visibility, white-out 423 *opacity*; mistiness, fogginess, nebulosity; murk, gloom 418 *darkness*; shadowiness, shadow; spectre 440 *visual fallacy*.

half-light, semidarkness, bad light; gloaming 129 *evening*; twilight, dusk, crepuscule; owl-light; daybreak, grey dawn; penumbra, half-shadow, partial eclipse.

glimmer, flicker 417 *flash*; firefly 420 *glow-worm*; sidelights, dipped l., dips; candlelight, firelight, ember; moonlight, starlight.

Adj. *dim*, darkish 418 *dark*; dusky, twilight, crepuscular; grey, pale 426 *colourless*; faint, faded, waning; indistinct, blurred, bleary; glassy, dull, lustreless, lacklustre, leaden; flat, matt; filmy, misty, nebulous 423 *opaque*; dingy, unpolished 649 *dirty*.

shadowy, umbrageous, shady, shaded, overspread, overshadowed, overcast, overclouded 418 *unlit*; vague, indistinct, undefined, obscure, fuzzy, blurry, looming; deceptive; half-seen, half-glimpsed 444 *invisible*; dreamlike, ghostly 4 *insubstantial*.

Vb. *be dim*, – faint etc. adj.; be indistinct, loom; fade, wane 426 *lose colour*; lour, gloom, darkle; glimmer, flicker, gutter, sputter.

bedim, dim, dip; fade out 418 *snuff out*; obscure, blear 440 *blur*; smirch, smear, besmirch, besmear, sully 649 *make unclean*; fog, mist; overshadow, shade, shadow, veil 418 *darken*.

420. Luminary: source of light – N. *luminary*, illuminant 417 *light*; naked light 379 *fire*; sun, moon, starlight 321 *star*; Milky Way, northern lights 321 *heavens*; lightning, bolt of l., sheet l., forked l., ball l., summer l. 417 *flash*.

glow-worm 417 *glow*; firefly, ignis fatuus, will-o'-the-wisp; fireball, St Elmo's fire, corposant.

torch, brand, ember; torchlight, link, flambeau, cresset, match 385 *lighter*; candle, taper, spill, wick, dip, rushlight, nightlight, naked light, flare, gas jet, burner; torchbearer, linkboy.

lamp, lamplight; lantern, bull's eye; safety lamp, Davy l., miner's l., acetylene l.; oil lamp, hurricane l., paraffin l., spirit l.; gas lamp, gas mantle; electric lamp, flash l., flash gun, torch, flashlight, searchlight, arc light, floodlight; headlamp, headlight, foglamp; stop-light, tail light, reflector; bulb, flashbulb, flashcube, photoflood, electric bulb, light b., filament; strobe light, stroboscope, strobe; vapour light, neon l., strip l., Chinese lantern, fairy lights; magic lantern, projector; light fitting, chandelier, gaselier, lustre, electrolier, candelabra, girandole; standard lamp, table l.; lamppost, standard; socket, bracket, pricket; sconce, candle holder, candlestick; lamplighter.

lighting, illumination 417 *light*; artificial lighting, street l.; floodlighting, son et lumière, limelight, spotlight, footlights, houselights.

signal light, warning l. 665 *danger signal*; traffic light; stop-light, trafficator,

winker; Very light, Bengal l.; rocket, star shell, flare; flare path, beacon, balefire 547 *signal*; lighthouse, lightship.

fireworks, firework display, pyrotechnics; rocket, Roman candle, Catherine wheel, sparkler; banger 723 *explosive*.

Adj. *luminescent*, self-luminous; incandescent, shining; phosphorescent, fluorescent, neon; radiant, bright 417 *luminous*; illuminated, well-lit.

Vb. *illuminate*, light up, light 417 *shine*, make bright.

421. Screen – N. *screen*, shield, mask 660 *protection*; bower 194 *arbour*; sunshade, parasol 226 *shade*; awning, visor; curtain, blind; lampshade; eyeshade, blinkers; eyelid, eyelashes; dark glasses, tinted g. 442 *eyeglass*; smoked glass, frosted g. 424 *semitransparency*; stained glass 437 *variegation*; filter, shutter, deadlight; hood, veil, mantle 228 *cloak*.

Adj. *screened*, sheltered; shady, bowery 419 *shadowy*; hooded 439 *blind*.

Vb. *screen*, shield, shelter 660 *safeguard*; keep out, filter out, cover up, veil, mask, shroud 525 *conceal*; blinker, blindfold; shade, curtain, canopy; cloud 419 *bedim*; smoke, frost, glaze.

422. Transparency – N. *transparency*, translucence, lucency, diaphaneity; thinness, gauziness; pellucidity, limpidity; clearness, clarity; hyaline, water, crystal, glass; window pane, gossamer, gauze 4 *insubstantial thing*.

Adj. *transparent*, diaphanous, revealing, sheer, see-through; thin, fine, filmy, gauzy, pellucid, translucent; lucent 424 *semitransparent*; liquid, limpid; crystal, crystalline, hyaline, vitreous, glassy; clear, crystal-clear.

Vb. *be transparent*, etc. adj.; transmit light, show through; shine through 417 *make bright*.

423. Opacity – N. *opacity*, opaqueness; solidity 324 *density*; filminess, frost; turbidity; devitrification; fog, mist 355 *cloud*; film, scale 421 *screen*; pall, smoke screen.

Adj. *opaque*, nontransparent, thick;

blank, windowless; not clear, unclarified, devitrified; cloudy, milky, turbid, muddied, puddled; foggy, hazy, misty, fuliginous 419 *dim*; frosted, misted, clouded.

424. Semitransparency – N. *semitransparency*, milkiness, lactescence; pearliness, opalescence; smoked glass, ground g., frosted g.; gauze, muslin, net; pearl, opal, horn.

Adj. *semitransparent*, semipellucid, semi-opaque, semidiaphanous, gauzy, filmy; translucent, opalescent, opaline, milky, lactescent, pearly; frosted, smoked 419 *dim*.

425. Colour – N. *colour*, primary c.; complementary colour, secondary c.; chromatism, chromatic aberration; prism, spectrum, rainbow 437 *variegation*; colour scheme, palette; coloration 553 *painting*; riot of colour 437 *variegation*; tincture, metal, fur 547 *heraldry*.

chromatics, science of colour, colorimetry, chromatology, spectrum analysis, spectrometer; colorimeter, tintometer; spectroscope, prism.

hue, colour quality, chroma, chromaticity, saturation, tone, value; brilliance, intensity, warmth, loudness; softness, deadness, dullness; coloration, livery; pigmentation, colouring, complexion, natural colour; flush, blush, glow; sickly hue, pallor 426 *achromatism*; discoloration; tint, shade, nuance, cast, dye; tinge, patina; half-tone, half-light, mezzotint.

pigment, colouring matter; warpaint 843 *cosmetic*; dyestuff, dye, fast d.; natural dye, vegetable d.; artificial dye, synthetic d., aniline d.; stain, fixative, mordant; wash, colourwash, whitewash, distemper; paint 553 *art equipment*.

Adj. *coloured*, in colour, painted, tinted etc. vb.; tinct, tinged, dyed, double-d.; colorific, tinctorial; fast, unfading; colourful, chromatic, polychromatic; prismatic, spectroscopic; technicoloured, kaleidoscopic 437 *variegated*.

florid, colourful, high-coloured, bright-hued; ruddy 431 *red*; intense, deep, strong; unfaded, vivid, brilliant 417 *lumi-nous*; warm, glowing, rich, gorgeous; painted, gay, bright; jazzy, gaudy, garish, showy, flashy; harsh, crude; lurid, loud, screaming, shrieking; clashing, discordant 25 *disagreeing*.

soft-hued, soft, quiet, tender, delicate; pearly, creamy 427 *whitish*; light, pale, pastel, muted; sober, dull, flat, matt, dead; sombre, dark 428 *black*; drab, dingy, faded; weathered, mellow; matching, toning, harmonious.

Vb. *colour*, colour in 553 *paint*; rouge 843 *primp*; pigment, tattoo; dye, dip, imbue; tint, touch up; tincture, tinge; wash, colourwash 226 *coat*; stain, run, discolour; come off on; tan, weather, mellow; illuminate, miniate, emblazon 437 *variegate*.

426. Achromatism: absence of colour – N. *achromatism*, achromaticity, colourlessness; decoloration, discoloration, etiolation, fading, bleaching 427 *whiteness*; overexposure 551 *photography*; pallor, pallidity; paleness, faintness etc. adj.; anaemia, bloodlessness; pigment deficiency, albinism; neutral tint; monochrome; black and white; albino, blond(e), peroxide b.

bleacher, decolorant, peroxide, bleach, lime.

Adj. *colourless*, hueless, toneless, neutral; uncoloured, achromatic; decoloured, discoloured; bleached, etiolated, overexposed; faint, faded; unpigmented, albino, light-skinned, fair, blond 433 *yellow*, 427 *whitish*; lustreless, glossless, mousy; bloodless, anaemic; drained of colour, washed out, washy; pale, pallid 427 *white*; ashy, ashen, livid, whey-faced; pasty, sallow, sickly 651 *unhealthy*; dingy, dull, leaden, glassy, lacklustre; lurid, ghastly, wan 419 *dim*; deathly, cadaverous.

Vb. *lose colour*, pale, fade, bleach, blanch, turn pale; run, come out in the wash.

decolorize, achromatize, fade, etiolate; blanch, bleach 427 *whiten*; deprive of colour, drain of c., wash out; tone down, deaden, weaken; pale, dim 419 *bedim*; dull, tarnish, discolour 649 *make unclean*.

427. Whiteness – N. *whiteness*, albescence; lack of pigment 426 *achromatism*; whitishness, creaminess, pearliness; white man *or* woman, white, paleface; albino.

white thing, alabaster, marble; snow, driven s.; chalk, paper, milk, flour, salt, ivory, lily, swan; silver, pewter, platinum; pearl, teeth; white patch, blaze.

whiting, blanco, white lead, pipeclay; whitewash.

Adj. *white*, albescent; dazzling, light 417 *luminous*; silvered, silvery, silver, argent, argentine; chalky, snowy, frosty; spumy, foam-flecked; white hot 379 *hot*; lily-white, milk-w., snow-w., white-skinned, Caucasian; albinic; whitened, whitewashed, bleached.

whitish, pearly, milky, creamy 424 *semi-transparent*; ivory, waxen 426 *colourless*; off-white, mushroom, magnolia; ecru 430 *brown*; blond(e), fair, Nordic; ash-blond(e), platinum b., fair-haired, flaxen-h., tow-headed; dusty.

Vb. *whiten*, white, blanco, whitewash; blanch, bleach; pale, fade 426 *decolorize*; frost, silver, grizzle.

428. Blackness – N. *blackness*, nigrescence, nigritude 418 *darkness*; inkiness, lividity, black, sable; melanism, swarthiness, duskiness, pigmentation; depth, deep tone; blackening, darkening 418 *obscuration*; black man *or* woman, black, Negro, Negrillo, Negrito; coloured man *or* woman.

black thing, coal, charcoal, soot, pitch, tar; ebony, jet, ink, smut; blackberry, sloe; raven, blackbird; mourning.

black pigment, blacking, lampblack, blacklead; Indian ink, printer's i.; japan, niello; burnt cork; melanin.

Adj. *black*, sable; ebon; inky, pitchy; sooty, fuliginous, smoky, smudgy, smutty; blackened, singed, charred; black-haired, raven-h.; black-eyed, sloe-e.; dark, brunette; black-skinned, negroid; pigmented, coloured; melanistic; sombre, gloomy; coal-black, jet-b., pitch-b.; nocturnal 418 *dark*.

blackish, nigrescent; swarthy, swart, black-faced, dusky, dark, dark-skinned;

coloured, pigmented; livid, black and blue.

Vb. *blacken*, black, japan, ink in; smudge, smirch; deepen 418 *darken*; singe, char 381 *burn*.

429. Greyness – N. *greyness*, grey, neutral tint; pewter, silver; gunmetal, ashes, slate; oyster, taupe.

Adj. *grey*, neutral, leaden, livid; greying, grizzled, hoary, hoar; silvery, silvered, frosted 427 *whitish*; light-grey, dove-g., pearl-g.; mousy, dun, drab, donkey-grey; steely, steel-grey; charcoal-g.; bluish-grey, slate-coloured; greyish, ashen, ashy, smoky, cinereous; dapple-grey.

430. Brownness – N. *brownness*, brown, bronze, copper, amber; cinnamon, coffee, chocolate; butterscotch, caramel, toffee, burnt almond; walnut, mahogany; dark complexion, suntan; brunette.

brown pigment, bistre, ochre, sepia, sienna, raw umber, burnt u., Vandyke brown.

Adj. *brown*, bronze, mahogany etc. n.; browned, toasted; bronzed, tanned, sunburnt; dark, brunette; nut-brown, hazel; light brown, ecru, oatmeal, beige, buff, fawn, biscuit, mushroom, café-au-lait; brownish, greyish-brown, dun, drab, mud-coloured; yellowish-brown, snuff-coloured, feuille morte, khaki; tawny, tan, foxy; reddish-brown, bay, roan, sorrel, chestnut, auburn, copper-coloured; russet, rust-coloured, liver-c., maroon 431 *red*; purple-brown, puce; dark brown, peat-b., mocha, chocolate, coffee-coloured etc. n.

Vb. *embrown*, brown, bronze, tan, sunburn; singe, char.

431. Redness – N. *redness*, rubescence, blush, flush 417 *glow*; rubefaction, reddening; rosiness, ruddiness, bloom, red cheeks, apple c.; high colour, floridness, rubicundity; crimson, scarlet, red etc. adj.; rose, poppy; cherry, tomato; burgundy, port, claret; gore 335 *blood*; ruby, garnet, cornelian; flame 379 *fire*; redbreast, robin r.; redskin, Red Indian; red-head, gingernob.

red pigment, red dye, murex, cochineal, carmine, kermes; cinnabar, vermilion; ruddle, madder, rose m.; alizarin, crimson lake, Venetian red, rosaniline; red ochre, red lead, minium; rouge 843 *cosmetic*.

Adj. *red*, reddish; ruddy, rubicund, sanguine, florid, blowzy; fiery, red-hot 379 *hot*; rubescent, flushing, blushing; red-cheeked, rosy-c.; bright red, red as a lobster, red as a beetroot; red-haired, ginger-h.; carroty, sandy, auburn, titian-red, flame-coloured; rufous, ferruginous, rubiginous 430 *brown*; pink, rose-p., roseate, rosy, rose-coloured; flesh-pink, shell-p., salmon-p., shocking-p.; coral, carnation, damask, crushed strawberry; crimson, cherry-red, cerise, carmine, cramoisy; fuchsine, maroon 436 *purple*; wine-coloured, wine-dark; oxblood, sang-de-boeuf; sanguine, murrey, gules; scarlet, cardinal-red, vermilion, pillarbox red, Turkey r.; reddened, rouged, painted.

bloodstained, bloodshot; blood-red; sanguine; ensanguined, incarnadine, bloody, gory.

Vb. *redden*, rouge 843 *primp*; incarnadine, dye red, stain with blood; flush, blush, glow; mantle, colour, crimson, go red.

432. Orange – N. *orange*, red and yellow, gold, old gold; or; copper, amber; marigold; apricot, tangerine; marmalade; ochre, Mars orange, cadmium o., henna.

Adj. *orange*, apricot etc. n.; ochreous, luteous, cupreous, coppery, ginger, tan; orangish, orangy, orange-coloured, flame-c., copper-c., brassy.

433. Yellowness – N. *yellowness*, yellow, brass, gold, old gold, topaz, amber, old ivory; sulphur, brimstone; buttercup, daffodil; lemon, honey; saffron, mustard; jaundice, yellow fever; sallow skin, fair hair; blond(e), strawberry b.

yellow pigment, gamboge, cadmium yellow, chrome y., orpiment; yellow ochre, massicot, luteolin, xanthin.

Adj. *yellow*, gold, amber etc. n.; tawny,

fulvous, sandy; fair-haired, golden-h. 427 *whitish*; creamy, cream-coloured, buff-c.; butter-c., honey-c., straw-c., fallow; acid yellow, lemon y.; primrose y., jasmine, citrine; canary yellow, sunshine y., sulphur y., mustard; golden, aureate, gilt, gilded; deep yellow, luteous; yellowy, yellowish, flavescent, xanthic.

Vb. *gild*, yellow.

434. Greenness – N. *greenness*, green etc. adj.; verdancy, greenery 366 *foliage*; verdure, viridity, viridescence; jade, emerald, malachite, beryl, chrysoprase, verd antique; verdigris, patina; celadon, reseda, mignonette; loden; vert.

green pigment, viridian, bice, Paris green; chlorophyll.

Adj. *green*, viridescent, verdant; verdurous, grassy, leafy; grass-green, leaf-g., moss-g.; emerald, sea-green; jade green, sap g., bottle g.; sage g.; pea g., apple g., lime g., chartreuse; eau-de-Nil, avocado, olive, olive-green, olivaceous; glaucous, greenish, virescent; vert.

435. Blueness – N. *blueness*, blue, cyan, azure; sapphire, aquamarine, turquoise, lapis lazuli; gentian, bluebell, cornflower, forget-me-not; bluishness, cyanosis; lividness, lividity.

blue pigment, blue dye, indigo, woad; Prussian blue, ultramarine, cobalt, zaffre, smalt; blue-bag.

Adj. *blue*, cyanic, azure; cerulean, sky-blue; duck-egg blue, eggshell b., turquoise; pale blue, ice-b., powder-b., Cambridge-b.; air-force b., Saxe-b., slate-b., steel-b., electric-b.; sapphire, aquamarine, peacock-blue, kingfisher-b., royal-b., ultramarine, deep blue, Oxford-b., midnight-b., navy-b., navy; indigo, perse; blue-black, black and blue, livid; cold, steely, bluish, blue with cold.

436. Purpleness – N. *purpleness*, purple, blue and red; imperial purple; amethyst; lavender, violet, heliotrope, heather; plum, aubergine; Tyrian purple, gentian violet; amaranth, lilac, mauve; purpure.

Adj. *purple*, plum etc. n.; purplish, purpled; violet, violaceous, mauve, lavender, lilac; purple-red, fuchsia, magenta, plum-coloured, puce; hyacinthine, heliotrope; mulberry, murrey; livid, black and blue.

Vb. *empurple*, purple.

437. Variegation – N. *variegation*, variety, diversity 15 *difference*; dancing light, play of colour, shot colours, iridescence 417 *light*; tiger's eye, opal, nacre, mother-of-pearl; shot silk, moiré; dichromatism, trichromatism; dichroism, trichroism, polychromy 425 *colour*; peacock's tail, tortoiseshell; Joseph's coat, motley, harlequin, patchwork; medley of colour, riot of c.; enamelwork, stained glass, kaleidoscope; rainbow, spectrum, prism.

chequer, check, hound's-tooth check, pepper-and-salt; plaid, tartan; chessboard; marquetry, parquetry, inlaid work 844 *ornamental art*; mosaic, tessellation, tesserae, crazy paving 43 *medley*.

stripe, stria, striation; line, streak, band, bar; agate; zebra, tiger; mackerel sky; crack 222 *network*.

maculation, mottle, dappling, stippling, marbling; spottiness, patchiness 17 *non-uniformity*; patch, speck, speckle, macula, spots, freckle, foxing 845 *blemish*; fleck, dot, polka d.; blotch, splotch, splodge, splash; leopard, Dalmatian.

Adj. *variegated*, fretted etc. vb.; diversified, daedal; patterned, embroidered 844 *ornamental*; polychromatic, colourful 425 *florid*; bicolour, tricolour; dichroic, dichromatic, trichromatic, trichroic, many-hued, many-coloured, multi-c., parti-c., motley; patched, random 82 *multiform*; kaleidoscopic; plaid, tartan; rainbow-coloured, rainbow, prismatic, spectral; mosaic, tessellated.

iridescent, versicoloured, chameleon; nacreous, mother-of-pearl; opalescent, opaline, pearly 424 *semitransparent*; shot, shot through with, pavonine, moiré, watered, chatoyant.

pied, parti-coloured, black-and-white, pepper-and-salt, grizzled, piebald, skewbald, roan, pinto, chequered, check, dappled, patchy.

mottled, marbled, jaspered, veined, reticulated; studded, spotted, spotty, patchy; speckled, speckledy, freckled; streaky, streaked, banded, striped 222 *crossed*; brindled, tabby.

Vb. *variegate*, diversify, fret, pattern; punctuate; chequer, check, counterchange; patch 656 *repair*; embroider 844 *decorate*; braid, quilt; damascene, inlay, tessellate; stud, pepper, dot with, mottle, speckle, freckle, spangle, spot; stipple, dapple; streak, stripe, striate; marble, vein, cloud; stain, blot, discolour 649 *make unclean*; make iridescent; interchange colour, play.

438. Vision – N. *vision*, sight, power of s., eyesight; seeing, visualization; perception, recognition; acuity (of vision), good sight; defective vision 440 *dim sight*; oculist, ophthalmologist 442 *eyeglass*.

eye, eyeball, iris, pupil, white, cornea, retina, optic nerve; optics, orbs, sparklers, peepers, weepers; windows of the soul; saucer eyes, goggle e.; eyelashes 421 *screen*; naked eye, unaided e.; weak eyes 440 *dim sight*; evil eye 983 *sorcery*; hawk, eagle, cat, lynx; Argus.

look, regard, glance, side g., squint; tail *or* corner of the eye; glint, blink, flash; gaze, steady g.; observation, contemplation, watch; stare, fixed s.; come-hither look 889 *wooing*; ogle, leer, wink 524 *hint*; grimace, dirty look, scowl, peep, peek, glimpse, half an eye.

inspection, ocular i., ocular demonstration 443 *visibility*; examination 459 *inquiry*; view, preview 522 *manifestation*; supervision 689 *management*; review, survey, overview; sweep, reconnaissance, reconnoitre, recce, tour of inspection; sightseeing, rubbernecking; look, butcher's, lookaround, look-see, dekko, once-over, coup d'oeil, rapid survey, rapid glance; second glance, double take; viewing, home v. 445 *cinema*, 531 *broadcasting*; espial, view, first v.; first sight; observation, prying, spying; peeping, voyeurism, peeping Tom.

view, full v., eyeful; vista, prospect, outlook, perspective; aspect 445 *appearance*; panorama, bird's-eye view, commanding v.; horizon, false h.; line of sight, line of vision; purview, ken; field of view; scene, setting 594 *theatre*; angle of vision, slant; viewpoint, standpoint; observation point, vantage p., lookout 209 *high structure*; belvedere, gazebo; camera obscura; astrodome, conning tower; observatory, observation balloon; grandstand, ringside seat 441 *onlookers*; loophole, peephole 263 *window*.

Adj. *seeing*, glimpsing etc. vb.; visual, perceptible 443 *visible*; panoramic, perspectival; ocular, ophthalmic; optical; stereoscopic, binocular; orthoptic; perspicacious, clear-sighted, sharp-s., sharp-eyed, gimlet-e., eagle-e.; vigilant, all eyes; second-sighted, visionary 513 *imaginative*.

Vb. *see*, behold, visualize, use one's eyes; perceive, discern, distinguish, make out, recognize 490 *know*; descry, discover 484 *detect*; sight, espy, spy, spot, observe 455 *notice*; lay *or* clap eyes on, catch sight of, raise land; catch a glimpse of, glimpse; view, hold in view, have in sight; see with one's own eyes, witness, look on 441 *watch*; see visions 513 *imagine*.

gaze, regard, gaze at, look, look at, eye; look full in the face, look in the eyes; stare, peer, goggle, gape, gawp; focus, rivet one's eyes, fix one's gaze; glare, glower, look daggers 891 *be angry*; glance, glance at; squint, look askance; make eyes at, ogle, leer 889 *court*; feast one's eyes on, gloat over; steal a glance, peep, peek, take a peep; cast *or* turn one's eyes on, bend one's looks on; look up, look round; look away, drop one's eyes, avert one's e. 439 *be blind*; exchange glances, make eye contact.

scan, scrutinize, inspect, examine, take stock of, look one up and down; contemplate, pore over 536 *study*; look over *or* through, read t., riffle t., leaf t., skim t.; take a look at, have a dekko *or* a butcher's, take a gander *or* a squint at, run one's eye over; view, survey, reconnoitre; scout, spy out the land; snoop 453 *be curious*; watch 457 *invigilate*; watch out for, keep watch, look out, keep an eye out for, keep a weather eye open for, keep

one's eye skinned *or* peeled; strain one's eyes, peer; squint at, squinny; crane, crane one's neck.

Int. look! view halloo! land ahoy!

439. Blindness – N. *blindness*, lack of vision; sightlessness, eyelessness; glaucoma, river blindness, cataract; night blindness, snow b., colour b.; dim-sightedness 440 *dim sight*; blind side, blind spot 444 *invisibility*; tunnel vision; blind eye 456 *inattention*; word blindness, dyslexia; glass eye, artificial e.; blind man *or* woman, the blind; braille, talking book; guide dog.

Adj. *blind*, sightless, eyeless, visionless, dark; unseeing 456 *inattentive*; blinded, blindfold, blinkered; glaucomatous 440 *dim-sighted*; blind as a bat.

Vb. *be blind*, not see, not use one's eyes; go blind, lose one's sight, lose one's eyes; grope 461 *be tentative*; wear blinkers, have a blind spot, not see for looking, not see what is under one's nose; shut one's eyes to 458 *disregard*; not bear the light, blink, wink, squint 440 *be dimsighted*.

blind, deprive of sight; put *or* gouge one's eyes out; dazzle, daze; blinker, blindfold 421 *screen*; throw dust in one's eyes 495 *mislead*.

440. Dim-sightedness: imperfect vision – N. *dim sight*, weak s., failing s., dim-sightedness, dull-sightedness; near-blindness, purblindness 439 *blindness*; half-vision, partial v., defective v.; weak eyes, eyestrain, bleariness; amblyopia; short sight, near s., near-sightedness, myopia; presbyopia, long sight, far s.; double vision; astigmatism, cataract, film; glaucoma; scotoma, dizziness, swimming; colour-blindness, dichromatism; snow-blindness, day-b. night-b., nyctalopia; ophthalmia, conjunctivitis, pink eye; cast; strabismus, squint; miosis; wink, blink, nictitation, nystagmus; blind side 444 *invisibility*.

visual fallacy, anamorphosis 246 *distortion*; refraction 417 *reflection*; illusion, optical i. 542 *deception*; trick of light, phantasm, phantasmagoria, will-o'-the-wisp, mirage; phantom, spectre, apparition 970 *ghost*; vision, dream 513 *fantasy*; distorting mirror, magic m. 442 *optical device*.

Adj. *dim-sighted*, purblind, half-blind, gravel-b.; weak-eyed, bespectacled; myopic, short-sighted, near-s.; presbyopic, long-sighted; astigmatic; colour-blind, dichromatic; dim-eyed, one-e., monocular; wall-eyed, squinting; strabismic, cross-eyed; boss-eyed, cock-e., swivel-e., goggle-e., bug-e. 845 *blemished*; miotic, nystagmic; bleary-eyed, blinking; dazzled, blinded 439 *blind*; amaurotic, glaucomatous.

Vb. *be dim-sighted*, – myopic etc. adj.; peer, screw up one's eyes, squint; blink, wink, nictitate; see double, grow dazzled, swim; grow blurred, dim, fail.

blur, confuse; dazzle, bedazzle 417 *shine*; darken, dim, smudge 419 *bedim*.

441. Spectator – N. *spectator*, beholder; seer 513 *visionary*; looker, viewer, observer, watcher; inspector, examiner, scrutator, scrutinizer 690 *manager*; attendant 742 *servant*; witness, eyewitness; passerby, bystander, onlooker; looker-on, gazer, starter, gaper, goggler; eyer, ogler, voyeur, peeping Tom; window shopper; sightseer, rubberneck 268 *traveller*; stargazer, astronomer; bird watcher, train spotter; lookout 484 *detector*; watch, night w. 664 *warner*; scout, spy 459 *detective*; filmgoer 445 *cinema*; theatregoer 594 *playgoer*; viewer, captive audience.

onlookers, audience, auditorium, sea of faces; box office, gate; house, gallery, gods, circle, dress c., pit, stalls; grandstand, terraces; supporters, fans 707 *patron*, 504 *enthusiast*.

Vb. *watch*, spectate, look on, view 438 *see*; witness 189 *be present*; follow, follow with one's eyes, observe, attend 455 *be attentive*; eye, ogle, gape, stare; spy, spy out 438 *scan*.

442. Optical instrument – N. *optical device*, optical instrument; glass 422 *trans-*

parency; optic, lens, meniscus; telephoto lens, zoom, l., wide-angle l., fisheye l. 551 *photography*; eyepiece, ocular, objective; sunglass, burning glass; optometer, ophthalmoscope; prism, spectroscope, spectrometer, grating, polariscope; kaleidoscope; stroboscope; photometer, light meter, exposure m., actinometer, radiometer; visual display unit, VDU 86 *data processing*; projector, overhead p., epidiascope, episcope, magic lantern, stereoscope, microfilm reader, slide viewer.

eyeglass, spectacles, specs, glasses, reading g.; pince-nez, sunglasses, dark glasses, Polaroid (tdmk) g., photochromic g., bifocals; thick glasses, pebble g.; contact lens; lorgnette, monocle; magnifying glass, hand lens, loupe; optician; optometrist.

telescope, refractor, reflector 321 *astronomy*; collimator; sight, finder, viewfinder, rangefinder; periscope; spyglass, night glass; binoculars, field glasses, opera g.

microscope, electron m., photomicroscope, ultramicroscope 196 *microscopy*.

mirror, reflector, mirror, speculum; rear-view mirror, wing m.; glass, looking g., pier g., cheval g.

camera, camera lucida, camera obscura, spectrograph 321 *astronomy*; pin-hole camera, box c., reflex c., hand-held c., cinecamera, television camera, videopack, ENG; electric eye, closed-circuit television 484 *detector*; shutter, aperture, stop; flashgun 420 *lamp*; film 551 *photography*.

443. Visibility – N. *visibility*, perceptibility, observability; sight, exposure; distinctness, clearness, clarity, definition, conspicuousness, prominence; ocular proof, visible evidence 522 *manifestation*; visual aid 534 *teaching*; scene, field of view 438 *view*; high visibility, low v.; ceiling, horizon 183 *range*.

Adj. *visible*, seeable, viewable; perceptible, perceivable, discernible, observable, noticeable, detectable; recognizable, unmistakable; symptomatic 547 *indicating*; apparent 445 *appearing*; evident, showing 522 *manifest*; exposed, open, naked, outcropping, open to view; sighted, in view, in full v.; before one's eyes; visible to the naked eye, macroscopic; telescopic; panoramic, stereoscopic; periscopic.

obvious, showing, for all to see; plain, clear, clear-cut, well-defined, well-marked; distinct, unblurred, in focus; unclouded, undisguised, uncovered, unhidden; spectacular, conspicuous, prominent; eye-catching, striking, shining 417 *luminous*; glaring, staring; pronounced, in bold relief, highlighted, spotlit; visualized, vivid, eidetic; under one's nose, staring one in the face, plain to see, plain as a pikestaff.

Vb. *be visible*, etc. adj.; show, show through 422 *be transparent*; meet the eye 455 *attract notice*; catch the eye, stand out; come to light; loom, heave in sight, come into view 445 *appear*; show up 295 *arrive*; surface 298 *emerge*; stick out, project 254 *jut*; manifest itself, be plain; shine forth 417 *shine*; make visible 522 *manifest*.

444. Invisibility – N. *invisibility*, nonappearance 190 *absence*; vanishing 446 *disappearance*; imperceptibility, indistinctness, indefiniteness; poor visibility 419 *dimness*; smallness 196 *minuteness*; disguisement 525 *concealment*; mist, fog, veil, curtain 421 *screen*; blind spot 439 *blindness*; blind corner 663 *pitfall*; hidden menace 661 *danger*; impermeability 423 *opacity*; black light 417 *radiation*.

Adj. *invisible*, imperceptible, unapparent, unnoticeable, indiscernible; indistinguishable, unrecognizable; unseen, unsighted; viewless, sightless; unnoticed 458 *neglected*; out of sight 446 *disappearing*; not in sight 199 *distant*; hidden 523 *latent*; disguised, camouflaged 525 *concealed*; shadowy, dark, obscured.

indistinct, partly-seen, half-s.; unclear, ill-defined, ill-marked, indefinite, indistinct 419 *dim*; faint, inconspicuous, microscopic 196 *minute*; confused, vague, blurred, blurry, out of focus; fuzzy, misty, hazy 424 *semitransparent*.

445. Appearance – N. *appearance*, phenomenon; materialization, showing, 443 *visibility*; display, demonstration 522 *manifestation*; externals, outside, superficies 223 *exteriority*; appearance, look of things; visual impact, face value; impression, effect; image, pose, front 541 *duplicity*; veneer, show, seeming, semblance; side, aspect, facet; phase, guise; garb 228 *dressing*; colour, outline, shape 243 *form*; set, hang, look; respect, light, angle, slant, point of view 438 *view*; a manifestation, emanation, theophany; vision 513 *fantasy*; hallucination, illusion 440 *visual fallacy*; apparition 970 *ghost*; reflection 18 *similarity*; visual 551 *image*.

spectacle, feast for the eyes, eyeful, vision, sight, scene; scenery, landscape, seascape, cloudscape, townscape; panorama 438 *view*; display, pageantry 875 *ostentation*; revue, extravaganza 594 *stage show*; television, video 531 *broadcasting*; illuminations, son et lumière; pyrotechnics 420 *fireworks*; presentation, show, exhibition 522 *exhibit*; peep show, slide s., film s., home movies; phantasmagoria 437 *variegation*; panorama, diorama, cyclorama; staging, tableau, transformation scene; set, décor, backcloth 594 *stage set*.

cinema, cinematography; screen, big s., silver s., Hollywood, film industry; film studio, film-making, shooting 551 *photography*; direction, continuity, cutting, montage, projection; photoplay, screenplay, scenario, script, shooting s.; credits, titles; special effects, animation; voice-over, sound effects, soundtrack; cinematograph, projector 442 *optical device*; flea pit 594 *theatre*; film director, film star 594 *actor*; filmgoer, cineaste 504 *enthusiast*.

film, films, pictures, motion p., moving p., movies, flicks, celluloid; Technicolor (tdmk), 3-D, Cinerama (tdmk), Cinemascope (tdmk); silent film, sound f., talkie; big picture, B p., supporting film, short, newsreel, trailer; cartoon, animated c., travelogue, documentary, feature film, cinema verité; art film, new wave, nouvelle vague; epic, blockbuster; musical;

weepie, creepie, thriller, spine-chiller, cliffhanger, horror film; Western, spaghetti w., horse opera, space o.; oldie, remake; rush, preview; general release.

mien, look, face; play of features, expression; brow, countenance, looks; complexion, colour, cast; air, demeanour, carriage, bearing, deportment, poise, presence; posture, behaviour 688 *conduct*.

feature, trait, mark, lineament; lines, cut, shape, fashion, figure 243 *form*; outline, contour, relief, elevation, profile, silhouette; visage, physiognomy, cut of one's jib 237 *face*.

Adj. *appearing*, apparent, phenomenal; seeming, specious, ostensible; deceptive 542 *deceiving*; outward, external, superficial 223 *exterior*; showing, on view 443 *visible*; visual, video-; exhibited, hung; spectacular 875 *showy*; revealed 522 *manifest*; dreamlike 513 *imaginary*.

Vb. *appear*, show 443 *be visible*; seem, look so 18 *resemble*; have the look of, present the appearance of, assume the guise of, take the shape of; cut a figure 875 *be ostentatious*; figure in, star in; exhibit 522 *manifest*; rise, arise 68 *begin*; materialize 295 *arrive*, 970 *haunt*.

Adv. *apparently*, manifestly, visibly; ostensibly, seemingly, to all appearances, to the eye, at first sight, on the face of it; on view, on show.

446. Disappearance – **N.** *disappearance*, vanishing; vanishing trick 542 *sleight*; exit 296 *departure*; evanescence, evaporation; dematerialization, dissipation; extinction 2 *nonexistence*; eclipse 418 *obscuration*; fadeout; vanishing point 444 *invisibility*.

Adj. *disappearing*, vanishing; evanescent 114 *transient*; dissipated, dispersed; missing, vanished 190 *absent*; lost, lost to sight, lost to view 444 *invisible*; gone to earth 525 *concealed*; gone 2 *extinct*.

Vb. *disappear*, vanish; dematerialize, melt into thin air; evanesce, evaporate 338 *vaporize*; dissolve, melt away; wear away, wear off, dwindle 37 *decrease*; fade, pale 419 *be dim*; fade away 114 *be transient*; disperse, scatter 75 *be dispersed*; go, be gone 296 *decamp*; hide, lie low 523 *lurk*; leave no trace 525 *conceal*; sink from view, be lost to sight; become extinct 2 *pass away*.

INTELLECT: THE EXERCISE OF THE MIND

4.1 FORMATION OF IDEAS

Section 1: General

447. Intellect – N. *intellect*, mind, psyche, mentality; understanding, intellection, conception; rationality, reasoning power; reason 475 *reasoning*; philosophy 449 *thought*; awareness, consciousness, self-c., stream of c. 455 *attention*; cognition, perception, apperception, percipience, insight; extrasensory perception, instinct 476 *intuition*; flair, judgement 463 *discrimination*; intellectualism, intellectuality; mental capacity, wits, senses 498 *intelligence*; mental evolution, psychogenesis; brain, cerebrum, cerebellum, cortex 213 *head*; electroencephalograph; alpha waves; sensorium 818 *feeling*.

spirit, soul, geist, mind; heart, breast, bosom, inner man *or* woman 5 *essential part*; double, ka, ba 80 *self*; psyche, pneuma, id, ego, superego, animus, anima; the unconscious, the subconscious; personality, dual p. 503 *psychopathy*; spiritualism 984 *occultism*; spiritualist, occultist.

psychology, metapsychology; parapsychology 984 *psychics*; abnormal psychology 503 *psychopathy*; behaviourism; crowd psychology; psychometry 459 *inquiry*; psychopathology, psychiatry, antipsychiatry, psychotherapy, psychoanalysis 658 *therapy*; psychosurgery 658 *surgery*; psychophysiology, psychobiology, psychophysics.

psychologist, psychoanalyst, psychiatrist, psychotherapist 658 *doctor*; head shrinker, shrink.

Adj. *mental*, thinking, endowed with reason 475 *rational*; cerebral, intellective, intellectual, conceptive, noological, noetic, conceptual, abstract; theoretical 512 *suppositional*; perceptual, percipient, perceptive; cognitive 490 *knowing*; conscious, self-c., subjective.

psychic, psychological; psychogenic, psychosomatic; subconscious, subliminal; spiritualistic 984 *psychical*; spiritual, otherworldly 320 *immaterial*.

Vb. *cognize*, perceive, apperceive 490 *know*; realize, sense, become aware of, become conscious of; objectify 223 *externalize*; note 438 *see*, 455 *notice*; ratiocinate 475 *reason*; understand 498 *be wise*; conceptualize, intellectualize 449 *think*; conceive, invent 484 *discover*; ideate 513 *imagine*; appreciate 480 *estimate*.

448. Absence of intellect – N. *absence of intellect*, unintelligence; brute creation 365 *animality*; vegetation 366 *vegetable life*; inanimate nature, stocks and stones; brainlessness, mindlessness 450 *absence of thought*; brain damage 503 *insanity*.

Adj. *mindless*, unintelligent; animal, vegetable; mineral, inanimate 359 *inorganic*; unreasoning 450 *unthinking*; brainless 499 *foolish*.

449. Thought – N. *thought*, mental process, thinking; mental act, ideation; intellectual exercise, mentation, cogitation 447 *intellect*; cerebration, lucubration, headwork, thinking cap; brainwork, brainfag; hard thinking, hard thought, concentration 455 *attention*; deep thought, profundity 498 *wisdom*; thoughts, ideas 451 *idea*; conception, workings of the mind

513 *ideality*; flow of ideas, current of thought, train of t.; association of ideas, reason 475 *reasoning*; brown study, reverie, musing 456 *abstractedness*; thinking out, excogitation (**see** *meditation*); invention, inventiveness 513 *imagination*; second thoughts, afterthought, reconsideration 67 *sequel*; retrospection, hindsight 505 *memory*; forethought 669 *preparation*, 510 *foresight*.

meditation, thoughtfulness, speculation 459 *inquiry*; lateral thinking; reflection, deep r., brooding, rumination, consideration, pondering; contemplation 438 *inspection*; absorption, pensiveness; introspection, self-communing; transcendental meditation, TM; religious contemplation, retreat, mysticism 979 *piety*; deliberation, excogitation 480 *judgement*; examination, close study, concentration, application 536 *study*.

philosophy, ontology, teleology, metaphysics, ethics; speculation, systematic thought; scientific thought, science, natural philosophy; ideology, school of philosophy 485 *opinion*; philosopher, thinker 492 *intellectual*; metaphysician.

Adj. *thoughtful*, conceptive; cogitative, deliberative; pensive, meditative, ruminant, ruminative, contemplative, reflective; self-communing, introspective; wrapt in thought, lost in t., deep in t.; absorbed, musing 456 *abstracted*; concentrating, studious 455 *attentive*; considerate 901 *philanthropic*; prudent 510 *foreseeing*.

philosophic, metaphysical, ontological, speculative, abstract, conceptual, ideological, systematic, rational, logical.

Vb. *think*, ween, trow 512 *suppose*; conceive, form ideas, ideate; fancy 513 *imagine*; think about, cogitate (**see** *meditate*); use one's brain, put on one's thinking cap; concentrate, collect one's thoughts 455 *be attentive*; bend *or* apply one's mind to, trouble one's head about, lucubrate, cerebrate, mull over, puzzle over; think hard, beat *or* cudgel *or* rack one's brains, worry at; think through, reason out 475 *reason*; think out, think up, excogitate, invent 484 *discover*; devise 623 *plan*; take into one's head, entertain *or* harbour a notion, have

an idea 485 *believe*; toy with an i., kick an i. around; think on 505 *remember*.

meditate, ruminate, chew over, digest; wonder about, debate 459 *inquire*; reflect, contemplate, study; speculate, philosophize, theorize; intellectualize 447 *cognize*; think about, consider, take stock of, ponder, weigh 480 *estimate*; think over, turn o., revolve, run over in the mind; reconsider, review, reexamine, have second thoughts, think better of; sleep on it 691 *consult*; commune with oneself, introspect; brood, muse, fall into a brown study; go into retreat.

dawn upon, occur to, flash into one's mind, cross one's m., come to m.; come into one's head, strike one; suggest itself, present itself; cause thought, provoke t., make one think 821 *impress*; penetrate, sink in.

engross, absorb, preoccupy, run in one's head, fill one's mind, be uppermost in one's thoughts; prey on one's mind, haunt, obsess.

450. Absence of thought – N. *absence of thought*, inability to think 448 *absence of intellect*; blank mind 491 *ignorance*; abstraction 456 *abstractedness*; inanity, vacuity 499 *unintelligence*; thoughtlessness 456 *inattention*; conditioned reflex, automatism; knee-jerk response, gut reaction; instinct 476 *intuition*.

Adj. *unthinking*, unreflecting 448 *mindless*; idealess, unidea'd, unimaginative 20 *imitative*; automatic, instinctive 476 *intuitive*; vacant, empty-headed, not thinking 456 *inattentive*; unoccupied, relaxed; inconsiderate 932 *selfish*; irrational 477 *illogical*; stupid 499 *unintelligent*.

451. Idea – N. *idea*, noumenon, notion, abstraction, a thought, concept; theory 512 *supposition*; percept, image, mental i.; archetype 23 *prototype*; reflection, observation 449 *thought*; impression, conceit, fancy 513 *ideality*; invention, brainchild, brain wave 484 *discovery*; wheeze, wrinkle 623 *contrivance*; view, point of v. 485 *opinion*; leading idea, main idea; one idea 481 *prejudgement*.

Adj. *ideational*, conceptual 449 *thoughtful*; theoretical 512 *suppositional*; notional, ideal 513 *imaginary*.

452. Topic – N. *topic*, food for thought, mental pabulum; subject matter, subject; argument, plot, theme, message; text, burden, motif; concern, interest, human i.; matter, affair; shop 622 *business*; agenda, order paper; motion 761 *request*; problem 459 *question*; heart of the question, gist, pith; theorem, proposition 512 *supposition*; thesis, case, point 475 *argument*; issue, moot point, point at issue; field of inquiry 536 *study*.

Adj. *topical*, thematic; challenging, thought-provoking; mooted, debatable 474 *uncertain*; fit for consideration.

Adv. *in question*, in the mind, on the brain, in one's thoughts; on foot, on the agenda; before the house, under consideration.

Section 2: Precursory conditions and operations

453. Curiosity: desire for knowledge – N. *curiosity*, intellectual c., speculativeness, inquiring mind, thirst for knowledge 536 *study*; interest, inquisitiveness, curiousness 459 *inquiry*; nosiness 678 *overactivity*; sightseeing 267 *land travel*; morbid curiosity, ghoulishness; voyeurism 951 *impurity*.

inquisitive person, questioner, enfant terrible 459 *inquirer*; nosey parker, stickybeak; busybody 678 *meddler*; newshound, gossip columnist 529 *news reporter*; seeker, searcher, explorer 461 *experimenter*; sightseer, globetrotter 441 *spectator*; snoop, snooper, spy 459 *detective*; eavesdropper, interceptor, phone-tapper 415 *listener*.

Adj. *inquisitive*, curious, interested; avid for knowledge 536 *studious*; morbidly curious, ghoulish, prurient; newsmongering, agog, all ears 455 *attentive*; wanting to know, burning with curiosity, consumed *or* eaten up with c.; overcurious, nosey, snoopy, prying, etc. vb.; inquisitorial 459 *inquiring*; meddlesome 678 *meddling*.

Vb. *be curious*, want to know; seek, look for 459 *search*; research 461 *experiment*; be interested, take an interest 455 *be attentive*; mosey around, dip into; dig up, nose out; peep, peek, spy 438 *scan*; snoop, pry, nose into 459 *inquire*; eavesdrop, tap, intercept, bug, listen in 415 *hear*; poke *or* stick one's nose in, be nosey 678 *meddle*; quiz, question 459 *interrogate*; stare, gawp 438 *gaze*.

454. Incuriosity – N. *incuriosity*, lack of interest, incuriousness, no questions, mental inertia; uninterest, unconcern 860 *indifference*; apathy 820 *moral insensibility*.

Adj. *incurious*, uninquisitive, unreflecting 450 *unthinking*; without interest, uninterested; unconcerned 860 *indifferent*; listless, inert, apathetic 820 *impassive*.

Vb. *be incurious*, etc. adj.; have no curiosity, take no interest 456 *be inattentive*; not trouble oneself, not bother with 860 *be indifferent*; mind one's own business; look the other way 458 *disregard*.

455. Attention – N. *attention*, notice, regard, consideration 449 *thought*; heed, alertness, attentiveness; solicitude, watchfulness 457 *surveillance*; intentness, undivided attention; concentration, application, studiousness 536 *study*; examination, scrutiny 438 *inspection*; close attention, meticulousness, finicalness 457 *carefulness*; diligence, pains, trouble 678 *assiduity*; exclusive attention, single-mindedness; interest 453 *curiosity*.

Adj. *attentive*, intent, diligent, assiduous 678 *industrious*; considerate, thoughtful, heedful, mindful, regardful 457 *careful*; alert, on the ball, with it; open-eyed, awake, wide-a.; awake to, alive to, aware, conscious 449 *thoughtful*; sharp-eyed, watchful 457 *vigilant*; rapt, all ears, all eyes; undistracted, concentrating, deep in; serious, earnest 536 *studious*; meticulous, particular 494 *accurate*; finical, pedantic 862 *fastidious*.

obsessed, single-minded, possessed, engrossed, wrapped up in, taken up with, into, hooked on; rapt, spellbound;

haunted by 854 *fearing*; monomaniacal 503 *crazy*.

Vb. *be attentive*, attend, pay attention; look to, heed, mind 457 *be careful*; take trouble, take pains, bother 682 *exert oneself*; listen, prick up one's ears, sit up and take notice; take seriously, fasten on 638 *make important*; give one's attention to, give *or* bend one's mind to 449 *think*; keep one's eye on the ball, concentrate, miss nothing; watch, be all eyes 438 *gaze*; drink in, hang on the lips of 415 *hear*; focus one's mind on, concentrate on; scrutinize, vet, review 438 *scan*; pore, mull, digest 536 *study*; glance at, dip into, flip through.

notice, note, take n., register; mark, recognize, spot; take cognizance of; take account of, consider; comment upon, mention 584 *converse*; recall, revert to; have time for, find time f.; acknowledge 884 *greet*.

attract notice, draw the attention, engage the a.; stick out like a sore thumb, arrest one's notice, interest 821 *impress*; excite attention, catch the eye 443 *be visible*; bring to one's notice, call attention to 528 *publish*; point out 547 *indicate*; stress, underline 532 *emphasize*; alert, warn 665 *raise the alarm*.

Int. see! mark! lo! behold! look! look here! look out! look alive! look to it! hark! oyez! hey! mind out! nota bene, NB, take notice! take care! watch your step!

456. Inattention – N. *inattention*, inadvertence, oversight, aberration; lapse 495 *error*; lack of interest 454 *incuriosity*; unconcern 860 *indifference*; disregard 458 *negligence*; thoughtlessness, heedlessness, want of thought 481 *misjudgement*; desultoriness, superficiality, flippancy; light-mindedness, levity, volatility 604 *caprice*; deaf ears, unseeing eyes, blind spot; distraction, red herring 612 *inducement*; absent-mindedness, wandering wits 450 *absence of thought*; stargazer, daydreamer, woolgatherer, Walter Mitty; jaywalker; scatterbrain, grasshopper mind, butterfly.

abstractedness, abstraction, absent-mindedness, absence of mind; wool-gathering, daydreaming, stargazing, doodling; reverie, brown study; distraction, preoccupation, divided attention.

Adj. *inattentive*, careless 458 *negligent*; off one's guard 508 *inexpectant*; unobservant, unnoticing 454 *incurious*; unseeing 439 *blind*; unhearing 416 *deaf*; undiscerning 464 *indiscriminating*; unmindful, unheeding, inadvertent, not thinking, unreflecting 450 *unthinking*; not concentrating, half asleep, only half awake; uninterested 860 *indifferent*; apathetic, unaware 820 *impassive*; oblivious 506 *forgetful*; inconsiderate, thoughtless, tactless, heedless; regardless 857 *rash*; cavalier, offhand, cursory, superficial, shallow.

abstracted, distrait(e), absent-minded, absent, far away, not with it, miles away; lost, lost in thought, rapt, absorbed; stargazing, bemused, in a brown study, deep in reverie, pensive, dreamy, daydreaming, mooning, woolgathering; nodding 679 *sleepy*.

distracted, preoccupied, engrossed; otherwise engaged, diverted 282 *deviating*; dazed, disconcerted, put out, thrown out of one's stride, put off, put off one's stroke; rattled, unnerved 854 *nervous*.

light-minded, wandering, desultory, trifling; frivolous, flippant, insouciant, light-headed; airy, volatile, mercurial, bird-witted, flighty, giddy, dizzy, scatty, scatterbrained, harebrained, featherbrained 503 *crazy*; inconstant 604 *capricious*.

Vb. *be inattentive*, not attend, pay no attention, pay no heed, not listen; not register, not notice, not use one's eyes; not click, not catch; overlook 495 *blunder*; be off one's guard, let slip, be caught out; lose track of, lose sight of; not remember 506 *forget*; dream, nod 679 *sleep*; not concentrate, trifle, play at; be abstracted, wander, let one's mind w., go woolgathering 513 *imagine*; fall into a brown study, muse, be lost in thought, moon, stargaze; idle, doodle 679 *be inactive*; be distracted, digress, lose the thread 282 *stray*; disregard, ignore 458 *neglect*; have no time for 922 *hold cheap*.

distract, divert; put out of one's head,

drive out of one's mind; confuse, muddle 63 *derange*; disturb, disconcert, discompose, fluster, put off one's stroke 318 *agitate*; dazzle 439 *blind*; bewilder, flummox 474 *puzzle*.

escape notice, escape attention, blush unseen, be overlooked 523 *lurk*; fall on deaf ears, pass over one's head, meet a blind spot, not click; go in at one ear and out at the other, slip one's memory 506 *be forgotten*.

457. Carefulness. Vigilance – N. *carefulness*, mindfulness, attentiveness 678 *assiduity*; heed, care, solicitude 455 *attention*; tidiness, neatness 60 *order*; attention to detail, thoroughness, meticulousness, minuteness; nicety, exactness 494 *accuracy*; overnicety, perfectionism 862 *fastidiousness*; conscience, scrupulosity 929 *probity*; vigilance, alertness 669 *preparedness*; circumspection, prudence, wariness 858 *caution*; forethought 510 *foresight*.

surveillance, an eye on, watching 660 *protection*; vigilance, invigilation, inspection; babysitting, chaperonage; lookout, weather eye; vigil, watch, deathwatch; doomwatch; guard, sentry-go; watchful eye, unsleeping e. 438 *eye*; sentry 660 *protection*, 749 *keeper*.

Adj. *careful*, thoughtful, considered, mindful, regardful, heedful 455 *attentive*; taking care, painstaking; solicitous, anxious; cautious, afraid to touch; loving, tender; conscientious, scrupulous 929 *honourable*; diligent, assiduous 678 *industrious*; thorough, meticulous, minute, exact 494 *accurate*; perfectionist 862 *fastidious*; tidy, neat, clean 60 *orderly*.

vigilant, alert, on guard, ready 669 *prepared*; on the alert, on guard, on the qui vive, on one's toes; watching, watchful, wakeful, wideawake; observant, sharp-eyed; all eyes, Argus-eyed., eagle-e. 438 *seeing*; prudent, provident, far-sighted 510 *foreseeing*; circumspect, guarded, wary 858 *cautious*.

Vb. *be careful*, mind, heed, beware 455 *be attentive*; take precautions, think twice, check 858 *be cautious*; have one's eyes open, have one's wits about one, keep a

lookout, watch one's step 461 *be tentative*; be on one's guard, mind one's P's and Q's; tidy, keep t. 62 *arrange*; take a pride in, take pains, be meticulous, dot one's i's and cross one's t's; try, do one's best 682 *exert oneself*.

look after, look to, see to, take care of 689 *manage*; take charge of, accept responsibility for; care for, mind, tend, keep 660 *safeguard*; baby-sit; nurse, foster, cherish; have regard for 920 *respect*; keep an eye on, keep tabs on, monitor; escort, chaperon, play gooseberry.

invigilate, stay awake, sit up; keep vigil, watch; stand sentinel; keep watch, look out, keep a sharp lookout, watch out for; keep one's eyes peeled, keep one's weather-eye open, sleep with one eye open, keep one's ear to the ground; mount guard, set watch, post sentries, stand to 660 *safeguard*.

Adv. *carefully*, attentively, diligently; studiously, thoroughly; lovingly, tenderly; painfully, anxiously; with care, gingerly, with kid gloves.

458. Negligence – N. *negligence*, carelessness 456 *inattention*; neglectfulness, forgetfulness 506 *oblivion*; remissness, neglect, oversight, omission; nonobservance, default, laches, culpable negligence 918 *undutifulness*; unguarded hour, unpreparedness 670 *nonpreparation*; disregard, noninterference, laissez faire; unconcern, insouciance, nonchalance 860 *indifference*; procrastination 136 *delay*; supineness, slackness 679 *inactivity*; slovenliness, sluttishness, untidiness 61 *disorder*; sloppiness, inaccuracy 495 *inexactness*; laxness 734 *laxity*; perfunctoriness, superficiality; trifling, scamping; scamped work 728 *failure*; trifler, shirker, slacker, waster 679 *idler*; sloven, slut.

Adj. *negligent*, neglectful, careless 456 *inattentive*; remiss 918 *undutiful*; thoughtless 450 *unthinking*; oblivious 506 *forgetful*; uncaring, insouciant 860 *indifferent*; regardless, reckless 857 *rash*; casual, offhand 734 *lax*; sloppy, slipshod, slaphappy, slapdash, unthorough, perfunctory, superficial; hurried 680 *hasty*;

inaccurate 495 *inexact*; slack, supine 679 *lazy*; procrastinating 136 *late*; sluttish, untidy, slovenly 649 *dirty*; unwary, off guard 508 *inexpectant*; improvident 670 *unprepared*.

neglected, uncared for, untended; unkempt 649 *dirty*; unprotected, deserted; unattended 621 *relinquished*; lost sight of, unthought of; disregarded, ignored, out in the cold; unconsidered, overlooked, omitted; unnoticed, unremarked; unread, unscanned, unexplored; half-done, perfunctory 726 *uncompleted*.

Vb. *neglect*, omit, pass over; lose sight of 456 *be inattentive*; leave undone, do by halves 726 *not complete*; skimp, scamp; skip, skim, skim through; not mention, skate over 525 *conceal*; not take seriously, dabble in, trifle, fribble.

disregard, ignore, pass over 620 *avoid*; let pass, wink at, connive at, take no notice 734 *be lax*; turn a blind eye to, dismiss 439 *be blind*; overlook, discount 483 *underestimate*; pass by, turn one's back on; turn a deaf ear to 416 *be deaf*; take lightly, not trouble oneself with, not trouble one's head about 860 *be indifferent*; treat as of no account 922 *hold cheap*; leave to their own devices 621 *relinquish*.

be neglectful, doze, drowse 679 *sleep*; be off one's guard, be caught napping *or* with one's pants down; drift, laissez faire, procrastinate, let slide, let slip 677 *not act*; not bother, let things go 679 *be inactive*; shelve, pigeonhole, put aside 136 *put off*; make neglectful, lull, throw off one's guard; catch napping 508 *surprise*.

459. Inquiry – N. *inquiry*, asking, questioning (see *interrogation*); witch-hunt (see *search*); inquisition, examination, investigation, visitation; checkup, medical; inquest, post mortem, autopsy, audit; trial 959 *legal trial*; public inquiry, commission of inquiry, working party (see *inquirer*); census, canvass, survey, market research; poll, opinion p., straw p. 605 *vote*; probe, test, means t., check, spot c.; trial run 461 *experiment*; review, scrutiny 438 *inspection*; introspection, self-examination; personality testing, Rorschach *or* inkblot test;

research, fundamental r., applied r. 536 *study*; analysis, dissection; exploration, reconnaissance, recce, survey 484 *discovery*; discussion, airing, sounding 584 *conference*; inquiring mind 453 *curiosity*.

interrogation, questioning, interpellation; forensic examination, examination-in-chief; leading question, cross-examination; reexamination; quiz, brains trust; catechism; inquisition, third degree, grilling; dialogue, dialectic, question and answer, Socratic method; question time.

question, question mark 547 *punctuation*; query, request for information; questions, questionnaire 87 *list*; question paper, examination p.; interrogatory, Parliamentary question; challenge, fair question; loaded q., catch; feeler, leading question; rhetorical q.; moot point, quodlibet 452 *topic*; crucial question, sixty-four-thousand-dollar q.; problem, poser, headache 530 *enigma*.

exam, examination, oral e., viva voce e., viva; interview, audition 415 *hearing*; test, battery of tests; intelligence test, IQ test; catechumen 460 *respondent*; examinee, entrant, sitter 461 *testee*.

search, probe, investigation, inquiry; quest, hunt, witch-h., treasure h. 619 *pursuit*; house-search, domiciliary visit; frisking; rummaging, turning over; exploration, excavation, dig; search party.

secret service, espionage, counter-e., spying, intelligence; informer, spy, undercover agent, secret a., cloak-and-dagger man; double agent, inside a.; counterspy; spy ring.

detective, plain-clothes d.; investigator, criminologist; private detective, private eye; tec, sleuth, bloodhound, dick, snooper, spy 524 *informer*; graphologist, handwriting expert; Sherlock Holmes.

inquirer, investigator, prober; journalist 529 *news reporter*; student, seeker, thinker 449 *philosophy*; searcher, search party; inventor, discoverer 484 *detector*; prospector, gold-digger; talent scout; scout, spy; surveyor, inspector, visitor 438 *inspection*; checker, screener, scrutineer, censor, ombudsman 480 *estimator*; examiner, board of examiners; tester, test pilot, researcher, research worker, dissector 461 *experimenter*; sampler, pollster, canvasser; explorer 268 *traveller*.

questioner, cross-examiner, catechizer; interrogator, inquisitor, Grand I.; interpellator, interlocutor, interviewer; challenger, heckler; quizzer, enfant terrible 453 *inquisitive person*; question *or* quiz master; riddler, enigmatist.

Adj. *inquiring*, curious, prying, nosey 453 *inquisitive*; quizzing, quizzical; interrogatory, interrogative; examining, inquisitional, cross-questioning; elenctic, dialectic, maieutic, heuristic, zetetic; investigative, fact-finding, exploratory 461 *experimental*; analytic, diagnostic.

moot, in question, questionable, debatable; problematic, doubtful 474 *uncertain*; knotty, puzzling 700 *difficult*; undecided, left open.

Vb. *inquire*, ask, demand 761 *request*; canvass, agitate, air, ventilate, discuss, query 475 *argue*; inquire into, make inquiries, probe, delve into, sound, look into, investigate, hold an inquiry; try, hear 959 *try a case*; review, overhaul, audit, scrutinize, monitor, screen; analyse, dissect, parse, sift, winnow, thrash out; research 536 *study*; consider, examine 449 *meditate*; check, check on; feel the pulse, take the temperature, take soundings; get to the bottom of, fathom, see into, X-ray 438 *scan*; snoop, pry, nose around 453 *be curious*; survey, reconnoitre, case, sus out; explore 461 *be tentative*; try, sample, taste 461 *experiment*.

interrogate, interpellate, question; cross-question, cross-examine, reexamine; badger, challenge, heckle; interview, examine, subject to questioning, sound out, probe, quiz, catechize, grill, give the third degree; put to the question 963 *torture*; pump, pick one's brains, suck one dry; put the question, pop the q.; pose a q., propound a q., moot.

search, seek, look for; rummage, ransack, comb; scrabble, forage, fossick, root about; scour, turn over, rake o., pick o., turn inside out, rifle through, go t., search t., look into every nook and corner; look high and low; quarter the ground, go over

with a fine-tooth comb; pry into, peer i., peep i., peek i.; frisk, search one's pockets; feel for, grope for, hunt for, drag for, fish for, dig for; leave no stone unturned 682 *exert oneself*; cast about, follow the trail 619 *pursue*; probe, explore, go in quest of 461 *be tentative*; dig, excavate, archaeologize; prospect, dowse.

460. Answer – N. *answer*, reply, response; reaction; acknowledgement 588 *correspondence*; official reply, rescript; returns, results 548 *record*; feedback 524 *information*; echo, antiphon; password 547 *identification*; back-chat, repartee; retort, riposte 714 *retaliation*; question and answer 584 *interlocution*; clue, key, explanation 520 *interpretation*; solution 658 *remedy*; oracle 530 *enigma*.

rejoinder, reply, rebuttal, rebutter, surrejoinder 479 *confutation*; refutation, contradiction 533 *negation*, 467 *counterevidence*; countercharge 928 *accusation*.

respondent, defendant; answerer, responder, replier, correspondent; examinee 461 *testee*; candidate, applicant 716 *contender*.

Adj. *answering*, replying etc. vb.; respondent, responsive; counter 182 *counteracting*; corresponding, antiphonal 12 *correlative*; contradicting 533 *negative*; oracular.

Vb. *answer*, give a., return an a.; reply, write back, acknowledge, respond; echo, reecho 106 *repeat*; react, answer back, flash back, come back at, retort, riposte 714 *retaliate*; rejoin, rebut, counter 479 *confute*; field; parry, refuse to answer 620 *avoid*; contradict 533 *negate*; defend, have the right of reply; solve 520 *interpret*.

461. Experiment – N. *experiment*, controlled e.; experimentalism, experimentation, verification; exploration, probe; analysis, examination 459 *inquiry*; proof 478 *demonstration*; assay 480 *estimate*; check, test, acid t., test case; probation; double-blind test; practical test, trial, tryout, trial run, practice r., dry r., test flight 671 *attempt*; audition, voice test; ordeal

959 *legal trial*; pilot scheme, teething troubles 68 *debut*.

empiricism, tentativeness, speculation 512 *conjecture*; experience, practice, rule of thumb, trial and error, hit and miss; shot in the dark, gamble 618 *gambling*; instinct 476 *intuition*; sampling, random sample; feeler 459 *question*; kite-flying, trial balloon.

experimenter, experimentalist, empiricist, researcher, research worker, analyst, analyser, vivisector; assayer, chemist; tester; test driver, test pilot; speculator, prospector, sourdough; explorer, adventurer 459 *inquirer*.

testing agent, criterion, touchstone; standard, yardstick 465 *gauge*; breathalyser; control; reagent, litmus paper; cupel, test tube, crucible; pyx, pyx chest; proving ground, wind tunnel; simulator, flight s., test track; laboratory.

testee, examinee 460 *respondent*; probationer 538 *beginner*; candidate 716 *contender*; subject, patient; guinea pig.

Adj. *experimental*, analytic, analytical, verificatory, probative; probationary, probational; provisional, tentative 618 *speculative*; trial, exploratory 459 *inquiring*; empirical, experiential; in the experimental stage 474 *uncertain*.

Vb. *experiment*, experimentalize, make experiments; check, check on, verify; prove, put to the proof; assay, analyse; research; dabble; experiment on, vivisect; make a guinea pig of, practise on; test, put to the t., run a t. on 459 *inquire*; try out 671 *attempt*; sample 386 *taste*.

be tentative, be empirical, feel one's way, proceed by trial and error; feel, probe, grope, fumble; get the feel of, put out a feeler, dip a toe in, fly a kite, see how the land lies *or* the wind blows; fish for, angle for, cast one's net; wait and see, see what happens; try it on, see how far one can go; try one's luck, speculate 618 *gamble*; venture, explore, prospect 672 *undertake*; probe, sound 459 *inquire*.

Adv. *experimentally*, on test, on trial, on approval, on probation; empirically, by rule of thumb, by trial and error, by the light of nature, by guess and by God; on spec.

462. Comparison – N. *comparison*, comparing, likening; confrontation, collation, juxtaposition; check 459 *inquiry*; comparability, points of comparison, analogy, parallel, likeness 18 *similarity*; identification 13 *identity*; antithesis 14 *contrariety*; contrast 15 *differentiation*; simile, allegory 519 *metaphor*; criterion, pattern, check list, control 23 *prototype*; comparer, collator.

Adj. *compared*, collated etc. vb.; likened, set against, contrasted; comparative, comparable, analogical; relative, correlative; allegorical, metaphorical 519 *figurative*.

Vb. *compare*, collate, confront; set side by side, bring together 202 *juxtapose*; parallel; draw a p. *or* a comparison 18 *liken*; contrast 15 *differentiate*; compare and contrast 463 *discriminate*; match, pair 28 *equalize*; check with 12 *correlate*; institute a comparison, compare with; compare notes, match ideas.

463. Discrimination – N. *discrimination*, distinction 15 *differentiation*; discernment, insight, perception, acumen, flair 498 *intelligence*; appreciation, appraisal 480 *estimate*; sensitivity, tact, delicacy, refinement 846 *good taste*; sense of timing, sense of occasion; nicety, particularity 862 *fastidiousness*; subtlety, hair-splitting 475 *reasoning*; sifting 62 *sorting*; selection 605 *choice*.

Adj. *discriminating*, discriminative, selective, judicious, discerning; sensitive 494 *accurate*; fine, delicate, nice, particular 862 *fastidious*; thoughtful, tactful 513 *imaginative*; critical 480 *judicial*; distinguishing 15 *distinctive*.

Vb. *discriminate*, distinguish, contradistinguish 15 *differentiate*; compare and contrast 462 *compare*; sort, sift; severalize, separate the sheep from the goats, sort the wheat from the chaff 46 *set apart*; pick out 605 *select*; make a distinction, draw the line 468 *qualify*; refine upon, split hairs 475 *reason*; appraise 480 *esti-*

mate; weigh, consider 480 *judge*; discern, have insight; have a feel for, have an eye *or* an ear for 490 *know*.

464. Indiscrimination – N. *indiscrimination*, lack of discrimination, promiscuousness, universality 79 *generality*; lack of judgement, uncriticalness; indiscretion 857 *rashness*; imperceptivity, unimaginativeness, tactlessness, insensitiveness 820 *moral insensibility*; tastelessness, lack of refinement 847 *bad taste*; inaccuracy, vagueness, loose terms 495 *inexactness*.

Adj. *indiscriminate*, unsorted 61 *orderless*; rolled into one, undistinguished, undifferentiated 16 *uniform*; random, haphazard, unaimed, undirected; confused, undefined 474 *uncertain*; promiscuous, wholesale, blanket 79 *general*.

indiscriminating, unselective, undiscerning, uncritical 499 *unintelligent*; imperceptive, obtuse; tactless, insensitive, unimaginative; unrefined, coarse 847 *vulgar*; indiscreet, ill-judged 857 *rash*; tone-deaf 416 *deaf*; colour-blind 439 *blind*; inaccurate 495 *inexact*.

Vb. *not discriminate*, be indiscriminate, make no distinction, see no difference, swallow whole; lump together, jumble, confuse, confound 63 *derange*.

465. Measurement – N. *measurement*, quantification; mensuration, surveying, triangulation, cadastral survey; geodetics, geodesy; metage 322 *weighing*; posology, dose, dosage 26 *finite quantity*; rating, valuation, evaluation; appraisement, assessment, estimation 480 *estimate*; calculation, computation, reckoning 86 *numeration*; check, reading; metrics, micrometry 203 *long measure*; trigonometry 247 *angular measure*.

geometry, plane g., planimetry; solid geometry, stereometry; altimetry, hypsometry; geometer.

metrology, dimensions, length, breadth, height, depth, thickness 195 *size*; weights and measures, metric system; weights 322 *weighing*; linear measure 203 *long measure*; volume, cubic contents 183 *measure*; liquid measure, gill, pint, quart,

gallon; litre; barrel, hogshead 194 *vessel*; minim, dram; peck, bushel, quarter; ohm, watt 160 *electricity*; horse power 160 *energy*; candlepower 417 *light*; decibel, sone 398 *sound*.

coordinate, ordinate and abscissa, polar coordinates, latitude and longitude, right ascension and declination, altitude and azimuth; grid reference.

gauge, measure, scale, graduated s.; time scale 117 *chronometry*; balance 322 *scales*; nonius, vernier, micrometer; footrule, yardstick, metre bar; tape measure; chain, link, pole, perch, rod; lead, log, log-line; fathometer, echo sounder; ruler, slide rule; straight-edge, T-square, try s., set s.; dividers, callipers, compass, protractor; sextant, quadrant 269 *sailing aid*; theodolite, alidade; astrolabe 321 *astronomy*; index, Plimsoll line, bench mark 547 *indicator*; high-water mark, water line 236 *limit*; axis, coordinate; standard 23 *prototype*; milestone 547 *signpost*.

surveyor, land s., quantity s. 480 *estimator*; topographer, cartographer, oceanographer, hydrographer, geodesist.

Adj. *metrical*, mensural; imperial, metric; metrological, modular; dimensional, three-d.; cubic, volumetric, linear, micrometric; cadastral, topographical; geodetic.

measured, surveyed, etc. vb.; graduated, calibrated; mensurable, measurable, meterable, assessable, computable, calculable.

Vb. *measure*, survey, triangulate; compute, calculate 86 *number*; quantify, size up; beat the bounds, pace out; tape, span; take soundings, heave the lead 313 *plunge*; pace 117 *time*; balance 322 *weigh*.

gauge, meter, take a reading, read off; standardize 16 *make uniform*; calibrate 27 *graduate*; draw to scale, map 551 *represent*.

Section 3:
Materials for reasoning

466. Evidence – N. *evidence*, facts, data, case history; grounds, reasons; hearsay 524 *report*; circumstantial evidence, internal e., proof 478 *demonstration*; corroboration, confirmation 473 *certainty*; document, exhibit, fingerprints 548 *record*; clue 524 *hint*; symptom, sign 547 *indication*; reference, citation, chapter and verse; documentation; authority, scripturality, canonicity.

testimony, witness; statement, evidence in chief 524 *information*; admission, confession 526 *disclosure*; one's case, plea 614 *pretext*; assertion, allegation 532 *affirmation*; Bible evidence, evidence on oath; sworn evidence, deposition, affidavit, attestation 532 *oath*; State's evidence, Queen's e.; word of mouth; compurgation 927 *vindication*; case record, dossier 548 *record*.

credential, testimonial, chit, character, recommendation, references; seal, signature, countersignature, endorsement; voucher, warranty 767 *security*; visa 756 *permit*.

witness, eye w. 441 *spectator*, 415 *listener*; informant 524 *informer*; deponent, testifier, attestor 765 *signatory*; witness to character, compurgator, referee.

Adj. *evidential*, evidentiary; prima facie 445 *appearing*; indicative, symptomatic 547 *indicating*; indirect, secondary, circumstantial; firsthand, direct; supporting, corroborative, confirmatory; presumptive, reliable 473 *certain*; probative, demonstrative, conclusive 478 *demonstrating*; factual, documentary, well-documented 473 *positive*; authentic, well-founded 494 *true*; weighty, authoritative 178 *influential*; testified, attested, witnessed; spoken to, sworn to; in evidence, on the record 548 *recorded*.

Vb. *evidence*, show, evince; show signs of, witness to 522 *manifest*; betoken, bespeak 551 *represent*; lend colour to 471 *be likely*; tell its own tale, speak for itself, speak volumes; carry weight 178 *influence*; suggest, imply, argue 547 *indicate*.

testify, witness; take one's oath 532 *affirm*; bear witness, give evidence, depose, swear to, vouch for; certify 473 *make certain*; attest, endorse, sign; plead 475 *argue*.

corroborate, support, uphold in evidence 927 *vindicate*; bear out, circumstantiate, verify; validate, confirm, ratify, make a case for 473 *make certain*; lead evidence, adduce e.; document; give chapter and verse.

467. Counterevidence – N. *counterevidence*, defence, rebuttal 460 *answer*; refutation 479 *confutation*; denial 533 *negation*; justification 927 *vindication*; counteroath, conflicting evidence; mitigating e. 468 *qualification*; hostile witness 603 *change of allegiance*.

Adj. *countervailing*, rebutting 460 *answering*; cancelling out 182 *counteracting*; converse, negatory 533 *negative*; damaging, telling against; qualificatory 468 *qualifying*.

Vb. *tell against*, weigh against, countervail; contravene, run counter, contradict; rebut 479 *confute*; point the other way 14 *be contrary*; cancel out 182 *counteract*; cut both ways 518 *be equivocal*; fail to confirm, tell another story, alter the case; weaken, undermine; turn the tables, turn the scale; contradict oneself.

468. Qualification – N. *qualification*, specification 80 *speciality*; modification 143 *change*; mitigation 177 *moderation*; stipulation 766 *conditions*; limitation 747 *restriction*; proviso, reservation; exception, salvo, saving clause, escape c.; exemption 919 *nonliability*; demur, objection 704 *opposition*; consideration, concession, allowance; extenuating circumstances; redeeming feature 31 *offset*.

Adj. *qualifying*, qualificative, qualificatory; restricting, limiting; modifying, altering the case; mitigatory 177 *lenitive*; extenuating, palliative, excusing, colouring; contingent, provisional 766 *conditional*; discounting, allowing for; exempted 919 *nonliable*.

Vb. *qualify*, condition, limit, restrict 747 *restrain*; colour, alter 143 *modify*; temper, palliate, mitigate 177 *moderate*; excuse 927 *extenuate*; grant, concede, make allowance for, take into account;

make exceptions 919 *exempt*; take exception, demur 762 *deprecate*.

Adv. *provided*, with the proviso that, subject to, conditionally, so *or* as long as.

469. Possibility – N. *possibility*, potentiality 160 *ability*; best one can do; what may be 124 *futurity*; contingency, eventuality, chance 159 *fair chance*; practicability, feasibility; availability, accessibility; risk of.

Adj. *possible*, potential, hypothetical; arguable, reasonable; viable, feasible, practicable, workable, achievable; attainable, approachable, accessible, obtainable, realizable; superable, surmountable; not impossible, within the bounds of possibility; available, still open, not excluded, not too late; conceivable, credible, imaginable; allowable 756 *permitted*; contingent 124 *future*; liable, tending.

Vb. *be possible*, etc. adj.; may, might, maybe, might be; might have been; admit of, allow 756 *permit*; be open to; stand a chance.

Adv. *possibly*, potentially; conceivably, in posse; perhaps, perchance, peradventure, mayhap; may be, could be; God willing.

470. Impossibility – N. *impossibility*, inconceivability etc. adj.; no chance, not a cat's chance, not a hope 853 *hopelessness*; what can never be; irrevocability; unfeasibility, impracticability; unavailability, inaccessibility, unobtainability, the moon; sour grapes, no go.

Adj. *impossible*, not possible; ruled out 757 *prohibited*; not to be thought of, out of the question, hopeless; unnatural, against nature; contrary to reason 477 *illogical*; incredible, inconceivable, unthinkable, unheard of 486 *unbelieved*; miraculous 864 *wonderful*; unrealistic 513 *imaginary*; irrevocable, beyond recall.

impracticable, unfeasible, unworkable, unrealizable, unviable; too much for, beyond one 700 *difficult*; insuperable, insurmountable; impassable, unbridgeable, impenetrable, unnavigable, not motorable, unscalable; unapproachable, inaccessible, unattainable, unavailable, out of reach.

Vb. *be impossible*, etc. adj., exceed possibility, defy nature, fly in the face of reason, have no chance whatever, eat one's hat if.

attempt the impossible, labour in vain 641 *waste effort*; grasp at shadows; be in two places at once, square the circle, find a needle in a haystack; weave a rope of sand, skin a flint, gather grapes from thorns, get blood from a stone, fetch water in a sieve; make bricks without straw, make a silk purse out of a sow's ear, change a leopard's spots; have one's cake and eat it; write on water, set the Thames on fire.

471. Probability – N. *probability*, likelihood, likeliness 159 *chance*; good chance, sporting c. 469 *possibility*; prospect 507 *expectation*; real risk of 661 *danger*; natural course 179 *tendency*; presumption; credibility, plausibility, good reason; verisimilitude, colour 445 *appearance*.

Adj. *probable*, likely 180 *liable*; on the cards, in a fair way to; natural, to be expected, foreseeable; presumable, presumptive; hopeful, promising.

plausible, specious, colourable; apparent, ostensible 445 *appearing*; logical, reasonable 475 *rational*; convincing, persuasive 485 *credible*; well-founded 494 *true*; ben trovato 24 *apt*.

Vb. *be likely*, etc. adj.; have a chance, be on the cards, run a good chance; bid fair to, be in danger of 179 *tend*; show signs, have the makings of, promise 852 *give hope*.

Adv. *probably*, presumably; in all probability, very likely, ten to one, Lombard Street to a China orange.

472. Improbability – N. *improbability*, unlikelihood, doubt 474 *uncertainty*; chance in a million, off-chance, outside c., long shot; forlorn hope 508 *lack of expectation*; rarity 140 *infrequency*; implausibility 541 *falsehood*.

Adj. *improbable*, unlikely, dubious 474

uncertain; unforeseeable, unforeseen 508 *unexpected*; hard to believe, fishy, unconvincing, implausible 474 *uncertified*; unheard of, incredible, too good to be true 486 *unbelieved*.

Vb. *be unlikely*, etc. adj.; have little hope, offer small chance; be implausible, not wash, strain one's credulity 486 *cause doubt*.

473. Certainty – N. *certainty*, certitude 490 *knowledge*; inevitability, inexorability, irrevocability, necessity 596 *fate*; freedom from error, infallibility; reliability, unimpeachability 494 *truth*; unambiguity; indisputability, proof 478 *demonstration*; authentication, ratification, validation; certification, verification, confirmation; attestation 466 *testimony*; ascertainment 484 *discovery*; dead certainty, cert, dead c., sure thing, safe bet, cinch, open and shut case, foregone conclusion; fact, matter of f., fait accompli 154 *event*; dictum, ipse dixit, axiom.

positiveness, assurance, confidence, conviction, persuasion 485 *belief*; unshakable opinion, idée fixe 481 *bias*; dogmatism 602 *opinionatedness*; infallibility, self-confidence; pontification, laying down the law.

doctrinaire, dogmatist 602 *obstinate person*; bigot, frantic, zealot; oracle, knowall 500 *wiseacre*.

Adj. *certain*, sure, unshakable 3 *substantial*; authoritative, official; factual, historical 494 *true*; ascertained, attested, guaranteed; tested, tried, foolproof 660 *safe*; infallible 540 *veracious*; axiomatic, dogmatic, taken for granted 485 *creedal*; self-evident, evident, unmistakable 443 *obvious*; unequivocal, unambiguous, inevitable, unavoidable 596 *fated*; bound to be, in the bag; sure as fate, sure as death; inviolable, safe as houses 660 *invulnerable*; verifiable 478 *demonstrated*.

positive, confident, assured, self-assured, certain in one's mind, undoubting, convinced, persuaded, certified, sure 485 *believing*; self-opinionated, dogmatizing, oracular 532 *assertive*; dogmatic, doctrinaire 481 *biased*; unshaken, set, fixed

153 *unchangeable*; categorical, absolute, unqualified, unreserved.

undisputed, beyond doubt, without a shadow of doubt, axiomatic, uncontroversial; unquestioned, undoubted, uncontested, indubitable, unquestionable, incontrovertible, incontestable, undeniable, irrefutable.

Vb. *be certain*, etc. adj.; satisfy oneself, feel sure, be clear in one's mind, make no doubt 485 *believe*; hold to one's opinions, have made up one's mind; rely on, bank on, trust in, swear by; gamble on, put one's shirt on, lay one's bottom dollar.

dogmatize, pontificate, lay down the law 532 *affirm*; play the oracle, know all the answers.

make certain, certify, authenticate 488 *endorse*; guarantee, warrant, assure; settle 480 *judge*; make sure, check, double-check 466 *corroborate*; insure against 660 *safeguard*; make inevitable 596 *necessitate*.

Adv. *certainly*, definitely, certes, for sure, doubtless, as sure as eggs is eggs; of course; no two ways about it, no ifs or buts; without fail.

474. Uncertainty – N. *uncertainty*, unverifiability, incertitude, doubtfulness, dubiousness; ambiguity 518 *equivocalness*; indefiniteness, vagueness, haziness, fog 423 *opacity*; yes and no, indeterminacy, indetermination, borderline case; query, question mark 459 *question*; open question, anybody's guess; nothing to go on, guesswork, guestimate 512 *conjecture*; contingency, doubtful c. 159 *chance*; gamble, toss-up 618 *gambling*; leap in the dark, bow at a venture, pig in a poke, blind date.

dubiety, dubitation 486 *doubt*; open mind, suspended judgment, open verdict; doubt, indecision, hesitancy, shilly-shallying, vacillation 317 *fluctuation*; seesaw, floating vote 601 *irresolution*; embarrassment, perplexity, bewilderment, bafflement, nonplus, quandary; dilemma, cleft stick, Morton's fork 530 *enigma*.

unreliability, fallibility 495 *error*; insecurity, precariousness, touch and go 661 *danger*; untrustworthiness, treacherousness; unsteadiness 152 *changeableness*; unpredictability 508 *lack of expectation*; fickleness, capriciousness 604 *caprice*; slipperiness 930 *improbity*; lack of security, bare word, scrap of paper.

Adj. *uncertain*, unsure, doubtful, dubious; unverifiable; insecure, chancy, risky 661 *unsafe*; sporadic 140 *infrequent*; provisional 114 *transient*; fluid 152 *unstable*; contingent 766 *conditional*; unpredictable, unforeseeable 508 *unexpected*; indeterminate, undefined; indecisive, undecided; in question, open to question 459 *moot*; arguable, debatable, disputable, controvertible; controversial; suspicious 472 *improbable*; problematic, hypothetical, speculative 512 *suppositional*; undefinable, borderline; ambiguous 518 *equivocal*; enigmatic, obscure 517 *puzzling*; vague, hazy 517 *unintelligible*; perplexing, bewildering, confusing.

unreliable, undependable, untrustworthy; treacherous 930 *dishonest*; unsteady, unstable 152 *changeful*; unpredictable, fickle 604 *capricious*; fallible, open to error 495 *erroneous*; precarious, ticklish, touch and go.

doubting, in doubt, doubtful, dubious; agnostic, sceptical 486 *unbelieving*; in two minds; open-minded; distrustful, mistrustful 858 *cautious*; uncertain, unconfident, diffident; hesitant, undecided, wavering 601 *irresolute*; baffled, perplexed 517 *puzzled*; nonplussed, stumped, at one's wits' end, on the horns of a dilemma; lost, disorientated, guessing, in the dark, abroad, all at sea, adrift, astray, at a loss 491 *ignorant*.

uncertified, unverified, unchecked; unconfirmed, unauthenticated, unratified, unsigned, unattested; unwarranted, unguaranteed; unauthoritative, unofficial, apocryphal, uncanonical, unauthentic; unproved, undemonstrated; unascertained; untried, untested, in the experimental stage.

Vb. *be uncertain*, hinge on 157 *depend*; be touch and go, hang by a thread, tremble in the balance; be ambiguous 518 *be equivocal*; have one's doubts 486 *doubt*; wait and see; have a suspicion, suspect, wonder whether; dither, be in two minds, sit on the fence, waver, teeter; falter 601 *be irresolute*; flounder, grope, fumble, cast about 461 *be tentative*; get lost, lose the scent; not know which way to turn, be at one's wits' end, be at a loss, not know what to make of, have no answer, be in a quandary; wouldn't swear, could be wrong.

puzzle, perplex, confuse, befuddle, maze, daze, bewilder, baffle, nonplus, flummox, stump 727 *defeat*; mystify, keep one guessing; bamboozle 542 *befool*; fox, throw off the scent 495 *mislead*; make one think 486 *cause doubt*.

Section 4:
Reasoning processes

475. Reasoning – N. *reasoning*, ratiocination, reason, discursive r.; sweet reason, reasonableness, rationality; dialectics, logic; logical sequence, inference, generalization; a priori reasoning, deductive r., deduction; induction, inductive reasoning, a posteriori r., empirical r.; rationalism 449 *philosophy*; plain reason, simple arithmetic.

argumentation, dialectic, Socratic elenchus, dialogue, logical disputation; formal logic, symbolic l.; sorites, syllogism; premise, postulate, hypothesis; quodlibet, proposition, thesis, theorem, problem; predication, lemma, predicate; inference, corollary; conclusion, QED 478 *demonstration*; reductio ad absurdum, paradox.

argument, discussion, symposium, dialogue; give and take, cut and thrust; disputation, controversy, debate 489 *dissent*; appeal to reason, plea, pleading, case; arguments, pros and cons; reasons, submission; apologetics; polemic; war of words, propaganda 534 *teaching*; controversialism, argumentativeness; hairsplitting, logic-chopping; logomachy 477 *sophistry*; contentiousness, wrangling, jangling 709 *dissension*; legal argument

959 *litigation*; argumentum ad hominem, play on the feelings; argument by analogy, parity of reasoning; tu quoque argument, same to you.

reasoner, logician, dialectician, syllogizer; rationalist, euhemerist, demythologizer; philosopher; sophist, casuist; polemist, polemicist, apologist, controversialist, eristic, controverter; arguer, debater, disputant; proponent, pleader 958 *lawyer*; sea lawyer, barrack-room l., logomachist, quibbler; pedant 492 *intellectual*; mathematician.

Adj. *rational*, clear-headed, reasoning, reasonable; rationalistic, euhemeristic; ratiocinative, logical; cogent, to the point, well-argued 9 *relevant*; dianoetic, discursory, analytic, synthetic; consistent, systematic, methodological; dialectical, discursive, syllogistic, deductive, inductive, epagogic, maieutic, inferential, a posteriori, a priori, universal; axiomatic 473 *certain*; tenable 469 *possible*.

arguing, polemical, apologetic; disputatious, eristic, argumentative; quibbling 477 *sophistical*; disputable, debatable 474 *uncertain*.

Vb. *be reasonable* 471 *be likely*; stand to reason, follow, hang together, hold water; appeal to reason; listen to reason; admit, concede 488 *assent*; have a case.

reason, philosophize 449 *think*; syllogize, ratiocinate; rationalize, explain away; apply reason, put two and two together; infer, educe, deduce, induct; work out, figure o.; explain 520 *interpret*.

argue, argufy, bandy arguments, discuss 584 *confer*; debate, dispute, controvert; quibble, split hairs, chop logic; argue the point; put one's case, plead; propagandize; take up the case, defend; attack, polemicize; demur, cavil 489 *dissent*; analyse, pull to pieces 459 *inquire*; out-argue, bludgeon 479 *confute*; prove one's case 478 *demonstrate*; wrangle 709 *bicker*; answer back 460 *answer*; have the last word.

476. Intuition: absence of reason – N. *intuition*, instinct; association, Pavlovian response, automatic reaction, gut r. 450 *ab-*

sence of thought; light of nature, sixth sense, psi; telepathy, insight; second sight, clairvoyance 984 *psychics*; id, subconscious 447 *spirit*; intuitiveness, direct apprehension, a priori knowledge; divination, dowsing; inspiration, presentiment, impulse 818 *feeling*; rule of thumb; hunch, impression, sense, guesswork; value judgement 481 *bias*; self-deception, wishful thinking; irrationality, illogicality, illogic; unreason 503 *insanity*.

Adj. *intuitive*, instinctive, impulsive; devoid of logic 477 *illogical*; impressionistic, subjective; involuntary 609 *spontaneous*; subconscious 447 *psychic*; noumenal, inspirational, inspired, clairvoyant, direct, unmediated.

Vb. *intuit*, know by instinct, sense, feel in one's bones, have a funny feeling *or* a hunch; get the impression; react automatically; play it by ear, rely on intuition; guess.

477. Sophistry: false reasoning – N. *sophistry*, illogicalness, illogic; rationalization, doublethink, self-deception; equivocation, mystification 525 *concealment*; word fencing, casuistry; subtlety, oversubtlety; special pleading, hair-splitting, logic-chopping; logomachy, quibbling, quibble 515 *empty talk*; chicanery, evasion.

sophism, specious argument, fallacious a.; illogicality, fallacy, paralogism; bad logic, loose thinking; solecism, flaw; begging the question, circular reasoning; non sequitur, post hoc ergo propter hoc; contradiction in terms, antilogy.

sophist, casuist, quibbler, equivocator; caviller; devil's advocate.

Adj. *sophistical*, specious, plausible, ad captándum; evasive, insincere; deceptive, illusory; over-refined, oversubtle, fine-spun; pettifogging, captious, quibbling; sophisticated, tortuous; casuistic.

illogical, contrary to reason, irrational, unreasonable; unreasoned, arbitrary; paralogistic, fallacious, fallible; contradictory, self-c., inconsistent; untenable, unsound; groundless, inconsequent, inconsequential; unscientific, false 495 *erroneous*.

poorly reasoned, unrigorous, inconclusive; unproved; loose, woolly, muddled, confused.

Vb. *reason badly*, paralogize, argue in a circle, beg the question, not see the wood for the trees, strain at a gnat and swallow a camel; not have a leg to stand on.

sophisticate, mislead 535 *misteach*; mystify 542 *befool*; quibble, split hairs 475 *argue*; shuffle, equivocate 518 *be equivocal*; evade 667 *elude*; varnish, colour, gloss over 541 *cant*; pervert, misapply 675 *misuse*; twist the argument, torture logic; prove that white is black.

478. Demonstration – N. *demonstration*, documentation 466 *evidence*; proven fact 494 *truth*; proof, rigorous p. conclusive p.; irrefragability 473 *certainty*; verification 461 *experiment*; deduction, inference, argument 475 *reasoning*; exposition 522 *manifestation*; burden of proof, onus.

Adj. *demonstrating*, demonstrative, probative 466 *evidential*; deducible, inferential, consequential, following 9 *relevant*; apodictic 532 *affirmative*; convincing; conclusive, categorical, decisive, crucial; heuristic 534 *education*.

demonstrated, evident; taken as proved, established; unrefuted, unanswered; open and shut, unanswerable, undeniable, irrefutable, irrefragable, incontrovertible 473 *certain*; demonstrable.

Vb. *demonstrate*, prove; show, evince 522 *manifest*; justify, bear out 466 *corroborate*; document, substantiate, establish, verify 466 *evidence*; infer, deduce 475 *reason*; make out a case, prove one's point 485 *convince*.

479. Confutation – N. *confutation*, refutation, disproof, invalidation 533 *negation*; elenchus, exposure; rebuttal 460 *rejoinder*; clincher, finisher, knockdown argument; reductio ad absurdum 851 *ridicule*; exploded argument, proved fallacy 477 *sophism*.

Adj. *confuted*, disproved etc. vb.; silenced, without a leg to stand on; condemned out of one's own mouth; disprovable, refutable, confutable.

Vb. *confute*, refute, disprove, invalidate; rebut, retort, have an answer, explain away; deny 533 *negate*; give the lie to, force to withdraw; cut the ground from under; confound, reduce to silence, gravel, nonplus; condemn out of his *or* her own mouth; show up, expose; blow sky-high, shoot full of holes, puncture, explode, demolish one's arguments, knock the bottom out of 165 *demolish*; have in one's hand, have on the hip; squash, crush 727 *defeat*; get the better of, score off; stand, stand up to argument; dismiss, override, sweep aside.

be confuted, etc. adj.; fall to the ground, have not a leg to stand on; have nothing left to say, have no answer.

Section 5:
Results of reasoning

480. Judgement: conclusion – N. *judgement*, judging 463 *discrimination*; arbitrament 733 *authority*; arbitration, umpirage; verdict, finding; pronouncement, sentence 963 *punishment*; decision, adjudication, award; order, ruling 737 *decree*; res judicata; conclusion, result, upshot; value judgement 476 *intuition*; deduction, inference, corollary 475 *reasoning*; judgement of Solomon 498 *wisdom*, 913 *justice*; vox populi 605 *vote*.

estimate, estimation, view 485 *opinion*; axiology 449 *philosophy*; assessment, valuation, evaluation, consideration; comparing 462 *comparison*; appreciation, appraisal, appraisement 520 *interpretation*; criticism, critique, crit, review, notice, comment 591 *article*; survey 524 *report*; second opinion 691 *advice*.

estimator, judge, adjudicator; arbitrator, umpire, referee; surveyor, valuer, appraiser; inspector, examiner, ombudsman 459 *inquirer*; counsellor 691 *adviser*; critic, reviewer 591 *dissertator*; commentator, observer 520 *interpreter*; juror, assessor 957 *jury*; voter 605 *electorate*.

Adj. *judicial*, judicious, judgematic 463 *discriminating*; shrewd 498 *wise*; unbiased, dispassionate 913 *just*; juridical, juristic, arbitral; judicatory, decretal; determinative, conclusive; moralistic, sententious; censorious 924 *disapproving*; critical, appreciative.

Vb. *judge*, sit in judgement, hold the scales; arbitrate, referee; hear, try; rule, pronounce; find for *or* against; decree, award, adjudge, adjudicate; decide, settle, conclude; pass judgement, deliver j.; sentence 961 *condemn*; return a verdict 605 *vote*; deduce 475 *reason*; sum up, recapitulate; moralize 534 *teach*.

estimate, form an e., measure, gauge; value, evaluate, appraise; rate, rank, size up; conjecture 512 *suppose*; take stock, consider, ponder, weigh the pros and cons 449 *meditate*; examine 459 *inquire*; express an opinion, pass an o., report on; commentate, criticize, review 591 *dissertate*; pass under review 438 *scan*.

481. Misjudgement. Prejudice – N. *misjudgement*,
miscalculation, misreckoning, misconception, wrong impression 495 *error*; loose thinking 495 *inexactness*; poor judgement 464 *indiscrimination*; fallibility 499 *unintelligence*; misconstruction 521 *misinterpretation*; miscarriage of justice 914 *injustice*; overvaluation 482 *overestimation*; undervaluation 483 *underestimation*; wishful thinking 542 *deception*.

prejudgement, prejudication, foregone conclusion 608 *predetermination*; preconception, prenotion; parti pris, mind made up; preconceived idea; idée fixe, hangup 503 *mania*.

prejudice, prepossession, predilection; partiality, favouritism 914 *injustice*; bias, jaundiced eye; blind spot, mote in the eye 439 *blindness*; onesidedness, partisanship, clannishness, cliquishness, esprit de corps; sectionalism 978 *sectarianism*; chauvinism, xenophobia, my country right or wrong; snobbishness, class prejudice; ageism; sexism; racialism, racism; anti-Semitism; colour prejudice; discrimination 57 *exclusion*; intolerance, persecution, 888 *hatred*.

narrow mind, narrow-mindedness, small-m.; insularity, parochialism, provincialism; closed mind, one-track m.; onesidedness, overspecialization; legalism, pedantry, donnishness, hypercriticism; illiberality, intolerance, dogmatism; bigotry, fanaticism 602 *opinionatedness*; legalist, pedant 862 *perfectionist*; faddist 504 *crank*; zealot, bigot, fanatic 473 *doctrinaire*; racialist, racist, white supremacist, chauvinist.

bias, unbalance 29 *inequality*; warp, bent, slant 179 *tendency*; angle, point of view 485 *opinion*; parti pris (see *prejudgement*); infatuation, obsession 503 *eccentricity*; crankiness, fad, bee in one's bonnet 604 *whim*.

Adj. *misjudging*, misinterpreting etc. vb.; in error 495 *mistaken*; fallible, gullible 499 *foolish*; wrong, wrong-headed; misguided; short-sighted 440 *dim-sighted*; superstitious 487 *credulous*; subjective, unrealistic, impractical; faddy, whimsical 503 *crazy*; besotted, infatuated 887 *enamoured*; haunted, obsessed, hung up, eaten up with.

narrow-minded, petty-m., small-m., confined, cramped, hidebound; parochial, provincial, insular; pedantic, donnish, legalistic, literal, literal-minded, unimaginative, matter-of-fact; hypercritical 862 *fastidious*; stiff, unbending 602 *obstinate*; dictatorial, dogmatic 473 *positive*; opinionated, opinionative; self-opinionated.

biased, warped, twisted; jaundiced, embittered; prejudiced, snobbish 708 *sectional*; partisan, one-sided 978 *sectarian*; nationalistic, chauvinistic, jingoistic, xenophobic; racist, racialist; sexist; class-prejudiced, colour-p.; predisposed, prejudging; unreasoning 477 *illogical*; discriminatory 914 *unjust*; illiberal, intolerant 735 *oppressive*; bigoted, fanatic 602 *obstinate*.

Vb. *misjudge*, miscalculate 495 *blunder*; not take into account, reckon without 477 *reason badly*; undervalue 483 *underestimate*; overestimate 482 *overrate*; come to the wrong conclusion 521 *misinterpret*; overreach oneself, overplay one's hand; get the wrong sow by the ear 695 *act foolishly*; not see the wood for the trees;

not see beyond one's nose 499 *be foolish.*

prejudge, forejudge, prejudicate 608 *predetermine*; prejudice the issue, precondemn; preconceive, presuppose, presume, premise; rush to conclusions, jump to c., run away with a notion 857 *be rash.*

be biased, etc. adj.; see one side only, show favouritism; lean, favour, take sides, have a down on, have it in for, hold it against one, discriminate against 735 *oppress*; be obsessed with, lose one's sense of proportion; blind oneself to 439 *be blind.*

482. Overestimation – N. *overestimation*, overestimate, overenthusiasm, overvaluation 481 *misjudgement*; overstatement 546 *exaggeration*; boasting 877 *boast*; hype, buildup 528 *publicity*; gush 515 *empty talk*; storm in a teacup, much ado about nothing; megalomania, vanity 871 *pride*; overconfidence 857 *rashness*; overoptimism; defeatism 853 *hopelessness*; optimist 852 *hope*; pessimist, prophet of doom, doom merchant, defeatist; puffer, barker 528 *publicizer.*

Adj. *optimistic*, upbeat, sanguine, oversanguine, overconfident; high-pitched, overpitched; enthusiastic, overenthusiastic, raving.

overrated, overestimated, overvalued, overpraised; puffed-up, cracked-up, hyped-up, overdone 546 *exaggerated.*

Vb. *overrate*, overestimate, count all one's geese swans; overvalue, overprice, set too high a value on 811 *overcharge*; rave, idealize, overprize, think too much of; overpraise 546 *exaggerate*; overdo, play up, overpitch, inflate 197 *enlarge*; cry up, puff, panegyrize 923 *praise*; attach too much importance to, make mountains out of molehills.

483. Underestimation – N. *underestimation*, underestimate, undervaluation, minimization; conservative estimate 177 *moderation*; depreciation 926 *detraction*; understatement, litotes; euphemism 950 *prudery*; self-depreciation, over-modesty 872 *humility*; false modesty, mock m. 850 *affectation*; pessimism 853 *hopelessness*;

pessimist, minimizer, cynic 926 *detractor.*

Adj. *depreciating*, depreciative, depreciatory, derogatory, belittling, pooh-poohing 926 *detracting*; underestimating, conservative 177 *moderate*; modest 872 *humble*; pessimistic, despairing 853 *hopeless*; euphemistic 541 *hypocritical.*

Vb. *underestimate*, underrate, undervalue; depreciate, underpraise, run down 926 *detract*; disparage 922 *hold cheap*; misprize, not do justice to 481 *misjudge*; understate, spare one's blushes; euphemize; play down, soft-pedal, slur over; shrug off 458 *disregard*; make little of, minimize; deflate, make light of; belittle, make no account of 922 *despise.*

484. Discovery – N. *discovery*, finding, breakthrough; rediscovery; invention; detective instinct, nose, flair 619 *pursuit*; detection, spotting 438 *inspection*; dowsing, water divining; ascertainment 473 *certainty*; exposure, revelation 522 *manifestation*; illumination, realization, disenchantment; accidental discovery, serendipity; inspiration; strike, find, trouvaille, trover, treasure trove; eye-opener 508 *lack of expectation*; solution, explanation; key 263 *opener.*

detector, probe; space p., spy satellite 276 *spaceship*; asdic, sonar; early warning system; radar, radar trap; finder 442 *telescope*; lie detector; sensor; Geiger counter; metal detector; divining rod, dowsing r.; dowser, water diviner; spotter, scout, talent s.; discoverer, inventor; explorer 268 *traveller*; archaeologist 459 *inquirer*; prospector 461 *experimenter.*

Adj. *discovering*, exploratory 461 *experimental*; on the scent, on the track, on the trail, getting warm; near discovery, ripe for detection.

Vb. *discover*, rediscover, invent; explore, find a way 461 *experiment*; find out, have it; strike, hit upon; happen on, stumble on; realize, tumble to, see the light, see in its true colours 516 *understand*; find, locate 187 *place*; fish up, dig up, unearth, bring to light 522 *manifest*; elicit, worm out; ferret o., nose o., smell o. 459 *search*; get wind of.

detect, get at the facts; find a clue, be near the truth, be getting warm; put one's finger on, hit the nail on the head, saddle the right horse; spot 438 *see*; sense, trace, pick up; smell a rat; nose, scent, wind; track down 619 *hunt*.

Int. eureka! got it!

485. Belief – **N.** *belief*, credence, credit; assurance, conviction, persuasion; confidence, reliance, trust, faith; religious belief 973 *religious faith*; uncritical belief 487 *credulity*; obsession, blind belief 481 *prejudice*; self-persuasion, self-conviction; expectation 852 *hope*; common belief, public opinion; credibility 471 *probability*.

creed, formulated belief, credo; dogma, Ark of the Covenant 976 *orthodoxy*; precepts, principles, tenets, articles; catechism; declaration of faith, belief, profession, confession; doctrine, system, ideology, ism 449 *philosophy*, 973 *theology*.

opinion, conviction, persuasion; sentiment, mind; point of view, viewpoint, stand, position, attitude 438 *view*; impression 818 *feeling*; thought 451 *idea*; thinking, way of thinking, body of opinions, outlook on life, Weltanschauung 449 *philosophy*; principle, premise; theory, hypothesis 512 *supposition*; surmise 512 *conjecture*; conclusion 480 *judgement*.

Adj. *believing*, maintaining, etc. vb.; confident 473 *certain*; sure 473 *positive*; convinced, persuaded, satisfied, converted, sold on, wedded to; trustful, trusting, unquestioning 487 *credulous*; conforming 976 *orthodox*; opinionated 481 *biased*.

credible, plausible, believable, tenable, reasonable 469 *possible*; likely 471 *probable*; reliable, trustworthy; persuasive, convincing 178 *influential*; trusted, believed, accepted; putative 512 *suppositional*.

creedal, doctrinal, dogmatic, confessional; canonical, orthodox, authoritative, accredited, ex cathedra; accepted on trust; sacrosanct, unquestioned, implicit; undeniable, unshakable 473 *undisputed*.

Vb. *believe*, be a believer; credit, put faith in; hold, maintain, take for gospel, firmly believe; profess, confess; receive, accept 488 *assent*; take on trust, buy, swallow; swallow whole 487 *be credulous*; take for granted, have no doubt, know for certain, be convinced 473 *be certain*; rest assured, be easy in one's mind about, be secure in the belief, rest in the b.; have confidence in, trust, rely on, depend on, take at his *or* her word; give one credit for; pin one's hopes on; have faith in, believe in, swear by, reckon on, count on, calculate on, bank on; take as proven, grant, allow.

opine, think, conceive, fancy; surmise 512 *suppose*; suspect, be under the impression 818 *feel*; deem, assume, presume, take it that, hold; embrace an opinion, get hold of an idea, get it into one's head; view as, take as, consider as, account; express an opinion 532 *affirm*.

convince, make believe, assure, persuade, satisfy; bring home to 478 *demonstrate*; convert, win over, bring round; evangelize, propagandize 534 *teach*; sell an idea to, put over *or* across 178 *influence*; compel belief.

be believed, be widely b.; go down well, be swallowed; find ready listeners, find willing ears; carry conviction; find credence, pass current, pass for truth.

486. Unbelief. Doubt – **N.** *unbelief*, non-belief, disbelief, incredulity 489 *dissent*; want of faith, atheism 974 *irreligion*; misbelief, heresy; loss of faith, reversal of opinion 603 *recantation*; implausibility 472 *improbability*.

doubt 474 *dubiety*; half-belief; wavering, uncertainty; misgiving, distrust, mistrust; suspiciousness; scepticism, agnosticism, pyrrhonism; scruple, reservation 468 *qualification*.

unbeliever, no believer, disbeliever; heathen, infidel, heretic; atheist 974 *irreligionist*; sceptic, pyrrhonist, agnostic; doubter, doubting Thomas; dissenter 489 *dissentient*; recanter 603 *turncoat*; denier 533 *negation*; cynic, nobody's fool; scoffer 926 *detractor*.

Adj. *unbelieving*, disbelieving, incredulous, sceptical, creedless; heathen, infidel; lapsed 603 *trimming*; doubtful, undecided, wavering 474 *doubting*; suspicious, oversuspicious; slow to believe, distrustful, mistrustful, jealous; impervious, hard to convince; cynical, hard-boiled.

unbelieved, disbelieved, discredited, exploded; distrusted, mistrusted etc. vb.; incredible, unbelievable 470 *impossible*; inconceivable, unimaginable, staggering 864 *wonderful*; hard to believe, hardly credible; untenable, undeserving of belief; open to suspicion, open to doubt, unreliable, suspect, suspicious, questionable, disputable, far-fetched 474 *uncertified*.

Vb. *disbelieve*, be incredulous, find hard to believe; discredit, refuse to credit, greet with scepticism, disagree 489 *dissent*; not fall for, not buy; scoff at 851 *ridicule*; deny outright 533 *negate*; retract, lapse, relapse 603 *recant*.

doubt, half-believe 474 *be uncertain*; demur, object, cavil, question, stick at, have reservations 468 *qualify*; pause, hesitate, waver 601 *be irresolute*; distrust, mistrust, suspect 854 *be nervous*; be sceptical, take leave to doubt; not trust, set no store by; have one's doubts, harbour d., cherish scruples; entertain suspicions, smell a rat; hold back 598 *be unwilling*.

cause doubt, cast d., raise questions; call in question, discredit 926 *defame*; shake, undermine; stagger 508 *surprise*; pass belief 472 *be unlikely*; argue against 613 *dissuade*; impugn 479 *confute*.

487. Credulity – N. *credulity*, credulousness; gullibility 612 *persuadability*; uncritical acceptance 485 *belief*; blind faith; infatuation, dotage; self-delusion, wishful thinking 481 *misjudgement*; superstition, superstitiousness; simpleton, sucker, mug 544 *dupe*.

Adj. *credulous*, believing, persuasible, persuadable, amenable; easily taken in 544 *gullible*; uncynical, unworldly; naive, simple, unsophisticated; green 499 *foolish*; doting, infatuated; superstitious 481 *misjudging*; confiding, trustful, unsuspecting.

Vb. *be credulous*, kid oneself; suspend one's judgement 477 *reason badly*; believe every word, fall for, buy it, take on trust 485 *believe*; take the bait, rise to the b., accept, swallow, swallow anything; not hear a word against 481 *be biased*.

488. Assent – N. *assent*, yes, yea, amen; agreement, concurrence 758 *consent*; acceptance, agreement in principle 597 *willingness*; acquiescence 721 *submission*; acknowledgement, recognition; admission, avowal 526 *disclosure*; sanction, nod, OK, imprimatur, thumbs up, go-ahead, green light 756 *permission*; approval 923 *approbation*; corroboration, confirmation, ratification; endorsement, signature; visa, pass 756 *permit*; stamp, rubber s. 706 *cooperation*; assentation 925 *flattery*.

consensus, consentience, same mind 24 *agreement*; concordance, harmony, unison 710 *concord*; unanimity, solid vote, general consent, common c., universal agreement; consentaneity, popular belief, public opinion, vox populi; chorus, single voice; likemindedness 18 *similarity*; bipartisanship; understanding, bargain 765 *compact*.

assenter, follower 83 *conformist*; cooperator 707 *collaborator*; yes-man 925 *flatterer*; the ayes; supporter 703 *aider*; seconder, assentor 707 *patron*; ratifier, authenticator; subscriber, endorser 765 *signatory*; party, consenting p., covenanter.

Adj. *assenting*, assentient 758 *consenting*; consentient, concurring, party to 24 *agreeing*; aiding and abetting, collaborating 706 *cooperative*; likeminded, consentaneous 710 *concordant*; unanimous, with one voice, in chorus; acquiescent 597 *willing*; allowing, granting 756 *permitting*; sanctioning, ratificatory; not opposed.

assented, voted, carried, agreed on all hands; unopposed, unanimous; unquestioned, uncontested 473 *undisputed*; admitted, granted, conceded 756 *permitted*; ratified, confirmed, signed, sealed; uncontroversial, nonparty, bipartisan.

Vb. *assent*, concur, agree with 24

accord; agree on all points, accept in toto, go all the way with, have no reservations 473 *be certain*; accept, agree in principle, like the idea, buy it; not deny, concede, admit, own, acknowledge, grant, allow 475 *be reasonable*; plead guilty 526 *confess*; nod assent, say yes, agree to, go along with 758 *consent*; sanction 756 *permit*; see eye to eye; chime in with, echo, ditto, say amen, chorus; rubber-stamp 925 *flatter*; collaborate 706 *cooperate*; agree upon, come to an understanding 765 *contract*.

acquiesce, not oppose, accept 739 *obey*; tolerate, not mind, put up with, suffer, endure, wear it; toe the line 721 *submit*; yield, defer to, withdraw one's objections; let the ayes have it, allow 756 *permit*; look on 441 *watch*; go with the stream 83 *conform*.

endorse, second, support, vote for 703 *patronize*; subscribe to, attest 547 *sign*; seal, stamp, rubber-stamp, confirm, ratify, sanction 758 *consent*; authenticate 473 *make certain*; countersign.

Adv. *unanimously*, with one accord, with one voice, one and all, in chorus, to a man, nem. con.; by show of hands, by acclamation; on the nod.

Int. amen! hear, hear! well said! as you say! you said it! you can say that again! how right you are! I couldn't agree more! yes indeed! yes.

489. Dissent – N. *dissent*, dissidence, difference 704 *opposition*; dissentience, difference of opinion, disagreement, discordance, controversy 709 *dissension*; faction 708 *party*; disaffection 829 *discontent*; dissatisfaction, disapproval 924 *disapprobation*; repudiation 607 *rejection*; protestantism, nonconformism 978 *schism*; counterculture, alternative life style 84 *nonconformity*; walkout, withdrawal, secession 621 *relinquishment*; reluctance 598 *unwillingness*; noncompliance 738 *disobedience*; denial, lack of consent 760 *refusal*; contradiction 533 *negation*; objection, demurrer, reservation 468 *qualification*; protest, expostulation 762 *deprecation*; challenge 711

defiance; passive resistance, noncooperation.

dissentient, objector, caviller, critic 926 *detractor*; interrupter, heckler 702 *hinderer*; dissident, dissenter, protester, protestant; separatist, seceder 978 *schismatic*; rebel 738 *revolter*; dropout 84 *nonconformist*; grouser 829 *malcontent*; odd man out, minority; splinter group, faction 708 *party*; the noes 704 *opposition*; noncooperator, conscientious objector 705 *opponent*; challenger, revolutionary 149 *revolutionist*.

Adj. *dissenting*, dissentient, differing, dissident 709 *quarrelling*; sceptical, unconvinced, unconverted 486 *unbelieving*; separatist, schismatic 978 *sectarian*; nonconformist 84 *unconformable*; malcontent, dissatisfied 829 *discontented*; unconsenting 760 *refusing*; protesting 762 *deprecatory*; noncompliant 769 *nonobservant*; reluctant 598 *unwilling*; challenging 711 *defiant*; resistant 704 *opposing*.

Vb. *dissent*, differ, agree to d. 25 *disagree*; beg to differ, make bold to d., take one up on 479 *confute*; demur, object, raise objections, have reservations, cavil, boggle, scruple 468 *qualify*; protest 762 *deprecate*; resist 704 *oppose*; challenge 711 *defy*; show reluctance 598 *be unwilling*; withhold assent, say no, shake one's head, not wear it 760 *refuse*; contradict 533 *negate*; repudiate, hold no brief for; not hold with 924 *disapprove*; secede, withdraw 621 *relinquish*; argue 709 *quarrel*.

Int. God forbid! not on your life! not on your nelly! over my dead body! never again! not likely!

490. Knowledge – N. *knowledge*, ken; knowing, cognition, cognizance, recognition, realization; intellection, apprehension, comprehension, perception, understanding, grasp, mastery 447 *intellect*; conscience, consciousness, awareness; consciousness raising; insight 476 *intuition*; precognition 510 *foresight*; illumination 975 *revelation*; lights, enlightenment 498 *wisdom*; acquired knowledge, learning, lore (**see** *erudition*); folk wisdom, folklore; occult lore 983 *sorcery*;

education, background; experience, acquaintance; acquaintanceship, familiarity, intimacy; private knowledge, privity 524 *information*; no secret, common knowledge, open secret 528 *publicity*; complete knowledge, omniscience; partial knowledge, intimation, sidelight, glimpse, glimmering, inkling; suspicion, scent; sensory knowledge, impression 818 *feeling*; self-knowledge, introspection; detection 484 *discovery*; specialism, savoir faire, savvy, know-how, expertise 694 *skill*; half-knowledge, semi-ignorance, smattering 491 *sciolism*; knowableness 516 *intelligibility*; science of knowledge, epistemology.

erudition, lore, wisdom, scholarship, letters 536 *learning*; general knowledge; universal k., polymathy; smattering, dilettantism 491 *sciolism*; reading, book-learning, bookishness; pedantry, donnishness; information, mine of i., encyclopedia 589 *library*; faculty 539 *academy*; scholar 492 *intellectual*.

culture, letters 557 *literature*; the humanities, the arts; education, instruction 534 *teaching*; literacy, numeracy; liberal education, scientific e.; self-education, self-instruction; civilization, cultivation; sophistication, acquirements, accomplishments, proficiency, mastery.

science, exact s., natural s., metascience; natural philosophy, experimental p.; scientific knowledge, body of k.; applied science, technology; ologies and isms.

Adj. *knowing*, all-k., encyclopedic, omniscient 498 *wise*; cognizant, cognitive 447 *mental*; conscious, aware, mindful of 455 *attentive*; alive to, sensible of 819 *impressible*; experienced, no stranger to, at home with 610 *habituated*; intimate, privy to, wise to, on to, in the know, in on 524 *informed*; fly, canny, shrewd 498 *intelligent*; conversant, practised, versed in, proficient 694 *expert*.

instructed, briefed, primed 524 *informed*; taught, trained, bred to; lettered, literate; numerate; schooled, educated, well-e.; learned, book-l., bookish, literary; erudite, scholarly 536 *studious*; well-read, widely-r., well-informed, knowledgeable; donnish, scholastic, pedantic; highbrow, intellectual, blue-stocking; cultured, cultivated, sophisticated; well-qualified, professional, specialized 694 *expert*.

known, cognized, perceived; verified 473 *certain*; discovered, explored; celebrated 866 *renowned*; notorious 528 *well-known*; familiar, intimate, dear; household, commonplace 610 *usual*; memorized 505 *remembered*; knowable, cognizable, discoverable.

Vb. *know*, savvy, ken, wot, ween; apprehend, conceive, catch, grasp, twig, click, have, take in, get 516 *understand*; comprehend, master; come to know, realize; get to know, acquaint oneself, familiarize o.; recognize, appreciate; be conscious of, be aware 447 *cognize*; discern 463 *discriminate*; perceive 438 *see*; study, mull, con 438 *scan*; know well, know full w.; see through, read one like a book, have one's measure, have one taped, know inside out; know down to the ground, know like the back of one's hand; know for a fact 473 *be certain*; be in the know, be informed; know by heart 505 *memorize*; have it pat, have at one's finger tips, be master of 694 *be expert*; experience 536 *learn*; know all the answers, be omniscient 498 *be wise*.

491. Ignorance – N. *ignorance*, unknowing, nescience; lack of news, no word of; unawareness, unconsciousness 375 *insensibility*; incognizance, nonrecognition, nonrealization; incomprehension, incapacity 499 *unintelligence*; inappreciation, philistinism 439 *blindness*; false knowledge, superstition 495 *error*; lack of knowledge, lack of education, no schooling; blank mind, tabula rasa; unacquaintance, unfamiliarity, inexperience, greenness, rawness; inexpertness, amateurishness 695 *unskilfulness*; innocence 699 *artlessness*; nothing to go on, lack of information, anybody's guess 474 *uncertainty*; unwisdom 499 *folly*; darkness, benightedness, unenlightenment; savagery, heathenism, paganism 982 *idolatry*;

ignorant person 493 *ignoramus*; autodidact, amateur 697 *bungler*; obscurantist; philistine.

unknown thing, unknown quantity; sealed book, Greek; Dark Continent; terra incognita; frontiers of knowledge; dark horse 530 *secret*; unidentified flying object, UFO; anonymity 562 *no name*.

sciolism, smattering, glimmering, glimpse, half-glimpse 524 *hint*; vagueness, half-knowledge 495 *inexactness*; superficiality, dilettantism, dabbling; quackery, charlatanism, bluff 850 *affectation*.

Adj. *ignorant*, nescient, unknowing, blank; incognizant, unrealizing, uncomprehending; in ignorance, unwitting; unaware, oblivious 375 *insensible*; unhearing, unseeing; unfamiliar with, unacquainted, a stranger to, not at home with; in the dark (see *uninstructed*); mystified 474 *uncertain*; clueless, without a clue; blinkered 439 *blind*; lay, amateurish, inexpert 695 *unskilful*; unversed, inexperienced, uninitiated, green, raw; naive, simple, unworldly 699 *artless*; unenlightened, benighted; savage, uncivilized; pagan, heathenish 982 *idolatrous*; backward 499 *unintelligent*; foolish 499 *unwise*; obscurantist, unscientific; dark, superstitious 481 *misjudging*; out of touch, behind the times 125 *retrospective*; wilfully ignorant 454 *incurious*.

uninstructed, unbriefed, uninformed, unapprized, not told, no wiser, kept in the dark; misinformed, mistaught, misled, hoodwinked; ill-informed 474 *uncertain*; unschooled, untaught, untutored, untrained; unlettered, illiterate, innumerate, uneducated; uncultivated, uncultured, lowbrow; unscholarly, unread; philistine.

unknown, unbeknown, untold, unheard; unspoken, unuttered; unseen 444 *invisible*; hidden, veiled 525 *concealed*; unrecognized, unapprehended, unrealized, unperceived; unexplained 517 *unintelligible*; dark, enigmatic, mysterious 523 *occult*; strange, unfamiliar, unprecedented; unnamed 562 *anonymous*; unidentified, unclassified, uninvestigated 458 *neglected*; undiscovered, unexplored,

uncharted, unplumbed, unfathomed; untried, untested; virgin 126 *new*; unknowable, undiscoverable; unpredictable 124 *future*; unheard of, obscure, humble 639 *unimportant*.

dabbling, smattering, sciolistic; unqualified, quack, bluffing; half-educated, semiliterate; shallow, superficial, dilettante.

Vb. *not know*, be ignorant, be in the dark, lack information, have nothing to go on; be unacquainted, not know from Adam; be innocent of, be green, know no better; not know the half of, have no idea, not have the foggiest, not have an inkling; have everything to learn 695 *be unskilful*; not know chalk from cheese 464 *not discriminate*; misunderstand 517 *not understand*; misconstrue 481 *misjudge*; half know, dabble in; half glimpse, guess, suspect 486 *doubt*; unlearn 506 *forget*; ignore 458 *disregard*; profess ignorance, shrug one's shoulders.

Adv. *ignorantly*, in ignorance, unawares; unconsciously; amateurishly, unscientifically; dimly, through a glass darkly; for all one knows.

492. Scholar – N. *scholar*, savant(e), man *or* woman of learning *or* of letters; connoisseur 846 *people of taste*, 504 *enthusiast*; don, doctor, professor, pedagogue 537 *teacher*; pedant, bookworm; classicist, humanist; polymath, encyclopedist; prodigy of learning, walking encyclopedia *or* dictionary; student 538 *learner*; graduate, professional, specialist 696 *proficient person*; academic circles, senior common room, professoriate.

intellectual, academic; brain worker; mastermind, brain, genius, prodigy 500 *sage*; know-all; highbrow, egghead, bluestocking, brahmin, longhair; culture vulture; intelligentsia, literati, illuminati; man *or* woman of science, scientist, technologist; boffin, backroom boy *or* girl; academician, Immortal.

493. Ignoramus – N. *ignoramus*, know-nothing, illiterate, analphabet, no scholar, lowbrow; philistine 847 *vulga-*

rian; duffer, wooden spoon, thickhead 501 *dunce*; greenhorn, novice 538 *beginner*; simpleton, babe, innocent 544 *dupe*; bigot 481 *narrow mind*.

sciolist, smatterer, half-scholar, pedant 500 *wiseacre*; dabbler, dilettante; quack, charlatan 545 *impostor*.

494. Truth – N. *truth*, verity; rightness, intrinsic truth; basic truth, truism 496 *axiom*; accordance with fact; truth of the matter, honest truth, simple t.; light, gospel 975 *revelation*; actuality, historicity 1 *reality*; factualness, fact, matter of f. 3 *substantiality*; home truth, candour, frankness; truthfulness 540 *veracity*.

authenticity, validity, realness, genuineness; the real McCoy, the real thing, the genuine article, it 13 *identity*.

accuracy, attention to fact; verisimilitude, realism, naturalism, local colour, warts and all; fine adjustment, sensitivity, fidelity, high f., exactness, precision; micrometry 465 *measurement*; mot juste; meticulousness 455 *attention*; pedantry, rigour, letter of the law; literality, literalness, the very words 540 *veracity*; chapter and verse 466 *evidence*.

Adj. *true*, veritable; correct, right, so; real, actual, factual, historical; well-grounded, well-founded; 478 *demonstrated*; literal, truthful 540 *veracious*; true to the facts, true to scale (see *accurate*); ascertained 473 *certain*; unquestionable 473 *undisputed*; true to life, undistorted, faithful; realistic, objective, unbiased; unromantic, unideal, down to earth; candid, honest, unflattering 522 *undisguised*.

genuine, authentic, veritable, bona fide, valid, guaranteed, official; sound, reliable, honest 929 *trustworthy*; natural, pure; sterling, hallmarked; pukka, dinkum; true-born, by birth; rightful, legitimate; unadulterated.

accurate, exact, precise, definite, defined; well-adjusted, high-fidelity, dead-on 24 *adjusted*; well-aimed, dead-centre 281 *directed*; unerring, undeviating; punctual, right, correct, true, spot on; never wrong, infallible; close, faithful, representative, photographic; fine, nice, delicate, sensitive; mathematical, scientific, electronic, micrometric; scrupulous, punctilious, meticulous 455 *attentive*; word for word, literal; literal-minded 862 *fastidious*.

Vb. *be true*, be so, be the case 1 *be*; hold true, hold good, hold water, wash, stand the test, ring true; conform to fact, prove true, hold together, be consistent; speak the truth 540 *be truthful*; copy nature 551 *represent*; square, set, trim 24 *adjust*; substantiate 466 *corroborate*; be right, be correct, have the right answer; hit the nail on the head 484 *detect*.

Adv. *truly*, verily, undeniably, really, veritably, genuinely, indeed; as a matter of fact 1 *actually*; to tell the truth, strictly speaking; sic, literally, to the letter, word for word; exactly, accurately, precisely, to a nicety, to a T, just right.

495. Error – N. *error*, erroneousness, wrongness, unsoundness; untruth, unreality; falsity, unfactualness, nonhistoricity 2 *nonexistence*; errancy, straying from the truth 282 *deviation*; fallacy 477 *sophism*; misbelief, unorthodoxy 977 *heterodoxy*; superstition 491 *ignorance*; fallibility 481 *misjudgement*; wishful thinking, doublethink, self-deception; misunderstanding, misconception, misconstruction 521 *misinterpretation*; misguidance 535 *misteaching*; falseness, untruthfulness 541 *falsehood*; illusion 440 *visual fallacy*; false dawn 509 *disappointment*; delusion 503 *insanity*; dream 513 *fantasy*; false impression, wrong idea (see *mistake*); prejudice 481 *bias*.

inexactness, inexactitude, inaccuracy, imprecision, nonadjustment; faultiness; unrigorousness, looseness, laxity, broadness, generalization 79 *generality*; sloppiness, carelessness 458 *negligence*; mistiming 118 *anachronism*; misstatement, misreport, misinformation 552 *misrepresentation*; misquotation (see *mistake*); malapropism 565 *solecism*.

mistake, miscalculation 481 *misjudgement*; blunder, botch-up 695 *bungling*; bloomer, clanger, howler, gaffe 497 *absurdity*; oversight 456 *inattention*; mishit 728 *failure*; bungle, slipup, boob, goof; slip, slip of the pen, slip of the tongue, spoonerism 565 *solecism*; misprint, erratum, corrigendum; inadvertency, trip, stumble; bad tactics; faux pas, solecism 847 *bad taste*.

Adj. *erroneous*, erring, wrong; solecistic 565 *ungrammatical*; unfactual, unhistorical 2 *unreal*; aberrant 282 *deviating*; devoid of truth 543 *untrue*; unsound, unscientific 477 *illogical*; baseless, unsubstantiated, uncorroborated, unfounded, ungrounded 479 *confuted*; exploded, discredited, disproved 924 *disapproved*; fallacious, misleading; unauthentic, apocryphal, unscriptural, unbiblical; unorthodox 977 *heterodox*; untruthful 541 *false*; not genuine, illusory, deceptive 542 *deceiving*; subjective, unrealistic 513 *imaginary*; crackpot 497 *absurd*; fallible, wrongheaded 481 *biased*; superstitious 491 *ignorant*.

mistaken, misunderstood, misconceived; misrepresented, perverted; misread, misprinted; miscalculated, misjudged; in error, misled, misguided; misinformed, ill-informed, deluded 491 *uninstructed*; wide, misdirected, off-target 25 *unapt*; at fault, out, cold, off the scent, off the track, on the wrong tack, at sea.

inexact, inaccurate; not strict, free; broad 79 *general*; not factual, incorrect, misreported, garbled; imprecise, erratic, wild, hit or miss; insensitive, clumsy; out, badly adjusted, out of tune, unsynchronized; uncorrected, unrevised; faulty, flawed 695 *bungled*; misprinted, misread, mistranslated.

Vb. *err*, commit an error, go wrong, make a mistake; labour under a misapprehension, bark up the wrong tree; be in the wrong, be mistaken; delude oneself 481 *misjudge*; be misled, be misguided; get hold of the wrong end of the stick, be at cross-purposes, misunderstand, misapprehend, get it wrong 517 *not understand*; miscount, misreckon 482 *overrate*, 483 *underestimate*; go astray 282 *stray*.

blunder, trip, stumble 695 *be clumsy*; slip, slip up, drop a brick *or* a clanger,

boob, goof 481 *misjudge*; commit a faux pas, put one's foot in it; blot one's copybook; muff, bungle; blow it 728 *fail*; play into one's hands 695 *act foolishly*; misread, misquote, misapprehend 521 *misinterpret*.

mislead, misdirect 282 *deflect*; misinform, lead astray 535 *misteach*; beguile, befool 542 *deceive*; falsify, garble 541 *dissemble*; whitewash, cover up 525 *conceal*.

496. Maxim – N. *maxim*, apophthegm, gnome, adage, saw, proverb, byword, aphorism; dictum, tag, saying, truth; epigram 839 *witticism*; truism, cliché, commonplace, platitude, banality, statement of the obvious, bromide; motto, watchword, slogan, catchword; formula, mantra; golden rule 693 *precept*; moral, fable 590 *narrative*; phylactery, formulary; folklore.

axiom, self-evident truth, truism, tautology; principle, postulate, theorem, formula; Sod's Law, Murphy's Law.

Adj. *aphoristic*, gnomic, sententious, proverbial, moralizing 498 *wise*; epigrammatic, piquant, pithy 839 *witty*; enigmatic, oracular 517 *puzzling*; corny, platitudinous, clichéd 610 *usual*; axiomatic.

Adv. *proverbially*, as the saying goes, as they say, to coin a phrase; pithily, in a nutshell; aphoristically, epigrammatically.

497. Absurdity – N. *absurdity*, height of a. 849 *ridiculousness*; ineptitude, inconsequence 10 *irrelevance*; false logic 447 *sophistry*; foolishness 499 *folly*; senselessness, futility, fatuity 641 *lost labour*; rot, rubbish, nonsense, stuff and nonsense, gibberish, twaddle 515 *silly talk*; romancing, bombast 546 *exaggeration*; malapropism, howler 495 *mistake*; paradox, spoonerism; joke 839 *witticism*; pun, play on words 518 *equivocalness*; riddle 530 *enigma*; quibble 477 *sophism*; anticlimax, bathos; catch 542 *trickery*.

foolery, antics, fooling about, horsing around, silliness, tomfoolery, skylarking 837 *revel*; whimsy 604 *whim*; extravagance, extravaganza; escapade, scrape; practical joke, monkey tricks; drollery, clowning, buffoonery; burlesque, parody 851 *ridicule*; farce, pretence 850 *affectation*.

Adj. *absurd*, inept 25 *unapt*; ludicrous, laughable, comical, grotesque 849 *ridiculous*; rash, silly 499 *foolish*; nonsensical, senseless 515 *meaningless*; preposterous, without rhyme or reason 477 *illogical*; wild, overdone, extravagant 546 *exaggerated*; pretentious 850 *affected*; frantic 503 *frenzied*; crazy, crackpot 495 *erroneous*; fanciful, fantastic 513 *imaginative*; futile, fatuous 641 *useless*; paradoxical 508 *unexpected*; inconsistent 10 *irrelevant*; quibbling 477 *sophistical*.

Vb. *be absurd*, play the fool 499 *be foolish*; fool about, lark about, muck a., horse a., monkey around, play practical jokes 837 *amuse oneself*; be a laughing-stock 849 *be ridiculous*; clown, burlesque 851 *ridicule*; talk through one's hat 515 *mean nothing*.

498. Intelligence. Wisdom – N. *intelligence*, thinking power 447 *intellect*; brains, grey matter, head, loaf, upper storey; nous, wit, mother w., commonsense; lights, understanding, sense, good s., horse s., savvy, gumption, knowhow; wits, sharp w., quick thinking, quickness, readiness, esprit; ability, capacity, grasp; mental calibre, intelligence quotient, IQ; forwardness, brightness; braininess, cleverness 694 *aptitude*; giftedness, brilliance, talent, genius; ideas, inspiration 476 *intuition*; brainwave 451 *idea*.

sagacity, judgement, discretion, discernment 463 *discrimination*; perception, perspicacity, clear thinking; acumen, sharpness, acuity, penetration; practicality, shrewdness; level-headedness, balance 502 *sanity*; prudence, forethought 510 *foresight*; subtleness, subtlety 698 *cunning*; worldly wisdom, oneupmanship 694 *skill*; alertness, awareness 457 *carefulness*; tact, statesmanship 688 *tactics*.

wisdom, sageness, understanding, sapience; profundity 449 *thought*; depth of mind, breadth of m.; experience 490

knowledge; tolerance, broadmindedness, catholic outlook; soundness; sobriety, objectivity, enlightenment.

Adj. *intelligent*, brainy, clever, forward, bright, bright as a button; brilliant, scintillating, talented, of genius 694 *gifted*; capable, able, practical 694 *skilful*; apt, ready, quick, quick on the uptake, receptive; acute, sharp, quick-witted; alive, aware, with it 455 *attentive*; astute, shrewd, fly, smart, canny, not born yesterday, up to snuff, all there, on the ball; knowing, sophisticated, worldly-wise; too clever by half, clever clever; sagacious, provident, prudent 457 *careful*; farseeing, clear-sighted 510 *foreseeing*; discerning 463 *discriminating*; penetrating, perspicacious, clear-headed, hard-h; subtle, wily 698 *cunning*; politic, statesmanlike.

wise, sage, sapient; thinking, reflecting 449 *thoughtful*; reasoning 475 *rational*; knowledgeable 490 *instructed*; profound, deep, oracular; sound, sensible, reasonable 502 *sane*; experienced, unflappable; unperplexed, unbaffled; balanced, level-headed, realistic, objective; judicious 913 *just*; tolerant, fair-minded, enlightened, unbiased; unfanatical, unbigoted, unprejudiced; broad, broad-minded; tactful, politic 698 *cunning*; wise as a serpent, wise as an owl, wise as Solomon.

Vb. *be wise*, – intelligent etc. adj.; use one's wits, use one's head; have a fund of wisdom 490 *know*; sparkle, scintillate, shine 644 *be good*; have a head on one's shoulders, have one's wits about one, know how many beans make five, see with half an eye, see at a glance; have one's head screwed on the right way, know a thing or two, know what's what, get around, know the score; show foresight 510 *foresee*; know which side one's bread is buttered on, be prudent 858 *be cautious*; grasp 516 *understand*; discern, see through 438 *see*; distinguish 463 *discriminate*; listen to reason 475 *be reasonable*; plan well 698 *be cunning*; learn from one's mistakes.

499. Unintelligence. Folly – N. *unintelligence*, want of intellect 448 *absence of* *intellect*; lack of brains, low IQ, low mental age, immaturity, infantilism; hydrocephalus, Down's syndrome, mongolism, cretinism, mental deficiency; mental handicap, arrested development, retardation, backwardness; imbecility, idiocy; stupidity, slowness, dullness, obtuseness, denseness; oafishness, stolidity 820 *moral insensibility*; poor head, no head for; incapacity, incompetence 695 *unskilfulness*; naivety, gullibility 481 *misjudgement*; vacuousness, superficiality, shallowness; impercipience 464 *indiscrimination*.

folly, foolishness, eccentricity 849 *ridiculousness*; act of folly 497 *foolery*; levity, frivolity, giddiness 456 *inattention*; irrationality 477 *sophistry*; unwisdom, imprudence, indiscretion; fatuity, fatuousness, pointlessness; wild-goose chase 641 *lost labour*; silliness, asininity; brainlessness, idiocy, lunacy; recklessness, wildness 857 *rashness*; obsession, infatuation 481 *misjudgement*; puerility, childishness 130 *nonage*; second childhood, dotage 131 *old age*; drivelling, babbling, maundering; conceit, empty-headedness 873 *vanity*.

Adj. *unintelligent*, unintellectual, lowbrow; ungifted, untalented; not bright, dull; subnormal, ESN, mentally handicapped; undeveloped, immature; backward, retarded, feeble-minded, moronic, cretinous, imbecile; limited, deficient, wanting, not all there, vacant, a button short; impercipient, unperceptive, slow on the uptake; stupid, obtuse, dense, thick, crass, Boeotian, blockish, oafish, doltish, owlish; dumb, dim, dim-witted, dull-w., slow-w., thick-w., half-w.; dead from the neck up, thick as two short planks; clod-pated, bone-headed, muddle-h.; cracked, barmy 503 *crazy*; impenetrable, unteachable; prosaic, unimaginative.

foolish, silly, idiotic, imbecile, asinine; nonsensical, senseless, inane 497 *absurd*; ludicrous, laughable 849 *ridiculous*; like a fool 544 *gullible*; simple, naive 699 *artless*; tactless 695 *clumsy*; soft, wet, soppy, sawney; gumptionless, gormless; goofy, dopey; childish, puerile, infantile 132 *infantine*; gaga 131 *ageing*; besotted, fond,

doting; sentimental, spoony 887 *enamoured*; dazed, fuddled, maudlin 949 *drunk*; babbling, burbling, drivelling, maundering; mindless, witless, brainless (**see** *unintelligent*); shallow, superficial, frivolous, feather-brained 456 *lightminded*; eccentric, extravagant, wild, madcap; daft 503 *crazy*.

unwise, unenlightened 491 *ignorant*; unphilosophical, unintellectual; unreasoning 477 *illogical*, 464 *indiscriminating*; injudicious 481 *misjudging*; undiscerning, short-sighted 439 *blind*; unteachable, insensate; thoughtless 450 *unthinking*; indiscreet, incautious, foolhardy 857 *rash*; inconsistent, unbalanced, unreasonable; inept 643 *inexpedient*; ill-considered, ill-advised, ill-judged 495 *mistaken*.

Vb. *be foolish*, maunder, dote, drivel, babble, burble; talk through one's hat 515 *mean nothing*; lose one's wits, take leave of one's senses 503 *be insane*; be unintelligent, never learn; look foolish 849 *be ridiculous*; make a fool of oneself, play the fool 497 *be absurd*; burn one's fingers 695 *act foolishly*; go on a fool's errand 641 *waste effort*.

500. Sage – N. *sage*, nobody's fool; learned person 492 *scholar*; wise man *or* woman, statesman *or* -woman; elder statesman *or* -woman, counsellor 691 *adviser*; expert 696 *proficient person*; genius, mastermind; mentor, guide, guru, pundit 537 *teacher*, 973 *religious teacher*; seer, prophet 511 *oracle*; yogi, swami 945 *ascetic*; leading light, luminary; great soul, mahatma; doctor, thinker, philosopher; egghead, boffin, highbrow 492 *intellectual*; wizard, shaman, magus 983 *sorcerer*.

wiseacre, wise guy, know-all, smartypants 873 *vain person*; smart aleck, clever dick; brains trust; witling, wise fool.

501. Fool – N. *fool*, silly f., tomfool; buffoon, clown, comic, jester, zany 594 *entertainer*; perfect fool, complete idiot, ass, donkey, goose, cuckoo; idiot, natural, half-wit; mongol, cretin, moron, imbecile; stupid, silly, silly-billy; stooge, butt 851 *laughing-stock*; twit, clot 697 *bungler*;

scatterbrain, birdbrain, featherbrain; crackpot, eccentric 504 *crank*; dotard 133 *old man*.

ninny, simpleton, Simple Simon; tom noddy, charlie; noodle, noddy, nincompoop, juggins, muggins, booby, sap, softhead, big stiff, poor stick, dope, jerk, gowk, galoot, goof; greenhorn 538 *beginner*; weed, drip, softy 163 *weakling*; sucker, mug 544 *dupe*; gaper, gawker.

dunce, dullard; blockhead, woodenhead, numskull, duffer, dolt, dumb cluck 493 *ignoramus*; fathead, thickhead, bonehead, pinhead, blockhead, dunderhead, blunderhead, chucklehead, jobbernowl; nitwit, dimwit; mutt, chump, clot, clod, block, oaf, booby, loon, bumpkin.

502. Sanity – N. *sanity*, saneness, soundness, soundness of mind; reasonableness; rationality, reason; balance, mental equilibrium; sobriety, common sense; lucidity, lucid interval; normality, proper mind, senses; sound mind, mens sana; mental health.

Adj. *sane*, normal, not neurotic; of sound mind, mentally sound, all there; in one's senses, compos mentis, in one's right mind, in possession of one's faculties; rational, reasonable 498 *intelligent*; commonsensical, sober; lucid, not wandering, clear-headed; undisturbed, well-balanced; not certifiable.

503. Insanity – N. *insanity*, unsoundness of mind, lunacy, madness, certifiability; mental sickness, mental illness; mental instability, intellectual unbalance; psychopathic condition, abnormal psychology; loss of reason, sick mind, unsound m., clouded brain, brain damage; mental decay, softening of the brain 131 *age*; dementia; amentia, congenital idiocy 499 *unintelligence*; autism, derangement 84 *abnormality*; psychiatry 447 *psychology*; psychotherapy 658 *therapy*; psychiatrist 658 *doctor*.

psychopathy, sociopathy, maladjustment, personality disorder; identity crisis, personal anomie; emotional disturbance; neurosis, psychoneurosis, nerves, nervous disorder, neurasthenia; hysteria; attack of nerves, nervous breakdown, brainstorm; shellshock, combat fatigue; obsession, compulsion, claustrophobia, agarophobia 854 *phobia*; paranoia, delusions, hallucinations; psychosis; split personality, multiple p.; catatonia, schizophrenia; depression, manic d., cyclothymia, elation.

mania, megalomania, persecution mania, religious m.; kleptomania; homicidal mania; monomania. See *eccentricity*.

frenzy, ecstasy, delirium, raving, hysteria; distraction, wandering of the mind 456 *abstractedness*; incoherence 517 *unintelligibility*; delirium tremens 949 *alcoholism*; epilepsy, fit, paroxysm 318 *spasm*.

eccentricity, craziness, crankiness, faddishness; oddness, weirdness, strange behaviour; oddity, twist, kink 84 *abnormality*; a screw loose, bats in the belfry; fixation, hangup, inhibition, repression; complex, inferiority c., Oedipus c., Electra c.; obsession, infatuation, monomania, ruling passion 481 *bias*; hobbyhorse 604 *whim*.

lunatic asylum, mental home, mental hospital, psychiatric h.; madhouse, Bedlam; booby-hatch, loony-bin, nuthouse, funny farm; locked ward, padded cell 658 *hospital*.

Adj. *insane*, mad, lunatic, moon-struck; not in one's right mind, non compos mentis, out of one's mind, deranged, demented; certifiable; mental; abnormal, sick, mentally ill; unbalanced, maladjusted; psychopathic, psychotic; neurotic, hysterical; paranoiac, paranoid, schizophrenic, schizoid; manic, maniacal; catatonic, depressive; hyperactive; hypochondriac 834 *melancholic*; kleptomaniac; claustrophobic, agoraphobic; autistic; brain-damaged, shell-shocked; defective 499 *unintelligent*; raving mad, stark staring m. (see *frenzied*); certified.

crazy, bewildered, wandering, bemused 456 *abstracted*; not all there, not right in the head; off one's head *or* one's nut, round the bend *or* the twist, up the pole; crazed, demented, driven mad, maddened (see *frenzied*); unhinged, unbalanced, off one's rocker; bedevilled, be-

207

witched, deluded; infatuated, obsessed, eaten up with, possessed; besotted 887 *enamoured*; drivelling, gaga; touched, wanting; idiotic, crack-brained 499 *foolish*; crackers, cracked, scatty, screwy, nutty, nuts, bananas, batty, bats, cuckoo, barmy, bonkers, loco; daft, dippy, loony, loopy, potty, dotty; cranky, wacky, eccentric, funny, queer, odd 84 *abnormal*; crotchety, whimsical 604 *capricious*; dizzy, giddy 456 *light-minded*.

frenzied, rabid, maddened; furious 891 *angry*; haggard, wild, distraught 825 *suffering*; possessed, bedevilled, bacchic, corybantic; frantic, frenetic, demented, like one possessed, beside oneself, uncontrollable; berserk, seeing red 176 *violent*; epileptic, having fits; hysterical, delirious, hallucinating, raving, rambling, incoherent, fevered 651 *sick*.

Vb. *be insane*, etc. adj.; have bats in the belfry, have a screw loose; dote, drivel 499 *be foolish*; ramble, wander; babble, rave; foam at the mouth; be delirious, see things.

go mad, go off one's head *or* one's rocker, go crackers, have to be certified; lose one's mind *or* one's reason, lose one's marbles, go out of one's mind, crack up; go berserk, run amok 891 *get angry*.

make mad, drive m., send m., drive insane, madden; craze, derange, dement; send off one's head *or* out of one's mind; send round the bend *or* the twist, drive up the wall; turn one's brain; blow one's mind 821 *excite*; unhinge, unbalance, send off one's rocker; infuriate 891 *enrage*; infatuate; go to one's head, turn one's h.

504. Madman – N. *madman*, madwoman, lunatic, mental case; bedlamite; screwball, nut, nutcase, loon, loony; psychopath, psycho; sociopath; hysteric, neurotic, neuropath; psychotic; obsessive, paranoiac; schizoid; manic-depressive; maenad, bacchante; raving lunatic, maniac; kleptomaniac, pyromaniac, monomaniac, megalomaniac; dipsomaniac 949 *drunkard*; drug addict 949 *drug-taking*; hypochondriac, melancholic.

crank, crackpot, nut, nutter, crack-brain; eccentric, oddity, oddball 851 *laughing-stock*; freak 84 *nonconformist*; faddist, fanatic, extremist, nympholept, lunatic fringe; seer, dreamer 513 *visionary*; knight errant, Don Quixote.

enthusiast, energumen 678 *busy person*; zealot 602 *obstinate person*; devotee, aficionado, addict, fiend, nut, freak, bug, buff; fan, supporter 707 *patron*; connoisseur, fancier 846 *people of taste*; radio ham, discophile, balletomane, opera buff, film b., cineaste; collector, stamp c., philatelist, phillumenist, numismatist.

Section 6:
Extension of thought

505. Memory – N. *memory*, good m., retentiveness, retention; data bank 632 *storage*; collective memory, race m., atavism; Mnemosyne.

remembrance, recollection, recall, total r.; commemoration, evocation, mind's eye; rehearsal, recapitulation 106 *repetition*; memorization 536 *learning*; reminiscence, retrospection, review, retrospect, hindsight; flashback, recurrence, voice from the past; déjà vu 984 *psychics*; afterthought 67 *sequel*; nostalgia 830 *regret*; memorabilia, memoirs; history 590 *narrative*; place in history 866 *famousness*.

reminder, memorial, testimonial, commemoration 876 *celebration*; souvenir, keepsake, relic, memento; trophy, statue 548 *monument*; remembrancer, prompter; memorandum, memo, aide-mémoire, diary; alda, scrapbook, commonplace-book, promptbook; leading question, prompt, suggestion, cue 524 *hint*; mnemonic.

Adj. *remembered*, etc. vb.; unforgotten, green, fresh; missed, regretted; memorable, unforgettable, not to be forgotten; haunting, persistent, indelible, ineffaceable, stamped on one's memory; got by heart, memorized 490 *known*.

remembering, mindful, faithful to the memory, keeping in mind; evocative, memorial, commemorative 876 *celebratory*; reminiscent, recollecting, anecdotic, anecdotal; living in the past, nostalgic; unable to forget, haunted, obsessed; prompting, mnemonic.

Vb. *remember*, recall, mind, think of; call to m.; recognize 490 *know*; recollect, bethink oneself; not forget 778 *retain*; keep *or* hold in mind, keep alive in one's thoughts, treasure in one's heart, cherish the memory, never forget.

retrospect, reminisce, recollect, recall, recapture; reflect, review, think back, retrace, hark back, cast one's mind b.; summon up, conjure up, rake up the past, archaize; reopen old wounds; rack one's brains, tax one's memory.

remind, jog *or* refresh one's memory; put one in mind of, take one back; prompt 524 *hint*; not allow one to forget, haunt; make one think of, evoke the memory o.; commemorate, memorialize, toast 876 *celebrate*; recount 106 *repeat*.

memorize, commit to memory, con 490 *know*; get by heart 536 *learn*; fix in one's memory, grave on the mind, hammer *or* drive into one's head; burden the memory, stuff the mind.

be remembered, stay in the memory, stick in the mind, make a lasting impression; recur 106 *reoccur*; flash across one's mind, ring a bell; run in one's thoughts, haunt one's t., be at the back of one's mind; make history 866 *have a reputation*; live on 115 *be eternal*.

506. Oblivion – N. *oblivion*, blankness, no recollection; obliviousness, forgetfulness; absent-mindedness 456 *abstractedness*; amnesia, blackout, mental block; misrecollection, paramnesia; dim memory, hazy recollection; short memory, memory like a sieve; effacement 550 *obliteration*; Lethe, waters of L.

amnesty, burial of the hatchet; pardon, absolution 909 *forgiveness*.

Adj. *forgotten*, beyond recall; not missed; in limbo 458 *neglected*; on the tip of one's tongue; suppressed, repressed; out of mind, over and done with; amnestied 909 *forgiven*.

forgetful, forgetting, oblivious; amnesic; unmindful, heedless 458 *negligent*, 908

ungrateful; absent-minded 456 *abstracted*.

Vb. *forget*, clean f., not remember, disremember, have no recollection of; not give another thought to, think no more of; suppress the memory, consign to oblivion; let bygones be bygones 909 *forgive*; break with the past, unlearn, efface 550 *obliterate*; lose one's memory; misremember, misrecollect; be forgetful, need reminding; leave behind, overlook 456 *be inattentive*; forget one's lines, dry; have a memory like a sieve, go in at one ear and out of the other; not quite recall, draw a blank.

be forgotten, slip one's memory; sink into oblivion, be overlooked 456 *escape notice*.

507. Expectation – N. *expectation*, anticipation, expectancy 455 *attention*; contemplation 617 *intention*; presumption, confidence, trust 473 *certainty*; optimism 833 *cheerfulness*; eager expectation 859 *desire*, 852 *hope*; waiting, suspense 474 *uncertainty*; pessimism, dread, apprehension 854 *fear*; expectations, prospects; prospect, lookout, outlook 511 *prediction*; defeated expectation 509 *disappointment*.

Adj. *expectant*, expecting, in expectation, in hourly e.; in suspense, on the waiting list; confident 473 *certain*; anticipatory, anticipative; banking on, taking for granted; predicting 510 *foreseeing*; unsurprised 865 *unastonished*; forewarned 669 *prepared*; waiting for, awaiting; on the lookout, on the watch for, standing by 457 *vigilant*; tense, keyed up 821 *excited*; on tenterhooks, agog 859 *desiring*; optimistic, hopeful 852 *hoping*; apprehensive 854 *nervous*; pessimistic 853 *hopeless*.

expected, long e.; as one expected 865 *unastonishing*; anticipated, on the cards, foreseeable 471 *probable*; prospective 155 *impending*; promised, intended, in view, in prospect 617 *intending*.

Vb. *expect*, look for, face; contemplate, have in mind, hold in view, promise oneself 617 *intend*; reckon 480 *estimate*; predict 510 *foresee*; see it coming 865 *not wonder*; think likely, assume; rely on, bank on, count on 473 *be certain*; count one's chickens before they are hatched

509 *be disappointed*; anticipate, forestall 669 *prepare oneself*; look out for, be ready f. 457 *be careful*; dread 854 *fear*; look forward to 852 *hope*, 859 *desire*; hope and believe 485 *believe*.

await, be on the waiting list; queue up, mark time, bide one's t.; stand by, be on call; hold one's breath, be in suspense; lead one to expect 859 *cause desire*.

508. Lack of expectation – N. *lack of expectation*, no expectation 472 *improbability*; false expectation 509 *disappointment*; inexpectancy 853 *hopelessness*; lack of interest, apathy 454 *incuriosity*; unpreparedness 670 *nonpreparation*; unexpectedness, unforeseen contingency; lack of warning, surprise, surprisal, disconcertment; the unexpected, the unforeseen, surprise packet, Jack-in-the-box, afterclap; windfall 615 *benefit*; shock, nasty s., start, jolt, turn; blow, bolt from the blue, bombshell; revelation, eye-opener; culture shock; paradox, reversal 221 *inversion*; astonishment, amazement 864 *wonder*; anticlimax.

Adj. *unexpected*, unanticipated, unlooked for, unhoped for; unpredicted, unforeseen; unforeseeable 472 *improbable*; unheralded, unannounced; without warning, surprising; amazing 864 *wonderful*; shocking, startling 854 *frightening*; sudden 116 *instantaneous*; unbargained for 670 *unprepared*; contrary to expectation, against e.; unprecedented 84 *unusual*; unaccountable 517 *puzzling*.

inexpectant, unexpecting, unsuspecting, off guard 456 *inattentive*; unaware, uninformed 491 *ignorant*; surprised, disconcerted, taken by surprise, taken aback, caught bending *or* on the hop 670 *unprepared*; astonished, amazed, thunderstruck 864 *wondering*; startled, jolted, shocked; unhopeful 853 *hopeless*; apathetic 860 *indifferent*.

Vb. *surprise*, take by s., spring it on one; ambush 542 *ensnare*; catch unawares, catch off one's guard; startle, jolt, make one jump, give one a turn; stagger, stun; take one's breath away, knock one down with a feather, bowl one over, strike one

all of a heap; be one in the eye for 509 *disappoint*; give one a surprise, pull out of the hat; astonish, amaze 864 *be wonderful*; shock 821 *impress*; flutter the dovecotes, set the cat among the pigeons 63 *derange*; drop from the clouds, come out of the blue; fall upon, spring u., pounce on; steal up on, creep up on; come up from behind, appear from nowhere.

Adv. *unexpectedly*, suddenly 116 *instantaneously*.

509. Disappointment – N. *disappointment*, bitter d.; regrets 830 *regret*; tantalization, frustration, bafflement; frustrated expectations, blighted hopes 853 *hopelessness*; false expectation 482 *overestimation*; disenchantment, disillusionment 829 *discontent*; miscalculation 481 *misjudgement*; mirage, false dawn, fool's paradise; shock, blow, setback 702 *hitch*; bad luck 731 *misfortune*; anticlimax 508 *lack of expectation*; comedown, letdown 872 *humiliation*; damp squib 728 *failure*.

Adj. *disappointed*, expecting otherwise 508 *inexpectant*; frustrated, thwarted; baffled, foiled 728 *defeated*; disconcerted, crestfallen, chagrined 872 *humbled*; disgruntled 829 *discontented*; sick with disappointment 853 *hopeless*; heartbroken 834 *dejected*; let down, betrayed, jilted, turned away 607 *rejected*.

disappointing, unsatisfactory, not up to expectation 829 *discontenting*; abortive 728 *unsuccessful*; deceptive 542 *deceiving*.

Vb. *be disappointed*, etc. adj.; try in vain 728 *fail*; be let down, have hoped better of; find to one's cost 830 *regret*; be crestfallen 872 *be humbled*.

disappoint, not come up to expectations 307 *fall short*; dash one's hopes, crush one's h., blight one's h.; disillusion; serve badly, fail one, let one down, not come up to scratch; balk, foil, thwart, frustrate 702 *hinder*; dumbfound 508 *surprise*; disconcert 872 *humiliate*; play one false 930 *be dishonest*; tantalize, leave unsatisfied 829 *cause discontent*; refuse, deny, turn away 607 *reject*.

Adv. *disappointingly*, tantalizingly, so near and yet so far.

510. Foresight – N. *foresight*, prevision; anticipation; precognition, foreknowledge, prescience, second sight, clairvoyance; premonition, presentiment, foreboding 511 *omen*; prognostication 511 *prediction*; forethought, longsightedness 498 *sagacity*; premeditation 608 *predetermination*; prudence, providence 858 *caution*; provision 669 *preparation*.

Adj. *foreseeing*, foresighted; prognostic 511 *predicting*; clairvoyant, secondsighted, prophetic; prescient, farsighted 498 *wise*; provident, prudent 858 *cautious*; anticipatory 507 *expectant*.

Vb. *foresee*, forecast 511 *predict*; foreknow, see into the future, have second sight; see ahead, see it coming, feel in one's bones; look for 507 *expect*; anticipate, forestall 135 *be early*; plan ahead 623 *plan*; have an eye to the future, see how the wind blows 669 *prepare*; keep a sharp lookout 455 *be attentive*; lay up for a rainy day 633 *provide*; take precautions 858 *be cautious*.

511. Prediction – N. *prediction*, foretelling, forewarning, prophecy; apocalypse 975 *revelation*; forecast, weather f.; prognostication, prognosis 510 *foresight*; presage, prefiguration, prefigurement; warning 665 *danger signal*; prospect 507 *expectation*; shape of things to come, horoscope, fortune.

divination, clairvoyance; augury, taking the auspices; vaticination, soothsaying; astrology, horoscopy; fortune-telling, palmistry, chiromancy; crystal gazing; cartomancy; I Ching; sortilege, casting lots; bibliomancy; oneiromancy 984 *occultism*; dowsing 484 *discovery*.

omen, portent, presage, writing on the wall; prognostic, symptom, sign 547 *indication*; augury, auspice; forewarning 664 *warning*; harbinger, herald 529 *messenger*; prefigurement, foretoken; gathering clouds, signs of the times 661 *danger*; luck-bringer, black cat; bird of ill omen, owl, raven.

oracle, consultant 500 *sage*; meteorologist, weatherman; doom merchant, Cassandra 664 *warner*; prophet, prophetess, seer, vaticinator; futurologist, prognosticator, forecaster; soothsayer 983 *sorcerer*; clairvoyant 984 *occultist*; Delphic oracle, Pythian o., sibyl; Old Moore, Nostradamus; cards, tarot c., dice, lot; tripod, crystal ball, tea leaves, palm; Bible, sortes Biblicae.

diviner, water d., dowser; astrologer; fortune-teller, gipsy, palmist, crystalgazer; augur, haruspex.

Adj. *predicting*, predictive, foretelling; clairvoyant 510 *foreseeing*; fortunetelling; weather-wise; prophetic, vatic, mantic, fatidical, apocalyptic; oracular, sibylline; premonitory, foreboding 664 *cautionary*; heralding, prefiguring 66 *precursory*.

presageful, significant, ominous, portentous, pregnant with; augural, auspicial, haruspical; auspicious, favourable 730 *prosperous*; inauspicious, sinister 731 *adverse*.

Vb. *predict*, forecast, prognosticate; foretell, prophesy, vaticinate, forebode, bode, augur, spell; foretoken, presage, portend; foreshow, foreshadow, prefigure, shadow forth, herald 64 *come before*; point to, betoken 547 *indicate*; forewarn 664 *warn*; lour 900 *threaten*; promise, augur well, bid fair to 852 *give hope*.

divine, auspicate, haruspicate; read the entrails, take the auspices; soothsay, vaticinate; cast a horoscope, cast a nativity; cast lots 618 *gamble*; tell fortunes; read the future, read the cards, read one's hand.

Section 7: Creative thought

512. Supposition – N. *supposition*, supposal, notion 451 *idea*; fancy, conceit 513 *ideality*; pretence 850 *affectation*; presumption, assumption, presupposition, postulation, postulate, premise; condition, stipulation 766 *conditions*; proposition 759 *offer*; submission 475 *argument*; hypothesis, theory 452 *topic*; thesis, position, stand, standpoint 485 *opinion*; suggestion 524 *hint*; clue, datum 466 *evidence*; hunch, inkling (**see** *conjecture*); instinct

476 *intuition*; association of ideas 449 *thought*.

, *conjecture*, guess, surmise, suspicion; rough guess, crude estimate; shrewd idea 476 *intuition*; construction, reconstruction; guesswork, speculation; shot in the dark 618 *gambling*.

theorist, hypothesist, theorizer, theoretician, model builder, research worker; supposer, surmiser, guesser, armchair detective; thinker 449 *philosophy*; boffin 623 *planner*; speculator 618 *gambler*.

Adj. *suppositional*, suppositive, notional, conjectural, propositional, hypothetical, theoretical, speculative, academic, of academic interest; gratuitous, unverified; suggestive, stimulating, thought-provoking.

supposed, etc. vb.; assumed, premised, taken; proposed 452 *topical*; given, granted 488 *assented*; suppositive, putative, presumptive; pretended, so-called, quasi 2 *unreal*; alleged, fabled 543 *untrue*; surmisable, imaginable.

Vb. *suppose*, pretend, fancy 513 *imagine*; think, conceive 485 *opine*; divine, have a hunch 476 *intuit*; surmise, conjecture, guess; suppose so, dare say 485 *believe*; presume, assume, presuppose, premise; posit, lay down 532 *affirm*; take for granted, postulate 475 *reason*; speculate, hypothesize, theorize 449 *meditate*; sketch 623 *plan*.

propound, propose 759 *offer*; moot, move, propose a motion 761 *request*; submit 475 *argue*; make a suggestion 691 *advise*; suggest 524 *hint*; put an idea into one's head 612 *motivate*.

513. Imagination – **N.** *imagination*, power of i., fertile i., lively i.; imaginativeness, creativeness; inventiveness, creativity 21 *originality*; fancifulness, fantasy, fantasticalness, stretch of the imagination (**see** *ideality*); understanding, insight, empathy, sympathy 819 *moral sensibility*; poetic imagination, frenzy, ecstasy, inspiration, afflatus, divine a.; fancy, the mind's eye, visualization, objectification, image-building, imagery, word-painting.

ideality, conception 449 *thought*;

idealization, ego ideal; mental image, projection 445 *appearance*; concept, image, conceit, fancy, notion 451 *idea*; whim, whimsy 497 *absurdity*; vagary 604 *caprice*; figment, fiction 541 *falsehood*; science fiction, fairy tale 590 *novel*; flight of fancy, romance, fantasy, extravaganza, rhapsody 546 *exaggeration*; poetic licence 593 *poetry*; quixotry, knight-errantry.

fantasy, wildest dreams; vision, dream, nightmare; bogey, phantom 970 *ghost*; mirage, fata morgana 440 *visual fallacy*; delusion, hallucination, chimera 495 *error*; trance, reverie 456 *abstractedness*; sick fancy, delirium 503 *frenzy*; subjectivity, auto-suggestion; wishful thinking; make-believe, daydream, pipe dream 859 *desire*; romance, stardust; romanticism, escapism, idealism; Utopia, Erewhon; promised land, El Dorado; Cockaigne, Ruritania, Shangri-la; Atlantis, Lyonesse, San Serif; fairyland, wonderland; cloud-cuckoo-land, dream land, dream world, castles in Spain, castles in the air; pie in the sky, millennium 124 *future state*; myth 543 *fable*.

visionary, seer 511 *diviner*; dreamer, day-d., somnambulist 456 *inattention*; fantast, fantasist; idealist, Utopian 901 *philanthropist*; escapist 620 *avoider*; romantic, romancer, romanticist, rhapsodist, mythmaker; enthusiast, knight-errant, Don Quixote 504 *crank*; creative worker 556 *artist*.

Adj. *imaginative*, creative, lively, original, inventive, fertile, ingenious; resourceful 694 *skilful*; fancy-led, romancing, romantic; high-flown, rhapsodical 546 *exaggerated*; poetic, fictional; Utopian, idealistic; dreaming, in a trance; extravagant, grotesque, bizarre, fantastical, whimsical, airy-fairy, preposterous, impractical, Heath Robinson 497 *absurd*; visionary, otherworldly, quixotic; imaginal, visualizing, eidetic, eidotropic.

imaginary, unreal 4 *insubstantial*; subjective, notional, chimerical, illusory 495 *erroneous*; dreamy, visionary, not of this world, ideal; cloudy, vaporous 419 *shadowy*; unhistorical, fictitious, fabulous, fabled, legendary, mythic, mythological

543 *untrue*; fanciful, fancied, imagined, fabricated, hatched; dreamed-up; hypothetical 512 *suppositional*; pretended, make-believe.

Vb. *imagine*, ideate 449 *think*; fancy, dream; think up, dream up; make up, devise, invent, originate, create, improvise; coin, hatch, concoct, fabricate 164 *produce*; visualize, envisage 438 *see*; conceive, picture to oneself; paint, objectify, realize, capture, recapture 551 *represent*;

use one's imagination; pretend, make-believe, daydream 456 *be inattentive*; build castles in the air; see visions, dream dreams; fantasize, idealize, romanticize, fictionalize, rhapsodize 546 *exaggerate*; enter into, empathize, sympathize 516 *understand*.

Adv. *imaginatively*, in imagination, in the mind's eye; with one's head in the clouds.

4.2 COMMUNICATION OF IDEAS

Section 1: Nature of ideas communicated

514. Meaning – N. *meaning*, substance, essence, spirit, gist, pith; contents, matter 452 *topic*; sense, value, drift, tenor, purport, import, implication; force, effect, implication; force, effect; relevance, bearing, scope; meaningfulness (**see** *connotation*); expression, diction 566 *style*; semantics, semiology 557 *linguistics*.

connotation, denotation, signification, significance, reference, application; construction 520 *interpretation*; context; derivation 156 *source*; semantic field; intention, core meaning, leading sense; idiom 80 *speciality*; usage, accepted meaning 610 *practice*; unambiguity 516 *intelligibility*; ambiguity 518 *equivocalness*; many meanings, polysemy; same meaning, synonym, synonymousness, synonymity 13 *identity*; antonym, antonymy 14 *contrariety*; semantic shift; literality 573 *plainness*; metaphorical meaning 519 *metaphor*; hidden meaning 523 *latency*; no sense 497 *absurdity*.

Adj. *meaningful*, significant, of moment 638 *important*; substantial, pithy, meaty, pregnant; importing, purporting, significative, indicative 547 *indicating*; telling 516 *expressive*; pointed 839 *witty*; suggestive, evocative, allusive, implicit; express, explicit 573 *plain*; declaratory 532 *affirmative*; interpretative 520 *interpretive*.

semantic, semiological, philological, etymological 557 *linguistic*; connotational, connotative; denotational, denotative; literal, verbal 573 *plain*; metaphorical 519 *figurative*; univocal, unambiguous 516 *intelligible*; polysemous, ambiguous 518 *equivocal*; synonymous, homonymous 13 *identical*; tautologous 106 *repeated*; antonymous 14 *contrary*; idiomatic 80 *special*; paraphrastic 520 *interpretive*; obscure 568 *unclear*; clear 567 *perspicuous*; implied, constructive 523 *tacit*; nonsensical 497 *absurd*; without meaning 515 *meaningless*.

Vb. *mean*, mean something; get across 524 *communicate*; typify, symbolize 547 *indicate*; signify, denote, connote, stand for 551 *represent*; import, purport, intend; point to, add up to, boil down to, spell, involve 523 *imply*; convey, express 532 *affirm*; bespeak, tell of, breathe of, speak volumes 466 *evidence*; mean to say, be getting at, be driving at, have in mind; allude to, refer to; be synonymous, co-refer 13 *be identical*; tautologize 106 *repeat*; infer, understand by 516 *understand*.

Adv. *significantly*, meaningly, meaningfully, with meaning, to the effect that; in a sense, in the sense that *or* of; literally, verbally, word for word.

515. Lack of meaning – N. *Lack of meaning*, meaninglessness, unmeaningness, absence of meaning; no context, no bearing 10 *irrelevance*; nonsignificance 639 *un-*

213

importance; amphigory 497 *absurdity*; inanity, triteness; truism, platitude, cliché 496 *maxim*; mere words, verbalism; illogicality 477 *sophistry*; invalidity 161 *ineffectuality*; illegibility, scribble 586 *script*; daub 552 *misrepresentation*; jargon, rigmarole, gobbledygook, galimatias; abracadabra, hocus-pocus, mumbo jumbo; gibberish, gabble, double Dutch, Greek 517 *unintelligibility*; incoherence 503 *frenzy*; double-talk, mystification 530 *enigma*; insincerity 925 *flattery*.

silly talk, nonsense 497 *absurdity*; stuff, stuff and nonsense, balderdash, rubbish, rhubarb, rot, tommyrot; drivel, twaddle, bosh, tosh, tripe, piffle, bilge, bull.

empty talk, idle speeches, sweet nothings, wind, gas, hot air, vapouring, verbiage 570 *diffuseness*; rant, bombast, fustian, rodomontade 877 *boasting*; blether, blah, flapdoodle, flimflam; guff, pijaw, eyewash, claptrap, poppycock 543 *fable*; humbug 541 *falsehood*; moonshine, malarkey, hokum, bunkum, bunk, boloney, hooey; flannel, flummery, blarney 925 *flattery*; patter, sales p., spiel; prattle, babble, gabble, jabber, yak 581 *chatter*.

Adj. *meaningless*, unmeaning; Pickwickian, nonsensical 497 *absurd*; senseless, null; unexpressive, unidiomatic 25 *unapt*; inane, empty, trivial, trite 639 *unimportant*; fatuous, piffling, blithering; trashy, rubbishy; waffling, windy, ranting 546 *exaggerated*; incoherent, raving, gibbering 503 *frenzied*.

unmeant, unintentional, involuntary, unintended, unimplied, unalluded to; mistranslated 521 *misinterpreted*; insincere 925 *flattering*.

Vb. *mean nothing*, have no meaning, make no sense; scribble, scratch, daub, strum; babble, prattle, prate, gabble, gibber, jabber 581 *be loquacious*; talk gibberish 517 *be unintelligible*; rant 546 *exaggerate*; gush, drivel, drool, blether, waffle, twaddle; vapour, gas 499 *be foolish*; blarney 925 *flatter*; make nonsense of 521 *misinterpret*; be Greek to, pass over one's head 474 *puzzle*.

516. Intelligibility – N. *intelligibility*, comprehensibility, readability, legibility; clearness, clarity, coherence, lucidity 567 *perspicuity*; precision, unambiguity 473 *certainty*; simplicity, straightforwardness, plain speaking; plain English, mother tongue 573 *plainness*; paraphrase, simplification 701 *facility*; popularization, haute vulgarization 520 *interpretation*.

Adj. *intelligible*, understandable, penetrable, comprehensible, coherent, audible; recognizable 490 *known*; unambiguous, unequivocal 514 *meaningful*; explicit, unblurred, distinct, clear-cut, precise, definite; well-spoken, articulate; plain-spoken 573 *plain*; straightforward, simple 701 *easy*; obvious, self-explanatory, easy to grasp; explained, simplified, popularized; clear, limpid 422 *transparent*; pellucid, lucid 567 *perspicuous*; readable, legible, decipherable 443 *visible*.

expressive, telling, striking, vivid, graphic, highly coloured 590 *descriptive*; emphatic, forceful; illustrative 520 *interpretive*.

Vb. *be intelligible*, etc. adj.; make sense, add up 475 *be reasonable*; speak for itself 466 *evidence*; have no secrets 443 *be visible*; be understood, come over, get across; clarify, elucidate 520 *interpret*; simplify, popularize 701 *facilitate*; labour the obvious 532 *emphasize*.

understand, comprehend, apprehend 490 *know*; master 536 *learn*; have, hold, retain 505 *remember*; see through, penetrate, fathom, get to the bottom of 484 *detect*; discern, distinguish 438 *see*; grasp, get hold of, seize, be on to, cotton on to, dig; get the hang of, take in, register; be with one, follow, savvy; collect, get, catch on, twig; catch one's drift, get the idea, get the picture; realize, get wise to, tumble to, rumble; have one's eyes opened, see it all; be undeceived 830 *regret*.

Adv. *intelligibly*, plainly, simply, in words of one syllable; in plain English, for the layman.

517. Unintelligibility – N. *unintelligibility*, incomprehensibility, inconceivability; inexplicability, impenetrability; perplexity 474 *uncertainty*; obscurity 568 *imperspicuity*; ambiguity 518 *equivocalness*; incoherence 515 *lack of meaning*; double Dutch, gibberish; jargon, foreign tongue 560 *dialect, slang*; stammering 580 *speech defect*; undecipherability, illegibility, unreadability; scribble, scrawl 586 *lettering*; inaudibility 401 *faintness*; Greek, sealed book 530 *secret*; paradox, pons asinorum, crux, riddle 530 *enigma*.

Adj. *unintelligible*, incomprehensible, inapprehensible, inconceivable, inexplicable, unaccountable; undiscoverable 491 *unknown*; unfathomable, inscrutable, impenetrable; blank, poker-faced, expressionless 820 *impassive*; inaudible 401 *muted*; unreadable, illegible, undecipherable, crabbed; undiscernible 444 *invisible*; arcane 523 *occult*; cryptic, obscure, esoteric; Sphinx-like, enigmatic, oracular.

puzzling, hard to understand, complex 700 *difficult*; beyond one, over one's head, recondite, abstruse, elusive; enigmatic, mysterious 523 *occult*; half-understood, nebulous, hazy, obscure 419 *shadowy*; clear as mud 568 *unclear*; ambiguous, oracular 518 *equivocal*; paradoxical 508 *unexpected*; fishy, strange, odd 84 *abnormal*; unexplained, insoluble, unsolvable; unresolved 474 *uncertain*.

inexpressible, unspeakable, untranslatable; unpronounceable, unutterable, ineffable; incommunicable, indefinable; profound, deep; mystic, mystical, transcendental.

puzzled, mystified, wondering, out of one's depth, flummoxed, stumped, baffled, perplexed, nonplussed 474 *doubting*.

Vb. *be unintelligible*, etc. adj.; be hard, be difficult, make one's head ache *or* swim 474 *puzzle*; talk in riddles 518 *be equivocal*; talk double Dutch *or* gibberish 515 *mean nothing*; speak badly, write badly, scribble, scrawl; keep one guessing 486 *cause doubt*; perplex, confuse 63 *bedevil*; require explanation, have no answer; go over one's head, be beyond one's reach; escape one; pass comprehension.

not understand, not get it; not make out,

not know what to make of, make nothing of, make neither head nor tail of; puzzle over, be floored by, be stumped by, give up; be out of one's depth 491 *not know*; wonder 474 *be uncertain*; be at cross-purposes 495 *blunder*; get one wrong 481 *misjudge*; not register 456 *be inattentive*.

518. Equivocalness – N. *equivocalness*, two voices 14 *contrariety*; ambiguity, ambivalence 517 *unintelligibility*; vagueness 474 *uncertainty*; double meaning, amphibology 514 *connotation*; Newspeak, doubletalk, weasel word 515 *lack of meaning*; conundrum, riddle, oracle 530 *enigma*; mental reservation 525 *concealment*; prevarication, balancing act; equivocation, white lie 543 *untruth*; quibble 477 *sophistry*; word-play, play on words, paronomasia 574 *ornament*; pun, equivoque, double entendre 839 *witticism*; faux ami, confusible; anagram, acrostic; synonymy, homonymy, polysemy; homonym, homophone 18 *analogue*.

Adj. *equivocal*, ambiguous, ambivalent; double-tongued, two-edged; left-handed, back-h.; equivocating, prevaricating, facing both ways; vague, evasive, oracular; amphibolous, homonymous.

Vb. *be equivocal*, cut both ways; play on words, pun; speak with two voices 14 *be contrary*; fudge, waffle, stall, not give a straight answer 620 *avoid*; equivocate, prevaricate, weasel 541 *dissemble*.

519. Metaphor: figure of speech – N. *metaphor*, mixed m.; transference; allusion, application; misapplication, catachresis; extended metaphor, allegory; mystical interpretation, anagoge 520 *interpretation*; fable, parable 534 *teaching*; objective correlative, symbol; symbolism, figurativeness, imagery 513 *imagination*; image, simile, likeness 462 *comparison*; personification, prosopopeia.

trope, figure of speech, flourish; irony 851 *satire*; rhetorical figure 574 *ornament*; litotes, hyperbole, oxymoron, euphuism, euphemism, dysphemism 850 *affectation*; antithesis 462 *comparison*; metathesis 221 *inversion*; word-play 518 *equivocalness*.

Adj. *figurative*, metaphorical, tropical; catachrestic; allusive, symbolic, allegorical, anagogic; parabolical; comparative 462 *compared*; euphuistic, euphemistic 850 *affected*; hyperbolic 546 *exaggerated*; satirical, ironical 851 *derisive*; flowery, florid 574 *ornate*; oratorical 574 *rhetorical*.

Adv. *metaphorically*, figuratively, so to speak, in a manner of speaking.

520. Interpretation – N. *interpretation*, definition, explanation, explication, exposition, exegesis; elucidation, clarification, illumination; illustration 83 *example*; resolution, solution 460 *answer*; decipherment, decoding 484 *discovery*; application, twist, turn; construction, reading 514 *meaning*; subaudition 514 *connotation*; euhemerism, demythologization; allegorization 519 *metaphor*; accepted reading, vulgate; criticism, higher c., literary c., appreciation, structuralism 557 *literature*; critique, review 480 *estimate*; insight 819 *moral sensibility*.

commentary, comment; gloss, footnote; inscription, caption, legend 563 *phrase*; motto, moral 693 *precept*; annotation, notes, marginalia; exposition 591 *dissertation*; apparatus criticus, critical edition; glossary, lexicon 559 *dictionary*.

translation, version, rendering; faithful translation, literal t.; key, crib; paraphrase, metaphrase; précis 592 *compendium*; adaptation 516 *intelligibility*; transliteration, decoding, decipherment; lip-reading.

hermeneutics, exegetics; epigraphy, palaeography 557 *linguistics*; cryptanalysis, cryptology; diagnostics, symptomatology; semiology, semiotics; graphology.

interpreter, clarifier, explainer, exponent, expounder, expositor, exegete 537 *teacher*, 973 *religious teacher*; rationalizer, euhemerist, demythologizer; editor 528 *publicizer*; textual critic, emendator; commentator, annotator; critic, reviewer, structuralist, Leavisite 480 *estimator*; medium 984 *spiritualism*; polyglot 557 *linguist*; translator, paraphraser; cryptographer, encoder; code-breaker; decoder; cryptanalyst; lip-reader; epigraphist,

palaeographer 125 *antiquarian*; mouthpiece, representative 754 *delegate*; public relations officer 524 *informant*; executant, performer 413 *musician*; player 594 *actor*; poet, painter 556 *artist*.

guide, precedent 83 *example*; lamp, light, star, guiding s.; dragoman, courier, cicerone 690 *director*; demonstrator 522 *exhibitor*.

Adj. *interpretive*, interpretative, constructive; explanatory, explicatory, explicative, elucidatory, expositive, expository; exegetical, hermeneutic; defining, definitive; illuminating, illustrative, exemplary; glossarial, annotative, scholiastic, editorial; lip-reading, translational, paraphrastic, metaphrastic; mediumistic; literal, word-for-word 494 *accurate*; faithful 551 *representing*; free 495 *inexact*.

Vb. *interpret*, define, clarify; explain, unfold, expound, elucidate 516 *be intelligible*; illustrate 83 *exemplify*; demonstrate 522 *show*; comment on, edit, annotate, gloss; read, construe, make sense of 516 *understand*; illuminate, throw light on 524 *inform*; account for 475 *reason*; popularize, simplify 701 *facilitate*.

translate, render, do into, English; rehash, reword, rephrase, paraphrase; adapt; transliterate, transcribe; cipher, encode; lip-read.

decipher, crack the cipher, decode; read, spell out, puzzle o., make o.; piece together, find the key to; solve, resolve, unravel, disentangle, read between the lines.

521. Misinterpretation – N. *misinterpretation*, misunderstanding, misconstruction, misapprehension, wrong end of the stick; cross-purposes, crossed lines 495 *mistake*; wrong explanation 535 *misteaching*; mistranslation, false construction; perversion 246 *distortion*; false reading; false colouring; falsification 552 *misrepresentation*; depreciation 483 *underestimation*; parody, travesty 851 *ridicule*; misapplication 565 *solecism*.

Adj. *misinterpreted*, misconceived 515 *unmeant*; misconstrued 495 *mistaken*; misread, misquoted.

Vb. *misinterpret*, misunderstand, misapprehend 481 *misjudge*; get hold of the wrong end of the stick 495 *blunder*; misread, misspell 495 *err*; set in a false light 535 *misteach*; mistranslate, misconstrue, put a false sense *or* construction on; give a twist, pervert, strain, wrest, twist the words 246 *distort*; weasel, play on words 518 *be equivocal*; read into; leave out, suppress; misrepeat, misquote; falsify, garble 552 *misrepresent*; travesty, parody, caricature 851 *ridicule*.

Section 2:
Modes of communication

522. Manifestation – N. *manifestation*, revelation, exposure 526 *disclosure*; expression 532 *affirmation*; proof 466 *evidence*; presentation 551 *representation*; symbolization 547 *indication*; symptom 511 *omen*; prerelease, preview 438 *view*; showing, demonstration, exhibition, display; proclamation, publication; openness, flagrancy 528 *publicity*; candour, plain speaking 573 *plainness*; conspicuousness 443 *visibility*; apparition 445 *appearance*; séance 984 *occultism*; Shekinah, glory 965 *theophany*.

exhibit, specimen 83 *example, 466 *evidence*; model, mock-up 551 *image*; showpiece, collector's piece; display, show, parade 445 *spectacle*; scene 438 *view*; showplace, showroom, showcase 528 *advertisement*; sign 547 *label*; museum 632 *collection*; retrospective, exhibition, exposition; shop window 796 *market*.

exhibitor, publicist 528 *publicizer*; displayer, demonstrator; showman; impresario 594 *stage manager*; exhibitionist 873 *vain person*; model.

Adj. *manifest*, apparent 445 *appearing*; plain, clear 80 *definite*; explained 516 *intelligible*; unconcealed, showing 443 *visible*; conspicuous, noticeable, prominent, pronounced, signal, marked, striking, in relief, in the foreground, in the limelight 443 *obvious*; open, patent, evident; gross, crass, palpable; self-evident, written all over one, for all to see, unmistakable 473

certain; eye-catching 875 *showy*; glaring, flagrant.

undisguised, overt, explicit 532 *affirmative*; in the open, public; exoteric; unreserved, open, candid, off the record 540 *veracious*; frank, straightforward, outspoken, blunt, no-nonsense 573 *plain*; bold, daring 711 *defiant*; brazen, shameless, barefaced; bare, naked 229 *uncovered*; flaunting, unconcealed.

Vb. *manifest*, reveal 526 *disclose*; evince 466 *evidence*; unearth 484 *discover*; explain 520 *interpret*; expose, lay bare 229 *uncover*; lay open 263 *open*; elicit 304 *extract*; incarnate, personify; typify, symbolize 547 *indicate*; throw light on 420 *illuminate*; highlight, spotlight 532 *emphasize*; express, formulate 532 *affirm*; bring up, mention; bring to the fore 638 *make important*; produce, proclaim, publicize 528 *publish*.

show, exhibit, display; set out, expose to view, dangle; wave, flourish 317 *brandish*; sport 228 *wear*; flaunt, parade 875 *be ostentatious*; present 551 *represent*; put on, stage 594 *dramatize*; televise, screen; put on show, hang (a picture); show off, model (garments); put through his *or* her paces; demonstrate 534 *teach*; point out 547 *indicate*; confront, bring face to face; hold up the mirror to 20 *imitate*; show up, expose 526 *disclose*.

Adv. *manifestly*, openly, publicly, for all to see; externally, on the face of it; in full view, in broad daylight.

523. Latency – N. *latency*, no signs of 525 *concealment*; treachery 930 *perfidy*; dormancy, potentiality 469 *possibility*; esotericism, mysticism 984 *occultism*; hidden meaning 517 *unintelligibility*; symbolism, allegory 519 *metaphor*; implication, adumbration; mystery 530 *secret*; shadowiness 419 *dimness*; imperceptibility 444 *invisibility*; more than meets the eye; deceptive appearance, hidden depths; iron hand in a velvet glove; Red under the bed, snake in the grass, mole 663 *pitfall*; hidden hand, wirepuller, strings, friends in high places, éminence grise 178 *influence*; old-boy network, Freemasonry;

undercurrent; unsoundness, something rotten; innuendo, insinuation, overtone 524 *hint*; sealed lips 582 *taciturnity*; undertone, aside 401 *faintness*; clandestineness, secret society 623 *plot*; ambushment 527 *ambush*; code, invisible writing.

Adj. *latent*, lurking, skulking 525 *concealed*; dormant 679 *inactive*; in abeyance; potential, undeveloped 469 *possible*; unguessed, unsuspected 491 *unknown*; submerged, below the surface 211 *deep*; in the background, behind the scenes, backroom, undercover 421 *screened*; unseen, undetected 444 *invisible*; obscure 418 *dark*; arcane, impenetrable 517 *unintelligible*; tucked away, sequestered 883 *secluded*; undiscovered, unexplored.

tacit, unsaid, unspoken, unexpressed; unavowed, sneaking; unvoiced, unmentioned; undivulged, unprofessed, undeclared; unwritten, unpublished; understood, implied, inferred, implicit, between the lines; implicative, suggestive; inferential, allusive.

occult, mysterious, mystic; symbolic, allegorical 519 *figurative*; cryptic, esoteric 984 *cabbalistic*; veiled, muffled, covert; indirect 220 *oblique*; clandestine, secret, kept quiet; insidious, treacherous 930 *perfidious*; underhand 525 *stealthy*; undiscovered, hush-hush, top-secret; off the record; coded, cryptographic.

Vb. *lurk*, burrow, hide, be a stowaway; lie in ambush, lie low; lie doggo 266 *be quiescent*; avoid notice, escape observation; laugh in one's sleeve 541 *dissemble*; creep, slink 525 *be stealthy*; pull the strings, be at the bottom of 156 *cause*; smoke, smoulder 175 *be inert*.

imply, insinuate, whisper, murmur 524 *hint*; understand, infer, allude; symbolize, connote, carry a suggestion, spell 514 *mean*.

524. Information – N. *information*, communication of knowledge, transmission, dissemination, diffusion; information technology; computerized information, data base, viewdata 86 *data processing*; tradition, hearsay; enlightenment, briefing 534 *teaching*; intercommunica-

tion, communication; mass media 528 *the press*, 531 *broadcasting*; narration 590 *narrative*; notification, announcement, intimation, warning, advice, notice, mention (see *hint*); advertisement 528 *publicity*; common knowledge, general information, gen, info; background, facts, the goods, documentary 494 *truth*; material, literature 589 *reading matter*; inside information, dope, lowdown, confidence 530 *secret*; scoop; acquaintance 490 *knowledge*; file, dossier 548 *record*; word, report, intelligence 529 *news*; communicativeness 581 *loquacity*; unauthorized communication, leak 526 *disclosure*.

report, review 459 *inquiry*; paper, Green Paper, White P., Black P.; account, eyewitness a. 590 *narrative*; statement, return 86 *statistics*; specification 480 *estimate*; progress report, confidential r.; bulletin, communiqué 529 *news*; representation, case; letters, dispatches 588 *correspondence*.

hint, whisper, aside; broad hint, wink, nudge 547 *gesture*; cue 505 *reminder*; suggestion, lead; caution 664 *warning*; tip, tip-off; word in the ear 691 *advice*; insinuation, innuendo 926 *calumny*; clue 520 *interpretation*; glimpse, inkling 419 *glimmer*; suspicion, inference, guess 512 *conjecture*; wheeze, dodge, wrinkle 623 *contrivance*.

informant, teller 590 *narrator*; spokesperson 579 *speaker*; mouthpiece 754 *delegate*; announcer 531 *broadcaster*; advertiser 528 *publicizer*; herald 529 *messenger*; testifier 466 *witness*; authority, source; quarter, channel, circle, grapevine; go-between, contact 231 *intermediary*; information centre; news agency 528 *the press*; correspondent, reporter 529 *news reporter*; tipper, tipster; bigmouth, blabbermouth; little bird.

informer 928 *accuser*; spy, snoop 459 *detective*; inside agent, mole; stool pigeon, nark; snitcher, sneak, blabber, squealer, squeaker, grass, supergrass; eavesdropper, telltale, talebearer, gossip 581 *chatterer*.

guidebook, Baedeker; travelogue,

topography; handbook, manual, vade mecum; timetable, Bradshaw; roadbook, itinerary 551 *map*; gazetteer 589 *reference book*; telephone directory, phone book; catalogue 87 *directory*; courier 520 *guide*.

Adj. *informative*, communicative, newsy, chatty, gossipy; informatory, informational, instructive, instructional, documentary 534 *educational*; expository 520 *interpretive*; annunciatory 528 *publishing*; advisory 691 *advising*; monitory 664 *cautionary*; explicit 80 *definite*; indiscreet 581 *loquacious*.

informed, well-i., kept i.; posted, primed, briefed, instructed 490 *knowing*; told, au courant, genned-up, clued-up, wised-up; in the know, in on, in the picture; brought up to date.

Vb. *inform*, certify, advise; intimate, impart, convey; apprise, acquaint; give to understand; brief, instruct 534 *teach*; put one in the picture, fill one in on; enlighten 534 *educate*; point out 547 *indicate*; confide; put one right, correct, disabuse, undeceive, disillusion; state, name 80 *specify*; mention, refer to 579 *speak*; gossip, spread rumours; blurt out, talk 581 *be loquacious*; reveal 526 *disclose*; tell, blab, split, grass, snitch, peach, squeal, blow the gaff 526 *confess*; rat, turn State's evidence 603 *tergiversate*; blow the whistle on, sell one down the river; tell tales, tell on, inform against, shop, denounce 928 *accuse*.

communicate, transmit, pass on; report, cover; keep posted; get through, get across, put it over; contact, get in touch; convey, bring word, write 588 *correspond*; flash, beam, speak 547 *signal*; wire, telegraph, telex, radio; telephone, phone, call, ring; broadcast, telecast, televise; announce, notify 528 *advertise*; give out, publicize 528 *publish*; retail, recount, narrate 590 *describe*; commune 584 *converse*; swap news, exchange information.

hint, suggest, put an idea in one's head; prompt 505 *remind*; caution 664 *warn*; tip off 691 *advise*; wink, tip the wink; nudge 547 *gesticulate*; insinuate, breathe, whisper, mention in passing, let fall, imply, allude, leave one to gather, intimate.

525. Concealment – N. *concealment*, hiding 523 *latency*; cache 527 *hiding-place*; fig leaf 226 *covering*; disguise, camouflage 542 *deception*; masquerade, anonymity, incognito 562 *no name*; smoke screen 421 *screen*; reticence, reserve 582 *taciturnity*; mental reservation, arrière pensée, ulterior motive; evasiveness 518 *equivocalness*; mystification, obfuscation; subterfuge 542 *trickery*; suppression, D notice; cover-up 543 *untruth*; deceitfulness 541 *duplicity*.

secrecy 399 *silence*; mystery 530 *secret*; secret society, clandestineness, secretiveness, furtiveness, stealthiness, low profile; conspiracy 623 *plot*; cipher, code 517 *unintelligibility*.

Adj. *concealed*, crypto-, hidden; hiding, lost; ensconced, in ambush 523 *latent*; incommunicado 747 *imprisoned*; mysterious, recondite 517 *unintelligible*; cryptic 523 *occult*; private 883 *secluded*; privy, confidential, off the record, unattributable; secret, top secret, restricted, hush-hush, inviolable; inviolate, unrevealed, ex-directory; undisclosed, untold; unsigned 562 *anonymous*; covert, behind the scenes; covered 364 *buried*; hooded, veiled 421 *screened*; stifled, suppressed, clandestine, undercover, underground.

stealthy, silent, furtive, sneaking; catlike, on tiptoe; prowling, skulking, lurking; clandestine, hugger-mugger, conspiratorial, cloak-and-dagger; hole-and-corner, backdoor, underhand, surreptitious 930 *dishonest*.

reticent, reserved, withdrawn; noncommittal, uncommunicative, cagey, evasive; silent 582 *taciturn*; tight-lipped, pokerfaced; close, secretive, buttoned-up, clamlike.

Vb. *conceal*, hide, hide away, secrete, ensconce, confine; keep in purdah 883 *seclude*; stow away, lock up, bottle up 632 *store*; bury 364 *inter*; sweep under the carpet, cover up, whitewash, paper over the cracks 226 *cover*; gloss over 226 *overlay*; blot out 550 *obliterate*; slur over, not mention 458 *disregard*; smother, stifle 165 *suppress*; veil, muffle, mask, disguise, camouflage; shroud 421 *screen*; shade, obscure, obfuscate 419 *bedim*; masquerade 541 *dissemble*; encode, use a cipher.

keep secret, keep it dark, keep under wraps, keep under one's hat; look blank, keep a straight face; keep one's mouth shut 582 *be taciturn*; be discreet, make no comment; reserve, withhold; hush up, cover up, suppress; keep in the dark 542 *deceive*.

be stealthy, etc. adj.; conspire 623 *plot*; snoop, sneak, slink, creep; glide, steal, tiptoe; prowl, skulk, loiter; assume a disguise 541 *dissemble*; lie doggo 523 *lurk*; dodge 620 *avoid*; cover one's tracks, go to earth 446 *disappear*; lay an ambush 527 *ambush*.

Adv. *secretly*, hugger-mugger; confidentially, sotto voce, between ourselves; aside, in petto; in one's sleeve; sub rosa, privately, in camera, behind closed doors, anonymously, incognito, with nobody any the wiser.

stealthily, furtively, like a thief in the night; by the back door, on the sly, on the quiet, on the QT.

526. Disclosure – N. *disclosure*, revealment, revelation; daylight; discovery; disillusionment 509 *disappointment*; denouement 154 *event*; lid off, exposé, divulgence 528 *publication*; exposure 522 *manifestation*; explanations, showdown; leak, indiscretion 524 *hint*; betrayal, giveaway; tell-tale sign, blush; acknowledgement, admission, avowal, confession; clean breast, cards on the table 494 *truth*.

Adj. *disclosing*, revelatory; revealing 422 *transparent*; expository 520 *interpretive*; divulging 528 *publishing*; communicative 524 *informative*; leaky, indiscreet 581 *loquacious*; tell-tale, indicative 547 *indicating*; tale-bearing, betraying; confessional.

Vb. *disclose*, reveal, expose 522 *manifest*; bare, lay b. 229 *doff*; unfold, unroll, unpack, unwrap 229 *uncover*; unveil, lift the veil; unseal, unclose 263 *open*; open up 484 *discover*; catch out 484 *detect*; give away, betray, blow one's cover; uncloak, unmask, tear off the mask; give oneself

away 495 *blunder*; declare oneself, drop the mask; disabuse, correct, undeceive, disillusion, open one's eyes 524 *inform*; take the lid off.

divulge, declare, express, give vent to 579 *speak*; ventilate, air, canvass, publicize 528 *publish*; let on, blurt out, blow the gaff, talk out of turn, spill the beans, let the cat out of the bag, give the show *or* the game away; talk, let out, leak 524 *communicate*; let drop 524 *hint*; come out with 573 *speak plainly*; get it off one's chest, unbosom oneself, unburden o.; confide, let one into the secret, open one's mind *or* heart to, bare one's soul to; declare one's intentions, show one's hand, put one's cards on the table; report, tell, name names 928 *accuse*; split, peach 524 *inform*; rat 603 *tergiversate*.

confess, admit, avow, acknowledge; concede, grant, allow 488 *assent*; own up, cough up; plead guilty; talk, sing, come out with, come clean 540 *be truthful*; make a clean breast of it 939 *be penitent*; turn Queen's evidence 603 *tergiversate*.

be disclosed, come out, come to light 445 *appear*; show its true colours, stand revealed; transpire, become known; leak out 298 *emerge*; show 443 *be visible*; give oneself away, there speaks . . .

527. Hiding. Disguise – N. *hiding-place*, hide, hideout, hideaway, hole, hidey-h., priesthole 662 *refuge*; lair, den 192 *retreat*; cache; oubliette 194 *cellar*; closet, safe, safe deposit 632 *storage*; recess, nook, cranny, niche; secret passage; cover, underground 662 *shelter*; backroom, inmost recesses 224 *interiority*.

ambush, ambuscade, ambushment 525 *concealment*; spider's web 542 *trap*; catch 663 *pitfall*; stalking horse. Trojan h., decoy 545 *impostor*; agent provocateur 663 *troublemaker*.

disguise, blind, masquerade 542 *deception*; camouflage, protective colouring 20 *mimicry*; dummy 542 *sham*; veneer 226 *covering*; mask, visor, veil 228 *cloak*; fancy dress; smoke screen, cover 421 *screen*.

hider, lurker, skulker, stowaway;

dodger 620 *avoider*; masker, masquerader; wolf in sheep's clothing 545 *impostor*.

Vb. *ambush*, waylay 523 *lurk*; set a trap for 542 *ensnare*; assume a disguise, wear a mask.

528. Publication – N. *publication*, dissemination, divulgation 526 *disclosure*; promulgation, proclamation; edict 737 *decree*; call-up, summons; cry, rallying c. 547 *call*; beat of drum, flourish of trumpets 400 *loudness*; press conference, press release; advance publicity; notification, bulletin; announcement, pronouncement, manifesto, programme, platform; the media, mass m.; publishing, book trade 589 *book*; broadcasting 531 *telecommunication*; broadcast, telecast, newscast 529 *news*; kite-flying 529 *rumour*; circulation, circular, encyclical.

publicity, limelight, spotlight, public eye; common knowledge 490 *knowledge*; ventilation, canvassing; open secret 522 *manifestation*; notoriety, fame 866 *famousness*; currency, circulation; readership, audience; viewing figures, listening f.; public relations, PR, propaganda; display, showmanship, window dressing 875 *ostentation*; sensationalism, ballyhoo 546 *exaggeration*; publicization, advertising, skywriting; public address system, tannoy 415 *hearing aid*; journalism, reporting, coverage, report, write-up (**see** *the press*); investigative journalism 459 *inquiry*; newsreel, newsletter 529 *news*; sounding board, correspondence column, open letter, letters to the editor; editorial 591 *article*; pulpit, platform, hustings, soapbox 539 *rostrum*; printing press 587 *print*; blaze of publicity, letters of gold, letters a foot high.

advertisement, notice, insertion, advert, ad, small a., classified a.; personal column; agony c.; headline, banner h., streamer, spread; puff, blurb, buildup, hype; promotional literature, unsolicited mail, handout, handbill; bill, affiche, poster 522 *exhibit*; billboard, hoarding, placard, sandwich board, notice b.; yellow pages; advertising copy, slogan, jingle; plug, trailer, commercial 531

broadcasting; hard sell, soft s., subliminal advertising.

the press, fourth estate, Fleet Street, the papers; newspaper, newssheet, sheet, paper, rag, tabloid, comic; serious press, underground p., gutter p., yellow p.; organ, journal, daily, quality d., broadsheet, heavy; issue, edition, extra; magazine section, feuilleton, supplement, colour s., trade s.; leaflet, pamphlet, brochure, newsletter.

journal, review, magazine, glossy m., pulp m.; part-work, periodical, monthly, quarterly, annual; gazette, trade journal, house magazine 589 *reading matter*.

publicizer, notifier, announcer 529 *messenger*; proclaimer, crier, town crier; barker, tout; bill sticker, bill poster, sandwichman; promoter, publicist, press agent, advertising a.; adman, advertiser, hidden persuader; copywriter, blurb writer, commercial artist, public relations officer, PRO; propagandist, pamphleteer 537 *preacher*; printer, publisher 589 *bookperson*; reporter, journalist 529 *news reporter*.

Adj. *published*, in print; in circulation, current; in the news, public 490 *known*; distributed, circularized, disseminated, broadcast; ventilated, well-v.; on the air, on television; multimedia, mixed media; declaratory, notificatory.

well-known, public, celebrated, famous, notorious; crying, flagrant, blatant, glaring, sensational 522 *manifest*.

Vb. *publish*, make public 524 *communicate*; report, cover, write up; reveal 526 *divulge*; highlight, spotlight 532 *emphasize*; radio, broadcast, televise, relay 524 *inform*; spread, circulate, diffuse, distribute, disseminate, circularize; canvass, ventilate, discuss 475 *argue*; pamphleteer, propagate 534 *teach*, 587 *print*; syndicate, serialize, edit, subedit, sub; issue, release, get out, put o., give o., bring to public notice, let it be known; spread a rumour, fly a kite; bruit about, noise abroad; talk about, retail, pass round 581 *be loquacious*; voice 579 *speak*.

proclaim, announce, herald, promulgate, notify; ban, denounce 928 *accuse*;

pronounce, declare, go on record 532
affirm; celebrate, sound, noise, trumpet,
blazon, blaze abroad, cry 400 *be loud*;
declaim, shout from the rooftops 415 *be
heard*; beat the big drum.

advertise, publicize; bill, placard,
poster; tell the world, headline, splash;
spotlight, build up, promote; make much
of, feature; sell, boost, puff, cry up, crack
up, hype up 482 *overrate*; plug 106
repeat.

be published, get into the papers, come
out; hit the headlines, make the front
page; circulate, go the rounds, get about,
spread like wildfire.

529. News – N. *news*, tidings; gospel 973
religion; dispatches, diplomatic bag; intelligence, report, dispatch, word, titbit
524 *information*; bulletin, communiqué,
handout; newspaper report, press notice;
news flash 531 *broadcast*; hot news, latest
n., stop-press n.; sensation, scoop, exclusive; copy, filler; newscast, newsreel 528
publicity; news value.

rumour, unconfirmed report; on dit,
hearsay, gossip, talk 584 *chat*; scandal 926
calumny; whisper, buzz, noise, bruit; false
report, hoax, canard; grapevine, bush
telegraph.

message, word of mouth, word 524 *information*; communication 547 *signal*;
wireless message, cable, wire 531 *telecommunication*; postcard, letters, dispatches
588 *correspondence*, 531 *postal communications*; ring, phone call; errand,
embassy 751 *commission*.

news reporter, newspaperman *or*
-woman, reporter, cub r., journalist, correspondent, legman, stringer 589 *author*;
gentleman *or* lady of the press, pressman
or -woman, press representative 524 *informant*; newsreader 531 *broadcaster*; news-
monger, quidnunc, gossip, talker 584 *interlocutor*; tattler, chatterer; muckraker,
scandalmonger 926 *defamer*; newsagent,
newsvendor, newspaper boy *or* girl.

messenger, forerunner 66 *precursor*;
harbinger 511 *omen*; announcer 528 *publicizer*; ambassador 754 *envoy*; apostle,
emissary; herald, trumpet; process-server

955 *law officer*; go-between 231 *intermediary*.

courier, runner, Queen's Messenger,
express m., dispatch rider; postman *or*
-woman 531 *postal communications*;
errand boy *or* girl, call-boy, bellhop, page;
carrier pigeon 273 *carrier*; Mercury, Ariel.

530. Secret – N. *secret*, mystery, secret
lore, esotericism, arcanum 984 *occultism*;
sealed orders, state secret; confidential
communication, confidence; sphinx, man
or woman of mystery, enigmatic personality, Gioconda smile; Mr *or* Miss X 562
no name; dark horse, unknown quantity;
skeleton in the cupboard; sealed book;
terra incognita 491 *unknown thing*.

enigma, mystery, puzzle, Chinese p.,
tangram; problem, poser, brain-twister,
teaser; knotty point, vexed question, crux
700 *difficulty*; code, hieroglyphics 517 *unintelligibility*; anagram, acrostic, crossword; riddle, riddle-me-ree, conundrum,
rebus; charade, dumb c.; labyrinth, maze
61 *complexity*.

531. Communications – N. *telecommunication*, long-distance c., telephony,
telegraphy, radio *or* wireless t., comsat;
semaphore, morse 547 *signal*; cable, telegram, wire 529 *message*; bush telegraph
529 *rumour*; radar 484 *discovery*; loran,
Decca (tdmk); telex, teleprinter; intercom, walkie-talkie, bleeper; microphone
400 *megaphone*; headset 415 *hearing aid;*
telephone, radio t., videophone; line,
land-l., trunk l., party l., hot l.; telephone
exchange, switchboard; wireless operator, radio ham, telegrapher, telephonist.

postal communications, postal services,
GPO; post, mail, letters 588 *correspondence*; surface mail, sea m., air m.; parcel
post, registered p., recorded delivery, express d.; postcode, postage stamp; pillarbox, postbox, letterbox; post office, sorting o., mailbag; postmaster *or* -mistress,
postman *or* -woman 529 *messenger*;
pigeon post; diplomatic bag, dispatch box.

broadcasting, the media 528 *publicity*;
BBC, Beeb, Auntie; IBA, ITA; independent radio *or* television; commercial r. *or*

t., local r. *or* t., cable r. *or* t., pirate r.; Citizen's Band r., CB; transmitter, booster; aerial, antenna; radio waves, modulation, AM, FM 417 *radiation*; radio station, television channel, network; wireless, radio, steam r., cat's whisker, crystal set; portable, transistor, tranny; television, telly, TV, the box, gogglebox, small screen; videorecorder, videotape 549 *recording instrument*; Teleprompter (tdmk), autocue; teletext 524 *information*; Open University; radio listener 415 *listener*; viewer 441 *spectator*.

broadcast, outside b., telecast, simulcast, transmission, relay, live r. 528 *publication*; recording, repeat, transcription 548 *record*; programme, request p., phone-in, telethon, quiz, chat show 837 *amusement*; news roundup 529 *news*; time signal, pips; talk, feature, documentary 524 *report*; soap opera, sitcom 594 *drama*; commercial 528 *advertisement*.

broadcaster, announcer, commentator, talking head, newsreader, newscaster 524 *informant*; presenter, front man, anchorman, linkman, compère, question master; disc jockey, DJ, deejay; media personality 866 *person of repute*.

532. Affirmation – N. *affirmation*, predication, statement; proposition, subject and predicate; saying, dictum 496 *maxim*; submission, thesis 512 *supposition*; conclusion 480 *judgement*; voice, choice, ballot 605 *vote*; expression, formulation; one's position; declaration, profession; allegation 928 *accusation*; assertion, ipse dixit, say-so; asseveration, averment; admission, avowal 526 *disclosure*; corroboration, confirmation, assurance, avouchment 466 *testimony*; insistence, vehemence, peremptoriness 571 *vigour*; stress, accent on, emphasis, overstatement; reiteration 106 *repetition*; challenge 711 *defiance*; protest 762 *deprecation*; representation 761 *entreaty*; observation, remark, interjection 579 *speech*; comment, criticism 480 *estimate*; dogmatism 473 *positiveness*.

oath, Bible o., oath-taking, swearing, adjuration, deposition, affidavit 466 *testimony*; word of honour, pledge 764 *promise*.

Adj. *affirmative*, affirming, etc. vb.; not negative 473 *positive*; predicative; declaratory, declarative 526 *disclosing*; pronouncing, enunciative 528 *publishing*; committed 764 *promissory*; earnest, meaning 617 *intending*; solemn, sworn, on oath, formal; affirmable, predicable.

assertive, saying, telling; assured, dogmatic 473 *positive*; trenchant, incisive, pointed, decisive, decided 571 *forceful*; distinct 80 *definite*; express, peremptory, categorical, absolute, emphatic, insistent, vehement; flat, broad, round, blunt, strong, outspoken, strongly-worded, straight from the shoulder 573 *plain*; pontifical, ex cathedra 485 *creedal*; provocative 711 *defiant*.

Vb. *affirm*, state, express, formulate, set down; declare, pronounce 528 *proclaim*, 579 *orate*; voice 579 *speak*; remark, comment, observe, say; be bound, dare swear 485 *opine*; vow, protest; assert, predicate; maintain, hold, contend 475 *argue*; make one's point 478 *demonstrate*; advance, urge 512 *propound*; represent, put one's case, submit; claim 761 *request*; allege, asseverate, avouch, aver 466 *testify*; certify, confirm 466 *corroborate*; commit oneself, pledge 764 *promise*; hold out 759 *offer*; profess, avow; admit 526 *confess*; abide by 599 *stand firm*; challenge 711 *defy*; repudiate 533 *negate*; speak up, speak out, make no bones about 573 *speak plainly*; brook no denial, lay down the law, pontificate 473 *dogmatize*; have one's say, have the last word.

swear, take one's oath; attest 466 *corroborate*; outswear 533 *negate*; cross one's heart, kiss the book, swear by all that is holy.

emphasize, stress, lay stress on, accent, accentuate; underline, italicize, dot the i's and cross the t's; raise one's voice, shout, fulminate 400 *be loud*; bang one's fist down, thump the table; be insistent, urge, enforce, insist; drive home, impress on, rub in; dwell on, reassert, labour 106 *repeat*; single out, point up 638 *make important*.

Adv. *affirmatively*, positively, ex cathedra; seriously, joking apart; on oath, on the Bible; in all conscience, upon one's word.

Int. As I stand here! As God is my witness! Cross my heart and hope to die!

533. Negation – N. *negation*, negative, nay; denial 760 *refusal*; disbelief 486 *unbelief*; disagreement 489 *dissent*; rebuttal 460 *rejoinder*; refutation, disproof 479 *confutation*; emphatic denial, contradiction, gainsaying; the lie, démenti; challenge 711 *defiance*; demurrer 468 *qualification*; protest 762 *deprecation*; repudiation, disclaimer, disavowal, disownment, dissociation 607 *rejection*; abnegation, renunciation 621 *relinquishment*; retraction, abjuration 603 *recantation*; noncorroboration, inability to confirm; refusal of consent 757 *prohibition*; cancellation, revocation 752 *abrogation*.

Adj. *negative*, denying, negating, negatory; adversative, contradictory 14 *contrary*; protesting 762 *deprecatory*; abrogative, revocatory; denied, disowned.

Vb. *negate*, negative; deny, gainsay, give the lie to, belie, contradict; issue a démenti; deny the possibility, eat one's hat if; disaffirm, repudiate, disavow, disclaim, disown 607 *reject*; demur, object 468 *qualify*; disagree 489 *dissent*; dissociate oneself 704 *oppose*; controvert, traverse, impugn, question, call in q. 479 *confute*, 486 *disbelieve*; appeal against 762 *deprecate*; stand up to 711 *defy*; thwart 702 *obstruct*; shake one's head, disallow 760 *refuse*, 757 *prohibit*; revoke 752 *abrogate*; abnegate 621 *relinquish*; abjure, forswear 603 *recant*.

Int. never! a thousand times no! nothing of the kind! quite the contrary! far from it! anything but! no such thing!

534. Teaching – N. *teaching*, pedagogy, pedagogics; education, schooling, upbringing; tutelage, tutoring; direction, guidance, instruction, edification; spoonfeeding; chalk and talk; programmed learning; tuition, preparation, coaching, cramming; seminar, teach-in, clinic, workshop, tutorial; initiation, introduction; training, discipline, drill; inculcation, indoctrination; preaching, pulpitry, homiletics; proselytism, propagandism; persuasion, conversion; conditioning, brainwashing; propaganda, agitprop 528 *publicity*.

curriculum, course of study 536 *learning*; core curriculum, common core; propaedeutics, ABC, three R's 68 *beginning*; foundation course; set books, text 589 *textbook*; project, exercise; homework, prep; liberal studies 490 *culture*; correspondence course, evening classes 539 *school*.

lecture, talk, illustrated t., radio t.; reading, prelection, discourse, disquisition; sermon, homily 579 *oration*; lesson, apologue, parable; lecturer 537 *teacher*.

Adj. *educational*, pedagogic, tutorial; scholastic, scholarly, academic; instructional, informational; audiovisual, instructive 524 *informative*; educative, didactic; doctrinal, normative; edifying, moralizing, homiletic; coeducational, comprehensive, all-ability; set, streamed, creamed, mixed-ability; extramural, intramural; extracurricular; cultural, humane; practical, utilitarian; multidisciplinary.

Vb. *educate*, edify; breed, rear, nurse, nurture, bring up, develop, form, mould, shape, lick into shape; tutor, teach, school; ground, coach, cram, prime 669 *prepare*; guide 689 *direct*; instruct 524 *inform*; enlighten, illumine; sharpen one's wits, open one's eyes; knock into one's head, inculcate, indoctrinate, imbue, instil, implant, sow the seeds of; disabuse, unteach; chasten.

teach, give lessons, hold classes; lecture, tutor, preach, harangue, discourse, hold forth; moralize; elucidate, expound 520 *interpret*; pamphleteer, propagandize, proselytize; condition, indoctrinate, brainwash 178 *influence*.

train, coach 669 *prepare*; take in hand, tame 369 *break in*; nurse, foster, cultivate; put through the mill, keep one's nose to the grindstone; drill, exercise, practise, make second nature, familiarize, accustom, groom for 610 *habituate*; show the ropes; house-train, teach how to behave.

535. Misteaching – N. *misteaching*, misinstruction, misguidance, misleading, misdirection; quackery, the blind leading the blind; false intelligence, misinformation 552 *misrepresentation*; mystification, obfuscation; miscorrection 495 *mistake*; obscurantism 491 *ignorance*; propaganda 541 *falsehood*; perversion 246 *distortion*; false logic 477 *sophistry*.

Adj. *misteaching*, misguiding etc. vb.; unedifying, propagandist; obscurantist 491 *ignorant*; mistaught, misled, misdirected 495 *mistaken*.

Vb. *misteach*, miseducate, bring up badly; misinstruct, misinform, misdirect, misguide 495 *mislead*; corrupt 934 *make wicked*; pervert 246 *distort*, 552 *misrepresent*; put on a false scent 542 *deceive*; lie 541 *be false*; leave no wiser, keep in ignorance, unteach; propagandize, brainwash; explain away.

536. Learning – N. *learning*, lore, wide reading, scholarship, attainments 490 *erudition*; acquisition of knowledge, thirst for k. 453 *curiosity*; pupillage, tutelage, apprenticeship, novitiate 669 *preparation*; first steps 68 *beginning*; docility, teachability 694 *aptitude*; self-instruction, self-education, self-improvement; culture, cultivation; late learning, opsimathy; learned person 492 *scholar*.

study, studying; application, studiousness; cramming, grind, mugging up; studies, lessons, class; homework, prep, preparation; revision, refresher course; perusal, reading, close r. 455 *attention*; research, field work 459 *inquiry*.

Adj. *studious*, academic; bookish, well-read, scholarly, erudite, learned, scholastic 490 *knowing*; diligent 678 *industrious*; receptive, teachable 455 *attentive*; self-taught, self-instructed, autodidactic.

Vb. *learn*, pursue one's education, go to school, sit at the feet of, take a course; acquire knowledge 490 *know*; imbibe, drink in; learn one's trade, serve an apprenticeship, article oneself 669 *prepare*

oneself; train, practise 610 *be wont*; get the feel *or* the hang of, master; get by heart 505 *memorize*.

study, apply oneself, burn the midnight oil; do, take up; research into 459 *inquire*; specialize, major in; swot, cram, mug up; get up, bone up on; revise, go over, brush up; read, peruse, pore over, wade through; thumb, browse, dip into; be studious, always have one's nose in a book.

537. Teacher – N. *teacher*, preceptor, mentor 520 *guide*; minister 986 *pastor*; guru 500 *sage*; instructor, educator; tutor, crammer, coach; governor, governess 749 *keeper*; educationist, educationalist, pedagogue; pedant 500 *wiseacre*; dominie, beak, schoolmarm; master *or* mistress, school teacher, supply t., class t.; year tutor, house master *or* mistress; assistant teacher, deputy head, head teacher, head, headmaster *or* -mistress, principal; usher, monitor; prefect, proctor; dean, don, fellow; lecturer, demonstrator 520 *interpreter*; prelector, reader, professor, Regius p.; catechist, catechizer; initiator, mystagogue; consultant 691 *adviser*; staff, faculty, professoriate.

trainer, instructor, coach; choirmaster; disciplinarian; animal trainer, lion-tamer 369 *breeder*.

preacher, lay p. 986 *pastor*; pulpiteer, orator 579 *speaker*; hot gospeller, evangelist; apostle, missionary; seer, prophet 511 *oracle*; propagandist 528 *publicizer*.

538. Learner – N. *learner*, disciple, follower; proselyte, convert, initiate, catechumen; late learner, opsimath; self-taught person, autodidact; empiricist 461 *experimenter*; swotter, bookworm; pupil, scholar, schoolboy *or* -girl; day pupil, boarder; sixth-former; schoolfellow, classmate, fellow student; gifted child, fast learner, high flyer; slow learner, late developer, underachiever; school-leaver; old boy, old girl.

beginner, novice, debutant; new boy *or* girl, tyro, greenhorn, tenderfoot, neophyte; amateur; recruit, raw r., rookie; colt, cadet, trainee, apprentice, articled clerk; probationer, L-driver.

student, collegian, seminarist; undergraduate, undergrad, freshman, fresher, sophomore; alumnus, alumna; commoner, pensioner, foundationer, exhibitioner; graduand, graduate, postgraduate, fellow; mature student; researcher, specialist.

class, form, grade, remove; set, band, stream; age group, tutor g., vertical grouping, house; study group, workshop; colloquium 584 *conference*; seminar, discussion group 534 *teaching*.

539. School – N. *academy*, institute, institution; conservatoire, ballet school, art s.; academy of dramatic art; charm school, finishing school; college, university, varsity, Open University; redbrick university, Oxbridge; college of further *or* higher education; polytechnic, poly; Academy, Lyceum, Stoa; alma mater, groves of academe.

school, nursery s., crèche, playgroup, kindergarten; private school, independent s., public s., state s., free s.; preparatory school, crammer; primary school, middle s., secondary s., high s.; secondary modern s., grammar s., comprehensive s.; sixth form college; boarding school, day s.; special school.

training school, nursery; training ship, training college, technical c., tech; college of commerce, secretarial college; theological college, seminary; law school, medical school, teaching hospital; military college, staff college.

classroom, schoolroom; study; lecture hall, auditorium, amphitheatre; resources area, library; desk, workshop, laboratory, lab, language lab; gymnasium, playing fields; campus.

rostrum, tribune, dais, forum; platform, stage, podium, estrade; hustings, soapbox; chair 534 *lecture*; pulpit, lectern, bema; microphone 531 *broadcasting*; leader page, column 528 *publicity*.

540. Veracity – N. *veracity*, veraciousness, truthfulness; fidelity, verisimilitude, realism, exactitude 494 *accuracy*; openness, frankness, candour 522 *manifestation*; honesty, sincerity 929 *probity*; simplicity, ingenuousness 699 *artlessness*; downrightness, plain speaking 573 *plainness*; baldness, plain words, home truth, unambiguity 494 *truth*; gate of horn.

Adj. *veracious*, truthful 494 *true*; telling the truth, veridical, not lying; as good as one's word 929 *trustworthy*; factual, ungarbled, undistorted, bald, unembroidered, unvarnished, unexaggerated, just 494 *accurate*; full, particular, circumstantial 570 *diffuse*; simple, ingenuous 699 *artless*; bona fide; unaffected, unfeigned 522 *undisguised*; candid, unreserved, forthcoming; blunt, free, downright, forthright, plain-speaking, outspoken, straightforward, straight from the shoulder, honest to goodness, honest to God 573 *plain*; honest, sincere 929 *honourable*; infallible, prophetic 511 *presageful*.

Vb. *be truthful*, tell the truth, tell no lies; stick to the facts 494 *be true*; speak in earnest, mean it; speak one's mind, keep nothing back 522 *show*; come clean 526 *confess*; appear in one's true colours 526 *disclose*; be prophetic 511 *predict*.

541. Falsehood – N. *falsehood*, falseness, falsity; treachery, bad faith 930 *perfidy*; untruthfulness, unveracity, mendacity, deceitfulness, malingering; lying, oathbreaking, perjury 543 *untruth*; fabrication, fiction; faking, forgery, falsification 542 *deception*; disingenuousness, prevarication, equivocation, shuffling, fencing 518 *equivocalness*; suppressio veri, suggestio falsi; whitewashing, cover-up; casuistry 477 *sophistry*; overstatement 546 *exaggeration*; perversion 246 *distortion*; false colouring, misrepresentation 521 *misinterpretation*; meretriciousness 875 *ostentation*; humbug, bunkum 515 *empty talk*; cant, eyewash; soft soap 925 *flattery*; liar 545 *deceiver*.

duplicity, double life, double-dealing 930 *improbity*; guile 542 *trickery*; front, façade, show 875 *ostentation*; pretence, hollow p., bluff, fake, counterfeit, imposture 542 *sham*; hypocrisy, Tartuffery; acting, play-a., simulation, dissimulation, dissembling, insincerity, tongue in cheek, cant; lip service, cupboard love, crocodile tears; pharisaism, false piety; fraud, pious f., legal fiction, diplomatic illness; collusion, nod and a wink; put-up job, frame-up 930 *foul play*; quackery, charlatanism 850 *pretension*; artfulness 698 *cunning*.

Adj. *false*, not true, truthless; imagined, made-up; untruthful, lying, unveracious, mendacious 543 *untrue*; perfidious, treacherous, forsworn, perjured; sneaky, artful 698 *cunning*; disingenuous, dishonest, uncandid, unfair; evasive, shuffling 518 *equivocal*; falsified, garbled; meretricious, embellished, touched up, varnished, painted; overdone 546 *exaggerated*; imitated, fake, phoney, sham, snide, quack, bogus 542 *spurious*; deceptive, fraudulent 542 *deceiving*; fiddled, engineered, rigged, packed; trumped up.

hypocritical, hollow, empty, insincere, diplomatic; put on, feigned; make-believe, acting; two-faced, double-dealing, designing, Machiavellian 930 *perfidious*; sanctimonious, Tartuffian, Pecksniffian, pharisaic; casuistic, plausible, smooth, smooth-tongued, oily; creepy, goody-goody; mealy-mouthed 850 *affected*; canting, gushing 925 *flattering*.

Vb. *be false*, etc. adj.; perjure oneself, bear false witness; palter, trifle with the truth, fib; lie, tell lies, lie in one's teeth *or* one's throat; strain, stretch the truth 546 *exaggerate*; invent, make up 513 *imagine*; put a false construction on 521 *misinterpret*; garble, doctor, tamper with, falsify 246 *distort*; overstate, understate 552 *misrepresent*; misreport, misinform 535 *misteach*; play false 930 *be dishonest*; run with the hare and hunt with the hounds; break faith 603 *tergiversate*.

dissemble, dissimulate, disguise 525 *conceal*; simulate, counterfeit 20 *imitate*; put on, affect, go through the motions, make a show of 594 *act*; feign, sham, pretend, sail under false colours; malinger 542 *deceive*; lack candour, be less than honest, say one thing and mean another;

keep something back, fail to declare; fudge, prevaricate, beat about the bush, shuffle 518 *be equivocal*.

fake, fabricate, forge, counterfeit 20 *imitate*; get up, trump up, frame; manipulate, fiddle, wangle, rig, pack (a jury); spin, weave, cook up, concoct, hatch, invent 623 *plot*.

542. Deception – N. *deception*, kidding, tongue in cheek; circumvention, outwitting; self-deception 487 *credulity*; fallacy 477 *sophistry*; illusion, delusion 495 *error*; deceptiveness, speciousness 523 *latency*; mirage 440 *visual fallacy*; outward show, meretriciousness; hollowness 4 *insubstantiality*; falseness, deceit, quackery, imposture 541 *falsehood*; deceitfulness, guile 698 *cunning*; hypocrisy 541 *duplicity*; treachery 930 *perfidy*; machination, collusion, hanky-panky, jiggery-pokery 623 *plot*; fraudulence, cheating, diddling; cheat 545 *deceiver*.

trickery, dupery, swindling, skulduggery; sharp practice, chicane, chicanery, pettifoggery; swindle, racket, wangle, fiddle, swiz, sell, fraud, cheat 930 *foul play*; trick, dirty t., confidence trick, fast one 698 *stratagem*; wrinkle 623 *contrivance*; bait, gimmick, diversion, red herring, tub to a whale; hoax, bluff, spoof, leg-pull; practical joke, rag 839 *witticism*; April fooling.

sleight, sleight of hand, legerdemain, prestidigitation, conjuring, hocus-pocus, illusion, ventriloquism; juggling, jugglery; thimblerig, three-card trick; magic 983 *sorcery*.

trap, deathtrap 527 *ambush*; catch 530 *enigma*; plant, frame-up 930 *foul play*; hook, noose, snare, springe, gin, man trap; net, meshes, toils, web; diversion, blind, decoy, bait, lure, sprat to catch a mackerel; flypaper, birdlime; booby trap, mine, tripwire 663 *pitfall*; trapdoor, false bottom 530 *secret*; poisoned apple, Trojan horse.

sham, veneer 541 *duplicity*; lip service, tokenism; pretence 850 *affectation*; paint, whitewash, varnish, gloss; paper tiger; wolf in sheep's clothing 545 *impostor*;

dummy, scarecrow; imitation, simulacrum, facsimile 22 *copy*; trompe-l'oeil, film set 4 *insubstantial thing*; mockery, hollow m.; counterfeit, forgery, fake; masquerade, mummery, borrowed plumes, false colours 525 *concealment*; tinsel, paste.

Adj. *deceiving*, deceitful, lying 543 *untrue*; deceptive 523 *latent*; hallucinatory, illusive, delusive, illusory; specious 445 *appearing*; glib, slick, oily, slippery, smooth; fraudulent, cheating; beguiling 925 *flattering*; insidious 930 *perfidious*; trumped-up 541 *false*; feigned, pretended 541 *hypocritical*; guileful 698 *cunning*; collusive, plotting; painted, whitewashed.

spurious, ungenuine, false, faked, fake; sham, counterfeit 541 *false*; mock, ersatz, bogus, phoney; pseudo-, so-called; artificial, plastic, paste, imitation, synthetic; tinsel, pinchbeck, pasteboard 812 *cheap*.

Vb. *deceive*, delude, dazzle; beguile, sugar the pill, gild the p., give a false impression, belie; let down 509 *disappoint*; pull the wool over one's eyes 439 *blind*; kid, bluff, bamboozle, hoodwink, hoax, spoof, humbug, hornswoggle; lead up the garden path 495 *mislead*; mystify 535 *misteach*; play false, betray, two-time, double-cross 930 *be dishonest*; pull a fast one, take for a ride, be too smart for 698 *be cunning*; cheat, con, swindle, sell, rook, do down; bilk, gyp, fleece, short-change 788 *defraud*; juggle, conjure, force a card, palm off, foist o.; try it on, practise chicanery; gerrymander, tinker with, fiddle, wangle; load the dice, stack the cards; impose upon 541 *dissemble*; counterfeit 541 *fake*.

befool, fool, make a fool of, make one look silly; mock 851 *ridicule*; sport with, trifle w.; take in, have, dupe, victimize, gull, outwit; trick, trap, catch out, take advantage of; kid, string along (**see** *deceive*); cajole, get round 925 *flatter*; let down, play fast and loose with, leave holding the baby 509 *disappoint*; send on a fool's errand *or* on a wild-goose chase 495 *mislead*.

ensnare, snare, trap, entrap, lay a trap for; emmesh, entangle, net; trip up, catch out, hook; bait the hook, lure, decoy 612 *tempt*; lie in wait, waylay 527 *ambush*.

543. Untruth – N. *untruth*, reverse of the truth 541 *falsehood*; less than the truth 483 *underestimation*; overstatement 546 *exaggeration*; lie, downright l., barefaced l.; taradiddle, fib, whopper; terminological inexactitude; broken word 930 *perfidy*; perjury, false oath; pack of lies, tissue of l., frame-up; concoction, fabrication 513 *ideality* (**see** *fable*); false excuse, Bunbury; misstatement 535 *misteaching*; misrepresentation, perversion 246 *distortion*; garbling, falsification 521 *misinterpretation*; lie factory, propaganda machine; gate of ivory.

mental dishonesty, disingenuousness, half-truth, partial t., white lie, mental reservation 468 *qualification*, 525 *concealment*; tongue in cheek, pretence, excuse 614 *pretext*; evasion, subterfuge, doublethink 518 *equivocalness*; self-depreciation, irony, backhanded compliment 850 *affectation*; artificiality, unnaturalness; empty words 541 *duplicity*; Judas kiss 930 *perfidy*.

fable, invention, fiction 513 *ideality*; tall story, fishy s. 546 *exaggeration*; fairy tale, romance, tale, yarn, story, cock-and-bull s. 497 *absurdity*; claptrap, guff 529 *rumour*; old wives' tales; myth, mythology; moonshine, farce, mare's nest; humbug 515 *empty talk*.

Adj. *untrue*, lying, mendacious 541 *false*; trumped-up, cooked, hatched, concocted; mythological, fabulous; unfounded, empty; fictitious, make-believe; artificial, factitious; phoney, bogus 542 *spurious*; overstated 546 *exaggerated*; ironical 851 *derisive*.

Vb. *be untrue*, be wide of the mark; not ring true 472 *be unlikely*; lie, be a liar 541 *be false*, 546 *exaggerate*; make-believe 513 *imagine*; pretend, sham 541 *dissemble*.

544. Dupe – N. *dupe*, fool, April f. 851 *laughingstock*; Simple Simon 501 *ninny*; credulous fool, gobe-mouche, gudgeon; easy prey, sitting duck, soft touch, pushover, cinch; fair game, victim, fall guy, patsy, stooge, mug, sucker; dude, green-horn, innocent; cat's-paw 628 *instrument*; admass.

Adj. *gullible* 487 *credulous*; duped, deceived, taken in, had, done, sold a pup.

545. Deceiver – N. *deceiver*, ragger, leg-puller; practical joker 839 *humorist*; dissembler, shammer, hypocrite, whited sepulchre; false friend, fair-weather f., jilter 603 *turncoat*; two-timer, double-crosser, double agent; traitor 938 *knave*; seducer 952 *libertine*; snake in one's bosom 663 *troublemaker*; conspirator 623 *planner*; counterfeiter, forger, faker 20 *imitator*.

liar, pathological l., mythomaniac; fibber, storyteller, yarn-spinner; fabricator, equivocator; oath-breaker, perjurer.

impostor, shammer, ringer, malingerer; carpetbagger 59 *intruder*; usurper; wolf in sheep's clothing; boaster, bluffer; charlatan, quack, mountebank 850 *affecter*; fake, fraud, humbug; pseud, pseudo, phoney; pretender, masquerader; front man 525 *concealment*.

trickster, hoaxer, hoodwinker; cheat, cheater; sharper, cardsharp, rook, thimblerigger 542 *trickery*; shyster, pettifogger; swindler, shark 789 *defrauder*; slicker, twister, jobber 938 *knave*; confidence trickster, con man; decoy, agent provocateur; fiddler, manipulator, rigger, fixer; wily bird, fox 698 *slyboots*.

conjuror, illusionist, prestidigitator, juggler, ventriloquist; magician 983 *sorcerer*.

546. Exaggeration – N. *exaggeration*, magnification, enlargement 197 *expansion*; extravagance, exaggerated lengths, extremes; excess, inordinacy, exorbitance, overdoing it; histrionics 875 *ostentation*; sensationalism, ballyhoo 528 *publicity*; overstatement, hyperbole, colouring, embroidery 38 *addition*; disproportion 246 *distortion*; caricature, burlesque; ranting 877 *boasting*; rodomontade, grandiloquence 574 *magniloquence*; tall story, traveller's tale 543 *fable*; teratology; flight of fancy, stretch of the imagination 513 *imagination*; storm in a teacup, much ado about nothing 318 *commotion*; extremist, exaggerator; sensationalist, Baron Munchausen.

Adj. *exaggerated*, blown up, out of all proportion 197 *expanded*; embroidered; strained, overstated, inflated; hyperbolical 574 *rhetorical*; overacted, histrionic; melodramatic; bombastic 877 *boastful*; tall, high-flown, steep, outrageous, farfetched 497 *absurd*; vaulting, extravagant, excessive, immoderate 32 *exorbitant*; fulsome, inordinate 637 *superfluous*.

Vb. *exaggerate*, inflate 197 *enlarge*; overelaborate, pile it on 38 *add*; touch up, heighten, embroider 844 *decorate*; lay it on thick *or* with a trowel, depict in glowing terms; overdo, overdraw, overcharge; overpraise, hype up, cry up 482 *overrate*; make much of 925 *flatter*; stretch, strain 246 *distort*; caricature; speak in superlatives, hyperbolize; overact, out-Herod Herod; rant 877 *boast*; go to extremes, go too far 306 *overstep*; spin a yarn 541 *be false*; make mountains out of molehills.

Section 3: Means of communicating ideas

547. Indication – N. *indication*, pointing out, showing 522 *manifestation*; signification, meaning 514 *connotation*; notification 524 *information*; symbolization, symbolism 551 *representation*; symbol, image, type, figure; token, emblem, figurehead (**see** *badge*); symptom, sign 466 *evidence*; blush 526 *disclosure*; nudge, wink 524 *hint* (**see** *gesture*); straw in the wind, sign of the times 511 *omen*; clue, scent, whiff 484 *discovery*; semiotics 520 *hermeneutics*; pointer, finger (**see** *indicator*); guide, index 87 *directory*; key 520 *interpretation*; marker, mark, blaze; stamp, print, impression; scar, stigma, stigmata; prick, tattoo 263 *perforation*; line, score, stroke; note, catchword (**see** *punctuation*); legend, caption 590 *description*; inscription, epitaph; motto, cipher, monogram.

identification, naming 561 *nomenclature*, 77 *classification*; brand, earmark, trademark, imprint (**see** *label*); signature, hand 586 *script*; fingerprint, footprint 548 *trace*; password, watchword, countersign, shibboleth; diagnostic, markings; characteristic, trait 445 *feature*; personal characteristic, trick of speech; mole, birthmark 845 *blemish*.

gesture, gesticulation, sign language, dactylology; deaf-and-dumb language; sign 524 *hint*; pantomime, dumb show, mime; body language, kinesics; demeanour 445 *mien*; motion, move; tic, twitch 318 *spasm*; shrug, nod, wink, grimace 438 *look*; smile, laugh 835 *laughter*; touch, kick, nudge 279 *knock*; hug, squeeze of the hand, handshake; push, shove; pointing, signal, wave; wringing one's hands, tearing one's hair; clenched fist 711 *defiance*; flag-waving 876 *celebration*; clap, clapping 923 *applause*; hiss, boo, catcall 924 *disapprobation*; stuck-out tongue 878 *sauciness*; frown, scowl 893 *sullenness*; pout, moue.

signal 529 *message*; sign 522 *manifestation*; flash, rocket, maroon; signalling, smoke signal, heliograph, semaphore, tick-tack; telegraph, morse 531 *telecommunication*; flashlamp 420 *lamp*; beacon 379 *fire*; red flag, red light 420 *signal light*; alarm 665 *danger signal*; whistle, siren, hooter; bleeper; buzzer, knocker, bell, gong; church bells; time signal, pip 117 *timekeeper*.

indicator, index, pointer, arrow, needle; arm, finger, hand, hour h.; Plimsoll line 465 *gauge*; traffic indicator, winker; cat's-eyes 305 *traffic control*; wind sock 340 *weather*.

signpost, fingerpost, guidepost; milestone, milepost, waymark; buoy 662 *safeguard*; compass 269 *sailing aid*; lodestar, guiding star, pole s.; landmark, seamark; cairn 253 *earthwork*; triangulation point, benchmark; tidemark 236 *limit*.

call, proclamation, hue-and-cry 528 *publication*; shout, hail; invitation; church bell, muezzin's cry 981 *worship*; summons, word 737 *command*; distress call, May-day; bugle-call, reveille, lights out,

last post; call to arms; battle cry, war c., rallying c., slogan, watchword.

badge, token, emblem, symbol, sign, totem (**see** *indication*); insignia (**see** *heraldry*); markings; badge of sovereignty 743 *regalia*; badge of office 743 *badge of rule*; baton, pips 743 *badge of rank*; medal, gong, cross, order, ribbon 729 *decoration*; laurels, bays 729 *trophy*; colours, blue, cap, oar; favour, rosette, love knot.

livery, dress, national d. 228 *uniform*; tartan, tie, old school t., blazer; brassard, epaulette; flash, hackle, cockade, rosette.

heraldry, armory, blazonry; Roll of Arms; armorial bearings, coat of arms, blazon; achievement, hatchment; shield, escutcheon; crest, wreath, mantling; supporters, motto; charge, device, bearing; marshalling, quartering, impaling, dimidiation; differencing; animal charge, griffin, eagle, falcon, martlet; floral charge, Tudor rose, cinquefoil, trefoil; badge, rebus; national device, lion and unicorn, spread eagle, bear, hammer and sickle; heraldic, tincture, gules, azure, vert, sable, purpure; metal, or, argent; fur, ermine, vair; College of Arms, herald, pursuivant.

flag, ensign, white e., blue e.; red ensign, Red Duster; jack; flag of convenience; colours, regimental c.; guidon, standard, vexillum, labarum, banner, gonfalon; banneret, bannerol, banderole, oriflamme; pennon, streamer, pennant, swallowtail, triple tail; pendant, burgee; bunting; Blue Peter, yellow flag; white flag 721 *submission*; eagle, Roman e.; tricolour; Union Jack; Stars and Stripes, Old Glory, Star Spangled Banner; Red Flag; black flag, Jolly Roger, skull and crossbones; hoist, fly, canton; flagpole, flagstaff.

label, mark of identification, tattoo, caste mark (**see** *identification*); ticket, bill, docket, chit, counterfoil, stub, duplicate; tally, counter, chip; tick, check, mark, countermark; sticker; tie-on label, tab, tag; name tape, nameplate, nameboard, signboard, fascia; sign, plate, brass p.; trade sign, trademark, logotype, logo, hallmark, cachet, rebus; earmark, brand, stigma, broad arrow; seal, signet, sigil, stamp, impression; masthead, caption, heading, title, superscription, rubric; imprint, colophon, watermark; bookplate, ex libris; card, visiting c.; passport 756 *permit*; endorsement, signature, mark, cross, initials, paraph; thumbprint 548 *trace*.

punctuation, point, stop, full s., period; comma, colon, semicolon; inverted commas, quotation marks, apostrophe, quotes; exclamation mark, question mark; parentheses, brackets, square b.; crotchet, crook, brace; hyphen, dash, swung d., dot, caret, omission mark, blank; reference mark, asterisk, star; obelus, dagger, squiggle; accent, diaeresis, cedilla, tilde; diacritical mark, sigla, stroke, paragraph, virgule; plus sign, minus s., decimal point; underlining, sublineation; italics 587 *print-type*.

Adj. *indicating*, indicative, indicatory, pointing; significative, connotative, denotative; suggesting 514 *meaningful*; figuring, typical, token, symbolic, emblematic 551 *representing*; tell-tale 526 *disclosing*; symptomatic 466 *evidential*; semiological, semiotic 520 *interpretive*; diagnostic, characteristic 80 *special*; prophetic 511 *presageful*; gesticulatory, pantomimic.

heraldic, emblematic; crested, armorial, blazoned, emblazoned; dexter, sinister; fleury, semé, pommé; rampant, couchant, sejant, passant.

Vb. *indicate*, point, point out, exhibit 522 *show*; mark out, blaze, waymark, signpost; register 548 *record*; name, identify 80 *specify*; index, reference; point the way, guide, direct; signify, connote, suggest 514 *mean*; symbolize, typify, betoken 551 *represent*; highlight 532 *emphasize*; bear the marks of, bear the stamp of 466 *evidence*; intimate, smack of, smell of 524 *hint*; betray 526 *disclose*; prefigure 511 *predict*.

mark, mark off, mark out, flag o., lay o. 236 *limit*; label, ticket, docket, tag, tab; earmark, designate; note, annotate, score, underline; number, letter, page; tick, tick off; nick, scratch, scribe 260 *notch*; chalk, chalk up; blot, stain 649 *make unclean*; scar 842 *make ugly*; punctuate, dot, cross out; blaze, brand, burn in; tattoo 263 *pierce*; stamp, punch, impress, emboss; imprint, overprint; etch 555 *engrave*; emblazon, blazon.

sign, countersign 488 *endorse*; autograph, subscribe, undersign; initial, put one's mark, put one's cross.

gesticulate, pantomime, mime, mimic, suit the action to the word 20 *imitate*; wave one's hands, saw the air; wave, waggle 318 *agitate*; gesture, motion, sign; point, beckon 455 *attract notice*; nod, wink, shrug; jog, nudge, poke, prod, dig in the ribs, clap on the back; leer, ogle 438 *gaze*; smile 835 *laugh*; raise one's eyebrows 924 *disapprove*; wring one's hands, grit one's teeth; gnash one's teeth 891 *be angry*; grimace, pout, scowl, frown; curl one's lip; shuffle, scrape one's feet, paw the ground.

signal, exchange signals 524 *communicate*; flag down, thumb; wave on *or* by *or* through; break the flag, fly the f., strike the f., dip the f., dip, salute; alert, sound the alarm 665 *raise the alarm*; beat the drum, sound the trumpets.

548. Record – N. *record*, documentation; memoir, chronicle, annals, history 590 *narrative*; case history, curriculum vitae 590 *biography*; photograph, portrait 551 *representation*; file, dossier, rogues' gallery; public record, gazette, Hansard; blue book, White Paper; minutes, transactions, acta; notes, marginalia, jottings, cuttings, press c.; memorabilia, memorandum 505 *reminder*; reports, returns, statements 524 *report*; tally, scoresheet, scoreboard; form, document, muniment; voucher, certificate, diploma, charter 466 *credential*, 767 *title deed*; copy 22 *duplicate*; archives, papers, correspondence; book, roll, register, registry, cartulary; notebook, minutebook, logbook, log, diary, journal, commonplace book, scrapbook, album; ledger 808 *account book*; index 87 *list*; card, index c., microcard, microfilm 196 *miniature*; tape, computer t. 86 *data processing*; magnetic tape, pressing 414 *gramophone*; inscription, caption 547 *indication*.

registration, registry, record-keeping; recording, sound r., tape r.; engraving, epigraphy; enrolment, enlistment; booking, reservation; entering, entry, bookkeeping 808 *accounts*; filing, indexing.

monument, memorial 505 *reminder*; mausoleum 364 *tomb*; statue, bust 551 *image*; brass, tablet, slab, stela 364 *obsequies*; column, obelisk; ancient monument, cromlech, dolmen, menhir 125 *antiquity*; cairn 253 *earthwork*.

trace, vestige, relic, remains 41 *leavings*; tracks, footstep, footprint, footmark, hoofmark, pug, tread; spoor, slot; scent, smell, piste; wake, wash, trail, vapour t.; furrow, swath, path; scuffmark, skidmark, fingermark 547 *indication*; fingerprint, dabs 466 *evidence*; mark, tidemark; scar 845 *blemish*.

Adj. *recording*, etc. vb.; clerical; annalistic, record-making; self-recording; recordable; monumental, epigraphic, inscriptional.

recorded, on record, documented; filmed, taped; canned, in the can, on wax; filed, indexed, entered, booked, registered; down, put d.; in writing 586 *written*; in print, in black and white; traceable, vestigial, extant.

Vb. *record*, tape-record, telerecord, tape, videotape; film 551 *photograph*; paint 551 *represent*; document, place on record; docket, file, index, catalogue; inscribe, take down, set down 586 *write*; capture on film, preserve for posterity; note, make a note of; minute, calendar; chronicle 590 *describe*.

register, mark up, tick off, tally, notch up, score; tabulate, table; enrol, enlist 87 *list*; fill in, fill up, enter, post, book 505 *remember*.

549. Recorder – N. *recorder*, registrar, record-keeper, archivist, remembrancer; Master of the Rolls; amanuensis, stenographer, scribe; secretary, receptionist; writer, penpusher; clerk, record clerk, book-keeper 808 *accountant*; draughtsman *or* -woman 556 *artist*; photographer

551 *photography*; sound recordist; filing cabinet, Record Office; Recording Angel.

chronicler, annalist, diarist, historian, historiographer 590 *narrator*; archaeologist 125 *antiquarian*; journalist, gossipwriter 529 *news reporter*; press photographer.

recording instrument, recorder, tape r., videotape r., VTR; record, disc 414 *gramophone*; teleprinter 531 *telecommunication*; cash register, till, checkout; turnstile; seismograph, anemometer, speedometer; flight recorder, black box; stopwatch 117 *timekeeper*; camera, photocopier; pen, pencil 586 *stationery*.

550. Obliteration – N. *obliteration*, wiping out etc. vb.; erasure, effacement; defacement; crossing out, deletion, blue pencil, censorship; cancellation, annulment 752 *abrogation*; burial, oblivion 506 *amnesty*; blot, stain; tabula rasa, clean slate; rubber, eraser 648 *cleaning utensil*.

Adj. *obliterated*, wiped out; out of print, leaving no trace, unrecorded, unregistered; intestate.

Vb. *obliterate*, remove the traces, cover up 525 *conceal*; overpaint, overprint, deface, make illegible; efface, eliminate, erase, scratch out, rub o.; expunge, wipe out; blot, blot o.; rub off, wipe o., wash o.; take out, cancel, delete; strike out, cross out, score through, censor, blue-pencil; raze 165 *demolish*; wipe off the map; bury 364 *inter*; sink in oblivion 506 *forget*; drown 399 *silence*; leave no trace 446 *disappear*.

551. Representation – N. *representation*, personification, incarnation, embodiment; figuration, symbolization 547 *indication*; diagram, hieroglyphics 586 *writing*; presentation, evocation 522 *manifestation*; personation, impersonation; enactment, role-playing 594 *acting*; mimesis, mimicry 20 *imitation*; depiction, characterization 590 *description*; delineation, drawing, illustration, artwork, graphics 553 *painting*; creation, work of art 164 *product*; impression, likeness, identikit 18 *similarity*; trace, tracing 233 *outline*;

reflection (**see** *image*); portraiture, portrayal; true picture, striking likeness, realism 553 *picture*; bad likeness 552 *misrepresentation*; reproduction 555 *printing*; etching 555 *engraving*; design, blueprint, draft, croquis, cartoon, sketch, outline 623 *plan*; projection, isometric drawing.

image, very i. 22 *duplicate*; mental image 451 *idea*; projection, hologram, silhouette; visual, visual aid 445 *spectacle*; idol, graven image 982 *idolatry*; putto, cherub; statuary, statue 554 *sculpture*; effigy, figure, stick f., figurine, figurehead; wax figure, waxwork; dummy, tailor's d., lay figure, manikin; maquette, model, working m.; marionette, fantoccini, puppet, finger p.; snowman, gingerbread man; scarecrow, guy, Guy Fawkes; robot, Dalek, automaton; type, symbol, epitome.

art, architecture 243 *form*; fine arts, beaux arts; graphic arts 553 *painting*; plastic art 554 *sculpture*; baroque, rococo; art deco, modern art, abstract art; op art, pop a.; kitsch 847 *bad taste*; aestheticism, functionalism; commercial art; decorative a. 844 *ornamental art*; minor arts, calligraphy, weaving, tapestry, embroidery, pottery.

photography, radiography; microphotography; cinematography 445 *cinema*; telecine 531 *broadcasting*; photograph, photo, picture, snapshot, snap; negative, print, contact p.; colour p.; slide, diapositive, transparency; frame, still; filmstrip 445 *film*; spectrogram, hologram; radiograph, X-ray 417 *radiation*; photocopy 22 *copy*; photogravure 555 *printing*; shot, take, close-up, mug shot, pan, zoom, tracking shot, dissolve, fade; lens 442 *camera*; cameraman, cinematographer, photographer, snapshotter; radiographer.

map, chart, plan, outline, cartogram; sketch map, relief m., survey m., road m.; Admiralty chart; ground plan, ichnography; elevation, side-e.; projection, Mercator's p., orthographic p., conic p.; atlas; globe; planisphere 321 *astronomy*; mapmaking, cartography.

Adj. *representing*, representative 590 *descriptive*; iconic, pictorial, graphic, vivid; symbolic, totemic, hieroglyphic 547 *indicating*; figurative, illustrative, diagrammatic; representational, realistic, naturalistic, true-to-life; impressionistic, surrealistic; abstract, nonfigurative, conceptual; artistic 694 *well-made*; paintable, photogenic; photographic.

Vb. *represent*, stand for, symbolize 514 *mean*; typify, incarnate, embody, personify, epitomize; personate, impersonate 542 *deceive*; pose, model; present, enact 594 *dramatize*; project, shadow forth, adumbrate, suggest; reflect, image, hold the mirror up to nature; mimic, copy 20 *imitate*; depict, characterize 590 *describe*; delineate, limn, draw, picture, portray, figure; illustrate 553 *paint*; hit off, catch a likeness, capture, realize 548 *record*; carve, cast 554 *sculpt*; cut 555 *engrave*; mould, shape 243 *form*; design, draft, sketch out 623 *plan*; diagrammatize 233 *outline*; sketch, doodle, dash off 609 *improvise*; map, chart, survey, plot.

photograph, take a photo *or* a picture; snap; take, shoot, film; X-ray, radiograph; expose, develop, process, print.

552. Misrepresentation – N. *misrepresentation*, not a true picture 19 *dissimilarity*; false light 541 *falsehood*; unfair picture, bad likeness; travesty, parody 546 *exaggeration*; caricature, burlesque, guy 851 *ridicule*; daub, botch, scrawl; distorted image 246 *distortion*.

Adj. *misrepresented*, travestied etc. vb.; misrepresenting, unrepresentative, flat, cardboard.

Vb. *misrepresent*, deform 246 *distort*; tone down 925 *flatter*; overdramatize 546 *exaggerate*; overdraw, caricature, guy, burlesque, parody, travesty; daub, botch; lie 541 *be false*.

553. Painting – N. *painting*, graphic art, colouring, illumination; daubing, finger painting; depicting, drawing 551 *representation*; artistry, composition, design, technique, draughtsmanship, brushwork; line, perspective, golden section; tone, values; highlight, local colour, shading, contrast; monotone, monochrome, polychrome 425 *colour*; black and white, chiaroscuro, grisaille.

art style, style of painting; grand style, grand manner; intimate style, genre painting (**see** *art subject*); pasticcio, pastiche; trompe l'oeil; iconography, portrait-painting, portraiture; scenography, scene painting, sign p., poster p., miniature p.; oil painting, watercolour, tempera, gouache; fresco painting, mural p., encaustic p., impasto, secco.

art subject, landscape, seascape, skyscape, cloudscape; scene, prospect, diorama, panorama 438 *view*; interior, conversation piece, still life, pastoral, nocturne, nude; crucifixion, pietà, nativity.

picture, pictorial equivalent 551 *representation*; tableau, mosaic, tapestry; collage, montage, photomontage; frottage, brass rubbing; painting, pastiche; icon, triptych, diptych, panel; fresco, mural; poster; canvas, daub; drawing, line d.; sketch, outline; oil painting, oleograph, gouache, watercolour, aquarelle, pastel, wash drawing, pen-and-ink d.; design, pattern, doodle; cartoon, chad, caricature, silhouette; miniature, vignette, thumbnail sketch; old master, masterpiece; study, portrait, head, profile; photogravure, chromolithograph, reproduction, halftone; aquatint, woodcut 555 *engraving*; print, plate; illustration, picture postcard, cigarette card; picture book, scrapbook 589 *book*.

art equipment, palette, palette knife, spatula, paintbrush, paintbox; paints, oils, poster paint, acrylic p.; watercolours, tempera, gouache, gesso; ink, crayon, pastel, chalk, charcoal, heelball; pen, pencil; sketchbook 631 *paper*; canvas, easel, picture frame, mount; studio, atelier.

Adj. *painted*, daubed, etc. vb.; graphic, pictorial, scenic, picturesque, decorative 844 *ornamental*; pastel 425 *coloured*; linear, black-and-white, chiaroscuro, sfumato; painterly, paintable 551 *representing*.

Vb. *paint*, wash, lay *or* float a w. 425 *colour*; tint, touch up, retouch; daub,

scumble 226 *coat*; splash on, slap on; portray 551 *represent*; miniate, illuminate; ink, crayon, shade, stipple; block in, rough in; pinxit.

554. Sculpture – N. *sculpture*, plastic arts 551 *representation*; modelling, figuring 243 *form*; carving, moulding; ceroplastics; paper modelling, origami; petroglyph, scrimshaw; toreutics 844 *ornamental art*; construction, stabile, mobile; kinetic art; statuary; group; statue, colossus; statuette, figurine, bust, torso, head; model, maquette, cast, plaster c. 551 *image*; objet trouvé; ceramics 381 *pottery*; glyph, anaglyph, medallion, cameo, intaglio; repoussé, relief, bas-relief; stone, marble, bronze, clay, wax, plasticine, papier-mâché; armature; chisel, burin.

Adj. *glyptic*, sculptured, carved; statuary, sculpturesque, statuesque, marmoreal; anaglyptic, in relief 254 *projecting*; plastic, ceroplastic; toreutic, glyphic.

Vb. *sculpt*, sculpture, sculp, block out, rough-hew 243 *form*; cut, carve, whittle, chisel, chip, scrimshaw; chase, engrave, emboss; model, mould, cast; sculpsit.

555. Engraving. Printing – N. *engraving*, etching, line engraving, plate e.; photogravure; zincography, cerography, glyptography, gem engraving; glass engraving; mezzotint, aquatint; wood engraving, woodcut; linoprinting, linocut; scraperboard; chisel, graver, burin, needle, drypoint, style.

printing, type 587 *print*; plate printing, lithography, photolithography, photogravure, chromolithography, colour printing; fabric printing, batik; silk-screen printing, serigraphy; die, punch, stamp.

Vb. *engrave*, grave, incise, cut; etch, stipple, scrape; impress, stamp; lithograph 587 *print*; mezzotint, aquatint.

556. Artist – N. *artist*, craftsman *or* -woman 686 *artisan*; architect 164 *producer*; art master *or* mistress, designer, draughtsman *or* -woman; fashion artist, dress-designer, couturier, couturière; drawer, sketcher, delineator, limner;

copyist; caricaturist, cartoonist; illustrator, commercial artist; painter, colourist, luminist; dauber, amateur; pavement artist; scene-painter, sign-p.; oil-painter, watercolourist, pastellist; illuminator, miniaturist; Academician, RA; old master; art historian, iconographer; aesthetician.

sculptor, sculptress, carver, statuary, monumental mason, modeller, moulder.

engraver, etcher, aquatinter; lapidary, chaser, gem-engraver; typographer 587 *printer*.

557. Language – N. *language*, tongue, speech, idiom, parlance, talk; patter, lingo 560 *dialect*; personal language, idiolect; mother tongue, native t.; vernacular, vulgar tongue; English as she is spoken 579 *speech*; correct speech, Standard English, Queen's English; lingua franca, pidgin; sign language 547 *gesture*; artificial language, Esperanto; officialese 560 *neology*; machine language 86 *data processing*; metalanguage; Babel 61 *confusion*.

linguistics, language study, dialectology, philology, comparative p.; comparative grammar, syntax 564 *grammar*; phonetics 577 *pronunciation*; lexicology, lexicography; etymology; morphology; semantics 514 *meaning*; onomasiology 561 *nomenclature*; sociolinguistics; palaeography; speech community; polyglottism, bilingualism.

literature, creative writing, belles lettres 589 *reading matter*; letters, classics, arts, humanities 654 *civilization*; literary circles, republic of letters, PEN 589 *author*; literary genre, fiction, nonfiction 590 *narrative, description*; poetry 593 *poem*; plays 594 *drama*; criticism 480 *estimate*; literary criticism 520 *interpretation*.

linguist, philologist, etymologist, lexicographer; logophile; semanticist; grammarian 564 *grammar*; phonetician 398 *acoustics*; man *or* woman of letters 492 *scholar*; classical scholar 125 *antiquarian*; polyglot, bilingual.

Adj. *linguistic*, lingual, philological, etymological, grammatical, morphologi-

cal; diachronic, synchronic; lexicographical, semiological, semantic; written, literary; spoken, living, idiomatic; vulgar, colloquial, vernacular 560 *dialectal*; local, enchorial; demotic; bilingual, multilingual, polyglot.

558. Letter – N. *letter*, part of the alphabet; sign, symbol, character 586 *writing*; alphabet, ABC; initial teaching alphabet, i.t.a., International Phonetic Alphabet, IPA; phonogram 398 *speech sound*; ideograph, hieroglyph 586 *lettering*; ampersand; big letter, capital l., majuscule; small letter, minuscule; block letter, uncial; cursive; printed letter, letterpress 587 *print-type*; orthography, spelling.

initials, first letter; monogram, cipher; anagram, acrostic, acronym.

Adj. *literal*, in letters, lettered; alphabetical; in syllables, syllabic; hieroglyphic 586 *written*; capital, initial; lexigraphical, spelt, orthographic; monogrammatic; anacrostic, anagrammatic; phonetic 577 *vocal*.

Vb. *spell*, spell out, read, syllable; alphabetize; transliterate; letter 586 *write*; initial 547 *sign*; anagrammatize.

559. Word – N. *word*, expression, locution 563 *phrase*; term, vocable 561 *name*; phoneme, syllable; semanteme 514 *meaning*; synonym 13 *identity*; homonym, homograph, homophone; weasel word 518 *equivocalness*; antonym 14 *contrariety*; etymon, root, back-formation; folk etymology; derivation, derivative, paronym, doublet; morpheme, stem, inflection; part of speech 564 *grammar*; diminutive, pejorative, intensive; enclitic, abbreviation, acronym, portmanteau word 569 *conciseness*; cliché, catchword, vogue word, buzz w., trigger w.; nonce w., new w., loan w. 560 *neology*; assonant 18 *similarity*; four-letter word 573 *plainness*; swearword 899 *malediction*; hard word, jawbreaker, mouthful; long word, polysyllable; short word, monosyllable; verbosity 570 *pleonasm*.

dictionary, lexicon, wordbook, wordstock, word list, glossary, vocabulary; gradus, thesaurus, wordhoard; compilation, concordance, index.

Adj. *verbal*, literal; titular, nominal; etymological, lexical; philological, lexicographical, glossarial; synonymous 514 *semantic*.

560. Neology – **N.** *neology*, neologism 126 *newness*; coinage, new word, nonce w., vogue w.; catch phrase; borrowing, loan word 559 *word*; jargon, technical term; barbarism, hybrid, corruption; novelese, reporterese, journalese, officialese, telegraphese; baby talk; Newspeak, doubletalk 518 *equivocalness*; archaism 565 *solecism*; word-play, spoonerism 839 *witticism*; word-coiner, neologist.

dialect, idiom, lingo, patois, vernacular 557 *language*; burr, brogue, accent 577 *pronunciation*; cockney, Geordie, broad Scots, Lallans; broken English, pidgin E., pidgin; lingua franca, hybrid language; Strine, franglais; anglicism, Americanism, Irishism, gallicism, Teutonism; provincialism; iotacism 580 *speech defect*; dialectology 557 *linguistics*.

slang, vulgarism, colloquialism; jargon, argot, cant, patter; gipsy lingo, Romany; rhyming slang, back slang, pig Latin; backchat, Billingsgate 899 *scurrility*; gibberish, gobbledygook 515 *empty talk*.

Adj. *neological*, neoteric, newfangled, newly coined, not in the dictionary; barbaric, unidiomatic, hybrid, corrupt, pidgin; loaned, borrowed; archaic, obsolete; irregular 565 *ungrammatical*.

dialectal, vernacular; cockney, broad; guttural, nasal, burred; provincial, local; homely, colloquial; nonstandard, slangy, canting; jargonistic, journalistic.

Vb. *neologize*, coin words; talk slang, jargonize, cant; speak with an accent 577 *voice*.

561. Nomenclature – **N.** *nomenclature*, naming etc. vb.; eponymy; toponymy; onomastics, terminology; description, designation, appellation, denomination; addressing 583 *allocution*; christening 988 *Christian rite*.

name, nomen, first name, forename, Christian name, praenomen; middle name(s), surname, patronymic, matronymic, cognomen; maiden name, married n.; appellation, moniker; nickname, pet name, diminutive, byname, sobriquet, agnomen; epithet, description; handle, style, title; designation, appellative; name and address 547 *label*; term, trade name; namesake; eponym, tautonym; pen name 562 *misnomer*; noun, proper n. 564 *part of speech*.

nomenclator, terminologist; namer, name-giver; roll-caller, announcer.

Adj. *named*, called etc. vb.; titled, entitled, christened; known as, alias; nominal, titular; binominal; named after, eponymous; namable.

naming, denominative, appellative, terminological, onomastic.

Vb. *name*, call, give a name; christen, baptize 988 *perform ritual*; surname, nickname, dub; give his *or* her title, sir, be-madam; title, entitle, style, term 80 *specify*; call the roll, announce.

be named, own *or* bear *or* go by the name of; rejoice in the name of, answer to.

562. Misnomer – **N.** *misnomer*, misnaming; malapropism 565 *solecism*; false name, alias, assumed title; nom de guerre, nom de plume, pen name, stage n., pseudonym, allonym; nickname 561 *name*; pseudonymity.

no name, anonymity; anon, anonym, certain person, so-and-so, what's his/her name; Richard Roe, Jane Doe, N or M, Sir or Madam; X, A. N. Other; what d'you call it, thingummy, thingamajig, whatsit; and co., etc.; some, any, what-have-you.

Adj. misnamed, miscalled; self-christened, self-styled, soi-disant, would-be, so-called, quasi, pseudonymous.

anonymous, unknown, faceless, nameless, without a name; incognito, innominate, unnamed, unsigned.

Vb. *misname*, miscall, misterm, mistitle; nickname 561 *name*; assume an alias; pass oneself off as 541 *dissemble*.

563. Phrase – N. *phrase*, subject and predicate; clause, sentence, period, paragraph; collocation, expression, locution; idiom, mannerism 80 *speciality*; formula, verbalism; set phrase, set terms; euphemism, metaphor 519 *trope*; catch phrase, slogan; hackneyed expression, well-worn phrase, cliché, commonplace; saying 496 *maxim*; lapidary phrase, epitaph 364 *obsequies*; inscription, legend, caption; empty phrases 515 *empty talk*; surface structure, deep s.; phraseology, phrasing, diction, wording, choice of words, choice of expression, turn of e.; well-turned phrase 575 *elegance*; periphrasis, circumlocution 570 *pleonasm*; paraphrase 520 *translation*; phraseogram 586 *script*; phrasemonger, phrasemaker, epigraphist, epigrammatist, proverbialist.

Adj. *phraseological*, sentential, periodic; idiomatic; well-rounded, well-couched.

Vb. *phrase*, word, articulate; reword, rephrase 520 *translate*; express, formulate, put in words, find words for; sloganize, talk in clichés; turn a sentence, round a period 566 *show style*.

564. Grammar – N. *grammar*, comparative g., philology 557 *linguistics*; analysis, parsing, construing; paradigm; accidence, inflection, case, declension; conjugation, mood, voice, tense; number, gender; accentuation, pointing 547 *punctuation*; syntax, word order, ellipsis, apposition; bad grammar 565 *solecism*; good grammar, grammaticalness, Standard English.

part of speech, substantive, noun, pronoun; adjective; adverb; preposition, copula, conjunction, interjection; subject, object; article, particle, affix, suffix, infix, prefix; inflection, case-ending; morpheme, semanteme; diminutive, augmentative.

Adj. *grammatical*, correct; syntactic, inflectional; heteroclite, irregular, anomalous; masculine, feminine, neuter; singular, dual, plural; substantival, adjectival, attributive, predicative; verbal, adverbial; participial; prepositional; conjunctive, copulative; comparative, superlative.

Vb. *parse*, analyse, inflect, conjugate, decline; punctuate; construe 520 *interpret*.

565. Solecism – N. *solecism*, bad grammar, incorrectness, misusage; faulty syntax, anacoluthon; antiphrasis 574 *ornament*; catachresis, cacology; irregularity 560 *dialect*; impropriety, barbarism 560 *neology*; malapropism, bull, slip, Freudian s. 495 *mistake*; mispronunciation 580 *speech defect*; misspelling, cacography; verbicide.

Adj. *ungrammatical*, solecistic; faulty, improper, incongruous; misapplied, catachrestic.

Vb. *be ungrammatical*, violate grammar, commit a solecism; murder the Queen's English; mispronounce 580 *stammer*; misspell 495 *blunder*.

566. Style – N. *style*, mode, tone, manner, vein, strain, idiom; idiosyncrasy, mannerism 80 *speciality*; mode of expression, diction, parlance, phrasing 563 *phrase*; choice of words, vocabulary; literary style, command of idiom, raciness, power 571 *vigour*; feeling for words, Sprachgefühl; grace 575 *elegance*; word magic, word-spinning 579 *oratory*; weak style 572 *feebleness*; severe style 573 *plainness*; elaborate style 574 *ornament*; clumsy style 576 *inelegance*.

Adj. *stylistic*, mannered, literary, elegant; rhetorical; expressive, eloquent, fluent; racy, idiomatic; forceful.

Vb. *show style*, care for words, spin w.; measure one's words 563 *phrase*.

567. Perspicuity – N. *perspicuity*, perspicuousness, clarity, lucidity, limpidity 516 *intelligibility*; directness 573 *plainness*; definiteness, exactness 494 *accuracy*.

Adj. *perspicuous*, lucid, limpid 422 *transparent*; clear, unambiguous 516 *intelligible*; explicit, clear-cut 80 *definite*; exact 494 *accurate*; direct 573 *plain*.

568. Imperspicuity – N. *imperspicuity*, obscurity 517 *unintelligibility*, 423 *opacity*; abstraction, abstruseness; complexity 574 *ornament*; hard words 700 *difficulty*; imprecision, impreciseness 495 *inexactness*; ambiguity 518 *equivocalness*; mysteriousness, profundity 530 *enigma*; ellipsis 569 *conciseness*; cloud of words, verbiage 570 *diffuseness*.

Adj. *unclear*, imperspicuous 423 *opaque*; obscure, oracular, enigmatic 517 *unintelligible*; abstruse, profound; allusive, indirect 523 *latent*; vague, imprecise 474 *uncertain*; ambiguous 518 *equivocal*; muddled, confused, tortuous, involved 61 *complex*, 576 *inelegant*; hard, full of long words 700 *difficult*.

569. Conciseness – N. *conciseness*, concision, succinctness, brevity, soul of wit; pithiness, aphorism, epigram 839 *witticism*; few words, terseness, laconicism; telegraphese; overconciseness, brachylogy; ellipsis 204 *shortening*; compendiousness 592 *compendium*; monostich, haiku; clipped speech, monosyllabism 582 *taciturnity*; the long and the short of it.

Adj. *concise*, brief, short and sweet 204 *short*; laconic, monosyllabic 582 *taciturn*; irreducible, succinct, crisp, brisk, to the point; trenchant, incisive; terse, curt, brusque 885 *ungracious*; compendious, condensed, tight-knit, compact; pithy, pregnant, sententious, neat, exact, pointed, aphoristic, epigrammatic; elliptic, telegraphic; summary, abbreviated.

Vb. *be concise*, etc. adj.; need few words, not beat about the bush, come straight to the point, cut a long story short; telescope, compress, condense 204 *shorten*; summarize, sum up 592 *abstract*; be short with, cut short; be sparing with words 582 *be taciturn*; express pithily, epigrammatize 839 *be witty*.

Adv. *concisely*, pithily, in brief, in short, in fine, in a word, in a nutshell.

570. Diffuseness – N. *diffuseness*, verboseness etc. adj.; profuseness, expatiation, circumstantiality, minuteness, blow-by-blow account; inspiration, vein, flow, outpouring; exuberance, richness, wealth of terms; verbosity, wordiness, verbiage; fluency 581 *loquacity*; long-windedness, prolixity; repetitiveness, reiteration 106

repetition; gush, rigmarole, waffle 515 *empty talk*; effusion, tirade 579 *oration*; descant, disquisition 591 *dissertation*.

pleonasm, superfluity, tautology 637 *redundance*; circumlocution, roundabout phrases, periphrasis; ambages 518 *equivocalness*; padding, expletive, filler; digression 10 *irrelevance*.

Adj. *diffuse*, verbose, nonstop 581 *loquacious*; profuse, copious, voluminous 171 *prolific*; inspired, flowing, fluent, exuberant; expatiating, circumstantial, detailed, minute; gushing, effusive; windy, turgid, bombastic 574 *rhetorical*; polysyllabic 574 *ornate*.

prolix, long-winded, wordy, prosy, prosing; spun out, protracted; boring 838 *tedious*; lengthy, epic, never-ending 203 *long*; diffusive, discursive, excursive, digressing, episodic; rambling, maundering 282 *deviating*; loose-knit, incoherent 61 *orderless*; desultory 10 *irrelevant*; indirect, circumlocutory, periphrastic, ambagious, roundabout; pleonastic, repetitious 106 *repeated*; tautologous, tautological; padded.

Vb. *be diffuse*, etc. adj.; dilate, expatiate, amplify, particularize, detail, expand, enlarge upon; descant, discourse at length; tautologize 106 *repeat oneself*; pad, pad out, draw o., spin o. 203 *lengthen*; gush 581 *be loquacious*; perorate 579 *orate*; use long words, swallow the dictionary; waffle, digress 282 *deviate*; ramble, maunder, drivel, yarn, never end; not come to the point 518 *be equivocal*.

571. Vigour – N. *vigour*, power, strength, drive, forcefulness 174 *vigorousness*; incisiveness, trenchancy, vim, punch; sparkle, verve, élan, panache, vivacity, liveliness, vividness, raciness; spirit, fire, fervour, enthusiasm 818 *feeling*; bite, piquancy, poignancy 388 *pungency*; strong language, stress 532 *affirmation*; reiteration 106 *repetition*; seriousness, solemnity, gravity, weight; impressiveness, sublimity, grandeur 574 *magniloquence*; rhetoric 579 *eloquence*.

Adj. *forceful*, powerful 162 *strong*; peppy, punchy 174 *vigorous*; racy, idiomatic; bold, dashing, spirited, sparkling 819 *lively*; glowing, fiery, ardent, impassioned 818 *fervent*; vehement, emphatic, insistent 532 *affirmative*; cutting, incisive, trenchant 256 *sharp*; pointed, pungent, mordant, salty 839 *witty*; grave, sententious, strongly-worded 834 *serious*; heavy, meaty, solid; weighty, forcible, cogent 740 *compelling*; vivid, graphic, effective 551 *representing*; flowing, inspired 579 *eloquent*; high-toned, lofty, grand, sublime 821 *impressive*.

572. Feebleness – N. *feebleness*, weak style, enervated s. 163 *weakness*; prosiness, frigidity, ineffectiveness, flatness, staleness, vapidity 387 *insipidity*; jejuneness, poverty, thinness, enervation, lack of sparkle, lack of conviction; baldness 573 *plainness*; anticlimax.

Adj. *feeble*, weak, thin, flat, vapid, insipid 387 *tasteless*; wishy-washy, watery; sloppy, sentimental, schmaltzy, novelettish; meagre, jejune, exhausted; colourless, bald 573 *plain*; languid, flaccid, nerveless, emasculated, tame, conventional; undramatic, uninspired, unimpassioned, unemphatic; ineffective, cold, prosaic, uninspiring, unexciting; monotonous, prosy, pedestrian, dull 838 *tedious*; cliché-ridden, hackneyed, platitudinous, stale, pretentious, flatulent; forced, forcible-feeble; inane, empty; juvenile, childish; careless, slovenly, slipshod; limping, lame, unconvincing 477 *poorly reasoned*; limp, loose, lax, inexact, disconnected, disjointed, rambling 570 *prolix*; poor, trashy 847 *vulgar*.

573. Plainness – N. *plainness*, naturalness, simplicity 699 *artlessness*; austerity, severity, baldness, starkness; matter-of-factness 593 *prose*; plain words, plain English 516 *intelligibility*; home truths 540 *veracity*; homespun, household words; vernacular, common speech, vulgar parlance; unaffectedness 874 *modesty*; bluntness, frankness, coarseness, four-letter word, Anglo-Saxon monosyllable.

Adj. *plain*, simple 699 *artless*; austere, severe, disciplined; bald, spare, stark,

bare, unfussy; neat 648 *clean*; pure, unadulterated 44 *unmixed*; unadorned, uncoloured, unembellished 540 *veracious*; unemphatic, undramatic, unsensational, played down; unassuming, unpretentious; uninflated, chaste, restrained; unaffected, honest, natural, straightforward; homely, homey, homespun, vernacular; prosaic, sober 834 *serious*; dry, stodgy 838 *tedious*; humdrum, workaday, everyday, commonplace 610 *usual*; unimaginative, uninspired, unpoetical 593 *prosaic*.

Vb. *speak plainly*, call a spade a spade, use plain English 516 *be intelligible*; say outright, tell it like it is, spell it out, tell one straight *or* to his *or* her face; not mince one's words, not beat about the bush, come to the point, come down to brass tacks, talk turkey.

Adv. *plainly*, simply 516 *intelligibly*; prosaically, in prose; in the vernacular, in plain words; not to put too fine a point upon it, in words of one syllable.

574. Ornament – N. *ornament*, embellishment, colour, decoration, embroidery, frills 844 *ornamentation*; floridness, floweriness, flowers of speech, arabesques 563 *phrase*; euphuism, preciosity; rhetoric, purple patch *or* passage, dithyramb; figurativeness, figure of speech 519 *trope*; alliteration, assonance; metaphor, simile, antithesis.

magniloquence, high tone 579 *eloquence*; grandiloquence, declamation, orotundity 571 *vigour*; extravagance, hyperbole 546 *exaggeration*; turgidity, flatulence, inflation; pretentiousness, affectation, pomposity; talking big 877 *boasting*; bombast, rant, fustian, rodomontade 515 *empty talk*; Johnsonese, long words 570 *diffuseness*.

phrasemonger, fine writer, wordspinner; euphuist, stylist; rhetorician, orator 579 *speaker*.

Adj. *ornate*, florid, flowery 844 *ornamented*; precious, euphuistic 850 *affected*; flamboyant, frothy 875 *showy*; alliterative 519 *figurative*; overloaded, stiff, stilted; pedantic, long-worded, sesquipedalian, Johnsonian.

rhetorical, declamatory, oratorical 579 *eloquent*; resonant, sonorous 400 *loud*; ranting, orotund; high-flown, highfalutin; grandiose, stately; bombastic, pompous, fustian, Ossianic; grandiloquent, magniloquent; inflated, turgid, swollen, dithyrambic; metaphorical 519 *figurative*.

575. Elegance – N. *elegance*, style, perfect s.; grace, gracefulness 841 *beauty*; refinement 846 *good taste*; restraint, distinction, dignity; clarity 567 *perspicuity*; purity, simplicity; naturalness 573 *plainness*; classicism, Atticism; harmony, euphony, concinnity 245 *symmetry*; rhythm, flow, fluency, felicity, the right word in the right place; neatness, polish, finish, well-turned period 574 *ornament*; classic, purist.

Adj. *elegant*, majestic, stately 841 *beautiful*; graced, graceful; stylish 846 *tasteful*; distinguished, dignified; good, correct, idiomatic; expressive 567 *perspicuous*; simple, natural, unaffected 573 *plain*; unlaboured, ready, easy, smooth, flowing, fluent, tripping, rhythmic, mellifluous, euphonious; harmonious, well-proportioned 245 *symmetrical*; neat, felicitous, happy, right, well-turned 694 *well-made*; artistic, elaborate, artificial; polished, finished, soigné; restrained, controlled; classic, flawless 646 *perfect*.

576. Inelegance – N. *inelegance*, inconcinnity; uncouthness 699 *artlessness*; coarseness, lack of finish, lack of polish 647 *imperfection*; harshness, cacophony 411 *discord*; stiffness, stiltedness, cumbrousness; impropriety, barbarism; incorrectness 565 *solecism*; vulgarism 847 *bad taste*; mannerism, unnaturalness, artificiality 850 *affectation*; turgidity, pomposity 574 *magniloquence*.

Adj. *inelegant*, ungraceful, graceless 842 *ugly*; faulty, incorrect; crabbed, tortuous 568 *unclear*; longwinded 570 *diffuse*; unfinished, unpolished, unrefined; bald 573 *plain*; coarse, crude, uncouth, barbarous 699 *artless*; impolite, tasteless 847 *vulgar*; unrestrained, immoderate, excessive; turgid, pompous 574 *rhetorical*; forced, laboured, artificial 850 *affected*; grotesque, bathetic; jarring, grating; heavy, ponderous; rough, harsh, abrupt; halting, cramped, unready, unfluent; clumsy, awkward; wooden, stiff, stilted 875 *formal*.

577. Voice – N. *voice*, speaking 579 *speech*; singing voice 412 *vocal music*; vociferation, lung power 400 *loudness*; tongue, vocal cords; lungs, bellows; larynx, voice box; syrinx; vocalization 398 *speech sound*; articulation, distinctness; utterance, enunciation, delivery, attack; exclamation 408 *cry*; ejaculation, gasp; whisper 401 *faintness*; accents, timbre, pitch, tone, intonation, modulation.

pronunciation, articulation, elocution, enunciation, inflexion, accentuation, stress, emphasis; accent, burr, brogue, drawl, twang 560 *dialect*; aspiration, glottal stop; lisping 580 *speech defect*; mispronunciation 565 *solecism*.

Adj. *vocal*, voiced, oral, aloud, out loud; vocalic, sonant 398 *sounding*; phonetic, enunciative; articulate, distinct, clear; in good voice 410 *melodious*; pronounced, uttered; accented, tonal; guttural 407 *hoarse*; shrill 407 *strident*; wheezy 406 *sibilant*.

Vb. *voice*, pronounce, verbalize 579 *speak*; mouth, give tongue, give voice, express, utter, enunciate, articulate; vocalize; inflect, modulate; breathe, aspirate; trill, roll, burr; accent 532 *emphasize*; exclaim, ejaculate 408 *cry*; drone, intone 413 *sing*; shout 400 *be loud*; lisp, drawl 580 *stammer*.

578. Voicelessness – N. *voicelessness*, aphonia, no voice, loss of v.; difficulty in speaking, inarticulation; thick speech, hoarseness, huskiness; muteness 399 *silence*; dumbness, mutism, deaf-m.; harsh voice 407 *stridor*; treble, falsetto; sob, sobbing; undertone, low voice, small v., muffled tones, whisper 401 *faintness*; sign language 547 *gesture*; mute, deaf-mute.

Adj. *voiceless*, aphonic; unvoiced, surd; breathed, whispered, muffled, inaudible 401 *muted*; mute, dumb, deaf and dumb;

speechless, wordless, at a loss for words; inarticulate, unvocal, tongue-tied 582 *taciturn*; silenced, gagged; dry, hollow, sepulchral, breaking, cracked, croaking 407 *hoarse*.

Vb. *be mute*, keep mum 582 *be taciturn*; hold one's tongue 525 *keep secret*; check oneself, dry up, shut up; lose one's voice *or* one's tongue, be struck dumb, lose the power of speech; talk with one's hands 547 *gesticulate*.

make mute, strike dumb, dumbfound, take one's breath away, rob one of words; stick in one's throat, choke on; muffle, hush, deaden 401 *mute*; shout down, drown one's voice; muzzle, gag, stop one's mouth, cut out one's tongue; shut one up, cut one short, hang up on; still, hush 399 *silence*.

579. Speech – N. *speech*, tongue, lips 577 *voice*; parlance 557 *language*; spoken word, accents, tones; discourse, conversation 584 *interlocution*; ready speech, fluency 581 *loquacity*; prolixity 570 *diffuseness*; elocution, voice production; utterance, delivery 577 *pronunciation*; ventriloquism; speech, dictum, utterance, remark, observation, comment, interjection 532 *affirmation*; fine words 515 *empty talk*; spiel, patter 542 *trickery*.

oration, speech; one's say, one's piece, a word in edgeways; discourse, disquisition, address, talk; panegyric, eulogy; valedictory; after-dinner speech, toast, vote of thanks; broadcast 534 *lecture*; recitation, recital, reading; set speech, declamation (**see** *eloquence*); sermon, preachment, homily, exhortation; harangue, tub-thumping, rodomontade, earful, mouthful; tirade, diatribe, philippic, invective; monologue 585 *soliloquy*; paper 591 *dissertation*; proem, preamble, prologue, peroration.

oratory, rhetoric, public speaking, tub-thumping; speech-making, speechifying; declamation, vapouring, ranting; vituperation, invective; soapbox 539 *rostrum*; Hyde Park Corner.

eloquence, gift of the gab, fluency, articulacy; glossolalia 821 *excitation*;

command of words, way with w., word-spinning 566 *style*; power 571 *vigour*; grandiloquence, orotundity, sublimity 574 *magniloquence*; elocution, good delivery; rolling periods, torrent of words, peroration, purple passage.

speaker, sayer, etc. vb.; gossiper 581 *chatterer*; conversationalist, deipno-sophist 584 *interlocutor*; speechifier, speech-maker, speech-writer, rhetorician, elocutionist; orator, Public O.; public speaker, after-dinner s., toastmaster; improviser, ad-libber; ranter, soap-box orator, tub-thumper, haranguer, demagogue 738 *agitator*; word-spinner, spellbinder; lecturer, dissertator; pulpiteer, Boanerges 537 *preacher*; presenter 531 *broadcaster*; prologue, narrator, chorus 594 *actor*; mouthpiece, spokesman *or* -woman, spokesperson 754 *delegate*.

Adj. *speaking*, talking; anglophone, francophone, bilingual, polyglot; articulate, fluent, outspoken, free-speaking 581 *loquacious*; oral 577 *vocal*; well-spoken, soft-s., loud-s.; audible, spoken, verbal; plummy, fruity 404 *resonant*.

eloquent, spellbinding, silver-tongued, trumpet-t.; smooth-t. 925 *flattering*; elocutionary, oratorical 574 *rhetorical*; grandiloquent, declamatory 571 *forceful*; fire-and-brimstone, ranting, rousing 821 *exciting*.

Vb. *speak*, mention, say; utter, articulate 577 *voice*; pronounce, declare 532 *affirm*; let out, blurt out 526 *divulge*; whisper, breathe 524 *hint*; talk, put in a word 584 *converse*; give utterance, deliver oneself of; break silence, open one's mouth *or* lips, find one's tongue; pipe up, speak up, raise one's voice; rattle on, gossip, chatter 581 *be loquacious*; patter, jabber, gabble; sound off, speak one's mind, tell a thing or two, have one's say 570 *be diffuse*; trot out, reel off, recite; read out, dictate; have a tongue in one's head, speak for oneself.

orate, speechify; declaim, deliver a speech; hold forth, spout, be on one's legs; take the floor, rise to speak; preach, preachify, sermonize, harangue; lecture, address 534 *teach*; invoke, apostrophize 583 *speak to*; perorate, mouth, rant, rail;

spellbind, be eloquent, have the gift of the gab; ad-lib 609 *improvise*.

580. Speech defect – N. *speech defect*, aphasia, loss of speech; aphonia 578 *voicelessness*; idioglossia, idiolalia; stammer, stutter, lallation, lisp; sigmatism 406 *sibilation*; speech impediment, drawl, slur; indistinctness, inarticulateness, thick speech, cleft palate; burr, brogue 560 *dialect*; accent, twang 577 *pronunciation*; affectation, plum in one's mouth 246 *distortion*; speech therapy.

Adj. *stammering*, stuttering etc. vb.; nasal, adenoidal; indistinct, inarticulate; tongue-tied, aphasic; breathless 578 *voiceless*.

Vb. *stammer*, stutter, trip over one's tongue; drawl, hesitate, falter, quaver, hem and ha, hum and haw; mumble, mutter; lisp; lallate; snuffle, snort, splutter, sibilate; nasalize, speak through the nose, drone; clip one's words, swallow one's w., gabble, slur; mispronounce.

581. Loquacity – N. *loquacity*, loquaciousness, garrulity, talkativeness, communicativeness; volubility, runaway tongue, flow of words 570 *diffuseness*; verbosity, wordiness, prolixity; logorrhoea, verbal diarrhoea; patter, spiel, gift of the gab 579 *eloquence*; anecdotage 505 *remembrance*.

chatter, chattering, gossiping, gabble, jabber, palaver, jaw-jaw, yakkety-yak; clack, quack, cackle, babble, prattle; small talk, gossip, tittle-tattle; waffle, blether, gush, guff 515 *empty talk*.

chatterer, nonstop talker; chinwag, chatterbox; gossip, blabber, tattler 529 *news reporter*; talker, quacker, bletherskite; proser, windbag, gasbag; conversationalist 584 *interlocutor*.

Adj. *loquacious*, talkative, garrulous, tongue-wagging, gossiping; communicative, chatty, gossipy, newsy; gabbing, babbling, gassy, windy, prosing, verbose 570 *prolix*; nonstop, voluble, fluent, glib; effusive, gushing.

Vb. *be loquacious*, etc. adj.; chatter, rattle, run on, reel off, talk nineteen to the dozen; gossip, tattle 584 *converse*; clack, quack, gabble, jabber 515 *mean nothing*; talk, jaw, yak, gab, prate, prose, gas, waffle, haver, blether, twitter, ramble on, rabbit on; drone, maunder, drivel; launch out, start talking, shoot; effuse, spout 570 *be diffuse*; outtalk, talk down; talk one's head off, talk the hind leg off a donkey; talk shop 838 *be tedious*; monopolize the conversation, not let one get a word in edgeways, never stop talking.

582. Taciturnity – N. *taciturnity*, incommunicativeness, reserve, reticence 525 *secrecy*; curtness, gruffness 885 *rudeness*; muteness 578 *voicelessness*; laconism, few words 569 *conciseness*; no speaker, no orator; not a gossip; clam, oyster, statue; Trappist.

Adj. *taciturn*, mute, mum 399 *silent*; sparing of words, short, curt, laconic, brusque, gruff 569 *concise*; vowed to silence; incommunicative, guarded, with sealed lips 525 *reticent*; close, not to be drawn 858 *cautious*; inarticulate, tongue-tied 578 *voiceless*.

Vb. *be taciturn*, etc. adj.; use few words 569 *be concise*; say nothing, have little to say; observe silence, make no answer; not be drawn, neither confirm nor deny; keep one's counsel 525 *keep secret*; hold one's peace, hold one's tongue, keep one's mouth *or* trap shut; fall silent, pipe down, dry up 145 *cease*; be speechless, lose one's tongue 578 *be mute*; waste no words on, save one's breath, not mention, leave out 458 *disregard*.

Int. hush! shut up! mum's the word! no comment! verb. sap.! a word to the wise!

583. Allocution – N. *allocution*, apostrophe; address, pep talk 579 *oration*; greeting, salutation, hail; invocation, appeal, interjection, interpellation; word in the ear, aside; hearers, audience 415 *listener*.

Adj. *vocative*, salutatory, invocatory.

Vb. *speak to*, speak at; address, talk to, lecture to; turn to, direct one's words at, apostrophize; appeal to, pray to, invoke; approach, accost; hail, call to 884 *greet*;

pass the time of day 584 *converse*; take aside, buttonhole.

584. Interlocution – N. *interlocution*, parley, colloquy, converse, conversation, causerie, talk; dialogue, question and answer; exchange, repartee, banter, badinage; slanging match 709 *quarrel*; confabulation, confab, verbal intercourse 882 *sociality*; communion, intercommunication 524 *information*; duologue, tête-à-tête.

chat, causerie, chinwag, natter; chit-chat, talk, small t., prattle, gossip 529 *rumour*; tattle, tittle-tattle, tongue-wagging 581 *chatter*; tête-à-tête, heart-to-heart.

conference, colloquy, talks, pourparler, parley, pow-wow, indaba, palaver; discussion, debate, forum, symposium, seminar, teach-in; talkfest, gabfest; polemics 475 *argument*; exchange of views, summit meeting, summit; negotiations 765 *treaty*; conclave, convention 74 *assembly*; working lunch; reception, conversazione 882 *social gathering*; interview, audition 415 *listening*; consultation, huddle, council 691 *advice*.

interlocutor, collocutor, dialogist, symposiast; examiner, interviewer 459 *questioner*; answerer 460 *respondent*; partner, conversationalist 581 *chatterer*.

Adj. *conversing*, interlocutory, confabulatory; dialogistic, dialogic; conversational; chatty 581 *loquacious*; communicative 524 *informative*; conferring, conferential.

Vb. *converse*, colloquize, confabulate, pass the time of day; lead one on, draw one out; buttonhole, engage in conversation, carry on a c., bandy words; chat, have a chat *or* a natter 579 *speak*; buzz, natter, chinwag, chew the fat, gossip, tattle 581 *be loquacious*; commune with, go into a huddle.

confer, talk it over, take counsel, pow-wow, palaver; discuss, debate 475 *argue*; parley, negotiate, hold talks; consult with 691 *consult*.

585. Soliloquy – N. *soliloquy*, monologue, monody; interior monologue, stream of

consciousness; apostrophe; aside; one-man/-woman show, onehander.

soliloquist, soliloquizer, monologist, monodist.

Vb. *soliloquize*, talk to oneself, say aside, think aloud; apostrophize, pray aloud; have an audience of one.

586. Writing – N. *writing*, creative w., composition, literary c., authorship, journalism 590 *description*; writings 589 *reading matter*; ink-slinging, quill-driving, penpushing, hackwork, Grub Street; paperwork 548 *record*; transcription, rewriting; handwriting, stylography, cerography; longhand, shorthand, stenography, lexigraphy, speedwriting, phonography, stenotypy; phonogram, phraseogram, logogram; typewriting, typing 587 *print*; braille; cipher 530 *secret*; picture writing, ideography, hieroglyphics; inscribing, epigraphy 555 *engraving*; study of handwriting, graphology.

lettering, stroke of the pen, up-stroke, down-s., pothook; flourish 251 *convolution*; handwriting, hand, fist; calligraphy, penmanship; script, italic, copperplate; printing, block letters; cacography, scribble, scrawl, hen tracks 517 *unintelligibility*; characters, alphabet 558 *letter*; runes, pictogram, ideogram; hieroglyph; palaeography.

script, written matter; illuminated address; specimen, calligraph; writing, screed, scrawl, scribble; manuscript, palimpsest, codex 589 *book*; original, autograph, holograph; copy, transcript 22 *duplicate*; typescript, stencil; newsprint; printed matter 587 *letterpress*; letter 588 *correspondence*; inscription, epigraph, graffito 548 *record*.

stationery, writing materials, pen and paper, pen and ink; stylus, quill, pen, felt-tip, ballpoint, biro (tdmk); nib; stylograph; pencil, crayon, chalk; papyrus, parchment, vellum; foolscap 631 *paper*; writing paper, notepaper; notebook, pad, jotter; slate, blackboard; blotting paper, blotter; ribbon, stencil.

calligrapher, calligraphist, penman *or*

-woman; cacographer, scribbler, scrawler; pen-pusher, scrivener, scribe, clerk 549 *recorder*; copyist, transcriber; signwriter 528 *publicizer*; epigraphist, inscriber; writer 589 *author*; letter writer 588 *correspondent*; graphologist, handwriting expert.

stenographer, shorthand writer, typist, shorthand t., stenotypist, audiotypist.

Adj. *written*, inscribed, inscriptional, epigraphic; in writing, in black and white 548 *recorded*; logographic, stenographic; handwritten, manuscript; penned, pencilled, scribbled etc. vb.; cursive, copybook, copperplate; italic, calligraphic; demotic, hieratic; ideographic, hieroglyphic, cuneiform; lettered, alphabetical; runic, Gothic, uncial, roman, italic 558 *literal*; upright, sloping, spidery.

Vb. *write*, be literate; engrave, inscribe; letter, block, print; flourish, scroll; scribble, scrawl; interline, overwrite; put in writing, set down, write d. 548 *record*; transcribe, copy, copy out, write out, engross; take down, take dictation; stenotype, typewrite, type, type out; draft, formulate, redact; compose, concoct, indite; pen, pencil, dash off; write letters 588 *correspond*; write one's name 547 *sign*; take up the pen, put pen to paper 590 *describe*, 591 *dissertate*, 593 *poetize*.

587. Print – N. *print*, printing, typing 586 *writing*; typography, printing from type, block printing, plate p., offset process, web offset; lithography, litho, photo-lithography, photolitho 555 *printing*; photocopying 551 *photography*; photo-composition, photosetting, cold type; composition, cold c., hot c., typesetting, hand-setting, make-up; Monotype, Linotype, stereotype, electrotype; plate, shell; makeready, printing off, running off.

letterpress, linage, printed matter, print, impression, presswork; pressrun; printout, run-off; copy, pull, proof, galley p., page p., revise; colophon, imprint 589 *edition*; offprint.

print-type, type, stereotype, plate; flong, matrix; broken type, pie; upper case, lower c.; fount, face, typeface, boldface, bold, clarendon, lightface, old face, bastard type; roman, italic, Gothic, black letter 558 *letter*; lead, rule, en, em; space, hairspace, quad; type bar, slug, logotype.

press, printing p., printing works, printers; typefoundry; composing room, press r., machining r.; handpress, flatbed, platen press, rotary p., Linotype (tdmk), Monotype (tdmk), offset press; galley, chase, forme, quoin, composing stick; roller, brayer, web.

printer, book p., jobbing p., typographer, compositor, typesetter; typefounder, printer's devil, pressman, printer's reader, proof r.

Vb. *print*, stamp; typeset, compose, photocompose; align, register, justify; set up, make ready, impose, machine, run off, print off; collate, foliate; lithograph, litho, offset, stereotype; send to press, put to bed; see through the press, proofread, correct; have printed, bring out 528 *publish*.

588. Correspondence – N. *correspondence*, exchange of letters; communication 524 *information*; mailing list, distribution l.; letters, mail, post, postbag 531 *postal communications*; letter, epistle, missive, dispatch, bulletin; love letter, billet doux, greetings card, Valentine 889 *endearment*; postcard, picture p., card, notelet; air letter; bill, account, enclosure; open letter 528 *publicity*; unsolicited mail, circular, round robin, chain letter; note, line; answer, acknowledgement; envelope, cover.

correspondent, letter writer, penfriend, poison pen; recipient, addressee; foreign correspondent 529 *news reporter*; contact 524 *informant*.

Adj. *epistolary*, postal, by post; under cover of, enclosed.

Vb. *correspond*, exchange letters, keep in touch 524 *communicate*; write to, send a letter, drop a line; acknowledge, reply, write back 460 *answer*; circularize 528 *publish*; post off, forward, mail, airmail; stamp, seal, frank, address.

589. Book – N. *book*, title, volume, tome, roll; manuscript, MS; script, typescript, unpublished work; publication, bestseller, potboiler; unsold book, remainder; work, standard w., classic; magnum opus; opuscule, booklet, bouquin; illustrated work, picture book, coffee-table b.; brochure, pamphlet 528 *the press*; hardback, softback, paperback.

reading matter, printed word 586 *writing*; forms, papers, bumf 548 *record*; script, copy; text, the words, libretto, lyrics, scenario, screenplay, book of words; proof 587 *letterpress*; writings 557 *literature*; books for children, juveniles; history, biography, travel 590 *description*; fiction 590 *novel*; memoirs 590 *biography*; essay 591 *dissertation*; occasional pieces 591 *article*; miscellanea, marginalia, jottings; selections 592 *anthology*; dedicatory volume, Festschrift; early works, juvenilia; oeuvre, corpus; newspaper, magazine 528 *journal*; issue, number, back n.; fascicle, part, instalment.

textbook, school book, reader 539 *classroom*; primer, grammar, gradus; text, required reading; handbook, manual, enchiridion; pocket book.

reference book, encyclopedia, cyclopedia 490 *erudition*; lexicon 559 *dictionary*; gazetteer, yearbook, annual 87 *directory*; calendar 117 *chronology*; guide 524 *guidebook*; diary 548 *record*; bibliography, reading list.

edition, impression, issue, run; series, set, collection, library; omnibus edition, complete works; incunabula, editio princeps, first edition, reissue, reprint; abridgement 592 *compendium*; octodecimo, sextodecimo, duodecimo, octavo, quarto, folio; layout, format; house style; front matter, prelims; dedication, acknowledgements; title, bastard t., half-t.; flyleaf, title page, endpaper, colophon 547 *label*; errata, corrigenda, addenda; appendix, supplement, index, thumb i.; bibliography; caption, heading, headline, running h., footnote; guide word, catchword; margin, gutter; sheet, forme, signature, quire; illustration 553 *picture*.

library, book collection; national library, public l., branch l., reference l., mobile l., lending l., circulating l., book club; bookshelf, bookcase, bookends; bookstall, bookshop, booksellers.

bookperson, litterateur, literary person; reader, bookworm 492 *scholar*; bibliophile, book lover, book collector, bibliomaniac; bibliographer; librarianship, librarian; bookselling, bibliopole, bookseller, antiquarian b., book dealer, bouquinist; publisher, printer 528 *publicizer*; editor, redactor; reviewing, reviewer 480 *estimator*.

author, authoress, writer, creative w., word-painter, wordsmith; man *or* woman of letters; fiction-writer, novelist, historian, biographer 590 *narrator*; essayist, editorialist 591 *dissertator*; verse writer 593 *poet*; playwright 594 *dramatist*; freelance; copywriter 528 *publicizer*; pressman *or* -woman 529 *news reporter*; editor, subeditor, copy editor, contributor, correspondent, columnist, paragraphist, gossip writer, diarist; scribbler, penpusher, hack, penny-a-liner, inkslinger, potboiler; ghost, ghost writer; reviser, translator, adapter.

590. Description – N. *description*, account, exposé 524 *report*; inscription, caption 592 *compendium*; narration, relation, rehearsal, recital, version; reportage, nonfiction; specification, characterization, details, particulars 87 *list*; portrayal, delineation; depiction; portrait, sketch, character s., profile, prosopography 551 *representation*; psychic profile, case history 548 *record*; faction, documentary drama; evocation, word-painting, local colour; picture, true p., realism, naturalism; travelogue; vignette, cameo, thumbnail sketch; obituary 364 *obsequies*.

narrative, storyline, plot, subplot, scenario 594 *stage play*; episode 154 *event*; dramatic irony, comic relief; fantasia 513 *fantasy*; fiction, story, tale, conte, romance, fairytale, folk tale; tradition, legend, legendry, mythology, myth, saga, epic; ballad 593 *poem*; allegory, parable, apologue, cautionary tale; yarn 543 *fable*; anecdote, reminiscence;

annals, chronicle, history, historiography.

biography, real-life story, human interest; life, curriculum vitae, life story *or* history; experiences, adventures, fortunes; hagiology, hagiography, martyrology; obituary, necrology; rogue's gallery, Newgate calendar; autobiography 505 *remembrance*; diary, journals, letters.

novel, fiction; roman à clef, Bildungsroman, roman fleuve; antinovel; historical novel, fictional biography, novelization; short story, novelette, novella; light reading, bedside r.; romance, love story, fairy s., adventure s., Western, science fiction, sci-fi, SF; Gothic novel, ghost story; crime story, detective s., whodunit; cliffhanger, thriller, shocker; paperback, pulp literature; potboiler, trash; blockbuster, bestseller 589 *book*.

narrator, describer, delineator; reporter, relater; raconteur, anecdotist; yarnspinner, story-teller, fabler, fabulist, mythologist, allegorist; romancer, novelist, fictionist 589 *author*; biographer, hagiographer, martyrologist, autobiographer, memoir writer, diarist; historian 549 *recorder*.

Adj. *descriptive*, representational; graphic, colourful, vivid; well-drawn 551 *representing*; true-to-life, naturalistic, realistic, real-life, photographic; picturesque, striking; impressionistic, suggestive, evocative, emotive; moving, thrilling 821 *exciting*; traditional, legendary, storied, mythological 519 *figurative*; epic, heroic, romantic, cloak-and-dagger; picaresque, low-life, kitchen-sink; narrative, historical, biographical, autobiographical; full, detailed 570 *diffuse*; factual, documentary 494 *accurate*; fictitious, fictional 513 *imaginary*.

Vb. *describe*, delineate, depict 551 *represent*; evoke, bring to life, make one see; characterize, particularize 80 *specify*; sketch, adumbrate 233 *outline*; relate, recount, rehearse, recite 524 *communicate*; write about 548 *record*; narrate, tell, tell a story, yarn, spin a y., unfold a tale; construct a plot; fictionalize, novelize; romance, mythicize, mythologize 513 *imagine*; review, recapitulate; reminisce.

591. Dissertation – N. *dissertation*, treatise, tract, tractate; exposition, summary 592 *compendium*; theme, thesis 475 *argument*; disquisition, essay, examination, survey 459 *inquiry*; discourse, discussion; excursus, memoir, paper, monograph, study; screed, harangue, homily, sermon 534 *lecture*; commentary.

article, column; leading article, leader, editorial; essay, causerie, belles-lettres; comment, review, notice, critique, criticism, write-up 480 *estimate*.

dissertator, essayist, expositor; pamphleteer 528 *publicizer*; editor, leader writer, editorialist; writer, belletrist, contributor 589 *author*; reviewer, critic, commentator, pundit 520 *interpreter*.

Vb. *dissertate*, treat, handle, write about, deal with, do justice to; descant, discourse upon 475 *argue*; set out, discuss, air one's views; notice, criticize, comment upon, write up; commentate 520 *interpret*.

592. Compendium – N. *compendium*, epitome, resumé, summary, brief; contents, heads, analysis; abstract, digest, sum and substance, gist; multum in parvo, précis, aperçu, conspectus, synopsis, bird's-eye view, survey; review, recapitulation, recap; rundown, runthrough; draft, minute 548 *record*; sketch, outline, skeleton; syllabus, prospectus; abridgement 204 *shortening*; contraction, compression 569 *conciseness*.

anthology, treasury, garland, flowers; selections, extracts; collection, compilation, collectanea, miscellanea, miscellany; analects, ephemera; gleanings, leaves, pages; scrapbook, notebook, commonplace book; anthologist.

epitomizer, abridger, abbreviator; abstracter, summarizer, précis-writer, shortener, cutter.

Adj. *compendious*, pithy 569 *concise*; analytical, synoptic; abstracted, abridged 204 *short*; potted; collected.

Vb. *abstract*, sum up, resume, summarize; epitomize, reduce 204 *shorten*; capsulize, encapsulate; condense 569 *be concise*; compile, collect 74 *bring together*;

conflate 50 *combine*; excerpt, glean, select, anthologize.

593. Poetry. Prose – N. *poetry*, poesy, balladry, minstrelsy, song; poetic art, poetics; verse, rhyme, numbers; poetic licence; poetic inspiration, afflatus, divine a.; Muses, tuneful Nine; Parnassus.

poem, lines, verses, stanzas, strains; epic, epos, Edda; dramatic poem, verse drama; light verse, vers de société, lyric verse, melic v.; ode, epode, palinode; dithyramb; monody, dirge, elegy; idyll, eclogue; georgic, bucolics; prothalamion, epithalamium; song, lay, ballad 412 *vocal music*; collected poems 592 *anthology*; canto; cycle, sequence.

doggerel, lame verse, balladry; jingle, ditty, nursery rhyme; nonsense verse; clerihew, limerick; cento, macaronics; mock epic, burlesque.

verse form, sonnet, sestet; ballade, rondeau, virelay, triolet, villanelle; burden, refrain, envoi; couplet, distich; haiku, tanka; triplet, tercet, terza rima, quatrain; ghazal; sestina, rhyme royal, ottava rima; metrical verse, blank v.; concrete poetry; limping iambics, scazon; free verse, vers libres; verse, versicle, stanza, stave, laisse, strophe, antistrophe; stichomythia; broken line, hemistich.

prosody, versification, metrics, metre, measure, numbers, scansion; rhyme, masculine r., feminine r., internal r., eye r.; rhyme scheme; assonance, alliteration; cadence, rhythm, sprung r.; metrical unit, foot; iamb, trochee, spondee, dactyl, anapaest; pentameter, hexameter, heptameter, octameter; alexandrine, heroic couplet; anacrusis, arsis, thesis, ictus, beat, stress, accent, accentuation; elision; enjambment, caesura.

poet, poet laureate; versemonger, poetaster; prosodist, versifier, metrist, vers-librist; rhymer, rhymester, rhymist, jingler; bard, minstrel, balladeer, skald, troubadour, jongleur, minnesinger; epic poet, lyric p., lyrist, dithyrambist, elegist; sonneteer, ballad-monger; songwriter, librettist; reciter, rhapsode, rhapsodist.

prose, not verse; prose poem; prosaic-ness, prosaism, prosiness, prose-writing 573 *plainness*; prosaist 589 *author*.

Adj. *poetic*, poetical, bardic; songful, tuneful; Parnassian, Pierian; heroic, Homeric, Dantesque, Miltonic *or* Miltonian; mock-heroic, satiric; elegiac, lyrical, dithyrambic, rhapsodic; lyric, anacreontic, Pindaric, Sapphic, Horatian; bucolic, eclogic, Virgilian; rhyming, jingling, etc. vb.; prosodic, accentual, metrical, measured, rhythmic, scanning; octosyllabic, hendecasyllabic, iambic, trochaic, spondaic, dactylic, anapaestic; catalectic; Petrarchan, Byronic, Shakespearian, Spenserian.

prosaic, pedestrian, unpoetical, unversified; in prose, matter-of-fact 573 *plain*.

Vb. *poetize*, sing, tune one's lyre; syllabize, scan; rhyme, chime; versify, make verses; berhyme; lampoon 851 *satirize*.

594. Drama. Ballet – N. *drama*, the theatre, the stage, the boards, the footlights; theatreland, Broadway, West End; silver screen, Hollywood 445 *cinema*; show business, show biz, dramatic entertainment, straight drama, legitimate theatre, live t.; intimate t., total t., alternative t., street t.; repertory, rep; theatricals, amateur t.; masque, charade, dumb show, puppetry, tableau 551 *representation*; tragic mask, comic m., sock, buskin, cothurnus; Melpomene, Thalia, Thespis.

dramaturgy, play construction, dramatic form; the unities; dramatization, theatricals, dramatics; melodramatics, histrionics; theatricality, staginess; bardolatry; stagecraft, theatrecraft, histrionic art; production, revival; auditions, casting; walk-through, rehearsal, dress r.; direction, stage management; showmanship; staging, stage directions; stage whisper, aside, cue; gagging, business, byplay; entrance, exit; rising of the curtain, prologue, chorus; act, scene; coup de théâtre, deus ex machina; curtain, drop of the c., blackout; finale, epilogue; curtain call, encore; interval, intermission, break; enactment, performance, command p., première, preview, first night; matinée, first house, second h.; one-night stand, road show; hit, smash h., long run.

stage play, play, drama, work; libretto, scenario, script, book of words, prompt book; part, lines; playlet, sketch, skit; double bill; curtain-raiser, entr'acte, intermezzo, divertissement; monologue, dramatic m.; duologue, two-hander; masque, mystery play, miracle play, morality p., passion p.; commedia dell'arte; No, Kabuki; Greek drama, trilogy, tetralogy, cycle; poetic drama, verse d.; melodrama, blood and thunder; tragedy, classical t.; tragicomedy, comédie larmoyante; comedy, comedy of manners, Restoration comedy; well-made play, problem p., slice-of-life drama, kitchen-sink d., theatre of the absurd, t. of cruelty; black comedy, Grand Guignol, farce, slapstick, burlesque, extravaganza 849 *ridiculousness*; pantomime, panto, harlequinade; musical comedy, musical, light opera, comic o., grand opera 412 *vocal music*; radio drama, drama-documentary, television play 531 *broadcast*; photoplay, screenplay 445 *cinema*; shadow play, puppet show, Punch and Judy show.

stage show, show 445 *spectacle*; ice show, circus 837 *amusement*; variety, music hall, vaudeville; revue, intimate r.; Follies, leg show, strip s.; floor show, cabaret; song and dance, act, turn; star turn; set piece, tableau.

ballet, dance, ballet dancing 837 *dancing*; choreography; classical ballet, Russian b., romantic b., modern dance; toe dance, tap d., clog d. 837 *dance*; solo, pas seul, pas de deux; chassé, glissade; arabesque; fouetté, plié, pirouette 315 *rotation*; entrechat, jeté 312 *leap*.

stage set, set, setting, décor, mise-en-scène, scenery, scene 445 *spectacle*; drop, backdrop, backcloth, cyclorama; screen, wings, flat; background, foreground; stage, boards; apron, proscenium, proscenium arch, picture-frame stage; gauze, curtain, fire c., safety c.; trap, star t.; prompt box (see *theatre*); properties, props, costume; make-up, greasepaint.

theatre, amphitheatre, stadium, circus,

hippodrome; fleapit, picture palace 445 *cinema*; theatre in the round, open-air t.; showboat, pier, pavilion; big top; playhouse, opera house, music hall; night club, boîte, cabaret; wings, coulisses, flies (see *stage set*); dressing room, green r.; footlights, floats, battens, spotlight, spot, limelight, floodlight, flood, houselights; auditorium, orchestra; seating, stalls, orchestra s.; pit, parterre; box, loge, circle, dress c., upper c.; gallery, balcony, gods; front of house, foyer, box office, stage door.

acting, impersonation 551 *representation*; interpretation, improvisation, impression, miming 20 *mimicry*; histrionics, play-acting; the Method; ham-acting, hamming, barnstorming; overacting, staginess, theatricality; repertoire; character, personage, role; starring role, leading r.; part, fat p.; vignette, cameo; supporting part, bit p., speaking p.; walk-on p.; stock part; principal boy *or* girl; stage fever; stage fright.

actor, actress, Thespian; mimic, mime; mummer, masker; play-actor, player, strolling p., trouper, cabotin(e); barnstormer, ham; rep player, character actor; actor-manager, star, film star, starlet, matinée idol 890 *favourite*; tragedian, tragedienne; comedian, comedienne; opera singer, prima donna, diva; ballet dancer, ballerina, prima b., coryphée; danseur, danseuse, figurant(e); protagonist, lead, leading man *or* lady, juvenile lead; understudy, stand-in 150 *substitute*; lookalike 18 *analogue*; supernumerary, super, extra, bit player; chorus, corps de ballet, troupe, company, repertory c., stock c.; dramatis personae, characters, cast; presenter, narrator; prologue 579 *speaker*.

entertainer, performer; artiste, artist, quick-change a., drag a., striptease a.; diseur, diseuse, monologist; impressionist, impersonator; troubadour, minstrel; street musician, busker; crooner, pop singer 413 *vocalist*; comic, stand-up c. 839 *humorist*; ventriloquist, fire-eater, juggler 545 *conjuror*; ropewalker, acrobat; clown, buffoon 501 *fool*; pierrot, pierrette;

hoofer, dancer, show girl, chorus g., belly dancer, gogo d.

stagehand, scene shifter; property man; scene painter; electrician, machinist; sound recordist, special effects man, continuity girl; costumier, wardrobe mistress, wigmaker, make-up artist; prompter, callboy; programme seller, usher, usherette, doorman.

stage manager, producer, director, regisseur; designer, manager, actor m., business m., press agent; impresario, showman; backer, sponsor, angel.

dramatist, dramaturge; playwright, script writer, lyric w., librettist; farceur 839 *humorist*; choreographer.

playgoer, theatregoer, operagoer 504 *enthusiast*; first-nighter; stage-door Johnny; audience, house, packed h., full h.; groundling, pittite 441 *spectator*; claque; dramatic critic, play *or* film reviewer.

Adj. *dramatic*, dramaturgical; scenic, theatrical, stagy 551 *representing*; operatic, balletic, Terpsichorean, choreographic; live, legitimate; Thespian, Roscian; histrionic, mimetic 20 *imitative*; tragic, buskined; Thalian, comic, tragicomic; farcical, burlesque, knockabout, slapstick 849 *funny*; cathartic, melodramatic, sensational 821 *exciting*; Brechtian, Shavian, Pinteresque, avant-garde; dramatized, acted; hammed up, camped up; hammy, barnstorming; on the stage, acting; cast, cast as, miscast; featured, starred, top of the bill; stagestruck, filmstruck, theatregoing.

Vb. *dramatize*, be a dramatist, write for the stage; adapt for the stage *or* for radio; stage, mount, produce, direct, stagemanage; rehearse; cast, typecast; star, feature, bill; present, put on, release 522 *show*; open, ring up the curtain.

act, go on the stage, tread the boards; face the cameras; perform, enact, play, playact; personify, personate, impersonate 551 *represent*; mime, take off 20 *imitate*; create a role, play the lead; play opposite, support; star, co-star, steal the show, upstage; play to the gallery, ham it up, camp it up, send up, barnstorm, overact, overdramatize 546 *exaggerate*; underact, throw away; walk on; understudy, stand in 150 *substitute*; rehearse, say one's lines; cue in; fluff, dry; ad-lib, gag; dramatize oneself 875 *be ostentatious*.

Adv. *on stage*, offstage, upstage, downstage, backstage; behind the footlights, in the limelight; dramatically.

Class Five

VOLITION: THE EXERCISE OF THE WILL

5.1 INDIVIDUAL VOLITION

Section 1:
Volition in general

595. Will – N. *will*, willing, volition; velleity; disposition 597 *willingness*; conation, act of will 682 *exertion*; strength of will, willpower 599 *resolution*; self control; intent, purpose 617 *intention*; decision 608 *predetermination*; one's will and pleasure; appetence 859 *desire*; one's own sweet will 932 *selfishness*; self-will, wilfulness 602 *obstinacy*; whimsicality 604 *caprice*; acte gratuit; free will, free choice 605 *choice*; voluntariness, spontaneity; voluntarism.

Adj. *volitional*, willing, volitive, conative; unprompted, freewill, spontaneous, 597 *voluntary*; discretional, discretionary, optional; minded, so m. 617 *intending*; self-willed, wilful 602 *obstinate*; arbitrary, autocratic, dictatorial 735 *authoritarian*; independent, self-determined 744 *free*; determined 599 *resolute*; intentional, willed 608 *predetermined*.

Vb. *will*, impose one's will, have one's way 737 *command*; be so minded 605 *choose*; purpose, determine 617 *intend*; wish 859 *desire*; have a mind *or* a will of one's own, go one's own way, be one's own man *or* woman 744 *be free*; be self-willed, take the law into one's own hands 602 *be obstinate*; know one's own mind 599 *be resolute*; volunteer 597 *be willing*; originate 156 *cause*.

Adv. *at will*, at pleasure, ad libitum, ad lib; voluntarily, of one's own free will, of one's own accord; spontaneously, for the heck of it.

596. Necessity – N. *necessity*, stern n.; no alternative 606 *no choice*; last resort 700

predicament; the inevitable, what must be 155 *destiny*; necessitation, dictation, determinism, fatalism 608 *predetermination*; pressure of events, force of circumstances, c. beyond one's control, act of God 154 *event*; no freedom 745 *subjection*; physical necessity, law of nature; force, superior f. 740 *compulsion*; logical necessity 478 *demonstration*; moral necessity, obligation 917 *duty*; necessitude, indispensability 627 *requirement*; involuntariness, reflex, conditioned r.; instinct, blind i. 476 *intuition*; fatalist, determinist, necessitarian.

fate, lot, cup, portion; weird, karma, kismet; doom, foredoom, predestination, preordination, election 155 *destiny*; book of fate, will of heaven; fortune 159 *chance*; stars, planets; the Fates, Parcae, Norns; Fatal Sisters, Lachesis, Clotho, Atropos.

Adj. *necessary*, indispensable 627 *required*; logical, unanswerable; imperative 740 *compelling*; overriding, irresistible, resistless; compulsory, mandatory 917 *obligatory*; necessitated, inevitable, inescapable, inexorable 473 *certain*; dictated, imposed, necessitarian, deterministic 606 *choiceless*.

involuntary, instinctive 476 *intuitive*; unpremeditated, unintended 618 *unintentional*; unconscious, unthinking, unwitting, blind, impulsive 609 *spontaneous*; unassenting 598 *unwilling*; under a spell 983 *bewitched*; automatic, machinelike, mechanistic, mechanical.

fated, karmic, fatal; appointed, destined, predestined, preordained 608 *predetermined*; elect 605 *chosen*; doomed, foredoomed; bound, obliged 745 *subject*.

Vb. *be forced*, etc. adj.; incur the necessity, lie under the n.; bow to fate, dree one's weird; be cornered 700 *be in* *difficulty*; have no choice, have no option, needs must; be unable to help it, be made that way.

necessitate, dictate, oblige 740 *compel*; bind by fate, destine, doom, foredoom 155 *predestine*; insist, leave no choice, demand 627 *require*.

Adv. *necessarily*, of necessity, of course, perforce; nothing for it, no help for it, no two ways about it; willy-nilly.

597. Willingness – N. *willingness*, voluntariness; spontaneousness 609 *spontaneity*; free choice 605 *choice*; disposition, mind, inclination 179 *tendency*; facility 694 *aptitude*; predisposition, readiness, right mood; cordiality, good will 897 *benevolence*; acquiescence 488 *assent*; compliance 758 *consent*; zeal, ardour, enthusiasm; impatience, overeagerness; dedication, sacrifice 931 *disinterestedness*; helpfulness 706 *cooperation*; pliancy, docility, tractability 612 *persuadability*.

volunteer, unpaid worker; ready w., willing horse 678 *busy person*, 901 *philanthropist*.

Adj. *willing*, ungrudging, acquiescent 488 *assenting*; compliant, agreeable, game for 758 *consenting*; in the mood, receptive, favourable, inclined, disposed, predisposed, amenable; pleased, glad, charmed, delighted; ready 669 *prepared*; ready and willing, prompt, quick; forward, anticipating; alacritous, zealous, eager, enthusiastic, dedicated, keen as mustard; overeager, impatient, spoiling for, raring to go; earnest, trying 671 *attempting*; helpful 706 *cooperative*; docile, biddable, easy-going 24 *agreeing*; fain, dying to 859 *desiring*; would-be 617 *intending*.

voluntary, offered, unprompted, unforced, unasked 609 *spontaneous*; unsolicited, self-imposed; supererogatory, beyond the call of duty; nonmandatory, discretionary, optional 605 *chosen*; volunteering, on one's own initiative, off one's own bat, of one's own free will; gratuitous, free, honorary 812 *uncharged*.

Vb. *be willing*, etc. adj.; not mind, have half a mind to; feel like, have a good mind

to 595 *will*; yearn to 859 *desire*; mean to 617 *intend*; agree, show willing, comply 758 *consent*; be found willing 739 *obey*; try, do one's best 671 *attempt*; go out of one's way, lean over backwards, collaborate 706 *cooperate*; anticipate, meet halfway; swallow, jump at, leap at; can't wait; stomach, make no bones about, not scruple, not hesitate, not hold back; volunteer 759 *offer oneself*.

Adv. *willingly*, with a will, readily, cordially, heartily; without being asked 595 *at will*; readily, like a shot, at the drop of a hat; with a good grace, nothing loath; gladly, with pleasure.

598. Unwillingness – N. *unwillingness*, disinclination, indisposition, reluctance; demur, objection 489 *dissent*; protest 762 *deprecation*; recalcitrance 704 *opposition*; rejection 760 *refusal*; unhelpfulness, noncooperation, dissociation, abstention; unenthusiasm, lack of zeal 860 *indifference*; backwardness 278 *slowness*; hesitation 858 *caution*; scruple, qualm 486 *doubt*; repugnance 861 *dislike*; aversion, no stomach for 620 *avoidance*; bashfulness 874 *modesty*; noncompliance 738 *disobedience*; indocility, refractoriness, fractiousness 893 *sullenness*; postponement 136 *delay*; remissness 458 *negligence*; slacker, shirker.

Adj. *unwilling*, indisposed, loath, reluctant, averse; not so minded, not in the mood 760 *refusing*; unconsenting, unreconciled 489 *dissenting*; opposed, irreconcilable 704 *opposing*; demurring, protesting 762 *deprecatory*; with no stomach for 861 *disliking*; regretful 830 *regretting*; hesitant 858 *cautious*; shy, bashful 874 *modest*; shirking 620 *avoiding*; unenthusiastic, half-hearted, lukewarm; backward, dragging 278 *slow*; unhelpful, uncooperative 702 *hindering*; fractious, recalcitrant, kicking 738 *disobedient*; not trying, perfunctory 458 *negligent*; grudging, sulky 893 *sullen*; unspontaneous, forced.

Vb. *be unwilling*, etc. adj.; not have the heart to, not stomach 861 *dislike*; disagree 489 *dissent*; object, demur, protest 762 *deprecate*; resist 704 *oppose*; reject 760 *refuse*; recoil, back away, duck, shirk 620 *avoid*; skimp, scamp 458 *neglect*; drag one's feet, look over one's shoulder, hang back 278 *move slowly*; slack, not pull one's weight 679 *be inactive*; not play, non-cooperate, dissociate oneself, abstain; grudge, begrudge 893 *be sullen*; force oneself, make o.

Adv. *unwillingly*, reluctantly, under protest, under pressure, with a bad grace, in spite of oneself, against one's will, against the grain; regretfully; not for the world.

599. Resolution – N. *resolution*, determination; earnestness, seriousness; resolve, fixed r., mind made up; decision 608 *predetermination*; drive, vigour 174 *vigorousness*; energy, thoroughness; fixity of purpose, concentration, iron will, willpower 595 *will*; strength of character, self-control, self-restraint, self-mastery, self-possession; tenacity 600 *perseverance*; aplomb, mettle, daring; guts, pluck, spunk, grit, backbone, spirit; fortitude, stiff upper lip, moral fibre 855 *courage*; single-mindedness, devotedness, devotion, dedication; staunchness, steadiness 153 *stability*; insistence, relentlessness, ruthlessness, inflexibility, steeliness 326 *hardness*; iron, steel, rock; clenched teeth, hearts of oak, bulldog breed 600 *stamina*; Mr Standfast.

Adj. *resolute*, resolved, made up, determined 595 *volitional*; desperate, stopping at nothing; serious, earnest, concentrated; intent upon, set u. 617 *intending*; pressing, urgent, forceful, energetic, heroic 174 *vigorous*; zealous 455 *attentive*; steady, staunch, constant 153 *unchangeable*; iron-willed, strong-w., strong-minded, decisive, decided, unbending, immovable, unyielding, inflexible 602 *obstinate*; stern, grim, inexorable, implacable, relentless, ruthless, steely 326 *hard*; stalwart 855 *unfearing*; steadfast, unwavering, unshakable, unshrinking, unflinching 600 *persevering*; indomitable 727 *unbeaten*; steeled, armoured, proof; self-controlled, self-possessed, self-reliant,

self-confident; purposive, purposeful, single-minded, whole-hearted, devoted, dedicated.

Vb. *be resolute*, etc. adj.; steel oneself, brace o., set one's face, clench *or* grit one's teeth; make up one's mind, will, resolve, determine 617 *intend*; insist 532 *emphasize*; cut through, override, put one's foot down, stand no nonsense; mean business, stick at nothing, not stop at trifles, go to all lengths, go the whole hog, see it through 725 *carry through*; face 661 *face danger*; outface, dare 711 *defy*; endure, go through fire and water 825 *suffer*; face the issue, take the bull by the horns; take the plunge, cross the Rubicon, burn one's boats; nail one's colours to the mast; be single-minded, set one's heart on, devote *or* dedicate oneself, commit oneself, give oneself to; set to, buckle to, go to it, put one's heart into 682 *exert oneself*.

stand firm, not be moved, dig one's toes *or* heels in, stand one's ground; not yield, not give an inch; stand fast 600 *persevere*; have what it takes, soldier on, stick it out, grin and bear it, endure 825 *suffer*.

Adv. *resolutely*, seriously, in good earnest; at any price, at all costs; in spite of everything, quand même; come what may, live or die, neck or nothing, once and for all.

600. Perseverance – N. *perseverance*, persistence, tenacity 602 *obstinacy*; staunchness, constancy, steadfastness 599 *resolution*; single-mindedness 455 *attention*; application, tirelessness 678 *assiduity*; doggedness, plodding 682 *exertion*; endurance, patience, fortitude; maintenance 146 *continuance*; ceaselessness 144 *permanence*.

stamina, staying power, indefatigability 162 *strength*; grit, true g., backbone, gameness, pluck 855 *courage*; old guard 602 *obstinate person*; trier, stayer 686 *worker*.

Adj. *persevering*, persistent, tenacious, stubborn 602 *obstinate*; game, plucky; patient, plodding, dogged 678 *industrious*; steady, unfaltering, unwavering, unflagging, indefatigable; unsleeping 457 *vigil-*

ant; unfailing, constant 146 *unceasing*; renewed, reiterated 106 *repeated*; indomitable, unconquerable 727 *unbeaten*; undaunted, undiscouraged 599 *resolute*.

Vb. *persevere*, persist, keep at it, not take no for an answer, hold out for; not despair, never say die 852 *hope*; endure 825 *suffer*; keep on trying 671 *attempt*; keep up 146 *sustain*; plod, peg away, plug a., hammer a. at 682 *work*; continue, go on, keep on, keep the ball rolling, keep going; not let go, hang on like grim death 778 *retain*; stick it out, sweat it out, stay the course, stick with it, see it through, see one buried first; not budge 602 *be obstinate*; stick to one's guns, hold out 599 *stand firm*; move heaven and earth 682 *exert oneself*; see the end of 725 *carry through*.

Adv. *persistently*, perseveringly, never say die; through thick and thin, to the bitter end.

601. Irresolution – N. *irresolution*, faintheartedness 856 *cowardice*; nonperseverance, broken resolve 603 *change of allegiance*; indecision, uncertainty 474 *dubiety*; hesitation 858 *caution*; inconstancy, fluctuation, vacillation 152 *changeableness*; fickleness 604 *caprice*; lack of willpower, lack of drive 175 *inertness*; passivity 679 *inactivity*; easygoingness, compromise 734 *laxity*; half-heartedness, half measures 726 *noncompletion*; lukewarmness 860 *indifference*; no will of one's own 163 *weakness*; impressibility, suggestibility, pliancy 612 *persuadability*.

waverer, shilly-shallyer; shuttlecock, butterfly; weathercock, chameleon 603 *turncoat*; faintheart, compromiser.

Adj. *irresolute*, undecided, indecisive, of two minds, vacillating; unable to make up one's mind 474 *doubting*; squeamish, hesitating 598 *unwilling*; timid, fainthearted, unheroic, nerveless 856 *cowardly*; shaken 854 *nervous*; half-hearted 860 *indifferent*; wobbling, unreliable; compromising, weak-willed, weak-kneed, spineless 163 *weak*; suggestible, pliant; easygoing, good-natured 734 *lax*; variable, temperamental 152 *changeful*;

whimsical 604 *capricious*; emotional 152 *unstable*; irresponsible 456 *light-minded*; impatient, unpersevering; unfaithful 603 *trimming*.

Vb. *be irresolute*, etc. adj.; back away 620 *avoid*; palter, shuffle 518 *be equivocal*; fluctuate, vacillate, seesaw, wobble, waver, sway, hover, teeter, dither 317 *oscillate*; not know one's own mind, blow hot and cold, hum and haw, be in two minds 474 *be uncertain*; leave in suspense 136 *put off*; debate, balance 475 *argue*; have second thoughts, hesitate 858 *be cautious*; falter, give up 621 *relinquish*; take half measures 770 *compromise*; give way 721 *submit*; change sides 603 *apostatize*.

602. Obstinacy – N. *obstinacy*, mind of one's own 599 *resolution*; tenacity, pertinacity 600 *perseverance*; stubbornness, obduracy; self-will, pigheadedness; inelasticity, inflexibility; intransigence, hard line, no compromise; fixity 152 *stability*; stiff neck 715 *resistance*; indocility, intractability, mulishness; perversity, wrongheadedness, cussedness, bloodymindedness.

opinionatedness, opiniativeness 473 *positiveness*; dogmatism, bigotry, zealotry; rigorism, intolerance, fanaticism 735 *severity*; ruling passion, obsession 481 *bias*; illiberality; old school, ancien régime.

obstinate person, mule; stick-in-the-mud, Blimp; hard-liner, hard core; fanatic, rigorist, stickler, pedant, dogmatist, zealot, bigot; last-ditcher, die-hard, bitter-ender 600 *stamina*; old fogy 504 *crank*.

Adj. *obstinate*, stubborn; bull-headed, pig-headed, mulish; pertinacious, unyielding 599 *resolute*; dogged, tenacious 600 *persevering*; adamant, inflexible, unbending; obdurate, hard-nosed, hardened, case-h.; uncompromising, intransigent; unmoved, immovable 153 *unchangeable*; unappeasable, implacable; wedded to, set in one's ways, hidebound, ultraconservative, blimpish 610 *habituated*; unteachable, impervious, blind, deaf; opinionated, dogmatic, pedantic 473 *positive*; obsessed, bigoted, fanatical

481 *biased*; dour, grim 893 *sullen*; hard-mouthed, stiff-necked 940 *impenitent*; perverse, incorrigible, bloody-minded.

wilful, self-willed, wayward, arbitrary; headstrong, perverse; unruly, jibbing, restive, refractory; irrepressible, ungovernable, intractable 738 *disobedient*; unpersuadable, incorrigible, contumacious; cross-grained, crotchety 892 *irascible*.

Vb. *be obstinate*, etc. adj.; persist 600 *persevere*; brazen it out 940 *be impenitent*; stick to one's guns, not budge 599 *stand firm*; go one's own way 734 *please oneself*; not change one's mind 473 *dogmatize*; not listen, stop up one's ears, take the bit between one's teeth, damn the consequences 857 *be rash*.

603. Change of allegiance – N. *change of allegiance*, change of mind; second thoughts 67 *sequel*; conversion, break with the past; backsliding, recidivism 657 *relapse*; change of direction, reversal, about-face, about-turn, U-turn, volte-face 286 *return*; slipperiness, suppleness, unreliability 930 *improbity*; tergiversation, apostasy, recreancy (see *recantation*); defection, desertion 918 *undutifulness*; secession, withdrawal 621 *relinquishment*; coquetry 604 *caprice*.

recantation, palinode, eating one's words, retraction, withdrawal, apology; renunciation, abjuration, forswearing, swearing off; disavowal, disclaimer; revocation 752 *abrogation*.

turncoat, rat; weathercock 152 *changeable thing*; opportunist, time-server, trimmer, Vicar of Bray 518 *equivocalness*; double-dealer 545 *deceiver*; jilt, flirt, coquette 604 *caprice*; tergiversator, recanter, recreant, apostate, renegade, forswearer, traitor, quisling 707 *collaborator*; lost leader, deserter, defector, quitter, ratter; squealer 524 *informer*; blackleg, scab; secessionist 978 *schismatic*; recidivist, backslider; convert, proselyte.

Adj. *trimming*, shuffling 518 *equivocal*; slippery, treacherous 930 *perfidious*; double-dealing 541 *hypocritical*; reactionary 286 *regressive*; fickle 604 *capricious*;

timeserving 925 *flattering*; vacillating 601 *irresolute*; apostate, recanting, renegade; recidivist, relapsed; false, unfaithful 918 *undutiful*.

Vb. *tergiversate*, change one's mind, think better of it 601 *be irresolute*; change one's tune, shift one's ground 152 *vary*; get cold feet, back out; back down (see *recant*); swerve, wheel about, turn one's back on; turn over a new leaf 939 *be penitent*; backslide 657 *relapse*; trim, shuffle, face both ways 518 *be equivocal*; jilt, desert, walk out on 621 *relinquish*; turn against, play false.

apostatize, turn one's coat, change sides, change one's allegiance; switch over, cross over, cross the floor; desert, defect, fall away; blackleg, rat; be off with the old love.

recant, unsay, eat one's words, eat one's hat; eat humble pie, apologize; take back, go back on, backpedal, backtrack, do a U-turn; recall one's words, resile, withdraw, retract, disavow 533 *negate*; renounce, abjure, forswear, swear off; revoke, rescind 752 *abrogate*.

604. Caprice – N. *caprice*, capriciousness, arbitrariness; whimsicality, freakishness, crankiness 497 *absurdity*; faddishness 481 *bias*; inconsistency, changeability, variability, fickleness, unreliability, levity, giddiness 152 *changeableness*; inconstancy, coquettishness, flirtatiousness; playfulness; pettishness.

whim, whimsy, caprice, fancy, megrim 513 *ideality*; passing fancy, impulse 609 *spontaneity*; vagary, sweet will, humour, mood, fit, crotchet, bee in the bonnet, maggot, quirk, kink, fad, craze, freak 503 *eccentricity*; escapade, prank 497 *foolery*; coquetry, flirtation.

Adj. *capricious*, motiveless, purposeless; whimsical, fanciful, fantastic; eccentric, humoursome, temperamental, crotchety, maggoty, freakish; prankish, mischievous, wanton, wayward, perverse; faddy, faddish 862 *fastidious*; captious, arbitrary, unreasonable; fretful, moody, contrary 892 *irascible*; undisciplined, refractory 602 *wilful*; erratic, unpredict-

able 508 *unexpected*; volatile, mercurial
456 *light-minded*; inconsistent 152 *unstable*; irresponsible, unreliable, fickle 603
trimming; flirtatious, coquettish, playful.

Vb. *be capricious*, etc. adj.; take it into
one's head; pick and choose, chop and
change, blow hot and cold 152 *vary*; have a
bee in one's bonnet 481 *be biased*; vacillate 601 *be irresolute*; flirt, coquette 837
amuse oneself.

Adv. *capriciously*, fitfully, as the mood
takes one, on impulse.

605. Choice – N. *choice*, election 463
discrimination; picking and choosing 862
fastidiousness; picking out, selection; co-
option, co-optation, adoption; nomination 751 *commission*; option; discretion, pick; decision 480 *judgement*;
preference, predilection, partiality 179
tendency; taste 859 *liking*; selection, list,
short l.; alternative, embarras de choix;
difficult choice, dilemma 474 *dubiety*; no
real alternative; nothing for it but 606 *no
choice*; greater good, lesser evil 642 *good
policy*; fancy, first choice, top seed; selection, pickings, gleanings, excerpts 592
anthology.

vote, voice 485 *opinion*; representation,
proportional r., cumulative vote, transferable v., majority v., first past the post;
casting vote; ballot, secret b., open vote,
postal v.; card vote; vote of confidence; show of hands, division, poll, plebiscite, referendum; suffrage, universal s.,
adult s.; franchise, right of representation;
parliamentary system, electoral s., ballot
box, vox populi; straw vote, Gallup poll
(tdmk), opinion p.; election, general e.;
by-election; primary; polls, hustings, candidature; return; psephology, psephol-
ogist; suffragette, suffragist.

electorate, voters, balloter, elector,
electoral college; quorum; electoral roll,
voting list; constituent, constituency, marginal c.; borough, pocket b., rotten b.;
polling booth, ballot box; slate, ticket,
manifesto.

Adj. *choosing*, optional, discretional
595 *volitional*; choosy 463 *discriminating*;
preferential, favouring 923 *approving*;

selective, eclectic; co-optative, elective,
electoral; voting, enfranchised; vote-
catching, electioneering, canvassing;
psephological.

chosen, preferable, better 642 *advisable*; select, choice 644 *excellent*; seeded
62 *arranged*; elect, designate; elected, returned; adopted, selected; preferred,
favourite, pet; by appointment.

Vb. *choose*, have a voice 595 *will*; make
one's choice; shop around, be choosy;
exercise one's discretion, opt for, take up
an option; elect, co-opt, adopt 923
approve; favour, fancy, like best; incline,
lean 179 *tend*; prefer, like better, would
rather; might as well, might do worse; go
in for, take up, be into; decide, make up
one's mind 480 *judge*; settle on, fix on,
come out for, plump f.; commit oneself,
take the plunge 599 *be resolute*; range
oneself, take sides, side, back, support,
embrace, espouse 703 *patronize*.

select, pick, pick out, single o.; pass 923
approve; nominate 751 *commission*; designate, mark out, mark down 547 *mark*;
preselect, earmark, reserve 46 *set apart*;
recommend 703 *patronize*; cull 592 *abstract*; glean, winnow, sift 463 *discriminate*; draw the line, separate; skim off,
cream; pick and choose 862 *be fastidious*.

vote, have a v., have a voice; be enfranchised; poll, cast a vote, register one's
v., raise one's hand, divide; vote for, vote
in, elect, return; vote down 607 *reject*;
electioneer, canvass; stand 759 *offer oneself*; put to the vote, hold a referendum;
count heads, count noses; hold an election, go to the country.

Adv. *optionally*, alternatively, either
. . . or; preferably, rather, sooner; à la
carte.

606. Absence of choice – N. *no choice*,
Hobson's choice, no alternative 596 *necessity*; dictation 740 *compulsion*; first that
comes 464 *indiscrimination*; impartiality,
first come first served 913 *justice*; no preference, noncommitment, nonalignment
neutrality 860 *indifference*; no difference,
six of one and half a dozen of the other, 'a
plague on both your houses' 28 *equality*;

indecision, open mind 474 *dubiety*; floating vote 601 *irresolution*; abstention 598 *unwillingness*; disfranchisement, disqualification, no vote, no voice.

Adj. *choiceless*, without alternative 596 *necessary*; without a preference, unable to choose, happy either way 625 *neutral*; open-minded, open to conviction, unresolved 601 *irresolute*; uninterested, apathetic 860 *indifferent*; disinterested, motiveless; impartial 913 *just*; abstaining 598 *unwilling*; nonvoting, voteless, unenfranchised, disfranchised, disqualified.

Vb. *be neutral*, take no sides, make no choice, not vote, abstain; sit on the fence 601 *be irresolute*; not care 860 *be indifferent*.

have no choice, have no alternative, take it or leave it, make a virtue of necessity 596 *be forced*; have no voice, have no vote.

Adv. *neither*, neither . . . nor.

607. Rejection – N. *rejection*, nonacceptance; nonapproval 924 *disapprobation*; repudiation, denial 533 *negation*; rebuff, repulse, frozen mitt, cold shoulder 760 *refusal*; spurn, kick, more kicks than ha'pence; lost election, nonelection 728 *defeat*; elimination 300 *ejection*; nonconsideration, counting out 57 *exclusion*; discarding 674 *nonuse*; discard, reject; unpopular cause, lost c.

Adj. *rejected*, thrown out etc. vb.; unsuitable, ineligible, unchosen 860 *unwanted*; unaccepted, sent back, tried and found wanting, declined with thanks 924 *disapproved*; kept out 57 *excluded*; not be thought of, out of the question 643 *inexpedient*; discarded 674 *disused*.

Vb. *reject*, not accept, decline, draw the line at, rebuff, repulse, spurn, dismiss out of hand 760 *refuse*; not approve, not pass, return, send back 924 *disapprove*; not consider, pass over 458 *disregard*; vote against 489 *dissent*; scrap, ditch, junk 674 *stop using*; set aside 752 *depose*; expel 300 *eject*; sort out 44 *eliminate*; count out 57 *exclude*; blackball, cold-shoulder, give the brush-off 885 *be rude*; not want 883 *make unwelcome*; disclaim, disavow, deny 533

negate; abnegate, repudiate 603 *recant*; scorn, disdain 851 *ridicule*; look a gift horse in the mouth 922 *hold cheap*.

608. Predetermination – N. *predetermination*, predestination 596 *necessity*; foreordination, preordination; premeditation, resolve 617 *intention*; prearrangement 669 *preparation*; order paper, agenda; frame-up, put-up job, packed jury 623 *plot*; parti pris, closed mind 481 *prejudice*; foregone conclusion.

Adj. *predetermined*, decreed, premeditated etc. vb.; predestined, foreordained 596 *fated*; willed, aforethought, prepense 617 *intending*; studied, weighed, considered, advised; contrived 623 *planned*; put-up, framed, prearranged 669 *prepared*.

Vb. *predetermine*, destine, appoint 155 *predestine*; premeditate, preconceive 617 *intend*; preconcert; settle, fix 156 *cause*; contrive, arrange, prearrange 623 *plan*; stack the cards 541 *fake*.

609. Spontaneity – N. *spontaneity*, unpremeditation; improvisation; extemporization, impromptu 670 *nonpreparation*; involuntariness, reflex, automatic r. 476 *intuition*; impulsiveness, impulse; spur of the moment; snap decision; inspiration, hunch, flash 451 *idea*.

improviser, extemporizer, improvisatore, improvisatrice; creature of impulse.

Adj. *spontaneous*, offhand, ad hoc, improvised, extemporaneous, extempory, sudden, snap; makeshift, catch-as-catch-can 670 *unprepared*; impromptu, unpremeditated, unrehearsed 618 *unintentional*; unprompted, unmotivated, unprovoked; unforced 597 *voluntary*; unguarded, incautious 857 *rash*; involuntary, automatic 476 *intuitive*; untaught 699 *artless*; impulsive, emotional 818 *feeling*.

Vb. *improvise*, extemporize, vamp, adlib 670 *be unprepared*; obey an impulse, act on the spur of the moment 604 *be capricious*; blurt, come out with, say whatever comes into one's head; rise to the occasion.

Adv. *extempore*, extemporaneously, impromptu, ad hoc, on the spur of the moment, offhand, off the cuff, off the top of one's head.

610. Habit – N. *habit*, habitude, force of habit; familiarity, second nature; addiction, confirmed habit; trait, idiosyncrasy; knack, trick, mannerism; usage, long habit, consuetude, custom; use, wont 146 *continuance*; prescription 127 *tradition*; law, precedent; way, ways, the old w.; lifestyle, way of life; beaten track; groove, rut; fixed ways, round, daily r. 16 *uniformity*; regularity 141 *periodicity*; run, routine 60 *order*; traditionalism, conservatism, old school 83 *conformity*.

practice, common p., usual custom, usual policy, matter of course; conformism, conventionalism 83 *conformity*; mores, manners and customs, social usage, behaviour patterns; institution, ritual, observance 988 *rite*, 981 *cult*; mode, vogue, craze 848 *fashion*; convention, protocol, done thing, usual thing; recognized procedure, drill; form, good f. 848 *etiquette*; manners, table m.; rules and regulations, standing order, routine 688 *conduct*; spit and polish 60 *order*.

habituation, training 534 *teaching*; inurement 669 *maturation*; naturalization, acclimatization; acquired taste; conditioning, association, fixation; drill 106 *repetition*.

habitué, creature of habit, addict, drug a. 949 *drug-taking*; traditionalist, conventionalist 83 *conformist*; customer, regular, client 792 *purchaser*; frequenter, devotee, fan 504 *enthusiast*.

Adj. *habitual*, customary, familiar 490 *known*; routine, stereotyped 81 *regular*; conventional, traditionary, traditional; orthodox; inveterate, prescriptive, time-honoured 113 *lasting*; occupational; haunting, besetting, obsessive; habit-forming 612 *inducing*; ingrained, dyed-in-the-wool 5 *intrinsic*; deep-rooted, deep-seated 153 *fixed*.

usual, accustomed, wonted, consuetudinary, traditional; in character, natural; household, familiar, well-known 490 *known*; unoriginal, trite, well-worn, hackneyed; banal, commonplace, common,

ordinary 79 *general*; set, stock 83 *typical*; prevalent, current 79 *universal*; daily, everyday 139 *frequent*; practised, done; settled, established, hallowed by custom 923 *approved*; de rigueur 740 *compelling*; invariable 153 *unchangeable*; in the fashion 848 *fashionable*.

habituated, in the habit of, accustomed to; given to, addicted to; used to, familiar with, at home with 490 *knowing*; inveterate, confirmed; practised, seasoned, trained, tame.

Vb. *be wont*, be used to; have the habit of; haunt, frequent; make a habit of, take up, go in for; be set in one's ways, cling to custom; become a habit, catch on, grow on one, take hold of o., stick; settle, take root; obtain, hold good 178 *prevail*.

habituate, accustom oneself, get used to, get into the way of, get the knack *or* the feel *or* the hang of, play oneself in, get into one's stride; take to, acquire the habit, cultivate a h.; get into a habit, catch oneself doing; keep one's hand in, practise 106 *repeat*; accustom, inure 534 *train*; domesticate, tame 369 *break in*; naturalize, acclimatize; imbue 534 *teach*; condition 178 *influence*.

611. Desuetude – N. *desuetude*, discontinuance, disuse 674 *nonuse*; rustiness, lack of practice 695 *unskilfulness*; outgrown custom; weaning 134 *adultness*; unwontedness, nonprevalence; not the thing, unconventionality 84 *nonconformity*; want of habit, inexperience, unfamiliarity 491 *ignorance*.

Adj. *unwonted*, not customary, not current, nonprevalent; unpractised, not observed, not done; unfashionable, bad form 847 *vulgar*; out of fashion 125 *past*; outgrown, discarded 674 *disused*; against custom, unconventional 84 *unconformable*; untraditional, unprecedented; unhackneyed 21 *original*.

unhabituated, unaccustomed, not used to, not in the habit of; untrained, not broken in, untamed, undomesticated; unfamiliar, inexperienced, new to, raw, green 491 *uninstructed*; disaccustomed, weaned; dried out; rusty 695 *unskilful*.

Vb. *disaccustom*, wean from, cure of 656 *cure*; break a habit, lose a h., kick the h.; wean oneself from, outgrow; give up, throw off, slough off, shed.

be unpractised, etc. adj.; not catch on; not be done, infringe protocol; lapse, fall into disuse.

612. Motive – N. *motive*, what is behind it 156 *cause*; rationale, reasons 156 *reason why*; motivation, driving force, impetus, mainspring, what makes one tick 156 *causation*; intention 617 *objective*; ideal, principle, guiding p. 689 *directorship*; aspiration, ambition 859 *desire*; calling, call 622 *vocation*; personal reasons, ulterior motive 932 *selfishness*; impulse 609 *spontaneity*.

inducement, pressure, insistence; lobbying 178 *influence*; provocation, incitement, encouragement, instigation, inspiration 821 *excitation*; solicitation, invitation 761 *request*; temptation, enticement, allurement, seduction, seductiveness, tantalization, witchery, bewitchment, fascination, charm, sex appeal, magnetism 291 *attraction*; cajolery, blandishment 925 *flattery*; coaxing, wheedling 889 *endearment*; persuasion, persuasiveness, salesmanship, sales talk 579 *eloquence*; pep talk, trumpet call, rallying cry 547 *call*; exhortation 534 *lecture*; pleading, advocacy 691 *advice*; propaganda, agitprop; advertising, soft sell, hard s. 528 *advertisement*; promises, election p.; bribery, b. and corruption 962 *reward*; castigation, tongue-lashing; honeyed words, siren song, winning ways.

persuadability, docility, tractability 597 *willingness*; pliancy, susceptibility, susceptivity, suggestibility, impressibility 819 *moral sensibility*; credulousness 487 *credulity*.

incentive, inducement; stimulus, fillip, tickle, prod, spur, goad, lash, whip 174 *stimulant*; rod, big stick, crack of the whip 900 *threat*; carrot, sop, sop to Cerberus; charm 983 *spell*; attraction 291 *magnet*; will-o'-the wisp 440 *visual fallacy*; lure, decoy, bait 542 *trap*; come-on, loss leader, special offer; profit 771 *gain*; pay, perks,

rise, bonus 804 *payment*; gratuity, tip, bribe 962 *reward*; slush fund, pork barrel; offer one cannot refuse 759 *offer*.

motivator, mover, prime m. 156 *cause*; manipulator, manager 178 *influence*; tactician, strategist 623 *planner*; instigator, prompter, inspirer, muse, counsellor 691 *adviser*; abettor 703 *aider*; agent provocateur 545 *deceiver*; tantalizer, tempter, seducer; seductress, temptress, vamp, femme fatale, siren; persuader, orator, rhetorician 579 *speaker*; advocate, pleader; coaxer, wheedler 925 *flatterer*; votecatcher, vote-snatcher; salesman *or* -woman, advertiser, propagandist 528 *publicizer*; ringleader 690 *leader*; rabblerouser 738 *agitator*; lobbyist, lobby, pressure group, ginger g.

Adj. *inducing*, inciting; incentive, provocative, persuasive; hortatory, directive; motivating, wire-pulling 178 *influential*; stimulating, challenging, rousing, inflaming 821 *exciting*; teasing, tantalizing; inviting, tempting, alluring 291 *attracting*; magnetic, fascinating, bewitching 983 *sorcerous*; irresistible, hypnotic, mesmeric; habit-forming 610 *habitual*.

induced, brought on 157 *caused*; inspired, motivated, goal-oriented; incited, egged on, spurred on 821 *excited*; receptive, tractable 597 *willing*; spellbound 983 *bewitched*; persuasible 487 *credulous*.

Vb. *motivate*, move, actuate 173 *operate*; manipulate, work upon, play u. 178 *influence*; weigh, count, sway 178 *prevail*; call the tune 34 *predominate*; work on the feelings, appeal, shame into (**see** *incite*); infect, inject with, infuse into 534 *educate*; interest, intrigue 821 *impress*; charm, fascinate, captivate, hypnotize, spellbind 983 *bewitch*; pull 291 *attract*; push 279 *impel*; pressurize 740 *compel*; bend, incline, dispose, predispose; lead, direct 689 *manage*; give a lead, set an example, set the pace 283 *precede*.

incite, energize, galvanize, stimulate 174 *invigorate*; encourage, cheer on, root for 855 *give courage*; inspirit, inspire, animate, provoke, rouse, rally 821 *excite*; evoke, call forth, challenge; exhort, invite, urge, insist, press, bring pressure to bear, lobby; nag, needle, goad, prod, jog, jolt; spur, prick, tickle; whip, lash; spur on, set on, egg on; drive, hurry 680 *hasten*; instigate, prompt, put up to; suggest, advocate 691 *advise*; kindle 68 *initiate*.

induce, instigate, bring about 156 *cause*; persuade, carry with one 485 *convince*; carry one's point, prevail upon, talk into, bully i., browbeat (**see** *motivate*); twist one's arm 740 *compel*; wear down, soften up; bring round, talk round 147 *convert*; win over, talk over, sweet-talk into 925 *flatter*; conciliate, appease 719 *pacify*.

tempt, entice, dangle before one, make one's mouth water; tantalize, tease; allure, lure, inveigle 542 *ensnare*; coax, wheedle; pander to.

bribe, suborn, seduce, corrupt; square, buy off; grease one's palm, tip 962 *reward*.

613. Dissuasion – N. *dissuasion*, contrary advice; caution 664 *warning*; discouragement 702 *hindrance*; deterrence 854 *intimidation*; objection, remonstrance 762 *deprecation*; rebuff 715 *resistance*; no encouragement, disincentive; deterrent 665 *danger signal*; contraindication, countersymptom 14 *contrariety*; cold water, damper, wet blanket; killjoy, spoilsport 702 *hinderer*.

Adj. *dissuasive*, discouraging, chilling, damping; reluctant 598 *unwilling*; expostulatory 762 *deprecatory*; monitory, warning against 664 *cautionary*.

Vb. *dissuade*, persuade against, advise a., argue a., talk out of 479 *confute*; caution 664 *warn*; remonstrate, expostulate 762 *deprecate*; shake 486 *cause doubt*; intimidate 900 *threaten*; deter, daunt 854 *frighten*; choke off, head off, steer one away from 282 *deflect*; wean away from 611 *disaccustom*; hold one back 747 *restrain*; disenchant, disillusion, disincline, indispose, disaffect; set against, turn a., put off 861 *cause dislike*; dishearten, discourage 834 *depress*; crush, squash, throw cold water on, quench, cool, chill, damp one's ardour; take the edge off 257 *blunt*; calm, quiet 177 *moderate*.

614. Pretext – N. *pretext*, ostensible motive, alleged m.; allegation, claim 532 *affirmation*; plea, excuse 927 *vindication*; let-out, loophole 667 *means of escape*; leg to stand on, peg to hang something on 218 *prop*; thin excuse, lame e.; special pleading, quibble; proviso 468 *qualification*; subterfuge 698 *stratagem*; pretence, previous engagement, diplomatic illness 543 *untruth*; blind, dust in the eyes; stalking horse, cloak, cover 421 *screen*; apology for, simulacrum, makeshift 150 *substitute*; colour, gloss, guise 445 *appearance*; bluff, sour grapes.

Adj. *ostensible*, alleged, pretended; specious, plausible; seeming.

Vb. *plead*, allege, claim, profess 532 *affirm*; make a plea of 475 *argue*; excuse oneself, defend o. 927 *justify*; gloss over, palliate 927 *extenuate*; shelter under, take hold as a handle for 137 *profit by*; find a loophole, wriggle out of 667 *escape*; varnish, colour; bluff, blind, throw dust in one's eyes 542 *befool*; pretend, affect 541 *dissemble*.

615. Good – N. *good*, what is good for one; the best, supreme good, summum bonum; public weal, common good; balance of interest, lesser evil, greatest happiness of the greatest number 642 *good policy*; weal, well-being, welfare 730 *prosperity*; riches, gravy 800 *wealth*; luck, good l., fortune, good f. 824 *happiness*; blessing, benison, world of good.

benefit, advantage, interest 640 *utility*; harvest, return 771 *acquisition*; profit 771 *gain*; betterment 654 *improvement*; boon 781 *gift*; good turn 897 *kind act*; favour, blessing, blessing in disguise; turn-up for the book, godsend, windfall, piece of luck, find; the very thing 859 *desired object*.

Adj. *good*, goodly, fine; gainful 640 *profitable*; advantageous, heaven-sent 644 *beneficial*; worthwhile 644 *valuable*; helpful 706 *cooperative*; commendable 923 *approved*; pleasure-giving 826 *pleasurable*.

Vb. *benefit*, favour, bless; help, be of service 640 *be useful*; advantage, profit;

pay, repay 771 *be profitable*; do one good 654 *make better*; turn out well, be for the best.

flourish, thrive, do well; rise in the world 730 *prosper*; arrive 727 *succeed*; improve 654 *get better*; cash in on 137 *profit by*, 771 *gain*.

Adv. *well*, satisfactorily, favourably, profitably; all to the good; for the best, in one's best interests; in fine style, on the up and up.

616. Evil – N. *evil*, disservice, injury; dirty trick 930 *foul play*; wrong, outrage 914 *injustice*; shame, abuse; curse, scourge, running sore 659 *bane*; ill, ills that flesh is heir to, Pandora's box; sad world, vale of tears; trouble 731 *adversity*; affliction, distress 825 *suffering*; grief 825 *sorrow*; malaise, discomfort 825 *worry*; nuisance 827 *annoyance*; hurt, bodily harm 377 *pain*; blow, buffet 279 *knock*; slings and arrows, calamity, bad luck 731 *misfortune*; accident 154 *event*; fatality 361 *death*; catastrophe, tragedy 165 *ruin*; mischief, harm, damage 772 *loss*; ill effect, bad result; disadvantage, drawback, fly in the ointment 647 *defect*; setback 702 *hitch*; indigence 801 *poverty*; grievance 829 *discontent*; cause of evil 898 *malevolence*.

Adj. *evil*, bad, too bad 645 *damnable*; unlucky, inauspicious 731 *adverse*; insidious, injurious, prejudicial, disadvantageous 645 *harmful*; trouble-making 898 *maleficent*; troublous 827 *distressing*; fatal 362 *deadly*; ruinous, disastrous 165 *destructive*; catastrophic, calamitous, tragic 731 *unfortunate*; all wrong, awry, out of joint.

Adv. *amiss*, wrong, awry, sour; unfortunately, unhappily, unluckily; to one's cost, for one's sins; worse luck!

Section 2:
Prospective volition

617. Intention – N. *intention*, intent; intentionality, deliberateness; calculation, calculated risk 480 *estimate*; purpose,

determination, predetermination 599 *resolution*; animus, mind 447 *intellect*; criminal intent 936 *guilt*; good intentions 897 *benevolence*; view, prospect, purview; study, pursuit, occupation 622 *business*; proposal; project, design 623 *plan*; enterprise 672 *undertaking*; ambition 859 *desire*; decision 480 *judgement*; ultimatum 900 *threat*; bid 671 *attempt*; engagement 764 *promise*; destination 69 *end*; teleology 156 *causation*; be-all and end-all, raison d'être 156 *reason why*; trend 179 *tendency*; tendentiousness 523 *latency*.

objective, destination, object, end, aim; axe to grind; mark, butt, target; bull's-eye; winning post 295 *goal*; place of pilgrimage, Mecca; quarry, game, prey 619 *chase*; prize, crown 729 *trophy*; dream, aspiration, vision 513 *ideality*; heart's desire, Promised Land, El Dorado 859 *desired object*.

Adj. *intending*, intent on, hell-bent 599 *resolute*; intentional, deliberate 595 *volitional*; out to, out for; purposive, teleological; minded, so m. 597 *willing*; prospective, would-be 859 *desiring*.

intended, for a purpose, tendentious; deliberate, intentional, studied, designed, purposeful, aforethought 608 *predetermined*.

Vb. *intend*, purpose, propose; have in mind *or* in view, have an eye to, contemplate, meditate; study, calculate; look for 507 *expect*; mean to, have every intention 599 *be resolute*; resolve, determine, premeditate 608 *predetermine*; project, design 623 *plan*; take on oneself, shoulder 672 *undertake*; engage 764 *promise*, 900 *threaten*; intend for, destine f., mark down for; keep for, reserve f.

aim at, go for, go after, go all out for, drive at, strive after 619 *pursue*; try for, endeavour 671 *attempt*; be after, have an eye on, have designs on, promise oneself, aspire to 859 *desire*; train one's sights on 281 *aim*.

Adv. *purposely*, on purpose, with one's eyes open, in cold blood, deliberately, intentionally; designedly, advisedly, knowingly; with malice aforethought; for a purpose, in order to; with the intention of, with a view *or* an eye to, with the object of, in pursuance of; by design.

618. Nondesign. Gamble – N. *nondesign*, indetermination, unpredictability 159 *chance*; involuntariness 609 *spontaneity*; coincidence, accident, fluke, luck 154 *event*; lottery, luck of the draw; drawing lots 159 *equal chance*; lot, wheel of Fortune 596 *fate*; mascot 983 *talisman*.

gambling, risk-taking; risk, hazard, Russian roulette 661 *danger*; gamble, potluck 159 *chance*; venture, speculation, flutter 461 *experiment*; shot, random s., shot in the dark 474 *uncertainty*; bid, throw; toss of a coin, turn of a card; wager, bet, stake, ante, psychic bid; last throw 857 *rashness*; dice, die, bones, ivories; game of chance; bingo; fruit machine, one-armed bandit; roulette, rouge et noir; betting, turf 716 *racing*; football pool, pools; draw, lottery, raffle, tombola, sweepstake; premium bond; futures.

gaming-house, hell, gambling den; betting shop; casino; amusement arcade; totalizator, tote.

gambler, gamester, player, dicer; better, layer, backer, punter; turf accountant, bookmaker, bookie, tout, tipster; venturer, merchant v., adventurer, undertaker, entrepreneur 672 *undertaking*; speculator, manipulator; bear, bull, stag; experimentalist 461 *experimenter*.

Adj. *unintentional*, nonintentional, inadvertent, unintended, unmeant 596 *involuntary*; unpurposed, unpremeditated 609 *spontaneous*; accidental, fortuitous, coincidental 159 *casual*.

designless, aimless, purposeless; motiveless 159 *causeless*; happy-go-lucky, devil-may-care; unselective 464 *indiscriminate*; undirected, random, haphazard 282 *deviating*.

speculative, experimental 474 *uncertain*; hazardous, risky, chancy, dicey, aleatory; risk-taking, venturesome, adventurous, enterprising.

Vb. *gamble*, game, play, do the pools; throw, dice, bet, stake, wager, lay; call one's hand, overcall; play high, play for high stakes, double the s.; take bets, offer odds, make a book; back, punt; cover a bet, hedge; play the market, speculate 461 *experiment*; hazard, risk, run a r., push one's luck 857 *be rash*; venture, chance it, chance one's arm, try one's luck, trust to chance; spin the wheel, draw lots, cut straws, spin a coin, toss up.

619. Pursuit – N. *pursuit*, pursuance, follow-up; hunting, quest 459 *search*; tracking, trailing, dogging 284 *following*; hounding, persecution, witch-hunt; prosecution, execution; activities 622 *business*.

chase, run, run for one's money; steeplechase, paperchase 716 *racing*; hunt, hue and cry, tally-ho; beat, drive, battue; hunting, shooting and fishing 837 *sport*; blood sport, fox hunt, stag h.; pigsticking; stalking, deer s.; hawking, fowling, falconry; fishing, angling, fly fishing, coarse f.; whaling; beagling, coursing, ratting, trapping, ferreting, rabbiting; tackle, rod and line, bait, fly; fowlingpiece 723 *firearm*; manhunt, dragnet 542 *trap*; quarry, victim 617 *objective*.

hunter, quester, seeker 459 *inquirer*; search party; pursuer, tracker, trailer, shadow; huntsman, huntress; whip, whipper-in; beater; Nimrod, Diana; sportsman, sportswoman 837 *player*; gun, shot, good s., marksman *or* -woman 287 *shooter*; headhunter 362 *killer*; big-game hunter; deer stalker; poacher, trout-tickler; trapper, rat-catcher, rodent officer; bird catcher, fowler, falconer, hawker; fisherman *or* -woman, piscator, angler; shrimper; trawler, trawlerman, whaler; field, pack, hounds; bloodhound 365 *dog*; hawk 365 *bird*; beast of prey, man-eater; mouser.

Adj. *pursuing*, pursuant, seeking 459 *inquiring*; in quest of, sent after; on one's tail, in pursuit, in hot p., in full cry, on the scent 284 *following*; piscatorial.

Vb. *pursue*, seek, look for, cast about for; be gunning for, hunt for 459 *search*; send after; stalk, shadow, dog, track, trail, tail, dog one's footsteps, follow the scent 284 *follow*; scent out 484 *discover*; witch-hunt, harry 735 *oppress*; chase, give c., hunt, whoop, halloo; run down, ride d.

712 *charge*; jump at, snatch at 786 *take*; set one's course 617 *aim at*; run after 889 *court*; mob, swarm over; be after, make it one's business; follow up, persist 600 *persevere*; press on 285 *progress*.

hunt, go hunting, ride to hounds; go fishing, cast one's net, fish, trawl; net, catch 542 *ensnare*; play cat and mouse; stalk; hawk; course; start game, flush, beat, start; set snares, poach.

620. Avoidance – N. *avoidance*, abstinence, abstention; forbearance, refraining 177 *moderation*; refusal 607 *rejection*; inaction, cop-out 679 *inactivity*; passivity 266 *quiescence*; nonintervention, noninvolvement; evasiveness, evasive action, dodge, duck, sidestep; delaying action, noncooperation; retreat, withdrawal 286 *regression*; evasion, flight 667 *escape*; jibbing, shrinking 854 *fear*; shunning, safe distance; shyness 598 *unwillingness*; revulsion 280 *recoil*; defence mechanism, repression, suppression; nonattendance 190 *absence*; escapism.

avoider 942 *abstainer*; dodger, sidestepper, evader, bilker, welsher 545 *trickster*; shrinker, quitter 856 *coward*; shirker, skiver, scrimshanker 679 *idler*; skulker 527 *hider*; draft-dodger, truant, deserter 918 *undutifulness*; runaway, fugitive 667 *escaper*; escapist 513 *visionary*; head in the sand, ostrich.

Adj. *avoiding*, shunning; evasive, elusive, slippery, hard to catch; untamed, wild; shy, shrinking 854 *nervous*; reluctant, noncooperative 598 *unwilling*; noncommittal, unforthcoming; passive, inert 679 *inactive*; not involved 625 *neutral*; fugitive, hunted, runaway, fly-by-night 667 *escaped*; hiding, skulking 523 *latent*.

avoidable, avertable, escapable, preventable.

Vb. *avoid*, not go near, keep away; bypass, circumvent 282 *deviate*; turn aside, look the other way; hold aloof, have no hand in, not soil one's fingers, keep one's hands clean; shun, eschew, leave *or* let alone, have nothing to do with, not touch with a bargepole; give a miss, give the go-by; fight shy, back away 290 *recede*;

keep one's distance, keep a respectful d., give a wide berth; keep *or* get out of the way, keep clear, make way for; forbear, spare; refrain, abstain, do without, not touch; hold back, not attempt, balk at 598 *be unwilling*; shelve, postpone; pass the buck, get out of; cop out, funk; shrink, jib, refuse, shy 854 *be nervous*; lead one a dance, throw off the scent, play hide-and-seek; sidestep, dodge, duck; deflect, ward off 713 *parry*; obviate; fudge the issue, get round, fence, hedge, pussyfoot 518 *be equivocal*; evade, escape, give one the slip 667 *elude*; cower, hide 523 *lurk*; bury one's head in the sand.

run away, desert, play truant, jump bail, take French leave 918 *fail in duty*; abscond, welsh, flit, elope 667 *escape*; absent oneself; retreat, turn tail, turn round; flee, fly, take to flight, run for one's life; be off, make o., scamper o., bolt, run, cut and run, show a clean pair of heels, take to one's h., beat it, make oneself scarce, scoot, scram 277 *move fast*; break away, steal a., sneak off, creep o.; scuttle, do a bunk 296 *decamp*.

621. Relinquishment – N. *relinquishment*, abandonment 296 *departure*; dereliction, desertion, defection 918 *undutifulness*; withdrawal 978 *schism*; walkout 620 *avoidance*; yielding, cession 780 *transfer*; waiver, renunciation 779 *nonretention*; retirement 753 *resignation*; disuse 674 *nonuse*; discontinuance 611 *desuetude*; cancellation 752 *abrogation*; world well lost 883 *seclusion*.

Adj. *relinquished*, forsaken, cast-off, abandoned etc. vb.; waived, forgone 779 *not retained*.

Vb. *relinquish*, drop, let go, leave hold of 779 *not retain*; surrender, resign, give up, yield; waive, forgo; lower one's sights; cede, hand over 780 *assign*; forfeit 772 *lose*; renounce, recant 603 *tergiversate*; not proceed with, give up the idea, forget it; wean oneself 611 *disaccustom*; forswear, abstain 620 *avoid*; shed, slough, cast off; drop, discard, write off 674 *stop using*; lose interest, have other fish to fry; back down, scratch, stand down, drop out

263

753 *resign*; give in, throw up the game 721 *submit*; leave, quit, vacate, evacuate 296 *depart*; forsake, abandon, run out on 918 *fail in duty*; go over, sell out; throw over, ditch, jilt, go back on one's word 542 *deceive*; shelve, postpone 136 *put off*; annul, cancel.

622. Business – N. *business*, affairs, interests, irons in the fire; occupation, concern, care 617 *intention*; business on hand, case, agenda; enterprise, venture, undertaking, pursuit 678 *activity*; routine, daily round 610 *practice*; business circles, City; economics, the economy; art, technology, industry, commerce, big business; company 708 *corporation*; agriculture, agribusiness; cottage industry, home-based i.; industrialism, industrialization, industrial arts, manufacture 164 *production*; trade, craft, handicraft 694 *skill*; guild, union 706 *association*; employment, work; avocation, sideline, hobby 837 *amusement*.

vocation, calling, life work 751 *commission*; life, walk of life, career; labour of love, self-imposed task; living, livelihood, daily bread, one's bread and butter; profession, craft, trade.

job, work, task 678 *activity*; chores, odd jobs 682 *labour*; duty, charge, commission 751 *mandate*; employ, service, employment; working day, manhour; occupation, situation, position, berth, incumbency, appointment, post, office; regular employment, full-time job, permanency; temporary job, part-time j.; situation wanted; opening, vacancy; labour exchange, employment agency, Job Centre.

function, capacity, office, duty; area, realm, province, domain, orbit, sphere; scope, field, terms of reference 183 *range*; beat, round; department, line, line of country; role, part; business, job; responsibility, concern, lookout, baby, pigeon.

Adj. *businesslike*, efficient 694 *skilful*; busy 678 *active*; vocational, professional, career; industrial, technological, commercial, financial, mercantile; labour-intensive, capital-i.; occupational, functional; official, governmental; routine,

workaday 610 *habitual*; earning, employed, self-e., freelance; in hand, on h., on foot 669 *preparatory*.

Vb. *employ*, busy, occupy, take up one's time; engage, recruit, hire 751 *commission*; take on the payroll 804 *pay*; give a situation to, offer a job to, fill a vacancy, staff; industrialize.

function, work, go 173 *operate*; play one's part, carry on; officiate, act, perform, do the offices, discharge the functions, serve as, do duty for, do the work of; stand in for 755 *deputize*; hold office, hold a portfolio, hold down a job.

do business, ply a trade, follow a calling; engage in, carry on, keep shop; deal with 791 *trade*; go about one's business; pursue one's vocation, earn one's living; set up in business, open a shop, put up one's plate.

623. Plan – N. *plan*, scheme, design; planning, contrivance; organization, systematization, rationalization 60 *order*; programme, project, proposal 617 *intention*; proposition, suggestion, motion, resolution; master plan, five-year p.; scale drawing, blueprint 551 *map*; diagram 86 *statistics*; sketch, outline, draft, first d., memorandum; skeleton, roughcast; pilot scheme 23 *prototype*; drawing board, planning office, back room, operations r., headquarters.

policy, forethought 510 *foresight*; statesmanship 498 *wisdom*; plan of attack, procedure, strategy 688 *tactics*; operational research 459 *inquiry*; approach, attack 624 *way*; scenario, forecast 511 *prediction*; programme, prospectus, platform, plank, ticket, slate; line, party l.; formula 81 *rule*; schedule, order of the day 622 *business*.

contrivance, expedient, resource, resort, card, trump c. 629 *means*; recipe, nostrum 658 *remedy*; loophole, way out, alternative, answer 667 *means of escape*; artifice, device, gimmick, dodge, ploy, shift 698 *stratagem*; wangle, fiddle 930 *foul play*; knack, trick 694 *skill*; stunt, wheeze; inspiration, happy thought, bright idea 451 *idea*; notion, invention; contraption, gadget 628 *instrument*; improvisation 609 *spontaneity*; makeshift 150 *substitute*; feat, bold move, masterstroke 676 *deed*.

plot, deep-laid p., intrigue; web of i.; cabal, conspiracy, inside job; scheme, racket, game 698 *stratagem*; frame-up, machination; manipulation 523 *latency*; counterplot.

planner, contriver, framer, inventor, originator, hatcher; proposer, promoter, projector; founder, author, architect, designer; backroom boy *or* girl 696 *expert*; brains, mastermind; organizer, strategist, tactician, manoeuvrer; politician, Machiavellian; wheeler-dealer, schemer, axe-grinder; plotter, intriguer, intrigant(e), spinner, spider, cabal; conspirator 545 *deceiver*.

Adj. *planned*, blueprinted, schematic, worked out 669 *prepared*; organized, systematized 60 *orderly*; under consideration, in draft, in proof; strategic, tactical; plotted.

planning, contriving 698 *cunning*; purposeful, scheming, up to something; intriguing, plotting, conspiratorial.

Vb. *plan*, form a p., resolve 617 *intend*; draw up, design, draft, blueprint; frame, shape; revise, recast; project, plan out, work o., map o., lay o.; programme, organize, systematize, rationalize, schematize, methodize; schedule, phase; invent, think up 484 *discover*, 513 *imagine*; find a way, make shift to; contrive, devise, engineer; hatch, concoct 669 *prepare*; arrange, prearrange 608 *predetermine*; calculate, think ahead, look a. 498 *be wise*; have a policy, follow a plan; have an axe to grind.

plot, scheme, have designs, be up to something, wheel and deal; manipulate 178 *influence*; cabal, conspire, intrigue, machinate; concoct, cook up, brew; hatch a plot 698 *be cunning*; dig a pit for 542 *ensnare*; frame 541 *fake*.

624. Way – N. *way*, route, itinerary; manner, wise, guise; fashion, style, form; method, mode, line, approach, address, attack; procedure, process, modus operandi 688 *tactics*; operation, treatment; modus vivendi, working arrangement 770

compromise; usual way 610 *practice*; technique 694 *skill*; going, gait 265 *motion*; way forward 285 *progression*; way of life 688 *conduct*. **See** route.

access, means of a., right of way, communications; way to 289 *approach*; entrance 263 *doorway*; adit, drive, gangway, corridor; way through 305 *passage*.

bridge, way over; footbridge, flyover, aqueduct; viaduct, span; pontoon bridge; drawbridge; causeway, stepping-stone, gangway, gangplank, catwalk, duckboards; ford, ferry; underpass 263 *tunnel*; isthmus, neck.

route, direction, line, course, march, tack, track; trajectory, orbit; lane, bus l.; air l., sea l., seaway, fairway, waterway 351 *conduit*; trade route; short cut; bypass, detour 626 *circuit*.

path, pathway, footway, footpath, pavement, sidewalk; towpath, bridlepath, bridleway, ride; byway, lane, track, trail; right of way, public footpath; walk, promenade, esplanade, parade, mall; pedestrian precinct; running track 724 *arena*; fairway, runway.

road, high r., highway, highways and byways; dirt road, cinder track; corniche, switchback; toll road, turnpike; thoroughfare, through road; main road, trunk r., arterial r., artery; bypass, ring road; motorway, M-way; clearway; slip road, acceleration lane; crossroads, junction, turn-off; intersection, roundabout, cloverleaf; crossing 305 *traffic control*; roadway, carriageway, dual c.; cycle track, cycleway; street, high s., back s.; alleyway, wynd, alley, blind a., cul de sac; close 192 *housing*; pavement, kerb, kerbstone; paving, cobbles, setts; hard shoulder, verge; macadam, tarmac, asphalt, road metal; road building, traffic engineering.

railway, railroad, line; permanent way, track; main line, branch l., loop l.; tramlines, tramway; monorail, rack and pinion, funicular, cableway, ropeway; overhead railway, underground r., tube 274 *train*; light railway, narrow gauge, standard g.; junction, crossover, level crossing; siding, marshalling yard, goods y., turntable; station, halt 145 *stopping place*; signal, gantry, signal box; rails, points.

Adj. *communicating*, granting access; through, arterial, trunk; bridged, crossed; paved, metalled, cobbled, tarmac; signposted, waymarked; well-lit; well-used, busy; trodden, beaten.

625. Middle way – N. *middle way*, middle course, middle of the road; balance, golden mean 30 *average*; moderateness, intermediate technology; central position, halfway, mid-stream; direct course, straight line, short cut, beeline 249 *straightness*; noncommittal, neutrality 177 *moderation*; mutual concession 770 *compromise*.

moderate, nonextremist, Minimalist, Menshevik; middle-of-the-roader, half-and-halfer; neutral.

Adj. *neutral*, noncommittal, uncommitted, unattached, free-floating 860 *indifferent*; moderate, nonextreme, unextreme, middle-of-the-road; sitting on the fence, lukewarm, half-and-half; neither one thing nor the other, grey.

undeviating, unswerving, direct 249 *straight*; in between, halfway, midway, intermediate.

626. Circuit – N. *circuit*, roundabout way, circuitous route, detour, loop 282 *deviation*; ambages 251 *convolution*; circulation 314 *circuition*; circumference 250 *circle*; full circle.

Adj. *roundabout*, circuitous, indirect, out of the way 251 *convoluted*; circulatory, rounding, skirting 230 *circumjacent*.

Vb. *circuit*, round, go round 314 *circle*; make a detour, go out of one's way 282 *deviate*; turn, bypass, short-circuit 620 *avoid*; skirt, edge round.

627. Requirement – N. *requirement*, essential, sine qua non, a necessary, a must 596 *necessity*; needs, necessities; indent, order, requisition, shopping list; stipulation, prerequisite 766 *conditions*; desideratum, want, lack, need 636 *insufficiency*;

gap 190 *absence*; demand, call for, run on; consumption, input, intake; shortage 307 *shortfall*; balance due, claim 761 *request*; injunction 737 *command*.

needfulness, case of need; necessity for, essentiality, indispensability, desirability; necessitousness 801 *poverty*; exigency 137 *crisis*; matter of life and death 638 *important matter*; obligation 917 *duty*; bare minimum, least one can do.

Adj. *required*, requisite, prerequisite, needful, needed; necessary, essential, vital, indispensable; called for, in request, in demand; reserved, booked; wanted, lacking, missing 190 *absent*.

demanding, crying out for, calling for, imperative, urgent, instant, pressing, compulsory 740 *compelling*.

Vb. *require*, need, want, lack; not have, be without, feel the need for, have occasion for; miss, need badly, crave 859 *desire*; call for, cry out f., clamour f.; claim, apply for 761 *request*; find necessary, be unable to do without, must have; consume 634 *waste*, 673 *use*; necessitate, oblige 740 *compel*, 737 *demand*; stipulate 766 *give terms*; order, indent, requisition; reserve, book, earmark.

628. Instrumentality – N. *instrumentality*, operation 173 *agency*; occasion 156 *cause*; pressure 178 *influence*; efficacy 160 *power*; services, help, assistance, midwifery 703 *aid*; support 706 *cooperation*; intervention, intermediacy, interference 678 *activity*; subservience 739 *obedience*; medium 629 *means*; application, serviceability, handiness 640 *utility*; instrumentation, mechanization, automation 630 *machine*.

instrument, hand, handmaid, slave of the lamp 742 *servant*; agent, midwife, assistant 703 *aider*; go-between 720 *mediator*; catalyst; vehicle; pawn, piece on the board; cat's paw, stooge, puppet, creature; appliance 630 *tool*; key, master k. 263 *opener*; password, safeconduct 756 *permit*; stepping-stone; highway; push button, switch.

Adj. *instrumental*, working 173 *operative*; hand-operated, manual; automatic, push-button 630 *mechanical*; effective, efficacious 160 *powerful*; telling, weighty 178 *influential*; conducive 156 *causal*; practical, applied; serviceable, handy 640 *useful*; promoting, assisting, helpful 703 *aiding*; Socratic, maieutic; functional, agential, subservient, ministering; mediational, intermediate, intervening.

Vb. *be instrumental*, work, act 173 *operate*; perform 676 *do*; serve, subserve, work for, lend oneself *or* itself to 703 *minister to*; help, assist 703 *aid*; advance, promote; have a hand in 775 *participate*; be to blame for 156 *cause*; be the instrument, pull another's chestnuts out of the fire 640 *be useful*; intermediate, intervene 720 *mediate*; pull strings 178 *influence*; tend 156 *conduce*; achieve 725 *carry through*.

Adv. *through*, per, by the hand of, by means of, with the help of, thanks to.

629. Means – N. *means*, ways and m., wherewithal; power, capacity 160 *ability*; strong hand, trumps, aces; conveniences, facilities; appliances, tools of the trade, bag of tricks 630 *tool*; technology 490 *knowledge*; technique, know-how 694 *skill*; wherewithal, matériel, equipment, supplies, stock, munitions, ammunition 633 *provision*; resources, raw material 631 *materials*; nuts and bolts 630 *machine*; pool of labour, manpower 686 *personnel*; financial resources 800 *wealth*; liquidity 797 *money*; capital, assets, stock-in-trade; line of credit 802 *credit*; reserves, standby, shot in one's locker, card up one's sleeve, two strings to one's bow 662 *safeguard*; method, measures, steps 624 *way*; cure 658 *remedy*; expedient, device 623 *contrivance*; makeshift, ad hoc measure 150 *substitute*; letout 667 *means of escape*; desperate remedy, last resort.

Vb. *find means*, provide the wherewithal 633 *provide*; equip, fit out 669 *make ready*; finance, promote, float; be in a position to 160 *be able*; contrive, find a way 623 *plan*; beg, borrow or steal, get by hook or by crook 771 *acquire*.

Adv. *by means of*, with, wherewith; by, using, through; with the aid of; by dint of; by fair means or foul.

630. Tool – N. *tool*, precision t., machine t., implement 628 *instrument*; apparatus, appliance, utensil; weapon 723 *arms*; device, contraption, gadget 623 *contrivance*; doodah, thingummy, whatsit; leverage 218 *pivot*; pulley, wheel; switch, stopcock; trigger 218 *handle*; pedal 287 *propulsion*; tools of the trade, tool-kit.

machine, mechanical device; machinery, mechanism, works; clockwork, wheelwork; nuts and bolts 58 *component*; spring, mainspring, hairspring; gears, gearing, synchromesh; motor, engine, internal combustion e.; turbine, dynamo 160 *sources of energy*; servomechanism, servomotor; robot, automaton; computer 86 *data processing*.

mechanics, engineering; electrical e. 160 *electronics*; cybernetics; automation, robotics; technology, advanced t., high t.

equipment, furniture, appointments; gear, tackle, harness; fittings 40 *adjunct*; outfit, kit; upholstery, furnishing; trappings, accoutrements 228 *dress*; utensils, impedimenta, paraphernalia; wares, stock-in-trade 795 *merchandise*; plant 687 *workshop*.

machinist, operator, operative; driver, minder, machine-m.; engineer, technician, mechanician, mechanic, fitter; tool-user, craftsman *or* -woman 686 *artisan*.

Adj. *mechanical*, mechanized, motorized, powered, power-driven; labour-saving, automatic 628 *instrumental*; robotlike, automated; machine-minded, tool-using.

631. Materials – N. *materials*, resources, building blocks 629 *means*; material, stuff, staple, stock; raw material, grist; meat, fodder 301 *food*; chemical feedstock; ore, mineral, metal, pig iron, ingot 385 *fuel*; clay 344 *soil*; glass, plastic, polythene, polystyrene, latex, celluloid (tdmk), fibreglass; yarn 208 *fibre*; hide 226 *skin*; timber, wood; plank 207 *lamina*; stuffing 227 *lining*; cloth, fabric 222 *textile*.

building material, bricks and mortar, lath and plaster, wattle and daub 331 *structure*; slate, tile 226 *roof*; stone, masonry; rendering 226 *facing*; cement,

concrete, reinforced c.; hard core 226
paving.

paper, pulp, wood p., newsprint; card,
Bristol board; cartridge paper, tissue p.;
papier mâché, cardboard, pasteboard;
chipboard, hardboard, plasterboard;
sheet, notepaper 586 *stationery.*

632. Store – N. *store*, stack, stockpile,
buildup 74 *accumulation*; packet, bundle,
bagful 26 *quantity*; harvest, crop, haystack; stock 795 *merchandise*; assets, investment 777 *property*; fund, reserves,
something in hand, backlog; savings, nest
egg; deposit, hoard, cache 527 *hiding-
place*; bottom drawer 633 *provision*; pool,
kitty 775 *joint possession*; quarry, mine,
goldmine; natural resources, deposit;
coalfield, gasfield, oilfield; coal mine, colliery; coalface, seam, stringer, lode, pipe,
vein, rich v.; well, oil w., gusher; fountain
156 *source*; supply, stream; tap, pipeline,
artesian well; milch cow, treacle well, cornucopia, abundance 635 *plenty.*

storage, stowage 74 *accumulation*; conservation 666 *preservation*; safe deposit
660 *protection*; stabling, warehousing;
storage space, shelfroom 183 *room*; box-
room, loft; hold, bunker 194 *cellar*;
storeship, supply base, storehouse,
storeroom, stockroom; warehouse, goods
shed, godown; depository, depot, entrepôt; dock 192 *stable*; magazine, arsenal,
armoury, gunroom; treasure house 799
treasury; strongroom, vault, night safe;
blood bank, sperm b.; data bank 86 *data
processing*, 505 *memory*; hive, honeycomb; granary, barn, silo; water tower,
reservoir, cistern, tank, gasholder, gasometer; battery, storage b.; cesspool 649
sink; pantry, larder, buttery, stillroom 194
chamber; cupboard, shelf, refrigerator
194 *cabinet*; packing case 194 *box*; container 194 *receptacle.*

collection, set, complete s.; archives 548
record; folder, portfolio 74 *accumulation*;
museum, gallery, art g.; library; menagerie 369 *zoo*; exhibition 522 *exhibit*;
repertory, repertoire.

Adj. *stored*, hoarded etc. vb.; in store,
in deposit; in hand, held; in reserve, unex-

pended; banked; available, in stock.

Vb. *store*, stow 193 *load*; lay up, stow
away, put in mothballs; dump, garage,
stable, warehouse; garner, gather, harvest
370 *cultivate*; stack, accumulate 74 *bring
together*; stock up, lay in, bulk-buy, panic
buy, stockpile, build up one's stocks 36
augment; take on *or* in 633 *provide*; fill up,
top up 633 *replenish*; put by, save, keep,
file, hang on to, keep by one 778 *retain*;
conserve 666 *preserve*; set aside, lay by,
keep back, reserve; bank, deposit, invest;
hoard, treasure; squirrel away, stash a.
525 *conceal*; husband, save up, salt away,
prepare for a rainy day 814 *economize*;
equip oneself 669 *prepare oneself.*

633. Provision – N. *provision*, logistics,
equipment 669 *fitting out*; purveyance,
catering; service, delivery; self-service;
feeding, entertainment, bed and breakfast, board and lodging, maintenance;
assistance 703 *subvention*; supply, constant s., feed; pipeline 272 *transference*;
commissariat, provisioning, supplies,
stores, rations, emergency r. 632 *store*;
reinforcement, replenishment 54 *plenitude*; food, provender 301 *provisions*;
helping, portion; grist to the mill, fuel to
the flame; budgeting, resource management 814 *economy.*

provider, donor 781 *giver*; wet nurse,
feeder; purser 798 *treasurer*; steward,
butler; commissary, quartermaster,
storekeeper; supplier, victualler, sutler;
provision merchant, retailer 794 *tradespeople.*

caterer, purveyor, hotelier, hotelkeep-
er, restaurateur; innkeeper, landlord,
landlady, mine host, publican; housekeeper, housewife; cook, chef.

Adj. *provisioning*, commissarial; self-
service; sufficing 635 *sufficient*; supplied,
provided, all found; well-appointed, three
star; available, on tap, on the menu.

Vb. *provide*, afford, offer, lend 781
give; provision, find; equip, furnish 669
make ready; supply, keep supplied; yield
164 *produce*; cater, purvey; service an
order 793 *sell*; deliver; hand out *or* round,
serve, serve up, dish up; victual, feed,

water; cook for, board, put up, maintain, keep, clothe; stock, keep a s.; budget, make provision; provide for oneself 632 *store*.

replenish, reinforce, make good, make up; top up, refill 54 *fill*; revictual, restock, refuel, reload.

634. Waste – N. *waste*, wastage 42 *decrement*; leakage 298 *outflow*; inroads, consumption; intake 627 *requirement*; outlay, expense 806 *expenditure*; depletion, exhaustion 300 *voidance*; dissipation 75 *dispersion*; damage 772 *loss*; wear and tear, built-in obsolescence 655 *deterioration*; wastefulness, improvidence 815 *prodigality*; overproduction 637 *superfluity*; misapplication 675 *misuse*; vandalism, sabotage 165 *destruction*; waste product 641 *rubbish*.

Adj. *wasteful*, extravagant, unnecessary, uneconomic 815 *prodigal*; throwaway 637 *superfluous*; labour-consuming, time-c., energy-c.; damaging 165 *destructive*.

wasted, exhausted, depleted, consumed; gone to waste, gone down the drain; fruitless, bootless 641 *profitless*; ill-spent, misapplied; of no avail, futile, in vain.

Vb. *waste*, consume, make a dent in, make inroads on, wade into; swallow, devour, gobble up 301 *eat*; spend, lay out 806 *expend*; use up, exhaust, deplete, drain, suck dry 300 *empty*; dissipate, throw to the four winds 75 *disperse*; abuse, overcrop, overfish, overgraze 675 *misuse*; wear out, damage 655 *impair*; misapply, fritter away, cast pearls before swine; make no use of 674 *not use*; labour in vain 641 *waste effort*; squander, throw away, pour down the drain 815 *be prodigal*; be careless, slop, spill; ruin, destroy, sabotage, vandalize 165 *lay waste*; leak, ebb away 298 *flow out*; run to seed 655 *deteriorate*; run to waste, go down the drain.

635. Sufficiency – N. *sufficiency*, adequacy, enough; competence, living wage; subsistence farming; self-sufficiency, autarky; no surplus; minimum, bare m.; full measure, satisfaction, contentment, all

that could be desired; repletion, one's fill 863 *satiety*.

plenty, horn of p., cornucopia 171 *abundance*; outpouring, showers of, flood, streams; lots, lashings, galore 32 *great quantity*; fullness, copiousness, amplitude 54 *plenitude*; affluence 800 *wealth*; fat of the land, feast, banquet 301 *feasting*; orgy, riot, profusion 815 *prodigality*; fertility, productivity 171 *productiveness*; harvest, rich h., bumper crop; rich vein, bonanza, ample store, endless supply, more where it came from 632 *store*; superabundance 637 *redundance*.

Adj. *sufficient*, sufficing 633 *provisioning*; self-sufficient 54 *complete*; enough, adequate, competent; enough to go round; satisfactory; commensurate, up to the mark; just right.

plenteous, plentiful, ample, enough and to spare 637 *superfluous*; openhanded, generous, lavish 813 *liberal*; extravagant 815 *prodigal*; wholesale, without stint, unsparing, inexhaustible 32 *great*; luxuriant, lush, rank, fertile 171 *prolific*; profuse, abundant, copious, overflowing 637 *redundant*; rich, affluent.

Vb. *suffice*, be enough, do, serve, answer 642 *be expedient*; make the grade, pass muster; measure up to, meet requirements, fill the bill; fill up 54 *fill*; refill 633 *replenish*; prove acceptable, satisfy, content; satiate 863 *sate*.

abound, be plentiful, proliferate, teem, swarm 104 *be many*; riot, luxuriate 171 *be fruitful*; flow, shower, snow, pour, stream 350 *rain*; brim, overflow 637 *superabound*; roll in, wallow in, swim in.

636. Insufficiency – N. *insufficiency*, not enough, drop in the bucket; minginess, nothing to spare 33 *small quantity*; inadequacy, deficiency, imperfection 647 *defect*; deficit 55 *incompleteness*; half measures, tinkering 307 *shortfall*; bankruptcy 805 *insolvency*; subsistence level, pittance, dole; stinginess 816 *parsimony*; short commons, iron rations, half r.; starvation diet 945 *asceticism*; fast day 946 *fasting*; malnutrition, vitamin deficiency 651 *disease*.

scarcity, scarceness, paucity 105 *few-ness*; dearth, lean years; drought, famine, starvation; infertility 172 *unproductive-ness*; shortage 307 *short-fall*; power cut 37 *decrease*; none to spare, short supply; scantiness, meagreness; deprivation 801 *poverty*; lack, want, need 627 *needfulness*.

Adj. *insufficient*, not satisfying, unsatisfactory, disappointing; inadequate, not enough, too little; scant, scanty, skimpy, slender 33 *small*; deficient, light on, lacking 55 *incomplete*; wanting, found w., poor 35 *inferior*; unequal to, not up to 695 *unskilful*; niggardly 816 *parsimonious*.

unprovided, unsupplied, unfurnished, bare 190 *empty*; empty-handed, unsatisfied, unsated; unprovided for; deficient in, starved of; hard up 801 *poor*; under-capitalized, underfinanced, understaffed, undermanned, shorthanded, under establishment, under strength; stinted, rationed, skimped; unavailable 190 *absent*.

underfed, undernourished, half-starved; famished; starved, famine-stricken 946 *fasting*; skinny, macerated, stunted 206 *lean*.

scarce, rare 140 *infrequent*; sparse 105 *few*; in short supply, at a premium, hard to get, hard to come by, not to be had for love or money, not to be had at any price, unavailable, unobtainable, out of stock.

Vb. *not suffice*, be insufficient 647 *be imperfect*; cramp one's style 747 *restrain*; want, lack, need, leave a gap 627 *require*; fail 509 *disappoint*; fall below 307 *fall short*; run out, dry up.

make insufficient, ask *or* expect too much; overcrop, impoverish 655 *impair*; exhaust, run down 634 *waste*; grudge, hold back, stint, skimp, ration 816 *be parsimonious*.

637. Redundance – N. *redundance*, overflow 298 *outflow*; abundance, super-abundance, profusion 635 *plenty*; avalanche, spate 32 *great quantity*; saturation 54 *plenitude*; excess 634 *waste*; excessiveness, nimiety, exorbitance, extremes 546 *exaggeration*; overdoing it, overexten-sion, overexpansion 678 *overactivity*; over-

measure, overpayment, overweight; lion's share 32 *main part*; overindulgence 943 *intemperance*; engorgement, plethora, congestion 863 *satiety*; more than enough, glut (**see** *superfluity*); fat, obesity 651 *disease*.

superfluity, luxury, luxuriousness; gilt on the gingerbread, frills, luxuries, nones-sentials, luxury article; overfulfilment, supererogation; overkill, duplication; something over, bonus, money to burn 40 *extra*; margin, overlap, excess, surplus 41 *remainder*; superfluousness, excrescence, accessory, fifth wheel 641 *inutility*; taut-ology 570 *pleonasm*; redundancy, unemployment 679 *inactivity*; overmanning 678 *activity*; too much of a good thing, embarras de richesses, glut, drug on the market; surfeit, sickener, overdose 863 *satiety*.

Adj. *redundant*, too many, one too m. 104 *many*; overmuch, excessive, immoderate 32 *exorbitant*; overdone 546 *exaggerated*; overflowing, running over, brimming over 54 *full*; flooding, streaming 350 *flowing*; snowed under, saturated 341 *drenched*; cloying 838 *tedious*; replete, gorged, crammed, stuffed, bursting; overcharged, overloaded; congested, plethoric; bloated 197 *expanded*.

superfluous, supererogatory; supernumerary; adscititious; needless, unnecessary, unrequired, uncalled for 641 *useless*; excessive 634 *wasteful*; luxury, luxurious, with all the trimmings; surplus, extra, over and above 41 *remaining*; spare, to spare 38 *additional*; de trop 860 *unwanted*; dispensable, expendable, replaceable.

Vb. *superabound*, riot, luxuriate 635 *abound*; run riot, overproduce, overpopulate 171 *be fruitful*; bristle with, meet one at every turn 104 *be many*; overflow, brim over 54 *be complete*; stream, flood, inundate, overwhelm 350 *flow*; engulf 299 *absorb*; know no bounds 306 *overstep*; soak, saturate 341 *drench*; stuff, cram 54 *fill*; congest, choke, overdose, glut, cloy, sicken 863 *sate*; overfeed 943 *be intemperate*; overfulfil, oversubscribe; flood the market; overstock, pile up; overdo, go over the top, overegg the pudding, pile it on, lay it on thick *or* with a trowel 546 *exaggerate*; overload, overburden; lavish upon 813 *be liberal*; make a splash 815 *be prodigal*.

be superfluous, etc. adj.; go begging; exceed requirements, duplicate; carry coals to Newcastle, gild the lily, teach one's grandmother to suck eggs; labour the obvious, take a sledgehammer to crack a nut, break a butterfly on a wheel 641 *waste effort*.

638. Importance – N. *importance*, first i., primacy, priority, urgency 64 *precedence*; paramountcy, supremacy 34 *superiority*; import, consequence, significance, weight; weightiness, gravity, seriousness, solemnity; substance, moment; interest, consideration, concern 622 *business*; notability, mark, prominence, eminence 866 *repute*; influence 866 *prestige*; magnitude 32 *greatness*; value 644 *goodness*.

important matter, vital concern; turning point 137 *crisis*; breath of life, be-all and end-all; no laughing matter, matter of life and death; big news 529 *news*; great doings, exploit 676 *deed*; landmark, milestone; red-letter day, great d. 876 *special day*.

chief thing, what matters, the thing, great t., main t.; issue, crux 452 *topic*; fundamentals, bedrock; essential, priority 627 *requirement*; gist, substance 5 *essential part*; highlight, main feature; cream, salt, pick 644 *elite*; keynote, cornerstone, mainstay, linchpin, kingpin; head, spearhead; heart of the matter, core, kernel, nub 225 *centre*; hub 218 *pivot*; cardinal point, main p., half the battle 32 *main part*; chief hope, trump card.

bigwig, personage, personality, heavyweight, somebody 866 *person of repute*; local worthy, pillar of the community; great man *or* woman, VIP, brass hat; his *or* her nibs, big shot, big noise, big wheel, big chief, big Daddy; high muck-a-muck, great panjandrum; leading light, kingpin, first fiddle, prima donna, star, lion; uncrowned king *or* queen 34 *superior*; grandee 868 *aristocrat*; magnate, mogul, mandarin; baron, tycoon 741 *auto-crat*; captains of industry, big battalions, top brass, top people; superpower 178 *influence*.

Adj. *important*, weighty, grave, solemn, serious; pregnant, big; of consequence, considerable, worth considering; world-shattering, earth-shaking, momentous, critical, fateful 137 *timely*; chief, capital, cardinal, major, main, paramount 34 *supreme*; crucial, essential, material 9 *relevant*; pivotal, central; basic, fundamental, radical; primary, prime, foremost, leading; overriding, overruling, uppermost; not to be despised, not to be sneezed at 644 *valuable*; necessary, vital, indispensable, irreplaceable, key 627 *required*; significant, telling; imperative, urgent, high-priority; high-level, top-l. 213 *topmost*; top-secret; high, grand, noble 32 *great*.

notable, remarkable; memorable, signal, unforgettable; first-rate, outstanding 34 *superior*; top-rank, top-flight 644 *excellent*; conspicuous, prominent, eminent, distinguished 866 *noteworthy*; imposing, commanding 821 *impressive*; formidable, powerful 178 *influential*; newsworthy, eventful, stirring, breathtaking, shattering, earth-shaking, epoch-making.

Vb. *be important*, matter, be a consideration, bulk large 612 *motivate*; weigh, carry, tell, count, cast a long shadow 178 *influence*; import, signify 514 *mean*; concern, interest, affect 9 *be related*; be somebody 920 *command respect*.

make important, give weight to, attach *or* ascribe importance to; seize on, fasten on; bring to the fore, enhance, highlight; rub in, stress, make a point of 532 *emphasize*; headline, splash 528 *advertise*; put on the map 528 *proclaim*; write in letters of gold 876 *celebrate*; magnify 197 *enlarge*; make much of, lionize, glorify 920 *show respect*; take seriously, make a fuss about; value, esteem, make much of, set store by; overestimate 482 *overrate*.

639. Unimportance – N. *unimportance*, inconsequence; insignificance, secondariness 35 *inferiority*; nothingness, lack of substance 4 *insubstantiality*; pettiness 33 *smallness*; paltriness, meanness, triviality, superficiality; flippancy, snap of the fingers, frivolity; worthlessness 812 *cheapness*; irrelevance, red herring 10 *unrelatedness*.

trifle, inessential, triviality, technicality; nothing, mere n., no great matter; accessory, sideshow; nothing in particular, not the end of the world; no great shakes, nothing to boast of, nothing to worry about, storm in a teacup 482 *overestimation*; bagatelle, floccinaucity, tinker's cuss, fig, damn, straw, pin, button; small change, small beer, small potatoes; paltry sum, peanuts, chickenfeed, fleabite; pinprick, scratch; nothing to it, child's play 701 *easy thing*; peccadillo, venial sin; trivia, petty detail 80 *particulars*; whit, jot, tittle; trickle, drop in the ocean 33 *small quantity*; farce, nonsense 497 *absurdity*; piffle 515 *empty talk*.

bauble, toy 837 *plaything*; gewgaw, kickshaw, knick-knack, bric-à-brac; novelty, trinket; tinsel, trumpery, frippery, trash.

nonentity, nobody, obscurity; man of straw 4 *insubstantial thing*; figurehead, cipher, sleeping partner; fribble, trifler, smatterer; mediocrity, lightweight, small beer; small fry, small game; banana republic; other ranks 869 *commonalty*; second fiddle 35 *inferior*; underling, understrapper 742 *servant*; pawn, stooge, puppet 628 *instrument*; Cinderella, poor relation; pipsqueak, whippersnapper, squirt, squit, trash 867 *object of scorn*.

Adj. *unimportant*, immaterial 4 *insubstantial*; ineffectual, uninfluential, inconsequential, insignificant, of no consequence, of no great weight; off the point 10 *irrelevant*; inessential, nonessential, not vital; unnecessary, dispensable, expendable; small, petty, trifling, nugatory, flimsy, paltry 33 *inconsiderable*; negligible, not worth considering, out of the running; weak, puny, powerless 161 *impotent*; wretched, measly, miserable, pitiful, pitiable, pathetic; obscure, disregarded, overlooked 458 *neglected*; overrated, beneath notice 922 *contemptible*; jumped-

up, no-account, tinpot; low-level, secondary, minor, peripheral 35 *inferior*.

trivial, trifling, piffling, piddling, fiddling; pettifogging, nit-picking, technical; footling, frivolous, puerile 499 *foolish*; superficial 212 *shallow*; slight 33 *small*; lightweight 323 *light*; not serious, forgivable, venial; parish-pump, small-time; twopenny-halfpenny, one-horse, secondrate, third-r.; rubbishy, trumpery, trashy, tawdry, gimcrack 645 *bad*; two-a-penny 812 *cheap*; worthless, valueless 641 *useless*; not worth a thought 922 *contemptible*; toy, token, nominal; mediocre, nondescript, forgettable, eminently f.; commonplace 610 *usual*.

Vb. *be unimportant*, etc. adj.; not matter, carry no weight, not count, count for nothing, cut no ice, signify little; shrug off 458 *disregard*; snap one's fingers at 922 *hold cheap*; cut down to size 872 *humiliate*.

Int. no matter! never mind! so what! too bad!

640. Utility – N. *utility*, use, usefulness; serviceability 628 *instrumentality*; efficacy 160 *ability*; adaptability, applicability, suitability 642 *good policy*; service, avail, help 703 *aid*; value, worth, merit 644 *goodness*; function, capacity, potency 160 *power*; profitability, earning capacity 171 *productiveness*; profit, mileage 771 *gain*; advantage, convenience, benefit 615 *good*; utilitarianism, functionalism; utilization 673 *use*.

Adj. *useful*, utile, of use, helpful, of service 703 *aiding*; practical, applied, functional; versatile, multipurpose, allpurpose, of all work; practicable, convenient, expedient 642 *advisable*; handy, ready, available, on tap; serviceable, fit for, good for, disposable, adaptable, applicable; fit for use, usable, reusable, employable; good, valid, current; subservient 628 *instrumental*; efficacious, effective 160 *powerful*; conducive 179 *tending*; adequate 635 *sufficient*; pragmatic, utilitarian.

profitable, economic, paying 771 *gainful*; prolific 164 *productive*; beneficial, advantageous, to one's advantage, worthwhile 615 *good*; worth one's salt *or* one's keep 644 *valuable*.

Vb. *be useful*, etc. adj.; avail, prove helpful, stand one in good stead; come in handy, have some use; function, work 173 *operate*; perform 676 *do*; serve, subserve, serve one's turn, suit one's purpose 642 *be expedient*; further, help 703 *aid*; do service, do yeoman s. 742 *serve*; conduce 179 *tend*; benefit, profit, advantage 644 *do good*; bear fruit 171 *be fruitful*; pay off 771 *be profitable*.

641. Inutility – N. *inutility*, uselessness; no purpose, superfluousness 637 *superfluity*; futility, inanity, vanity 497 *absurdity*; worthlessness, unemployability; inadequacy 636 *insufficiency*; inefficacy 161 *impotence*; inefficiency, incompetence, ineptitude 695 *unskilfulness*; unserviceableness, inconvenience 643 *inexpedience*; inapplicability, unadaptability; unprofitability 172 *unproductiveness*; disservice, detriment.

lost labour, game not worth the candle; waste of breath, waste of time, dead loss 728 *failure*; labour in vain, wild-goose chase, fool's errand; half measures, tinkering.

rubbish, trash; waste, refuse, lumber, junk, scrap, litter; spoilage, wastage, waste products; sweepings 41 *leavings*; chaff, husks, bran; scraps, bits; crumbs; offal, carrion; dust, muck, debris, slag, clinker, dross, scum 649 *dirt*; stubble, weeds; rags and bones, old clothes, castoffs; reject, throwout; midden, rubbish heap, scrap h., dustheap, slag heap, dump.

Adj. *useless*, purposeless, pointless, Sisyphean; futile 497 *absurd*; unpractical, impracticable, unworkable, no go; nonfunctional 844 *ornamental*; redundant, nonreturnable 637 *superfluous*; unnecessary, unneeded 860 *unwanted*; unfit, unapt, inapplicable 643 *inexpedient*; unusable, unemployable, unadaptable; unqualified, incompetent 695 *unskilful*; ineffective, ineffectual 161 *impotent*; nonfunctioning, inoperative, dud, kaput; invalid 752 *abrogated*; unserviceable, out

of order, not working; worn out, hors de combat; obsolete, outmoded 127 *antiquated*; hopeless, vain.

profitless, bootless, unavailing; lossmaking, unprofitable, not worthwhile, wasteful, ill-spent; vain 728 *unsuccessful*; nothing to show for 634 *wasted*; unrewarding, thankless, fruitless, barren, sterile 172 *unproductive*; idle 679 *lazy*; worthless, good for nothing, valueless, no earthly use; rubbishy, trashy, not worth powder and shot, not worth the paper it is written on 645 *bad*; unsalable, dear at any price 811 *dear*.

Vb. *be useless*, have no use; waste one's time, be on a hiding to nothing; not help 702 *hinder*.

waste effort, labour the obvious; waste one's breath, talk to a brick wall; preach to the converted 637 *be superfluous*; labour in vain, flog a dead horse, tilt at windmills; cry for the moon 470 *attempt the impossible*; paper over the cracks, spoil the ship for a ha'porth of tar 726 *not complete*; rearrange the deckchairs on the Titanic 497 *be absurd*.

Adv. *uselessly*, to no purpose; to no avail, until one is blue in the face.

642. Good policy – N. *good policy*, expedience; answer, right a., advisability, desirability, worthwhileness, suitability 640 *utility*; fitness, propriety 915 *dueness*; high time, right t. 137 *occasion*; convenience, pragmatism, utilitarianism, opportunism, timeserving; profit, advantage 615 *benefit*.

Adj. *advisable*, commendable; better to, desirable, worthwhile 644 *beneficial*; acceptable 923 *approved*; suitable 24 *fit*; fitting, befitting, seemly, proper, right; owing 915 *due*; well-timed 137 *timely*; prudent, politic, judicious 498 *wise*; expedient, advantageous, profitable 640 *useful*; convenient, handy, workable, practical, pragmatic, practicable; qualified, cut out for; to the purpose, applicable.

Vb. *be expedient*, suit the occasion, befit; be to the purpose, help 703 *aid*; forward, advance, promote 640 *be useful*; answer, have the desired effect 156 *conduce*; do, serve, be better than nothing 635 *suffice*; qualify for, fit, be just the thing 24 *accord*; profit, advantage, benefit 644 *do good*.

643. Inexpedience – N. *inexpedience*, no answer, not the a.; bad policy, counsel of despair 495 *error*; inadvisability, undesirability; unsuitability, unfitness 25 *inaptitude*; impropriety, unfittingness 916 *undueness*; inopportuneness 138 *untimeliness*; disqualification, disability, handicap 702 *obstacle*; inconvenience, disadvantage, detriment; doubtful advantage, mixed blessing, pis aller; last resort 596 *necessity*.

Adj. *inexpedient*, better not, inadvisable, undesirable, not recommended; illadvised, impolitic 499 *unwise*; inappropriate, malapropos, out of place, unseemly, improper 916 *undue*; not right 914 *wrong*; beneath one's dignity, infra dig; unfit, inadmissible, unsuitable, infelicitous, inept 25 *unapt*; unseasonable, inopportune 138 *ill-timed*; unsatisfactory 636 *insufficient*; disadvantageous 645 *harmful*; unprofitable 641 *useless*; inconvenient, unhelpful 702 *hindering*.

Vb. *be inexpedient*, etc. adj.; won't do, won't answer; not help 641 *be useless*; disadvantage 645 *harm*; work against 702 *obstruct*; embarrass 700 *be difficult*.

644. Goodness – N. *goodness*, soundness, quality; long suit, good points, redeeming feature; merit, desert, title to fame; excellence, eminence, supereminence 34 *superiority*; virtue, worth, value 809 *price*; flawlessness 646 *perfection*; beneficence 897 *benevolence*; virtuous character 933 *virtue*.

elite, chosen few; pick, prime, flower; cream, crème de la crème, salt of the earth, pick of the bunch, meritocracy; crack troops, corps d'élite; top people 638 *bigwig*; charmed circle, aristocracy 868 *upper class*; choice bit, titbit, prime cut, pièce de résistance.

exceller, nonpareil, nonesuch; genius 864 *prodigy*; Admirable Crichton 646 *paragon*; one of the best 937 *good person*; one in a thousand, treasure 890 *favourite*;

jewel, pearl 844 *gem*; gold, pure g.; chefd'oeuvre 694 *masterpiece*; recordbreaker, best-seller; best ever, last word in, best thing since sliced bread; bee's knees, cat's whiskers; scorcher, humdinger, wow, knockout, hit, smash h.; smasher 841 *a beauty*; star 890 *favourite*; the tops, the greatest, top of the pops; top-notcher, first-rater; cock of the walk, toast of the town, pride of the north; champion 727 *victor*.

Adj. *excellent*, fine, braw; exemplary, worth imitating; good 933 *virtuous*; very good, first-rate 34 *superior*; prime, quality, fine, superfine; superlative, in a class by itself; all-star, rare, vintage, classic 646 *perfect*; choice, select, picked, handpicked, exclusive, exquisite, recherché 605 *chosen*; admirable 923 *approvable*; famous, great; lovely 841 *beautiful*; glorious, dazzling, splendid, splendiferous, magnificent, marvellous, wonderful, terrific, sensational, superb.

super, fantastic, fabulous, way-out; lovely, gorgeous, heavenly, out of this world 32 *prodigious*; smashing, stunning, swell, great, grand, hunky-dory; delicious 826 *pleasurable*.

best, very b., optimum, A1, champion, tip-top, top-notch, first-rate, crack; a cut above 34 *supreme*; unequalled, unparalleled, peerless, matchless, unbeatable, unsurpassable 646 *perfect*.

valuable, of value, invaluable, inestimable, priceless 811 *of price*; irreplaceable, unique, rare, precious, worth its weight in gold; sterling, gilt-edged, bluechip.

beneficial, salutary 652 *salubrious*; edifying, worthwhile 640 *useful*; favourable, kind, propitious 730 *prosperous*; harmless, innocuous.

not bad, tolerable, passable, respectable, standard, up to the mark, fair, satisfactory 635 *sufficient*; nice, decent, sound, all right, okay, OK; unexceptionable, unobjectionable; middling 30 *median*.

Vb. *be good*, etc. adj.; stand the test, pass muster 635 *suffice*; challenge comparison, vie, rival, equal the best; excel, transcend 34 *be superior*.

do good, have a good effect; do a world of good, be the making of, make a man *or* woman of 654 *make better*; help 615 *benefit*; favour, smile on 730 *prosper*; do a favour, do a good turn, put in one's debt 897 *be benevolent*; not hurt, do no harm.

645. Badness – N. *badness*, bad qualities, nastiness, foulness, rottenness; demerit; unworthiness, worthlessness; low quality, low standard 35 *inferiority*; faultiness, flaw 647 *imperfection*; shoddiness 641 *inutility*; clumsiness 695 *unskilfulness*; unsoundness, taint 655 *deterioration*; morbidity 651 *disease*; harmfulness, hurtfulness, ill, hurt, harm, injury, detriment, damage, mischief 616 *evil*; noxiousness, poisonousness 653 *insalubrity*; poison, blight, cancer 659 *bane*; pestilence, plague; contamination 651 *infection*; scandal 867 *slur*; filth 649 *uncleanness*; thorn in the flesh 377 *pain*; molestation, maltreatment, persecution 735 *severity*; malignity 898 *malevolence*; vice 934 *wickedness*; sin 936 *guilt*; bad influence, evil genius; ill wind 731 *misfortune*; black magic, evil eye 983 *sorcery*; curse 899 *malediction*; snake in the grass 663 *troublemaker*; bad character 904 *evildoer*.

Adj. *bad*, vile, base, evil, irredeemable; poor, mean, wretched, grotty, measly, low-grade, not good enough, execrable, awful 35 *inferior*; no good, worthless, cheapjack, shoddy, tacky, crummy, ropy, punk, pathetic 641 *useless*; unsatisfactory, faulty 647 *imperfect*; bad at, incompetent 695 *clumsy*; mangled, spoiled 695 *bungled*; scruffy, foul, filthy 649 *dirty*; gone bad, rank, tainted 655 *deteriorated*; decaying 51 *decomposed*; infected 651 *diseased*; irremediable, incurable; depraved 934 *wicked*; mean, shabby 930 *dishonest*; wrongful, unjust 914 *wrong*; undeserving, unworthy, contemptible; shameful, disgraceful 867 *discreditable*; lamentable, deplorable 827 *distressing*; onerous, burdensome; too bad 827 *annoying*.

harmful, hurtful, injurious, damaging, detrimental, prejudicial, deleterious 643 *inexpedient*; wasting, consuming 165

destructive; pernicious, fatal 362 *deadly*; costly 811 *dear*; disastrous, ruinous 731 *adverse*; noxious, malignant, unhealthy 653 *insalubrious*; polluting, poisonous, radioactive 653 *toxic*; unsafe, risky 661 *dangerous*; sinister, ominous 616 *evil*; malefic, mischief-making 898 *unkind*; persecuting 735 *oppressive*; monstrous 32 *exorbitant*.

not nice, unlikable, obnoxious, nasty, beastly, horrid, horrible, terrible, gruesome, grim, ghastly, awful, dreadful, perfectly d.; scruffy 867 *disreputable*; foul, rotten, lousy, putrid, stinking, sickening, revolting, nauseating 861 *disliked*; loathsome, detestable, abominable 888 *hateful*; vulgar, sordid, low, indecent, improper, gross, filthy, obscene 951 *impure*; shocking, disgusting 924 *disapproved*; plaguy, wretched 827 *annoying*.

damnable, damned, darned, blasted, confounded, blinking, dratted, bothersome, blankety-blank; execrable, accursed, cursed, hellish, infernal, devilish, diabolical.

Vb. *harm*, do h.; cost one dear 827 *hurt*; disagree with, make one ill; injure, damage, pollute 655 *impair*; corrupt 655 *pervert*; play havoc with 63 *derange*; do no good 641 *be useless*; worsen, make things worse; do evil 914 *do wrong*; molest, plague, vex 827 *trouble*; land one in trouble, queer one's pitch, do for; spite, be unkind 898 *be malevolent*.

ill-treat, maltreat, abuse 675 *misuse*; illuse, overburden, put upon, tyrannize, bear hard on, trample on, victimize, prey upon; persecute 735 *oppress*; wrong, aggrieve, distress 827 *torment*; outrage, violate 176 *be violent*; savage, maul 655 *wound*; batter, bruise 279 *strike*; rack, crucify 963 *torture*; spite 898 *be malevolent*; crush 165 *destroy*.

646. Perfection – N. *perfection*, sheer p.; finish, classic quality; the ideal; nothing wrong with, immaculateness, faultlessness, flawlessness, mint condition; correctness, irreproachability; transcendence 34 *superiority*; quintessence, essence; peak, pinnacle 213 *summit*; pitch of perfection, ne plus ultra, extreme, last word; chef d'oeuvre 694 *masterpiece*.

paragon, nonesuch 644 *exceller*; ideal, beau idéal, knight in shining armour, saint, plaster s.; classic, pattern of perfection, shining example 23 *prototype*; phoenix, superman, wonderwoman 864 *prodigy*.

Adj. *perfect*, perfected, brought to perfection, ripe 669 *matured*; just right, ideal, flawless, faultless; impeccable, infallible; correct, irreproachable; immaculate, unblemished, spotless, without a stain; uncontaminated, pure 44 *unmixed*; sound, sound as a bell, right as rain, in perfect condition; watertight, seaworthy; whole, entire, one hundred per cent; complete 52 *intact*; beyond praise 644 *excellent*; consummate 34 *supreme*; model, classic.

undamaged, safe and sound, with a whole skin, unhurt, unscathed, no harm done; unmarked, unspoilt; undiminished, whole, entire 52 *intact*; in the pink 650 *healthy*.

Vb. *perfect*, consummate, bring to perfection; ripen 669 *mature*; correct 654 *rectify*; put the finishing touch 213 *crown*; complete, leave nothing to be desired 725 *carry through*.

647. Imperfection – N. *imperfection*, imperfectness, not one hundred per cent; room for improvement, not one's best; perfectibility 654 *improvement*; faultiness 495 *error*; patchiness, unevenness, curate's egg 17 *nonuniformity*; immaturity 670 *undevelopment*; bit missing 55 *incompleteness*; deficiency, inadequacy 636 *insufficiency*; unsoundness 661 *vulnerability*; failing, weakness 307 *shortfall*; low standard, mediocrity 35 *inferiority*; second best 150 *substitute*.

defect, flaw, fault 495 *error*; loophole, crack 201 *gap*; deficiency, limitation 307 *shortfall*; weak point, soft spot, tragic flaw 661 *vulnerability*; feet of clay, weak link in the chain 163 *weakness*; scratch, stain 845 *blemish*; drawback 702 *obstacle*.

Adj. *imperfect*, not quite right, not ideal, less than perfect; fallible; uneven,

patchy, good in parts 17 *nonuniform*; faulty, flawed, cracked; wobbly, rickety 163 *flimsy*; leaky, unsound 661 *vulnerable*; soiled, shop-s. 845 *blemished*; overripe, underripe; past its best 655 *deteriorated*; below par, off form; off-colour 651 *unhealthy*; not good enough 636 *insufficient*; defective, not entire 55 *incomplete*; warped 246 *deformed*; mutilated, maimed 163 *weakened*; crude, untrained, scratch 670 *immature*; makeshift, make-do, rough and ready 150 *substituted*; second-best, second-rate 35 *inferior*; poor, unimpressive 645 *bad*; ordinary, much of a muchness, so-so; no great shakes, nothing to boast of; tolerable, bearable.

Vb. *be imperfect*, fall short of perfection, have a fault; not bear inspection, not pass muster 636 *not suffice*; not impress, not make the grade; have feet of clay 163 *be weak*.

648. Cleanness – N. *cleanness*, immaculateness 950 *purity*; freshness, dewiness, whiteness; shine, polish, spit and polish; cleanliness, daintiness 862 *fastidiousness*.

cleansing, clean, spring-cleaning, dry-c.; washing, wiping; refining, clarification, purification; lustration, purgation; flushing, dialysis; defecation 302 *excretion*; ventilation, fumigation, deodorization 395 *inodorousness*; antisepsis, sterilization, disinfection, decontamination, disinfestation, delousing; sanitation, drainage, sewerage, plumbing 652 *hygiene*, 649 *latrine*.

ablutions, washing; hygiene, oral h.; lavage, lavation, douche, flush; wash, cat-lick, lick and a promise; bathing, scrubbing etc. vb.; shampoo; dip 313 *plunge*; bath, tub; bidet; hot bath, blanket b., Turkish b., sauna; shower; hammam, sudatorium; laundry; washtub, copper, boiler, washing machine, launderette.

cleanser, purifier; disinfectant, carbolic, deodorant; soda, detergent, soap, shampoo, water, hot w.; mouth wash, gargle; lotion, hand l.; cleansing cream, cold c.; dentifrice, toothpaste; pumice stone; polish, furniture p., boot p., blacking; wax, varnish; whitewash, blacklead; aperient 658 *purgative*; drainpipe; waterworks.

cleaning utensil, broom, mop, sponge, swab, scourer; strigil; loofah; duster, feather d., whisk; brush, scrubbing b., nailbrush, toothbrush, toothpick, dental floss; comb, hair brush, clothes b.; dustpan and brush, waste bin, dustbin; carpet sweeper, vacuum cleaner; doormat, footscraper; squeegee; pipe cleaner, pullthrough, reamer; windscreen wiper; filter, strainer 263 *porosity*; eraser 550 *obliteration*; dishwasher.

cleaning cloth, duster; dishcloth, tea towel; leather, wash-l.; chamois, shammy; flannel, facecloth, towel; handkerchief, tissue; bib, apron, napkin.

cleaner, refiner, distiller; dry cleaner, launderer, laundress, washerwoman; fuller; washer-up, dishwasher; charwoman, charlady, cleaner, help, home help; scavenger, sweeper, dustman, refuse collector; lavatory attendant; chimneysweep, window cleaner; bootblack; barber 843 *beautician*; gleaner, picker, scavenger.

Adj. *clean*, dirt-free; snowy 427 *white*; polished, shining 417 *undimmed*; cleanly, dainty 862 *fastidious*; dewy, fresh; bright as a new pin, fresh as a daisy; cleaned, scrubbed, etc. vb.; shaven, shorn, barbered, trimmed; cleaned up, laundered, starched; spruce, natty, spick and span, neat, tidy, well-groomed 60 *orderly*; deodorized, disinfected, aseptic, hygienic, sterilized 652 *salubrious*; pure, purified, refined, immaculate, spotless, speckless, stainless, unsoiled, untarnished, clean as a whistle 646 *perfect*; untouched, blank; ritually clean, kosher.

cleansing, lustral, purificatory; disinfectant; hygienic, sanitary; purgative, purgatory; detergent, abstersive; ablutionary, balneary.

Vb. *clean*, spring-clean, clean up; groom, valet, spruce, neaten, trim 62 *arrange*; wash, wipe, dry; sponge, mop, swab; scrub, scour; flush; sandblast, holystone 333 *rub*; launder, starch, iron; bleach, dry-clean; soap, lather, shampoo; bathe, dip, rinse, swill down, sluice,

douche, shower 341 *drench*; dust, whisk, sweep, beat, vacuum; brush, comb, rake; buff, polish; shine, blacklead 417 *make bright*; whitewash 427 *whiten*; erase 550 *obliterate*; strip, pick, pick clean, clean out, clear out, make a clean sweep 300 *eject*.

purify, purge, clean up; bowdlerize, expurgate; sublimate, elevate 654 *make better*; cleanse, lave, lustrate, asperge; wash one's hands of; freshen, ventilate, deodorize, fumigate; edulcorate, desalinate; decontaminate, disinfect 652 *sanitate*; free from impurities, depurate, refine, distil, clarify, rack, skim; decarbonize; strain, filter, percolate, lixiviate, leach; sift, sieve 44 *eliminate*; flush, wash out 350 *make flow*.

649. Uncleanness – N. *uncleanness*, uncleanliness, dirty habits; dirtiness (**see** *dirt*); muckiness, scruffiness, filthiness; pediculosis, phthiriasis; squalor, slumminess 801 *poverty*; untidiness, sluttishness, slovenliness 61 *disorder*; stink 397 *stench*; pollution, defilement; corruption, putrescence 51 *decomposition*; contamination 651 *infection*; scatology, obscenity 951 *impurity*.

dirt, filth, stain; crud, yuk, muck, mud, sludge, slime; quagmire 347 *marsh*; night soil 302 *excrement*; snot, mucus; dust, cobweb, grime, smut, smudge; grouts, dregs, draff 41 *leavings*; sediment, deposit, precipitate, fur; scum, dross; slag 381 *ash*; drainage, sewerage, effluent; cast skin, exuviae, slough; scurf, dandruff; tartar, plaque; pus, matter, feculence; refuse, garbage, litter 641 *rubbish*; rot, mildew, mould 51 *decay*; vermin, flea, nit 365 *insect*.

swill, pig-s., hogwash; bilge, bilgewater; ditch-w., dish-w., slops; sewage; wallow, slough.

latrine, privy, heads, jakes, bog, john, loo; closet, water c., WC; cloakroom, powder room, rest r., washroom, lavatory, toilet; urinal, public convenience, comfort station, Ladies, Gents; commode, bedpan, chamber pot, jerry 302 *defecation*.

sink, kitchen s., cesspit, cesspool, sump, septic tank, soakaway; gutter, sewer, main, cloaca 351 *drain*; dunghill, midden, rubbish heap, compost h.; Augean stables, pigsty; slum 192 *housing*; shambles 362 *slaughterhouse*; plague-spot 651 *infection*.

dirty person, sloven, slattern, drab, traipse, slut; litterbug, litter lout; mudlark, street arab; scavenger 648 *cleaner*; beast, pig, wallower; ratbag, fleabag.

Adj. *unclean*, unhallowed 980 *profane*; smutty, scatological 951 *impure*; coarse, unrefined, unpurified; septic, festering, poisonous 653 *toxic*; unsterilized, nonsterile 653 *infectious*; sordid, squalid, slummy, insanitary, unhygienic 653 *insalubrious*; foul, offensive, nasty, grotty 645 *not nice*; noisome, nauseous, nauseating, stinking, malodorous 397 *fetid*; uncleanly, beastly, hoggish; grubby, scruffy; scurfy, scabby; flea-ridden, lousy, crawling; faecal 302 *excretory*; carious, rotting, tainted, high; flyblown, maggoty 51 *decomposed*.

dirty, filthy; dusty, grimy, sooty, smoky; befouled, polluted; littered, rubbish-strewn; thick with dust, unswept; untidy, unkempt, slatternly, sleazy, slovenly, sluttish, bedraggled, frowzy 61 *orderless*; unsoaped, unwashed; black, dingy, uncleaned, unpolished; tarnished, stained, soiled; greasy, oily; clotted, caked, matted, muddied, dirt-encrusted; messy, mucky, muddy 347 *marshy*; furred up, scummy; musty, fusty, cobwebby; mouldy, rotten 655 *dilapidated*.

Vb. *be unclean*, etc. adj.; get dirty, collect dust, foul up, clog; rust, moulder, fester, rot 51 *decompose*; smell 397 *stink*; wallow, roll in the mud.

make unclean, foul, befoul; dirty, soil; grime, begrime; stain, blot, sully, tarnish; muck up, make a mess, untidy; daub, smirch, besmirch, smudge 419 *bedim*; spot, patch, streak, smear, besmear, grease; cake, clog, muddy, roil; draggle, drabble; spatter, bespatter, splash 341 *moisten*; taint, corrupt, pollute, contaminate 655 *impair*; defile, desecrate 980 *be impious*.

650. Health – N. *health*, rude h., robust h., glowing h., good h.; healthiness, good constitution 162 *vitality*; fitness, condition, pink of c.; bloom, rosiness, rosy cheeks, ruddy complexion; well-being, physical w.; eupepsia 376 *euphoria*; whole skin, soundness; long life, longevity 131 *age*; clean bill of health; hygiene.

Adj. *healthy*, healthful, hygienic, sanitary 652 *salubrious*; in good health, eupeptic, euphoric; blooming, ruddy, rosy, rosy-cheeked; lusty, bouncing, strapping, hale and hearty, sound, fit, well, fine, bonny, full of beans 174 *vigorous*; never ill, robust, hardy, strong 162 *stalwart*; fighting fit, in condition, in the pink, in good nick, in good shape, in good heart, in fine fettle *or* trim *or* feather; feeling fine, feeling great; sound in wind and limb, sound as a bell, fit as a fiddle, A1; a picture of health, getting well, convalescent, on the mend, on the up-grade, on the up and up, up and about 656 *restored*; pretty well, no worse, as well as can be expected; unharmed 646 *undamaged*.

Vb. *be healthy*, etc. adj.; look after oneself; feel fine, thrive, flourish, enjoy good health; be in the pink, have never felt better; wear well, look young; keep fit, keep well, have a clean bill of health.

651. Ill health. Disease – N. *ill health*, bad h., poor h., delicate h., failing h.; delicacy, weak constitution; unhealthiness, infirmity, debility 163 *weakness*; seediness, loss of condition; morbidity, indisposition, cachexia; chronic complaint, allergy; chronic ill health; valetudinarianism, hypochondria; nerves 503 *psychopathy*.

illness, affliction, disability, handicap, infirmity 163 *weakness*; sickness, indisposition, ailment, complaint, complication; symptoms, syndrome 547 *indication*; condition, history of; visitation, attack; spasm, stroke, seizure, fit; shock; poisoning, metal p., food p.; radiation sickness; nausea, waves of n., queasiness, heaving stomach, vomiting; dizziness, vertigo; headache, migraine 377 *pain*; temperature, feverishness, fever, ague, shivers, shakes; hypothermia, hyperthermia; delirium 503 *frenzy*; breakdown, collapse; fainting 375 *insensibility*; prostration, coma; terminal disease, fatal illness 361 *decease*; sickbed, deathbed.

disease, malady, disorder; epidemic disease, endemic d.; infectious disease, communicable d., notifiable d.; congenital d.; occupational d., industrial d.; alcoholism, obesity; deficiency disease, malnutrition, pellagra, rickets, scurvy; degenerative disease, wasting d., marasmus, atrophy; traumatic disease, trauma; organic disease, functional d., circulatory d., neurological d., nervous d., heart d.; endocrine disease, diabetes; urogenital disease; respiratory d; gastro-intestinal d.; cancer; hydrocele, dropsy; fibrosis; brain disease 503 *insanity*.

plague, pestilence, infection, contagion; epidemic, pandemic; bubonic plague, Black Death.

infection, contagion, bug; miasma, pollution, taint; infectiousness 653 *insalubrity*; suppuration, festering, purulence, gangrene; toxicity, sepsis 659 *poison*; plague spot, hotbed; vector, carrier, host; parasite 659 *bane*; virus, bacillus, bacteria, germ, pathogen; blood-poisoning, toxaemia, septicaemia, pyaemia; food-poisoning (**see** *digestive disorders*); parasitical disease, toxocariasis (**see** *tropical disease*); infectious disease, cold, common c., influenza, flu; tuberculosis; measles, German measles; whooping-cough, mumps; chickenpox, smallpox; scarlet fever; fever (**see** *tropical disease*); typhus; glandular fever; encephalitis, meningitis; sleepy sickness; tetanus, lockjaw, rabies, hydrophobia.

tropical disease, fever, malaria, ague; cholera, Asiatic c.; yellow fever, blackwater f., Lassar f.; leishmaniasis; sleeping sickness; bilharzia; hookworm; trachoma, glaucoma, river blindness; yaws; leprosy; beri-beri, kwashiorkor.

digestive disorders, indigestion, dyspepsia, liverishness; biliousness, nausea, vomiting, retching; colic, gripes; stomach ache, tummy a., belly a., guts ache; stomach upset, collywobbles, diarrhoea,

gutrot, the runs, the trots 302 *defecation*; diarrhoea and vomiting, D and V, gastroenteritis; dysentery, cholera, typhoid; food poisoning, botulism, Legionnaire's disease; flatulence, wind, belching 300 *voidance*; acidosis, heartburn; hiatus hernia; ulcer, peptic u.; enteritis, colitis, appendicitis, perforated appendix; jaundice, hepatitis, cirrhosis, cystitis, nephritis, kidney failure; gallstones, haemorrhoids, piles; constipation.

respiratory disease, cough, cold, sore throat, catarrh; sinusitis, adenoids, tonsillitis, pharyngitis; laryngitis, croup, bronchitis; emphysema, asthma; pleurisy, pneumonia; silicosis, asbestosis, farmer's lung; diphtheria; whooping cough; lung cancer; smoker's cough; cystic fibrosis; pulmonary tuberculosis, consumption.

cardiovascular disease, angina pectoris; palpitation, dyspnoea; murmur, heart m.; heart condition, bad heart, weak h., heart trouble; congenital heart disease, hole in the heart; rheumatic heart disease, coronary h. d.; heart failure; heart attack, coronary thrombosis, coronary; cerebral thrombosis, brain haemorrhage, stroke; blood pressure, high b. p., hypertension; hypotension, low blood pressure; vascular disease; arteriosclerosis; arteritis, phlebitis, varicose veins; thrombosis, clot, blood c., embolism, infarction.

blood disease, anaemia, pernicious a., sickle-cell a.; leukaemia, Hodgkin's disease; haemophilia; haemorrhage.

cancer, neoplasm, growth; tumour, benign t.; malignant t., cancerous growth; sarcoma, melanoma; rodent ulcer.

skin disease, skin lesion; mange; lupus; yaws; leprosy; erythema; erysipelas, St Anthony's fire; impetigo, tetters, herpes; shingles; dermatitis, eczema; ringworm; prurigo, pruritus, itch 378 *formication*; hives, urticaria, nettlerash; thrush; athlete's foot; rash, eruption; acne, spots, blackheads; pustule, pimple; blister, wart, verruca 253 *swelling*; birthmark 845 *blemish*.

venereal disease, VD, pox; syphilis, gonorrhoea, the clap; venereal ulcer, chancre, syphilitic sore.

ulcer, ulceration, gathering, festering, purulence; inflammation, lesion 655 *wound*; scald, burn; sore, boil, abscess, fistula; cyst; blain, chilblain, kibe; corn 253 *swelling*; gangrene 51 *decay*; discharge, pus, matter.

rheumatism, rheumatics; rheumatic fever; fibrositis; frozen shoulder, tennis elbow, housemaid's knee, pulled muscle; arthritis, rheumatoid a.; gout 377 *pang*; osteoarthritis; lumbago, sciatica; slipped disc.

nervous disorders, nervous breakdown 503 *psychopathy*; brain tumour; brain haemorrhage, stroke, seizure; hemiplegia, diplegia, paraplegia 375 *insensibility*; palsy, cerebral p., spasticity; involuntary movements, tremor, tic 318 *spasm*; petit mal, grand mal, epilepsy, falling sickness; infantile paralysis, poliomyelitis, polio; spina bifida; Parkinson's disease; Huntington's chorea, St Vitus's dance; multiple sclerosis; muscular dystrophy.

animal disease, distemper; foot-and-mouth disease, swine fever; myxomatosis; rinderpest, murrain; anthrax, sheeprot, bloat; liver fluke, worms; megrims, staggers; glanders, farcy, spavin, thrush; Newcastle disease, fowl pest; psittacosis; hard pad; mange; rabies.

sick person, sufferer; patient, in-p., out-p.; case, stretcher c., hospital c.; mental case 504 *madman*; invalid, chronic i.; valetudinarian, hypochondriac, martyr to ill health; consumptive, asthmatic, bronchitic, dyspeptic, diabetic; haemophiliac, bleeder; insomniac; neuropath, addict, alcoholic; spastic, arthritic, paralytic; paraplegic, disabled person; crock, old c., cripple 163 *weakling*; walking wounded; sick list.

pathology, forensic p.; diagnosis, prognosis; aetiology, nosology, epidemiology, bacteriology, parasitology 658 *therapy*.

Adj. *unhealthy*, unsound, sickly; infirm, decrepit, weakly 163 *weak*; delicate, always ill; in bad health, in poor h.; in poor condition, mangy; undernourished, malnourished 636 *underfed*; peaked, emaciated; sallow, pale, peaky, anaemic 426 *colourless*; bilious 434 *green*; jaundiced

433 *yellow*; invalid, valetudinarian; pill-popping, hypochondriac.

sick, ill, unwell, not well, indisposed, out of sorts, under the weather, off-colour, below par; queasy, nauseated, green around the gills; in poor shape, in a bad way, poorly, seedy, squeamish, groggy, grotty, queer, ailing; sickening for, showing symptoms of; feverish, headachy, off one's food *or* one's oats; confined, laid up, bedridden, on one's back, in bed, in hospital, on the sick list, invalided, hospitalized; run down, exhausted 684 *fatigued*; seized, taken ill, taken bad; prostrate, collapsed; in a coma 375 *insensible*; on the danger list; critical, serious, comfortable; chronic, incurable, inoperable; moribund 361 *dying*; wasting away, in a decline.

diseased, pathological, disordered, distempered; infected, plague-stricken; contaminated, tainted, gangrenous 51 *decomposed*; peccant, morbid, pathogenic; iatrogenic; psychosomatic 447 *mental*; infectious, contagious; festering, purulent 653 *toxic*; degenerative, consumptive, tuberculous, tubercular; diabetic; anaemic; leukaemic, haemophiliac; arthritic, rheumatic, rheumatoid, rheumaticky, creaking; palsied, paralysed, paralytic, spastic, epileptic; leprous; carcinomatous, cancerous, cankered; syphilitic, venereal; swollen, oedematous; gouty; bronchial, throaty, bronchitic, croupy, sniffly, full of cold, bunged up; asthmatic; allergic; febrile, fevered, shivering, aguish, feverish, delirious; sore, tender; ulcerous, ulcerated, inflamed; spotty, pimply; spavined, broken-winded; mangy.

Vb. *be ill*, etc. adj.; enjoy poor health; ail, suffer, labour under, undergo treatment; not feel well, complain of; feel queer etc. adj.; feel sick 300 *vomit*; lose one's health, sicken, fall sick, fall ill; catch an infection *or* a bug, contract a disease; break out with, go down with; be seized, be stricken, be taken with, not feel so good; have a stroke, collapse; be laid up, take to one's bed; be invalided out; languish, pine, peak, droop, waste away, go into a decline; fail, get worse, sink, fade away 655 *deteriorate*, 163 *be weak*.

652. Salubrity – N. *salubrity*, healthiness, well-being 650 *health*; salubriousness, healthfulness, wholesomeness; whole food, health food; smokeless zone, fresh air, sea a. 340 *air*; sunshine, outdoors; benign climate, health resort.

hygiene, sanitation, cleanliness 648 *cleanness*; preventive medicine, prophylaxis; quarantine, cordon sanitaire 660 *protection*; immunity, immunization, inoculation, vaccination; pasteurization; antisepsis, sterilization, disinfection, chlorination; sanatorium, spa 658 *hospital*; hot springs 658 *therapy*; keeping fit, jogging, cycling, constitutional 682 *exercise*; hygienics.

sanitarian, hygienist, sanitationist; public health inspector; sanitary engineer; medical officer; fresh-air fiend, sun-worshipper, naturist, nudist.

Adj. *salubrious*, healthful, healthy, wholesome; pure, fresh 648 *clean*; ventilated, well-v., air-conditioned; tonic, bracing, invigorating 656 *restorative*; hygienic, sanitary, disinfected, etc. vb.; sterile, aseptic, antiseptic; sanative, sanatory; prophylactic, protective 658 *remedial*; good for, salutary, what the doctor ordered 644 *beneficial*; nutritious, nourishing, body-building, health-giving; noninjurious, harmless, benign, nonmalignant; uninfectious, innoxious; immune, protected 660 *invulnerable*.

Vb. *sanitate*, disinfect, boil, sterilize, antisepticize, chlorinate, pasteurize; immunize, inoculate, vaccinate; quarantine, put in q., isolate 883 *seclude*; ventilate 340 *aerate*; freshen 648 *purify*; cleanse 648 *clean*; drain 342 *dry*; conserve 666 *preserve*.

653. Insalubrity – N. *insalubrity*, unhealthiness, unwholesomeness; uncleanliness, lack of hygiene, lack of sanitation; verminousness 649 *uncleanness*; unhealthy conditions, condemned housing, slum; mephitis, bad air, bad climate; smoke haze, smog; infectiousness,

contagiousness; carrier, vector; germ, microbe 196 *microorganism*; miasma, contagion 651 *infection*; pollution, radioactivity, fallout; poisonousness 659 *bane*.

Adj. *insalubrious*, unwholesome, unhealthy; bad for one's health, insanitary, unhygienic 649 *unclean*; bad, nasty, noxious, miasmal 645 *harmful*; radioactive, carcinogenic; verminous, flea-ridden, rat-infested, undrained 347 *marshy*; stagnant, foul, polluted, undrinkable, inedible; indigestible, unnutritious; unsound, not fresh, stale, gone bad 655 *deteriorated*; unventilated, windowless, airless 264 *sealed off*; smoke-filled, stuffy, overheated; underheated.

infectious, morbific, pathogenic; infective, germ-carrying; contagious, catching, taking, communicable; pestiferous, pestilent, plague-stricken; malarious, malarial; epidemic, pandemic, endemic; epizootic, enzootic, sporadic; unsterilized, nonsterile, infected 649 *dirty*.

toxic, poisonous, mephitic, pestilential, germ-laden; venomous, envenomed, poisoned; gathering, festering, septic, pussy, purulent, suppurating; lethal 362 *deadly*.

654. Improvement – N. *improvement*, betterment, amelioration, melioration; uplift, regeneration; good influence 178 *influence*; change for the better, transfiguration 143 *transformation*; conversion, new leaf 939 *penitence*; revival, recovery 656 *restoration*; evolution, development, perfectibility; elaboration, enrichment; advance, onward march, progress 285 *progression*; furtherance, advancement, preferment, promotion, kick upstairs 308 *ascent*; upturn, upswing 310 *elevation*; revaluation, enhancement 36 *increase*.

amendment, mending etc. vb.; renovation 656 *repair*; reorganization 62 *arrangement*; reformation, reform (**see** *reformism*); purification 648 *cleansing*; refining, rectification, correction, redaction, revision, red ink, blue pencil; emendation, recension, revised edition, improved version 589 *edition*; second thoughts, review, reconsideration 67 *sequel*; polish, finishing touch 725 *completion*.

civilization, culture, kultur; Western civilization, Eastern c.; black culture, Negritude; civility, refinement 846 *good taste*; training, upbringing, education; cultivation, polish, improvement of the mind 490 *culture*.

reformism, meliorism, perfectionism, idealism; Moral Re-Armament; liberalism, socialism, radicalism; extremism, revolution 738 *sedition*; feminism, progressivism; gradualism, Fabianism; social engineering 901 *sociology*.

reformer, improver, restorer 656 *mender*; emender, corrector, editor, reviser; progressive, gradualist, Fabian 625 *moderate*; liberal, radical, feminist; extremist, revolutionary 738 *agitator*; socialist, communist, Marxist, Red; reformist, idealist, Utopian 513 *visionary*; sociologist, social worker 901 *philanthropist*.

Adj. *improved*, bettered, enhanced; touched up 843 *beautified*; reformed, revised 34 *superior*; better, all the better for; looking up, on the mend; improvable, corrigible, curable, reformable, perfectible.

improving, reformative, remedial 656 *restorative*; reforming, reformist, progressive, radical; civilizing, cultural; idealistic, perfectionist, Utopian, millenarian, chiliastic.

Vb. *get better*, grow b., improve, mend, take a turn for the better, turn the corner; pick up, rally, revive, recover 656 *be restored*; make progress, make headway, develop, evolve 285 *progress*; mellow, ripen 669 *mature*; better oneself 730 *prosper*; mend one's ways, reform, turn over a new leaf, go straight; improve oneself, learn by experience 536 *learn*.

make better, better, improve, ameliorate, meliorate, reform; improve upon, refine u.; polish, elaborate, enrich, enhance; do one a power of good 644 *do good*; improve out of all recognition, transfigure 147 *transform*; make, be the making of 178 *influence*; uplift, regenerate; refine, elevate, sublimate 648 *purify*; civilize, socialize, teach manners; mend

656 *repair*; restore 656 *cure*; infuse fresh blood into 685 *refresh*; mitigate 177 *moderate*; forward, advance, upgrade 285 *promote*; foster, encourage, bring to fruition 669 *mature*; make the most of, get the best out of 673 *use*; develop, open up, reclaim 370 *cultivate*; tidy up 62 *arrange*; spruce up 648 *clean*; do up, vamp up, tone up; renovate, refurbish, renew, give a facelift; bring up to date 126 *modernize*; touch up 841 *beautify*; improve on nature 843 *primp*; embellish, adorn 844 *decorate*.

rectify, put *or* set right, straighten out 24 *adjust*; mend, patch 656 *repair*; correct, debug, blue-pencil, proof-read, revise, redact, edit, amend, emend; rewrite, redraft, retell, recast, remould, refashion, remodel, recreate, reform; reorganize, streamline 62 *regularize*; review, re-examine, reconsider; think better of, have second thoughts.

655. Deterioration – N. *deterioration*, debasement, coarsening; cheapening, devaluation; retrogression, slipping back, losing ground 286 *regression*; reversion to type, throwback; decline, ebb 37 *decrease*; twilight, fading 419 *dimness*; falling off, downtrend, downturn, slump, depression, recession 801 *poverty*; law of diminishing returns; exhaustion 634 *waste*; corruption, perversion, degeneration, degeneracy 934 *wickedness*; downward course, primrose path 309 *descent*; recidivism; setback 657 *relapse*.

dilapidation, collapse, ruination 165 *destruction*; planning blight; disrepair, neglect 458 *negligence*; ravages of time, wear and tear, erosion, corrosion, rust, moth, rot 51 *decay*; mildew 659 *blight*; decrepitude 131 *old age*; atrophy 651 *disease*; ruin, wreck, physical w., shadow of one's former self.

impairment, spoiling 675 *misuse*; detriment, damage 772 *loss*; discoloration, weathering; pollution, contamination, defilement 649 *uncleanness*; ulceration, poisoning, contamination 651 *infection*; adulteration, sophistication, watering down 43 *mixture*; assault, outrage 712 *attack*; ruination, demolition 165 *destruc-*

tion; injury, mischief, harm 165 *havoc*; disablement, crippling, laming; mutilation, weakening 163 *weakness*; sprain, strain, dislocation; sabotage, demoralization 63 *derangement*; exacerbation 832 *aggravation*.

wound, injury, trauma; open wound; bloody nose; sore, running s. 651 *ulcer*; laceration, lesion; cut, gash, abrasion, nick, snick, scratch 46 *scission*; stab, prick, jab, puncture 263 *perforation*; contusion, bruise, bump, discoloration, black eye, shiner, thick ear 253 *swelling*; burn, scald; rupture, hernia; broken bones, fracture; scar, cicatrice 845 *blemish*.

Adj. *deteriorated*, not improved, the worse for; exacerbated 832 *aggravated*; spoilt, impaired, hurt, etc. vb.; worn out, effete, exhausted 641 *useless*; stale, gone bad, rotten 645 *bad*; corked, flat 387 *tasteless*; undermined, sapped 163 *weakened*; tired, done in, washed up 684 *fatigued*; no better, worse, getting w., in a bad way, far gone, on one's last legs; failing, in decline 131 *ageing*; on the downgrade, on the downward path 309 *descending*; faded, withered, decaying 51 *decomposed*; wasting away, ebbing; falling off 37 *decreasing*; degenerative, retrogressive, retrograde, unprogressive 286 *regressive*; lapsed 603 *trimming*; degenerate, depraved 934 *vicious*; come down in the world 801 *poor*.

dilapidated, the worse for wear, falling to pieces, in disrepair, in shreds, in ruins; broken, cracked, leaking; battered, weather-beaten, storm-tossed; decrepit, ruinous, ramshackle, shaky, rickety, tumbledown, rundown, on its last legs 163 *weakened*; slummy, condemned; worn, well-w., frayed, shabby, tatty, dingy, holey, in tatters, in rags, out-at-elbows; worn out, worn to a frazzle *or* a shadow, done for 641 *useless*; seedy, down at heel, down and out 801 *poor*; rusty, rotten, mildewed, mouldering, moss-grown, moth-eaten, worm-e. 51 *decomposed*.

Vb. *deteriorate*, not improve, get no better; worsen, get worse, go from bad to worse, take a turn for the worse; slip, slide, go downhill; have seen better days

657 *relapse*; fall off, slump, decline, wane 37 *decrease*; slip back, revert 286 *regress*; lapse 603 *tergiversate*; degenerate, let oneself go, go to pieces, run to seed, hit the skids 165 *be destroyed*; go to the bad 934 *be wicked*; disintegrate, fall apart, collapse, break down 309 *tumble*; contract, shrink 198 *become small*; wear out, age 131 *grow old*; fade, wither, wilt, shrivel, perish, crumble, moulder, mildew, grow moss; go to rack and ruin; rust, rot, decay 51 *decompose*; spoil, stale, lose its taste, go flat, go off, go sour, turn 391 *be unpalatable*; go bad, smell 397 *stink*; corrupt, putrefy, rankle, fester, suppurate, gangrene 51 *decompose*; sicken 651 *be ill*; jump from the frying pan into the fire, go farther and fare worse 832 *aggravate*.

pervert, warp, twist 246 *distort*; abuse, prostitute 675 *misuse*; deprave 951 *debauch*; vitiate, corrupt 934 *make wicked*; degrade, debase; brutalize, dehumanize, barbarize; denature 147 *transform*; denationalize, detribalize; brainwash 535 *misteach*.

impair, damage, hurt, injure, scathe 645 *harm*; play havoc with 63 *derange*; dismantle, dismast; spoil, mar 695 *be clumsy*; tinker, tamper, meddle with, monkey w. 678 *meddle*; exacerbate 832 *aggravate*; do no good, kill with kindness; degrade, devalue, debase 812 *cheapen*; spot, stain, mark 845 *blemish*; deface 246 *distort*; mutilate, maim 161 *disable*; clip one's wings 702 *hinder*; castrate 161 *unman*; expurgate, eviscerate, bowdlerize; curtail, dock 204 *shorten*; cream off, skim, take the heart out of; adulterate 43 *mix*; denature, deactivate; subvert, demoralize 163 *weaken*; gnaw at the roots, eat away, fret, erode, corrode 51 *decompose*; blight, blast, wither; ravage, overrun 165 *lay waste*; vandalize, wreck 165 *destroy*; crumble 332 *pulverize*; wear out, exhaust, consume, use up 634 *waste*; infect, contaminate, poison, ulcerate; taint, foul, pollute 649 *make unclean*.

wound, scotch, draw blood, let b.; tear, lacerate, mangle, rip 46 *disunite*; maul, savage 176 *be violent*; black one's eye, bloody one's nose; bite, scratch, claw;

gash, hack, incise 46 *cut*; sting, prick, stab, gore, run through 263 *pierce*; bruise, contuse 279 *strike*; crush 332 *pulverize*; chafe 333 *rub*; smash 46 *break*; graze, pepper, wing.

656. Restoration – N. *restoration*, reparation, reparations 941 *atonement*; retrieval, recovery; re-establishment, reinstallation, rehabilitation; replanting, reafforestation, reclamation, recycling; rescue, salvage, redemption 668 *deliverance*; reconstitution, re-erection, rebuilding, reformation, reconstruction, reorganization; remodelling 654 *amendment*; reconversion, reaction; resumption, return to normal, derestriction; reinforcement 162 *strengthening*; replenishment 633 *provision*.

repair, repairs, running r., renovation, renewal, reconditioning, redintegration, reassembling; rectification, emendation; restoration, making like new; mending, patching up, etc. vb.; patch, darn, insertion, reinforcement; facelift 843 *beautification*.

revival, recovery 685 *refreshment*; renewal, reawakening, resurgence, recovery, rally, comeback; fresh spurt, new energy; economic miracle 730 *prosperity*; reactivation, revivification, reanimation, resuscitation, artificial respiration, kiss of life; rejuvenation, rejuvenescence, second youth, Indian summer; facelift, new look; rebirth, renaissance; palingenesis, regeneration, resurrection.

recuperation, recovery, pulling through, cure; healing, mending, cicatrization; convalescence, restoration to health 658 *remedy*; moderation, easing 831 *relief*; psychological cure, catharsis, abreaction; curability.

mender, repairer, renovator, painter, decorator, interior d.; emendator, rectifier; rebuilder, restorer, refurbisher; patcher, darner, cobbler, shoe-repairer; knife grinder, tinker, plumber, fixer, handyman; curer, healer, bonesetter 658 *doctor*; faith healer; psychiatrist; reformist 654 *reformer*.

Adj. *restored*, revived, etc. vb.; re-made, reconditioned, reproofed; rectified 654 *improved*; like new, renewed; saved, born again 979 *sanctified*; reborn, renascent, resurgent, like a phoenix from the ashes; alive and kicking 650 *healthy*; cured, none the worse, better, convalescent, on the mend, pulling through; in one's right mind, back to normal, oneself again; retrievable, restorable, recoverable; mendable, amendable; medicable, curable, operable.

restorative, reparative, analeptic, recuperative, curative, sanative, healing, medicated 658 *remedial*.

Vb. *be restored*, recover, come round *or* to, revive, rally 685 *be refreshed*; pull through, get over, get well, convalesce, recuperate; turn the corner 654 *get better*; weather the storm, survive, live through; live again, resurrect, arise from the dead, return from the grave; reappear, make a comeback, take on a new lease of life; sleep off, be oneself again, bounce back, snap out of it, come up smiling; pick oneself up, find one's feet again; get back to normal, go on as before.

restore, re-establish, rehabilitate; reconstitute, reconstruct, reform, reorganize 654 *make better*; renovate, renew, rebuild, re-erect, remake, redo; overhaul, service, refit, refurbish, make like new 126 *modernize*; make whole; redintegrate; reafforest, replant, reclaim; recycle, reprocess; reinforce, build up one's strength 162 *strengthen*; rescue, salvage, retrieve, recapture.

revive, revivify, revitalize, resuscitate, regenerate, recall to life, resurrect, reanimate, rekindle; breathe fresh life into, rejuvenate 685 *refresh*.

cure, heal, make well, cure of, break of; nurse, medicate 658 *doctor*; bandage, bind up one's wounds; nurse through, work a cure, snatch from the grave, restore to health, set up, set on one's feet again; set (a bone); cicatrize, heal over, skin o., scab o., close, knit together; right itself, work its own cure.

repair, do repairs; put right, remedy 654 *rectify*; overhaul, mend, fix; cobble, resole, heel; reface, retread, recover, resurface 226 *cover*; darn, patch, patch up; stop, fill (teeth); do up, touch up, freshen up, retouch, revamp, plaster up, fill in the cracks, paper over; seal, stop a gap 350 *staunch*; caulk 264 *close*; pick up the pieces, piece together, refit, reassemble, cannibalize 45 *join*; give a facelift, refurbish, recondition, renovate.

657. Relapse – N. *relapse*, lapse, falling back; throwback, return 148 *reversion*; retrogression 286 *regression*; sinking, falling off 655 *deterioration*; backsliding, recidivism, apostasy 603 *change of allegiance*; recrudescence, reinfection, recurrence, fresh outbreak.

Vb. *relapse*, slip back, slide b., sink b., fall b.; retrogress 286 *regress*; degenerate 655 *deteriorate*; backslide, recidivate, lapse, fall from grace 603 *apostatize*; fall off again, revert to 148 *revert*; have a relapse.

658. Remedy – N. *remedy*, succour, help 703 *aid*; oil on troubled waters 177 *moderator*; remedial measure, corrective 654 *amendment*; cure 656 *recuperation*; medicinal value, healing gift, healing quality; sovereign remedy, specific; prescription, formula, nostrum; quack remedy, patent medicine; sovereign remedy, panacea, heal-all, cure-all, catholicon; elixir, elixir vitae, philosopher's stone.

medicine, materia medica, pharmacopoeia; Galenical, herb, medicinal h., simple; balm, balsam; medication, medicament, patent medicine, proprietary drug, ethical d. (see *drug*); placebo; pill, bolus, tablet, capsule, lozenge; physic, draught, potion, elixir; decoction, infusion; dose, booster d.; drench; drops, drip; injection, jab, shot; preparation, mixture, powder, electuary, linctus; plaster (see *surgical dressing*); spray, inhaler; medicine chest.

antidote, counterirritant, antihistamine; counterpoison, antiserum, antitoxin, mithridate; antiemetic; antipyretic, febrifuge, quinine; vermifuge, anthelmintic; antigen, antibody, interferon; antibiotic; immunosuppressant; anti-spasmodic, anticonvulsant; sedative, muscle relaxant; anticoagulant; antacid, analgesic, painkiller. See *drug*.

purgative, purge, laxative, aperient; diuretic; expectorant, emetic, nauseant; carminative, digestive; douche, enema.

tonic, restorative; cordial, reviver, refresher, pick-me-up 174 *stimulant*; caffeine, nicotine, alcohol; spirits, smelling salts, sal volatile; infusion, tisane, herb tea; coca, betel nut, ginseng; vitamin tablet, iron pill.

drug, synthetic drug, wonder d., miracle d.; antibiotic, sulpha drug, sulphonomide; penicillin; aureomycin, streptomycin, insulin, cortisone; hormone, steroid; progesterone, oestrogen; analgesic, aspirin, codeine 375 *anaesthetic*; tranquillizer, antidepressant, sedative; barbiturate, sleeping pill 679 *soporific*; narcotic, dope, morphine, opium, cocaine; intoxicant, stimulant 949 *drug-taking*.

balm, balsam, oil, emollient 177 *moderator*; salve, ointment, cream; lanolin, liniment, embrocation, lotion, wash; eyewash, collyrium; placebo.

surgical dressing, dressing, lint, gauze; swab; bandage, roller, sling, splint, cast, plaster of Paris; tourniquet; fingerstall; patch; plaster, sticking p.; fomentation, poultice, compress; tampon, pledget; pessary, suppository.

medical art, therapeutics, healing touch 656 *recuperation*; medical practice, allopathy, homoeopathy, naturopathy, nature cure; medicine, clinical m., preventive m., fringe m., folk m.; acupuncture; radiography, tomography; diagnosis, prognosis 651 *pathology*; healing, gift of h., laying on of hands, faith healing, Christian Science; gynaecology, midwifery 167 *obstetrics*; geriatrics, paediatrics; orthopaedics, ophthalmology, neurology, dermatology, ear, nose and throat, ENT, cardiology, oncology; radiotherapy; psychodiagnostics, psychopathology; bacteriology, microbiology, virology, immunology; pharmaceutics, pharmacology, posology; veterinary medicine.

surgery, plastic s., cosmetic s., rhinoplasty, prosthetics; manipulative surgery, chiropractic; operation, surgical o., op.; phlebotomy, venesection; transfusion, perfusion; dialysis; D and C, dilatation and curettage; transplant; cauterization; amputation, trephination, lobotomy, tonsillectomy, appendicectomy, colostomy, laparotomy; mastectomy, vasectomy; dentistry, stopping, filling, crowning; massage, chiropody, pedicure, manicure; electrolysis.

therapy, therapeutics, medical care, treatment; nursing, bedside manner; first aid, aftercare; course, cure, nature c., hydrotherapy; regimen, diet; bonesetting, orthopaedics, osteopathy, osteotherapy; hypnotherapy; hormone therapy; immunotherapy; chemotherapy; physiotherapy, occupational therapy; radiotherapy, phototherapy; heat treatment; electrotherapy, shock treatment, ECT, EST; psychotherapy 447 *psychology*; group therapy, behaviour t., aversion t.; acupuncture; catheterization; intravenous injection, dripfeed.

hospital, infirmary; mental hospital 503 *lunatic asylum*; dispensary, clinic, antenatal c.; nursing home, convalescent h., rest h.; home for the dying, hospice; stretcher, ambulance; ward, sick bay, sickroom, sickbed; oxygen tent, iron lung; respirator, life-support system, heart-lung machine, kidney m.; incubator, intensive care unit; X-ray machine, scanner; dressing station, first-aid s., casualty s.; operating theatre, operating table; consulting room, surgery, clinic, community health centre; sanatorium, spa, hydro, watering place; hot springs, thermae; solarium, sun lamp.

doctor, physician; leech, quack, charlatan; veterinary surgeon, vet, horsedoctor; faith healer, layer-on of hands, Christian Scientist; allopath, homoeopath, naturopath; acupuncturist; hakim, barefoot doctor, flying d.; witch-doctor, medicine man 983 *sorcerer*; medic, medical student; houseman, intern, registrar; medical practitioner, general p., GP; locum tenens, locum; clinician, therapeutist, healer; surgeon, plastic s., neuro-

surgeon; sawbones; medical officer, sanitary inspector; medical adviser, consultant, specialist; diagnostician, pathologist, forensic p.; psychiatrist, psychoanalyst, neurologist; paramedic, anaesthetist, radiographer; physiotherapist, occupational therapist, speech t.; paediatrician, geriatrician; obstetrician, midwife; gynaecologist; dermatologist, haematologist; biochemist, microbiologist; radiotherapist; orthopaedist, osteopath, bonesetter, chiropractor, masseur, masseuse; pedicurist, chiropodist, manicurist; ophthalmologist, optician, oculist; dentist, dental surgeon, orthodontist; nutritionist, dietitian; medical profession, Harley Street, National Health Service; Red Cross, St John's Ambulance.

druggist, apothecary, chemist, pharmacist, dispenser, posologist, pharmacologist; chemist's, pharmacy.

nurse, male n., probationer n., student n., staff n.; charge n., sister, night s., ward s., theatre s.; matron; State Enrolled Nurse, State Registered Nurse, district nurse, health visitor; nursing auxiliary, ward orderly, dresser, stretcher-bearer, ambulanceman; almoner, hospital social worker 901 *sociology*; Florence Nightingale, lady with a lamp.

Adj. *remedial*, corrective, analeptic, curative, first-aid 656 *restorative*; helpful 644 *beneficial*; therapeutic, medicinal, healing, curing 652 *salubrious*; specific, sovereign; all-healing; soothing, demulcent, emollient 177 *lenitive*; anodyne, analgesic, narcotic, hypnotic, anaesthetic 375 *insensible*; peptic, digestive; purging 648 *cleansing*; emetic, vomitory, laxative; antidotal 182 *counteracting*; prophylactic, disinfectant, antiseptic; antipyretic, febrifugal; tonic, stimulative.

medical, surgical, pathological, physicianly; Hippocratic, Galenic, allopathic, homoeopathic, herbal; orthopaedic; vulnerary, traumatic; obstetric; clinical; medicable, operable, curable.

Vb. *remedy*, put right 656 *restore*; succour, help 703 *aid*; treat, heal 656 *cure*; palliate, soothe, neutralize 831 *relieve*.

doctor, be a d., practise, have a practice; treat, prescribe; attend 703 *minister to*; tend, nurse 656 *revive*; hospitalize, put on the sick list; physic, medicate, dose, purge; inject, give a jab; dress, bind, swathe, bandage; apply a tourniquet 350 *staunch*; poultice, plaster, foment; set, put in splints; drug, dope, anaesthetize; operate, cut open; amputate; trepan, trephine; curette; cauterize; bleed, phlebotomize; transfuse, perfuse; massage, manipulate; stop, fill, crown; pedicure, manicure; antisepticize, disinfect 652 *sanitate*.

659. Bane – N. *bane*, curse, plague, infestation, pest, scourge 616 *evil*; malady 651 *disease*; weakness, bad habit 934 *vice*; visitation, affliction 731 *adversity*; cross, trial 825 *sorrow*; bugbear, bête noire 827 *annoyance*; burden, imposition, white elephant; thorn in the flesh, stone round one's neck; stress, strain, torment 825 *worry*; running sore; gall, wormwood 393 *sourness*; poison dart, fang 256 *sharp point*; source of trouble, hornet's nest 663 *pitfall*; viper 365 *reptile*; snake in the grass 663 *troublemaker*; parasite, leech 365 *insect*, *creepy-crawly*; locust 168 *destroyer*; oppressor, holy terror 735 *tyrant*.

blight, rot, dry r., wet r.; mildew, mould, rust, fungus; moth, woodworm, canker, cancer 51 *decay*; visitation 651 *plague*; frost, drought.

poison, poisonousness, virulence, venomousness, toxicity; pollution; bacteria 651 *infection*; teratogen, carcinogen; chemical weapon, biological w.; venom, toxicant, toxin; germicide, insecticide, pesticide; fungicide, herbicide, weedkiller, defoliant, dioxin, paraquat, derris, DDT; acid, corrosive; hemlock, atropine, arsenic, strychnine, cyanide, prussic acid, vitriol; nicotine 388 *tobacco*; asphyxiant, poison gas, nerve g., lewisite, mustard gas, tear g., CS gas; carbon monoxide, choke damp; foul air, mephitis, miasma, effluvium 653 *insalubrity*; atmospheric pollution, smog; lead pollution; uranium, plutonium; radioactivity, radioactive cloud, fallout 417 *radiation*; dope 658 *drug*, 949 *drug-taking*; intoxicant, depressant 949 *alcoholism*; lethal dose, overdose; toxicology.

Adj. *baneful*, pestilent, noisome 645 *harmful*; blighting, withering, virulent, poisonous, venomous 653 *toxic*; cursed, accursed 616 *evil*.

660. Safety – N. *safety*, safeness, security; invulnerability, impregnability, immunity, charmed life; social security, welfare state 901 *sociology*; safe distance, wide berth 620 *avoidance*; all clear, coast c.; guarantee 473 *certainty*; sense of security, assurance, confidence; safety valve 667 *means of escape*; close shave 667 *escape*; rescue 668 *deliverance*.

protection, conservation 666 *preservation*; insurance 858 *caution*; patronage, auspices, aegis, fatherly eye 703 *aid*; protectorate, guardianship, wardenship, wardship, tutelage, custody, protective c. 747 *restraint*; custodianship, safekeeping, keeping, charge, safe hands 778 *retention*; ward, watch and w. 457 *surveillance*; safeguard, precaution, preventive measure; immunization, cordon sanitaire 652 *hygiene*; quarantine 883 *seclusion*; cushion, buffer; screen, cover; umbrella 662 *shelter*; deterrent 723 *weapon*; safeconduct 756 *permit*; escort, guard 722 *armed force*; defence, bastion, tower of strength 713 *defences*; haven, asylum 662 *refuge*; sheet anchor 662 *safeguard*; shield 713 *armour*.

protector, protectress, guardian, tutor; guardian angel, patron saint 707 *patron*; defender, preserver; shepherd; bodyguard, lifeguard; bouncer; vigilante 713 *defender*; conservator, custodian, curator, warden; warder, guard, security g., coastguard; chaperon, babysitter 749 *keeper*; lookout, watch, night w. 664 *warner*; firewatcher, fire fighter; constable 955 *police*; sentry, sentinel, garrison, security forces 722 *soldiery*; watchdog, guard dog 457 *surveillance*.

Adj. *safe*, without risk, unhazardous; assured, secure, sure, snug; safe and sound, spared 666 *preserved*; unharmed 646 *undamaged*; garrisoned, welldefended; insured, covered; immunized;

disinfected, hygienic 652 *salubrious*; in safety, on sure ground; out of the wood, out of danger, out of harm's way; clear, in the clear, unthreatened, unexposed; under shelter, sheltered, etc. vb.; under the wing of; in safe hands, under lock and key; guaranteed 929 *trustworthy*; benign, harmless 615 *good*.

invulnerable, immune, impregnable, sacrosanct; unassailable, unchallengeable; founded on a rock, defensible, tenable 162 *strong*; proof, foolproof; waterproof, fireproof, bulletproof, bombproof; seaworthy, airworthy; armoured, steel-clad.

tutelary, custodial, guardian, protective, shepherdlike; ready to die for 931 *disinterested*; watchful 457 *vigilant*; failsafe; doubly sure, belt and braces; protecting 666 *preserving*.

Vb. *be safe*, etc. adj.; find safety, come through 667 *escape*; land on one's feet, keep one's head above water, weather the storm, ride it out; keep a whole skin, bear a charmed life, have nine lives; be snug, nestle 523 *lurk*; keep a safe distance 620 *avoid*.

safeguard, keep safe, guard, protect; cover up for, shield; champion 703 *patronize*; grant asylum, afford sanctuary; keep, conserve 666 *preserve*; treasure 632 *store*; watch over, care for, mother, take under one's wing; nurse, foster, cherish; take charge of 457 *look after*; put in a safe place 525 *conceal*; cushion, cocoon 218 *support*; insulate, earth; cover 421 *screen*; take in, shelter; enfold 235 *enclose*; make safe, secure, fortify 162 *strengthen*; arm, armour, armour-plate; shepherd, convoy, escort; flank, support; garrison; immunize, vaccinate; pasteurize 652 *sanitate*; guarantee 473 *make certain*; police, patrol.

seek safety, take precautions, play safe 858 *be cautious*; lie low 523 *lurk*; run away 667 *escape*; live to fight another day; run for port.

661. Danger – N. *danger*, peril; shadow of death, lion's mouth, dragon's lair; Scylla and Charybdis; dangerous situation 700

predicament; emergency 137 *crisis*; insecurity, jeopardy, risk, hazard, razor's edge 474 *uncertainty*; black spot 663 *pitfall*; trap, death t. 527 *ambush*; endangerment, dangerous course 857 *rashness*; forlorn hope, risky venture 672 *undertaking*; leap in the dark 618 *gambling*; slippery slope, road to ruin 655 *deterioration*; sword of Damocles, menace 900 *threat*; sense of danger 854 *nervousness*; cause for alarm, cloud on the horizon 665 *danger signal*; narrow escape, near thing 667 *escape*.

vulnerability, susceptibility 180 *liability*; security risk; nakedness, defencelessness 161 *helplessness;* instability, insecurity; easy target, sitting duck; chink in the armour, Achilles' heel, soft underbelly 163 *weakness*; unsoundness, human error 647 *imperfection*; weaker brethren.

Adj. *dangerous*, perilous, fraught, treacherous; unlit, unfrequented; risky, hazardous, dicey, dodgy, chancy 618 *speculative*; serious, ugly, nasty, critical, at flashpoint; at stake, in question; menacing, ominous 900 *threatening*; poisonous 645 *harmful*; unhealthy 653 *insalubrious*; inflammable, explosive, radioactive.

unsafe, not safe, slippery, treacherous, untrustworthy 474 *unreliable*; insecure, unsound, precarious, dicky; unsteady 152 *unstable*; shaky, tottering, crumbling, rickety, frail 655 *dilapidated*; jerry-built 163 *weak*; built on sand, leaky, waterlogged; critical, ticklish, touch and go, hanging by a thread, trembling in the balance, on the brink.

vulnerable, in danger of 180 *liable*; open to, wide open, exposed, naked 229 *uncovered*; unarmoured, unfortified, undefended, unprotected, at the mercy of 161 *defenceless*; unshielded, shelterless, helpless, unguarded, unescorted, unshepherded, unsupported, isolated, out on a limb; unwarned, off one's guard 508 *inexpectant*.

endangered, in danger, etc. n.; facing death, in a bad way; slipping, drifting; on the rocks, on thin ice; in a tight corner, surrounded, trapped, under fire; in the lion's den, on the razor's edge; between two fires, between the devil and the deep blue sea, between Scylla and Charybdis; on the run, not out of the wood; at bay, with one's back to the wall; with a noose round one's neck 961 *condemned*.

Vb. *be in danger*, run the risk of 180 *be liable*; enter the lion's den, walk into a trap; tread on dangerous ground, skate on thin ice, get out of one's depth, sail too near the wind, ride the tiger, play with fire; hang by a thread, tremble in the balance 474 *be uncertain*; totter 309 *tumble*.

face danger, dice with death; take one's life in one's hands 855 *be courageous*; expose oneself, lay oneself open to; stand in the breach 711 *defy*; look down a gun barrel; have the odds against one; challenge fate, tempt Providence, court disaster; take a tiger by the tail, put one's head in the lion's mouth 857 *be rash*; run the gauntlet, venture, dare, stick one's neck out 618 *gamble*.

endanger, be dangerous, spell danger; put in jeopardy, face with, confront w.; imperil, hazard, jeopardize, compromise; risk, stake, venture 618 *gamble*; put in fear of one's life; menace 900 *threaten*; warm up, hot up.

662. Refuge. Safeguard – N. *refuge*, sanctuary, asylum, retreat, safe place; funk-hole, bolthole, foxhole, burrow; trench, dugout, airraid shelter, fallout s.; earth, hole, den, lair, nest 192 *home*; defensible space, privacy; sanctum 194 *chamber*; cloister, hermitage, ivory tower 192 *retreat*; sanctum sanctorum, temple, ark, acropolis, citadel; stronghold, keep 713 *fort*; secret place 527 *hiding-place*; rock, tower, mainstay 218 *prop*.

shelter, cover, roof over one's head; covert, hole; fold, sheepfold; lee; windbreak, hedge 235 *fence*; camp, stockade 235 *enclosure*; shield, wing; fireguard, fender, bumper, windscreen 421 *screen*; umbrella, oilskins; goggles, ear muffs, ear plugs; shinguard, pads; protective clothing, overalls; haven, harbour, port; harbourage, anchorage 192 *stable*; padded cell 503 *lunatic asylum*; halfway house,

sheltered housing; almshouse, home, hospice.

safeguard, protection 660 *safety*; precautions 702 *hindrance*; crush barrier, guardrail, railing; mail 713 *armour*; respirator, gas mask; safety device, dead man's handle, safety catch, safety valve; lightning conductor, fuse, earth; crash helmet; ejector-seat, parachute; safety net; lifeboat 275 *raft*; life belt, life jacket, Mae West; lifeline, breeches buoy 667 *means of escape*; anchor, grapnel, grappling iron; lead, reins, brake 748 *fetter*; bolt, bar, lock 264 *stopper*; mole, embankment; lighthouse, lightship; spare parts.

663. Pitfall: source of danger – N. *pitfall*, pit, trap for the unwary, catch; snag 702 *obstacle*; booby trap, death t., minefield 542 *trap*; surprise 527 *ambush*; sleeping dog; thin ice; quagmire 347 *marsh*; quicksands, breakers, shallows, reef, rock; chasm, abyss, precipice; crosscurrent, undertow 350 *current*; whirlpool 350 *wave*; storm, squall 352 *gale*; volcano, dynamite, time bomb, powder keg 723 *explosive*; trouble-spot 661 *danger*; hornet's nest 659 *bane*.

troublemaker, mischiefmaker, stirrer, wrecker; ill-wisher 881 *enemy*; firebrand 738 *agitator*; ugly customer, undesirable 904 *ruffian*; nigger in the woodpile, snake in the grass 178 *influence*.

664. Warning – N. *warning*, caution, caveat; example, lesson, object l.; notice, advance n. 524 *information*; word in the ear, word to the wise, tip-off, wink 524 *hint*; whistle-blowing 528 *publication*; ultimatum 737 *demand*; admonishment 924 *reprimand*; deterrent 613 *dissuasion*; protest 762 *deprecation*; warning shot, shot across the bows; foreboding, premonition 511 *prediction*; voice of conscience, warning voice; alarm, siren, alert 665 *danger signal*; gathering cloud 661 *danger*; signs of the times, writing on the wall 547 *indication*; knell, death k.; beacon 547 *signal, indicator*; menace 900 *threat*.

warner, admonisher 691 *adviser*;

prophet, Cassandra 511 *diviner*; flagman, signaller; lighthouse-keeper; lookout, watch 457 *surveillance*; scout, spy; picket, sentinel, sentry 600 *protector*; advance guard, rearguard; watchdog.

Adj. *cautionary*, hinting, warning, monitory, admonitory; protesting 762 *deprecatory*; exemplary, instructive 524 *informative*; symptomatic, prognostic 547 *indicating*; premonitory, ominous 511 *presageful*; menacing, minatory 900 *threatening*; deterrent 854 *frightening*.

Vb. *warn*, caution; give fair warning, give notice, notify 524 *inform*; tip off 524 *hint*; counsel 691 *advise*; put one in mind of 505 *remind*; admonish 924 *reprove*; forewarn 511 *predict*; put on one's guard, alert 669 *prepare*; menace 900 *threaten*; advise against 613 *dissuade*; remonstrate, protest 762 *deprecate*; sound the alarm 665 *raise the alarm*.

Int. look out! watch out! take care!

665. Danger signal – N. *danger signal*, note of warning 664 *warning*; murmur, muttering 829 *discontent*; writing on the wall, black cap, evil omen 511 *omen*; storm cone, gale warning; alarm clock, alarm bell, burglar alarm, fire alarm, fire bell, foghorn, fog signal, bell buoy, motor horn, klaxon, bicycle bell, police whistle; blast, honk 400 *loudness*; church bell, curfew, tocsin; siren, alert, red a.; tattoo, trumpet-call 547 *call*; war cry, battle c., rallying cry; fiery cross; warning light, red l., Very l., beacon; red flag; distress signal, SOS 547 *signal*; sign of alarm, start, tremor 854 *fear*.

false alarm, cry of 'wolf', scare, hoax; bugbear, bugaboo, bogey, nightmare, bad dream 854 *intimidation*; blank cartridge, flash in the pan 4 *insubstantiality*; canard 543 *untruth*; scaremonger 854 *alarmist*.

Vb. *raise the alarm*, sound the a., give the a., dial 999, alert, arouse 854 *frighten*; sound one's horn, honk, toot; turn out the guard, raise a hue and cry, cry blue murder 528 *proclaim*; give a false alarm, cry 'wolf', cry too soon; toll, knell.

666. Preservation – N. *preservation*, safekeeping; safe conduct 660 *protection*; salvation 668 *deliverance*; conservation, conservancy; perpetuation, prolongation 144 *permanence*; upkeep, maintenance, support 633 *provision*; service, servicing, valeting 648 *cleansing*; insulation, heat retention; saving up 632 *storage*, 814 *economy*; game reserve, nature r., bird sanctuary, conservation area, listed building; protected species; taxidermy, mummification, embalmment; cold storage, freezing 382 *refrigeration*; dehydration 342 *desiccation*; canning, tinning; sterilization 652 *hygiene*; quarantine, cordon sanitaire.

preserver, life-saver, saviour, rescuer, deliverer 668 *deliverance*; amulet, charm 983 *talisman*; preservation order; preservative, ice, amber, formaldehyde; mothball, lavender; pickle, brine, aspic; freezer 384 *refrigerator*; silo; cannery, bottling plant; seat belt, gas mask 662 *safeguard*; incubator, respirator, iron lung, life-support system; embalmer, mummifier; canner, bottler; conservationist, environmentalist 660 *protector*.

Adj. *preserving*, conserving etc. vb.; energy-saving; preservative, conservative; prophylactic, protective, preventive 652 *salubrious*.

preserved, well-p., kept, well-k., undecayed 646 *perfect*; frozen, on ice; pickled, potted, bottled, etc. vb.; mummified, embalmed; laid up in lavender 632 *stored*; conserved, protected 660 *safe*.

Vb. *preserve*, conserve; keep fresh, freeze 382 *refrigerate*; embalm, mummify, stuff; pickle, salt 388 *season*; souse, marinade; cure, smoke, kipper, dehydrate 342 *dry*; pot, bottle, tin, can; protect, paint, creosote, waterproof; maintain, keep up, keep in good repair 656 *repair*; prop up, shore up 218 *support*; keep alive, sustain 633 *provide*; keep safe 660 *safeguard*; save up, bottle up 632 *store*; reserve 814 *economize*; nurse, tend 658 *doctor*; cherish, treasure 457 *look after*; rescue 668 *deliver*.

667. Escape – N. *escape*, rescue 668 *deliverance*; getaway, breakout; decampment, flight, flit, moonlight f., French leave 296 *departure*; hasty retreat 286 *regression*; disappearing trick 446 *disappearance*; elopement, evasion, truancy 620 *avoidance*; narrow escape, hairbreadth e., close shave, close call, narrow squeak, near thing 661 *danger*; let-off, discharge 960 *acquittal*; immunity, impunity 919 *nonliability*; escapology, escapism.

means of escape, exit, emergency e., back door, secret passage 298 *egress*; ladder, fire escape; vent, safety valve 662 *safeguard*; dodge, device, trick 623 *contrivance*; loophole, escape clause, let-out, get-out 468 *qualification*.

escaper, escapee, runaway; truant, escaped prisoner, prison-breaker; fugitive, refugee; survivor; escapist; escapologist, Houdini.

Adj. *escaped*, fled, flown, stolen away; eloping, truant; fugitive, runaway; slippery, elusive 620 *avoiding*; free, at large, scot free, acquitted; well out of.

Vb. *escape*, effect one's escape 746 *achieve liberty*; make a getaway, break gaol, break out; abscond, jump bail, flit, elope, skip, go AWOL 620 *run away*; steal away, sneak off, duck and run, make oneself scarce 296 *decamp*; slip through, break away, get free, slip one's lead; get out 298 *emerge*; get away, slip through one's fingers; get off, go scot-free; scrape through, save one's bacon; wriggle out of 919 *be exempt*.

elude, evade, abscond, dodge 620 *avoid*; lie low 523 *lurk*; give one the slip, shake off, throw off the scent, give a run for his *or* her money; be found to be missing 190 *be absent*.

668. Deliverance – N. *deliverance*, delivery, extrication 304 *extraction*; disencumberment, riddance 831 *relief*; emancipation 746 *liberation*; rescue, life-saving; salvage, retrieval 656 *restoration*; salvation, redemption, ransom; release, amnesty; discharge, reprieve 960 *acquittal*; respite 136 *delay*; truce 145 *cessation*; way out, let-out 667 *escape*; dispensation, exemption 919 *nonliability*.

Adj. *extricable*, rescuable, deliverable, redeemable.

Vb. *deliver*, save, rescue, come to the r., snatch from the jaws of death, throw a lifeline; get one out of 304 *extract*; extricate 62 *unravel*; unloose, untie, unbind 46 *disunite*; disburden 701 *disencumber*; release, emancipate, set free 746 *liberate*; get one off 960 *acquit*; deliver oneself 667 *escape*; rid oneself, get rid of; redeem, ransom, buy off 792 *purchase*; salvage, retrieve 656 *restore*; excuse, dispense from 919 *exempt*.

669. Preparation – N. *preparation*, making ready; clearance, clearing the decks; preliminaries, tuning, priming, loading; mobilization; trial run 461 *experiment*; practice, rehearsal; brief, briefing; training 534 *teaching*; novitiate 68 *beginning*; study, homework 536 *learning*; spadework 682 *labour*; groundwork 218 *basis*; planning, blueprint, pilot scheme 623 *plan*; shadow cabinet; arrangement, prearrangement 608 *predetermination*; consultation 691 *advice*; forethought, anticipation, precautions 510 *foresight*.

fitting out, logistics 633 *provision*; appointment, commission, equipment, array, armament; promotion; inauguration, flotation 68 *debut*.

maturation, ripening, bringing to a head; seasoning, hardening, acclimatization; gestation, incubation 167 *propagation*; nursing, nurture; cultivation 370 *agriculture*; bloom, florescence, efflorescence; fructification, fruition 725 *completion*.

preparedness, readiness, ripeness, mellowness; maturity 134 *adultness*; fitness, shipshape condition 646 *perfection*.

preparer, coach 537 *trainer*; torchbearer, trail-blazer, pioneer, bridgebuilder 66 *precursor*; sappers and miners 722 *soldiery*; fitter, equipper 633 *provider*; cultivator 370 *farmer*.

Adj. *preparatory*, preparative; preparing etc. adj.; precautionary, preliminary 64 *preceding*; brooding, maturing; in embryo; in preparation, on foot, on the stocks, on the anvil; in store 155 *impending*; under consideration, mooted 623 *planned*; under training 536 *studious*.

prepared, ready, alert 457 *vigilant*; in readiness, at the ready; mobilized, standing by, on call; all set, raring to go; teed up, keyed up, psyched up, spoiling for; trained, qualified, well-prepared, practised, at concert pitch, word-perfect; primed, briefed 524 *informed*; forewarned, warned; in the saddle; battened down; groomed, in full feather, dressed to kill, got up to k. 228 *dressed*; accoutred, in harness, armed, armed to the teeth; rigged out, equipped, furnished 633 *provisioning*; in hand 632 *stored*; in reserve, ready to hand, ready for use; in working order, operational.

matured, ripened etc. vb.; ripe, mellow, mature, seasoned, weathered, hardened; tried, experienced, veteran 694 *expert*; adult, grown, full-g., full-fledged 134 *grown-up*; out, in flower, florescent, flowering, fruiting; overripe, overmature; elaborated, wrought, worked up, laboured, smelling of the lamp; deep-laid; perfected 725 *completed*.

ready-made, ready-mixed, cut and dried, ready to use, ready-to-wear, off the peg; ready-formed, ready-furnished; prefabricated; processed, oven-ready; predigested, precooked, instant.

Vb. *prepare*, take steps *or* measures; make preparations, make ready, pave the way, pioneer 64 *come before*; lay the foundations, do the groundwork; predispose, incline, soften up; prepare the ground, sow the seed 370 *cultivate*; set to work, address oneself to 68 *begin*; roughhew, cut out, block o.; sketch, outline 623 *plan*; plot, prearrange 608 *predetermine*; forearm, guard against 660 *seek safety*; anticipate 507 *expect*.

make ready, ready, set in order, put in readiness; stow away, pack 632 *store*; batten down the hatches; commission, put in c.; put one's house in order, bring up to scratch; tune up, adjust 62 *arrange*; clear the decks, close the ranks; array, mobilize 74 *bring together*; whet the knife, shuffle the cards, tee up; set, cock, prime, load;

raise steam, warm up, crank up, rev up; equip, crew, man; fit, fit out, furnish, kit out, rig out, dress; arm 633 *provide*; improvise, rustle up; rehearse, drill, groom, lick into shape 534 *train*; inure, acclimatize 610 *habituate*; coach, brief 524 *inform*.

mature, mellow, ripen, bring to fruition 646 *perfect*; force, bring on 174 *invigorate*; bring to a head 725 *climax*; stew, brew 301 *cook*; gestate, hatch, incubate, breed 369 *breed stock*; grow, farm 370 *cultivate*; fledge, nurse, nurture; elaborate, work out 725 *carry through*; season, weather, cure, temper, season 326 *harden*.

prepare oneself, brace o., compose o.; qualify oneself, serve an apprenticeship; study, train, rehearse, practise 536 *learn*; gird up one's loins, roll up one's sleeves; limber up, warm up, flex one's muscles; shoulder arms; be prepared, stand ready, stand by, keep one's powder dry.

Adv. *in preparation*, in anticipation, in readiness, just in case; in hand, in train, under way, under construction.

670. Nonpreparation – N. *nonpreparation*, lack of preparation; potluck; unpreparedness, unreadiness; lack of training, want of practice; disqualification, unfitness; rawness, immaturity, greenness 126 *newness*; belatedness 136 *lateness*; improvidence, nonprovision 458 *negligence*; no deliberation 857 *rashness*; hastiness, rush 680 *haste*; improvisation 609 *spontaneity*; surprise 508 *lack of expectation*; forwardness, precocity 135 *earliness*; imperfection 55 *incompleteness*.

undevelopment, delayed maturity; state of nature, native state, virgin soil; raw material, unlicked cub, rough diamond; late developer; rough copy, unfinished attempt; embryo, abortion.

Adj. *unprepared*, unready, not ready, backward, behindhand 136 *late*; unorganized, unarranged, makeshift; without preparation, ad hoc, ad lib, improvised, impromptu, snap, catch-as-catch-can, off the top of one's head 609 *spontaneous*; unstudied 699 *artless*; careless 458 *negligent*; rush, overhasty 680 *hasty*; unguarded, exposed 661 *vulnerable*; caught unawares, taken off guard, caught napping, on the wrong foot 508 *inexpectant*; at sixes and sevens 61 *orderless*; shiftless, improvident, unthrifty, happy-go-lucky 456 *light-minded*; scratch, untrained, untutored 491 *uninstructed*; undrilled, unpractised, unrehearsed 611 *unhabituated*; in a state of nature, uncultivated, unworked, untilled, virgin 674 *unused*.

immature, ungrown, half-grown, unripe, green, underripe, half-ripe, unripened, unmellowed, unseasoned; unfledged, unlicked, callow, wet behind the ears; nonadult, adolescent, juvenile 130 *young*; undeveloped, half-developed, half-baked, raw 647 *imperfect*; underdeveloped, backward 136 *late*; unhatched, unborn, embryonic, rudimentary 68 *beginning*; half-formed, roughhewn, unpolished, unfinished; undigested, illdigested; before time, premature, abortive, at half-cock 728 *unsuccessful*; untrained, apprentice 695 *unskilled*; crude, uncivilized 699 *artless*; forced, precocious.

Vb. *be unprepared*, etc. adj.; lack preparation; want practice, need training; offer potluck 609 *improvise*; live from day to day, let tomorrow take care of itself; go off at half-cock 135 *be early*; take no precautions, drop one's guard 456 *be inattentive*; catch unawares 508 *surprise*.

671. Attempt – N. *attempt*, essay, bid; step, move, gambit 676 *deed*; endeavour, effort 682 *exertion*; tackle, try, good try, valiant effort; one's level best, best one can do; set, dead s. 712 *attack*; trial 461 *experiment*; go at, shot at, stab at, jab at, crack at, whack at, bash at; first attempt 68 *debut*; last bid, last throw; venture 672 *undertaking*; perfectionism 862 *fastidiousness*.

trier, bidder, tackler 852 *hoper*; tester 461 *experimenter*; searcher 459 *inquirer*; fighter 716 *contender*; idealist 862 *perfectionist*; lobbyist, activist 654 *reformer*; undertaker, contractor, entrepreneur, jobber.

Adj. *attempting*, tackling, doing one's

best 597 *willing*; game 599 *resolute*; questing 459 *inquiring*; tentative, testing; probationary 461 *experimental*; ambitious, venturesome, daring 672 *enterprising*.

Vb. *attempt*, essay, try; seek to, aim 617 *intend*; angle for, seek 459 *search*; offer, bid, make a b.; make an attempt, make shift to, make the effort, do something about, not just stand there; endeavour, struggle, strive, try and try again 599 *be resolute*; do one's best, do one's damnedest 682 *exert oneself*; strain, sweat 682 *work*; tackle, take on, try one's hand at, have a go, give it a try *or* a whirl, have a shot *or* a crack *or* a stab at 672 *undertake*; get down to, get to grips with, take the bull by the horns; chance one's arm, try one's luck, venture, speculate 618 *gamble*; test, make trial of 461 *experiment*; fly a kite 461 *be tentative*.

Int. Here goes! Nothing venture, nothing gain!

672. Undertaking – N. *undertaking*, job, task, assignment; self-imposed task, lavour of love; contract, engagement, obligation 764 *promise*; operation, exercise; programme, project 623 *plan*; tall order 700 *hard task*; enterprise, adventure 459 *inquiry*; venture, speculation 618 *gambling*; matter in hand 622 *business*; struggle, effort, campaign 671 *attempt*.

Adj. *enterprising*, pioneering, adventurous, venturesome, daring; go-ahead, progressive; opportunist, ambitious 859 *desiring*; overambitious 857 *rash*.

Vb. *undertake*, engage in, apply oneself to, take up, go in for; venture on, take on, tackle 671 *attempt*; go about, take in hand, set one's hand to; set going 68 *initiate*; embark on, launch into, plunge into; fall to, buckle to, put one's best foot forward, set one's shoulder to the wheel 68 *begin*; grasp the nettle 855 *be courageous*; assume responsibility, take charge of 689 *manage*; execute 725 *carry out*; set up shop 622 *do business*; take on one's shoulders, take upon oneself 917 *incur a duty*; engage to 764 *promise*; get involved, let oneself in for, volunteer 597 *be willing*; take on too much, bite off more than one can chew, have too many irons in the fire 678 *be busy*; show enterprise, pioneer; venture, dare 661 *face danger*.

673. Use – N. *use*, usufruct, enjoyment 773 *possession*; conversion, utilization, exploitation; employment, application, appliance; exercise 610 *practice*; resort, recourse; treatment, good usage 457 *carefulness*; ill-treatment 675 *misuse*; wear, wear and tear 655 *dilapidation*; exhaustion, consumption 634 *waste*; reuse, palimpsest; usefulness, benefit, service 642 *good policy*; serviceability, practicality 640 *utility*; office, purpose, point 622 *function*; long use, wont 610 *habit*.

Adj. *used*, applied etc. vb.; in service, in use, in practice; used up, worn, threadbare, second-hand, well-used, well-thumbed, dog-eared 655 *dilapidated*; beaten, well-trodden 490 *known*; hackneyed, stale; practical, utilitarian 642 *advisable*; makeshift, provisional 150 *substituted*; subservient 628 *instrumental*; available, usable, employable 640 *useful*; at one's service, disposable.

Vb. *use*, employ, exercise, practise, put into practice; apply, exert, bring to bear, administer; utilize, make use of, harness, convert; reuse, recycle, exploit, get mileage out of, get the best out of, make the most of; milk, drain 304 *extract*; put to good use, turn to account, make capital out of, use to advantage 137 *profit by*; make play with, play on, trade on, cash in on; play off against; make a tool *or* handle of; make a cat's-paw of, take advantage of 542 *befool*; put to use, wear out, use up 634 *waste*; handle, thumb 378 *touch*; tread, follow, beat (a path); work, drive 173 *operate*; wield, ply; overwork, tax 684 *fatigue*; work on, work up.

avail oneself of, take up, adopt, try; resort to, have recourse to, fall back on, draw on; impose on, presume on; press into service, make do with, make shift w., make the best of.

dispose of, command; have at one's disposal, control; allot 783 *apportion*; spare, have to s.; requisition, call in; call into play, set in motion, deploy 612 *motivate*;

enjoy 773 *possess*; consume, expend, absorb, use up 634 *waste*.

674. Nonuse – N. *nonuse*, abeyance 677 *inaction*; nonavailability 190 *absence*; stagnation, unemployment 679 *inactivity*; abstinence 620 *avoidance*; savings 632 *store*; disuse, obsolescence, superannuation 611 *desuetude*; dismissal 300 *ejection*; waiver 621 *relinquishment*; unsuitability 643 *inexpedience*; uselessness, write-off 641 *inutility*.

Adj. *unused*, unutilized; not available 190 *absent*; out of order, not in service 641 *useless*; unpracticable 643 *inexpedient*; nonconvertible, nonreturnable; undisposed of 632 *stored*; on the spike, pigeonholed; spare, extra; unconsumed 666 *preserved*; unexploited, untapped, lying idle *or* fallow; unessayed, untried; unexercised, in abeyance; untrodden, unbeaten; untouched, unopened 126 *new*; ungathered, left to rot 634 *wasted*; unnecessary, redundant 860 *unwanted*; unrequired, free, vacant; dispensed with, waived; underused, resting, unemployed 679 *inactive*; jobless, out of work.

disused, derelict, discarded, cast-off, jettisoned, scrapped, written off; sacked, laid off etc. vb.; laid up, in mothballs, out of commission, rusting, on the scrap heap; in limbo 458 *neglected*; done with, used up, run down, worn out; on the shelf, retired; out of use, superseded, obsolete 127 *antiquated*.

Vb. *not use*, hold in abeyance; have no use for; do without, dispense with 621 *relinquish*; overlook 458 *neglect*; underuse, underutilize; spare, reserve 632 *store*.

stop using, leave off 145 *cease*; outgrow 611 *disaccustom*; lay up, dismantle; have done with, lay aside, hang up; pension off, put out to grass; discard, dump, ditch, scrap, write off 300 *eject*; lay off, pay off 300 *dismiss*; drop, replace 150 *substitute*; be unused, rust 655 *deteriorate*.

675. Misuse – N. *misuse*, abuse, wrong use; misemployment, misapplication; mismanagement, maladministration 695 *bungling*; misappropriation 788 *pecula-*

tion; perversion 246 *distortion*; prostitution, violation; pollution 649 *uncleanness*; overuse 634 *waste*; misusage, mishandling, mistreatment, maltreatment, illtreatment, force 176 *violence*.

Vb. *misuse*, abuse; misemploy, put to bad use, misdirect; divert, misappropriate 788 *defraud*; violate, desecrate 980 *be impious*; prostitute 655 *pervert*; pollute 649 *make unclean*; do violence to 176 *force*; 246 *distort*; take advantage of, exploit 673 *use*; manhandle 645 *ill-treat*; mishandle, mismanage 695 *be unskilful*; overwork 684 *fatigue*; wear out 655 *impair*; fritter away 634 *waste*; misapply 641 *waste effort*.

Section 3: Voluntary action

676. Action – N. *action*, doing, performance; steps, measures 623 *policy*; transaction, enactment, perpetration; dispatch, execution, effectuation 725 *completion*; procedure, praxis 610 *practice*; behaviour 688 *conduct*; movement, play 265 *motion*; operation, interaction, evolution 173 *agency*; pressure 178 *influence*; work, labour 682 *exertion*; activism, activeness 678 *activity*; campaign, crusade, war on 671 *attempt*; implementation, handling 689 *management*.

deed, act, action, exploit, beau geste, feat, achievement 855 *prowess*; crime 930 *foul play*; stunt, tour de force 875 *ostentation*; gesture, move 623 *policy*; manoeuvre 688 *tactics*; stroke, blow, coup 623 *contrivance*; task, exercise 672 *undertaking*; proceeding, transaction 154 *affairs*; work, handiwork; acts 590 *narrative*.

doer, man *or* woman of action 678 *busy person*; practical person, realist; hero, heroine 855 *brave person*; practitioner 696 *expert*; stunt man *or* woman, player 594 *actor*; executant, performer; perpetrator, committer 904 *evildoer*; mover, manipulator 612 *motivator*; operator 686 *agent*; contractor, undertaker, entrepreneur; action group, campaigner, canvasser; executive 690 *director*; hand, operative 686 *worker*; craftsman, craftswoman 686 *artisan*; creative worker 556 *artist*.

Adj. *doing*, acting, operating, etc. vb.; in the act, red-handed; working, at work, in action, in harness 173 *operative*; up and doing, industrious 678 *active*; occupational 610 *habitual*.

Vb. *do*, act, perform; come into operation 173 *operate*; militate, act upon 178 *influence*; manipulate 612 *motivate*; manoeuvre 698 *be cunning*; do something, lift a finger; proceed with, get on with, move, take action, take steps; try 671 *attempt*; tackle 672 *undertake*; do the deed, perpetrate, commit; achieve, accomplish 725 *carry through*; take care of, execute, implement, put into practice 725 *carry out*; solemnize, observe; make history 866 *have a reputation*; practise, exercise, carry on, discharge, prosecute, pursue, ply one's trade; officiate, do one's stuff 622 *function*; transact 622 *do business*; administer 689 *direct*; have to do with, deal with; sweat, labour 682 *work*; strike a blow for 703 *aid*; have a hand in 775 *participate*; have a finger in 678 *meddle*; conduct oneself, indulge in 688 *behave*.

Adv. *in the act*, in flagrante delicto, red-handed; in the midst of, in the thick of; while one is about it.

677. Inaction – N. *inaction*, nonaction, inertia 175 *inertness*; inability to act 161 *impotence*; failure to act 458 *negligence*; abstention 620 *avoidance*; passive resistance 711 *defiance*; suspension, dormancy 674 *nonuse*; deadlock, stalemate 145 *stop*; paralysis 375 *insensibility*; stagnation 266 *quiescence*; idle hours 681 *leisure*; rest 683 *repose*; nonemployment, underemployment, unemployment; no work, sinecure; idleness 679 *inactivity*; Fabian policy 136 *delay*; nonintervention 860 *indifference*; head in the sand, defeatism 856 *cowardice*.

Adj. *nonactive*, inoperative, idle 679 *inactive*; passive 175 *inert*; unoccupied 681 *leisurely*; unprogressive, ostrich-like; Fabian, cunctative; defeatist 853 *hopeless*; stationary, motionless 266 *quiescent*; cold, extinct; not stirring, without a sign of life, dead-and-alive 361 *dead*; laid off, unemployed, jobless, out of work 674 *unused*; paralysed 375 *insensible*; apathetic 820 *impassive*; neutral 860 *indifferent*.

Vb. *not act*, fail to a., hang fire 598 *be unwilling*; pass the buck 620 *avoid*; look on, stand by 441 *watch*; bide one's time 136 *wait*; procrastinate 136 *put off*; live and let live, let things take their course, laissez aller, laissez faire, let sleeping dogs lie, let well alone; sit on the fence 860 *be indifferent*; turn a blind eye 458 *disregard*; sit tight, not move, not budge, not stir, show no sign, not lift a finger 175 *be inert*; rest on one's oars *or* one's laurels, relax one's efforts; drift, slide, coast, freewheel; let pass 458 *neglect*; keep quiet 266 *be quiescent*; relax 683 *repose*; pause 145 *cease*.

678. Activity – N. *activity*, activism, militancy 676 *action*; activation 612 *motive*; agitation, excitation 174 *stimulation*; life, stir 265 *motion*; nimbleness, briskness, alacrity; quickness, dispatch; spurt, burst, fit 318 *spasm*; hurry, flurry, hurry-scurry, bustle 680 *haste*; fuss, bother, ado, to-do, frenzy 61 *turmoil*; whirl, scramble, rat race; drama, much ado; thick of things, thick of the action, the fray; irons in the fire 622 *business*; call on one's time, pressure of work; high street, marketplace; hum, hive 687 *workshop*.

restlessness, pottering, fiddling, aimless activity 456 *inattention*; unquiet, fidgets 318 *agitation*; jumpiness 822 *excitability*; fever, fret 503 *frenzy*; eagerness, enthusiasm 818 *warm feeling*; vigour, energy, dynamism, militancy, enterprise, initiative, push, drive, go 174 *vigorousness*; vivacity, animation, vitality 360 *life*; wakefulness, vigilance 457 *carefulness*; sleeplessness, insomnia.

assiduity, application 455 *attention*; sedulity, industry, legwork 682 *labour*; earnestness 599 *resolution*; tirelessness, indefatigability 600 *perseverance*; studiousness, painstaking, diligence; wholeheartedness, devotedness.

overactivity, overexpansion 637 *redundance*; Parkinson's law; displacement activity, chasing one's own tail 641 *lost labour*; song and dance 318 *commotion*; hyperthyroidism, overexertion; officiousness, interference, meddling, finger in every pie.

busy person, new broom, enthusiast, bustler, hustler; activist, militant, zealot, fanatic; slogger, no slouch, hard worker, Stakhanovite, workaholic 686 *worker*; factotum, maid-of-all-work, drudge, dogsbody, fag, slave, galley s., Trojan; eager beaver, busy bee, ant; workhorse; man *or* woman of action 676 *doer*; participator; live wire, dynamo, powerhouse, whizz kid, go-getter, pusher, thruster; careerist.

meddler, dabbler, stirrer, interferer, spoilsport; officious person, nosey parker, busybody 453 *inquisitive person*; kibitzer, back-seat driver 691 *adviser*; fusspot, nuisance.

Adj. *active*, stirring 265 *moving*; going, working, incessant 146 *unceasing*; expeditious 622 *businesslike*; able, able-bodied 162 *strong*; live, brisk, nippy, spry, smart 277 *speedy*; nimble, lightfooted, lightsome, tripping; energetic, thrustful 174 *vigorous*; pushing, go-getting, up-and-coming 672 *enterprising*; frisky, coltish, dashing, sprightly, alive and kicking, full of beans 819 *lively*; eager 818 *fervent*; fierce, desperate 599 *resolute*; enthusiastic, zealous, prompt, on one's toes 597 *willing*; alert 457 *vigilant*; sleepless, restless, feverish, fretful, tossing, fidgety, fussy, nervy 318 *agitated*; frantic, demonic 503 *frenzied*; hyperactive, overactive 822 *excitable*; involved, engagé; militant, up in arms 718 *warlike*.

busy, bustling, hustling, humming, lively, eventful; coming and going, pottering; up and doing, stirring, astir, afoot, on the move, on the go, on the trot, in full swing; hard at it, up to one's eyes; in harness, at work, at one's desk; occupied, fully o., employed; busy as a bee.

industrious, studious, sedulous, assiduous 600 *persevering*; labouring, hardworking, plodding, slogging 682 *laborious*; unflagging, tireless, indefatigable; efficient, workmanlike 622 *businesslike*.

meddling, officious, pushy, interfering, meddlesome, intrusive, intriguing; dabbling.

Vb. *be active*, trouble oneself, join in 775 *participate*; be stirring 265 *move*; run riot 61 *rampage*; rouse oneself, bestir o., stir one's stumps, be up and doing; hum, thrive 730 *prosper*; keep moving, keep on the go; thrust, drive 279 *impel*; dash, run 277 *move fast*; buckle to 682 *exert oneself*; beaver away 600 *persevere*; polish off, make short work of, not let the grass grow under one's feet; jump to it, make the sparks fly, make things hum 676 *do*, 597 *be willing*; be on one's toes 457 *be careful*; seize the opportunity 137 *profit by*; not take it lying down, be up in arms 711 *defy*; protest, agitate, demonstrate, kick up a shindy, raise the dust 762 *deprecate*.

be busy, bustle, scurry; live in a whirl, run round in circles; chase one's own tail 641 *waste effort*; not know which way to turn; have one's hands full, be rushed off one's feet, have not a moment to spare *or* to call one's own; fuss, fret, fume 822 *be excitable*; have other fish to fry, be engaged; slave, slog 682 *work*; overwork, make work, make heavy weather of, never stop.

meddle, interpose, intervene, interfere, be officious, not mind one's own business, have a finger in every pie; poke one's nose in, shove one's oar in, butt in 297 *intrude*; pester, bother 827 *trouble*; boss around 735 *oppress*; tinker, tamper, touch 655 *impair*.

Adv. *actively*, on the go, on one's toes; full tilt; with might and main, for all one is worth, for dear life.

679. Inactivity – N. *inactivity*, inactiveness 677 *inaction*; inertia, torpor 175 *inertness*; lull, suspended animation 145 *cessation*; immobility, stillness, slack period, doldrums, grave, morgue 266 *quiescence*; no progress 655 *deterioration*; rustiness 674 *nonuse*; slump 37 *decrease*; unemployment, shutdown; absenteeism 598 *unwillingness*; procrastination, mañana 136 *delay*; idleness, loafing 681 *leisure*.

sluggishness, lethargy, laziness, indol-

ence, sloth; remissness 458 *negligence*; dawdling 278 *slowness*; debility 163 *weakness*; lifelessness; languor, dullness, listlessness 820 *moral insensibility*; stupor, torpor, torpidity 375 *insensibility*; apathy 860 *indifference*; phlegm, impassivity 823 *inexcitability*.

sleepiness, weariness, lassitude 684 *fatigue*; somnolence, doziness, drowsiness, nodding, yawning, heavy lids; dreaminess 513 *fantasy*.

sleep, slumber, kip, bye-byes; deep sleep, beauty s.; drowse; nap, catnap, forty winks, shut-eye, snooze, doze 683 *repose*; hibernation, aestivation; unconsciousness 375 *insensibility*; sleepwalking, somnambulism; dreams, gate of ivory, g. of horn; Morpheus, sandman; dreamland, Land of Nod; cradle, pillow, bed.

soporific, sleeping draught, nightcap; sleeping pill; opiate 375 *anaesthetic*; lullaby, cradle song.

idler, drone, lazybones, lie-abed, loafer, lounger, flâneur, slouch, sluggard; slacker, skiver, clock-watcher; Weary Willie, moper, sleepyhead; dawdler 278 *slowcoach*; hobo, bum, tramp 268 *wanderer*; sponger, scrounger, freeloader 763 *beggar*; layabout, good-for-nothing, ne'er-do-well, wastrel, slubber-degullion; drifter, free-wheeler; opium-eater, lotus-e.; sinecurist, rentier; fainéant, dummy, passenger, sleeping partner, absentee landlord; idle rich, leisured classes; dreamer, sleeper; hibernator; Sleeping Beauty.

Adj. *inactive*, motionless, stationary, at a standstill 266 *quiescent*; suspended, not working, not in use, laid up 674 *disused*; inanimate, lifeless 175 *inert*; torpid, dopey, drugged 375 *insensible*; sluggish, stiff, rusty 677 *nonactive*; listless, lackadaisical 834 *dejected*; languid, languorous 684 *fatigued*; dull, lumpish 820 *impassive*; apathetic 860 *indifferent*; lethargic 823 *inexcitable*; non-participating 190 *absent*; idle, disengaged 681 *leisurely*.

lazy, do-nothing, fainéant; slothful, work-shy, indolent, idle, bone-idle, parasitical; loafing 681 *leisurely*; dawdling 278 *slow*; dilatory 136 *late*; slack, remiss 458 *negligent*.

sleepy, ready for bed, tired 684 *fatigued*; half-awake, half-asleep; slumberous, somnolent, heavy-eyed, drowsy, dozy, dopey, groggy, nodding, yawning; napping, dozing; asleep, fast asleep, sound a., dead to the world; unconscious, out; dormant, hibernating, comatose.

soporific, somniferous, sleep-inducing, sedative, hypnotic.

Vb. *be inactive*, do nothing, rust, stagnate, vegetate 677 *not act*; let the grass grow under one's feet 136 *put off*; take it easy, let things go 458 *be neglectful*; hang about, kick one's heels 136 *wait*; slouch, lag, loiter, dawdle 278 *move slowly*; dally, drag one's feet 136 *be late*; loll, lounge, laze, rest 683 *repose*; lie down on the job, slack, skive 620 *avoid*; have nothing to do, loaf, idle, mooch about, moon a., while away the time, kill t., twiddle one's thumbs; droop, languish, slump 266 *be quiescent*; strike, come out 145 *cease*.

sleep, slumber, snooze, nap, catnap; aestivate, hibernate; sleep soundly, sleep like a log *or* a top *or* a little child; dream; go to sleep, nod off, drop off, fall asleep, take a nap, have a kip, have forty winks; close one's eyes, yawn, nod, doze, drowse; go to bed, turn in, doss down, kip d., shake d., hit the hay; settle down, bed d., roost, perch.

make inactive, put to bed, send to sleep, lull, rock, cradle; soothe 177 *assuage*; paralyse, drug, put out 375 *render insensible*; cramp, immobilize 747 *fetter*; lay up 674 *stop using*; dismantle; pay off, stand o., lay o. 300 *dismiss*.

680. Haste -- **N.** *haste*, hurry, scurry, hustle, bustle, flurry, whirl, scramble 678 *activity*; flap, flutter, fidget, fuss 318 *agitation*; rush, rush job 670 *nonpreparation*; race against time, no time to lose 136 *lateness*; immediacy, urgency 638 *importance*; expedition, dispatch 277 *velocity*; hastening, acceleration 277 *spurt*; overhaste, precipitateness 857 *rashness*; hastiness, impatience 822 *excitability*.

Adj. *hasty*, overhasty, impetuous, impulsive, hot-headed, precipitant 857 *rash*; feverish, impatient 818 *fervent*; pushing, shoving 176 *violent*; precipitate, headlong, breathless, breakneck 277 *speedy*; expeditious, prompt, without delay; in haste, hotfoot; in a hurry, unable to wait, pressed for time, hard-pressed, driven; scamped, slapdash, cursory 458 *negligent*; rough and ready, rushed, last-minute 670 *unprepared*; rushed into, railroaded; urgent, immediate 638 *important*.

Vb. *hasten*, expedite, dispatch; urge, drive, spur 612 *incite*; bundle off, hustle away; rush, allow no time, brook no delay; be hasty, be precipitate, rush headlong 857 *be rash*; haste, make haste; dash off, tear off 277 *move fast*; spurt, dash 277 *accelerate*; hurry, scurry, hustle, bustle 678 *be active*; be in a hurry, have no time to spare *or* to lose, act without ceremony, cut short the preliminaries, brush aside; cut corners, rush one's fences; dash through, make short work of; be pressed for time, work against time *or* to a deadline, work under pressure, think on one's feet; lose no time, make every minute count; hasten away, not be seen for dust 296 *decamp*.

Adv. *hastily*, hurriedly, precipitately, pell-mell, feverishly, post-haste, hotfoot 277 *swiftly*; at short notice, immediately, urgently, with not a moment to lose.

Int. hurry up! be quick! buck up! look lively! look sharp! get a move on! step on it! quick march! at the double!

681. Leisure – **N.** *leisure*, spare time, free t.; time on one's hands, time to kill; sinecure; idleness, dolce far niente; time off, holiday 679 *inactivity*; time to spare, no hurry; rest, ease, relaxation 683 *repose*; retirement 753 *resignation*.

Adj. *leisurely*, deliberate, unhurried 278 *slow*; at one's convenience, in one's own time; at leisure, unoccupied 683 *reposeful*; at a loose end, at ease; off duty, on holiday; retired, in retirement; affording leisure, labour-saving.

Vb. *have leisure*, have plenty of time, have time to spare; take one's ease, spend, pass, while away; be in no hurry, take one's time 278 *move slowly*; take a holiday 683 *repose*; give up work, retire 753 *resign*.

682. Exertion – N. *exertion*, effort, struggle 671 *attempt*; strain, stress; tug, pull, stretch, heave; drive, force, pressure 160 *energy*; ergonomics; ado, trouble, the hard way; muscle, elbow grease, sweat of one's brow; taking pains 678 *assiduity*; overexertion 678 *overactivity*; overtime, busman's holiday.

exercise, practice, regular p., drill, training, work-out 669 *preparation*; keeping fit, jogging, constitutional; gymnastics, athletics; yoga, isometrics, eurhythmics, callisthenics; games, sports 837 *sport*.

labour, industry, work, hard w., uphill w., long haul; spadework, donkeywork; manual labour, sweat of one's brow; housework, chores, daily grind, toil, drudgery, slavery, sweat, fag, grind, strain, treadmill, grindstone; hack work; bull; hard labour 963 *penalty*; forced labour, corvée; fatigue, fatigue duty 917 *duty*; piecework, taskwork, homework, outwork; journeywork; task, chore, job 676 *deed*; shift, stint 110 *period*; job of work, stroke of w., hand's turn; man-hours, woman-hours.

Adj. *labouring*, born to toil, hornyhanded; working, sweating, etc. vb.; on the go, hard at it 678 *busy*; hardworking, laborious 678 *industrious*; slogging, plodding 600 *persevering*; strenuous, energetic 678 *active*; painstaking, thorough 455 *attentive*; exercising, practising; gymnastic, athletic.

laborious, crushing, killing, backbreaking; gruelling, punishing, exhausting; toilsome, troublesome, weary, wearisome, burdensome; heroic, Herculean; arduous, hard, heavy, uphill 700 *difficult*; hardfought, hard-won; thorough, painstaking, laboured; elaborate, artificial; detailed, fiddling.

Vb. *exert oneself*, apply oneself, put one's best foot forward, try 671 *attempt*; struggle, strain, strive, sweat blood; trouble oneself, bestir oneself, put oneself out, bend over backwards; spare no effort, do

one's utmost, go to any lengths, move heaven and earth; go all out, pull out all the stops, put one's heart and soul into, put one's back into it, strain every nerve, use every muscle 678 *be active*; force one's way, drive through, wade t.; hammer at, slog at 600 *persevere*; battle, campaign 676 *do*.

work, labour, toil, moil, drudge, fag, grind, slog, sweat, work up a lather; pull, haul, tug, shove, hump, heave; dig, spade; soil one's hands; get down to it 68 *begin*; keep at it 600 *persevere*; work hard, moonlight, work double shift, work all hours, work night and day, burn the midnight oil 678 *be busy*; slave, slave away, work one's fingers to the bone, work like a Trojan; work oneself to death; overwork 684 *fatigue*.

Adv. *laboriously*, the hard way; manually, by hand; by the sweat of one's brow; heart and soul, with might and main, with all one's might, for all one is worth.

683. Repose – N. *repose*, rest from one's labours 679 *inactivity*; restfulness, ease 376 *euphoria*; peace and quiet 266 *quiescence*; happy dreams 679 *sleep*; relaxation, breathing space, breather 685 *refreshment*; pause, respite, let-up 145 *lull*; holiday, break, vacation, leave, furlough, day off, sabbatical year 681 *leisure*; day of rest, Sabbath, Lord's day.

Adj. *reposeful*, restful, easeful, relaxing; slippered, unbuttoned, in one's shirtsleeves, carefree, casual, relaxed, laidback, at ease 828 *content*; cushioned, pillowed 376 *comfortable*; peaceful, quiet 266 *tranquil*; leisured, sabbatical 681 *leisurely*; post-prandial, after-dinner.

Vb. *repose*, rest, take it easy, take one's ease, sit back, put one's feet up; loll, lounge, laze, sprawl 216 *be horizontal*; perch, roost 311 *sit down*; go to bed 679 *sleep*; relax, wind down, unwind, take a breather 685 *be refreshed*; slack off, let up, slow down 266 *come to rest*; take time off *or* out, take a holiday, go on leave 681 *have leisure*.

Adv. *at rest*, reposefully, restfully, peacefully, on holiday, on vacation.

684. Fatigue – N. *fatigue*, tiredness, weariness, lassitude, languor, lethargy; brain-fag, staleness; jadedness, distress; exhaustion, collapse, prostration; strain, over-tiredness 682 *exertion*; shortness of breath, palpitations 352 *respiration*; faintness, swoon 375 *insensibility*.

Adj. *fatigued*, tired, ready for bed 679 *sleepy*; asleep on one's feet, tired out, exhausted, spent; done, done up, done in, pooped, fagged, fagged out, knocked up, washed up, washed out, clapped o., tuckered o., worn to a frazzle; dull, stale; strained, overworked, overtired; dog-tired, bone-weary, tired to death, dropping, ready to drop, on one's last legs, all in, dead beat, whacked, knackered, flaked out, flat o.; more dead than alive, prostrate; stiff, aching, sore, toilworn; way-worn, footsore, footweary, walked off one's feet; tired-eyed, hollow-e.; haggard, worn; faint, drooping, flagging, languid, languorous; jaded, tired of 838 *bored*.

panting, out of breath, short of b.; breathless, gasping, puffing and blowing, winded 352 *puffing*.

fatiguing, gruelling, punishing 682 *laborious*; tiresome, wearisome; wearing, exacting, demanding; irksome, trying 838 *tedious*.

Vb. *be fatigued*, etc. adj.; tire oneself out, overdo it, overtax one's strength; ache in every muscle *or* limb, gasp, pant 352 *breathe*; languish, droop, flag 163 *be weak*; stagger, faint, swoon; nod 679 *sleep*; drop, collapse, flake out, crack up, crock up, pack up; be at the end of one's strength; can go no further, can do no more; overwork, get stale, need a holiday.

fatigue, tire, tire out, wear out, exhaust, do up, fag, whack, knock up, crock up, prostrate; double up, wind; task, tax, strain, work, drive, flog, overwork, overtax, overburden, overstrain; enervate, drain, take it out of 827 *trouble*; weary, bore, send to sleep 838 *be tedious*.

685. Refreshment – N. *refreshment*, breather 683 *repose*; break, recess 145 *lull*; renewal, recreation, recuperation 656 *restoration*; refresher, reviver, nineteenth hole 174 *stimulant*; refreshments 301 *food*; wash and brush up 648 *cleansing*.

Adj. *refreshing*, thirst-quenching; cooling 380 *cold*; comforting 831 *relieving*; bracing, reviving, recreational 656 *restorative*.

refreshed, freshened up, recovered, revived 656 *restored*; like a giant refreshed, twice the man *or* woman one was; perked up, ready for more.

Vb. *refresh*, freshen, freshen up 648 *clean*; air, fan, ventilate 340 *aerate*; shade, cool 382 *refrigerate*; brace, stimulate 174 *invigorate*; revive, reanimate, reinvigorate 656 *restore*; ease 831 *relieve*; give a breather; offer food 301 *feed*.

be refreshed, breathe, draw breath, get one's breath back, regain *or* recover one's breath, take a deep b., fill one's lungs; respire, clear one's head; come to, perk up, get one's second wind; recuperate, revive 656 *be restored*; mop one's brow, stretch one's legs, refresh oneself, take a breather, sleep it off; have a change, have a rest 683 *repose*.

686. Agent – N. *agent*, operator, actor, performer, player, executant, practitioner; perpetrator 676 *doer*; tool 628 *instrument*; functionary 741 *officer*; representative 754 *delegate*; spokesman *or* -woman 755 *deputy*; proxy 150 *substitute*; executor, executrix, executive, administrator; dealer, middleman 794 *merchant*; employer, manufacturer, industrialist 164 *producer*.

worker, voluntary w. 901 *philanthropist*; freelance, self-employed person; trade unionist 775 *participator*; toiler, moiler, drudge, dogsbody, hack; menial, factotum, wallah 742 *servant*; hewer of wood and drawer of water 742 *slave*; ant, beaver 678 *busy person*; professional person, business man *or* woman, career w., breadwinner, earner, employee, wage slave, clerical worker, desk w., office w., white-collar w.; shop assistant 793 *seller*; labourer, casual l., day l., agricultural l., farm worker 370 *farmer*; piece-worker, manual w., blue-collar w.; working man *or* woman, workman, hand, operative.

artisan, artificer, technician; skilled worker, semi-skilled w., master 696 *proficient person*; journeyman, apprentice 538 *learner*; craftsman *or* -woman, potter, turner, joiner, cabinet-maker, carpenter, sawyer, cooper; wright, shipwright, boat-builder; builder, architect, mason; metalworker, smith; miner, steelworker, foundryman; mechanic, machinist, fitter; engineer, civil e., mining e.; power-worker, waterworker; plumber, welder, electrician, gas-fitter; weaver, spinner, tailor 228 *clothier*.

personnel, staff, force, company, gang, squad, crew, complement, cadre 74 *band*; dramatis personae 594 *actor*; co-worker, colleague, associate, partner 707 *colleague*; workpeople, hands, men, payroll; labour, casual l.; labour pool, labour force, manpower.

687. Workshop – N. *workshop*, studio, atelier; workroom, study, library; laboratory, research l.; plant, installation; works, factory; workshop, yard; sweatshop; mill, loom; sawmill, paper mill; foundry, metalworks; steelyard, steelworks, smelter; blast furnace, smithy 383 *furnace*; power station, gasworks 160 *energy*; quarry, mine 632 *store*; colliery, coalmine; tin mine, stannary; mint; arsenal, armoury; dockyard, shipyard, slips; construction site, building s.; refinery, distillery, brewery, maltings; shop, shop-floor, bench, production line; nursery 370 *farm*; dairy 369 *stock farm*; office, bureau; firm, company; offices, secretariat, Whitehall; hive of industry 678 *activity*.

688. Conduct – N. *conduct*, behaviour, deportment; bearing, carriage, port; demeanour, attitude, posture 445 *mien*; aspect, look 445 *appearance*; tone, delivery 577 *voice*; motion, action, gesticulation 547 *gesture*; mode of behaviour, fashion, style; manner, guise, air; manners 884 *courtesy*; pose, role-playing 850 *affectation*; outlook 485 *opinion*; misbehaviour, misconduct 934 *wickedness*; track record, history; way of life, ethos,

morals, principles, ideals, customs, manners, lifestyle 610 *habit*; line of action 623 *policy*; career, course, race, walk of life 622 *vocation*; observance, routine 610 *practice*; procedure, method, modus operandi 624 *way*; treatment, handling, manipulation 689 *management*; dealings, transactions 154 *affairs*; deeds 676 *deed*.

tactics, strategy, campaign, plan of c. 623 *plan*; line, party l. 623 *policy*; art of the possible, politics, realpolitik, statesmanship 733 *governance*; lifemanship, gamesmanship, one-upmanship 698 *cunning*; brinkmanship 694 *skill*; manoeuvres, jockeying for position; tactical advantage 34 *advantage*; playing for time 136 *delay*; manoeuvre, shift 623 *contrivance*; move, gambit 676 *deed*; game, little g. 698 *stratagem*.

Adj. *behaving*, behavioural, behaviouristic; psychological; tactical, strategic; political, statesmanlike 622 *businesslike*.

Vb. *behave*, act 676 *do*; play the game 933 *be virtuous*; break all the rules, misbehave, try it on, carry on 934 *be wicked*; keep out of mischief, be on one's best behaviour; gesture 547 *gesticulate*; posture, pose 850 *be affected*; conduct oneself, behave o., carry o., bear o., deport o., acquit o., comport o., demean o.; set an example; indulge in 678 *be active*; play one's part, follow one's career, shape a course; paddle one's own canoe, shift for oneself; manoeuvre, jockey, twist, turn; behave towards, treat.

689. Management – N. *management*, conduct, running, handling; stewardship, agency 751 *commission*; care, charge, control 733 *authority*; superintendence, oversight 457 *surveillance*; art of management, tact, way with 694 *skill*; business management, work study, time and motion s., operational research, cost-benefit analysis; organization, decision-making 623 *policy*; housekeeping, housewifery, husbandry, economics, political economy; statecraft, statesmanship; government 733 *governance*; ménage, regimen, regime, dispensation; regulation, lawmaking 953 *legislation*; reins, reins of government, ministry, cabinet, inner c.; staff work, administration; bureaucracy, civil service; secretariat 687 *workshop.*

directorship, direction, responsibility, control, supreme c. 737 *command*; leadership, premiership, chairmanship, captaincy 34 *superiority*; guidance, steerage, pilotage, steersmanship; pole star 520 *guide*; controls, helm, rudder, wheel, tiller, joystick; needle, compass, binnacle; gyrocompass, gyropilot, autopilot 269 *sailing aid*; beam, radar 281 *direction*; remote control.

Adj. *directing*, directorial, leading, hegemonic; directional, guiding, steering, at the helm; governing, gubernatorial, holding the reins, in the chair 733 *authoritative*; dictatorial 735 *authoritarian*; supervisory, managing, managerial; executive, administrative; legislative, nomothetic; high-level, top-l. 638 *important*; economic, political; official, bureaucratic 733 *governmental.*

Vb. *manage*, manipulate, pull the strings 178 *influence*; have taped, have the measure of 490 *know*; handle, conduct, run, carry on; minister, administer, prescribe; supervise, superintend, oversee, caretake 457 *invigilate*; nurse 457 *look after*; have charge of, hold the portfolio, hold the purse strings (**see** *direct*); keep order, police, regulate; legislate 953 *make legal*; control, govern 733 *rule*; know how to manage, have a way with.

direct, lead 64 *come before*; boss, dictate 737 *command*; be in charge, wear the trousers; hold office, have responsibility; mastermind, have overall responsibility; assume r. 917 *incur a duty*; preside, take the chair; head, captain, skipper, stroke; pilot, steer, take the helm 269 *navigate*; point, show the way 547 *indicate*; shepherd, guide, conduct, lead on; introduce, compère; escort 89 *accompany*; channel, canalize, funnel, route.

690. Director – N. *director*, governing body 741 *governor*; steering committee; cabinet 692 *council*; board of directors, board, chair; staff, top brass, management; manager, controller; legislator,

law-giver; employer, boss 741 *master*; headman, chief 34 *superior*; principal, head, dean, vice-chancellor, chancellor; president, vice-p.; chairperson, chairman, chairwoman, speaker; premier, prime minister; captain, skipper; stroke, cox, master 270 *mariner*; steersman, helmsman 270 *navigator*; pilot 520 *guide*; director of studies 537 *teacher*; backseat driver 691 *adviser*; king-maker 612 *motivator*; hidden hand 178 *influence.*

leader, leader of the House; spearhead, centre forward; bell-wether; fugleman, file-leader; pace-maker; toastmaster; high priest, mystagogue; coryphaeus, chorusleader, conductor; precentor; drum major; führer 741 *autocrat*; demagogue, tribune; ringleader 738 *agitator.*

manager, man *or* woman in charge, key person, kingpin 638 *bigwig*; administrator, executive 676 *doer*; statesman *or* -woman, politician; economist, political e.; housekeeper, chatelaine, housewife; steward, bailiff, farm manager; agent 754 *consignee*; superintendent, supervisor, inspector, overseer, foreman *or* -woman, ganger, gaffer; warden, matron; proctor, disciplinarian; party manager, whip; custodian, caretaker, curator 749 *keeper*; master of hounds, whipper-in; circus manager, ringmaster; compère.

official, office-holder, office-bearer; Jack-in-office, tin god; marshal, steward; shop steward; government servant, public s., civil s., apparatchik 742 *servant*; officer of state, vizier, minister, secretary of state, secretary-general, secretary, unders.; permanent s., bureaucrat, Eurocrat, mandarin 741 *officer*; magistrate 733 *position of authority*; commissioner, prefect, intendant; consul, proconsul, praetor, quaestor, aedile, tribune; counsellor 754 *envoy*; alderman 692 *councillor*; functionary, clerk; school prefect, monitor.

691. Advice – N. *advice*, piece of a., counsel; words of wisdom 498 *wisdom*; counselling 658 *therapy*; criticism, constructive c. 480 *estimate*; didacticism, moralizing, moral injunction 693 *precept*; caution 664 *warning*; recommendation 512 *supposi-*

tion; suggestion, submission; tip, word to the wise 524 *hint*; guidance, briefing, instruction 524 *information*; charge to the jury 959 *legal trial*; deliberation, consultation, heads together 584 *conference*; seeking advice, referment 692 *council*; advice against 762 *deprecation*.

adviser, counsellor, consultant, troubleshooter 696 *expert*; referee, arbiter 480 *estimator*; advocate, recommender 612 *motivator*; therapist 658 *doctor*; counsel 958 *lawyer*; guide, mentor, confidant(e) 537 *teacher*; admonisher 505 *reminder*; Dutch uncle; oracle 500 *sage*; busybody 678 *meddler*.

Adj. *advising*, advisory, consultative, deliberative; hortative, recommendatory 612 *inducing*; advising against 613 *dissuasive*; admonitory, warning 664 *cautionary*; didactic; moral, moralizing.

Vb. *advise*, give advice, counsel, offer c.; think best, recommend, prescribe, advocate, commend; propose, move, suggest 512 *propound*; prompt 524 *hint*; press, urge, exhort 612 *incite*; advise against 613 *dissuade*; admonish 664 *warn*; enjoin, charge 737 *command*.

consult, seek advice, refer; call in, call on; refer to arbitration, hold a public inquiry; confide in, be closeted with, have at one's elbow; take advice, listen to, be advised; sit in council *or* conclave, put heads together, hold a council of war, deliberate, parley, sit round a table, compare notes 584 *confer*.

692. Council – N. *council*, council chamber, board room; court 956 *tribunal*; Privy Council, praesidium; Curia, consistory, Bench of Bishops; vestry; cabinet, kitchen c.; panel, quango, think tank, board, advisory b., consultative body, Royal Commission; conclave, convocation 985 *synod*; convention, congress, meeting, summit; diet, moot; United Nations, Security Council; municipal council, county c., district c., town c., parish c.; soviet; sitting, session, audience, hearing 584 *conference*.

parliament, European P.; Mother of Parliaments, Westminster, Upper House, House of Lords, House of Peers, 'another place'; Lower House, House of Commons; senate, senatus; legislature, legislative assembly, deliberative a., consultative a.; Duma, Reichsrat, Reichstag; States-General, National Assembly, Chambre des Députés, Bundesrat, Bundestag; Rigsdag, Storting, Folketing, Cortes, Dail, Seanad, Knesset, Majlis; Supreme Soviet; Congress, Senate; House of Representatives; quorum, division.

councillor, privy councillor; senator; peer, life peer; Lords Spiritual, L. Temporal; representative, deputy, congressman *or* -woman, Member of Parliament, MP 754 *delegate*; backbencher, lobby fodder; parliamentarian, legislator; mayor, alderman 690 *official*.

Adj. *parliamentary*, senatorial, congressional; unicameral, bicameral; conciliar; convocational, synodal.

693. Precept – N. *precept*, firm advice 691 *advice*; direction, instruction; injunction, charge 737 *command*; commission 751 *mandate*; order, writ 737 *warrant*; prescript, prescription, ordinance, regulation 737 *decree*; canon, norm, formula, formulary, rubric; guidelines 81 *rule*; principle, rule, golden r., moral 496 *maxim*; recipe, receipt; commandment, act, code, corpus juris 953 *legislation*; tenet, article, constitution; ticket, party line; Ten Commandments, Twelve Tables; canon law, common l., unwritten l. 953 *law*; rule of custom, convention 610 *practice*; technicality, nice point; precedent, leading case, text 83 *example*.

Adj. *preceptive*, prescriptive, decretal, mandatory, binding; canonical, rubrical, statutory 953 *legal*; moralizing 496 *aphoristic*.

694. Skill – N. *skill*, skilfulness, dexterity, dexterousness, handiness, ambidexterity; grace, style 575 *elegance*; neatness, deftness, adroitness, address; ease 701 *facility*; proficiency, competence, efficiency; faculty, capability, capacity 160 *ability*; many-sidedness, versatility, amphibiousness; touch, grip, control; mastery, wizardry, virtuosity, prowess 644 *goodness*; métier, forte, strong suit; acquirement, attainment, accomplishment, skills; seamanship, airmanship, horsemanship, marksmanship; experience, expertise, professionalism; specialism; know-how, technique 490 *knowledge*; practical ability, clever fingers; craftsmanship, art, artistry; finish 646 *perfection*; ingenuity, resourcefulness, craftiness 698 *cunning*; cleverness, sharpness, nous, worldly wisdom, sophistication, lifemanship 498 *sagacity*; savoir faire, finesse, tact 463 *discrimination*; feat of skill, trick 623 *contrivance*; sleight of hand, conjuring 542 *sleight*; tightrope walking; brinkmanship 688 *tactics*.

aptitude, innate ability, good head for; bent 179 *tendency*; faculty, endowment, gift, flair; turn, knack, green fingers; talent, genius, genius for; aptness, fitness, qualification.

masterpiece, chef-d'oeuvre, a beauty; pièce de résistance, masterwork, magnum opus; stroke of genius, masterstroke, feat, exploit, hat trick 676 *deed*; tour de force, bravura, fireworks; ace, trump, clincher 644 *exceller*; work of art, objet d'art, curio, collector's piece *or* item.

Adj. *skilful*, good, good at, top-flight, first-rate 644 *excellent*; skilled, crack; apt, handy, dexterous, ambidextrous, deft, slick, adroit, agile, nimble, neat; nimble-fingered, green-f.; surefooted; cunning, clever, quick, shrewd, smart, ingenious 498 *intelligent*; politic, diplomatic, statesmanlike 498 *wise*; adaptable, flexible, resourceful; many-sided, versatile; able, competent, efficient; wizard, masterly, magisterial, accomplished, finished 646 *perfect*.

gifted, naturally g.; of many parts, talented, endowed, well-e; born for, cut out for.

expert, experienced, veteran, seasoned, tried, versed in, well up in, au fait 490 *instructed*; skilled, trained 669 *prepared*; proficient, qualified, competent, up to the mark; efficient, professional 622 *businesslike*.

well-made, well-crafted; finished, felicitous, happy; artistic, artificial, sophisticated, stylish 575 *elegant*; daedal, cunning; shipshape, workmanlike.

Vb. *be skilful*, etc. adj.; be good at, do well 644 *be good*; shine, excel 34 *be superior*; have a turn *or* a gift for, show aptitude; have the knack, have the trick of, have the right touch; be in practice, be in good form, have one's eye *or* hand in; play one's cards well, not put a foot wrong; exploit 673 *use*; take advantage of 137 *profit by*; live by one's wits, get around, know all the answers, know what's what, have one's wits about one 498 *be wise*.

be expert, turn professional; be master *or* mistress of one's profession, be good at one's job, know one's stuff *or* one's onions, have the know-how; qualify 536 *learn*; be an old hand, know the ropes, know all the ins and outs, know backwards, be up to every trick 490 *know*.

695. Unskilfulness – N. *unskilfulness*, no gift for; rustiness 674 *nonuse*; inexperience, inexpertness 491 *ignorance*; incapacity, inability, incompetence, inefficiency 161 *ineffectuality*; Peter principle; charlatanism 850 *pretension*; clumsiness, lubberliness, awkwardness, gaucherie (see *bungling*); backwardness 499 *unintelligence*; booby prize, wooden spoon.

bungling, botching, tinkering 726 *noncompletion*; bungle, botch, dog's breakfast, pig's ear, cock-up, shambles; off day; poor show, bad job 728 *failure*; missed chance 138 *untimeliness*; hamhandedness, dropped catch, fumble, muff, fluff, miss, mishit, slice, own goal 495 *mistake*; tactlessness, heavy-handedness; infelicity, indiscretion 464 *indiscrimination*; mishandling 675 *misuse*; too many cooks; mismanagement, misrule; wild-goose chase 641 *lost labour*.

Adj. *unskilful*, ungifted, untalented, unendowed, unaccomplished; unversatile, unadaptable, inept 25 *unapt*; unable, incapable 161 *impotent*; incompetent, inefficient, ineffectual; unpractical, unbusinesslike, unstatesmanlike, undiplomatic; impolitic, ill-considered 499 *unwise*; thoughtless, giddy 456 *light-minded*; feckless, futile; not up to scratch, inadequate.

unskilled, raw, green 670 *immature*; uninitiated, untrained 670 *unprepared*; unqualified, inexpert, inexperienced, ignorant 491 *uninstructed*; nonprofessional, ham, lay, amateurish, amateur; unscientific, unsound, quackish.

clumsy, awkward, gauche, gawkish; boorish, uncouth 885 *discourteous*; stuttering, stammering; tactless 464 *indiscriminating*; bumbling, bungling; lubberly, unhandy, maladroit, all thumbs, butterfingered; left-handed, cack-h., ham-h., heavy-footed; ungainly, lumbering, hulking, gangling, shambling; stiff, rusty 674 *unused*; out of practice, off form 611 *unhabituated*; losing one's touch, slipping; slapdash 458 *negligent*; fumbling, groping 461 *experimental*; ungraceful, graceless, clownish 576 *inelegant*; top-heavy, lopsided 29 *unequal*; cumbersome, ponderous, ungainly, unmanageable 195 *unwieldy*; unadjusted 495 *inexact*.

bungled, botched, mismanaged vb.; faulty 647 *imperfect*; misguided, ill-considered, ill-judged; ill-prepared 670 *unprepared*; ill-contrived, ill-devised, cobbled together; unhappy, infelicitous; crude, rough and ready, inartistic, amateurish 699 *artless*; half-baked 726 *uncompleted*.

Vb. *be unskilful*, etc. adj.; not know how 491 *not know*; show one's ignorance, go the wrong way about it; tinker 726 *not complete*; burn one's fingers; mishandle, mismanage; misapply 675 *misuse*; misdirect 495 *blunder*; miss one's cue 506 *forget*; lose one's cunning, go rusty 611 *disaccustom*; come a cropper, come unstuck 728 *fail*.

act foolishly, not know what one is about, act in one's own worst interests, stand in one's own light, cut one's own throat, cut off one's nose to spite one's face, throw out the baby with the bath water, make a fool of oneself 497 *be absurd*; quarrel with one's bread and butter,

bite the hand that feeds one, kill the goose that lays the golden eggs, spoil the ship for a ha'porth of tar, bring one's house about one's ears, put the cart before the horse, put all one's eggs in one basket; bite off more than one can chew, have too many irons in the fire; spoil one's chances 138 *lose a chance*; labour in vain 470 *attempt the impossible*; go on a fool's errand 641 *waste effort*; strain at a gnat and swallow a camel.

be clumsy, lumber, bumble, get in the way, stand in the light; trip, stumble, blunder 456 *be inattentive*; stutter 580 *stammer*; fumble, grope, flounder 461 *be tentative*; take two bites at a cherry, muff, fluff; mishit, misthrow; overthrow, overshoot; play into the hands of; spill, slop, drop a catch 311 *let fall*; catch a crab; bungle, drop a brick, put one's foot in it, make a faux pas, get egg on one's face 495 *blunder*; botch 655 *impair*; fool with 678 *meddle*; make a mess or a hash of 728 *miscarry*; make a poor fist at 728 *fail*.

696. Proficient person – N. *proficient person*, expert, adept, dab hand, dabster; do-it-yourself type, all-rounder, jack of all trades, handyman 646 *paragon*; Renaissance man, person of many parts; master, past m., graduate, cordon bleu; genius 500 *sage*; wizard 864 *prodigy*; magician 545 *conjuror*; maestro, virtuoso; prima donna 413 *musician*; gold-medallist, title-holder; dan, black belt, ace, crack shot 644 *exceller*; seeded player, white hope.

expert, no novice, practitioner; professional, pro, specialist, authority, doyen 537 *teacher*; pundit, savant, polymath, walking encyclopedia 492 *scholar*; veteran, old hand, old stager, old soldier, warhorse, sea dog, shellback; practised hand or eye; sophisticate, smart customer 698 *slyboots*; sharp, sharper 545 *trickster*; cosmopolitan, citizen of the world, man or woman about town, man or woman of the world; artist, craftsman or -woman 686 *artisan*; experienced hand, right person for the job, key man or woman; consultant 691 *adviser*; boffin 623 *planner*; cognoscente, connoisseur, fancier.

697. Bungler – N. *bungler*, failure 728 *loser*; one's despair; incompetent, botcher; bumbler, blunderer, blunderhead, bungling idiot; fumbler, muffer, muff, butterfingers; lump, lout, hulk, lubber, bull in a china shop; duffer, clown, buffoon, booby, galoot, clot 501 *fool*; scribbler, dauber; bad shot, poor s.; rabbit, amateur, dabbler; jack of all trades and master of none; novice, greenhorn, sorcerer's apprentice 538 *beginner*; quack 545 *impostor*; landlubber, fair-weather sailor; fish out of water 25 *misfit*.

698. Cunning – N. *cunning*, craft 694 *skill*; lore 490 *knowledge*; resourcefulness, ingenuity 513 *imagination*; guile, gamesmanship, craftiness, artfulness, subtlety, wiliness, slyness, foxiness; cageyness 525 *secrecy*; suppleness, slipperiness, shiftiness; chicanery 930 *foul play*; finesse 542 *sleight*; cheating 542 *deception*; smoothness 925 *flattery*; disguise 525 *concealment*; wheeling and dealing 688 *tactics*; policy, diplomacy, Machiavellianism, realpolitik; jobbery, gerrymandering 930 *improbity*; underhand dealing, sharp practice; intrigue 623 *plot*.

stratagem, ruse, wiles, art, artifice, resource, resort, device, ploy, shift, dodge 623 *contrivance*; machination, little game 623 *plot*; subterfuge, evasion; excuse, white lie 543 *mental dishonesty*; cheat, trick 542 *trickery*; feint, catch 542 *trap*; blind, dust thrown in the eyes, flag of convenience 542 *sham*; thin end of the wedge, manoeuvre 688 *tactics*.

slyboots, crafty fellow, artful dodger, wily person, serpent, snake, fox; snake in the grass 663 *troublemaker*; fraud, hypocrite 545 *deceiver*; cheat, sharper 545 *trickster*; juggler 545 *conjuror*; smoothie, glib tongue 925 *flatterer*; diplomatist, Machiavelli, intriguer, schemer 623 *planner*; strategist, tactician, manoeuvrer, wheeler-dealer; wire-puller 612 *motivator*.

Adj. *cunning*, learned, knowledgeable 498 *wise*; crafty, artful, sly, wily, subtle, foxy; tricky, tricksy; secret 525 *stealthy*; scheming, Machiavellian 623 *planning*; knowing, fly, slick, smart, sophisticated, urbane; canny, pawky, sharp, astute, shrewd, acute; too clever for, too clever by half, no flies on, not born yesterday 498 *intelligent*; cagey 525 *reticent*; experienced 694 *skilful*; resourceful, ingenious; shifty, slippery; deceitful, flattering 542 *deceiving*; crooked, devious 930 *dishonest*.

Vb. *be cunning*, etc. adj.; finesse, dodge, juggle, manoeuvre, jockey, double-cross, twist, turn 251 *wriggle*; lie low 523 *lurk*; intrigue, scheme, play a deep game, spin a web, weave a plot, have an axe to grind, have an eye to the main chance 623 *plot*; contrive, wangle, devise 623 *plan*; tinker, gerrymander; pull a fast one, steal a march on, trick, cheat 542 *deceive*; sweet-talk, blarney 925 *flatter*; temporize, play for time; be one up on, outsmart, outwit 306 *outdo*; dig a pit for 527 *ambush*; match in cunning, see the catch; know all the answers, live by one's wits.

699. Artlessness – N. *artlessness*, simplicity, simple-mindedness; naivety, ingenuousness, guilelessness 935 *innocence*; inexperience, unworldliness; unaffectedness, unsophistication, naturalness, freedom from artifice 573 *plainness*; sincerity, candour, frankness; bluntness, matter-of-factness, outspokenness 540 *veracity*; truth, honesty 929 *probity*; primitiveness, savagery; darkness, barbarism 491 *ignorance*.

ingenue, unsophisticated person, Candide; child of nature, savage, noble s.; enfant terrible; lamb, babe in arms 935 *innocent*; simpleton 501 *ninny*; greenhorn 538 *beginner*; rough diamond; plain man *or* woman, simple soul; yokel, rustic, country cousin 869 *country-dweller*.

Adj. *artless*, without art, without artifice; unstudied, unprepared; uncontrived 44 *simple*; unvarnished 573 *plain*; native, natural, unartificial, homespun, homemade; do-it-yourself 695 *unskilled*; in a state of nature, uncivilized, savage, primitive, unscientific 491 *ignorant*; Arcadian, unsophisticated, ingenuous, naive, childlike 935 *innocent*;

unworldly, simple-minded, callow, wet behind the ears; guileless, unsuspicious, confiding; unaffected, unconstrained, unreserved, uninhibited 609 *spontaneous*; candid, frank, open, straightforward 540 *veracious*; true, honest, sincere 929 *honourable*; above-board, on the level; blunt, outspoken, free-spoken; transparent 522 *undisguised*; prosaic, no-nonsense, matter-of-fact 494 *accurate*; unassuming, unpretentious 874 *modest*; unrefined, unpolished.

Vb. *be artless*, etc. adj.; live in a state of nature, know no better; have no guile 935 *be innocent*; have no affectations, eschew artifice; wear one's heart upon one's sleeve; look one in the face, look one straight in the eyes, call a spade a spade, say what is in one's mind 573 *speak plainly*; not mince one's words 540 *be truthful*.

Section 4: Antagonism

700. Difficulty – N. *difficulty*, hardness, arduousness, laboriousness, the hard way 682 *exertion*; impracticability, nonstarter 470 *impossibility*; intricacy, perplexity, inextricability 61 *complexity*; complication 832 *aggravation*; obscurity, impenetrability 517 *unintelligibility*; inconvenience, awkwardness, embarrassment 643 *inexpedience*; rough ground, hard going, bad patch; quagmire 347 *marsh*; knot, Gordian k.; problem, thorny p., crux, hard nut to crack, poser, teaser, puzzle, headache 530 *enigma*; impediment, handicap, obstacle, snag, rub, where the shoe pinches 702 *hindrance*; maze, crooked path 251 *convolution*; impasse, blank wall 264 *closure*; deadlock 145 *stop*; stress, brunt, burden 684 *fatigue*; trial, tribulation 825 *suffering*; trouble 731 *adversity*; difficult person, handful, one's despair, kittle cattle; hot potato.

hard task, test, trial of strength; Herculean task, superhuman t., thankless t., Sisyphean labour; task, job, work cut out, hard row to hoe, no picnic; tall order, tough assignment 682 *labour*.

predicament, embarrassment, false position, delicate situation; quandary, dilemma, cleft stick; borderline case 474 *dubiety*; catch-22 situation; fix, jam, hole, scrape, hot water, trouble, fine kettle of fish, pickle, stew, imbroglio, mess, muddle; pinch, straits, pass, pretty p.; sticky wicket, tight corner, ticklish situation, hot seat 661 *danger*; critical situation, exigency, emergency 137 *crisis*.

Adj. *difficult*, hard, tough, formidable; steep, arduous, uphill; inconvenient, onerous, irksome, toilsome 682 *laborious*; exacting, demanding 684 *fatiguing*; insuperable 470 *impossible*; problematic, more easily said than done; delicate, ticklish, tricky; embarrassing, awkward; unwieldy, unmanageable; intractable, refractory 738 *disobedient*; stubborn, perverse 602 *obstinate*; ill-behaved, naughty 934 *wicked*; perplexing, obscure 517 *unintelligible*; knotty, complex, complicated, intricate; impenetrable, impassable, trackless, pathless; thorny, craggy 259 *rough*; sticky, critical 661 *dangerous*.

in difficulties, hampered 702 *hindered*; in a quandary, in a dilemma, in a cleft stick, between two stools 474 *doubting*; baffled, nonplussed 517 *puzzled*; in a jam, in a fix, on the hook, up a gum tree, in a spot, in a hole, in a scrape, in hot water, in the soup, in a pickle; out of one's depth, under fire; in the hot seat 661 *endangered*; worried, harassed 825 *suffering*; under pressure, up against it, hard pressed; in dire straits, at one's wits' end, cornered; stuck, stuck fast 728 *grounded*.

Vb. *be difficult*, etc. adj.; make things difficult, complicate matters 63 *bedevil*; put one on the spot 827 *trouble*; baffle 474 *puzzle*; hamper 702 *hinder*; make things worse 832 *aggravate*.

be in difficulty, have a problem; tread carefully, walk among eggs 461 *be tentative*; have one's hands full 678 *be busy*; be at a loss 474 *be uncertain*; have one's work cut out, be put to it; run into trouble; be asking for trouble, fish in troubled waters; let oneself in for, cop it 731 *have trouble*; feel the pinch 825 *suffer*; make heavy weather of, flounder; come unstuck 728 *miscarry*; live dangerously 661 *face danger*; labour under difficulties, be handicapped by.

Adv. *with difficulty*, hardly; the hard way, uphill; against the grain; in the teeth of; at a pinch.

701. Facility – N. *facility*, easiness, ease, convenience, comfort; flexibility 327 *softness*; capability, feasibility 469 *possibility*; comprehensibility 516 *intelligibility*; facilitation, simplification, smoothing, disentanglement; free hand, full scope 744 *scope*; provision for 703 *aid*; simplicity, straightforwardness, an open-and-shut case; easy going, calm seas 258 *smoothness*; fair wind, straight road, downhill.

easy thing, no trouble, a pleasure, child's play, kid's stuff; soft option, short work, light w. 679 *inactivity*; picnic, doddle 837 *amusement*; chickenfeed, piece of cake; plain sailing, easy ride; nothing to it; easy meat, soft touch; pushover, walkover 727 *victory*; cinch, sure thing, dead cert 473 *certainty*.

Adj. *easy*, facile, undemanding, cushy; effortless, painless; frictionless 258 *smooth*; uncomplicated 44 *simple*; not hard, not difficult, foolproof; easy as pie, no sooner said than done; as easy as falling off a log, as simple as ABC; feasible 469 *possible*; facilitating 703 *aiding*; with the current, with the tide; convenient 376 *comfortable*; approachable 289 *accessible*; comprehensible 516 *intelligible*.

tractable, manageable, easy-going 597 *willing*; submissive 721 *submitting*; malleable 327 *flexible*; smooth-running, well-oiled, frictionless; handy, manoeuvrable.

Vb. *be easy*, etc. adj.; present no difficulties, give no trouble, make no demands; be had for the asking; go like clockwork 258 *go smoothly*.

do easily, have no trouble, see one's way to; make light of, make no bones about, make short work of, do standing on one's head *or* with one hand tied behind one's back; have it all one's own way, have a walkover 727 *win*; sail home, coast h.; be at home, be in one's element, take in one's stride, take to like a duck to water; save

oneself trouble, take the easy way out, take the line of least resistance.

facilitate, ease, make easy; iron out 258 *smooth*; grease, oil 334 *lubricate*; simplify 520 *interpret*; enable 160 *empower*; allow 756 *permit*; put one in the way of, help on, speed, expedite 703 *aid*; pioneer, open up 64 *come before*; pave the way, bridge the gap; give full play to 744 *give scope*.

disencumber, free, liberate, unshackle, unfetter 668 *deliver*; clear away, unclog 648 *clean*; derestrict, deobstruct; disengage, disentangle, extricate 62 *unravel*; untie 46 *disunite*; ease, lighten, unburden 831 *relieve*.

Adv. *easily*, swimmingly, like clockwork; effortlessly, just like that; without a hitch.

702. Hindrance – N. *hindrance*, impediment, rub; inhibition, hangup, block; obstruction, frustration; blockage 264 *closure*; blockade 712 *attack*; restriction, control 747 *restraint*; arrest 747 *detention*; check, retardation 278 *slowness*; drag 333 *friction*; interference, meddling, interception, intervention 231 *interjacency*; obstructiveness 704 *opposition*; countermeasure 182 *counteraction*; defence 715 *resistance*; disincentive 613 *dissuasion*; hostility 924 *disapprobation*; blacking, boycott 620 *avoidance*; forestalling, prevention, sterilization 652 *hygiene*; ban, embargo 757 *prohibition*.

obstacle, impediment, hindrance, nuisance, drawback, inconvenience, handicap 700 *difficulty*; bunker, hazard; bottleneck, logjam; tie, tether 47 *bond*; red tape, regulations; snag, block, stop, stymie; stumbling block, tripwire, hurdle; barrier, wall, groyne, boom, dam, dike, embankment, bulwark, buffer 713 *defences*; fence, blockade 235 *enclosure*; curtain, Iron Curtain 231 *partition*; stile, gate, turnstile, tollgate; crosswind, headwind; impasse, deadlock, stalemate, vicious circle, catch-22; cul-de-sac, blind alley, dead end.

hitch, snag, catch; contretemps, spot of trouble; teething troubles; technical hitch, breakdown, failure; puncture, flat; leak, burst pipe; fuse, short circuit; stoppage, holdup, setback 145 *stop*; screw loose, spanner in the works, fly in the ointment.

encumbrance, handicap, liability; drag, shackle 748 *fetter*; trammels, meshes, toils; impedimenta, baggage, lumber; cross, millstone, albatross; dead weight, burden, load, last straw; onus, incubus; family commitments, dependants; debts.

hinderer, hindrance; wet blanket, damper, spoilsport, killjoy; dog in the manger; interceptor, fielder; obstructionist, filibuster, saboteur; heckler, interrupter, barracker; interferer 678 *meddler*; interloper 59 *intruder*; mischiefmaker, poltergeist, gremlin 663 *troublemaker*; challenger 705 *opponent*.

Adj. *hindering*, impeding, obstructive, stalling, delaying, frustrating, thwarting etc. vb.; cross, contrary, unfavourable 731 *adverse*; restrictive, cramping 747 *restraining*; prohibitive, preventive 757 *prohibiting*; prophylactic 182 *counteracting*; intrusive 59 *extraneous*; interfering 678 *meddling*; in the way, in the light; inconvenient 643 *inexpedient*; snaggy 700 *difficult*; onerous, burdensome, cumbrous 322 *weighty*; tripping, entangling; choking, strangling, stifling; disheartening 613 *dissuasive*; unhelpful, uncooperative 598 *unwilling*, 704 *opposing*.

Vb. *hinder*, hamper, obstruct, impede; inconvenience 827 *trouble*; upset 63 *derange*; trip, get under one's feet; tangle 542 *ensnare*; get in the way, stand in one's light; come between 678 *meddle*; intercept, cut off, head off, undermine; nip in the bud, stifle, choke 165 *suppress*; gag, muzzle 578 *make mute*; shoot down, kill stone dead; hamper, burden, cumber, encumber; press 322 *weigh*; load with, saddle w. 193 *load*; cramp, handicap; tie hand and foot 747 *fetter*; restrict 236 *limit*; be a drag on, hold back 747 *restrain*; hold up 278 *retard*; hobble, hamstring 161 *disable*; wing 655 *wound*; intimidate 854 *frighten*; discourage 613 *dissuade*; mar, spoil 655 *impair*; throw cold water on; snub, rebuff 760 *refuse*.

obstruct, interpose, interfere 678 *meddle*; obtrude 297 *intrude*; stymie, snooker, stand in the way; buzz, jostle, crowd, squeeze; stop, intercept, block, wall up 264 *close*; foul up, bring to a standstill; dam, earth up, embank; fend off 713 *parry*; barricade 235 *enclose*; hedge in, blockade 232 *circumscribe*; keep out 57 *exclude*; prevent, inhibit, bar 757 *prohibit*.

be obstructive, give trouble, play up 700 *be difficult*; put off, stall, stonewall; not play ball 598 *be unwilling*; baffle, foil, stymie, balk; counter 182 *counteract*; check, thwart, frustrate 704 *oppose*; interrupt, interject, heckle, barrack; shout down; take evasive action 620 *avoid*; talk out, filibuster 581 *be loquacious*; play for time 113 *spin out*; picket 145 *halt*; sabotage, throw a spanner in the works, put a spoke in one's wheel; take the wind out of one's sails.

703. Aid – **N.** *aid*, assistance, help, helping hand, leg-up, lift, boost; succour, rescue 668 *deliverance*; comfort, support, moral s., backing, abetment, encouragement; reinforcement 162 *strengthening*; helpfulness 706 *cooperation*; service, ministration 897 *kind act*; interest, good offices; patronage, auspices, sponsorship 660 *protection*, 178 *influence*; good will, charity, sympathy 897 *benevolence*; intercession 981 *prayers*; advocacy, championship; promotion, furtherance 654 *improvement*; nursing, spoonfeeding; first aid 658 *medical art*; relief 685 *refreshment*; preferential treatment; favourable circumstances 730 *prosperity*; fair wind, tail w.; facilities 701 *facility*; self-help, do-it-yourself.

subvention, economic aid; donation 781 *gift*; charity 901 *philanthropy*; social security, benefit, supplementary b.; loan 802 *credit*; subsidy, hand-out, bounty, grant, allowance, expense account; stipend, bursary, scholarship 962 *reward*; keep 633 *provision*; manna, soup kitchen.

aider, help, helper, assister, assistant, lieutenant, henchman, aide, right-hand man, man *or* girl Friday; stand-by, support, prop, mainstay; tower of strength 660 *protector*; hand-holder, ministering angel; district nurse, social worker, counsellor 691 *adviser*; good neighbour, good

Samaritan, friend in need; ally 707 *collaborator*; reinforcements 707 *auxiliary*; fairy godmother 903 *benefactor*; promoter, sponsor 707 *patron*; booster 923 *commender*; abettor 612 *motivator*; factor 58 *component*; springboard 628 *instrument*.

Adj. *aiding*, helpful, obliging 706 *cooperative*; kind 897 *benevolent*; neighbourly 880 *friendly*; favourable, propitious; supportive, encouraging 612 *inducing*; of service 640 *useful*; constructive, well-meant; morale-boosting; assistant, auxiliary, subsidiary, ancillary, accessory; in aid of, contributory, promoting; subservient 742 *serving*; assisting 628 *instrumental*.

Vb. *aid*, help, assist, lend a hand 706 *cooperate*; take under one's wing, take in tow; hold one's hand, spoonfeed; be kind to 897 *be benevolent*; help one out, tide one over, see one through; oblige, accommodate 784 *lend*; subsidize; facilitate, speed, boost 285 *promote*; abet, instigate, foment 612 *induce*; contribute to 156 *conduce*; lend support to, back up, stand by 218 *support*; comfort, sustain, hearten, rally 855 *give courage*; succour, bail out, help o., relieve 668 *deliver*; step into the breach 162 *strengthen*; ease 685 *refresh*.

patronize, favour, smile on 730 *be auspicious*; sponsor, back, guarantee, go bail for; recommend, put up for; propose, second; protect 660 *safeguard*; join 78 *be included*; subscribe to 488 *endorse*; take an interest in 880 *befriend*; take one's part, side with, champion, stick up for, stand up f. 713 *defend*; vote f. 605 *vote*; pray for, intercede; cherish, foster 889 *pet*; buy from 792 *purchase*.

minister to, wait on, help, oblige 742 *serve*; nurse 658 *doctor*; squire, valet, mother; be of service to 640 *be useful*; pander to 925 *flatter*.

Adv. *in aid of*, for the sake of, on behalf of; under the aegis *or* auspices of; thanks to.

704. Opposition – N. *opposition*, antagonism, hostility; conflict, friction 709 *dis-*

sension; recalcitrance 602 *obstinacy*; counterargument 479 *confutation*; contradiction 533 *negation*; challenge 711 *defiance*; stand 715 *resistance*; headwind, crosscurrent 702 *obstacle*; tug of war, battle of wills; rivalry, competition 716 *contention*; the Opposition, the other side; underground, alternative society 84 *nonconformity*.

opposites, opposite poles 14 *contrariety*; duellists 716 *contender*; factions, cat and dog 709 *quarreller*; town and gown, the right and the left.

Adj. *opposing*, oppositional; in opposition; anti, against; antagonistic, antipathetic 881 *inimical*; unfavourable, unpropitious 731 *adverse*; thwarting 702 *hindering*; contradictory 14 *contrary*; cussed 602 *obstinate*; recalcitrant 738 *disobedient*; resistant 182 *counteracting*; at variance, at odds with 709 *quarrelling*; at daggers drawn 716 *contending*; fronting, facing, eyeball to eyeball 237 *frontal*; polarized 240 *opposite*; mutually opposed 911 *jealous*.

Vb. *oppose*, go against, militate a. 14 *be contrary*; stand against, hold out a. 715 *resist*; set one's face against 607 *reject*; object, protest against 762 *deprecate*; vote against 924 *disapprove*; not support, dissociate oneself; contradict, belie 533 *negate*; counter 479 *confute*; work against 182 *counteract*; countermine 702 *be obstructive*; stand up to, challenge 711 *defy*; fly in the face of 738 *disobey*; rebuff, spurn, slam the door in one's face 760 *refuse*; compete with 716 *contend*; set against, pit a., match a.

withstand, confront, face, stand up to 661 *face danger*; rise against 738 *revolt*; take on, cross swords with 716 *fight*; struggle against, breast the tide; grapple with, wrestle w. 599 *stand firm*; hold one's own 715 *resist*.

Adv. *in opposition*, against, versus, agin; in conflict with, against the grain, in the teeth of, in the face of, in spite of, despite.

705. Opponent – N. *opponent*, opposer, adversary, antagonist 881 *enemy*; assailant 712 *attacker*; the opposition, opposite camp; obstructionist 702 *hinderer*; cross benches; die-hard, bitter-ender, reactionary, counter-revolutionary; objector 489 *dissentient*; resister, passive r.; dissident, noncooperator 829 *malcontent*; challenger, rival; contestant, duellist 716 *contender*; common enemy, public e.

706. Cooperation – N. *cooperation*, helpfulness 597 *willingness*; contribution, coagency, synergy, symbiosis; duet, double harness, tandem; collaboration, joint effort, combined operation; team work, concerted effort; relay, relay race; team spirit, esprit de corps; lack of friction, bipartisanship 710 *concord*; clannishness, cliquishness, partisanship, old school tie; connivance, collusion 612 *inducement*; conspiracy 623 *plot*; complicity; participation; sympathy 880 *friendliness*; fraternity, solidarity, fellowship, freemasonry; common cause, mutual assistance, networking, back-scratching, log-rolling; reciprocity, give and take; consultation 584 *conference*.

association, coming together; partnership 775 *participation*; nationalization, internationalization 775 *joint possession*; pool, kitty; membership, affiliation 78 *inclusion*; connection, hookup 9 *relation*; consociation, ecosystem; combination 45 *union*; integration, solidarity 52 *whole*; unification 88 *unity*; amalgamation, fusion, merger; coalition, alliance, league, federation, confederation, confederacy, umbrella organization; axis, united front 708 *political party*; fellowship, club 708 *community*; set, clique 708 *party*; workers' association, trade union, chapel; business association, company, consortium 708 *corporation*; housing association, economic community, cooperative, commune.

Adj. *cooperative*, helpful 703 *aiding*; symbiotic, synergic 710 *concordant*; collaborating, in tandem; associated, in league, hand in glove with; bipartisan; federal 708 *corporate*.

Vb. *cooperate*, collaborate, work together, work as a team; team up, join forces 775 *participate*; show willing, play ball, reciprocate, respond; lend oneself to, espouse 703 *patronize*; join in, take part, pitch in; rally round 703 *aid*; row in the same boat, stand shoulder to shoulder; make common cause with, take in each other's washing; network, band together, associate, confederate, federate; unite, combine, make common cause, club together; lay heads together 691 *consult*; collude, connive, play another's game; treat with 766 *make terms*.

707. Auxiliary – N. *auxiliary*, relay, recruit, reinforcement 722 *soldiery*; ally, brother- *or* sister-in-arms (**see** *colleague*); adjuvant, assistant, helpmate, helping hand 703 *aider*; right-hand man, second; adjutant, lieutenant, aide-de-camp; amanuensis; midwife, handmaid; dogsbody 742 *servant*; acolyte, server; friend in need 880 *friend*; hanger-on, sidekick 742 *dependant*; disciple, adherent 978 *sectarian*; cat's-paw 628 *instrument*; shadow, familiar 89 *concomitant*; jackal, running dog, creature, âme damnée.

collaborator, cooperator, co-worker, fellow w.; team-mate, yoke-fellow; sympathizer, fellow traveller, fifth columnist.

colleague, associate, confrère, fellow, brother, sister; co-director, partner 775 *participator*; comrade, companion, boon c., playmate, mate, chum 880 *friend*; helpmate 894 *spouse*; standby, stalwart; ally, confederate; accomplice, accessory, aider and abettor, fellow conspirator, partner in crime; co-religionist; one's fellows, one's own side.

patron, defender 660 *protector*; well-wisher, sympathizer; champion, advocate, friend at court; supporter, sponsor, backer, guarantor; proposer, seconder; partisan, votary, aficionado, fan; friend in need, deus ex machina; rich uncle 903 *benefactor*; promoter, founder; patron of art, Maecenas; customer, client.

708. Party – N. *party*, movement; group, class 77 *classification*; confession, communion 978 *sect*; faction, cabal, cave, splinter group 489 *dissentient*; circle, inner c., charmed c.; set, clique, in-crowd, coterie; caucus, junta, camarilla, politburo, committee, club, cell, cadre; ring, closed shop; team, troupe, company; gang, bunch, outfit 74 *band*; side, camp.

political party, right, left, centre; coalition, popular front, bloc; Red, commie, Trot; socialist, labourite, Fabian, syndicalist; anarchist 738 *revolter*; right-winger, rightist, true blue; left-winger, leftist, pinko; radical, populist, democrat; moderate, centrist; party worker; liberal; politician, politico; militant, activist 676 *doer*.

society, partnership 706 *association*; league, alliance, axis; economic association, cooperative, free trade area; private society, club; secret society, Freemasonry, lodge, cell; friendly society, trade union; chapel; group, division, branch; movement, fellow, associate, member; paid-up m., card-carrying m.; comrade, trade unionist; affiliate.

community, fellowship, body, congregation, brotherhood, fraternity, confraternity, sorority, sisterhood; guild, sodality; tribe, clan 11 *family*, 371 *social group*; state 371 *nation*.

corporation, body; mayor and corporation 692 *council*; company, jointstock c.; multinational c., firm, concern; joint c., partnership; house, business h.; establishment, organization, institute; trust, combine, monopoly, cartel, syndicate, conglomerate 706 *association*; chamber of commerce, guild, cooperative society; consumers' association.

Adj. *corporate*, incorporate, corporative; joint, partnered, bonded, banded, leagued, federal, federative; allied, federate, confederate; social 882 *sociable*; fraternal 880 *friendly*; cooperative, syndicalist; communal 775 *sharing*.

sectional, factional, denominational 978 *sectarian*; partisan, clannish, cliquish, cliquey, exclusive; class-conscious; nationalistic 481 *biased*; rightist, rightwing; leftist, left-wing, pink, red; radical, conservative.

Vb. *join a party*, subscribe; join, sign on, enlist, enrol oneself; belong to 78 *be included*; align oneself, side with, take sides, team up with 706 *cooperate*; club together, associate, ally, league, federate; merge.

Adv. *in league*, in cahoots with, hand in glove w.; hand in hand, side by side, shoulder to shoulder; en masse, collectively.

709. Dissension – N. *dissension*, disagreement 489 *dissent*; noncooperation 704 *opposition*; disharmony, disaccord 411 *discord*; recrimination 714 *retaliation*; bickering, cat-and-dog life; differences, odds, variance, friction, tension, unpleasantness; no love lost 888 *hatred*; disunity, disunion, infighting, house divided against itself 25 *disagreement*; rift, cleavage 294 *divergence*; split, faction 978 *schism*; breach, rupture; challenge 711 *defiance*.

quarrelsomeness, factiousness, litigiousness; aggressiveness 718 *bellicosity*; provocativeness 711 *defiance*; cantankerousness, prickliness 892 *irascibility*; shrewishness, sharp tongue 899 *scurrility*; contentiousness 716 *contention*; spite 898 *malevolence*.

quarrel, open q.; feud, vendetta 910 *revenge*; war 718 *warfare*; strife 716 *contention*; conflict, clash 279 *collision*; controversy, dispute, wrangle, argy-bargy 475 *argument*; stormy exchange, altercation, set-to, slanging match 899 *scurrility*; spat, tiff, squabble, barney, storm in a teacup; rumpus, row, shindy, scrimmage, fracas, brawl, fisticuffs 61 *turmoil*; gang warfare, riot 716 *fight*.

casus belli, root of the trouble; flashpoint, breaking point; tender spot, sore point; apple of discord, bone of contention, bone to pick; point at issue, area of disagreement, battleground.

quarreller, disputer, wrangler; controversialist 475 *reasoner*; duellist 716 *contender*; Kilkenny cats; quarrelmonger 663 *troublemaker*; scold 892 *shrew*; aggressor 712 *attacker*.

Adj. *quarrelling*, clashing 14 *contrary*; at odds, at sixes and sevens, at loggerheads, at variance, at daggers drawn 881 *inimical*; divided, factious, schismatic 489 *dissenting*; mutinous, rebellious 738 *disobedient*; uncooperative 704 *opposing*; sore 891 *resentful*; cantankerous 892 *irascible*; sulky 893 *sullen*; implacable 910 *revengeful*; litigious 959 *litigating*; quarrelsome 718 *warlike*; spoiling for a fight 712 *attacking*; abusive 899 *cursing*; argumentative, contentious, disputatious 475 *arguing*.

Vb. *quarrel*, disagree 489 *dissent*; clash, conflict 279 *collide*; cross swords with, be at one another's throats; be at variance, have differences; recriminate; fall out, part company, split, break with; break away 978 *schismatize*; break off relations 718 *go to war*; take it to court 959 *litigate*; dispute 479 *confute*.

make quarrels, pick q., start something, pick a fight; look for trouble, challenge 711 *defy*; irritate, provoke 891 *enrage*; have a bone to pick; set at odds, set by the ears 888 *excite hate*; create discord, sow dissension, make trouble, put the cat among the pigeons; come between 46 *sunder*; set against, pit a., match with; egg on, incite 612 *motivate*.

bicker, squabble; nag, henpeck, spar with, live a cat-and-dog life; wrangle, dispute with, go at it hammer and tongs 475 *argue*; scold 899 *cuss*; have words with, altercate, row with; kick up a shindy, disturb the peace, make the fur fly 61 *rampage*.

710. Concord – N. *concord*, harmony, unison 24 *agreement*; unanimity 488 *consensus*; understanding, rapport; solidarity, team spirit 706 *cooperation*; reciprocity 12 *correlation*; sympathy, fellow feeling 887 *love*; compatibility, coexistence, amity 880 *friendship*; rapprochement, détente, conciliation 719 *pacification*; arbitration 720 *mediation*; entente cordiale, happy family, best of friends, sweetness and light, love and peace 717 *peace*; goodwill, honeymoon period.

Adj. *concordant*, harmonious; en rapport, unanimous, of one mind, bipartisan 24 *agreeing*; coexistent, compatible, united, allied; fraternal, amicable 880 *friendly*; frictionless 717 *peaceful*; conciliatory 719 *pacificatory*.

Vb. *concord*, harmonize; agree 24 *accord*; hit it off, see eye to eye, pull together 706 *cooperate*; reciprocate, respond 181 *concur*; fraternize 880 *be friendly*; keep the peace.

711. Defiance – N. *defiance*, dare, challenge, gage, gauntlet; bold front, brave face 855 *courage*; war dance, battle cry 900 *threat*; brazenness 878 *insolence*; bravura 875 *ostentation*.

Adj. *defiant*, defying, challenging, provocative, bellicose 718 *warlike*; saucy 878 *insolent*; mutinous, rebellious 738 *disobedient*; daring 855 *courageous*; stiffnecked 871 *proud*; reckless 857 *rash*.

Vb. *defy*, challenge, take one up on 489 *dissent*; stand up to 704 *oppose*; caution 664 *warn*; throw in one's teeth, throw down the gauntlet, throw one's hat in the ring; demand satisfaction, call out; dare, outdare, beard; brave, run the gauntlet 661 *face danger*; laugh in one's face, snap one's fingers at 922 *hold cheap*; bid defiance to, hurl d.; call one's bluff; show fight, bare one's teeth 900 *threaten*; wave a banner 317 *brandish*; march, demonstrate, stage a sit-in, not be moved; cock a snook 878 *be insolent*; ask for trouble 709 *make quarrels*; crow, bluster, brag 877 *boast*.

712. Attack – N. *attack*, aggressiveness, aggro 718 *bellicosity*; aggression, unprovoked a.; stab in the back 930 *foul play*; mugging, assault, assault and battery, grievous bodily harm 176 *violence*; armed attack, offensive, drive, push, thrust; run at, dead set at; onslaught, onset, rush, charge; sally, sortie, breakout, breakthrough; counterattack 714 *retaliation*; shock tactics, blitzkrieg, coup de main; encroachment, infringement 306 *overstepping*; invasion, incursion 297 *ingress*; raid, foray 788 *brigandage*; blitz, air raid; taking by storm, escalade; boarding; investment, siege, blockade; challenge, tilt.

terror tactics, war of nerves 854 *in-*

timidation; war to the knife 735 *severity*; whiff of grapeshot, shot across the bows; bloodbath 362 *slaughter*; laying waste 165 *havoc*.

bombardment, cannonade, barrage, strafe, blitz; broadside, volley, salvo; bombing, strategic b., tactical b., saturation b.; firing, shooting, fire, gunfire; fusillade, burst of fire, rapid f., cross-f.; enfilade; flak; sharpshooting, sniping.

lunge, thrust, pass; cut, cut and thrust, stab, jab; bayonet, cold steel; punch, swipe 279 *knock*.

attacker, assailant, aggressor; hawk, militant; spearhead, storm troops, shock t., strike force; fighter pilot 722 *armed force*; sharpshooter, sniper; terrorist, guerrilla; invader, raider; besieger, blockader, stormer, escalader.

Adj. *attacking*, assailing, etc. vb.; aggressive, on the offensive 718 *warlike*; hawkish, militant, spoiling for a fight 881 *inimical*; up in arms, on the warpath 718 *warring*.

Vb. *attack*, start a fight 718 *go to war*; strike the first blow, fire the first shot; assault, assail, go for, set on, pounce on, fall o., pitch into; attack tooth and nail, savage, maul 655 *wound*; launch out at, let fly, let one have it, round on; take by surprise; invade 306 *encroach*; raid, foray 297 *burst in*; take the offensive; counterattack 714 *retaliate*; thrust, push 279 *impel*; erupt, sally 298 *emerge*; board, grapple; escalade, storm 727 *overmaster*; ravage 165 *lay waste*; harry, drive, corner, bring to bay 619 *hunt*; enter the lists 711 *defy*; take up the cudgels 716 *fight*.

besiege, lay siege to, beleaguer, invest, beset, blockade 235 *enclose*; sap, mine, undermine, spring a mine.

strike at, raise one's hand against; lay about one 279 *strike*, *kick*; go berserk 176 *be violent*; fetch a blow, lash out at; beat up, mug; clash, ram 279 *collide*; lunge; close with, grapple w., fight hand to hand; cut and thrust, stab, bayonet, run through 263 *pierce*; strike home, bring down.

charge, sound the c., advance, go over the top; bear down on, come upon; mob 61 *rampage*; make a rush, rush at, run at,

dash at, ride full tilt at; ride down, run down, ram 279 *collide*.

fire at, shoot at, pick off 287 *shoot*; shoot down, bring d.; torpedo, sink; soften up, strafe, bombard, blitz, cannonade, shell, fusillade, pepper; bomb, plaster; open fire, let fly, volley; rake, straddle, enfilade; take aim 281 *aim*.

lapidate, stone, throw a stone, heave a brick; shy, sling, pelt; hurl at 287 *propel*.

713. Defence – N. *defence*, the defensive, self-defence 715 *resistance*; counterstroke, parry 182 *counteraction*; defensiveness 854 *nervousness*; posture of defence, guard; safekeeping 666 *preservation*; self-protection 660 *protection*; rampart, bulwark, screen, buffer, fender, bumper 662 *safeguard*; deterrent 723 *weapon*.

defences, lines, entrenchment, fieldwork, redoubt, redan, lunette; breastwork, parados; outwork, earthwork, embankment; sandbags; mole, boom; barricade 235 *barrier*; abatis, palisade, paling, stockade; moat, ditch, dike, fosse; trench, dugout; tripwire, booby trap 542 *trap*; barbed wire; spike, caltrop, chevaux de frise; dragon's teeth; Maginot Line, Siegfried L., Hadrian's Wall, Great Wall of China; bunker 662 *shelter*; barrage, flak; barrage balloon; wooden walls; minefield; smokescreen 421 *screen*.

fortification (**see** *fort*); circumvallation, bulwark, rampart, wall; parapet, battlements, machicolation, embrasure, loophole; vallum, scarp, escarp, counterscarp, glacis; curtain, bastion; buttress 218 *prop*.

fort, fortress, stronghold, fastness; citadel 662 *refuge*; castle, keep, ward, barbican, tower, turret, bartizan, donjon; portcullis, drawbridge; gate, postern, sally port; peel, Martello tower, pillbox; blockhouse; laager 235 *enclosure*; camp 253 *earthwork*.

armour, harness; full armour, panoply; mail, chain m.; armour plate; breastplate, backplate, cuirass; hauberk, coat of mail, corslet; helmet, helm, casque; visor, beaver; steel helmet, tin hat; shako, bearskin, busby 228 *headgear*; greaves, gauntlet, vambrace; shield, buckler, target; protective clothing, riot shield 662 *safeguard*.

defender, champion 927 *vindicator*; patron 703 *aider*; knight-errant, paladin; loyalist, legitimist, patriot; bodyguard, lifeguard 722 *soldier*; watch, sentry, sentinel; patrol, patrolman; garrison, picket, guard, escort, rearguard; militia, thin red line 722 *soldiery*; firefighter, firewatcher; civil defence corps; guardian, warden 660 *protector*; warder, custodian 749 *keeper*; deliverer, rescuer 668 *deliverance*.

Adj. *defending*, on the defensive 715 *resisting*; defensive, protective 660 *tutelary*.

defended, armoured, armour-plated; mailed, mail-clad, iron-c; panoplied, accoutred, armed to the teeth 669 *prepared*; moated, barricaded, walled, fortified; entrenched, dug in; defensible, bombproof, bulletproof 660 *invulnerable*.

Vb. *defend*, guard, protect 660 *safeguard*; fence, hedge 232 *circumscribe*; barricade 235 *enclose*; block 702 *obstruct*; shield, curtain 421 *screen*; cloak 525 *conceal*; provide with arms, munition, arm, accoutre 669 *make ready*; armour, armour-plate; fortify 162 *strengthen*; entrench, dig in 599 *stand firm*; garrison, man the defences, stop the gap; champion 927 *vindicate*; fight for, take up arms for, break a lance for, take up the cudgels for 703 *patronize*; come to the rescue 668 *deliver*.

parry, counter, riposte, fence, fend off, ward o., hold o., keep o., fight o., stave o., hold *or* keep at bay 620 *avoid*; turn, avert 282 *deflect*; stall, block 702 *obstruct*; play for a draw; fight back 715 *resist*; repulse 292 *repel*; bear the brunt, hold one's own 704 *withstand*; survive, live to fight another day 667 *escape*.

714. Retaliation – N. *retaliation*, reprisal, lex talionis 910 *revenge*; requital, recompense, quittance, comeuppance 962 *reward*; deserts 915 *dueness*; poetic justice, retribution, Nemesis 963 *punishment*; reaction, boomerang, backlash 280 *recoil*; counterstroke, counterblast, counterplot 182 *counteraction*; counterattack 712 *attack*; recrimination, riposte, retort 460 *rejoinder*; reciprocation, tit for tat, quid pro quo, eye for an eye; biter bit, game at which two can play.

Adj. *retaliatory*, in reprisal, in self-defence; retaliative, retributive, punitive, recriminatory; like for like; rightly served.

Vb. *retaliate*, take reprisals 963 *punish*; counter, riposte 713 *parry*; pay one out, pay off old scores, be quits, get even with, get one's own back 910 *avenge*; requite, reward; teach one a lesson; return good for evil; reciprocate, return like for like; return the compliment, give as good as one gets, pay in his *or* her own coin; return, retort, cap 460 *answer*; recriminate 928 *accuse*; react, boomerang 280 *recoil*; round on, kick back 715 *resist*; turn the tables on, hoist with his *or* her own petard, make one laugh on the other side of his *or* her face, have the last laugh.

be rightly served, serve one right; find one's match, get one's deserts, get what was coming to one, get a dose of one's own medicine 963 *be punished*.

Int. take that! put that in your pipe and smoke it! the laugh's on you! now who's laughing!

715. Resistance – N. *resistance*, stand 704 *opposition*; intractability 602 *obstinacy*; reluctance 598 *unwillingness*; repugnance 861 *dislike*; objection, demur 468 *qualification*; recalcitrance, protest 762 *deprecation*; noncooperation, passive resistance, civil disobedience; rising, insurrection, resistance movement 738 *revolt*; self-defence 713 *defence*; repulse, rebuff, bloody nose 760 *refusal*.

Adj. *resisting*, standing firm against 704 *opposing*; protesting, reluctant 598 *unwilling*; recalcitrant, mutinous 738 *disobedient*; stubborn 602 *obstinate*; holding out, unyielding, indomitable, unsubdued 727 *unbeaten*; resistant, proof.

Vb. *resist*, offer resistance, stand against 704 *withstand*; obstruct 702 *hinder*; stand out against 711 *defy*; confront, outface 704 *oppose*; protest 762 *deprecate*; demur, object 468 *qualify*; mutiny, not take it lying down 738 *revolt*; make a stand, fight off 713 *parry*; make a fight of it 716 *contend*; not give way 599 *stand firm*; be proof against 760 *refuse*.

716. Contention – N.

contention, strife, tussle, conflict, clash, running battle 709 *dissension*; combat, fighting 718 *warfare*; debate, dispute, polemics, ink-slinging 475 *argument*; altercation, words 709 *quarrel*; stakes, bone of contention 709 *casus belli*; competition, rivalry, emulation 911 *jealousy*; competitiveness, gamesmanship, survival of the fittest, rat race; cut-throat competition, war to the knife; sports, athletics 837 *sport*.

contest, trial, trial of strength; pentathlon, decathlon, tug-of-war 682 *exertion*; tussle, struggle 671 *attempt*; bitter struggle, needle match; equal contest, ding-dong fight; close finish, photo f.; competition, open c., free-for-all; knockout competition, tournament; tourney, joust, tilt; prize competition, stakes, Ashes; match, test m.; concours, rally; event, handicap, run-off; heat, final, semifinal, quarter-final, Cup tie; set, game, rubber; sporting event 837 *sport*; field day 837 *amusement*; athletics, gymnastics; gymkhana, rodeo; games, Olympic G., Olympics.

racing, race, sprint, dash 277 *speeding*; road race, marathon, crosscountry; slalom, obstacle race; relay race; the Turf, horse racing, sport of kings; point-to-point, steeplechase, hurdles, sticks; dirt-track racing, stockcar r., speedway, motocross; cycle race, Tour de France; boat race, yacht r., regatta; racecourse, track, stadium 724 *arena*.

pugilism, self-defence, boxing, shadow b., sparring, fisticuffs; prize fighting, boxing match; clinch, in-fighting; round, bout; the ring, the fancy 837 *sport*.

wrestling, jujitsu, judo, karate, kung fu; all-in wrestling, catch-as-catch-can, no holds barred; catch, hold; wrestle, grapple, wrestling match.

duel, triangular d.; affair of honour; gladiatorial combat; jousting, tilting, tourney, tournament; fencing, swordplay, quarterstaff, kendo; hand-to-hand

fighting, close grips; bullfight, tauromachy; cockfight.

fight, hostilities 718 *warfare*; battle royal, free fight, free-for-all, rough and tumble, roughhouse, horse-play, shindy, scuffle, scrum, scrimmage, scramble, dogfight, mêlée, fracas, uproar 61 *turmoil*; gang warfare, street fight, riot, rumble; brawl 709 *quarrel*; punch-up, fisticuffs, blows; affray, set-to, tussle; running fight, dingdong f.; close grips, close quarters; combat, fray, clash 279 *collision*; encounter, dustup, scrap, brush; skirmishing; stand-up fight, shoot-out 718 *battle*; feat of arms 676 *deed*; campaign, struggle; fight to the death; Armageddon 724 *battleground*.

contender, fighter, gamecock; gladiator, bullfighter 722 *combatant*; prizefighter 722 *pugilist*; duellist 709 *quarreller*; fencer, swordsman; candidate, entrant, examinee; competitor, rival, emulator; challenger, runner-up, finalist; front runner, favourite, top seed; starter, also-ran, the field, all comers; contestant, pothunter; racer, runner, sprinter.

Adj. *contending*, struggling, etc. vb.; rival, competing; agonistic, sporting; athletic, palaestric, pugilistic, gladiatorial; contentious 709 *quarrelling*; combative 718 *warlike*; at loggerheads, at odds 718 *warring*; competitive, keen, cut-throat; hand-to-hand, close, at close quarters; close-run; well-fought, fought to the finish.

Vb. *contend*, combat, strive, struggle, battle, fight, tussle, wrestle, grapple 671 *attempt*; put up a fight 715 *resist*; argue for, insist 532 *emphasize*; contest, compete, challenge, stake, wager, bet; play, play against, match oneself, vie with, race; emulate, rival; take on, enter the lists, take up the challenge, pick up the gauntlet; couch one's lance, break a lance w.; take on, try a fall, try conclusions with 712 *strike at*.

fight, scuffle, scrimmage, scrap, set to 176 *be violent*; pitch into, sail i. 712 *attack*; lay about one 712 *strike at*; mix it, join in; square up to, come to blows, exchange b., box, spar, pummel 279 *strike*; join issue with 709 *quarrel*; duel, call out; have a brush with, skirmish; take on 718 *give battle*; come to grips, close with, grapple, lock horns; fence, cross swords, measure s.; appeal to arms 718 *go to war*; fight to the last man 599 *be resolute*.

717. Peace – N. *peace*, peacefulness, peace and quiet, a quiet life 266 *quiescence*; harmony 710 *concord*; universal peace, Pax Romana 730 *palmy days*; law and order 60 *order*; end of hostilities, demobilization 145 *cessation*; truce, armistice 145 *lull*; cold war, coexistence, armed neutrality; neutrality, noninvolvement, nonintervention 620 *avoidance*; peaceableness, nonaggression 177 *moderation*; cordial relations 880 *friendship*; pacifism, peace at any price, nonviolence; disarmament, peacemaking 719 *pacification*; pipe of peace, calumet; peace treaty, nonaggression pact 765 *treaty*; burial of the hatchet 506 *amnesty*.

pacifist, man *or* woman of peace, peacelover, peacemonger, dove; peace party 177 *moderator*; neutral, civilian, noncombatant, nonbelligerent; passive resister, conscientious objector, conchie; peacemaker 720 *mediator*.

Adj. *peaceful*, quiet 266 *tranquil*; without bloodshed, bloodless; harmless, dovelike 935 *innocent*; mild-mannered, easygoing 884 *amiable*; uncompetitive, uncontentious; peaceable, law-abiding, peaceloving, pacific, unwarlike, unaggressive, war-weary; pacifist, nonviolent; unarmed, noncombatant, civilian; unresisting 721 *submitting*; peacemaking 720 *mediatory*; without enemies, at peace; not at war, neutral; postwar, prewar, interwar; peacetime.

Vb. *be at peace*, observe neutrality, keep out of trouble; mean no harm, keep the peace; work for peace 720 *mediate*; beat swords into ploughshares, smoke the pipe of peace.

718. War – N. *war*, arms, the sword; appeal to arms, arbitrament of war; cold war, armed neutrality; paper war 709 *quarrel*; war of nerves 854 *intimidation*;

intervention, armed i.; real war, hot w.; civil war; holy war, crusade, jihad; limited war, localized w.; war on all fronts; world war, global w.; total war, blitzkrieg, atomic war, nuclear w., push-button war; war of attrition, war to the death, no holds barred; Armageddon; drums, bugle, trumpet; call to arms 547 *call*; battle cry, war whoop 711 *defiance*; Ares, Mars.

belligerency, state of war; resort to arms, declaration of war, outbreak of w., militancy, hostilities; call-up, mobilization; wartime, war footing.

bellicosity, war fever; pugnacity, combativeness, aggressiveness, hawkishness, militancy 709 *quarrelsomeness*; militarism, expansionism; jingoism 481 *prejudice*.

art of war, strategy 688 *tactics*; castrametation 713 *fortification*; generalship 694 *skill*; ballistics, gunnery, musketry; drill 534 *teaching*; staffwork, logistics 623 *plan*; manoeuvres.

warfare, war, warpath; bloodshed 176 *violence*; soldiering, active service; bombing 712 *bombardment*; besieging, blockading 235 *enclosure*; chemical warfare, germ w., atomic w., nuclear w., theatre nuclear w., tactical n. w.; blockade, attrition, scorched earth policy; bush-fighting, guerrilla warfare; campaign, expedition; operations, combined o.; incursion, invasion, raid; plan of campaign, battle orders 623 *plan*.

battle, pitched b., battle royal 716 *fight*; line of battle, order of b., array; line, firing l., front, battle f., battle station; action, scrap, skirmish, brush, collision, clash; offensive 712 *attack*; stand 713 *defence*; engagement, dogfight; battlefield, theatre of war 724 *battleground*.

Adj. *warring*, on the warpath; at war, in a state of w.; belligerent, militant, mobilized, under arms, on active service; sword in hand 669 *prepared*; arrayed, embattled; at loggerheads 709 *quarrelling*; on the offensive 712 *attacking*.

warlike, militaristic, bellicose, hawkish, unpacific; militant, aggressive, pugnacious, combative; war-loving, fierce, bloodthirsty 898 *cruel*; military, paramilitary, martial; veteran, battle-scarred; soldierly, soldierlike; military, naval; operational, strategic, tactical.

Vb. *go to war*, declare war, open hostilities; appeal to arms 716 *fight*; rise, rebel 738 *revolt*; raise one's banner, set up one's standard, call to arms; arm, militarize, mobilize, put on a war footing; call up, recruit, conscript; join up, enlist, enrol.

wage war, make w., go on the warpath, war against; campaign, take the field; go on active service, soldier; take the offensive 712 *attack*; keep the field 713 *defend*; manoeuvre, march, countermarch; blockade, beleaguer 230 *surround*; put to the sword 362 *slaughter*; ravage 165 *lay waste*; press the button 165 *demolish, be destroyed*.

give battle, offer b.; join battle, engage, combat, fight it out 716 *fight*; choose one's ground, dig in; rally, close the ranks, make a stand 715 *resist*; sound the charge 712 *charge*; open fire 712 *fire at*; skirmish 716 *contend*.

719. Pacification – N. *pacification*, peacemaking; conciliation, appeasement 177 *moderation*; reconciliation, reconcilement, rapprochement; accommodation 24 *agreement*; composition of differences 770 *compromise*; good offices 720 *mediation*; peace treaty, nonaggression pact 765 *treaty*; suspension of hostilities, cease-fire 145 *lull*; disarmament, demobilization, disbanding; nonproliferation; nuclear disarmament, nuclear-free zone.

peace offering, eirenicon, irenics 177 *moderator*; propitiation 736 *leniency*; olive branch, overture, hand of friendship 880 *friendliness*; flag of truce, white flag, pipe of peace 717 *peace*; blood money, compensation 787 *restitution*; amnesty, mercy 909 *forgiveness*.

Adj. *pacificatory*, conciliatory, placatory, propitiatory; irenic 880 *friendly*; disarming, soothing 177 *lenitive*; peacemaking, mediatory.

Vb. *pacify*, make peace; mollify 177 *assuage*; smooth one's ruffled feathers, pour balm into one's wounds 656 *cure*; hold out the olive branch, return a soft answer 880 *be friendly*; conciliate, propitiate, disarm, reconcile, placate, appease, satisfy 828 *content*; pour oil on troubled waters 266 *bring to rest*; win over 770 *compromise*; settle differences 24 *adjust*; bring together 720 *mediate*; keep the peace 717 *be at peace*.

make peace, stop fighting, cry quits, break it up 145 *cease*; bury the hatchet, forgive and forget 506 *forget*; shake hands, make it up, patch up a quarrel, come to an understanding, agree to differ; lay down one's arms, suspend hostilities; demilitarize, disarm, demobilize.

720. Mediation – N. *mediation*, good offices, intercession; umpirage, arbitration; intervention; statesmanship, diplomacy; parley, negotiation 584 *conference*.

mediator, go-between, negotiator 231 *intermediary*; arbitrator, umpire, referee 480 *estimator*; diplomat, diplomatist spokesperson 754 *delegate*; intercessor, pleader, propitiator 177 *moderator*; pacifier, troubleshooter, ombudsman; marriage guidance counsellor 691 *adviser*; peacemaker, dove.

Adj. *mediatory*, mediatorial, intercessory, intercessorial, propitiatory 719 *pacificatory*.

Vb. *mediate*, intervene, step in; intercede for, beg off, propitiate; bring together, negotiate; arbitrate, umpire 480 *judge*; compose differences 719 *pacify*.

721. Submission – N. *submission*, submissiveness 739 *obedience*; subservience 745 *servitude*; acquiescence, compliance 488 *assent*; peace at any price, line of least resistance, nonresistance, resignation, fatalism 679 *inactivity*; capitulation, surrender, unconditional s. 621 *relinquishment*; deference 872 *humility*; homage 739 *loyalty*; genuflexion, obeisance; defeatist, quitter; mouse, doormat 856 *coward*.

Adj. *submitting*, meek, unresisting; law-abiding 717 *peaceful*; submissive 739 *obedient*; fatalistic, resigned 488 *assenting*; pliant, malleable 327 *soft*; weak-kneed, supine, prostrate; on bended knees 872 *humble*.

Vb. *submit*, yield, give in; not resist, not insist, defer to; bow to, make a virtue of necessity, yield with a good grace, admit defeat 728 *be defeated*; resign oneself 488 *acquiesce*; not contest 679 *be inactive*; give up, cry quits, have had enough, throw up the sponge, throw in the towel, surrender, show the white flag, ask for terms; capitulate; give oneself up, throw down one's arms; haul down the flag, strike one's colours.

knuckle under, succumb, cave in, collapse; show no fight, take the line of least resistance, bow before the storm; be submissive 745 *be subject*; take one's medicine 963 *be punished*; eat humble pie 872 *be humble*; take it, take it lying down, pocket the insult, grin and bear it, stomach, put up with 825 *suffer*; bend, bow, kowtow, cringe, crawl 311 *stoop*; grovel, lick the boots of, kiss the rod; throw oneself at the feet of, beg for mercy.

722. Combatant. Army. Navy. Air Force –
N. *combatant*, fighter 716 *contender*; aggressor, assailant 712 *attacker*; stormtroops, shock troops; warrior, brave; bodyguard, strongarm man 713 *defender*; gunman 362 *killer*; bully, bravo 904 *ruffian*; swashbuckler, swaggerer 877 *boaster*; duellist, swordsman, fencer; gladiator, retiarius; fighting cock, gamecock; bullfighter, toreador, matador, picador; wrestler, judoist 716 *wrestling*; competitor 716 *contender*; champion 644 *exceller*; jouster, tilter; knight, knight-errant, paladin.

pugilist, boxer, bruiser, sparring partner; flyweight, bantamweight, featherweight, welterweight, middleweight, cruiserweight, heavyweight; slogger 716 *pugilism*.

militarist, jingoist, chauvinist, expansionist, militant, warmonger, hawk; crusader, Ghazi; Samurai, Mameluke; professional soldier, freelance, mercenary (**see** *soldier*); soldier of fortune, adventurer, condottiere; freebooter, marauder 789 *robber*.

soldier, regular; campaigner, old soldier, veteran, Chelsea pensioner; warrior, brave, myrmidon; man-at-arms, redcoat, legionary, centurion; vexillary, standardbearer, colour escort, colour sergeant, ensign, cornet; hoplite, peltast; sharpshooter, sniper, franc-tireur 287 *shooter*; auxiliary, Territorial, Home Guard, militiaman; yeoman; irregular, irregular troops, moss-trooper, kern, rapparee; raider, tip-and-run r.; guerrilla, partisan, freedom fighter, fedayeen; underground fighter, Maquis; picked troops 644 *elite*; guards, housecarls 660 *protector* (**see** *armed force*); effective, reservist; conscript, recruit, rookie; serviceman, Tommy, Tommy Atkins, GI, doughboy, Aussie, Anzac, poilu, sepoy, Gurkha, askari; female warrior, Amazon; battlemaid, Valkyrie; servicewoman, Wren.

soldiery, cannon fodder; the ranks, other r.; private, private soldier, man-at-arms; slinger, archer, bowman; pikeman, halberdier, lancer; musketeer, fusilier, rifleman, pistoleer, grenadier, bombardier, gunner, machine gunner, artilleryman; sapper, miner, engineer; signalman; corporal 741 *army officer*.

army, host; phalanx, legion; cohorts, big battalions; horde 104 *multitude*; general levy, arrière-ban; ·Home Guard; militia, yeomanry; regular army, Territorial A., draft; the services, armed forces, air arm, fleet air arm, fleet.

armed force, forces, troops, contingents, effectives, men, personnel; armament, armada; corps d'élite, ceremonial troops, guards, household cavalry; janissaries; picked troops, crack t., shock t., storm t.; spearhead, expeditionary force; parachute troops, paratroops, Commandos, task force, raiding party; combat troops, field army, line, front-line troops, first echelon; wing, van, vanguard, rear, rearguard; second echelon, base troops, reserves, reinforcements 707 *auxiliary*; base, staff; detachment, picket, party, detail; patrol, night patrol, night watch, sentry 660 *protector*; garrison, army of occupation.

formation, array, line; square, phalanx;

legion, cohort, century, decury, maniple; column, file, rank; unit, group, detachment, corps, division; brigade, artillery b., battery; regiment, squadron, troop; battalion, company, platoon, section, squad, detail, party 74 *band.*

infantry, foot regiment, infantryman, foot soldier, foot-slogger, PBI.

cavalry, sabres, horse; horseman, cameleer; mounted police, mounted infantry, horse artillery; cavalryman, yeoman; Ironsides, trooper; knight; lancer, hussar, cuirassier, dragoon; cossack; rough-rider; armoured car, armoured personnel carrier; tank, Panzer; charger 273 *warhorse.*

navy, sea power, Admiralty; fleet arm, armada; fleet, flotilla, squadron.

naval man, navy, senior service; Sea Lord 741 *naval officer*; sailor 270 *mariner*; bluejacket, man-o'-war man, able seaman, rating, pressed man; foretopman; powder monkey; cabin boy; marine, leatherneck, limey; submariner, naval airman.

warship, galleon 275 *ship*; raider, privateer, pirate ship; man-o'-war, ship of the line, armoured vessel, battleship, dreadnought; monitor, ironclad; cruiser, battle c.; frigate, corvette; mosquito boat, fast patrol b., PT b.; gunboat, motor torpedo boat, E-boat; destroyer; fire ship, blockship; minelayer, minesweeper; submarine, nuclear s., U-boat; Q-ship, mystery s.; aircraft carrier, fleet c.; landing craft, duck, amphibian; transport, troopship; tender, store ship, hospital s.; flagship.

air force, air arm, fleet air arm; squadron, flight, group, wing; warplane 276 *aircraft*; bomber, fighter b., fighter, interceptor, interdictor; flying boat, patrol plane; troop-carrier; Zeppelin 276 *airship*; airborne division; parachute troops, paratroopers; aircraftman *or* -woman, ground staff; fighter pilot, bomber p., navigator, observer, air crew.

723. Arms – N. *arms* (**see** *weapon*); armament, munitions; armaments, arms race; nuclear deterrent 713 *defence*; arms

traffic, gun-running; ballistics, rocketry, gunnery, musketry, archery.

arsenal, armoury, gun room, ammunition chest; arms depot 632 *storage*; magazine, powder keg; caisson, ammunition box; cartridge belt, bandolier; quiver; scabbard, sheath; holster 194 *receptacle.*

weapon, arm; armour 713 *defence*; conventional weapon, nuclear w., theatre n. w., tactical n. w. 718 *warfare*; secret weapon, death ray, laser; germ warfare, chemical w.; gas, mustard g., nerve g. 659 *poison*; teeth, claws 256 *sharp point.*

missile weapon, javelin, harpoon, dart; bolas, lasso; boomerang, throwstick; arrow, shaft, bolt, quarrel; arrowhead, barb; brickbat; slingstone, shot (**see** *ammunition*); whizzbang, rocket, MIRV; bow, longbow, crossbow, arbalest, ballista, catapult, mangonel, sling; blowpipe; bazooka, rocket-thrower (**see** *gun*); cruise missile, guided m., ballistic m., ICBM, intercontinental ballistic missile, surface-to-air m. 287 *missile*; antimissile missile, ABM.

club, mace, knobkerrie 279 *hammer*; battering ram 279 *ram*; staff, stave, stick, switch, lathi, quarterstaff; life-preserver, bludgeon, truncheon, cudgel, shillelagh, blackjack, sandbag, knuckle-duster, cosh, bicycle chain.

spear, harpoon, gaff; lance, javelin, pike, assegai; partisan, bill, halberd 256 *sharp point.*

axe, battleaxe, tomahawk, hatchet, halberd, bill; poleaxe, chopper 256 *sharp edge.*

sidearms, sword; steel, cold steel, naked s.; broadsword, glaive, claymore; cutlass, sabre, scimitar, falchion, snickersnee; blade, bilbo, Toledo; rapier, foil; dagger, bayonet, dirk, poniard, stiletto 256 *sharp point*; machete, kukri, kris, panga; knife, bowie k., flick k., switchblade 256 *sharp edge.*

firearm, small arms, hand gun, arquebus, hackbut; matchlock, wheel-lock, flintlock, fusil, musket; blunderbuss, muzzleloader, smoothbore, carbine; breechloader, needlegun; rifle, magazine r., repeating r.; fowling piece, shotgun, sawn-off s.; bore, calibre; muzzle; trigger, lock; magazine; breech, butt, gunstock; sight, backsight; ramrod.

pistol, duelling p., horse p.; petronel, pistolet; six-shooter, revolver, repeater, gat, shooting iron, automatic.

gun, guns, ordnance, cannonry, artillery; battery, broadside; artillery park, gun p.; cannon, culverin; mortar; piece, field piece, field gun, siege g.; heavy metal; howitzer, trench-mortar, minethrower; antiaircraft gun, ack-ack, Bofors gun, bazooka; Gatling g., mitrailleuse, pom-pom, machine gun, M 60 machine g., submachine g., tommy g.; flamethrower; guncarriage, limber, caisson; gun emplacement, launching pad, silo.

ammunition, live a.; powder and shot; shot, buckshot; ball, cannonball, bullet, expanding b., soft-nosed b., dumdum b.; projectile 287 *missile*; slug, pellet; shell, shrapnel; flak, ack-ack; cartridge, cartridge belt.

explosive, propellant; powder, gunpowder; saltpetre, cordite, gun cotton, dynamite, gelignite, TNT, nitroglycerine; cap, detonator, fuse; priming, charge, warhead, atomic w.

bomb, shell, bombshell; grenade, hand g., pineapple, Molotov cocktail; atom bomb, A-bomb, nuclear b., hydrogen b., H-bomb; neutron b., enhanced radiation b.; mushroom cloud, fallout; blockbuster; cluster bomb, fragmentation b.; firebomb, incendiary bomb, napalm b.; Greek fire; mine, landmine; limpet; depth charge, torpedo, tin fish; flying bomb, V-1, doodlebug, V-2; rocket bomb; time bomb, infernal machine.

724. Arena – N. *arena*, field, field of action; ground, terrain; centre, scene, stage, theatre; hustings, platform, floor; amphitheatre, coliseum, stadium, stand, grandstand; campus, parade ground; forum, marketplace 76 *focus*; hippodrome, circus, course, racecourse; track, running t.; cinder t., dog t.; ring, bullring, boxing r.; ropes; rink, ice r.; palaestra, gymnasium, gym; range, rifle r., butts; playground 837 *pleasure ground*; playing field, football f.,

pitch, cricket p.; court, tennis c.; badminton c., squash c.; putting green, bowling g., bowling alley, skittle a.; lists, tiltyard; cockpit, beargarden; chessboard.

battleground, battlefield, field of battle; field of blood, Aceldama; theatre of war, combat zone, no-go area; front, front line, trenches, no-man's-land; sector, salient, bulge, pocket; beachhead, bridgehead; disputed territory 718 *battle*.

Section 5: Results of action

725. Completion – N. *completion*, conclusion, end of the matter 69 *end*; issue, upshot, result, end r. 157 *effect*; fullness 54 *completeness*; fulfilment 635 *sufficiency*; maturity, fruition, readiness 669 *preparedness*; consummation, culmination 646 *perfection*; rounding off, finishing off, mopping up, winding up; topping out; top, crown 213 *summit*; missing link; last touch, last stroke, crowning s., final s., finishing s., coup de grâce, clincher; achievement, fait accompli; finished product; climax, payoff; resolution, solution, denouement 69 *finality*.

effectuation, execution, discharge, implementation; dispatch, performance 676 *action*; accomplishment, achievement, realization 727 *success*; elaboration, working out.

Adj. *completive*, crowning, culminating 213 *topmost*; conclusive, final 69 *ending*; thorough, thoroughgoing 599 *resolute*.

completed, full, full-blown 54 *complete*; done, achieved, etc. vb.; highly wrought 646 *perfect*; sewn up, buttoned up, in the can, under one's belt, secured 727 *successful*.

Vb. *carry through*, follow t., drive home, clinch, seal, set the seal on; clear up, mop up, wipe up, finish off, polish off; dispose of, give the coup de grâce; complete, consummate, put the finishing touch 54 *make complete*; hammer out 646 *perfect*; ripen 669 *mature*; see out, see it through; get shot of, dispose of, wrap up 69 *terminate*.

carry out, see through, effect, enact 676

do; dispatch, execute, discharge, implement, effectuate, realize, accomplish, fulfil, achieve 727 *succeed*; make short work of; do thoroughly, not do by halves, go the whole hog; deliver the goods, bring home the bacon, be as good as one's word.

climax, cap 213 *crown*; culminate, reach its peak; scale the heights; reach boiling point, come to a head; touch bottom; put the lid on, add the last straw; touch one's goal 295 *arrive*.

726. Noncompletion – N. *noncompletion*, no success 728 *failure*; nonexecution 458 *negligence*; nonfulfilment 636 *insufficiency*; deficiency 307 *shortfall*; lack 55 *incompleteness*; unripeness, immaturity 670 *undevelopment*; never-ending task, painting the Forth Bridge, Penelope's web, Sisyphean labour 71 *continuity*; a lick and a promise 456 *inattention*; job half-done, loose ends; drawn game; stalemate, deadlock.

Adj. *uncompleted*, partial, fragmentary 55 *incomplete*; unachieved, unaccomplished; half-finished 458 *neglected*; half-baked, unripe 670 *immature*; perfunctory, superficial; left hanging, left in the air; not worked out, inchoate, sketchy 647 *imperfect*; never-ending 71 *continuous*.

Vb. *not complete*, leave undone 458 *neglect*; skip, scamp, do by halves 636 *not suffice*; scotch the snake not kill it; give up, not follow up *or* through; fall out, drop o., not stay the course; fall short 728 *fail*; defer 136 *put off*.

727. Success – N. *success*, sweet smell of s.; glory 866 *famousness*; happy ending, favourable issue; success story, progress, steady advance 285 *progression*; breakthrough; good fortune 730 *prosperity*; lead, first blood 34 *advantage*; flash in the pan; exploit, feat, achievement 676 *deed*; accomplishment 725 *completion*; feather in one's cap, triumph, hit; beginner's luck 618 *nondesign*; hat trick, stroke of genius, masterstroke; trump card, winning c. 34 *superiority*.

victory, infliction of defeat 728 *defeat*; conquest 745 *subjection*; taking by storm

712 *attack*; the best of it; win, game and match; checkmate; Pyrrhic victory; walkover, pushover 701 *easy thing*; slam, grand s.; kill, knockout, KO; mastery, ascendancy, upper hand, whip h. 34 *advantage*; triumph 876 *celebration*.

victor, winner, champion, top dog, medallist, prizewinner, first, double f. 644 *exceller*; winning side, the winners; conquering hero, conqueror, conquistador; master, mistress, master *or* mistress of the field; self-made man *or* woman, rising star 730 *prosperous person*.

Adj. *successful*, effective, efficacious; sovereign 658 *remedial*; well-spent, fruitful 640 *profitable*; happy, lucky; felicitous, masterly 694 *skilful*; unbeatable (**see** *unbeaten*); never-failing, surefire, foolproof; unerring, infallible 473 *certain*; home and dry 725 *completed*; prizewinning, victorious, world-beating 644 *excellent*; winning, one up 34 *superior*; on top, in the ascendant, on the up and up, going places 730 *prosperous*; triumphant, crowning; triumphal, victorious; crowned with success, flushed with victory; glorious 866 *renowned*.

unbeaten, undefeated, unbowed, unvanquished 599 *resolute*; unbeatable, unconquerable, invincible.

Vb. *succeed*, succeed in, effect, accomplish, achieve, compass 725 *carry through*; be successful, make out, win one's spurs; make a success *or* a go of; make good, rise, do well, come to the top 730 *prosper*; pass, make the grade, qualify, graduate, give a good account of oneself, come well out of it, come off with flying colours, come out on top, have the best of it 34 *be superior*; break through 285 *progress*; gain one's end, secure one's object, attain one's purpose; pull it off, bring it off; score a success, make the big time, make a hit, go over big; hit the jackpot; arrive, make one's mark, click.

be successful, come off; answer the purpose, do the trick; turn up trumps, rise to the occasion, do oneself proud; do wonders, do marvels; work, work like magic, act like a charm 173 *operate*; tell 178 *influence*; pay off, bear fruit; get it, hit the nail on the head; not put a foot wrong; have the ball at one's feet, hold all the trumps; brush obstacles aside 701 *do easily*; hold one's own 599 *stand firm*.

triumph, have one's day, be crowned with success 876 *celebrate*; crow 877 *boast*; score off, be one up on; make it, win through; surmount, overcome; reap the fruits 771 *gain*.

overmaster, be too much for 34 *be superior*; master, overcome, overpower, override 306 *outdo*; have the advantage, prevail 34 *predominate*; have one on the hip *or* by the short hairs; checkmate, trump, ruff; conquer, vanquish, crush 745 *subjugate*; capture, carry, take 712 *attack*.

defeat, discomfit, put another's nose out of joint; repulse 292 *repel*; best, be too good for, get the better of 34 *be superior*; worst, outplay, outpoint, outshine 306 *outdo*; cut the ground from under one's feet, lay by the heels; baffle, nonplus 474 *puzzle*; knock spots off, wipe the floor with; beat, lick, thrash, whip, trounce, overwhelm, crush, trample on; beat hollow; rout 75 *disperse*; silence, put hors de combat 165 *suppress*; flatten, put out for the count, knock out; knock for six; bowl out, skittle o.; put an end to, wipe out, do for, settle, fix, dish 165 *destroy*.

win, carry the day, be victorious, claim the victory; come off best, win hands down, sweep all before one, have it all one's own way, romp home, walk *or* waltz away with 701 *do easily*; win on points, scrape home; take the prize *or* the cup, gain the palm, wear the crown; beat all comers, rule OK 34 *be superior*.

Adv. *successfully*, to some purpose, to good effect; with flying colours, in triumph.

728. Failure – N. *failure*, nonsuccess, negative result; no luck 731 *misfortune*; nonfulfilment 726 *noncompletion*; frustration 702 *hindrance*; ineffectiveness 161 *ineffectuality*; vain attempt 641 *lost labour*; mess, muddle 695 *bungling*; miscarriage 172 *unproductiveness*; damp squib, washout, fiasco, flop, non-event; no ball, misfire 495 *mistake*; no go, dead stop, halt;

fault, breakdown 702 *hitch*; collapse, incapacity; anticlimax 509 *disappointment*; losses, bankruptcy 805 *insolvency*.

defeat, bafflement; nonplus, deadlock 145 *stop*; lost battle, repulse, rebuff, bloody nose, check, reverse; checkmate; the worst of it, discomfiture, beating, drubbing, hiding, licking, thrashing, trouncing; retreat; stampede, rout, landslide; fall, downfall, collapse, debacle; perdition 165 *ruin*; lost cause, losing battle; deathblow, quietus; Waterloo; conquest, subjugation 745 *subjection*.

loser, also-ran, non-starter; has-been, extinct volcano; dud, failure, flop, lemon 697 *bungler*; victim 544 *dupe*; born loser 731 *unlucky person*; underdog 35 *inferior*; dropout 25 *misfit*; bankrupt 805 *nonpayer*; losing side, the vanquished.

Adj. *unsuccessful*, ineffective; inglorious, unrewarded, empty-handed; unlucky 731 *unfortunate*; vain, bootless, negative, fruitless, profitless; dud, hanging fire, miscarried, stillborn, aborted, abortive, premature; manqué, failed, ploughed; unplaced; out of one's depth 474 *uncertain*.

defeated, beaten, bested, worsted, pipped, dished, done for; baffled, thwarted, foiled 702 *hindered*; disconcerted, dashed, discomfited, hoist with one's own petard; outmanoeuvred, outmatched, outplayed, outvoted; outclassed 35 *inferior*; thrashed, licked; unplaced, out of the running; routed, put to flight; swamped, overwhelmed, sunk; overborne, overthrown, struck down, knocked out, brought low.

grounded, stranded, wrecked, washed up, left high and dry; on the rocks, on one's beam-ends 165 *destroyed*; unhorsed, dismounted, thrown; ruined 700 *in difficulties*.

Vb. *fail*, not succeed, have no success, get no results; fall down on, bungle 495 *blunder*; flunk, not make the grade 636 *not suffice*; fail one, let one down 509 *disappoint*; miss the boat 138 *lose a chance*; go wide, miss, fall between two stools 282 *deviate*; get nothing out of it, draw a blank, back the wrong horse, return empty-handed, lose one's pains 641 *waste effort*; kiss goodbye to 772 *lose*; overreach

323

oneself, come a cropper 309 *tumble*; break down, malfunction, come to pieces *or* unstuck; falter, stall, seize up, crock up, pack up, conk out; come to a dead stop, come up against a blank wall; get bogged down, come to a sticky end 655 *deteriorate*; go on the rocks 313 *founder*; crash, bust 805 *not pay*.

miscarry, be stillborn, abort; misfire, hang fire, fizzle out; not come off, come to nothing 641 *be useless*; fail to succeed, fall flat; come to grief; burst, bust, explode, blow up, go up in smoke; flop; go wrong, go awry, gang agley, take a turn for the worse; do no good 832 *aggravate*; dash one's hopes 509 *disappoint*.

be defeated, lose, lose out, suffer defeat, take a beating, lose the day; just miss, get pipped at the post; get the worst of it, come off second best, go off with one's tail between one's legs, lick one's wounds; lose hands down; take the count, bite the dust; fall, succumb 745 *be subject*; lose ground 290 *recede*; admit defeat 721 *submit*; go to the wall 165 *be destroyed*.

729. Trophy – N. *trophy*, spoils 790 *booty*; scalp, head; triumphal arch 548 *monument*; triumph, ovation 876 *celebration*; plum, glittering prizes; benefit, benefit match; prize 962 *reward*; sports trophy, Ashes, cup, pot, plate, shield; award, Oscar; bays, laurels, crown, coronal, chaplet, garland, wreath, palm of victory; epinician ode, pat on the back; feather in one's cap 547 *badge*; glory 866 *repute*.

decoration, honour 870 *title*; battle honours, spurs 866 *honours*; citation, mention in dispatches; rosette, ribbon, sash; blue, oar; medal, gong, star, cross, garter, order; service stripe, long-service medal, war m., campaign m.; Victoria Cross, VC.

730. Prosperity – N. *prosperity*, thriving, health and wealth 727 *success*; well-being, welfare, weal 824 *happiness*; booming economy, boom; roaring trade, seller's market; affluence, Easy Street 800 *wealth*; golden touch, Midas t.; fleshpots, fat of the land, milk and honey 635 *plenty*; favour, smiles of fortune, good f. 615

good; bonanza, winning streak, luck 159 *chance*; honour and glory, renown 866 *prestige*.

palmy days, heyday, prime, floruit; halcyon days, summer, sunshine; Indian summer, Edwardian s.; piping times 717 *peace*; life of Riley, place in the sun, bed of roses 376 *euphoria*; golden times, Golden Age, Saturnia Regna 824 *happiness*.

prosperous person, man *or* woman of property 800 *rich person*; successful person, rising man *or* woman; favourite of the gods, child of fortune, lucky dog; arriviste, upstart, parvenu, nouveau riche; celebrity, hero 866 *person of repute*.

Adj. *prosperous*, thriving, flourishing, booming 727 *successful*; doing well, up and coming, on the up and up; on the make, profiteering; well set-up, established, well-to-do, well-off, comfortably off 800 *moneyed*; riding high, riding on the crest of a wave, buoyant; fortunate, lucky, born with a silver spoon in one's mouth, born under a lucky star; in clover, on velvet; at ease 824 *happy*; fat, sleek, euphoric.

palmy, balmy, halcyon, golden, couleur de rose, rosy; blissful, blessed; favourable, promising, auspicious, propitious, cloudless, clear, fine, fair, set f.; euphoric 376 *comfortable*.

Vb. *prosper*, thrive, flourish, have one's day; do well, have a good time of it 376 *enjoy*; bask in, make hay, live in clover, have it easy, have it made, live off the fat of the land, 'never have had it so good'; batten on, grow fat 301 *eat*; blossom, bloom, flower 171 *be fruitful*; win glory 866 *have a reputation*; drive a roaring trade; profiteer 771 *gain*; get on, go far, rise in the world, arrive 727 *succeed*; make a fortune, strike it rich 800 *get rich*; run on oiled wheels 258 *go smoothly*; keep afloat, keep one's head above water, not do badly.

have luck, have all the l., have a stroke of luck *or* a lucky break, have a run of luck; strike lucky, strike oil; be on to a good thing, get on the gravy train; fall on one's feet, bear a charmed life; have the ball at one's feet.

be auspicious, promise well, augur well; favour, prosper, profit 615 *benefit*; look kindly on, smile on, bless; turn out well, take a good turn, take a favourable t. 644 *do good*.

Adv. *prosperously*, swimmingly 727 *successfully*; beyond one's wildest dreams; in luck's way.

Int. good luck! all the best! best of British!

731. Adversity – N. *adversity*, misfortune, mixed blessing; struggle 700 *difficulty*; hardship, hard life, no bed of roses 825 *suffering*; bad times, hard t., iron age, ice a., hell on earth 616 *evil*; burden, load, pressure; ups and downs of life 154 *event*; troubles, sea of t. 825 *worry*; wretchedness, misery 834 *dejection*; bitter cup, bitter pill 872 *humiliation*; cross 825 *sorrow*; curse, blight, scourge 659 *bane*; bleakness, chill; ill wind, cross w.; blow, setback, reverse 728 *defeat*; plight, funeral 700 *predicament*; poor lookout; trough, bad patch 655 *deterioration*; slump, recession, depression 679 *inactivity*; gathering clouds 900 *threat*; downfall 165 *ruin*; want, need 801 *poverty*.

misfortune, bad fortune, ill f.; bad luck, hard luck; no luck, evil star 645 *badness*; raw deal, rotten hand; hard lot, hard fate, hard lines; ill hap, mishap 159 *chance*; disaster, calamity, catastrophe, the worst.

unlucky person, poor unfortunate, poor risk; star-crossed lover, sport of fortune, plaything of fate, Jonah; down-and-out 728 *loser*; underdog 35 *inferior*; lame dog 163 *weakling*; wretch, poor w. 825 *sufferer*; scapegoat, victim 544 *dupe*.

Adj. *adverse*, hostile, frowning, ominous, sinister, inauspicious, unfavourable; bleak, cold, hard; opposed, cross 704 *opposing*; malign 645 *harmful*; dire, ruinous 165 *destructive*; disastrous, calamitous, catastrophic; too bad 645 *bad*.

unprosperous, inglorious 728 *unsuccessful*; unwell, in poor shape; in low

water, badly off 801 *poor*; in trouble, up against it 700 *in difficulties*; on the wane, on the down grade 655 *deteriorated*; in the wars, in a bad way, in an evil plight, in dire straits, in extremities.

unfortunate, ill-fated, unlucky, ill-starred, star-crossed, blasted; unblest, luckless, hapless, poor, wretched, miserable, unhappy; stricken, doomed, accursed; out of luck, down on one's luck; out of favour, under a cloud 924 *disapproved*; born under an evil star; accident-prone.

Vb. *have trouble*, be born to t.; be one's own worst enemy, stew in one's own juice; be the victim of fate, have no luck, get more kicks than ha'pence; be hard pressed, be up against it, fall foul of 700 *be in difficulty*; strike a bad patch 825 *suffer*; come to grief 728 *miscarry*; feel the pinch, fall on evil days 801 *be poor*; go downhill, go down in the world 655 *deteriorate*; go to rack and ruin, go to the dogs 165 *be destroyed*.

732. Averageness – N. *averageness*, mediocrity 30 *average*; common lot, average circumstances; enough to get by; plain living, no excess 177 *moderation*; respectability, bourgeoisie 869 *middle classes*; Main Street, suburbia, subtopia, villadom; man *or* woman in the street 869 *commoner*.

Adj. *middling*, average, mediocre; neither good nor bad, betwixt and between; ordinary, commonplace 30 *median*; common, representative 83 *typical*; nonextreme 177 *moderate*; decent 874 *modest*; undistinguished, inglorious, nothing to boast of; minor, second-rate 35 *inferior*; fair, fair to middling; so-so, all right, OK, adequate; unobjectionable, tolerable, passable; colourless, grey 625 *neutral*.

Vb. *be middling*, etc. adj.; pass muster 635 *suffice*; jog on, manage well enough; never set the Thames on fire; leave something to be desired 647 *be imperfect*.

5.2 SOCIAL VOLITION

Section 1:
General social volition

733. Authority – N. *authority*, power; powers that be, 'they', the Establishment, ruling classes 741 *master*; the Government 690 *director*; right, divine r., prerogative, royal p.; dynasticism, legitimacy; law, lawful authority 953 *legality*; legislative assembly 692 *parliament*; delegated authority 751 *commission*; portfolio 955 *jurisdiction*; power behind the throne 178 *influence*; indirect authority, patronage, prestige, credit; leadership, hegemony 689 *directorship*; ascendancy, supremacy 34 *superiority*; seniority, priority 64 *precedence*; majesty, royalty, crown 868 *nobility*; succession, legitimate s., accession; seizure of power, usurpation.

governance, rule, sway; reins of government, direction, command 689 *directorship*; control, supreme c.; hold, grip, clutches 778 *retention*; domination, mastery, whip hand, reach, long arm; dominion, condominium, sovereignty, suzerainty, raj, overlordship 34 *superiority*; reign, regency, dynasty; foreign rule, heteronomy, empery, empire, rod of e. 745 *subjection*; imperialism, colonialism, neocolonialism; white supremacy, black power; regime; state control, statism, dirigisme; bureaucracy, apparat, civil service, officialism, bumbledom, red tape.

despotism, benevolent d., paternalism; one-man rule, monocracy, tyranny; dictatorship, tsarism, Stalinism; absolutism, autocracy, autarchy, absolute monarchy; dictatorship of the proletariat; totalitarianism; police state, rule of terror 735 *brute force*.

government, direction 689 *management*; state system, polity; politics, politicking; constitutional government, rule of law 953 *legality*; misgovernment 734 *anarchy*; theocracy 985 *ecclesiasticism*; monarchy, kingship; republicanism, federalism; tribalism; patriarchy, matriarchate; feudalism; benevolent despotism, paternalism; squirearchy, aristocracy, meritocracy, oligarchy, minority rule, elitism; gynarchy, gynocracy 373 *womankind*; gerontocracy, senatorial government; duumvirate, triumvirate; plutocracy; representative government, parliamentary g., party system 708 *political party*, 605 *vote*; democracy, egalitarianism, government of the people, by the people, for the people; demagogy, demagoguery, vox populi; majority rule, one man one vote; isocracy, pantisocracy; collectivism, proletarianism; communism, Marxism-Leninism, party rule, Bolshevism, Fascism, National Socialism; committee rule, sovietism; stratocracy, military government, martial law; mobocracy, mob rule; syndicalism, socialism, Fabianism, statism; bureaucracy, technocracy; self-government, autonomy, home rule 744 *independence*; puppet government, caretaker g., regency; sphere of influence, mandate.

position of authority, post, place, office, high o.; kingship, kinghood, tsardom, royalty, regality; regency, regentship; protectorship; rulership, chieftainship, sheikhdom, emirate, principate, lordship, seigniory; rajahship, sultanate, caliphate, governorship, viceroyalty; satrapy, ethnarchy; consulate, consulship, proconsulate, prefecture, tribunate, aedileship; magistrature, magistracy; mayoralty, aldermanship; headship, presidency, premiership 689 *directorship*; overlordship, superintendency, inspectorship; masterdom, mastership; government post, Cabinet seat.

political organization, body politic; state, nation s., commonwealth; country, realm, kingdom, republic, city state; temple state; federation, confederation; principality, duchy, archduchy, dukedom, palatinate; empire, dominion, colony, dependency, protectorate, mandate 184 *territory*; free world, Communist bloc, Third World 184 *region*; superpower;

province, county 184 *district*; corporative state, welfare s.; laws, constitution.

Adj. *authoritative*, empowered, competent; in office, in authority, magisterial, official, ex officio; mandatory 740 *compelling*; magistral, masterful, domineering; commanding, lordly, dignified, majestic; imperious, bossy; absolute, autocratic, dictatorial, totalitarian 735 *authoritarian*; powerful, puissant 162 *strong*; hegemonic, leading 178 *influential*; dominant, paramount 34 *supreme*.

ruling, reigning, regnant; sovereign, on the throne; royal, regal, majestic, kinglike, kingly, queenly, princely, lordly; dynastic; imperial.

governmental, gubernatorial, political, constitutional; administrative, ministerial, official, bureaucratic, centralized; technocratic; matriarchal, patriarchal; monarchical, feudal, aristocratic, oligarchic, plutocratic, democratic, popular, republican; self-governing, autonomous, autarchic 744 *independent*.

Vb. *rule*, hold sway, reign, reign supreme, sit on the throne, wear the crown; govern, control 737 *command*; hold the reins, hold office 689 *direct*; be in power, have authority; tyrannize 735 *oppress*; dictate, lay down the law; legislate for; keep order, police.

dominate, preponderate, hold all the aces 34 *predominate*; lord it over, boss, rule the roost, wear the trousers 737 *command*; have the mastery, call the tune 727 *overmaster*; have in one's power, have over a barrel; lead by the nose, twist round one's little finger, have under one's thumb, hold in the palm of one's hand 178 *influence*; drill, drive 735 *be severe*; dictate 740 *compel*; hold down 745 *subjugate*; override, overrule, overawe; have it all one's own way.

734. Laxity: absence of authority – N. *laxity*, slackness, indifference 458 *negligence*; laissez faire 744 *scope*; informality, lack of ceremony 769 *nonobservance*; loosening, relaxation 746 *liberation*; decentralization 46 *disunion*; connivance 756 *permission*; licence, overindulgence,

permissiveness 736 *leniency*; weak will, feeble grasp 163 *weakness*; no control, noninterference, abdication of authority 753 *resignation*; concession 770 *compromise*.

anarchy, breakdown of law and order, no authority, free-for-all, disorganization, chaos 61 *turmoil*; licence, insubordination, indiscipline 738 *disobedience*; anarchism, nihilism; interregnum, power vacuum; misrule, misgovernment; mob law, lynch l. 954 *lawlessness*; defiance of authority, usurpation 916 *arrogation*.

Adj. *lax*, loose, slack; devolved, decentralized; disorganized 61 *orderless*; feeble, soft 163 *weak*; slipshod 458 *negligent*; uncaring 860 *indifferent*; relaxed, unstrict, informal, not standing on ceremony; free-and-easy 744 *unconfined*; permissive, tolerant, undemanding, overindulgent 736 *lenient*; weak-willed 601 *irresolute*; unassertive, unmasterful, lacking authority.

anarchic, ungoverned, uncontrolled, unbridled; insubordinate, rebellious 738 *disobedient*; disorderly, unruly 738 *riotous*; unauthorized 954 *illegal*; lawless, anarchistic 769 *nonobservant*.

Vb. *be lax*, not enforce; hold a loose rein 744 *give scope*; waive the rules, stretch a point, connive at; tolerate, suffer; laisser aller 677 *not act*; let one get away with, not say boo to a goose; spoonfeed, indulge, spoil 736 *be lenient*; make concessions 770 *compromise*; lose control, renounce authority; misrule, misgovern, mismanage, reduce to chaos 63 *derange*.

please oneself, be a law unto oneself, defy authority 738 *disobey*; take on oneself, act without authority 916 *be undue*.

735. Severity – N. *severity*, strictness, stringency; formalism; high standards 862 *fastidiousness*; rigidity, inflexibility 326 *hardness*; discipline, firm control, strong hand, tight grasp 733 *authority*; rod of iron, heavy hand, Draconian laws; harshness, rigour, extremes; no concession, letter of the law, pound of flesh; intolerance, rigorism 602 *opinionatedness*; puritanism 950 *prudery*; infliction, visitation, inquisition, persecution, exploitation, harassment, oppression, Rachmanism; victimization, callousness, inclemency 906 *pitilessness*; harsh treatment, tender mercies, cruelty 898 *inhumanity*.

brute force, naked f.; big battalions, gunboat diplomacy 160 *power*; coercion 740 *compulsion*; bloodiness 176 *violence*; subjugation 745 *subjection*; absolutism, dictatorship 733 *despotism*; tyranny, liberticide; Fascism, Nazism; totalitarianism; militarism; martial law, iron rule, iron hand, mailed fist, jackboot.

tyrant, rigorist, stickler; petty tyrant, Jack-in-office; disciplinarian, martinet; militarist; hanging judge; heavy father, Dutch uncle; Big Brother, authoritarian, despot, dictator 741 *autocrat*; boss, commissar, gauleiter; inquisitor, persecutor; oppressor, bully, hard master, taskmaster, slave-driver; extortioner, bloodsucker, tax-gatherer; predator, harpy; vulture; ogre 938 *monster*; hardliner.

Adj. *severe*, Spartan 945 *ascetic*; strict, rigorous, extreme; strait-laced, puritanical; formalistic, pedantic; bigoted, fanatical; hypercritical 862 *fastidious*; intolerant, censorious 924 *disapproving*; unbending, rigid 326 *hard*; hard as nails, hard-headed, hard-boiled, flinty, dour; obdurate 602 *obstinate*; inexorable, relentless, implacable 906 *pitiless*; heavy, stern, stiff; punitive; stringent, Draconian, drastic, savage.

authoritarian, masterful, domineering, lordly, arrogant, haughty 878 *insolent*; despotic, absolute, arbitrary; totalitarian, fascist; dictatorial, autocratic; undemocratic; coercive 740 *compelling*; fussy, bossy.

oppressive, hard on 914 *unjust*; tyrannical, despotic; tyrannous, harsh; grinding, withering, exigent, exacting; exploitive, predatory; persecuting, inquisitorial; high-handed, overbearing, domineering; heavy-handed, ungentle 176 *violent*; brutal 898 *cruel*.

Vb. *be severe*, etc. adj.; stand no nonsense, be cruel to be kind; exert authority, put one's foot down, discipline; bear hard on, keep a tight rein on 747 *restrain*; be down on, come down like a ton of bricks,

crack down on, stamp on, put a stop to 165 *suppress*; persecute 619 *pursue*; ill-treat 675 *misuse*; get tough with, pull no punches; visit with 963 *punish*; exact reprisals 714 *retaliate*; harden one's heart, give no quarter 906 *be pitiless*.

oppress, tyrannize, abuse one's authority 734 *please oneself*; domineer, lord it; terrorize 854 *frighten*; bludgeon 740 *compel*; shove around, boss a., put upon; bully, bait 827 *torment*; persecute, victimize 898 *be malevolent*; task, tax, drive 684 *fatigue*; exploit, extort, squeeze, grind the faces of the poor; trample, tread underfoot, hold down 165 *suppress*; enslave 745 *subjugate*; ride roughshod, injure 914 *do wrong*; rule with a rod of iron; burden, crush.

736. Leniency – N. *leniency*, softness 734 *laxity*; mildness, gentleness, forbearance, soft answer 823 *patience*; pardon 909 *forgiveness*; quarter, lenity, clemency 905 *pity*; indulgence, toleration; sufferance, allowance; justice with mercy 177 *moderation*; light rein, light hand, velvet glove, kid gloves; wet, liberal, soggy l.

Adj. *lenient*, soft, gentle, mild; indulgent, tolerant, easy, easy-going, undemanding 734 *lax*; forbearing, longsuffering 823 *patient*; clement 909 *forgiving*; tender 905 *pitying*.

Vb. *be lenient*, show consideration; deal gently, go easy, pull one's punches 177 *moderate*; indulge, humour; tolerate, allow 756 *permit*; stretch a point 734 *be lax*; not press, refrain, forbear 823 *be patient*; pity, spare, give quarter 905 *show mercy*; pardon 909 *forgive*; relax, humanize 897 *be benevolent*.

737. Command – N. *command*, summons; commandment, ordinance; injunction, imposition; dictation, bidding, behest, will and pleasure; say-so; charge 751 *mandate*; instructions, regulations; directive, order; word of command, word; beck, nod 547 *gesture*, 547 *call*; whip, three-line w.; dictate 740 *compulsion*; negative command, taboo, ban 757 *prohibition*; countermand, counterorder.

decree, edict, fiat, ukase, ipse dixit; law, canon, rescript 693 *precept*; bull, papal decree, decretal; circular, encyclical; ordinance, order in council; decision 480 *judgement*; act 953 *legislation*; electoral mandate 605 *vote*; dictate, diktat, dictation.

demand, claim, revendication 915 *dueness*; requisition 761 *request*; notice, final n., final demand, ultimatum; blackmail 900 *threat*; imposition 809 *tax*.

warrant, search w., commission, brevet, authorization, written authority, letters patent, passport 756 *permit*; writ, summons, subpoena 959 *legal process*.

Adj. *commanding*, imperative, categorical, dictatorial; jussive, mandatory, obligatory, peremptory, compulsive 740 *compelling*; decretory, decretal 733 *authoritative*.

Vb. *command*, bid, invite; order, tell, give an order; call, nod, beck, motion 547 *gesticulate*; direct, give a directive, send round instructions; rule, lay down, enjoin; charge, call upon 751 *commission*; impose, lay upon 917 *impose a duty*; detail, tell off; send for, summon; subpoena 959 *litigate*; dictate 740 *compel*; countermand 752 *abrogate*; lay an embargo 757 *prohibit*.

decree, pass a d., pass an order in council; promulgate 528 *proclaim*; declare, say so, lay down the law 532 *affirm*; prescribe, ordain, appoint 608 *predetermine*; legislate 953 *make legal*; give a ruling 480 *judge*.

demand, requisition 627 *require*; order, indent 761 *request*; make demands on, give final notice, present an ultimatum 900 *threaten*; reclaim 915 *claim*; demand payment, dun, bill, invoice; exact, levy 809 *tax*.

738. Disobedience – N. *disobedience*, indiscipline, unbiddableness 598 *unwillingness*; naughtiness, misbehaviour; delinquency 934 *wickedness*; insubordination, mutinousness; noncompliance 711 *defiance*, 769 *nonobservance*; disloyalty 918 *undutifulness*; infraction, infringement 936 *guilty act*; civil disobedience, passive resistance 715 *resistance*; con-

scientious objection 704 *opposition*; murmuring, restlessness 829 *discontent*; seditiousness (**see** *sedition*); wildness 954 *lawlessness*, 788 *brigandage*.

revolt, mutiny; direct action 145 *strike*; faction 709 *dissension*; breakaway, secession 978 *schism*; defection 603 *change of allegiance*; restlessness, restiveness 318 *agitation*; sabotage 165 *destruction*; disturbance, disorder, riot, streetfighting, barricades 61 *turmoil*; rebellion, insurrection, rising, uprising 176 *outbreak*; putsch, coup d'état; insurgency 715 *resistance*; subversion 149 *revolution*; terrorism 954 *lawlessness*; civil war 718 *war*; regicide, tyrannicide 362 *homicide*.

sedition, seditiousness; agitation, cabal, intrigue ~~623~~ *plot*; agitprop, subversion, infiltration, fifth-columnism; underground activities 523 *latency*; terrorism, anarchism, nihilism; treason, high t., lesemajesty 930 *perfidy*.

revolter, awkward person, handful 700 *difficulty*; naughty child, scamp, scapegrace, little monkey 938 *bad person*; mutineer, rebel, frondeur; demonstrator, striker 705 *opponent*; secessionist, splinter group; deviationist, dissident 829 *malcontent*; nonstriker 84 *nonconformist*; independent, maverick, lone wolf; seditionary, seditionist; traitor 603 *turncoat*; tyrannicide, regicide; insurrectionist, insurgent; guerrilla, partisan; resistance, underground; extremist, Jacobin, sansculotte, Bolshevist, Trotskyist 149 *revolutionist*; counter-revolutionary, reactionary, monarchist; terrorist, anarchist, nihilist; antinomian.

agitator, disruptive influence, agent provocateur; protester, demonstrator, counterdemonstrator, marcher; tubthumper, ranter, rabble-rouser, demagogue; firebrand 663 *troublemaker*; seditionist, seditionmonger; suffragette, women's libber; ringleader.

rioter, street r., brawler, rowdy 904 *ruffian*; saboteur, wrecker, Luddite; secret society, Ku Klux Klan.

Adj. *disobedient*, undisciplined, naughty, mischievous, misbehaving; unfilial, undaughterly; unbiddable, awkward, difficult, self-willed, wayward, restive, unruly, unmanageable 176 *violent*; intractable, ungovernable 598 *unwilling*; insubordinate, mutinous, rebellious, bolshie, bloody-minded 704 *opposing*; nonconformist 84 *unconformable*; uncompliant 769 *nonobservant*; recalcitrant 715 *resisting*; challenging 711 *defiant*; refractory 602 *obstinate*; subversive, revolutionary, reactionary; seditious, troublemaking; traitorous, disloyal 918 *undutiful*; antinomian 734 *anarchic*; wild, untamed.

riotous, rioting, out of control; anarchic, rowdy, unruly, wild, rackety 61 *disorderly*; law-breaking 954 *lawless*; mutinous, insurrectionary, rebellious, up in arms 715 *resisting*.

Vb. *disobey*, be disobedient, misbehave, get into mischief; flout authority, not comply with 769 *not observe*; not do as one is told, show insubordination 711 *defy*; defy the whip, cross-vote; snap one's fingers, fly in the face of 704 *oppose*; break the law 954 *be illegal*; violate, infringe, transgress, trespass; kick, chafe, fret, champ at the bit, play up; kick over the traces, take the bit between one's teeth, take the law into one's own hands 734 *please oneself*.

revolt, rebel, mutiny; down tools, come out 145 *cease*; sabotage 702 *obstruct*; secede, break away 978 *schismatize*; betray 603 *tergiversate*; agitate, demonstrate, protest 762 *deprecate*; kick up a stink, raise Cain, start a riot 715 *resist*; rise, throw off the yoke 746 *achieve liberty*; overthrow, upset, revolutionize.

739. Obedience – N. *obedience*, compliance 768 *observance*; goodness, meekness, tractability, malleability 327 *softness*; readiness 597 *willingness*; nonresistance, submissiveness, passiveness 721 *submission*; dutifulness, discipline 917 *duty*; deference, tameness, docility; dumb driven cattle 742 *slave*.

loyalty, constancy, devotion, fidelity, faithfulness 929 *probity*; allegiance, fealty, homage, service, deference, submission; vote of confidence.

Adj. *obedient*, compliant, cooperating, conforming 768 *observant*; loyal, faithful, constant; devoted, dedicated, sworn; submissive 721 *submitting*; law-abiding 717 *peaceful*; complaisant, amenable, docile; good, well-behaved; filial, daughterly; ready 597 *willing*; acquiescent, resigned, unresisting 679 *inactive*; meek, biddable, dutiful, under discipline; at one's beck and call 917 *obliged*; disciplined, regimented; trained, manageable, tame; respectful, deferential 879 *servile*.

Vb. *obey*, comply, act upon 768 *observe*; toe the line, come to heel 83 *conform*; assent 758 *consent*; listen, hearken, heed, mind, obey orders, do as one is told; hold oneself ready 597 *be willing*; vote to order, follow the party line; do one's bidding 742 *serve*; be loyal, bear allegiance 768 *keep faith*; pay tribute 745 *be subject*; know one's duty 917 *do one's duty*; yield 721 *submit*; grovel 879 *be servile*; play second fiddle 35 *be inferior*.

740. Compulsion – N. *compulsion*, spur of necessity 596 *necessity*; law of nature 953 *law*; act of God, force majeure; moral compulsion 917 *conscience*; Hobson's choice 606 *no choice*; dictation, coercion; arm-twisting, blackmail 900 *threat*; sanctions 963 *penalty*; enforcement, constraint, duress, force, main force; mailed fist, big stick, bludgeon, strong arm, strongarm tactics 735 *brute force*; forcefeeding; pressgang, conscription, call-up, draft; exaction, extortion 786 *taking*; forced labour 745 *servitude*.

Adj. *compelling*, compulsive, involuntary, of necessity, unavoidable, inevitable 596 *necessary*; imperative, dictatorial 737 *commanding*; compulsory, mandatory, binding 917 *obligatory*; urgent, pressing; overriding, constraining, coercive; omnipotent, irresistible 160 *powerful*; forcible, forceful, cogent; high-pressure, sledge-hammer, strongarm 735 *oppressive*.

Vb. *compel*, constrain, coerce 176 *force*; enforce, put into force; dictate, necessitate, oblige, bind 917 *impose a duty*; order 737 *command*; make one, leave no option; draft, conscript; drive, dragoon, regiment, discipline; bulldoze, steamroller, railroad, pressgang, bully into; bludgeon 735 *oppress*; requisition, commandeer 786 *take*; apply pressure, lean on, squeeze, turn the heat on, put the screws on, twist one's arm 963 *torture*; blackmail, hijack, hold to ransom 900 *threaten*; be peremptory, insist, not take no for an answer 532 *affirm*; force upon, ram down one's throat; force-feed.

Adv. *by force*, perforce, compulsorily, of necessity, under pressure, under protest, under duress; forcibly, at gunpoint.

741. Master – N. *master*, mistress; sire, lord, lady, dame; liege, lord, overlord, suzerain 707 *patron*; lord of the manor, squire, laird 868 *aristocrat*; senator, oligarch, plutocrat; sir, madam 870 *title*; senior, head, principal 34 *superior*; president, chairperson 690 *director*; employer, captain of industry, capitalist, boss, governor, guvnor, guv 690 *manager*; leader, führer (**see** *autocrat*); cock of the walk, lords of creation 638 *bigwig*; ruling class, the Establishment; the authorities, principalities and powers, the powers that be 733 *government*; staff, High Command 689 *directorship*.

autocrat, absolute ruler, despot, tyrant, dictator, duce, führer, Big Brother; tycoon, boss, shogun 638 *bigwig*; petty tyrant, satrap, gauleiter, commissar, Jack-in-office, tin god, little Hitler 690 *official*.

sovereign, suzerain, crowned head, anointed king *or* queen; Majesty, Highness, Royal H., Excellency; dynasty, house, royal line; royalty, monarch, king, queen, Rex, Regina; divine king, Pharaoh, Inca; imperator, emperor, empress; Caesar, Kaiser, Tsar, prince, princess; shah, Sophy; khan; Mikado; Mogul, Sultan, Sultana; Prester John; Caliph, Dalai Lama, Aga Khan.

potentate, dynast, ruler; chief, chieftain, headman, induna, sheikh; prince, pendragon, princeling, rajah, ranee, maharajah, maharanee; emir, sirdar, sherif; nawab, begum; archduke, duke, duchess, burgrave, margrave, margra-

vine, Palatine, Elector, Electress; regent, Prince Regent.

governor, High Commissioner, Governor-General; viceroy, vicereine, khedive; grand vizier; patriarch 986 *ecclesiarch*; imam, ayatollah 690 *leader*.

officer, functionary, mandarin, nabob, bureaucrat 690 *official*; civil servant, public s.; gauleiter, commissar; chief officer, prime minister, vizier, chancellor, vice-c.; burgomaster, mayor, mayoress, alderman, provost, bailie, city father, councillor; dignitary 866 *person of repute*; sheriff, bailiff; justice 957 *judge*; president, doge; consul, proconsul, praetor, quaestor, aedile; prefect, intendant, commissioner; lictor, mace-bearer, beadle; tipstaff 955 *law officer*; sexton 986 *church officer*.

naval officer, Sea Lord; admiral, vice-a., rear-a., commodore, captain, commander, lieutenant-c., lieutenant, flag-l., sub-l., petty officer, leading seaman.

army officer, staff, High Command, brass hat; commissioned officer, brevet o.; marshal, field m., commander-in-chief, generalissimo, general, lieutenant-g., major-g.; brigadier, colonel, lieutenant-c., major, captain, lieutenant, second l., subaltern; ensign, cornet; warrant officer, noncommissioned o., NCO, sergeant major, company s. m., staff s., colour s., sergeant, corporal, lance corporal; adjutant, aide-de-camp, quartermaster, orderly officer; tribune, legate, centurion 722 *soldiery*; war minister, warlord, commanding officer, commander, commandant.

air officer, air marshal, air commodore, group captain, wing commander, squadron leader, flight lieutenant, flying officer, pilot o., warrant o., flight sergeant 722 *air force*.

742. Servant – N. *servant*, menial, fag, slave; factotum, chief cook and bottle washer 678 *busy person*; orderly, attendant; underling, understrapper 35 *inferior*; assistant, secretary 703 *aider*; mercenary, hireling, employee, hand, hired man; odd-job man, handyman, labourer, peon 686 *worker*; hack, drudge, dogsbody, erk; cowherd, milkmaid 369 *herdsman*; shop assistant 793 *seller*; steward, stewardess, cabin boy; waiter, waitress, bartender, barman, barmaid; ostler, groom, stable lad *or* girl; errand boy *or* girl, messenger 529 *courier*; commissionaire 264 *doorkeeper*; porter, night p.; caddy 273 *bearer*; sweeper 648 *cleaner*; caretaker (see *domestic*); help, daily, char, charwoman, cleaning lady; universal aunt.

domestic, staff 686 *personnel*; servitor, domestic servant, manservant, footman, flunkey, lackey; abigail, maid, maidservant, handmaid, parlour maid, housemaid, chambermaid; tweeny, skivvy, slavey; kitchen maid; turnspit, scullion, washerup; housekeeper, butler, cook; steward, chaplain, governess, tutor, nurse, nanny; personal servant, body s., page, squire, valet, batman *or* -woman; lady's maid, waiting woman; nursemaid, au pair; gardener, groom; coachman, chauffeur 268 *driver*.

retainer, follower, following, suite, train 67 *retinue*; court, courtier; attendant, usher; bodyguard, housecarl; squire, page; majordomo, chamberlain, equerry, steward, bailiff, seneschal; chatelaine, housekeeper; cellarer, butler, cup-bearer; chaplain; lady-in-waiting, companion, confidante; nanny 749 *keeper*.

dependant, clientèle, client; hanger-on, parasite, satellite 284 *follower*; stooge, puppet; subordinate 35 *inferior*; minion, myrmidon, lackey (see *domestic*); man, liegeman, vassal; pensioner; apprentice, protégé(e), ward, charge, foster child.

subject, national, citizen 191 *native*; liege, vassal; people, citizenry 869 *commonalty*; dependency, colony, satellite.

slave, thrall, bondman, bondwoman, bondmaid; helot, helotry; serf, villein; galley slave, sweated labour 686 *worker*; odalisque, eunuch; chattel, puppet, pawn; machine, robot 628 *instrument*; chaingang 750 *prisoner*.

Adj. *serving*, ministering 703 *aiding*; in service, menial; working, on the payroll; on the staff, in the train of; at one's beck and call 739 *obedient*; in captivity, in bonds 745 *subject*.

Vb. *serve*, wait upon 703 *minister to*; be on hand 89 *accompany*; attend on, follow 739 *obey*; tend, squire, valet, dress; do chores, oblige; fag for, dogsbody for, work for, make oneself useful 640 *be useful*, 622 *function*.

743. Badge of rule – N. *regalia*, emblem of royalty, crown, orb, sceptre; coronet, tiara, diadem; rod of empire, sword of state 733 *authority*; coronation robes; ermine, purple; throne, seat of kings; ensign 547 *flag*; royal standard 547 *heraldry*; lion, eagle, fleur-de-lis; uraeus.

badge of rule, emblem of authority, staff, wand, verge, rod, baton, truncheon, gavel; herald's wand, caduceus; signet, seal, privy s., keys, ring; sword of state, mace, fasces, axes; pastoral staff, crosier; ankh, ansate cross; woolsack, chair, bench; triple crown, mitre 989 *canonicals*; judge's cap, black c.; cap of maintenance, cap of dignity; robe, mantle, toga.

badge of rank, sword, belt, sash, spurs, cocked hat, epaulette, tab 547 *badge*; uniform 547 *livery*; brass, star, pips, crown, crossed batons; gold braid, scrambled egg; chevron, stripe, anchor, curl, brassard, armlet; garter, order 729 *decoration*.

744. Freedom – N. *freedom*, liberty, free will 595 *will*; civil rights, equal r. 915 *dueness*; privilege, prerogative, exemption, immunity 919 *nonliability*; liberalism, libertarianism, latitudinarianism; licence, artistic l.; indiscipline 738 *disobedience*; laissez faire, nonintervention; noninvolvement 860 *indifference*; nonalignment, cross benches; emancipation 746 *liberation*; women's liberation, women's lib; gay l.; enfranchisement, naturalization, citizenship; franchise 605 *vote*.

independence, freedom of action 605 *choice*; emancipation, bohemianism 84 *nonconformity*; bachelorhood 895 *celibacy*; individualism, self-expression 80 *speciality*; self-determination, nationhood 371 *nation*; autonomy, autarchy, self-government, self-rule, home r.; autarky, self-sufficiency 635 *sufficiency*; independent means 800 *wealth*.

scope, play, full p. 183 *range*; swing, rope, long r.; manoeuvrability, leverage; field, room, living space 183 *room*; latitude, liberty, Liberty Hall; permissive society; informality, unconstraint; licence, excess 734 *laxity*; ball at one's feet 137 *opportunity*; facilities, the run of, free hand, blank cheque, carte blanche; free-for-all, free enterprise, free trade; open country, high seas.

free person, freeman, burgess, burgher, citizen; freedman, freedwoman; ex-convict, released prisoner; escapee 667 *escaper*; free agent, freelance; independent, cross-bencher; isolationist, neutral 625 *moderate*; free-trader; freethinker, latitudinarian, liberal; libertarian, Bohemian, individualist 84 *nonconformist*; lone wolf 883 *solitary*.

Adj. *free*, freeborn, enfranchised; heartwhole, fancy-free; scot-free 960 *acquitted*; on the loose, at large 667 *escaped*; released, freed 746 *liberated*; free as air, free as a bird; footloose, go-as-you-please, ranging 267 *travelling*; licensed, chartered, privileged 756 *permitted*; exempt, immune 919 *nonliable*; free-speaking; free-thinking, emancipated, broad, broadminded, latitudinarian (**see** *independent*); unprejudiced, independent 913 *just*; free and easy, all things to all men 882 *sociable*; loose, unbridled 951 *impure*; at leisure, out of harness 681 *leisurely*; unclaimed, going begging 860 *unwanted*.

unconfined, uncribbed, uncabined, untrammelled, unbridled, uncurbed, unchecked, unrestrained, ungoverned; unprevented, unhindered, uninhibited, informal, dégagé(e), casual; free-range, wandering; left to one's own devices.

independent, uninduced, unilateral 609 *spontaneous*; unattached 860 *indifferent*; free to choose, uncommitted, uninvolved; nonpartisan, unaffiliated 625 *neutral*; isolationist 883 *unsociable*; unconquered 727 *unbeaten*; autonomous, autarchic, self-governing; autarkic, self-sufficient, self-supporting, self-contained, self-

motivated, inner-directed; self-reliant, one's own master; owning no master 734 *anarchic*; self-employed, one's own boss, free-lance; unofficial, cowboy, wildcat; single 895 *unwedded*; individualistic, unconventional 84 *unconformable*; breakaway 489 *dissenting*.

unconditional, unconditioned, no strings attached; catch-as-catch-can, free-for-all; unrestricted, unlimited, absolute; discretionary, arbitrary.

Vb. *be free*, go free 667 *escape*; have the run of, range, have scope, have play, have a free hand; have plenty of rope; feel at home, feel free, be oneself, let oneself go, let it all hang out, let one's hair down 683 *repose*; have one's fling, have one's way, cut loose, drop out 734 *please oneself*; follow one's bent, do one's own thing; drift, wander, roam 282 *stray*; go it alone, shift *or* fend for oneself, paddle one's own canoe; have a will of one's own 595 *will*; call no man master, be one's own man *or* woman; stand on one's own feet, ask no favours 635 *suffice*; take liberties, make free with; make bold to, permit oneself.

give scope, give one his *or* her head, allow full play, give free rein to 734 *be lax*; give a free hand, give the run of 701 *facilitate*; set free 746 *liberate*; license 756 *permit*; let alone, live and let live, leave to his *or* her own devices; leave the door open.

745. Subjection – N. *subjection*, subordination; inferior rank, juniority 35 *inferiority*; creaturehood; dependence, tutelage, guardianship, wardship, apron strings, leading s.; apprenticeship, subjecthood, allegiance; subjugation, conquest, colonialism; disfranchisement, enslavement 721 *submission*; constraint 747 *restraint*; oppression 735 *severity*; yoke 748 *fetter*.

service, employ, employment; servitorship, flunkeydom 739 *obedience*; tribute, suit and service; vassalage, feudality 739 *loyalty*; forced labour 740 *compulsion*.

servitude, slavery, enslavement, captivity, thraldom, bondage, yoke; helotry, serfdom, villeinage, peonage.

Adj. *subjected*, dominated etc. vb.; subjugated 728 *defeated*; subdued, pacified; in chains 747 *restrained*; discriminated against, underprivileged, disfranchised; colonized, enslaved, sold into slavery; in harness 742 *serving*; under the yoke; oppressed, downtrodden, underfoot; treated like dirt, henpecked, browbeaten; the sport of, the plaything of; brought to heel, quelled, tamed; eating out of one's hand, submissive 721 *submitting*; subservient, slavish 879 *servile*.

subject, unfree, unfranchised; satellite, satellitic; bond, bound, tributary, colonial; owing fealty, feudal 739 *obedient*; under, subordinate, junior, cadet 35 *inferior*; dependent, in chancery, in statu pupillari; tied to one's apron strings; subject to 180 *liable*; a slave to 610 *habituated*; in the hands of, in the clutches of, under the control of, in the power of, at the mercy of, under the sway of, under one's thumb; having no say in, voiceless; parasitical 879 *servile*; in the pay of.

Vb. *be subject*, live under 739 *obey*; depend on 35 *be inferior*; let oneself be trampled on *or* kicked around; serve, live in subjection, be a slave 721 *submit*; have no will of one's own 628 *be instrumental*; cringe, fawn 879 *be servile*.

subjugate, subdue 727 *overmaster*; colonize, annex; take captive, lead in triumph; take, capture, enslave, sell into slavery; fetter, bind 747 *imprison*; disfranchise; trample on, treat like dirt 735 *oppress*; keep down, hold d., repress, sit on 165 *suppress*; dominate 178 *influence*; discipline, regiment; tame, quell 369 *break in*; have eating out of one's hand, bring to heel, have at one's beck and call; make one's plaything, do what one likes with 673 *dispose of*.

746. Liberation – N. *liberation*, setting free, release, discharge 960 *acquittal*; free expression, abreaction, catharsis 818 *feeling*; extrication, disinvolvement 46 *separation*; riddance, good r. 831 *relief*; rescue, redemption, salvation 668 *deliverance*; manumission, emancipation, enfranchisement; parole, bail; liberaliz-

ation, relaxation (of control) 734 *laxity*; decontrol, derationing 752 *abrogation*; demobilization, disbandment 75 *dispersion*; absolution 909 *forgiveness*; quittance, quitclaim.

Adj. *liberated*, rescued, delivered, saved; rid of, relieved; paroled, set free, freed, manumitted 744 *unconfined*; released, etc. vb.

Vb. *liberate*, rescue, save 668 *deliver*; dispense 919 *exempt*; pardon 909 *forgive*; discharge, absolve, let off the hook 960 *acquit*; make free, emancipate, manumit; enfranchise, give the vote; grant equal rights, end discrimination; release, free, set free, set at liberty, let out; parole 766 *give terms*; unfetter, unshackle, unchain; unlock 263 *open*; loosen, unloose, loose, unbind, extricate, disengage 62 *unravel*; unstop, uncork, ungag, unmuzzle; uncage, unleash, let off the lead; let loose, turn adrift; license, charter 744 *give scope*; let out, give vent to 300 *empty*; unhand, let go 779 *not retain*; relax, liberalize 734 *be lax*; lift off 831 *relieve*; decontrol, deration 752 *abrogate*; demobilize, disband 75 *disperse*; unyoke, unharness 701 *disencumber*.

achieve liberty, gain one's freedom, breathe freely; assert oneself 738 *revolt*; free oneself, shake oneself free; break loose, burst one's bonds, throw off the yoke, kick over the traces 667 *escape*.

747. Restraint – N. *restraint*, self-r., self-control 942 *temperance*; reserve, inhibitions; suppression, repression, coercion, constraint 740 *compulsion*; cramp, check 702 *hindrance*; curb 748 *fetter*; arrest, retardation 278 *slowness*; prevention 757 *prohibition*; control, discipline 733 *authority*; censorship, press laws 735 *severity*; binding over 963 *penalty*.

restriction, limitation 236 *limit*; localization 232 *circumscription*; speed limit, restricted area; no-go area, curfew; constriction, squeeze 198 *compression*; duress, pressure 740 *compulsion*; control, rationing; restrictive practice 57 *exclusion*; monopoly, price ring, cartel, closed shop; ring, circle; protectionism, tariff;

retrenchment, cuts 814 *economy*; freeze, price control, credit squeeze; blockade; monopolist, protectionist, restrictionist, monetarist.

detention, preventive d., custody, protective c. 660 *protection*; arrest, house a.; custodianship, keep, charge, ward; quarantine, internment; remand; lettre de cachet; captivity, duress, durance; bondage 745 *servitude*; impoundment, immurement, confinement, incarceration, imprisonment; sentence, time, a stretch, porridge; penology, penologist.

Adj. *restraining*, etc. vb.; restrictive, conditional, with strings; limiting, limitary; custodial, keeping; unbending, strict 735 *severe*; stiff 326 *rigid*; tight 206 *narrow*; close, confined, poky; coercive 740 *compelling*; repressive, inhibiting 757 *prohibiting*; monopolistic, protectionist.

restrained, self-r. 942 *temperate*; pent up, bottled up; disciplined 739 *obedient*; on a lead; pinned down, kept under 745 *subjected*; on parole 917 *obliged*; protected, rationed, limited, restricted; cramped, hampered, hindered; tied, bound, gagged; held up, weatherbound, fogbound, snowbound.

imprisoned, confined, detained, kept in; landlocked; entombed, confined 364 *buried*; in quarantine; interned, under detention, under house arrest, incommunicado; under arrest, laid by the heels, in custody; refused bail, on remand; behind bars, incarcerated, locked up 750 *captive*; inside, in jug, in clink, in quod; gated, confined to barracks; corralled, penned up, impounded; pilloried, in the stocks; serving a sentence, doing time, doing porridge; caged, in captivity, trapped.

Vb. *restrain*, hold back; arrest, check, curb, rein in, put a brake on 278 *retard*; cramp, clog, hamper 702 *hinder*; swathe, bind, tie hand and foot 45 *tie*; put a stop to 145 *halt*; ban, bar 757 *prohibit*; bridle, discipline, control 735 *be severe*; subdue 745 *subjugate*; restrain oneself, control o. 823 *keep calm*; grip, hold, hold in check 778 *retain*; hold in, keep in, fight down, fight back, bottle up; restrict, tighten,

hem in, limit, keep within bounds 232 *circumscribe*; damp down, assuage 177 *moderate*; hold down, slap d., clamp *or* crack down on, sit on, jump on, repress 165 *suppress*; muzzle, gag, silence 578 *make mute*; censor 550 *obliterate*; restrict access 57 *exclude*; withhold, keep back, stint; ration 814 *economize*; resist 704 *oppose*; police, patrol, keep order.

arrest, make an a., apprehend, lay by the heels, catch, cop, nab, collar, pinch, nick, pick up; haul in, run in; put the handcuffs on, snap the bracelets on (**see** *fetter*); take, take prisoner, capture; kidnap, seize, take hostage; put under arrest, take into custody, clap in goal.

fetter, manacle, bind, pinion, tie up, handcuff, put in irons; pillory, put in the stocks, tether, picket 45 *tie*; shackle, trammel, hobble, chain; make conditions, attach strings.

imprison, confine, immure, quarantine, intern; hold, detain, keep in, gate; cloister 883 *seclude*; entomb 364 *inter*; wall up, seal up, coop up, cage, kennel, impound, corral, herd, pen, cabin, box up, shut in, trap 235 *enclose*; put in a straitjacket; incarcerate, commit to prison, remand, give in charge; jug, lock up; turn the key on, keep under lock and key, put behind bars, clap in irons; refuse bail.

748. Prison – N. *prison*, prison-house, house of correction; open prison, prison without bars; penitentiary, reformatory, Borstal; approved school, remand home, community h.; assessment centre, detention c.; sin bin; prison ship, hulks; dungeon, oubliette, black hole; Broadmoor.

gaol, jail, quod, clink, jug, can, stir; glasshouse, brig.

lockup, chokey, calaboose, nick, police station; guardroom, guardhouse, roundhouse; cooler, cell, condemned c., Death Row; dungeon, oubliette, torture chamber; prison van, Black Maria; dock, bar; pound, pen 235 *enclosure*; stocks, pillory; lock, bolt, bar.

prison camp, detention c., internment c., prison of war c., stalag; concentration camp, Belsen, Auschwitz; labour camp, re-education camp; penal settlement.

fetter, shackle, trammels, bond, chain, ball and c., ring-bolt, irons, gyves, bilboes, hobble; manacle, pinion, handcuff, bracelet, darbies; straitjacket, corset; muzzle, gag, bit, bridle, snaffle, headstall, halter; rein, bearing r., martingale; reins, ribbons, traces; yoke, collar, harness; curb, brake, skid, clog, drag 702 *hindrance*; lead, tether, rope 47 *halter*.

749. Keeper – N. *keeper*, custodian, curator; archivist 549 *recorder*; charge officer; caretaker, concierge, housekeeper; warden, ranger, gamekeeper; guard, escort, convoy; garrison 713 *defender*; watchdog, sentry, watchman, coastguard, lighthouse keeper 660 *protector*; invigilator, tutor, chaperon, duenna, governess, nanny, nursemaid, baby-sitter 742 *domestic*; foster parent, adoptive p.; guardian, legal g.; probation officer 901 *philanthropist*.

gaoler, jailer, turnkey, warder, wardress, prison guard, prison officer, screw; prison governor.

750. Prisoner – N. *prisoner*, captive, capture, prisoner of war, POW; parolee, ticket-of-leave man; person under arrest; political prisoner, prisoner of conscience; detainee, prisoner of state; prisoner at the bar, defendant 928 *accused person*; first offender; persistent o., old lag, gaolbird 904 *offender*; inmate, guest of Her Majesty; convict; lifer; trusty; chain gang, galley slave 742 *slave*; hostage, kidnap victim 767 *security*.

Adj. *captive*, imprisoned, chained, fettered, shackled, in chains, in irons, behind bars, under lock and key, cooling one's heels; jailed, in prison, inside 747 *imprisoned*; in custody, under arrest; remanded; detained.

751. Commission: vicarious authority – N. *commission*, vicarious authority; committal, delegation; devolution, decentralization; deputation, legation, mission, embassy 754 *envoy*; regency, regentship 733 *authority*; representation, procurat-

ory, proxy; card vote; agency, factorage, trusteeship, executorship 689 *management*.

mandate, trust, charge 737 *command*; commission, assignment, appointment, office, task, errand, mission; enterprise 672 *undertaking*; nomination 605 *vote*; posting 272 *transference*; investiture, installation, induction, ordination, enthronement, coronation; power of attorney 737 *warrant*; brevet 756 *permit*; terms of reference 766 *conditions*; responsibility, care, ward, charge.

Adj. *commissioned*, empowered, etc. vb.; deputed, accredited; vicarious, representational, agential.

Vb. *commission*, empower, authorize, charge, charter 756 *permit*; post, accredit, appoint, assign, name, nominate; engage, hire 622 *employ*; invest, induct, install, ordain; enthrone, crown, anoint; commit, turn over to, leave it to; consign, entrust, trust with; delegate, depute; return, elect, give a mandate 605 *vote*.

752. Abrogation – N. *abrogation*, annulment, invalidation; voidance, nullification; cancellation, cassation, suppression; recall, repeal, revocation, rescission; abolition, dissolution; retractation 603 *recantation*; suspension, discontinuance, dead letter 674 *nonuse*; reversal, counterorder, countermand, nolle prosequi.

deposal, deposition, dethronement; demotion, degradation; disestablishment, disendowment; deconsecration, secularization; dismissal, sack 300 *ejection*; unfrocking 963 *punishment*; ousting, deprivation 786 *expropriation*; replacement, recall, supersession 150 *substitution*.

Adj. *abrogated*, quashed, etc. vb.; void, null and void; functus officio, dead; dormant; revoked.

Vb. *abrogate*, annul, disannul, cancel; scrub 550 *obliterate*; invalidate, abolish, dissolve, nullify, void, vacate; quash, set aside, reverse, overrule; repeal, revoke, recall, rescind, tear up; countermand, counterorder; repudiate, retract 603 *recant*; suspend 674 *stop using*; not proceed with 621 *relinquish*.

depose, uncrown, dethrone; unseat; divest 786 *deprive*; unfrock; disbench, disbar 57 *exclude*; disaffiliate, disestablish, disendow; deconsecrate, secularize; suspend, cashier 300 *dismiss*; ease out, edge o., oust 300 *eject*; demote, degrade; recall, supersede, replace, remove 272 *transfer*.

753. Resignation – N. *resignation*, demission; retirement, retiral; withdrawal 296 *departure*; pension, golden handshake 962 *reward*; waiver, surrender, abdication 621 *relinquishment*; abjuration, disclaimer.

Adj. *resigning*, abdicating; outgoing, former, retired, quondam, onetime, ci-devant; emeritus.

Vb. *resign*, tender one's resignation, demit, lay down one's office, break one's staff; be relieved, hand over, vacate; apply for the Chiltern Hundreds; stand down *or* aside, make way for; sign off, declare (cricket); scratch, withdraw, back out, throw in one's hand 721 *submit*; quit, chuck it; ask for one's cards; abdicate, renounce 621 *relinquish*; retire, go into retirement; be pensioned off; waive, disclaim, abjure 533 *negate*.

754. Consignee – N. *consignee*, committee, steering c., panel, quango 692 *council*; working party 691 *adviser*; bailee, stakeholder; nominee, appointee, licensee; trustee 686 *agent*; factor, bailiff, steward 690 *manager*; caretaker, curator 749 *keeper*; representative (see *delegate*); attorney 958 *law agent*; proxy 755 *deputy*; negotiator, broker 231 *intermediary*; underwriter, insurer; office-bearer 741 *officer*; functionary 690 *official*.

delegate, shop steward; nominee, representative; commissary, commissioner; man *or* woman on the spot 588 *correspondent*; emissary 529 *messenger*; plenipotentiary (see *envoy*); delegation, mission.

envoy, emissary, legate, nuncio, resident, ambassador, ambassadress, High Commissioner, chargé d'affaires; corps diplomatique, diplomatic corps; minister, diplomat; consul, vice-c.; attaché; embassy, legation, mission, consulate, High Commission; diplomatist, negotiator, plenipotentiary.

755. Deputy – N. *deputy*, surrogate, proxy; scapegoat, substitute, understudy, stand-in 150 *substitution*; second-in-command, righthand man 703 *aider*; caretaker government; heir apparent, successor designate 776 *beneficiary*; spokesperson, mouthpiece 529 *messenger*; second, champion 707 *patron*; agent, factor, attorney 754 *consignee*.

Adj. *deputizing*, representing, acting for; vice-, pro-; diplomatic, ambassadorial, plenipotentiary; standing-in for 150 *substituted*.

Vb. *deputize*, act for 622 *function*; represent, hold a mandate for, appear f., answer f.; hold in trust 689 *manage*; negotiate, be broker for, stand for 150 *substitute*; be the whipping boy, act as scapegoat.

Section 2:
Special social volition

756. Permission – N. *permission*, leave, sanction, clearance 744 *freedom*; grant; licence, authorization, warrant; allowance, indulgence 736 *leniency*; acquiescence 758 *consent*; connivance 703 *aid*; blessing, approval 923 *approbation*; concession, dispensation.

permit, authority, law 737 *warrant*; commission 751 *mandate*; brevet, grant, charter, patent, letters p.; pass, password; passport, passbook, visa, safe-conduct; ticket, chit; licence, driving l.; carte blanche 744 *scope*; leave, parole; clearance, all clear, green light, go-ahead; nihil obstat, imprimatur.

Adj. *permitting*, complaisant 736 *lenient*; conniving 703 *aiding*.

permitted, allowed etc. vb.; licit 953 *legal*; unforbidden, optional, discretional 744 *unconditional*; permissible, allowable; passed.

Vb. *permit*, let, make possible; give permission, grant, accord, vouchsafe; say yes 758 *consent*; give one's blessing; sanction, pass 923 *approve*; entitle, authorize, warrant, charter, patent, license; ratify, legalize 953 *make legal*; decontrol; dispense 919 *exempt*; clear, give the go-ahead, give the green light; concede, allow 488 *assent*; leave the way open 701 *facilitate*; foster, encourage 156 *conduce*; humour, suffer, tolerate 736 *be lenient*; shut one's eyes to, wink at 734 *be lax*; laissez aller 744 *give scope*.

757. Prohibition – N. *prohibition*, interdiction, disallowance, injunction; countermand, counterorder; intervention, interference; interdict, veto, ban, embargo; restriction, curfew 747 *restraint*; proscription, taboo, Index; thumbs down 760 *refusal*; nonrecognition, intolerance 924 *disapprobation*; licensing laws 942 *temperance*; censorship, press laws, repression, suppression 735 *severity*; blackout, news b.; forbidden fruit 859 *desired object*.

Adj. *prohibiting*, prohibitory, forbidding, prohibitive, excessive 470 *impossible*; repressive 747 *restraining*; penal 963 *punitive*; hostile 881 *inimical*; exclusive 57 *excluding*.

prohibited, forbidden, not allowed; barred, banned; censored, blacked-out; illicit, outlawed, against the law 954 *illegal*; verboten, taboo; untouchable, blacked; frowned on, not done; unmentionable, unprintable; out of bounds 57 *excluded*.

Vb. *prohibit*, forbid; disallow, veto 760 *refuse*; withdraw permission, countermand, counterorder 752 *abrogate*; inhibit, prevent 702 *hinder*; restrict, stop 747 *restrain*; ban, interdict, taboo, proscribe, outlaw; black, place out of bounds 57 *exclude*; repress 165 *suppress*; censor, blue-pencil 550 *obliterate*; not tolerate 735 *be severe*; frown on, not countenance 924 *disapprove*; draw the line, block; intervene, interpose, interfere.

758. Consent – N. *consent*, full c. 597 *willingness*; agreement 488 *assent*; compliance 768 *observance*; concession, grant, accord; acquiescence, acceptance, allowance 756 *permission*; sanction, endorsement, ratification, confirmation.

Adj. *consenting*, agreeable, compliant 597 *willing*; winking at 703 *aiding*; yielding 721 *submitting*.

Vb. *consent*, say yes, nod; ratify, confirm 488 *endorse*; sanction, pass 756 *permit*; give one's approval 923 *approve*; tolerate, recognize, allow, connive 736 *be lenient*; agree, accede 488 *assent*; have no objection 488 *acquiesce*; be persuaded, come round 612 *be induced*; yield, give way 721 *submit*; comply; grant, accord, concede 781 *give*; deign, condescend; listen, hearken 597 *be willing*; accept, jump at; settle 766 *make terms*.

759. Offer – N. *offer*, tender, bid; proposition, proposal; approach, overture, advance, invitation; feeler; presentation, offering 781 *gift*; candidature, application 761 *request*.

Adj. *offering*, inviting; offered, advertised; open, available; on offer, on the market, up for grabs; to let, for sale; open to bid, up for auction.

Vb. *offer*, proffer, hold out, make an offer, bid, tender; present, lay at one's feet 781 *give*; dedicate, consecrate; sacrifice to; propose, put forward, suggest 512 *propound*; make overtures, make advances; induce 612 *bribe*; hawk about, invite tenders 793 *sell*; auction; cater for 633 *provide*; make available, place at one's disposal.

offer oneself, sacrifice o.; stand, run for, enter 716 *contend*; volunteer, come forward 597 *be willing*; apply, put in for 761 *request*; be on offer, look for takers, go begging.

760. Refusal – N. *refusal*, nonacceptance, thumbs down 607 *rejection*; denial, no 533 *negation*; flat refusal 711 *defiance*; repulse, rebuff, slap in the face 292 *repulsion*; withholding 778 *retention*; recalcitrance 738 *disobedience*; noncompliance 769 *nonobservance*; recusancy 598 *unwillingness*; objection 762 *deprecation*; renunciation 621 *relinquishment*.

Adj. *refusing*, denying, etc. vb.; uncompliant 769 *nonobservant*; jibbing, objecting, demurring 762 *deprecatory*; deaf to 598 *unwilling*.

Vb. *refuse*, say no, shake one's head; deny, disclaim 533 *negate*; decline, turn down, spurn 607 *reject*; repulse, rebuff, tell one where to get off 292 *repel*; turn away 300 *dismiss*; harden one's heart 602 *be obstinate*; turn a deaf ear 416 *be deaf*; close one's hand, turn one's back on; hang back 598 *be unwilling*; beg off, back down; shy at, jib at 620 *avoid*; debar, keep out 57 *exclude*; not hear of 924 *disapprove*; not allow 757 *prohibit*; not consent 715 *resist*; oppose 704 *withstand*; protest 762 *deprecate*; not comply 769 *not observe*; withhold 778 *retain*; waive, renounce 621 *relinquish*.

761. Request – N. *request*, asking; negative request 762 *deprecation*; canvass, canvassing; requisition 737 *demand*; claim, counterclaim 915 *dueness*; consumer demand, seller's market 627 *requirement*; proposition, proposal, motion, suggestion; overture, approach 759 *offer*; bid, application, suit; petition, round robin; prayer, appeal, plea (**see** *entreaty*); pressure, instance, insistence, urgency 740 *compulsion*; clamour, cry, cri de coeur; dunning, importunity; accosting, solicitation, invitation, temptation; mendicancy, begging; small ad, 'wanted' column; wish, want 859 *desire*.

entreaty, beseeching; submission, supplication, prayer 981 *prayers*; appeal, invocation, apostrophe; adjuration, conjuration; incantation, imprecation.

Adj. *requesting*, asking, etc. vb.; mendicant, alms-seeking; claiming 627 *demanding*; insistent, clamorous, importunate, pressing, urgent, instant.

supplicatory, suppliant, prayerful; on bended knees, cap in hand; precatory; imploratory, beseeching, with tears in one's eyes; invocatory, imprecatory.

Vb. *request*, ask, invite, solicit; approach, accost 759 *offer*; sue for; woo 889 *court*; seek, look for 459 *search*; fish for, angle for; need, call for, clamour f. 627 *require*; crave, beg a favour, trouble one for 859 *desire*; apply, put in for, bid

for; apply to, call on, appeal to; tout, hawk, canvass 793 *sell*; petition; expect 915 *claim*; make demands 737 *demand*; urge 612 *induce*; coax, wheedle, cajole; importune, ply, press, dun, besiege, beset; touch for 785 *borrow*; requisition 786 *take*; state one's terms 766 *give terms*.

beg, cadge, crave, sponge; bum, scrounge, thumb a lift, hitchhike; panhandle; pass the hat 786 *levy*.

entreat, beg hard; supplicate, pray, implore, beseech, appeal, conjure, adjure; invoke, imprecate; apostrophize, appeal to, call on; kneel to, go down on one's knees.

762. Deprecation: negative request – N. *deprecation*, negative request 613 *dissuasion*; intercession, mediation 981 *prayers*; murmur, complaint 829 *discontent*; exception, demur, expostulation, remonstrance, protest 704 *opposition*; reaction, backlash; tut-tut, raised eyebrows, groans, jeers 924 *disapprobation*; demonstration, indignation meeting, march; noncompliance 760 *refusal*.

Adj. *deprecatory* 613 *dissuasive*; protesting, expostulatory; clamant, vocal; intercessory, mediatorial; averting, apotropaic.

Vb. *deprecate*, advise against 613 *dissuade*; avert the omen, touch wood, keep one's fingers crossed; beg off, plead for, intercede 720 *mediate*; appeal 761 *entreat*; shake one's head 924 *disapprove*; remonstrate, expostulate 924 *reprove*; jeer, groan 926 *detract*; murmur, complain 829 *be discontented*; object, take exception to; demur, jib, kick, squeal, protest against, appeal a., petition a., lobby a., campaign a., cry out a., cry blue murder 704 *oppose*; demonstrate, walk out.

763. Petitioner – N. *petitioner*, suppliant, supplicant; appealer, appellant; claimant, pretender; postulant, aspirant; seeker, inquirer; customer, bidder; suitor, wooer; canvasser, hawker, touter, tout, barker, spieler; dun; pressure group, lobby, lobbyist; applicant, candidate 716 *contender*; complainer 829 *malcontent*.

beggar, panhandler; mendicant, mendicant friar, fakir, sannyasi; tramp, bum 268 wanderer; cadger, scrounger; sponger, parasite 879 toady.

Section 3: Conditional social volition

764. Promise – N. promise, undertaking, commitment; engagement 894 marriage; troth, word, word of honour, vow 532 oath; declaration 532 affirmation; profession, assurance, pledge, credit, honour 767 security; gentlemen's agreement 765 compact; covenant, bond 803 debt; debt of honour 917 duty; firm date 672 undertaking; promise-maker, votary; party 765 signatory.

Adj. promissory, promising, votive; on oath, under hand and seal; on credit, on parole.

Vb. promise, say one will 532 affirm; hold out 759 offer; make a promise, give one's word, vow 532 swear; vouch for, go bail for 767 give security; pledge, stake; engage 672 undertake; commit oneself, bind oneself, covenant 765 contract; take on oneself 917 incur a duty; exchange vows 894 wed.

765. Compact – N. compact, contract, bargain, agreement 672 undertaking; gentleman's agreement 764 promise; exchange of vows; engagement 894 marriage; covenant, bond 767 security; league, alliance 706 cooperation; pact, understanding 24 agreement; private understanding, something between them; conspiracy 623 plot; deal, give and take 770 compromise; adjustment, composition, arrangement, settlement; ratification 488 assent; seal, signature, countersignature; indenture 767 title deed.

treaty, international agreement; peace treaty, nonaggression pact 719 pacification; convention, concordat, protocol; Geneva Convention.

signatory, signer, countersigner, subscriber, the undersigned; attestor 466 witness; endorser, ratifier; adherent, party

488 assenter; covenanter, contractor; treaty-maker, negotiator 720 mediator.

Adj. contractual, conventional 488 assenting; bilateral, multilateral; agreed to, signed, countersigned, ratified; covenanted, signed, sealed and delivered; under one's hand and seal.

Vb. contract, engage 672 undertake; precontract 764 promise; covenant, make a compact, strike a bargain, shake hands on, do a deal; adhere; league, ally 706 cooperate; treat, negotiate 791 bargain; give and take 770 compromise; stipulate 766 give terms; agree 766 make terms; conclude, close, settle; indent, execute, sign, ratify 488 endorse; insure, underwrite 767 give security.

766. Conditions – N. conditions, treaty-making, diplomacy, negotiation, bargaining, collective b.; hard bargaining, horse-trading 791 barter; formula, terms, set t.; final terms, ultimatum 900 threat; condition, set of terms, frame of reference; articles of agreement; provision, clause, entrenched c., proviso, limitation, strings, reservation, exception, small print 468 qualification; stipulation, sine qua non 627 requirement; rule 693 precept; contractual terms 765 treaty; terms of reference 751 mandate.

Adj. conditional, with strings attached, stipulatory, provisory 468 qualifying; limiting, subject to terms, conditioned, contingent, provisional; safeguarded, entrenched; binding 917 obligatory.

Vb. give terms, propose conditions; bind, tie down; insist on 737 demand; stipulate 627 require; insert a proviso 468 qualify; add a clause, write in.

make terms, negotiate, parley 584 confer; deal with, treat w.; make overtures 461 be tentative; haggle 791 bargain; give and take 770 compromise; negotiate a treaty, hammer out a formula 765 contract.

767. Security – N. security, guarantee, warranty 737 warrant; word of honour 764 promise; sponsorship, patronage 660 protection; surety, bail, replevin, recognizance, parole; gage, pledge, pawn, hostage; stake, stake money, deposit, earnest, handsel, token, instalment; down payment 804 *payment*; indemnity, insurance, underwriting 660 *safety*; hypothecation 780 *transfer*; collateral, sponsor, underwriter 707 *patron*.

title deed, deed, instrument; deed poll; indenture; charter, covenant 765 *compact*; receipt, IOU, voucher, quittance; certificate, authentication, marriage lines; verification, seal, stamp, endorsement 466 *credential*; banknote, treasury note, promissory n., note of hand; blue chip, gilt-edged security; portfolio, scrip, share, debenture; mortgage deed, insurance policy; will, testament, codicil.

Adj. *pledged*, pawned, popped, deposited; up the spout, in hock, in pawn, on deposit; on lease, on mortgage; on bail, on recognizance.

secured, covered, hedged, insured; gilt-edged, copper-bottomed; guaranteed.

Vb. *give bail*, go b., bail one out, go surety; take recognizance, release on bail; hold in pledge, keep in pawn.

give security, offer collateral, hypothecate, mortgage; pledge, pawn 785 *borrow*; guarantee, warrant 473 *make certain*; authenticate 466 *corroborate*; seal, stamp, sign, countersign 488 *endorse*; grant a receipt, write an IOU; vouch for 764 *promise*; indemnify, insure, assure, underwrite 660 *safeguard*.

768. Observance – N. *observance*, fulfilment, satisfaction 610 *practice*; diligence, conscientiousness; adherence to, attention to; performance, discharge, acquittal 676 *action*; compliance 739 *obedience*; conformance 83 *conformity*; good faith 739 *loyalty*; dependability, reliability 929 *probity*.

Adj. *observant*, practising 676 *doing*; attentive to 455 *attentive*; conscientious, diligent, religious, punctilious; over-conscientious 862 *fastidious*; pedantic, exact 494 *accurate*; responsible, reliable, dependable 929 *trustworthy*; loyal, compliant 739 *obedient*; adhering to 83 *conformable*; faithful 929 *honourable*.

Vb. *observe*, heed, respect, have regard to, acknowledge, attend to 455 *be attentive*; keep, practise, adhere to, cling to, follow, abide by, be loyal to 83 *conform*; comply 739 *obey*; fulfil, discharge, perform, execute 676 *do*; satisfy 635 *suffice*.

keep faith, be faithful to 917 *do one's duty*; honour one's obligations, be as good as one's word, keep one's promise, be true to the spirit of, stand by 929 *be honourable*; redeem one's pledge, pay one's debt; give one his *or* her due 915 *grant claims*.

769. Nonobservance – N. *nonobservance*, inobservance; indifference 734 *laxity*; inattention, omission 458 *negligence*; nonadherence 84 *nonconformity*; abhorrence 607 *rejection*; anarchism 734 *anarchy*; nonperformance, nonfeasance 679 *inactivity*; nonfulfilment 726 *noncompletion*; infringement, violation 306 *overstepping*; noncompliance, disloyalty 738 *disobedience*; disregard 921 *disrespect*; bad faith, breach of promise 930 *perfidy*; retractation 603 *change of allegiance*; repudiation 533 *negation*; bankruptcy 805 *insolvency*.

Adj. *nonobservant*, nonpractising, lapsed; nonconformist 84 *unconformable*; disregarding 458 *negligent*; unprofessional, uncanonical; maverick, cowboy; indifferent, informal 734 *lax*; noncompliant 738 *disobedient*; infringing 954 *lawbreaking*; disloyal 918 *undutiful*; unfaithful 930 *perfidious*; anarchical 734 *anarchic*.

Vb. *not observe*, not practise 607 *reject*; not conform, not follow 84 *be unconformable*; discard 674 *stop using*; set aside 752 *abrogate*; omit 458 *neglect*; disregard 921 *not respect*; stretch a point 734 *be lax*; violate, do violence to, drive a coach and horses through, trample underfoot 176 *force*; transgress 306 *overstep*; not comply with 738 *disobey*; desert 918 *fail in duty*; break faith, break one's promise *or* one's word, dishonour 533 *negate*; renege on, go back on 603 *tergiversate*; prove unreliable 930 *be dishonest*; give the go-by, cut, shirk 620 *avoid*; palter, quibble, fob off 518 *be equivocal*.

770. Compromise – N. *compromise*, concession; mutual concession, give and take, formula 765 *compact*; second best, pis aller, half a loaf 35 *inferiority*; modus vivendi, working arrangement 624 *way*; splitting the difference 30 *average*; halfway 625 *middle way*; balancing act.

Vb. *compromise*, find a formula, find a basis; give and take, meet one halfway; not insist, stretch a point 734 *be lax*; go half and half, split the difference 30 *average out*; compound, commute; compose differences, go to arbitration; patch up 719 *pacify*; take the good with the bad, make the best of a bad job.

Section 4:
Possessive relations

771. Acquisition – N. *acquisition*, getting, earning; acquirement, obtainment, procurement; collection 74 *assemblage*; money-grubbing 816 *avarice*; pool, scoop, jackpot 74 *accumulation*; trover 484 *discovery*; recovery, retrieval, revendication, recoupment; redemption 792 *purchase*; appropriation 786 *taking*; subreption 788 *stealing*; inheritance, patrimony; find, trouvaille, windfall, treasure trove; legacy, bequest 781 *gift*; gratuity 962 *reward*; prize, plum 729 *trophy*; plunder 790 *booty*.

earnings, income, wage, salary 804 *pay*; rate for the job, pay scale, differential; pension, superannuation, compensation, golden handshake; remuneration, emolument 962 *reward*; perquisite, perks, fringe benefits; salvage, totting; commission, rake-off 810 *discount*; return, receipts, proceeds, turnover, takings 807 *receipt*; harvest, vintage, crop, gleanings.

gain, thrift, savings 814 *economy*; credit side, profit, capital gain, winnings; dividend, share-out; usury, interest 36 *increment*; pay increase, rise 36 *increase*; advantage, benefit; personal benefit, main chance 932 *selfishness*.

Adj. *acquiring*, acquisitive, accumulative; on the make, winning 730 *prosperous*; hoarding, saving; greedy 816 *avaricious*.

gainful, paying, money-making, money-spinning, lucrative, remunerative 962 *rewarding*; advantageous 640 *profitable*; fruitful, fertile 164 *productive*; stipendiary, paid, remunerated, breadwinning.

acquired, had, got; ill-gotten; inherited, patrimonial; on the credit side.

Vb. *acquire*, get, come by; earn, gain, obtain, procure; find, come across, pick up, light on 484 *discover*; get hold of, lay one's hands on, make one's own 786 *appropriate*; win, capture 786 *take*; pick, glean, gather, reap, crop, harvest; tap, milk, mine 304 *extract*; collect, accumulate, pile up 74 *bring together*; scrape together, rake t.; raise, levy, raise the wind; save up, hoard 632 *store*; buy 792 *purchase*; beg, borrow or steal; get a living, turn an honest penny; draw a salary, be in receipt of 782 *receive*; convert, cash, encash, realize, clear, make; get back, recover, salvage, recycle, regain, redeem, retrieve; reclaim; attain, reach.

inherit, come into, be left; succeed to, step into the shoes of, be the heir of.

gain, make a profit; make, win 730 *prosper*; make a fortune *or* a killing 800 *get rich*; scoop, win the jackpot, break the bank.

be profitable, profit, repay, pay well; bring in, gross, yield 164 *produce*; pay a dividend, show a profit 730 *prosper*; accrue, roll in, stick to one's fingers.

772. Loss – N. *loss*, deprivation, privation, bereavement; dispossession 786 *expropriation*; sacrifice, forfeiture 963 *penalty*; perdition 165 *ruin*; depreciation 655 *deterioration*; diminishing returns 42 *decrement*; setback, check, reverse; overdraft 805 *insolvency*; consumption 806 *expenditure*; wastage, leakage 634 *waste*; dissipation, evaporation, drain 37 *decrease*.

Adj. *losing*, unprofitable 641 *profitless*; squandering 815 *prodigal*; the worse for wear 655 *deteriorated*; forfeiting, sacrificial; deprived, dispossessed, robbed; denuded, stripped of, shorn of, bereft, bereaved; minus, without, lacking; rid of, quit of; out of pocket, in the red, overdrawn, insolvent; non-profitmaking.

lost, gone, vanished 446 *disappearing*; missing 188 *misplaced*; untraceable, lost, stolen or strayed 190 *absent*; off one's hands; lacking 307 *deficient*; irrecoverable, irreclaimable, irretrievable, irredeemable, unsalvageable, nonrecyclable 634 *wasted*; spent, squandered; forfeit, sacrificed.

Vb. *lose*, mislay 188 *misplace*; miss, let slip, kiss good-bye to 138 *lose a chance*; have nothing to show for, throw away 634 *waste*; forfeit, sacrifice; spill, pour down the drain; throw good money after bad 806 *expend*; be down, be out of pocket; incur losses, sell at a loss; go bankrupt 805 *not pay*; be overdrawn, be in the red.

773. Possession – N. *possession*, ownership, proprietorship, rightful possession, enjoyment, usufruct, uti possidetis; seisin, occupancy, nine points of the law, bird in the hand; mastery, hold, grasp, grip 778 *retention*; tenancy, holding; tenure, fee, fief; prescription 610 *habit*; sole possession, monopoly, corner; preoccupancy, preemption, squatting; future possession, expectations, heirship, inheritance, heritage, patrimony; taking possession, claiming 786 *taking*.

Adj. *possessing*, having, holding, etc. vb.; proprietorial, propertied, landed; in possession, occupying; endowed with, blest w.; monopolistic, possessive.

possessed, enjoyed, etc. vb.; in the possession of, in one's hand, in one's grasp; in one's account, to one's name, to one's credit; at one's disposal; proper, personal 80 *special*; one's own, unshared, private; engaged, occupied; inherent, appertaining.

Vb. *possess*, be possessed of, own, have; hold in one's grasp 778 *retain*; command 673 *dispose of*; call one's own, boast of 915 *claim*; contain, include 78 *comprise*; fill, occupy; squat, inhabit; enjoy 673 *use*; have all to oneself, corner the market; get, make one's own 786 *take*; recover,

retrieve, preempt 135 *be early*; come into 771 *inherit*.

774. Nonownership – N. *nonownership*, nonpossession, nonoccupancy, vacancy; tenancy, lease; pauperism 801 *poverty*; deprivation, disentitlement 772 *loss*; no-man's-land 190 *emptiness*.

Adj. *not owning*, dependent 745 *subject*; dispossessed, disentitled; destitute, penniless 801 *poor*; unblest with; minus, without 627 *required*.

unpossessed, not belonging; ownerless, nobody's; international, common; unclaimed, disowned; up for grabs, anybody's; unheld, unoccupied, vacant 190 *empty*; derelict 779 *not retained*; going begging 860 *unwanted*.

775. Joint possession – N. *joint possession*, joint ownership, common o.; common land, common, global commons; public property; joint stock, pool, kitty 632 *store*; cooperative system, mutualism 706 *cooperation*; nationalization, public ownership, state o., socialism, communism, collectivism; collective farm, collective, commune, kolkhoz, kibbutz; sharecropping, métayage.

participation, membership 78 *inclusion*; sharing, co-sharing, partnership, profit-sharing 706 *association*; Dutch treat, bottle party; dividend, shareout; share, fair s. 783 *portion*; complicity, involvement, sympathy, fellow feeling, joint action.

participator, member, partner, co-p., sharer 707 *colleague*; parcener, coheir, joint h.; shareholder, stockholder 776 *possessor*; co-tenant, flat-mate, room-m., housing association; sharecropper, métayer; cooperator, mutualist; trade unionist; collectivist, socialist, communist; commune-dweller, kibbutznik; sympathizer, contributor 707 *patron*.

Adj. *sharing*, joint, profit-sharing, cooperative; common, communal, international, global; collective, socialistic, communistic; partaking, participating, in on, involved 708 *corporate*; in the swim, in the thick of things; sympathetic, condoling.

Vb. *participate*, have a hand in, join in, be in on 706 *cooperate*; partake of, share in; share, go shares, go fifty-fifty 783 *apportion*; share expenses, go Dutch.

communalize, socialize, mutualize, nationalize, internationalize, communize; put in the kitty, pool, hold in common.

776. Possessor – N. *possessor*, holder, person in possession; taker, captor, conqueror; trespasser, squatter; monopolizer, dog in the manger; occupant, occupier, incumbent; mortgagee, lessee, leaseholder, copyholder, tenant; householder, freeholder; yeoman.

owner, monarch of all one surveys; master, mistress, proprietor, proprietress; buyer 792 *purchaser*; lord of the manor, landed interest; squire, laird 868 *aristocracy*; man *or* woman of property, property-holder, shareholder, stockholder, landowner, landlord, landlady; testator 781 *giver*.

beneficiary, feoffee 782 *recipient*; devisee, legatee; inheritor, successor, next of kin; heir, heiress.

777. Property – N. *property*, meum et tuum, suum cuique; possession, possessions, one's all; personalty, personal property; church property, temporalities; real property, immovables (**see** *lands*); movables, personal estate, goods and chattels, appurtenances, belongings, paraphernalia, effects, personal e., impedimenta, baggage, things, what one stands up in; goods, wares 795 *merchandise*; plant, fixtures, furniture.

estate, assets, frozen a., liquid a., assets and liabilities; what one is worth; resources 629 *means*; substance, capital 800 *wealth*; revenue, income 807 *receipt*; valuables, securities, stocks and shares, portfolio; stake, holding, investment; copyright, patent; right, title, interest; lease, tenure, freehold, copyhold; tenement, hereditament.

lands, acres, grounds; estate, property; real estate, realty; holding, tenure, allodium, domain, demesne; messuage, toft,

plot 184 *territory*; crown lands, common land.

dower, dowry, dot, portion, marriage p., marriage settlement; allotment, allowance; alimony, patrimony, birthright 915 *dueness*; heritage, inheritance, legacy, bequest; heirloom; expectations, remainder, reversion; limitation, entail; mortmain.

Adj. *proprietary*, branded, patented; propertied, landed, predial, manorial, seigniorial, feudal, allodial, freehold, leasehold, copyhold; patrimonial, hereditary, heritable, testamentary.

Vb. *dower*, endow 781 *give*; devise 780 *bequeath*; grant, allot 780 *assign*; establish, found.

778. Retention – N. *retention*, prehensility, tenacity; tenaciousness, retentiveness, holding on, hanging on; handhold, foothold, toehold 218 *support*; bridgehead, beachhead 34 *advantage*; clutches, grip, iron g., grasp, hold, stranglehold, half-nelson; squeeze, clinch, lock; hug, bear h., embrace, clasp 889 *endearment*; keep, keeping in 747 *detention*; finders keepers 760 *refusal*; containment, holding action, pincer movement 235 *enclosure*; plug, stop 264 *stopper*; ligament 47 *bond*.

nippers, pincers, tweezers, pliers, wrench, tongs, forceps, vice, clamp 47 *fastening*; talon, claw, nails 256 *sharp point*; tentacle, hook, tendril 378 *feeler*; teeth, fangs 256 *tooth*; paw, hand 378 *finger*; fist, clenched f.

Adj. *retentive*, tenacious, prehensile; vice-like, retaining 747 *restraining*; clinging, adhesive 48 *cohesive*; firm, tight, strangling, throttling; tight-fisted 816 *parsimonious*.

retained, in the grip of, pinioned, pinned; fast, stuck f., bound, held; detained 747 *imprisoned*; held in, contained; saved, kept 666 *preserved*; kept back, withheld; nontransferable, inalienable; entailed, in mortmain.

Vb. *retain*, hold; grab, buttonhole 702 *obstruct*; hold up, catch 218 *support*; hold on, hold fast, hold tight, not let go; cling to, hang on to, stick to 48 *agglutinate*;

fasten on, grip, grasp, clench; hug, clasp, clutch, embrace; pin down, hold d.; have by the throat, tighten one's grip 747 *restrain*; fix one's teeth in, dig one's nails in, dig one's toes in, hang on like a bulldog, hang on for dear life; detain; contain, keep within limits 235 *enclose*; keep to oneself, keep back; not dispose of 632 *store*; save, keep 666 *preserve*; not part with, withhold 760 *refuse*.

779. Nonretention – N. *nonretention*, parting with, disposal 780 *transfer*; selling off 793 *sale*; letting go, release 746 *liberation*; unfreezing, decontrol; dispensation, exemption 919 *nonliability*; dissolution (of a marriage) 896 *divorce*; abandonment, renunciation 621 *relinquishment*; availability, salability, disposability.

derelict, deserted village, abandoned position; jetsam, flotsam 641 *rubbish*; castoff, slough; waif, stray, foundling, orphan; outcast, pariah.

Adj. *not retained*, not kept; disposed of, sold off; left behind 41 *remaining*; dispensed with, abandoned 621 *relinquished*; released 746 *liberated*; derelict, unappropriated 774 *unpossessed*; disowned, disinherited; heritable, transferable; available 793 *salable*.

Vb. *not retain*, part with, transfer 780 *assign*; dispose of 793 *sell*; be openhanded 815 *be prodigal*; free, let go, unhand, relax one's grip; unlock, unclench 263 *open*; unbind, untie 46 *disunite*; forgo, dispense with, do without, spare, give up 621 *relinquish*; renounce, abjure 603 *recant*; cancel, revoke 752 *abrogate*; derestrict 746 *liberate*; replace 150 *substitute*; disown, disclaim; divorce; disinherit 801 *impoverish*; get rid of, cast off, ditch, jettison 300 *eject*; cast away, abandon; pension off, invalid out; discharge, give notice 300 *dismiss*; lay off, stand o.; drop, discard 674 *stop using*.

780. Transfer (of property) – N. *transfer*, transmission, consignment, delivery, handover 272 *transference*; impropriation; settlement, limitation; conveyancing, conveyance; bequeathal; assignment; alienation 779 *nonretention*; demise, devise, bequest 781 *gift*; lease, let, rental, hire; trade 791 *barter*; conversion, exchange 151 *interchange*; nationalization, privatization; change of hands, changeover; succession, reversion, inheritance; pledge, pawn, hostage.

Adj. *transferred*, made over; transferable, conveyable, alienable, exchangeable, negotiable; heritable, reversional, reversionary; givable, bestowable.

Vb. *assign*, convey, transfer by deed; sign away, give a. 781 *give*; let, rent, hire 784 *lease*; alienate 793 *sell*; negotiate, barter 791 *trade*; exchange, convert 151 *interchange*; confer ownership, impropriate, invest with; deliver, hand over 272 *transfer*; pledge, pawn 784 *lend*; nationalize, municipalize 775 *communalize*.

bequeath, will and bequeath, devise, demise; grant, assign; leave, make a bequest; make a will, add a codicil.

781. Giving – N. *giving*, bestowal, donation; alms-giving, charity 901 *philanthropy*; generosity 813 *liberality*; contribution 703 *subvention*; presentation 962 *reward*; endowment, settlement 777 *dower*; grant, accordance, conferment; bequeathal.

gift, keepsake, token; present, birthday p.; Christmas box, whip-round, tip, honorarium, baksheesh, gratuity 962 *reward*; token, consideration; bribe 612 *inducement*; prize, award 729 *trophy*; benefit; alms 901 *philanthropy*; bounty, manna; largesse, donation, hand-out; bonus, bonanza; perks, perquisites; grant, allowance, subsidy 703 *subvention*; grace, favour, service, labour of love; free gift, ex gratia payment; windfall 771 *acquisition*; bequest, legacy 780 *transfer*.

offering, votive. 979 *piety*; peace offering, thank o., offertory, collection 981 *oblation*; widow's mite; contribution, subscription, flag day; ante, stake.

giver, donor, bestower; rewarder, tipper, briber; presenter, awarder, prizegiver; testator, legator, devisor, bequeather; subscriber, contributor; tribute-payer 742 *subject*; almsgiver, blood donor 903 *benefactor*; generous giver, Lady Bountiful, Father Christmas 813 *good giver*.

Adj. *giving*, granting etc. vb.; subscribing, contributory 703 *aiding*; alms-giving, charitable, eleemosynary 897 *benevolent*; votive, oblatory 981 *worshipping*; generous, bountiful 813 *liberal*.

Vb. *give*, bestow, render; afford, provide; grant, accord 756 *permit*; gift, donate, make a present of; leave 780 *bequeath*; dower, endow, enrich; present, award 962 *reward*; confer, bestow upon, invest with; dedicate, consecrate, vow to 759 *offer*; offer up, immolate, sacrifice 981 *offer worship*; tip, remember, cross one's palm with silver; grease one's palm 612 *bribe*; bestow alms 897 *philanthropize*; give freely, put one's hand in one's pocket, lavish, pour out, shower upon 813 *be liberal*; spare, give away; treat, entertain 882 *be hospitable*; give out, dispense 783 *apportion*; contribute, subscribe, subsidize 703 *aid*; pay one's share *or* whack, chip in 775 *participate*; part with, fork out, shell o. 804 *pay*; share, impart 524 *communicate*; pay tribute; hand over, make o., deliver 780 *assign*; commit, consign 272 *send*.

782. Receiving – N. *receiving*, admittance, acceptance 299 *reception*; getting 771 *acquisition*; inheritance, succession, heirship; collection, collectorship, receivership; a receipt, windfall 781 *gift*; toll, tribute, dues, receipts, proceeds, winnings, takings 771 *earnings*; receiving end.

recipient, acceptor, receiver, taker; trustee 754 *consignee*; addressee 588 *correspondent*; buyer 792 *purchaser*; donee, grantee, assignee, allottee, licensee, patentee, concessionnaire, lessee, releasee; heir 776 *beneficiary*; payee, earner, stipendiary; pensioner, annuitant; winner, prize-w.; object of charity 763 *beggar*.

receiver, official r., liquidator 798 *treasurer*; payee, collector, debt-c., rent-c., tax-c., tax-farmer, publican; income-tax officer, excise o., customs officer;

booking clerk; shareholder, bond-holder, rentier.

Adj. *receiving*, recipient; receptive, welcoming; paid, stipendiary, wage-earning; pensioned; awarded, given.

Vb. *receive*, be given, get 771 *acquire*; collect, levy 786 *take*; gross, net, pocket, pouch; be in receipt of; accept, take in 299 *admit*; draw, encash, be paid; inherit, succeed to, come into; receipt, acknowledge.

be received, be credited 38 *accrue*; come to hand, come in, roll in; stick to one's fingers; fall to one's share.

783. Apportionment – N. *apportionment*, allocation, division, partition, sharing out; shares, fair s., distribution, deal; dispensation, administration.

portion, share, share-out, cut, split; dividend; allocation, allotment; lot, contingent; proportion, ratio; quantum, quota; moiety 53 *part*; deal, hand (at cards); modicum, pittance, allowance; ration, dose, dosage, measure, dollop, whack, helping, slice of the cake 53 *piece*; rake-off, commission 810 *discount*.

Vb. *apportion*, allot, allocate; appoint, assign; assign a place, detail, billet; partition, zone; demarcate, delimit 236 *limit*; divide, carve up, split, cut; go shares 775 *participate*; share, share out, divvy up, distribute, spread around; dispense, administer, serve, deal, deal out, portion out, dole out, parcel out, dish out 781 *give*; mete out, measure, ration, dose.

Adv. *pro rata*, to each according to his *or* her share; proportionately, respectively, per head.

784. Lending – N. *lending*, hiring, leasing, farming out; letting, subletting; usury 802 *credit*; investment; mortgage, bridging loan; advance, imprest, loan, accommodation; pawnbroking; lease, let, sub-let.

pawnshop, pawnbroker's, mont-de-piété, pop-shop, hock s.; bank, credit company, finance c., building society.

lender, creditor; investor, financier, banker; money-lender, usurer, loan shark; pawnbroker, uncle; mortgagee, lessor, hirer, renter; backer, angel; tallyman; hire-purchase dealer.

Adj. *lending*, investing, laying out; usurious, extortionate; lent, loaned, on credit.

Vb. *lend*, loan, put out at interest; advance, accommodate, allow credit 802 *credit*; put up the money, back, finance; invest 791 *speculate*.

lease, let, hire out, farm out; sublet.

785. Borrowing – N. *borrowing*, touching; loan application; mortgage 803 *debt*; credit account, credit card; hire purchase, HP, instalment plan, the never-never; pledging, pawning; loan 784 *lending*; plagiarism, copying 20 *imitation*.

Vb. *borrow*, borrow from, touch for 761 *request*; hypothecate, mortgage, pawn, pledge, pop, hock; take a loan, exact a benevolence; get credit, take on tick; buy on hire purchase 792 *purchase*; run into debt 803 *be in debt*; promise to pay, apply for a loan, raise the wind; invite investment, accept deposits; beg, borrow, or steal 771 *acquire*; plagiarize 20 *copy*.

hire, rent, farm, lease, take on lease, charter.

786. Taking – N. *taking*, seizure, capture; grasp, apprehension 778 *retention*; appropriation, assumption 916 *arrogation*; requisition, commandeering, compulsory purchase 771 *acquisition*; exaction, taxation 809 *tax*; recovery, retrieval, recoupment; removal 188 *displacement*, 788 *stealing*; abduction, kidnapping, raid; haul, catch 790 *booty*; takings 771 *earnings*.

expropriation, dispossession, angary; forcible seizure, attachment, distraint, distress, foreclosure; eviction, expulsion 300 *ejection*; takeover, deprivation, divestment 752 *abrogation*; hiving off, asset-stripping; confiscation; exaction, extortion; swindle, rip-off; impounding, sequestration.

rapacity, rapaciousness 859 *hunger*; greed 816 *avarice*; blood-sucking, extortion, blackmail.

taker, appropriator, remover; seizer, snatcher, grabber; spoiler, raider 789 *robber*; kidnapper, abductor, press gang; slave-raider, slaver; captor 741 *master*; usurper, arrogator; extortioner, blackmailer; locust 168 *destroyer*; bloodsucker, leech, parasite, vampire, harpy, vulture, wolf, shark; predator; confiscator, sequestrator; expropriator; asset-stripper.

Adj. *taking*, abstractive, deductive; grasping, extortionate, rapacious, wolfish, vulturine; devouring, all-engulfing, voracious, ravening; raptorial, predatory 788 *thieving*; expropriatory, confiscatory; commandeering, requisitory; acquisitive, possessive 771 *acquiring*.

Vb. *take*, accept, be given 782 *receive*; take in 299 *admit*; take up, snatch up; take hold 778 *retain*; lay lands upon, seize, snatch, grab, pounce on; snatch at, reach out for, make a long arm; grasp at, clutch at, grab at, scramble for; capture 727 *overmaster*; conquer 745 *subjugate*; catch, intercept, apprehend, nobble 747 *arrest*; hook, trap 542 *ensnare*; net, land, bag, pocket, pouch 771 *acquire*; gather, cull, pick, pluck; reap, harvest; scrounge, pick up, snap up, snaffle; help oneself 788 *steal*; pick clean, strip; withdraw (**see** *take away*); draw off 304 *extract*; sweep the board, scoop the pool.

appropriate, take for oneself, make one's own, annex; pirate, plagiarize 20 *copy*; take possession, stake one's claim; take over, assume ownership; overrun, people, populate, occupy, settle, colonize; win, conquer; take back, recover, repossess, retrieve, reclaim; commandeer, requisition 737 *demand*; nationalize, secularize 775 *communalize*; denationalize, privatize; trespass, squat; make free with; monopolize, hog; engulf 299 *absorb*.

levy, raise, extort, exact, wrest from 304 *extract*; exact tribute, collect a toll 809 *tax*; overtax, suck dry (**see** *fleece*); draw off, drain 300 *empty*; wring, squeeze 735 *oppress*.

take away, remove 188 *displace*; hive off, abstract, relieve of 788 *steal*; remove bodily, kidnap, shanghai, impress, abduct, ravish, carry off, bear away; elope with, clear off w. 296 *decamp*; loot, plunder 788 *rob*.

deprive, bereave, orphan, widow; divest, denude, strip 229 *uncover*; dispossess 916 *disentitle*; oust, evict, expel 300 *eject*; expropriate, confiscate, sequestrate, distrain, foreclose; disinherit, cut out of one's will.

fleece, skin, strip bare; take to the cleaners, rip off; swindle 542 *deceive*; blackmail, bleed, sponge, suck dry; soak, sting; mulct 788 *defraud*; eat out of house and home 301 *eat*; leave one without a penny 801 *impoverish*.

787. Restitution – N. *restitution*, giving back, return; reinstatement, rehabilitation 656 *restoration*; rescue 668 *deliverance*; recuperation, replevin, recovery; compensation, indemnification; repayment, recoupment; refund, reimbursement; indemnity, damages 963 *penalty*; amends, reparation 941 *atonement*.

Adj. *restoring*, restitutory, refunding; indemnificatory, compensatory 941 *atoning*.

Vb. *restitute*, make restitution 656 *restore*; return, render, give back 779 *not retain*; pay up, cough up 804 *pay*; refund, repay, recoup, reimburse; indemnify, compensate, make it up to; make reparation 941 *atone*; bring back, repatriate; ransom, redeem 668 *deliver*; reinstate, reinvest, rehabilitate, raise one to his *or* her feet; recover, retrieve.

788. Stealing – N. *stealing*, theft, larceny; pilfering, pickpocketing, shoplifting; burglary, house-breaking, breaking and entering; safe-blowing, s.-breaking; robbery, highway r., gang r.; robbery with violence, stickup, holdup, mugging; smash and grab raid; cattle-raiding, c.-rustling; abduction, kidnapping, hijack; slave-raiding; body-snatching; abstraction, removal 786 *taking*; cribbing, pirating 20 *imitation*; joyride 785 *borrowing*; job, fiddle.

brigandage, banditry, outlawry, piracy, buccaneering, filibustering; privateering,

letters of marque 718 *warfare*; raiding 712 *attack*.

spoliation, plundering, looting, pillage; sack, depredations, rapine 165 *havoc*.

peculation, embezzlement, misappropriation, malversation, breach of trust, fraudulent conversion; blackmail, extortion, protection racket; daylight robbery, rip-off; moonlighting, tax evasion, fraud, fiddle, swindle, cheating; confidence trick, skin game 542 *deception*.

thievishness, thievery, light fingers, kleptomania; predacity 786 *rapacity*; dishonesty, crookedness 930 *improbity*; den of thieves, thieves' kitchen.

Adj. *thieving*, with intent to steal; thievish, light-fingered; kleptomaniac; larcenous, burglarious; predatory, predacious, raptorial; piratical, buccaneering, filibustering; scrounging, foraging; fraudulent, on the fiddle 930 *dishonest*.

Vb. *steal*, lift, thieve, pilfer, shoplift, help oneself; be light-fingered, pick pockets, have a finger in the till; pick locks, blow a safe; burgle, burglarize, housebreak; rob, relieve of; rifle, sack, clean out; swipe, nobble, nick, pinch, half-inch, pocket, snaffle, snitch, knock off 786 *take*; forage, scrounge; lift cattle, rustle, make off with; abduct, kidnap, shanghai; abstract, purloin, filch; sneak off with, walk off w., spirit away; crib, plagiarize, pirate 20 *copy*; smuggle, run, bootleg, poach, hijack.

defraud, embezzle, peculate, misappropriate, purloin, let stick to one's fingers; fiddle, cook the books, obtain money on false pretences; con, swindle, cheat, diddle, chisel, do out of 542 *deceive*; rook, gull, dupe; rip off 786 *fleece*.

rob, rob with violence, mug; hold up, stick up; buccaneer, filibuster, maraud, raid; foray, forage, scrounge; strip, gut, ransack, rifle; plunder, pillage, loot, sack, despoil, ravage 165 *lay waste*; victimize, blackmail, demand money with menaces; extort, screw, squeeze 735 *oppress*.

789. Thief – N. *thief*, swell mob, light-fingered gentry, den of thieves; crook, Artful Dodger; pickers and stealers, light fingers; kleptomaniac, stealer, lifter, filcher, purloiner, pilferer, petty thief, larcenist; sneak thief, shoplifter; pickpocket, dip, cutpurse, bag-snatcher; cattle thief, rustler; burglar, cat b., housebreaker, safe-b., safe-blower, cracksman, picklock, yegg; poacher, bootlegger, smuggler, runner, gun r.; abductor, kidnapper 786 *taker*; slaver, slave-raider; body-snatcher, resurrectionist; fence, receiver of stolen property; plagiarist, infringer, pirate.

robber, robber band, forty thieves; brigand, bandit, outlaw, Robin Hood; footpad, highwayman, knight of the road, Dick Turpin; mugger, thug, gang-robber 904 *ruffian*; gangster, racketeer; gunman, hijacker; sea rover, pirate, buccaneer, picaroon, corsair, filibuster, privateer; Captain Kidd, Long John Silver; marauder, raider, freebooter; plunderer, pillager, sacker, ravager, despoiler, wrecker.

defrauder, embezzler, peculator, fiddler, diddler; defaulter, welsher; swindler, sharper, cheat, shark, con man, chevalier d'industrie 545 *trickster*; forger, counterfeiter, coin-clipper.

790. Booty – **N.** *booty*, spoils 729 *trophy*; plunder, loot, pillage; prey, victim, quarry; find, prize, haul, catch 771 *gain*; pickings, tottings; stolen goods, swag; moonshine, hooch, bootleg, contraband; illicit gains, graft, boodle.

791. Barter – **N.** *barter*, exchange, fair e., swap 151 *interchange*; exchange of goods, payment in kind, truck system; traffic, trading, dealing, buying and selling; factorage, brokerage, jobbing, stockjobbing, share-pushing; negotiation, bargaining, higgling, haggling, horse-trading.

trade, trading, exporting 272 *transference*; protection, trade restrictions; free trade 796 *market*; traffic, drug t., slave trade; smuggling, black market; retail trade 793 *sale*; free enterprise 744 *scope*; profit-making, mutual profit; tied aid, dollar diplomacy 612 *inducement*; commerce 622 *business*; private enterprise, state e.; private sector, public s.; transaction, deal,

business d., bargain 765 *compact*; clientele, custom 792 *purchase*.

Adj. *trading*, trafficking, exchanging; swapping; commercial, mercantile; wholesale, retail; exchangeable, marketable 793 *salable*; for profit 618 *speculative*.

Vb. *trade*, exchange 151 *interchange*; barter, truck, swap, do a s.; traffic in, buy and sell, export and import; trade in, deal in, handle 622 *do business*; deal in stolen property, fence; turn over one's stock 793 *sell*; commercialize, put on a business footing; trade with, do business w., deal w., open an account w.; finance, back, promote; have an eye to business.

speculate, venture, risk 618 *gamble*; invest, sink one's capital in, put one's money to work; rig the market, racketeer, profiteer; deal in futures, dabble in shares, play the market, go bust; operate, bull, bear, stag.

bargain, negotiate, chaffer; push up, beat down; huckster, haggle, higgle, dicker 766 *make terms*; bid for, preempt; outbid 759 *offer*; overbid, underbid; stickle, stick out for, hold out for 766 *give terms*; settle for, take; drive a bargain 765 *contract*.

792. Purchase – **N.** *purchase*, buying; buying up, takeover, cornering, forestalling, preemption; redemption, ransom 668 *deliverance*; hire purchase 785 *borrowing*; spending, shopping spree 806 *expenditure*; mail order; custom, patronage, consumer demand 627 *requirement*; buying over, bribery 612 *inducement*; bid, takeover b. 759 *offer*; first refusal, right of purchase; a purchase, buy, bargain, one's money's worth; purchases, shopping list.

purchaser, buyer; vendee, consignee; shopper, window-s.; customer, patron, client, clientele, consumer; bidder, highest b.; bargainer, haggler; share-buyer, bull, stag.

Adj. *buying*, redemptive, purchasing, shopping, marketing; cash and carry, cash on delivery, COD; preemptive, bidding, bargaining, in the market for; bullish.

Vb. *purchase*, make a p., buy 771 *ac-*

quire; shop, market, go shopping; buy outright, pay cash for; buy on credit, buy on hire purchase; buy on account 785 *borrow*; buy in 632 *store*; buy up, preempt, corner, make a corner in; buy out, make a take-over bid; buy over, suborn 612 *bribe*; buy back, redeem, ransom; pay for 804 *defray*; invest in 791 *speculate*; bid for 759 *offer*; buy shares, bull, stag.

793. Sale – N. *sale*, selling, marketing; disposal 779 *nonretention*; clearance, sell-out; jumble sale, bazaar; sale of office, simony 930 *improbity*; monopoly, oligopoly 747 *restraint*; public sale, auction, roup, Dutch auction, vendue; good market, market for; boom 730 *prosperity*; salesmanship, sales talk, pitch, patter, spiel; hard sell, soft s. 528 *advertisement*; market research 459 *inquiry*; salability, marketability; vendible, seller, best-s., selling line 795 *merchandise*.

seller, vendor, consignor, transferor; shareseller, bear; auctioneer; market trader, barrow boy 794 *pedlar*; shopkeeper, dealer 633 *caterer*; wholesaler, marketer, retailer 794 *tradespeople*; sales representative, rep, door-to-door salesman *or* -woman; traveller, commercial t., knight of the road; agent, canvasser, tout; shop walker, shop assistant, salesman, saleswoman; clerk, booking c., ticket agent; roundsman *or* -woman.

Adj. *salable*, vendible, marketable, on sale; sold, sold out; in demand, sought after, called for; available, up for sale; bearish; on auction, under the hammer.

Vb. *sell,* make a sale; flog, dispose of; market, put on sale, vend; unload on the market, dump; hawk, peddle, push; canvass, tout; cater for 633 *provide*; put up for sale, auction, auction off, bring under the hammer, knock down to; wholesale; retail 791 *trade*; realize one's capital, encash; undercut, sell off, remainder; sell up *or* out, wind up 145 *cease*.

be sold, be on sale, sell, have a market, meet a demand, sell like hot cakes, sell out.

794. Merchant – N. *merchant*, merchant venturer; livery company, guild, chamber of commerce; concern, firm 708 *corporation*; businessman *or* -woman; entrepreneur; trafficker, fence; importer, exporter; wholesaler; merchandiser, dealer, chandler; middleman, broker, stockbroker; stock-jobber, share-pusher; financier 784 *lender*.

tradespeople, tradesfolk; tradesman, retailer, middleman; shopkeeper, storekeeper 793 *seller*; monger, provision merchant 633 *caterer*.

pedlar, peddler 793 *seller*; rag-and-bone man; street seller, hawker, huckster, colporteur, bagman, chapman, cheapjack; costermonger, market trader, stallkeeper.

795. Merchandise – N. *merchandise*, line, staple; article, commodity, vendible, stock, stock-in-trade, range, repertoire 632 *store*; freight, cargo 193 *contents*; stuff, supplies, wares, goods; shop goods, consumer g., consumer durables; perishable goods, canned g., dry g., white g., sundries.

796. Market – N. *market*, mart; open market, free trade area, Common Market; free market, open-door policy 791 *trade*; black market, underground economy, black e.; marketplace 76 *focus*; street market, flea m.; auction room; fair, trade f., industries f., motor show; exhibition, shop window 522 *exhibit*; corn exchange; exchange, Stock E., Change, bourse, kerb market, bucket shop.

emporium, entrepôt, depot, warehouse 632 *storage*; wharf, quay; trading centre, trading post; bazaar, arcade, pedestrian precinct, shopping centre.

shop, retailer's; store, multiple s., department s., chain s.; emporium, bazaar, boutique, bargain basement, supermarket, hypermarket, superstore, cash and carry; concern, firm, establishment, house, trading h.; corner shop, stall, booth, stand, newstand, kiosk, barrow, vending machine, slot m.; counter; premises 687 *workshop*.

797. Money – N. *money*, Lsd, pounds, shillings and pence; pelf, Mammon 800 *wealth*; lucre, filthy l.; medium of exchange, cash nexus; currency, hard c., soft c.; honest money, legal tender; money of account, sterling, pound s.; precious metal (**see** *bullion*); ready money, the ready, cash, hard c., petty c.; change, small c., coppers; pocket money, pin m.; spending m.; paltry sum, chickenfeed, peanuts.

shekels, dibs, spondulicks, brass, tin, dough, lolly, bread; boodle, swag, loot.

funds, temporary f., hot money; liquidity, account, annuities; liquid assets; wherewithal, the needful 629 *means*; sinews of war, finances, exchequer, cash flow, cash supplies, monies, treasure 633 *provision*; remittance 804 *payment*; capital; reserves, balances, sterling b.; amount, figure, sum, round s., lump s.; pound, quid, smacker, oncer; fiver, tenner, pony, monkey, grand; mint of money, wads, scads, pile, packet, stacks 32 *great quantity*; moneybags, purse, bottomless p. 632 *store*.

finance, high f., world of finance; financial control, purse strings; money dealings, cash transaction; money market, exchange 796 *market*; exchange rate, valuta, parity; snake; floating pound; devaluation, depreciation, falling exchange rate; rising exchange rate, strong pound; bimetallism; gold standard; green pound; equalization fund, sinking f., revolving f.; deficit finance, inflation, inflationary spiral; disinflation, deflation; stagflation; reflation.

coinage, minting, issue; specie, minted coinage, coin, piece, coin of the realm; guinea, sovereign, half s.; crown; decimal coinage; numismatics, numismatology.

paper money, fiat m., fiduciary currency, assignat; bankroll, wad; note, banknote, treasury note, bill; draft, order, postal o., cheque, giro c., traveller's c., letter of credit; promissory note, note of hand, IOU; coupon, certificate, bond, premium b. 767 *security*.

false money, bad m., counterfeit m., base coin; flash note, forgery; dud cheque 805 *nonpayment*; clipped coinage, depreciated currency, devalued c.; demonetized coinage, obsolete c.

bullion, bar, ingot, nugget; solid gold, solid silver; precious metal, yellow m., platinum, gold, white g., electrum, silver, billon.

minter, moneyer, mint master; coiner, forger; money-dealer, money-changer, cambist 794 *merchant*; cashier 798 *treasurer*; financier, capitalist; moneybags 800 *rich person*.

Adj. *monetary*, numismatic; pecuniary, financial, fiscal, budgetary, coined, stamped, minted, issued; nummary, fiduciary; sterling; inflationary, deflationary; clipped, devalued, depreciated; withdrawn, demonetized.

Vb. *mint*, coin, stamp; monetize, issue; circulate; pass, utter; forge, counterfeit.

demonetize, withdraw, call in; devalue 812 *cheapen*.

798. Treasurer – N. *treasurer*, honorary t.; bursar, purser; cashier, teller, croupier; depositary, stakeholder, trustee, steward 754 *consignee*; liquidator 782 *receiver*; bookkeeper 808 *accountant*; banker, financier; paymaster, almoner, controller, Chancellor of the Exchequer; mint master 797 *minter*; giro, bank 799 *treasury*.

799. Treasury – N. *treasury*, treasure house; exchequer, public purse; reserves, fund 632 *store*; counting house, custom house; bursary, almonry; bank, Bank of England, Old Lady of Threadneedle Street; savings bank, Post Office savings b., penny b., building society; coffer, chest 194 *box*; treasure chest, depository 632 *storage*; strongroom, strongbox, safe, safe deposit, cash box, moneybox, piggybank, stocking, mattress; till, cash register, slot machine; box office, gate, turnstile; moneybag, purse, wallet, wad, rouleau 194 *case*.

800. Wealth – N. *wealth*, Mammon, lucre, pelf, brass, moneybags 797 *money*;

moneymaking, golden touch, Midas t., philosopher's stone; riches, fleshpots, fat of the land 635 *plenty*; luxury 637 *superfluity*; opulence, affluence 730 *prosperity*; easy circumstances 376 *euphoria*; solvency, soundness, credit-worthiness 802 *credit*; solidity, substance; independence, competence, self-sufficiency; high income, surtax bracket; well-lined purse, capital 629 *means*; liquid assets, bank account; bottomless purse, goose that lays golden eggs; nest egg 632 *store*; tidy sum, mint of money, pots of m., scads, wads, packet 32 *great quantity*; fortune, inheritance; estates 777 *property*; bonanza, mine, gold m.; El Dorado, riches of Solomon, king's ransom; plutocracy, capitalism.

rich person, wealthy p., well-to-do p., man *or* woman of means; baron, tycoon, magnate, nabob, moneybags, millionaire, multi-m., millionairess, Croesus, Midas; moneymaker, moneyspinner, fat cat, capitalist, plutocrat, bloated p.; heir, heiress 776 *beneficiary*; the haves, moneyed class, leisured c. 848 *beau monde*; new rich, nouveau riche, parvenu, self-made man *or* woman 730 *prosperous person*.

Adj. *rich*, fertile, abundant; luxurious, plushy, ritzy, slap-up; diamond-studded, glittering 875 *ostentatious*; wealthy, well-endowed, well-provided for; opulent, affluent 730 *prosperous*; well-off, well-to-do, comfortably off, well-paid, overpaid.

moneyed, propertied, worth a packet, worth millions; made of money, lousy with m., rolling in m., dripping, loaded; stinking rich, filthy r., disgustingly r.; in funds, in cash, in credit, in the black; well-heeled, flush, in the money, in the dough, quids in, doing nicely thankyou; credit-worthy, solvent, able to pay.

Vb. *afford*, have the means *or* the wherewithal, make both ends meet, keep one's head above water, keep the wolf from the door, keep up with the Joneses.

get rich, come into 771 *inherit*; do all right for oneself 730 *prosper*; make money, mint m., spin m., rake in the shekels, laugh all the way to the bank;

make a packet *or* a pile, make a bomb, make a fortune, feather one's nest, line one's pocket, strike it rich, hit the jackpot 771 *gain*.

801. Poverty – N. *poverty*, Lady Poverty 945 *asceticism*; renunciation of wealth, voluntary poverty 931 *disinterestedness*; impecuniosity, financial embarrassment, difficulties, Queer Street 805 *insolvency*; impoverishment, beggary, mendicancy; penury, pennilessness, pauperism, destitution; privation, indigence, neediness, necessitousness, need 627 *requirement*; wolf at the door, famine 946 *fasting*; light pocket, empty purse, slender means, meagre resources, reduced circumstances, low water 636 *insufficiency*; straits, distress, belt-tightening 825 *suffering*; grinding poverty, subsistence level, hand-to-mouth existence, bare e.; poorness, meanness, beggarliness, shreds and tatters; recession, slump, depression 655 *deterioration*; squalor, public s., slum 655 *dilapidation*; workhouse, poorhouse.

poor person, bankrupt, insolvent 805 *nonpayer*; hermit 945 *ascetic*; pauper, indigent, rag-picker, starveling, vagrant, tramp, down-and-out 763 *beggar*; slum-dweller, underdog; the poor, new poor, the have-nots, the underprivileged 869 *lower classes*; poor white, white trash; Cinderella 867 *object of scorn*; poor relation.

Adj. *poor*, not well-off, badly o., hard up; lowpaid, underpaid; impecunious, short of funds, out of pocket, in the red; skint, cleaned out, bust, broke, flat b., stony b., bankrupt 805 *nonpaying*; reduced to poverty, on the breadline, in the dole queue; impoverished, dispossessed, deprived, stripped, fleeced, robbed; penurious, poverty-stricken; needy, indigent, in want, necessitous; homeless, shelterless; hungry 636 *underfed*; in distress, straitened, pinched, hard put to it, on one's uppers, on one's beam ends, not knowing which way to turn 700 *in difficulties*; unable to make both ends meet, unable to pay one's way *or* keep the wolf from the door; unprovided for, penniless, moneyless, destitute; down to one's last penny, without a bean, with nothing to hope for.

beggarly, shabby, seedy, down at heel, out at elbows, down and out, in rags, tattered, patched, barefoot, threadbare, tatty 655 *dilapidated*; scruffy, squalid, mean, slummy, back-street 649 *dirty*; poverty-stricken, poor as a church mouse, poor as Job.

Vb. *be poor*, earn little or nothing, live on a pittance, eke out a livelihood, scratch a living, scrape an existence, live from hand to mouth; feel the pinch, fall on hard times, be in dire straits, have to watch the pennies, be unable to afford; beg for one's bread; starve 859 *be hungry*; want, lack 627 *require*; not have two halfpennies to rub together; go broke 805 *not pay*; come down in the world 655 *deteriorate*.

impoverish, reduce to poverty, leave destitute, beggar, pauperize; ruin 165 *destroy*; rob, strip 786 *fleece*; dispossess, disinherit 786 *deprive*.

802. Credit – N. *credit*, repute 866 *prestige*; creditworthiness, reliability, sound proposition 929 *probity*; borrowing capacity, limit of credit; line of credit, tick; letter of credit, credit card, credit note; credit account, the black; account, score, tally, bill 808 *accounts*; loan, mortgage 784 *lending*.

creditor, dun; mortgagee, pledgee 784 *lender*; depositor, investor.

Vb. *credit*, give c., grant a loan 784 *lend*; credit one's account; grant, vote; take credit, open an account 785 *borrow*.

803. Debt – N. *debt*, indebtedness 785 *borrowing*; liability, obligation, commitment; encumbrance, mortgage; debit, charge; debts, bills; national debt, floating d.; promise to pay, debt of honour 764 *promise*; bad debt, write-off 772 *loss*; tally, account; deficit, overdraft, balance to pay 307 *shortfall*; inability to pay 805 *insolvency*; blocked account, frozen assets 805 *nonpayment*; deferred payment 802 *credit*; arrears, foreclosure.

interest, simple i., compound i.; excess-

ive i., usury, pound of flesh 784 *lending*; premium, rate of interest, bank rate.

debtor, loanee, borrower, loan applicant; obligor, drawee; mortgagor, pledgor; bad debtor, defaulter 805 *nonpayer*.

Adj. *indebted*, in debt, in hock, borrowing; liable, answerable; owing, overdrawn, in the red; encumbered, mortgaged; deep in debt, in Queer Street 700 *in difficulties*; unable to pay 805 *nonpaying*; in the hands of the receiver.

owed, unpaid; owing, due, overdue, in arrears; outstanding; on the debit side, chargeable, payable, debited; repayable, returnable, COD.

Vb. *be in debt*, owe money, pay interest; get credit, overdraw; get on tick 785 *borrow*; use a credit card, keep an account with; run up an account, run into debt; be in the red; cheat one's creditors, do a moonlight flit 805 *not pay*.

804. Payment – N. *payment*, paying for, defrayment; paying off, discharge, quittance, acquittance, satisfaction, liquidation, clearance, settlement; cash payment, down p. 797 *money*; first payment, earnest, deposit; instalment, standing order; voluntary payment, contribution 781 *offering*; payment in lieu, composition 150 *substitution*; repayment, compensation 787 *restitution*; disbursement, remittance 806 *expenditure*.

pay, payout, payoff, pay packet, pay day, wages, salary 771 *earnings*; grant, subsidy 703 *subvention*; salary, pension, annuity, remuneration, emolument, fee, bribe 962 *reward*; cut, commission 810 *discount*; contribution, subscription, collection, tribute 809 *tax*; damages, indemnity 963 *penalty*; compensation, redundancy pay, golden handshake; paymaster 798 *treasurer*.

Vb. *pay*, disburse 806 *expend*; contribute 781 *give*; pay in kind 791 *trade*; pay out, shell o., fork o., stump up, cough up; come across, do the needful, unloose the purse strings; pay a high price, pay through the nose; pay back, repay, reimburse 787 *restitute*; tickle *or* grease one's palm 612 *bribe*; remunerate, tip 962 *reward*; pay in advance, ante up; pay by cheque *or* by giro; pay on the nail, pay on the dot, pay cash; honour (a bill), pay up, meet, satisfy, redeem, discharge; liquidate, settle, settle an account, clear accounts with 808 *account*.

defray, pay for, bear the cost, put up funds; pay one's way, pay one's shot; foot the bill, meet the b., pick up the b., pay the piper; buy a round, stand treat 781 *give*; go Dutch 775 *participate*.

805. Nonpayment – N. *nonpayment*, default; defalcation 930 *improbity*; stoppage, deduction 963 *penalty*; moratorium, embargo, freeze; dishonouring, repudiation 760 *refusal*; tax avoidance, tax evasion 620 *avoidance*; deferred payment, hire purchase 785 *borrowing*; cancellation of debts 752 *abrogation*; protested bill, dishonoured cheque, dud c., bouncing c.; depreciation, devaluation.

insolvency, inability to pay, failure to meet one's obligations; crash, failure; bankruptcy; nothing in the kitty, overdrawn account, overdraft 636 *insufficiency*.

nonpayer, defaulter, defalcator, embezzler, tax dodger 789 *defrauder*; bilker, welsher, absconder; failure, lame duck; bankrupt, undischarged b.

Adj. *nonpaying*, defaulting, behindhand, in arrears; unable to pay, insolvent, bankrupt; hopelessly in debt 803 *indebted*; ruined 801 *poor*.

Vb. *not pay*, default, embezzle, swindle 788 *defraud*; fall into arrears, get behindhand; stop payment, freeze, block; refuse payment, protest a bill; fiddle one's income tax, practise tax evasion 930 *be dishonest*; divert, sequester 786 *deprive*; bounce one's cheque, dishonour, repudiate; become insolvent, go bankrupt, get whitewashed; sink, fail, break, go bust, crash, wind up, go into liquidation; welsh, bilk 542 *deceive*; abscond 296 *decamp*; be unable to pay 801 *be poor*; go off the gold standard, devalue 797 *demonetize*; cancel a debt, wipe the slate clean 752 *abrogate*.

806. Expenditure – N. *expenditure*, spending, disbursement 804 *payment*; cost of living; outgoings, overheads, costs, expenses; expense account; expense, outlay, investment; disinvestment, run on savings; fee, tax 804 *pay*; spending spree 815 *prodigality*.

Adj. *expending*, spending, sumptuary; generous 813 *liberal*; extravagant 815 *prodigal*; out of pocket.

Vb. *expend*, spend; buy 792 *purchase*; lay out, invest, sink money; be out of pocket, incur expenses; afford, stand, bear the cost 804 *pay*; run down one's account, draw on one's savings, disinvest; open one's purse, empty one's pocket; donate 781 *give*; spare no expense 813 *be liberal*; splash out 815 *be prodigal*; use up, consume, run through, get t. 634 *waste*.

807. Receipt – N. *receipt*, voucher, acknowledgement of payment; money received, credits, revenue, royalty, rents, rent-roll, dues; customs, taxes 809 *tax*; turnover, takings, proceeds, returns, receipts, box-office r., gate money, gate; income, privy purse; emolument, pay, salary, wages 771 *earnings*; remuneration 962 *reward*; pension, annuity; allowance, pocket money; alimony, maintenance; interest, return, rake-off; winnings, profits, capital gain 771 *gain*; bonus, premium 40 *extra*; prize 729 *trophy*; legacy 777 *dower*.

Adj. *received*, paid, receipted, acknowledged, acknowledged with thanks.

Vb. see 711 *acquire*, 782 *receive*, be received, 786 *take*.

808. Accounts – N. *accounts*, accountancy, commercial arithmetic; bookkeeping, entry, double e., single e.; audit, inspection of accounts; account, profit and loss a., balance sheet, debit and credit, receipts and expenditures; budgeting, budget 633 *provision*; running account, current a., cash a., suspense a., expense a.; statement of account, account rendered, compte rendu, statement, bill, waybill, invoice, manifest 87 *list*; account paid 804 *payment*; reckoning, score, tally, facts and figures 86 *numeration*.

account book, pass b., cheque b.; cash b., day b.; journal, ledger, register, books 548 *record*.

accountant, chartered a., certified public a.; cost accountant, bookkeeper, storekeeper; cashier 798 *treasurer*; inspector of accounts, auditor; actuary, statistician.

Adj. *accounting*, bookkeeping; actuarial, inventorial, budgetary; accountable.

Vb. *account*, keep the books, keep accounts; budget; cost, value, write up, write down 480 *estimate*; book, enter, journalize, post, carry over, debit, credit 548 *register*; prepare a balance sheet, balance accounts; settle accounts, square a., finalize a., wind up a.; prepare a statement, charge, bill, invoice; cook the books, fiddle 788 *defraud*; audit, inspect accounts, go through the books; take stock, inventory 87 *list*.

809. Price – **N.** *price*, selling p., market p., standard p., list p.; rate, going r., rate for the job; piece rate, flat r.; high rate, ceiling; low rate, floor; price control, fixed price; value, face v., par v., fair v., worth, money's w., what it will fetch; scarcity value, famine price; price list, tariff; quoted price, quotation; amount, figure, sum; ransom, fine 963 *penalty*; demand, dues, charge; surcharge, supplement 40 *extra*; excessive charge, extortion; fare, flat f., hire, rental, rent; fee, entrance *or* admission fee; refresher, commission, rake-off; freightage, wharfage, lighterage; salvage; postage; cover charge, corkage; bill, invoice, reckoning, shot.

cost, purchase price; damage, expenses 806 *expenditure*; running costs, overheads; wage bill; legal costs, damages 963 *penalty*; cost of living.

tax, taxes, dues; taxation, tax demand 737 *demand*; rating, assessment, appraisement 480 *estimate*; cess, rate, general r., water r.; levy, toll, duty; imposition, impost; charge, scot and lot (**see** *price*); exaction, forced loan 740 *compulsion*; tribute, danegeld, ransom 804 *payment*; Peter's pence, tithe; National Insurance; poll tax, capitation t.; estate duty, death duty; direct taxation, income tax, PAYE, sur-

tax, supertax, company tax, corporation t.; capital levy, capital gains tax; indirect taxation, excise, customs, tariff, tonnage and poundage; local tax, octroi; purchase tax, sales t., value-added tax, VAT.

Adj. *priced*, charged, fixed; chargeable, leviable, taxable, assessable, ratable, customable, dutiable, excisable; ad valorem; to the tune of, for the price of; taxed, assessed.

Vb. *price*, cost, assess, value, rate 480 *estimate*; put a price on, place a value on; charge 737 *demand*; bill, invoice.

cost, be worth, fetch, bring in; amount to, come to; bear a price, have its p.; sell for, go f., realize.

tax, lay a tax on; fix a tariff, levy a rate, assess for tax, value; toll, excise, subject to duty; raise taxes 786 *levy*; fine 963 *punish*.

810. Discount – **N.** *discount*, something off, reduction, rebate, cut 42 *decrement*; stoppage, deduction; concession, allowance, margin; tare, tare and tret; drawback, backwardation, contango; cut rate, special offer 612 *incentive*; bargain price 812 *cheapness*; poundage, percentage; brokerage; one's cut, commission, rake-off.

Vb. *discount*, deduct 39 *subtract*; allow a margin, tare; reduce, rebate 37 *abate*; offer a discount, mark down, cut, slash 812 *cheapen*.

811. Dearness – **N.** *dearness*, costliness, expensiveness; value, high worth, pricelessness; scarcity value, rarity; exorbitance, extortion, rack rents, rip-off; overcharge, unfair price, bad value; bad bargain, high price, fancy p.; cost, heavy c., pretty penny; rising costs, sellers' market; inflation, bullish tendency.

Adj. *dear*, high-priced, pricy, expensive, ritzy, upmarket; costly, extravagant, dearly-bought; overrated, overcharged, overpriced; exorbitant, excessive, extortionate; steep, stiff, sky-high; beyond one's means, prohibitive, more than one can afford, more than one's pocket can stand.

of price, of worth 644 *valuable*; priceless, beyond price; invaluable, inestimable, worth a king's ransom, worth its weight in gold, worth a fortune; precious, rare, scarce, like gold dust; at a premium, not to be had for love or money.

Vb. *be dear*, cost a lot, cost a packet, hurt one's pocket, make a hole in one's p.; gain in value, rise in price, harden; go up, appreciate, escalate, soar, climb; price itself out of the market; prove expensive, cost one dear, cost the earth.

overcharge, overprice, ask too much; profiteer, soak, sting, bleed, rip off, short-change, hold to ransom 786 *fleece*.

pay too much, pay through the nose, pay the devil, be stung, be had, be done; pay high, pay dear, achieve a Pyrrhic victory.

812. Cheapness – N. *cheapness*, inexpensiveness, good value, value for money, money's worth, snip, bargain; sale goods, seconds, rejects; cheap rate, off-peak r., concessional r. 810 *discount*; nominal price, cut p., bargain p., sale p., rockbottom p.; peppercorn rent, easy terms; buyers' market; Dutch auction; falling prices, bearishness; depreciation, fall, slump; deflation; glut, drug on the market.

no charge, nominal c. 781 *gift*; gratuitousness, labour of love; free quarters, grace and favour.

Adj. *cheap*, inexpensive, moderate, reasonable, fair; affordable, within one's means, easy on the pocket; low-budget; substandard, shop-soiled; economical, economy size; worth the money; low-priced, cheap at the price, dirt-cheap, going for a song; bargain-rate, down-market, cut-price, sale-price, reduced, marked down; tourist-class, off-season; two-a-penny; cheap and nasty, cheapjack, catchpenny 641 *useless*; falling, slumping; underpaid, underpriced.

uncharged, gratuitous, complimentary; gratis, for nothing, for love, for kicks, for the asking; free, scot-f., free of charge, for free; zero-rated, rent-free, post-paid,

f.o.b.; unpaid, honorary 597 *voluntary*; free, gratis and for nothing.

Vb. *be cheap*, etc. adj.; cost little, be easy on the pocket; be free, be had for the asking; get cheaper, depreciate, come down, fall, slump, plunge, plummet.

cheapen, lower, reduce the price, mark down, cut, slash; undercharge, give away, make a present of 781 *give*; beat down, undercut, undersell; dump, unload; flood the market.

813. Liberality – N. *liberality*, bountifulness, munificence, generosity 931 *disinterestedness*; open-handedness, hospitality, open house 882 *sociability*; blank cheque 744 *scope*; cornucopia 635 *plenty*; lavishness 815 *prodigality*; bounty, largesse 781 *gift*; charity 897 *kind act*.

good giver, cheerful g.; blood donor, kidney d.; good spender, good tipper; Lady Bountiful, Santa Claus 903 *benefactor*.

Adj. *liberal*, free-spending, open-handed, lavish 815 *prodigal*; bountiful, charitable 897 *benevolent*; hospitable 882 *sociable*; handsome, generous, munificent, splendid, slap-up; lordly, princely, royal, right royal; ungrudging, unstinting, unsparing; abundant, ample, bounteous, profuse 635 *plenteous*.

Vb. *be liberal*, etc. adj.; lavish, shower upon 781 *give*; give generously, give till it hurts 897 *philanthropize*; pay well, tip w.; keep open house 882 *be hospitable*; do one proud, not count the cost, spare no expense; give a blank cheque 744 *give scope*; throw one's money around 815 *be prodigal*.

814. Economy – N. *economy*, thrift, thriftiness, frugality; prudence, carefulness; husbandry, good housekeeping, good management; economy drive, credit squeeze 747 *restriction*; time-saving, labour-s., time and motion study; economizing, saving, paring, cheese-p.; retrenchment, economies, cuts; savings 632 *store*; conservation, energy-saving; economizer; economist; conservationist 666 *preserver*.

Adj. *economical*, time-saving, labour-s., energy-s., money-s., cost-cutting; money-conscious 816 *parsimonious*; thrifty, careful, prudent, canny, frugal, sparing, spare; unlavish, meagre, Spartan, sparse; with nothing to spare.

Vb. *economize*, husband one's resources, avoid extravagance, keep costs down, waste nothing, find a use for everything, recycle, reuse; keep within one's budget, cut one's coat according to one's cloth; cut costs, cut back, make economies, retrench, tighten one's belt; pinch, scrape, look after the pennies 816 *be parsimonious*; save, hoard 632 *store*; plough back, reinvest, make every penny work.

815. Prodigality – N. *prodigality*, lavishness, profusion 637 *redundance*; conspicuous consumption 875 *ostentation*; extravagance, wastefulness, profligacy, dissipation, squandering, spending spree, splurge 634 *waste*; unthriftiness, improvidence, uncontrolled expenditure, deficit finance; money burning a hole in one's pocket.

prodigal, prodigal son, spender, big s., free s., waster, wastrel, profligate, spendthrift, scattergood, squanderer.

Adj. *prodigal*, lavish 813 *liberal*; profuse, overlavish, extravagant, wasteful, profligate; uneconomic, thriftless, spendthrift, improvident, dissipative, reckless; penny wise and pound foolish.

Vb. *be prodigal*, blow one's money, blue one's m.; overspend, splash money around, splurge, spend money like water; squander 634 *waste*; play ducks and drakes, fritter away, gamble a., dissipate; not count the cost, think money grows on trees; misspend, throw good money after bad; eat up one's capital, put nothing by.

Int. hang the expense! a short life and a merry one! easy come, easy go!

816. Parsimony – N. *parsimony*, parsimoniousness; false economy, misplaced e., policy of penny wise and pound foolish; cheese-paring, scrimping, scraping, penny-pinching; tightfistedness, niggardliness, meanness, minginess, stinginess, miserliness; illiberality, ungenerosity, uncharitableness 932 *selfishness*.

avarice, cupidity, acquisitiveness, possessiveness; money-grubbing, itching palm; rapacity, avidity, greed 859 *desire*; mercenariness, venality.

niggard, skinflint, screw, scrimp, scraper, pinchfist, penny pincher, pinchpenny, tightwad, meanie; miser, money-grubber, lickpenny, muckworm; cadger; saver, hoarder, squirrel, magpie; churl, codger, curmudgeon; usurer 784 *lender*; Harpagon, Scrooge.

Adj. *parsimonious*, careful 814 *economical*; overeconomical, overfrugal; money-conscious, penny-wise, miserly, niggardly, mean, mingy, stingy, near, close, tight; tight-fisted, close-f. 778 *retentive*; grudging, curmudgeonly, churlish, shabby, illiberal, ungenerous, uncharitable, empty-handed, giftless; penurious, chary, pinching, scraping, scrimping.

avaricious, grasping 932 *selfish*; possessive, acquisitive 771 *acquiring*; hoarding, saving, miserly; money-grubbing, covetous 859 *greedy*; usurious, rapacious, extortionate; mercenary, venal, sordid.

Vb. *be parsimonious*, etc. adj.; grudge, begrudge 760 *refuse*; stint, skimp 636 *make insufficient*; scrape, scrimp, pinch 814 *economize*; screw, rack-rent, skin a flint 786 *fleece*; be penny-wise, spoil the ship for a ha'porth of tar; beat down 791 *bargain*; cadge, beg, borrow; hoard, sit on, keep for oneself 932 *be selfish*.

Class Six

EMOTION, RELIGION AND MORALITY

Section 1: General

817. Affections – N. *affections*, qualities, instincts; passions, feelings, emotions, emotional life; nature, disposition 5 *character*; spirit, temper, tone 5 *temperament*; personality, psychology, mentality, outlook, make-up; being, innermost b., breast, bosom, heart, soul, core, inmost soul, heart of hearts 5 *essential part*, 447 *spirit*; animus, attitude, frame of mind, state of m., humour, mood; predilection, inclinations 179 *tendency*; passion, heartstrings 818 *feeling*; fullness of heart; heyday of the blood; force of character.

Adj. *with affections*, affected, characterized, formed, moulded, instinct with, imbued w., eaten up w., possessed w.; inborn 5 *genetic*; emotional, demonstrative 818 *feeling*.

818. Feeling – N. *feeling*, experience, affect; sentience, sensation, sense of 374 *sense*; emotion, sentiment; impulse 609 *spontaneity*; intuition, instinct; responsiveness, response, reaction, fellow feeling, sympathy, involvement 880 *friendliness*; vibrations, vibes; empathy, understanding 490 *knowledge*; impression, deep sense of 819 *moral sensibility*; thrill, kick 318 *spasm*; shock, turn 508 *lack of expectation*; pathos 825 *suffering*; catharthis, abreaction; emotionalism, affectivity 822 *excitability*; sentimentality, romanticism; blush, flush, suffusion; tingling, gooseflesh, tremor, quiver, flutter, palpitation 318 *agitation*; swelling heart, lump in one's throat.

warm feeling, glow; cordiality, empressement, effusiveness, heartiness; hot head, impatience; unction, earnestness; fervour, ardour, enthusiasm 174 *vigorousness*; emotion, passion, ecstasy, inspiration 822 *excitable state*.

Adj. *feeling*, affective, sensible 374 *sentient*; spirited, vivacious, lively 819 *sensitive*; sensuous 944 *sensual*; experiencing, living; enduring, bearing 825 *suffering*; intuitive, sensitive, vibrant, responsive, reacting; involved, sympathetic, condoling 775 *sharing*; tender-hearted 819 *impressible*; emotional, passionate; unctuous, soulful; intense 821 *excited*; cordial, hearty; gushing, effusive; sentimental, romantic; mawkish, maudlin, schmaltzy, treacly, soppy, sloppy, slushy.

fervent, fervid, perfervid, passionate, ardent, intense; eager, breathless, panting, throbbing; impassioned, vehement, earnest, zealous; enthusiastic, exuberant, bubbling; warm-blooded 822 *excitable*; fiery, glowing 379 *hot*; overwrought, worked up 503 *frenzied*; uncontrollable 176 *violent*.

felt, experienced; heartfelt, cordial, hearty, warm, sincere 540 *veracious*; deeply-felt, visceral 211 *deep*; stirring, soul-s., heart-warming, heart-swelling; emotive, traumatic 821 *impressive*; acute, keen, poignant 256 *sharp*; caustic, burning 388 *pungent*; penetrating, absorbing; thrilling, tingling, rapturous, ecstatic 826 *pleasurable*; pathetic, affecting 827 *distressing*.

Vb. *feel*, sense; feel deeply, take to heart; experience, taste; smart under 825 *suffer*; feel with, sympathize; react, warm to 821 *be excited*.

show feeling, show signs of emotion; demonstrate, not hide one's feelings 522 *manifest*; enthuse, go into ecstasies 824 *be pleased*; fly into a passion 891 *get angry*; blench, turn pale; colour, blush 431 *redden*; quiver, tremble 318 *be agitated*; tingle, thrill, throb 317 *oscillate*.

Adv. *feelingly*, con amore, heart and soul; cordially, heartily, devoutly, from the bottom of one's heart.

819. Sensibility – N. *moral sensibility*, sensitivity, soul; touchiness 892 *irascibility*; raw feelings, thin skin, soft spot; sore point, where the shoe pinches 891 *resentment*; impressibility, affectibility, susceptibility; finer feelings, sentiments; sentimentality; tenderness 887 *love*; spirit, spiritedness, vivacity 571 *vigour*; emotionalism, ebullience 822 *excitability*; aestheticism 463 *discrimination*; temperament 152 *changeableness*; sensitive plant, bundle of nerves.

Adj. *impressible*, alive to, responsive 374 *sentient*; persuasible; moody, impressionable 822 *excitable*; susceptible, susceptive; romantic, sentimental; emotional, warm-hearted; tender-hearted, soft-h.

sensitive, sensitized 374 *sentient*; aesthetic 463 *discriminating*; hypersensitive 822 *excitable*; touchy 892 *irascible*.

lively, alive, vital, vivacious, animated; irrepressible, ebullient, effervescent; spirited, high-s.; lively-minded, spirituel(le); alert 455 *attentive*; highly-strung, temperamental; mobile, changeable; enthusiastic 818 *fervent*.

Adv. *on the raw*, to the quick, to the heart.

820. Insensibility – N. *moral insensibility*, insensitiveness; numbness 375 *insensibility*; inertia 175 *inertness*; woodenness, obtuseness, no imagination 499 *unintelligence*; slowness, delayed reaction 456 *inattention*; nonchalance, insouciance, unconcern, apathy 860 *indifference*; imperturbation, phlegm, stolidness, coolness, sangfroid 823 *inexcitability*; no feelings, aloofness, impassibility, impassivity; poker face, deadpan expression; insensitivity, coarseness, philistinism; imperception, thick skin, rhinoceros hide; cold heart, unsusceptibility, unimpressibility, dourness; callousness 326 *hardness*; dry eyes, no heart, heart of stone 898 *inhumanity*.

unfeeling person, iceberg, icicle, cold fish, cold heart; stock, stone, block, marble.

Adj. *impassive*, unconscious 375 *insensible*; unsusceptible, insensitive, unimaginative; unresponsive, unimpressionable 823 *inexcitable*; phlegmatic, stolid; wooden, blockish; bovine; dull, slow 499 *unintelligent*; unemotional, passionless, impassible; proof against, steeled a.; stoical, ascetic, undemonstrative; detached 860 *indifferent*; unaffected, unruffled, unshockable; imperturbable, cool; blank, expressionless, deadpan, poker-faced; impersonal, dispassionate, reserved, stony, frigid; cold-hearted, unfeeling, heartless, soulless, inhuman.

apathetic, unenthusiastic, uninspired, unexcited, unmoved, untouched, unaroused; half-hearted, lukewarm 860 *indifferent*; uninterested 454 *incurious*; nonchalant, insouciant, pococurante; spiritless, lackadaisical; vegetative 266 *quiescent*; supine 679 *inactive*; passive 175 *inert*; torpid 375 *insensible*.

thick-skinned, pachydermatous; impenetrable, impervious; blind to, deaf to, dead to, closed to; obtuse, unimaginative, insensitive; callous 326 *hard*; hard-bitten, hard-boiled, inured 669 *matured*; shameless, unblushing.

Vb. *make insensitive*, benumb 375 *render insensible*; steel 326 *harden*; sear, dry up 342 *dry*; deafen 399 *silence*; shut the eyes of 439 *blind*; brutalize 655 *pervert*; stale, coarsen 847 *vulgarize*; cloy 863 *sate*; deaden 257 *blunt*.

Adv. *in cold blood*, with dry eyes, without emotion; without enthusiasm.

821. Excitation – N. *excitation*, arousal; galvanization, electrification 174 *stimulation*; possession, inspiration, afflatus, exhilaration, intoxication; encouragement, animation, incitement; provocation; impression, impact 178 *influence*; bewitchment 983 *sorcery*; rapture 824 *joy*; human interest, sentiment, sob-stuff, pathos; sensationalism, melodrama; scandalmongering; excitement, high pressure, tension 160 *energy*; fuss, drama, perturbation 822 *excitable state*; shock, thrill, kicks 318 *spasm*; tizzy, flurry, furore 318 *commotion*; fever pitch, climax 503 *frenzy*;

passion, emotion, enthusiasm, lyricism 818 *feeling*; temper, fury 891 *anger*.

excitant, agent provocateur 738 *agitator*; sensationalist, sob sister, scandalmonger; headline 528 *publicity*; fillip 174 *stimulant*; upper, pep pill 949 *drug-taking*; sting, spur 612 *incentive*; fan; irritant, gadfly.

Adj. *excited*, stung etc. vb.; ebullient, seething 355 *bubbly*; tense, wrought up, strung up, keyed up, wound up; overheated, feverish, frantic 503 *frenzied*; glowing 379 *hot*; hot under the collar, hot and bothered; seeing red, wild, mad, foaming at the mouth 891 *angry*; avid, eager, itching, agog 859 *desiring*; tingling 818 *feeling*; flurried 318 *agitated*; restless, overexcited, overwrought, distraught; freaked out, on a high, on a trip; beside oneself, hysterical, uncontrollable, carried away, turned on, hyped up; inspired, possessed, enthusiastic, lyrical, raving 822 *excitable*.

exciting, stimulating, sparkling, intoxicating, heady, exhilarating; provocative, piquant, tantalizing; salty, spicy; alluring 887 *lovable*; evocative, emotive, suggestive; cliff-hanging, hair-raising, spinechilling; thrilling, moving, inspiring; rousing, stirring, soul-s; sensational, dramatic, melodramatic; gripping, absorbing, enthralling.

impressive, imposing, grand, stately; majestic 868 *noble*; awe-inspiring, sublime; overwhelming, overpowering; picturesque, scenic; striking, arresting, dramatic; telling, forceful.

Vb. *excite*, affect 178 *influence*; warm the heart 833 *cheer*; touch, move 834 *sadden*; impassion, stir the feelings; quicken the pulse, electrify, galvanize; make one's blood boil; inflame, enkindle; sting, pique, tantalize, tease 827 *torment*; touch on the raw, cut to the quick; work on, work up, whip up 612 *incite*; enthuse, inspire, possess; stir, rouse, arouse, awaken, turn on (**see** *animate*); evoke, summon up, call forth; thrill, exhilarate, intoxicate; transport 826 *delight*.

animate, enliven, quicken 360 *vitalize*; revive, rekindle, breathe fresh life into

656 *restore*; inspire, inspirit, put one on his *or* her mettle; encourage, hearten 855 *give courage*; give an edge, whet 256 *sharpen*; urge, spur 277 *accelerate*; jolt, jog, shake up; give a fillip to, stimulate, ginger 174 *invigorate*; foster, foment 162 *strengthen*; fuel, intensify, fan the flame, stir the embers.

impress, sink in, leave an impression; hold, grip, absorb; intrigue, strike 455 *attract notice*; affect 178 *influence*; bring home to 532 *emphasize*; come home to, penetrate; arrest, amaze 864 *be wonderful*; dazzle, fill with admiration; inspire with awe, humble; take one's breath away, overwhelm; upset, unsettle 827 *trouble*.

be excited, lose one's cool; flare up 379 *be hot*; sizzle, seethe, explode; thrill to, tingle, tremble 822 *be excitable*; quiver, flutter, palpitate 318 *be agitated*; mantle, flush 818 *show feeling*; squirm, writhe 251 *wriggle*; toss and turn.

Adv. *excitedly*, frenziedly; all agog, with one's heart in one's mouth, with beating heart, aquiver, atremble.

822. Excitability – N. *excitability*, inflammability; instability, temperament, emotionalism; hot blood, hot temper 892 *irascibility*; impatience, incontinence; vehemence, impetuosity 857 *rashness*; turbulence, restlessness, fidgets, nerves 318 *agitation*.

excitable state, exhilaration, elevation, elation, intoxication, abandon; thrill, transport, trip, high, ecstasy, inspiration, lyricism 818 *feeling*; fever, fever of excitement, whirl 318 *agitation*; ferment, pother, stew; outburst, explosion, scene, song and dance 318 *commotion*; brainstorm, hysterics, delirium, fit, agony 503 *frenzy*; distraction, madness, mania, passion; rage, towering r., fury 176 *violence*; temper, tantrums 891 *anger*.

Adj. *excitable*, oversensitive, raw 819 *sensitive*; passionate, emotional; susceptible, romantic; out for thrills, looking for kicks; suggestible, inflammable, like tinder; unstable, impressionable 819 *impressible*; temperamental, mercurial, volatile 152 *changeful*; fitful 604 *capricious*; restless, unquiet, nervy, fidgety, edgy 318 *agitated*; highly-strung, nervous, skittish, mettlesome 819 *lively*; hotheaded 892 *irascible*; impatient, trigger-happy 680 *hasty*; impetuous, impulsive 857 *rash*; savage, fierce; boisterous, rumbustious 176 *violent*; restive 738 *riotous*; effervescent, simmering, seething; volcanic, explosive, electric; fanatical, unbalanced; rabid 176 *furious*; feverish, febrile 503 *frenzied*; like a cat on hot bricks, like a cat on a hot tin roof 821 *excited*.

Vb. *be excitable*, etc. adj.; show impatience, fret, fume, stamp; shuffle, chafe, fidget, champ at the bit 818 *show feeling*; tingle with, be itching to; be on edge 318 *be agitated*; start, jump 854 *be nervous*; have a temper 892 *be irascible*; foam, froth, have hysterics 503 *go mad*; go wild, run riot, see red; storm 61 *rampage*; ramp, rage 176 *be violent*; fly into a temper, fly off the handle, burst out, break o., explode, create 891 *get angry*; kindle, burn, smoulder, catch fire, flare up 821 *be excited*.

823. Inexcitability – N. *inexcitability*, imperturbability, composure; coolness, sangfroid, nonchalance; frigidity, impassibility 820 *moral insensibility*; tranquillity, serenity, placidity; equanimity, even temper; self-possession, self-control 942 *temperance*; stoicism; detachment, dispassionateness 860 *indifference*; gravity, staidness, demureness, sobriety 834 *seriousness*; quietism, Quakerism.

patience, forbearance, endurance, long-suffering; tolerance, toleration; stoicism; resignation 721 *submission*.

Adj. *inexcitable*, dispassionate, cold, dull 820 *impassive*; stable 153 *unchangeable*; unworried, cool, imperturbable, unflappable; cool-headed, level-h.; steady, composed, controlled; deliberate, unhurried, unhasty; even, level, equable 16 *uniform*; good-tempered, even-t.; staid, sedate, sober, reserved 834 *serious*; quiet, placid, unruffled, calm, serene 266 *tranquil*; mild, meek 177 *moderate*; unwarlike

717 *peaceful*; easygoing, undemanding; resigned, submissive 739 *obedient*; passive 175 *inert*; unenthusiastic, unsentimental, unromantic, unpoetic, earthbound.

patient, tolerant, long-suffering; stoic, stoical, philosophical, uncomplaining.

Vb. *keep calm*, compose oneself, collect o., keep cool, keep a cool head; master one's feelings, swallow one's resentment, keep one's cool, keep one's hair *or* shirt on; not turn a hair, not bat an eyelid; relax, stop worrying, take things easy *or* as they come 683 *repose*; resign oneself, take in good part.

be patient, show restraint, forbear; put up with, stand for, tolerate, bear, endure, support, suffer, abide; resign oneself, grin and bear it, put a brave face on it; stomach, pocket 721 *knuckle under*; turn the other cheek 909 *forgive*; turn a blind eye 734 *be lax*; ignore provocation, keep the peace.

Section 2:
Personal Emotion

824. Joy – N. *joy* 376 *pleasure*; enjoyment, thrill, kick 826 *pleasurableness*; joyfulness 835 *rejoicing*; delight, gladness, rapture, exaltation, exhilaration, transports of delight; abandonment, ecstasy, enchantment, bewitchment, ravishment; unholy joy, schadenfreude 898 *malevolence*; rose-strewn path; halcyon days 730 *palmy days*.

happiness, felicity; wellbeing 376 *euphoria*; unalloyed delight, rose without a thorn; flourishing time, golden age 730 *prosperity*; blessedness, bliss, beatitude; seventh heaven, cloud nine, nirvana, Paradise, Elysium, Garden of Eden, Arcadia 513 *fantasy*.

enjoyment, gratification, satisfaction, fulfilment 828 *content*; delectation, relish, zest, gusto; indulgence, luxuriation, wallowing 943 *intemperance*; full life, hedonism, epicureanism 944 *sensualism*; merry-making, lark, frolic 833 *merriment*; fun, treat, buting 837 *amusement*; good cheer, cakes and ale, beer and skittles.

Adj. *pleased*, well-p., glad, not sorry; satisfied, happy 828 *content*; gratified, flattered, chuffed, pleased as Punch; over the moon, on top of the world; loving it, tickled pink 837 *amused*; exhilarated 833 *merry*; euphoric, walking on air; overjoyed 833 *jubilant*; delighted, transported, enraptured, ravished, rapturous, ecstatic, raving 923 *approving*; in raptures, in ecstasies, in transports, in the seventh heaven, on cloud nine; charmed, enchanted 818 *impressed*; gloating.

happy, happy as a sandboy, happy as a lark; blithe, joyful, joyous, gladsome 833 *merry*; beaming, smiling 835 *laughing*; radiant, sparkling, starry-eyed; lucky, fortunate 730 *prosperous*; blissful, blest, blessed; in bliss, in paradise.

Vb. *be pleased*, etc. adj.; have the pleasure; hug oneself, congratulate o., purr with pleasure, dance with p., jump for joy 833 *be cheerful*; laugh, smile 835 *rejoice*; get a kick out of, take pleasure in, delight in, rejoice in 376 *enjoy*; go into ecstasies, rave about 818 *show feeling*; have fun 837 *amuse oneself*; gloat, savour, appreciate, relish, smack one's lips.

825. Suffering – N. *suffering*, heartache, lacrimae rerum 834 *melancholy*; homesickness, nostalgia 859 *desire*; weariness 684 *fatigue*; nightmare, incubus; affliction, distress, dolour, anguish, angst, agony, torture, torment 377 *pain*; twinge, stab 377 *pang*; bitter cup 827 *painfulness*; crucifixion, martyrdom; rack 963 *punishment*; purgatory, hell, damnation; bed of thorns, no bed of roses 700 *difficulty*; unpleasantness, mauvais quart d'heure; inconvenience, discomfort, malaise; trial, ordeal; tribulation 659 *bane*; living death, fate worse than death 616 *evil*; dystopia; evil days, unhappy times 731 *adversity*.

sorrow, grief, sadness 834 *dejection*; woe, wretchedness, misery; prostration, despair, desolation 853 *hopelessness*; unhappiness 731 *adversity*; weariness of spirit, heavy heart, bleeding h., broken h.; dissatisfaction 829 *discontent*; vexation, bitterness, chagrin 830 *regret*.

worry, uneasiness, discomfort, disquiet, inquietude, fretting 318 *agitation*; discomposure, dismay, distress; phobia, hangup; weight on one's mind, anxiety, concern, solicitude, thought, care; responsibility, load, burden; strain, tension, premenstrual t., PMT; worries, cares of the world; trouble 616 *evil*; bother, annoyance, irritation, thorn in the flesh, death of 659 *bane*; something to worry about, lookout, funeral; headache, problem 530 *enigma*.

sufferer, victim, scapegoat, sacrifice; prey, shorn lamb 544 *dupe*; martyr; wretch 731 *unlucky person*; patient 651 *sick person*.

Adj. *suffering*, ill 651 *sick*; agonizing, writhing, in pain, bleeding, harrowed, on the rack, in torment, in hell 377 *pained*; uncomfortable, ill at ease; anguished, distressed, upset; worked up 818 *fervent*; anxious, unhappy about, worried, troubled, apprehensive 854 *nervous*; sick with worry, cut up about, in a state 318 *agitated*; discomposed, disconcerted; ill-used, maltreated; longsuffering, downtrodden, victimized 745 *subjected*; stricken, wounded; heavy-laden, crushed 684 *fatigued*; careworn, harassed; woeful, woebegone, haggard, wild-eyed.

unhappy, unlucky 731 *unfortunate*; despairing 853 *hopeless*; doomed 961 *condemned*; pitiable, poor, wretched, miserable; sad, melancholy, despondent, disconsolate; cut up, heart-broken, broken-hearted, heavy-h., sick at heart; sorrowful, sorrowing, grief-stricken, woebegone 834 *dejected*; weeping, weepy, wet-eyed, tearful 836 *lamenting*; nostalgic, longing 859 *desiring*; dissatisfied, disappointed 829 *discontented*; sorry, remorseful 830 *regretting*.

Vb. *suffer*, undergo, endure 818 *feel*; bear, put up with; suffer torments, agonize, bleed; hurt oneself 377 *feel pain*; take up one's cross, become a martyr; take it on the chin; have a thin time, go through it 731 *have trouble*; distress oneself, worry, worry to death, fret 318 *be agitated*; mind, take it badly, take it to heart; weep, sigh 836 *lament*; pity oneself, be despondent 834 *be dejected*.

826. Pleasurableness – N. *pleasurableness*, pleasantness, delightfulness, amenity; sunny side, bright s.; attractiveness, appeal 291 *attraction*; winning ways 925 *flattery*; amiability, winsomeness, charm, fascination, enchantment, witchery, loveliness 841 *beauty*; honeymoon 824 *joy*; a little of what one fancies, a delight, a treat, a joy; novelty, pastime, fun 837 *amusement*; melody, harmony 412 *music*; tastiness 390 *savouriness*; spice, zest, relish; dainty, titbit 392 *sweetness*; balm 685 *refreshment*; land flowing with milk and honey 635 *plenty*; peace, perfect p. 266 *quietude*, 681 *leisure*; pipe-dream 513 *fantasy*.

Adj. *pleasurable*, pleasant, nice, good; pleasure-giving 837 *amusing*; pleasing, agreeable, gratifying, flattering; acceptable, welcome; well-liked, to one's taste, to one's liking, just what the doctor ordered 644 *excellent*; frictionless, painless 376 *comfortable*; easeful, refreshing 683 *reposeful*; peaceful 266 *tranquil*; voluptuous 376 *sensuous*; genial, warm, sunny 833 *cheering*; delightful, delectable, delicious, exquisite; luscious, juicy; tasty 390 *savoury*; sweet, dulcet, musical, harmonious 410 *melodious*; picturesque, scenic, lovely 841 *beautiful*; amiable, winning, endearing 887 *lovable*; attractive, fetching, appealing, interesting 291 *attracting*; seductive, enticing, inviting, captivating; charming, enchanting, bewitching, ravishing; haunting, thrilling, heart-warming 821 *exciting*; homely, cosy; idyllic, paradisal, heavenly, out of this world; blissful 824 *happy*.

Vb. *please*, give pleasure, afford p., agree with; lull, soothe 177 *assuage*; comfort 833 *cheer*; put at ease 831 *relieve*; sugar, gild the pill 392 *sweeten*; pat, pet 889 *caress*; indulge, pander to 734 *be lax*; charm, interest 837 *amuse*; rejoice, gladden, make happy; gratify, satisfy 828 *content*; bless, raise to the seventh heaven.

delight, surprise with joy; rejoice, exhilarate, elate, elevate, uplift; rejoice one's heart, warm the cockles of one's h., do one's heart good; thrill, intoxicate, ravish; transport, turn on, send one into raptures *or* ecstasies 821 *excite*; make music in one's ears 925 *flatter*; take one's fancy 887 *excite love*; tickle one's palate, regale, refresh; tickle, titillate, tease, tantalize; entrance, enrapture; enchant, charm 983 *bewitch*; take one's breath away 821 *impress*; allure, seduce 291 *attract*.

827. Painfulness – N. *painfulness*, harshness, harassment 735 *severity*; hurtfulness, harmfulness 645 *badness*; disagreeableness, unpleasantness 616 *evil*; friction, chafing, irritation, inflammation 832 *aggravation*; soreness 377 *pain*; sore point, rub 819 *moral sensibility*; sore, running s., thorn in the flesh, where the shoe pinches 659 *bane*; shock 508 *lack of expectation*; unpalatability, disgust; sharpness, bitterness, bitter cup, bitter pill, gall and wormwood 393 *sourness*; bread of affliction 731 *adversity*; tribulation, ordeal, cross 825 *suffering*; trouble, care 825 *worry*; dreariness, cheerlessness; pitifulness, pathos; sorry sight, sad spectacle; disenchantment, disillusionment 509 *disappointment*; hornet's nest, hot water 700 *predicament*.

annoyance, vexation, pest, curse, pain in the neck 659 *bane*; botheration, embarrassment 825 *worry*; interference, nuisance, pinprick; burden, drag 702 *encumbrance*; grievance, complaint; hardship, troubles 616 *evil*; last straw, limit; offence, affront 921 *indignity*; molestation, persecution 898 *malevolence*; displeasure, mortification 891 *resentment*; menace, enfant terrible.

Adj. *paining*, hurting, sore, tender; agonizing, racking, purgatorial 377 *painful*; scathing, searing, burning, shooting, gnawing, throbbing; caustic, corrosive, vitriolic; harsh, hard 735 *severe*; gruelling, punishing, excruciating; harmful 659 *baneful*.

unpleasant, unpleasing, disagreeable; uncomfortable, joyless 834 *cheerless*; uninviting, unappealing 842 *ugly*; unwelcome 860 *unwanted*; displeasing, distasteful, unpalatable; nasty, beastly 645 *not nice*; bitter, sharp 393 *sour*; offensive, objectionable 861 *disliked*.

annoying, troublesome, embarrassing, worrying; bothersome, tiresome 838 *tedious*; burdensome, onerous 322 *weighty*; unfortunate, untoward 731 *adverse*; awkward, unaccommodating, pesky, plaguy 702 *hindering*; importunate, pestering; trying, irritating, vexatious, provoking, maddening, infuriating; galling, mortifying.

distressing, afflicting, crushing, grievous; shocking, traumatic; harrowing, heart-rending, tear-jerking; pathetic, tragic, lamentable, deplorable 905 *pitiable*; ghastly, grim, horrific, nerve-racking 854 *frightening*.

intolerable, insufferable, impossible, insupportable, unendurable, unbearable 32 *exorbitant*; past bearing, not to be endured, more than flesh and blood can stand.

Vb. hurt, injure 645 *harm*; pain 377 *give pain*; wound one's feelings, gall, mortify 891 *huff*; rub up the wrong way, tread on one's corns; cut to the quick, grieve, afflict, distress 834 *sadden*; rub salt in the wound, gnaw, chafe, rankle, fester 832 *aggravate*; offend, aggrieve (**see** *displease*); affront 921 *not respect*.

torment, martyr; harrow, rack 963 *torture*; put through the hoop, bait, bully 735 *oppress*; beset, besiege 737 *demand*; haunt, obsess; annoy, tease, pester, plague, nag, henpeck, badger, worry, chivvy, harass, harry, heckle; molest, bother, provoke, needle, sting, bug, gall, irk, roil 891 *enrage*.

trouble, discomfort, disquiet, disturb, agitate, discompose, disconcert, upset, incommode 63 *derange*; worry, embarrass 474 *puzzle*; tire 684 *fatigue*; weary 838 *be tedious*; obsess, haunt, bedevil; prey on the mind 834 *depress*; infest, get in one's hair, get under one's feet 702 *obstruct*.

displease, not appeal, find no favour 924 *incur blame*; grate, jar, disagree with, grate on, jar on, get on one's nerves, set one's teeth on edge, go against the grain, give one the pip, give one a pain, get one's goat, get under one's skin; disenchant 509

disappoint; aggrieve 829 *cause discontent*; offend, shock, horrify, scandalize, disgust, revolt, repel, sicken, nauseate, stick in the throat, make one's gorge rise 861 *cause dislike*; make one's flesh creep, appal 854 *frighten*.

828. Content – N. *content*, contentment, satisfaction, complacency; self-satisfaction, smugness 873 *vanity*; measure of content, ray of comfort; serenity 266 *quietude*; easy mind, peace of m., heart's ease, nothing left to worry about 376 *euphoria*; snugness, cosiness, comfort, sitting pretty 730 *prosperity*; acquiescence, resignation 721 *submission*.

Adj. content, contented, satisfied, well-s. 824 *happy*; appeased, pacified; cosy, snug 376 *comfortable*; at ease 683 *reposeful*; smiling 833 *cheerful*; flattered 824 *pleased*; with nothing left to wish for, with no desire unfulfilled; unrepining, uncomplaining, with no regrets; unenvious 931 *disinterested*; philosophical 823 *inexcitable*; resigned, acquiescent; easily pleased, easygoing; untroubled, unafflicted, unvexed; thankful 907 *grateful*.

contenting, satisfying, satisfactory 635 *sufficient*; tolerable, bearable, endurable; unobjectionable, passable, acceptable 923 *approvable*; desirable, all that is wished for 859 *desired*.

Vb. be content, etc. adj.; purr with content 824 *be pleased*; rest satisfied, count one's blessings; have much to be thankful for 907 *be grateful*; have all one could ask for 730 *prosper*; congratulate oneself, hug o. 835 *rejoice*; be at ease, sit pretty 376 *enjoy*; be reconciled 719 *make peace*; get over it, take comfort 831 *be relieved*; rest content, take in good part; take things as they come, make the best of, have no complaints, not repine; put up with 721 *submit*.

content, satisfy, gratify, make one's day 826 *please*; meet with approval, go down well; make happy, bless with contentment; leave no desire unfulfilled 863 *sate*; comfort 833 *cheer*, 831 *relieve*; lull, set at ease; conciliate, appease 719 *pacify*.

829. Discontent – N. *discontent*, discontentment, displeasure, dissatisfaction 924 *disapprobation*; cold comfort, not what one expected 509 *disappointment*; soreness, irritation, chagrin, mortification 891 *resentment*; uneasiness, disquiet 825 *worry*; grief 825 *sorrow*; maladjustment, strain, tension; restlessness, unrest 738 *disobedience*; faddiness 862 *fastidiousness*; querulousness 709 *quarrelsomeness*; ill will 912 *envy*; chip on one's shoulder, grievance, grudge, gripe, complaint 709 *quarrel*; weariness, melancholy, ennui 834 *dejection*; sulkiness, dirty look, scowl, frown 893 *sullenness*; groan, curse 899 *malediction*; cheep, squeak, murmur, whispering campaign 762 *deprecation*.

malcontent, grumbler, grouch, grouser, mutterer, croaker, whiner, bleater, bellyacher 834 *moper*; plaintiff 763 *petitioner*; faultfinder, critic 709 *quarreller*; angry young man; dissident, dropout 738 *revolter*; murmurer 738 *agitator*; indignation meeting, protest m. 705 *opponent*; hard taskmaster 735 *tyrant*.

Adj. *discontented*, displeased, not best pleased; dissatisfied 924 *disapproving*; unsatisfied, frustrated 509 *disappointed*; defeated 728 *unsuccessful*; malcontent, dissident 489 *dissenting*; restive 738 *disobedient*; disgruntled, weary, browned off, fed up 838 *bored*, 825 *unhappy*; repining 830 *regretting*; unconsoled, disconsolate 834 *dejected*; grudging, jealous, envious; bitter, soured 393 *sour*; cross, sulky 893 *sullen*; grouchy, grumbling, grousing, whining, swearing 899 *cursing*; protesting 762 *deprecatory*; smarting, sore, mortified, insulted, affronted, piqued, vexed, put out, annoyed 891 *resentful*; fretful, querulous, petulant, complaining; hard to please, never satisfied 862 *fastidious*; hypercritical, censorious 926 *detracting*; irreconcilable 704 *opposing*.

Vb. *be discontented*, etc. adj.; be critical, crab, carp, criticize, find fault 862 *be fastidious*; lack, miss 627 *require*; sneer, groan, jeer 924 *disapprove*; take offence, take in bad part, take amiss, take to heart, take on, be offended 891 *resent*; sulk 893

be sullen; look blue, look glum, make a wry face 834 *be dejected*; moan, mutter, murmur, whine, whinge, bleat, complain 762 *deprecate*; bellyache, grumble, grouse, croak; wail 836 *lament*; cherish a grievance, have a chip on one's shoulder; rise up 738 *revolt*; grudge 912 *envy*; quarrel with one's bread and butter 709 *quarrel*; not know when one is well off; repine 830 *regret*.

cause discontent, dissatisfy 509 *disappoint*; get one down 834 *depress*; discourage 613 *dissuade*; sour, embitter; upset, put out of humour 891 *huff*; mortify 872 *humiliate*; offend 827 *displease*; shock, scandalize, disgust; sow dragon's teeth, make trouble 738 *revolt*.

830. Regret – N. *regret*, regretfulness; mortification 891 *resentment*; soul-searching, self-reproach, remorse, contrition, compunction, qualms, regrets, apologies 939 *penitence*; disillusion, second thoughts; longing, homesickness, nostalgia 859 *desire*; sense of loss; matter of regret, pity of it.

Adj. *regretting*, homesick, nostalgic, wistful; harking back 125 *retrospective*; repining, bitter 891 *resentful*; irreconcilable, inconsolable 836 *lamenting*; regretful, remorseful, rueful, conscience-stricken, sorry, apologetic, penitent 939 *repentant*; undeceived, disillusioned, sadder and wiser.

regretted, sadly missed, badly wanted; regrettable, deplorable, too bad, a shame, a crying s.

Vb. *regret*, rue, deplore; curse one's folly, never forgive oneself, blame o., accuse o., reproach o., kick o., bite one's tongue; unwish, wish undone, repine, wring one's hands, cry over spilt milk 836 *lament*; sigh for the good old days, fight one's battles over again 505 *retrospect*; look back, look over one's shoulder; miss, long for, pine for 859 *desire*; apologize, feel remorse, be sorry 939 *be penitent*; deplore 924 *disapprove*; feel mortified, gnash one's teeth 891 *resent*; have cause for regret, have had one's lesson 963 *be punished*.

831. Relief – N. *relief*, rest 685 *refreshment*; easing, alleviation, mitigation, palliation 177 *moderation*; good riddance; exemption 668 *deliverance*; solace, consolation, comfort, crumb of c.; silver lining, break in the clouds 852 *hope*; load off one's mind, sigh of relief 656 *revival*; lullaby, cradle song; salve 658 *balm*; painkiller, sedative 679 *soporific*; comforter, consoler, ray of sunshine.

Adj. *relieving*, soothing, balsamic 685 *refreshing*; lulling, assuaging, pain-killing 177 *lenitive*; restorative 658 *remedial*; consoling, consolatory, comforting.

Vb. *relieve*, ease, soften, cushion; relax, lessen the strain; temper 177 *moderate*; lift, raise, lighten, take a load off one's mind 701 *disencumber*; spare, save 668 *deliver*; console, dry one's eyes, wipe away the tears, solace, comfort; cheer up, encourage 833 *cheer*; shade, cool 685 *refresh*; bandage, bind up; calm, soothe, nurse; palliate, moderate 177 *assuage*; smooth one's brow, stroke, pat 889 *caress*; cradle, lull; anaesthetize 375 *render insensible*; take pity on, put out of one's misery.

be relieved, obtain relief; heave a sigh of relief, breathe again; console oneself, take comfort, feel better, dry one's eyes 833 *be cheerful*; get over it, pull oneself together 656 *be restored*.

832. Aggravation – N. *aggravation*, exacerbation, exasperation, irritation; intensification 162 *strengthening*; making worse 655 *deterioration*; complication 700 *difficulty*; irritant 821 *excitant*.

Adj. *aggravated*, intensified; exacerbated, made worse 655 *deteriorated*.

Vb. *aggravate*, intensify, enhance, heighten, deepen 36 *augment*; worsen, make worse, not improve matters 655 *deteriorate*; add insult to injury, rub salt in the wound, rub it in; exacerbate, embitter, sour, envenom, inflame 821 *excite*; exasperate, irritate 891 *enrage*; add fuel to the flames, go from bad to worse, jump from the frying pan into the fire.

833. Cheerfulness – N. *cheerfulness*, optimism, hopefulness 852 *hope*; cheeriness 824 *joy*; geniality, sunniness, breeziness, smiles, good humour; alacrity, vitality, animal spirits, high s., joie de vivre; light-heartedness, light heart 828 *content*; liveliness, sparkle, vivacity, animation 822 *excitable state*; life and soul of the party, party spirit 882 *sociability*; optimist, perennial o., Pollyanna.

merriment, laughter and joy; cheer, good c.; exhilaration, high spirits, abandon; jollity, joviality, jocularity, gaiety, glee, mirth, hilarity 835 *laughter*; levity, frivolity; merry-making, fun and games, sport, good s. 837 *amusement*; jubilation 876 *celebration*.

Adj. *cheerful*, cheery, blithe, blithesome 824 *happy*; hearty, genial, convivial 882 *sociable*; sanguine, optimistic; smiling, sunny, bright, beaming, radiant 835 *laughing*; breezy, in high spirits, in a good humour; in good heart, unrepining, optimistic, upbeat, hopeful, buoyant, resilient, irrepressible; carefree, light-hearted, happy-go-lucky, debonair; jaunty, perky, chirpy, chipper, spry, sprightly, sparkling, full of beans 819 *lively*; alacritous 597 *willing*.

merry, joyous, joyful; sparkling, mirth-loving, waggish, jocular 839 *witty*; gay, frivolous 456 *light-minded*; playful, sportive, frisky, gamesome, frolicsome, kittenish, roguish, arch, sly, full of tricks; mirthful, jocund, jovial, jolly, joking; wild, rackety, hilarious, uproarious, rip-roaring, rollicking 837 *amused*.

jubilant, overjoyed, gleeful, delighted 824 *pleased*; chuffed, elated, flushed, exultant, triumphant, cock-a-hoop 727 *successful*.

Vb. *be cheerful*, be in good spirits; look on the bright side 852 *hope*; make the best of it; take heart, snap out of it, cheer up, perk up, buck up 831 *be relieved*; brighten, liven up, smile, beam, sparkle; dance, sing 835 *rejoice*; whoop, cheer 876 *celebrate*; have fun, enjoy oneself 837 *amuse oneself*.

cheer, gladden, warm the heart 828 *content*; comfort 831 *relieve*; put in a good humour 826 *please*; enliven 821 *animate*; exhilarate, elate 826 *delight*; encourage, inspirit, hearten, raise the spirits, buck up, jolly along, bolster 855 *give courage*; act like a tonic, energize 174 *invigorate*.

Adv. *cheerfully*, willingly, joyfully, gladly; gaily, without a care in the world; airily, breezily; allegro, con brio.

834. Dejection. Seriousness – N. *dejection*, unhappiness, cheerlessness, dejectedness, low spirits, dumps, doldrums; spiritlessness, dispiritedness, sinking heart; disillusion 509 *disappointment*; defeatism, pessimism, cynicism, despair, death wish 853 *hopelessness*; weariness 684 *fatigue*; sadness, misery, wretchedness, disconsolateness, dolefulness 825 *sorrow*; despondency, prostration, languishment; Slough of Despond, grey dawn; gloominess, glumness, long face, face as long as a fiddle; depressant 838 *bore*; gloom and doom, trouble 825 *worry*.

melancholy, melancholia, hypochondria; neurosis, neurasthenia; depression, cafard, black mood, blue devils, blues, mopes, mopishness, sighing; world-weariness, taedium vitae, Weltschmerz, angst, nostalgia 825 *suffering*.

seriousness, earnestness; gravity, solemnity, sobriety, demureness, staidness; grimness 893 *sullenness*; primness, humourlessness, dullness; straight face, poker f.; earnest, dead e.; no laughing matter, chastening thought.

moper, complainer 829 *malcontent*; sourpuss, crosspatch, bear with a sore head; pessimist, damper, wet blanket, killjoy, spoilsport; Job's comforter, misery, sobersides; death's-head, skeleton at the feast, gloom and doom merchant; hypochondriac.

Adj. *dejected*, joyless, dreary, cheerless, unhappy, sad (**see** *melancholic*); gloomy, despondent, downbeat, pessimistic, defeatist, despairing 853 *hopeless*; beaten 728 *defeated*; discouraged, disheartened, dismayed; dispirited, troubled 825 *suffering*; downcast, downhearted, droopy, low, down, down in the mouth, low-spirited, depressed; not oneself, out of spirits; listless 679 *inactive*; lacklustre 419 *dim*; discountenanced, chapfallen, crestfallen 509 *disappointed*; cheesed off,

sick as a parrot 829 *discontented*; in the doldrums; chastened, subdued, sadder and wiser 830 *regretting*; chagrined, mortified, cut up; disillusioned.

melancholic, atrabilious, vapourish, hypochondriac; blue, feeling blue, down in the dumps; jaundiced, sour; thoughtful, pensive; melancholy, sad; heavy-hearted, sick at heart 825 *unhappy*; rueful 830 *regretting*; mournful, doleful, woeful 836 *lamenting*; forlorn, miserable, wretched, disconsolate; sorry for oneself, wallowing in self-pity; moody 893 *sullen*; mopish, dull, dismal, gloomy, morose, glum, sunk in gloom; long in the face, woebegone; wan, haggard, careworn.

serious, sober, sobersided, solemn, sedate, stolid, staid, demure, muted, grave, stern 735 *severe*; sour, dour, grim, saturnine 893 *sullen*; unlaughing, unsmiling; inscrutable, straight-faced, po-f., poker-f., deadpan; prim, humourless; unfunny, heavy, dull, solid 838 *tedious*; chastening, sobering.

cheerless, comfortless, unconsoling; uncongenial, uninviting; depressing, dreary 838 *tedious*; dismal, lugubrious, funereal, gloomy, dark, forbidding; drab, grey, sombre; cold.

Vb. *be dejected*, despond, lose heart 853 *despair*; succumb, languish, droop, flag 684 *be fatigued*; hang one's head, pull a long face; mope, brood 449 *think*; sulk 893 *be sullen*; eat one's heart out, yearn 859 *desire*; sigh, grieve 829 *be discontented*; groan 825 *suffer*; weep 836 *lament*; repine 830 *regret*.

be serious, not smile, repress a s.; not laugh, keep a straight face, keep one's countenance, maintain one's gravity, sober up; look grave, look glum; lack sparkle, not see the joke, take oneself seriously 838 *be tedious*; sober, chasten.

sadden, grieve, break one's heart, make one's heart bleed; draw tears, melt one's heart; pain 829 *cause discontent*; drive to despair, crush, prostrate.

depress, deject, get one down; dismay, dishearten, discourage, dispirit, unman 854 *frighten*; cast a gloom over 418 *darken*; dampen, put a damper on, throw cold water, dash one's hopes 509 *disappoint*; dull the spirits, prey on the mind, weigh on; weary 684 *fatigue*; bore 838 *be tedious*.

835. Rejoicing – N. *rejoicing*, jubilation 837 *festivity*; jubilee 876 *celebration*; felicitation 886 *congratulation*; cheers, hurrah, hallelujah 923 *praise*; thanksgiving 907 *thanks*; paean, Te Deum; raptures, elation 824 *joy*; revelling 837 *revel*; merrymaking, abandon 833 *merriment*.

laughter, risibility; loud laughter, Homeric l.; roar of laughter, shrieks of l., cachinnation; mocking laughter 851 *ridicule*; laugh, belly l., horse l., guffaw; chuckle, chortle, cackle, crow, coo; giggle, snigger, snicker, titter, tee-hee; fit of laughing, the giggles; smile, simper, smirk, grin; twinkle, half-smile; humour, sense of h. 839 *wit*; laughing matter, comedy, farce.

laugher, chuckler, etc. vb.; Cheshire cat; mocker 926 *detractor*; rollicker 837 *reveller*; comic muse, Thalia.

Adj. *rejoicing*, cheering etc. vb.; exultant, elated 833 *jubilant*; lyrical, ecstatic 923 *approving*.

laughing, guffawing etc. vb.; splitting one's sides, creased, doubled up, convulsed, rolling in the aisles; humorous; mocking 851 *derisive*; laughable, risible 849 *ridiculous*; comic, comical, funny, farcical 497 *absurd*.

Vb. *rejoice*, be joyful, shout for joy; dance, skip 312 *leap*; clap one's hands, whoop, cheer 923 *applaud*; yell oneself hoarse 408 *vociferate*; carol 413 *sing*; exult, crow 876 *celebrate*; felicitate 886 *congratulate*; thank one's lucky stars 907 *thank*; let one's hair down; dance in the streets, make merry 833 *be cheerful*, 837 *revel*; have a party 882 *be sociable*; congratulate oneself, hug o., gloat 824 *be pleased*; purr, coo, gurgle; cry for joy.

laugh, get the giggles; hoot, chuckle, chortle, crow, cackle; giggle, snigger, snicker, titter; laugh at 851 *ridicule*; fall about, hold one's sides, be in stitches, burst with laughter, shriek with l.; kill oneself laughing, laugh fit to burst.

smile, break into a s., grin, show one's teeth; grimace, curl one's lip; smirk, simper; twinkle, beam, flash a smile.

836. Lamentation – N. *lamentation*, lamenting, ululation, wail, weeping and wailing; mourning 364 *obsequies*; sackcloth and ashes; widow's weeds, crepe, black; cypress, willow; crying, sobbing, etc. vb.; tears, tearfulness 834 *dejection*; wet eyes, red e., swollen e.; breakdown, hysterics; cry, good c.; sob, sigh, groan, moan, whimper, whine, grizzle, bawl, boo-hoo.

lament, plaint, complaint, jeremiad, dirge, knell, requiem, threnody, elegy, epicedium, swansong 364 *obsequies*; keen, coronach, wake 905 *condolence*; howl 409 *ululation*; sobstuff, sob-story, hard-luck s.; tale of woe; de profundis, cri de coeur; show of grief, crocodile tears 542 *sham*.

weeper, wailer, keener, lamenter, threnodist, elegist; mourner, mute; grizzler, sniveller, whimperer, whiner, crybaby; Jeremiah, Niobe.

Adj. *lamenting*, crying etc. vb.; lachrymatory; in tears, bathed in t., dissolved in t.; tearful, lachrymose; wet-eyed, red-e.; close to tears, ready to cry; mournful, doleful, lugubrious 825 *unhappy*; woeful, haggard, wild-eyed, wringing one's hands 834 *dejected*; complaining, plangent, plaintive, singing the blues; elegiac, epicedial, threnodic, dirgelike 364 *funereal*; in mourning, in black; at half-mast; whining, fretful, querulous; pathetic, pitiful, tear-jerking 905 *pitiable*.

Vb. *lament*, grieve, sorrow, sigh, heave a s. 825 *suffer*; deplore 830 *regret*; condole, commiserate 905 *pity*; grieve for, sigh for, bewail, bemoan, elegize, threnodize; mourn, wail, keen; go into mourning; wring one's hands, beat one's breast, tear one's hair; take on, carry on, take it badly 829 *be discontented*.

weep, wail, greet; shed tears, burst into t.; give way to t., break down, cry, bawl, cry one's eyes out; cry out, shriek 409 *ululate*; sob, sigh, moan, groan 825 *suffer*; snivel, grizzle, blubber, pule, whine, whinge, whimper.

837. Amusement – N. *amusement*, pleasure, interest, delight 826 *pleasurableness*; diversion, divertissement, entertainment; pastime, hobby; solace, recreation 685 *refreshment*; relaxation 683 *repose*; holiday 681 *leisure*; April Fool's Day; play, sport, fun, good clean f., good cheer, jollity, joviality, jocundity 833 *merriment*; occasion, do, junket 876 *celebration*; outing, excursion, jaunt; treat, Sunday school t., picnic (see *festivity*); conversazione, garden party, bunfight, fête, flower show, gymkhana, jamboree 74 *assembly*; game.

festivity, playtime, holiday-making; visiting 882 *social round*; fun 835 *laughter*; beer and skittles 824 *enjoyment*; social whirl, high life; good time; living it up, a short life and a merry one 943 *intemperance*; festival, fair, fun-fair, carnival, fiesta, gala; festivities, fun and games, merrymaking, revels, saturnalia 833 *merriment*; high day, feast d. 876 *special day*; carousal, wassail 301 *feasting*; conviviality, party 882 *social gathering*; bender, orgy, carouse 949 *drunkenness*; bust, binge, beano, blowout; barbecue, beanfeast 301 *meal*.

revel, rout, rave-up, knees-up, jollification, whoopee, fun, high old time; high jinks, spree, junket, junketing, horseplay; night out, night on the tiles; play, game, romp, rollick, frolic, lark, skylarking, escapade, prank, rag 497 *foolery*.

pleasure ground, park, chase; green, common; arbour, gardens; seaside, beach, holiday camp; playground, recreation ground, playing field, links, golf course; rink, skating r.; tennis court 724 *arena*; circus, fair, merry-go-round.

place of amusement, fairground, funfair, shooting gallery, amusement arcade; skittle alley; billiard room, pool r., assembly r., pump r.; concert hall, vaudeville, hippodrome, playhouse 594 *theatre*, 445 *cinema*; ballroom, dance floor; discotheque, disco; cabaret, night club, clip joint; bingo hall, casino.

sport, outdoor life; sportsmanship 694 *skill*; sports, field s., track events; games, gymnastics 162 *athletics*, 312 *leap*, 716 *contest*, *racing*, *pugilism*, *wrestling*; outdoor

sports, cycling, hiking, rambling, orienteering, camping, picnicking; running, jogging; riding, pony-trekking; archery, shooting, clay-pigeon s.; hunting, shooting and fishing 619 *chase*; water sports, swimming, boating 269 *aquatics*; rock-climbing, mountaineering 308 *ascent*; caving 309 *descent*; winter sports, skiing, tobogganning, skating; flying, gliding 271 *aeronautics*.

ball game, King Willow, cricket, French c.; baseball, soft-ball, rounders; tennis, table t., pingpong; badminton, squash; handball, volleyball; fives, pelota; netball, basketball; football, soccer; Rugby football, rugger; lacrosse, hockey, ice h.; polo, water polo; croquet, putting, golf; skittles, ninepins, bowls, curling; marbles, dibs; quoits; billiards, snooker, pool; bagatelle, pinball.

indoor game, nursery g., parlour g., panel g., party g.; charades; I-spy; word game, spelling bee, Scrabble (tdmk); riddles, crosswords, acrostics; consequences, noughts and crosses, battleships, boxes; darts, dominoes, mah-jong, tiddly-winks, jigsaw puzzle.

board game, chess, draughts, checkers, Chinese c., halma, fox and hounds; backgammon; ludo, snakes and ladders, Monopoly (tdmk), go.

children's games, ring-a-ring-o'-roses; leapfrog, hopscotch; touch, tag, he, hide-and-seek, follow-my-leader, blind man's buff, cowboys and Indians, cops and robbers, prisoner's base.

card game, cards, game of cards, rubber of whist *or* bridge; boston, whist, bridge; nap, loo, cribbage, bezique; rummy, gin r., canasta; solo, solitaire, patience; snap, beggar-my-neighbour, old maid, Happy Families, pelmanism; bingo; pontoon, black jack; brag, poker; banker, baccarat, chemin de fer, monte 618 *gambling*.

dancing, dance, ball; masquerade; thé dansant, tea dance, ceilidh, square dance, hoe-down; hop, jam session, disco; ballet dancing 594 *ballet*; folk dancing, country d., Scottish c. d., old-time d., sequence d., ballroom d.; Terpsichore.

dance, war dance, sword d., corroboree; shuffle, soft-shoe s., cakewalk; pas seul; clog dance, step d., tap d., toe d.; fan dance, dance of the seven veils, hula-hula; high kicks, cancan; belly dance, gipsy dance, flamenco; country dance, morris d., barn d., square d., hay; hornpipe, keel row; folk dance, polonaise, mazurka; fling, Highland f.; reel, Strathspey, Gay Gordons, strip the willow, Dashing White Sergeant; tarantella, bolero, fandango, galliard, écossaise, gavotte, quadrille, cotillion, minuet, pavane, saraband, schottische, polka; waltz, valeta, lancers; foxtrot, quickstep; Charleston, black bottom, two-step, paso-doble, tango, rumba, samba, mambo, bossa nova, habanera, beguine, conga, cha-cha; hokey-cokey, Palais Glide; stomp, bop, bebop, shimmy, jive, rock 'n' roll, twist; Paul Jones, snowball; dancer, corps de ballet 594 *actor*; high-kicker 594 *entertainer*; hoofer, jiver, jitterbug, disco dancer 312 *jumper*.

plaything, bauble, knick-knack, trinket, toy 639 *bauble*; teddy bear, doll, top, yo-yo; jacks, fivestones, marbles; ball, balloon 252 *sphere*; hoop, skipping rope, stilts, pogo stick, rocking horse, tricycle; roller skates; popgun, water pistol; toy soldier, model yacht, model railway; magic lantern, peep show 522 *exhibit*; puppet show, Punch and Judy 551 *image*; cards, pack, deck; domino, tile; draught, counter, chip; tiddly-wink; chess piece, pawn.

player, sportsman *or* -woman; competitor 716 *contender*; all-rounder; footballer, forward, striker, defence, goalkeeper; cricketer, batsman, fielder, wicketkeeper, bowler; hockey-player, tennis-p.; marksman *or* -woman; archer 287 *shooter*; shot-putter 287 *thrower*; dicer, gamester 618 *gambler*; card-player, chess-p.; fellow sportsman *or* -woman, playmate 707 *colleague*.

reveller, merry-maker, rioter, roisterer, gamboller, rollicker, frolicker; drinker 949 *drunkard*; feaster 301 *eater*; partygoer 882 *sociable person*; pleasure-seeker, playboy, good-time girl; holidaymaker, tripper 268 *traveller*; master of the revels, master of ceremonies, MC, toastmaster;

symposiarch, arbiter elegantiarum.

Adj. *amusing*, entertaining, diverting etc. vb.; sportive, full of fun 833 *merry*; pleasant 826 *pleasurable*; laughable, clownish 849 *funny*; recreational 685 *refreshing*; festal, festive, holiday.

amused, entertained, tickled 824 *pleased*; festive, sportive, rollicking, roisterous, prankish, playful, kittenish, roguish, waggish, jolly, jovial; in festal mood 835 *rejoicing*; sporty, games-playing 162 *athletic*; playing, at play; easy to please.

Vb. *amuse*, interest, entertain, beguile, divert, make one laugh, take one out of oneself; please 826 *delight*; recreate 685 *refresh*; enliven 833 *cheer*; treat, regale, take out; raise a smile, set the table in a roar, have them rolling in the aisles, wow, slay, be the death of 849 *be ridiculous*; humour, keep amused; give a party 882 *be hospitable*.

amuse oneself, while away the time 681 *have leisure*; pursue one's hobby, dabble in; play, play at, enjoy oneself 833 *be cheerful*; take a holiday, have an outing, have a field day, have a ball; sport, disport oneself; frisk, frolic, rollick, romp, gambol, caper; cut capers, lark around, skylark, play the fool 497 *be absurd*; jest 839 *be witty*; play cards, game, dice 618 *gamble*; play games.

dance, go dancing; waltz, foxtrot, tango, jive; whirl 315 *rotate*; jig about 312 *leap*; shuffle, hoof, trip, tread a measure, trip the light fantastic toe.

revel, make merry, make whoopee, celebrate 835 *rejoice*; drive dull care away, let oneself go, let one's hair down, let off steam; go on the razzle *or* on a bender, have a night out *or* on the tiles, live it up, paint the town red; junket, roister; feast, banquet, quaff, carouse, wassail, make the rafters ring; drown one's sorrows 949 *get drunk*; sow one's wild oats, burn the candle at both ends.

Int. carpe diem! eat, drink and be merry! on with the dance!

838. Tedium – N. *tedium*, ennui 834 *melancholy*; lack of interest 860 *indiffer-*

ence; weariness, languor 684 *fatigue*;
wearisomeness, tediousness, irksome-
ness; stodginess, heaviness; too much of a
good thing 863 *satiety*; flatness, staleness
387 *insipidity*; stuffiness 840 *dullness*; lon-
gueurs 570 *diffuseness*; monotony, dull m.
106 *repetition*; time to kill 679 *inactivity*.

bore, no fun; irk, drag, bind, chore;
daily round 610 *habit*; grindstone, treadmill 682 *labour*; boring person, bromide,
pain in the neck, dryasdust, proser, pub
bore; killjoy, misery 834 *moper*; frump,
Mrs Grundy.

Adj. *tedious*, uninteresting, strictly for
the birds; unenjoyable, unexciting, uneventful, unentertaining, unamusing, unfunny; slow, dragging, leaden, heavy; dry,
arid; flat, stale, insipid 387 *tasteless*; bald
573 *plain*; humdrum, soulless, mundane;
dreary, stuffy, bourgeois 840 *dull*; stodgy,
prosaic, uninspired, unreadable; long-
winded, drawn out 570 *prolix*; somnific
679 *soporific*; boring, wearisome, tiresome, irksome; wearing, chronic 684 *fatiguing*; repetitive, monotonous 16 *uniform*; cloying, satiating; nauseating.

bored, unamused; twiddling one's
thumbs 679 *inactive*; fed up to the back
teeth, browned off, had it up to here 829
discontented; stale, weary, jaded 684 *fatigued*; world-weary 834 *melancholic*; blasé
860 *indifferent*; satiated, nauseated, sick
of, sick and tired 861 *disliking*.

Vb. *be tedious*, pall, lose its novelty;
jade 863 *sate*; bore, irk, try, weary 684
fatigue; bore to death *or* to tears, bore the
pants off, bore stiff; weary to distraction,
tire out; get one down, try one's patience,
outstay one's welcome, stay too long; send
one to sleep; drag 278 *move slowly*; go on
and on, never end; harp on 106 *repeat
oneself*.

839. Wit – N. *wit*, wittiness, esprit,
ready wit; salt, Attic s. 575 *elegance*;
sparkle 498 *intelligence*; humour, sense of
h.; wry humour, dryness, slyness, drollery, pleasantry, waggishness, facetious-
ness; jocularity, jocosity 833 *merriment*;
comicalness, absurdity 849 *ridiculousness*;
joking, jesting, tomfoolery, buffoonery,

clowning, funny business 497 *foolery*;
comic turn, laugh a minute; broad
humour, low h., vulgarity 847 *bad taste*;
farce, broad f., knockabout comedy, slapstick, high camp 594 *dramaturgy*; whimsicality, fancy 604 *whim*; cartoon, comic
strip, caricature; biting wit, satire, sarcasm 851 *ridicule*; irony 850 *affectation*;
black comedy, gallows humour; word-
fencing 477 *sophistry*; wordplay, play on
words, punning 518 *equivocalness*.

witticism, witty remark, stroke of wit,
jeu d'esprit, sally, bon mot; epigram, conceit; pun, play on words; feed line, punch
l.; banter, chaff, persiflage; retort, repartee, quid pro quo, backchat, backtalk; sarcasm 851 *satire*; joke, standing j.; family
j., in-joke; jest, good one, rib-tickler,
side-splitter; quip, gag, crack, wisecrack,
one-liner; old joke, corny j.; chestnut, Joe
Miller; practical joke, hoax, legpull; dirty
joke, blue j., sick j.; story, funny s., shag-
gy-dog s.; limerick, clerihew.

humorist, wit, bel esprit, epigrammatist; conversationalist; card, character,
wag, wisecracker, joker; funny man, gagman, gagster, punster; ragger, teaser;
practical joker 545 *deceiver*; satirist, lampooner 926 *detractor*; comedian, comedienne, comic 594 *entertainer*; cartoonist, caricaturist; parodist 20 *imitator*;
raconteur, raconteuse; jester, court j., cap
and bells, clown, farceur, buffoon, stooge
501 *fool*.

Adj. *witty*, spirituel(le), nimble-witted,
quick; Attic 575 *elegant*; pointed, ben trovato, epigrammatic; brilliant, sparkling
498 *intelligent*; salty, racy, piquant; fruity,
risqué; snappy, biting, pungent, keen,
sharp, sarcastic; ironic, dry, sly, pawky;
facetious, flippant; jocular, jocose, joking, joshing, jokey, waggish, roguish; lively, pleasant, gay 833 *merry*; comic 849
funny; comical, humorous, droll; whimsical 604 *capricious*; playful, sportive.

Vb. *be witty*, scintillate, sparkle, flash;
jest, joke, crack a j., quip, gag, wisecrack;
raise a laugh 837 *amuse*; pun, play on
words; fool, jape; tease, chaff, rag, banter, twit, pull one's leg, have one on, make
fun of 851 *ridicule*; ham up, camp up;

caricature, burlesque 851 *satirize*; retort, flash back; enjoy a joke.

840. Dullness – N. *dullness*, heaviness, stuffiness, dreariness, deadliness; monotony 838 *tedium*; colourlessness, drabness; lack of sparkle, lack of inspiration, want of originality; stodginess, unreadability, prosiness; staleness, flatness 387 *insipidity*; banality, triteness, superficiality; no sense of humour, inability to see a joke 834 *seriousness*; prosaicness 573 *plainness*.

Adj. *dull*, unamusing, uninteresting, unstimulating, uninspiring; unfunny, uncomical, straight; deadly dull, dull as ditchwater; stuffy, dreary, pointless, meaningless 838 *tedious*; colourless, drab; flat, bland, vapid, insipid 387 *tasteless*; unimaginative, uninventive, derivative, superficial; stupid 499 *unintelligent*; humourless, frumpish 834 *serious*; unwitty, graceless 576 *inelegant*; heavy, ponderous; stodgy, prosaic, matter-of-fact, pedestrian, unreadable; stale, trite, platitudinous 610 *usual*.

841. Beauty – N. *beauty*, pulchritude 646 *perfection*; sublimity, grandeur, magnificence; splendour, gorgeousness, brilliance; transfiguration 843 *beautification*; landscape, seascape, cloudscape 445 *spectacle*; fair proportions, regular features 245 *symmetry*; physical beauty, loveliness, comeliness, prettiness; attractiveness 826 *pleasurableness*; glamour, sex appeal, cuteness; attractions, charms, graces, perfections; good looks, pretty face, beaux yeux; cherry lips, schoolgirl complexion, peaches and cream c.; shapeliness, curvaceousness, vital statistics; gracefulness, grace 575 *elegance*; chic, style 848 *fashion*; refinement 846 *good taste*; aesthetics, aestheticism.

a beauty, thing of beauty, work of art; garden, beauty spot; jewel, pearl 646 *paragon*; rose, lily; fair one, belle, beau idéal 890 *favourite*; beauty queen, bathing belle, pin-up girl, cover girl; beefcake, cheesecake; hunk, muscleman, Mr Universe; fine figure of a man *or* woman;

blond(e), brunette, redhead; English rose; dream, vision, poem, picture, perfect p., sight for sore eyes; charmer, dazzler; stunner, knockout, eyeful, goodlooker; doll, dolly bird, cookie; glamour puss, glamour girl *or* boy; heartthrob, dreamboat; enchantress, femme fatale, vamp, seductress, siren, witch; smasher, scorcher, lovely, cutie, honey, beaut, peach, dish; sylph, fairy, peri, houri; Venus, Aphrodite; Hyperion, Adonis.

Adj. *beautiful*, pulchritudinous, beauteous; lovely, fair, bright, radiant; comely, goodly, bonny, pretty; sweet, nice; pretty as a picture, photogenic; handsome, goodlooking, well-favoured; well-built, husky, manly; tall, dark and handsome; gracious, stately, majestic, statuesque, Junoesque; adorable, godlike, divine; picturesque, scenic, ornamental; landscaped; artistic, harmonious, well-composed 694 *well-made*; aesthetic 846 *tasteful*; exquisite, choice 605 *chosen*; unblemished 646 *perfect*.

splendid, superb, fine 644 *excellent*; grand 868 *noble*; glorious, ravishing, rich, gorgeous, highly-coloured 425 *florid*; bright, resplendent; glossy, magnificent; ornate 844 *ornamented*.

shapely, well-proportioned, regular, classic; well-formed, well-turned; buxom, bosomy, curvaceous 248 *curved*; slinky, callipygous; clean-limbed, slender, slim, lissom, svelte, willowy 206 *lean*; lightsome, graceful, elegant, chic; petite, dainty, delicate; undeformed 646 *perfect*.

personable, prepossessing, agreeable; comfortable, buxom, sonsy; attractive, dishy, taking, fetching, appealing 826 *pleasurable*; sexy, cute, kissable; charming, entrancing, enchanting, glamorous; lovesome, winsome 887 *lovable*; freshfaced, wholesome, lusty, blooming; rosy, rosy-cheeked, bright-eyed; sightly, becoming, fit to be seen, easy on the eye, passable, presentable, proper, decent, neat, natty, tidy, trim; spruce, snappy, dapper, glossy, sleek; well-dressed, well turned out, smart, soigné(e) 848 *fashionable*; elegant, dainty 846 *tasteful*.

Vb. *beautify*, improve; prettify, bejewel

844 *decorate*; set off, grace, become, flatter; enhance, glamorize, transfigure; give a facelift, smarten up; prink 843 *primp*.

842. Ugliness – N. *ugliness*, unsightliness, hideousness, repulsiveness; lack of beauty, gracelessness 576 *inelegance*; want of symmetry, unshapeliness 246 *deformity*; mutilation, disfigurement 845 *blemish*; uglification, disfiguration, defacement; squalor 649 *uncleanness*; homeliness, plainness, not much to look at, no beauty, no oil painting; haggardness, wrinkles, crowsfeet, hand of time 131 *age*.

eyesore, hideosity, blot 845 *blemish*; offence to the eyes; blot on the landscape, architectural monstrosity, satanic mills; ugly person, fright, sight, frump; scarecrow, horror, gargoyle, grotesque; monster, abortion; harridan, witch; plain Jane, ugly duckling; satyr, Caliban; gorgon, Medusa; Beast.

Adj. *ugly*, lacking beauty, unlovely, uncomely, unhandsome; coarse-looking, blowzy, frowzy; ugly as sin, hideous 649 *unclean*; frightful, shocking, monstrous; repulsive, repellent, loathsome 861 *disliked*; beastly, nasty 645 *not nice*; not much to look at, unprepossessing, homely, plain, plain-featured, without any looks; mousy, frumpish, frumpy; torbidding, ill-favoured, hard-featured, villainous, grim, saturnine 893 *sullen*.

unsightly, faded, worn, ravaged, wrinkled 131 *ageing*; not worth looking at, not fit to be seen; marred 845 *blemished*; unshapely, shapeless, formless, asymmetrical 244 *amorphous*; grotesque, twisted, deformed, disfigured 246 *distorted*; defaced, shapeless, litter-strewn; badly made, ill-proportioned, misshapen; dumpy, squat 196 *dwarfish*; bloated 195 *fleshy*; stained, discoloured, washed out 426 *colourless*; ghastly, wan, grisly, gruesome; tousled 61 *orderless*.

graceless, ungraceful 576 *inelegant*; inartistic, unaesthetic; unflattering, unbecoming, unattractive; squalid, dingy, poky, dreary, drab; lank, dull, mousy; dowdy, badly dressed, lacking clothes-

sense; garish, gaudy, coarse 847 *vulgar*; rude, crude, uncouth 699 *artless*; clumsy, awkward, ungainly, cumbersome, clodhopping 195 *unwieldy*.

Vb. *make ugly*, uglify; wither 655 *deteriorate*; sully 649 *make unclean*; spoil, deface, disfigure, mar, blemish, blot; misshape, deform; grimace 893 *be sullen*; torture, twist 246 *distort*; mutilate, vandalize 655 *impair*.

843. Beautification – N. *beautification*, beautifying 844 *ornamentation*; transfiguration 143 *transformation*; landscape gardening 844 *ornamental art*; plastic surgery, cosmetic s., nose job, facelift; beauty treatment, facial; massage; manicure, pedicure; tattooing 844 *ornamental art*; toilet, grooming, make-up, cosmetology; wash and brush up 648 *ablutions*.

hairdressing, trichology, scalp massage; barbering, shaving; depilation, plucking; haircut, shave; hair style, coiffure, crop, bob, shingle, pageboy, crewcut, urchin cut; styling, curling, frizzing, waving, setting, hair-straightening, defrizzing; hairdo, shampoo and set, blow wave; permanent w., perm; curl 251 *coil*; bang, fringe, ponytail, chignon, bun; beehive, Afro 259 *hair*; false hair, hairpiece, toupee, switch, wig; curlers, rollers; bandeau, Alice band; comb, hairpin, hairgrip, slide; hairnet, snood 228 *headgear*.

cosmetic, aid to beauty; patch, beauty spot; make-up, paint, greasepaint, warpaint; rouge, cream, face c. 357 *unguent*; lipstick, lip gloss; nail polish, nail varnish, powder, face p., talcum p.; kohl, mascara, eye shadow, eyeliner; hand lotion, aftershave l.; soap, shampoo 648 *cleanser*; antiperspirant, deodorant; scent, perfume, cologne, eau de c., lavender water, toilet w.; eyebrow pencil, false eyelashes; powder puff, compact; vanity case, nail file; shaver, razor, depilatory; toiletries, beauty parlour.

beautician, beauty specialist; plastic surgeon; make-up artist, tattooer; cosmetician; barber, hairdresser, stylist, coiffeur, coiffeuse; trichologist; manicurist, pedicurist, chiropodist.

Adj. *beautified*, transfigured, transformed; prettified, glamorized; made-up, rouged, raddled, painted, powdered, scented; curled, primped; dressed up, dolled up, tarted up, done up like a dog's dinner 841 *beautiful*.

Vb. *primp*, prettify, dress up, bedizen, ornament 844 *decorate*; prink, prank, trick out; preen; titivate, make up, rouge, paint, shadow, highlight; powder; curl, wave 841 *beautify*.

844. Ornamentation – N. *ornamentation*,

decoration, adornment, garnish; ornate style 574 *ornament*; art deco, art nouveau, baroque, rococo; chinoiserie; gilt, gaudiness 875 *ostentation*; enhancement, enrichment, embellishment; setting, background; centrepiece, epergne; floral decoration, flower arrangement, wreath, garland, bouquet, nosegay, posy, buttonhole; objet d'art, bric-à-brac, curio, bibelot.

ornamental art, landscape gardening, topiarism; architecture; interior decoration, painting, decorating; statuary 554 *sculpture*; frieze, dado; capital, acanthus; pilaster, caryatid, figurehead; boss, cornice, corbel, gargoyle; astragal, moulding, beading, fluting, reeding, chamfering, strapwork, linenfold; fretting, tracery; varnishing 226 *facing*; pargeting, veneering, panelling, graining; ormolu, gilding, gilt, gold leaf; illumination, illustration 551 *art*; stained glass; tie-dyeing, batik; tattooing; etching 555 *engraving*; work, handiwork, handicraft, fancywork, woodwork, fretwork, frostwork; pokerwork, pyrography; open-work, filigree; whittling, carving, embossing, chasing; inlay, enamelling, marquetry 437 *variegation*; toreutics; cut glass, engraved g.; wrought iron.

pattern, motif, print, design, composition 331 *structure*; detail; spandrel, ogee; crocket, finial, tracery, scrollwork, flourish 251 *coil*; swag, festoon; weave, diaper 331 *texture*; chevron, key pattern; check 437 *chequer*; spot, dot 437 *maculation*; watermark 547 *identification*.

needlework, stitchery, tapestry; cross-stitch, sampler; patchwork, appliqué; open work, drawn-thread w.; embroidery, smocking; crochet, lace; tatting, knitting 222 *network*; stitch, purl, plain; gros point, petit p., needle p.

trimming, passementerie, piping, valance, border, fringe, frill, flounce 234 *edging*; binding, trappings; braid, cockade 547 *badge*; bow 47 *fastening*; bobble, pompom; tassel, dangler, bead; feather, plume 259 *plumage*; streamer, ribbon.

finery, Sunday best 228 *clothing*; frippery, frills and furbelows, froufrou; gaudery, gaud, trinket, knick-knack, gewgaw, fandangle; tinsel, spangle, sequin 639 *bauble*.

jewellery, bijouterie; diadem, tiara 743 *regalia*; pendant, locket 217 *hanging object*; charm 983 *talisman*; rope, string, necklet, necklace, choker; torque, armlet, anklet, bracelet, wristlet, bangle; ring, earring, signet ring; brooch, clasp; stud, pin, tie p., cufflinks 47 *fastening*; medal, medallion.

gem, jewel, stone, precious s., semiprecious s.; brilliant, sparkler, diamond, rock, ice; ruby, pearl, sapphire, emerald, amethyst; coral, ivory, jet, amber, jade, lapis lazuli.

Adj. *ornamental*, decorative, nonfunctional, fancy, arty-crafty; intricate, elaborate, quaint, daedal; scenic, picturesque, pretty-pretty; geometric; baroque, rococo.

ornamented, richly o., luxuriant; adorned, decorated, embellished, ornate; patterned, inlaid, enamelled, chryselephantine 437 *variegated*; worked, embroidered; wreathed, festooned, garlanded; overcoloured 425 *florid*; luscious, plush, gilt, gilded 800 *rich*; gorgeous, garish, glittering, flashy, gaudy 875 *showy*.

Vb. *decorate*, adorn; ornament; embellish, enhance, enrich; grace, set off; paint, tart up 841 *beautify*; garnish, trim; array, deck, bedeck 228 *dress*; deck out, trick o. 843 *primp*; garland, crown 866 *honour*; stud, spangle 437 *variegate*; colourwash, whitewash 226 *coat*; enamel, gild, silver; blazon, illuminate, illustrate 553 *paint*, 425 *colour*; border 234 *hem*; work, pick out, embroider; pattern, inlay, engrave; enchase, encrust, emboss, bead, mould; fret, carve 262 *groove*, 260 *notch*; enlace, wreathe, festoon 251 *twine*.

845. Blemish – N. *blemish*, scar, cicatrice, weal, welt, pockmark; flaw, defect 647 *imperfection*; disfigurement 246 *distortion*; stigma, blot on the landscape 842 *eyesore*; scribbling, graffiti; blur, blotch, smudge 550 *obliteration*; smut, smear, stain 649 *dirt*; spot, speck 437 *maculation*; freckle, mole, birthmark, strawberry mark; excrescence, pimple, blackhead, wart 253 *swelling*; acne, eczema 651 *skin disease*; harelip, cleft palate; cast, squint; cut, scratch, bruise, black eye, cauliflower ear, broken nose 655 *wound*.

Adj. *blemished*, defective, flawed 647 *imperfect*; tarnished, stained, soiled, flyblown 649 *dirty*; shop-soiled 655 *deteriorated*; marked, scarred, marred; foxed, spotted, pitted, pockmarked; spotty, freckled; squinting 440 *dimsighted*; bandy, crooked 246 *deformed*.

Vb. *blemish*, flaw, crack, damage 655 *impair*; blot, smudge, sully 649 *make unclean*; scar, pit, pockmark 547 *mark*; mar, spoil the look of 842 *make ugly*; deface, disfigure, scribble on.

846. Good taste – N. *good taste*, tastefulness, taste, refined t., cultivated t.; restraint, simplicity 573 *plainness*; choiceness, excellence 644 *goodness*; refinement, delicacy, euphemism 950 *purity*; fine feeling, discernment, palate 463 *discrimination*; daintiness 862 *fastidiousness*; decency, seemliness 848 *etiquette*; tact, consideration, manners, breeding, civility, urbanity, social graces 884 *courtesy*; correctness, propriety, decorum; grace, polish, finish, sophistication, elegance; cultivation, culture, virtu, connoisseurship, amateurship, dilettantism; epicureanism, epicurism; aestheticism, aesthetics 480 *judgement*; artistry, virtuosity, flair 694 *skill*.

people of taste, sophisticate, connoisseur, cognoscente, amateur, dilettante; epicurean, epicure, gourmet, aesthete 480 *estimator*; arbiter of taste, arbiter el-

egantiarum; purist, precisian; euphemist 950 *prude*.

Adj. *tasteful*, gracious, dignified; in good taste, in the best of t.; choice, exquisite 644 *excellent*; simple 573 *plain*; graceful, Attic, classical 575 *elegant*; chaste, refined, delicate, euphemistic 950 *pure*; aesthetic, artistic 819 *sensitive*; discerning, epicurean 463 *discriminating*; nice, dainty, choosy 862 *fastidious*; critical, appreciative 480 *judicial*; decent, seemly, becoming 24 *apt*; proper, correct, comme il faut 848 *fashionable*; mannerly 848 *well-bred*.

847. Bad taste – N. *bad taste*, tastelessness, poor taste 645 *badness*; no taste, lack of t.; bad art, kitsch; commercialism, commercialization, prostitution of talent; yellow press, gutter p.; coarseness, barbarism, vulgarism, philistinism, Babbittry 699 *artlessness*; vulgarity, gaudiness, garishness, loudness; shoddy, frippery, tinsel, glitter 639 *bauble*; lack of feeling, insensitivity, crassness, grossness; tactlessness, indelicacy, impropriety, unseemliness; untimely jest, misplaced wit; obscenity 951 *impurity*; unfashionableness, dowdiness, frumpishness; frump, square.

ill-breeding, vulgarity, commonness; loudness, heartiness, rusticity, provinciality, unfashionableness; bad form, incorrectness; bad manners, no manners, gaucherie, boorishness 885 *discourtesy*; ungentlemanliness, caddishness; brutishness, savagery; misbehaviour, indecorum, ribaldry; rough behaviour, rowdyism 61 *disorder*.

vulgarian, snob, social climber; cad, bounder; rough diamond, unlicked cub; arriviste, parvenu, nouveau riche; proletarian 869 *commoner*; Goth, Vandal, Philistine, Babbitt; barbarian, savage; yob, punk.

Adj. *vulgar*, undignified; unrefined, inelegant; tasteless, in bad taste, in the worst possible t.; gross, crass, coarse, coarse-grained; unfastidious, not particular; knowing no better, philistine, barbarian 699 *artless*; commercialized; tawdry, cheap, cheap and nasty, kitschy, ersatz;

flashy 875 *showy*; loud, screaming, gaudy, garish, raffish; flaunting, shameless, tarted up; fulsome, excessive; schmaltzy, novelettish; overdressed, underdressed; shabby genteel 850 *affected*; not respectable, common, low, gutter, sordid 867 *disreputable*; improper, indelicate, indecorous; going too far, beyond the pale, scandalous, indecent; obscene 951 *impure*.

ill-bred, underbred, badly brought up; unpresentable, not to be taken anywhere; ungentlemanly, unladylike; hoydenish; ungenteel, non-U 869 *plebeian*; tactless, insensitive; uncivil, impolite, unmannerly, ill-mannered 885 *discourteous*; unfashionable, frumpish, dowdy; provincial, countrified, gone native; crude, rude, boorish, yobbish, loutish, clod-hopping, uncouth, uncultured, uncultivated, unrefined 491 *ignorant*; unsophisticated 699 *artless*; unlettered, uncivilized, barbaric; awkward, gauche 695 *clumsy*; rowdy, ruffianly 61 *disorderly*; snobbish 850 *affected*.

Vb. *vulgarize*, cheapen, coarsen, debase, lower, lower the tone; commercialize, popularize; show bad taste, know no better 491 *not know*; be unfashionable, be out of date.

848. Fashion. Etiquette – N. *fashion*, style, mode; vogue, cult; prevailing taste 126 *modernism*; rage, fad, craze; new look, latest fashion; dernier cri, last word, ne plus ultra; height of fashion; fashionableness, stylishness, flair, chic; dress sense, fashion s.; fashion show; haute couture, elegance, foppishness, dressiness; foppery 850 *affectation*; Vanity Fair, passing show, way of the world.

etiquette, point of e. 875 *formality*; protocol, convention 610 *practice*; snobbery, done thing, good form; convenances, proprieties, appearances; decency, decorum, propriety, right note, correctness 846 *good taste*; civilized behaviour 884 *courtesy*; breeding, good b., polish; gentility, gentlemanliness, ladylike behaviour; manners, good m., best behaviour; poise, dignity, savoir faire.

beau monde, society, high s.; court, drawing room, salon; top drawer, right people, smart set 868 *upper class*; cream, upper crust 644 *elite*; jeunesse dorée, gilded youth, beautiful people, jet set; hipster, swinger; man *or* woman about town, man *or* woman of fashion; high stepper, classy dame; slave to fashion; man *or* woman of the world, mondaine, socialite, playboy, clubman, clubwoman, cosmopolitan 882 *sociable person*.

fop, buck, belle; debutante, deb; coxcomb, dandy, exquisite, beau; popinjay, peacock, clothes-horse, fashion plate; swell, toff, dude; Ted, mod; spark, blood, blade, gay dog; lounge lizard, carpet knight, gallant; ladykiller, squire of dames.

Adj. *fashionable*, modish, stylish, voguish; correct, comme il faut; in, in vogue, in fashion, à la mode; chic, elegant, well-dressed, well-groomed 846 *tasteful*; clothes-conscious, foppish, dressy; high-stepping, dashing, rakish, snazzy, flashy 875 *showy*; dandy, smart, classy, swanky, swell, swish, posh; up-to-the-minute, ultrafashionable, all the rage 126 *modern*; hip, hep, trendy, swinging, with it; groomed, dandified, en grande tenue; in society, in the right set, knowing the right people; in the swim 83 *conformable*; snobbish 850 *affected*; conventional, done 610 *usual*.

well-bred, blue-blooded 868 *noble*; cosmopolitan, sophisticated, civilized, citified, urbane; polished, polite, well brought up, house-trained; gentlemanly, ladylike 868 *genteel*; civil, well-mannered 884 *courteous*; courtly, stately, dignified 875 *formal*; poised, easy, unembarrassed, smooth; correct, decorous, proper, decent; tactful, diplomatic; considerate 884 *amiable*; punctilious 929 *honourable*.

Vb. *be in fashion*, be done, catch on 610 *be wont*; be all the rage, be the latest 126 *modernize*; get with it, change with the times 83 *conform*; move in the best circles, be seen in the right c.; savoir faire, savoir vivre; entertain 882 *be hospitable*; keep up appearances; cut a dash *or* a figure, set the fashion, give a lead; look right, pass; have

style, show flair, dress well; dandify 843
primp.

849. Ridiculousness – N. *ridiculousness*,
ludicrousness, risibility, laughability 497
absurdity; funniness, comicality, drollery
839 *wit*; quaintness, oddness, queerness,
eccentricity 84 *nonconformity*; bathos,
anticlimax; extravagance, bombast 546
exaggeration; doggerel, limerick 839 *witticism*; spoonerism, malapropism; comic
turn, comedy, farce, burlesque, slapstick,
knockabout, clowning, buffoonery 594
stage play; paradox, paradoxicality 508
lack of expectation.

Adj. *ridiculous*, ludicrous, preposterous, grotesque, fantastic, cock-eyed, inappropriate 497 *absurd*; awkward, clownish 695 *clumsy*; silly 499 *foolish*; derisory
639 *unimportant*; laughable, risible; bizarre, rum, quaint, odd, queer 84 *unusual*;
mannered 850 *affected*; bombastic, extravagant 546 *exaggerated*; crazy, crackpot,
fanciful 513 *imaginary*; paradoxical.
funny, funny-peculiar 84 *abnormal*;
funny-ha-ha, laughter-inducing. good for
a laugh, comical, droll, humorous 839 *witty*; rich, priceless, hilarious, a real hoot,
too funny for words; light, comic, serio-
comic, tragicomic; mocking, ironical 851
derisive; burlesque, mock-heroic; doggerel; farcical, slapstick, clownish.

Vb. *be ridiculous*, make one laugh, raise
a laugh; tickle, disturb one's gravity, give
one the giggles 837 *amuse*; look silly, be a
figure of fun, cut a ridiculous figure, be a
laughingstock, play the fool 497 *be
absurd*; pass from the sublime to the
ridiculous; make an exhibition of oneself
695 *act foolishly*.

850. Affectation – N. *affectation*, cult, fad
848 *fashion*; affectedness, pretentiousness
875 *ostentation*; grand airs, posing, posturing, attitudinizing, striking attitudes, high
moral tone; pose, public image; artificiality, mannerism, trick; grandiloquence 574
magniloquence; preciosity 574 *ornament*;
pout, moue 547 *gesture*; coquetry 604
caprice; conceitedness, foppery, foppishness, dandyism, coxcombry 873 *vanity*;

euphemism, mock modesty; irony, back-
handed compliment 851 *ridicule*; insincerity, play-acting, tongue in cheek 541
duplicity; staginess, theatricality.
pretension, pretensions, false p.; artifice, sham, humbug 542 *deception*; superficiality, shallowness, starchiness 875
formality; pedantry, purism; prunes and
prisms 950 *prudery*; sanctimoniousness.
affecter, humbug, charlatan 545 *impostor*; play-actor 594 *actor*; hypocrite,
flatterer 545 *deceiver*; bluffer 877 *boaster*;
coquette, flirt; attitudinizer, poser,
poseur, poseuse 873 *vain person*; ironist
839 *humorist*; coxcomb 848 *fop*; purist,
pedant; know-all 500 *wise guy*; prig,
goody-goody 950 *prude*; euphuist.

Adj. *affected*, self-conscious; studied,
mannered, euphuistic, precious, chichi;
artificial, unnatural, stilted 875 *formal*;
prim, priggish, prudish, mealy-mouthed,
euphemistic, sanctimonious, self-
righteous, holier than thou; arch, sly,
nudging, winking; coquettish, coy, cute,
twee, too-too, mock-modest, niminy-
piminy, mincing, simpering; canting,
hypocritical 542 *deceiving*; bluffing 877
boastful; specious, pretentious, high-
sounding, gushing, fulsome, stagy 875 *ostentatious*; dandified, foppish, poncy,
camp; conceited, la-di-da, giving oneself
airs, showing off, swanking, posturing,
striking poses, attitudinizing 873 *vain*;
stuck-up, snobbish 871 *prideful*; bogus 541
false; for effect, put on, insincere, phoney
546 *exaggerated*.

Vb. *be affected*, affect, assume; pretend, feign 541 *dissemble*; act a part 594
act; ham, barnstorm 546 *exaggerate*; try
for effect, camp it up, play to the gallery;
strike attitudes, posture, pose, strike a p.;
prance, mince, ponce about 875 *be ostentatious*; put on airs, show off 873 *be
vain*; talk big 877 *boast*; pout, moue,
simper 835 *smile*; coquette, flirt; play the
hypocrite, save appearances.

851. Ridicule – N. *ridicule*, derision,
mockery 921 *disrespect*; raillery, teasing,
ribbing, banter, persiflage, badinage, leg-
pull; practical joke 497 *foolery*; grin, snig-

ger 835 *laughter*; irony, tongue in cheek, sarcasm, barbed shaft; catcall 924 *censure*; personal remarks; ribaldry 839 *witticism*.

satire, parody, burlesque, travesty, caricature, cartoon 552 *misrepresentation*; skit, spoof, send-up, take-off 20 *mimicry*; squib, lampoon, pasquinade 926 *detraction*.

laughingstock, object of ridicule, figure of fun, butt, universal b., by-word; sport, game, fair g.; Aunt Sally; April fool, buffoon, clown 501 *fool*; stooge, foil, feed, straight man; guy, caricature, travesty, mockery of, apology for; eccentric 504 *crank*; original, card, caution, queer fish; old fogey, geezer, museum piece, back number, square.

Adj. *derisive*, ridiculing, etc. vb.; flippant 456 *light-minded*; sardonic, sarcastic; disparaging 926 *detracting*; ironical, quizzical; satirical, Hudibrastic 839 *witty*; ribald 847 *vulgar*; burlesque, mock-heroic.

Vb. *ridicule*, deride, pour scorn on, laugh at; snigger, laugh in one's sleeve; banter, chaff, rally, twit, josh, rib, tease, roast, rag, pull one's leg, poke fun, make merry with, make fun of, make sport of, make a monkey of, take the mickey out of, have one on, kid, fool, make a fool of 542 *befool*; mock, scoff 926 *detract*; turn to ridicule; take down, deflate, debunk, make one look silly 872 *humiliate*.

satirize, lampoon 921 *not respect*; mock, gibe; mimic, send up, take off 20 *imitate*; parody, travesty, spoof, burlesque, caricature, guy 552 *misrepresent*; pillory 928 *accuse*.

852. Hope – N. *hope*, hopes, expectations, assumption 507 *expectation*; high hopes, hope and belief 485 *belief*; confidence, faith; anchor, mainstay, staff 218 *support*; ray of hope, gleam *or* glimmer of h. 469 *possibility*; good omen, favourable auspices, promise 511 *omen*; hopefulness, buoyancy, breeziness, optimism 833 *cheerfulness*; wishful thinking, self-deception; rose-coloured spectacles, rosy picture.

aspiration, ambition 617 *intention*;

pious hope, fond h.; vision, pipe dream, heart's desire; utopianism, chiliasm, millenarianism; castles in Spain, fool's paradise 513 *fantasy*; promised land, utopia, millennium 617 *objective*.

hoper, aspirant, candidate, waiting list; hopeful, young h.; heir apparent 776 *beneficiary*; optimist; utopian, millenarian, chiliast 513 *visionary*.

Adj. *hoping*, aspiring, starry-eyed; ambitious, would-be 617 *intending*; dreaming 513 *imaginative*; hopeful, in hopes 507 *expectant*; sanguine, confident 473 *certain*; buoyant, optimistic, airy; undespairing, undiscouraged; Micawberish; not unhopeful, reasonably confident.

promising, favourable, auspicious 730 *prosperous*; bright, fair, golden, roseate, rosy, rose-coloured; hopeful, encouraging, likely; utopian, visionary.

Vb. *hope*, trust, have faith; rest assured, feel confident, hope in, put one's trust in, rely, lean on, bank on, count on, pin one's hopes on, presume, hope and believe 485 *believe*; look forward 507 *expect*; hope for, dream of, promise oneself 617 *intend*; have hopes, live in h., keep one's fingers crossed; buck up, take heart; remain hopeful, see no cause for despair; hope on, hope against hope; catch at a straw, keep one's spirits up 833 *be cheerful*; keep smiling 600 *persevere*; see life through rose-coloured spectacles; flatter oneself, delude o., anticipate, count one's chickens before they are hatched 135 *be early*; indulge in wishful thinking 513 *imagine*.

give hope, inspirit, encourage 833 *cheer*; show signs of, have the makings of, promise well, shape up w., augur w. 471 *be likely*.

Int. nil desperandum! never say die! while there's life, there's hope!

853. Hopelessness – N. *hopelessness*, no hope, discouragement, despondency, dismay 834 *dejection*; pessimism, cynicism, despair, desperation, no way out, last hope gone; dashed hopes, cheated h. 509 *disappointment*; resignation 508 *lack of expectation*; not a hope 470 *impossibility*;

chimera, vain hope, forlorn h. 513 *fantasy*; poor lookout, no prospects; hopeless case, dead duck; hopeless situation, bad business 700 *predicament*; counsel of despair, pessimist, defeatist 834 *moper*.

Adj. *hopeless*, bereft of hope, in despair, desperate, suicidal; unhopeful, pessimistic, cynical, looking on the black side; defeatist, expecting the worst; disconsolate 834 *dejected*.

unpromising, holding out no hope, hopeless, comfortless 834 *cheerless*; desperate 661 *dangerous*; unpropitious, inauspicious 731 *adverse*; ill-omened, ominous 511 *presageful*; immitigable, irremediable, remediless, incurable; past cure, beyond hope, despaired of; irreparable, irrevocable, irredeemable, irreclaimable; irreversible, inevitable; impracticable 470 *impossible*.

Vb. *despair*, lose heart, lose hope; give way to despair 834 *be dejected*; have shot one's last bolt, give up hope, abandon h.; hope for nothing more from, write off; give up, turn one's face to the wall 721 *submit*.

leave no hope, offer no h.; drive to despair, shatter one's last hope 509 *disappoint*.

854. Fear – N. *fear*, healthy f., dread, awe 920 *respect*; abject fear 856 *cowardice*; fright, stage f.; wind up, funk, blue funk; terror, mortal t.; trepidation, alarm; shock, flutter 318 *agitation*; scare, stampede, panic; flight, sauve qui peut; horror, horripilation, hair on end, cold sweat; consternation, dismay 853 *hopelessness*.

nervousness, want of courage, lack of confidence, cowardliness 856 *cowardice*; self-distrust, diffidence, shyness 874 *modesty*; defensiveness, blustering, bluster; timidity, timorousness, fearfulness, hesitation, fighting shy 620 *avoidance*; loss of nerve, cold feet, fears, misgivings, qualms, mistrust, apprehension, uneasiness, disquietude, anxiety 825 *worry*; perturbation, trepidation, fear and trembling, flutter, tremor, palpitation, quaking, shaking; nerves, willies, butterflies, collywobbles, creeps, shivers, jumps, jitters,

heebie-jeebies 318 *agitation*; gooseflesh, hair on end, knees knocking.

phobia, claustrophobia, agoraphobia, aerophobia, acrophobia, pyrophobia, frigophobia, pogonophobia, autophobia, phobophobia; racial prejudice 888 *hatred*; McCarthyism, spy mania, witch-hunting.

intimidation, deterrence, war of nerves, war cry, sabre-rattling, arms buildup 900 *threat*; caution 664 *warning*; terrorization, terrorism 735 *severity*; alarmism, scaremongering; sword of Damocles, suspended sentence 963 *punishment*; deterrent 723 *weapon*; object of terror, hobgoblin, spook 970 *ghost*; Gorgon, Medusa; bugbear, bugaboo, ogre 938 *monster*.

alarmist, scaremonger, doom merchant, spreader of alarm and despondency, Calamity Jane; defeatist, pessimist; terrorist, terrorizer, intimidator, sabre-rattler.

Adj. *fearing*, afraid, frightened, funky, panicky; overawed 920 *respectful*; intimidated, terrorized, demoralized; in fear, in trepidation, in a fright, in a cold sweat, in a flat spin, in a panic; terror-crazed, panic-stricken; scared, alarmed, startled; hysterical, in hysterics; dismayed, consternated, flabbergasted; frozen, petrified, stunned; appalled, shocked, horrified, aghast, horror-struck, unmanned, scared out of one's wits, numbed with fear, paralysed by f., frightened to death, white as a sheet, pale as death, ashen-faced; suffering from shock.

nervous, defensive, on the d., tense, uptight; waiting for the bomb to drop; timid, timorous, shy, diffident 874 *modest*; wary, hesitating 858 *cautious*; doubtful, misdoubting, suspicious 474 *doubting*; windy, faint-hearted 601 *irresolute*; apprehensive, uneasy, fearful, anxious 825 *unhappy*; haunted, a prey to fears, highly-strung, afraid of one's own shadow, jittery, jumpy, nervy; tremulous, shaky, trembling 856 *cowardly*; with one's heart in one's mouth, shaking like a leaf; on pins and needles 318 *agitated*.

frightening, shocking, etc. vb.; formidable, redoubtable; hazardous, hairy 661 *dangerous*; tremendous, dreadful, awe-inspiring, numinous, fearsome, awesome 821 *impressive*; grim, grisly, hideous, ghastly, lurid, frightful, revolting, horrifying, horrific, horrible, terrible, awful, appalling, mind-boggling, mind-blowing; hair-raising, blood-curdling; weird, eerie, creepy, scary, ghoulish, nightmarish, gruesome, macabre, sinister; ominous, direful 511 *presageful*; intimidating, hectoring 735 *oppressive*; minatory, menacing; nerve-racking 827 *distressing*.

Vb. *fear*, be afraid; stand in awe, dread 920 *respect*; get the wind up, take fright, take alarm; start, jump, flutter 318 *be agitated*.

quake, shake, tremble, quiver, shiver, shudder, stutter, quaver; quake in one's shoes, be frightened to death, be scared out of one's wits; change colour, blench, pale; wince, flinch 620 *avoid*; quail, cower, crouch; stand aghast, be horrified, be chilled with fear, freeze with horror, feel one's blood run cold *or* turn to water.

be nervous, etc. adj.; feel shy; have misgivings 486 *doubt*; shrink, shy, quail, funk it, not face it; be anxious, dread; hesitate, get cold feet, think twice 858 *be cautious*; get the wind up, be on edge 318 *be agitated*.

frighten, fright, affright; make faces, grimace; scare, panic, stampede; intimidate, put in fear, menace 900 *threaten*; alarm, cause a., raise the a.; scare the living daylights out of, scare stiff, scare half to death; make one jump, give one a fright *or* a turn, startle, flutter, flurry 318 *agitate*; start, flush 619 *hunt*; disquiet, disturb, perturb 827 *trouble*; put the wind up, make nervous, rattle, shake, unnerve, play on one's nerves; unman, demoralize; put the fear of God into, overawe 821 *impress*; quell, subdue, cow 727 *overmaster*; shock 508 *surprise*; dismay, confound 63 *derange*; frighten off, deter 613 *dissuade*; terrorize 735 *oppress*; browbeat, bully 827 *torment*; terrify, horrify, chill, freeze, paralyse, petrify, rivet, turn to stone; appal, freeze the blood, make one's blood run cold, turn one's blood to water;

make one's hair stand on end, make one's flesh creep, make one's knees knock, make one's teeth chatter, frighten out of one's wits.

855. Courage – N. *courage*, bravery, valiance, valour; moral courage, courage of one's convictions 929 *probity*; heroism, gallantry, chivalry; self-confidence, self-reliance, fearlessness, intrepidity, daring, nerve; defiance of danger, boldness, hardihood, audacity 857 *rashness*; spirit, mettle 174 *vigorousness*; tenacity, bulldog courage; high morale, stoutness of heart 599 *resolution*; manliness, gameness, pluck, spunk, cojones, guts, heart, heart of oak, backbone, grit 600 *stamina*; sham courage, Dutch c., pot valour; desperate courage, courage of despair; brave face, bold front 711 *defiance*.

prowess, derring-do, chivalry, knightliness, heroism; act of courage, feat of arms, emprise, exploit, stroke, bold s. 676 *deed*; heroics.

brave person, hero, heroine, VC, GC; knight, paladin; good soldier, beau sabreur, brave, warrior 722 *soldier*; man *or* woman of mettle, man *or* woman of spirit, plucky fellow, game dog, bulldog; daredevil, risk-taker 857 *desperado*; Greatheart, Lionheart; Joan of Arc, Boadicea; knight of the Round Table; gallant knight, preux chevalier; band of heroes, gallant company; forlorn hope, picked troops 644 *elite*; lion, tiger, game-cock, fighting c.

Adj. *courageous*, brave, valorous, valiant, gallant, heroic; chivalrous, knightly; soldierly, martial, amazonian 718 *warlike*; stout, doughty, manful, manly, red-blooded; fierce, bold 711 *defiant*; dashing, hardy, audacious, daring, venturesome, bold as brass 857 *rash*; adventurous, mettlesome, spirited; full of fight, full of spirit, spunky; dogged, indomitable 600 *persevering*; game, plucky, ready for anything, unflinching, unshrinking.

unfearing, unafraid, intrepid, nerveless, with nerves of steel *or* of iron; danger-loving; sure of oneself, confident, self-c.; fearless, dauntless; undismayed, undaunted, unabashed, unapprehensive, unshakable.

Vb. *be courageous*, have what it takes, show spirit; venture, adventure, bell the cat, take the bull by the horns 672 *undertake*; dare 661 *face danger*; show fight, brave 711 *defy*; confront, look in the face; speak out, stand up and be counted 532 *affirm*; face the music, brave it out 599 *stand firm*; laugh at danger; show valour, win one's spurs; grin and bear it 825 *suffer*.

take courage, pluck up c., muster c., nerve oneself, take one's courage in both hands; put a brave face on it, show fight, screw up one's courage 599 *be resolute*; rally 599 *stand firm*.

give courage, put heart into, hearten, nerve; embolden, encourage, inspirit 612 *incite*; buck up, rally 833 *cheer*; pat on the back, keep in spirits, raise morale; bolster up, give confidence.

856. Cowardice – N. *cowardice*, abject fear, funk 854 *fear*; cowardliness, craven spirit, no guts 601 *irresolution*; pusillanimity, timidity; faint-heartedness, chicken-heartedness; unmanliness, poltroonery, dastardliness; defeatism 853 *hopelessness*; desertion 918 *undutifulness*; white feather, yellow streak, low morale, faint heart, chicken liver; pot valiance, Dutch courage 877 *boasting*; overcaution 858 *caution*; moral cowardice 603 *change of allegiance*.

coward, faintheart, no hero; poltroon, craven, dastard, yellow-belly, lily-liver, chickenheart, wheyface; scaredycat, fraidycat, cowardy custard; sneak, rat 524 *informer*; runaway 603 *turncoat*; coward at heart, bully, braggart 877 *boaster*; cissy, milksop, baby, cry-b. 163 *weakling*; quitter, shirker, flincher, deserter; cur, chicken, rabbit, mouse, invertebrate, doormat; defeatist 854 *alarmist*.

Adj. *cowardly*, coward, craven, poltroonish; not so brave, pusillanimous, timid, timorous, fearful, niddering, afraid of one's own shadow, unable to say boo to a goose 854 *nervous*; soft, unmanly 163 *weak*; spiritless, spunkless, faint-hearted, chicken-livered, white-l., lily-l., yellow-

bellied, chicken; sneaking, skulking, cowering; dastardly, yellow, abject, recreant, caitiff; unsoldierly; cowed 721 *submitting*; defeatist 853 *hopeless*; unheroic, unvaliant, uncourageous 858 *cautious*; funky 601 *irresolute*.

Vb. *be cowardly*, lack courage, have no pluck *or* grit *or* guts, have no heart *or* stomach for, not dare 601 *be irresolute*; lose one's nerve, have cold feet 854 *be nervous*; shrink, funk, chicken out 620 *avoid*; slink, skulk, sneak; quail, cower, cringe 721 *knuckle under*; show the white feather, turn tail, cut and run, panic, scuttle, show one's back, desert 620 *run away*; lead from behind 858 *be cautious*.

857. Rashness – N. *rashness*, incaution, incautiousness 456 *inattention*; carelessness, imprudence, improvidence, indiscretion 499 *folly*; irresponsibility, frivolity, flippancy, light-mindedness; wildness, indiscipline 738 *disobedience*; recklessness, foolhardiness, temerity, audacity, presumption, overconfidence; hotheadedness 822 *excitability*; impetuosity 680 *haste*; brinkmanship, game of chicken; desperation, courage of despair; leap in the dark 661 *danger*.

desperado, daredevil, tearaway, madcap, harum-scarum, hothead, Hotspur, fire-eater; adventurer 618 *gambler*; one who sticks at nothing, gunman, terrorist; bully, bravo 904 *ruffian*.

Adj. *rash*, ill-considered, ill-advised, harebrained, foolhardy, wildcat, injudicious, indiscreet, imprudent 499 *unwise*; careless, hit-and-miss, slapdash, accident-prone 458 *negligent*; unforeseeing, incautious, unwary, heedless, thoughtless; airy, breezy, flippant, giddy, devil-may-care, harum-scarum, slaphappy, trigger-happy 456 *light-minded*; irresponsible, reckless, regardless, couldn't-care-less, don't-care, foolhardy, lunatic, wanton, wild, cavalier; bold, daring, temerarious, audacious; overdaring, overbold, madcap, daredevil, do-or-die, neck or nothing, breakneck, suicidal; overambitious, oversure 852 *hoping*; presumptuous 878 *insolent*; precipitate, Gadarene, headlong, hellbent, desperate 680 *hasty*; headstrong 602 *wilful*; impulsive, impatient, hot-blooded, hot-headed 822 *excitable*; danger-loving 855 *unfearing*; venturesome, adventurous, risk-taking 672 *enterprising*; improvident, thriftless 815 *prodigal*.

Vb. *be rash*, etc. adj.; lack caution, expose oneself, drop one's guard, stick one's neck out, take unnecessary risks; go bullheaded at, rush at 680 *hasten*; ignore the consequences, damn the c.; not be insured 618 *gamble*; play fast and loose 815 *be prodigal*; play with fire, burn one's fingers; go out on a limb, risk one's neck 661 *face danger*; play a desperate game, ask for trouble, push one's luck, rush in where angels fear to tread 695 *act foolishly*.

858. Caution – N. *caution*, care, heed 457 *carefulness*; hesitation 854 *nervousness*; looking before one leaps, circumspection; reticence 525 *secrecy*; calculation, counting the risk, safety first 669 *preparation*; deliberation, sobriety 834 *seriousness*; prudence, discretion 498 *wisdom*; insurance, precaution 662 *safeguard*; forethought 510 *foresight*; Fabianism, one step at a time, festina lente 278 *slowness*; wait-and-see policy.

Adj. *cautious*, chary, wary, watchful 455 *attentive*; heedful 457 *careful*; doubtful, suspicious 854 *nervous*; taking no risks, insured; guarded, cagey 525 *reticent*; once bitten, twice shy; on one's guard, circumspect, gingerly, stealthy, tentative 461 *experimental*; conservative 660 *safe*; prudent, prudential 498 *wise*; noncommittal 625 *neutral*; counting the cost, canny, timid, overcautious, unadventurous; unhasty, deliberate 823 *patient*; coolheaded, level-h., cool 823 *inexcitable*.

Vb. *be cautious*, beware 457 *be careful*; take no risks, go by the book, play safe, play for a draw; play a waiting game 498 *be wise*; ca' canny, go slow; cover one's tracks 525 *conceal*; keep under cover, hide 523 *lurk*; see how the land lies 438 *scan*; see how the wind blows 461 *be tentative*; be on one's guard, tread warily, watch one's

step 525 *be stealthy*; look twice, think t.; calculate, count the cost; take one's time; let well alone, let sleeping dogs lie 620 *avoid*; take precautions, make sure, cover oneself, insure, hedge 660 *seek safety*; leave nothing to chance 669 *prepare*.

859. Desire – N. *desire*, wish; want, need 627 *requirement*; nostalgia, homesickness 830 *regret*; wistfulness, longing, hankering, yearning; daydream 513 *fantasy*; ambition, aspiration 852 *hope*; appetence, yen, urge 279 *impulse*; cacoethes, itch; avidity, eagerness, zeal 597 *willingness*; passion, ardour 822 *excitability*; fury, frenzy 503 *mania*; craving, lust for (**see** *hunger*); covetousness, cupidity 816 *avarice*; greed 786 *rapacity*; voracity, insatiability; concupiscence (**see** *libido*); incontinence 943 *intemperance*.

hunger, famine, empty stomach 946 *fasting*; appetite, keen a.; thirst, thirstiness 342 *dryness*; dipsomania 949 *alcoholism*.

liking, fancy, fondness 887 *love*; stomach, appetite, zest; relish, tooth, sweet t. 386 *taste*; leaning, penchant, propensity 179 *tendency*; weakness, partiality; inclination, predilection 605 *choice*; whim, whimsy 604 *caprice*; fascination 612 *inducement*.

libido, Eros, life instinct, sexual urge; erotism, eroticism; concupiscence, sexual desire, passion, rut, heat, oestrus; mating season; lust 951 *unchastity*; nymphomania, satyriasis 84 *abnormality*.

desired object, desideratum 627 *requirement*; catch, prize, plum 729 *trophy*; lion 890 *favourite*; forbidden fruit, torment of Tantalus; envy, temptation; magnet, lure 291 *attraction*; princesse lointaine 887 *loved one*; aim, goal, star, ambition, aspiration, dream 617 *objective*; ideal 646 *perfection*; height of one's ambition.

desirer, coveter, envier; wooer 887 *lover*; glutton, sucker for; fancier, amateur, dilettante, collector; votary 981 *worshipper*; aspirant 852 *hoper*; claimant, pretender; candidate 763 *petitioner*; ambitious person, careerist.

Adj. *desiring*, appetent, desirous,

wishing, wishful, tempted; lustful, concupiscent 951 *lecherous*; craving 627 *demanding*; nostalgic 830 *regretting*; set upon, bent upon 617 *intending*; ambitious 852 *hoping*; aspiring, would-be, wistful, longing, yearning, hungry for; anxious, eager, ardent, agog, breathless, impatient, dying for; itching, spoiling for; avid, mad for; liking, fond, partial to.

greedy, acquisitive, possessive 932 *selfish*; ambitious; voracious, openmouthed 947 *gluttonous*; unsatisfied, unquenchable, insatiable; grasping 816 *avaricious*; extortionate 735 *oppressive*.

hungry, unfilled, empty, supperless 946 *fasting*; half-starved, starving, famished 636 *underfed*; peckish, ready for; ravenous, hungry as a hunter; thirsty, dry, parched.

desired, likable, desirable, enviable, in demand; acceptable, welcome; appetizing 826 *pleasurable*; fetching, attractive, appealing 291 *attracting*; invited 597 *voluntary*.

Vb. *desire*, want, feel the lack of 627 *require*; cry out for 737 *demand*; wish, pray, wish otherwise, unwish 830 *regret*; covet 912 *envy*; set one's heart on 617 *intend*; aspire, raise one's eyes to, dream of, aim high 852 *hope*; cry for the moon; invoke, wish on, call down on; welcome, be glad of, jump at; lean towards, favour, prefer 605 *choose*; crave, itch for, hanker after, long for; yearn, pine, languish; pant for, gasp f., burn f., be dying f.; like, have a taste for 887 *love*; take to, warm to, moon after, sigh a., burn 887 *be in love*; ogle, make eyes at, make passes 889 *court*; set one's cap at, make a dead set at, run after, chase 619 *pursue*; lust after 951 *be impure*.

be hungry, hunger, famish, starve; water at the mouth; thirst, be dry *or* thirsty.

cause desire, incline 612 *motivate*; fill with longing 887 *excite love*; stimulate 821 *excite*; whet the appetite, make the mouth water 390 *make appetizing*; parch, raise a thirst; dangle, tease, titillate, tantalize 612 *tempt*; allure, seduce 291 *attract*.

860. Indifference – N. *indifference*, unconcern 454 *incuriosity*; lukewarmness, coolness, faint praise, two cheers 823 *inexcitability*; unsurprise 865 *lack of wonder*; mutual indifference, nothing between them; anorexia, no appetite, loss of a.; inappetence, no desire for; apathy; nonchalance, insouciance 458 *negligence*; carelessness 456 *inattention*; don't-care attitude 734 *laxity*; heedlessness 857 *rashness*; amorality, indifferentism 464 *indiscrimination*; nil admirari; six of one and half a dozen of the other; indifferentist, neutral; object of indifference, wallflower.

Adj. *indifferent*, uncaring, unconcerned, insolicitous; uninterested 454 *incurious*; lukewarm, Laodicean 598 *unwilling*; impersonal, passionless, phlegmatic 820 *impassive*; unimpressed, blasé 865 *unastonished*; cold 823 *inexcitable*; nonchalant, insouciant, pococurante 458 *negligent*; lackadaisical, listless 679 *inactive*; unambitious, unaspiring; don't-care, easy-going 734 *lax*; unresponsive, unmoved, insensible to 625 *undeviating*; loveless, heart-whole, fancy-free, uninvolved; disenchanted, cooling off; amoral, cynical.

unwanted, unwelcome, de trop; undesired, unwished for, uninvited, unbidden, unprovoked; loveless, unmissed 458 *neglected*; unchosen, on the shelf; all one to 606 *choiceless*; unattractive, undesirable 861 *disliked*.

Vb. *be indifferent*, etc. adj.; see nothing wonderful 865 *not wonder*; not have one's heart in it, take no interest 456 *be inattentive*; not mind, care nothing for, not give a fig *or* a thankyou for; have no taste for 861 *dislike*; couldn't care less, take it or leave it; not think twice about, not care, not give a hoot, shrug, make light of 922 *hold cheap*; hold no brief for 606 *be neutral*; grow indifferent, fall out of love, cool off; fail to move, leave one cold 820 *make insensitive*.

Int. never mind! what does it matter! who cares! so what!

861. Dislike – N. *dislike*, disinclination, no fancy for, no stomach for; reluctance 598 *unwillingness*; aversion 620 *avoidance*; antipathy, allergy; distaste, disrelish; repugnance, repulsion, disgust, abomination, abhorrence, detestation, loathing; horror 854 *fear*; xenophobia 888 *hatred*; nausea, heaving stomach 300 *voidance*; sickener, one's fill 863 *satiety*; bitterness 393 *sourness*; object of dislike, not one's type, bête noire, pet aversion, Dr Fell.

Adj. *disliking*, disinclined 598 *unwilling*; squeamish, qualmish, queasy; allergic, antipathetic; averse, hostile 881 *inimical*; repelled, loathing 888 *hating*; unfriendly, unsympathetic, out of sympathy; disillusioned; sick of 863 *sated*; nauseated 300 *vomiting*.

disliked, undesired 860 *unwanted*; unchosen 607 *rejected*; unpopular, out of favour, avoided; disagreeing, not to one's taste, bitter, repugnant, antipathetic, repulsive 292 *repellent*; revolting, loathsome 888 *hateful*; abominable, disgusting 924 *disapproved*; nauseous, nauseating, sickening 391 *unsavoury*; disagreeable, insufferable 827 *intolerable*; loveless, unlovable; unlovely 842 *ugly*.

Vb. *dislike*, mislike, disrelish, find not to one's taste; not care for, have no stomach for; object 762 *deprecate*; mind 891 *resent*; take a dislike to, have a down on; react against 280 *recoil*; want to heave 300 *vomit*; shrink from, have no time for 620 *avoid*; look askance at, turn up one's nose at 922 *despise*; make a face, can't stand, detest 888 *hate*; shudder at 854 *fear*; unwish, wish undone 830 *regret*.

cause dislike, disincline; go against the grain, rub up the wrong way 891 *enrage*; pall, jade 863 *sate*; disagree with, upset; put off, revolt 292 *repel*; offend, grate, jar 827 *displease*; get one's goat 827 *torment*; disgust, stick in one's throat, nauseate, sicken, make one's gorge rise, turn one's stomach, make one sick.

862. Fastidiousness – N. *fastidiousness*, niceness, daintiness, delicacy; discernment, perspicacity 463 *discrimination*; refinement 846 *good taste*; connoisseurship, epicurism; meticulousness 457 *carefulness*; idealism, artistic conscience; perfec-

tionism, fussiness, nit-picking, over-refinement, hypercriticalness, donnishness, pedantry, rigorism 735 *severity*.

perfectionist, idealist, purist, precisian, rigorist, fusspot, pedant, stickler, hard taskmaster; picker and chooser, gourmet, epicure.

Adj. *fastidious*, nice, dainty, delicate, epicurean; perspicacious, discerning 463 *discriminating*; particular, demanding, choosy, finicky, finical; overparticular, scrupulous 455 *attentive*; punctilious, painstaking, conscientious, overconscientious, critical, hypercritical, overcritical, fussy, pernickety, hard to please 924 *disapproving*; pedantic, donnish, precise, exacting, difficult 735 *severe*; puritanical 950 *prudish*.

Vb. *be fastidious*, etc. adj.; have only the best; pick and choose 605 *choose*; refine, split hairs 463 *discriminate*; find fault, fuss, turn up *or* wrinkle one's nose, disdain 922 *despise*.

863. Satiety – N. *satiety*, fullness, repletion 54 *plenitude*; overfulness, saturation point 637 *redundance*; glut, surfeit, too much of a good thing 838 *tedium*; overdose, excess; spoiled child, enfant gâté.

Adj. *sated*, replete 54 *full*; overfull, surfeited, glutted, cloyed, sick of; jaded, blasé.

Vb. *sate*, satiate; satisfy, quench, slake 635 *suffice*; saturate, soak; stuff, gorge, glut, surfeit, cloy, jade, pall; overdose, overfeed, sicken 861 *cause dislike*; spoil, kill with kindness; bore, weary 838 *be tedious*.

864. Wonder – N. *wonder*, wonderment; admiration, awe, fascination; cry of wonder, gasp of admiration, whistle, exclamation, exclamation mark; surprise 508 *lack of expectation*; astonishment, astoundment, amazement; stupefaction.

thaumaturgy, wonder-working, miracle-w., spellbinding, magic 983 *sorcery*; thaumatology, teratology; feat, exploit 676 *deed*; transformation scene, coup de théâtre 594 *dramaturgy*.

prodigy, portent 511 *omen*; something incredible, quite something, phenomenon, miracle, marvel, wonder; drama, sensation, cause célèbre, nine-days' wonder, annus mirabilis; wonderland, fairyland 513 *fantasy*; seven wonders of the world; sight 445 *spectacle*; infant prodigy, genius 696 *proficient person*; miracle-worker, thaumaturge, wizard 983 *sorcerer*; hero, heroine, superwoman, bionic man, whizzkid 646 *paragon*; freak, sport, monster, monstrosity 84 *rara avis*.

Adj. *wondering*, marvelling etc. vb.; awestruck, fascinated, spellbound; surprised 508 *inexpectant*; astonished, amazed, astounded; rapt, lost in wonder, lost in amazement, unable to believe one's eyes *or* senses; wide -eyed, round-e., pop-e.; open-mouthed, agape; dazzled, dumbfounded; dumb, struck d. 399 *silent*; bowled over, struck all of a heap, thunderstruck; transfixed, rooted to the spot; shocked, aghast, flabbergasted.

wonderful, wondrous, marvellous, miraculous, monstrous, prodigious, phenomenal; stupendous, fearful 854 *frightening*; admirable, exquisite 644 *excellent*; overwhelming, awesome, awe-inspiring, breathtaking 821 *impressive*; dramatic, sensational; shocking; exceptional, unprecedented 84 *unusual*; remarkable, noteworthy; strange, odd, weird and wonderful, mysterious 517 *puzzling*; exotic, outlandish, unheard of; fantastic 513 *imaginary*; hardly possible, too good *or* bad to be true 472 *improbable*; unbelievable, incredible, inconceivable, unimaginable, indescribable; unutterable, unspeakable, ineffable 517 *inexpressible*; mind-boggling, mind-blowing, astounding, amazing 508 *unexpected*; wonder-working, thaumaturgic; magic, like m. 983 *magical*.

Vb. *wonder*, marvel, admire, whistle; hold one's breath, gasp with admiration; gaze, goggle at, gawk, rub one's eyes, not believe one's e.; gape, look aghast; be overwhelmed, not know what to say.

be wonderful, etc. adj.; do wonders, work miracles, achieve marvels; surpass belief 486 *cause doubt*; beggar all description, baffle d., beat everything; spellbind, enchant 983 *bewitch*; dazzle, strike dumb, awe 821 *impress*; take one's breath away; bowl over, stagger; stun, stupefy, astound, astonish, amaze, flabbergast 508 *surprise*; baffle, startle, shock, scandalize.

Int. amazing! incredible! I don't believe it! well I never! blow me down! did you ever! gosh! wow! how about that! goodness gracious! whatever next!

865. Lack of wonder – N. *lack of wonder*, unastonishment, unsurprise; irreverence, nil admirari; blankness 860 *indifference*; composure, imperturbability, equability 820 *moral insensibility*; unimaginativeness; disbelief; nothing to wonder at, nothing in it.

Adj. *unastonished*, unamazed, unsurprised; collected, composed; unimpressionable 820 *apathetic*; blasé, unimpressed, unmoved 860 *indifferent*; unimaginative; blind to; taking for granted 507 *expectant*.

unastonishing, unsurprising 507 *expected*; common, ordinary, all in the day's work 610 *usual*.

Vb. *not wonder*, see nothing remarkable; be blind and deaf to; not believe 486 *disbelieve*; see through 516 *understand*; treat as a matter of course, take for granted; see it coming 507 *expect*.

Int. no wonder! nothing to it! of course! why not! quite so, naturally.

866. Repute – N. *repute*, good r., reputation, good report; title to fame, name, good n., character, reputability, respectability 802 *credit*; regard, esteem 920 *respect*; opinion, good o., good odour, favour, popularity; approval, stamp of a., cachet 923 *approbation*.

prestige, aura, mystique, magic; glamour, dazzle, éclat, lustre, splendour; brilliance, prowess; illustriousness, glory, honour, kudos, succès d'estime (**see** *famousness*); esteem, estimation, high account 638 *importance*; rank, status 73 *serial place*; position, top of the ladder *or* the tree 34 *superiority*; prominence, eminence; distinction, greatness 868 *nobility*; impressiveness, dignity, stateliness, solemnity, grandeur; name to conjure with 178 *influence*; paramountcy, primacy 733 *authority*; prestigiousness, snob value.

famousness, title to fame, celebrity, notability, illustriousness, renown, stardom, fame; household name, synonym for; glory 727 *success*; notoriety 867 *disrepute*; talk of the town 528 *publicity*; place in history, undying name, immortality.

honours, honour, blaze of glory; crown, martyr's c.; halo, aureole, nimbus, glory; blushing honours, battle h.; laurels, bays, wreath, garland, favour; feather in one's cap 729 *trophy*; order, medal 729 *decoration*; shield, arms 547 *heraldry*; signal honour, distinction, accolade 962 *reward*; compliment, flattery 923 *praise*; memorial, monument 505 *reminder*; dignity, handle, title; knighthood, peerage 868 *nobility*; academic honour, doctorate, degree, diploma 870 *academic title*; honours list, roll of honour 87 *list*.

dignification, glorification, lionization; honouring, crowning 876 *celebration*; sanctification, dedication, canonization, beatification; deification, apotheosis; enshrinement, enthronement; promotion, advancement, aggrandizement 285 *progression*; exaltation 310 *elevation*; ennoblement, knighting.

person of repute, honoured sir *or* madam, gentle reader; worthy, pillar of society, man *or* woman of honour 929 *honourable person*; peer 868 *person of rank*; somebody, VIP 638 *bigwig*; notable, celebrity, figure, public f.; champion 644 *exceller*; star, rising star, luminary; man *or* woman of the hour, heroine, hero; idol 890 *favourite*; cynosure 646 *paragon*; cream 644 *elite*; choice spirit, leading light 500 *sage*; galaxy, constellation.

Adj. *reputable*, of repute; creditworthy 929 *trustworthy*; gentlemanly 929 *honourable*; worthy, creditable, meritorious, prestigious 644 *excellent*; esteemed, respectable, well-regarded, well thought of 920 *respected*; in good odour, in favour 923 *approved*.

worshipful, reverend, honourable; admirable 864 *wonderful*; heroic, impos-

ing, dignified, august, stately, grand 821 *impressive*; lofty, high, high and mighty 32 *great*; majestic, regal 868 *noble*; high-caste, heaven-born; glorious, full of honours; time-honoured, sacrosanct 979 *sanctified*; honorific.

noteworthy, notable, remarkable 84 *unusual*; of mark, of distinction, distinguished 638 *important*; conspicuous, prominent, in the public eye 443 *obvious*; eminent, preeminent, supereminent; peerless 34 *superior*; brilliant 417 *luminous*; illustrious, splendid, glorious 875 *ostentatious*.

renowned, celebrated, acclaimed, sung; of glorious name; famous, fabled, legendary, far-famed; historic, illustrious, great, glorious 644 *excellent*; notorious 867 *disreputable*; well-known, on the map 490 *known*; of note, noted (**see** *noteworthy*); on every tongue, in the news 528 *published*; imperishable, immortal 115 *perpetual*.

Vb. *have a reputation*, have a good name, have a name to lose; rank, stand high, have status, be looked up to 920 *command respect*; stand well with, do oneself credit, gain prestige, build a reputation, acquire a character; make one's mark 730 *prosper*; win one's spurs, gain one's laurels 727 *succeed*; cover oneself with glory 875 *be ostentatious*; rise to fame, flash to stardom; shine, excel 644 *be good*; outshine, eclipse, steal the show 34 *be superior*; bask in glory, hand down one's name to posterity; make history.

honour, revere, regard, look up to 920 *respect*; stand in awe of 854 *fear*; bow down to 981 *worship*; appreciate, prize, value, treasure 887 *love*; pay one's respects to 920 *show respect*, 884 *be courteous*; compliment 925 *flatter*; grace with, honour w., dedicate to, inscribe to; glorify 923 *applaud*; grant the palm, make much of, lionize, chair; credit, honour for 907 *thank*; commemorate 505 *remember*; celebrate, blazon 528 *proclaim*; reflect honour, redound to one's credit, lend distinction *or* lustre to, be a credit to.

dignify, glorify, exalt; canonize 979 *sanctify*; enthrone, crown 751 *commis-*

sion; signalize, mark out, distinguish 547 *indicate*; aggrandize 285 *promote*; honour, decorate; elevate, raise to the peerage, ennoble; dub, knight, give the accolade; sir, bemadam.

867. Disrepute – N. *disrepute*, disreputableness, bad reputation, bad name, bad character, shady reputation, past; notoriety, infamy, ill repute, ill fame, succès de scandale; no reputation, ingloriousness, obscurity; bad odour, disfavour, discredit, bad light 888 *odium*; dishonour, disgrace, shame 926 *detraction*; ignominy, loss of honour, Watergate; departed glory, Ichabod; loss of face, loss of rank, demotion, degradation 872 *humiliation*; baseness, turpitude 934 *wickedness*.

slur, reproach, imputation, aspersion, reflection, slander, obloquy, opprobrium, abuse 926 *calumny*; slight, insult 921 *indignity*; scandal, disgrace, shame; stain, smear, stigma, black mark, spot, blot 845 *blemish*; bar sinister, blot on one's scutcheon, badge of infamy, scarlet letter, mark of Cain.

object of scorn, reproach, byword 938 *bad person*; reject, the dregs 645 *badness*; Cinderella 639 *nonentity*.

Adj. *disreputable*, not respectable, shady 930 *rascally*; notorious, infamous, nefarious 645 *bad*; doubtful, dubious, questionable 645 *not nice*; improper, indecent 951 *impure*; held in contempt 922 *contemptible*; characterless, without references, of no reputation; abject, despicable 888 *hateful*; mean, cheap, low 847 *vulgar*; shabby, squalid, dirty, scruffy 649 *unclean*; down at heel 655 *dilapidated*; in a bad light, under a cloud, in one's bad *or* black books, in the doghouse, unable to show one's face, in disgrace; reproached 924 *disapproved*; unpopular 861 *disliked*.

discreditable, no credit to, reflecting on one, damaging, compromising; ignoble, unworthy; improper, unbecoming 643 *inexpedient*; dishonourable 930 *dishonest*; despicable 922 *contemptible*; shameful, disgraceful, infamous 924 *blameworthy*; scandalous, shocking, outrageous, disgusting; too bad 645 *not nice*.

degrading, lowering, demeaning, ignominious, opprobrious; derogatory; beneath one, infra dig.

inglorious, without repute, without a name; unheroic, unaspiring, unambitious 874 *modest*; unremarked, unnoticed 458 *neglected*; unknown to fame, unheard of, obscure 491 *unknown*; unseen, unheard 444 *invisible*; unhymned, unsung; titleless 869 *plebeian*; debunked, humiliated 872 *humbled*; shorn of glory, faded, withered, tarnished; discredited, disgraced, dishonoured, out of favour, in eclipse; degraded, demoted, reduced to the ranks.

Vb. *lose repute*, go out of fashion, pass from the public eye; come down in the world, fall, sink; fade, wither; fall into disrepute, achieve notoriety, get a bad name for oneself 924 *incur blame*; spoil one's record, blot one's copybook, disgrace oneself, compromise one's name, risk one's reputation, outlive one's r.; forfeit one's honour, lose one's good name, forfeit one's good opinion, lose prestige, lose face; look silly, cut a sorry figure, blush for shame, laugh on the wrong side of one's mouth; be exposed, be brought to book 963 *be punished*.

demean oneself, lower o., degrade o.; derogate, condescend, stoop, marry beneath one; compromise one's dignity, make oneself cheap, behave unworthily, have no sense of one's position; sacrifice one's pride, forfeit self-respect; have no pride, feel no shame.

shame, hold up to s.; pillory, expose, show up; mock 851 *ridicule*; snub 872 *humiliate*; discompose, disconcert, put out of countenance, deflate, debunk; strip of one's honours, downgrade, demote 963 *punish*; malign, disparage 926 *defame*; destroy one's reputation, take away one's good name; put in a bad light, reflect upon, taint; sully, mar, blacken, tarnish, stain, blot 649 *make unclean*; stigmatize, brand, cast a slur on 547 *mark*; dishonour, disgrace, discredit, give a bad name, bring into disrepute, bring shame upon 924 *incur blame*; heap shame upon, drag through the mire; tread underfoot; make one blush, not spare one's blushes.

868. Nobility – N. *nobility*, nobleness, distinction, rank, station, order 27 *degree*; royalty, kingliness, queenliness, majesty 733 *authority*; birth, high b., gentle b.; descent, ancestry, lineage, pedigree 169 *genealogy*; noble house, royal h., dynasty 11 *family*; blood, blue b.; bloodstock, caste, high c.; coat of arms, crest 547 *heraldry*.

aristocracy, patriciate, patrician order; nobility, noblesse, ancien régime; lordship, lords, peerage, lords spiritual and temporal; dukedom, earldom, viscountcy, baronetcy; baronage, knightage; landed interest, squirearchy, squiredom; county family, county set, gentry, gentlefolk; life peerage.

upper class, upper classes, upper ten, upper crust, top drawer; first families, best people, betters 644 *elite*; high society, high life 848 *beau monde*; ruling class, the twice-born, the Establishment 733 *authority*; high-ups, Olympians; the haves 800 *rich person*.

aristocrat, patrician, Olympian; person of high caste, Brahmin, Rajput; bloodstock, thoroughbred; senator, magnifico, dignitary; don, grandee, gentleman, gentlewoman, armiger; squire, laird; boyar, junker; prince 741 *sovereign*; nob, swell, gent 848 *fop*; panjandrum 638 *bigwig*.

person of rank, titled person, noble, nobleman *or* -woman, noble lord *or* lady, atheling, seigneur; princeling, lordling; lordship, milord; ladyship, milady; peer, hereditary p., life p.; peer of the realm, peeress; duke, grand d., archduke, duchess; marquis, marchioness, marquise, margrave, margravine, count, countess, contessa; earl, viscount, viscountess, baron, baroness, thane, baronet, knight; rajah, emir 741 *potentate*, *governor*.

Adj. *noble*, chivalrous, knightly; gentlemanly, gentlemanlike, ladylike (**see** *genteel*); majestic, royal, regal, every inch a king *or* queen; kingly, queenly, princely, lordly; ducal, baronial, seigneurial; of royal blood, of high birth, of good family, well-born, high-b., born in the purple; thoroughbred, pur sang, blue-blooded; ennobled, titled; high-up, grand 32 *great*.

genteel, patrician, senatorial, aristocratic; superior, top-drawer, high-class, upper-c.; classy, posh, U, comme il faut 848 *well-bred*.

869. Commonalty – N. *commonalty*, commons, third estate, bourgeoisie, middle classes, lower c.; plebs, plebeians; citizenry, townsfolk, countryfolk; silent majority, grass roots; general public; populace, the people, the common p.; vulgar herd, great unwashed; the many, the multitude, hoi polloi; the masses, admass, lumpenproletariat, proletariat; rank and file, ragtag and bobtail, Tom, Dick and Harry 79 *everyman*.

rabble, mob, horde 74 *crowd*; clamjamphrie, rabble rout, rascal multitude; riffraff, scum, dregs of society, canaille, cattle, vermin.

lower classes, lower orders 35 *inferior*; small fry, humble folk; working class, servant c.; second-class citizens, the have-nots, the under-privileged; proletariat, proles; submerged tenth, slum population; down-and-outs, outcasts, white trash; demi-monde, underworld, low life.

middle classes, bourgeoisie 732 *averageness*; professional classes, salaried c., salariat; whitecollar workers; Brown, Jones and Robinson.

commoner, bourgeois(e), plebeian, pleb; plain Mr *or* Mrs; citizen, Joe Public; man *or* woman of the people, democrat, republican; proletarian, prole; working man *or* woman 686 *worker*; town-dweller, country-d. 191 *native*; man *or* woman in the street 79 *everyman*; backbencher, private; underling 35 *inferior*; upstart, parvenu; a nobody 639 *nonentity*.

country-dweller, countryman *or* -woman, yeoman; rustic, Hodge, swain, peasant, son *or* daughter of the soil 370 *farmer*; boor, churl, yokel, hind, chawbacon, clod, clodhopper, rube, hayseed, hick, backwoodsman; bumpkin, country b., country cousin, provincial, hillbilly; village idiot 501 *ninny*.

low fellow, fellow, varlet 938 *cad*; slum-dweller 801 *poor person*; guttersnipe, mudlark, street arab, gamin, ragamuffin, tatterdemalion; down-and-out, tramp, bum, vagabond 268 *wanderer*; gaberlunzie, panhandler 763 *beggar*; bully, ugly customer, roughneck 904 *ruffian*; rascal 938 *knave*; gangster, hood; criminal 904 *offender*; vandal, yahoo.

Adj. *plebeian*, common, simple, untitled, without rank, titleless; ignoble, below the salt; below-stairs, servant-class; lower-deck, rank and file 732 *middling*; mean, low 867 *disreputable*; lowly, baseborn, low-born, low-caste, of mean extraction; slave-born, servile; humble, of low estate 35 *inferior*; unaristocratic, middle-class, working-c., cloth-cap, non-U, proletarian; homely, homespun; obscure 867 *inglorious*; unpolished 847 *ill-bred*; unfashionable, bourgeois, Main Street, suburban, provincial, rustic; risen from the ranks; boorish 847 *vulgar*; churlish 885 *ungracious*.

barbaric, barbarous, barbarian, wild, savage, brutish, yobbish; uncivilized, uncultured, primitive 699 *artless*.

870. Title – N. *title*, courtesy title, academic t., honorific, handle; honour, knighthood 866 *honours*; dignified style 875 *formality*.

871. Pride – N. *pride*, proper p.; self-esteem, amour propre; self-respect, self-confidence; conceit 873 *vanity*; snobbery, inverted s. 850 *affectation*; false pride, touchiness, prickliness 819 *moral sensibility*; dignity, reputation 866 *prestige*; stateliness, loftiness; condescension, hauteur 922 *contempt*; overweening pride, arrogance, hubris 878 *insolence*; pomposity 875 *ostentation*; vainglory 877 *boasting*; class-consciousness, race-prejudice 481 *prejudice*; boast, pride and joy 890 *favourite*; cynosure 646 *paragon*.

proud person, vain p., snob, parvenu; swelled head, swank, swankpot; prima donna, high muckamuck 638 *bigwig*; fine gentleman, grande dame 848 *fop*; turkey cock, swaggerer 877 *boaster*.

Adj. *proud*, haughty, lofty, sublime 209 high; plumed, crested 875 *showy*; fine, grand 848 *fashionable*; grandiose, dignified, stately, statuesque 821 *impressive*; majestic, lordly, aristocratic 868 *noble*; proud-hearted, high-souled 855 *courageous*; high-stepping, high-spirited 819 *lively*; stiff-necked 602 *obstinate*; mighty, overmighty 32 *great*; imperious, high-handed 733 *authoritative*; overweening, overbearing 878 *insolent*.

prideful, flushed with pride, puffed-up, inflated, swelling, swollen; high and mighty, stuck-up, toffee-nosed, snobbish, nose-in-the-air; uppish, uppity; on one's dignity, on one's high horse; haughty, disdainful, superior, supercilious, hoity-toity, patronizing, condescending 922 *despising*; standoffish, aloof, distant; unapproachable, stiff, starchy 885 *ungracious*; taking pride in, purse-proud, house-p; proud of, bursting with pride; strutting, swaggering 877 *boastful*; pleased with oneself, like the cat that got the cream; conceited 873 *vain*; pretentious 850 *affected*; pompous 875 *showy*; proud as a peacock.

Vb. *be proud*, hold one's head high; stand on one's dignity, mount one's high horse; give oneself airs, think it beneath one; show off, swagger, strut 875 *be ostentatious*; condescend, patronize; look down on, disdain 922 *despise*; lord it, queen it, come it over 735 *oppress*.

872. Humility. Humiliation – N. *humility*, humbleness 874 *modesty*; abasement, lowliness; meekness, submissiveness 721 *submission*; self-knowledge, self-depreciation, self-abasement; condescension, stooping; no boaster, mouse, violet.

humiliation, abasement, humbling, let-down, setdown, climbdown, comedown 921 *indignity*; crushing retort; rebuke 924 *reprimand*; shame, disgrace 867 *disrepute*; blush, confusion; shamefaced look, hang-dog expression; chastening thought, mortification, hurt pride, injured p. 891 *resentment*.

Adj. *humble*, not proud, self-deprecating, poor in spirit, lowly; meek, submissive 721 *submitting*; self-effacing

931 *disinterested*; self-abasing, stooping, condescending 884 *courteous*; mouselike, harmless, inoffensive; unassuming, unpretentious 874 *modest*; mean, low 639 *unimportant*, 869 *plebeian*.

humbled, broken-spirited, bowed down; chastened, crushed, dashed, abashed, crestfallen 834 *dejected*; humiliated, squashed, deflated; ashamed 939 *repentant*; mortified, shamed; brought low, discomfited 728 *defeated*.

Vb. *be humble*, humble oneself 867 *demean oneself*; play second fiddle 874 *be modest*; put others first 931 *be disinterested*; condescend 884 *be courteous*; stoop, crawl, sing small, eat humble pie 721 *knuckle under*; turn the other cheek 909 *forgive*.

be humbled, be taken down a peg; be ashamed, colour up 431 *redden*; feel small, hide one's face, hang one's head, avert one's eyes, have nothing to say for oneself, wish the earth would swallow one up.

humiliate, humble, chasten, abash, disconcert, put to the blush; lower, take down a peg, debunk, deflate; make one feel small, teach his *or* her place, rub one's nose in the dirt; snub, squash, sit on 885 *be rude*; slight, mortify, hurt one's pride, put to shame 867 *shame*; score off, put one's nose out of joint, make one look silly 542 *befool*; put in the shade 306 *outdo*; outstare, frown down, wither, daunt 854 *frighten*; get the better of 727 *overmaster*.

873. Vanity – N. *vanity*, vain pride 871 *pride*; immodesty, conceit, self-importance, megalomania; swank, side, puffed-up chest, swollen head; cockiness, self-assurance; self-conceit, self-esteem; self-satisfaction, smugness; self-admiration, narcissism; self-complacency, self-praise, self-congratulation, vainglory 877 *boasting*; self-centredness 932 *selfishness*; exhibitionism 875 *ostentation*; Vanity Fair 848 *beau monde*.

vain person, self-admirer, Narcissus; self-centred person, egotist, coxcomb 848 *fop*; exhibitionist, peacock, show-off; knowall, bighead, God's gift to women;

smart aleck, cleverstick, Mr *or* Miss Clever 500 *wiseacre*; stuffed shirt, pompous twit 4 *insubstantial thing*.

Adj. *vain*, conceited 871 *prideful*; self-satisfied, self-complacent, full of oneself, self-important 932 *selfish*; smug, complacent, pleased with oneself; self-admiring, narcissistic; swollen-headed, big-h., too big for one's boots, bumptious, cocky, perky, smart-ass 878 *insolent*; swaggering, vainglorious 877 *boastful*; pretentious, pompous 875 *ostentatious*; putting on airs 850 *affected*.

Vb. *be vain*, etc. adj.; have one's head turned; have a high opinion of oneself, think too much of o., think oneself the cat's pyjamas *or* God Almighty; blow one's own trumpet 877 *boast*; admire oneself, flatter o.; plume oneself, preen o., pride o.; swank, show off, put on airs 875 *be ostentatious*; fish for compliments; get above oneself, give oneself airs 850 *be affected*.

874. Modesty – N. *modesty*, shyness, retiring disposition; diffidence, timidity 854 *nervousness*; overmodesty 950 *prudery*; bashfulness, blushing, blush; chastity 950 *purity*; self-depreciation, self-effacement 872 *humility*; unobtrusiveness, unpretentiousness; demureness, reserve; modest person, shrinking violet.

Adj. *modest*, without vanity, free from pride, self-effacing, unobtrusive 872 *humble*; self-deprecating, unboastful; unassertive, unambitious; quiet, unassuming, unpretentious, unimposing 639 *unimportant*; shy, retiring, diffident 854 *nervous*; overshy, awkward, inarticulate; bashful, blushful, blushing, rosy; shamefaced, sheepish; reserved, demure, coy; shockable, prudish; chaste 950 *pure*.

Vb. *be modest*, efface oneself 872 *be humble*; play second fiddle, keep in the background, take a back seat, know one's place; blush unseen, shun the limelight 456 *escape notice*; not look for praise; creep into one's shell 620 *avoid*; blush, colour 431 *redden*; preserve one's modesty 933 *be virtuous*.

Adv. *modestly*, unpretentiously, sans

façon, without fuss, without ceremony, privately, without beat of drum.

875. Ostentation. Formality – N. *ostentation*, display, parade, show 522 *manifestation*; exhibitionism 528 *publicity*; showiness, magnificence, grandiosity; splendour, brilliance; self-importance 873 *vanity*; fuss, swagger, pretension, airs and graces; swank, side; bravado, heroics 877 *boast*; theatricality, histrionics, dramatics, sensationalism 546 *exaggeration*; showmanship, window-dressing; grandeur, solemnity (**see** *formality*); declamation, rhetoric 574 *magniloquence*; flourish of trumpets, fanfaronade 528 *publication*; pageantry, pomp, panache, dash, splash 844 *finery*; glitter, tinsel 844 *ornamentation*; idle show, false glitter, mockery, hollow m. 4 *insubstantiality*; gloss, veneer, polish; lip service 542 *deception*.

formality, state, stateliness, dignity; ceremoniousness, stiffness, starchiness; royal we, editorial we 870 *title*; ceremony, ceremonial, ritual; drill, spit and polish; correctitude, protocol, form, good f. 848 *etiquette*; punctilio 455 *attention*; solemnity, formal occasion, function 876 *celebration*; robes, regalia 228 *formal dress*, 228 *uniform*.

pageant, show 522 *exhibit*; fête, gala, tournament, tattoo; field day 876 *celebration*; son et lumière 445 *spectacle*; set piece, tableau 594 *stage set*; display, bravura, stunt; pyrotechnics 420 *fireworks*; carnival 837 *festivity*, *revel*; procession, march-past, flypast; changing the guard, trooping the colour; turnout, review, parade 74 *assembly*.

Adj. *ostentatious*, showy, pompous; done for effect; window-dressing, for show; prestige, specious 542 *spurious*; consequential, self-important; pretentious 850 *affected*; swanky 873 *vain*; orotund, magniloquent, high-sounding 574 *rhetorical*; grand, highfalutin, splendiferous, splendid, brilliant, magnificent, grandiose, posh; superb, royal 813 *liberal*; sumptuous, diamond-studded, luxurious, de luxe, plushy, ritzy 811 *dear*.

showy, flashy, dressy, dressed to kill 848 *fashionable*; lurid, gaudy, gorgeous 425 *florid*; tinsel, glittering, garish 847 *vulgar*; flaming, flaring, flaunting, flagrant, blatant; brave, dashing, gallant, gay, jaunty, rakish, sporty; spectacular, scenic, dramatic, theatrical, stagy; sensational, daring.

formal, dignified, solemn, stately, majestic, grand, fine; ceremonious, punctilious, correct, precise, stiff, starchy; black-tie, white-tie, full-dress; of state, official; ceremonial, ritual; for a special occasion 876 *celebratory*.

Vb. *be ostentatious*, observe the formalities, stand on ceremony; cut a dash, make a splash; glitter, dazzle 417 *shine*; flaunt, sport 228 *wear*; wave, flourish 317 *brandish*; blazon, trumpet 528 *proclaim*; demonstrate, exhibit 522 *show*; put on a show *or* a front, window-dress, stage-manage; see to the outside, paper the cracks, polish; strive for effect, sensationalize; shoot a line 877 *boast*; take the centre of the stage, grab the limelight 455 *attract notice*; put oneself forward, dramatize o. 850 *be affected*; show off, show one's paces, promenade, swan around; parade, peacock, strut, swank, put on side 873 *be vain*; make an exhibition of oneself.

876. Celebration – N. *celebration*, performance, solemnization 676 *action*; commemoration 505 *remembrance*; observance 988 *ritual*; ceremony, function, formal occasion; coronation 751 *commission*; reception, welcome, hero's w., tickertape w., red-carpet treatment 875 *formality*, 923 *applause*; fête, jubilee 837 *festivity*; jubilation, cheering, ovation, triumph, salute, salvo, tattoo, roll of drums, fanfare, flourish of trumpets, flag-waving 835 *rejoicing*; decorations, illuminations; firework display 420 *fireworks*; bonfire 379 *fire*; triumphal arch 729 *trophy*; thanksgiving 907 *thanks*; paean, hosanna, hallelujah; congratulation; health, toast.

special day, day to remember, great day, red-letter d., flag d.; saint's day 988 *holy day*; birthday, wedding anniversary; centenary, sesquicentenary 141 *anniversary*.

Adj. *celebratory*, commemorative 505 *remembering*; occasional, anniversary, centennial, bicentennial 141 *seasonal*; festive, jubilant 835 *rejoicing*; triumphant, triumphal; welcoming 886 *congratulatory*.

Vb. *celebrate*, solemnize, perform; hallow, keep holy 979 *sanctify*; commemorate 505 *remember*; honour, observe, keep; make it an occasion, mark the o.; make much of, welcome 882 *be hospitable*; fête; chair, carry shoulder-high; mob, rush 61 *rampage*; garland, crown 962 *reward*; lionize, give a hero's welcome, roll out the red carpet, hang out the flags, beat a tattoo, fire a salute 884 *pay one's respects*; cheer, jubilate 835 *rejoice*, 837 *revel*.

toast, pledge, clink glasses; drink to, raise one's glass to, drink a health 301 *drink*.

877. Boasting – N. *boasting*, boastfulness, vainglory, braggadocio 875 *ostentation*; self-glorification, self-advertisement, swagger 873 *vanity*; puffery 528 *publicity*; grandiloquence 515 *empty talk*; swaggering, swashbuckling, heroics, bravado; flagwagging; chauvinism, jingoism 481 *bias*; bluster 854 *nervousness*; sabre-rattling 900 *threat*.

boast, brag, vaunt; puff, hype 528 *advertisement*; gasconade, flourish, fanfaronade, bravado, bombast, rant, rodomontade, tall talk 546 *exaggeration*; hot air, bluff 515 *empty talk*; bluster, hectoring.

boaster, vaunter, swaggerer, braggart, braggadocio, macho; brag, big-mouth, loud-mouth, shouter, prater, gasbag; blagueur, blusterer, bluffer 545 *impostor*; swank, show-off 873 *vain person*; swashbuckler, gascon; trumpeter, puffer 528 *publicizer*; ranter, hot air merchant; jingoist, chauvinist; sabre-rattler.

Adj. *boastful*, bragging, big-mouthed; braggart 875 *ostentatious*; vainglorious 873 *vain*; sabre-rattling, jingoistic, chauvinistic 718 *warlike*; pretentious 542 *spurious*; bombastic, grandiloquent 546 *exaggerated*; cock-a-hoop.

Vb. *boast*, brag, vaunt, talk big, shoot a line, bluff, huff and puff, bluster, hector,

shout; prate, rant 515 *mean nothing*; magnify 546 *exaggerate*; trumpet, parade, flaunt, show off 528 *publish*; puff, crack up 528 *advertise*; sell oneself, blow one's own trumpet 875 *be ostentatious*; show off, swagger, swank 873 *be vain*; pat oneself on the back, boast of, plume oneself on 871 *be proud*; glory in, crow over 727 *triumph*.

878. Insolence – N. *insolence*, hubris, arrogance, haughtiness 871 *pride*; bravado 711 *defiance*; bluster 900 *threat*; disdain 922 *contempt*; sneer 926 *detraction*; contumely 899 *scurrility*; self-assurance, self-assertion, brashness; presumption 916 *arrogation*; audacity, boldness, effrontery, chutzpah, shamelessness, brazenness, face, front.

sauciness, disrespect, impertinence, impudence, pertness; flippancy, nerve, gall, brass; cheek, cool c., neck; lip, mouth, sauce, snook, V-sign 547 *gesture*; taunt, insult 921 *indignity*; rudeness, incivility, throwaway manner 885 *discourtesy*; defiance, answering back, backchat 460 *rejoinder*.

insolent person, saucebox, impertinent, jackanapes, cheeky devil; minx, hussy, baggage, madam; whippersnapper, pup, puppy; upstart, beggar on horseback, Jack-in-office 639 *nonentity*; braggart 877 *boaster*; bantam-cock, cockalorum 871 *proud person*; hoodlum, roisterer, fire-eater 904 *ruffian*.

Adj. *insolent*, rebellious 711 *defiant*; sneering 926 *detracting*; insulting 921 *disrespectful*; injurious, scurrilous 899 *cursing*; supercilious, disdainful, contemptuous 922 *despising*; haughty, snooty, high-hat, high and mighty 871 *proud*; hubristic, arrogant, presumptuous; brash, bumptious, bouncing 873 *vain*; flagrant, blatant; shameless, lost to shame, unblushing, unabashed, brazen, brazenfaced, bold as brass; overweening, overbearing 735 *oppressive*; blustering.

impertinent, pert, forward, fresh; impudent, saucy, cheeky, brassy, cool, jaunty, perky, cocky, cocksure, flippant, flip; cavalier, offhand, familiar, overfamiliar, devil-may-care, breezy, airy 921 *disre-*

spectful; rude 885 *discourteous*; defiant, provocative, offensive.

Vb. *be insolent*, forget one's manners, get personal 885 *be rude*; have a nerve, cheek, sauce, give lip, taunt, provoke; have the audacity *or* the cheek to; answer back 460 *answer*; get above oneself, teach one's grandmother to suck eggs; not know one's place, take on oneself, make bold to, make free with, get fresh; put on airs 871 *be proud*; sneer at 922 *despise*; rally 851 *ridicule*; sniff, snort; not give a fig 860 *be indifferent*; cock a snook, put one's tongue out, give the V-sign, send to blazes 711 *defy*; outstare, outface; take a high tone, queen it, lord it over; hector, bully, browbeat, treat with a high hand 735 *oppress*; swank, swagger 873 *be vain*; talk big 877 *boast*; be a law unto oneself 738 *disobey*.

879. Servility – N. *servility*, slavishness, no pride, lack of self-respect 856 *cowardice*; subservience 721 *submission*; submissiveness, obsequiousness 739 *obedience*; abasement 872 *humility*; prostration, genuflexion, obeisance; toadyism, sycophancy 925 *flattery*; flunkeyism 745 *service*.

toady, time-server, yes-man, rubber stamp 488 *assenter*; lickspittle, bootlicker, backscratcher, bumsucker, crawler, creep; hypocrite, creeping Jesus 850 *affecter*; spaniel, fawner 925 *flatterer*; sycophant, parasite, leech, sponger, freeloader; hanger-on 742 *dependant*; flunkey, lackey 742 *retainer*; lapdog, poodle; tool, creature, cat's-paw 628 *instrument*.

Adj. *servile*, not free, dependent 745 *subject*; slavish 856 *cowardly*; mean, abject, base 745 *subjected*; subservient, deferential 721 *submitting*; pliant, supple 739 *obedient*; time-serving 603 *trimming*; grovelling, etc. vb.; toadying, sycophantic, parasitical; creepy, obsequious, unctuous, oily 925 *flattering*.

Vb. *be servile*, forfeit one's self-respect, stoop to anything 867 *demean oneself*; squirm, cringe, creep, crawl, grovel, truckle, lick the boots of 721 *knuckle*

under; bow, kowtow 311 *stoop*; swallow insults 872 *be humble*; make up to, toady to, suck up to, spaniel, fawn 925 *flatter*; dance attendance on 742 *serve*; comply 739 *obey*; do one's dirty work 628 *be instrumental*; whine, wheedle 761 *beg*; batten on, sponge on; run with the hare and hunt with the hounds 83 *conform*; serve the times 603 *tergiversate*.

Section 3:
Interpersonal emotion

880. Friendship – N. *friendship*, bonds of f., amity 710 *concord*; compatibility, mateyness; friendly relations, hobnobbing 882 *sociality*; companionship, togetherness; fellowship, brotherhood, sisterhood 706 *association*; solidarity, support 706 *cooperation*; acquaintanceship, acquaintance, familiarity; fast friendship 887 *love*; making friends, introduction, recommendation; overtures, rapprochement 289 *approach*; reconciliation.

friendliness, amicability, kindliness, kindness, neighbourliness 884 *courtesy*; cordiality, warmth 897 *benevolence*; camaraderie, mateyness; hospitality 882 *sociability*; greeting, welcome 884 *courteous act*; regard, mutual r. 920 *respect*; goodwill, fellow feeling, sympathy, understanding, same wavelength, entente 710 *concord*; support 703 *aid*.

friend, girlfriend, boyfriend 887 *loved one*; acquaintance, intimate a.; mutual friend, crony, old c. (**see** *chum*); neighbour, fellow countryman *or*-woman; well-wisher 707 *patron*; second 660 *protector*; fellow, sister, brother, soul brother *or* sister; partner, associate 707 *colleague*; ally 707 *auxiliary*; friend in need 703 *aider*; guest, welcome g., persona grata; young friend, protégé(e); host 882 *sociable person*; former friend, fairweather f.

close friend, best f.; soul mate, kindred spirit; best man, bridesmaid; dear friend, intimate, bosom pal, confidant(e); alter ego, other self, shadow; comrade, companion, boon c.; inseparables, band of brothers *or* sisters; two minds with but a single thought.

chum, crony; pal, mate, amigo, cobber, buddy, butty, sidekick; fellow, comrade 707 *colleague*; playmate, classmate, school-fellow; pen friend, pen pal; hearties, my h.

Adj. *friendly*, nonhostile, amicable 887 *loving*; loyal, faithful, staunch 929 *trustworthy*; fraternal, brotherly, sisterly, cousinly; harmonious 710 *concordant*; compatible, congenial, sympathetic, understanding; well-wishing, well-meaning 897 *benevolent*; hearty, cordial, warm, welcoming 882 *sociable*; comradely, chummy, pally, matey; friendly with, at home w.; acquainted 490 *knowing*; on familiar terms, well in with, intimate, inseparable, thick as thieves.

Vb. *be friendly*, get on well, have dealings with, rub along w.; fraternize, hobnob, keep company with 882 *be sociable*; have friends, make f., win f.; shake hands 884 *greet*; welcome 882 *be hospitable*; sympathize 516 *understand*; like, warm to 887 *love*; mean well 897 *be benevolent*.

befriend, take up 703 *patronize*; make welcome; strike up an acquaintance, scrape an a.; break the ice 289 *approach*; cultivate one's friendship 889 *court*; take to, warm to, click with, hit it off; fraternize with, hobnob, get pally with, chum up w., make friends w.; make acquainted, introduce, present.

881. Enmity – N. *enmity*, hostility, antagonism 704 *opposition*; no love lost, unfriendliness, incompatibility, antipathy 861 *dislike*; loathing 888 *hatred*; animosity, animus, ill feeling, bad blood 898 *malevolence*; jealousy 912 *envy*; coldness, estrangement, alienation, strain, tension 709 *dissension*; bitterness, hard feelings 891 *resentment*; disloyalty 930 *perfidy*; breach 709 *quarrel*; hostilities 718 *belligerency*; vendetta, feud.

enemy, no friend, unfriend; ex-friend 603 *turncoat*; traitor, viper in one's bosom 663 *troublemaker*; bad neighbour, ill-wisher; antagonist 705 *opponent*; rival 716 *contender*; foe 722 *combatant*; aggressor 712 *attacker*; enemy within the gates, fifth column, Trojan Horse; public enemy, outlaw; personal enemy, sworn e., arch e.; misanthropist, misogynist 902 *misanthrope*; xenophobe, negrophobe, racialist, anti-Semite 481 *narrow mind*; persona non grata, bête noire 888 *hateful object*.

Adj. *inimical*, unfriendly, ill-disposed, disaffected; disloyal 930 *perfidious*; aloof, distant 883 *unsociable*; antipathetic, incompatible, unsympathetic 861 *disliking*; loathing 888 *hating*; hostile 704 *opposing*; antagonized, estranged, alienated, unreconciled, irreconcilable; bitter 891 *resentful*; jealous 912 *envious*; spiteful 898 *malevolent*; on bad terms, not on speaking t.; at variance, at loggerheads, at daggers drawn 709 *quarrelling*; at war with; intolerant 735 *oppressive*.

Vb. *be inimical*, show hostility 883 *make unwelcome*; bear ill will 898 *be malevolent*; grudge 912 *envy*; hound, persecute 735 *oppress*; make war 718 *wage war*; fall out, come to blows, be incompatible, collide, clash 709 *quarrel*.

make enemies, be unpopular 883 *be unsociable*; antagonize 891 *enrage*; estrange, alienate, make bad blood 709 *make quarrels*.

882. Sociality – N. *sociality*, relations, community r., race r.; membership, intercommunity 706 *association*; making one of, belonging; team spirit, esprit de corps; fellowship, comradeship, companionship, society; camaraderie, fraternization, social intercourse, familiarity 880 *friendship*; social circle, home c., family c., one's friends and acquaintances 880 *friend*; society, social climbing.

sociability, compatibility 83 *conformity*; sociableness, gregariousness 880 *friendliness*; social success, popularity; social tact, common touch; social graces, savoir vivre 884 *courtesy*; urbanity 846 *good taste*; ability to mix, clubbability; affability, welcome, greeting, glad hand 884 *courteous act*; hospitality, entertaining, home from home, Liberty Hall 813 *liberality*; good company, geniality, cordiality, bonhomie; conviviality, joviality 824 *enjoyment*; gaiety 837 *revel*; cheer, good c., loving cup 301 *feasting*.

social gathering, meeting 74 *assembly*; reunion, get-together, conversazione, social; reception, at home, soirée, levee; entertainment 837 *amusement*; singsong, camp fire; party, hen p., stag p., partie carrée, tête-à-tête; housewarming; house party; banquet 301 *feasting*; love feast 988 *ritual act*; coffee morning, tea party, bun fight, drinks, cocktail party, dinner p., garden p. 837 *festivity*; dance, ball, hop, disco 837 *dancing*.

social round, social whirl, season; visiting, calling, dropping in; stay, visit; frequentation 880 *friendship*; engagement, rendezvous, assignation, date, blind d.; meeting place, club, pub, local 76 *focus*.

sociable person, caller, visitor, habitué; bon vivant, good fellow; good mixer, good company, life and soul of the party; catch, lion 890 *favourite*; boon companion, hobnobber, clubman; hostess; host; diner-out, parasite, freeloader, gate-crasher; gadabout, social butterfly; socialite, social climber 848 *beau monde*.

Adj. *sociable*, gregarious, social, extrovert, outgoing, party-minded; companionable, affable, chatty, gossipy, clubbable; cosy, folksy; neighbourly 880 *friendly*; hospitable, cordial, hearty, back-slapping, hail-fellow-well-met; convivial, jolly, jovial 833 *merry*; urbane 884 *courteous*; easy, free-and-easy 683 *reposeful*.

Vb. *be sociable*, like company; socialize, mix 880 *be friendly*; get around, go out, live it up 837 *amuse oneself*; join in 775 *participate*; crack a bottle 301 *drink*; carouse 837 *revel*; make oneself at home, unbend 683 *repose*; chat to 584 *converse*; date, make a date; make friends 880 *befriend*; introduce oneself, enlarge one's circle; keep up with 588 *correspond*.

visit, sojourn, stay, weekend; keep in touch, look one up, call in, look in, drop in.

be hospitable, keep open house 813 *be liberal*; invite, have round, receive; welcome, make w. 884 *greet*; do the honours, preside; do proud, kill the fatted calf 876

celebrate; entertain, regale 301 *feed*; throw a party 837 *revel*.

883. Unsociability, seclusion – N. unsociability, unsociableness; shyness 620 *avoidance*; introversion, autism; refusal to mix, staying at home; singleness 895 *celibacy*; inhospitality 816 *parsimony*; unapproachability, aloofness 871 *pride*; unfriendliness, coldness 885 *discourtesy*; ostracism 57 *exclusion*; blacklist 607 *rejection*.

seclusion, privacy, private world, world of one's own; peace and quiet 266 *quietude*; home life, domesticity; loneliness, solitude; retreat, retirement, withdrawal; confinement, purdah 525 *concealment*; isolation, estrangement 46 *separation*; sequestration, segregation, quarantine 57 *exclusion*; reserve, reservation, ghetto; harem; gaol 748 *prison*; godforsaken hole, back of beyond; backwater; island, desert, wilderness; hide-out 527 *hiding-place*; study, cloister, cell 192 *retreat*; ivory tower, hermitage, shell.

solitary, unsocial person, iceberg; lonely person, lonely heart; loner, lone wolf, rogue elephant; isolationist, island; introvert; stay-at-home, home-body; recluse, hermit; maroon, castaway.

outcast, pariah, leper, outsider; outcaste, untouchable, harijan; expatriate, alien 59 *foreigner*; exile, deportee, evacuee, refugee, homeless person, stateless p.; outlaw, bandit; vagabond 268 *wanderer*; waif, stray 779 *derelict*.

Adj. *unsociable*, unsocial, antisocial, introverted, morose, not fit to live with; unassimilated 59 *extraneous*; unclubbable, stay-at-home; inhospitable, unwelcoming, unneighbourly, unfriendly, misanthropic; distant, aloof, stand-offish 871 *prideful*; frosty, icy 893 *sullen*; unforthcoming, uncommunicative 582 *taciturn*; solitary, lonely 88 *alone*; shy, retiring, withdrawn 620 *avoiding*; celibate; anchoretic, eremetic.

friendless, forlôrn, desolate, forsaken; lonely, lonesome, solitary; on one's own 88 *alone*; cold-shouldered, unpopular, avoided 860 *unwanted*; blacklisted, blackballed, ostracized, sent to Coventry 57 *excluded*; expelled, exiled 757 *prohibited*.

secluded, private, sequestered, cloistered; hidden, buried, tucked away 523 *latent*; behind the veil, in purdah 421 *screened*; quiet, lonely, isolated, enisled; remote, out of the way; godforsaken, unvisited, unfrequented, off the beaten track 491 *unknown*; uninhabited, deserted 190 *empty*.

Vb. *be unsociable*, keep oneself to oneself, shun company; go it alone, play a lone hand; stay in one's shell, stand aloof 620 *avoid*; stay at home, vegetate 266 *be quiescent*; make a retreat, take the veil.

make unwelcome, repel, keep at arm's length, make one keep his *or* her distance; not acknowledge, ignore, cut dead 885 *be rude*; cold-shoulder, turn one's back on; rebuff, give one the brush-off; turn out, turf o. 300 *eject*; ostracize, send to Coventry 57 *exclude*; have no time for, refuse to associate with, have nothing to do with 620 *avoid*; banish, exile 963 *punish*.

seclude, sequester, island, isolate, quarantine, segregate; confine, shut up 747 *imprison*.

884. Courtesy – **N.** *courtesy*, chivalry; deference 920 *respect*; consideration, condescension 872 *humility*; graciousness, politeness, civility, urbanity, mannerliness, manners, good m., good behaviour; gentlemanliness, ladylikeness 846 *good taste*; tactfulness, diplomacy; courtliness 875 *formality*; amenity, amiability, kindliness 897 *benevolence*; gentleness, mildness; good humour, complaisance, affability, suavity 882 *sociability*.

courteous act, courtesy, civility, favour 897 *kind act*; soft answer 736 *leniency*; compliment, kind words 886 *congratulation*; introduction 880 *friendliness*; welcome, acknowledgement, recognition, salutation, salute, greeting, handclasp, handshake 920 *respects*; bow, curtsy; farewell 296 *valediction*.

Adj. *courteous*, chivalrous 868 *noble*; courtly, gallant, old-world 875 *formal*; polite, gentlemanly, ladylike, well-mannered 848 *well-bred*; gracious, con-

descending 872 *humble*; deferential, mannerly 920 *respectful*; on one's best behaviour, anxious to please 455 *attentive*; obliging, complaisant 897 *benevolent*; suave, bland, smooth, well-spoken 925 *flattering*; obsequious 879 *servile*.

amiable, affable, friendly 882 *sociable*; considerate, kind 897 *benevolent*; inoffensive, gentle, easy, mild, soft-spoken 736 *lenient*; good-tempered, sweet-t. 823 *inexcitable*; well-behaved, good 739 *obedient*; peaceable 717 *peaceful*.

Vb. *be courteous*, be on one's best behaviour, mind one's P's and Q's; show courtesy 920 *respect*; oblige 703 *aid*; condescend, have time for; keep a civil tongue in one's head, return a soft answer 823 *be patient*; mend one's manners.

pay one's respects, send one's regards; do one the honour 925 *flatter*; drink to 876 *toast*; pay homage 920 *show respect*; honour 876 *celebrate*.

greet, accost, acknowledge; nod, wave, smile; say hallo, bid good morning 583 *speak to*; salute, raise one's hat; touch one's cap, tug one's forelock; bend, bow, bob, duck, curtsy, salaam 920 *show respect*; shake hands, press the flesh; escort 89 *accompany*; present arms, parade, turn out 876 *celebrate*; receive, do the honours; welcome 882 *be sociable*; embrace 889 *caress*.

885. Discourtesy – **N.** *discourtesy*, impoliteness, bad manners, sheer bad m.; no manners, scant courtesy, incivility, inurbanity; churlishness, uncouthness, boorishness 847 *ill-breeding*; misbehaviour, misconduct; tactlessness, inconsiderateness, want of consideration.

rudeness, ungraciousness, gruffness, bluntness; sharpness, tartness, acerbity, asperity; harshness 735 *severity*; offhandedness, brusquerie; sarcasm 851 *ridicule*; unparliamentary language 899 *scurrility*; insult 921 *indignity*; personalities, lip, truculence 878 *insolence*; impatience, interruption; scowl 893 *sullenness*; a discourtesy, piece of bad manners.

rude person, no gentleman, no lady; savage, barbarian, brute, lout, boor, loudmouth, mannerless brat, unlicked cub 878 *insolent person*; curmudgeon, crab, bear; sourpuss, crosspatch 829 *malcontent*.

Adj. *discourteous*, ungallant, unchivalrous, unhandsome; ungentlemanly, unladylike; impolite, uncivil, rude; mannerless, ill-mannered, boorish, uncouth 847 *ill-bred*; insolent, impudent 878 *impertinent*; unpleasant, disagreeable; unaccommodating, uncomplaisant; offhanded, cavalier; tactless, inconsiderate.

ungracious, unsmiling, gruff 893 *sullen*; peevish, testy 892 *irascible*; difficult, surly, churlish 883 *unsociable*; ungentle, rough, harsh 735 *severe*; frank, overfrank, blunt, brusque, short; tart, sharp, biting, acrimonious; sarcastic, uncomplimentary 926 *detracting*; abusive, vituperative 899 *cursing*; contumelious, injurious 921 *disrespectful*.

Vb. *be rude*, have no manners 878 *be insolent*; show no thought for others 921 *not respect*; have no time for 456 *be inattentive*; snub, turn one's back on, cut, look right through, cut dead 883 *make unwelcome*; show one the door, send away with a flea in his *or* her ear 300 *eject*; cause offence 891 *huff*; insult, abuse; take liberties; stare, ogle; make one blush 867 *shame*; lose one's temper 891 *get angry*; curse 899 *cuss*; snarl, scowl 893 *be sullen*.

886. Congratulation – N. *congratulation*, felicitation; congratulations, felicitations, compliments, compliments of the season; good wishes, best w., happy returns; salute, toast; welcome, official reception 876 *celebration*; thanks 907 *gratitude*.

Adj. *congratulatory*, complimentary; honorific, triumphal 876 *celebratory*.

Vb. *congratulate*, felicitate, compliment; offer one's congratulations, wish one joy; send one's compliments 884 *pay one's respects*; sanction a triumph, accord an ovation, give three cheers 923 *applaud*; fête, lionize 876 *celebrate*; congratulate oneself, thank one's lucky stars 824 *be pleased*; thank heaven 907 *be grateful*.

887. Love – N. *love*, affection, friendship, charity, Eros; agape, brotherly love,

sisterly l., Christian l.; true love, real thing; natural affection, mother-love; conjugal love, uxoriousness; closeness, intimacy; sentiment 818 *feeling*; kindness, tenderness 897 *benevolence*; Platonic love 880 *friendship*; two hearts that beat as one, mutual love, compatibility, sympathy, fellow feeling; fondness, liking, predilection, fancy 179 *tendency*; attachment, devotion 739 *loyalty*; courtly love, gallantry; sentimentality, susceptibility 819 *moral sensibility*; lovesickness, Cupid's sting; eroticism, lust 859 *libido*; regard 920 *respect*; hero worship; first love, calf l., puppy l.; crush, pash, infatuation; romantic love, passion, rapture, ecstasy 822 *excitable state*; love-hate, odi et amo.

lovableness, amiability, attractiveness, popularity; winsomeness, charm, fascination, appeal, sex a.; attractions, charms, winning ways, coquetry, flirtatiousness; sentimental value.

love affair, affaire de coeur; romance, flirtation, amour, amourette, entanglement; free love; liaison, intrigue, adultery 951 *illicit love*; falling in love, something between them; course of love, the old old story; love-making 889 *wooing*; wedding bells 894 *marriage*; broken romance, broken heart.

lover, love, true l., Romeo; sweetheart; young man, boyfriend, swain, beau, gallant, cavalier, escort, date; steady, fiancé; wooer, courter, suitor, admirer; adorer, worshipper; fan, fan club; sugar daddy; gigolo, ladies' man, lady-killer, seducer; flirt, coquette, philanderer 952 *libertine*; lovers, turtledoves, lovebirds.

loved one, beloved, love, true love, heart's desire, light of one's life 890 *darling*; intimate 880 *close friend*; intended, fiancée, bride-to-be 894 *spouse*; conquest, inamorata, lady-love, girlfriend, girl, bird, baby; sweetheart, valentine, flame, old f.; idol, hero; heartthrob, maiden's prayer, dream girl 859 *desired object*; mistress 952 *kept woman*; femme fatale.

love god, goddess of love, Venus, Aphrodite; Amor, Eros, Cupid, blind boy; cupidon, amoretto.

Adj. *loving*, brotherly, sisterly; courting, making love 889 *caressing*; affectionate, demonstrative; tender, motherly, conjugal; lover-like, loverly, gallant, romantic, sentimental, lovesick; lovelorn, languishing 834 *dejected*; attached to, fond of, uxorious, doting; possessive 911 *jealous*; adoring, devoted, enslaved (**see** *enamoured*); flirtatious, coquettish 604 *capricious*; amorous, amative, ardent, passionate 818 *fervent*; yearning 859 *desiring*; lustful 951 *lecherous*.

enamoured, in love, sweet on, soft on, stuck on, gone on, sold on; struck with, taken w., smitten, bitten, caught, hooked; charmed, enchanted 983 *bewitched*; mad on, infatuated, besotted, crazy about, wild a., head over heels in love 503 *crazy*; rapturous, ecstatic 824 *happy*.

lovable, likeable, congenial, to one's liking, after one's own heart 859 *desired*; lovesome, winsome 884 *amiable*; sweet, angelic, divine, adorable; lovely 841 *beautiful*; attractive, seductive, alluring 291 *attracting*; prepossessing, appealing, engaging, winning, endearing, captivating, irresistible; cuddly, desirable, kissable; charming, enchanting, bewitching 983 *sorcerous*; liked, beloved, dear, darling, pet, fancy, favourite.

erotic, aphrodisiac, erotogenic, erogenous; sexy, pornographic 951 *impure*; amatory 821 *excited*.

Vb. *love*, like, care for, take pleasure in, be partial to; be fond of, have a soft spot for; be susceptible, have a heart; hold dear, care for, cherish, cling to; appreciate, value, prize, treasure, think the world of; admire 920 *respect*; adore, worship, idolize, only have eyes for; live for, live only f. (**see** *be in love*); make love 45 *unite with*; pet, fondle 889 *caress*.

be in love, burn, faint, die of love; glow with ardour, flame with passion; love to distraction, dote 503 *be insane*; take a fancy *or* a shine to, take to, be taken with, be sweet on; carry a torch for 859 *desire*; form an attachment, fall for, get hooked on, have it bad; be nuts on 503 *go mad*; set one's heart on, lose one's heart, bestow one's affections; declare one's love, woo,

sue, press one's suit 889 *court*; set one's cap at 619 *pursue*.

excite love, arouse desire 859 *cause desire*; warm, inflame 381 *heat*; enrapture, enthral 821 *excite*; dazzle, bedazzle, enchant 983 *bewitch*; allure 291 *attract*; make oneself attractive 843 *primp*; lure, seduce 612 *tempt*; lead on, flirt, coquette, philander; make eyes at 889 *court*; catch one's eye, take one's fancy, steal one's heart; make a hit, bowl over, sweep off one's feet, turn one's head; make a conquest, captivate; lead to the altar 894 *wed*; endear oneself, ingratiate o., insinuate o., wind oneself into one's affections; steal every heart.

888. Hatred – N. *hatred*, hate, no love lost; love-hate; aversion, antipathy 861 *dislike*; repugnance, detestation, loathing, abhorrence, abomination; disaffection, estrangement 709 *dissension*; hostility, antagonism 881 *enmity*; animosity, bad blood 891 *resentment*; malice, ill will, grudge 898 *malevolence*; jealousy 912 *envy*; wrath 891 *anger*; execration 899 *malediction*; phobia, xenophobia 481 *prejudice*; misogyny 902 *misanthropy*.

odium, disfavour, unpopularity 924 *disapprobation*; bad odour, black books 867 *disrepute*; odiousness, hatefulness, loathsomeness, obnoxiousness; despicability 922 *contemptibility*.

hateful object, anathema; unwelcome necessity, bitter pill; abomination; object of one's hate 881 *enemy*; not one's type, one's aversion, pet a., bête noire, bugbear, Dr Fell, nobody's darling; pest, menace, good riddance 659 *bane*; rotter 938 *cad*; blackleg, scab 603 *turncoat*.

Adj. *hating*, loathing; loveless; antipathetic 861 *disliking*; set against 704 *opposing*; averse, abhorrent, antagonistic, hostile 881 *inimical*; envious, spiteful, malicious 898 *malevolent*; bitter, rancorous 891 *resentful*; implacable; vindictive 910 *revengeful*; virulent 899 *cursing*.

hateful, odious, unlovable, unloved; invidious, obnoxious, pestilential 659 *baneful*; beastly, nasty, horrid 645 *not nice*; abhorrent, loathsome, abominable;

accursed, execrable, cursed; offensive, repulsive, repellent, revolting 861 *disliked*; bitter, sharp 393 *sour*; unwelcome 860 *unwanted*.

hated, loathed etc. vb.; out of favour, unpopular 861 *disliked*; in one's bad books, discredited 924 *disapproved*; loveless, unloved; unregretted, unlamented, unmourned; unchosen, spurned, jilted, crossed in love 607 *rejected*.

Vb. *hate*, bear hatred, have no love for; hate one's guts; loathe, abominate, detest, abhor; turn away from, revolt from 280 *recoil*; can't bear, can't stand 861 *dislike*; spurn, contemn 922 *despise*; execrate 899 *curse*; bear malice, have a down on 898 *be malevolent*; bear a grudge, have it in for 910 *be revengeful*, 891 *resent*; snap, snarl, bare one's fangs 893 *be sullen*; fall out of love, turn to hate.

excite hate, cause loathing, disgust, nauseate, stink in the nostrils 861 *cause dislike*; shock, horrify 924 *incur blame*; antagonize, destroy goodwill, estrange, alienate, sow dissension, set at each other's throats, create bad blood, end friendship 881 *make enemies*; poison, envenom, embitter; exasperate, incense 891 *enrage*.

889. Endearment – N. *endearment*, blandishments 925 *flattery*; soft nothings, sweet n., lovers' vows; dalliance, billing and cooing, slap and tickle, footsie; caress, embrace, clasp, hug, bear h.; cuddle, squeeze; kiss, smacker; slap and tickle, pat, pinch, nip 378 *touch*; familiarity, overfamiliarity, pass.

wooing, courting, play, lovemaking; glad eye, come hither look, ogle, sheep's eyes, fond look; flirtation, coquetry, gallantry, amorous intentions, honourable i.; courtship, suit, love s., addresses, advances; serenade, love song; love letter, billet-doux; sonnet; proposal, engagement, betrothal 894 *marriage*.

love token, true lover's knot; ring, wedding r.; valentine, red roses; arrow, heart; tattoo.

Adj. *caressing*, etc. vb.; demonstrative, affectionate 887 *loving*; soppy, spoony,

lovey-dovey; cuddlesome, flirtatious, coquettish.

Vb. *pet*, pamper, spoil, spoonfeed, mother, smother, kill with kindness; cosset, coddle; make much of, be all over one; treasure 887 *love*; cherish, foster 660 *safeguard*; nurse, lap, rock, cradle, baby; coo, croon over; coax, wheedle 925 *flatter*.

caress, love, fondle, dandle, take in one's lap; play with, stroke, smooth, pat, paw, pinch one's cheek, pat on the head, chuck under the chin; kiss, embrace, enlace, enfold, press to one's bosom, hang on one's neck; clasp, hug, not let go 778 *retain*; squeeze, press, cuddle; snuggle, nestle, nuzzle, nibble; play, romp, wanton, toy, trifle, dally; make love, carry on, canoodle, spoon, bill and coo, hold hands, pet, neck, snog, smooch, play footsie; vamp 887 *excite love*; (of animals) lick, fawn, rub against.

court, give the glad eye, make eyes at 438 *gaze*; get off with, get fresh, make a pass at; flirt, coquette 887 *excite love*; be sweet on 887 *be in love*; set one's cap at 619 *pursue*; squire, escort 89 *accompany*; hang round 284 *follow*; date, make a date, take out; walk out with, go steady; woo, pay court to, pay one's addresses to; whisper sweet nothings, serenade; sigh at the feet of, pine, languish; offer one's heart *or* one's hand; propose, pop the question, become engaged 894 *wed*.

890. Darling. Favourite – N. *darling*, dear, my dear; dearest, dear one, only one; one's own, one's all; truelove, love, beloved 887 *loved one*; heart, dear h.; sweetheart, sweeting, sweetie, sugar, honey, honeybaby, honeybunch; precious, jewel, treasure; chéri(e), mavourneen; angel, angel child, cherub; pippin, poppet, popsy, moppet, mopsy; pet, petkins, lamb, chick, chicken, ducks, ducky, dearie, lovey.

favourite, darling, mignon; spoiled child, enfant gâté, mother's darling, teacher's pet; jewel, heart's-blood, apple of one's eye, blue-eyed boy; someone after one's own heart, one of the best; first choice 644 *exceller*; boast, pride and joy;

national figure, favourite son, grand old man, man *or* woman of the hour 866 *person of repute*; hero, heroine, golden girl *or* boy; screen goddess, matinée idol, star; general favourite, universal f., cynosure, toast of the town; world's sweetheart, Queen of Hearts 841 *a beauty*; centre of attraction, honeypot 291 *attraction*; catch, lion 859 *desired object*.

891. Resentment. Anger – N. *resentment*, displeasure 829 *discontent*; huffiness, ill humour 893 *sullenness*; heart-burning, rancour, soreness, painful feelings; indignation (**see** *anger*); umbrage, offence, huff, pique; bile, gall; acrimony, bitterness, hard feelings; animosity, grudge 881 *enmity*; vindictiveness, spite 910 *revenge*; cause of offence, red rag to a bull, sore point; irritation 827 *annoyance*; provocation, last straw 921 *indignity*; wrong, injury.

anger, irritation, exasperation, vexation, indignation; high dudgeon, wrath, ire, choler; rage, tearing r., fury, passion 822 *excitable state*; temper, tantrum, tizzy, paddy, paddywhack, fume, fret, pet, fit of temper, burst of anger, outburst, explosion, taking, paroxysm 318 *agitation*; rampage, roar 400 *loudness*; fierceness, glare, frown, scowl; snarl, bark, snap 892 *irascibility*; warmth, heat, high words 709 *quarrel*.

Adj. *resentful*, piqued, stung, galled, miffed; sore, smarting 829 *discontented*; pained, hurt, offended; warm, indignant; reproachful, bitter, embittered, acrimonious, rancorous 888 *hating*; spleenful 898 *malevolent*; vindictive 910 *revengeful*; jealous 912 *envious*; grudging 598 *unwilling*.

angry, displeased, not amused, stern, frowning 834 *serious*; impatient, cross, waxy, ratty, wild, mad, livid; wroth, wrathful, irate; peeved, nettled, rattled, annoyed, irritated, provoked, stung; worked up, het up, hot under the collar; indignant, incensed, infuriated, beside oneself; shirty, in a temper, in a paddy, in a wax, in a huff, in a rage, in a fury, in a

taking; fuming, speechless, spitting with fury; savage, violent 176 *furious*; apoplectic, rabid, hopping mad 503 *frenzied*; seeing red, berserk; glaring, glowering 893 *sullen*; red with anger, flushed with rage; fierce 892 *irascible*.

Vb. *resent*, be piqued, – offended etc. adj.; be unable to stomach; feel, mind, smart under 829 *be discontented*; take amiss, take the wrong way, not see the joke; take offence, take umbrage, take exception to; get sore, cut up rough; burn, smoulder, simmer, boil; vent one's spleen 898 *be malevolent*; take to heart, bear malice.

get angry, get cross, get wild, get sore, go spare; kindle, grow heated, flush with anger; flare up; bridle, bristle; lose one's temper, forget oneself; throw a tantrum, stamp, shout; get one's dander *or* one's monkey up, fly into a temper, fly off the handle; let fly, boil over, blow up, flip one's lid, blow one's top, explode; see red, go berserk 822 *be excitable*.

be angry, chafe, fret, fume, fuss, flounce, ramp, stamp, champ at the bit, paw the ground; carry on, create, make a scene; go on the warpath 61 *rampage*; turn nasty, cut up rough, raise Cain; rage, rant, bellow, bluster, fulminate 400 *be loud*; look black, look daggers, frown, scowl 893 *be sullen*; spit, snap, lash out; gnash one's teeth, grind one's t., weep with rage, swell with fury, burst with indignation, stamp with rage, lash one's tail 821 *be excited*.

huff, miff, pique, sting, nettle, rankle, smart; ruffle one's dignity, wound 827 *hurt*; put one's back up, rub up the wrong way, get across, give umbrage, offend, cause offence 888 *excite hate*; affront, outrage 921 *not respect*.

enrage, upset, ruffle, disturb one's equanimity, irritate, rile, peeve; annoy, vex, pester, bother 827 *trouble*; do it to annoy 827 *torment*; fret, nag, gnaw; try one's patience, exasperate; push too far, anger, incense, infuriate, madden, drive mad; goad, sting, taunt; whip up one's anger, kindle one's wrath, excite indignation, raise one's hackles, make one's blood boil, make one see red; cause resentment, embitter, envenom, poison; exasperate 832 *aggravate*.

892. Irascibility – N. *irascibility*, irritability, impatience 822 *excitability*; grumpiness, gruffness 883 *unsociability*; asperity 393 *sourness*; sensitivity 819 *moral sensibility*; huffiness, touchiness, prickliness; pugnacity 709 *quarrelsomeness*; temperament, testiness, petulance; captiousness, uncertain temper, short t.; hot temper, limited patience; hot blood, inflammable nature; bad temper, foul t.

shrew, scold, fishwife; spitfire, termagant, virago, vixen, battleaxe, harridan, fury; Tartar, hornet; bear, crosspatch.

Adj. *irascible*, impatient, choleric, irritable, peppery, testy, crusty, peevish, crotchety, cranky, cross-grained; short-tempered, hot-t.; prickly, touchy, tetchy, huffy, thin-skinned 819 *sensitive*; hot-blooded, fiery 822 *excitable*; hasty 857 *rash*; quick-tempered 709 *quarrelling*; scolding, shrewish, vixenish; petulant, cantankerous, querulous; captious, bitter 393 *sour*; splenetic, spleenful, bilious, liverish, gouty; scratchy, snuffy, snappy, snappish, waspish; tart, sharp, short; uptight, edgy; fractious, fretful, moody, temperamental, changeable; gruff, grumpy, ratty, like a bear with a sore head 829 *discontented*; cross, stroppy 893 *sullen*.

Vb. *be irascible*, have a temper 893 *be sullen*; snap *or* bite one's head off, jump down one's throat 891 *get angry*.

893. Sullenness – N. *sullenness*, grimness 834 *seriousness*; sulkiness, ill humour; surliness, churlishness 883 *unsociability*; pout, grimace 829 *discontent*; gruffness 885 *discourtesy*; crossness, peevishness, ill temper 892 *irascibility*; spleen, bile, liver; sulks, bouderie, moodiness 834 *melancholy*; black look, hangdog l.; glare, glower, lour, frown, scowl; growl, snarl, snap, bite.

Adj. *sullen*, gloomy, saturnine; glowering, scowling; unsmiling 834 *serious*; sulky, sulking, cross, cross as two sticks, out of temper, out of humour, out of sorts 883 *unsociable*; surly, morose, crabbed,

cross-grained, difficult; cantankerous, stroppy 709 *quarrelling*; refractory 738 *disobedient*; grouchy, grumpy 829 *discontented*; vinegary 393 *sour*; gruff, abrupt, brusque 885 *discourteous*; temperamental, moody 152 *changeful*; bilious, jaundiced, dyspeptic; blue, down, depressed 834 *melancholic*; petulant, peevish, shirty, bad-tempered 892 *irascible*; smouldering, sultry.

Vb. *be sullen*, glower, glare, lour; scowl, frown, knit one's brows; spit, snap, snarl, growl, snort; make a face, pout, sulk 883 *be unsociable*; mope 834 *be dejected*; get out of bed on the wrong side; grouch, grouse, carp, crab 829 *be discontented*.

894. Marriage – N. *marriage*, matrimony, holy m., sacrament of m., one flesh; wedlock, wedded state; match, union; conjugal knot, marriage tie; cohabitation; living as man and wife; husbandhood, wifehood; banns, marriage certificate, marriage lines; Hymen.

type of marriage, monogamy, monandry, bigamy, polygamy, polygyny, polyandry; second marriage, remarriage; endogamy, exogamy; arranged match, marriage of convenience; love-match; mixed marriage, intermarriage, miscegenation; mismarriage, mésalliance; morganatic marriage, left-handed m.; companionate marriage, trial m., open m.; free union, free love; ménage à trois; shotgun wedding.

wedding, getting married; matchmaking, betrothal, engagement; bridal, nuptials; marriage rites, nuptial mass; church wedding, white w., civil marriage, registry-office m.; run-away match, elopement; prothalamium, epithalamium; wedding breakfast, reception; honeymoon; silver wedding 876 *special day*.

spouse 887 *loved one*; Mr and Mrs, Darby and Joan; married couple, young marrieds, newlyweds, honeymooners; bride, bridegroom; consort, partner, mate, yoke-mate, helpmate, helpmeet, better half; married man, husband, hubbie, man, old man; married woman, wife, matron, feme covert, woman, old w., missus; monogamist, digamist; polygamist, polygynist, bigamist; common-law husband *or* wife, wife *or* husband in all but name.

Adj. *married*, paired, mated, matched; spliced, hitched, in double harness; espoused, wedded, united, made man and wife, made one, joined in holy matrimony; monogamous; remarried, digamous; just married, newly-wed; mismarried, ill-matched.

matrimonial, marital, connubial, concubinary; premarital, postmarital, extramarital; nuptial, bridal, hymeneal, epithalamial; conjugal, wifely, matronly, husbandly; bigamous; polygamous, polygynous, polyandrous; endogamous, exogamous; morganatic.

Vb. *marry*, marry off, find a husband *or* wife for, match, mate; matchmake, arrange a match; betroth, affiance, espouse, publish the banns, announce the engagement; give in marriage, give away; join in marriage, declare man and wife; splice, hitch, tie the knot.

wed, marry, espouse; find a wife *or* a husband 889 *court*; take the plunge, get married, get hitched, get spliced; bestow one's hand, accept a proposal, plight one's troth, become engaged, put up the banns; lead to the altar, take for better or worse; pair off, mate, couple 45 *unite with*; cohabit, set up house together, live as man and wife, live together, live in sin; marry well, make a good match; mismarry; elope; make an honest woman of, go through a form of marriage; marry again, remarry; intermarry.

895. Celibacy – N. *celibacy*, single state 744 *independence*; bachelorhood, bachelordom; misogamy, misogyny 883 *unsociability*; spinsterhood, spinsterdom; maidenhood, virginity 950 *purity*.

celibate, unmarried man, single m., bachelor; confirmed bachelor, not the marrying kind; misogamist, misogynist 902 *misanthrope*; monastic 986 *monk*; hermit 883 *solitary*.

spinster, unmarried woman, feme sole,

bachelor girl; maid, maiden, virgo intacta; maiden aunt, old maid; vestal virgin, nun.

Adj. *unwedded*, unwed, unmarried, single; spouseless; on the shelf; heartwhole, fancy-free 744 *independent*; maidenly, virgin 950 *pure*; spinster, spinsterlike, spinsterish; bachelor, bachelorlike; celibate.

896. Divorce. Widowhood – N. *divorce*, divorcement, repudiation; decree nisi, decree absolute; separation, legal s., judicial s.; annulment; nonconsummation; desertion, living apart; alimony; marriage on the rocks, broken marriage; divorcee, divorcé(e); corespondent; single parent.

widowhood, widowerhood, dowagerhood; grass widowhood; widows' weeds 228 *formal dress*; widower, widow, relict; dowager; war widow; grass w., grass widower, Merry Widow.

Adj. *divorced*, deserted, separated, living apart.

widowed, husbandless, wifeless.

Vb. *divorce*, separate, split up, live apart; desert 621 *relinquish*; untie the knot 46 *disunite*; put away, sue for divorce, file a divorce suit; get a divorce; grant a divorce, pronounce a decree absolute.

897. Benevolence – N. *benevolence*, good will 880 *friendliness*; ahimsa, harmlessness 935 *innocence*; benignity, kindly disposition, heart of gold; amiability 882 *sociability*; milk of human kindness, warmheartedness, kind-heartedness, kindliness, kindness, loving-k., charity 887 *love*; brotherly love 880 *friendship*; consideration, caring, concern, fellow feeling, sympathy 818 *feeling*, 905 *pity*; decent feeling, humanitarianism 901 *philanthropy*; charitableness, beneficence, generosity, magnanimity 813 *liberality*; gentleness, mildness, tolerance 734 *laxity*; mercy 909 *forgiveness*; grace of God; blessing, benediction.

kind act, kindness, favour, service; good deed; charity, alms 781 *giving*; prayers, good offices, good turn 703 *aid*; labour of love, voluntary work.

kind person, bon enfant, true Christian;

good sort, good neighbour, good Samaritan; well-wisher 880 *friend*; sympathizer 707 *patron*; do-gooder 901 *philanthropist*.

Adj. *benevolent*, well meant, well-intentioned, for the best 880 *friendly*; out of kindness, to oblige; out of charity, eleemosynary; sympathetic, wishing well; benign, benignant, kindly, kind-hearted, warm-h.; kind, good, human, decent, Christian; affectionate 887 *loving*; fatherly, paternal; motherly, maternal; brotherly, fraternal; sisterly, cousinly; good-natured, easy 884 *amiable*; merciful 909 *forgiving*; tolerant, indulgent 734 *lax*; humane, considerate 736 *lenient*; soft-hearted, tender 905 *pitying*; genial 882 *sociable*; bountiful 813 *liberal*; generous, magnanimous 931 *disinterested*; beneficent, charitable 901 *philanthropic*; obliging, accommodating 703 *aiding*; complaisant 884 *courteous*.

Vb. *be benevolent*, feel the springs of charity, have one's heart in the right place; show concern, care for, feel for; sympathize, enter into another's feelings, do as one would be done by; return good for evil, love one's enemy 909 *forgive*; wish well, pray for, bless, give one's blessing; have the best intentions, mean well; favour 703 *patronize*; benefit 644 *do good*; be a good Samaritan, do a good turn, put one under an obligation 703 *aid*.

philanthropize, do good, have a social conscience, serve the community, show public spirit, care; get involved 678 *be active*; reform, improve; relieve the poor, visit, nurse 703 *minister to*.

898. Malevolence – N. *malevolence*, ill will 881 *enmity*; evil intent, worst intentions; spite, gall, viciousness, malignity, malignancy, malice; bad blood, hate 888 *hatred*; venom, virulence, balefulness 659 *bane*; acrimony 393 *sourness*; envy, rancour, spleen 891 *resentment*; gloating, Schadenfreude, unholy joy; evil eye 983 *spell*.

inhumanity, misanthropy, inconsiderateness, lack of concern; uncharitableness; intolerance 735 *severity*; harshness, implacability, obduracy, heart of marble *or* of stone 906 *pitilessness*; unkindness,

callousness 326 *hardness*; cruelty, barbarity, bloodlust; barbarism, savagery, ferocity; sadism, fiendishness 934 *wickedness*; truculence, brutality; vandalism 165 *destruction*.

cruel act, brutality; ill-treatment 675 *misuse*; unkindness, disservice, ill turn; victimization, bullying 735 *severity*; foul play, bloodshed 176 *violence*; excess, extremes; atrocity, outrage, devilry; cruelty, torture, barbarity; cannibalism, genocide 362 *slaughter*.

Adj. *malevolent*, evil-intentioned, ill-disposed 661 *dangerous*; ill-natured, churlish 893 *sullen*; nasty, bloody-minded, bitchy, cussed 602 *wilful*; malicious, catty, spiteful 926 *detracting*; mischievous (**see** *maleficent*); baleful, malign, malignant 645 *harmful*; vicious, viperous; black-hearted 888 *hating*; jealous 912 *envious*; treacherous 930 *perfidious*; bitter, rancorous 891 *resentful*; implacable 906 *pitiless*; vindictive, gloating 910 *revengeful*; hostile, fell 881 *inimical*; intolerant 735 *oppressive*.

maleficent, malefic 645 *harmful*; poisonous, venomous 659 *baneful*; working evil, mischief-making 645 *bad*.

unkind, ill-natured 893 *sullen*; unkindly, unaffectionate, unbrotherly, undaughterly, unfilial, unchristian; cold, unfriendly 881 *inimical*; uncooperative, disobliging; ungenerous, uncharitable, unforgiving; mean, nasty; rude 885 *ungracious*; unsympathetic, unresponsive, uncaring 820 *impassive*; stern 735 *severe*; tough, hardboiled, hardbitten 326 *hard*; inhuman, unnatural.

cruel, grim, fell; steely, grim-faced, cold-eyed, hard-hearted, stony-h.; callous, cold-blooded; heartless, ruthless 906 *pitiless*; tyrannical 735 *oppressive*; gloating, sadistic; blood-thirsty 362 *murderous*; bloody 176 *violent*; feral, tigerish, wolfish; unnatural, subhuman, brutalized, brutish; brutal, rough, truculent, fierce, ferocious; savage, barbarous, wild, untamed, untamable; inhuman, fiendish 969 *diabolic*.

Vb. *be malevolent*, bear malice, cherish a grudge 888 *hate*, 912 *envy*; disoblige, spite, do one a bad turn; go to extremes, do one's worst, wreak one's spite 906 *be pitiless*; take one's revenge, victimize, gloat, be revengeful; take it out on, bully, maltreat 645 *ill-treat*; molest, annoy 645 *harm*; malign 926 *detract*; harry, persecute, tyrannize 735 *oppress*; raven, thirst for blood 362 *slaughter*; rankle, fester, poison, be a thorn in the flesh; blight, blast 165 *lay waste*; cast the evil eye 983 *bewitch*

899. Malediction – N. *malediction*, curse, imprecation, anathema 898 *malevolence*; evil eye 983 *spell*; execration, fulmination 900 *threat*; ban, proscription, excommunication.

scurrility, ribaldry, vulgarity; profanity, cursing and swearing, effing and blinding; bad language, foul l., strong l., unparliamentary l., Limehouse, Billingsgate; naughty word, expletive, swearword, oath, swear, damn, curse, cuss; invective, vituperation, abuse, slanging match, stormy exchange; more bark than bite 900 *threat*; vilification 926 *calumny*; cheek, sauce 878 *sauciness*; epithet, insult 921 *indignity*; contumely 922 *contempt*; rough edge of one's tongue, tongue-lashing 924 *reproach*.

Adj. *maledictory*, cursing, maledictive, imprecatory, fulminatory, denunciatory, damnatory.

cursing, swearing; profane, foul-mouthed, foul-spoken, scurrilous 847 *vulgar*; vituperative, abusive, vitriolic 924 *disapproving*; contumelious 922 *despising*.

Vb. *curse*, cast the evil eye 983 *bewitch*; accurse, wish ill 898 *be malevolent*; wish on, call down on; curse up hill and down dale; anathematize, imprecate, execrate; fulminate, thunder against 924 *reprove*; excommunicate, damn; round upon, confound, send to the devil *or* to blazes; abuse, revile 924 *reprobate*.

cuss, curse, swear, damn, blast; blaspheme 980 *be impious*; swear like a trooper, curse and swear, eff and blind, turn the air blue; slang, blackguard 924 *reprobate*; rail at, scold, give the rough edge of one's tongue.

900. Threat – N. *threat*, menace; commination 899 *malediction*; challenge 711 *defiance*; blackmail 737 *demand*; battle cry, sabre-rattling 854 *intimidation*; deterrent, big stick 723 *weapon*; gathering clouds 511 *omen*; secret weapon 663 *pitfall*; sword of Damocles 661 *danger*; fair warning, writing on the wall 664 *warning*; bluster 877 *boast*.

Adj. *threatening*, menacing, minatory, minacious; sabre-rattling 711 *defiant*; bullying 877 *boastful*; muttering, grumbling 893 *sullen*; portentous, ominous, foreboding 511 *presageful*; louring 155 *impending*; ready to spring, growling, snarling 891 *angry*; abusive 899 *cursing*; comminatory 899 *maledictory*; deterrent 854 *frightening*; nasty, unpleasant 661 *dangerous*.

Vb. *threaten*, menace, utter threats; demand with menaces, blackmail 737 *demand*; hijack, hold to ransom; frighten, deter, intimidate, bully, wave the big stick 854 *frighten*; roar, bellow 408 *vociferate*; fulminate, thunder 899 *curse*; bark, talk big, bluster, hector 877 *boast*; shake 317 *brandish*; clench one's fist, draw one's sword 711 *defy*; bare one's fangs, snarl, growl 893 *be sullen*; bristle, spit 891 *get angry*; pull a gun on, hold at gunpoint; gather, mass, hang over 155 *impend*; bode ill, presage disaster, spell danger 511 *predict*; serve notice, caution 664 *warn*; threaten reprisals.

901. Philanthropy – N. *philanthropy*, humanitarianism, humanity 897 *benevolence*; humanism, cosmopolitanism, internationalism; altruism 931 *disinterestedness*; idealism, ideals; the greatest happiness of the greatest number, utilitarianism; common good, socialism, communism; chivalry, knight-errantry; dedication, crusading spirit, nonconformist conscience, social c. 654 *reformism*; good works, mission, 'white man's burden'; Holy War, jihad, crusade, campaign, cause, good c.; voluntary agency, charity 703 *aid*.

sociology, social science, social engineering, social planning; poor relief, benefit, dole; social services, Welfare State; community service, social work, slumming, good works.

patriotism, civic ideals, good citizenship, public spirit, concern for the community, love of one's country; local patriotism, parochialism; nationalism, chauvinism, my country right or wrong; irredentism, Zionism.

philanthropist, friend of the human race 903 *benefactor*; humanitarian, do-gooder, social worker, slummer 897 *kind person*; community service worker 597 *volunteer*; paladin, champion, crusader, knight, knight errant; messiah 690 *leader*; missionary, bodhisattva; Utopian, idealist, altruist, flower people 513 *visionary*; utilitarian, reformist 654 *reformer*; populist, humanist, cosmopolite, citizen of the world, internationalist.

patriot, lover of one's country, fighter for one's c.; father *or* mother of the people; nationalist, chauvinist 481 *narrow mind*; irredentist, Zionist.

Adj. *philanthropic*, humanitarian, humane 897 *benevolent*; charitable, aid-giving 703 *aiding*; enlightened, humanistic, liberal; cosmopolitan, internationally minded; altruistic 931 *disinterested*; visionary, dedicated; sociological, socialistic; utilitarian.

patriotic, public-spirited, community-minded; irredentist, nationalistic, chauvinistic; loyal, true, true-blue.

Vb. see 897 *philanthropize*.

Adv. pro bono publico.

902. Misanthropy – N. *misanthropy*, hatred of mankind, cynicism 883 *unsociability*; misandry, misogyny; moroseness 893 *sullenness*; inhumanity; egotism.

misanthrope, misanthropist, man-hater, woman-h., misogynist; cynic; Diogenes; egotist; no patriot, defeatist; unsocial animal 883 *solitary*; sulker 829 *malcontent*.

Adj. *misanthropic*, inhuman, antisocial 883 *unsociable*; cynical; uncivic, unpatriotic, defeatist.

Vb. *misanthropize*, become a misanthrope, lose faith in humankind.

903. Benefactor – N. *benefactor*, benefactress 901 *philanthropist*; Lady Bountiful, Father Christmas, Santa Claus 781 *giver*; fairy godmother, guardian angel, good genius 660 *protector*; founder, foundress, supporter 707 *patron*; saviour, rescuer 668 *deliverance*; champion 713 *defender*; Lady Godiva 897 *kind person*; good neighbour 880 *friend*; salt of the earth, saint 937 *good person*.

904. Evildoer – N. *evildoer*, malefactor 934 *wickedness*; villain, blackguard, bad lot, baddy; one up to no good 663 *trouble-maker*; slanderer 926 *detractor*; obstructionist, saboteur 702 *hinderer*; wrecker, vandal 168 *destroyer*; terrorist, arsonist 738 *rioter*.

ruffian, blackguard, rogue, scoundrel 938 *knave*; lout, hooligan, hoodlum, larrikin 869 *low fellow*; Hell's Angel, yob, yobbo, punk; bully, terror; rough, tough, rowdy, ugly customer, plug-ugly, bruiser; thug; bravo, desperado, assassin, gunman 362 *murderer*; brute, beast, savage, barbarian, caveman.

offender, sinner 938 *bad person*; suspect; culprit, guilty person, law-breaker; criminal, villain, crook, malefactor, malfeasant, wrongdoer, misdemeanant, felon; delinquent, juvenile d., first offender; recidivist, backslider, old lag, convict, ex-c., gaolbird; lifer; parolee, probationer; mafioso, mobster, gangster, racketeer; housebreaker 789 *thief*; forger 789 *defrauder*; blackmailer, bloodsucker; poisoner 362 *murderer*; outlaw, public enemy 881 *enemy*; intruder, trespasser; underworld, Mafia 934 *wickedness*.

hellhag, hellhound, fiend, devil incarnate; bitch, virago 892 *shrew*; she-devil, fury, harpy; ogre, ogress, vampire, werewolf 938 *monster*.

noxious animal, brute, beast, wild b.; beast of prey, man-eater; serpent, viper 365 *reptile*; basilisk 84 *rara avis*; scorpion, hornet; pest, locust, deathwatch beetle 365 *insect*; rat 659 *bane*; wild cat, mad dog, rogue elephant.

905. Pity – N. *pity*, springs of p., ruth; remorse, compunction 830 *regret*; charity, compassion 897 *benevolence*; soft heart, tender h., bleeding h.; gentleness 736 *leniency*; commiseration, melting mood 825 *sorrow*; sympathy, empathy.

condolence, commiseration, sympathy, fellow feeling; consolation, comfort 831 *relief*; keen, wake 836 *lament*.

mercy, quarter, grace; second chance; mercifulness, clemency 909 *forgiveness*; light sentence; let-off 960 *acquittal*.

Adj. *pitying*, compassionate, sympathetic, understanding, condolent, commiserating; sorry for, feeling for; merciful, clement 736 *lenient*; tender-hearted, soft-hearted 819 *impressible*; weak 734 *lax*; unhardened, easily moved; placable 909 *forgiving*; humane, charitable 897 *benevolent*; forbearing 823 *patient*.

pitiable, pitiful, piteous, pathetic, heartrending; deserving pity; arousing compassion.

Vb. *pity*, feel p., show compassion, take pity on; sympathize with, enter into one's feelings, feel for, share the grief of 775 *participate*; sorrow, grieve, bleed for, feel sorry for, weep f., commiserate, condole with; yearn over 836 *lament*; console, comfort, wipe away one's tears 833 *cheer*; have pity, melt, thaw, relent 909 *forgive*.

show mercy, spare the life of, give quarter; commute (a sentence), pardon, amnesty 909 *forgive*; give one a break *or a* second chance 736 *be lenient*; relent, not be too hard upon, go easy on, let one down gently; put out of one's misery, give the coup de grâce, be cruel to be kind.

ask mercy, beg for m., fall at one's feet; excite pity, move to compassion, disarm, melt, thaw, soften 719 *pacify*.

906. Pitilessness – N. *pitilessness*, heartlessness, mercilessness 735 *severity*; callousness 898 *inhumanity*; inflexibility, inexorability, relentlessness 910 *revengefulness*; letter of the law, pound of flesh; no pity, short shrift, no quarter.

Adj. *pitiless*, unfeeling 820 *impassive*; unsympathetic, unmoved, dry-eyed; hard-hearted, stony-h.; callous, hardened; harsh 735 *severe*; brutal, sadistic 898 *cruel*; merciless, ruthless, heartless; un-

merciful, unrelenting, remorseless, implacable; unforgiving 910 *revengeful*.

Vb. *be pitiless*, have no heart, not be moved, turn a deaf ear; show no pity, give no quarter, spare none; harden one's heart, stand on the letter of the law, insist on one's pound of flesh 735 *be severe*; take one's revenge 910 *avenge*.

907. Gratitude – N. *gratitude*, gratefulness, thankfulness, sense of obligation; appreciativeness, appreciation.

thanks, hearty t.; vote of thanks, thankyou; thanksgiving, Te Deum 876 *celebration*; grace before meals; thankyou letter, bread-and-butter l.; credit, credit title, acknowledgement; recognition, tribute 923 *praise*; thank-offering, parting present, recognition of one's services, token of one's gratitude, tip 962 *reward*; requital, favour returned.

Adj. *grateful*, thankful, appreciative; acknowledging favours, giving credit; obliged, much o., under obligation, beholden, indebted.

Vb. *be grateful*, thank one's lucky stars, praise heaven; feel an obligation; pocket thankfully, receive with open arms, not look a gift horse in the mouth; be privileged, have the honour to.

thank, give thanks; praise, bless; acknowledge, credit, give full c. 158 *attribute*; show appreciation, tip 962 *reward*; return a favour, requite, repay 787 *restitute*.

908. Ingratitude – N. *ingratitude*, lack of appreciation, ungratefulness, unthankfulness; thanklessness; more kicks than ha'pence; no sense of obligation, indifference to favours; no reward, thankless task; ingrate, ungrateful wretch.

Adj. *ungrateful*, unthankful 885 *discourteous*; unobliged, unbeholden; unmindful 506 *forgetful*.

unthanked, unappreciated, thankless, without credit, unacknowledged, forgotten; rewardless, bootless, unrewarding, unrewarded, unrequited, ill-requited, untipped.

Vb. *be ungrateful*, show ingratitude, admit no obligation; take for granted, take as one's due; not thank, omit to t., forget to t.; see no reason to thank, not give a thankyou for; forget a kindness, return evil for good.

909. Forgiveness – N. *forgiveness*, pardon, free p., full p., reprieve 506 *amnesty*; indemnity, grace, indulgence 905 *mercy*; remission, absolution 960 *acquittal*; exculpation, exoneration 927 *vindication*; mutual forgiveness, reconciliation 719 *pacification*; forgiving nature 905 *pity*; longsuffering, forbearance 823 *patience*; forgiver, pardoner.

Adj. *forgiving*, merciful, placable, condoning, conciliatory 736 *lenient*; magnanimous 897 *benevolent*; unreproachful, longsuffering 823 *patient*; more in sorrow than in anger.

forgiven, pardoned, amnestied, reprieved; remitted; let off 960 *acquitted*; absolved, shriven; unavenged, unpunished; pardonable, forgivable, venial, excusable.

Vb. *forgive*, pardon, reprieve, amnesty, forgive and forget 506 *forget*; remit, absolve, shrive; wipe the slate clean 550 *obliterate*; relent, unbend, accept an apology 736 *be lenient*; be merciful, let one off the hook 905 *show mercy*; bear with, make allowances 823 *be patient*; take no offence, bear no malice, take in good part, not hold it against one; overlook, pass over, turn the other cheek; return good for evil 897 *be benevolent*; condone, not make an issue of 458 *disregard*; excuse 927 *justify*; exculpate, exonerate 960 *acquit*; bury the hatchet, let bygones be bygones, make it up, be reconciled; restore to favour.

910. Revenge – N. *revengefulness*, vindictiveness 898 *malevolence*; ruthlessness 906 *pitilessness*; implacability, irreconcilability, unappeasability 891 *resentment*.

revenge, sweet r.; crime passionel 911 *jealousy*; vengeance, avengement, day of reckoning 963 *punishment*; reprisals, punitive expedition 714 *retaliation*; eye for an eye, tooth for a tooth; vendetta, feud, blood f. 881 *enmity*.

avenger, vindicator, punisher, revanchist; Nemesis, Eumenides.

Adj. *revengeful*, vengeful, thirsting for revenge; avenging 714 *retaliatory*; at feud 881 *inimical*; unforgiving, unforgetting, implacable, unappeasable, unrelenting 906 *pitiless*; vindictive 898 *malevolent*; rancorous 891 *resentful*.

Vb. *avenge*, take one's revenge, take vengeance, take the law into one's own hands; get one's own back, repay, pay out, settle old scores, square an account, give one what was coming to him *or* her; get back at 714 *retaliate*; have one's fill of revenge, gloat.

911. Jealousy – N. *jealousy*, pangs of j.; jaundiced eye, green-eyed monster; distrust, mistrust 486 *doubt*; heart-burning 891 *resentment*; enviousness 912 *envy*; hate 888 *hatred*; inferiority complex; emulation, competitiveness, rivalry 716 *contention*; possessiveness 887 *love*; eternal triangle, crime passionel 910 *revenge*; rival, the other man *or* woman; Othello.

Adj. *jealous*, green-eyed, jaundiced 912 *envious*; eaten up with jealousy; possessive 887 *loving*; suspicious, mistrusting, distrustful 474 *doubting*; emulative, competitive, rival, competing.

912. Envy – N. *envy*, envious eye, enviousness, covetousness 859 *desire*; rivalry 911 *jealousy*; ill will, spite 898 *malevolence*; mortification, unwilling admiration, grudging praise.

Adj. *envious*, envying, green with envy 911 *jealous*; greedy 829 *discontented*; covetous 859 *desiring*; grudging; mortified 891 *resentful*.

Vb. *envy*, view with e., cast envious looks, covet, crave, must have for oneself, long to change places with 859 *desire*.

Section 4: Morality

913. Right – N. *right*, rightness, fitness, what ought to be; obligation 917 *duty*; seemliness, propriety, decency 848 *eti-*

quette; normality 83 *conformity*; rules and regulations 693 *precept*; ethicalness, morality 917 *morals*; righteousness 933 *virtue*; rectitude 929 *probity*; one's due 915 *dueness*.

justice, freedom from wrong, justifiability; redress; reform 654 *reformism*; process of law 953 *legality*; retribution, poetic justice 962 *reward*; lex talionis 714 *retaliation*; fair-mindedness, objectivity, disinterestedness, detachment, impartiality, equality, equity, equitableness, reasonableness, fairness; fair deal, square d., fair play; no discrimination, equal opportunity; Queensberry rules; Astraea.

Adj. *right*, rightful, proper, right and p., meet and right; fitting 24 *fit*; good 917 *ethical*; put right, redressed 654 *improved*; standard, classical 83 *conformable*.

just, upright, righteous, on the side of the angels 933 *virtuous*; fair-minded, disinterested, unprejudiced, unbiased 625 *neutral*; detached, impersonal, dispassionate, objective, open-minded; equal, egalitarian, impartial, even-handed; fair, fair and square, equitable, reasonable; in the right, justifiable; legitimate 953 *legal*; sportsmanlike 929 *honourable*; deserved 915 *due*.

Vb. *be right*, behove 915 *be due*; have good cause, be in the right, have right on one's side.

be just, play the game 929 *be honourable*; do justice, give the devil his due 915 *grant claims*; see justice done, see fair play, hear both sides 480 *judge*; temper justice with mercy 905 *show mercy*; right a wrong, put right 654 *rectify*; serve one right 714 *retaliate*; declare one's interest.

Adv. *rightly*, justly, with justice; in the right, within one's rights; impartially, without respect of persons, without fear or favour, fairly, on its merits.

914. Wrong – N. *wrong*, something wrong 84 *abnormality*; curse, scandal 645 *badness*; disgrace, dishonour 867 *slur*; impropriety, indecorum 847 *bad taste*; unreasonableness 481 *misjudgement*; unjustifiability, what ought not to be 916 *undueness*; culpability 936 *guilt*; immorality,

vice, sin 934 *wickedness*; dishonesty, unrighteousness 930 *improbity*; irregularity, criminality 954 *illegality*; wrongfulness, misdeed 936 *guilty act*; a wrong, injustice 930 *foul play*; sense of wrong, grievance, just g. 891 *resentment*; wrong-doer 938 *bad person*.

injustice, miscarriage of justice 481 *misjudgement*; warped judgement, packed jury 481 *bias*; one-sidedness, inequity, unfairness; discrimination; partiality, favouritism, nepotism; preferential treatment, positive discrimination; party spirit, old school tie 481 *prejudice*; unlawfulness 954 *illegality*; unfair advantage, 'heads I win, tails you lose' 916 *undueness*; no equality, wolf and the lamb 29 *inequality*; not cricket 930 *foul play*; imposition, robbing Peter to pay Paul.

Adj. *wrong*, not right 645 *bad*; odd, queer, suspect 84 *abnormal*; unfitting, unseemly, improper 847 *vulgar*; wrong-headed 481 *misjudging*; out of court, inadmissible; irregular, against the rules 757 *prohibited*; wrongful, illicit, criminal 954 *illegal*; culpable, in the wrong 936 *guilty*; unwarrantable, inexcusable, unjustifiable (**see** *unjust*); open to objection 861 *disliked*; injurious 645 *harmful*; unrighteous 930 *dishonest*; iniquitous, immoral 934 *wicked*.

unjust, unjustifiable; weighted 29 *unequal*; inequitable, iniquitous, unfair; hard on 735 *severe*; below the belt, unsportsmanlike; discriminatory, one-sided, partisan, prejudiced 481 *biased*.

Vb. *do wrong*, wrong, injure 645 *harm*; be hard on 735 *be severe*; not play the game, hit below the belt; break the rules, commit a foul; break the law 954 *be illegal*; wink at, connive at; leave unrighted, deny justice; load the scales, pack *or* rig the jury; lean to one side, discriminate against 481 *be biased*; overcompensate, lean over backwards; commit, perpetrate.

915. Dueness – N. *dueness*, what is due, what is owing; accountability, responsibility, obligation 917 *duty*; from each according to his *or* her ability and to each according to his *or* her need; the least one can do, bare minimum; expectations; dues 804 *payment*; indebtedness 803 *debt*; recognition, acknowledgement 907 *thanks*; case for; qualification, merits, deserts, just d. 913 *right*; justification 927 *vindication*; entitlement, claim, title; birthright 777 *dower*; interest, vested i., prescriptive right, inalienable r.; easement, prescription, ancient lights; human rights, women's r. 744 *freedom*; constitutional right, civil rights, bill of r., Magna Carta; immunity 919 *nonliability*; prerogative, privilege; charter 756 *permit*; liberty, franchise; bond 767 *title deed*; patent, copyright; owner, title-holder 776 *possessor*; plaintiff 763 *petitioner*.

Adj. *due*, payable 803 *owed*; ascribable, attributable, assignable; merited, deserved, earned, coming to one; sanctioned, lawful 756 *permitted*; constitutional, entrenched, unimpeachable, inviolable, sacrosanct; confirmed, vested, prescriptive, inalienable; legitimate, rightful, of right 953 *legal*; claimable, earmarked, reserved; expected, fitting, befitting 913 *right*.

deserving, worthy of, meritorious, emeritus, honoris causa; grant-worthy, credit-w.; justifiable, justified; entitled, having the right.

Vb. *be due*, ought to be, should be, should have been; be one's due, have it coming; be the least one can do; behove, befit, beseem 917 *be one's duty*.

claim, claim as a right, lay claim to, stake a c. 786 *appropriate*; demand one's rights, stand on one's r.; draw on, come down on for, take one's toll; call in (debts), reclaim; sue, demand redress 761 *request*; exercise a right; patent, copyright.

deserve, merit, be worthy, have a claim on; earn, receive one's due, get one's deserts; have it coming to one, have only oneself to thank; sow the wind and reap the whirlwind.

grant claims, give everyone his *or* her due 913 *be just*; credit 158 *attribute*; hand it to, acknowledge 907 *thank*; authorize 756 *permit*; pay one's dues, honour 804 *pay*; legitimize 953 *make legal*.

916. Undueness – N. *undueness*, not the thing, impropriety, unseemliness 847 *bad taste*; illegitimacy 954 *illegality*; no thanks to 908 *ingratitude*; absence of right, nonentitlement; no claim, no right; courtesy title; gratuitousness, gratuity, bonus; inordinacy, excessiveness 637 *redundance*; imposition 735 *severity*; unfair share, lion's s. 32 *main part*.

arrogation, assumption, presumption, unwarranted p., swollen claims; pretendership, usurpation; misappropriation 786 *expropriation*; encroachment, trespass 306 *overstepping*.

loss of right, disentitlement, disfranchisement, disqualification; denaturalization, detribalization; forfeiture 772 *loss*; dismissal, deprivation 752 *deposal*; ouster, dispossession 786 *expropriation*; seizure, forcible s. 788 *stealing*; cancellation 752 *abrogation*; waiver, abdication 621 *relinquishment*.

usurper, arrogator 735 *tyrant*; pretender 545 *impostor*; trespasser, squatter, cuckoo in the nest.

Adj. *undue*, not owing; gratuitous, by favour; unlooked for, uncalled for 508 *unexpected*; inappropriate, improper, unseemly, unbefitting 643 *inexpedient*; preposterous, not to be thought of, out of the question 497 *absurd*.

unwarranted, unwarrantable; unauthorized, unsanctioned, unlicensed, unconstitutional; unrightful, illicit, ultra vires 954 *illegal*; arrogated, usurped; presumptuous 878 *insolent*; unjustified, unjustifiable 914 *wrong*; undeserved, unmerited; invalid; forfeited, forfeit; fictitious, false 542 *spurious*.

unentitled, without title, without qualifications; unworthy, undeserving; underprivileged, unprivileged, without rights, unchartered, unfranchised, voteless; disentitled, dethroned, deposed; disqualified, invalidated, disfranchised, defrocked.

Vb. *be undue*, not be due; misbecome 847 *vulgarize*; presume, arrogate, usurp; trespass, squat 306 *encroach*; infringe, violate 954 *be illegal*.

disentitle, dethrone 752 *depose*; disqualify, disfranchise, alienize, denaturalize, detribalize, denationalize; invalidate, disallow 752 *abrogate*; dispossess 786 *deprive*; declare; forfeit, illegalize 954 *make illegal*; bastardize, debase 655 *impair*.

917. Duty – N. *duty*, the right thing, the decent t.; one's duty, bounden d., obligation, onus, responsibility 915 *dueness*; fealty, allegiance 739 *obedience*; sense of duty, dutifulness; discharge of duty 768 *observance*; call of duty, claims of conscience, case of c.; bond, tie, commitment 764 *promise*; task, office, charge 751 *commission*.

conscience, categorical imperative, inner voice, 'still, small voice', 'stern daughter of the voice of God'.

code of duty, code of honour, unwritten code, professional c.; Ten Commandments, Hippocratic oath 693 *precept*.

morals, morality 933 *virtue*; honour 929 *probity*; moral principles, ideals, standards; ethics; ethology, deontology, casuistry, moral philosophy, moral science; idealism, humanism.

Adj. *obliged*, duty-bound; on duty; in the line of duty; obligated, beholden, under obligation; sworn, pledged; unexempted, liable, answerable, responsible, accountable; in honour bound, bound in conscience; conscientious 768 *observant*; duteous, dutiful 739 *obedient*; under a vow.

obligatory, incumbent, up to one; binding, de rigueur, compulsory 740 *compelling*; inescapable, unavoidable; strict, unconditional, categorical.

ethical, moral 933 *virtuous*; honest, decent 929 *honourable*; moralistic, ethological, casuistical; humanistic, idealistic.

Vb. *be one's duty*, be incumbent, behove, become, befit 915 *be due*; devolve on, belong to, be up to, pertain to, fall to, be part of the job; lie at one's door, rest with.

incur a duty, take on oneself, accept responsibility, shoulder one's r.; commit oneself 764 *promise*; owe it to oneself, feel duty's call, submit to one's vocation.

do one's duty, fulfil one's d. 739 *obey*;

discharge, acquit, perform 676 *do*; do one's bit, play one's part; discharge one's functions 768 *observe*; be on duty, stay at one's post, go down with one's ship; come up to what is expected, not be found wanting; meet one's obligations, make good one's promise, be as good as one's word.

impose a duty, require, oblige, look to, call upon; call to office 751 *commission*; saddle with, detail, order 737 *command*; tax, exact; bind, condition 766 *give terms*.

918. Undutifulness – N. *undutifulness*, default, dereliction of duty; laches, culpable negligence 458 *negligence*; unduteousness 921 *disrespect*; malingering, cop-out 620 *avoidance*; nonpractice 769 *nonobservance*; idleness, laziness 679 *sluggishness*; forgetfulness 506 *oblivion*; noncooperation 598 *unwillingness*; truancy, absenteeism; absconding 667 *escape*; infraction, indiscipline, mutiny, rebellion 738 *disobedience*; desertion, defection 603 *change of allegiance*; disloyalty 930 *perfidy*; irresponsibility, escapism; truant, absentee, malingerer, defaulter 620 *avoider*; slacker 679 *idler*; deserter, absconder 667 *escaper*; traitor 603 *turncoat*; mutineer 738 *revolter*.

Adj. *undutiful*, uncooperative 598 *unwilling*; unduteous, unfilial, undaughterly 921 *disrespectful*; mutinous, rebellious 738 *disobedient*; disloyal, treacherous 930 *perfidious*; irresponsible, unreliable; truant 190 *absent*; absconding 667 *escaped*.

Vb. *fail in duty*, neglect one's d., ignore one's obligations 458 *disregard*; oversleep 679 *sleep*; default, let one down, leave one in the lurch 509 *disappoint*; mismanage, bungle 495 *blunder*, 506 *forget*; shirk, wriggle out of, malinger 620 *avoid*; wash one's hands of, pass the buck 919 *be exempt*; play truant 190 *be absent*; abscond 667 *escape*; quit, scarper 296 *decamp*; abandon, desert, desert the colours 621 *relinquish*; disobey orders, exceed one's instructions 738 *disobey*; mutiny 738 *revolt*; be disloyal 603 *tergiversate*; noncooperate, withdraw, walk out.

919. Nonliability – N. *nonliability*, nonresponsibility, exemption, dispensation; conscience clause, force majeure 468 *qualification*; immunity, impunity, privilege, special treatment; extraterritoriality, diplomatic immunity; licence, leave 756 *permission*; aegrotat, certificate of exemption 756 *permit*; excuse 960 *acquittal*; pardon, amnesty 909 *forgiveness*; discharge, release 746 *liberation*; renunciation 621 *relinquishment*; evasion of responsibility 753 *resignation*.

Adj. *nonliable*, not responsible, not answerable, unaccountable; excused 960 *acquitted*; dispensed, exempted, privileged; shielded, protected; untouched, exempt, immune; unaffected, well out of; independent, free-born 744 *free*; tax-free 812 *uncharged*.

Vb. *exempt*, set apart, set aside; count out, rule o. 57 *exclude*; excuse 960 *acquit*; absolve, pardon 909 *forgive*; spare 905 *show mercy*; grant immunity 756 *permit*; license, dispense; amnesty, set at liberty 746 *liberate*; pass over, stretch a point 736 *be lenient*.

be exempt, have no liability, not come within the scope of; enjoy immunity; spare oneself the necessity, exempt oneself, excuse oneself; pass the buck, shift the blame 272 *transfer*; escape liability, get away with 667 *escape*; admit no responsibility 918 *fail in duty*.

920. Respect – N. *respect*, regard, consideration, esteem 923 *approbation*; high standing, honour, favour 866 *repute*; attentions 884 *courtesy*; due respect, deference 872 *humility*; obsequiousness 879 *servility*; humble service 739 *loyalty*; admiration, awe 864 *wonder*, 854 *fear*; reverence 981 *worship*.

respects, regards, duty, kind regards, greetings 884 *courteous act*; red carpet, guard of honour, address of welcome, salutation, salaam; bob, bow, curtsy, genuflexion, obeisance; reverence, homage; salute, presenting arms.

Adj. *respectful*, deferential, cap in hand 872 *humble*; obsequious 879 *servile*; submissive 721 *submitting*; reverent 981

worshipping; admiring, awestruck 864 *wondering*; polite 884 *courteous*; ceremonious, at the salute, cap in hand, bareheaded; on one's knees, prostrate; bowing, scraping; rising, standing, on one's feet.

respected, esteemed, revered 866 *reputable*; respectable, reverend, venerable; time-honoured 866 *worshipful*; imposing 821 *impressive*.

Vb. *respect*, entertain r. for, hold in r., think well of, rank high, look up to, esteem, regard, value; admire 864 *wonder*; reverence, venerate 866 *honour*; adore 981 *worship*; revere, stand in awe of, have a wholesome respect for 854 *fear*; know one's place, defer to 721 *submit*; pay tribute to, take one's hat off to 923 *praise*; make much of, lionize, carry shoulder-high 876 *celebrate*.

show respect, pay homage 884 *pay one's respects*; welcome, hail, salute, present arms, turn out the guard, roll out the red carpet; cheer, drink to 876 *toast*; bob, duck, bow, bow and scrape, curtsy, kneel, kowtow, prostrate oneself 884 *greet*; stand on ceremony, rise to one's feet, uncover.

command respect, awe, impose 821 *impress*; rank high 866 *have a reputation*; command admiration 864 *be wonderful*; dazzle 875 *be ostentatious*; gain a reputation.

921. Disrespect – N. *disrespect*, want of respect, irreverence, impoliteness 885 *rudeness*; disfavour 924 *disapprobation*; undervaluation 483 *underestimation*; low esteem 867 *disrepute*; disparagement 926 *detraction*; contumely 899 *scurrility*; scorn 922 *contempt*; mockery 851 *ridicule*; desecration 980 *impiety*.

indignity, humiliation, affront, insult, slight, snub, slap in the face, outrage 878 *insolence*; snook, V-sign 878 *sauciness*; gibe, taunt, jeer 922 *contempt*; quip, sarcasm 851 *ridicule*; catcall, brickbat, rotten eggs 924 *disapprobation*.

Adj. *disrespectful*, neglectful 458 *negligent*; insubordinate 738 *disobedient*; irreverent 980 *profane*; rude, impolite 885 *discourteous*; offhand, offhanded, familiar, cheeky, saucy 878 *impertinent*; insulting 878 *insolent*; sarcastic 851 *derisive*; injurious, contumelious 899 *cursing*; denigratory, depreciative, pejorative 483 *depreciating*; supercilious 922 *despising*; uncomplimentary 924 *disapproving*.

unrespected, held in low esteem, of no account 867 *disreputable*; ignored, disregarded 458 *neglected*; underrated, undervalued; looked down on 922 *contemptible*.

Vb. *not respect*, be disrespectful; have no respect for, have no regard f. 924 *disapprove*; misprize 483 *underestimate*; have a low opinion of 922 *despise*; denigrate, disparage 926 *defame*; show disrespect, lack courtesy, remain seated, remain covered; crowd, jostle 885 *be rude*; ignore, snub, slight 872 *humiliate*; dishonour, disgrace, drag in the mud 867 *shame*; trifle with 922 *hold cheap*; cheapen, lower, degrade 847 *vulgarize*; desecrate, profane 980 *be impious*; call names 899 *curse*; taunt, twit 878 *be insolent*; guy, mock 851 *ridicule*; make mouths at, jeer, hiss, boo 924 *disapprove*; mob 619 *pursue*; pelt, stone, heave a brick 712 *lapidate*.

922. Contempt – N. *contempt*, scorn; disdain, disdainfulness, superiority 871 *pride*; contemptuousness, sniffiness; snobbishness 850 *affectation*; curl of the lip, snort, sniff; slight 921 *indignity*; sneer, dig at 926 *detraction*; derision 851 *ridicule*; snub, rebuff 885 *discourtesy*.

contemptibility, unworthiness, insignificance, futility 639 *unimportance*; pettiness, meanness, paltriness 33 *smallness*; cause for shame, byword of reproach.

Adj. *despising*, contemptuous, disdainful, holier than thou, snooty, snuffy, sniffy, snobbish; haughty, supercilious 871 *proud*; scornful, withering, sneering 924 *disapproving*; disrespectful, impertinent 878 *insolent*; pooh-poohing 483 *depreciating*.

contemptible, despicable, beneath contempt; abject, worthless 645 *bad*; petty, paltry, mean; spurned, spat on 607 *rejected*; scorned, despised 921 *unrespected*; trifling, pitiable, futile 639 *unimportant*.

Vb. *despise*, contemn, hold in contempt

921 *not respect*; look down on, consider beneath one, be too good for 871 *be proud*; disdain, spurn, sniff at 607 *reject*; come it over, turn up one's nose, wrinkle one's n., curl one's lip, toss one's head, snort; snub 885 *be rude*; whistle, hiss, boo, point at 924 *reprobate*; to scorn, scoff, jeer, mock, deride 851 *ridicule*; ride roughshod over 735 *oppress*.

hold cheap, have a low opinion of 921 *not respect*; ignore, dismiss, discount, take no account of 458 *disregard*; belittle, disparage 483 *underestimate*; decry 926 *detract*; set no value on, set no store by, think nothing *or* small beer of, not care a rap *or* a straw; snap one's fingers at, shrug away, pooh-pooh; slight, trifle with, treat like dirt 872 *humiliate*.

923. Approbation – N. *approbation*, approval, satisfaction 828 *content*; appreciation 907 *gratitude*; good opinion, kudos, credit 866 *prestige*; regard, admiration, esteem 920 *respect*; good books, good graces, grace, favour 887 *love*; adoption, acceptance, welcome, favourable reception; sanction 756 *permission*; nod of approval, blessing; thumbs up, consent 488 *assent*; patronage, advocacy 703 *aid*; friendly notice, favourable review 480 *estimate*; good word, kind w., testimonial, reference 466 *credential*.

praise, laud, laudation, benediction, blessing; compliment, encomium, eulogy, panegyric; adulation 925 *flattery*; hero worship 864 *wonder*; overpraise 482 *overestimation*; faint praise, two cheers; shout of praise, hosanna, alleluia; song of praise, paean of p., dithyramb, doxology, Gloria; tribute, credit, due credit 907 *thanks*; bouquet, accolade, citation, honourable mention, commendation, glowing terms; hagiography; self-praise 877 *boasting*; puff, blurb 528 *advertisement*.

applause, acclaim, universal a.; enthusiasm 821 *excitation*; hero's welcome 876 *celebration*; acclamation, plaudits, clapping, stamping, whistling, cheering; clap, three cheers; thunderous applause, round of a., ovation, standing o.; encore, curtain call; pat on the back.

commender, praiser, laudator, encomiast, eulogist, panegyrist; claqueur, claque; approver, admirer, heroworshipper, fan club; advocate, supporter 707 *patron*; blurbwriter, puffer, booster 528 *publicizer*; canvasser, electioneer.

Adj. *approving*, uncomplaining, satisfied 828 *content*; favouring, supporting; appreciative 907 *grateful*; approbatory, favourable, friendly, well-inclined; complimentary, commendatory, laudatory, eulogistic, encomiastic, panegyrical, lyrical; admiring; idolatrous; fulsome, uncritical, undiscriminating; acclamatory, clapping, thunderous 400 *loud*; dithyrambic, ecstatic, in raptures 821 *excited*.

approvable, admissible, permissible, acceptable; worthwhile 640 *useful*; deserving, meritorious, commendable, laudable, estimable, worthy, praiseworthy, creditable, admirable, unimpeachable 646 *perfect*; enviable, desirable 859 *desired*.

approved, passed, tested, tried; stamped with approval, blessed; popular, in favour, in the good graces of, in good odour, thought well of 866 *reputable*; favoured, backed 605 *chosen*.

Vb. *approve*, think highly of 920 *respect*; like well 887 *love*; think well of, admire, esteem, set store by 866 *honour*; appreciate, give credit, salute, take one's hat off to, hand it to, give full marks; count it to one's credit; think the best, award the palm; pronounce good, give the seal *or* stamp of approval; accept, pass, tick; nod one's approval 488 *assent*; sanction, give one's blessing 756 *permit*; ratify 488 *endorse*; commend, recommend, advocate, support, back, favour, put in a good word for 703 *patronize*.

praise, compliment 925 *flatter*; speak well of, speak highly of, swear by; bless 907 *thank*; pay tribute to, commend, laud, eulogize, panegyrize, praise to the skies, hymn the praises, doxologize, exalt, extol, glorify, magnify; wax lyrical, get carried away; not spare one's blushes 546 *exaggerate*; puff, inflate 482 *overrate*; lionize 982 *idolatrize*; trumpet, cry up, hype up, crack up 528 *advertise*.

applaud, welcome, hail, acclaim; clap,

give a big hand, stamp, whistle, bring the house down, raise the roof; cheer, give three cheers; cheer to the echo, shout for, root for; clap *or* pat on the back; congratulate, garland, chair 876 *celebrate*; drink to 876 *toast*.

924. Disapprobation – N. *disapprobation*, disapproval 829 *discontent*; nonapproval, return 607 *rejection*; no permission 760 *refusal*; disfavour, unpopularity 861 *dislike*; low opinion 921 *disrespect*; bad books 867 *disrepute*; disparagement 926 *detraction*; fault-finding 862 *fastidiousness*; hostility 881 *enmity*; cavil 468 *qualification*; outcry, protest, tut-tut 762 *deprecation*; indignation 891 *anger*; hiss, boo, slow handclap, whistle, catcall 851 *ridicule*; ostracism, boycott, bar 57 *exclusion*; blackball, blacklist, Index.

censure, dispraise, blame 928 *accusation*; home truth, left-handed compliment, back-handed c.; criticism, hostile c., stricture; fault-finding; bad press, critical review, slating; open letter, tirade, jeremiad, philippic, diatribe 704 *opposition*; insinuation, innuendo 926 *calumny*; brand, stigma.

reproach, recriminations 709 *quarrel*; home truths, invective, vituperation 899 *scurrility*; execration 899 *malediction*; personal remarks 921 *indignity*; taunt 878 *insolence*; dig, cut 851 *ridicule*; tonguelashing, hard words (see *reprimand*); disapproving look, dirty l., black l.

reprimand, remonstrance 762 *deprecation*; stricture, animadversion, reprehension, reprobation; censure, rebuke, reproof, snub; rocket, raspberry; piece of one's mind; black mark; castigation, rap over the knuckles 963 *punishment*; admonition, admonishment, tonguelashing, scolding, dressing down, roasting, wigging, carpeting, mauvais quart d'heure; talking to, lecture, jobation.

disapprover, no admirer; nonsupporter; damper, wet blanket, spoilsport, misery 834 *moper*; puritan, rigorist 950 *prude*; opposer 705 *opponent*; critic, hostile c., knocker, fault-finder; reprover, castigator, censurer 926 *detractor*; misogynist 902 *misanthrope*; grouser 829 *malcontent*.

Adj. *disapproving*, not amused, shocked, scandalized; unadmiring, unimpressed; disapprobatory, unfavourable, hostile 881 *inimical*; objecting 762 *deprecatory*; reproachful, chiding, scolding; critical, unflattering, uncomplimentary; withering, hard-hitting; overcritical, hypercritical, captious, fault-finding, niggling, carping; disparaging 926 *detracting*; caustic, trenchant, mordant; sarcastic 851 *derisive*; censorious, holier than thou; censuring, recriminative 928 *accusing*.

disapproved, blacklisted, blackballed 607 *rejected*; unsatisfactory, ploughed, failed 728 *unsuccessful*; deleted, censored 550 *obliterated*; out of favour, under a cloud; dispraised, criticized, decried, run down; lectured, henpecked, nagged; on the mat, on the carpet; unlamented 861 *disliked*; hooted, hissed off the stage; discredited, disowned, out; in bad odour 867 *disreputable*.

blameworthy, not good enough, too bad; open to criticism, censurable 645 *bad*; reprehensible, dishonourable, unjustifiable 867 *discreditable*; unpraiseworthy, not to be recommended, not to be thought of; culpable, to blame 928 *accusable*.

Vb. *disapprove*, not admire, hold no brief for, fail to appreciate, not think much of, take a dim view of; think the worse of, think ill of 922 *despise*; not pass, fail, plough; return 607 *reject*; disallow 757 *prohibit*; cancel 752 *abrogate*; censor 550 *obliterate*; withhold approval, shake one's head, not hold with 489 *dissent*; reprehend, deplore 830 *regret*; abhor, reprobate 861 *dislike*; wash one's hands of, disown; keep at a distance, draw the line, blacklist 57 *exclude*; protest, remonstrate, take exception to 762 *deprecate*; discountenance, show disapproval, shout down, bawl d., hoot, boo, bay, heckle, hiss, whistle, give the bird; throw bricks 712 *lapidate*; make a face, make a moue; look daggers 891 *be angry*.

dispraise, not recommend, damn with faint praise; criticize, find fault, pick

holes, niggle, crab, cavil, depreciate, run down, belittle, pan 926 *detract*; tilt at, shoot at, throw the book at 712 *attack*; weigh in, pitch into, hit out at, lay into, savage, maul, slash, slate, scourge, flay, put the boot in; inveigh, thunder, fulminate, storm against 61 *rampage*; shout down, cry shame, slang, call names; gird, rail, revile, abuse 899 *curse*; vilify, blacken 926 *defame*; stigmatize, brand, pillory; expose, denounce 928 *accuse*; twit, taunt 921 *not respect*.

reprove, reprehend, reproach, rebuke, snub; call to order, caution, wag one's finger, read the Riot Act 664 *warn*; book, give one a black mark; censure, reprimand, take to task, rap over the knuckles, box the ears; tick off, tell off, have one's head for, carpet, have on the carpet, haul over the coals; remonstrate, expostulate, admonish, castigate, chide, correct; lecture, give one a talking to *or* a wigging, give one a dressing-down, lambaste, trounce, roast, browbeat, blow up, tear a strip off, come down hard on, come down on like a ton of bricks, chastise 963 *punish*.

blame, find fault, carp, pick holes in; get at, henpeck 709 *bicker*; reprehend, hold to blame, pick on, hold responsible; inculpate, incriminate 928 *accuse*; round on, recriminate 714 *retaliate*.

reprobate, reproach, upbraid, slate, rate, berate, rail, revile, abuse, blackguard 899 *curse*; go for, inveigh against, bawl out, scold, tongue-lash, excoriate, give the rough edge of one's tongue, rail in good set terms against, give one a piece of one's mind, give one what for, give it to one straight from the shoulder, not pull one's punches.

incur blame, take the blame, take the rap, carry the can, catch it; be held responsible, have to answer for; blot one's copy book, get a bad name 867 *lose repute*; be up on a charge, stand accused; stand corrected; scandalize 861 *cause dislike*.

925. Flattery – N. *flattery*, cajolery, taffy, blarney, blandishments, sweet talk; flannel, soft soap, soft sawder, salve, lipsalve, rosewater, incense, adulation; honeyed words, sweet nothings 889 *endearment*; compliment, pretty speeches; coquetry; winning ways; fawning, backscratching; sycophancy 879 *servility*; unctuousness, insincerity 542 *sham*.

flatterer, adulator, cajoler, wheedler; coquette, charmer; claque 923 *commender*; courtier, yes-man 488 *assenter*; creep, sycophant, hanger-on 879 *toady*; fair-weather friend, hypocrite 545 *deceiver*.

Adj. *flattering*, overpraising 546 *exaggerated*; complimentary, fulsome, adulatory; sugary, saccharine; smooth-tongued, honey-t., bland; smooth, oily, unctuous, soapy, slimy, smarmy; obsequious, sycophantic 879 *servile*; ingratiating, insinuating; lulling, soothing; vote-catching, vote-snatching; insincere 541 *hypocritical*.

Vb. *flatter*, compliment 923 *praise*; overdo it, lay it on thick *or* with a trowel, not spare one's blushes; cry up 482 *overrate*; adulate, turn one's head; butter up, soft-soap; blarney, flannel; sweet-talk, sugar; wheedle, coax, cajole; lull, soothe, beguile 542 *deceive*; humour, jolly along, pander to; blandish, smarm; press the flesh, make much of, be all over one 889 *caress*; fawn on, cultivate, court, massage one's ego; curry favour, make up to, suck up to; toady to 879 *be servile*; insinuate oneself, get on the right side of, creep into one's good graces; flatter oneself 873 *be vain*.

926. Detraction – N. *detraction*, faint praise, two cheers 483 *underestimation*; criticism, bad press 924 *disapprobation*; vivisection, hatchet job; exposure, bad light 867 *disrepute*; decrial, disparagement, depreciation, running down; slighting language, scorn 922 *contempt*; contumely, obloquy, vilification 899 *scurrility*; calumniation, defamation 543 *untruth*; backbiting, cattiness, spite 898 *malevolence*; aspersion, reflection, snide remark (**see** *calumny*); innuendo, insinuation, imputation, whispering campaign; smear campaign, mud-slinging, denigration, character assassination; brand, stigma; muck-raking, scandal-mongering; nil admirari 865 *lack of wonder*.

calumny, slander, libel, false report 543 *untruth*; defamatory remark, smear, dirty word 867 *slur*; offensive remark, personal r., personality, insult 921 *indignity*; sneer, sarcasm 851 *ridicule*; caricature 552 *misrepresentation*; lampoon 851 *satire*; scandal, malicious gossip, bad mouth.

detractor, decrier, disparager, depreciator; nonadmirer, debunker, deflater; mocker, scoffer, satirizer, satirist, lampooner; castigator, denouncer 924 *disapprover*; no respecter of persons, no flatterer; critic, attacker 928 *accuser*; knocker, fault-finder, caviller, nit-picker; heckler, barracker.

defamer, calumniator, traducer, hatchet man; slanderer, libeller; backbiter, gossiper, scandal-monger, muck-raker; gossip columnist, gutter press; denigrator, mud-slinger; poison pen.

Adj. *detracting*, derogatory, pejorative; disparaging, depreciatory, slighting 922 *despising*; denigratory, smearing; compromising, damaging; scandalous, calumnious, calumniatory, defamatory, slanderous, libellous; insulting 921 *disrespectful*; contumelious, injurious; denunciatory, castigatory 924 *disapproving*; sarcastic, sneering, snide 851 *derisive*; catty, spiteful 898 *malevolent*; unflattering, candid.

Vb. *detract*, derogate, depreciate, disparage, run down, sell short; debunk, deflate, puncture, cut down to size 921 *not respect*; minimize 483 *underestimate*; belittle, slight 922 *hold cheap*; sneer at, sniff at 922 *despise*; decry, cry down, damn with faint praise 924 *disapprove*; criticize, knock, slam, fault, find f., slate, pull to pieces, tear to ribbons 924 *dispraise*; caricature, guy 552 *misrepresent*; lampoon 851 *satirize*; scoff, mock, get in a dig at 851 *ridicule*; whisper, insinuate, cast aspersions.

defame, dishonour, damage, compromise 867 *shame*; give a dog a bad name, destroy one's good name; denounce, expose, pillory, stigmatize, brand 928 *accuse*; calumniate, libel, slander, traduce, malign; vilify, denigrate, speak ill of, gossip, badmouth, talk about, backbite, talk behind one's back; discredit 486 *cause doubt*; smear, smirch, drag in the gutter 649 *make unclean*; witch-hunt, muckrake.

927. Vindication – N. *vindication,* restoration, rehabilitation; triumph of justice, right triumphant; exoneration, exculpation 960 *acquittal*; justification, good grounds, just cause, every excuse; compurgation, apologia, defence; alibi, excuse 614 *pretext*; extenuation, palliation, mitigation, mitigating circumstance 468 *qualification*; counterargument 479 *confutation*; rebuttal 460 *rejoinder*.

vindicator, punisher 910 *avenger*; apologist, advocate, defender, champion; justifier, excuser; compurgator 466 *witness*.
   Adj. *vindicating,* vindicatory, vindicative, avenging; apologetic, exculpatory; extenuatory, mitigating, palliative.

vindicable, justifiable, defensible, arguable; specious, plausible; allowable, excusable, pardonable, venial; justified, within one's rights; not guilty 935 *innocent*.
   Vb. *vindicate,* do justice to 915 *grant claims*; set right, restore, rehabilitate; maintain, speak up for 475 *argue*; bear out, confirm 478 *demonstrate*; champion 713 *defend*, 703 *patronize*.

justify, warrant, give grounds for, furnish an excuse, give a handle, give one cause; put one in the right *or* in the clear, clear, exonerate, exculpate 960 *acquit*; give colour to, whitewash; salve one's conscience 614 *plead*; plead ignorance.

extenuate, excuse, make excuses for, make allowances; palliate, mitigate, slur over, gloss over; take the will for the deed 736 *be lenient*.

928. Accusation – N. *accusation,* complaint, charge, home truth; censure, blame, stricture 924 *reproach*; challenge 711 *defiance*; inculpation, crimination; countercharge, recrimination 460 *rejoin-*

der; imputation, allegation, information, denunciation; plaint 959 *litigation*; prosecution, impeachment, arraignment, indictment, summons; case to answer.

false charge, faked c., cooked-up c., trumped-up c., put-up job, frame-up; false information, counterfeit evidence, plant; lie, libel 926 *calumny*.

accuser, complainant, plaintiff, petitioner, appellant, libellant, litigant; challenger, denouncer, charger; grass, nark 524 *informer*; impeacher, indicter, prosecutor, public p., procurator fiscal; libeller, slanderer 926 *defamer*; hostile witness 881 *enemy*; the finger of suspicion.

accused person, the accused, prisoner, prisoner at the bar; defendant, respondent, corespondent; culprit, suspect; libellee, victim.
   Adj. *accusing,* accusatory, denunciatory, criminatory, recriminatory; incriminating, pointing to; imputative; talebearing, calumnious, defamatory 926 *detracting*; suspicious 924 *disapproving*.

accused, informed against, suspect; under suspicion, under a cloud; up on a charge, hauled up, booked, summoned; awaiting trial; slandered 924 *disapproved*.

accusable, imputable; actionable, suable, chargeable, justiciable; unjustifiable 924 *blameworthy*; undefended 661 *vulnerable*.
   Vb. *accuse,* challenge 711 *defy*; point a finger at, cast the first stone, throw in one's teeth, reproach 924 *reprove*; cast a slur on 926 *defame*; impute, charge with, saddle w., tax w., hold against, lay to one's charge, lay at one's door, put the blame on, pin on 924 *blame*; point at, expose, show up, name names 526 *divulge*; denounce, inform against, tell on 524 *inform*; involve, implicate, inculpate, incriminate; recriminate, countercharge 479 *confute*.

indict, impeach, arraign, inform against, lodge a complaint, lay an information against; charge, bring a charge 959 *litigate*; book, cite, summon, prosecute, sue; bring an action, haul up, put on trial, put in the dock; throw the book at; frame, trump up a charge 541 *fake*.

929. Probity – N. *probity*, rectitude, uprightness, goodness 933 *virtue*; stainlessness 950 *purity*; good character, moral fibre, honesty, incorruptibility, integrity; nobleness, nobility; decent feelings, tender conscience; honour, principles; conscientiousness, scrupulosity; trustworthiness, reliability; truthfulness 540 *veracity*; sincerity, good faith 494 *truth*; fidelity 739 *loyalty*; clean hands 935 *innocence*; impartiality 913 *justice*; respectability 866 *repute*; gentlemanliness, chivalry; principle, point of honour, punctilio, code, bushido 913 *right*.

honourable person, honest p., man of honour, woman of her word, sound character, trusty soul 937 *good person*; true lady, perfect gentleman, preux chevalier; fair fighter, clean f., good loser, sportsman, sportswoman, sport, good sport, good sort, true Brit.

Adj. *honourable*, upright, erect 933 *virtuous*; correct, strict; law-abiding, honest, on the level; principled, high-p., on the up-and-up; scrupulous, conscientious; incorruptible, unbribable; immaculate 935 *innocent*; stainless, unsullied 648 *clean*; noble, high-minded 950 *pure*; guileless 699 *artless*; good, straight, on the square; fair 913 *just*; sporting, sportsmanlike; gentlemanly, chivalrous; respectable 866 *reputable*; saintly 979 *pious*.

trustworthy, reliable, dependable, tried, tested, proven; trusty, true, true-blue, sure, staunch, constant, faithful, loyal 739 *obedient*; responsible, duteous 768 *observant*; conscientious, scrupulous 457 *careful*; candid, frank, open, open and above-board, open-hearted 494 *true*; straightforward, truthful, as good as one's word 540 *veracious*.

Vb. *be honourable*, behave well 933 *be virtuous*; deal honourably, play fair 913 *be just*; fear God 979 *be pious*; keep faith, keep one's promise; speak the truth 540 *be truthful*; go straight 654 *get better*.

930. Improbity – N. *improbity*, dishonesty; lack of principle, suppleness, laxity; unconscientiousness 456 *inattention*; unscrupulousness, opportunism; insincerity,

disingenuousness, untrustworthiness, unreliability, undependability, untruthfulness 541 *falsehood*; unfairness 914 *injustice*; shuffling, slipperiness; deviousness, crooked paths; corruption, venality, graft, jobbery, nepotism, simony, barratry; Tammanyism; baseness, shabbiness, shame 867 *disrepute*; worthlessness, villainy, knavery, roguery; spivvery, skulduggery, racketeering; criminality 954 *lawbreaking*; turpitude, moral t. 934 *wickedness*.

perfidy, unfaithfulness, infidelity 543 *untruth*; bad faith; divided allegiance, disloyalty 738 *disobedience*; double-dealing, Judas kiss 541 *duplicity*; volte-face 603 *change of allegiance*; defection, desertion 918 *undutifulness*; treachery, stab in the back, sellout; treason 738 *sedition*; breach of faith, broken word, broken promise, breach of p., scrap of paper.

foul play, dirty trick, foul 914 *wrong*; professional foul 623 *contrivance*; trick, chicanery 542 *trickery*; practice, sharp p., heads I win tails you lose; fishy transaction, dirty work, job, deal, ramp, racket; fiddle, wangle, gerrymandering, hanky-panky, monkey business; tax evasion 620 *avoidance*; malversation 788 *peculation*; crime, felony 954 *lawbreaking*.

Adj. *dishonest*, not on the level 914 *wrong*; unprincipled, unscrupulous, conscienceless; shameless, lost to shame; unethical, immoral 934 *wicked*; untrustworthy, unreliable, undependable, not to be trusted; supple, flexible 603 *trimming*; disingenuous, untruthful 543 *untrue*; two-faced 541 *hypocritical*; tricky, opportunist, slippery 698 *cunning*; shifty 518 *equivocal*; designing, scheming; underhand 523 *latent*; up to something, on the fiddle; not straight, bent, crooked, devious; sinister, shady, fishy, suspicious, doubtful, questionable; fraudulent 542 *spurious*; illicit 954 *illegal*; foul 645 *bad*; mean, shabby, dishonourable 867 *disreputable*; unworthy, inglorious 867 *degrading*; ignoble, unchivalrous, ungentlemanly; unsporting, unsportsmanlike, unfair.

rascally, criminal 954 *lawless*; knavish, picaresque, spivvish; infamous, blackguard, villainous; scurvy, low, base, vile; mean, shabby, paltry, wretched, contemptible.

venal, corruptible, purchasable, bribable, hireling, mercenary, bought; corrupt, jobbing, grafting, simoniacal, nepotistic; barratrous.

perfidious, treacherous, faithless 541 *false*; double-crossing, time-serving 541 *hypocritical*; disloyal 603 *tergiversating*; false-hearted, guileful, traitorous, treasonous, treasonable, disloyal, untrue 738 *disobedient*; plotting, scheming; insidious, dark, Machiavellian; cheating 542 *deceiving*.

Vb. *be dishonest*, have no morals, forget one's principles, yield to temptation; live by one's wits, lead a life of crime 954 *be illegal*; fiddle, finagle, wangle, gerrymander, racketeer; peculate 788 *defraud*; cheat, swindle 542 *deceive*; betray, play false, do the dirty on, stab in the back; double-cross 541 *dissemble*; fawn 925 *flatter*; break faith, break one's word, tell lies 541 *be false*; shuffle 518 *be equivocal*; sell out 603 *apostatize*; stoop to 867 *lose repute*; smack of dishonesty, smell fishy.

931. Disinterestedness – N. *disinterestedness*, impartiality 913 *justice*; unselfishness, selflessness, self-effacement 872 *humility*; self-control, self-abnegation, self-denial, self-sacrifice, self-immolation, martyrdom; heroism, stoicism 855 *courage*; idealism, high ideals; sublimity, loftiness, nobility, magnanimity; chivalry, quixotry; generosity, liberality 897 *benevolence*; dedication, consecration, labour of love; loyalty, faithfulness 929 *probity*; patriotism 901 *philanthropy*; altruism, thought for others, consideration 884 *courtesy*; charity 887 *love*.

Adj. *disinterested*, impartial 913 *just*; incorruptible, honest 929 *honourable*; self-effacing 872 *humble*; unpossessive, unenvious, unselfish, selfless, self-forgetful; self-sacrificing, ready to die for, devoted, dedicated; loyal, faithful; heroic 855 *courageous*; thoughtful, considerate 884 *courteous*; altruistic, philanthropic 897 *benevolent*; undesigning; non-

profitmaking; idealistic, quixotic, high-minded, lofty, elevated, sublime, noble, great-hearted, magnanimous, chivalrous, knightly; generous, liberal 781 *giving*.

Vb. *be disinterested*, make a sacrifice, sacrifice oneself, devote o., live for, die f.; do as one would be done by, think of others, take a back seat 872 *be humble*; rise above oneself; have no axe to grind, have nothing to gain, do for its own sake.

932. Selfishness – N. *selfishness*, self-love, self-admiration, narcissism, self-worship 873 *vanity*; self-pity, self-indulgence, ego trip 943 *intemperance*; self-absorption, egocentricity; egoism, egotism, individualism, particularism; self-preservation, everyone for themselves; axe to grind, private ends, personal advantage; self-seeking, self-serving, self-aggrandizement, self-interest, concern for number one; no thought for others, 'I'm all right, Jack'; cupboard love; illiberality, mean-mindedness; miserliness 816 *parsimony*; acquisitiveness 816 *avarice*; possessiveness 911 *jealousy*; worldliness, worldly wisdom; careerism, naked ambition, power politics.

egotist, egoist, self-centred person, narcissist 873 *vain person*; particularist, individualist; self-seeker; careerist, arriviste, go-getter, adventurer, gold-digger, fortune-hunter; miser 816 *niggard*; monopolist, dog in the manger, hog, road h.; opportunist, time-server, worldling.

Adj. *selfish*, egocentric, self-centred, self-absorbed, wrapped up in oneself; egoistic, egotistic; individualistic; self-regarding, self-considering, self-seeking; self-indulgent 943 *intemperate*; self-admiring, narcissistic 873 *vain*; unphilanthropic, unneighbourly; unpatriotic, uncharitable, unsympathetic 898 *unkind*; mean-minded, ungenerous 816 *parsimonious*; acquisitive, mercenary 816 *avaricious*; venal 930 *dishonest*; covetous 912 *envious*; hoggish 859 *greedy*; possessive, dog-in-the-manger 911 *jealous*; self-serving, designing; go-getting, on the make, opportunist, careerist; unidealistic, materialistic, worldly.

Vb. *be selfish*, put oneself first, think only of oneself, take care of number one; indulge oneself, cosset o.; feather one's nest, look out for oneself, have an eye to the main chance; keep for oneself, hang on to, hog, monopolize, be a dog in the manger 778 *retain*; have personal motives, have an axe to grind, have one's own game to play; advance one's own interests, sacrifice the interests of others.

933. Virtue – N. *virtue*, virtuousness, goodness; saintliness 979 *sanctity*; righteousness 913 *justice*; uprightness, rectitude, moral r., integrity 929 *probity*; stainlessness, irreproachability; guiltlessness 935 *innocence*; morality, ethics 917 *morals*; temperance, chastity 950 *purity*; straight and narrow, virtuous conduct, good behaviour, good conscience.

virtues, cardinal v., moral v., moral laws; theological virtues, faith, hope, charity; natural virtues, prudence, justice, temperance, fortitude; qualities, saving grace; a virtue, good fault, fault on the right side; worth, merit, desert; excellence 646 *perfection*; idealism, ideals 931 *disinterestedness*; self-control 942 *temperance*.

Adj. *virtuous*, moral 917 *ethical*; good, good as gold 644 *excellent*; stainless, without a spot on one's character 950 *pure*; guiltless 935 *innocent*; irreproachable, impeccable, above temptation 646 *perfect*; saintly 979 *sanctified*; well-principled, right-minded, on the side of the angels 913 *right*; righteous 913 *just*; upright, sterling, honest 929 *honourable*; dutiful 739 *obedient*; unselfish 931 *disinterested*; well-intentioned 897 *benevolent*; sober, chaste 942 *temperate*; proper, edifying, improving, exemplary; elevated, sublimated; meritorious, worthy 923 *approved*.

Vb. *be virtuous*, have all the virtues, be a shining light 644 *be good*; behave, be on one's best behaviour; resist temptation 942 *be temperate*; keep to the straight and narrow, follow one's conscience; discharge one's obligations 917 *do one's duty*; go straight 929 *be honourable*; hear no evil, see no evil, speak no evil; set a good example 644 *do good*.

934. Wickedness – N. *wickedness*, evil 645 *badness*; Devil, cloven hoof 969 *Satan*; fallen nature, Old Adam; unrighteousness, iniquity, sinfulness, sin 914 *wrong*; loss of innocence 936 *guilt*; ungodliness 980 *impiety*; no morals; amorality, amoralism; hardness of heart 898 *malevolence*; wilfulness 602 *obstinacy*; waywardness, naughtiness, bad behaviour 738 *disobedience*; immorality, turpitude, moral t.; loose morals, profligacy 951 *impurity*; demoralization, degeneracy 655 *deterioration*; recidivism, backsliding 603 *change of allegiance*; vice, corruption, depravity 645 *badness*; heinousness, shamelessness; bad character, viciousness, baseness, vileness; villainy 930 *foul play*; dishonesty 930 *improbity*; crime 954 *lawbreaking*; devilry 898 *inhumanity*; devil worship, diabolism 982 *idolatry*; shame, scandal, abomination 867 *disrepute*; misbehaviour, delinquency, wrongdoing, evil-doing, transgression; primrose path, slippery slope; low life, criminal world, underworld, demi-monde; den of vice, sink of iniquity.

vice, fault, demerit; human weakness, moral w., infirmity, frailty, foible 163 *weakness*; imperfection, shortcoming, defect, deficiency, failing, flaw, weak point; trespass 914 *wrong*; sin, seven deadly sins, pride, covetousness, lust, anger, gluttony, envy, sloth; venial sin, peccadillo, scrape; impropriety 847 *bad taste*; offence 936 *guilty act*; crime 954 *illegality*.

Adj. *wicked*, unvirtuous, immoral; amoral, lax, unprincipled 930 *dishonest*; unblushing, hardened, shameless, brazen; ungodly 980 *impious*; iniquitous, unrighteous 914 *unjust*; evil 645 *bad*; black-hearted 898 *malevolent*; misbehaving, bad, naughty 738 *disobedient*; weak (**see** *frail*); peccant, sinful 936 *guilty*; unworthy, unmeritorious; graceless, reprobate; hopeless, incorrigible, irredeemable; accursed, godforsaken; devilish 969 *diabolic*.

vicious, good-for-nothing, ne'er-do-well; hopeless, past praying for; worthless, graceless 924 *disapproved*; villainous, miscreant, double-dyed 930 *rascally*; improper, unseemly, indecent 847 *vulgar*; without morals, immoral; unvirtuous 951 *unchaste*; profligate, abandoned, characterless 867 *disreputable*; corrupt, degraded, debauched, ruined, depraved, degenerate, sick, rotten 655 *deteriorated*; brutalized 898 *cruel*.

frail, infirm, feeble 163 *weak*; human, only h. 734 *lax*; suggestible, easily tempted 661 *vulnerable*; not above temptation, fallen 647 *imperfect*; recidivous 603 *trimming*.

heinous, heavy, grave, serious, deadly; black, scarlet, of deepest dye; hellish, infernal; sinful, immoral 914 *wrong*; demoralizing, unedifying; criminal, nefarious 954 *lawbreaking*; monstrous, flagrant, scandalous, infamous, shameful, disgraceful, shocking, outrageous, obscene; gross, foul, rank; base, vile, abominable, accursed; mean, shabby, despicable 645 *bad*; blameworthy, reprehensible, indefensible, unjustifiable; atrocious, brutal 898 *cruel*; unforgivable, unpardonable, inexcusable, unatonable.

Vb. *be wicked*, etc. adj.; fall from grace, blot one's copybook, lapse, relapse, backslide 603 *tergiversate*; fall into evil ways, go to the bad *or* to the dogs 655 *deteriorate*; do wrong, transgress, misbehave, misdemean oneself, carry on, be naughty, sow one's wild oats; trespass, offend, sin, commit s.; leave the straight and narrow, err, stray, slip, trip, stumble, fall.

make wicked, corrupt, demoralize, brutalize 655 *pervert*; mislead, lead astray, seduce 612 *tempt*; set a bad example; dehumanize, brutalize.

935. Innocence – N. *innocence*, guiltlessness, clean hands; clear conscience, nothing to declare; blamelessness, freedom from blame 960 *acquittal*; inexperience, unworldliness 699 *artlessness*; playfulness, harmlessness, innocent intentions; freedom from sin, unfallen state, state of grace 933 *virtue*; stainlessness 950 *purity*; incorruptibility 929 *probity*; impeccability 646 *perfection*; golden age 824 *happiness*.

innocent, babe, newborn babe, babes and sucklings; child, ingenue; lamb, dove;

angel, pure soul; milksop, goody-goody; innocent party.

Adj. *innocent*, pure, unspotted, stainless, unblemished, spotless, immaculate 648 *clean*; incorrupt, uncorrupted, undefiled; unfallen, sinless, impeccable 646 *perfect*; naive 491 *ignorant*; unworldly 699 *artless*; well-meaning 897 *benevolent*; innocuous, harmless, inoffensive, playful, gentle, lamb-like, dove-like, child-like, angelic; wide-eyed, looking as if butter would not melt in one's mouth; shockable, goody-goody; Arcadian.

guiltless, free from guilt, not responsible, not guilty 960 *acquitted*; more sinned against than sinning; falsely accused, blameless; faultless, irreproachable, above suspicion; with every excuse, pardonable, forgivable, excusable.

Vb. *be innocent*, know no wrong 929 *be honourable*; live in a state of grace 933 *be virtuous*; have clean hands, have a clear conscience, have nothing to be ashamed of, have nothing to confess; have the best intentions, mean no harm; know no better 699 *be artless*; stand above suspicion.

936. Guilt – N. *guilt*, guiltiness, redhandedness; culpability; criminality 954 *illegality*; sinfulness, original sin 934 *wickedness*; involvement, complicity; liability, one's fault; blame, censure 924 *reproach*; guilt complex; guilty feelings, guilty conscience, bad c.; guilty behaviour, suspicious conduct, blush, stammer, embarrassment; confession 526 *disclosure*; twinge of conscience, remorse, shame 939 *penitence*.

guilty act, sin 934 *vice*; misdeed, misdoing, transgression, trespass, offence, crime, corpus delicti 954 *illegality*; misdemeanour, felony; misconduct, misbehaviour, malpractice, malversation; infamous conduct, unprofessional c.; indiscretion, impropriety, peccadillo; naughtiness, scrape; lapse, slip 495 *mistake*; culpable omission, laches 458 *negligence*; dereliction of duty 918 *undutifulness*; injustice, tort, injury 914 *wrong*; enormity, atrocity, outrage 898 *cruel act*.

Adj. *guilty*, found g. 961 *condemned*; suspected, blamed 924 *disapproved*; responsible, in the wrong, at fault, to blame 928 *accusable*; blameful 924 *blameworthy*; peccant, sinful 934 *wicked*; criminal 954 *illegal*; blood-guilty 362 *murderous*; red-handed, caught in the act, surprised in the attempt; hangdog, sheepish, shamefaced, ashamed.

Vb. *be guilty*, be at fault, bear the blame; have crimes to answer for, have blood on one's hands; be caught in the act *or* red-handed; plead guilty 526 *confess*; have no excuse, stand condemned; transgress, sin 934 *be wicked*.

Adv. *guiltily*, criminally; red-handed, in the very act, flagrante delicto.

937. Good person – N. *good person*, sterling character, exemplary c. 929 *honourable person*; pillar of society, model of virtue, salt of the earth, shining light 646 *paragon*; saint 979 *pietist*; mahatma, maharishi; angel 935 *innocent*; heart of gold 897 *kind person*; good neighbour 903 *benefactor*; idealist 901 *philanthropist*; one in a million; hero, heroine 855 *brave person*; goody, good guy, good sort, brick, trump, sport.

938. Bad person – N. *bad person*, no saint, sinner, hardened s., limb of Satan, Antichrist 904 *evildoer*; fallen angel, lost sheep, lost soul, âme damnée; immoralist; reprobate, slubberdegullion, scapegrace, good-for-nothing, ne'er-do-well, black sheep, the despair of; scallywag, scamp; profligate 952 *libertine*; wanton 952 *loose woman*; wastrel 815 *prodigal*; reproach, outcast, dregs, riffraff, trash, scum 867 *object of scorn*; nasty type, ugly customer, undesirable, bad 'un, badmash 904 *ruffian*; bad lot, bad hat, bad guy, baddy, villain; bad influence, bad example; bad child, naughty c., terror, holy t., enfant terrible, whelp, monkey, little devil 663 *troublemaker*.

knave, varlet, varmint, rascal, rapscallion 869 *low fellow*; rogue, criminal 904 *offender*; pirate 789 *robber*; villain, blackguard, scoundrel, miscreant; cheat, liar,

crook; impostor, twister 545 *trickster*; sneak, rat 524 *informer*; renegade, recreant 603 *turncoat*; traitor, quisling, Judas; snake, reptile, vermin 904 *noxious animal*.

cad, nasty bit of work; rotter, blighter, bastard, dastard, bounder, heel, slob, scab, son of a bitch; stinker, skunk, dirty dog, filthy beast; pervert, degenerate; cur, hound, swine, rat, louse; pig, beast, bitch; the end, absolute e.

monster, horror, unspeakable villain; brute, savage, sadist; ogre 735 *tyrant*; Juggernaut, Moloch; public enemy number one; monster of depravity, fiend 969 *devil*; hellhound, fury 904 *hellhag*; devil incarnate, fiend i.; King Kong, Frankenstein's monster, bogey, terror, nightmare.

939. Penitence – N. *penitence*, repentance, contrition, attrition, compunction, remorse, self-reproach 830 *regret*; self-accusation 526 *disclosure*; confession 988 *Christian rite*; weight on one's mind, uneasy conscience 936 *guilt*; deathbed repentance 603 *recantation*; sackcloth and ashes 941 *penance*; apology 941 *atonement*.

penitent, confessor; flagellant 945 *ascetic*; magdalen, returned prodigal, a sadder and a wiser man; reformed character, brand plucked from the burning.

Adj. *repentant*, contrite, remorseful, sorry, apologetic 830 *regretting*; ashamed 872 *humbled*; softened, weeping 836 *lamenting*; compunctious, relenting, conscience-stricken, pricked by conscience; self-reproachful, self-accusing, self-condemned; confessing, penitent 941 *atoning*; chastened, sobered; reclaimed, reformed, converted, regenerate, born again.

Vb. *be penitent*, repent, show compunction, feel shame, express regrets, apologize; reproach oneself, blame o.; go to confession, acknowledge one's faults 526 *confess*; do penance 941 *atone*; bewail one's sins 836 *lament*; eat humble pie 721 *knuckle under*; rue, wish undone 830 *regret*; think again, learn one's lesson; reform, turn over a new leaf 654 *get better*; see the light, be converted, put on the new man, turn from sin 603 *recant*.

Int. sorry! mea culpa!

940. Impenitence – N. *impenitence*, contumacy, obduracy 602 *obstinacy*; hardness of heart 326 *hardness*; no apologies, no regrets 906 *pitilessness*; incorrigibility; hardened sinner 938 *bad person*.

Adj. *impenitent*, unregretting, unrecanting; contumacious, obdurate, stubborn 602 *obstinate*; unconfessing, unrepentant, without regrets; unrelenting, relentless 600 *persevering*; without compunction, heartless 898 *cruel*; unsoftened, unmoved; hard, hardened; conscienceless, unashamed, unblushing, brazen; incorrigible, hopeless, despaired of, lost 934 *wicked*; unconfessed, unshriven; unchastened, unreformed, unconverted.

Vb. *be impenitent*, make no excuses, offer no apologies, have no regrets, would do it again; not see the light 602 *be obstinate*; make no confession, die in one's sins; feel no compunction, harden one's heart 906 *be pitiless*.

941. Atonement – N. *atonement*, making amends, amende honorable, apology, full a., satisfaction; reparation, compensation, indemnity, indemnification, blood money, conscience m. 787 *restitution*; repayment, quittance, quits.

propitiation, expiation, conciliation 719 *pacification*; reclamation, redemption 965 *divine function*; sacrifice, offering, peace o. 981 *oblation*; scapegoat, whipping boy 150 *substitute*.

penance, shrift, confession 939 *penitence*; penitential exercise, fasting, flagellation 945 *asceticism*; lustration, purgation 648 *cleansing*; purgatory; stool of repentance, corner 964 *pillory*; white sheet, sanbenito; sackcloth and ashes 836 *lamentation*.

Adj. *atoning*, making amends 939 *repentant*; reparatory, compensatory, indemnificatory 787 *restoring*; conciliatory, apologetic; propitiatory, expiatory, piacular, purgatorial, lustral 648 *cleans-*

ing; sacrificial 759 *offering*; penitential, penitentiary 963 *punitive*.

Vb. *atone*, salve one's conscience, make amends, make reparation, indemnify, compensate, pay compensation, make it up to; apologize, offer one's apologies; propitiate, conciliate 719 *pacify*; give satisfaction 787 *restitute*; repair one's fault, make up for, make matters right; offer sacrifice, expiate, pay the penalty 963 *be punished*; reclaim, redeem.

do penance, undergo p.; pray, fast, flagellate oneself, scourge o.; purge one's contempt, suffer purgatory; put on sackcloth and ashes; take one's punishment, swallow one's medicine 963 *be punished*.

942. Temperance – N. *temperance*, temperateness, nothing in excess 177 *moderation*; self-denial 931 *disinterestedness*; self-control, self-discipline, stoicism 747 *restraint*; continence, chastity 950 *purity*; soberness 948 *sobriety*; forbearance 620 *avoidance*; abstemiousness, abstinence, abstention, teetotalism; prohibitionism 747 *restriction*; vegetarianism, veganism; dieting 946 *fasting*; frugality 814 *economy*; plain living, simple life 945 *asceticism*.

abstainer, teetotaller 948 *sober person*; nonsmoker; vegetarian, fruitarian, vegan; dropout; dieter, faster 945 *ascetic*.

Adj. *temperate*, not excessive, measured 177 *moderate*; plain, sparing 814 *economical*; frugal 816 *parsimonious*; abstemious 620 *avoiding*; dry, teetotal 948 *sober*; vegan, vegetarian; self-controlled, continent 747 *restrained*; chaste 950 *pure*; self-denying 945 *ascetic*.

Vb. *be temperate*, keep within bounds, avoid excess, know when to stop 177 *be moderate*, 948 *be sober*; forbear, refrain, abstain 620 *avoid*; control oneself, deny o. 747 *restrain*; go dry, give up, swear off; ration oneself 946 *starve*.

943. Intemperance – N. *intemperance*, immoderation, unrestraint, abandon; excess 637 *redundance*; extravagance 815 *prodigality*; want of self-control, indiscipline, incontinence 734 *laxity*; indulgence, self-i., overindulgence; bad habit 610 *habit*; addiction 949 *drug-taking*; high living, dissipation 944 *sensualism*; overeating 947 *gluttony*; hangover 949 *drunkenness*.

Adj. *intemperate*, immoderate 637 *redundant*; unfrugal, extravagant 815 *prodigal*; luxurious 637 *superfluous*; unascetic, unspartan, self-indulgent, overindulgent; unrestrained, undisciplined 738 *riotous*; incontinent 951 *unchaste*; unsober 949 *drunk*; animal 944 *sensual*.

Vb. *be intemperate*, luxuriate, plunge, wallow; lack self-control 734 *be lax*; deny oneself nothing, indulge oneself, give oneself up to 734 *please oneself*; have one's fling 815 *be prodigal*; not know when to stop, overindulge, burn the candle at both ends 837 *revel*; drink like a fish 949 *get drunk*; overeat, pig it, make oneself sick 947 *gluttonize*; become a slave to habit.

Adv. *intemperately*, immoderately, excessively, with abandon; not wisely but too well.

944. Sensualism – N. *sensualism*, life of the senses, unspirituality, earthiness, materialism; sensuality, carnality, sexuality, the flesh; grossness, bestiality; love of pleasure, hedonism, epicurism, epicureanism, eudaemonism 376 *pleasure*; sybaritism, voluptuousness, luxuriousness, dolce vita; luxury, lap of l. 637 *superfluity*; high living, fast l., wine, women and song 824 *enjoyment*; dissipation 943 *intemperance*; licentiousness 951 *impurity*; overindulgence, gourmandise 947 *gluttony*; eating and drinking 301 *feasting*; orgy, saturnalia, Bacchanalia 837 *revel*.

sensualist, animal, pig, swine; no ascetic, hedonist, pleasure-lover, thrill-seeker; luxury-lover, sybarite, voluptuary; epicurean, bon viveur; epicure, gourmet, gourmand 947 *glutton*; hard drinker 949 *drunkard*; loose liver 952 *libertine*; drug addict 949 *drug-taking*; degenerate, decadent.

Adj. *sensual*, earthy, gross, unspiritual 319 *material*; fleshly, carnal, bodily; sexual, venereal 887 *erotic*; animal, bestial; pleasure-giving 826 *pleasurable*; sybaritic,

voluptuous, pleasure-loving, thrill-seeking, living for kicks; hedonistic, epicurean, Lucullan, luxury-loving, luxurious; pampered, indulged, overindulged; overfed 947 *gluttonous*; high-living 943 *intemperate*; licentious 951 *impure*; orgiastic, Bacchanalian 949 *drunken*.

Vb. *be sensual*, cultivate one's senses, be the slave of one's desires, live for pleasure, wallow in luxury; indulge oneself, pamper o., do oneself proud 943 *be intemperate*.

945. Asceticism – N. *asceticism*, austerity, self-mortification, self-chastisement; flagellation 941 *penance*; ascetic practice, yoga; anchoritism, eremitism 883 *seclusion*; holy poverty 801 *poverty*; plain living, simple fare, dinner of herbs 946 *fasting*; self-denial, Puritanism 942 *temperance*; sackcloth, hair shirt, cilice.

ascetic, spiritual athlete, gymnosophist, yogi, sannyasi, fakir, dervish, fire-walker; hermit, eremite, anchorite, anchoress, recluse; flagellant 939 *penitent*; water-drinker 948 *sober person*; faster 942 *abstainer*; Puritan, Plymouth Brethren.

Adj. *ascetic*, yogic; hermit-like, eremitical, anchoretic; puritanical; Spartan, austere 735 *severe*; water-drinking 942 *temperate*.

946. Fasting – N. *fasting*, abstinence from food; no appetite, anorexia, a. nervosa 651 *ill health*; cutting down 301 *dieting*; strict fast, xerophagy; Lenten fare, bread and water, starvation diet, soupe maigre 945 *asceticism*; iron rations, short commons 636 *scarcity*; no food, starvation, inanition 859 *hunger*.

fast, fast day, Friday, Lent, Ramadan; meatless day, fish d., jour maigre 945 *asceticism*; hunger strike.

Adj. *fasting*, not eating, off one's food; abstinent, keeping Lent; unfed, empty, dinnerless, supperless; half-starved 636 *underfed*; starving, famished, wasting away 206 *lean*, 859 *hungry*; frugal, scanty, meagre; Spartan; Lenten.

Vb. *starve*, famish, clem 859 *be hungry*; macerate, show one's bones; have nothing to eat 801 *be poor*; fast, go without food;

keep Lent, keep Ramadan; refuse one's food, go on hunger strike; eat less, diet, reduce 37 *abate*; tighten one's belt, go on short commons; eat sparingly 942 *be temperate*; keep a poor table 816 *be parsimonious*.

947. Gluttony – N. *gluttony*, greediness, gulosity, voracity, edacity; good living, indulgence, overeating 943 *intemperance*; guzzling, gormandizing, belly worship, gourmandise, pleasures of the table 301 *gastronomy*; blowout 301 *feasting*.

glutton, guzzler, gormandizer; locust, wolf, vulture, cormorant, pig, hog; good trencherman *or* -woman, hearty eater 301 *eater*; greedy-guts, greedy pig; gourmand, bon vivant, Lucullus.

Adj. *gluttonous*, rapacious, ventripotent 859 *greedy*; voracious, edacious, wolfish; omnivorous 464 *indiscriminating*; insatiable 859 *hungry*; pampered, overfed, guzzling, gormandizing; bellyworshipping; gastronomic, epicurean.

Vb. *gluttonize*, gormandize; guzzle, bolt, wolf, scoff, gobble up 301 *eat*; gorge, cram, stuff; glut oneself, overeat; eat one's head off, eat out of house and home; have a good appetite, ply a good knife and fork; eat like a pig, make a beast of oneself, have eyes bigger than one's stomach; indulge one's appetite, tickle one's palate; savour one's food, lick one's lips *or* one's chops, water at the mouth; keep a good table, live only for eating.

948. Sobriety – N. *sobriety*, soberness 942 *temperance*; water-drinking, tea-d., teetotalism; clear head, no hangover; dry area.

sober person, moderate drinker, no toper; nonaddict, nonalcoholic; waterdrinker, teetotaller 942 *abstainer*; Band of Hope, temperance society, Alcoholics Anonymous; prohibitionist, pussyfoot.

Adj. *sober*, abstinent 620 *avoiding*; water-drinking 942 *temperate*; not drinking, off drink, on the wagon; teetotal, dry; unintoxicated, clear-headed, sober as a judge; come to one's senses, sobered up; dried out, off the bottle; unfermented, nonalcoholic, soft.

Vb. *be sober*, drink water; not drink, keep off liquor, drink moderately 942 *be temperate*; dry out, come off (drugs); go on the wagon, give up alcohol, sign the pledge; carry one's liquor, keep a clear head; sober up, sleep it off.

949. Drunkenness. Drug-taking – N. *drunkenness*, excessive drinking 943 *intemperance*; insobriety, inebriety; bibulousness, wine-bibbing; sottishness, beeriness; Dutch courage 821 *excitation*; intoxication, inebriation, befuddlement; tipsiness, staggering 317 *oscillation*; one over the eight, drop too much, hard drinking; compotation, potation, libations; hair of the dog that bit one; flowing bowl, booze 301 *alcoholic drink*; drinking bout, jag, blind, binge, spree, bender, pubcrawl, Bacchanalia 837 *revel*; Bacchus, Dionysus.

crapulence, crapulousness; morning after the night before, hangover, thick head, sick headache.

alcoholism, dipsomania; delirium tremens, dt's, the horrors, heebiejeebies, jimjams, pink elephants; grog-blossom, red nose.

drug-taking, glue-sniffing, pill-popping; hard drug, soft d.; joint, reefer, roach; shot, fix; narcotic, dope; nicotine 388 *tobacco*; cannabis, marijuana, ganja, hemp, hashish, hash, bhang, pot, grass; cocaine, coke, snow; heroin, horse, smack; methadone 658 *drug*; downers; pep pill, amphetamine, uppers 821 *excitant*; intoxicant, hallucinogen, LSD, acid, mescalin; drug addiction, drug abuse 943 *intemperance*; drying out, withdrawal symptoms, cold turkey; drug addict, dope fiend, freak; head, junkie, mainliner; pusher.

drunkard, habitual d., inebriate, drunk, sot, lush; slave to drink, wino, alcoholic, dipsomaniac; drinker, social d., secret d.; bibber, tippler, toper, boozer, swiller, soaker, old soak, sponge, wineskin; tosspot, frothblower; bacchant(e), maenad; carouser, pubcrawler 837 *reveller*.

Adj. *drunk*, inebriated, intoxicated, under the influence; in one's cups, the worse for liquor; half-seas over, three sheets in the wind, one over the eight; boozed up, liquored up, happy, high 821 *excited*; mellow, well-primed, tanked up, bevvied up; gloriously drunk, roaring d., pot-valiant 61 *disorderly*.

tipsy, tiddly, squiffy, tight, half-cut, pissed, Brahms and Liszt; well-oiled, pickled, canned, bottled, stewed, well-lubricated; smashed, sloshed, sozzled, soaked, soused, plastered; pixilated, fuddled; maudlin, tearful, tired and emotional; drunken, boozy, muzzy, woozy; glassy-eyed, pie-e., seeing double; reeling 317 *oscillating*; hiccupping 580 *stammering*.

dead drunk, stinking d., stoned; blind drunk, blotto; legless, paralytic; under the table, dead to the world; drunk as a lord, pissed as a newt, fou as a coot.

crapulous, crapulent, with a hangover, with a thick head; dizzy, giddy, sick.

drugged, doped, high, zonked out, spaced o., freaked o.; stoned, incapacitated 375 *insensible*; turned on, hooked on drugs, addicted.

drunken, inebriate 943 *intemperate*; habitually drunk, never sober; sottish, gin-sodden, boozy, beery, vinous; bibulous, fond of a drink; tippling, boozing, etc. vb.; red-nosed, bloodshot, liverish; on the bottle, alcoholic, dipsomaniac.

intoxicating, inebriative; heady, like wine 821 *exciting*; stimulant, intoxicant; opiate, narcotic; hallucinatory, psychedelic, psychotropic, mind-blowing; addictive, habit-forming; alcoholic, spirituous, vinous, beery; hard, potent, stiff 162 *strong*.

Vb. *be drunk*, be under the influence of liquor, have had too much; not hold one's liquor, pass out; hiccup, stutter 580 *stammer*; see double, not walk straight 317 *oscillate*.

get drunk, liquor up, tank up, crack a bottle, knock back a few, bend one's elbow, tipple, booze, tope, swig, swill, hit the bottle 301 *drink*; go on the spree, go on a blind *or* a bender, go pub-crawling; drown one's sorrows, quaff, carouse, wassail 837 *revel*.

drug oneself, smoke, sniff, snort, inject oneself, shoot, mainline; turn on, trip, take a trip; freak out.

inebriate, exhilarate, elevate 821 *excite*; go to one's head, make one's head swim, fuddle, befuddle, stupefy; tipsify; drink one under the table.

950. Purity – N. *purity*, faultlessness 646 *perfection*; sinlessness, immaculacy 935 *innocence*; moral purity, morals 933 *virtue*; decency, delicacy 846 *good taste*; pudency 874 *modesty*; chastity, continence 942 *temperance*; frigidity 820 *moral insensibility*; honour, one's h.; virginity, maidenhood 895 *celibacy*.

prudery, prudishness, shockability; false modesty 874 *modesty*; demureness 834 *seriousness*; priggishness, primness, coyness 850 *affectation*; sanctimoniousness 979 *pietism*; Puritanism 735 *severity*; euphemism, genteelism, mealy-mouthedness; censorship, expurgation, bowdlerization 550 *obliteration*.

virgin, maiden, vestal virgin, virgo intacta, maid 895 *celibate*; religious celibate 986 *monk, nun*.

prude, prig, Victorian, euphemist 850 *affecter*; Puritan, wowser; guardian of morality, censor, Mrs Grundy.

Adj. *pure*, faultless 646 *perfect*; undefiled, unfallen, sinless 935 *innocent*; maidenly, virgin, virginal 895 *unwedded*; blushing, rosy 874 *modest*; coy, shy 620 *avoiding*; chaste, continent 942 *temperate*; unassailable, impregnable 929 *honourable*; frigid 820 *impassive*; immaculate, spotless, snowy 427 *white*; moral 933 *virtuous*; Platonic, sublimated, purified; decent, decorous 846 *tasteful*; printable, quotable, repeatable 648 *clean*; censored, bowdlerized.

prudish, squeamish, shockable, Victorian; prim 850 *affected*; overdelicate, overmodest; old-maidish, straitlaced, narrowminded, puritan, priggish; sanctimonious 979 *pietistic*.

951. Impurity – N. *impurity*, defilement 649 *uncleanness*; indelicacy 847 *bad taste*; indecency, immodesty, shamelessness, exhibitionism; coarseness, grossness; ribaldry, bawdry, bawdiness, salaciousness; loose talk, filthy t.; double entendre, equivoque; smut, dirt, filth, obscenity, obscene literature, adult l., erotica; pornography, hard-core p., soft porn; blue film, skin flick; prurience, voyeurism.

unchastity, promiscuity, wantonness; incontinence, easy virtue, amorality; permissive society 734 *laxity*; vice, immorality, sexual delinquency; roving eye; concupiscence, lust 859 *libido*; carnality, eroticism, erotism, the flesh 944 *sensualism*; lewdness, salacity, lubricity; dissipation, debauchery, licentiousness, licence, libertinism, libertinage; seduction, defloration; venery, lechery, fornication, womanizing; harlotry, whorishness.

illicit love, unlawful desires, forbidden fruit; extramarital relations; incestuous affection, incest; homosexuality 84 *abnormality*; perversion, pederasty, buggery, sodomy, bestiality; adultery, unfaithfulness, infidelity, cuckoldry; wife-swapping; eternal triangle, liaison, intrigue 887 *love affair*; free love, irregular union 894 *type of marriage*.

rape, ravishment, violation, indecent assault, grope; gang bang; sex crime, sex murder.

social evil, harlotry, whoredom; oldest profession; streetwalking, prostitution; indecent exposure, flashing; pimping, pandering, white slave traffic; vice squad.

brothel, bordello, bagnio, stews; whorehouse, bawdy-house, house of ill fame; knocking-shop; red-light district.

Adj. *impure*, unclean, nasty 649 *dirty*; unwholesome 653 *insalubrious*; indelicate, vulgar, coarse, gross; ribald, broad, free, loose; strong, racy, bawdy, Rabelaisian; uncensored, unexpurgated; suggestive, piquant, titillating, near the knuckle; spicy, juicy, fruity; immoral, risqué, equivocal, nudge-nudge wink-wink; naughty, wicked, blue; unmentionable, unquotable, unprintable; smutty, filthy; scabrous, scatological, offensive; indecent, obscene, lewd, salacious, lubricious; licentious, pornographic; prurient, erotic; sexual, sexy, hot.

unchaste, unvirtuous 934 *vicious*; susceptible 934 *frail*; fallen, seduced, prostituted, taken advantage of; of easy virtue, of loose morals, amoral, immoral; light, wanton, loose, fast, naughty; wild, rackety; immodest, daring; shameless, flaunting, scarlet; whorish, tarty; promiscuous, sleeping around; streetwalking, on the game.

lecherous, carnal, voluptuous 944 *sensual*; libidinous, lascivious, lustful; prurient, concupiscent 859 *desiring*; on heat, ruttish, randy; sex-conscious, man-c., woman-c.; oversexed, sex-mad; perverted, bestial; lewd, licentious, libertine, rakish; depraved, debauched, dissolute, dissipated 934 *vicious*; whoremongering, brothel-haunting.

extramarital, irregular, unlawful; incestuous; homosexual 84 *abnormal*; adulterous, unfaithful; bed-hopping, promiscuous.

Vb. *be impure*, have no morals; be unfaithful, commit adultery, cuckold; be dissipated 943 *be intemperate*; fornicate, womanize, whore, wench; keep a mistress, have a lover; lech, lust, be on heat 859 *desire*; be promiscuous, sleep around; streetwalk, be on the streets; pimp, pander, procure.

debauch, defile 649 *make unclean*; proposition, seduce, lead astray; take advantage of, have one's way with; dishonour, deflower, disgrace 867 *shame*; prostitute, make a whore of; lay, knock off, bed 45 *unite with*; rape, ravish, violate, molest, abuse, outrage, interfere with, assault.

952. Libertine – N. *libertine*, philanderer, flirt; gay dog, rake, roué, profligate 944 *sensualist*; lady-killer, gallant, squire of dames; fancy man, gigolo, sugar daddy; seducer, deceiver; corespondent, adulterer, cuckolder, wife-swapper; immoralist, amorist, Don Juan, Casanova; wolf, woman-chaser, kerb-crawler; womanizer, fornicator; whoremonger; voyeur, lecher, flasher, satyr, goat, dirty old man; sex maniac, rapist; catamite, male prostitute; pederast, sodomite 84 *nonconformist*.

cuckold, deceived husband, injured h., complaisant h.; wearer of horns.

loose woman, light o'love, wanton, easy lay; fast woman, sexpot, hot stuff; woman of easy virtue *or* of doubtful reputation, demi-rep, one no better than she should be; bint, wench, floosie, jade, hussy; nymphet, sex kitten, Lolita, groupie; trollop, trull, slut; tart, chippy, scrubber, pick-up; vamp, adventuress, temptress, seductress, femme fatale, scarlet woman, painted w., Jezebel, Delilah; adultress, other woman; nymphomaniac.

kept woman, fancy w., mistress, paramour, leman, hetaera, concubine 887 *loved one*; bit of fluff, floosie, doxy, moll.

prostitute, pro; white slave, fallen woman, erring sister; frail sisterhood, demi-monde; harlot, trollop, whore, strumpet; streetwalker, woman of the streets, broad, hustler, hooker, scrubber; pick-up, casual conquest, call girl; fille de joie, poule, cocotte, courtesan; demi-mondaine, demi-rep; odalisque 742 *slave*.

bawd, go-between, pimp, ponce, pander, procurer, procuress, mack, brothel-keeper, madam; white slaver.

953. Legality – N. *legality*, formality, form, formula, rite, due process 959 *litigation*; letter of the law (**see** *law*); constitutionality, constitutionalism; good law 913 *justice*; lawfulness, legitimacy, validity.

legislation, legislature, legislatorship, law-giving, law-making, codification, legalization, legitimization, ratification; enactment, regulation; plebiscite 605 *vote*; law, statute, ordinance, order 737 *decree*; edict, rescript 693 *precept*; legislator, lawgiver, lawmaker.

law, law and equity, the law; body of law, corpus juris, constitution, charter; statute book, legal code, pandect, penal code, civil c.; written law, statute l., common l.; international law, jus gentium, law of nations; law of the land; legal process 955 *jurisdiction*; jurisprudence, science of law; law consultancy, legal advice.

Adj. *legal*, lawful 913 *just*; law-abiding 739 *obedient*; legitimate, licit 756 *permitted*; within the law, de jure, legally

sound; statutable, statutory, constitutional; nomothetic, law-giving, legislatorial, legislational, legislative, decretal; legislated, enacted, made law; legalized, legitimized; liable *or* amenable to law, actionable, justiciable, triable 928 *accusable*; jurisprudential, learned in the law.

Vb. *be legal*, stand up in law; come *or* keep within the law, stay the right side of the law.

make legal, legalize, legitimize, ratify 488 *endorse*; vest, establish 153 *stabilize*; legislate, pass, enact 737 *decree*.

954. Illegality – N. *illegality*, bad law, loophole, irregularity, error of law; wrong verdict 481 *misjudgement*; contradictory law, antinomy; miscarriage of justice 914 *injustice*; unlawfulness, illicitness, illegitimacy.

lawbreaking, breach of law, transgression, contravention 306 *overstepping*; trespass, offence, tort, civil wrong; champerty, malpractice 930 *foul play*; dishonesty 930 *improbity*; criminality 936 *guilt*; criminal offence, indictable o., crime, capital c., misdemeanour, felony; misprision, misfeasance, malfeasance 914 *wrong*; criminology; criminal 904 *offender*.

lawlessness, antinomianism; outlawry, disfranchisement; no law, breakdown of law and order, crime wave 734 *anarchy*; summary justice, vigilantism; kangaroo court, gang rule, mob law, lynch l.; riot, hooliganism, rebellion 738 *revolt*; usurpation 916 *arrogation*; arbitrary rule; martial law 735 *brute force*.

bastardy, bar *or* bend *or* baton sinister; bastardization, illegitimacy; bastard, illegitimate child, natural c., love c., by-blow.

Adj. *illegal*, illegitimate, illicit; contraband, black-market, hot; impermissible 757 *prohibited*; unauthorized, unofficial; unlawful 914 *wrong*; unlegislated, not covered by law; unchartered, unconstitutional, unstatutory; null and void 752 *abrogated*; irregular, contrary to law; on the wrong side of the law, against the l.; outside the law, outlawed; tortious, cognizable 928 *accusable*.

lawbreaking, offending 936 *guilty*; criminal, felonious, fraudulent, shady 930 *dishonest.*

lawless, antinomian 734 *anarchic*; ungovernable 738 *riotous*; violent, summary; arbitrary, irresponsible, unanswerable, unaccountable; unofficial, cowboy; above the law, despotic, tyrannical 735 *oppressive.*

bastard, illegitimate, spurious; misbegotten, baseborn; born out of wedlock, born on the wrong side of the blanket; without a father, without benefit of clergy.

Vb. *be illegal,* break the law, offend against the l.; wrest the law, defy the law, drive a coach and horses through; take the law into one's own hands 734 *please oneself*; stand above the law.

make illegal, put outside the law, outlaw; illegalize 757 *prohibit*; penalize 963 *punish*; bastardize, illegitimize; make the law a dead letter 752 *abrogate.*

955. Jurisdiction – N. *jurisdiction,* portfolio 622 *function*; judicature, magistracy, commission of the peace; competence, legal c., legal authority, arm of the law 733 *authority*; administration of justice, Home Office; local jurisdiction, local authority, corporation, municipality 692 *council*; watch committee 956 *tribunal*; legal authority 751 *mandate.*

law officer, legal administrator, Lord Chancellor, Attorney General; Crown Counsel, public prosecutor; procurator fiscal 957 *judge*; mayor, sheriff 733 *position of authority*; court officer, clerk of the court, tipstaff, bailiff; summoner, process-server; apparitor 690 *official.*

police, forces of law and order, long arm of the law; police force, constabulary, the fuzz; Scotland Yard; police officer, policeman *or* -woman, constable, special c., copper, cop, traffic c., patrolman *or* -woman; bobby, flatfoot, rozzer, dick; watch, posse comitatus; Special Patrol Group, SPG; plain-clothes man 459 *detective.*

Adj. *jurisdictional,* competent; executive, administrative 689 *directing*; justiciary, judiciary, juridical; justiciable, subject to jurisdiction.

956. Tribunal – N. *tribunal,* seat of justice, woolsack, throne; judgement seat, bar; confessional; forum 692 *council*; public opinion; judicatory, bench, board, panel of judges, judge and jury; commission of the peace.

lawcourt, court, open c.; court of law, court of justice, criminal court, civil c.; appellate court, Court of Appeal, C. of Cassation; Court of Exchequer, Star Chamber; House of Lords 692 *parliament*; High Court of Justice, Queen's Bench; assizes; sessions, quarter s., petty s.; Old Bailey; magistrate's court, juvenile c., police c.; coroner's court; court-martial, drumhead court, summary c.

courtroom, courthouse, lawcourts, bench, woolsack, jury box; judgement seat, mercy s.; dock, bar; witness box.

957. Judge – N. *judge,* justice, justiceship; your Lordship, my lud, m'lud; justiciary; Lord Chancellor, Lord Chief Justice, Master of the Rolls, Lords of Appeal; military judge, Judge Advocate General; puisné judge, county court j., recorder, Common Serjeant; sessions judge, assize j., circuit j.; magistrate, stipendiary m.; coroner; honorary magistrate, justice of the peace, JP; bench, judiciary.

magistracy, the beak, his *or* her Worship, his *or* her Honour; arbiter, ombudsman 480 *estimator*; Recording Angel 549 *recorder*; Solomon.

jury, grand jury, petty j., trial j., coroner's j.; juror's panel, jury list; juror, juryman *or* -woman; foreman *or* forewoman of the jury.

958. Lawyer – N. *lawyer,* legal practitioner, man *or* woman of law; common lawyer, canon l., civil l., criminal l.; barrister, barrister-at-law, advocate, counsel, learned c.; stuff gown, junior counsel; senior barrister, bencher; silk gown, silk, leading counsel, Queen's C., QC; serjeant, serjeant-at-law; circuit barrister, circuiteer; Philadelphia lawyer 696 *expert*; shyster, pettifogger, crooked lawyer.

law agent, attorney, public a., attorney

at law, proctor, procurator; Writer to the Signet, solicitor before the Supreme Court; solicitor, legal adviser; legal representative, legal agent, pleader, advocate; equity draftsman; conveyancer.

notary, notary public, commissioner for oaths; scrivener, petition-writer; clerk of the court 955 *law officer*; solicitor's clerk, barrister's devil.

jurist, jurisconsult, legal adviser, legal expert, legal light, master of jurisprudence, pundit, legist, legalist, canonist; law student.

bar, civil b., criminal b.; Inns of Chancery, Inns of Court; legal profession, the Robe; barristership, advocacy; solicitorship, attorneyship; legal consultancy.

Adj. *jurisprudential*, learned in the law, called to the bar, at the b., barristerial, forensic; notarial.

959. Litigation – N. *litigation*, going to law, legal dispute, issue; lawsuit, suit at law, suit, case, cause, action; prosecution, charge 928 *accusation*; test case 461 *experiment*; claim, counter c. 915 *dueness*; plea, petition; affidavit, pleading 532 *affirmation*.

legal process, proceedings, course of law 955 *jurisdiction*; citation, subpoena, summons 737 *warrant*; arrest, detention, committal 747 *restraint*; habeas corpus, bail, surety, security, recognizance; injunction, stay order; writ.

legal trial, trial, trial by jury, justice seen to be done; assize, sessions 956 *lawcourt*; inquest, examination 459 *inquiry*; hearing, prosecution, defence; hearing of evidence; examination, cross-e. 466 *testimony*; pleadings, arguments, counterargument, rebutter, rebuttal; proof, disproof; ruling, finding, decision, verdict 480 *judgement*; majority verdict, hung jury; favourable verdict 960 *acquittal*; unfavourable verdict 961 *condemnation*; appeal, retrial; precedent, case law; law reports; cause list; case record, dossier 548 *record*.

litigant, libellant, party, suitor 763 *petitioner*; claimant, plaintiff, defendant, appellant, respondent, objector, in-

tervener; accused, prisoner at the bar 928 *accused person*; informer, prosecutor 928 *accuser*.

Adj. *litigating*, at law with, litigant, suing 928 *accusing*; litigious 709 *quarrelling*.

litigated, on trial, coram judice; disputed, contested; up for trial, brought before the court; sub judice, on the cause list, down for hearing; litigable, disputable, suable 928 *accusable*.

Vb. *litigate*, go to law, appeal to l., institute legal proceedings, file a suit; prepare a case, brief counsel; file a claim 915 *claim*; have the law on one, take one to court, haul before the c., make one a party, implead, prefer charges 928 *indict*; cite, summon, serve notice on; prosecute, bring to justice.

try a case, take cognizance, empanel a jury, hear a cause; call witnesses, cross-examine; sit in judgment 480 *judge*; sum up, charge the jury; bring in a verdict, pronounce sentence; commit for trial.

960. Acquittal – N. *acquittal*, verdict of not guilty, benefit of the doubt; clearance, exculpation, exoneration 935 *innocence*; absolution, discharge; let-off, thumbs up 746 *liberation*; justification 927 *vindication*; successful defence, case dismissed; reprieve, pardon; nonprosecution 919 *nonliability*.

Adj. *acquitted*, not guilty 935 *guiltless*; cleared, in the clear, exonerated, exculpated, vindicated; exempt 919 *nonliable*; let off, discharged, without a stain on one's character 746 *liberated*; reprieved 909 *forgiven*.

Vb. *acquit*, find *or* pronounce not guilty; prove innocent, get one off 927 *vindicate*; clear, absolve, exonerate, exculpate; find there is no case to answer, not press charges 919 *exempt*; discharge, let go, let off 746 *liberate*; reprieve, pardon; quash, set aside the sentence 752 *abrogate*.

961. Condemnation – N. *condemnation*, unfavourable verdict, hostile v.; finding of guilty, conviction; damnation, perdition; blacklist 924 *disapprobation*; excommunication 899 *malediction*; doom, judgement, sentence 963 *punishment*; outlawry, proscription; death warrant, condemned cell, Death Row; black cap, thumbs down.

Adj. *condemned*, found guilty, made liable; convicted, sentenced; proscribed, outlawed, with a price on one's head; nonsuited 924 *disapproved*.

Vb. *condemn*, find liable, find against, nonsuit; find guilty, convict, sentence; reject one's defence *or* one's appeal; proscribe, outlaw 954 *make illegal*; blacklist 924 *disapprove*; damn, excommunicate 899 *curse*.

962. Reward – N. *reward*, guerdon, remuneration, recompense; meed, deserts, just d. 913 *justice*; recognition, thanks 907 *gratitude*; tribute 923 *praise*; prize-giving, award, presentation, prize; cup, medal 729 *trophy*; consolation prize, booby p.; honour 729 *decoration*, 866 *honours*; letters after one's name 870 *title*; prize money, jackpot; prize fellowship, exhibition 703 *subvention*; reward for service, fee 804 *pay*; productivity bonus 612 *incentive*; perquisite, perks, fringe benefits; income, turnover 771 *earnings*; return, profit 771 *gain*; compensation, indemnification; quid pro quo 31 *offset*; reparation 787 *restitution*; bounty, gratuity, golden handshake; commission, rake-off, kickback; tip, douceur, baksheesh 781 *gift*; bribe 612 *incentive*; hush money, protection m.

Adj. *rewarding*, generous 813 *liberal*; profitable 771 *gainful*; promising 759 *offering*; reparatory 787 *restoring*; retributive 714 *retaliatory*.

Vb. *reward*, recompense; award, present; bestow a medal 866 *honour*; thank, show one's gratitude 907 *be grateful*; remunerate 804 *pay*; tip 781 *give*; tip well 813 *be liberal*; repay, requite; make reparation 787 *restitute*; win over 612 *bribe*.

Adv. *rewardingly*, profitably; for a consideration, as a reward, in compensation, for one's pains.

963. Punishment – N. *punishment*, sentence 961 *condemnation*; penalization, victimization; chastisement, heads rolling; carpeting 924 *reprimand*; disciplinary action, discipline; dose, pill, bitter p. 731 *adversity*; just deserts, comeuppance 915 *dueness*; doom, judgement 913 *justice*; poetic justice, retribution, Nemesis; requital, reprisal 714 *retaliation*; avengement 910 *revenge*; penance, self-mortification 941 *atonement*; penology, penologist.

corporal punishment, beating, thrashing, etc. vb.; scourging, flagellation; slap, smack, rap over the knuckles; drubbing, blow, cuff, clout 279 *knock*; third degree, torture, peine forte et dure, strappado, death by a thousand cuts 377 *pain*.

capital punishment, extreme penalty 361 *death*; death sentence; execution 362 *killing*; decapitation, decollation; traitor's death, hanging, drawing and quartering; strangulation, garrotte; hanging, long drop; electrocution; lapidation; crucifixion, impalement; burning at the stake, auto-da-fé; mass execution, purge 362 *slaughter*; martyrdom; illegal execution, lynch law; judicial murder.

penalty, damage 772 *loss*; infliction, imposition, task, lines; sentence, penalization; liability 915 *dueness*; damages, costs 787 *restitution*; amercement, mulct, fine 804 *payment*; ransom 809 *price*; forfeit, forfeiture, sequestration, confiscation 786 *expropriation*; gating, imprisonment 747 *detention*; suspension, rustication; binding over; penal servitude, hard labour, galleys; transportation, expulsion, deportation 300 *ejection*; banishment, exile, proscription, ban, outlawing 57 *exclusion*; reprisal 714 *retaliation*.

punisher, vindicator 910 *avenger*; chastiser, corrector, chastener, discipliner; persecutor 735 *tyrant*; justiciary, magistrate 957 *judge*; whipper, caner, flogger, flagellator; torturer, inquisitor; executioner, hangman; firing squad; lyncher 362 *murderer*.

Adj. *punitive*, penological, penal, punitory; castigatory, disciplinary, corrective;

retributive 910 *revengeful*; in reprisal 714 *retaliatory*; penalizing, confiscatory 786 *taking*; torturing 377 *painful*.

punishable, liable, amerceable, mulctable; indictable 928 *accusable*; asking for it.

Vb. *punish*, visit, afflict 827 *hurt*; persecute, victimize, make an example of 735 *be severe*; take disciplinary action; give one a lesson, chasten, discipline, chastise; reprimand, rebuke, have one's head for 924 *reprove*; throw the book at, come down hard on, come down on like a ton of bricks, give one what for; penalize, sentence 961 *condemn*; exact retribution, settle with, pay one out 714 *retaliate*; bring to book 910 *avenge*; amerce, mulct, fine, confiscate 786 *take away*; unfrock, demote, degrade, reduce to the ranks, suspend 867 *shame*; tar and feather, pillory, set in the stocks; masthead; duck, keelhaul; picket, spread-eagle; lock up 747 *imprison*.

spank, slap, smack, slipper, paddle; cuff, clout, box on the ears, rap over the knuckles; drub, trounce, beat, belt, strap, leather, larrup, wallop, welt, tan, cane, birch, switch, whack, dust, tan one's hide, beat black and blue 279 *strike*.

flog, whip, horsewhip, thrash 279 *strike*; scourge, give one the cat; lash, flay, flagellate.

torture, give the third degree; give one the works 377 *give pain*; put to the torture, thumbscrew, rack, break on the wheel, mutilate, kneecap; persecute, martyrize 827 *torment*.

execute, put to death 362 *kill*; lynch 362 *murder*; dismember, tear limb from limb; decimate; crucify, impale; flay alive; stone to death 712 *lapidate*; shoot, fusillade; burn alive, send to the stake, bow-string, garrotte, strangle; gibbet, hang, string up; send to the scaffold, bring to the block; behead, decapitate, guillotine; electrocute, gas; purge 362 *slaughter*.

be punished, take the consequences, be for the high jump, have it coming to one, catch it; take the rap, stand the racket, face the music; take one's medicine, hold one's hand out; get what one was asking for, get one's deserts; regret it, smart for it; lay one's head on the block; dance upon nothing, swing; pay for it with one's head, die the death.

964. Means of punishment – N. *scourge*, birch, cat, cat-o'-nine-tails, rope's end, knout, cowhide; whip, horsewhip, switch; lash, strap, tawse, thong, belt; cane, stick, rod, ferule, ruler 723 *club*.

pillory, stocks, whipping post, ducking stool; corner, dunce's cap; stool of repentance, cutty stool; irons 748 *fetter*; prison 748 *gaol*.

instrument of torture, rack, thumbscrew, iron boot, pilliwinks; Iron Maiden, triangle, wheel, treadmill; torture chamber.

means of execution, scaffold, block, gallows, gibbet, Tyburn tree; cross; stake; hemlock 659 *poison*; bullet, wall; axe, guillotine, widow-maker; hempen collar, halter, rope, noose; garrotte, bowstring; electric chair, hot seat; death chamber, gas c.; condemned cell.

Section 5: Religion

965. Divineness – N. *divineness*, divinity, deity; godhead; divine principle, Brahma; numen, numinousness, mana; divine essence, perfection, the Good the True and the Beautiful; Brahmahood, nirvana; Atman, world soul; primum mobile 156 *source*; divine nature, God's ways, Providence.

the Deity, God, Supreme Being, Alpha and Omega; the Eternal, the All-wise, the Almighty, the Most High; the All-holy, the All-merciful; Creator, Preserver; Allah; Elohim, Yahweh, Jehovah, Adonai, I AM; God of Abraham, Lord of Hosts; Demiurge; All-Father, Great Spirit; Ahura Mazda.

Trinity, triad, Hindu Triad, Brahma, Siva, Vishnu; Holy Trinity, Hypostatic Union; Triune God, Three in One and One in Three; God the Father, God the Son, God the Holy Ghost.

Holy Ghost, Holy Spirit, Spirit of Truth; Paraclete, Comforter, Consoler; Dove.

God the Son, Word, Logos, Son of God, the Only Begotten; Messiah, Son of David, Lord's Anointed, Christ; Immanuel; Lamb of God, Son of Man; Jesus, Jesu, Jesus Christ; Holy Infant, Christ Child; Jesus of Nazareth, the Galilean; the Good Shepherd, Saviour, Redeemer, Friend; Lord, Master; Light of the World, King of Kings, Prince of Peace.

divine function, creation, preservation; judgement, mercy; inspiration, unction, grace, prevenient g.; propitiation, atonement, redemption, salvation, mediation, intercession.

theophany, divine manifestation, divine emanation; incarnation; transfiguration; Shekinah, Glory of the Lord; avatar.

Adj. *divine*, holy, hallowed, sanctified, sacred, heavenly, celestial; transcendental, sublime, ineffable; numinous, mystical, religious, spiritual, superhuman, supernatural, transcendent; unearthly, supramundane, not of this world; providential; theophanic; theocratic.

godlike, divine, superhuman; transcendent, immanent; omnipresent 189 *ubiquitous*; immeasurable 107 *infinite*; absolute, self-existent; timeless, eternal, immortal 115 *perpetual*; immutable, changeless; almighty, omnipotent 160 *powerful*; providential, all-wise, omniscient; all-merciful 909 *forgiving*; compassionate 887 *loving*; holy, all-h., worshipped 979 *sanctified*; sovereign 866 *worshipful*; theomorphic, incarnate, in the image of God.

redemptive, intercessional, mediatory, propitiatory; incarnational; soteriological, messianic.

966. Deities in general – N. *deity*, mythic d., god, goddess, deva, devi; the gods, the immortals; Olympian 967 *Olympian deity*; pagan god, false g., idol; godling, petty god; demigod, half-god, divine hero; object of worship, fetish, totem 982 *idol*; theogony; pantheon.

Adj. *mythological*, mythical; theogonic; deiform, theomorphic, deific, deified.

967. Pantheon – N. *classical deities*, gods and goddesses of Greece and Rome; Homeric deities, Hesiodic theogony; primeval deities, Erebus, Nox; Gaia, Tellus, Uranus, Cronus, Saturn; Pontus, Oceanus, Tethys; Helios, Sol, Hyperion, Phaëthon; Titan, Atlas, Prometheus; Giant, Enceladus; the Fates, Clotho, Lachesis, Atropos.

Olympian deity, Olympian, Zeus, Jupiter, Jove, president of the immortals; Chthonian deity, Pluto, Hades; Poseidon, Neptune; Apollo, Phoebus; Hermes, Mercury; Ares, Mars; Hephaestus, Vulcan; Dionysus, Bacchus; Hera, Juno; Demeter, Ceres; Persephone, Proserpina; Athena, Minerva; Aphrodite, Venus; Artemis, Diana; Eros, Cupid; Iris; Hebe; Eumenides, Erinys, Furies.

lesser deity, Pan, Flora; Aurora, Eos; Luna, Selene; Aeolus; Triton, Nereus, Proteus, Glaucus; Ate, Bellona; Astraea; Muses, tuneful Nine; Aesculapius; Somnus, Morpheus; Hymen; Hestia, Vesta; Lares, Penates; local god, genius loci.

nymph, wood n., tree n., dryad, hamadryad; mountain nymph, oread; water nymph, naiad; sea nymph, nereid; Oceanid; Pleiades; siren 970 *mythical being*.

968. Angel. Saint. Madonna. – N. *angel*, archangel, heavenly host, angelic h., choir invisible; thrones, principalities and powers; seraph, seraphim, cherub, cherubim; ministering spirit, guardian angel; angelophany; angelolatry; angelology.

saint, patron s., s. and martyr, the blessed . . .; soul, soul in bliss, Church triumphant.

Madonna, Our Lady, Blessed Virgin Mary, Mother of God, Mater Dolorosa; Queen of Heaven, Queen of Angels, Stella Maris; Mariolatry.

Adj. *angelic*, angelical, archangelic; seraphic, cherubic; saintly, glorified, celestial.

Vb. *angelize*, angelify; beatify 979 *sanctify*.

969. Devil – N. *Satan*, Lucifer, fallen angel; Archfiend, Prince of Darkness,

Prince of this world; serpent, Tempter, Adversary, Antichrist; Diabolus, Father of Lies; angel of the bottomless pit, Apollyon, Abaddon; the foul fiend, the Devil, the Evil One; spirit of evil, Ahriman.

Mephisto, Mephistopheles, His Satanic Majesty, the Old Gentleman, Old Nick, Old Harry, Old Scratch, Auld Hornie, Clootie.

devil, fiend; familiar, imp, imp of Satan, devil's spawn 970 *demon*; malevolent spirit, unclean s., dybbuk; powers of darkness; fallen angel, lost soul, sinner, denizen of Hell; Mammon, Belial, Beelzebub, Lord of the Flies; devildom, devilship; horns, cloven hoof.

diabolism, devilry, demonry, diablerie 898 *inhumanity*; Satanism, devilism; devil worship, demonism, polydaemonism, demonolatry; demoniac possession; witchcraft, black magic, Black Mass 983 *sorcery*; Satanology, demonology.

diabolist, Satanist, devil-worshipper, demonolater, demonist; demonologist.

Adj. *diabolic*, diabolical, devil-like, satanic, Mephistophelean, fiendish, demonic, demoniacal, devilish 898 *malevolent*; infernal, hellish, hell-born; devil-worshipping, demonolatrous; demoniac, possessed; demonological.

970. Mythical being – N. *fairy*, faerie, elfland, fairyland; fairy folk, good f., little people; fay, peri; good fairy, fairy godmother; bad fairy, witch; fairy queen, Mab, Titania; Oberon, Erl King; Ariel; elemental spirit, sylph, sylphid; genius; fairy ring, pixie r.; fairyism, fairy lore, fairy tales, folklore.

elf, elves, elfin folk, alfar; pixie, piskie, brownie, kobold; gnome, dwarf; troll, orc, goblin; imp, sprite, hobgoblin; changeling; leprechaun; pigwidgin; poltergeist, gremlin, dybbuk; Puck, Hob, Robin Goodfellow; elvishness, goblinry.

ghost, spirit, departed s.; shades, Manes; revived corpse, zombie; visitant, revenant, poltergeist, duppy; spook, spectre, apparition, phantom, wraith, presence, doppelgänger, fetch 440 *visual fallacy*; control 984 *spiritualism*.

demon, cacodemon; imp, familiar 969 *devil*; afreet; she-demon, banshee; ogre, ogress, giant, giantess, Baba Yaga; bugbear, bugaboo, bogle, bogey, bogey man 938 *monster*; ghoul, vampire, lycanthrope, werewolf; incubus, succuba; fury, harpy; Gorgon; ogreishness, ghoulishness.

mythical being 968 *angel*, 969 *devil*; demon, genie, jinn; houri; Valkyrie, battlemaid; centaur, satyr, faun; water elf, kelpie, nix, nixie; merfolk, merman, mermaid; Lorelei, siren; water spirit 967 *nymph*; Merlin 983 *sorcerer*; Wayland Smith, Green Man, Wodwose; yeti, Abominable Snowman 84 *rara avis*.

Adj. *fairylike*, fairy, nymphean; dwarflike 196 *dwarfish*; monstrous, ogreish, devilish, demonic 969 *diabolic*; vampirish, lycanthropic; gorgonian; elf-like, elfin, elvish, impish, Puckish 898 *maleficent*; magic 983 *magical*; mythical, mythic, folklorish 513 *imaginary*.

spooky, spookish, ghostly, ghoulish; haunted, hagridden; nightmarish, macabre 854 *frightening*; weird, uncanny, unearthly, eldritch 84 *abnormal*; eerie, numinous, supernatural, supernormal; spectral, wraith-like; disembodied, discarnate 320 *immaterial*; spiritualistic 984 *psychical*.

Vb. *haunt*, visit, walk; ghost, gibber, mop and mow.

971. Heaven – N. *heaven*, kingdom of God, kingdom of heaven, heavenly kingdom, kingdom come; Paradise, abode of the blest, land of the leal; Abraham's bosom, eternal rest, celestial bliss; nirvana, seventh heaven; the Millennium, earthly paradise, Zion, New Jerusalem, Holy City, Celestial C.; afterlife, resurrection; assumption, translation, glorification; deification, apotheosis.

mythic heaven, Olympus; Valhalla, Asgard; Elysium, Elysian fields, happy hunting grounds; Earthly Paradise, Garden of Eden, Hesperides, Islands of the Blest 513 *fantasy*.

Adj. *paradisiac*, paradisal; heavenly, celestial, supernal, eternal; beatific, blessed, blissful 824 *happy*; resurrectional, glorified; Elysian, Olympian; millennial.

972. Hell – N. *hell*, place of the dead, lower world, nether regions, infernal r., underworld; grave, limbo, Sheol, Hades; purgatory; perdition, place of the damned, inferno, Pandemonium; abyss, bottomless pit; place of torment, lake of fire and brimstone; hellfire.

mythic hell, Hel, Niflheim; Hades, Tartarus, Avernus, Erebus; Acheron, Styx, Lethe; Charon; Cerberus; Pluto, Osiris.

Adj. *infernal*, hellish, Chthonian, Plutonian; Stygian, Lethean; damned, devilish 969 *diabolic*.

973. Religion – N. *religion*, religious feeling 979 *piety*; Messianism 507 *expectation*; search for truth; natural religion, deism; primitive religion, early faith; paganism 982 *idolatry*; nature religion, orgiastic r., mystery r., mysteries; dharma, revealed religion, historical r., incarnational r., sacramental r.; mysticism, Sufism; Yoga; Eightfold Path; theosophy 449 *philosophy*; theolatry 981 *worship*.

deism, belief in a god, theism; animism, pantheism, polytheism, henotheism, monotheism, dualism; gnosticism.

religious faith, faith 485 *belief*; Christianity, the Cross; Judaism; Islam, Mohammedanism, the Crescent; Baha-'ism, Zoroastrianism; Vedic religion, Dharma; Hinduism, Brahminism, Vedantism, Tantrism; Sikhism; Jainism; Buddhism, Theravada, Hinayana, Mahayana, Zen; Shintoism; Taoism, Confucianism.

theology, study of religion; natural theology, revealed t.; religious learning, divinity; scholasticism, Thomism; Rabbinism; isagogics, theological exegesis; typology; demythologization; Christology; soteriology, theodicy; eschatology; hagiology, hagiography, iconology; dogmatics; symbolics, creedal theology; tradition, deposit of faith; teaching, doctrine; definition, canon; doxy, dogma, tenet; articles of faith, credo 485 *creed*; confession, Thirty-nine Articles; Bibli-

ology, higher criticism; comparative religion.

theologian, divine; doctor of the Church; doctor of the Law, rabbi, mufti, mullah; schoolman, scholastic, Thomist, Talmudist, canonist; theogonist, hagiologist, hagiographer, iconologist; textualist, Masorete; Bible critic, higher c.; scripturalist, fundamentalist, rabbinist.

religious teacher, prophet, rishi, inspired writer; guru, maharishi 500 *sage*; evangelist, apostle, missionary; reformer, religious r.; expected leader, Messiah; expounder, hierophant, catechist 520 *interpreter*.

religionist, deist, theist; monotheist, henotheist, polytheist, pantheist; animist, fetishist 982 *idolater*; pagan, gentile 974 *heathen*; people of the book; adherent, believer 976 *the orthodox*; militant 979 *zealot*.

Adj. *religious*, divine, holy, sacred, spiritual, sacramental; deistic, theistic, animistic, pantheistic, henotheistic, monotheistic, dualistic; Christian, Muslim, Jewish; Buddhist, Hindu; yogic, mystic, Sufic; devotional 981 *worshipping*.

theological, theosophical, scholastic, rabbinical; doctrinal, dogmatic, creedal, canonical; Christological, soteriological; doxological 988 *ritualistic*; hagiological, iconological.

974. Irreligion – N. *irreligion*, unreligiousness, unspirituality; nothing sacred, profaneness, ungodliness, godlessness 980 *impiety*; false religion, heathenism 982 *idolatry*; atheism, nullifidianism 486 *unbelief*; agnosticism, scepticism 486 *doubt*; probabilism, euhemerism 449 *philosophy*; lack of faith; lapse from faith 603 *change of allegiance*; paganization, dechristianization; indifferentism 860 *indifference*.

antichristianity, antichristianism 704 *opposition*; paganism, heathenism; Satanism 969 *diabolism*; free thought, rationalism, positivism, nihilism 449 *philosophy*; hylotheism, materialism; secularism, worldliness 944 *sensualism*; Mammonism 816 *avarice*.

irreligionist, Antichrist; nullifidian, dissenter, atheist 486 *unbeliever*; rationalist, euhemerist, freethinker; agnostic, sceptic; nihilist, materialist, positivist; secularist, Mammonist, Mammonite, worldling.

heathen, non-Christian, pagan; misbeliever, infidel, giaour; gentile, the uncircumcised, the unbaptized; apostate.

Adj. *irreligious*, without religion; godless, altarless, profane 980 *impious*; nihilistic, atheistic; creedless, nullifidian, agnostic 486 *unbelieving*; free-thinking, rationalistic, euhemeristic; nonreligious, nonworshipping, nonpractising 769 *nonobservant*; unreligious, unspiritual, ungodly 934 *wicked*; amoral 860 *indifferent*; secular, worldly, materialistic 932 *selfish*; Mammonistic 944 *sensual*; faithless, backsliding 603 *trimming*; unchristian, non-Christian; antireligious, anticlerical.

heathenish, unholy 980 *profane*; unchristian, unbaptized, unconfirmed; gentile, uncircumcised; heathen, pagan, infidel; unconverted 491 *uninstructed*.

975. Revelation – N. *revelation*, divine r., apocalypse 526 *disclosure*; illumination 417 *light*; afflatus, inspiration; prophecy; mysticism; the Law, Mosaic L., Ten Commandments; divine message, God's word, gospel; theophany, epiphany, incarnation, Word made flesh; avatar, emanation, divine e.

scripture, Word of God, inspired text, sacred writings; Holy Scripture, Holy Writ, Bible, Holy B., the Good Book; Vulgate, Septuagint; canonical writings; canon; Old Testament, Torah, the Law and the Prophets, Hagiographa; New Testament, Gospels, Epistles, Acts, Revelation; Apocrypha, agrapha; psalter, psalmbook, breviary, missal 981 *prayers*; fundamentalism, scripturalism.

non-Biblical scripture, Koran; Hadith, Sunna; Veda, Bhagavad Gita; smriti, shastra, sutra, tantra; Granth; Avesta, Zend-Avesta.

Adj. *revelational*, inspirational, mystic; inspired, prophetic, revealed, epiphanous; visional; apocalyptic; prophetic, evangelical; mystagogic.

scriptural, sacred, holy; hierographic, hieratic; revealed, inspired, prophetic; canonical 733 *authoritative*; biblical, gospel, evangelistic, apostolic; subapostolic, patristic, homiletic; Talmudic, Mishnaic; Koranic, uncreated; Vedic, Upanishadic, Puranic; textual, Masoretic.

976. Orthodoxy – N. *orthodoxy*, sound theology; religious truth, pure Gospel 494 *truth*; scripturality, canonicity; the Faith, the true faith; primitive faith, early Church; ecumenicalism, catholicity, Catholicism; credo 485 *creed*; catechism.

orthodoxism, strict interpretation; scripturalism, textualism, fundamentalism; traditionalism, institutionalism, ecclesiasticism 985 *the church*; sound churchmanship; Christian practice 768 *observance*; intolerance, heresy-hunting, persecution; Counter-Reformation; Inquisition; guaranteed orthodoxy, imprimatur 923 *approbation*.

Christendom, Christian world, the Church; Christian fellowship, communion of saints; Holy Church, Mother C.; Bride of Christ; Body of Christ; Church militant, Church on earth; Church triumphant; World Council of Churches.

Catholicism, Orthodoxy, Eastern O.; Roman Catholicism, Romanism; popery, papistry, ultramontanism, Scarlet Woman; Counter-Reformation; Anglicanism, Episcopalianism, prelacy; Anglo-Catholicism, High Church; Tractarianism, Oxford Movement.

Protestantism, the Reformation, Anglicanism, Lutheranism, Calvinism; Presbyterianism, Congregationalism, United Reformed Church; Baptists; Society of Friends; Wesleyanism, Methodism.

church member, churchman *or* -woman, church-goer, pillar of the church; the baptized, the confirmed; practising Christian, communicant 981 *worshipper*; the saints, the faithful; church people, chapel p.; congregation, co-religionist, fellow-worshipper.

the orthodox, the faithful; born-again

Christian, evangelical; believer, true b.; pillar of orthodoxy, conformist; traditionalist, scripturalist, fundamentalist.

Adj. *orthodox*, holding the faith 485 *believing*; right-minded, sound; nonheretical, unschismatical 488 *assenting*; loyal, devout 739 *obedient*; practising, conforming; churchy 979 *pietistic*; strict, pedantic; hyperorthodox; intolerant, witch-hunting, heresy-h., inquisitional; doctrinal 485 *creedal*; authoritative, canonical, biblical, scriptural, evangelical, gospel 494 *genuine*; fundamentalist; Trinitarian; catholic, ecumenical, universal.

977. Heterodoxy – N. *heterodoxy*, other men's doxy; unorthodoxy, unauthorized belief, personal judgement; erroneous opinion, wrong belief 495 *error*; doubtful orthodoxy, heretical tendency, latitudinarianism, Modernism; unscripturality, noncatholicity; heresy, rank h.; heretic, heresiarch.

Adj. *heterodox*, differing, unconventional 15 *different*; dissentient 489 *dissenting*; nondoctrinaire, nonconformist; uncatholic, antipapal; unorthodox, unbiblical, unscriptural, unauthorized, unsanctioned; heretical, damnable.

Vb. *declare heretical*, anathematize 961 *condemn*.

978. Sectarianism – N. *sectarianism*, particularism, clannishness, sectionalism 481 *prejudice*; bigotry 481 *bias*; separatism, schismaticalness 738 *disobedience*; denominationalism, nonconformism, nonconformity 489 *dissent*.

schism, division, differences 709 *quarrel*; dissociation, breakaway, secession, withdrawal 46 *separation*; nonrecognition, mutual excommunication; recusancy 769 *nonobservance*; Great Schism.

sect, division, off-shoot 708 *party*; order 708 *community*; chapel, conventicle 976 *Protestantism*; Friends, Quakers; Unitarians; Moravians; Plymouth Brethren; Churches of Christ; Sabbatarians, Seventh-day Adventists; Church of Christ

Scientist; Latter-Day Saints, Mormons; Jehovah's Witnesses; Salvation Army, Salvationists; Moonies; Scientologists; Oxford Group.

non-Christian sect, Orthodox Jews, Reform J.; Pharisees, Sadducees; Hasidim, Rabbinists; Karaites; Essenes; Gnostics; Sunnis, Shi'ites, Sufis, Wahhabis; Black Muslims; Rastafarians, Rastas; Hare Krishna sect.

sectarian, particularist; Dissenter, Nonconformist, Independent; Puritan; Covenanter.

schismatic, separated brother *or* sister; separatist, seceder, secessionist; rebel, recusant, nonjuror; dissident, dissenter, nonconformist 489 *dissentient*; wrong believer, heretic.

Adj. *sectarian*, particularist; partisan 481 *biased*; exclusive 708 *sectional*.

schismatic, secessionist, breakaway 46 *separate*; excommunicated, excommunicable, heretical; dissentient, nonconformist 489 *dissenting*; recusant 769 *nonobservant*; apostate 603 *trimming*.

Vb. *schismatize*, commit schism, separate, secede, break away; be in a state of schism.

979. Piety – N. *piety*, goodness 933 *virtue*; reverence, veneration 920 *respect*; dutifulness, loyalty, conformity 768 *observance*; churchmanship 976 *orthodoxy*; religion, religious feeling; fear of God, submissiveness, humbleness 872 *humility*; faith, trust 485 *belief*; devotion, dedication 931 *disinterestedness*; devoutness, unction; enthusiasm, fervour, zeal, muscular Christianity; inspiration, exaltation, speaking in tongues, glossolalia; adoration, prostration 981 *worship*; prayerfulness, meditation, retreat; contemplation, mysticism, communion with God 973 *religion*; faith healing; act of piety, pious duty, charity; pilgrimage, hadj.

sanctity, holiness, sacredness; goodness 933 *virtue*; synergism; state of grace, odour of sanctity 950 *purity*; godliness, saintliness; spirituality, unworldliness, otherworldliness; sainthood, blessedness; enlightenment, Buddhahood; conversion, regeneration 656 *revival*; sanctification 965 *divine function*; canonization, beatification.

pietism, show of piety, sanctimony; sanctimoniousness, unction 542 *sham*; religionism, religiosity, religious mania; scrupulosity, overpiety 976 *orthodoxism*; formalism, Puritanism 481 *narrow mind*; literalness, fundamentalism; Bible-worship, bibliolatry; Sabbatarianism 978 *sectarianism*; churchiness 985 *ecclesiasticism*; preachiness, unctuousness; odium theologicum, bigotry, fanaticism 481 *prejudice*; persecution, witch-hunting 735 *severity*; salvation 901 *philanthropy*.

pietist, pious person, real saint 937 *good person*; children of God, c. of light; the good, the righteous, the just; conformist 488 *assenter*; communicant 981 *worshipper*; confessor, martyr; saint, bodhisattva; man *or* woman of prayer, contemplative, mystic, Sufi; holy man, sadhu, sannyasi, fakir, dervish 945 *ascetic*; hermit, anchorite 883 *solitary*; religious 986 *clergy*; devotee; convert, believer 976 *church member*; the chosen people, the elect; pilgrim, palmer, hadji; votary.

zealot, religionist; fanatic, bigot, iconoclast; Puritan; Pharisee, scribe; the unco guid; fundamentalist, Bible-worshipper, Sabbatarian 978 *sectarian*; Bible-puncher 537 *preacher*; evangelical, salvationist, hot-gospeller; missionary 901 *philanthropist*; revivalist, speaker in tongues; champion of the faith, crusader, Ghazi.

Adj. *pious*, good 933 *virtuous*; reverent 920 *respectful*; faithful, loyal 739 *obedient*; conforming 768 *observant*; believing 976 *orthodox*; practising, professing, confessing; pure, pure in heart; unworldly, spiritual; godly, God-fearing, religious, devout; prayerful 981 *worshipping*; meditative, contemplative, mystic; holy, saintly, saintlike, sainted; full of grace.

pietistic, fervent, enthusiastic, inspired; austere, anchoretic 945 *ascetic*; earnest, pi, religiose, overreligious, overpious; self-righteous, holier than thou; overstrict, formalistic, Pharisaic, ritualistic 978 *sectarian*; priest-ridden, churchy;

preachy, sanctimonious 850 *affected*; goody-goody 933 *virtuous*; crusading, evangelical.

sanctified, made holy, consecrated; holy, sacred, solemn, sacrosanct 866 *worshipful*; sainted, canonized, beatified; chosen; saved, redeemed, regenerate, born again 656 *restored*.

Vb. *be pious*, fear God 854 *fear*; have faith 485 *believe*; keep the faith, fight the good fight; walk humbly with one's God 872 *be humble*; go to church *or* chapel, attend divine worship; pray, say one's prayers 981 *worship*; give to the poor 897 *be benevolent*; glorify God 923 *praise*; show reverence 920 *show respect*; hearken 739 *obey*; sermonize, preach at 534 *teach*.

become pious, be converted, get religion; go over 603 *tergiversate*; see the light, mend one's ways, reform; repent, receive Christ 939 *be penitent*.

make pious, bring to God, proselytize, convert 485 *convince*; Christianize, win for Christ, baptize; Islamize, Judaize; depaganize, spiritualize; edify, inspire, uplift 654 *make better*.

sanctify, hallow, make holy 866 *honour*; consecrate, dedicate, enshrine 866 *dignify*; canonize, beatify; bless, make the sign of the cross.

980. Impiety – N. *impiety*, irreverence 921 *disrespect*; lack of piety, godlessness 974 *irreligion*; scoffing, derision 851 *ridicule*; sacrilegiousness, profanity; blasphemy 899 *malediction*; sacrilege, desecration, violation, profanation 675 *misuse*; unrighteousness, consciencelessness 934 *wickedness*; stubbornness 940 *impenitence*; apostasy 603 *change of allegiance*; profaneness, unholiness, worldliness; amoralism, indifferentism; paganism, heathenism 982 *idolatry*.

false piety, solemn mockery 542 *sham*; sanctimony, sanctimoniousness 979 *pietism*; hypocrisy, lip service 541 *duplicity*; cant 850 *affectation*.

impious person, blasphemer, curser, swearer 899 *malediction*; mocker, scorner 926 *detractor*; desecrator, violator, profaner; nonworshipper, unbeliever 974 *heathen*; disbeliever 974 *irreligionist*; indifferentist, amoralist; worldling, materialist 944 *sensualist*; sinner, reprobate, children of darkness 938 *bad person*; backslider, apostate 603 *turncoat*; fallen angel 969 *Satan*; hypocrite, Tartuffe 545 *deceiver*.

Adj. *impious*, ungodly, antireligious, anti-Christian, anticlerical 704 *opposing*; dissenting, heretical; unbelieving, godless, irreligious; nonworshipping, nonpractising 769 *nonobservant*; misbelieving 982 *idolatrous*; scoffing 851 *derisive*; blasphemous, swearing 899 *cursing*; irreligious, irreverent 921 *disrespectful*; sacrilegious, iconoclastic; unawed, brazen 855 *unfearing*; sinful, unregenerate 934 *wicked*; apostate 603 *trimming*; canting, Pharisaical 541 *hypocritical*.

profane, unholy, unhallowed, unsanctified, unblest; accursed; unconsecrated, deconsecrated, secularized; dechristianized 974 *heathenish*.

Vb. *be impious*, etc. adj.; rebel against God 871 *be proud*; sin 934 *be wicked*; swear, blaspheme, take the name of the Lord in vain 899 *curse*; have no reverence 921 *not respect*; profane, desecrate, violate 675 *misuse*; commit sacrilege, defile 649 *make unclean*; cant 541 *dissemble*; backslide 603 *apostatize*; harden one's heart 655 *deteriorate*.

981. Worship – N. *worship*, honour, reverence, homage 920 *respect*; awe 854 *fear*; veneration, adoration; humbleness 872 *humility*; devotion 979 *piety*; prayer, meditation, contemplation, communion.

cult, mystique; supreme worship, latria; inferior worship, dulia, hyperdulia; Christolatry, Mariolatry; iconolatry, image-worship; false worship 982 *idolatry*.

act of worship, rites, mysteries 988 *rite*; laud 923 *praise*; glorification, extolment 866 *dignification*; hymn-singing, psalmody 412 *vocal music*; thanksgiving, blessing, benediction 907 *thanks*; offering, almsgiving (see *oblation*).

prayers, orisons, devotions; retreat, contemplation 449 *meditation*; prayer, impetration 761 *request*; invocation 583 *allocution*; intercession, intercessory prayer, arrow p.; prayers for the dead, vigils; special prayer, intention; rogation, supplication, litany; commination, imprecation; exorcism 300 *ejection*; benediction, benedicite, benison, grace 907 *thanks*; prayer for the day, collect; Lord's Prayer, Paternoster, Our Father; Ave, Ave Maria, Hail Mary; rosary, beads; prayer wheel; prayer book, missal, breviary, book of hours; call to prayer, muezzin's cry.

hymn, song, psalm; religious song, spiritual; processional, recessional; introit; plainsong 412 *vocal music*; anthem, canticle; song of praise, doxology, Gloria; paean, hallelujah, hosanna; hymnody, psalmody; hymnbook, hymnal, psalter; hymnology, hymnography.

oblation, offertory, collection, alms 781 *offering*; libation, incense 988 *rite*; votive offering, de voto o.; thank-offering 907 *gratitude*; burnt offering, holocaust; sacrifice, devotion; immolation; self-sacrifice 931 *disinterestedness*; a humble and a contrite heart 939 *penitence*.

public worship, common prayer; agape, love-feast; service, divine office 988 *church service*; church, church-going, chapel-g. 979 *piety*; prayer meeting, revival m. 74 *assembly*; open-air service, evangelism, revivalism.

worshipper, fellow w. 976 *church member*; adorer, venerator; votary, devotee 979 *pietist*; glorifier, hymner, praiser 923 *commender*; follower 742 *servant*; image-worshipper 982 *idolater*; sacrificer 781 *giver*; invoker, supplicant, intercessor 763 *petitioner*; man *or* woman of prayer, contemplative, mystic, visionary; dervish, enthusiast, revivalist 973 *religious teacher*; celebrant 986 *clergy*; communicant, churchgoer, chapelgoer, temple worshipper; congregation 976 *church member*; psalm-singer, hymn-s.; psalmist, hymn-writer; pilgrim, palmer, hadji 268 *traveller*.

Adj. *worshipping*, devout 979 *pious*; reverent 920 *respectful*; prayerful, fervent 761 *supplicatory*; on one's knees, at one's prayers; church-going, chapel-g., communicant 976 *orthodox*; hymn-singing, psalm-s.; mystic, mystical.

devotional, worshipful, solemn 979 *sanctified*; sacramental, mystic, mystical; invocatory; precatory, intercessory, petitionary 761 *supplicatory*; imprecatory 899 *maledictory*; sacrificial; oblationary, votive 759 *offering*; praising, doxological.

Vb. *worship*, honour, revere, venerate, adore 920 *respect*; honour and obey 854 *fear*; pay homage to, make a god of, deify, apotheosize 982 *idolatrize*; bow down before, kneel to, genuflect, humble oneself, prostrate o.; lift up one's heart, extol, magnify, glorify 923 *praise*; hymn, celebrate; burn incense before; pray, say one's prayers, commune with God 979 *be pious*.

offer worship, celebrate 988 *perform ritual*; sacrifice, offer up 781 *give*; propitiate, appease 719 *pacify*; vow, dedicate, consecrate 979 *sanctify*; go to church *or* chapel, meet for prayer 979 *be pious*; hear Mass, take the sacraments, communicate; deny oneself, fast 946 *starve*; chant psalms, sing praises 923 *praise*.

Int. Alleluia! Hallelujah! Hosanna! Glory be to God!

982. Idolatry – N. *idolatry*, idolatrousness, superstition 981 *worship*; heathenism, paganism 973 *religion*; fetishism, anthropomorphism, zoomorphism; iconolatry, image worship; idol worship, mumbo jumbo; hocus-pocus 983 *sorcery*; cult, cargo c.; sacrifice, human s. 981 *oblation*; heliolatry, sun worship; necrolatry, demonolatry, devil worship 969 *diabolism*; Mammonism.

deification, god-making, apotheosis; idolization, hero worship 920 *respect*; king worship, emperor w.

idol, image, graven i.; cult image, fetish, totem pole; lingam, yoni; golden calf; godling, joss; teraphim, lares et penates, totem; Juggernaut, Baal, Moloch.

idolater, idolatress; idol-worshipper, idolatrizer; fetishist, totemist; iconolater, image-worshipper 981 *worshipper*; heliolater, sunworshipper; bibliolater 979 *pietist*; Mammonist; demonolater, devil-

worshipper 969 *diabolist*; pagan 974 *heathen*; idolizer, deifier 923 *commender*.

Adj. *idolatrous*, pagan 974 *heathenish*; fetishistic; anthropomorphic, theriomorphic; fire-worshipping, sun-w.; devil-worshipping 969 *diabolic*.

Vb. *idolatrize*, worship idols; anthropomorphize, make God in one's own image; deify, apotheosize 979 *sanctify*; idealize, idolize, put on a pedestal 923 *praise*.

983. Sorcery – N. *sorcery*, spellbinding, witchery, magic arts, enchantments; witchcraft; gramarye, magic lore 490 *knowledge*; wizardry 694 *skill*; wonderworking 864 *thaumaturgy*; magic, illusionism 542 *sleight*; white magic, theurgy; black magic, black art, necromancy 969 *diabolism*; priestcraft, superstition, shamanism; obeah, voodooism, voodoo, hoodoo; spirit-raising 984 *occultism*; exorcism 988 *rite*; magic rite, incantation; coven, witches' sabbath; Walpurgisnacht; Hallowe'en; witching hour.

spell, charm, enchantment, cantrip, hoodoo, curse; evil eye, jinx, hex; bewitchment, fascination 291 *attraction*; obsession, possession, demoniacal p., bedevilment; incantation, rune; magic sign, magic formula, open sesame, abracadabra; hocus pocus, mumbo jumbo.

talisman, charm, countercharm; cross, phylactery; St Christopher medal 662 *safeguard*; juju, obeah, fetish 982 *idol*; periapt, amulet, mascot, lucky charm; luck-bringer, four-leaf clover, horseshoe, black cat; pentacle, pentagram; swastika, fylfot, gammadion; scarab; birthstone; relic, holy r.

magic instrument, bell, book and candle, wizard's cap, witch's broomstick; witches' brew, philtre, portion; wand, ring; Aladdin's lamp; flying carpet, seven-league boots; cap of darkness, cloak of invisibility; wishing well, wishbone, merrythought.

sorcerer, wise man, seer, soothsayer 511 *diviner*; astrologer, alchemist 984 *occultist*; Druid, Druidess; magus, mage, the Magi; thaumaturgist, wonder-worker, miracle-w. 864 *thaumaturgy*; shaman, witchdoctor, medicine man, fetishist 982 *idolater*; obeah man, voodooist, hoodooist, spirit-raiser, exorcist; snake-charmer; illusionist 545 *conjuror*; spell-binder, enchanter, wizard, warlock; magician, theurgist; necromancer 969 *diabolist*; Merlin, Prospero, Gandalf.

sorceress, wise woman, sibyl 511 *diviner*; enchantress, witch; hag, hellcat; succubus, succuba; fairy godmother 970 *fairy*; Circe, Medea.

Adj. *sorcerous*, wizardly, witch-like; thaumaturgic 864 *wonderful*; theurgic; necromantic 969 *diabolic*; shamanistic, voodooistic; incantatory, runic; spell-binding, enchanting 291 *attracting*; occult, esoteric 984 *cabbalistic*.

magical, witching; otherworldly, super-natural, uncanny, eldritch, weird 970 *fairylike*; talismanic 660 *tutelary*; magic, charmed, enchanted.

bewitched, enchanted, charmed, fey; hypnotized, fascinated, spellbound, under a spell; under a curse, blighted, blasted; hag-ridden, haunted.

Vb. *practise sorcery*, etc. n.; do magic, weave spells; make wax effigies; wave a wand, recite a spell *or* an incantation, say the magic word; conjure, call up; raise spirits; exorcize, lay ghosts.

bewitch, charm, enchant 291 *attract*; hypnotize; magic, magic away; spellbind, cast a spell on, lay under a spell; hoodoo, voodoo; cast the evil eye 898 *be malevolent*; lay under a curse 899 *curse*.

984. Occultism – N. *occultism*, esotericism, hermeticism, mysticism 973 *religion*; mystical interpretation, cabbala; theosophy; yogism; supernaturalism, psychicism, pseudopsychology; occult lore, alchemy, astrology, psychomancy, spiritualism, magic 983 *sorcery*; crystal-gazing 511 *divination*; sixth sense 476 *intuition*; animal magnetism, mesmerism, hypnotism.

psychics, parapsychology, psychism 447 *psychology*; psychical research; paranormal perception, extrasensory p., ESP; telaesthesia, clairaudience, clairvoyance, second sight 476 *intuition*; psychokinesis,

fork-bending; telepathy, telergy; thought-reading, mind-r., thought transference; precognition, psi faculty; déjà vu.

spiritualism, spiritism; psychomancy 983 *sorcery*; mediumship, séance; astral body 320 *immateriality*; materialization, ectoplasm 319 *materiality*; apport, telekinesis; poltergeists; spirit-rapping, table-tapping, table-turning; automatism, automatic writing, spirit w.; psychograph, planchette, ouija board; control 970 *ghost*; ghost-hunting; psychical research.

occultist, mystic, transcendentalist, supernaturalist; esoteric, cabbalist; reincarnationist; theosophist, yogi; spiritualist, Rosicrucian; alchemist 983 *sorcerer*; astrologer, fortune-teller 511 *diviner*.

psychic, clairvoyant, clairaudient; telepath, telepathist; mind reader, thought r.; mesmerist, hypnotist; medium; prophet 511 *oracle*; dowser 484 *detector*.

Adj. *cabbalistic*, esoteric, hermetic 523 *occult*; mystic, transcendental, supernatural; astrological; alchemic, necromantic 983 *sorcerous*.

psychical, psychic, fey, second-sighted; telepathic, clairvoyant; thought-reading, mind-r.; spiritualistic, mediumistic; mesmeric, hypnotic.

paranormal, parapsychological, super-natural, preternatural, hyperphysical, supranormal.

Vb. *practise occultism*, alchemize 147 *transform*; astrologize 511 *divine*; hypnotize, mesmerize; practise spiritualism, hold a séance, go into a trance; materialize, dematerialize.

985. The Church – N. *the church*, church-dom 976 *Christendom*; priestly government, hierocracy, theocracy 733 *authority*; papalism, papacy, popedom; prelatism, prelacy; episcopacy, episcopalianism; presbyterianism, congregationalism 978 *sectarianism*; ecclesiology, ecclesiologist.

ecclesiasticism, clericalism, sacerdotalism; priesthood, brahmanhood; priestdom, priestcraft; Brahmanism; ecclesiastical privilege 919 *nonliability*; ecclesiastical censorship, Holy Office 757 *prohibition*.

monasticism, monastic life, monachism 895 *celibacy*; cenobitism 883 *seclusion*; monkhood 945 *asceticism*.

church ministry, ecclesiastical vocation, call 622 *vocation*; apostleship, apostolate, mission, overseas m., inner-city m. 147 *conversion*; industrial priesthood; pastorate, pastorship, cure of souls 901 *philanthropy*; spiritual guidance 988 *ministration*.

church office, holy orders; priesthood; apostolate, apostleship; pontificate, papacy, Holy See, Vatican; cardinalate, cardinalship; patriarchate, exarchate, metropolitanate; primacy, primateship; archiepiscopate, episcopate, episcopacy, prelacy, prelature; abbotship, abbacy; priorate, priorship; archdeaconry, archdeaconate, archdeaconship; deanery, deanship; canonry, canonicate; prebendaryship; deaconate, deaconship; diaconate, subdiaconate; presbyterate, presbytership, eldership, moderatorship; ministership, pastorship, pastorate; rectorship, vicarship, vicariate; curacy; chaplainship, chaplaincy; incumbency, tenure, benefice 773 *possession*.

parish, deanery; presbytery; diocese, bishopric, see, archbishopric; metropolitanate, patriarchate, province 184 *district*.

benefice, incumbency, tenure; living, rectorship; glebe, tithe; prebend, canonry; temporalities 777 *property*; patronage, advowson.

synod, convocation 692 *council*; college of cardinals, consistory, conclave; bench of bishops; chapter, vestry; kirk session, presbytery, Sanhedrin 956 *tribunal*; consistorial court, Court of Arches.

Adj. *ecclesiastical*, ecclesiastic; theocratic; hierocratic, priest-ridden; apostolic; hierarchical, pontifical, papal; patriarchal, metropolitan; episcopal 986 *clerical*; episcopalian, presbyterian 978 *sectarian*; prioral, abbatial; conciliar, synodic, presbyteral, capitular; diocesan, parochial.

priestly, sacerdotal, hieratic, Aaronic,

Levitical; Brahminic; sacramental, spiritual; apostolic, pastoral.

Vb. *be ecclesiastical*, be churchly, be priestly etc. adj.; episcopize, prelatize; frock, ordain; nominate, present; prefer 781 *give*; enter the church 986 *take orders*.

986. Clergy – N. *clergy*, hierarchy; the cloth, the pulpit, the ministry; priesthood, secular clergy, regular c., religious.

cleric, clerk in holy orders, priest, deacon, subdeacon, acolyte, exorcist, lector, ostiary; churchman *or* -woman, ecclesiastic, divine; Doctor of Divinity; clergyman, man *or* woman of the cloth; reverend, father; padre, sky pilot, Holy Joe; parson, rector, incumbent; hedge priest, priestling 639 *nonentity*; ordinand, seminarist 538 *learner*.

pastor, shepherd, minister, woman m., parish priest, rector, vicar, curate; chaplain; confessor, father c.; spiritual director *or* adviser; lay preacher 537 *preacher*; missioner, missionary 901 *philanthropist*; evangelist, revivalist, salvationist, hotgospeller.

ecclesiarch, ecclesiastical potentate 741 *governor*; pope, Supreme Pontiff, Holy Father, Vicar of Christ, Bishop of Rome; cardinal, prince of the church; patriarch, exarch, metropolitan, primate, archbishop; prelate, diocesan, bishop; suffragan, assistant bishop; episcopate, Lords Spiritual; archpriest, archpresbyter; archdeacon, deacon; dean, canon; prebendary, capitular; elder, presbyter, moderator.

monk, monastic 895 *celibate*; hermit, cenobite 883 *solitary*; Orthodox monk, caloyer; Islamic monk, santon, marabout; Sufi 979 *pietist*; dervish, fakir 945 *ascetic*; Buddhist monk, pongye, bonze; brother, regular, conventual; superior, archimandrite, abbot, prior; novice, lay brother; friar, mendicant f.; religious; fraternity, brotherhood, lay b.; order, religious o.

nun, anchoress, recluse; religious, bride of Christ; novice, postulant; lay sister; Mother Superior, abbess, prioress, canoness, deaconess; sisterhood.

church officer, elder, presbyter, deacon 741 *officer*; priest, chaplain; minister; lay preacher, lay reader; acolyte 988 *ritualist*; chorister, precentor 413 *choir*; sidesman *or* -woman; churchwarden; clerk, vestry c., parish c.; beadle, verger, pew-opener; sacristan, sexton; grave digger, bell-ringer.

priest, chief p., high p., archpriest, hierophant; priestess, vestal; rabbi; imam, mufti; Brahmin; bonze, lama; pontifex, flamen; Druid, Druidess, shaman, witch doctor.

monastery, monkery, lamasery; friary, priory, abbey; cloister, convent, nunnery, beguinage; ashram, hermitage 192 *retreat*; cell 194 *chamber*.

parsonage, presbytery, rectory, vicarage; manse; deanery 192 *abode*; palace, bishop's p.; close, precincts 235 *enclosure*.

Adj. *clerical*, in orders, in holy o.; ordained, consecrated; prebendal, beneficed; parsonical, rectorial, vicarial; pastoral, ministerial, presbyteral 985 *priestly*; diaconal, subdiaconal, archidiaconal, prelatical 985 *ecclesiastical*.

monastic, monasterial, cloistral; cloistered, conventual, enclosed; monkish, monachic, celibate; contemplative, in retreat; cowled, veiled; tonsured.

Vb. *take orders*, be ordained, enter the church *or* the ministry; take vows, take the veil.

987. Laity – N. *laity*, people, flock, fold; diocesans, parishioners; congregation 976 *church member*; lay brethren, lay sisterhood 708 *community*.

secularity, laicity; secularization, deconsecration.

lay person, layman *or* -woman; lay brother, lay sister; ordinand, seminarist, novice, postulant 538 *learner*; lay preacher, lay reader; elder, deacon, deaconess 986 *church officer*; parishioner, diocesan 976 *church member*.

Adj. *laical*, congregational, parochial; laic, lay, nonclerical, unordained; non-ecclesiastical, unclerical, unpriestly, secular; temporal, of the world; laicized, secularized, deconsecrated.

Vb. *laicize*, secularize, undedicate, deconsecrate.

988. Ritual – N. *ritual*, procedure, prescribed p.; form, order, liturgy 610 *practice*; symbolization, symbolism 519 *metaphor*; ceremonial, ceremony 875 *formality*.

ritualism, ceremonialism, ceremony, formalism; liturgics.

rite, mode of worship 981 *cult*; institution, observance 610 *practice*; rubric, formula 693 *precept*; ceremony, solemnity, sacrament, mystery 876 *celebration*; rites, mysteries; initiatory rite, rite of passage, circumcision, initiation, baptism 299 *reception*.

ministration, functioning, officiation, performance 676 *action*; administration, celebration, solemnization; the pulpit, preaching 534 *teaching*; homiletics; pastorship, pastoral care; confession, shrift, absolution.

Christian rite, sacrament; baptism, christening; confirmation, First Communion; Holy Communion, Eucharist; absolution 960 *acquittal*; Holy Matrimony 894 *marriage*; Holy Orders 985 *the church*; Holy Unction, chrism; visitation of the sick, extreme unction, last rites, viaticum; burial of the dead; requiem mass; ordination, consecration; exorcism, excommunication; bell, book and candle; canonization, beatification; dedication, undedication.

church service, office, duty, service 981 *act of worship*; liturgy, celebration, concelebration; mass, high m., communion, the Lord's Supper; matins, lauds, prime, terce, sext, none, vespers, compline; morning prayer, matins; evening prayer, evensong; Tenebrae; vigil; watch-night service; novena.

ritual act, symbolic act 551 *representation*; lustration, thurification, incense-burning; procession, stations of the Cross; obeisance, genuflexion, prostration; sign of the cross 547 *gesture*; Eucharistic rite, breaking the bread; elevating of the Host; kiss of peace.

ritualist, ceremonialist, formalist; liturgist, litanist; sacramentarian, sacramentalist; celebrant 986 *priest*; server, acolyte; thurifer.

office-book, service-b., ordinal, lectionary; liturgy, litany; book of hours, breviary; missal, prayer book; beads, rosary.

hymnal, hymn book, psalter, psalmbook 981 *hymn*.

holy day, feast, feast day, festival 837 *festivity*; fast day, meatless d. 946 *fast*; high day, day of observance, day of obligation 876 *celebration*; Sabbath, Lord's Day; saint's day 141 *anniversary*.

Adj. *ritual*, procedural; solemn, ceremonial, liturgical; processional, recessional; symbolic 551 *representing*; sacramental, Eucharistic; baptismal; sacrificial, paschal; festal, pentecostal; fasting, Lenten; prescribed, ordained; unleavened; kosher; consecrated, blessed.

ritualistic, ceremonious, ceremonial, formulistic.

Vb. *perform ritual*, celebrate, officiate; lead worship 981 *offer worship*; baptize, christen, confirm, ordain, lay on hands; minister, administer the sacraments, give communion; sacrifice, make s.; offer prayers, bless, give benediction; anathematize, ban; excommunicate, unchurch, unfrock; dedicate, consecrate, deconsecrate; purify, lustrate; cense, burn incense; anoint, give extreme unction; confess, absolve, shrive; take communion, receive the sacraments; kneel, genuflect, prostrate oneself; sign oneself, cross o.; tell one's beads, say one's rosary; process, circumambulate; fast, do penance.

ritualize, ceremonialize, institute a rite; sacramentalize, observe, keep holy.

989. Canonicals – N. *canonicals*, clerical dress, cloth; frock, soutane, cassock, scapular; gown, Geneva g.; cowl, hood; lappet, bands; clerical collar, dog c.; apron, gaiters, shovel hat; cardinal's hat; priest's cap, biretta; skull-cap, calotte, zucchetto; Salvation Army bonnet; tonsure; tallith.

vestments, ephod, canonical robes; pontificalia, pontificals; cassock, surplice,

rochet; cope, tunicle, dalmatic, alb 228 *robe*; amice, chasuble; stole, pallium; maniple, fanon; mitre, tiara, triple crown 743 *regalia*; crosier, crook 743 *badge of rule*; pectoral 222 *cross*; episcopal ring; orphrey.

Adj. *vestmental*, vestiary; canonical, pontifical.

vestured, robed 228 *dressed*; cowled, hooded, veiled 986 *monastic*; gaitered, aproned 986 *clerical*; mitred, crosiered; tiara'd.

990. Temple – N. *temple*, fane, pantheon; shrine, joss house 982 *idolatry*; tabernacle, the Temple, House of the Lord; place of worship 981 *worship*; mosque; house of prayer, oratory; sacred edifice, pagoda, stupa, ziggurat 164 *edifice*.

holy place, holy ground; sacrarium, sanctuary, adytum, altar, high a.; Ark of the Covenant, Mercy-seat, Sanctum, Holy of Holies, oracle; martyry, sacred tomb, sepulchre; God's Acre 364 *cemetery*; place of pilgrimage; Holy City, Zion; Mecca, Benares.

church, house of God; parish church, daughter c., chapel of ease; cathedral, minster, procathedral; basilica; abbey; kirk, chapel, tabernacle, temple, bethel, ebenezer; conventicle, meeting house, prayer h.; oratory, chantry; synagogue, mosque.

church utensil, font, baptistery; stoup, piscina; chalice, paten; altar table, communion t.; pulpit, lectern; Bible, hymnal, prayer book; hassock, kneeler; salver, collection plate, offertory bag; bell 412 *campanology*.

church interior, nave, aisle, apse, ambulatory, transept; chancel, choir, sanctuary; hagioscope, squint; rood screen, rood loft; pew, stall, choir s., sedilia, misericord; chapel, side c., Lady c.; confessional; clerestory, triforium; stained glass, rose window, stations of the Cross, Easter sepulchre; baptistery; sacristy, vestry; undercroft, crypt; rood, cross, crucifix.

church exterior, porch, narthex; tower, steeple, spire; bell tower, bellcote, belfry, campanile; buttress, flying b. 218 *prop*; cloister, ambulatory; chapter house; churchyard, kirkyard, lychgate; close 235 *enclosure*.

Adj. *churchlike*, basilican; cruciform; apsidal; Romanesque, Norman, Gothic, Early English, Decorated, Perpendicular, baroque, Puginesque, Gothic revival.

INDEX

For a note on how to use the index, see p. x

447

abroad
abroad 59 adv.
afar 199 adv.
abrogate
abrogate 752 vb.
abrupt
instantaneous
116 adj.
vertical 215 adj.
sullen 893 adj.
abscess
ulcer 651 n.
abscission
scission 46 n.
abscond
decamp 296 vb.
escape 667 vb.
fail in duty 918 vb.
abseil
descend 309 vb.
absence
nonexistence 2 n.
absence 190 n.
avoidance 620 n.
absent
absent 190 adj.
disappearing
446 adj.
unprovided 636 adj.
absenteeism
absence 190 n.
inactivity 679 n.
undutifulness 918 n.
absent-minded
abstracted 456 adj.
forgetful 506 adj.
absent oneself
depart 296 vb.
disappear 446 vb.
absinth, absinthe
alcoholic drink
301 n.
sourness 393 n.
absolute
unrelated 10 adj.
consummate 32 adj.
complete 54 adj.
positive 473 adj.
authoritative
733 adj.
unconditional
744 adj.
absoluteness
simpleness 44 n.
unity 88 n.
absolution
forgiveness 909 n.

Christian rite 988 n.
absolutism
despotism 733 n.
absolve
forgive 909 vb.
exempt 919 vb.
acquit 960 vb.
absorb
consume 165 vb.
absorb 299 vb.
drink 301 vb.
eat 301 vb.
dry 342 vb.
engross 449 vb.
appropriate 786 vb.
absorbed
abstracted 456 adj.
absorbing
exciting 821 adj.
abstain
be neutral 606 vb.
avoid 620 vb.
not act 677 vb.
abstainer
abstainer 942 n.
sober person
948 n.
abstemious
temperate 942 adj.
sober 948 adj.
abstention
no choice 606 n.
abstinence
temperance 942 n.
abstract
insubstantial 4 adj.
subtract 39 vb.
immaterial 320 adj.
mental 447 adj.
compendium 592 n.
take away 786 vb.
steal 788 vb.
abstract art
art 551 n.
abstracted
thoughtful 449 adj.
abstracted 456 adj.
abstraction
insubstantial thing
4 n.
idea 451 n.
abstruse
puzzling 517 adj.
unclear 568 adj.
absurd
absurd 497 adj.
foolish 499 adj.

meaningless
515 adj.
witty 839 adj.
ridiculous 849 adj.
abundance
great quantity 32 n.
abundance 171 n.
plenty 635 n.
abundant
many 104 adj.
liberal 813 adj.
abuse
evil 616 n.
waste 634 vb.
misuse 675 n.vb.
be rude 885 vb.
scurrility 899 n.
not respect 921 vb.
dispraise 924 vb.
debauch 951 vb.
impiety 980 n.
—one's authority
oppress 735 vb.
abusive
ungracious 885 adj.
cursing 899 adj.
abut
be contiguous
202 vb.
abutment
prop 218 n.
abysmal
deep 211 adj.
heinous 934 adj.
abyss
depth 211 n.
cavity 255 n.
academic
irrelevant 10 adj.
intellectual 492 n.
scholar 492 n.
suppositional
512 adj.
educational 534 adj.
Academy
philosopher 449 n.
ᶜacademy 539 n.
accede
approach 289 vb.
assent 488 vb.
— to the throne
take authority
733 vb.
accelerate
accelerate 277 vb.
hasten 680 vb.
accent

sound 398 n.
punctuation 547 n.
pronunciation
577 n.
prosody 593 n.
accentuate
emphasize 532 vb.
accept
admit 299 vb.
believe 485 vb.
acquiesce 488 vb.
submit 721 vb.
receive 782 vb.
approve 923 vb.
—responsibility (for)
incur a duty 917 vb.
acceptability
sufficiency 635 n.
acceptable
advisable 642 adj.
pleasurable 826 adj.
approvable 923 adj.
accepted
usual 610 adj.
orthodox 976 adj.
access
approach 289 n.
spasm 318 n.
access 624 n.
accessible
near 200 adj.
accessible 289 adj.
admitting 299 adj.
easy 701 adj.
accession
addition 38 n.
arrival 295 n.
authority 733 n.
accessories
dressing 228 n.
accessory
extrinsic 6 adj.
adjunct 40 n.
concomitant 89 n.
superfluity 637 n.
colleague 707 n.
accident
event 154 n.
chance 159 n.
collision 279 n.
nondesign 618 n.
accidental
casual 159 adj.
unintentional
618 adj.
accident-prone
unfortunate 731 adj.

accidie
inertness 175 n.
acclaim
repute 866 n.
applaud 923 vb.
acclimatize
habituate 610 vb.
acclivity
incline 220 n.
accolade
honours 866 n.
accommodate
adjust 24 vb.
comprise 78 vb.
place 187 vb.
aid 703 vb.
accommodating
benevolent 897 adj.
accommodation
room 183 n.
quarters 192 n.
accompaniment
accompaniment 89 n.
musical piece 412 n.
accompanist
instrumentalist 413 n.
accompany
accompany 89 vb.
synchronize 123 vb.
follow 284 vb.
accomplice
colleague 707 n.
accomplish
do 676 vb.
carry out 725 vb.
succeed 727 vb.
accomplished
skilful 694 adj.
accomplishments
culture 490 n.
accord
agreement 24 n.
accord 24 vb.
conform 83 vb.
assent 488 vb.
concord 710 vb.
consent 758 n.
give 781 vb.
according as
provided 468 adv.
accordion
organ 414 n.
accost
approach 289 vb.
speak to 583 vb.

accouchement
obstetrics 167 n.
account
report 524 n.
description 590 n.
accounts 808 n.
prestige 866 n.
account for
cause 156 vb.
account for 158 vb.
interpret 520 vb.
accountability
dueness 915 n.
duty 917 n.
accountancy
numeration 86 n.
accounts 808 n.
accountant
recorder 549 n.
treasurer 798 n.
accountant 808 n.
accounts
accounts 808 n.
accoutrements
dressing 228 n.
equipment 630 n.
accredited
creedal 485 adj.
commissioned 751 adj.
accretion
increment 36 n.
addition 38 n.
accrue
accrue 38 vb.
be received 782 vb.
accumulate
grow 36 vb.
bring together 74 vb.
store 632 vb.
acquire 771 vb.
accuracy
carefulness 457 n.
accuracy 494 n.
veracity 540 n.
accurate
adjusted 24 adj.
accursed
damnable 645 adj.
unfortunate 731 adj.
hateful 888 adj.
accusation
accusation 928 n.
accuse
blame 924 vb.
accuse 928 vb.

litigate 959 vb.
accused, the
prisoner 750 n.
accused person 928 n.
accuser
informer 524 n.
detractor 926 n.
accuser 928 n.
accustom
train 534 vb.
habituate 610 vb.
accustomed
usual 610 adj.
unastonished 865 adj.
ace
unit 88 n.
masterpiece 694 n.
proficient person 696 n.
ace in the hole
advantage 34 n.
acerbity
sourness 393 n.
rudeness 885 n.
malevolence 898 n.
acetylene
fuel 385 n.
ache
pang 377 n.
feel pain 377 vb.
suffer 825 vb.
achievable
possible 469 adj.
achieve
do 676 vb.
carry out 725 vb.
succeed 727 vb.
achievement
heraldry 547 n.
deed 676 n.
Achilles' heel
weakness 163 n.
vulnerability 661 n.
achromatism
achromatism 426 n.
acid
sour 393 adj.
poison 659 n.
sullen 893 adj.
drug-taking 949 n.
acidity
pungency 388 n.
sourness 393 n.
acid test
experiment 461 n.

acknowledge
attribute 158 vb.
answer 460 vb.
assent 488 vb.
confess 526 vb.
correspond 588 vb.
observe 768 vb.
greet 884 vb.
thank 907 vb.
grant claims 915 vb.
acknowledgement
attribution 158 n.
reward 962 n.
acme
summit 213 n.
perfection 646 n.
acne
skin disease 651 n.
blemish 845 n.
acolyte
auxiliary 707 n.
church officer 986 n.
acoustics
acoustics 398 n.
acquaint
inform 524 vb.
acquaintance
knowledge 490 n.
friendship 880 n.
acquiescence
conformity 83 n.
assent 488 vb.
willingness 597 n.
acquire
acquire 771 vb.
receive 782 vb.
acquired
extrinsic 6 adj.
acquired taste
habituation 610 n.
acquirements
culture 490 n.
skill 694 n.
acquisitive
acquiring 771 adj.
avaricious 816 adj.
greedy 859 adj.
acquit
liberate 746 vb.
forgive 909 vb.
acquit 960 vb.
—oneself
behave 688 vb.
acquittal
vindication 927 n.
acquittal 960 n.

acquittance
payment 804 n.
acreage
measure 183 n.
acres
land 344 n.
lands 777 n.
acrid
pungent 388 adj.
fetid 397 adj.
acrimonious
ungracious 885 adj.
resentful 891 adj.
acrobat
athlete 162 n.
entertainer 594 n.
acrobatic
flexible 327 adj.
acronym
initials 558 n.
word 559 n.
across
across 222 adv.
across-the-board
general 79 adj.
acrostic
enigma 530 n.
acrylic fibre
fibre 208 n.
act
dissemble 541 vb.
dramaturgy 594 n.
act 594 vb.
function 622 vb.
deed 676 n.
do 676 vb.
behave 688 vb.
decree 737 n.
—a part
be affected 850 vb.
—for
deputize 755 vb.
—upon
operate 173 vb.
motivate 612 vb.
acting
substituted 150 adj.
acting 594 n.
actinism
radiation 417 n.
actinometer
optical device 442 n.
action
agency 173 n.
action 676 n.
deed 676 n.
activity 678 n.

conduct 688 n.
battle 718 n.
litigation 959 n.
actionable
accusable 928 adj.
illegal 954 adj.
activation
stimulation 174 n.
activity 678 n.
activator
alterer 143 n.
active
operative 173 adj.
vigorous 174 adj.
doing 676 adj.
active 678 adj.
active service
warfare 718 n.
activist
busy person 678 n.
political party 708 n.
activity
motion 265 n.
agitation 318 n.
job 622 n.
activity 678 n.
act of God
ruin 165 n.
necessity 596 n.
actor, actress
cinema 445 n.
actor 594 n.
actual
real 1 adj.
present 121 adj.
true 494 adj.
actuary
enumerator 86 n.
accountant 808 n.
actuate
operate 173 vb.
move 265 vb.
motivate 612 vb.
acuity
sharpness 256 n.
sagacity 498 n.
acumen
discrimination
463 n.
sagacity 498 n.
acupuncture
anaesthetic 375 n.
therapy 658 n.
acute
keen 174 adj.
violent 176 adj.
sharp 256 adj.

sentient 374 adj.
strident 407 adj.
intelligent 498 adj.
felt 818 adj.
adage
maxim 496 n.
adagio
slowly 278 adv.
adagio 412 adv.
Adam and Eve
precursor 66 n.
humankind 371 n.
adamant
obstinate 602 adj.
adamantine
hard 326 adj.
adapt
adjust 24 vb.
modify 143 vb.
translate 520 vb.
adaptable
conformable 83 adj.
skilful 694 adj.
adaptation
musical piece 412 n.
edition 589 n.
add
add 38 vb.
affix 45 vb.
do sums 86 vb.
enlarge 197 vb.
insert 303 vb.
—insult to injury
aggravate 832 vb.
—up
be intelligible
516 vb.
—up to
mean 514 vb.
addendum
adjunct 40 n.
extra 40 n.
adder
reptile 365 n.
addict
enthusiast 504 n.
habitué 610 n.
drug-taking 949 n.
addictive
intoxicating
949 adj.
addition
increment 36 n.
addition 38 n.
adjunct 40 n.
numerical operation
86 n.

additional
extrinsic 6 adj.
additional 38 adj.
superfluous 637 adj.
additive
food content 301 n.
addle
make sterile 172 vb.
addle-head
fool 501 n.
address
locality 187 n.
abode 192 n.
send 272 vb.
oration 579 n.
speak to 583 vb.
correspond 588 vb.
skill 694 n.
—oneself to
begin 68 vb.
addressee
resident 191 n.
correspondent
588 n.
recipient 782 n.
addresses
wooing 889 n.
adduce
corroborate 466 vb.
adenoids
respiratory disease
651 n.
adept
proficient person
696 n.
adequate
sufficient 635 adj.
middling 732 adj.
adhere
accrue 38 vb.
cohere 48 vb.
assent 488 vb.
—to
observe 768 vb.
adherent
follower 284 n.
auxiliary 707 n.
adhesive
adhesive 47 n.
retentive 778 adj.
ad hoc
specially 80 adv.
spontaneous
609 adj.
unprepared 670 adj.
adieus
valediction 296 n.

adipose
fatty 357 adj.
adit
excavation 255 n.
access 624 n.
adjacent
near 200 adj.
contiguous 202 adj.
adjective
part of speech 564 n.
adjoin
be contiguous
202 vb.
adjourn
put off 136 vb.
pause 145 vb.
adjudicate
judge 480 vb.
try a case 959 vb.
adjudicator
estimator 480 n.
adjunct
adjunct 40 n.
adjure
affirm 532 vb.
entreat 761 vb.
adjust
adjust 24 vb.
regularize 62 vb.
make conform
83 vb.
modify 143 vb.
rectify 654 vb.
adjutant
auxiliary 707 n.
army officer 741 n.
ad-lib
improvise 609 vb.
unprepared 670 adj.
ad lib, ad libitum
at will 595 adv.
admass
dupe 544 n.
commonalty 869 n.
administer
use 673 vb.
manage 689 vb.
Administration, the
authority 733 n.
administrative
directing 689 adj.
governmental
733 adj.
jurisdictional
955 adj.
administrator
agent 686 n.

manager 690 n.
admirable
excellent 644 adj.
wonderful 864 adj.
approvable 923 adj.
admiral
naval officer 741 n.
Admiralty
navy 722 n.
authority 733 n.
admiration
wonder 864 n.
respect 920 n.
approbation 923 n.
admirer
lover 887 n.
admissible
apt 24 adj.
approvable 923 adj.
admission
inclusion 78 n.
reception 299 n.
assent 488 n.
disclosure 526 n.
admit
admit 299 vb.
assent 488 vb.
confess 526 vb.
receive 782 vb.
admittance
ingress 297 n.
admixture
tincture 43 n.
admonish
warn 664 vb.
reprove 924 vb.
ad nauseam
repeatedly 106 adv.
ado
activity 678 n.
exertion 682 n.
adobe
pottery 381 n.
adolescence
youth 130 n.
adolescent
youngster 132 n.
immature 670 adj.
Adonis
a beauty 841 n.
adopt
choose 605 vb.
avail oneself of
673 vb.
adoption
parentage 169 n.
adorable

lovable 887 adj.
adoration
worship 981 n.
adore
love 887 vb.
worship 981 vb.
adorn
decorate 844 vb.
adrift
apart 46 adv.
doubting 474 adj.
adroit
skilful 694 adj.
adulation
flattery 925 n.
adult
adult 134 n.
matured 669 adj.
adulterate
mix 43 vb.
modify 143 vb.
impair 655 vb.
adultery
love affair 887 n.
illicit love 951 n.
adultness
middle age 131 n.
adultness 134 n.
adumbrate
predestine 155 vb.
darken 418 vb.
represent 551 vb.
advance
increase 36 n.
early 135 adj.
motion 265 n.
progress 285 vb.
promote 285 vb.
approach 289 n.vb.
affirm 532 vb.
be expedient 642 vb.
improvement 654 n.
lend 784 vb.
—against
charge 712 vb.
advanced
modern 126 adj.
advance guard
front 237 n.
warner 664 n.
advance notice
warning 664 n.
advances
approach 289 n.
wooing 889 n.
advantage
advantage 34 n.

benefit 615 n.vb.
utility 640 n.
good policy 642 n.
gain 771 n.
advent
approach 289 n.
arrival 295 n.
adventitious
additional 38 adj.
casual 159 adj.
adventure
event 154 n.
undertaking 672 n.
adventurer
traveller 268 n.
impostor 545 n.
gambler 618 n.
desperado 857 n.
adventures
biography 590 n.
novel 590 n.
adventurous
enterprising
672 adj.
rash 857 adj.
adverb
part of speech 564 n.
adversary
opponent 705 n.
adverse
contrary 14 adj.
inexpedient 643 adj.
harmful 645 adj.
hindering 702 adj.
adverse 731 adj.
adversity
evil 616 n.
bane 659 n.
adversity 731 n.
suffering 825 n.
advertise
attract notice
455 vb.
advertise 528 vb.
advertisement
advertisement
528 n.
inducement 612 n.
sale 793 n.
boasting 877 n.
advertising
publicity 528 n.
advice
hint 524 n.
message 529 n.
advice 691 n.
precept 693 n.

advisable
advisable 642 adj.
advise
inform 524 vb.
advise 691 vb.
—against
dissuade 613 vb.
warn 664 vb.
adviser
adviser 691 n.
expert 696 n.
advocate
motivator 612 n.
advise 691 vb.
patron 707 n.
approve 923 vb.
lawyer 958 n.
adze
sharp edge 256 n.
aegis
protection 660 n.
aegrotat
nonliability 919 n.
aeon, eon
era 110 n.
aerate
aerate 340 vb.
sanitate 652 vb.
aerated
bubbly 355 adj.
aerial
high 209 adj.
flying 271 adj.
broadcasting 531 n.
aerie, aery
(*see* eyrie)
aeroballistics
aeronautics 271 n.
aerobatics
aeronautics 271 n.
aerodynamics
aeronautics 271 n.
pneumatics 340 n.
aerofoil
wing 271 n.
aeronaut
traveller 268 n.
aeronaut 271 n.
aeronautics
aeronautics 271 n.
sport 837 n.
aeroplane
aircraft 276 n.
aerosol
propellant 287 n.
vaporizer 338 n.
aerospace

aeronautics 271 n.
atmosphere 340 n.
aerostat
airship 276 n.
aesthete
people of taste
846 n.
aestheticism
sensibility 374 n.
moral sensibility
819 n.
beauty 841 n.
good taste 846 n.
aetiology
causation 156 n.
pathology 651 n.
afar
afar 199 adv.
affability
sociability 882 n.
courtesy 884 n.
affair
topic 452 n.
love affair 887 n.
affairs
affairs 154 n.
business 622 n.
affect
be related 9 vb.
modify 143 vb.
influence 178 vb.
dissemble 541 vb.
impress 821 vb.
be affected 850 vb.
affectation
mimicry 20 n.
magniloquence
574 n.
affectation 850 n.
affecting
felt 818 adj.
exciting 821 adj.
distressing 827 adj.
affection
love 887 n.
affectionate
loving 887 adj.
caressing 889 adj.
affections
temperament 5 n.
affections 817 n.
affidavit
testimony 466 n.
oath 532 n.
affiliation
association 706 n.
participation 775 n.

affinity
relation 9 n.
consanguinity 11 n.
tendency 179 n.
attraction 291 n.
liking 859 n.
affirm
affirm 532 vb.
plead 614 vb.
promise 764 vb.
affirmation
testimony 466 n.
affirmation 532 n.
affirmative
positive 473 adj.
affirmative 532 adj.
affix
add 38 vb.
affix 45 vb.
part of speech 564 n.
afflatus
poetry 593 n.
excitation 821 n.
afflict
hurt 827 vb.
punish 963 vb.
affliction
bane 659 n.
suffering 825 n.
affluence
plenty 635 n.
prosperity 730 n.
wealth 800 n.
afford
provide 633 vb.
give 781 vb.
afford 800 vb.
afforestation
forestry 366 n.
affray
turmoil 61 n.
fight 716 n.
affront
hurt 827 vb.
huff 891 vb.
indignity 921 n.
not respect 921 vb.
aficionado
enthusiast 504 n.
patron 707 n.
aflame
luminous 417 adj.
impressed 818 adj.
afloat
happening 154 adj.
seafaring 269 adj.
aforesaid

preceding 64 adj.
repeated 106 adj.
prior 119 adj.
aforethought
predetermined
608 adj.
intended 617 adj.
a fortiori
eminently 34 adv.
afraid
fearing 854 adj.
afresh
again 106 adv.
newly 126 adv.
Africanize
transform 147 vb.
aft
rearward 238 adv.
after
after 65 adv.
subsequent 120 adj.
rearward 238 adv.
behind 284 adv.
after, be
aim at 617 vb.
pursue 619 vb.
afterbirth
obstetrics 167 n.
aftercare
therapy 658 n.
after-dinner
culinary 301 adj.
reposeful 683 adj.
aftereffect
sequel 67 n.
afterglow
sequel 67 n.
glow 417 n.
afterlife
future state 124 n.
heaven 971 n.
aftermath
sequel 67 n.
effect 157 n.
afternoon
evening 129 n.
afterpart
rear 238 n.
aftertaste
sequel 67 n.
afterthought
sequel 67 n.
lateness 136 n.
afterwards
after 65 adv.
subsequently
120 adv.

again
again 106 adv.
again and again
repeatedly 106 adv.
often 139 adv.
against
against 240 adv.
opposing 704 adj.
against one's will
unwillingly 598 adv.
against the grain
unwillingly 598 adv.
with difficulty
  700 adv.
in opposition
  704 adv.
against the law
prohibited 757 adj.
illegal 954 adj.
agape
open 263 adj.
wondering 864 adj.
love 887 n.
public worship
  981 n.
agate
stripe 437 n.
gem 844 n.
age
date 108 n.
pass time 108 vb.
era 110 n.
long duration 113 n.
chronology 117 n.
oldness 127 n.
age 131 n.
deteriorate 655 vb.
aged
ageing 131 adj.
age group
contemporary
  123 n.
class 538 n.
ageism
prejudice 481 n.
ageless
perpetual 115 adj.
young 130 adj.
agelong
lasting 113 adj.
agency
agency 173 n.
instrumentality
  628 n.
management 689 n.
commission 751 n.
agenda

affairs 154 n.
topic 452 n.
business 622 n.
agent
cause 156 n.
instrument 628 n.
doer 676 n.
agent 686 n.
deputy 755 n.
seller 793 n.
agent provocateur
motivator 612 n.
agitator 738 n.
excitant 821 n.
agglomeration
coherence 48 n.
accumulation 74 n.
agglutinate
affix 45 vb.
agglutinate 48 vb.
aggrandizement
greatness 32 n.
increase 36 n.
expansion 197 n.
dignification 866 n.
aggravate
augment 36 vb.
aggravate 832 vb.
enrage 891 vb.
aggravating
annoying 827 adj.
aggregate
all 52 n.
numerical result
  85 n.
solid body 324 n.
aggregation
accumulation 74 n.
aggression
attack 712 n.
aggressive
violent 176 adj.
active 678 adj.
quarrelling 709 adj.
attacking 712 adj.
warlike 718 adj.
aggressor
attacker 712 n.
enemy 881 n.
aggrieve
displease 827 vb.
hurt 827 vb.
aghast
fearing 854 adj.
wondering 864 adj.
agile
speedy 277 adj.

skilful 694 adj.
agitate
move 265 vb.
brandish 317 vb.
agitate 318 vb.
distract 456 vb.
inquire 459 vb.
gesticulate 547 vb.
revolt 738 vb.
trouble 827 vb.
cause discontent
  829 vb.
agitation
derangement 63 n.
changeableness
  152 n.
agitation 318 n.
restlessness 678 n.
sedition 738 n.
excitation 821 n.
excitable state 822 n.
worry 825 n.
fear 854 n.
agitator
motivator 612 n.
troublemaker 663 n.
agitator 738 n.
excitant 821 n.
agitprop
teaching 534 n.
inducement 612 n.
aglow
fiery 379 adj.
luminous 417 adj.
agnostic
doubting 474 adj.
unbeliever 486 n.
irreligious 974 adj.
ago
formerly 125 adv.
agog
inquisitive 453 adj.
expectant 507 adj.
desiring 859 adj.
agonize
feel pain 377 vb.
suffer 825 vb.
agony
pain 377 n.
excitable state 822 n.
suffering 825 n.
agony column
advertisement
  528 n.
agoraphobia
phobia 854 n.
agrarian

agrarian 370 adj.
agree
accord 24 vb.
concur 181 vb.
concord 710 vb.
consent 758 vb.
contract 765 vb.
agreeable
agreeing 24 adj.
pleasant 376 adj.
willing 597 adj.
pleasurable 826 adj.
personable 841 adj.
courteous 884 adj.
agreement
similarity 18 n.
agreement 24 n.
conformity 83 n.
concurrence 181 n.
consensus 488 n.
cooperation 706 n.
compact 765 n.
agribusiness
agriculture 370 n.
business 622 n.
agricultural
agrarian 370 adj.
agriculturalist,
  agriculturist
producer 164 n.
farmer 370 n.
agricultural worker
farmer 370 n.
agriculture
agriculture 370 n.
agronomics
agriculture 370 n.
ague
spasm 318 n.
tropical disease
  651 n.
ahead
superior 34 adj.
future 124 adj.
in front 237 adv.
ahead 283 adv.
ahimsa
peace 717 n.
benevolence 897 n.
aid
support 218 n.vb.
instrumentality
  628 n.
be expedient 642 vb.
facilitate 701 vb.
aid 703 n.vb.
philanthropy 901 n.

aide-de-camp
auxiliary 707 n.
army officer 741 n.
aiguillette
livery 547 n.
aileron
wing 271 n.
aircraft 276 n.
ailment
illness 651 n.
aim
aim 281 vb.
objective 617 n.
fire at 712 vb.
desired object 859 n.
—at
aim at 617 vb.
pursue 619 vb.
desire 859 vb.
aimless
orderless 61 adj.
designless 618 adj.
air
insubstantial thing
4 n.
element 319 n.
air 340 n.
dry 342 vb.
ventilation 352 n.
tune 412 n.
mien 445 n.
divulge 526 vb.
air base
air travel 271 n.
airborne
flying 271 adj.
ascending 308 adj.
airbus
aircraft 276 n.
air commodore
air officer 741 n.
air-conditioned
cooled 382 adj.
salubrious 652 adj.
air-conditioner
ventilation 352 n.
aircraft
aircraft 276 n.
aircraft carrier
warship 722 n.
air crew
aeronaut 271 n.
air force 722 n.
airdrop
transference 272 n.
airer
hanger 217 n.

drier 342 n.
airfield
air travel 271 n.
air force
air force 722 n.
air freight
transport 272 n.
airgun
propellant 287 n.
air hostess
aeronaut 271 n.
airing
inquiry 459 n.
airlane
air travel 271 n.
route 624 n.
airless
insalubrious
653 adj.
air letter
correspondence
588 n.
airlift
air travel 271 n.
transport 272 n.
airline
air travel 271 n.
airliner
aircraft 276 n.
air lock
intermediary 231 n.
air mail
postal
communications
531 n.
airman, airwoman
aeronaut 271 n.
air marshal
air officer 741 n.
air pipe
air pipe 353 n.
airplane
aircraft 276 n.
air pocket
emptiness 190 n.
airport
air travel 271 n.
air raid
attack 712 n.
airraid shelter
refuge 662 n.
air route
air travel 271 n.
airs
affectation 850 n.
ostentation 875 n.
air shaft

air pipe 353 n.
airship
airship 276 n.
airspace
territory 184 n.
air stream
wind 352 n.
airstrip
air travel 271 n.
airtight
sealed off 264 adj.
air travel
air travel 271 n.
airway
air travel 271 n.
air pipe 353 n.
airworthy
aviational 276 adj.
airy
insubstantial 4 adj.
airy 340 adj.
light-minded
456 adj.
disrespectful
921 adj.
airy-fairy
imaginative 513 adj.
aisle
path 624 n.
church interior
990 n.
ajar
open 263 adj.
akimbo
angular 247 adj.
akin
akin 11 adj.
similar 18 adj.
alabaster
white thing 427 n.
alacrity
velocity 277 n.
willingness 597 n.
cheerfulness 833 n.
Aladdin's lamp
magic instrument
983 n.
à la mode
fashionable 848 adj.
alarm
loudness 400 n.
megaphone 400 n.
danger signal 665 n.
frighten 854 vb.
alarmist
false alarm 665 n.
alarmist 854 n.

alb
vestments 989 n.
albedo
reflection 417 n.
albino
colourless 426 adj.
white thing 427 n.
album
gramophone 414 n.
reminder 505 n.
record 548 n.
albumen
organism 358 n.
alchemist
alterer 143 n.
occultist 984 n.
alchemy
conversion 147 n.
alcohol
stimulant 174 n.
alcoholic drink
301 n.
alcoholic
drunkard 949 n.
intoxicating
949 adj.
alcoholism
disease 651 n.
alcoholism 949 n.
alcove
arbour 194 n.
cavity 255 n.
alderman
councillor 692 n.
ale
alcoholic drink
301 n.
aleatory
casual 159 adj.
speculative 618 adj.
alert
attentive 455 adj.
vigilant 457 adj.
warn 664 vb.
danger signal 665 n.
lively 819 adj.
alexandrine
prósody 593 n.
alfresco
externally 223 adv.
alfresco 340 adv.
algae
microorganism
196 n.
plant 366 n.
algebra
mathematics 86 n.

algorithm
  mathematics 86 n.
  numeration 86 n.
alias
  misnomer 562 n.
alibi
  pretext 614 n.
  vindication 927 n.
alidade
  gauge 465 n.
alien
  foreigner 59 n.
  extraneous 59 adj.
alienate
  set apart 46 vb.
  make enemies
    881 vb.
alienation
  transfer 780 n.
  enmity 881 n.
alight
  place oneself
    187 vb.
  land 295 vb.
  descend 309 vb.
  sit down 311 vb.
  fiery 379 adj.
align
  make uniform
    16 vb.
  arrange 62 vb.
  print 587 vb.
  —oneself
  join a party 708 vb.
alignment
  direction 281 n.
alike
  similar 18 adj.
aliment
  food 301 n.
alimentary
  nourishing 301 adj.
alimony
  dower 777 n.
  divorce 896 n.
aliquot
  numerical element
    85 n.
alive
  existing 1 adj.
  alive 360 adj.
  lively 819 adj.
alive to
  impressible
    819 adj.
alkahest
  liquefaction 337 n.

all
  all 52 n.
  completeness 54 n.
  universal 79 adj.
Allah
  the Deity 965 n.
all and sundry
  everyman 79 n.
all anyhow
  nonuniformly
    17 adv.
  orderless 61 adj.
allay
  assuage 177 vb.
all clear
  signal 547 n.
  safety 660 n.
all ears
  inquisitive 453 adj.
  attentive 455 adj.
allegation
  testimony 466 n.
  affirmation 532 n.
  accusation 928 n.
alleged
  supposed 512 adj.
  ostensible 614 adj.
allegiance
  loyalty 739 n.
  duty 917 n.
allegory
  comparison 462 n.
  metaphor 519 n.
  narrative 590 n.
allegro
  adagio 412 adv.
  cheerfully 833 adv.
alleluia!
  981 int.
all-embracing
  comprehensive
    52 adj.
  general 79 adj.
allergy
  sensibility 374 n.
  ill health 651 n.
  dislike 861 n.
alleviate
  assuage 177 vb.
  relieve 831 vb.
alley
  road 624 n.
alliance
  relation 9 n.
  association 706 n.
  compact 765 n.
  marriage 894 n.

alligator
  reptile 365 n.
all-in
  inclusive 78 adj.
all in
  fatigued 684 adj.
all in all
  on the whole 52 adv.
alliteration
  recurrence 106 n.
  ornament 574 n.
  prosody 593 n.
all manner of
  different 15 adj.
  multiform 82 adj.
allocation
  arrangement 62 n.
  apportionment
    783 n.
  portion 783 n.
allocution
  allocution 583 n.
all of a piece
  uniform 16 adj.
  one 88 adj.
all one
  equivalent 28 adj.
allopathy
  medical art 658 n.
allot
  dispose of 673 vb.
  apportion 783 vb.
allotment
  garden 370 n.
all over one, be
  pet 889 vb.
  flatter 925 vb.
allow
  acquiesce 488 vb.
  confess 526 vb.
  facilitate 701 vb.
  be lenient 736 vb.
  permit 756 vb.
  —for
  set off 31 vb.
  —to pass
  disregard 458 vb.
allowable
  possible 469 adj.
  permitted 756 adj.
allowance
  offset 31 n.
  qualification 468 n.
  subvention 703 n.
  receipt 807 n.
  discount 810 n.
alloy

a mixture 43 n.
  impair 655 vb.
all-purpose
  useful 640 adj.
all right
  not bad 644 adj.
  middling 732 adj.
all-rounder
  proficient person
    696 n.
  player 837 n.
all set
  prepared 669 adj.
all sorts
  medley 43 n.
allspice
  condiment 389 n.
all there
  intelligent 498 adj.
  sane 502 adj.
all thumbs
  clumsy 695 adj.
allude
  mean 514 vb.
  imply 523 vb.
allure
  attraction 291 n.
  tempt 612 vb.
  cause desire 859 vb.
allusion
  referral 9 n.
  metaphor 519 n.
allusive
  meaningful 514 adj.
  figurative 519 adj.
  tacit 523 adj.
alluvium
  soil 344 n.
ally
  join 45 vb.
  aider 703 n.
  join a party 708 vb.
  friend 880 n.
alma mater
  academy 539 n.
almanac
  directory 87 n.
  chronology 117 n.
almighty
  powerful 160 adj.
Almighty, the
  the Deity 965 n.
almond
  fruit 301 n.
almoner
  nurse 658 n.
  giver 781 n.

almost
  almost 33 adv.
  nearly 200 adv.
alms
  gift 781 n.
  kind act 897 n.
almshouse
  retreat 192 n.
  shelter 662 n.
aloft
  aloft 209 adv.
  up 308 adv.
alone
  alone 88 adj.
  friendless 883 adj.
along
  longwise 203 adv.
alongside
  near 200 adv.
  sideways 239 adv.
aloof
  distant 199 adj.
  impassive 820 adj.
  unsociable 883 adj.
aloud
  loudly 400 adv.
  vocal 577 adj.
alpaca
  fibre 208 n.
  textile 222 n.
alphabet
  letter 558 n.
  lettering 586 n.
alphanumeric
  computerized
  86 adj.
alpha plus
  excellent 644 adj.
alpha ray
  radiation 417 n.
alpha waves
  intellect 447 n.
alpine
  alpine 209 adj.
Alps
  high land 209 n.
already
  before 119 adv.
  at present 121 adv.
also
  in addition 38 adv.
also-ran
  inferior 35 n.
  loser 728 n.
altar
  holy place 990 n.
altazimuth

astronomy 321 n.
alter
  modify 143 vb.
alteration
  difference 15 n.
  change 143 n.
altercation
  quarrel 709 n.
  contention 716 n.
alter ego
  analogue 18 n.
  close friend 880 n.
alternate
  correlate 12 vb.
  be discontinuous
  72 vb.
  vary 152 vb.
  deputy 755 n.
alternative
  substitute 150 n.
  choice 605 n.
alternative life style
  dissent 489 n.
alternative reading
  interpretation 520 n.
although
  although 182 adv.
  provided 468 adv.
altimetry
  altimetry 209 n.
altitude
  height 209 n.
alto
  vocalist 413 n.
altogether
  on the whole 52 adv.
  completely 54 adv.
altruism
  philanthropy 901 n.
altruistic
  benevolent 897 adj.
  disinterested
  931 adj.
alumnus, alumna
  student 538 n.
alveolus
  cavity 255 n.
always
  while 108 adv.
a.m.
  morning 128 n.
amalgam
  a mixture 43 n.
amalgamate
  combine 50 vb.
amalgamation
  association 706 n.

amanuensis
  recorder 549 n.
  auxiliary 707 n.
amass
  bring together
  74 vb.
  store 632 vb.
amateur
  beginner 538 n.
  unskilled 695 adj.
  people of taste
  846 n.
amateurish
  bungled 695 adj.
  unskilled 695 adj.
amative
  loving 887 adj.
amatory
  erotic 887 adj.
  loving 887 adj.
amaurotic
  dim-sighted 440 adj.
amaze
  surprise 508 vb.
  impress 821 vb.
  be wonderful
  864 vb.
Amazon
  athlete 162 n.
  soldier 722 n.
  brave person 855 n.
ambassador,
ambassadress
  envoy 754 n.
amber
  resin 357 n.
  yellow 433 adj.
  gem 844 n.
ambergris
  resin 357 n.
  scent 396 n.
ambidextrous
  double 91 adj.
  skilful 694 adj.
ambience
  surroundings 230 n.
ambiguity
  equivocalness
  518 n.
ambiguous
  uncertain 474 adj.
  equivocal 518 adj.
  unclear 568 adj.
ambition
  intention 617 n.
  aspiration 852 n.
  desired object 859 n.

ambitious
  attempting 671 adj.
  enterprising
  672 adj.
ambivalence
  contrariety 14 n.
  equivocalness
  518 n.
amble
  gait 265 n.
  ride 267 vb.
  wander 267 vb.
  move slowly 278 vb.
ambrosia
  savouriness 390 n.
ambrosial
  sweet 392 adj.
  fragrant 396 adj.
ambulance
  hospital 658 n.
ambulatory
  travelling 267 adj.
  path 624 n.
  church interior
  990 n.
ambush
  ambush 527 n.vb.
  trap 542 n.
  pitfall 663 n.
ameliorate
  make better 654 vb.
amen
  assent 488 n.
amenable
  willing 597 adj.
  obedient 739 adj.
amend
  rectify 654 vb.
amende honorable
  atonement 941 n.
amends
  compensation 31 n.
  restitution 787 n.
  atonement 941 n.
amenity
  pleasurableness
  826 n.
  courtesy 884 n.
amentia
  insanity 503 n.
amercement
  penalty 963 n.
Americanism
  dialect 560 n.
amethyst
  purpleness 436 n.
  gem 844 n.

AMI

amiable
amiable 884 adj.
lovable 887 adj.
benevolent 897 adj.
amicable
concordant 710 adj.
friendly 880 adj.
amid, amidst
between 231 adv.
amino acid
food 301 n.
amiss
amiss 616 adv.
amity
friendship 880 n.
ammonite
coil 251 n.
ammunition
means 629 n.
ammunition 723 n.
amnesia
oblivion 506 n.
amnesty
amnesty 506 n.
forgive 909 vb.
amoeba
microorganism
196 n.
among, amongst
between 231 adv.
amoral
indifferent 860 adj.
wicked 934 adj.
amorous
loving 887 adj.
amorphous
incomplete 55 adj.
amorphous 244 adj.
amount
quantity 26 n.
amount to
number 86 vb.
cost 809 vb.
amour
love affair 887 n.
amour propre
pride 871 n.
vanity 873 n.
amp, ampere
electronics 160 n.
amphetamine
drug-taking 949 n.
amphibian
vehicle 274 n.
amphibian 365 n.
amphibious
double 91 adj.

ANA

amphitheatre
arena 724 n.
ample
great 32 adj.
many 104 adj.
spacious 183 adj.
large 195 adj.
broad 205 adj.
plenteous 635 adj.
liberal 813 adj.
amplification
expansion 197 n.
amplifier
megaphone 400 n.
amplitude
plenitude 54 n.
range 183 n.
plenty 635 n.
ampoule
receptacle 194 n.
amputate
subtract 39 vb.
amulet
talisman 983 n.
amuse
amuse 837 vb.
amusement
enjoyment 824 n.
amusement 837 n.
amusing
amusing 837 adj.
funny 849 adj.
anachronism
anachronism 118 n.
different time 122 n.
anacoluthon
solecism 565 n.
anacreontic
poetic 593 adj.
merry 833 adj.
anaemia
weakness 163 n.
anaemic
unhealthy 651 adj.
anaesthesia
insensibility 375 n.
anaesthetic
anaesthetic 375 n.
remedial 658 adj.
soporific 679 n.
anaesthetize
render insensible
375 vb.
anagoge
metaphor 519 n.
anagram
initials 558 n.

ANC

anal
excretory 302 adj.
analeptic
restorative 656 adj.
analgesia
insensibility 375 n.
analgesic
anaesthetic 375 n.
remedial 658 adj.
relieving 831 adj.
analogous
relative 9 adj.
similar 18 adj.
analogue
analogue 18 n.
computerized
86 adj.
analogy
comparison 462 n.
analyse
decompose 51 vb.
class 62 vb.
inquire 459 vb.
analysis
numerical operation
86 n.
grammar 564 n.
analyst
experimenter 461 n.
analytic, -al
rational 475 adj.
anamorphosis
distortion 246 n.
anarchic, anarchical
anarchic 734 adj.
nonobservant
769 adj.
lawless 954 adj.
anarchist
revolutionist 149 n.
revolter 738 n.
anarchy
disorder 61 n.
anarchy 734 n.
anathema
malediction 899 n.
anatomical
structural 331 adj.
anatomist
zoologist 367 n.
anatomize
sunder 46 vb.
anatomy
structure 331 n.
biology 358 n.
ancestor
precursor 66 n.

ANG

paternity 169 n.
ancestral
immemorial
127 adj.
parental 169 adj.
ancestry
heredity 5 n.
source 156 n.
genealogy 169 n.
anchor
sailing aid 269 n.
safeguard 662 n.
anchorage
station 187 n.
shelter 662 n.
anchored
fixed 153 adj.
anchorite, anchoress
ascetic 945 n.
ancien régime
archaism 127 n.
aristocracy 868 n.
ancient
former 125 adj.
olden 127 adj.
ancients, the
precursor 66 n.
ancillary
aiding 703 adj.
andante
slowness 278 n.
tempo 410 n.
anecdote
narrative 590 n.
anemometry
anemometry 352 n.
angel
darling 890 n.
good person 937 n.
angel 968 n.
angelic, angelical
virtuous 933 adj.
angelus
signal 547 n.
anger
anger 891 n.
angle
angularity 247 n.
opinion 485 n.
hunt 619 vb.
—for
attempt 671 vb.
request 761 vb.
Anglicanism
Protestantism 976 n.
anglicism
dialect 560 n.

angry
  angry 891 adj.
angst
  suffering 825 n.
  melancholy 834 n.
anguish
  pain 377 n.
  suffering 825 n.
angular
  angular 247 adj.
angularity
  obliquity 220 n.
  angularity 247 n.
anility
  old age 131 n.
anima
  spirit 447 n.
animal
  animal 365 n.adj.
  sensual 944 adj.
animal husbandry
  animal husbandry
    369 n.
animality
  animality 365 n.
  absence of intellect
    448 n.
animal spirits
  vitality 162 n.
animal trainer
  breeder 369 n.
  trainer 537 n.
animate
  invigorate 174 vb.
  animate 821 vb.
animated
  active 678 adj.
  lively 819 adj.
animation
  life 360 n.
  cinema 445 n.
  excitation 821 n.
animism
  deism 973 n.
animosity
  enmity 881 n.
animus
  spirit 447 n.
  affections 817 n.
ankh
  cross 222 n.
ankle
  foot 214 n.
  angularity 247 n.
annalist
  chronicler
    549 n.

annals
  chronology 117 n.
  record 548 n.
  narrative 590 n.
anneal
  be tough 329 vb.
annex
  connect 45 vb.
  appropriate 786 vb.
annexe
  adjunct 40 n.
annihilate
  nullify 2 vb.
  destroy 165 vb.
anniversary
  date 108 n.
  anniversary 141 n.
  celebratory 876 adj.
annotate
  mark 547 vb.
annotation
  commentary 520 n.
announce
  proclaim 528 vb.
  name 561 vb.
announcer
  broadcaster 531 n.
annoy
  torment 827 vb.
  enrage 891 vb.
annoyance
  bane 659 n.
  annoyance 827 n.
annoyed
  discontented
    829 adj.
annual
  periodic 110 adj.
  seasonal 141 adj.
  reference book
    589 n.
annuity
  receipt 807 n.
annul
  abrogate 752 vb.
  divorce 896 vb.
annular
  round 250 adj.
anodyne
  lenitive 177 adj.
  remedial 658 adj.
anoint
  lubricate 334 vb.
  perform ritual
    988 vb.
anomalous
  abnormal 84 adj.

anonymity
  concealment 525 n.
anonymous
  anonymous 562 adj.
anorak
  jacket 228 n.
anorexia
  fasting 946 n.
another
  different 15 adj.
  additional 38 adj.
answer
  numerical result
    85 n.
  answer 460 n.vb.
  confutation 479 n.
  be useful 406 vb.
  be successful
    727 vb.
—**back**
  argue 475 vb.
  be insolent 878 vb.
—**for**
  deputize 755 vb.
—**to**
  correlate 12 vb.
  be named 561 vb.
ant
  insect 365 n.
  busy person 678 n.
antacid
  antidote 658 n.
antagonism
  opposition 704 n.
  enmity 881 n.
antagonist
  opponent 705 n.
antagonize
  cause dislike 861 vb.
  make enemies
    881 vb.
  huff 891 vb.
ante
  gambling 618 n.
  offering 781 n.
antecedence
  precedence 64 n.
  priority 119 n.
antecedent
  precursor 66 n.
antedate
  come before 64 vb.
antediluvian
  antiquated 127 adj.
antelope
  speeder 277 n.
  mammal 365 n.

antenatal
  fertilized 167 adj.
antenna
  feeler 378 n.
  broadcasting 531 n.
anterior
  preceding 64 adj.
  prior 119 adj.
anteroom
  lobby 194 n.
anthem
  hymn 981 n.
anthill
  small hill 209 n.
anthology
  anthology 592 n.
  choice 605 n.
anthracite
  coal 385 n.
anthrax
  animal disease
    651 n.
anthropocentric
  human 371 adj.
anthropoid
  animal 365 n.
  human 371 adj.
anthropology
  anthropology
    371 n.
anthropomorphic
  idolatrous 982 adj.
anti-
  contrary 14 adj.
  opposing 704 adj.
antibiotic
  antidote 658 n.
  drug 658 n.
antibody
  antidote 658 n.
Antichrist
  bad person 938 n.
  Satan 969 n.
anticipate
  be early 135 vb.
  expect 507 vb.
  foresee 510 vb.
  prepare 669 vb.
anticlerical
  irreligious 974 adj.
  impious 980 adj.
anticlimax
  disappointment
    509 n.
  feebleness 572 n.
  ridiculousness
    849 n.

anticline
dome 253 n.

anticoagulant
liquefaction 337 n.

anticonvulsant
antidote 658 n.

antics
foolery 497 n.
revel 837 n.

anticyclone
weather 340 n.

antidepressant
drug 658 n.

antidote
contrariety 14 n.
counteraction 182 n.
antidote 658 n.

antifreeze
heating 381 adj.

antigen
antidote 658 n.

antihero
acting 594 n.

antihistamine
antidote 658 n.

antilogy
sophism 477 n.

antinomian
anarchic 734 adj.

antinomy
contrariety 14 n.
illegality 954 n.

antipathy
dislike 861 n.
hatred 888 n.

antiperspirant
cosmetic 843 n.

antiphon
hymn 981 n.

antipodes
farness 199 n.
contraposition
240 n.

antiquarian
antiquarian 125 n.

antiquated
antiquated 127 adj.
disused 674 adj.

antique
archaism 127 n.

antiquity
antiquity 125 n.
monument 548 n.

anti-Semitism
prejudice 481 n.

antiseptic
salubrious 652 adj.

remedial 658 adj.

antisocial
unsociable 883 adj.
misanthropic
902 adj.

antispasmodic
antidote 658 n.

antithesis
contrariety 14 n.
difference 15 n.
trope 519 n.

antitoxin
antidote 658 n.

antitype
prototype 23 n.

antonomasia
trope 519 n.

antonym
contrariety 14 n.
word 559 n.

anus
buttocks 238 n.

anvil
stand 218 n.

anxious
careful 457 adj.
suffering 825 adj.
nervous 854 adj.

any
universal 79 adj.
anonymous 562 adj.
no choice 606 n.

anyone
everyman 79 n.

apart
separate 46 adj.

apartheid
exclusion 57 n.

apartment
flat 192 n.

apathetic
inert 175 adj.
incurious 454 adj.
nonactive 677 adj.
apathetic 820 adj.

apathy
indifference 860 n.

ape
imitate 20 vb.
mammal 365 n.

ape-man
humankind 371 n.

aperçu
compendium 592 n.
witticism 839 n.

aperient
purgative 658 n.

aperitif
prelude 66 n.
alcoholic drink
301 n.

aperture
opening 263 n.

apex
summit 213 n.

aphasia
speech defect 580 n.

aphid
insect 365 n.

aphonia, aphony
voicelessness 578 n.

aphorism
maxim 496 n.
conciseness 569 n.

aphrodisiac
stimulant 174 n.
erotic 887 adj.

apiary
nest 192 n.
stock farm 369 n.

aplomb
stability 153 n.
resolution 599 n.

apocalypse
ruin 165 n.
revelation 975 n.

Apocrypha
scripture 975 n.

apocryphal
uncertified 474 adj.

apodictic
demonstrating
478 adj.

apogee
distance 199 n.
summit 213 n.

Apollo
musician 413 n.

apologetic
regretting 830 adj.
repentant 939 adj.
atoning 941 adj.

apologetics, apologia
argument 475 n.
pretext 614 n.

apologist
vindicator 927 n.

apologize
recant 603 vb.
be penitent 939 vb.

apology
penitence 939 n.

apology for
copy 22 n.

laughingstock
851 n.

apophthegm
maxim 496 n.

apoplectic
angry 891 adj.

apoplexy
insensibility 375 n.
illness 651 n.

apostasy
change of mind
603 n.
rejection 607 n.
impiety 980 n.

apostate
turncoat 603 n.

apostle
messenger 529 n.
religious teacher
973 n.

apostolate
church ministry
985 n.

apostolic
ecclesiastical
985 adj.

apostrophe
punctuation 547 n.
entreaty 761 n.

apothecary
druggist 658 n.

apotheosis
deification 982 n.

appal
displease 827 vb.
frighten 854 vb.

apparat
governance 733 n.

apparatchik
official 690 n.

apparatus
tool 630 n.

apparel
clothing 228 n.

apparent
visible 443 adj.
appearing 445 adj.
manifest 522 adj.

apparition
visual fallacy 440 n.
ghost 970 n.

appeal
attract 291 vb.
allocution 583 n.
motivate 612 vb.
entreaty 761 n.
deprecate 762 vb.

pleasurableness
826 n.
beauty 841 n.
lovableness 887 n.
legal trial 959 n.
appear
begin 68 vb.
appear 445 vb.
—for
deputize 755 vb.
appearance
similarity 18 n.
form 243 n.
appearance 445 n.
appearances
etiquette 848 n.
appease
assuage 177 vb.
pacify 719 vb.
appellant
petitioner 763 n.
appellation
name 561 n.
append
add 38 vb.
place after 65 vb.
appendage
adjunct 40 n.
part 53 n.
appendicitis
digestive disorders
651 n.
appendix
adjunct 40 n.
appertaining
relative 9 adj.
appertain to
be included 78 vb.
appetence, appetency
will 595 n.
desire 859 n.
appetite
eating 301 n.
desire 859 n.
hunger 859 n.
appetizer
prelude 66 n.
hors d'oeuvres
301 n.
appetizing
tasty 386 adj.
savoury 390 adj.
applaud
applaud 923 vb.
apple
fruit 301 n.
apple of one's eye

favourite 890 n.
appliance
tool 630 n.
applicable
relevant 9 adj.
useful 640 adj.
advisable 642 adj.
applicant
respondent 460 n.
petitioner 763 n.
application
relevance 9 n.
attention 455 n.
connotation 514 n.
perseverance 600 n.
use 673 n.
assiduity 678 n.
request 761 n.
apply
relate 9 vb.
use 673 vb.
offer oneself 759 vb.
request 761 vb.
—oneself
study 536 vb.
exert oneself 682 vb.
appoint
select 605 vb.
employ 622 vb.
commission 751 vb.
appointed
predetermined
608 adj.
appointment
job 622 n.
mandate 751 n.
apportion
apportion 783 vb.
appositeness
relevance 9 n.
apposition
contiguity 202 n.
appraise
estimate 480 vb.
appreciate
grow 36 vb.
know 490 vb.
be dear 811 vb.
honour 866 vb.
appreciation
discrimination
463 n.
estimate 480 n.
interpretation 520 n.
approbation 923 n.
appreciative
tasteful 846 adj.

grateful 907 adj.
apprehend
expect 507 vb.
understand 516 vb.
arrest 747 vb.
apprehensive
nervous 854 adj.
apprentice
beginner 538 n.
artisan 686 n.
apprise
inform 524 vb.
approach
nearness 200 n.
approach 289 n.vb.
policy 623 n.
offer 759 n.vb.
approachable
accessible 289 adj.
approbation
approbation 923 n.
appropriate
relevant 9 adj.
apt 24 adj.
appropriate 786 vb.
approval
permission 756 n.
approbation 923 n.
approve
consent 758 vb.
be pleased 824 vb.
approved
usual 610 adj.
approximate
similar 18 adj.
approach 289 vb.
approximately
almost 33 adv.
nearly 200 adv.
appurtenance(s)
adjunct 40 n.
concomitant 89 n.
appurtenant
relative 9 adj.
April fool
dupe 544 n.
laughingstock
851 n.
a priori
rational 475 n.
apron
apron 228 n.
stage set 594 n.
apron strings
subjection 745 n.
apropos
concerning 9 adv.

apse
church interior
990 n.
apt
relevant 9 adj.
apt 24 adj.
opportune 137 adj.
intelligent 498 adj.
aptitude
fitness 24 n.
ability 160 n.
aptitude 694 n.
apt to
tending 179 adj.
liable 180 adj.
aquamarine
blueness 435 n.
gem 844 n.
aquanaut
diver 313 n.
aquaplane
swim 269 vb.
aquarelle
picture 553 n.
aquarium
zoo 369 n.
aquatic
swimming
269 adj.
watery 339 adj.
aquatics
aquatics 269 n.
sport 837 n.
aquatint
picture 553 n.
engraving 555 n.
aqueduct
conduit 351 n.
aquiline
curved 248 adj.
arabesque
pattern 844 n.
arable
agrarian 370 adj.
Aran
pattern 844 n.
arbiter
adviser 691 n.
arbitrament
judgement 480 n.
arbitrary
unconformable
84 adj.
wilful 602 adj.
authoritarian
735 adj.
unconditional

744 adj.
lawless 954 adj.
arbitrate
judge 480 vb.
mediate 720 vb.
arbitrator
mediator 720 n.
arboreal
arboreal 366 adj.
arboretum
wood 366 n.
arbour
arbour 194 n.
arc
arc 250 n.
arcade
path 624 n.
emporium 796 n.
Arcadian
artless 699 adj.
innocent 935 adj.
arcane
unintelligible
517 adj.
latent 523 adj.
arch
supreme 34 adj.
prop 218 n.
curve 248 n.
be convex 253 vb.
affected 850 adj.
archaeologist
antiquarian 125 n.
excavator 255 n.
archaeology
palaeology 125 n.
archaic
antiquated 127 adj.
olden 127 adj.
archaism
archaism 127 n.
neology 560 n.
archbishop
ecclesiarch 986 n.
archbishopric
church office 985 n.
archduke
potentate 741 n.
archer
shooter 287 n.
archery
sport 837 n.
archetypal
orginal 21 adj.
archetype
prototype 23 n.
idea 451 n.

archipelago
island 349 n.
architect
producer 164 n.
planner 623 n.
architectonics
structure 331 n.
architectural
architectural
192 adj.
eyesore 842 n.
architecture
form 243 n.
structure 331 n.
art 551 n.
architrave
summit 213 n.
archives
record 548 n.
title deed 767 n.
archivist
recorder 549 n.
archway
doorway 263 n.
arctic
cold 380 adj.
ardent
forceful 571 adj.
hasty 680 adj.
fervent 818 adj.
desiring 859 adj.
loving 887 adj.
ardour
heat 379 n.
arduous
laborious 682 adj.
difficult 700 adj.
area
measure 183 n.
region 184 n.
function 622 n.
arena
battle 718 n.
arena 724 n.
argon
air 340 n.
argosy
merchant ship
275 n.
argot
slang 560 n.
arguable
possible 469 adj.
uncertain 474 adj.
argue
argue 475 vb.
bicker 709 vb.

—against
cause doubt 486 vb.
dissuade 613 vb.
—for
contend 716 vb.
argument
topic 452 n.
argument 475 n.
dissertation 591 n.
contention 716 n.
argumentative
quarrelling 709 adj.
aria
tune 412 n.
arid
unproductive
172 adj.
dry 342 adj.
arise
become 1 vb.
begin 68 vb.
be visible 443 vb.
appear 445 vb.
—from
result 157 vb.
aristocracy
social group 371 n.
aristocracy 868 n.
aristocrat
aristocrat 868 n.
arithmetic
mathematics 86 n.
ark
box 194 n.
refuge 662 n.
arm
adjunct 40 n.
empower 160 vb.
prop 218 n.
tool 630 n.
make ready 669 vb.
weapon 723 n.
armada
navy 722 n.
armament
fitting out 669 n.
arms 723 n.
armature
sculpture 554 n.
armband
belt 228 n.
armchair
seat 218 n.
suppositional
512 adj.
armed force(s)
armed force 722 n.

arm in arm
joined 45 adj.
with 89 adv.
armistice
peace 717 n.
armless
crippled 163 adj.
armlet
belt 228 n.
badge of rank 743 n.
armorial
heraldic 547 adj.
armour
protection 660 n.
safeguard 662 n.
armour 713 n.
weapon 723 n.
armour-bearer
retainer 742 n.
armoured
invulnerable
660 adj.
armoured car
cavalry 722 n.
armour plate
protection 660 n.
armour 713 n.
armoury
arsenal 723 n.
armpit
cavity 255 n.
arms
arms 723 n.
arms buildup
intimidation 854 n.
arms depot
arsenal 723 n.
arm-twisting
compulsion 740 n.
army
multitude 104 n.
army 722 n.
aroma
odour 394 n.
aromatic
pungent 388 adj.
fragrant 396 adj.
around
nearly 200 adv.
around 230 adv.
arouse
cause 156 vb.
raise the alarm
665 vb.
excite 821 vb.
arraign
indict 928 vb.

arrange
  compose 56 vb.
  arrange 62 vb.
  predetermine
    608 vb.
  plan 623 vb.
arrangement
  musical piece 412 n.
array
  order 60 n.
  arrangement 62 n.
  multitude 104 n.
  dress 228 vb.
  decorate 844 vb.
arrears
  debt 803 n.
arrest
  cessation 145 n.
  arrest 747 vb.
arresting
  unexpected 508 adj.
  impressive 821 adj.
arrival
  arrival 295 n.
arrive
  be present 189 vb.
  arrive 295 vb.
  prosper 730 vb.
arriviste
  prosperous person
    730 n.
  vulgarian 847 n.
arrogance
  pride 871 n.
  insolence 878 n.
arrogate
  be undue 916 vb.
arrow
  speeder 277 n.
  indicator 547 n.
  missile weapon
    723 n.
arsenal
  accumulation 74 n.
  storage 632 n.
  arsenal 723 n.
arsenic
  poison 659 n.
arson
  incendiarism 381 n.
art
  composition 56 n.
  art 551 n.
  skill 694 n.
  stratagem 698 n.
  ornamental art
    844 n.

artefact, artifact
  product 164 n.
arterial
  communicating
    624 adj.
artery
  tube 263 n.
  life 360 n.
  road 624 n.
artesian well
  water 339 n.
art exhibition
  spectacle 445 n.
artful
  cunning 698 adj.
art gallery
  collection 632 n.
arthritic
  crippled 163 adj.
article
  product 164 n.
  object 319 n.
  part of speech 564 n.
  article 591 n.
  merchandise 795 n.
article oneself
  learn 536 vb.
articles
  conditions 766 n.
  creed 485 n.
articulate
  join 45 vb.
  intelligible 516 adj.
  phrase 563 vb.
  voice 577 vb.
  speak 579 vb.
artifice
  contrivance 623 n.
  stratagem 698 n.
artificial
  produced 164 adj.
  spurious 542 adj.
  affected 850 adj.
artificial
  insemination
  propagation 167 n.
artificial limb
  substitute 150 n.
artillery
  gun 723 n.
artisan
  producer 164 n.
  artisan 686 n.
artist
  artist 556 n.
artiste
  entertainer 594 n.

artistic
  elegant 575 adj.
  well-made 694 adj.
  tasteful 846 adj.
artistry
  skill 694 n.
artless
  ignorant 491 adj.
  veracious 540 adj.
  plain 573 adj.
  spontaneous
    609 adj.
  artless 699 adj.
  innocent 935 adj.
arts
  culture 490 n.
  literature 557 n.
arty-crafty
  ornamental 844 adj.
as
  similarly 18 adv.
ascend
  be high 209 vb.
  ascend 308 vb.
ascendancy,
  ascendance
  superiority 34 n.
  power 160 n.
  influence 178 n.
ascent
  incline 220 n.
  progression 285 n.
  ascent 308 n.
ascertain
  make certain
    473 vb.
  discover 484 vb.
ascertained
  known 490 adj.
ascetic
  abstainer 942 n.
  ascetic 945 n.adj.
asceticism
  poverty 801 n.
  asceticism 945 n.
ascribe
  attribute 158 vb.
  grant claims 915 vb.
aseptic
  clean 648 adj.
  salubrious 652 adj.
asexual
  simple 44 adj.
as good as one's word
  veracious 540 adj.
  trustworthy 929 adj.
ash

tree 366 n.
ash 381 n.
ashamed
  humbled 872 adj.
  repentant 939 adj.
ashen
  colourless 426 adj.
  grey 429 adj.
  fearing 854 adj.
ashes
  remainder 41 n.
  corpse 363 n.
ashlar
  building material
    631 n.
ashram
  retreat 192 n.
aside
  sideways 239 adv.
  hint 524 n.
  dramaturgy 594 n.
asinine
  foolish 499 adj.
ask
  inquire 459 vb.
  request 761 vb.
—for
  desire 859 vb.
askew
  oblique 220 adj.
  distorted 246 adj.
aslant
  oblique 220 adj.
asleep
  quiescent 266 adj.
  sleepy 679 adj.
as long as
  provided 468 adj.
aspect
  modality 7 n.
  situation 186 n.
  view 438 n.
  appearance 445 n.
asperity
  roughness 259 n.
  rudeness 885 n.
  irascibility 892 n.
aspersion
  slur 867 n.
  detraction 926 n.
asphalt
  paving 226 n.
  road 624 n.
asphyxiant
  poison 659 n.
aspic
  preserver 666 n.

aspirant
 hoper 852 n.
 desirer 859 n.
aspirate
 extract 304 vb.
 breathe 352 vb.
 speech sound 398 n.
 voice 577 vb.
aspiration
 objective 617 n.
 aspiration 852 n.
 desire 859 n.
aspire
 hope 852 vb.
aspirin
 drug 658 n.
ass
 beast of burden
  273 n.
 fool 501 n.
assail
 attack 712 vb.
assailant
 attacker 712 n.
assassin
 murderer 362 n.
 ruffian 904 n.
assassination
 homicide 362 n.
assault
 attack 712 n.vb.
 debauch 951 vb.
assay
 experiment
  461 n.vb.
assegai
 spear 723 n.
assemblage
 assemblage 74 n.
assemble
 join 45 vb.
 bring together
  74 vb.
 congregate 74 vb.
assembly
 assembly 74 n.
 social gathering
  882 n.
assembly line
 continuity 71 n.
 production 164 n.
assent
 assent 488 n.vb.
 willingness 597 n.
 consent 758 n.vb.
assert
 affirm 532 vb.

—oneself
 influence 178 vb.
 be active 678 vb.
 achieve liberty
  746 vb.
—one's rights
 claim 915 vb.
assertive
 assertive 532 adj.
assess
 appraise 465 vb.
 price 809 vb.
assessment
 estimate 480 n.
assessor
 estimator 480 n.
 magistracy 957 n.
assets
 means 629 n.
 estate 777 n.
asset-stripper
 taker 786 n.
asseverate
 affirm 532 vb.
assiduity
 carefulness 457 n.
 assiduity 678 n.
assign
 transfer 272 vb.
 dispose of 673 vb.
 commission 751 vb.
 assign 780 vb.
 apportion 783 vb.
—to
 attribute 158 vb.
assignation
 social round 882 n.
assignment
 undertaking 672 n.
 mandate 751 n.
assimilate
 make uniform
  16 vb.
 make conform
  83 vb.
 absorb 299 vb.
assimilation
 assimilation 18 n.
assist
 aid 703 vb.
assistance
 instrumentality
  628 n.
 aid 703 n.
assistant
 auxiliary 707 n.
assize(s)

 lawcourt 956 n.
 legal trial 959 n.
associate
 congregate 74 vb.
 colleague 707 n.
 society 708 n.
 join a party 708 vb.
—with
 accompany 89 vb.
association
 relation 9 n.
 group 74 n.
 concurrence 181 n.
 participation 775 n.
 sociality 882 n.
assonance
 prosody 593 n.
assorted
 different 15 adj.
assortment
 medley 43 n.
 accumulation 74 n.
assuage
 assuage 177 vb.
 pacify 719 vb.
 relieve 831 vb.
assume
 wear 228 vb.
 believe 485 vb.
 expect 507 vb.
 suppose 512 vb.
 dissemble 541 vb.
 appropriate 786 vb.
—responsibility
 undertake 672 vb.
 direct 689 vb.
assumption
 opinion 485 n.
 supposition 512 n.
assurance
 belief 485 n.
 affirmation 532 n.
 safety 660 n.
 promise 764 n.
assure
 make certain
  473 vb.
 convince 485 vb.
 give security 767 vb.
asterisk
 punctuation 547 n.
astern
 rearward 238 adv.
asteroid
 planet 321 n.
as the crow flies
 straight on 249 adv.

 towards 281 adv.
asthma
 respiratory disease
  651 n.
asthmatic
 puffing 352 adj.
 sibilant 406 adj.
astigmatic
 dim-sighted 440 adj.
astir
 busy 678 adj.
astonish
 surprise 508 vb.
 be wonderful
  864 vb.
astonishing
 prodigious 32 adj.
 unusual 84 adj.
astound
 surprise 508 vb.
 impress 821 vb.
astral
 celestial 321 adj.
astray
 deviating 282 adj.
astringent
 compressor 198 n.
 pungent 388 adj.
astrolabe
 astronomy 321 n.
astrologer
 diviner 511 n.
 occultist 984 n.
astronaut
 aeronaut 271 n.
 satellite 321 n.
astronomer
 astronomy 321 n.
astronomy
 astronomy 321 n.
astute
 intelligent 498 adj.
 cunning 698 adj.
asunder
 apart 46 adv.
asylum
 refuge 662 n.
asymmetrical
 distorted 246 adj.
at a loss, be
 not know 491 vb.
 be in difficulty
  700 vb.
atavism
 heredity 5 n.
ataxia
 helplessness 161 n.

at bay
endangered 661 adj.
in difficulties
737 700 adj.
at hand
impending 155 adj.
on the spot 189 adj.
atheism
unbelief 486 n.
irreligion 974 n.
athlete
athlete 162 n.
contender 716 n.
athletics
athletics 162 n.
contest 716 n.
sport 837 n.
at home
social gathering
882 n.
at intervals
discontinuously
72 adv.
periodically
141 adv.
atlas
map 551 n.
atmosphere
influence 178 n.
surroundings 230 n.
atmosphere 340 n.
atmospherics
discord 411 n.
atoll
island 349 n.
atom
small thing 33 n.
unit 88 n.
minuteness 196 n.
element 319 n.
atom bomb
bomb 723 n.
atomic
dynamic 160 adj.
atomize
decompose 51 vb.
demolish 165 vb.
atomizer
vaporizer 338 n.
atom-smasher
nucleonics 160 n.
atonal
harmonic 410 adj.
atonement
atonement 941 n.
divine function
965 n.

atony
weakness 163 n.
atrocious
cruel 898 adj.
heinous 934 adj.
atrocity
violence 176 n.
cruel act 898 n.
atrophy
helplessness 161 n.
disease 651 n.
attach
add 38 vb.
affix 45 vb.
connect 45 vb.
attaché
envoy 754 n.
attaché case
box 194 n.
attachment
adjunct 40 n.
love 887 n.
attack
outbreak 176 n.
spasm 318 n.
attempt 671 n.
attack 712 n.vb.
detraction 926 n.
attacker
opponent 705 n.
attacker 712 n.
attain
arrive 295 vb.
acquire 771 vb.
—one's purpose
succeed 727 vb.
attainable
accessible 289 adj.
possible 469 adj.
attainments
culture 490 n.
learning 536 n.
attempt
attempt 671 n.vb.
—the impossible
attempt the
impossible 470 vb.
waste effort 641 vb.
act foolishly 695 vb.
attend
accompany 89 vb.
be present 189 vb.
follow 284 vb.
be attentive 455 vb.
doctor 658 vb.
attendant
retainer 742 n.

attention
attention 455 n.
carefulness 457 n.
attenuate
make thin 206 vb.
rarefy 325 vb.
attest
testify 466 vb.
swear 532 vb.
attic
attic 194 n.
Attic
elegant 575 adj.
witty 839 adj.
attire
dressing 228 n.
attitude
form 243 n.
opinion 485 n.
affections 817 n.
attitudinize
be affected 850 vb.
attorney
law agent 958 n.
attract
bring together
74 vb.
attract 291 vb.
motivate 612 vb.
delight 826 vb.
attraction
focus 76 n.
influence 178 n.
attraction 291 n.
incentive 612 n.
desired object 859 n.
favourite 890 n.
attractive
personable 841 adj.
lovable 887 adj.
attribute
speciality 80 n.
concomitant 89 n.
attribute 158 vb.
grant claims 915 vb.
attrition
friction 333 n.
warfare 718 n.
atypical
nonuniform 17 adj.
abnormal 84 adj.
auburn
brown 430 adj.
auction
sale 793 n.
audacity
courage 855 n.

rashness 857 n.
insolence 878 n.
audible
sounding 398 adj.
loud 400 adj.
intelligible 516 adj.
speaking 579 adj.
audience
listener 415 n.
onlookers 441 n.
playgoer 594 n.
audio
sound 398 n.
audiotypist
stenographer 586 n.
audiovisual
auditory 415 adj.
educational 534 adj.
audit
inquiry 459 n.
accounts 808 n.
audition
hearing 415 n.
listening 415 n.
exam 459 n.
auditor
accountant 808 n.
auditorium
theatre 594 n.
auger
sharp point 256 n.
augment
augment 36 vb.
strengthen 162 vb.
augur
diviner 511 n.
—well
be auspicious
730 vb.
august
great 32 adj.
worshipful 866 adj.
aunt
kinsman 11 n.
Aunt Sally
laughingstock
851 n.
au pair
domestic 742 n.
aura
surroundings
230 n.
prestige 866 n.
aural
auditory 415 adj.
aurora
glow 417 n.

auscultation
listening 415 n.
auspice(s)
omen 511 n.
protection 660 n.
auspicious
opportune 137 adj.
presageful 511 adj.
palmy 730 adj.
austere
plain 573 adj.
ascetic 945 adj.
austerity
asceticism 945 n.
autarchy
despotism 733 n.
autarky
sufficiency 635 n.
independence 744 n.
authentic
genuine 494 adj.
authenticate
testify 466 vb.
endorse 488 vb.
authenticity
authenticity 494 n.
author
cause 156 n.
producer 164 n.
author 589 n.
narrator 590 n.
dissertator 591 n.
authoritarian
directing 689 adj.
authoritarian
735 adj.
authoritative
influential 178 adj.
certain 473 adj.
authoritative
733 adj.
commanding
737 adj.
authority
power 160 n.
influence 178 n.
informant 524 n.
expert 696 n.
authority 733 n.
commission 751 n.
permit 756 n.
jurisdiction 955 n.
authorize
empower 160 n.
commission 751 vb.
permit 756 vb.
autism

unsociability 883 n.
autobiography
biography 590 n.
autocracy
despotism 733 n.
autocrat
tyrant 735 n.
autocrat 741 n.
autocratic
authoritative
733 adj.
autocue
broadcasting 531 n.
autograph
sign 547 vb.
autolysis
death 361 n.
automate
computerize 86 vb.
empower 160 vb.
produce 164 vb.
automatic
unthinking 450 adj.
involuntary 596 adj.
mechanical 630 adj.
pistol 723 n.
automation
production 164 n.
automobile
automobile 274 n.
autonomous
independent
744 adj.
autopilot
aeronaut 271 n.
directorship 689 n.
autopsy
inquest 364 n.
inquiry 459 n.
autosuggestion
fantasy 513 n.
autumn
autumn 129 n.
auxiliary
additional 38 adj.
aiding 703 adj.
auxiliary 707 n.
avail
benefit 615 vb.
be useful 640 vb.
available
on the spot 189 adj.
accessible 289 adj.
possible 469 adj.
provisioning
633 adj.
offering 759 adj.

avalanche
revolution 149 n.
descent 309 n.
snow 380 n.
avant-garde
precursor 66 n.
modernist 126 n.
avarice
avarice 816 n.
avatar
theophany 965 n.
avenge
avenge 910 vb.
punish 963 vb.
avenue
housing 192 n.
road 624 n.
aver
affirm 532 vb.
average
average 30 n.
median 30 adj.
middle 70 n.
general 79 adj.
typical 83 adj.
not bad 644 adj.
middling 732 adj.
averages
statistics 86 n.
aversion
unwillingness 598 n.
dislike 861 n.
avert
deflect 282 vb.
parry 713 vb.
aviary
nest 192 n.
zoo 369 n.
aviation
aeronautics 271 n.
aviator
aeronaut 271 n.
avidity
rapacity 786 n.
desire 859 n.
avocation
business 622 n.
avoid
avoid 620 vb.
parry 713 vb.
be unsociable
883 vb.
avoirdupois
weighing 322 n.
avow
confess 526 vb.
affirm 532 vb.

avulsion
scission 46 n.
avuncular
akin 11 adj.
await
await 507 vb.
awake
attentive 455 adj.
awaken
have feeling 374 vb.
excite 821 vb.
award
judge 480 vb.
trophy 729 n.
honours 866 n.
reward 962 n.vb.
aware
sentient 374 adj.
attentive 455 adj.
knowing 490 adj.
impressible 819 adj.
awareness
intellect 447 n.
awash
drenched 341 adj.
away
absent 190 adj.
awe
fear 854 n.
wonder 864 n.
respect 920 n.
worship 981 n.
awe-inspiring
impressive 821 adj.
frightening 854 adj.
wonderful 864 adj.
awestruck
fearing 854 adj.
wondering 864 adj.
respectful 920 adj.
awful
not nice 645 adj.
awfully
extremely 32 adv.
awkward
unconformable
84 adj.
inelegant 576 adj.
clumsy 695 adj.
disobedient 738 adj.
graceless 842 adj.
ill-bred 847 adj.
awl
sharp point 256 n.
awning
canopy 226 n.
screen 421 n.

awry
orderless 61 adj.
oblique 220 adj.
amiss 616.adv.
axe
shorten 204 vb.
sharp edge 256 n.
dismiss 300 vb.
axe 723 n.
axe to grind
objective 617 n.
selfishness 932 n.
axial
central 225 adj.
directed 281 adj.
axiom
axiom 496 n.
axiomatic
certain 473 adj.
axis
pivot 218 n.
association 706 n.
axle
rotator 315 n.
ayatollah
governor 741 n.
ayes, the
assenter 488 n.
azure
blueness 435 n.
heraldry 547 n.

B

baa
ululation 409 n.
Baal
idol 982 n.
babble
flow 350 vb.
empty talk 515 n.
chatter 581 n.
babe
weakling 163 n.
innocent 935 n.
babel
confusion 61 n.
discord 411 n.
lack of meaning
515 n.
baby
child 132 n.
little 196 adj.
coward 856 n.
loved one 887 n.
babyhood
youth 130 n.

babyish
infantine 132 adj.
foolish 499 adj.
baby-sit
look after 457 vb.
baby-sitter
protector 660 n.
keeper 749 n.
Bacchanalia
drunkenness 949 n.
bacchic
disorderly 61 adj.
frenzied 503 adj.
bachelor
celibate 895 n.
unwedded 895 adj.
bachelor girl
woman 373 n.
spinster 895 n.
bacillus
microorganism
196 n.
infection 651 n.
back
prop 218 n.
line 227 vb.
rear 238 n.
back 238 adj.
regress 286 vb.
gamble 618 n.
patronize 703 vb.
approve 923 vb.
—away
be unwilling 598 vb.
avoid 620 vb.
—down
tergiversate 603 vb.
—out
resign 753 vb.
not observe 769 vb.
—up
support 218 vb.
aid 703 vb.
backbencher
inferior 35 n.
councillor 692 n.
backbite
defame 926 vb.
backbone
essential part 5 n.
prop 218 n.
stamina 600 n.
backbreaking
laborious 682 adj.
backchat
sauciness 878 n.
backcloth

stage set 594 n.
back door
stealthy 525 adj.
backer
gambler 618 n.
patron 707 n.
background
circumstance 8 n.
accompanying
89 adj.
surroundings 230 n.
rear 238 n.
information 524 n.
backhanded
equivocal 518 adj.
backing
lining 227 n.
aid 703 n.
backlash
reversion 148 n.
recoil 280 n.
retaliation 714 n.
backlog
store 632 n.
back of beyond
district 184 n.
farness 199 n.
seclusion 883 n.
backpack
bag 194 n.
travel 267 vb.
backpedal
recant 603 vb.
backroom boy/girl
intellectual 492 n.
planner 623 n.
expert 696 n.
back-scratching
cooperation 706 n.
flattery 925 n.
back seat
inferiority 35 n.
backside
buttocks 238 n.
back-slapping
sociability 882 n.
backslide
tergiversate 603 vb.
relapse 657 vb.
backstage
on stage 594 adv.
backtalk
sauciness 878 n.
back-to-front
inverted 221 adj.
backtrack
regress 286 vb.

backward
regressive 286 adj.
ignorant 491 adj.
unwilling 598 adj.
avoiding 620 adj.
immature 670 adj.
backward-looking
retrospective
125 adj.
backwards
backwards 286 adv.
**backwards and
forwards**
to and fro 317 adv.
backwash
effect 157 n.
wave 350 n.
backwater
lake 346 n.
seclusion 883 n.
backwoodsman
absence 190 n.
country-dweller
869 n.
bacon
meat 301 n.
bacteria
microorganism
196 n.
infection 651 n.
bacteriology
pathology 651 n.
bad
inferior 35 adj.
decomposed 51 adj.
evil 616 adj.
bad 645 adj.
deteriorated
655 adj.
adverse 731 adj.
wrong 914 adj.
bad books
disapprobation
924 n.
bad conscience
guilt 936 n.
penitence 939 n.
baddy
evildoer 904 n.
bad person 938 n.
bad faith
nonobservance
769 n.
perfidy 930 n.
bad form
ill-breeding
847 n.

badge
badge 547 n.
badge of rank
743 n.

badger
mammal 365 n.
torment 827 vb.

badinage
witticism 839 n.

bad job
bungling 695 n.
hopelessness 853 n.

bad language
rudeness 885 n.
scurrility 899 n.

bad luck
disappointment
509 n.
misfortune 731 n.

bad manners
ill-breeding 847 n.
discourtesy 885 n.

bad name
disrepute 867 n.

bad patch
difficulty 700 n.
adversity 731 n.

bad press
detraction 926 n.

bad taste
bad taste 847 n.
impurity 951 n.

bad temper
irascibility 892 n.
sullenness 893 n.

baffle
puzzle 474 vb.
be difficult 700 vb.
defeat 727 vb.

baffled
puzzled 517 adj.

bag
bag 194 n.
carrier 273 n.
take 786 vb.

bagatelle
trifle 639 n.

baggage
thing transferred
272 n.
encumbrance 702 n.
insolent person
878 n.

baggy
spacious 183 adj.
broad 205 adj.
hanging 217 adj.

bagpipes
flute 414 n.

bag-snatcher
thief 789 n.

Baha'ism
religious faith 973 n.

bail
security 767 n.

bailee
consignee 754 n.

bailiff
ejector 300 n.
manager 690 n.
officer 741 n.
consignee 754 n.

bail out
empty 300 vb.
give bail 767 vb.

bairn
child 132 n.

bait
attraction 291 n.
trap 542 n.
incentive 612 n.
torment 827 vb.

baize
textile 222 n.

bake
cook 301 vb.
dry 342 vb.
heat 381 vb.

baker
provider 633 n.

balance
correlate 12 vb.
adjust 24 vb.
equalize 28 vb.
remainder 41 n.
symmetry 245 n.
scales 322 n.
superfluity 637 n.
inexcitability 823 n.
account 808 vb.

balances
funds 797 n.
credit 802 n.

balance sheet
accounts 808 n.

balancing act
equivocalness
518 n.
compromise 770 n.

balcony
lobby 194 n.
projection 254 n.
theatre 594 n.

bald

hairless 229 adj.
smooth 258 adj.
plain 573 adj.

balderdash
silly talk 515 n.

bale
bunch 74 n.
stow 187 vb.

—out
fly 271 vb.

baleful
harmful 645 adj.
malevolent 898 adj.

baler
ladle 194 n.
farm tool 370 n.

balk, baulk
beam 218 n.
be obstructive
702 vb.

ball
sphere 252 n.
ammunition 723 n.
dancing 837 n.
plaything 837 n.

ballad
vocal music 412 n.
poem 593 n.

ballast
offset 31 n.
stabilizer 153 n.

ballet
ballet 594 n.
dancing 837 n.

ballet dancer
jumper 312 n.
actor 594 n.
dance 837 n.

ball game
ball game 837 n.

ballistic missile
missile weapon
723 n.

ballistics
propulsion 287 n.

balloon
expand 197 vb.
sphere 252 n.
be convex 253 vb.
airship 276 n.
plaything 837 n.

balloonist
aeronaut 271 n.

ballot
vote 605 n.

ballot box
electorate 605 n.

ballroom
place of amusement
837 n.

ballyhoo
publicity 528 n.
exaggeration 546 n.

balm
moderator 177 n.
lubricant 334 n.
scent 396 n.
balm 658 n.
pleasurableness
826 n.
relief 831 n.

balmy
warm 379 adj.
fragrant 396 adj.

balustrade
handle 218 n.

bamboo
grass 366 n.

bamboozle
puzzle 474 vb.
befool 542 vb.

ban
exclude 57 vb.
restrain 747 vb.
prohibition 757 n.
make unwelcome
883 vb.
malediction 899 n.
penalty 963 n.

banal
usual 610 adj.
dull 840 adj.

banana
fruit 301 n.

banana republic
nonentity 639 n.
political
organization
733 n.

bananas
crazy 503 adj.

band
bond 47 n.
ligature 47 n.
band 74 n.
strip 208 n.
loop 250 n.
orchestra 413 n.
stripe 437 n.
class 538 n.
party 708 n.
formation 722 n.

bandage
tie 45 vb.

ligature 47 n.
compressor 198 n.
strip 208 n.
wrapping 226 n.
surgical dressing
  658 n.
bandeau
hairdressing 843 n.
bandit
revolter 738 n.
robber 789 n.
outcast 883 n.
bandmaster
musician 413 n.
bandolier
belt 228 n.
arsenal 723 n.
bandsman
orchestra 413 n.
bandstand
pavilion 192 n.
band together
congregate 74 vb.
cooperate 706 vb.
bandy-legged
deformed 246 adj.
bane
bane 659 n.
annoyance 827 n.
hateful object 888 n.
bang
knock 279 n.
strike 279 n.
loudness 400 n.
bang 402 n.vb.
banger
automobile 274 n.
meat 301 n.
fireworks 420 n.
bangle
jewellery 844 n.
bang-on
super 644 adj.
banish
eject 300 vb.
make unwelcome
  883 vb.
banishment
penalty 963 n.
banister
pillar 218 n.
banjo
harp 414 n.
bank
high land 209 n.
incline 220 n.
edge 234 n.

shore 344 n.
treasury 799 n.
—on
be certain 473 vb.
expect 507 vb.
banker
lender 784 n.
treasurer 798 n.
Bank Holiday
amusement 837 n.
banknote
paper money 797 n.
bank rate
interest 803 n.
bankrupt
fleece 786 vb.
poor person 801 n.
nonpayer 805 n.
bankruptcy
loss 772 n.
insolvency 805 n.
banner
flag 547 n.
banns
marriage 894 n.
banquet
eat 301 vb.
plenty 635 n.
festivity 837 n.
banshee
demon 970 n.
bantam
dwarf 196 n.
poultry 365 n.
bantamweight
pugilist 722 n.
banter
witticism 839 n.
ridicule 851 n.vb.
baptism
reception 299 n.
moistening 341 n.
Christian rite 988 n.
Baptists
Protestantism 976 n.
baptize
name 561 vb.
bar
exclude 57 vb.
tavern 192 n.
line 203 n.
barrier 235 n.
close 264 vb.
stripe 437 n.
obstruct 702 vb.
prohibit 757 vb.
bar 958 n.

barb
sharp point 256 n.
missile weapon
  723 n.
barbarian
extraneous 59 adj.
vulgarian 847 n.
ruffian 904 n.
barbaric
barbaric 869 adj.
barbarism
neology 560 n.
solecism 565 n.
bad taste 847 n.
barbarity
violence 176 n.
inhumanity 898 n.
barbarous
barbaric 869 adj.
barbecue
meal 301 n.
festivity 837 n.
barbed wire
obstacle 702 n.
barber
beautician 843 n.
barbiturate(s)
soporific 679 n.
drug-taking 949 n.
bard
musician 413 n.
poet 593 n.
bare
unproductive
  172 adj.
empty 190 adj.
uncover 229 vb.
plain 573 adj.
vulnerable 661 adj.
barefaced
undisguised
  522 adj.
barefoot
uncovered 229 adj.
beggarly 801 adj.
bareheaded
uncovered 229 adj.
respectful 920 adj.
barely
slightly 33 adv.
bare minimum
needfulness 627 n.
dueness 915 n.
bargain
compact 765 n.
make terms 766 vb.
bargain 791 vb.

cheapness 812 n.
barge
carrier 273 n.
boat 275 n.
baritone
vocalist 413 n.
bark
skin 226 n.
ululate 409 vb.
be irascible 892 vb.
threaten 900 vb.
barker
publicizer 528 n.
barley
provender 301 n.
grass 366 n.
barm
leaven 323 n.
barmaid, barman
servant 742 n.
barmy
crazy 503 adj.
barn
storage 632 n.
barney
quarrel 709 n.
barnstorm
act 594 vb.
barnyard
farm 370 n.
barometer
weather 340 n.
baron
bigwig 638 n.
person of rank
  868 n.
baroque
art 551 n.
ornamental 844 adj.
barque
sailing ship 275 n.
barrack(s)
quarters 192 n.
be obstructive
  702 vb.
barrage
bombardment
  712 n.
defences 713 n.
barrel
cylinder 252 n.
barren
unproductive
  172 adj.
profitless 641 adj.
barricade
barrier 235 n.

obstruct 702 vb.
revolt 738 vb.

barrier
exclusion 57 n.
barrier 235 n.
obstacle 702 n.

barrister
lawyer 958 n.

barrow
earthwork 253 n.
pushcart 274 n.
monument 548 n.

barrow boy
seller 793 n.

bartender
servant 742 n.

barter
interchange
151 n.vb.
barter 791 n.

base
inferiority 35 n.
station 187 n.
base 214 n.
basis 218 n.
disreputable 867 adj.
rascally 930 adj.

baseball
ball game 837 n.

baseless
unreal 2 adj.
erroneous 495 adj.

basement
cellar 194 n.

bash
strike 279 vb.
attempt 671 n.

bashfulness
modesty 874 n.

basic
intrinsic 5 adj.
fundamental
156 adj.
important 638 adj.

BASIC
data processing
86 n.

basilica
church 990 n.

basin
bowl 194 n.
cavity 255 n.

basis
reason why 156 n.
basis 218 n.

bask
be hot 379 vb.

enjoy 376 vb.

basket
basket 194 n.

basketball
ball game 837 n.

bas relief
sculpture 554 n.

bass
resonance 404 n.
vocalist 413 n.

bassoon
flute 414 n.

bast
ligature 47 n.
fibre 208 n.

bastard
unwarranted
916 adj.
bastardy 954 n.

baste
tie 45 vb.
cook 301 vb.
grease 357 vb.

bastion
protection 660 n.
fortification 713 n.

bat
velocity 277 n.
hammer 279 n.
strike 279 vb.
propel 287 vb.
mammal 365 n.
club 723 n.

batch
group 74 n.

bath
vessel 194 n.
ablutions 648 n.

bathe
swim 269 vb.
plunge 313 vb.
drench 341 vb.
clean 648 vb.

bathetic
inelegant 576 adj.

bathos
absurdity 497 n.
ridiculousness
849 n.

bathroom
ablutions 648 n.

batik
textile 222 n.
printing 555 n.
ornamental art
844 n.

batman

domestic 742 n.

baton
badge of rule 743 n.

batsman
player 837 n.

battalion
formation 722 n.

batten
strip 208 n.
—down
close 264 vb.
—on
eat 301 vb.
prosper 730 vb.

batter
demolish 165 vb.
obliquity 220 n.
strike 279 vb.
pulpiness 356 n.
ill-treat 645 vb.

battered
dilapidated 655 adj.

battering ram
ram 279 n.

battery
electronics 160 n.
stock farm 369 n.
formation 722 n.
gun 723 n.

battle
slaughter 362 n.
exert oneself 682 vb.
contend 716 vb.
battle 718 n.

battleaxe
shrew 892 n.

battle cry
call 547 n.

battledress
uniform 228 n.

battlefield,
battleground
casus belli 709 n.
battleground 724 n.

battlements
summit 213 n.
fortification 713 n.

battleship
warship 722 n.

batty
crazy 503 adj.

bauble
bauble 639 n.
plaything 837 n.
finery 844 n.

bawdy
impure 951 adj.

bawl
vociferate 408 vb.
weep 836 vb.

bay
compartment 194 n.
gulf 345 n.
ululate 409 vb.
brown 430 adj.
disapprove 924 vb.

bayonet
pierce 263 vb.
sidearms 723 n.

bays
trophy 729 n.
honours 866 n.

bazaar
sale 793 n.
emporium 796 n.

bazooka
gun 723 n.

BBC
broadcasting 531 n.

be
be 1 vb.
live 360 vb.

beach
land 295 vb.
shore 344 n.

beachcomber
wanderer 268 n.

beachhead
battleground 724 n.

beacon
fire 379 n.
signal 547 n.
danger signal 665 n.

bead
sphere 252 n.
trimming 844 n.

beadle
law officer 955 n.

beads
prayers 981 n.

beagling
chase 619 n.

beak
prow 237 n.
protuberance 254 n.

beam
beam 218 n.
laterality 239 n.
direction 281 n.
flash 417 n.
radiate 417 vb.
communicate
524 vb.
smile 835 vb.

beanfeast
feasting 301 n.
beans
food 301 n.
vegetable 301 n.
bear
reproduce itself
167 vb.
be fruitful 171 vb.
support 218 vb.
carry 273 vb.
orientate 281 vb.
mammal 365 n.
speculate 791 vb.
be patient 823 vb.
—down on
approach 289 vb.
charge 712 vb.
—fruit
be useful 640 vb.
be successful
727 vb.
—malice
resent 891 vb.
—off
take away 786 vb.
—oneself
behave 688 vb.
—out
corroborate 466 vb.
vindicate 927 vb.
—up
support 218 vb.
resist 715 vb.
—upon
be related 9 vb.
influence 178 vb.
—with
forgive 909 vb.
beard
hair 259 n.
defy 711 vb.
beardless
young 130 adj.
hairless 229 adj.
bearer
bearer 273 n.
servant 742 n.
bearing
relation 9 n.
prop 218 n.
direction 281 n.
meaning 514 n.
heraldry 547 n.
conduct 688 n.
bearing on
concerning 9 adv.

beast
violent creature
176 n.
animal 365 n.
cad 938 n.
beastly
not nice 645 adj.
beast of burden
beast of burden
273 n.
worker 686 n.
beast of prey
killer 362 n.
animal 365 n.
beat
periodicity 141 n.
territory 184 n.
strike 279 vb.
outdo 306 vb.
oscillate 317 vb.
pulverize 332 vb.
tempo 410 n.
prosody 593 n.
fatigued 684 adj.
defeat 727 vb.
spank 963 vb.
—about the bush
dissemble 541 vb.
be diffuse 570 vb.
—down
bargain 791 vb.
—it
decamp 296 vb.
run away 620 vb.
—off
repel 292 vb.
—time
play music 413 vb.
—up
strike 279 vb.
thicken 354 vb.
beaten track
habit 610 n.
beatific
paradisiac 971 adj.
beatify
sanctify 979 vb.
beating
*corporal
punishment* 963 n.
beatitude
happiness 824 n.
beau
fop 848 n.
lover 887 n.
Beaufort scale
anemometry 352 n.

beautiful
beautiful 841 adj.
beautify
beautify 841 vb.
primp 843 vb.
decorate 844 vb.
beauty
symmetry 245 n.
elegance 575 n.
beauty 841 n.
exceller 644 n.
paragon 646 n.
a beauty 841 n.
beaux arts
art 551 n.
beaver
mammal 365 n.
busy person 678 n.
bebop
music 412 n.
dance 837 n.
because (of)
hence 158 adv.
beck
stream 350 n.
beckon
gesticulate 547 vb.
become
become 1 vb.
be turned to 147 vb.
becoming
personable
841 adj.
tasteful 846 adj.
bed
layer 207 n.
bed 218 n.
garden 370 n.
sleep 679 n.
debauch 951 vb.
bed and breakfast
inn 192 n.
provision 633 n.
bed bug
insect 365 n.
bedclothes
coverlet 226 n.
bedeck
decorate 844 vb.
bedevil
bedevil 63 vb.
trouble 827 vb.
bedim
darken 418 vb.
bedim 419 vb.
bedlam
turmoil 61 n.

lunatic asylum
503 n.
bed of nails
suffering 825 n.
bed of roses
euphoria 376 n.
bedouin
wanderer 268 n.
bedpan
latrine 649 n.
bedraggled
orderless 61 adj.
dirty 649 adj.
bedridden
sick 651 adj.
bedrock
reality 1 n.
source 156 n.
base 214 n.
chief thing 638 n.
bedroom
chamber 194 n.
bedside manner
therapy 658 n.
bed-sitter
flat 192 n.
bedtime
evening 129 n.
bee
insect 365 n.
busy person 678 n.
beef
meat 301 n.
be discontented
829 vb.
—up
strengthen 162 vb.
beefy
stalwart 162 adj.
beehive
nest 192 n.
stock farm 369 n.
bee in one's bonnet
bias 481 n.
eccentricity 503 n.
whim 604 n.
bee-keeping
animal husbandry
369 n.
beeline
short distance 200 n.
straightness 249 n.
beer
alcoholic drink
301 n.
beer and skittles
enjoyment 824 n.

festivity 837 n.

beery
drunken 949 adj.

beeswax
fat 357 n.

beetle
be high 209 vb.
insect 365 n.

beetle-browed
projecting 254 adj.

beetroot
vegetable 301 n.

befall
happen 154 vb.

befitting
fit 24 adj.
advisable 642 adj.

befool
befool 542 vb.

before
before 64 adv.
before (in time)
119 adv.
in front 237 adv.
ahead 283 adv.

before time
anachronistic
118 adj.
immature 670 adj.

befoul
make unclean
649 vb.

befriend
patronize 703 vb.
befriend 880 vb.

befuddle
puzzle 474 n.
inebriate 949 vb.

beg
borrow 785 vb.
beg 761 vb.
—, borrow or steal
find means 629 vb.
acquire 771 vb.
—off
mediate 720 vb.
refuse 760 vb.
deprecate 762 vb.
—the question
reason badly
477 vb.

beget
generate 167 vb.

begetter
paternity 169 n.

beggar
beggar 763 n.

poor person 801 n.

begin
become 1 vb.
begin 68 vb.
start out 296 vb.
undertake 672 vb.

beginner
beginner 538 n.

beginning
beginning 68 n.adj.
source 156 n.

begotten
born 360 adj.

begrudge
be unwilling 598 vb.
be parsimonious
816 vb.

beguile
deceive 542 vb.
amuse 837 vb.

behalf
benefit 615 n.

behave
behave 688 vb.
be virtuous 933 vb.

behaviour
mien 445 n.
conduct 688 n.

behaviourism
psychology 447 n.

behead
shorten 204 vb.
execute 963 vb.

behest
command 737 n.

behind
buttocks 238 n.
rear 238 n.
behind 284 adv.

behindhand
late 136 adj.
unprepared
670 adj.

behind one's back
not here 190 adv.
concealed 525 adj.

behind the times
antiquated 127 adj.

behold
see 438 vb.

beholden
grateful 907 adj.
obliged 917 adj.

beholder
spectator 441 n.

behove
be right 913 vb.

be one's duty
917 vb.

beige
brown 430 adj.

being
existence 1 n.
self 80 n.
person 371 n.

bejewel
decorate 844 vb.

belabour
strike 279 vb.
flog 963 vb.

belated
late 136 adj.

belay
tie 45 vb.

belch
eruct 300 vb.
breathe 352 vb.

beleaguer
besiege 712 vb.

belfry
church exterior
990 n.

belie
negate 533 vb.

belief
belief 485 n.
religious faith 973 n.

believable
plausible 471 adj.
credible 485 adj.

believe
be certain 473 vb.
believe 485 vb.
be credulous 487 vb.

believer
religionist 963 n.

belittle
underestimate
483 vb.
hold cheap 922 vb.
detract 926 vb.

bell
campanology 412 n.
gong 414 n.
signal 547 n.

belladonna
poisonous plant
659 n.

bell, book and candle
malediction 899 n.

bell-bottomed
broad 205 adj.

bellboy, bellhop
courier 529 n.

servant 742 n.

bell buoy
danger signal 665 n.

belle
a beauty 841 n.
fop 848 n.

belles lettres
literature 557 n.

bellicose
violent 176 adj.
quarrelling 709 adj.
warlike 718 adj.

belligerent
warring 718 adj.
combatant 722 n.

bellow
be loud 400 vb.
vociferate 408 vb.

bellows
blowing 352 n.

bell ringing
campanology 412 n.

bell-shaped
rotund 252 adj.

bell wether
sheep 365 n.
leader 690 n.

belly
maw 194 n.
insides 224 n.
swelling 253 n.
be convex 253 vb.

bellyacher
malcontent 829 n.

bellyflop
plunge 313 n.

bellyful
sufficiency 635 n.

belly worship
gluttony 947 n.

belong (to)
be intrinsic 5 vb.
be related 9 vb.
be included 78 vb.
join a party 708 vb.

belonging
friendship 880 n.

belongings
property 777 n.

beloved
loved one 887 n.
darling 890 n.

below
under 210 adv.

below par
imperfect 647 adj.
sick 651 adj.

below the belt
unjust 914 adj.
below the salt
plebeian 869 adj.
below the surface
latent 523 adj.
belt
region 184 n.
compressor 198 n.
belt 228 n.
loop 250 n.
strike 279 vb.
spank 963 vb.
belt and braces
tutelary 660 adj.
belt-tightening
poverty 801 n.
bemadam
dignify 866 vb.
bemedal
decorate 844 vb.
dignify 866 vb.
bemoan
lament 836 vb.
bemused
abstracted 456 adj.
bench
seat 218 n.
workshop 687 n.
tribunal 956 n.
bench mark
gauge 465 n.
signpost 547 n.
bench of bishops
synod 985 n.
bend
ligature 47 n.
modify 143 vb.
be oblique 220 vb.
distortion 246 n.
angularity 247 n.
curve 248 n.
deflect 282 vb.
stoop 311 vb.
knuckle under
  721 vb.
—over backwards
exert oneself 682 vb.
bendable
flexible 327 adj.
bended knees
entreaty 761 n.
bender
festivity 837 n.
drunkenness 949 n.
beneath
under 210 adv.

beneath one's dignity
degrading 867 adj.
benedicite
prayers 981 n.
Benedictine
monk 986 n.
benediction
thanks 907 n.
prayers 981 n.
benefaction
gift 781 n.
liberality 813 n.
benefactor,
  benefactress
patron 707 n.
benefactor 903 n.
benefice
benefice 985 n.
beneficence
benevolence 897 n.
beneficial
good 615 adj.
profitable 640 adj.
beneficial 644 adj.
salubrious 652 adj.
beneficiary
beneficiary 776 n.
recipient 782 n.
benefit
benefit 615 n.vb.
utility 640 n.
be expedient 642 vb.
do good 644 vb.
subvention 703 n.
gain 771 n.
sociology 901 n.
benefit of the doubt
acquittal 960 n.
benevolent
amiable 884 adj.
benevolent 897 adj.
philanthropic
  901 adj.
disinterested
  931 adj.
benighted
late 136 adj.
ignorant 491 adj.
benign
salubrious 652 adj.
benevolent 897 adj.
bent
abnormal 84 adj.
tendency 179 n.
curved 248 adj.
aptitude 694 n.
dishonest 930 adj.

benthos
marine life 365 n.
ben trovato
plausible 471 adj.
witty 839 adj.
bent upon
resolute 599 adj.
desiring 859 adj.
benumbed
insensible 375 adj.
inactive 679 adj.
bequeath
bequeath 780 vb.
bequest
dower 777 n.
berate
reprobate 924 vb.
bereave
deprive 786 vb.
bereavement
loss 772 n.
beret
headgear 228 n.
beribbon
decorate 844 vb.
dignify 866 vb.
berry
fruit 301 n.
berserk
frenzied 503 adj.
angry 891 adj.
berth
quarters 192 n.
dwell 192 vb.
arrive 295 vb.
job 622 n.
beseech
entreat 761 vb.
beset
besiege 712 vb.
torment 827 vb.
besetting sin
bane 659 n.
vice 934 n.
beside
near 200 adv.
beside oneself
frenzied 503 adj.
excited 821 adj.
beside the point
irrelevant 10 adj.
besiege
besiege 712 vb.
torment 827 vb.
besmear, besmirch
make unclean
  649 vb.

defame 926 vb.
besotted
foolish 499 adj.
enamoured 887 adj.
bespatter
moisten 341 vb.
make unclean
  649 vb.
bespeak
evidence 466 vb.
indicate 547 vb.
bespectacled
dim-sighted 440 adj.
bespoke
tailored 228 adj.
besprinkle
moisten 341 vb.
best
supreme 34 adj.
best 644 adj.
best behaviour
etiquette 848 n.
courtesy 884 n.
bested
defeated 728 adj.
bestial
animal 365 adj.
sensual 944 adj.
bestir oneself
be active 678 vb.
exert oneself 682 vb.
best one can do
attempt 671 n.
bestow
give 781 vb.
bestride
be broad 205 vb.
overlie 226 vb.
best-seller
book 589 n.
best wishes
congratulation
  886 n.
bet
gambling 618 n.
bête noire
bane 659 n.
hateful object 888 n.
betoken
evidence 466 vb.
betray
deceive 542 vb.
indicate 547 vb.
apostatize 603 vb.
fail in duty 918 vb.
betrothal
wooing 889 n.

wedding 894 n.
betrothed
loved one 887 n.
better
superior 34 adj.
gambler 618 n.
improved 654 adj.
restored 656 adj.
betterment
benefit 615 n.
improvement 654 n.
better not
inexpedient 643 adj.
betting
gambling 618 n.
between
between 231 adv.
between two stools
in difficulties
  700 adj.
bevel
obliquity 220 n.
beverage
draught 301 n.
bevy
group 74 n.
bewail
lament 836 vb.
beware
be careful 457 vb.
be cautious 858 vb.
bewilder
puzzle 474 vb.
bewitch
delight 826 vb.
excite love 887 vb.
bewitch 983 vb.
beyond
beyond 199 adv.
beyond doubt
undisputed 473 adj.
beyond one
impracticable
  470 adj.
beyond the pale
excluded 57 adj.
vulgar 847 adj.
bezel
obliquity 220 n.
bi-
dual 90 adj.
bias
influence 178 vb.
tendency 179 n.
obliquity 220 n.
distortion 246 n.
bias 481 n.

eccentricity 503 n.
motivate 612 vb.
biased
biased 481 adj.
unjust 914 adj.
bib
apron 228 n.
Bible
scripture 975 n.
bibliographer
bookperson 589 n.
bibliography
list 87 n.
edition 589 n.
bibliophile
bookperson 589 n.
bicentenary
fifth and over
  99 adj.
anniversary 141 n.
bicker
bicker 709 vb.
bicolour
variegated 437 adj.
bicycle
bicycle 274 n.
bid
gambling 618 n.
attempt 671 n.vb.
command 737 vb.
offer 759 n.vb.
biddable
willing 597 adj.
obedient 739 adj.
bidding
command 737 n.
bide one's time
wait 136 vb.
not act 677 vb.
bidet
ablutions 648 n.
biennial
seasonal 141 adj.
bier
bed 218 n.
bifocals
eyeglass 442 n.
bifurcate
bifurcate 92 vb.
diverge 294 vb.
big
great 32 adj.
large 195 adj.
important 638 adj.
bigamist
spouse 894 n.
Big Brother

tyrant 735 n.
big game
animal 365 n.
big-game hunter
hunter 619 n.
biggest slice of the
  cake
chief part 52 n.
bighead
vain person 873 n.
bigmouth
boaster 877 n.
big noise
bigwig 638 n.
person of repute
  866 n.
bigot
narrow mind 481 n.
zealot 979 n.
big shot
bigwig 638 n.
big spender
prodigal 815 n.
big stick
incentive 612 n.
threat 900 n.
bigwig
bigwig 638 n.
bike
ride 267 vb.
bicycle 274 n.
bikini
beachwear 228 n.
bilateral
dual 90 adj.
contractual 765 adj.
bile
resentment 891 n.
bilge
silly talk 515 n.
swill 649 n.
bilingual
speaking 579 adj.
bilious
unhealthy 651 adj.
sullen 893 adj.
bilk
defraud 788 vb.
not pay 805 vb.
bill
list 87 n.
advertise 528 vb.
paper money 797 n.
accounts 808 n.
bill and coo
caress 889 vb.
billboard

advertisement
  528 n.
billet
quarters 192 n.
apportion 783 vb.
billiards
ball game 837 n.
billion
over one hundred
  99 n.
bill of exchange
paper money 797 n.
bill of rights
dueness 915 n.
billon
bullion 797 n.
billowy
curved 248 adj.
convex 253 adj.
billycan
cauldron 194 n.
bimetallism
finance 797 n.
bin
vessel 194 n.
binary
computerized
  86 adj.
dual 90 adj.
binaural
sounding 398 adj.
bind
tie 45 vb.
combine 50 vb.
stabilize 153 vb.
doctor 658 vb.
compel 740 vb.
restrain 747 vb.
give terms 766 vb.
bore 838 n.
—oneself
promise 764 vb.
binding
ligature 47 n.
wrapping 226 n.
edging 234 n.
necessary 596 adj.
compelling 740 adj.
trimming 884 n.
obligatory 917 adj.
binding over
penalty 963 n.
binge
festivity 837 n.
drunkenness 949 n.
bingo
gambling 618 n.

binnacle
  sailing aid 269 n.
binoculars
  telescope 442 n.
biochemist
  doctor 658 n.
biochemistry
  biology 358 n.
biodegradable
  decomposable
    51 adj.
biogas
  fuel 385 n.
biogenic
  organic 358 adj.
biographer
  author 589 n.
biographical
  descriptive 590 adj.
biography
  biography 590 n.
biological
  biological 358 adj.
biological weapon
  poison 659 n.
biology
  biology 358 n.
biomass
  vegetable life 366 n.
  fuel 385 n.
bionic man
  prodigy 864 n.
bioplast
  life 360 n.
biorhythm
  regular return 141 n.
biosphere
  world 321 n.
biota
  organism 358 n.
biotechnology
  biology 358 n.
biotic
  alive 360 adj.
biotype
  organism 358 n.
bipartisan
  cooperative 706 adj.
  concordant 710 adj.
bipartite
  bisected 92 adj.
biped
  animal 365 n.
biplane
  aircraft 276 n.
birch
  tree 366 n.

scourge 964 n.
bird
  young creature
    132 n.
  bird 365 n.
  loved one 887 n.
bird-fancier
  breeder 369 n.
bird in the hand
  possession 773 n.
bird sanctuary
  preservation 666 n.
birds and the bees
  propagation 167 n.
bird's-eye view
  view 438 n.
  compendium 592 n.
birds of a feather
  analogue 18 n.
birdsong
  ululation 409 n.
biretta
  canonicals 989 n.
biro
  stationery 586 n.
birth
  origin 68 n.
  obstetrics 167 n.
  propagation 167 n.
  life 360 n.
birth certificate
  record 548 n.
birth control
  hindrance 702 n.
birthday
  anniversary 141 n.
birthmark
  identification 547 n.
birthplace
  source 156 n.
  home 192 n.
birth rate
  statistics 86 n.
birthright
  dueness 915 n.
biscuit
  pastries 301 n.
bisect
  bisect 92 vb.
bisexual
  abnormal 84 adj.
bishop
  ecclesiarch 986 n.
bishopric
  church office 985 n.
bistro
  café 192 n.

bit
  small quantity 33 n.
  piece 53 n.
  component 58 n.
  data processing
    86 n.
  perforator 263 n.
  fetter 748 n.
bit by bit
  by degrees 27 adv.
bitch
  dog 365 n.
  female animal
    373 n.
bitchiness
  malevolence 898 n.
bite
  small quantity 33 n.
  cut 46 vb.
  vigorousness 174 n.
  be sharp 256 vb.
  mouthful 301 n.
  chew 301 vb.
  pungency 388 n.
  wound 655 vb.
  hurt 827 vb.
  be irascible 892 vb.
—back
  restrain 747 vb.
—one's tongue
  regret 830 vb.
biter bit
  retaliation 714 n.
biting
  keen 174 adj.
  cold 380 adj.
  witty 839 adj.
  ungracious
    885 adj.
bits and pieces
  medley 43 n.
  rubbish 641 n.
bitter
  alcoholic drink
    301 n.
  cold 380 adj.
  sour 393 adj.
  unpleasant 827 adj.
  regretting 830 adj.
  resentful 891 adj.
bitterly
  painfully 32 adv.
bitter pill
  adversity 731 n.
bittersweet
  contrary 14 adj.
  painful 377 adj.

bitty
  fragmentary 53 adj.
  incomplete 55 adj.
bitumen
  resin 357 n.
bivalve
  marine life 365 n.
bivouac
  place oneself
    187 vb.
bizarre
  unusual 84 adj.
blab
  divulge 526 vb.
black
  exclude 57 vb.
  funereal 364 adj.
  dark 418 adj.
  black 428 adj.
  prohibit 757 vb.
  heinous 934 adj.
—out
  be insensible 375 vb.
  obliterate 550 vb.
black and white
  light contrast 417 n.
  pied 437 adj.
blackball
  exclude 57 vb.
blackberry
  fruit 301 n.
blackbird
  bird 365 n.
  vocalist 413 n.
blackboard
  classroom 539 n.
black books
  odium 888 n.
black box
  recording
    instrument 549 n.
black economy
  market 796 n.
blacked
  prohibited 757 adj.
blacken
  blacken 428 vb.
  defame 926 vb.
black eye
  wound 655 n.
blackguard
  cuss 899 vb.
  ruffian 904 n.
blackhead
  blemish 845 n.
black hole
  star 321 n.

blacking
black pigment
428 n.
blackjack
club 723 n.
card game 837 n.
black lead
lubricant 334 n.
blackleg
nonconformist 84 n.
black light
radiation 417 n.
blacklist
disapprove 924 vb.
black magic
sorcery 983 n.
blackmail
demand 737 n.vb.
compulsion 740 n.
threat 900 n.
black man/woman
blackness 428 n.
black mark
reprimand 924 n.
black market
trade 791 n.
illegal 954 adj.
Black Mass
diabolism 969 n.
Black Muslim
revolter 738 n.
blackness
darkness 418 n.
blackness 428 n.
blackout
insensibility 375 n.
obscuration 418 n.
Black Paper
report 524 n.
black power
governance 733 n.
black sheep
bad person 938 n.
blacksmith
artisan 686 n.
black spot
danger 661 n.
bladder
sphere 252 n.
blade
sharp edge 256 n.
foliage 366 n.
fop 848 n.
blame
blame 924 vb.
accusation 928 n.
guilt 936 n.

—for
attribute 158 vb.
—oneself
regret 830 vb.
be penitent 939 vb.
blameless
guiltless 935 adj.
blameworthy
discreditable
867 adj.
blameworthy
924 adj.
blanch
lose colour 426 vb.
bland
lenitive 177 adj.
smooth 258 adj.
flattering 925 adj.
blandishments
inducement 612 n.
endearment 889 n.
flattery 925 n.
blank
nonexistence 2 n.
zero 103 n.
empty 190 adj.
ignorant 491 adj.
impassive 820 adj.
blank cheque
scope 744 n.
blanket
general 79 adj.
coverlet 226 n.
screen 421 vb.
indiscriminate
464 adj.
blank verse
prosody 593 n.
blare
be loud 400 vb.
stridor 407 n.
blarney
empty talk 515 n.
flattery 925 n.
blasé
incurious 454 adj.
indifferent 860 adj.
unastonished
865 adj.
blaspheme
be impious 980 vb.
blast
outbreak 176 n.
gale 352 n.
loudness 400 n.
bang 402 n.vb.
fire at 712 vb.

blast furnace
furnace 383 n.
blast-off
space travel 271 n.
blatant
showy 875 adj.
insolent 878 adj.
blaze
fire 379 n.
shine 417 vb.
mark 547 vb.
—a trail
come before 64 vb.
blazer
jacket 228 n.
livery 547 n.
blazon
heraldry 547 n.
bleach
decolorize 426 vb.
whiten 427 vb.
bleak
wintry 129 adj.
empty 190 adj.
bleary
dim 419 adj.
bleat
ululate 409 vb.
be discontented
829 vb.
bleed
flow out 298 vb.
empty 300 vb.
doctor 658 vb.
fleece 786 vb.
suffer 825 vb.
bleeding
haemorrhage
302 n.
sanguineous
335 adj.
bleep
shrill 407 vb.
bleeper
signal 547 n.
blemish
defect 647 n.
impair 655 vb.
eyesore 842 n.
blemish 845 n.vb.
slur 867 n.
blench
show feeling 818 vb.
quake 854 vb.
blend
mix 43 vb.
compound 50 n.

bless
be auspicious
730 vb.
permit 756 vb.
thank 907 vb.
approve 923 vb.
worship 981 vb.
blessed
palmy 730 adj.
happy 824 adj.
paradisiac 971 adj.
blessing
benefit 615 n.
blether, blather
empty talk 515 n.
chatter 581 n.
blight
decay 51 n.
destroyer 168 n.
impair 655 vb.
blight 659 n.
blind
shade 226 n.
screen 421 vb.n.
blind 439 adj.vb.
inattentive 456 adj.
indiscriminating
464 adj.
misjudging 481 adj.
ignorant 491 adj.
trickery 542 n.
deceive 542 vb.
pretext 614 n.
stratagem 698 n.
impassive 820 adj.
drunkenness 949 n.
blind alley
lost labour 641 n.
obstacle 702 n.
blind corner
invisibility 444 n.
blindfold
screen 421 vb.
blind 439 adj.vb.
blind spot
blindness 439 n.
prejudice 481 n.
blink
flash 417 n.
gaze 438 vb.
be dim-sighted
440 vb.
blinker
screen 421 vb.
deceive 542 vb.
bliss
happiness 824 n.

blissful
palmy 730 adj.
paradisiac 971 adj.
blister
swelling 253 n.
blistered
rough 259 adj.
blithe
cheerful 833 adj.
blitz
havoc 165 n.
attack 712 n.vb.
bombardment 712 n.
blizzard
storm 176 n.
wintriness 380 n.
bloated
fleshy 195 adj.
convex 253 adj.
unsightly 842 adj.
bloc
political party 708 n.
block
housing 192 n.
bulk 195 n.
stand 218 n.
close 264 vb.
solid body 324 n.
dunce 501 n.
obstacle 702 n.
obstruct 702 vb.
parry 713 vb.
prohibit 757 vb.
—out
outline 233 vb.
represent 551 vb.
prepare 669 vb.
blockade
close 264 vb.
obstruct 702 vb.
besiege 712 vb.
restriction 747 n.
blockage
stop 145 n.
obstacle 702 n.
block and tackle
lifter 310 n.
blockbuster
destroyer 168 n.
bomb 723 n.
blockhead
dunce 501 n.
blockishness
unintelligence 499 n.

moral insensibility 820 n.
bloke
male 372 n.
blond(e)
whitish 427 adj.
yellowness 433 n.
blood
breed 77 n.
blood 335 n.
redness 431 n.
blood-and-thunder
dramatic 594 adj.
bloodbath
slaughter 362 n.
blood-curdling
frightening 854 adj.
blood donor
giver 781 n.
bloodhound
dog 365 n.
detective 459 n.
bloodless
insubstantial 4 adj.
colourless 426 adj.
peaceful 717 adj.
guiltless 935 adj.
blood lust
violence 176 n.
inhumanity 898 n.
blood money
peace offering 719 n.
atonement 941 n.
blood-poisoning
infection 651 n.
blood pressure
cardiovascular disease 651 n.
bloodshed
slaughter 362 n.
bloodshot
bloodstained 431 adj.
blood sports
chase 619 n.
bloodstained
sanguineous 335 adj.
bloodstained 431 adj.
bloodstock
thoroughbred 273 n.
nobility 868 n.
bloodsucker
taker 786 n.

bloodthirsty
murderous 362 adj.
cruel 898 adj.
bloody
violent 176 adj.
sanguineous 335 adj.
murderous 362 adj.
bloodstained 431 adj.
cruel 898 adj.
bloody-minded
obstinate 602 adj.
bloom
be fruitful 171 vb.
open 263 vb.
flower 366 n.
health 650 n.
bloomer
mistake 495 n.
blooming
vigorous 174 adj.
personable 841 adj.
blossom
grow 36 vb.
be fruitful 171 vb.
flower 366 n.
prosper 730 vb.
blot
absorb 299 vb.
dry 342 vb.
mark 547 vb.
obliterate 550 vb.
impair 655 vb.
blemish 845 n.vb.
slur 867 n.
—one's copybook
lose repute 867 vb.
incur blame 924 vb.
blotch
maculation 437 n.
blotter
stationery 586 n.
blouse
shirt 228 n.
blouson
jacket 228 n.
blow
expand 197 vb.
knock 279 n.
wind 352 n.
blow 352 vb.
disappointment 509 n.
deed 676 n.
adversity 731 n.
—down

fell 311 vb.
—it
blunder 495 vb.
—one's cover
disclose 526 vb.
—one's mind
make mad 503 vb.
—one's own trumpet
be vain 873 vb.
boast 877 vb.
—open
force 176 vb.
—out
extinguish 382 vb.
snuff out 418 vb.
—over
be past 125 vb.
cease 145 vb.
—sky-high
demolish 165 vb.
confute 479 vb.
—the whistle on
inform 524 vb.
warn 664 vb.
—up
demolish 165 vb.
force 176 vb.
enlarge 197 vb.
blow up 352 vb.
exaggerate 546 vb.
reprove 924 vb.
blower
ventilation 352 n.
blowhole
orifice 263 n.
blowlamp
furnace 383 n.
blown
panting 684 adj.
blowout
feasting 301 n.
blowpipe
propellant 287 n.
missile weapon 723 n.
blows
fight 716 n.
blowy
windy 352 adj.
blowzy
red 431 adj.
blubber
fat 357 n.
weep 836 vb.
bludgeon
club 723 n.
oppress 735 vb.

blue
 blueness 435 n.
 blue 435 adj.
 badge 547 n.
 melancholic
  834 adj.
Blue
 athlete 162 n.
blue blood
 genealogy 169 n.
 nobility 868 n.
blue-collar worker
 worker 686 n.
blue-eyed boy
 favourite 890 n.
blue joke
 witticism 839 n.
blue language
 scurrility 899 n.
blue moon
 neverness 109 n.
blue-pencil
 amendment 654 n.
blueprint
 plan 623 n.vb.
blues
 music 412 n.
 melancholy 834 n.
blue-stocking
 intellectual 492 n.
bluff
 high land 209 n.
 trickery 542 n.
 deceive 542 vb.
 pretext 614 n.
blunder
 blunder 495 vb.
 act foolishly 695 vb.
blunderer
 fool 501 n.
 bungler 697 n.
blunt
 moderate 177 vb.
 unsharpened
  257 adj.
 smooth 258 adj.
 undisguised
  522 adj.
 veracious 540 adj.
 artless 699 adj.
 make insensitive
  820 vb.
bluntness
 plainness 573 n.
 rudeness 885 n.
blur
 bedim 419 vb.

blur 400 vb.
blurb
 advertisement
  528 n.
blurred
 amorphous 244 adj
 indistinct 444 adj.
blurt out
 divulge 526 vb.
blush
 redden 431 vb.
 show feeling 818 vb
 be modest 874 vb.
bluster
 ineffectuality 161 n.
 be violent 176 vb.
 defy 711 vb.
 boast 877 n.vb.
 threaten 900 vb.
blustery
 windy 352 adj.
board
 lamina 207 n.
 shelf 218 n.
 stand 218 n.
 enter 297 vb.
 hardness 326 n.
 materials 631 n.
 provide 633 vb.
 council 692 n.
 attack 712 vb.
 tribunal 956 n.
—out
 dwell 192 vb.
board and lodging
 provision 633 n.
boarder
 resident 191 n.
boarding house
 quarters 192 n.
board of directors
 director 690 n.
boast
 exaggerate 546 vb.
 triumph 727 vb.
 boast 877 n.vb.
boasting
 empty talk 515 n.
 magniloquence
  574 n.
boat
 go to sea 269 vb.
 boat 275 n.
boater
 headgear 228 n.
boathouse
 stable 192 n.

boating
 aquatics 269 n.
 water travel 269 n.
 sport 837 n.
boatman
 boatman 270 n.
boatswain
 mariner 270 n.
 navigator 270 n.
bob
 oscillate 317 vb.
 hairdressing 843 n.
bobble
 hanging object
  217 n.
 trimming 844 n.
bobby
 police 955 n.
bode
 predict 511 vb.
bodhisattva
 pietist 979 n.
bodice
 garment 228 n.
bodiless
 insubstantial 4 adj.
 immaterial 320 adj.
bodily
 violently 176 adv.
body
 substance 3 n.
 main part 32 n.
 band 74 n.
 frame 218 n.
 object 319 n.
 structure 331 n.
 corpse 363 n.
 person 371 n.
 corporation 708 n.
—forth
 externalize 223 vb.
 manifest 522 vb.
body and soul
 wholly 52 adv.
body-building
 nourishing 301 adj.
bodyguard
 protector 660 n.
 retainer 742 n.
body language
 gesture 547 n.
body politic
 political
  organization
  733 n.
boffin
 intellectual 492 n.

expert 696 n.
bog
 marsh 347 n.
bogey, bogy, bogie
 fantasy 513 n.
 monster 938 n.
 demon 970 n.
boggle
 be unwilling 598 vb.
bogus
 spurious 542 adj.
 affected 850 adj.
Bohemian
 nonconformist 84 n.
boil
 swelling 253 n.
 cook 301 vb.
 bubble 355 vb.
 be hot 379 vb.
 ulcer 651 n.
 sanitate 652 vb.
 be excited 821 vb.
—down
 make smaller
  198 vb.
—down to
 mean 514 vb.
boiler
 cauldron 194 n.
 heater 383 n.
boiler suit
 suit 228 n.
boiling
 furious 176 adj.
 angry 891 adj.
boisterous
 disorderly 61 adj.
 excitable 822 adj.
bold
 undisguised
  522 adj.
 rash 857 adj.
 insolent 878 adj.
bold front
 defiance 711 n.
 courage 855 n.
bole
 soil 344 n.
 tree 366 n.
boll
 sphere 252 n.
bollard
 traffic control 305 n.
Bolshevist
 revolter 738 n.
bolshie
 disobedient 738 adj.

bolster (up)
  support 218 vb.
  give courage 855 vb.
bolt
  fastening 47 n.
  close 264 vb.
  move fast 277 vb.
  decamp 296 vb.
  run away 620 vb.
  gluttonize 947 vb.
bolthole
  refuge 662 n.
bolus
  mouthful 301 n.
  medicine 658 n.
bomb
  nucleonics 160 n.
  demolish 165 vb.
  bomb 723 n.
bombard
  shoot 287 vb.
  fire at 712 vb.
bombardment
  bombardment
    712 n.
bombast
  empty talk 515 n.
  magniloquence
    574 n.
bomber
  air force 722 n.
bombproof
  defended 713 adj.
bombshell
  lack of expectation
    508 n.
bona fide
  genuine 494 adj.
bonanza
  plenty 635 n.
  prosperity 730 n.
bond
  relation 9 n.
  bond 47 n.
  fetter 748 n.
  promise 764 n.
  title deed 767 n.
bondage
  servitude 745 n.
bone
  empty 300 vb.
  hardness 326 n.
  structure 331 n.
boneless
  impotent 161 adj.
bonemeal
  fertilizer 171 n.

bone of contention
  casus belli 709 n.
boner
  mistake 495 n.
bones
  remainder 41 n.
  corpse 363 n.
bone to pick
  casus belli 709 n.
  resentment 891 n.
bonfire
  fire 379 n.
  celebration 876 n.
bonhomie
  sociability 882 n.
bonkers
  crazy 503 adj.
bon mot
  witticism 839 n.
bonnet
  headgear 228 n.
bonny
  healthy 650 adj.
  beautiful 841 adj.
bonsai
  tree 366 n.
bonus
  extra 40 n.
  incentive 612 n.
  gift 781 n.
bon viveur
  sensualist 944 n.
bon voyage!
  296 int.
bony
  lean 206 adj.
  hard 326 adj.
boo
  vociferate 408 vb.
  not respect 921 vb.
  disapprove 924 vb.
boob
  · *mistake* 495 n.
booby
  ninny 501 n.
  bungler 697 n.
booby prize
  unskilfulness
    695 n.
booby trap
  trap 542 n.
  pitfall 663 n.
book
  book 589 n.
  account 808 vb.
bookcase
  library 589 n.

book-collector
  bookperson 589 n.
bookie
  gambler 618 n.
booking
  registration 548 n.
bookish
  instructed 490 adj.
  studious 536 adj.
bookkeeper
  enumerator 86 n.
  accountant 808 n.
booklet
  book 589 n.
bookmaker
  gambler 618 n.
bookplate
  label 547 n.
bookseller
  bookperson 589 n.
bookshop
  library 589 n.
bookworm
  scholar 492 n.
boom
  grow 36 vb.
  productiveness
    171 n.
  be loud 400 vb.
  resonance 404 n.
  prosper 730 vb.
boomerang
  recoil 280 n.vb.
  missile weapon
    723 n.
boon
  benefit 615 n.
boon companion
  close friend 880 n.
boorish
  ill-bred 847 adj.
boost
  augment 36 vb.
  invigorate 174 vb.
  advertise 528 vb.
  aid 703 n.vb.
booster
  rocket 276 n.
boot
  box 194 n.
  kick 279 vb.
—out
  repel 292 vb.
  eject 300 vb.
booth
  compartment 194 n.
  shop 796 n.

bootleg
  booty 790 n.
bootless
  profitless 641 adj.
bootlicker
  toady 879 n.
boots
  footwear 228 n.
booty
  booty 790 n.
booze
  alcoholic drink
    301 n.
  get drunk 949 vb.
bop
  music 412 n.
  dance 837 n.vb.
border
  contiguity 202 n.
  edging 234 n.
  limit 236 n.
  flank 239 vb.
  trimming 844 n.
borderer
  dweller 191 n.
borderline
  uncertain 474 adj.
bore
  breadth 205 n.
  pierce 263 vb.
  wave 350 n.
  firearm 723 n.
  bore 838 n.
  be tedious 838 vb.
borehole
  excavation 255 n.
  water 339 n.
borer
  perforator 263 n.
  insect 365 n.
born
  born 360 adj.
born again
  sanctified 979 adj.
born yesterday
  artless 699 adj.
borough
  district 184 n.
borrow
  copy 20 vb.
  borrow 785 vb.
Borstal
  prison 748 n.
bosh
  silly talk 515 n.
bosom
  interiority 224 n.

bosom 253 n.
  affections 817 n.
boss
  superior 34 n.
  swelling 253 n.
  director 690 n.
  dominate 733 vb.
  master 741 n.
bossy
  authoritarian
    735 adj.
bosun
  mariner 270 n.
botanical
  vegetal 366 adj.
botany
  botany 368 n.
botch, bodge
  misrepresent|
    552 vb.
  be clumsy 695 vb.
botch-up
  mistake 495 n.
both
  dual 90 adj.
bother
  commotion 318 n.
  distract 456 vb.
  hinder 702 vb.
  worry 825 n.
  torment 827 vb.
bottle
  vessel 194 n.
  preserve 666 vb.
—up
  remember 505 vb.
  restrain 747 vb.
bottleneck
  narrowness 206 n.
  obstacle 702 n.
bottom
  lowness 210 n.
  base 214 n.
  buttocks 238 n.
bottom drawer
  store 632 n.
  preparation 669 n.
bottomless
  deep 211 adj.
botulism
  digestive disorders
    651 n.
boudoir
  chamber 194 n.
bouffant
  convex 253 adj.
bough

branch 53 n.
  foliage 366 n.
boulder
  rock 344 n.
boulevard
  path 624 n.
bounce
  recoil 280 n.
  eject 300 vb.
  leap 312 vb.
  oscillate 317 vb.
  elasticity 328 n.
  be elastic 328 vb.
bouncer
  ejector 300 n.
bouncing
  vigorous 174 adj.
  healthy 650 adj.
bound
  tied 45 adj.
  limit 236 vb.
  leap 312 vb.
  certain 473 adj.
  fated 596 adj.
  restrained 747 adj.
  obliged 917 adj.
boundary
  limit 236 n.
bounder
  cad 938 n.
bound for
  directed 281 adj.
boundless
  infinite 107 adj.
  spacious 183 adj.
bounds
  outline 233 n.
bounteous
  liberal 813 adj.
bountiful
  giving 781 adj.
bounty
  subvention 703 n.
  liberality 813 n.
bouquet
  bunch 74 n.
  fragrance 396 n.
  praise 923 n.
bourgeois
  commoner 869 n.
bourgeois ethic
  conformity 83 n.
bourgeoisie
  middle classes
    869 n.
bout
  period 110 n.

labour 682 n.
  pugilism 716 n.
boutique
  clothier 228 n.
  shop 796 n.
bovine
  animal 365 adj.
  unintelligent|
    499 adj.
bow
  prow 237 n.
  curve 248 n.
  be convex 253 vb.
  propellant 287 n.
  stoop 311 vb.
  viol 414 n.
  knuckle under|
    721 vb.
  missile weapon
    723 n.
  trimming 844 n.
  show respect 920 vb.
—to
  be inferior 35 vb.
bowdlerize
  purify 648 vb.
bowels
  insides 224 n.
bower
  arbour 194 n.
bowl
  bowl 194 n.
  cavity 255 n.
  propel 287 vb.
  rotate 315 vb.
—along
  go smoothly 258 vb.
  move fast 277 vb.
—out
  dismiss 300 vb.
—over
  fell 311 vb.
  be wonderful|
    864 vb.
bow-legged
  deformed 246 adj.
bowler
  headgear 228 n.
  player 837 n.
bowline
  tackling 47 n.
bowling alley
  place of amusement
    837 n.
bowling green
  pleasure ground
    837 n.

bowls
  ball game 837 n.
bowman
  shooter 287 n.
  soldiery 722 n.
bowshot
  short distance 200 n.
bowsprit
  prow 237 n.
box
  box 194 n.
  compartment 194 n.
  enclose 235 vb.
  storage 632 n.
  fight 716 vb.
boxer
  dog 365 n.
  pugilist 722 n.
boxing
  pugilism 716 n.
box office
  onlookers 441 n.
  treasury 799 n.
box on the ears
  reprimand 924 n.
box room
  chamber 194 n.
  storage 632 n.
boy
  youngster 132 n.
  male 372 n.
boycott
  exclusion 57 n.
  make unwelcome
    883 vb.
  disapprobation
    924 n.
boy friend
  lover 887 n.
boyhood
  youth 130 n.
boyish
  infantine 132 adj.
  immature 670 adj.
bra
  underwear 228 n.
brace
  duality 90 n.
  strengthen 162 vb.
  prop 218 n.
—oneself
  prepare oneself
    669 vb.
brace and bit
  perforator 263 n.
braced
  rigid 326 adj.

bracelet
fetter 748 n.
jewellery 844 n.
braces
hanger 217 n.
bracing
salubrious 652 adj.
refreshing 685 adj.
bracken
plant 366 n.
bracket
equalize 28 vb.
classification 77 n.
pair 90 vb.
shelf 218 n.
—with
liken 18 vb.
brackets
punctuation 547 n.
brackish
salty 388 adj.
bradawl
perforator 263 n.
brag
card game 837 n.
boast 877 n.vb.
Brahma
divineness 965 n.
Brahmin, Brahman
aristocrat 868 n.
priest 986 n.
Brahminism
religious faith 973 n.
braid
ligature 47 n.
weave 222 vb.
trimming 844 n.
brail
elevate 310 vb.
braille
writing 586 n.
brain
head 213 n.
intellectual 492 n.
intelligence 498 n.
brainchild
idea 451 n.
brain damage
absence of intellect
448 n.
brainless
foolish 499 adj.
brainstorm
excitable state 822 n.
brain-twister
enigma 530 n.
brainwash

convert 147 vb.
misteach 535 vb.
brain wave
idea 451 n.
brainy
intelligent 498 adj.
braise
cook 301 vb.
brake
bring to rest 266 vb.
retard 278 vb.
safeguard 662 n.
restraint 747 n.
bran
cereals 301 n.
branch
branch 53 n.
descendant 170 n.
extend 183 vb.
foliage 366 n.
society 708 n.
—off
diverge 294 vb.
—out
deviate 282 vb.
brand
sort 77 n.
burn 381 vb.
lighter 385 n.
torch 420 n.
identification 547 n.
mark 547 vb.
slur 867 n.
defame 926 vb.
branded
proprietary 777 adj.
brandish
brandish 317 vb.
brandy
alcoholic drink
301 n.
brashness
insolence 878 n.
brass
orchestra 413 n.
horn 414 n.
yellowness 433 n.
monument 548 n.
wealth 800 n.
sauciness 878 n.
brass hat
bigwig 638 n.
army officer 741 n.
brassière
underwear 228 n.
brass plate
label 547 n.

brass rubbing
picture 553 n.
brass tacks
reality 1 n.
brassy
strident 407 adj.
brat
child 132 n.
bravado
ostentation 875 n.
boasting 877 n.
brave
defy 711 vb.
brave person 855 n.
courageous
855 adj.
bravo
desperado 857 n.
923 int.
bravura
musical skill 413 n.
braw
excellent 644 adj.
brawl
turmoil 61 n.
quarrel 709 n.
brawn
vitality 162 n.
meat 301 n.
bray
ululate 409 vb.
braze
agglutinate 48 vb.
brazen
strident 407 adj.
undisguised
522 adj.
insolent 878 adj.
impenitent 940 adj.
brazier
furnace 383 n.
breach
gap 201 n.
dissension 709 n.
breach of promise
perfidy 930 n.
breach of the peace
turmoil 61 n.
bread
cereals 301 n.
food 301 n.
shekels 797 n.
**bread-and-butter,
one's**
vocation 622 n.
breadth
breadth 205 n.

breadwinner
worker 686 n.
break
break 46 vb.
discontinuity 72 n.
opportunity 137 n.
lull 145 n.
continuance 146 n.
interval 201 n.
be brittle 330 vb.
repose 683 n.
oppress 735 vb.
—away
separate 46 vb.
run away 620 vb.
quarrel 709 vb.
schismatize 978 vb.
—down
decompose 51 vb.
fail 728 vb.
weep 836 vb.
—even
be equal 28 vb.
—in
burst in 297 vb.
break in 369 vb.
habituate 610 vb.
—of
cure 656 vb.
—off
discontinue 72 vb.
cease 145 vb.
—one's word
not observe 769 vb.
be dishonest 930 vb.
—out
begin 68 vb.
be violent 176 vb.
emerge 298 vb.
escape 667 vb.
—the law
do wrong 914 vb.
be illegal 954 vb.
—through
emerge 298 vb.
escape 667 vb.
—up
separate 46 vb.
decompose 51 vb.
disperse 75 vb.
demolish 165 vb.
breakable
brittle 330 adj.
breakaway
independent
744 adj.
schismatic 978 adj.

BRE

breakdown
stop 145 n.
illness 651 n.
hitch 702 n.
breakfast
meal 301 n.
breaking point
casus belli 709 n.
completion 725 n.
breakneck
sloping 220 adj.
hasty 680 adj.
rash 857 adj.
breakout
escape 667 n.
breakthrough
success 727 n.
breakup
finality 69 n.
ruin 165 n.
breakwater
safeguard 662 n.
breast
interiority 224 n.
bosom 253 n.
spirit 447 n.
withstand 704 vb.
affections 817 n.
breastplate
armour 713 n.
breath
insubstantial thing
  4 n.
life 360 n.
faintness 401 n.
breathalyser
testing agent 461 n.
breathe
breathe 352 vb.
live 360 vb.
hint 524 vb.
voice 577 vb.
be refreshed 685 vb.
—fresh life into
vitalize 360 vb.
revive 656 vb.
animate 821 vb.
breather
lull 145 n.
repose 683 n.
breathing
respiration 352 n.
breathless
agitated 318 adj.
puffing 352 adj.
voiceless 578 adj.
hasty 680 adj.

BRI

panting 684 adj.
breath of air
breeze 352 n.
breathtaking
notable 638 adj.
wonderful 864 adj.
breed
race 11 n.
breed 77 n.
produce 164 vb.
reproduce 166 vb.
reproduce itself
  167 vb.
breed stock 369 vb.
educate 534 vb.
breeder
breeder 369 n.
breeding
good taste 846 n.
etiquette 848 n.
breeding-ground
seedbed 156 n.
breeze
breeze 352 n.
breezy
windy 352 adj.
cheerful 833 adj.
disrespectful
  921 adj.
breve
notation 410 n.
brevet
mandate 751 n.
breviary
office-book 988 n.
brevity
conciseness 569 n.
brew
a mixture 43 n.
mix 43 vb.
alcoholic drink
  301 n.
mature 669 vb.
brewery
workshop 687 n.
brewing
impending 155 adj.
bribable
venal 930 adj.
bribe
incentive 612 n.
bribe 612 vb.
purchase 792 vb.
bric-à-brac
bauble 639 n.
brick
pottery 381 n.

BRI

building material
  631 n.
good person 937 n.
brickbat
missile 287 n.
indignity 921 n.
bricklayer
artisan 686 n.
bricks and mortar
housing 192 n.
building material
  631 n.
brick wall
obstacle 702 n.
brickwork
structure 331 n.
bridal
matrimonial
  894 adj.
bride, bridegroom
spouse 894 n.
bridesmaid
auxiliary 707 n.
bridge
connect 45 vb.
tooth 256 n.
pass 305 vb.
bridge 624 n.
card game 837 n.
bridgehead
front 237 n.
battleground 724 n.
bridle
break in 369 vb.
restraint 747 n.
get angry 891 vb.
bridlepath
path 624 n.
brief
brief 144 adj.
short 204 adj.
inform 524 vb.
concise 569 adj.
compendium 592 n.
make ready 669 vb.
briefcase
case 194 n.
briefing
advice 691 n.
briefs
underwear 228 n.
brig
sailing ship 275 n.
brigade
formation 722 n.
brigadier
army officer 741 n.

BRI

brigand
robber 789 n.
bright
luminous 417 adj.
intelligent 498 adj.
clean 648 adj.
cheerful 833 adj.
brighten
make bright 417 vb.
bright-eyed
personable 841 adj.
brilliance
light 417 n.
hue 425 n.
intelligence 498 n.
beauty 841 n.
ostentation 875 n.
brim
be complete 54 vb.
edge 234 n.
—over
superabound
  637 vb.
brine
ocean 343 n.
season 388 vb.
preserver 666 n.
bring
carry 273 vb.
—about
cause 156 vb.
carry out 725 vb.
—back
restitute 787 vb.
—down
fell 311 vb.
—forth
reproduce itself
  167 vb.
—home to
convince 485 vb.
impress 821 vb.
—in
admit 299 vb.
be profitable
  771 vb.
—it off
succeed 727 vb.
—on
cause 156 vb.
promote 285 vb.
—out
print 587 vb.
—round
convince 485 vb.
—to a head
mature 669 vb.

—to bear
use 673 vb.
—to book
punish 963 vb.
—together
bring together
74 vb.
mediate 720 vb.
—to light
discover 484 vb.
manifest 522 vb.
—up
vomit 300 vb.
educate 534 vb.
brink
extremity 69 n.
nearness 200 n.
edge 234 n.
brinkmanship
tactics 688 n.
rashness 857 n.
brisk
vigorous 174 adj.
speedy 277 adj.
active 678 adj.
bristle
prickle 256 n.
be rough 259 vb.
get angry 891 vb.
brittle
flimsy 163 adj.
brittle 330 adj.
broach
initiate 68 vb.
perforator 263 n.
make flow 350 vb.
broad
general 79 adj.
broad 205 adj.
inexact 495 adj.
dialectal 560 adj.
broadcast
disperse 75 vb,
communicate
524 vb.
published 528 adj.
broadcast, be
be heard 415 vb.
broadcasting
broadcasting 531 n.
broaden
expand 197 vb.
broad-minded
wise 498 adj.
free 744 adj.
broadsheet
the press 528 n.

broadside
laterality 239 n.
bombardment
712 n.
Broadway
drama 594 n.
brocade
textile 222 n.
brochette
sharp point 256 n.
brochure
the press 528 n.
book 589 n.
brogue
dialect 560 n.
broil
cook 301 vb.
broiler
poultry 365 n.
broke
poor 801 adj.
broken
discontinuous
72 adj.
rough 259 adj.
tamed 369 adj.
imperfect 647 adj.
broken in
habituated 610 adj.
broken thread
discontinuity 72 n.
broker
intermediary 231 n.
consignee 754 n.
merchant 794 n.
brokerage
discount 810 n.
bronchitis
respiratory disease
651 n.
bronze
brown 430 adj.
sculpture 554 n.
brooch
fastening 47 n.
jewellery 844 n.
brood
group 74 n.
young creature
132 n.
posterity 170 n.
meditate 449 vb.
be dejected 834 vb.
broody
fertilized 167 adj.
brook
stream 350 n.

permit 756 vb.
broom
cleaning utensil
648 n.
broth
hors-d'oeuvres
301 n.
brothel
brothel 951 n.
brother
kinsman 11 n.
analogue 18 n.
colleague 707 n.
monk 986 n.
brotherhood
family 11 n.
community 708 n.
friendship 880 n.
sect 978 n.
brow
head 213 n.
face 237 n.
mien 445 n.
browbeat
induce 612 vb.
frighten 854 vb.
browbeaten
subjected
745 adj.
brown
darken 418 vb.
brown 430 adj.
browned off
discontented
829 adj.
bored 838 adj.
brown study
abstractedness
456 n.
browse
graze 301 vb.
study 536 vb.
bruise
pulverize 332 vb.
pain 377 n.
wound 655 n.vb.
blemish 845 n.
bruiser
ruffian 904 n.
brunch
meal 301 n.
brunette
woman 373 n.
brown 430 adj.
brunt
difficulty 700 n.
brush

be contiguous
202 vb.
rub 333 vb.
touch 378 vb.
cleaning utensil
648 n.
fight 716 n.
—up
study 536 vb.
brush-off
repulsion 292 n.
brushwood
fuel 385 n.
brushwork
painting 553 n.
brusque
concise 569 adj.
ungracious 885 adj.
brutal
violent 176 adj.
oppressive 735 adj.
cruel 898 adj.
brutalize
pervert 655 vb.
make insensitive
820 vb.
brute
violent creature
176 n.
animal 365 n.
mindless 448 adj.
rude person 885 n.
ruffian 904 n.
brute force
brute force 735 n.
brutish
discourteous
885 adj.
bubble
insubstantial thing
4 n.
sphere 252 n.
be agitated 318 vb.
lightness 323 n.
brittleness 330 n.
bubble 355 n.vb.
bubbly
wine 301 n.
bubbly 355 adj.
excited 821 adj.
buccaneer
robber 789 n.
buck
leap 312 vb.
mammal 365 n.
paper money 797 n.
fop 848 n.

—up
relieve 831 vb.
cheer 833 vb.
bucket
vessel 194 n.
bucket shop
market 796 n.
buckle
fastening 47 n.
distort 246 vb.
make concave
255 vb.
buckshot
ammunition 723 n.
bucolic
agrarian 370 adj.
poetic 593 adj.
bud
grow 36 vb.
swelling 253 n.
flower 366 n.
Buddha
sage 500 n.
Buddhism
religious faith 973 n.
budding
beginning 68 adj.
young 130 adj.
buddy
chum 880 n.
budge
be in motion 265 vb.
budget
provide 633 vb.
accounts 808 n.
budget price
cheapness 812 n.
buff
rub 333 vb.
brown 430 adj.
enthusiast 504 n.
buffer
intermediary 231 n.
protection 660 n.
buffer state
contiguity 202 n.
buffet
café 192 n.
cabinet 194 n.
knock 279 n.
ill-treat 645 vb.
wound 655 vb.
buffoon
fool 501 n.
humorist 839 n.
buffoonery
foolery 497 n.

bug
microorganism
196 n.
insect 365 n.
hear 415 vb.
enthusiast 504 n.
infection 651 n.
torment 827 vb.
bugbear
hateful object 888 n.
buggery
illicit love 951 n.
buggy
automobile 274 n.
bugle
horn 414 n.
call 547 n.
build
produce 164 vb.
form 243 n.vb.
structure 331 n.
—up
strengthen 162 vb.
urbanize 192 vb.
make higher 209 vb.
advertise 528 vb.
builder
producer 164 n.
building
edifice 164 n.
housing 192 n.
building block
materials 631 n.
building society
pawnshop 784 n.
buildup
increase 36 n.
overestimation
482 n.
built-in
component 58 adj.
built-up
urban 192 adj.
bulb
swelling 253 n.
plant 366 n.
lamp 420 n.
bulbous
rotund 252 adj.
bulge
increment 36 n.
swelling 253 n.
be convex 253 vb.
bulging
full 54 adj.
bulk
main part 32 n.

greater number
104 n.
bulk 195 n.
—large
be important
638 vb.
bulkhead
partition 231 n.
bulky
substantial 3 adj.
large 195 adj.
bull
cattle 365 n.
solecism 565 n.
labour 682 n.
speculate 791 vb.
bulldog
dog 365 n.
brave person 855 n.
bulldoze
demolish 165 vb.
compel 740 vb.
bulldozer
destroyer 168 n.
flattener 216 n.
pulverizer 332 n.
bullet
ammunition 723 n.
bulletin
report 524 n.
news 529 n.
bulletproof
invulnerable
660 adj.
bull-headed
obstinate 602 adj.
bull in a china shop
bungler 697 n.
bullion
bullion 797 n.
bullish
buying 792 adj.
dear 811 adj.
bullock
beast of burden
273 n.
bullring
arena 724 n.
bull's-eye
centre 225 n.
objective 617 n.
bully
tyrant 735 n.
oppress 735 vb.
frighten 854 vb.
threaten 900 vb.
ruffian 904 n.

—into
compel 740 vb.
bulwark
protection 660 n.
defence 713 n.
fortification 713 n.
bum
wanderer 268 n.
idler 679 n.
bumbler
bungler 697 n.
bumf
reading matter
589 n.
bump
swelling 253 n.
protuberance
254 n.
collision 279 n.
nonresonance
405 n.
—into
meet 295 vb.
bumper
draught 301 n.
defence 713 n.
bumpkin
country-dweller
869 n.
bumptious
insolent 878 adj.
bumpy
nonuniform 17 adj.
rough 259 adj.
bun
pastries 301 n.
hairdressing 843 n.
bunch
bunch 74 n.
bring together
74 vb.
bundle
bunch 74 n.
bring together
74 vb.
bag 194 n.
collection 632 n.
bunfight
social gathering
882 n.
bung
stopper 264 n.
bungalow
house 192 n.
bungle
lose a chance
138 vb.

BUN

blunder 495 vb.
fail 728 vb.
bungler
bungler 697 n.
bunk
bed 218 n.
empty talk 515 n.
bunker
cellar 194 n.
storage 632 n.
defences 713 n.
bunkum
empty talk 515 n.
bunting
flag 547 n.
buoy
sailing aid 269 n.
signpost 547 n.
buoyancy
lightness 323 n.
elasticity 328 n.
buoyant
swimming 269 adj.
cheerful 833 adj.
burble
flow 350 vb.
be foolish 499 vb.
burden
load 193 vb.
make heavy 322 vb.
vocal music 412 n.
topic 452 n.
encumbrance 702 n.
oppress 735 vb.
annoyance 827 n.
burdened
bearing 273 adj.
bureau
cabinet 194 n.
workshop 687 n.
bureaucracy
management 689 n.
governance 733 n.
bureaucrat
official 690 n.
burgeon
grow 36 vb.
be fruitful 171 vb.
burgh
housing 192 n.
burglar
thief 789 n.
burglary
stealing 788 n.
burgundy
wine 301 n.
burial

BUR

interment 364 n.
burial service
obsequies 364 n.
buried
buried 364 adj.
concealed 525 adj.
secluded 883 adj.
burlesque
misrepresentation 552 n.
be witty 839 vb.
satire 851 n.
burly
stalwart 162 adj.
burn
stream 350 n.
burn 381 vb.
shine 417 vb.
blacken 428 vb.
desire 859 vb.
resent 891 vb.
—one's fingers
be rash 857 vb.
burner
furnace 383 n.
burning
painful 377 adj.
pungent 388 adj.
fervent 818 adj.
burnish
smooth 258 vb.
make bright 417 vb.
burnt offering
oblation 981 n.
burn-up
speeding 277 n.
burp
eruct 300 vb.
burr
perforator 263 n.
rasp 407 vb.
dialect 560 n.
burrow
dwelling 192 n.
excavation 255 n.
make concave 255 vb.
descend 309 vb.
refuge 662 n.
bursar
treasurer 798 n.
bursary
subvention 703 n.
burst
break 46 vb.
be dispersed 75 vb.
be violent 176 vb.

BUS

open 263 vb.
spurt 277 n.
be brittle 330 vb.
bang 402 vb.
activity 678 n.
—in
burst in 297 vb.
bursting
full 54 adj.
bury
insert 303 vb.
inter 364 vb.
conceal 525 vb.
bus
bus 274 n.
bush
plain 348 n.
tree 366 n.
bushel
metrology 465 n.
bushmen
humankind 371 n.
bush telegraph
rumour 529 n.
bushy
dense 324 adj.
arboreal 366 adj.
business
affairs 154 n.
topic 452 n.
intention 617 n.
business 622 n.
activity 678 n.
trade 791 n.
business house
corporation 708 n.
businesslike
businesslike 622 adj.
busker
musician 413 n.
entertainer 594 n.
bussing
transference 272 n.
bust
break 46 vb.
bosom 253 n.
sculpture 554 n.
miscarry 728 vb.
poor 801 adj.
bustle
garment 228 n.
commotion 318 n.
activity 678 n.
haste 680 n.
bustling
eventful 154 adj.

BUT

busy
eventful 154 adj.
busy 678 adj.
busybody
inquisitive person 453 n.
meddler 678 n.
but
qualification 468 n.
butane
fuel 385 n.
butch
male 372 adj.
butcher
killer 362 n.
butler
retainer 742 n.
butt
vat 194 n.
collide 279 vb.
firearm 723 n.
laughingstock 851 n.
—in
meddle 678 vb.
butter
fat 357 n.
—up
flatter 925 vb.
butterfingers
bungler 697 n.
butterflies
nervousness 854 n.
butterfly
insect 365 n.
inattention 456 n.
buttermilk
milk 301 n.
butterscotch
brownness 430 n.
buttocks
buttocks 238 n.
button
fastening 47 n.
close 264 vb.
buttoned-up
reticent 525 adj.
completed 725 adj.
buttonhole
fastening 47 n.
fragrance 396 n.
speak to 583 vb.
buttress
prop 218 n.
corroborate 466 vb.
butty
meal 301 n.

buxom
fleshy 195 adj.
personable 841 adj.
buy
purchase 792 n.vb.
—off
bribe 612 vb.
buyer
purchaser 792 n.
buzz
fly 271 vb.
resound 404 vb.
rumour 529 n.
obstruct 702 vb.
buzzer
signal 547 n.
buzz word
neology 560 n.
by
by means of
629 adv.
bygone
archaism 127 n.
by hand
laboriously 682 adv.
bylaw, byelaw
legislation 953 n.
bypass
road 624 n.
circuit 626 vb.
byplay
gesture 547 n.
by-product
effect 157 n.
product 164 n.
byre
stable 192 n.
cattle pen 369 n.
bystander
spectator 441 n.
byte
data processing
86 n.
byway
path 624 n.
byword
maxim 496 n.
object of scorn
867 n.

C

cab
cab 274 n.
locomotive 274 n.
cabal
plot 623 n.

cabaret
stage show 594 n.
place of amusement
837 n.
cabbage
inertness 175 n.
vegetable 301 n.
cabbala
occultism 984 n.
cabin
small house 192 n.
chamber 194 n.
cabinet
cabinet 194 n.
storage 632 n.
council 692 n.
cable
cable 47 n.
telecommunication
531 n.
cablecar
tram 274 n.
cache
hiding-place 527 n.
store 632 n.
cachet
label 547 n.
repute 866 n.
cachou
sweet thing 392 n.
scent 396 n.
cackle
ululate 409 vb.
laugh 835 vb.
cacophony
stridor 407 n.
cactus
prickle 256 n.
plant 366 n.
cad
cad 938 n.
cadastral
listed 87 adj.
metrical 465 adj.
cadaverous
lean 206 adj.
cadaverous 363 adj.
colourless 426 adj.
caddy, caddie
bearer 273 n.
servant 742 n.
cadence
melody 410 n.
cadenza
musical piece 412 n.
cadet
young 130 adj.

beginner 538 n.
cadge
beg 761 vb.
cadger
idler 679 n.
beggar 763 n.
cadre
personnel 686 n.
party 708 n.
caesarian section
obstetrics 167 n.
caesura
prosody 593 n.
café, cafeteria
café 192 n.
caffeine
tonic 658 n.
caftan, kaftan
robe 228 n.
shirt 228 n.
cage
stable 192 n.
compartment 194 n.
enclosure 235 n.
lockup 748 n.
cagey
reticent 525 adj.
cautious 858 adj.
cairn
signpost 547 n.
monument 548 n.
cajole
induce 612 vb.
flatter 925 vb.
cake
pastries 301 n.
solid body 324 n.
cakes and ale
enjoyment 824 n.
cakewalk
dance 837 n.
calamity
evil 616 n.
misfortune 731 n.
calcify
harden 326 vb.
calculate
do sums 86 vb.
measure 465 vb.
estimate 480 vb.
plan 623 vb.
calculated (to)
tending 179 adj.
predetermined
608 adj.
calculation
numeration 86 n.

caution 858 n.
calculator
counting instrument
86 n.
calculus
mathematics 86 n.
calendar
chronology 117 n.
record 548 vb.
calf
young creature
132 n.
skin 226 n.
leg 267 n.
cattle 365 n.
calibrate
graduate 27 vb.
gauge 465 vb.
calibre
sort 77 n.
size 195 n.
breadth 205 n.
firearm 723 n.
calico
textile 222 n.
call
cry 408 n.vb.
call 547 n.
name 561 vb.
motive 612 n.
visit 882 vb.
—a spade a spade
speak plainly
573 vb.
be artless 699 vb.
—for
require 627 vb.
request 761 vb.
—in
bring together
74 vb.
consult 691 vb.
—names
not respect 921 vb.
—off
halt 145 vb.
—on
consult 691 vb.
request 761 vb.
—out
fight 716 vb.
—the tune
motivate 612 vb.
dominate 733 vb.
—upon
command
737 vb.

callboy
stagehand 594 n.
caller
incomer 297 n.
sociable person
882 n.
call girl
prostitute 952 n.
calligraphy
lettering 586 n.
calling
vocation 622 n.
callipers
gauge 465 n.
callisthenics
athletics 162 n.
exercise 682 n.
callous
hard 326 adj.
thick-skinned
820 adj.
pitiless 906 adj.
callow
young 130 adj.
immature 670 adj.
call-up
belligerency 718 n.
calm
assuage 177 vb.
smoothness 258 n.
quietude 266 n.
inexcitable 823 adj.
relieve 831 vb.
unastonished
865 adj.
calmative
moderator 177 n.
calorie(s)
dieting 301 n.
thermometry 379 n.
calorific
heating 381 adj.
calumniate
defame 926 vb.
calumny
slur 867 n.
calumny 926 n.
false charge 928 n.
calypso
vocal music 412 n.
camaraderie
friendliness 880 n.
sociality 882 n.
camber
make oblique
220 vb.
curve 248 n.

cambric
textile 222 n.
camel
beast of burden
273 n.
cameo
acting 594 n.
jewellery 844 n.
camera
camera 442 n.
photography 551 n.
camouflage
mimicry 20 n.
disguise 527 n.
camp
place oneself
187 vb.
abode 192 n.
shelter 662 n.
party 708 n.
affected 850 adj.
campaign
marching 267 n.
undertaking 672 n.
exert oneself 682 vb.
tactics 688 n.
warfare 718 n.
—against
deprecate 762 vb.
campaigner
doer 676 n.
campanile
church exterior
990 n.
campanologist
campanology 412 n.
camper
traveller 268 n.
automobile 274 n.
campfire
focus 76 n.
camp follower
dependant 742 n.
camphor
preserver 666 n.
campus
focus 76 n.
academy 539 n.
can
be able 160 vb.
small box 194 n.
vessel 194 n.
preserve 666 vb.
canal
transport 272 n.
conduit 351 n.
canalize

direct 689 vb.
canard
rumour 529 n.
cancan
dance 837 n.
cancel
nullify 2 vb.
obliterate 550 vb.
abrogate 752 vb.
—out
counteract 182 vb.
tell against 467 vb.
cancer
cancer 651 n.
blight 659 n.
candid
veracious 540 adj.
artless 699 adj.
candidate
testee 461 n.
contender 716 n.
petitioner 763 n.
candidature
vote 605 n.
candle
torch 420 n.
candlelight
glimmer 419 n.
candle power
light 417 n.
candour
veracity 540 n.
artlessness 699 n.
candy
sweets 301 n.
cane
scourge 964 n.
canine
dog 365 n.
animal 365 adj.
canister
small box 194 n.
canker
blight 659 n.
cannabis
drug-taking 949 n.
canned
recorded 548 adj.
preserved 666 adj.
tipsy 949 adj.
cannibalism
eating 301 n.
cannibalize
repair 656 vb.
cannon,
gun 723 n.
cannonball

ammunition 723 n.
cannot
be impotent 161 vb.
canny
intelligent 498 adj.
cunning 698 adj.
cautious 858 adj.
canoe
rowing boat 275 n.
canoeing
aquatics 269 n.
canon
precept 693 n.
decree 737 n.
scripture 975 n.
ecclesiarch 986 n.
canonical
orthodox 976 adj.
canonical robes
vestments 989 n.
canonize
sanctify 979 vb.
canopy
canopy 226 n.
screen 421 n.vb.
cant
obliquity 220 n.
falsehood 541 n.
slang 560 n.
be affected 850 vb.
false piety 980 n.
cantankerous
irascible 892 adj.
cantata
vocal music 421 n.
canteen
café 192 n.
canter
ride 267 vb.
canticle
hymn 981 n.
cantilever
prop 218 n.
canting
affected 850 adj.
canto
poem 593 n.
cantonment
station 187 n.
cantor
choir 413 n.
canvas
textile 222 n.
sail 275 n.
picture 553 n.
canvass
argue 475 vb.

dissertate 591 vb.
vote 605 vb.
sell 793 vb.

canvasser
commender 923 n.

canyon
valley 255 n.

cap
be superior 34 vb.
crown 213 vb.
covering 226 n.
headgear 228 n.
stopper 264 n.
climax 725 vb.

capability
ability 160 n.
skill 694 n.

capable
possible 469 adj.
intelligent 498 adj.

capacious
great 32 adj.
spacious 183 adj.

capacity
plenitude 54 n.
inclusion 78 n.
ability 160 n.
room 183 n.
size 195 n.
intelligence 498 n.
function 622 n.

cape
cloak 228 n.

caper
leap 312 n.vb.
dance 837 vb.

capillary
tube 263 n.

capital
supreme 34 adj.
summit 213 n.
deadly 362 adj.
literal 558 adj.
important 638 adj.
super 644 adj.
funds 797 n.

capitalist
master 741 n.
rich person 800 n.

capitalize
profit by 137 vb.
use 673 vb.

capital punishment
capital punishment 963 n.

capitation
statistics 86 n.

capitulation
submission 721 n.

capon
poultry 365 n.

caprice
caprice 604 n.

capricious
light-minded 456 adj.
capricious 604 adj.

capsize
be inverted 221 vb.

capsule
receptacle 194 n.
medicine 658 n.

captain
navigate 269 vb.
direct 689 vb.
leader 690 n.
naval officer 741 n.

caption
label 547 n.

captious
sophistical 477 adj.
disapproving 924 adj.

captivate
motivate 612 vb.
excite love 887 vb.

captive
prisoner 750 n.

captivity
detention 747 n.

captor
possessor 776 n.
taker 786 n.

capture
represent 551 vb.
overmaster 727 vb.
trophy 729 n.
subjugate 745 vb.
take 786 vb.

car
automobile 274 n.

carafe
vessel 194 n.

caramel
sweets 301 n.
brownness 430 n.

carat
weighing 322 n.

caravan
procession 71 n.
small house 192 n.

caravanner
traveller 268 n.

carbohydrates
food 301 n.

carbolic
cleanser 648 n.

carbonate
gasify 336 vb.

carbon copy
duplicate 22 n.
record 548 n.

carboy
vessel 194 n.

carbuncle
swelling 253 n.

carcass
structure 331 n.
corpse 363 n.

carcinogen
poison 659 n.

carcinogenic
insalubrious 653 adj.

card
label 547 n.
record 548 n.
correspondence 588 n.
paper 631 n.
humorist 839 n.

cardboard
paper 631 n.

card game
card game 837 n.

cardigan
jersey 228 n.

cardinal
supreme 34 adj.
important 638 adj.
ecclesiarch 986 n.

card index
sorting 62 n.

card punch
data processing 86 n.

cards
oracle 511 n.
card game 837 n.

cardsharp
trickster 545 n.

cards on the table
disclosure 526 n.

card up one's sleeve
contrivance 623 n.

care
carefulness 457 n.
mandate 751 n.
worry 825 n.
caution 858 n.

philanthropize 897 vb.

—for
look after 457 vb.
love 887 vb.

career
move fast 277 vb.
progression 285 n.
vocation 622 n.

careerist
egotist 932 n.

career woman
worker 686 n.

carefree
reposeful 683 adj.
cheerful 833 adj.

careful
careful 457 adj.
economical 814 adj.
cautious 858 adj.

careless
inattentive 456 adj.
negligent 458 adj.
rash 857 adj.
indifferent 860 adj.

careless, be
waste 634 vb.

caress
endearment 889 n.
caress 889 vb.

caretaker
manager 690 n.
keeper 749 n.
consignee 754 n.

cargo
contents 193 n.
thing transferred 272 n.
merchandise 795 n.

cargo boat
merchant ship 275 n.

caricature
misinterpret 521 vb.
exaggerate 546 vb.
misrepresent 552 vb.
be witty 839 vb.
satire 851 n.
calumny 926 n.

caries
decay 51 n.

carillon
campanology 412 n.

carnage
slaughter 362 n.

carnal
sensual 944 adj.
lecherous 951 adj.
carnival
festivity 837 n.
pageant 875 n.
carnivore
eater 301 n.
animal 365 n.
carol
vocal music 412 n.
sing 413 vb.
carouse
revel 837 vb.
be sociable 882 vb.
get drunk 949 vb.
carp
fish 365 n.
be discontented
829 vb.
car park
enclosure 235 n.
traffic control 305 n.
carpet
floor-cover 226 n.
reprove 924 vb.
carpetbagger
impostor 545 n.
carrel
compartment 194 n.
carriage
gait 265 n.
transport 272 n.
carriage 274 n.
mien 445 n.
conduct 688 n.
carrier
prop 218 n.
carrier 273 n.
courier 529 n.
infection 651 n.
carrier pigeon
bearer 273 n.
courier 529 n.
carrion
decay 51 n.
corpse 363 n.
carrot
vegetable 301 n.
incentive 612 n.
carroty
red 431 adj.
carry
reproduce itself
167 vb.
be distant 199 vb.
support 218 vb.

wear 228 vb.
carry 273 vb.
—off
take away 786 vb.
—on
go on 146 vb.
do 676 vb.
behave 688 vb.
manage 689 vb.
be angry 891 vb.
—out
carry out 725 vb.
—through
terminate 69 vb.
persevere 600 vb.
carry through
725 vb.
carrying
loud 400 adj.
resonant 404 adj.
cart
carry 273 vb.
cart 274 n.
carte blanche
scope 744 n.
cartel
association 706 n.
compact 765 n.
carter
driver 268 n.
carrier 273 n.
cartilage
toughness 329 n.
cartogram
statistics 86 n.
map 551 n.
cartographer
surveyor 465 n.
carton
small box 194 n.
cartoon
film 445 n.
picture 553 n.
wit 839 n.
cartoonist
artist 556 n.
humorist 839 n.
cartridge
gramophone 414 n.
ammunition 723 n.
cartridge belt
arsenal 723 n.
cartwheel
overturning 221 n.
carve
cut 46 vb.
form 243 vb.

groove 262 vb.
sculpt 554 vb.
decorate 844 vb.
—up
apportion 783 vb.
cascade
descend 309 vb.
waterfall 350 n.
case
state 7 n.
event 154 n.
case 194 n.
cover 226 vb.
enclosure 235 n.
topic 452 n.
argument 475 n.
sick person 651 n.
litigation 959 n.
case-hardened
thick-skinned
820 adj.
impenitent 940 adj.
case history
record 548 n.
description 590 n.
case in point
relevance 9 n.
example 83 n.
casement
window 263 n.
cash
coinage 797 n.
money 797 n.
cash in on
profit by 137 vb.
use 673 vb.
cash and carry
buying 792 adj.
cashbook
account book 808 n.
cash box
treasury 799 n.
cash crop
agriculture 370 n.
cashier
depose 752 vb.
treasurer 798 n.
cashmere
textile 222 n.
cash register
treasury 799 n.
casino
gaming-house
618 n.
cask
vat 194 n.
casket

small box 194 n.
interment 364 n.
casserole
cauldron 194 n.
dish 301 n.
cassette
gramophone 414 n.
photography 551 n.
cassock
robe 228 n.
vestments 989 n.
cast
number 86 vb.
tendency 179 n.
doff 229 vb.
form 243 n.vb.
propel 287 vb.
hue 425 n.
dim sight 440 n.
sculpture 554 n.
actor 594 n.
blemish 845 n.
—off
navigate 269 vb.
not retain 779 vb.
—out
reject 607 vb.
castaway
solitary 883 n.
caste
classification 77 n.
nobility 868 n.
castigate
reprove 924 vb.
punish 963 vb.
casting lots
divination 511 n.
cast iron
hardness 326 n.
castle
house 192 n.
fort 713 n.
**castles in Spain/in the
air**
fantasy 513 n.
aspiration 852 n.
cast-offs
clothing 228 n.
rubbish 641 n.
castrate
unman 161 vb.
make sterile 172 vb.
castrato
eunuch 161 n.
vocalist 413 n.
casual
casual 159 adj.

CAS

negligent 458 adj.
unintentional
618 adj.
reposeful 683 adj.
casuals
informal dress
228 n.
casualty
misfortune 731 n.
death roll 361 n.
casualty ward
hospital 658 n.
casuist
reasoner 475 n.
sophist 477 n.
morals 917 n.
cat
cat 365 n.
cad 938 n.
cataclysm
havoc 165 n.
outbreak 176 n.
catacombs
cemetery 364 n.
catalepsy
insensibility 375 n.
catalogue
class 62 vb.
list 87 n.vb.
record 548 vb.
catalyst
alterer 143 n.
catamaran
raft 275 n.
catamite
libertine 952 n.
catapult
propellant 287 n.
missile weapon
723 n.
cataract
waterfall 350 n.
blindness 439 n.
catarrh
excretion 302 n.
respiratory disease
651 n.
catastrophe
ruin 165 n.
misfortune 731 n.
catcall
indignity 921 n.
disapprobation
924 n.
catch
fastening 47 n.
rub 333 vb.

CAT

vocal music 412 n.
hear 415 vb.
surprise 508 vb.
ensnare 542 vb.
represent 551 vb.
hunt 619 vb.
defect 647 n.
pitfall 663 n.
stratagem 698 n.
hitch 702 n.
arrest 747 vb.
booty 790 n.
favourite 890 n.
—on
understand 516 vb.
be in fashion
848 vb.
—one's eye
attract notice
455 vb.
—out
detect 484 vb.
befool 542 vb.
—up with
outstrip 277 vb.
approach 289 vb.
catch-22
predicament 700 n.
catch-all
receptacle 194 n.
catching
influential 178 adj.
infectious 653 adj.
catchpenny
spurious 542 adj.
catchphrase
neology 560 n.
catchword
maxim 496 n.
call 547 n.
catchy
melodious 410 adj.
catechism
creed 485 n.
orthodoxy 976 n.
categorical
assertive 532 adj.
**categorical
   imperative**
conscience 917 n.
categorization
arrangement 62 n.
category
classification 77 n.
catenary
curve 248 n.
cater

CAU

feed 301 vb.
provide 633 vb.
caterpillar
creepy-crawly
365 n.
caterwaul
ululate 409 vb.
cathartic
dramatic 594 adj.
remedial 658 adj.
cathedral
church 990 n.
catheter
drain 351 n.
catholic
universal 79 adj.
Catholicism
Catholicism 976 n.
catlike
stealthy 525 adj.
catnap
sleep 679 n.vb.
**cat on hot bricks, like
   a**
agitated 318 adj.
excitable 822 adj.
cat-o'-nine-tails
scourge 964 n.
cat's eye
traffic control 305 n.
cat's paw
dupe 544 n.
instrument 628 n.
cattle
cattle 365 n.
cattle farm
stock farm 369 n.
catty
malevolent 898 adj.
detracting 926 adj.
catwalk
bridge 624 n.
caucus
party 708 n.
caul
obstetrics 167 n.
cauldron
cauldron 194 n.
heater 383 n.
caulk
repair 656 vb.
causal
causal 156 adj.
instrumental
628 adj.
causation
causation 156 n.

CAV

agency 173 n.
cause
cause 156 n.vb.
produce 164 vb.
influence 178 n.
predetermine
608 vb.
motive 612 n.
be instrumental
628 vb.
philanthropy 901 n.
causeless
causeless 159 adj.
designless 618 adj.
causeway
bridge 624 n.
caustic
burning 381 n.
pungent 388 adj.
paining 827 adj.
disapproving
924 adj.
cauterize
doctor 658 vb.
caution
carefulness 457 n.
foresight 510 n.
hint 524 n.
warning 664 n.
caution 858 n.
cautionary
advising 691 adj.
cautious
slow 278 adj.
(see **caution***)*
cavalcade
procession 71 n.
cavalier
rider 268 n.
disrespectful 921 adj.
cavalry
cavalry 722 n.
cave
dwelling 192 n.
interiority 224 n.
cavity 255 n.
caveat
warning 664 n.
cave in
descend 309 vb.
knuckle under
721 vb.
cavern
cavity 255 n.
cavernous
spacious 183 adj.
deep 211 adj.

cavil
dissent 489 n.vb.
disapprobation
924 n.
caving
descent 309 n.
sport 837 n.
cavity
receptacle 194 n.
cavity 255 n.
opening 263 n.
cavort
leap 312 vb.
caw
ululation 409 n.
cease
cease 145 vb.
be inactive 679 vb.
cease-fire
lull 145 n.
pacification 719 n.
ceaseless
perpetual 115 adj.
cede
relinquish 621 vb.
not retain 779 vb.
ceilidh
dancing 837 n.
ceiling
vertex 213 n.
roof 226 n.
limit 236 n.
celebrant
worshipper 981 n.
celebrate
proclaim 528 vb.
rejoice 835 vb.
revel 837 vb.
celebrate 876 vb.
celebration
feasting 301 n.
merriment 833 n.
celebration 876 n.
celebrity
person of repute
866 n.
celestial
celestial 321 adj.
paradisiac 971 adj.
celibacy
celibacy 895 n.
celibate
celibate 895 n.
cell
electronics 160 n.
retreat 192 n.
compartment 194 n.

enclosure 235 n.
organism 358 n.
party 708 n.
lockup 748 n.
seclusion 883 n.
cellar
cellar 194 n.
storage 632 n.
cellist
instrumentalist
413 n.
cello
viol 414 n.
cellular
cellular 194 adj.
celluloid
film 445 n.
cement
adhesive 47 n.
bond 47 n.
agglutinate 48 vb.
solid body 324 n.
building material
631 n.
cemetery
cemetery 364 n.
cenotaph
tomb 364 n.
censer
scent 396 n.
censor
estimator 480 n.
obliterate 550 vb.
disapprover
924 n.
censorious
severe 735 adj.
disapproving
924 adj.
censurable
discreditable
867 adj.
blameworthy|
924 adj.
censure
censure 924 n.
reprimand 924 n.
census
statistics 86 n.
centaur
mythical being
970 n.
centenarian
old person 133 n.
centenary
hundred 99 n.
anniversary 141 n.

centimetre
long measure 203 n.
centipede
creepy-crawly
365 n.
central
middle 70 adj.
fundamental|
156 adj.
central 225 adj.
inland 344 adj.
important 638 adj.
centralized
governmental
733 adj.
centre
focus 76 n.
centre 225 n.
converge 293 vb.
political party 708 n.
centrepiece
ornamentation
844 n.
centrifugal
repellent 292 adj.
divergent 294 adj.
avoiding 620 adj.
centripetal
attracting 291 adj.
convergent 293 adj.
centurion
army officer 741 n.
century
hundred 99 n.
period 110 n.
ceramics
pottery 381 n.
sculpture 554 n.
cereals
cereals 301 n.
grass 366 n.
cerebral
mental 447 adj.
cerebral thrombosis
cardiovascular
disease 651 n.
cerebrate
think 449 vb.
ceremonial
formality 875 n.
formal 875 adj.
ritual 988 n.adj.
ceremonious
formal 875 adj.
respectful 920 adj.
ceremony
formality 875 n.

celebration 876 n.
rite 988 n.
certain
definite 80 adj.
certain 473 adj.
demonstrated
478 adj.
true 494 adj.
expectant 507 adj.
certain, a
one 88 adj.
certainty
safety 660 n.
easy thing 701 n.
(*see* **certain**)
certifiable
insane 503 adj.
certificate
credential 466 n.
record 548 n.
honours 866 n.
certify
make certain
473 vb.
inform 524 vb.
affirm 532 vb.
certitude
certainty 473 n.
cessation
finality 69 n.
cessation 145 n.
quiescence 266 n.
cession
relinquishment
621 n.
cesspit, cesspool
sink 649 n.
cetacean
marine life 365 n.
chafe
rub 333 vb.
hurt 827 vb.
be angry 891 vb.
chaff
leavings 41 n.
grass 366 n.
rubbish 641 n.
witticism 839 n.
ridicule 851 n.vb.
chagrin
sorrow 825 n.
discontent 829 n.
chain
bond 47 n.
cable 47 n.
series 71 n.
long measure 203 n.

fetter 748 n.
jewellery 844 n.
—together
connect 45 vb.
chaingang
slave 742 n.
prisoner 750 n.
chain reaction
continuity 71 n.
chair
seat 218 n.
rostrum 539 n.
director 690 n.
honour 866 vb.
applaud 923 vb.
**chairman,
  chairwoman**
director 690 n.
chairmanship
directorship 689 n.
chalet
small house 192 n.
chalice
cup 194 n.
chalk
white thing 427 n.
mark 547 vb.
stationery 586 n.
—out
limit 236 vb.
plan 623 vb.
—up
mark 547 vb.
register 548 vb.
challenge
question 459 n.
dissent 489 n.vb.
negation 533 n.
defy 711 vb.
threat 900 n.
chamber
chamber 194 n.
chamberlain
retainer 742 n.
chambermaid
domestic 742 n.
chamber pot
latrine 649 n.
chambers
quarters 192 n.
chameleon
changeable thing 152 n.
chamfer
groove 262 vb.
chamois
skin 226 n.

jumper 312 n.
cleaning cloth 648 n.
champ
chew 301 vb.
—at the bit
be excitable 822 vb.
champagne
wine 301 n.
champaign
plain 348 n.
champion
supreme 34 adj.
athlete 162 n.
exceller 644 n.
proficient person 696 n.
patron 707 n.
defender 713 n.
victor 727 n.
vindicator 927 n.
chance
opportunity 137 n.
happen 154 vb.
chance 159 n.vb.
possibility 469 n.
nondesign 618 n.
—it
gamble 618 vb.
chancel
church interior 990 n.
chancellor
director 690 n.
treasurer 798 n.
chancy
casual 159 adj.
uncertain 474 adj.
speculative 618 adj.
dangerous 661 adj.
chandelier
lamp 420 n.
chandler
merchant 794 n.
change
differ 15 vb.
change 143 n.
be turned to 147 vb.
vary 152 vb.
money 797 n.
—for
substitute 150 vb.
—into
become 1 vb.
—one's mind
tergiversate 603 vb.
—round
displace 188 vb.

—sides
apostatize 603 vb.
—the face of
transform 147 vb.
revolutionize 149 vb.
changeable
changeable 143 adj.
changeful 152 adj.
changeful
fitful 142 adj.
changeful 152 adj.
changeless
unchangeable 153 adj.
changeling
substitute 150 n.
change of life
middle age 131 n.
changeover
transfer 780 n.
channel
furrow 262 n.
passage 305 n.
gulf 345 n.
conduit 351 n.
informant 524 n.
access 624 n.
instrument 628 n.
direct 689 vb.
chant
vocal music 412 n.
sing 413 vb.
chaos
confusion 61 n.
anarchy 734 n.
chap
male 372 n.
chapel
society 708 n.
sect 978 n.
church 990 n.
chapelgoer
church member 976 n.
chaperon
accompany 89 vb.
look after 457 vb.
keeper 749 n.
chaplain
pastor 986 n.
chapped
rough 259 adj.
chapter
subdivision 53 n.
topic 452 n.
synod 985 n.

chapter and verse
evidence 466 n.
char
burn 381 vb.
blacken 428 vb.
servant 742 n.
character
character 5 n.
sort 77 n.
nonconformist 84 n.
credential 466 n.
acting 594 n.
affections 817 n.
repute 866 n.
virtue 933 n.
characteristic
characteristic 5 adj.
intrinsic 5 adj.
speciality 80 n.
special 80 adj.
identification 547 n.
characterization
representation 551 n.
description 590 n.
dramaturgy 594 n.
characterless
irresolute 601 adj.
charade(s)
sham 542 n.
representation 551 n.
indoor game 837 n.
charcoal
fuel 385 n.
art equipment 553 n.
charge
fill 54 vb.
empower 160 vb.
load 193 vb.
move fast 277 vb.
heraldry 547 n.
job 622 n.
management 689 n.
charge 712 vb.
explosive 723 n.
command 737 n.vb.
dependant 742 n.
commission 751 vb.
price 809 n.vb.
accusation 928 n.
chargé d'affaires
envoy 754 n.
charger
cavalry 722 n.
chariot
carriage 274 n.

charioteer
driver 268 n.

charisma
power 160 n.
influence 178 n.

charitable
philanthropic
901 adj.

charity
gift 781 n.
liberality 813 n.
love 887 n.
benevolence 897 n.
kind act 897 n.
philanthropy 901 n.

charlady
cleaner 648 n.

charlatan
sciolist 493 n.
impostor 545 n.

charm
attraction 291 n.
please 826 vb.
beauty 841 n.
jewellery 844 n.
lovableness 887 n.
spell 983 n.
talisman 983 n.
bewitch 983 vb.

charmed circle
elite 644 n.
party 708 n.

charmed life
safety 660 n.

charmer
a beauty 841 n.

charms
beauty 841 n.

charnel house
interment 364 n.

chart
sailing aid 269 n.
map 551 n.
represent 551 vb.

charter
record 548 n.
permit 756 n.vb.
title deed 767 n.
hire 785 vb.

chary
parsimonious
816 adj.
cautious 858 adj.

chase
groove 262 vb.
move fast 277 vb.
chase 619 n.

pursue 619 vb.
desire 859 vb.
court 889 vb.

—away
repel 292 vb.

chaser
draught 301 n.

chasm
depth 211 n.
cavity 255 n.

chassis
frame 218 n.
structure 331 n.

chaste
plain 573 adj.
elegant 575 adj.
tasteful 846 adj.
virtuous 933 adj.
pure 950 adj.

chasten
depress 834 vb.
punish 963 vb.

chastened
repentant 939 adj.

chastise
reprove 924 vb.
punish 963 vb.

chastity
temperance 942 n.

chat
chat 584 n.

chattel
slave 742 n.
property 777 n.

chatter
be cold 380 vb.
empty talk 515 n.
chatter 581 n.
chat 584 n.

chatterbox
chatterer 581 n.

chatty
informative 524 adj.
loquacious 581 adj.

chauffeur
driver 268 n.

chauvinism
prejudice 481 n.
patriotism 901 n.

chauvinist
militarist 722 n.

cheap
cheap 812 adj.
vulgar 847 adj.

cheapen
cheapen 812 vb.
vulgarize 847 vb.

not respect 921 vb.

—oneself
demean oneself
867 vb.

cheat
trickster 545 n.
slyboots 698 n.
defraud 788 vb.
be dishonest
930 vb.
knave 938 n.

check
delay 136 n.
halt 145 vb.
retard 278 vb.
chequer 437 n.
be careful 457 vb.
comparison 462 n.
make certain
473 vb.
hindrance 702 n.
defeat 728 n.
restraint 747 n.
pattern 844 n.

checkmate
overmaster 727 vb.

checkout
recording
instrument 549 n.

checkup
inquiry 459 n.

cheek
laterality 239 n.
sauciness 878 n.

cheeky
disrespectful
921 adj.

cheep
ululate 409 vb.

cheer
vociferate 408 vb.
relieve 831 vb.
merriment 833 n.
cheer 833 vb.
give courage 855 vb.
applaud 923 vb.

—on
incite 612 vb.

cheerful
cheerful 833 adj.

cheerless
cheerless 834 adj.
dejected 834 adj.

cheese
milk 301 n.

cheesecloth
textile 222 n.

cheesed off
discontented
829 adj.
bored 838 adj.

cheese-paring
parsimony 816 n.

chef
cookery 301 n.
caterer 633 n.

chef d'oeuvre
exceller 644 n.
masterpiece 694 n.

chemical warfare
poisoning 659 n.

chemise
dress 228 n.
underwear 228 n.

chemist
physics 319 n.
druggist 658 n.

cheque
paper money 797 n.

chequer
variegate 437 vb.

cherish
look after 457 vb.
preserve 666 vb.
love 887 vb.
pet 889 vb.

cherry
fruit 301 n.
redness 431 n.

cherub
child 132 n.
image 551 n.
angel 968 n.

chess
board game 837 n.

chest
box 194 n.
bosom 253 n.
treasury 799 n.

chesterfield
seat 218 n.

chestnut
horse 273 n.
fruit 301 n.
brown 430 adj.
witticism 839 n.

chest of drawers
cabinet 194 n.

chesty
puffing 352 adj.

chevron
heraldry 547 n.
badge of rank 743 n.
pattern 844 n.

chew
chew 301 vb.
—over
meditate 449 vb.
chiaroscuro
painting 553 n.
chiasmus
ornament 574 n.
chic
fashionable 848 adj.
chicanery
trickery 542 n.
cunning 698 n.
chicken
young creature
132 n.
meat 301 n.
poultry 365 n.
coward 856 n.
chickenfeed
trifle 639 n.
easy thing 701 n.
chicken run
stock farm 369 n.
chide
reprove 924 vb.
chief
supreme 34 adj.
important 638 adj.
director 690 n.
potentate 741 n.
chieftain
potentate 741 n.
chieftainship
position of authority
733 n.
chiffon
textile 222 n.
chignon
hairdressing 843 n.
chilblain(s)
ulcer 651 n.
child
child 132 n.
posterity 170 n.
innocent 935 n.
childbirth
obstetrics 167 n.
childhood
youth 130 n.
childish
young 130 adj.
infantine 132 adj.
foolish 499 adj.
childless
unproductive
172 adj.

childlike
artless 699 adj.
child's play
trifle 639 n.
easy thing 701 n.
chill
coldness 380 n.
refrigerate 382 vb.
frighten 854 vb.
chiller
refrigerator 384 n.
chilly
chilly 380 adj.
inimical 881 adj.
chime
resound 404 vb.
campanology 412 n.
chimera
insubstantial thing
4 n.
fantasy 513 n.
chimney
chimney 263 n.
air pipe 353 n.
chimneysweep
cleaner 648 n.
chimpanzee
mammal 365 n.
chin
face 237 n.
protuberance 254 n.
china
pottery 381 n.
china clay
materials 631 n.
chink
gap 201 n.
resonance 404 n.
**chink in one's
armour**
vulnerability 661 n.
chinoiserie
ornamentation
844 n.
chintz
textile 222 n.
chinwag
chat 584 n.
chip
cut 46 vb.
piece 53 n.
microelectronics
196 n.
be brittle 330 vb.
chipboard
paper 631 n.
chip off the old block

analogue 18 n.
descendant 170 n.
**chip on one's
shoulder**
discontent 829 n.
chips
vegetable 301 n.
chiromancy
divination 511 n.
chiropodist
beautician 843 n.
chirp, chirrup
ululate 409 vb.
chirpy
cheerful 833 adj.
chisel
cut 46 vb.
form 243 vb.
sharp edge 256 n.
sculpt 554 vb.
tool 630 n.
chit
youngster 132 n.
credential 466 n.
chivalrous
noble 868 adj.
courteous 884 adj.
honourable 929 adj.
chives
potherb 301 n.
chivvy
torment 827 vb.
chlorinate
sanitate 652 vb.
safeguard 660 vb.
chloroform
anaesthetic 375 n.
chlorophyll
green pigment
434 n.
chock
prop 218 n.
chocolate
sweets 301 n.
brown 430 adj.
choice
discrimination
463 n.
willingness 597 n.
choice 605 n.
excellent 644 adj.
tasteful 846 adj.
choiceless
choiceless 606 adj.
choir
choir 413 n.
choke

stopper 264 n.
close 264 vb.
extinguish 382 vb.
rasp 407 vb.
choker
jewellery 844 n.
cholera
infection 651 n.
choleric
irascible 892 adj.
choose
choose 605 vb.
choosy
fastidious 862 adj.
chop
cut 46 vb.
meat 301 n.
—and change
vary 152 vb.
—logic
argue 475 vb.
—up
cut 46 vb.
chopper
sharp edge 256 n.
aircraft 276 n.
axe 723 n.
choppy
rough 259 adj.
flowing 350 adj.
chop suey
dish 301 n.
choral
musical 412 adj.
chord
musical note 410 n.
chore
labour 682 n.
bore 838 n.
choreography
composition 56 n.
ballet 594 n.
chorister
choir 413 n.
chortle
laughter 835 n.
chorus
vociferate 408 vb.
vocal music 412 n.
choir 413 n.
sing 413 vb.
consensus 488 n.
actor 594 n.
chorus girl
entertainer 594 n.
chosen few
elite 644 n.

chosen people
pietist 979 n.
chow mein
dish 301 n.
Christ
God the Son 965 n.
christen
auspicate 68 vb.
name 561 vb.
Christendom
Christendom 976 n.
christening
Christian rite 988 n.
Christianity
religious faith 973 n.
chromatic
harmonic 410 adj.
coloured 425 adj.
chromosome
heredity 5 n.
organism 358 n.
chronic
lasting 113 adj.
sick 651 adj.
tedious 838 adj.
chronic invalid
sick person 651 n.
chronicle
record 548 n.vb.
narrative 590 n.
chronicler
chronicler 549 n.
chronological
chronological
117 adj.
chronology
date 108 n.
chronology 117 n.
chrysalis
young creature
132 n.
chubby
fleshy 195 adj.
chuck
propel 287 vb.
—out
eject 300 vb.
reject 607 vb.
chuckle
laugh 835 vb.
chuffed
pleased 824 adj.
chug
move slowly 278 vb.
chum
chum 880 n.
chump

dunce 501 n.
chunk
piece 53 n.
chunky
fleshy 195 adj.
church
church 990 n.
the church 985 n.
church-goer
worshipper 981 n.
churchman,
churchwoman
church member
976 n.
church office
church office 985 n.
church service
church service
988 n.
churchwarden
church officer 986 n.
churchyard
cemetery 364 n.
church exterior
990 n.
churlish
ungracious 885 adj.
churn
vessel 194 n.
agitate 318 vb.
—out
produce 164 vb.
chute
outlet 298 n.
descent 309 n.
waterfall 350 n.
chutney
sauce 389 n.
cider
alcoholic drink
301 n.
cigar, cigarette
tobacco 388 n.
cigar-shaped
rotund 252 adj.
cilium
filament 208 n.
hair 259 n.
cinch
certainty 473 n.
easy thing 701 n.
Cinderella
nonentity 639 n.
cinders
ash 381 n.
cinder track
arena 724 n.

cineaste
cinema 445 n.
enthusiast 504 n.
cinecamera
camera 442 n.
cinema
cinema 445 n.
cinemagoer
spectator 441 n.
cinnamon
condiment 389 n.
brownness 430 n.
cipher, cypher
number 85 n.
zero 103 n.
enigma 530 n.
indication 547 n.
initials 558 n.
nonentity 639 n.
circa
nearly 200 adv.
circle
group 74 n.
circle 250 n.
circuit 626 n.vb.
circuit
electricity 160 n.
outline 233 n.
circle 250 n.
circuition 314 n.
circuit 626 n.vb.
circuitous
deviating 282 adj.
circuitous 314 adj.
roundabout
626 adj.
circular
continuous 71 adj.
round 250 adj.
publication 528 n.
decree 737 n.
circularity
circularity 250 n.
circulate
pass 305 vb.
circle 314 vb.
be published
528 vb.
mint 797 vb.
circulation
blood 335 n.
circumcision
rite 988 n.
circumference
surroundings 230 n.
outline 233 n.
circle 250 n.

circumlocution
pleonasm 570 n.
circumnavigation
water travel 269 n.
circumscribe
circumscribe
232 vb.
limit 236 vb.
restrain 747 vb.
circumspect
vigilant 457 adj.
cautious 858 adj.
circumstance
circumstance 8 n.
concomitant 89 n.
circumstantial
circumstantial 8 adj.
evidential 466 adj.
diffuse 570 adj.
descriptive 590 adj.
circumvent
deceive 542 vb.
avoid 620 vb.
circus
zoo 369 n.
stage show 594 n.
pleasure ground
837 n.
cissy, sissy
weakling 163 n.
cistern
vat 194 n.
storage 632 n.
citadel
refuge 662 n.
fort 713 n.
citation
referral 9 n.
decoration 729 n.
cite
exemplify 83 vb.
repeat 106 vb.
citizen
native 191 n.
citizenry
inhabitants 191 n.
social group 371 n.
commonalty 869 n.
citizenship
freedom 744 n.
city
city 184 n.
housing 192 n.
City
business 622 n.
city state
political

organization
733 n.
civic
national 371 adj.
civil
national 371 adj.
well-bred 848 adj.
courteous 884 adj.
civil code
law 953 n.
civil disobedience
resistance 715 n.
civil engineering
production 164 n.
civilian
peaceful 717 adj.
civility
courtesy 884 n.
civilization
culture 490 n.
civilization
654 n.
civilize
make better 654 vb.
civilized
well-bred 848 adj.
civil rights
freedom 744 n.
dueness 915 n.
civil servant
official 690 n.
servant 742 n.
civil service
management 689 n.
governance 733 n.
clack
roll 403 n.vb.
chatter 581 n.
clad
dressed 228 adj.
cladding
facing 226 n.
claim
territory 184 n.
affirm 532 vb.
plead 614 vb.
require 627 vb.
demand 737 n.vb.
dueness 915 n.
claim 915 vb.
claimant
petitioner 763 n.
dueness 915 n.
litigant 959 n.
clairvoyance
intuition 476 n.
psychics 984 n.

clairvoyant
psychic 984 n.
clam
marine life 365 n.
taciturnity 582 n.
clamant
loud 400 adj.
desiring 859 adj.
clamber
climb 308 vb.
clammy
viscid 354 adj.
clamour
cry 408 n.
vociferate 408 vb.
clamp
affix 45 vb.
fastening 47 n.
nippers 778 n.
—down on
be severe 735 vb.
restrain 747 vb.
clan
race 11 n.
genealogy 169 n.
community 708 n.
clandestine
concealed 525 adj.
stealthy 525 adj.
clang
be loud 400 vb.
resonance 404 n.
clanger
mistake 495 n.
clank
resound 404 vb.
clannish
ethnic 11 adj.
sectional 708 adj.
clansman
kinsman 11 n.
clap
strike 279 vb.
bang 402 n.
applause 923 n.
clap, the
venereal disease
651 n.
clapped out
fatigued 684 adj.
claptrap
empty talk 515 n.
claque
playgoer 594 n.
flatterer 925 n.
claret
wine 301 n.

redness 431 n.
clarify
eliminate 44 vb.
interpret 520 vb.
purify 648 vb.
clarinet
flute 414 n.
clarity
intelligibility 516 n.
perspicuity 567 n.
clash
contrariety 14 n.
disagreement 25 n.
collide 279 vb.
discord 411 vb.
quarrel 709 n.vb.
contention 716 n.
be inimical 881 vb.
clasp
fastening 47 n.
cohere 48 vb.
retain 778 vb.
endearment 889 n.
class
class 62 vb.
group 74 n.
classification 77 n.
class 538 n.
class-conscious
sectional 708 adj.
classic
prototypal 23 adj.
symmetrical
245 adj.
elegant 575 adj.
excellent 644 adj.
classical
architectural
192 adj.
classification
relation 9 n.
classification 77 n.
identification 547 n.
classified ad
advertisement
528 n.
classify
class 62 vb.
classmate
chum 880 n.
classroom
classroom 539 n.
classy
fashionable
848 adj.
clatter
loudness 400 n.

clause
phrase 563 n.
conditions 766 n.
claustrophobia
phobia 854 n.
claw
rend 46 vb.
foot 214 n.
wound 655 vb.
nippers 778 n.
clay
softness 327 n.
soil 344 n.
materials 631 n.
clean
make bright 417 vb.
clean 648 adj.vb.
sanitate 652 vb.
pure 950 adj.
—out
empty 300 vb.
search 459 vb.
steal 788 vb.
cleaner
cleaner 648 n.
clean hands
innocence 935 n.
clean-limbed
shapely 841 adj.
cleanliness
hygiene 652 n.
cleanse
purify 648 vb.
sanitate 652 vb.
cleanser
cleaner 648 n.
clean-shaven
hairless 229 adj.
smooth 258 adj.
clean slate
obliteration 550 n.
clean sweep
revolution 149 n.
clear
unmixed 44 adj.
empty 300 vb.
leap 312 vb.
melodious 410 adj.
undimmed 417 adj.
transparent 422 adj.
obvious 443 adj.
intelligible 516 adj.
perspicuous
567 adj.
safe 660 adj.
permit 756 vb.
acquit 960 vb.

—away
displace 188 vb.
disencumber
 701 vb.
—off (with)
decamp 296 vb.
take away 786 vb.
clearance
room 183 n.
interval 201 n.
voidance 300 n.
permission 756 n.
clear-cut
definite 80 adj.
obvious 443 adj.
positive 473 adj.
clear field
opportunity 137 n.
clear-headed
intelligent 498 adj.
sober 948 adj.
clearing
open space 263 n.
clear-sighted
intelligent 498 adj.
clearway
road 624 n.
cleat
fastening 47 n.
cleavage
scission 46 n.
dissension 709 n.
cleave
sunder 46 vb.
cleaver
sharp edge 256 n.
clef
notation 410 n.
cleft
disunited 46 adj.
bisected 92 adj.
gap 201 n.
cleft stick
dubiety 474 n.
clemency
leniency 736 n.
mercy 905 n.
clench
close 264 vb.
retain 778 vb.
clenched fist
gesture 547 n.
nippers 778 n.
clergy
clergy 986 n.
clerical
recording 548 adj.

ecclesiastical
 985 adj.
clerical 986 adj.
clerihew
witticism 839 n.
clerk
scholar 492 n.
recorder 549 n.
calligrapher
 586 n.
official 690 n.
clever
intelligent 498 adj.
cliché
lack of meaning
 515 n.
neology 560 n.
click
crackle 402 vb.
know 490 vb.
befriend 880 vb.
client
habitué 610 n.
dependant 742 n.
purchaser 792 n.
clientele
trade 791 n.
cliff
high land 209 n.
cliff-hanging
exciting 821 adj.
climacteric
middle age 131 n.
climate
influence 178 n.
region 184 n.
weather 340 n.
climatology
weather 340 n.
climax
culminate 34 vb.
summit 213 n.
climax 725 vb.
excitation 821 n.
climb
ascend 308 vb.
climb 308 vb.
climbdown
humiliation 872 n.
climber
climber 308 n.
plant 366 n.
clinch
unite with 45 vb.
make certain
 473 vb.
pugilism 716 n.

carry through
 725 vb.
retain 778 vb.
clincher
confutation 479 n.
cling
cohere 48 vb.
caress 889 vb.
—to
retain 778 vb.
clinging
cohesive 48 adj.
clinic
hospital 658 n.
clinical
medical 658 adj.
clink
faintness 401 n.
clinker
ash 381 n.
clip
connect 45 vb.
cut 46 vb.
make smaller
 198 vb.
shorten 204 vb.
hairdressing 843 n.
—the wings
disable 161 vb.
clip joint
place of amusement
 837 n.
clipper
sailing ship 275 n.
clippers
sharp edge 256 n.
clique
party 708 n.
cliquish, cliquey
biased 481 adj.
sectional 708 adj.
cloak
cloak 228 n.
screen 421 n.
pretext 614 n.
cloak-and-dagger
stealthy 525 adj.
cloakroom
chamber 194 n.
latrine 649 n.
clobber
clothing 228 n.
strike 279 vb.
clock
timekeeper 117 n.
clock in
begin 68 vb.

arrive 295 vb.
—out
depart 296 vb.
clockmaker
timekeeper 117 n.
clock-watcher
idler 679 n.
clockwork
machine 630 n.
clockwork, like
periodical 141 adj.
easily 701 adv.
clod
solid body 324 n.
soil 344 n.
clog
footwear 228 n.
make unclean
 649 vb.
restrain 747 vb.
clogged up
closed 264 adj.
cloister
retreat 192 n.
seclusion 883 n.
monastery 986 n.
clone
reproduce 166 vb.
close
similar 18 adj.
join 45 vb.
end 69 n.vb.
cease 145 vb.
near 200 adj.
narrow 206 adj.
close 264 vb.
approach 289 vb.
dense 324 adj.
warm 379 adj.
taciturn 582 adj.
obstruct 702 vb.
—down
terminate 69 vb.
—in
converge 293 vb.
—with
converge 293 vb.
fight 716 vb.
closed circuit
electricity 160 n.
closed door
exclusion 57 n.
closed mind
narrow mind 481 n.
closed shop
exclusion 57 n.
restriction 747 n.

CLO

close-fisted
parsimonious
816 adj.
close-fitting
adjusted 24 adj.
closeness
(*see* **close**)
close quarters
short distance 200 n.
close season
lull 145 n.
close-set
firm 45 adj.
close shave
escape 667 n.
closet
chamber 194 n.
close-up
photography 551 n.
closure
closure 264 n.
clot
solid body 324 n.
blood 335 n.
thicken 354 vb.
fool 501 n.
bungler 697 n.
cloth
textile 222 n.
canonicals 989 n.
cloth, the
clergy 986 n.
clothe
dress 228 vb.
provide 633 vb.
clothes
clothing 228 n.
clothes-conscious
fashionable 848 adj.
clothier
clothier 228 n.
clothing
clothing 228 n.
cloud
cloud 355 n.vb.
make opaque
423 vb.
cloudburst
storm 176 n.
cloud-cuckoo-land
fantasy 513 n.
cloudless
dry 342 adj.
undimmed 417 adj.
palmy 730 adj.
cloudy
cloudy 355 adj.

CLU

dim 419 adj.
unclear 568 adj.
clout
influence 178 n.
strike 279 vb.
spank 963 vb.
clove(s)
condiment 389 n.
scent 396 n.
cloven
bisected 92 adj.
cloven hoof
devil 969 n.
clover
provender 301 n.
palmy days 730 n.
clown
be absurd 497 vb.
entertainer 594 n.
humorist 839 n.
cloy
sate 863 vb.
cloying
unsavoury 391 adj.
club
group 74 n.
meeting place 192 n.
hammer 279 n.
party 708 n.
club 723 n.
—together
cooperate 706 vb.
clubfoot
deformity 246 n.
clubhouse
meeting place 192 n.
clubman,
clubwoman
beau monde 848 n.
sociable person
882 n.
clue
evidence 466 n.
interpretation 520 n.
indication 547 n.
clueless
ignorant 491 adj.
clump
bunch 74 n.
wood 366 n.
clumsy
unwieldy 195 adj.
inelegant 576 adj.
clumsy 695 adj.
graceless 842 adj.
cluster
group 74 n.

COA

congregate 74 vb.
clutch
group 74 n.
retain 778 vb.
—at
take 786 vb.
clutter
confusion 61 n.
coach
bus 274 n.
carriage 274 n.
train 274 n.
educate 534 vb.
train 534 vb.
teacher 537 n.
trainer 537 n.
coachhouse
stable 192 n.
coachman
driver 268 n.
coagulate
thicken 354 vb.
coal
coal 385 n.
fuel 385 n.
coalesce
combine 50 vb.
coalfield
store 632 n.
coalition
association 706 n.
society 708 n.
coal measures
mineral 359 n.
coal mine
excavation 255 n.
coarse
rough 259 adj.
textural 331 adj.
unsavoury 391 adj.
inelegant 576 adj.
graceless 842 adj.
impure 951 adj.
coarsen
impair 655 vb.
vulgarize 847 vb.
coarseness
plainness 573 n.
moral insensibility
820 n.
bad taste 847 n.
coast
laterality 239 n.
go smoothly 258 vb.
travel 267 vb.
shore 344 n.
not act 677 vb.

COC

coastal
marginal 234 adj.
coastal 344 adj.
coaster
stand 218 n.
merchant ship
275 n.
coastguard
keeper 749 n.
coastline
shore 344 n.
coat
layer 207 n.
skin 226 n.
wrapping 226 n.
coat 226 vb.
jacket 228 n.
overcoat 228 n.
paint 553 vb.
coating
covering 226 n.
facing 226 n.
coat of arms
heraldry 547 n.
coax
tempt 612 vb.
flatter 925 vb.
cob
building material
631 n.
cobble(s)
paving 226 n.
road 624 n.
cobbled together
produced 164 adj.
bungled 695 adj.
cobbler
clothier 228 n.
mender 656 n.
cobra
reptile 365 n.
cobweb
weak thing 163 n.
filament 208 n.
network 222 n.
dirt 649 n.
cocaine
drug 658 n.
drug-taking 949 n.
cock
poultry 365 n.
make ready 669 vb.
—a snook
be insolent 878 vb.
—up
make vertical
215 vb.

cockade
livery 547 n.
cock-a-hoop
jubilant 833 adj.
cock and bull story
fable 543 n.
cock-eyed
oblique 220 adj.
distorted 246 adj.
cockney
native 191 n.
dialect 560 n.
cockpit
chamber 194 n.
aircraft 276 n.
arena 724 n.
cockroach
insect 365 n.
cocksure
impertinent 878 adj.
cocktail
a mixture 43 n.
draught 301 n.
cocktail party
social gathering
882 n.
cocky
prideful 871 adj.
vain 873 adj.
impertinent
878 adj.
coconut
fruit 301 n.
cocoon
young creature
132 n.
receptacle 194 n.
wrapping 226 n.
coda
end 69 n.
musical piece 412 n.
coddle
cook 301 vb.
pet 889 vb.
code
rule 81 n.
secrecy 525 n.
enigma 530 n.
probity 929 n.
code-breaker
interpreter 520 n.
codicil
adjunct 40 n.
title deed 767 n.
codification
law 953 n.
legislation 953 n.

codify :
class 62 vb.
coefficient
numerical element
85 n.
coerce
compel 740 vb.
coercion
brute force 735 n.
coeval
contemporary
123 n.
synchronous
123 adj.
coexistence
accompaniment
89 n.
synchronism 123 n.
concord 710 n.
coffee
soft drink 301 n.
brownness 430 n.
coffer
box 194 n.
treasury 799 n.
coffin
interment 364 n.
cog
tooth 256 n.
notch 260 n.vb.
cogent
powerful 160 adj.
forceful 571 adj.
compelling 740 adj.
cogitate
think 449 vb.
cognate
akin 11 adj.
cognition
knowledge 490 n.
cognitive
mental 447 adj.
cognizable
known 490 adj.
cognizance
knowledge 490 n.
cognoscente
expert 696 n.
people of taste
846 n.
cohabit
unite with 45 vb.
wed 894 vb.
cohere
cohere 48 vb.
coherence
coherence 48 n.

coherent
sane 502 adj.
intelligible 516 adj.
cohesion
coherence 48 n.
density 324 n.
cohesive
conjunctive 45 adj.
cohesive 48 adj.
retentive 778 adj.
cohort(s)
army 722 n.
coiffure
hairdressing 843 n.
coil
complexity 61 n.
coil 251 n.
pattern 844 n.
coin
fake 541 vb.
mint 797 vb.
—words
neologize 560 vb.
coincide
be identical 13 vb.
accompany 89 vb.
coincidence
synchronism 123 n.
event 154 n.
chance 159 n.
coitus
coition 45 n.
coke
coal 385 n.
cold
wintry 129 adj.
cold 380 adj.
respiratory disease
651 n.
impassive 820 adj.
indifferent 860 adj.
unkind 898 adj.
cold comfort
discontent 829 n.
cold feet
nervousness 854 n.
cold-shoulder
exclude 57 vb.
disregard 458 vb.
make unwelcome
883 vb.
cold storage
refrigeration
382 n.
cold water
moderator 177 n.
dissuasion 613 n.

colic
digestive disorders
651 n.
collaborate
cooperate 706 vb.
collaborator
turncoat 603 n.
collaborator 707 n.
collage
combination 50 n.
picture 553 n.
collapse
helplessness 161 n.
ruin 165 n.
descent 309 n.
illness 651 n.
dilapidation 655 n.
fatigue 684 n.
knuckle under
721 vb.
failure 728 n.
collar
halter 47 n.
garment 228 n.
arrest 747 vb.
collate
compare 462 vb.
collateral
akin 11 adj.
security 767 n.
collation
meal 301 n.
colleague
colleague 707 n.
collect
bring together
74 vb.
receive 782 vb.
—oneself
keep calm 823 vb.
collection
accumulation 74 n.
exhibit 522 n.
collection 632 n.
oblation 981 n.
collective
general 79 adj.
joint possession
775 n.
collectivism
joint possession
775 n.
collector
enthusiast 504 n.
desirer 859 n.
college
academy 539 n.

collide
collide 279 vb.

colliery
excavation 255 n.

collision
collision 279 n.
convergence 293 n.
quarrel 709 n.

collocation
location 187 n.

colloquial
dialectal 560 adj.

colloquialism
slang 560 n.

colloquy
conference 584 n.
interlocution 584 n.

collusion
deception 542 n.
cooperation 706 n.

colon
insides 224 n.
punctuation 547 n.

colonel
army officer 741 n.

colonial
settler 191 n.

colonialism
governance 733 n.
subjection 745 n.

colonist
settler 191 n.
incomer 297 n.

colonize
place oneself 187 vb.
subjugate 745 vb.
appropriate 786 vb.

colonnade
path 624 n.

colony
territory 184 n.
political organization 733 n.

colophon
label 547 n.

coloration
colour 425 n.
hue 425 n.

coloratura
vocal music 412 n.

colossal
enormous 32 adj.
huge 195 adj.
tall 209 adj.

colossus
giant 195 n.

colour
character 5 n.
sort 77 n.
modify 143 vb.
light 417 n.
colour 425 n.vb.
qualify 468 vb.
paint 553 vb.
pretext 614 n.
show feeling 818 vb.

colourable
plausible 471 adj.
deceiving 542 adj.

colour bar
exclusion 57 n.
prejudice 481 n.

colour-blind
dim-sighted 440 adj.
indiscriminating 464 adj.

coloured
coloured 425 adj.
painted 553 adj.

coloured man/woman
blackness 428 n.

colourful
florid 425 adj.
showy 875 adj.

colouring
hue 425 n.
meaning 514 n.
identification 547 n.
painting 553 n.

colourless
colourless 426 adj.
feeble 572 adj.
middling 732 adj.
dull 840 adj.

colours
badge 547 n.
flag 547 n.

colourwash
coat 226 vb.

colt
young creature 132 n.
horse 273 n.
beginner 538 n.

column
pillar 218 n.
cylinder 252 n.
monument 548 n.
article 591 n.
formation 722 n.

columnist
informant 524 n.
author 589 n.

coma
insensibility 375 n.
sleep 679 n.

comatose
insensible 375 adj.
apathetic 820 adj.

comb
smoother 258 n.
search 459 vb.
clean 648 vb.

combat
fight 716 n.vb.

combatant
combatant 722 n.

combative
quarrelling 709 adj.
warlike 718 adj.

combat zone
battleground 724 n.

combe
valley 255 n.

combination
union 45 n.
combination 50 n.
composition 56 n.
assemblage 74 n.
association 706 n.

combine
combine 50 vb.
(*see* **combination**)

combine harvester
farm tool 370 n.

combustible
fuel 385 n.
combustible 385 adj.

combustion
burning 381 n.

come
arrive 295 vb.

—**about**
happen 154 vb.

—**and go**
be active 678 vb.

—**apart**
separate 46 vb.

—**between**
make quarrels 709 vb.

—**by**
acquire 771 vb.

—**clean**
confess 526 vb.

—**down**

descend 309 vb.

—**down on**
be severe 735 vb.
punish 963 vb.

—**forward**
offer oneself 759 vb.

—**in**
enter 297 vb.

—**into**
inherit 771 vb.

—**it over**
be proud 871 vb.

—**of**
result 157 vb.

—**off**
happen 154 vb.
be successful 727 vb.

—**out**
be disclosed 526 vb.

—**out with**
divulge 526 vb.

—**round to**
consent 758 vb.

—**through**
be safe 660 vb.

—**to**
be restored 656 vb.
cost 809 vb.

—**to a head**
culminate 34 vb.

—**together**
congregate 74 vb.

—**to hand**
be received 782 vb.

—**to mind**
dawn upon 449 vb.

—**to nothing**
miscarry 728 vb.

—**to one's ears**
hear 415 vb.

—**to the point**
specify 80 vb.
speak plainly 573 vb.

—**under**
be included 78 vb.

—**upon**
meet 295 vb.
discover 484 vb.

comeback
revival 656 n.

comedian, comedienne
actor 594 n.
entertainer 594 n.
humorist 839 n.

comedown
humiliation 872 n.
comedy
stage play 594 n.
ridiculousness
849 n.
comely
beautiful 841 adj.
come-on
incentive 612 n.
comestibles
food 301 n.
comet
planet 321 n.
comeuppance
punishment 963 n.
comfort
euphoria 376 n.
repose 683 n.
aid 703 n.vb.
content 828 n.vb.
relieve 831 vb.
cheer 833 vb.
give hope 852 vb.
condolence 905 n.
comfortable
comfortable
376 adj.
easy 701 adj.
palmy 730 adj.
comforter
neckwear 228 n.
comfortless
cheerless 834 adj.
unpromising
853 adj.
comic
the press 528 n.
entertainer 594 n.
dramatic 594 adj.
humorist 839 n.
funny 849 adj.
coming
future 124 adj.
(*see* **come**)
coming to one
due 915 adj.
comity
courtesy 884 n.
comity of nations
social group 371 n.
comma
punctuation 547 n.
command
be superior 34 vb.
be high 209 vb.
dispose of 673 vb.

directorship 689 n.
dominate 733 vb.
command 737 n.vb.
commandant
army officer 741 n.
commandeer
appropriate 786 vb.
commander
army officer 741 n.
naval officer 741 n.
commanding
influential 178 adj.
authoritative|
733 adj.
commanding|
737 adj.
commandment
precept 693 n.
command 737 n.
commando
armed force 722 n.
commemorate
remind 505 vb.
honour 866 vb.
celebrate 876 vb.
commence
begin 68 vb.
commend
advise 691 vb.
praise 923 vb.
commendable
good 615 adj.
advisable 642 adj.
approvable 923 adj.
commensurate
relative 9 adj.
numerable 86 adj.
comment
commentary 520 n.
speech 579 n.
article 591 n.
commentator
interpreter 520 n.
broadcaster 531 n.
dissertator 591 n.
commerce
business 622 n.
trade 791 n.
commercial
advertisement
528 n.
trading 791 adj.
commercialize
vulgarize 847 vb.
commination
malediction
899 n.

comminute
break 46 vb.
pulverize 332 vb.
commiserate
pity 905 vb.
commissar
tyrant 735 n.
autocrat 741 n.
officer 741 n.
commissariat
provision 633 n.
commission
band 74 n.
job 622 n.
fitting out 669 n.
commission
751 n.vb.
earnings 771 n.
commissionaire
doorkeeper 264 n.
commissioner
official 690 n.
delegate 754 n.
notary 958 n.
commit
do 676 vb.
commission 751 vb.
do wrong 914 vb.
—**oneself**
affirm 532 vb.
undertake 672 vb.
promise 764 vb.
incur a duty 917 vb.
commitment
promise 764 n.
duty 917 n.
committal
transference 272 n.
legal process 959 n.
committee
band 74 n.
consignee 754 n.
commode
cabinet 194 n.
latrine 649 n.
commodious
spacious 183 adj.
useful 640 adj.
commodity
object 319 n.
merchandise 795 n.
commodore
naval officer 741 n.
common
general 79 adj.
typical 83 adj.
frequent 139 adj.

usual 610 adj.
sharing 775 adj.
vulgar 847 adj.
plebeian 869 adj.
common cause
cooperation 706 n.
commoner
commoner 869 n.
common knowledge
publicity 528 n.
common land
joint possession
775 n.
common man
everyman 79 n.
common ownership
joint possession
775 n.
commonplace
typical 83 adj.
topic 452 n.
maxim 496 n.
commons
provisions 301 n.
commonalty 869 n.
commonsense
intelligence 498 n.
common touch
sociability 882 n.
courtesy 884 n.
commonwealth
political
organization
733 n.
commotion
turmoil 61 n.
commotion 318 n.
excitable state
822 n.
communal
national 371 adj.
corporate 708 adj.
sharing 775 adj.
communalize
communalize
775 vb.
commune
joint possession
775 n.
commune with
converse 584 vb.
communicate|
524 vb.
communicable
transferable
272 adj.
infectious 653 adj.

communicant
church member
976 n.
worshipper 981 n.
communicate
connect 45 vb.
communicate[1]
524 vb.
correspond 588 vb.
offer worship[1]
981 vb.
communication
message 529 n.
interlocution 584 n.
communications
access 624 n.
communicative
informative 524 adj.
loquacious 581 adj.
communion
party 708 n.
church service
988 n.
communiqué
report 524 n.
news 529 n.
communism
government 733 n.
joint possession
775 n.
communist
reformer 654 n.
agitator 738 n.
communistic
sharing 775 adj.
community
inhabitants 191 n.
social group 371 n.
community 708 n.
community centre
focus 76 n.
meeting place 192 n.
community relations
sociality 882 n.
commutation
substitution 150 n.
commute
travel 267 vb.
show mercy 905 vb.
commuter
dweller 191 n.
traveller 268 n.
compact
small 33 adj.
little 196 adj.
dense 324 adj.
concise 569 adj.

compact 765 n.
compaction
coherence 48 n.
compression 198 n.
companion
analogue 18 n.
concomitant 89 n.
colleague 707 n.
close friend 880 n.
companionable
sociable 882 adj.
companionship
sociality 882 n.
companionway
doorway 263 n.
company
assembly 74 n.
band 74 n.
accompaniment
89 n.
personnel 686 n.
association 706 n.
corporation 708 n.
formation 722 n.
comparable
equivalent 28 adj.
comparative
comparative 27 adj.
compared 462 adj.
figurative 519 adj.
compare
liken 18 vb.
compare 462 vb.
comparison
comparison 462 n.
metaphor 519 n.
compartment
subdivision 53 n.
compartment 194 n.
compartmentalize
set apart 46 vb.
compass
ability 160 n.
range 183 n.
sailing aid 269 n.
direction 281 n.
compassion
leniency 736 n.
pity 905 n.
compassionate
impressible 819 adj.
compass point
compass point
281 n.
compatible
agreeing 24 adj.
concordant 710 adj.

friendly 880 adj.
compatriot
kinsman 11 n.
compeer
compeer 28 n.
contemporary
123 n.
compel
command 737 vb.
compel 740 vb.
compelling
causal 156 adj.
powerful 160 adj.
influential 178 adj.
forceful 571 adj.
necessary 596 adj.
compelling 740 adj.
obligatory 917 adj.
compendium
conciseness 569 n.
compendium 592 n.
compensate
compensate 31 vb.
restitute 787 vb.
atone 941 vb.
compensation
compensation 31 n.
compère
broadcaster 531 n.
direct 689 vb.
compete
contend 716 vb.
offer oneself 759 vb.
competence
ability 160 n.
skill 694 n.
wealth 800 n.
jurisdiction 955 n.
competent
expert 694 adj.
competition
opposition 704 n.
contention 716 n.
competitive
equal 28 adj.
competitor
compeer 28 n.
contender 716 n.
player 837 n.
compilation
anthology 592 n.
compile
compose 56 vb.
bring together
74 vb.
complacency
content 828 n.

complacent
vain 873 adj.
complain
deprecate 762 vb.
be discontented[1]
829 vb.
complainant
accuser 928 n.
complaint
illness 651 n.
discontent 829 n.
lament 836 n.
accusation 928 n.
complaisant
obedient 739 adj.
permitting 756 adj.
complement
analogue 18 n.
make complete[1]
54 vb.
personnel 686 n.
complementary
correlative 12 adj.
complete
make complete
54 vb.
perfect 646 adj.vb.
carry through
725 vb.
completeness
whole 52 n.
completeness 54 n.
completion
completion 725 n.
(*see* **complete**)
complex
whole 52 n.
complex 61 adj.
eccentricity 503 n.
difficult 700 adj.
complexion
hue 425 n.
mien 445 n.
complexity
complexity 61 n.
compliance
obedience 739 n.
observance 768 n.
complicate
bedevil 63 vb.
aggravate 832 vb.
complicated
complex 61 adj.
complication
complexity 61 n.
illness 651 n.
aggravation 832 n.

complicity
cooperation 706 n.
participation 775 n.
guilt 936 n.
compliment
honours 866 n.
congratulate 886 vb.
praise 923 n.vb.
flattery 925 n.
complimentary
uncharged 812 adj.
comply
obey 739 vb.
(*see* **compliance**)
component
component
58 n.adj.
element 319 n.
comport oneself
behave 688 vb.
compose
combine 50 vb.
compose 56 vb.
constitute 56 vb.
arrange 62 vb.
compose music
413 vb.
composed
inexcitable 823 adj.
unastonished
865 adj.
composer
musician 413 n.
composite
mixed 43 adj.
plural 101 adj.
composition
a mixture 43 n.
composition 56 n.
production 164 n.
structure 331 n.
compact 765 n.
compromise 770 n.
compositor
printer 587 n.
compost
fertilizer 171 n.
composure
inexcitability 823 n.
compound
a mixture 43 n.
combine 50 vb.
composition 56 n.
enclosure 235 n.
compromise 770 vb.
comprehend
comprise 78 vb.

know 490 vb.
understand 516 vb.
comprehensible
intelligible 516 adj.
comprehensive
comprehensive
52 adj.
complete 54 adj.
general 79 adj.
school 539 n.
compress
make smaller
198 vb.
be concise 569 vb.
surgical dressing
658 n.
compression
diminution 37 n.
compression 198 n.
narrowing 206 n.
compendium
592 n.
comprise
comprise 78 vb.
compromise
middle way 625 n.
compact 765 n.
compromise
770 n.vb.
defame 926 vb.
compromising
discreditable
867 adj.
compulsion
necessity 596 n.
compulsion 740 n.
compulsive
compelling 740 adj.
compulsory
authoritative
733 adj.
obligatory 917 adj.
compunction
regret 830 n.
penitence 939 n.
computation
data processing
86 n.
numeration 86 n.
compute
computerize 86 vb.
do sums 86 vb.
measure 465 vb.
computer
counting instrument
86 n.
computer program

data processing
86 n.
comrade
colleague 707 n.
political party 708 n.
chum 880 n.
comradeship
sociality 882 n.
con
memorize 505 vb.
defraud 788 vb.
concatenation
continuity 71 n.
concave
concave 255 adj.
conceal
conceal 525 vb.
dissemble 541 vb.
concealment
invisibility 444 n.
concealment 525 n.
concede
assent 488 vb.
permit 756 vb.
conceit
idea 451 n.
ideality 513 n.
affectation 850 n.
vanity 873 n.
conceivable
possible 469 adj.
conceive
be fruitful 171 vb.
vitalize 360 vb.
cognize 447 vb.
opine 485 vb.
imagine 513 vb.
concentrate
augment 36 vb.
focus 76 vb.
centralize 225 vb.
converge 293 vb.
think 449 vb.
be attentive 455 vb.
concentration
density 324 n.
(*see* **concentrate**)
concentric
parallel 219 adj.
central 225 adj.
concept
idea 451 n.
ideality 513 n.
conception
product 164 n.
intellect 447 n.
thought 449 n.

idea 451 n.
conceptual
mental 447 adj.
concern
be related 9 vb.
topic 452 n.
business 622 n.
function 622 n.
importance 638 n.
shop 796 n.
worry 825 n.
concert
agreement 24 n.
music 412 n.
concertina
organ 414 n.
concerto
musical piece 412 n.
concession
offset 31 n.
compromise 770 n.
concessional
cheap 812 adj.
concessionnaire
recipient 782 n.
concierge
keeper 749 n.
conciliate
pacify 719 vb.
be courteous 884 vb.
concise
concise 569 adj.
conclave
council 692 n.
synod 985 n.
conclude
terminate 69 vb.
judge 480 vb.
conclusion
sequel 67 n.
finality 69 n.
opinion 485 n.
completion 725 n.
conclusive
demonstrating
478 adj.
completive 725 adj.
concoct
imagine 513 vb.
fake 541 vb.
plan 623 vb.
concoction
a mixture 43 n.
draught 301 n.
untruth 543 n.
concomitant
concomitant 89 n.

concord
agreement 24 n.
concord 710 n.
concordance
dictionary 559 n.
concordat
treaty 765 n.
concourse
assembly 74 n.
convergence 293 n.
concrete
substantial 3 adj.
material 319 adj.
solid body 324 n.
building material
631 n.
concretion
substance 3 n.
condensation 324 n.
solid body 324 n.
concubine
kept woman 952 n.
concupiscence
libido 859 n.
concur
concur 181 vb.
assent 488 vb.
concurrence
agreement 24 n.
concurrence 181 n.
concuss
render insensible
375 vb.
condemn
condemn 961 vb.
punish 963 vb.
condemned
fated 596 adj.
dilapidated 655 adj.
condemned 961 adj.
condensation
condensation 324 n.
moisture 341 n.
condense
be dense 324 vb.
be concise 569 vb.
condescend
be humble 872 vb.
show respect 920 vb.
condescension
pride 871 n.
humility 872 n.
condiment
condiment 389 n.
condition
state 7 n.
teach 534 vb.

habituate 610 vb.
health 650 n.
conditional
qualifying 468 adj.
conditional 766 adj.
conditions
circumstance 8 n.
requirement 627 n.
conditions 766 n.
condolence
condolence 905 n.
condone
forgive 909 vb.
conduce
conduce 156 vb.
tend 179 vb.
aid 703 vb.
conduct
accompany 89 vb.
transfer 272 vb.
play music 413 vb.
mien 445 n.
action 676 n.
conduct 688 n.
manage 689 vb.
conductor
driver 268 n.
musician 413 n.
leader 690 n.
conduit
tube 263 n.
conduit 351 n.
cone
cone 252 n.
confection
a mixture 43 n.
product 164 n.
confectionery
pastries 301 n.
sweets 301 n.
confederacy
association 706 n.
confederate
colleague 707 n.
confederation
association 706 n.
political
organization
733 n.
confer
confer 584 vb.
consult 691 vb.
give 781 vb.
—an honour
dignify 866 vb.
conference
inquiry 459 n.

conference 584 n.
confess
believe 485 vb.
confess 526 vb.
be penitent 939 vb.
confession
disclosure 526 n.
ministration 988 n.
confessions
biography 590 n.
confessor
pastor 986 n.
confetti
small thing 33 n.
confidant(e)
adviser 691 n.
close friend 880 n.
confide
divulge 526 vb.
—in
consult 691 vb.
confidence
positiveness 473 n.
expectation 507 n.
information 524 n.
secret 530 n.
safety 660 n.
hope 852 n.
confidence trick
trickery 542 n.
confident
unfearing 855 adj.
(see **confidence***)*
confidential
concealed 525 adj.
configuration
form 243 n.
confine
limit 236 vb.
imprison 747 vb.
seclude 883 vb.
confinement
obstetrics 167 n.
confines
near place 200 n.
confirm
strengthen 162 vb.
corroborate 466 vb.
make certain
473 vb.
endorse 488 vb.
confirmation
Christian rite 988 n.
confirmed
habituated 610 adj.
confiscate
deprive 786 vb.

conflagration
fire 379 n.
conflict
contrariety 14 n.
disagreement 25 n.
quarrel 709 n.vb.
confluence
union 45 n.
convergence 293 n.
current 350 n.
conform
do likewise 20 vb.
conform 83 vb.
conformation
composition 56 n.
form 243 n.
conformity
uniformity 16 n.
conformity 83 n.
observance 768 n.
orthodoxism 976 n.
confound
derange 63 vb.
not discriminate|
464 vb.
confute 479 vb.
confounded
damnable 645 adj.
confraternity
community 708 n.
confrère
colleague 707 n.
confront
be present 189 vb.
be opposite
240 vb.
compare 462 vb.
show 522 vb.
withstand 704 vb.
resist 715 vb.
be courageous
855 vb.
confusable
identical 13 adj.
confuse
bedevil 63 vb.
puzzle 474 vb.
confused
mixed 43 adj.
orderless 61 adj.
indistinct 444 adj.
unclear 568 adj.
confusion
medley 43 n.
confusion 61 n.
psychopathy 503 n.
humiliation 872 n.

confutation
vindication 927 n.
confute
confute 479 vb.
negate 533 vb.
congeal
be dense 324 vb.
thicken 354 vb.
congenial
agreeing 24 adj.
pleasant 376 adj.
congenital
genetic 5 adj.
congestion
crowd 74 n.
redundance 637 n.
conglomerate
cohere 48 vb.
solid body 324 n.
rock 344 n.
corporation 708 n.
congratulate
congratulate 886 vb.
—oneself
feel pride 871 vb.
congratulation
rejoicing 835 n.
congratulation
886 n.
congregate
congregate 74 vb.
meet 295 vb.
congregation
assembly 74 n.
worshipper 981 n.
laity 987 n.
congress
union 45 n.
council 692 n.
parliament 692 n.
congruent
agreeing 24 adj.
congruity
similarity 18 n.
conformance 24 n.
symmetry 245 n.
conical
rotund 252 adj.
tapering 256 adj.
conifer
tree 366 n.
conjecture
uncertainty 474 n.
conjecture 512 n.
conjugal
matrimonial
894 adj.

conjugate
parse 564 vb.
conjunction
union 45 n.
concurrence 181 n.
part of speech 564 n.
conjure
deceive 542 vb.
entreat 761 vb.
—up
imagine 513 vb.
conjuror
conjuror 545 n.
entertainer 594 n.
con man
trickster 545 n.
connect
connect 45 vb.
continue 71 vb.
connection,
connexion
relation 9 n.
bond 47 n.
connivance
cooperation 706 n.
laxity 734 n.
permission 756 n.
connive at
disregard 458 vb.
connoisseur
enthusiast 504 n.
people of taste
846 n.
connotation
connotation 514 n.
connote
mean 514 vb.
imply 523 vb.
conquer
overmaster 727 vb.
conqueror
victor 727 n.
conquest
victory 727 n.
subjection 745 n.
consanguineous
akin 11 adj.
conscience
conscience 917 n.
conscienceless
wicked 934 adj.
conscience money
atonement 941 n.
conscience-stricken
regretting 830 adj.
repentant 939 adj.
conscientious

careful 457 adj.
observant 768 adj.
trustworthy 929 adj.
conscientious
objector
pacifist 717 n.
conscious (of)
sentient 374 adj.
mental 447 adj.
knowing 490 adj.
conscript
soldier 722 n.
compel 740 vb.
consecrate
sanctify 979 vb.
consecutive
sequential 65 adj.
continuous 71 adj.
consensus
agreement 24 n.
consensus 488 n.
consent
agreement 24 n.
assent 488 n.vb.
consent 758 n.vb.
consequence
sequel 67 n.
effect 157 n.
importance 638 n.
consequential
caused 157 adj.
conservancy
preservation 666 n.
conservation
storage 632 n.
protection 660 n.
preservation 666 n.
conservationist
preserver 666 n.
conservative
preserving 666 adj.
sectional 708 adj.
cautious 858 adj.
conservatoire
academy 539 n.
conservatory
garden 370 n.
conserve
sweet thing 392 n.
store 632 vb.
preserve 666 vb.
consider
meditate 449 vb.
inquire 459 vb.
estimate 480 vb.
considerable
substantial 3 adj.

great 32 adj.
many 104 adj.
important 638 adj.
considerate
thoughtful 449 adj.
disinterested
931 adj.
consideration
quid pro quo 150 n.
meditation 449 n.
courtesy 884 n.
respect 920n.
consign
send 272 vb.
consignee
consignee 754 n.
recipient 782 n.
consignment
thing transferred
272 n.
transfer 780 n.
consistency
uniformity 16 n.
density 324 n.
consistent
rational 475 adj.
consist of
comprise 78 vb.
consolation
relief 831 n.
condolence 905 n.
console
cabinet 194 n.
cheer 833 vb.
consolidate
bring together
74 vb.
centralize 225 vb.
be dense 324 vb.
consonance
agreement 24 n.
consonant
speech sound 398 n.
consort
concomitant 89 n.
spouse 894 n.
consortium
association 706 n.
conspectus
generality 79 n.
compendium 592 n.
conspicuous
obvious 443 adj.
conspiracy
secrecy 525 n.
plot 623 n.
compact 765 n.

conspirator
planner 623 n.
conspiratorial
stealthy 525 adj.
conspire
plot 623 vb.
constable
police 955 n.
constancy
uniformity 16 n.
stability 153 n.
perseverance 600 n.
loyalty 739 n.
constant
identity 13 n.
uniform 16 adj.
regular 81 adj.
frequent 139 adj.
unchangeable
153 adj.
trustworthy 929 adj.
constellation
star 321 n.
person of repute
866 n.
consternation
fear 854 n.
constipation
defecation 302 n.
digestive disorders
651 n.
constituency
electorate 605 n.
constituent(s)
component 58 n.
contents 193 n.
electorate 605 n.
constitute
constitute 56 vb.
constitution
character 5 n.
composition 56 n.
structure 331 n.
political
organization
733 n.
law 953 n.
constitutional
habit 610 n.
exercise 682 n.
legal 953 adj.
constraint
compulsion 740 n.
restraint 747 n.
constrict
make smaller
198 vb.

constriction
narrowing 206 n.
restriction 747 n.
construct
compose 56 vb.
produce 164 vb.
form 243 vb.
construction
arrangement 62 n.
structure 331 n.
interpretation 520 n.
sculpture 554 n.
constructive
productive 164 adj.
aiding 703 adj.
constructor
producer 164 n.
construe
interpret 520 vb.
parse 564 vb.
consulate
envoy 754 n.
consult
confer 584 vb.
consult 691 vb.
consultant
oracle 511 n.
doctor 658 n.
adviser 691 n.
expert 696 n.
consultation
advice 691 n.
consume
destroy 165 vb.
eat 301 vb.
waste 634 vb.
use 673 vb.
expend 806 vb.
consumer
eater 301 n.
purchaser 792 n.
consummate
consummate 32 adj.
complete 54 adj.
perfect 646 adj.
carry through
725 vb.
consummation
coition 45 n.
consumptive
sick person 651 n.
contact
union 45 n.
connect 45 vb.
contiguity 202 n.
touch 378 n.
informant 524 n.

contact lens
eyeglass 442 n.
contagion
infection 651 n.
contagious
influential 178 adj.
transferable
272 adj.
infectious 653 adj.
contain
comprise 78 vb.
surround 230 vb.
—oneself
be temperate 942 vb.
container
receptacle 194 n.
storage 632 n.
containerize
transpose 272 vb.
contaminate
make unclean
649 vb.
impair 655 vb.
contaminated
diseased 651 adj.
contemplate
scan 438 vb.
meditate 449 vb.
expect 507 vb.
contemplation
meditation 449 n.
prayers 981 n.
contemplative
thoughtful 449 adj.
monastic 986 adj.
contemporary
contemporary
123 n.
modern 126 adj.
contempt
pride 871 n.
contempt 922 n.
contemptible
inferior 35 adj.
unimportant
639 adj.
ridiculous 849 adj.
discreditable
867 adj.
contemptible
922 adj.
rascally 930 adj.
contemptuous
insolent 878 adj.
despising 922 adj.
contend
affirm 532 vb.

contend 716 vb.
contender
contender 716 n.
player 837 n.
content
structure 331 n.
euphoria 376 n.
willing 597 adj.
content 828 n.adj.
content 828 vb.
contention
argument 475 n.
quarrel 709 n.
contention 716 n.
contents
component 58 n.
contents 193 n.
topic 452 n.
conterminous
contiguous 202 adj.
contest
contest 716 n.
sport 837 n.
contestant
opponent 705 n.
contender 716 n.
context
circumstance 8 n.
relation 9 n.
concomitant 89 n.
connotation 514 n.
meaning 514 n.
contiguity
contiguity 202 n.
contiguous
near 200 adj.
continence
temperance 942 n.
continent
region 184 n.
land 344 n.
temperate 942 adj.
continental
regional 184 adj.
dweller 191 n.
inland 344 adj.
contingency
juncture 8 n.
chance 159 n.
contingent
extrinsic 6 adj.
casual 159 adj.
uncertain 474 adj.
conditional
766 adj.
contingents
armed force 722 n.

505

continual
continuous 71 adj.
unceasing 146 adj.
continuance
continuity 71 n.
course of time
111 n.
durability 113 n.
continuance 146 n.
continuation
sequel 67 n.
continue
run on 71 vb.
(*see* **continuance,**
continuity)
continuity
continuity 71 n.
continuance 146 n.
cinema 445 n.
continuo
melody 410 n.
continuous
continuous 71 adj.
(*see* **continuity**)
continuum
space 183 n.
contort
distort 246 vb.
contortionist
athlete 162 n.
contour
outline 233 n.
form 243 n.
feature 445 n.
indication 547 n.
contraband
prohibited 757 adj.
booty 790 n.
contraception
impotence 161 n.
unproductiveness
172 n.
contract
become small
198 vb.
shorten 204 vb.
undertaking 672 n.
contract 765 vb.
make terms 766 vb.
—a disease
be ill 651 vb.
contraction
obstetrics 167 n.
contraction 198 n.
word 559 n.
conciseness 569 n.
(*see* **contract**)

contractor
trier 671 n.
signatory 765 n.
contractual
contractual 765 adj.
contradict
be contrary 14 vb.
tell against 467 vb.
negate 533 vb.
oppose 704 vb.
contradiction
rejoinder 460 n.
contradictory
illogical 477 adj.
contradistinguish
discriminate 463 vb.
contraindicate
tell against 467 vb.
contralto
vocalist 413 n.
contraposition
contraposition
240 n.
contraption
contrivance 623 n.
tool 630 n.
contrapuntal
musical 412 adj.
contraries
polarity 14 n.
opposites 704 n.
contrariety
(*see* **contrary**)
contrary
contrary 14 adj.
disagreeing 25 adj.
counteracting
182 adj.
opposite 240 adj.
countervailing
467 adj.
negative 533 adj.
capricious 604 adj.
hindering 702 adj.
adverse 731 adj.
disobedient 738 adj.
contrast
contrariety 14 n.
difference 15 n.
compare 462 vb.
contravene
be contrary 14 vb.
contravention
lawbreaking 954 n.
contretemps
hitch 702 n.
contribute

give 781 vb.
—to
augment 36 vb.
conduce 156 vb.
tend 179 vb.
aid 703 vb.
contribution
cooperation 706 n.
giving 781 n.
payment 804 n.
contributor
correspondent
588 n.
participator 775 n.
contrition
regret 830 n.
penitence 939 n.
contrivance
contrivance 623 n.
plan 623 n.
means 629 n.
tactics 688 n.
stratagem 698 n.
contrive
predetermine
608 vb.
find means 629 vb.
control
be able 160 vb.
influence 178 n.
management 689 n.
governance 733 n.
rule 733 vb.
restrain 747 vb.
spiritualism 984 n.
—oneself
be temperate 942 vb.
controlled
impassive 820 adj.
inexcitable 823 adj.
controller
director 690 n.
controls
aircraft 276 n.
instrument 628 n.
directorship 689 n.
controversial
uncertain 474 adj.
arguing 475 adj.
controversy
question 459 n.
argument 475 n.
controvert
argue 475 vb.
negate 533 vb.
contumacious
wilful 602 adj.

contumely
insolence 878 n.
disrespect 921 n.
contusion
wound 655 n.
conundrum
enigma 530 n.
conurbation
city 184 n.
housing 192 n.
convalescence
recuperation 656 n.
convection
transference 272 n.
convene
bring together
74 vb.
convenience
opportunity 137 n.
euphoria 376 n.
utility 640 n.
good policy 642 n.
leisure 681 n.
facility 701 n.
convent
monastery 986 n.
conventicle
assembly 74 n.
sect 978 n.
convention
conformity 83 n.
conference 584 n.
practice 610 n.
compact 765 n.
etiquette 848 n.
conventional
conformable 83 adj.
fashionable 848 adj.
conventionalist
conformist 83 n.
converge
focus 76 vb.
converge 293 vb.
conversant (with)
knowing 490 adj.
conversation
speech 579 n.
interlocution
584 n.
conversationalist
speaker 579 n.
humorist 839 n.
converse
contrary 14 adj.
speak 579 vb.
converse 584 vb.
be sociable 882 vb.

conversion
conversion 147 n.
use 673 n.
convert
modify 143 vb.
changed person
147 n.
convert 147 vb.
convince 485 vb.
learner 538 n.
use 673 vb.
pietist 979 n.
converted
believing 485 adj.
repentant 939 adj.
convertible
automobile 274 n.
convex
convex 253 adj.
convexity
curvature 248 n.
convexity 253 n.
convey
move 265 vb.
transfer 272 vb.
carry 273 vb.
mean 514 vb.
communicate
524 vb.
assign 780 vb.
conveyance
transport 272 n.
vehicle 274 n.
transfer 780 n.
conveyancer
law agent 958 n.
conveyor belt
continuity 71 n.
convict
offender 904 n.
condemn 961 vb.
conviction
positiveness 473 n.
belief 485 n.
hope 852 n.
convince
convert 147 vb.
demonstrate 478 vb.
convince 485 vb.
convincing
plausible 471 adj.
credible 485 adj.
convivial
cheerful 833 adj.
sociable 882 adj.
conviviality
festivity 837 n.

convocation
council 692 n.
synod 985 n.
convoke
bring together
74 vb.
convoluted
convoluted 251 adj.
roundabout
626 adj.
convolution
complexity 61 n.
convolution 251 n.
convoy
accompany 89 vb.
keeper 749 n.
convulsion
turmoil 61 n.
derangement 63 n.
revolution 149 n.
spasm 318 n.
coo
ululate 409 vb.
pet 889 vb.
cook
cook 301 vb.
domestic 742 n.
—**the books**
defraud 788 vb.
—**up**
fake 541 vb.
plot 623 vb.
cooker
furnace 383 n.
cookery
cookery 301 n.
cookie, cooky
pastries 301 n.
cooking
impending 155 adj.
preparatory
669 adj.
cool
moderate 177 vb.
cold 380 adj.
refrigerate 382 vb.
wise 498 adj.
refreshing 685 adj.
inexcitable 823 adj.
indifferent 860 adj.
inimical 881 adj.
cooler
refrigerator 384 n.
cooling-off period
delay 136 n.
coop
stable 192 n.

cooperate
cooperate 706 vb.
cooperation
combination 50 n.
concurrence 181 n.
aid 703 n.
cooperation 706 n.
cooperative
willing 597 adj.
cooperative 706 adj.
corporate 708 adj.
sharing 775 adj.
cooperator
collaborator 707 n.
participator 775 n.
co-opt
choose 605 vb.
coordinate
regularize 62 vb.
coordinate 465 n.
cop
arrest 747 vb.
—**it**
be in difficulty
700 vb.
—**out**
avoid 620 vb.
cope
vestments 989 n.
cope (with)
withstand 704 vb.
coping
summit 213 n.
copious
diffuse 570 adj.
plenteous 635 adj.
copper
cauldron 194 n.
orange 432 n.
coinage 797 n.
police 955 n.
copperplate
engraving 555 n.
lettering 586 n.
coppice
wood 366 n.
copse
wood 366 n.
copula
bond 47 n.
copulation
coition 45 n.
propagation 167 n.
copy
copy 20 vb.
copy 22 n.
prototype 23 n.

conform 83 vb.
duplication 91 n.
reproduce 166 vb.
news 529 n.
sham 542 n.
represent 551 vb.
script 586 n.
copycat
imitator 20 n.
conformist 83 n.
copyhold
proprietary 777 adj.
copyright
dueness 915 n.
copywriter
publicizer 528 n.
coquetry
affectation 850 n.
coquette
affecter 850 n.
excite love 887 vb.
coral
marine life 365 n.
red 431 adj.
gem 844 n.
cord
cable 47 n.
ligature 47 n.
fibre 208 n.
cordage
tackling 47 n.
cordial
soft drink 301 n.
tonic 658 n.
feeling 818 adj.
sociable 882 adj.
cordite
explosive 723 n.
cordon
enclose 235 vb.
—**off**
circumscribe
232 vb.
restrain 747 vb.
cordon bleu
cookery 301 n.
proficient person
696 n.
cordon sanitaire
protection 660 n.
corduroy
textile 222 n.
core
essence 1 n.
essential part 5 n.
centre 225 n.
chief thing 638 n.

corespondent
divorce 896 n.

cork
stopper 264 n.
lightness 323 n.

corked
deteriorated
655 adj.

corkscrew
coil 251 n.
opener 263 n.
rotate 315 vb.

corn
cereals 301 n.
ulcer 651 n.

cornea
eye 438 n.

corner
place 185 n.
angularity 247 n.
cavity 255 n.
hiding-place 527 n.
defeat 727 vb.
purchase 792 vb.

cornered
in difficulties
700 adj.

cornerstone
prop 218 n.
chief thing 638 n.

cornet
cone 252 n.
horn 414 n.

corn exchange
market 796 n.

cornice
summit 213 n.

cornucopia
abundance 171 n.
plenty 635 n.
liberality 813 n.

corny
known 490 adj.
aphoristic 496 adj.

corollary
adjunct 40 n.

corona
light 417 n.

coronary
cardiovascular
disease 651 n.

coronation
dignification 866 n.

coronation robes
regalia 743 n.

coroner
judge 957 n.

coroner's court
lawcourt 956 n.

coronet
regalia 743 n.

corporal
soldiery 722 n.

corporal punishment
corporal
punishment 963 n.

corporate
corporate 708 adj.

corporation
business 622 n.
corporation 708 n.

corporeal
material 319 adj.

corps
formation 722 n.

corps de ballet
actor 594 n.

corps diplomatique
envoy 754 n.

corpse
corpse 363 n.

corpulence
bulk 195 n.
thickness 205 n.

corpus
whole 52 n.
reading matter
589 n.

corral
enclosure 235 n.
imprison 747 vb.

correct
accurate 494 adj.
true 494 adj.
grammatical
564 adj.
print 587 vb.
rectify 654 vb.
remedy 658 vb.
fashionable 848 adj.
formal 875 adj.
honourable 929 adj.
punish 963 vb.

correction
amendment 654 n.

correctitude
formality 875 n.

corrective
counteracting
182 adj.
remedial 658 adj.
punitive 963 adj.

correlate
compare 462 vb.

correlation
relativeness 9 n.
correlation 12 n.
statistics 86 n.

correlative
agreeing 24 adj.

correspond
be related 9 vb.
correlate 12 vb.
correspond 588 vb.

correspondence
similarity 18 n.
symmetry 245 n.
correspondence
588 n.

correspondent
informant 524 n.
news reporter 529 n.
correspondent
588 n.

corridor
lobby 194 n.
access 624 n.

corrigendum
mistake 495 n.

corroborate
corroborate 466 vb.
demonstrate 478 vb.

corrode
burn 381 vb.

corrosion
dilapidation 655 n.

corrosive
destroyer 168 n.
harmful 645 adj.

corrugate
crinkle 251 vb.
fold 261 vb.
groove 262 vb.

corrupt
decompose 51 vb.
misteach 535 vb.
pervert 655 vb.
venal 930 adj.
vicious 934 adj.
make wicked
934 vb.

corruption
decay 51 n.
improbity 930 n.

corsair
robber 789 n.

corset
underwear 228 n.

cortège
procession 71 n.
obsequies 364 n.

cortex
skin 226 n.

cortisone
drug 658 n.

coruscation
flash 417 n.

corvée
labour 682 n.
compulsion 740 n.

corvette
sailing ship 275 n.

corybantic
frenzied 503 adj.

cosh
strike 279 vb.
club 723 n.

cosmetic
cosmetic 843 n.

cosmetician
beautician 843 n.

cosmic
comprehensive
52 adj.
cosmic 321 n.

cosmonaut
aeronaut 271 n.

cosmopolitan
universal 79 adj.
urban 192 adj.
beau monde 848 n.
well-bred 848 adj.

cosmos
whole 52 n.
universe 321 n.

cosset
pet 889 vb.

cost
cost 809 n.vb.

costly
valuable 644 adj.
harmful 645 adj.
dear 811 adj.

cost of living
statistics 86 n.
expenditure 806 n.

costs
expenditure 806 n.
penalty 963 n.

costume
suit 228 n.

costumier
clothier 228 n.
stagehand 594 n.

cosy
comfortable
376 adj.
palmy 730 adj.

cot
bed 218 n.
coterie
band 74 n.
party 708 n.
cottage
small house 192 n.
cotton
textile 222 n.
couch
bed 218 n.
seat 218 n.
cough
eruct 300 vb.
breathe 352 vb.
respiratory disease 651 n.
couldn't care less
be indifferent 860 vb.
coulter
farm tool 370 n.
council
assembly 74 n.
adviser 691 n.
council 692 n.
tribunal 956 n.
synod 985 n.
councillor
councillor 692 n.
counsel
incite 612 vb.
advise 691 vb.
lawyer 958 n.
counsellor
sage 500 n.
adviser 691 n.
count
comprise 78 vb.
number 86 n.
measure 465 vb.
be important 638 vb.
person of rank 868 n.
—on
believe 485 vb.
expect 507 vb.
—out
exclude 57 vb.
exempt 919 vb.
countdown
start 68 n.
countenance
face 237 n.
mien 445 n.
patronize 703 vb.

approve 923 vb.
counter
contrary 14 adj.
enumerator 86 n.
counteract 182 vb.
stand 218 n.
answer 460 n.
parry 713 vb.
shop 796 n.
counteract
counteract 182 vb.
tell against 467 vb.
counterattack
retaliation 714 n.
counterbalance
offset 31 n.
counterblast
answer 460 n.
counterchange
interchange 151 vb.
countercharge
rejoinder 460 n.
counterespionage
secret service 459 n.
counterfeit
imitative 20 adj.
fake 541 vb.
sham 542 n.
spurious 542 adj.
counterfeiter
defrauder 789 n.
counterfoil
label 547 n.
counterirritant
antidote 658 n.
countermand
abrogate 752 vb.
countermarch
turn back 286 vb.
countermeasure
hindrance 702 n.
countermine
plot 623 n.vb.
defences 713 n.
counterpane
coverlet 226 n.
counterpart
analogue 18 n.
counterpoint
music 412 n.
counterpoise
equalize 28 vb.
offset 31 n.
gravity 322 n.
counter-revolution
revolution 149 n.

counter-revolutionary
opponent 705 n.
revolter 738 n.
countersign
endorse 488 vb.
sign 547 vb.
counterstroke
retaliation 714 n.
countervail
counteract 182 vb.
tell against 467 vb.
counterweight
offset 31 n.
countless
infinite 107 adj.
countrified
provincial 192 adj.
ill-bred 847 adj.
country
region 184 n.
political organization 733 n.
countryman, countrywoman
country-dweller 869 n.
countryside
district 184 n.
county
district 184 n.
political organization 733 n.
coup
deed 676 n.
coup de grâce
killing 362 n.
completion 725 n.
coup d'état
revolution 149 n.
coupé
automobile 274 n.
couple
analogue 18 n.
join 45 vb.
unite with 45 vb.
duality 90 n.
marry 894 vb.
couplet
verse form 593 n.
coupling
coition 45 n.
joining together 45 n.
bond 47 n.

courage
courage 855 n.
courageous
courageous 855 adj.
courier
bearer 273 n.
courier 529 n.
course
tendency 179 n.
layer 207 n.
motion 265 n.
direction 281 n.
dish 301 n.
flow 350 vb.
hunt 619 n.
route 624 n.
therapy 658 n.
arena 724 n.
course of events
affairs 154 n.
course of studies
curriculum 534 n.
course of time
course of time 111 n.
courser
speeder 277 n.
court
housing 192 n.
open space 263 n.
arena 724 n.
retainer 742 n.
court 889 vb.
lawcourt 956 n.
courteous
well-bred 848 adj.
courteous 884 adj.
respectful 920 adj.
courtesan
prostitute 952 n.
courtesy
etiquette 848 n.
(*see* **courteous**)
courthouse
courtroom 956 n.
courtier
retainer 742 n.
toady 879 n.
courting
wooing 889 n.
courtly
well-bred 848 adj.
courteous 884 adj.
court-martial
lawcourt 956 n.
court of law
lawcourt 956 n.

courtroom
  courtroom 956 n.
courtship
  wooing 889 n.
courtyard
  place 185 n.
  enclosure 235 n.
cousin
  kinsman 11 n.
couturier, couturière
  clothier 228 n.
cove
  gulf 345 n.
coven
  sorcery 983 n.
covenant
  compact 765 n.
  contract 765 vb.
  title deed 767 n.
covenanter
  sectarian 978 n.
cover
  offset 31 n.
  comprise 78 vb.
  extend 183 vb.
  receptacle 194 n.
  cover 226 vb.
  close 264 vb.
  meal 301 n.
  conceal 525 vb.
  hiding-place 527 n.
  obliterate 550 vb.
  pretext 614 n.
  shelter 662 n.
  defend 713 vb.
—oneself
  be cautious 858 vb.
—up
  conceal 525 vb.
coverage
  inclusion 78 n.
  publicity 528 n.
coverlet
  coverlet 226 n.
covert
  plumage 259 n.
  wood 366 n.
  concealed 525 adj.
cover-up
  concealment 525 n.
  falsehood 541 n.
covet
  desire 859 vb.
  envy 912 vb.
covetous
  avaricious 816 adj.
covey

group 74 n.
cow
  cattle 365 n.
  frighten 854 vb.
coward
  coward 856 n.
cowardice
  cowardice 856 n.
cowboy
  rider 268 n.
  herdsman 369 n.
  independent
    744 adj.
  lawless 954 adj.
cower
  stoop 311 vb.
  quake 854 vb.
cowherd, cowgirl
  herdsman 369 n.
cowl
  headgear 228 n.
  canonicals 989 n.
co-worker
  personnel 686 n.
  collaborator 707 n.
cowpuncher
  herdsman 369 n.
cowshed
  stable 192 n.
  cattle pen 369 n.
cox, coxswain
  navigator 270 n.
  direct 689 vb.
coxcomb
  fop 848 n.
coy
  affected 850 adj.
  modest 874 adj.
cozen
  deceive 542 vb.
crab
  fish food 301 n.
  dispraise 924 vb.
crabbed
  sour 393 adj.
  unclear 568 adj.
  sullen 893 adj.
crabwise
  sideways 239 adv.
crack
  break 46 vb.
  weakness 163 n.
  gap 201 n.
  narrowness 206 n.
  furrow 262 n.
  opening 263 n.
  knock 279 n.

  be brittle 330 vb.
  crackle 402 vb.
  decipher 520 vb.
  defect 647 n.
  skilful 694 adj.
  witticism 839 n.
—down on
  be severe 735 vb.
  restrain 747 vb.
—up
  go mad 503 vb.
  advertise 528 vb.
crack at
  attempt 671 n.
crack-brained
  crazy 503 adj.
cracked
  nonresonant
    405 adj.
  discordant 411 adj.
  imperfect 647 adj.
  (*see* **crack**)
crackers
  crazy 503 adj.
crackle
  crackle 402 vb.
crackpot
  absurd 497 adj.
  crank 504 n.
crack shot
  shooter 287 n.
crack troops
  elite 644 n.
cradle
  origin 68 n.
  nonage 130 n.
  seedbed 156 n.
  home 192 n.
  basket 194 n.
  bed 218 n.
  support 218 n.
  pet 889 vb.
cradle song
  soporific 679 n.
craft
  ship 275 n.
  vocation 622 n.
craftsman,
  craftswoman
  producer 164 n.
  artist 556 n.
  artisan 686 n.
  expert 696 n.
craftsmanship
  skill 694 n.
crafty
  intelligent 498 adj.

  cunning 698 adj.
crag
  high land 209 n.
  rock 344 n.
craggy
  sharp 256 adj.
  rough 259 adj.
cram
  fill 54 vb.
  load 193 vb.
  educate 534 vb.
  study 536 vb.
  gluttonize 947 vb.
crammer
  school 539 n.
cramp
  fastening 47 n.
  spasm 318 n.
  hinder 702 vb.
  restrain 747 vb.
cramped
  little 196 adj.
  narrow-minded
    481 adj.
crane
  lifter 310 n.
cranium
  head 213 n.
crank
  nonconformist
    84 n.
  rotate 315 vb.
  crank 504 n.
cranny
  compartment 194 n.
  hiding-place 527 n.
crapulence
  crapulence 949 n.
crash
  ruin 165 n.
  textile 222 n.
  collision 279 n.
  descent 309 n.
  bang 402 n.
  fail 728 vb.
  insolvency 805 n.
crash helmet
  safeguard 662 n.
crash landing
  aeronautics 271 n.
crass
  unintelligent
    499 adj.
  vulgar 847 adj.
crate
  basket 194 n.
  vehicle 274 n.

crater
cavity 255 n.
cravat
neckwear 228 n.
crave
require 627 vb.
request 761 vb.
desire 859 vb.
craven
cowardly 856 adj.
crawl
be in motion 265 vb.
move slowly 278 vb.
be servile 879 vb.
—with
be many 104 vb.
superabound
  637 vb.
crayon
art equipment 553 n.
craze
variegate 437 vb.
make mad 503 vb.
fashion 848 n.
crazy
obsessed 455 adj.
absurd 497 adj.
crazy 503 adj.
creak
stridor 407 n.
cream
milk 301 n.
fat 357 n.
select 605 vb.
elite 644 n.
cosmetic 843 n.
—off
impair 655 vb.
creamy
semiliquid 354 adj.
savoury 390 adj.
whitish 427 adj.
crease
jumble 63 vb.
fold 261 n.vb.
create
cause 156 vb.
produce 164 vb.
be angry 891 vb.
creation
originality 21 n.
production 164 n.
universe 321 n.
representation
  551 n.
creative
original 21 adj.

productive 164 adj.
imaginative 513 adj.
creator
cause 156 n.
producer 164 n.
the Deity 965 n.
creature
product 164 n.
animal 365 n.
person 371 n.
instrument 628 n.
dependant 742 n.
creature of habit
habitué 610 n.
crèche
school 539 n.
credence
belief 485 n.
credential
credential 466 n.
credible
plausible 471 adj.
credible 485 adj.
credit
attribute 158 vb.
believe 485 vb.
subvention 703 n.
lend 784 vb.
credit 802 n.vb.
account 808 vb.
repute 866 n.
thanks 907 n.
dueness 915 n.
creditable
excellent 644 adj.
approvable
  923 adj.
credit card
borrowing 785 n.
creditor
creditor 802 n.
credit side
gain 771 n.
credit squeeze
economy 814 n.
credit-worthy
reputable 866 adj.
deserving 915 adj.
credo
creed 485 n.
credulity
credulity 487 n.
persuadability
  612 n.
credulous
credulous 487 adj.
gullible 544 adj.

creed
creed 485 n.
orthodoxy 976 n.
creek
gulf 345 n.
creep
move slowly 278 vb.
itch 378 vb.
be stealthy 525 vb.
be servile 879 vb.
—out
emerge 298 vb.
—up on
surprise 508 vb.
creeper
plant 366 n.
creeps
formication 378 n.
nervousness 854 n.
creepy-crawly
creepy-crawly
  365 n.
bane 659 n.
cremation
interment 364 n.
burning 381 n.
crematorium
interment 364 n.
crenellate
notch 260 vb.
Creole
settler 191 n.
crescendo
increase 36 n.
loudness 400 n.
crescent
housing 192 n.
arc 250 n.
moon 321 n.
religious faith 973 n.
crest
superiority 34 n.
summit 213 n.
plumage 259 n.
heraldry 547 n.
nobility 868 n.
crestfallen
dejected 834 adj.
humbled 872 adj.
cretin
fool 501 n.
crevice
gap 201 n.
crew
band 74 n.
navigate 269 vb.
mariner 270 n.

personnel 686 n.
crib
copy 22 n.
bed 218 n.
translation 520 n.
borrow 785 vb.
crick
pang 377 n.
cricket
insect 365 n.
ball game 837 n.
cri de coeur
lament 836 n.
crier
publicizer 528 n.
crime
foul play 930 n.
lawbreaking 954 n.
crime passionel
revenge 910 n.
jealousy 911 n.
crime wave
lawlessness 954 n.
criminal
offender 904 n.
rascally 930 adj.
guilty 936 adj.
criminal offence
lawbreaking 954 n.
criminologist
detective 459 n.
crimp
crinkle 251 vb.
crimson,
red 431 adj.
cringe
stoop 311 vb.
be servile 879 vb.
crinkle
crinkle 251 vb.
fold 261 n.
crinoline
skirt 228 n.
cripple
disable 161 vb.
weaken 163 vb.
sick person 651 n.
crisis
crisis 137 n.
event 154 n.
predicament 700 n.
crisp
crinkle 251 vb.
brittle 330 adj.
concise 569 adj.
crisscross
crossed 222 adj.

criterion
testing agent 461 n.
comparison 462 n.
critic
estimator 480 n.
dissentient 489 n.
theorist 512 n.
interpreter 520 n.
dissertator 591 n.
malcontent 829 n.
people of taste
846 n.
detractor 926 n.
critical
crucial 137 adj.
discriminating
463 adj.
important 638 adj.
sick 651 adj.
dangerous 661 adj.
discontented
829 adj.
fastidious 862 adj.
disapproving
924 adj.
criticism
estimate 480 n.
interpretation 520 n.
article 591 n.
advice 691 n.
censure 924 n.
criticize
be discontented
829 vb.
(*see* **criticism**)
critique
estimate 480 n.
croak
rasp 407 vb.
ululate 409 vb.
croaker
malcontent 829 n.
crochet
needlework 844 n.
crock
vessel 194 n.
crockery
pottery 381 n.
crocodile
procession 71 n.
reptile 365 n.
crocodile tears
duplicity 541 n.
croft
farm 370 n.
crofter
farmer 370 n.

cromlech
monument 548 n.
crone
old woman 133 n.
crony
chum 880 n.
crook
prop 218 n.
make oblique
220 vb.
angularity 247 n.
offender 904 n.
knave 938 n.
crooked
oblique 220 adj.
distorted 246 adj.
deviating 282 adj.
dishonest 930 adj.
croon
sing 413 vb.
crooner
vocalist 413 n.
entertainer 594 n.
crop
product 164 n.
maw 194 n.
shorten 204 vb.
graze 301 vb.
agriculture 370 n.
store 632 n.
hairdressing 843 n.
—up
happen 154 vb.
cropper
descent 309 n.
croquet
ball game 837 n.
crosier
vestments 989 n.
cross
hybrid 43 n.
counteract 182 vb.
cross 222 n.vb.
pass 305 vb.
bane 659 n.
opposing 704 adj.
decoration 729 n.
angry 891 adj.
religious faith 973 n.
—oneself
perform ritual
988 vb.
—one's fingers
deprecate 762 vb.
—out
mark 547 vb.
obliterate 550 vb.

—over
pass 305 vb.
apostatize 603 vb.
—the Rubicon
overstep 306 vb.
cross-bencher
opponent 705 n.
free person 744 n.
crossbow
missile weapon
723 n.
cross-bred
mixed 43 adj.
cross-country
towards 281 adv.
pedestrianism
267 n.
crosscurrent
counteraction 182 n.
current 350 n.
opposition 704 n.
cross-examine
interrogate 459 vb.
cross-examiner
questioner 459 n.
cross-eyed
dim-sighted 440 adj.
cross-fire
bombardment
712 n.
cross-grained
wilful 602 adj.
sullen 893 adj.
cross-hatch
groove 262 vb.
darken 418 vb.
crossing
crossing 222 n.
water travel 269 n.
passage 305 n.
crosspatch
moper 834 n.
cross-purposes
misinterpretation
521 n.
cross-question
interrogate 459 vb.
cross-reference
referral 9 n.
class 62 vb.
crossroads
juncture 8 n.
divergence 294 n.
road 624 n.
cross-section
example 83 n.
crosswind

obstacle 702 n.
crosswise
obliquely 220 adv.
crossword
enigma 530 n.
crotch
angularity 247 n.
crotchet
angularity 247 n.
notation 410 n.
whim 604 n.
crotchety
irascible 892 adj.
crouch
be low 210 vb.
stoop 311 vb.
be servile 879 vb.
croup
buttocks 238 n.
respiratory disease
651 n.
croupier
treasurer 798 n.
crow
black thing 428 n.
triumph 727 vb.
boast 877 vb.
crowbar
tool 630 n.
crowd
crowd 74 n.
multitude 104 n.
be dense 324 vb.
onlookers 441 n.
rabble 869 n.
crown
completeness 54 n.
vertex 213 n.
crown 213 vb.
strike 279 vb.
climax 725 vb.
authority 733 n.
regalia 743 n.
crowned head
sovereign 741 n.
crucial
crucial 137 adj.
fundamental
156 adj.
important 638 adj.
crucial moment
juncture 8 n.
crisis 137 n.
crucible
heater 383 n.
crucifix
cross 222 n.

crucifixion
killing 362 n.
suffering 825 n.
cruciform
crossed 222 adj.
crucify
give pain 377 vb.
ill-treat 645 vb.
execute 963 vb.
crude
inelegant 576 adj.
immature 670 adj.
graceless 842 adj.
cruel
violent 176 adj.
cruel 898 adj.
pitiless 906 adj.
cruelty
inhumanity 898 n.
cruise
water travel 269 n.
cruiser
warship 722 n.
crumb(s)
small thing 33 n.
leavings 41 n.
powder 332 n.
crumble
break 46 vb.
decompose 51 vb.
be brittle 330 vb.
pulverize 332 vb.
crumbling
antiquated 127 adj.
weakened 163 adj.
unsafe 661 adj.
crumbly
fragmentary 53 adj.
crumple
jumble 63 vb.
crinkle 251 vb.
fold 261 n.vb.
crunch
chew 301 vb.
pulverize 332 vb.
rasp 407 vb.
crupper
buttocks 238 n.
crusade
action 676 n.
war 718 n.
crusader
militarist 722 n.
philanthropist 901 n.
zealot 979 n.
crush

jumble 63 vb.
crowd 74 n.
demolish 165 vb.
make smaller 198 vb.
pulverize 332 vb.
confute 479 vb.
defeat 727 vb.
oppress 735 vb.
humiliate 872 vb.
love 887 n.
crushing
destructive 165 adj.
laborious 682 adj.
completive 725 adj.
distressing 827 adj.
crust
exteriority 223 n.
covering 226 n.
skin 226 n.
cereals 301 n.
mouthful 301 n.
crustacean
marine life 365 n.
crusty
irascible 892 adj.
crutch
prop 218 n.
angularity 247 n.
crux
enigma 530 n.
chief thing 638 n.
cry
be loud 400 vb.
cry 408 n.vb.
proclaim 528 vb.
weep 836 vb.
—down
underestimate 483 vb.
detract 926 vb.
—for the moon
waste effort 641 vb.
desire 859 vb.
—out
vociferate 408 vb.
—up
advertise 528 vb.
exaggerate 546 vb.
—wolf
be false 541 vb.
raise the alarm 665 vb.
crybaby
weakling 163 n.
cryonic suspension
refrigeration 382 n.

crypt
cellar 194 n.
church interior 990 n.
cryptanalysis
hermeneutics 520 n.
cryptic
occult 523 adj.
concealed 525 adj.
cabbalistic 984 adj.
crypto-
latent 523 adj.
cryptogram
enigma 530 n.
cryptographer
interpreter 520 n.
crystal
solid body 324 n.
transparency 422 n.
crystal ball
oracle 511 n.
crystal-gazer
diviner 511 n.
occultist 984 n.
crystalline
hard 326 adj.
transparent 422 adj.
crystallization
conversion 147 n.
condensation 324 n.
cub
young creature 132 n.
youngster 132 n.
cubbyhole
retreat 192 n.
compartment 194 n.
cube
treble 94 vb.
angular figure 247 n.
cubic
spatial 183 adj.
metrical 465 adj.
cubicle
chamber 194 n.
compartment 194 n.
cuckold
cuckold 952 n.
cuckoo
repetition 106 n.
bird 365 n.
crazy 503 adj.
cuckoo in the nest
intruder 59 n.
cud
mouthful 301 n.

cuddle
caress 889 vb.
cudgel
hammer 279 n.
club 723 n.
cue
hint 524 n.
dramaturgy 594 n.
cuff
garment 228 n.
fold 261 n.
knock 279 n.
corporal punishment 963 n.
cuirass
armour 713 n.
cuisine
cookery 301 n.
cul-de-sac
closure 264 n.
obstacle 702 n.
culinary
culinary 301 adj.
cull
killing 362 n.
select 605 vb.
culminate
culminate 34 vb.
crown 213 vb.
climax 725 vb.
culottes
skirt 228 n.
culpable
wrong 914 adj.
blameworthy 924 adj.
guilty 936 adj.
culprit
offender 904 n.
accused person 928 n.
cult
fashion 848 n.
affectation 850 n.
cult 981 n.
cult image
idol 982 n.
cultivate
cultivate 370 vb.
make better 654 vb.
flatter 925 vb.
cultivated
instructed 490 adj.
cultivation
agriculture 370 n.
culture 490 n.
good taste 846 n.

cultivator
farmer 370 n.
cultural
educational 534 adj.
improving 654 adj.
culture
culture 490 n.
civilization 654 n.
cultured
instructed 490 adj.
culvert
drain 351 n.
cumbersome
unwieldy 195 adj.
weighty 322 adj.
clumsy 695 adj.
cumulative
increasing 36 adj.
cumulativeness
continuity 71 n.
cuneiform
lettering 586 n.
cunning
wise 498 adj.
skill 694 n.
cunning 698 n.adj.
dishonest 930 adj.
cup
cup 194 n.
support 218 vb.
cavity 255 n.
alcoholic drink 301 n.
trophy 729 n.
cupboard
cabinet 194 n.
storage 632 n.
cupful
contents 193 n.
cupidity
avarice 816 n.
desire 859 n.
cupola
roof 226 n.
dome 253 n.
cur
dog 365 n.
cad 938 n.
curable
restored 656 adj.
medical 658 adj.
curate
pastor 986 n.
curative
remedial 658 adj.
curator
protector 660 n.

keeper 749 n.
curb
moderate 177 vb.
retard 278 vb.
restrain 747 vb.
fetter 748 n.
curdle
be dense 324 vb.
thicken 354 vb.
curds
milk 301 n.
cure
cure 656 vb.
remedy 658 n.
therapy 658 n.
preserve 666 vb.
—of
disaccustom 611 vb.
cure-all
remedy 658 n.
curettage
voidance 300 n.
curfew
restriction 747 n.
curia
council 692 n.
curie
radiation 417 n.
curio
exhibit 522 n.
curiosity
curiosity 453 n.
curl
filament 208 n.
curve 248 n.
loop 250 n.
coil 251 n.
hairdressing 843 n.
curlicue
coil 251 n.
pattern 844 n.
curly
undulatory 251 adj.
hairy 259 adj.
currency
generality 79 n.
publicity 528 n.
money 797 n.
current
general 79 adj.
present 121 adj.
direction 281 n.
current 350 n.
published 528 adj.
usual 610 adj.
current affairs
affairs 154 n.

curriculum
curriculum 534 n.
curriculum vitae
biography 590 n.
curry
dish 301 n.
season 388 vb.
—favour
be servile 879 vb.
currycomb
rub 333 vb.
groom 369 vb.
curse
influence 178 n.
bane 659 n.
adversity 731 n.
malediction 899 n.
curse 899 vb.
be impious 980 vb.
bewitch 983 vb.
cursive
written 586 adj.
cursory
transient 114 adj.
inattentive 456 adj.
curt
concise 569 adj.
taciturn 582 adj.
curtail
subtract 39 vb.
cut 46 vb.
shorten 204 vb.
curtain
partition 231 n.
screen 421 vb.n.
stage set 594 n.
curtain call
recurrence 106 n.
curtain-raiser
beginning 68 n.
curtains
finality 69 n.
curtsy, curtsey
show respect 920 vb.
curvaceous
curved 248 adj.
shapely 841 adj.
curvature
curvature 248 n.
curve
make oblique 220 vb.
curve 248 n.
deviate 282 vb.
curvet
leap 312 n.vb.

cushion
moderate 177 vb.
cushion 218 n.
support 218 vb.
softness 327 n.
protection 660 n.
cushy
comfortable 376 adj.
easy 701 adj.
cusp
sharp point 256 n.
cussedness
obstinacy 602 n.
malevolence 898 n.
custard
dessert 301 n.
custodial
tutelary 660 adj.
custodian
protector 660 n.
keeper 749 n.
custody
protection 660 n.
detention 747 n.
custom
tradition 127 n.
habit 610 n.
purchase 792 n.
etiquette 848 n.
customary
general 79 adj.
habitual 610 adj.
customer
patron 707 n.
purchaser 792 n.
customs
conduct 688 n.
tax 809 n.
cut
diminution 37 n.
decrement 42 n.
cut 46 vb.
piece 53 n.
shorten 204 vb.
form 243 n.vb.
excavation 255 n.
be sharp 256 vb.
notch 260 vb.
meat 301 n.
fell 311 vb.
give pain 377 vb.
engrave 555 vb.
wound 655 n.vb.
portion 783 n.
discount 810 n.
cheapen 812 vb.

make unwelcome
883 vb.
be rude 885 vb.
—a dash
be ostentatious
875 vb.
—and run
move fast 277 vb.
decamp 296 vb.
—back
subtract 39 vb.
economize 814 vb.
—both ways
tell against 467 vb.
be equivocal 518 vb.
—corners
hasten 680 vb.
—down
fell 311 vb.
—down to size
detract 926 vb.
—in
converse 584 vb.
—no ice
be unimportant
639 vb.
—off
set apart 46 vb.
circumscribe
232 vb.
hinder 702 vb.
—out
form 243 vb.
extract 304 vb.
—through
pierce 263 vb.
cut above, a
superior 34 adj.
cut and dried
arranged 62 adj.
definite 80 adj.
cut and thrust
argument 475 n.
fight 716 n.
cutaneous
dermal 226 adj.
cute
personable 841 adj.
affected 850 adj.
cuticle
skin 226 n.
cutlass
sidearms 723 n.
cutlery
sharp edge 256 n.
cut out for
fit 24 adj.

cut price
discount 810 n.
cutter
sharp edge 256 n.
boat 275 n.
artisan 686 n.
cutthroat
destructive 165 adj.
murderer 362 n.
ruffian 904 n.
cutting
scission 46 n.
excavation 255 n.
sharp 256 adj.
plant 366 n.
cinema 445 n.
cuttings
anthology 592 n.
cyan
blueness 435 n.
cyanide
poison 659 n.
cybernetics
data processing
86 n.
mechanics 630 n.
cycle
recurrence 106 n.
era 110 n.
regular return 141 n.
ride 267 vb.
bicycle 274 n.
cyclist
rider 268 n.
cyclone
storm 176 n.
gale 352 n.
cyclostyle
copy 20 vb.
cygnet
young creature
132 n.
cylinder
cylinder 252 n.
cylindrical
rotund 252 adj.
tubular 263 adj.
cymbals
gong 414 n.
cynic
misanthrope 902 n.
detractor 926 n.
cynical
unbelieving
486 adj.
detracting 926 adj.
cynicism

moral insensibility
820 n.
hopelessness 853 n.
cynosure
prototype 23 n.
focus 76 n.
attraction 291 n.
favourite 890 n.
cyst
bladder 194 n.
ulcer 651 n.
cytology
biology 358 n.

D

dab
knock 279 n.
dabble
moisten 341 vb.
experiment 461 vb.
—in
not know 491 vb.
amuse onself
837 vb.
dab hand
proficient person
696 n.
dactyl
prosody 593 n.
dactylology
deafness 416 n.
dad, daddy
paternity 169 n.
dado
ornamental art
844 n.
daedal
ornamental 844 adj.
daft
foolish 499 adj.
crazy 503 adj.
dagger
sharp point 256 n.
sidearms 723 n.
daily
often 139 adv.
seasonal 141 adj.
the press 528 n.
usual 610 adj.
servant 742 n.
daily bread
food 301 n.
vocation 622 n.
daily round
regular return 141 n.
habit 610 n.

dainty
small 33 adj.
little 196 adj.
savoury 390 adj.
clean 648 adj.
personable 841 adj.
fastidious 862 adj.
dairy
chamber 194 n.
dairymaid
domestic 742 n.
dais
stand 218 n.
rostrum 539 n.
dale
valley 255 n.
dalliance
endearment 889 n.
dally
be inactive 679 vb.
amuse oneself
837 vb.
caress 889 vb.
dam
maternity 169 n.
lake 346 n.
dam (up)
close 264 vb.
obstruct 702 vb.
damage
break 46 vb.
harm 645 vb.
impair 655 vb.
damages
restitution 787 n.
penalty 963 n.
damaging
harmful 645 adj.
discreditable
867 adj.
damask
textile 222 n.
dame
lady 373 n.
person of repute
866 n.
damn
curse 899 vb.
cuss 899 vb.
condemn 961 vb.
damnable
damnable 645 adj.
damnation
condemnation
961 n.
damp
water 339 n.

moisture 341 n.
extinguish 382 vb.
dampen
moderate 177 vb.
mute 401 vb.
depress 834 vb.
damper
moderator 177 n.
stopper 264 n.
mute 414 n.
moper 834 n.
disapprover
　924 n.
damp-proof
dry 342 adj.
damp squib
disappointment
　509 n.
failure 728 n.
dance
be in motion 265 vb.
leap 312 vb.
shine 417 vb.
ballet 594 n.
be excited 821 vb.
dance 837 n.vb.
dancer
jumper 312 n.
entertainer 594 n.
dance 837 n.
dandified
fashionable 848 adj.
affected 850 adj.
dandle
caress 889 vb.
dandruff
dirt 649 n.
dandy
fop 848 n.
danger
probability 471 n.
danger 661 n.
danger-loving
unfearing 855 adj.
rash 857 adj.
dangerous
dangerous 661 adj.
frightening 854 adj.
malevolent 898 adj.
danger signal
warning 664 n.
danger signal 665 n.
dangle
come unstuck 49 vb.
hang 217 vb.
oscillate 317 vb.
tempt 612 vb.

dank
humid 341 adj.
dapper
personable 841 adj.
dapple
variegate 437 vb.
dare
face danger 661 vb.
undertake 672 vb.
defy 711 vb.
be courageous
　855 vb.
daredevil
brave person 855 n.
desperado 857 n.
rash 857 adj.
daring
showy 875 adj.
unchaste 951 adj.
(see **dare**)
dark
evening 129 n.
dark 418 adj.
black 428 adj.
invisible 444 adj.
latent 523 adj.
cheerless 834 adj.
sullen 893 adj.
cabbalistic 984 adj.
darken
darken 418 vb.
bedim 419 vb.
blur 440 vb.
depress 834 vb.
dark glasses
screen 421 n.
dark horse
unknown thing
　491 n.
darkness
darkness 418 n.
(see **dark**)
dark-skinned
blackish 428 adj.
darling
loved one 887 n.
darling 890 n.
darn
repair 656 n.
dart
move fast 277 vb.
missile 287 n.
darts
indoor game 837 n.
dash
small quantity 33 n.
tincture 43 n.

vigorousness 174 n.
spurt 277 n.
move fast 277 vb.
strike 279 vb.
punctuation 547 n.
hasten 680 vb.
racing 716 n.
defeat 727 vb.
courage 855 n.
ostentation 875 n.
—off
move fast 277 vb.
write 586 vb.
dastard
coward 856 n.
data
data processing
　86 n.
evidence 466 n.
data bank
data processing
　86 n.
memory 505 n.
data base
information 524 n.
data processing
data processing
　86 n.
microelectronics
　196 n.
date
date 108 n.
chronology 117 vb.
social round 882 n.
dated
antiquated 127 adj.
daub
coat 226 vb.
colour 425 vb.
picture 553 n.
make unclean
　649 vb.
dauber
artist 556 n.
bungler 697 n.
daughter
descendant 170 n.
daunt
dissuade 613 vb.
dauntless
unfearing 855 adj.
davit
hanger 217 n.
dawdle ·
be late 136 vb.
wander 267 vb.
move slowly 278 vb.

dawdler
slowcoach 278 n.
idler 679 n.
dawn
precursor 66 n.
beginning 68 n.
morning 128 n.
appear 445 vb.
—on
dawn upon 449 vb.
day
date 108 n.
period 110 n.
daybreak
morning 128 n.
day centre
meeting place
　192 n.
daydream
fantasy 513 n.
desire 859 n.vb.
abstractedness
　456 n.
daylight
interval 201 n.
light 417 n.
manifestation
　522 n.
disclosure 526 n.
day off
repose 683 n.
day of judgement
finality 69 n.
day of reckoning
revenge 910 n.
punishment 963 n.
day out
amusement 837 n.
daytime
morning 128 n.
daze
distract 456 vb.
puzzle 474 vb.
dazed
wondering 864 adj.
dazzle
light 417 n.
shine 417 vb.
blind 439 vb.
blur 440 vb.
distract 456 vb.
deceive 542 vb.
impress 821 vb.
be ostentatious
　875 vb.
command respect
　920 vb.

dazzling
excellent 644 adj.
splendid 841 adj.
D-day
start 68 n.
special day 876 n.
deacon, deaconess
church officer 986 n.
lay person 987 n.
deactivate
counteract 182 vb.
deactivated
inert 175 adj.
dead
extinct 2 adj.
inert 175 adj.
dead 361 adj.
nonresonant
405 adj.
abrogated 752 adj.
dead and buried
past 125 adj.
forgotten 506 adj.
dead beat
fatigued 684 adj.
dead body
corpse 363 n.
dead duck
hopelessness 853 n.
deaden
render insensible
375 vb.
mute 401 vb.
make mute 578 vb.
make insensitive
820 vb.
dead end
closure 264 n.
obstacle 702 n.
deadfall
trap 542 n.
dead heat
draw 28 n.
dead letter
ineffectuality 161 n.
abrogation 752 n.
deadline
limit 236 n.
deadlock
equilibrium 28 n.
stop 145 n.
inaction 677 n.
difficulty 700 n.
defeat 728 n.
dead loss
lost labour 641 n.
deadly

destructive 165 adj.
deadly 362 adj.
toxic 653 adj.
dull 840 adj.
malevolent 898 adj.
dead march
obsequies 364 n.
dead of night
midnight 129 n.
darkness 418 n.
dead-on
accurate 494 adj.
deadpan
impassive 820 adj.
dead reckoning
navigation 269 n.
dead set
attempt 671 n.
dead stop
stop 145 n.
dead weight
encumbrance 702 n.
dead wood
rubbish 641 n.
deaf
deaf 416 adj.
deaf-aid
hearing aid 415 n.
deaf and dumb
deaf 416 adj.
voiceless 578 adj.
deafen
be loud 400 vb.
deafen 416 vb.
deaf to
refusing 760 adj.
deal
great quantity 32 n.
deed 676 n.
compact 765 n.
apportionment
783 n.
—in
do 676 vb.
trade 791 vb.
—with
be related 9 vb.
dissertate 591 vb.
trade 791 vb.
dealer
merchant 794 n.
dealings
deed 676 n.
dean
director 690 n.
ecclesiarch 986 n.
dear

profitless 641 adj.
dear 811 adj.
lovable 887 adj.
darling 890 n.
dearth
scarcity 636 n.
death
extinction 2 n.
death 361 n.
deathbed
late 136 adj.
decease 361 n.
illness 651 n.
death blow
end 69 n.
killing 362 n.
defeat 728 n.
death chamber
means of execution
964 n.
death knell
warning 664 n.
deathless
perpetual 115 adj.
renowned 866 adj.
deathly
cadaverous 363 adj.
colourless 426 adj.
death of
worry 825 n.
annoyance 827 n.
death rate
statistics 86 n.
death roll 361 n.
death ray
weapon 723 n.
death sentence
capital punishment
963 n.
death's-head
intimidation 854 n.
death trap ·
danger 661 n.
pitfall 663 n.
death wish
dejection 834 n.
debacle
ruin 165 n.
debag
uncover 229 vb.
debar
exclude 57 vb.
prohibit 757 vb.
debase
pervert 655 vb.
vulgarize 847 vb.
demonetize 797 vb.

debatable
topical 452 adj.
moot 459 adj.
uncertain 474 adj.
debate
argue 475 vb.
conference 584 n.
debater
reasoner 475 n.
debauch
debauch 951 vb.
debauched
vicious 934 adj.
sensual 944 adj.
lecherous 951 adj.
debauchery
intemperance 943 n.
debenture
title deed 767 n.
debilitate
weaken 163 vb.
debility
weakness 163 n.
ill health 651 n.
debit
debt 803 n.
debonair
cheerful 833 adj.
debris
remainder 41 n.
rubbish 641 n.
debt
debt 803 n.
dueness 915 n.
debt-collector
receiver 782 n.
debtor
debtor 803 n.
debug
rectify 654 vb.
debunk
ridicule 851 vb.
humiliate 872 vb.
debus
land 295 vb.
debut
debut 68 n.
debutant(e)
beginner 538 n.
decade
period 110 n.
decadence
deterioration 655 n.
decadent
sensualist 944 n.
decamp
decamp 296 vb.

decant
transpose 272 vb.
make flow 350 vb.
decanter
vessel 194 n.
decapitate
execute 963 vb.
decay
decay 51 n.
decompose 51 vb.
oldness 127 n.
desuetude 611 n.
dirt 649 n.
dilapidation 655 n.
decease
decease 361 n.
deceit
deception 542 n.
deceitful
false 541 adj.
deceiving 542 adj.
deceive
mislead 495 vb.
deceive 542 vb.
defraud 788 vb.
be impure 951 vb.
deceiver
deceiver 545 n.
deceiving
appearing 445 adj.
disappointing
509 adj.
deceleration
slowness 278 n.
decency
good taste 846 n.
purity 950 n.
decent
not bad 644 adj.
middling 732 adj.
ethical 917 adj.
decentralization
nonuniformity 17 n.
dispersion 75 n.
deception
visual fallacy 440 n.
deception 542 n.
deceptive
simulating 18 adj.
erroneous 495 adj.
disappointing
509 adj.
deceiving 542 adj.
decibel
sound 398 n.
decide
cause 156 vb.

judge 480 vb.
be resolute 599 vb.
decided
assertive 532 adj.
volitional 595 adj.
deciduous
ephemeral 114 adj.
vegetal 366 adj.
decimal
numerical element
85 n.
decimate
render few 105 vb.
slaughter 362 vb.
execute 963 vb.
decipher
decipher 520 vb.
decipherable
intelligible 516 adj.
decision
judgement 480 n.
resolution 599 n.
choice 605 n.
intention 617 n.
decree 737 n.
decision-making
management 689 n.
decisive
crucial 137 adj.
causal 156 adj.
deck
layer 207 n.
overlay 226 vb.
gramophone 414 n.
decorate 844 vb.
deckhand
mariner 270 n.
declaim
orate 579 vb.
declamation
magniloquence
574 n.
oratory 579 n.
declaration
affirmation 532 n.
declare
divulge 526 vb.
proclaim 528 vb.
affirm 532 vb.
speak 579 vb.
declension
grammar 564 n.
declination
situation 186 n.
decline
decrease 37 n.vb.
weakness 163 n.

regression 286 n.
parse 564 vb.
reject 607 vb.
deteriorate 655 vb.
refuse 760 vb.
declivity
incline 220 n.
descent 309 n.
decoction
draught 301 n.
decode
decipher 520 vb.
décolleté
bareness 229 n.
decolorant
bleacher 426 n.
decomposable
decomposable
51 adj.
decompose
decompose 51 vb.
disperse 75 vb.
deconsecrate
laicize 987 vb.
deconsecrated
profane 980 adj.
decontaminate
purify 648 vb.
decontrol
liberate 746 vb.
nonretention 779 n.
décor
spectacle 445 n.
stage set 594 n.
decorate
coat 226 vb.
exaggerate 546 vb.
beautify 841 vb.
decorate 844 vb.
dignify 866 vb.
decoration
decoration 729 n.
badge of rank 743 n.
(*see* **decorate**)
decorative
ornamental 844 adj.
decorous
fit 24 adj.
well-bred 848 adj.
decorum
good taste 846 n.
decoy
trap 542 n.
trickster 545 n.
incentive 612 n.
decrease
decrease 37 n.vb.

deterioration 655 n.
decreasing
few 105 adj.
decree
judgement 480 n.
decree 737 n.vb.
divorce 896 n.
legislation 953 n.
decrement
decrement 42 n.
shortfall 307 n.
loss 772 n.
decrepit
ageing 131 adj.
unhealthy 651 adj.
dilapidated 655 adj.
decry
hold cheap 922 vb.
detract 926 vb.
dedicate
offer 759 vb.
give 781 vb.
dignify 866 vb.
sanctify 979 vb.
dedicated
resolute 599 adj.
obedient 739 adj.
disinterested
931 adj.
deduce
reason 475 vb.
deduct
subtract 39 vb.
deduction
decrement 42 n.
reasoning 475 n.
discount 810 n.
deed
deed 676 n.
title deed 767 n.
prowess 855 n.
deem
opine 485 vb.
deep
spacious 183 adj.
deep 211 adj.
ocean 343 n.
loud 400 adj.
inexpressible
517 adj.
latent 523 adj.
unclear 568 adj.
felt 818 adj.
deep down
inside 224 adv.
deepen
augment 36 vb.

be deep 211 vb.
blacken 428 vb.
aggravate 832 vb.
deep-freeze
refrigerator 384 n.
preservation 666 n.
deep in
attentive 455 adj.
deep-laid
matured 669 adj.
cunning 698 adj.
deep-rooted
lasting 113 adj.
fixed 153 adj.
deep 211 adj.
habitual 610 adj.
deep-sea
seafaring 269 adj.
deep-seated
intrinsic 5 adj.
lasting 113 adj.
interior 224 adj.
felt 818 adj.
deer
speeder 277 n.
mammal 365 n.
deface
destroy 165 vb.
obliterate 550 vb.
impair 655 vb.
make ugly 842 vb.
blemish 845 vb.
defalcate
be dishonest
930 vb.
defalcation
nonpayment 805 n.
defamation
detraction 926 n.
defamatory
detracting 926 adj.
defame
defame 926 vb.
accuse 928 vb.
default
deficit 55 n.
negligence 458 n.
nonpayment 805 n.
fail in duty 918 vb.
defeat
confute 479 vb.
defeat 727 vb.
defeat 728 n.
defeatism
dejection 834 n.
hopelessness 853 n.
cowardice 856 n.

defeatist
alarmist 854 n.
defecation
defecation 302 n.
defect
shortfall 307 n.
insufficiency 636 n.
defect 647 n.
defection
change of allegiance
603 n.
undutifulness 918 n.
perfidy 930 n.
defective
incomplete 55 adj.
insane 503 adj.
imperfect 647 adj.
defence
counterevidence
467 n.
defence 713 n.
legal trial 959 n.
defenceless
defenceless 161 adj.
vulnerable 661 adj.
defences
defences 713 n.
defend
patronize 703 vb.
defend 713 vb.
defendant
accused person
928 n.
litigant 959 n.
defender
protector 660 n.
patron 707 n.
defender 713 n.
defensible
defended 713 adj.
vindicable 927 adj.
defensive
defending 713 adj.
nervous 854 adj.
defer
put off 136 vb.
deference
submission 721 n.
respect 920 n.
deferential
servile 879 adj.
respectful 920 adj.
deferment
delay 136 n.
defiance
affirmation 532 n.
negation 533 n.

opposition 704 n.
defiance 711 n.
insolence 878 n.
defiant
unconformable
84 adj.
undisguised
522 adj.
deficiency
inferiority 35 n.
insufficiency 636 n.
defect 647 n.
deficient
deficient 307 adj.
unintelligent
499 adj.
deficit
deficit 55 n.
shortfall 307 n.
defile
narrowness 206 n.
make unclean
649 vb.
impair 655 vb.
debauch 951 vb.
be impious 980 vb.
define
specify 80 vb.
limit 236 vb.
interpret 520 vb.
definite
definite 80 adj.
limited 236 adj.
positive 473 adj.
accurate 494 adj.
assertive 532 adj.
definition
visibility 443 n.
perspicuity 567 n.
definitive
ending 69 adj.
interpretive 520 adj.
deflate
make smaller
198 vb.
ridicule 851 vb.
humiliate 872 vb.
detract 926 vb.
deflation
decrease 37 n.
finance 797 n.
cheapness 812 n.
deflect
make oblique
220 vb.
deflect 282 vb.
parry 713 vb.

deflection
deviation 282 n.
deflower
debauch 951 vb.
defoliant
poison 659 n.
defoliate
lay waste 165 vb.
deform
distort 246 vb.
misrepresent
552 vb.
impair 655 vb.
make ugly 842 vb.
deformed
abnormal 84 adj.
crippled 163 adj.
imperfect 647 adj.
defraud
defraud 788 vb.
be dishonest 930 vb.
defrauder
trickster 545 n.
defrauder 789 n.
defrock
shame 867 vb.
defrost
heat 381 vb.
deft
skilful 694 adj.
defunct
extinct 2 adj.
dead 361 adj.
defy
negate 533 vb.
be resolute 599 vb.
defy 711 vb.
disobey 738 vb.
degauss
counteract 182 vb.
degeneracy
deterioration 655 n.
wickedness 934 n.
degenerate
be turned to 147 vb.
deteriorate 655 vb.
relapse 657 vb.
vicious 934 adj.
cad 938 n.
degenerative
diseased 651 adj.
degrade
impair 655 vb.
pervert 655 vb.
depose 752 vb.
shame 867 vb.
not respect 921 vb.

degree
relativeness 9 n.
degree 27 n.
series 71 n.
angular measure
  247 n.
thermometry 379 n.
measurement 465 n.
importance 638 n.
honours 866 n.
dehumanize
pervert 655 vb.
make wicked
  934 vb.
dehydrate
dry 342 vb.
preserve 666 vb.
deification
deification 982 n.
deify
dignify 866 vb.
idolatrize 982 vb.
deign
consent 758 vb.
deism
deism 973 n.
religion 973 n.
deity
divineness 965 n.
deity 966 n.
déjà vu
bore 838 n.
psychics 984 n.
dejected
unhappy 825 adj.
dejected 834 adj.
de jure
due 915 adj.
legal 953 adj.
delay
delay 136 n.
lull 145 n.
inaction 677 n.
delectable
savoury 390 adj.
pleasurable 826 adj.
delegate
councillor 692 n.
commission
  751 vb.
delegate 754 n.
delete
obliterate 550 vb.
deleterious
harmful 645 adj.
deliberate
slow 278 adj.

predetermined
  608 adj.
intended 617 adj.
consult 691 vb.
deliberation
meditation 449 n.
caution 858 n.
delicacy
savouriness 390 n.
discrimination
  463 n.
ill health 651 n.
good taste 846 n.
fastidiousness
  862 n.
delicate
flimsy 163 adj.
brittle 330 adj.
soft-hued 425 adj.
difficult 700 adj.
delicatessen
food 301 n.
delicious
pleasant 376 adj.
savoury 390 adj.
sweet 392 adj.
pleasurable 826 adj.
delight
joy 824 n.
delight 826 vb.
amusement 837 n.
delightful
pleasant 376 adj.
pleasurable 826 adj.
delimit
limit 236 vb.
mark 547 vb.
delineate
outline 233 vb.
describe 590 vb.
delinquency
wickedness 934 n.
guilt 936 n.
delinquent
troublemaker 663 n.
offender 904 n.
delirious
frenzied 503 adj.
excited 821 adj.
delirium
frenzy 503 n.
fantasy 513 n.
lack of meaning
  515 n.
excitable state 822 n.
deliver
transfer 272 vb.

provide 633 vb.
deliver 668 vb.
disencumber
  701 vb.
liberate 746 vb.
restitute 787 vb.
relieve 831 vb.
deliverance
safety 660 n.
escape 667 n.
deliverer
defender 713 n.
benefactor 903 n.
delivery
obstetrics 167 n.
transference 272 n.
speech 579 n.
provision 633 n.
deliverance 668 n.
delta
land 344 n.
delude
deceive 542 vb.
—oneself
hope 852 vb.
deluge
drench 341 vb.
rain 350 n.
superabound
  637 vb.
delusion
error 495 n.
deception 542 n.
delusions
psychopathy
  503 n.
de luxe
comfortable
  376 adj.
ostentatious
  875 adj.
delve
make concave
  255 vb.
—into
inquire 459 vb.
demagnetize
counteract 182 vb.
demagogue
agitator 738 n.
demand
require 627 vb.
demand 737 n.vb.
—one's rights
claim 915 vb.
demanding
fatiguing 684 adj.

difficult 700 adj.
fastidious 862 adj.
demarcate
limit 236 vb.
mark 547 vb.
dematerialize
disembody 320 vb.
disappear 446 vb.
demeaning
degrading 867 adj.
demean oneself
behave 688 vb.
demean oneself
  867 vb.
demeanour
mien 445 n.
gesture 547 n.
conduct 688 n.
demented
insane 503 adj.
démenti
negation 533 n.
demerit
vice 934 n.
demi-
bisected 92 adj.
demigod
deity 966 n.
demilitarize
make peace 719 vb.
demi-monde
prostitute 952 n.
demise
decease 361 n.
demobilization
dispersion 75 n.
peace 717 n.
democracy
government 733 n.
commonalty 869 n.
democratic
equal 28 adj.
governmental
  733 adj.
demography
statistics 86 n.
anthropology 371 n.
demolish
demolish 165 vb.
confute 479 vb.
demon
violent creature
  176 n.
monster 938 n.
demon 970 n.
demonetize
demonetize 797 vb.

demoniac,
  demoniacal
  diabolic 969 adj.
demoniac possession
  spell 983 n.
demonic
  diabolic 969 adj.
  fairylike 970 adj.
demonstrable
  certain 473 adj.
demonstrate
  demonstrate 478 vb.
  show 522 vb.
  deprecate 762 vb.
  show feeling 818 vb.
demonstration
  assemblage 74 n.
demonstrative
  indicating 547 adj.
  caressing 889 adj.
demonstrator
  guide 520 n.
  exhibitor 522 n.
  agitator 738 n.
  revolter 738 n.
demoralize
  impair 655 vb.
  frighten 854 vb.
demote
  depose 752 vb.
demotic
  linguistic 557 adj.
demulcent
  remedial 658 adj.
demur
  qualification 468 n.
  dissent 489 n.vb.
  negate 533 vb.
  be unwilling 598 vb.
demure
  modest 874 adj.
den
  dwelling 192 n.
  chamber 194 n.
  hiding-place 527 n.
  refuge 662 n.
denationalize
  appropriate 786 vb.
  disentitle 916 vb.
denaturalize
  disentitle 916 vb.
denature
  weaken 163 vb.
  pervert 655 vb.
dendrology
  forestry 366 n.
denial

negation 533 n.
  refusal 760 n.
denier
  fibre 208 n.
  texture 331 n.
denigrate
  not respect 921 vb.
  defame 926 vb.
denim
  textile 222 n.
denims
  trousers 228 n.
denizen
  dweller 191 n.
denomination
  nomenclature 561 n.
  party 708 n.
denominational
  sectional 708 adj.
denominator
  numerical element
    85 n.
denotation
  connotation 514 n.
denote
  specify 80 vb.
  mean 514 vb.
denouement
  effect 157 n.
  completion 725 n.
denounce
  inform 524 vb.
  satirize 851 vb.
  defame 926 vb.
dense
  firm 45 adj.
  multitudinous
    104 adj.
  dense 324 adj.
  unintelligent
    499 adj.
density
  materiality 319 n.
  density 324 n.
  opacity 423 n.
dent
  concavity 255 n.
  notch 260 n.vb.
dental
  toothed 256 adj.
  speech sound 398 n.
dentist
  doctor 658 n.
denude
  uncover 229 vb.
  disclose 526 vb.
denunciation

accusation 928 n.
deny
  disbelieve 486 vb.
  negate 533 vb.
  refuse 760 vb.
—oneself
  be temperate 942 vb.
deodorant
  inodorousness
    395 n.
  cleanser 648 n.
deodorize
  purify 648 vb.
depart
  go away 190 vb.
  depart 296 vb.
department
  subdivision 53 n.
  classification 77 n.
  district 184 n.
  function 622 n.
departure
  start 68 n.
  deviation 282 n.
  departure 296 n.
depend
  depend 157 vb.
  be uncertain 474 vb.
dependable
  trustworthy 929 adj.
dependant
  inferior 35 n.
  dependant 742 n.
dependence
  subjection 745 n.
dependency
  political
    organization
    733 n.
dependent
  inferior 35 adj.
  subject 745 adj.
depict
  represent 551 vb.
  describe 590 vb.
depilatory
  stripper 229 n.
deplete
  waste 634 vb.
deplorable
  bad 645 adj.
  regretted 830 adj.
deplore
  regret 830 vb.
  lament 836 vb.
  disapprove 924 vb.
deploy

place 187 vb.
  open 263 vb.
  dispose of 673 vb.
depopulate
  lay waste 165 vb.
  empty 300 vb.
deport
  exclude 57 vb.
deportee
  outcast 883 n.
deportment
  mien 445 n.
  conduct 688 n.
deposal
  deposal 752 n.
depose
  testify 466 vb.
  depose 752 vb.
deposit
  leavings 41 n.
  place 187 vb.
  thing transferred
    272 n.
  store 632 n.vb.
  security 767 n.
deposition
  testimony 466 n.
  deposal 752 n.
depositor
  creditor 802 n.
depot
  station 187 n.
  storage 632 n.
depraved
  vicious 934 adj.
depravity
  wickedness 934 n.
deprecate
  deprecate 762 vb.
  be discontented
    829 vb.
  disapprove 924 vb.
depreciate
  abate 37 vb.
  underestimate
    483 vb.
  demonetize 797 vb.
  detract 926 vb.
depreciation
  decrement 42 n.
  loss 772 n.
depredations
  havoc 165 n.
  spoliation 788 n.
depress
  make concave
    255 vb.

lower 311 vb.
depress 834 vb.
depressing
  cheerless 834 adj.
depression
  valley 255 n.
  weather 340 n.
  melancholy 834 n.
deprivation
  separation 46 n.
  deposal 752 n.
  loss 772 n.
  expropriation 786 n.
  loss of right 916 n.
deprive
  deprive 786 vb.
  impoverish 801 vb.
depth
  depth 211 n.
  interiority 224 n.
  wisdom 498 n.
depth charge
  bomb 723 n.
deputation
  commission 751 n.
depute
  commission 751 vb.
deputize
  substitute 150 vb.
  deputize 755 vb.
deputy
  substitute 150 n.
  deputy 755 n.
deracinate
  eject 300 vb.
derail
  derange 63 vb.
  displace 188 vb.
derange
  derange 63 vb.
  make mad 503 vb.
  trouble 827 vb.
deranged
  insane 503 adj.
deration
  liberate 746 vb.
derelict
  disused 674 adj.
  unpossessed 774 adj.
  derelict 779 n.
  not retained 779 adj.
dereliction
  undutifulness 918 n.
derestrict
  revert 148 vb.
deride
  ridicule 851 vb.

de rigueur
  usual 610 adj.
  obligatory 917 adj.
derision
  ridicule 851 n.
derisive
  derisive 851 adj.
  disrespectful
    921 adj.
derisory
  ridiculous 849 adj.
derivation
  origin 68 n.
  attribution 158 n.
  etymology 559 n.
derivative
  imitative 20 adj.
  caused 157 adj.
derive (from)
  result 157 vb.
  attribute 158 vb.
  acquire 771 vb.
dermatitis
  skin disease 651 n.
derogatory
  degrading 867 adj.
  detracting 926 adj.
derrick
  lifter 310 n.
dervish
  ascetic 945 n.
desalinate
  purify 648 vb.
descant
  tune 412 n.
  be diffuse 570 vb.
  dissertate 591 vb.
descend
  land 295 vb.
  descend 309 vb.
descendant
  successor 67 n.
  descendant 170 n.
descending order
  series 71 n.
descent
  consanguinity 11 n.
  decrease 37 n.
  posteriority 120 n.
  source 156 n.
  genealogy 169 n.
  sonship 170 n.
  descent 309 n.
  plunge 313 n.
  deterioration 655 n.
describe
  represent 551 vb.

describe 590 vb.
description
  indication 547 n.
  representation
    551 n.
  name 561 n.
  description 590 n.
descriptive
  expressive 516 adj.
  descriptive 590 adj.
descry
  see 438 vb.
desecrate
  misuse 675 vb.
  be impious 980 vb.
desert
  desert 172 n.
  emptiness 190 n.
  dryness 342 n.
  plain 348 n.
  tergiversate 603 vb.
  relinquish 621 vb.
  fail in duty 918 vb.
deserted
  alone 88 adj.
  empty 190 adj.
  neglected 458 adj.
  secluded 883 adj.
deserter
  avoider 620 n.
  coward 856 n.
desertion
  disobedience 738 n.
  divorce 896 n.
  perfidy 930 n.
  (*see* **desert**)
deserts
  dueness 915 n.
  reward 962 n.
deserve
  deserve 915 vb.
deserved
  just 913 adj.
  due 915 adj.
deserving
  excellent 644 adj.
  approvable 923 adj.
déshabillé
  informal dress
    228 n.
  uncovering 229 n.
desiccation
  desiccation 342 n.
desideratum
  desired object 859 n.
design
  prototype 23 n.

composition 56 n.
  form 243 n.
  intend 617 vb.
  plan 623 n.vb.
  pattern 844 n.
designate
  specify 80 vb.
  future 124 adj.
  mark 547 vb.
  select 605 vb.
designation
  classification 77 n.
  nomenclature
    561 n.
designer
  artist 556 n.
  planner 623 n.
designing
  hypocritical
    541 adj.
designless
  designless 618 adj.
desirability
  good policy 642 n.
desirable
  advisable 642 adj.
  desired 859 adj.
  lovable 887 adj.
  approvable 923 adj.
desire
  motive 612 n.
  desire 859 n.vb.
desist
  cease 145 vb.
  not act 677 vb.
desk
  stand 218 n.
  classroom 539 n.
desolate
  unproductive
    172 adj.
  empty 190 adj.
  friendless 883 adj.
  secluded 883 adj.
desolation
  havoc 165 n.
  desert 172 n.
  sorrow 825 n.
despair
  hopelessness 853 n.
despatch
  (*see* **dispatch**)
desperado
  desperado 857 n.
  ruffian 904 n.
desperate
  resolute 599 adj.

hopeless 853 adj.
rash 857 adj.
despicable
contemptible
 922 adj.
despise
despise 922 vb.
despite
although 182 adv.
despoil
lay waste 165 vb.
rob 788 vb.
despondent
unhappy 825 adj.
dejected 834 adj.
hopeless 853 adj.
despot
tyrant 735 n.
autocrat 741 n.
despotic
authoritarian
 735 adj.
oppressive 735 adj.
lawless 954 adj.
despotism
despotism 733 n.
brute force 735 n.
dessert
dessert 301 n.
destination
stopping place
 145 n.
objective 617 n.
destined
future 124 adj.
impending 155 adj.
fated 596 adj.
destine for
intend 617 vb.
destiny
destiny 155 n.
fate 596 n.
predetermination
 608 n.
destitute
wanderer 268 n.
destitution
poverty 801 n.
destroy
nullify 2 vb.
destroy 165 vb.
destroyer
destroyer 168 n.
violent creature
 176 n.
warship 722 n.
destruction

extinction 2 n.
destruction 165 n.
destructive
destructive 165 adj.
violent 176 adj.
wasteful 634 adj.
desuetude
desuetude 611 n.
desultory
orderless 61 adj.
discontinuous
 72 adj.
fitful 142 adj.
light-minded
 456 adj.
detach
disunite 46 vb.
unstick 49 vb.
send 272 vb.
detached
unrelated 10 adj.
nonadhesive 49 adj.
neutral 625 adj.
independent
 744 adj.
impassive 820 adj.
detachment
armed force 722 n.
detail
small quantity 33 n.
specify 80 vb.
send 272 vb.
describe 590 vb.
trifle 639 n.
command 737 vb.
pattern 844 n.
detailed
complete 54 adj.
diffuse 570 adj.
descriptive 590 adj.
details
particulars 80 n.
detain
imprison 747 vb.
retain 778 vb.
detainee
prisoner 750 n.
detect
see 438 vb.
detect 484 vb.
understand 516 vb.
detectable
visible 443 adj.
detection
discovery 484 n.
detective
detective 459 n.

detector
detector 484 n.
détente
concord 710 n.
pacification 719 n.
detention
delay 136 n.
detention 747 n.
penalty 963 n.
deter
dissuade 613 vb.
hinder 702 vb.
frighten 854 vb.
detergent
cleanser 648 n.
deteriorate
decompose 51 vb.
deteriorate 655 vb.
deterioration
weakness 163 n.
regression 286 n.
deterioration 655 n.
relapse 657 n.
determinant
cause 156 n.
determinate
definite 80 adj.
determination
will 595 n.
resolution 599 n.
intention 617 n.
assiduity 678 n.
determine
terminate 69 vb.
cause 156 vb.
will 595 vb.
be resolute 599 vb.
intend 617 vb.
determined
resolute 599 adj.
obstinate 602 adj.
determinism
necessity 596 n.
deterrence
dissuasion 613 n.
intimidation 854 n.
deterrent
safeguard 662 n.
cautionary 664 adj.
defence 713 n.
intimidation 854 n.
detest
dislike 861 vb.
hate 888 vb.
detestable
not nice 645 adj.
dethrone

unthrone 734 vb.
depose 752 vb.
detonate
be violent 176 vb.
bang 402 vb.
detonator
explosive 723 n.
detour
deviation 282 n.
circuit 626 n.
detract (from)
underestimate
 483 vb.
hold cheap 922 vb.
detract 926 vb.
detraction
diminution 37 n.
detriment
impairment 655 n.
detrimental
inexpedient 643 adj.
harmful 645 adj.
detritus
leavings 41 n.
deuce
draw 28 n.
duality 90 n.
deus ex machina
dramaturgy 594 n.
aider 703 n.
devaluation
deterioration 655 n.
devalue
demonetize 797 vb.
devastate
lay waste 165 vb.
devastation
havoc 165 n.
develop
become 1 vb.
augment 36 vb.
produce 164 vb.
urbanize 192 vb.
photograph 551 vb.
development
production 164 n.
expansion 197 n.
progression 285 n.
improvement 654 n.
deviant
nonconformist 84 n.
deviate
deviate 282 vb.
deviation
irrelevance 10 n.
nonconformity
 84 n.

deviation 282 n.
error 495 n.
deviationist
nonconformist 84 n.
device
heraldry 547 n.
contrivance 623 n.
tool 630 n.
stratagem 698 n.
devil
season 388 vb.
monster 938 n.
devil 969 n.
Satan 969 n.
demon 970 n.
devilish
cruel 898 adj.
diabolic 969 adj.
infernal 972 adj.
devil-may-care
rash 857 adj.
devilry
cruel act 898 n.
diabolism 969 n.
devil's advocate
sophist 477 n.
devil worship
diabolism 969 n.
devious
deviating 282 adj.
circuitous 314 adj.
dishonest 930 adj.
devise
think 449 vb.
imagine 513 vb.
plan 623 vb.
devitalize
weaken 163 vb.
devoid
empty 190 adj.
devolution
commission 751 n.
transfer 780 n.
devolve
impose a duty
917 vb.
devote (to)
use 673 vb.
give 781 vb.
devoted
obedient 739 adj.
loving 887 adj.
disinterested
931 adj.
pious 979 adj.
devotee
enthusiast 504 n.

habitué 610 n.
worshipper 981 n.
devotion
loyalty 739 n.
love 887 n.
devotional
religious 973 adj.
devotional 981 adj.
devour
destroy 165 vb.
absorb 299 vb.
waste 634 vb.
gluttonize 947 vb.
devoured by
possessed 773 adj.
impressed 818 adj.
devout
religious 973 adj.
pious 979 adj.
dew
moisture 341 n.
dewy
humid 341 adj.
clean 648 adj.
dexterity
skill 694 n.
dexterous, dextrous
dextral 241 adj.
skilful 694 adj.
dharma
religion 973 n.
dhoti
loincloth 228 n.
dhow
sailing ship 275 n.
di-
dual 90 adj.
diabetes
disease 651 n.
diabolic, diabolical
damnable 645 adj.
cruel 898 adj.
diabolic 969 adj.
infernal 972 adj.
diadem
regalia 743 n.
jewellery 844 n.
diaeresis
punctuation 547 n.
diagnosis
classification 77 n.
pathology 651 n.
medical art 658 n.
diagnostic
characteristic 5 adj.
distinctive 15 adj.
special 80 adj.

identification 547 n.
diagonal
oblique 220 adj.
diagram
representation
551 n.
plan 623 n.
dial
timekeeper 117 n.
signal 547 vb.
dialect
language 557 n.
dialect 560 n.
dialectic(s)
reasoning 475 n.
dialogue
argumentation 475 n.
interlocution 584 n.
dialysis
cleansing 648 n.
diamante
finery 844 n.
diameter
dividing line 92 n.
breadth 205 n.
diamond
angular figure
247 n.
hardness 326 n.
gem 844 n.
diapason
loudness 400 n.
diaper
loincloth 228 n.
pattern 844 n.
diaphanous
transparent 422 adj.
diaphragm
partition 231 n.
musical instrument
414 n.
diarist
chronicler 549 n.
narrator 590 n.
diarrhoea
digestive disorders
651 n.
diary
chronology 117 n.
reminder 505 n.
record 548 n.
biography 590 n.
diatribe
oration 579 n.
censure 924 n.
dibble
farm tool 370 n.

dice
cut 46 vb.
oracle 511 n.
gamble 618 vb.
dicey
speculative 618 adj.
dangerous 661 adj.
dichotomy
disunion 46 n.
dicky, dickey
seat 218 n.
garment 228 n.
Dictaphone
recording
instrument 549 n.
dictate
speak 579 vb.
necessitate 596 vb.
dominate 733 vb.
rule 733 vb.
dictation
no choice 606 n.
dictator
tyrant 735 n.
autocrat 741 n.
dictatorial
authoritative
733 adj.
compelling 740 adj.
insolent 878 adj.
dictatorship
despotism 733 n.
diction
style 566 n.
dictionary
dictionary 559 n.
dictum
maxim 496 n.
didactic
educational 534 adj.
advising 691 adj.
diddle
deceive 542 vb.
defraud 788 vb.
die
mould 23 n.
die 361 vb.
— away
decrease 37 vb.
sound faint 401 vb.
—down
be quiescent 266 vb.
—out
pass away 2 vb.
diehard
obstinate person
602 n.

diesel engine
locomotive 274 n.
machine 630 n.
diet
dieting 301 n.
therapy 658 n.
dieter
abstainer 942 n.
dietitian, dietician
dieting 301 n.
doctor 658 n.
differ
quarrel 709 vb.
difference
difference 15 n.
disagreement 25 n.
inequality 29 n.
remainder 41 n.
dissent 489 n.
different
nonuniform 17 adj.
extraneous 59 adj.
special 80 adj.
converted 147 adj.
changeful 152 adj.
differential
numerical element
85 n.
earnings 771 n.
differentiate
specify 80 vb.
discriminate 463 vb.
difficult
unclear 568 adj.
laborious 682 adj.
difficult 700 adj.
disobedient
738 adj.
fastidious 862 adj.
difficulty
difficulty 700 n.
obstacle 702 n.
adversity 731 n.
diffidence
nervousness 854 n.
modesty 874 n.
diffident
doubting 474 adj.
diffraction
reflection 417 n.
diffuse
disperse 75 vb.
publish 528 vb.
diffusive
prolix 570 adj.
dig
excavation 255 n.

make concave
255 vb.
cultivate 370 vb.
reproach 924 vb.
—in
place oneself
187 vb.
stand firm 599 vb.
—up
extract 304 vb.
discover 484 vb.
digest
arrangement 62 n.
absorb 299 vb.
eat 301 n.
meditate 449 vb.
compendium 592 n.
digestion
reception 299 n.
eating 301 n.
digestive
remedial 658 adj.
digger
excavator 255 n.
gardener 370 n.
digit
number 85 n.
feeler 378 n.
digital
computerized
86 adj.
dignified
elegant 575 adj.
impressive 821 adj.
well-bred 848 adj.
worshipful 866 adj.
formal 875 adj.
courteous 884 adj.
dignify
dignify 866 vb.
dignitary
officer 741 n.
aristocrat 868 n.
dignity
conduct 688 n.
authority 733 n.
etiquette 848 n.
prestige 866 n.
pride 871 n.
formality 875 n.
digress
deviate 282 vb.
be diffuse 570 vb.
digression
deviation 282 n.
circuit 626 n.
digs

quarters 192 n.
dike, dyke
fence 235 n.
conduit 351 n.
obstacle 702 n.
diktat
decree 737 n.
dilapidated
weakened 163 adj.
unsafe 661 adj.
used 673 adj.
dilapidation
decay 51 n.
dilapidation 655 n.
dilate
expand 197 vb.
be diffuse 570 vb.
dilation
dilation 197 n.
dilatory
late 136 adj.
slow 278 adj.
dilemma
dubiety 474 n.
augmentation 475 n.
predicament 700 n.
dilettante
dabbling 491 adj.
people of taste
846 n.
diligence
attention 455 n.
assiduity 678 n.
observance 768 n.
diligent
studious 536 adj.
dilly-dally
be inactive 679 vb.
dilute
weaken 163 vb.
moisten 341 vb.
dim
bedim 419 vb.
blur 440 vb.
indistinct 444 adj.
unintelligent
499 adj.
dimension
measure 183 n.
dimensions
size 195 n.
metrology 465 n.
diminish
abate 37 vb.
render few 105 vb.
diminishing returns
loss 772 n.

diminution
diminution 37 n.
contraction 198 n.
diminutive
small 33 adj.
little 196 adj.
word 559 n.
dimness
dimness 419 n.
invisibility 444 n.
dimple
cavity 255 n.
dimwit
dunce 501 n.
din
commotion 318 n.
loudness 400 n.
dine
eat 301 vb.
—out
be sociable 882 vb.
diner
café 192 n.
eater 301 n.
dingdong
equal 28 adj.
contending 716 adj.
dinghy
rowing boat 275 n.
dingy
dim 419 adj.
colourless 426 adj.
dirty 649 adj.
graceless 842 adj.
dinner
meal 301 n.
festivity 837 n.
dinner party
social gathering
882 n.
dinosaur
archaism 127 n.
dint
make concave
255 vb.
knock 279 n.
diocesan
ecclesiastical
985 adj.
diocese
parish 985 n.
Dionysiac
disorderly 61 adj.
diorama
spectacle 445 n.
dioxin
poison 659 n.

dip
incline 220 n.
cavity 255 n.
valley 255 n.
lower 311 vb.
plunge 313 n.vb.
drench 341 n.
bedim 419 vb.
signal 547 vb.
ablutions 648 n.
—into
be curious 453 vb.
study 536 vb.
diphtheria
respiratory disease
  651 n.
diphthong
speech sound 398 n.
voice 577 n.
diploma
credential 466 n.
honours 866 n.
diplomacy
cunning 698 n.
diplomat
mediator 720 n.
envoy 754 n.
diplomatic
hypocritical
  541 adj.
skilful 694 adj.
diplomatic corps
envoy 754 n.
diplomatist
slyboots 698 n.
envoy 754 n.
dipper
ladle 194 n.
dipsomania
alcoholism 949 n.
dire
harmful 645 adj.
adverse 731 adj.
direct
straight 249 adj.
send 272 vb.
orientate 281 vb.
indicate 547 vb.
perspicuous
  567 adj.
direct 689 vb.
command 737 vb.
direct action
revolt 738 n.
direction
direction 281 n.
teaching 534 n.

dramaturgy 594 n.
directorship 689 n.
directive
command 737 n.
directly
instantaneously
  116 adv.
director
guide 520 n.
stage manager
  594 n.
director 690 n.
directory
directory 87 n.
direful
frightening 854 adj.
dirge
obsequies 364 n.
lament 836 n.
dirigible
airship 276 n.
dirt
excrement 302 n.
rubbish 641 n.
dirt 649 n.
slur 867 n.
dirty
opaque 423 adj.
neglected 458 adj.
dirty 649 adj.
dishonest 930 adj.
impure 951 adj.
dirty trick
foul play 930 n.
disability
illness 651 n.
disable
disable 161 vb.
impair 655 vb.
hinder 702 vb.
disabuse
inform 524 vb.
educate 534 vb.
disaccustom
disaccustom 611 vb.
stop using 674 vb.
disadvantage
inferiority 35 n.
inexpedience 643 n.
disadvantageous
harmful 645 adj.
disaffect
dissuade 613 vb.
disaffection
dissent 489 n.
disagree
disagree 25 vb.

dissent 489 vb.
cause dislike 861 vb.
disagreeable
unpleasant 827 adj.
discourteous
  885 adj.
disagreement
disagreement 25 n.
nonconformity
  84 n.
dissension 709 n.
(*see* **disagree**)
disallow
exclude 57 vb.
prohibit 757 vb.
disentitle 916 vb.
disallowed
refused 760 adj.
disappear
disappear 446 vb.
be lost 772 vb.
disappearance
absence 190 n.
disappearance
  446 n.
concealment 525 n.
disappoint
disappoint 509 vb.
miscarry 728 vb.
displease 827 vb.
disapprove
deprecate 762 vb.
dislike 861 vb.
disapprove 924 vb.
disarm
disable 161 vb.
weaken 163 vb.
assuage 177 vb.
make peace 719 vb.
disarmament
peace 717 n.
disarray
disorder 61 n.
disaster
ruin 165 n.
misfortune 731 n.
disaster area
havoc 165 n.
disastrous
evil 616 adj.
harmful 645 adj.
disavow
negate 533 vb.
recant 603 vb.
reject 607 vb.
disband
disperse 75 vb.

disbar
exclude 57 vb.
disbelief
unbelief 486 n.
negation 533 n.
lack of wonder
  865 n.
disburden
disencumber
  701 vb.
disburse
expend 806 vb.
disc, disk
lamina 207 n.
circle 250 n.
gramophone 414 n.
discard
reject 607 vb.
relinquish 621 vb.
stop using 674 vb.
not retain 779 vb.
discarnate
immaterial 320 adj.
discern
see 438 vb.
detect 484 vb.
understand 516 vb.
discerning
discriminating
  463 adj.
intelligent 498 adj.
tasteful 846 adj.
fastidious 862 adj.
discharge
propulsion 287 n.
outflow 298 n.
ejection 300 n.
dismiss 300 vb.
empty 300 vb.
deliverance 668 n.
carry out 725 vb.
deposal 752 n.
payment 804 n.
do one's duty
  917 n.
acquittal 960 n.
disciple
listener 415 n.
disciplinarian
trainer 537 n.
tyrant 735 n.
disciplinary
punitive 963 adj.
discipline
order 60 n.
teaching 534 n.
dominate 733 vb.

severity 735 n.
obedience 739 n.
restraint 747 n.
disc jockey
broadcaster 531 n.
disclaim
negate 533 vb.
resign 753 vb.
not retain 779 vb.
disclose
manifest 522 vb.
disclose 526 vb.
indicate 547 vb.
disclosure
disclosure 526 n.
disco, discotheque
dancing 837 n.
place of amusement
837 n.
discoloration
achromatism 426 n.
discoloured
unsightly 842 adj.
discomfited
humbled 872 adj.
discomfort
pain 377 n.
suffering 825 n.
worry 825 n.
discompose
derange 63 vb.
agitate 318 vb.
trouble 827 vb.
discomposure
disorder 61 n.
worry 825 n.
disconcert
derange 63 vb.
distract 456 vb.
disappoint 509 vb.
disconcerted
inexpectant 508 adj.
disconnect
disunite 46 vb.
discontinue 72 vb.
disconnected
unrelated 10 adj.
disconsolate
melancholic
834 adj.
hopeless 853 adj.
discontented
discontented
829 adj.
resentful 891 adj.
discontinuance
desuetude 611 n.

abrogation 752 n.
discontinue
terminate 69 vb.
discontinuity
disunion 46 n.
discontinuity 72 n.
fitfulness 142 n.
discord
disagreement 25 n.
discord 411 n.vb.
dissension 709 n.
discordant
strident 407 adj.
florid 425 adj.
discotheque
(*see* disco)
discount
decrement 42 n.
disregard 458 vb.
discount 810 n.vb.
discountenance
disapprove 924 vb.
discourage
dissuade 613 vb.
depress 834 vb.
frighten 854 vb.
discourse
lecture 534 n.
oration 579 n.
dissertation 591 n.
discourteous
impertinent 878 adj.
discourtesy
ill-breeding 847 n.
discourtesy 885 n.
disrespect 921 n.
discover
produce 164 vb.
see 438 vb.
discover 484 vb.
discoverer
precursor 66 n.
detector 484 n.
discovery
discovery 484 n.
knowledge 490 n.
disclosure 526 n.
discredit
cause doubt 486 vb.
disrepute 867 n.
defame 926 vb.
discreditable
bad 645 adj.
discreditable
867 adj.
discredited
erroneous 495 adj.

disapproved
924 adj.
discreet
reticent 525 adj.
cautious 858 adj.
discrepancy
difference 15 n.
disagreement 25 n.
discrete
separate 46 adj.
discretion
discrimination
463 n.
sagacity 498 n.
choice 605 n.
caution 858 n.
discretionary
voluntary 597 adj.
unconditional
744 adj.
discriminate
discriminate 463 vb.
be wise 498 vb.
select 605 vb.
discrimination
discrimination
463 n.
judgement 480 n.
prejudice 481 n.
injustice 914 n.
discursive
rational 475 adj.
prolix 570 adj.
discus
circle 250 n.
missile 287 n.
discuss
confer 584 vb.
dissertate 591 vb.
discussion
inquiry 459 n.
argument 475 n.
disdain
reject 607 vb.
pride 871 n.
despise 922 vb.
disease
disease 651 n.
disembark
land 295 vb.
disembarrassed
facilitated 701 adj.
disembodied
immaterial 320 adj.
spooky 970 adj.
disembowel
empty 300 vb.

disenchanted
disliking 861 adj.
disenchantment
discovery 484 n.
disappointment
509 n.
disencumber
disencumber
701 vb.
relieve 831 vb.
disengage
disunite 46 vb.
liberate 746 vb.
disengaged
inactive 679 adj.
disentangle
simplify 44 vb.
unravel 62 vb.
liberate 746 vb.
disestablish
depose 752 vb.
diseur, diseuse
entertainer 594 n.
disfavour
disrepute 867 n.
odium 888 n.
disfigure
make ugly 842 vb.
disfranchise
disentitle 916 vb.
disgorge
vomit 300 vb.
disgrace
disrepute 867 n.
shame 867 vb.
wrong 914 n.
disgraceful
bad 645 adj.
discreditable
867 adj.
disgruntled
disappointed
509 adj.
discontented
829 adj.
disguise
make unlike
19 vb.
conceal 525 vb.
disguise 527 n.
disgust
cause discontent
829 vb.
dislike 861 n.
disgusting
unsavoury 391 adj.
not nice 645 adj.

unpleasant 827 adj.
hateful 888 adj.

dish
dish 301 n.
defeat 727 vb.
a beauty 841 n.
—out
apportion 783 vb.
—up
provide 633 vb.

disharmony
discord 411 n.
dissension 709 n.

dishearten
depress 834 vb.

dishevelment
disorder 61 n.
derangement 63 n.

dishonest
false 541 adj.
dishonest 930 adj.

dishonour
disrepute 867 n.
not respect 921 vb.
improbity 930 n.

dishonourable
blameworthy
924 adj.

dishwasher
cleaner 648 n.

dishy
personable 841 adj.

disillusion
disappoint 509 vb.
dejection 834 n.

disillusioned
regretting 830 adj.
indifferent 860 adj.

disincentive
dissuasion 613 n.
hindrance 702 n.

disinclination
unwillingness 598 n.

disincline
dissuade 613 vb.
cause dislike 861 vb

disinfect
sanitate 652 vb.
safeguard 660 vb.

disinfectant
cleanser 648 n.

disinflation
finance 797 n.

disingenuous
false 541 adj.

disinherit
deprive 786 vb.

disintegrate
break 46 vb.
decompose 51 vb.
deteriorate 655 vb.

disinter
exhume 364 vb.
discover 484 vb.

disinterested
just 913 adj.
disinterested
931 adj.

disjointed
feeble 572 adj.

disjunctive
separate 46 adj.

disk
(*see* **disc**)

dislike
dislike 861 n.vb.
disapprove 924 vb.

dislocate
derange 63 vb.
force 176 vb.
displace 188 vb.

dislodge
displace 188 vb.
eject 300 vb.

disloyal
trimming 603 adj.
undutiful 918 adj.
perfidious 930 adj.

dismal
cheerless 834 adj.
melancholic
834 adj.

dismantle
break 46 vb.
demolish 165 vb.
make inactive
679 vb.

dismay
worry 825 n.
fear 854 n.

dismember
rend 46 vb.

dismiss
dismiss 300 vb.
disregard 458 vb.
reject 607 vb.
not retain 779 vb.

dismissal
valediction 296 n.
ejection 300 n.

dismount
descend 309 vb.

disobedience
disobedience 738 n.

disobedient
wilful 602 adj.
undutiful 918 adj.

disobey
please oneself
734 vb.

disorder
disorder 61 n.
derangement 63 n.
disease 651 n.
anarchy 734 n.

disorderly
riotous 738 adj.

disorganize
derange 63 vb.

disorganized
lax 734 adj.

disorientate
derange 63 vb.
displace 188 vb.

disown
negate 533 vb.
not retain 779 vb.
disapprove 924 vb.

disparage
hold cheap 922 vb.
detract 926 vb.

disparity
unrelatedness 10 n.
difference 15 n.
inequality 29 n.

dispassionate
impassive 820 adj.
just 913 adj.

dispatch, despatch
punctuality 135 n.
send 272 vb.
kill 362 vb.
report 524 n.
do 676 vb.
hasten 680 vb.
carry out 725 vb.

dispatch rider
courier 529 n.

dispel
disperse 75 vb.
repel 292 vb.

dispensable
superfluous 637 adj.

dispensary
hospital 658 n.

dispensation
management 689 n.
nonretention 779 n.
nonliability 919 n.

dispense
apportion 783 vb.

dispenser
druggist 658 n.

dispersal
dispersion 75 n.

disperse
disperse 75 vb.
disappear 446 vb.

dispersion
dispersion 75 n.
divergence 294 n.

dispirit
depress 834 vb.

displace
displace 188 vb.
transpose 272 vb.

displacement
gravity 322 n.
(*see* **displace**)

display
spectacle 445 n.
exhibit 522 n.
show 522 vb.
ostentation 875 n.

displease
displease 827 vb.

displeased
discontented
829 adj.
angry 891 adj.

disport oneself
amuse oneself
837 vb.

disposable
decomposable
51 adj.
ephemeral 114 adj.
used 673 adj.

disposal
arrangement 62 n.
use 673 n.
nonretention 779 n.

dispose
arrange 62 vb.
motivate 612 vb.
—of
dispose of 673 vb.
sell 793 vb.

disposition
temperament 5 n.
arrangement 62 n.
location 187 n.
willingness 597 n.

dispossess
eject 300 vb.
appropriate 786 vb.
impoverish 801 vb.
disentitle 916 vb.

dispraise
dispraise 924 vb.
disproof
counterevidence
467 n.
disproportion
unrelatedness 10 n.
inequality 29 n.
disproportionate
distorted 246 adj.
disprove
confute 479 vb.
disputable
uncertain 474 adj.
disputant
reasoner 475 n.
disputation
argument 475 n.
dispute
argue 475 vb.
quarrel 709 n.vb.
disqualification
loss of right 916 n.
disqualify
exclude 57 vb.
disable 161 vb.
disentitle 916 vb.
disquiet
worry 825 n.
trouble 827 vb.
disquisition
dissertation 591 n.
disregard
exclude 57 vb.
be incurious 454 vb.
disregard 458 vb.
not use 674 vb.
not respect 921 vb.
disrepair
dilapidation 655 n.
disreputable
vulgar 847 adj.
disreputable
867 adj.
dishonest 930 adj.
disrepute
disrepute 867 n.
odium 888 n.
disrespect
disrespect 921 n.
impiety 980 n.
disrespectful
impertinent 878 adj.
disrespectful
921 adj.
disruption
destruction 165 n.

disruptive influence
agitator 738 n.
dissatisfaction
discontent 829 n.
disapprobation
924 n.
dissatisfy
displease 827 vb.
dissect
sunder 46 vb.
decompose 51 vb.
class 62 vb.
dissemble
make unlike 19 vb.
conceal 525 vb.
dissemble 541 vb.
be affected 850 vb.
dissembler
deceiver 545 n.
disseminate
disperse 75 vb.
publish 528 vb.
dissension
dissent 489 n.
dissension 709 n.
dissent
nonconformity
84 n.
dissent 489 n.vb.
dissension 709 n.
sectarianism 978 n.
dissenter
schismatic 978 n.
dissertation
dissertation 591 n.
disservice
evil 616 n.
inutility 641 n.
dissident
nonconformist 84 n.
dissentient 489 n.
malcontent 829 n.
schismatic 978 n.
dissimilar
different 15 adj.
dissimilar 19 adj.
dissimulate
dissemble 541 vb.
dissimulation
mimicry 20 n.
duplicity 541 n.
dissipate
disperse 75 vb.
waste 634 vb.
be prodigal 815 vb.
dissipated
sensual 944 adj.

dissipation
intemperance
943 n.
dissociate oneself
be unwilling 598 vb.
oppose 704 vb.
dissociation
schism 978 n.
dissolution
decomposition 51 n.
finality 69 n.
destruction 165 n.
abrogation 752 n.
dissolve
decompose 51 vb.
liquefy 337 vb.
dissonance
discord 411 n.
dissuade
dissuade 613 vb.
deprecate 762 vb.
distaff
weaving 222 n.
distaff side
womankind 373 n.
distance
distance 199 n.
length 203 n.
outstrip 277 vb.
distant
extraneous 59 adj.
distant 199 adj.
prideful 871 adj.
unsociable 883 adj.
distaste
dislike 861 n.
distasteful
unpleasant 827 adj.
distemper
colour 425 vb.
animal disease
651 n.
distend
augment 36 vb.
expand 197 vb.
distich
verse form 593 n.
distil
extract 304 vb.
vaporize 338 vb.
purify 648 vb.
distillation
essential part 5 n.
alcoholic drink
301 n.
distillery
vaporizer 338 n.

distinct
separate 46 adj.
loud 400 adj.
obvious 443 adj.
distinction
differentiation 15 n.
discrimination
463 n.
elegance 575 n.
prestige 866 n.
distinctive
distinctive 15 adj.
special 80 adj.
distinguish
differentiate 15 vb.
see 438 vb.
discriminate 463 vb.
dignify 866 vb.
distinguished
elegant 575 adj.
notable 638 adj.
distort
transform 147 vb.
distort 246 vb.
misinterpret 521 vb.
misteach 535 vb.
misrepresent
552 vb.
make ugly 842 vb.
distortion
unrelatedness 10 n.
visual fallacy 440 n.
untruth 543 n.
(*see* **distort**)
distract
distract 456 vb.
distraction
abstractedness
456 n.
excitable state 822 n.
distrain
deprive 786 vb.
distress
give pain 377 vb.
fatigue 684 n.
adversity 731 n.
poverty 801 n.
worry 825 n.
distressing
distressing 827 adj.
distress signal
danger signal 665 n.
distribute
apportion 783 vb.
district
district 184 n.
regional 184 adj.

locality 187 n.
parish 985 n.
distrust
doubt 486 n. vb.
disturb
derange 63 vb.
agitate 318 vb.
trouble 827 vb.
disturbance
turmoil 61 n.
commotion 318 n.
disturbed
violent 176 adj.
nervous 854 adj.
disunion, disunity
dissension 709 n.
disunite
disunite 46 vb.
disuse
desuetude 611 n.
stop using 674 vb.
disused
antiquated 127 adj.
ditch
partition 231 n.
cavity 255 n.
drain 351 n.
stop using 674 vb.
not retain 779 vb.
dither
be irresolute 601 vb.
dithyrambic
rhetorical 574 adj.
ditto
repeat 106 vb.
assent 488 vb.
ditty
vocal music 412 n.
diuretic
purgative 658 n.
diurnal
seasonal 141 adj.
diva
vocalist 413 n.
divan
bed 218 n.
divaricate
diverge 294 vb.
dive
tavern 192 n.
swim 269 vb.
fly 271 vb.
plunge 313 n.vb.
diver
diver 313 n.
bird 365 n.
diverge

diverge 294 vb.
divergence,
   divergency
difference 15 n.
dissension 709 n.
diverse
different 15 adj.
nonuniform 17 adj.
multiform 82 adj.
diversify
modify 143 vb.
variegate 437 vb.
diversion
deviation 282 n.
trap 542 n.
amusement 837 n.
diversity
variegation 437 n.
(*see* **diverse**)
divert
deflect 282 vb.
distract 456 vb.
amuse 837 vb.
divertissement
musical piece 412 n.
stage play 594 n.
Dives
rich person 800 n.
divest
uncover 229 vb.
deprive 786 vb.
divide
sunder 46 vb.
do sums 86 vb.
bisect 92 vb.
partition 231 n.
limit 236 n.
vote 605 vb.
apportion 783 vb.
divided
disunited 46 adj.
quarrelling 709 adj.
schismatic 978 adj.
dividend
numerical element
  85 n.
portion 783 n.
dividers
gauge 465 n.
divination
divination 511 n.
occultism 984 n.
divine
foresee 510 vb.
divine 511 vb.
beautiful 841 adj.
divine 965 adj.

godlike 965 adj.
theologian 973 n.
diviner
diviner 511 n.
occultist 984 n.
divining rod
detector 484 n.
divinity
divineness 965 n.
theology 973 n.
divisible
severable 46 adj.
division
scission 46 n.
subdivision 53 n.
classification 77 n.
district 184 n.
vote 605 n.
formation 722 n.
apportionment
  783 n.
schism 978 n.
divorce
separation 46 n.
divorce 896 n.vb.
divulge
manifest 522 vb.
divulge 526 vb.
dizzy
high 209 adj.
rotary 315 adj.
light-minded
  456 adj.
crazy 503 adj.
do
operate 173 vb.
suffice 635 vb.
be useful 640 vb.
do 676 vb.
celebration 876 n.
—**as others do**
conform 83 vb.
—**away with**
destroy 165 vb.
kill 362 vb.
—**down**
deceive 542 vb.
—**duty for**
substitute 150 vb.
deputize 755 vb.
—**for**
destroy 165 vb.
murder 362 vb.
serve 742 vb.
—**one's duty**
do one's duty
  917 vb.

—**up**
modernize 126 vb.
close 264 vb.
make better 654 vb.
—**well**
flourish 615 vb.
prosper 730 vb.
—**without**
not use 674 vb.
refuse 760 vb.
dobbin
horse 273 n.
doch-an-doris
valediction 296 n.
draught 301 n.
docile
studious 536 adj.
willing 597 adj.
induced 612 adj.
obedient 739 adj.
docility
persuadability
  612 n.
dock
cut 46 vb.
stable 192 n.
shorten 204 vb.
arrive 295 vb.
courtroom 956 n.
docker
boatman 270 n.
docket
list 87 n.vb.
label 547 n.
record 548 vb.
docking
space travel 271 n.
doctor
mix 43 vb.
psychologist 447 n.
scholar 492 n.
mender 656 n.
doctor 658 n.vb.
theologian 973 n.
doctrinaire
doctrinaire 473 n.
positive 473 adj.
narrow mind
  481 n.
theorist 512 n.
doctrinal
creedal 485 adj.
doctrine
creed 485 n.
theology 973 n.
document
evidence 466 n.

DOC

corroborate 466 vb.
record 548 n.vb.
documentary
evidential 466 adj.
informative 524 adj.
broadcast 531 n.
descriptive 590 adj.
doddering
ageing 131 adj.
weak 163 adj.
doddle
easy thing 701 n.
dodge
trickery 542 n.
avoid 620 vb.
elude 667 vb.
stratagem 698 n.
dodgy
dangerous 661 adj.
doer
doer 676 n.
doff
doff 229 vb.
dog
follow 284 vb.
dog 365 n.
pursue 619 vb.
dog collar
canonicals 989 n.
dog-eared
folded 261 adj.
used 673 adj.
dogged
persevering 600 adj.
obstinate 602 adj.
courageous 855 adj.
doggerel
doggerel 593 n.
dog in the manger
hinderer 702 n.
egotist 932 n.
dogma
creed 485 n.
theology 973 n.
dogmatic
positive 473 adj.
creedal 485 adj.
assertive 532 adj.
dogmatist
doctrinaire 473 n.
obstinate person
602 n.
do-gooder
volunteer 597 n.
philanthropist
901 n.
dogsbody

DOM

busy person 678 n.
servant 742 n.
doing
agency 173 n.
doing 676 adj.
doings
affairs 154 n.
deed 676 n.
do-it-yourself
artless 699 adj.
doldrums
inactivity 679 n.
dejection 834 n.
dole
gift 781 n.
portion 783 n.
sociology 901 n.
doleful
melancholic
834 adj.
dole out
apportion 783 vb.
be parsimonious
816 vb.
doll
image 551 n.
plaything 837 n.
dollar
coinage 797 n.
dolled up
beautified 843 adj.
dollop
piece 53 n.
dolorous
paining 827 adj.
dolt
dunce 501 n.
doltish
unintelligent
499 adj.
domain
territory 184 n.
function 622 n.
lands 777 n.
dome
edifice 164 n.
roof 226 n.
dome 253 n.
domestic
native 191 adj.
provincial 192 adj.
interior 224 adj.
animal 365 n.
domestic 742 n.
domesticate
break in 369 vb.
domesticity

DON

unsociability 883 n.
domestic science
cookery 301 n.
domicile
abode 192 n.
dominance
influence 178 n.
dominant
supreme 34 adj.
influential 178 adj.
dominate
influence 178 vb.
dominate 733 vb.
domination
governance 733 n.
domineering
authoritarian
735 adj.
oppressive 735 adj.
dominion
governance 733 n.
political
organization
733 n.
dominoes
indoor game 837 n.
domino theory
continuity 71 n.
don
wear 228 vb.
scholar 492 n.
teacher 537 n.
donate
give 781 vb.
donation
subvention 703 n.
gift 781 n.
done
past 125 adj.
completed 725 adj.
done, be
pay too much
811 vb.
done for
dying 361 adj.
defeated 728 adj.
done in/up
fatigued 684 adj.
done thing
practice 610 n.
etiquette 848 n.
donkey
beast of burden
273 n.
fool 501 n.
donnish
instructed 490 adj.

DOR

fastidious 862 adj.
donor
propagation 167 n.
provider 633 n.
giver 781 n.
don't-care
rash 857 adj.
indifferent 860 adj.
doodle
be inattentive
456 vb.
picture 553 n.
doom
fate 596 n.
condemnation
961 n.
punishment 963 n.
doomed
unfortunate 731 adj.
unhappy 825 adj.
doomsday
future state 124 n.
doomwatch
surveillance 457 n.
door
doorway 263 n.
access 624 n.
doorman
doorkeeper 264 n.
doormat
weakling 163 n.
submission 721 n.
doorway
doorway 263 n.
dope
anaesthetic 375 n.
ninny 501 n.
information 524 n.
drug 658 n.
doctor 658 vb.
doped
insensible 375 adj.
drugged 949 adj.
dope fiend
drug-taking 949 n.
dopey, dopy
foolish 499 adj.
sleepy 679 adj.
dormancy
inaction 677 n.
dormant
inert 175 adj.
quiescent 266 adj.
abrogated 752 adj.
dormitory
quarters 192 n.
chamber 194 n.

dose
finite quantity 26 n.
medicine 658 n.
portion 783 n.
doss down
dwell 192 vb.
sleep 679 vb.
dosshouse
inn 192 n.
dossier
information 524 n.
record 548 n.
dot
small thing 33 n.
maculation 437 n.
punctuation 547 n.
pattern 844 n.
dotage
old age 131 n.
folly 499 n.
dote
be foolish 499 vb.
be in love 887 vb.
dottle
leavings 41 n.
dotty
foolish 499 adj.
crazy 503 adj.
double
analogue 18 n.
double 91 vb.
fold 261 vb.
gait 265 n.
turn back 286 vb.
hypocritical
541 adj.
double agent
secret service 459 n.
double-blind test
experiment 461 n.
double-check
make certain
473 vb.
double-cross
deceive 542 vb.
be dishonest 930 vb.
double-dealing
duplicity 541 n.
perfidy 930 n.
double Dutch
lack of meaning
515 n.
double-dyed
consummate 32 adj.
vicious 934 adj.
double-glazing
silencer 401 n.

double harness
duality 90 n.
cooperation 706 n.
double-jointed
flexible 327 adj.
double meaning
connotation 514 n.
equivocalness
518 n.
doublet
jacket 228 n.
double take
sequel 67 n.
inspection 438 n.
double-talk
lack of meaning
515 n.
equivocalness
518 n.
doublethink
mental dishonesty
543 n.
doubt
dubiety 474 n.
doubt 486 n.vb.
not know 491 vb.
doubtful
moot 459 adj.
uncertain 474 adj.
cautious 858 adj.
disreputable
867 adj.
doubtless
certainly 473 adv.
douche
ablutions 648 n.
dough
cereals 301 n.
softness 327 n.
pulpiness 356 n.
shekels 797 n.
doughty
courageous 855 adj.
dour
obstinate 602 adj.
serious 834 adj.
douse, dowse
drench 341 vb.
extinguish 382 vb.
dove
bird 365 n.
pacifist 717 n.
dovetail
join 45 vb.
dowager
old woman 133 n.
dowdy

graceless 842 adj.
dowel
fastening 47 n.
dower
dower 777 n.
down
under 210 adv.
hair 259 n.
down 309 adv.
softness 327 n.
recorded 548 adj.
dejected 834 adj.
down-and-out
unlucky person
731 n.
poor person 801 n.
down at heel
dilapidated 655 adj.
beggarly 801 adj.
downbeat
tempo 410 n.
dejected 834 adj.
downcast
dejected 834 adj.
downfall
ruin 165 n.
defeat 728 n.
downgrade
shame 867 vb.
downhearted
dejected 834 adj.
downhill
sloping 220 adj.
easy 701 adj.
downmarket
cheap 812 adj.
downpour
rain 350 n.
downright
consummate 32 adj.
veracious 540 adj.
downs
high land 209 n.
plain 348 n.
downstairs
under 210 adv.
downstream
towards 281 adv.
down 309 adv.
downthrow
descent 309 n.
down to earth
true 494 adj.
downtown
city 184 n.
downtrodden
subjected 745 adj.

suffering 825 adj.
downturn
deterioration 655 n.
down under
beyond 199 adv.
downy
fibrous 208 adj.
smooth 258 adj.
downy 259 adj.
soft 327 adj.
dowry
dower 777 n.
dowse
search 459 vb.
dowser
detector 484 n.
doyen
seniority 131 n.
expert 696 n.
doze
sleep 679 n.vb.
dozen
over five 99 n.
drab
soft-hued 425 adj.
cheerless 834 adj.
dull 840 adj.
graceless 842 adj.
drachm
weighing 322 n.
Draconian
severe 735 adj.
draft
compose 56 vb.
write 586 vb.
plan 623 n. vb.
army 722 n.
compulsion 740 n.
paper money 797 n.
draft-dodger
avoider 620 n.
drag
counteraction 182 n.
be long 203 vb.
slowness 278 n.
draw 288 vb.
friction 333 n.
encumbrance 702 n.
fetter 748 n.
bore 838 n.
—on
drag on 113 vb.
—one's feet
be unwilling 598 vb.
drag artist(e)
imitator 20 n.
entertainer 594 n.

drag-line
excavator 255 n.
dragnet
chase 619 n.
dragon
rara avis 84 n.
violent creature
176 n.
dragoon
cavalry 722 n.
compel 740 vb.
dragster
automobile 274 n.
drain
outflow 298 n.
empty 300 vb.
dry 342 vb.
drain 351 n.
waste 634 vb.
sink 649 n.
sanitate 652 vb.
fatigue 684 vb.
drainage
voidance 300 n.
cleansing 648 n.
swill 649 n.
dram
draught 301 n.
metrology 465 n.
drama
drama 594 n.
stage play 594 n.
activity 678 n.
excitation 821 n.
dramatic
dramatic 594 adj.
impressive 821 adj.
wonderful 864 adj.
showy 875 adj.
dramatis personae
actor 594 n.
personnel 686 n.
dramatist
author 589 n.
dramatist 594 n.
dramatize
represent 551 vb.
dramatize 594 vb.
dramaturgy
dramaturgy
594 n.
drape
hang 217 vb.
dress 228 vb.
draper
clothier 228 n.
draperies

hanging object
217 n.
robe 228 n.
drastic
vigorous 174 adj.
severe 735 adj.
draught
depth 211 n.
traction 288 n.
draught 301 n.
gravity 322 n.
wind 352 n.
medicine 658 n.
draughts
board game 837 n.
draughtsman,
　　draughtswoman
recorder 549 n.
artist 556 n.
draughtsmanship
painting 553 n.
draw
copy 20 vb.
draw 28 n.
be equal 28 vb.
draw 288 vb.
attract 291 vb.
extract 304 vb.
represent 551 vb.
paint 553 vb.
describe 590 vb.
receive 782 vb.
desired object 859 n.
—a blank
fail 728 vb.
—attention to
show 522 vb.
—back
recede 290 vb.
—in
make smaller
198 vb.
—lots
gamble 618 vb.
—off
extract 304 vb.
—out
spin out 113 vb.
extract 304 vb.
—the line
exclude 57 vb.
discriminate 463 vb.
disapprove 924 vb.
—the teeth
disable 161 vb.
—together
join 45 vb.

—up
compose 56 vb.
plan 623 vb.
drawback
decrement 42 n.
obstacle 702 n.
drawbridge
doorway 263 n.
drawer
compartment 194 n.
artist 556 n.
drawers
underwear 228 n.
drawing
picture 553 n.
drawing board
plan 623 n.
drawl
speech defect 580 n.
drawn
equal 28 adj.
lean 206 adj.
drawstring
fastening 47 n.
dray
cart 274 n.
dread
expect 507 vb.
fear 854 n.vb.
dreadful
not nice 645 adj.
frightening 854 adj.
dreadlocks
hair 259 n.
dream
insubstantial thing
4 n.
visual fallacy 440 n.
be inattentive
456 n.
fantasy 513 n.
sleep 679 vb.
desired object 859 n.
dreamer
crank 504 n.
visionary 513 n.
dreamland
fantasy 513 n.
sleep 679 n.
dreamlike
shadowy 419 adj.
dreamy
abstracted 456 adj.
dreary
dark 418 adj.
cheerless 834 adj.
tedious 838 adj.

dredge
extract 304 vb.
dredger
ship 275 n.
dregs
leavings 41 n.
rabble 869 n.
drench
drench 341 vb.
dress
dress 228 n.vb.
cook 301 vb.
livery 547 n.
doctor 658 vb.
make ready
669 vb.
—up
dissemble 541 vb.
primp 843 vb.
dressage
equitation 267 n.
dresser
cabinet 194 n.
shelf 218 n.
clothier 228 n.
dressing
condiment 389 n.
surgical dressing
658 n.
dressing down
reprimand 924 n.
dressmaker
clothier 228 n.
dress rehearsal
preparation 669 n.
dressy
fashionable
848 adj.
showy 875 adj.
dribble
small quantity 33 n.
propel 287 vb.
exude 298 vb.
flow 350 vb.
drier, dryer
drier 342 n.
drift
accumulation 74 n.
tendency 179 n.
thing transferred
272 n.
direction 281 n.
deviation 282 n.
be light 323 vb.
be uncertain 474 vb.
meaning 514 n.
not act 677 vb.

drifter
  wanderer 268 n.
  fishing boat 275 n.
driftwood
  thing transferred
   272 n.
drill
  make uniform
   16 vb.
  textile 222 n.
  perforator 263 n.
  farm tool 370 n.
  train 534 vb.
  habituation 610 n.
  formality 875 n.
drink
  drink 301 vb.
  get drunk 949 vb.
—to
  toast 876 vb.
drinker
  reveller 837 n.
  drunkard 949 n.
drinking bout
  drunkenness 949 n.
drinks
  social gathering
   882 n.
drip
  weakling 163 n.
  exude 298 vb.
  flow 350 vb.
  ninny 501 n.
dripfeed
  therapy 658 n.
dripping
  fat 357 n.
drive
  operate 173 vb.
  vigorousness 174 n.
  ride 267 vb.
  impel 279 vb.
  propel 287 vb.
  incite 612 vb.
  chase 619 n.
  path 624 n.
  haste 680 n.
  exertion 682 n.
  compel 740 vb.
—at
  aim at 617 vb.
—home
  emphasize 532 vb.
—off
  repel 292 vb.
drivel
  silly talk 515 n.

driver
  driver 268 n.
  machinist 630 n.
driving force
  motive 612 n.
drizzle
  rain 350 n.vb.
droll
  witty 839 adj.
  funny 849 adj.
drone
  roll 403 vb.
  voice 577 vb.
  idler 679 n.
drool (over)
  exude 298 vb.
  mean nothing
   515 vb.
  love 887 vb.
droop
  hang 217 vb.
  be ill 651 vb.
  be fatigued 684 vb.
  be dejected 834 vb.
drop
  small thing 33 n.
  decrease 37 vb.
  minuteness 196 n.
  depth 211 n.
  hanging object
   217 n.
  sphere 252 n.
  descend 309 vb.
  let fall 311 vb.
  moisture 341 n.
  stage set 594 n.
  stop using 674 vb.
  be fatigued 684 vb.
—a brick
  blunder 495 vb.
  be clumsy 695 vb.
—in
  arrive 295 vb.
  visit 882 vb.
—out
  not complete
   726 vb.
  be free 744 vb.
dropout
  nonconformist 84 n.
  dissentient 489 n.
droppings
  excrement 302 n.
drops
  medicine 658 n.
dropsy
  disease 651 n.

dross
  rubbish 641 n.
  dirt 649 n.
drought
  dryness 342 n.
  scarcity 636 n.
  blight 659 n.
drove
  group 74 n.
drover
  driver 268 n.
drown
  fill 54 vb.
  suppress 165 vb.
  founder 313 vb.
  drench 341 vb.
  perish 361 vb.
  silence 399 vb.
drowse
  be inattentive
   456 vb.
  sleep 679 n.vb.
drubbing
  defeat 728 n.
  corporal
   punishment 963 n.
drudge
  busy person 678 n.
  worker 686 n.
  servant 742 n.
drudgery
  assiduity 678 n.
  labour 682 n.
drug
  anaesthetic 375 n.
  drug 658 n.
  poison 659 n.
drug abuse
  drug-taking 949 n.
drug addict
  drug-taking 949 n.
drugget
  floor-cover 226 n.
druggist
  druggist 658 n.
Druid, Druidess
  sorcerer 983 n.
  priest 986 n.
drum
  cylinder 252 n.
  strike 279 vb.
  roll 403 vb.
  play music 413 vb.
  drum 414 n.
  call 547 n.
drunk
  reveller 837 n.

drunkard 949 n.
drunkenness
  intemperance
   943 n.
  drunkenness 949 n.
dry
  unproductive
   172 adj.
  dry 342 adj.vb.
  staunch 350 vb.
  sour 393 adj.
  clean 648 vb.
  preserve 666 vb.
  tedious 838 adj.
  witty 839 adj.
  hungry 859 adj.
  sober 948 adj.
—up
  decrease 37 vb.
  cease 145 vb.
  be mute 578 vb.
  not suffice 636 vb.
dryad
  nymph 967 n.
dry-clean
  clean 648 vb.
dry dock
  stable 192 n.
dry-eyed
  pitiless 906 adj.
dry rot
  dirt 649 n.
  blight 659 n.
dry run
  experiment 461 n.
dual
  dual 90 adj.
dual-purpose
  double 91 adj.
dub
  name 561 vb.
  dignify 866 vb.
dubiety
  dubiety 474 n.
dubious
  doubting 474 adj.
  uncertain 474 adj.
ducal
  noble 868 adj.
duck
  zero 103 n.
  textile 222 n.
  stoop 311 vb.
  plunge 313 vb.
  drench 341 vb.
  bird 365 n.
  avoid 620 vb.

duckboards
paving 226 n.

duct
tube 263 n.
conduit 351 n.

ductile
flexible 327 adj.

dud
useless 641 adj.
loser 728 n.

due
impending 155 adj.
owed 803 adj.
due 915 adj.

duel
duel 716 n.

duellist
quarreller 709 n.
combatant 722 n.

dueness
right 913 n.
dueness 915 n.

duenna
keeper 749 n.

dues
tax 809 n.

duet
duet 412 n.
cooperation 706 n.

due to
caused 157 adj.

duffer
dunce 501 n.
bungler 697 n.

dugout
excavation 255 n.
rowing boat 275 n.
refuge 662 n.

duke, duchess
potentate 741 n.
person of rank
868 n.

dulcet
melodious 410 adj.
pleasurable 826 adj.

dulia
cult 981 n.

dull
blunt 257 vb.
nonresonant
405 adj.
soft-hued 425 adj.
colourless 426 adj.
unintelligent
499 adj.
cheerless 834 adj.
serious 834 adj.

tedious 838 adj.
dull 840 adj.

dullness
inertness 175 n.

dumb
unintelligent
499 adj.
voiceless 578 adj.

dumbfound
surprise 508 vb.
be wonderful
864 vb.

dumb show
gesture 547 n.
drama 594 n.

dummy
copy 22 n.
substituted 150 adj.
sham 542 n.
image 551 n.

dump
storage 632 n.
rubbish 641 n.
stop using 674 vb.

dumps
dejection 834 n.

dumpy
fleshy 195 adj.
short 204 adj.
thick 205 adj.

dun
brown 430 adj.
demand 737 vb.

dunce
dunce 501 n.

dune
small hill 209 n.

dung
excrement 302 n.
cultivate 370 vb.

dungarees
trousers 228 n.

dungeon
cellar 194 n.
prison 748 n.

duo
duet 412 n.

duologue
interlocution 584 n.

dupe
befool 542 vb.
dupe 544 n.
loser 728 n.

duplicate
duplicate 22 n.
double 91 adj.vb.
reproduce 166 vb.

duplicity
duplicity 541 n.
perfidy 930 n.

durable
lasting 113 adj.
tough 329 adj.

durables
merchandise 795 n.

duration
time 108 n.
course of time
111 n.

duress
compulsion 740 n.

during
while 108 adv.

dusk
evening 129 n.
half-light 419 n.

dusky
blackish 428 adj.

dust
overlay 226 vb.
powder 332 n.
rubbish 641 n.
dirt 649 n.

dustbin
sink 649 n.

dustbowl
desert 172 n.

dust devil
gale 352 n.

duster
obliteration 550 n.
cleaning cloth 648 n.

dusting
corporal
punishment 963 n.

dustman
cleaner 648 n.

**dust thrown in the
eyes**
pretext 614 n.
stratagem 698 n.

dustup
fight 716 n.

dusty
powdery 332 adj.
dry 342 adj.
whitish 427 adj.
dirty 649 adj.

Dutch treat
participation 775 n.

Dutch uncle
adviser 691 n.

dutiable
priced 809 adj.

dutiful
obedient 739 adj.
trustworthy 929 adj.

duty
necessity 596 n.
job 622 n.
labour 682 n.
tax 809 n.
duty 917 n.

duty-bound
obliged 917 adj.

duty-free
nonliable 919 adj.

duvet
coverlet 226 n.

dwarf
dwarf 196 n.
elf 970 n.

dwarfish
dwarfish 196 adj.

dwell
be situated 186 vb.
dwell 192 vb.

—on
emphasize 532 vb.

dweller
dweller 191 n.

dwelling
dwelling 192 n.

dwindle
decrease 37 vb.
become small
198 vb.

dybbuk
devil 969 n.
elf 970 n.

dye
tincture 43 n.
pigment 425 n.
colour 425 vb.

dying
extinct 2 adj.
dying 361 adj.
(see **die***)*

dyke
(see **dike***)*

dynamic
dynamic 160 adj.
operative 173 adj.
vigorous 174 adj.

dynamics
science of forces
162 n.
motion 265 n.

dynamism
energy 160 n.
vigorousness 174 n.

dynamite
demolish 165 vb.
explosive 723 n.
dynamo
machine 630 n.
busy person 678 n.
dynasty
governance 733 n.
sovereign 741 n.
dysentery
digestive disorders
651 n.
dyslexia
blindness 439 n.
dyspepsia
digestive disorders
631 n.
dystopia
suffering 825 n.

E

each
universal 79 adj.
each other
correlation 12 n.
eager
willing 597 adj.
fervent 818 adj.
desiring 859 adj.
eagle
bird 365 n.
flag 547 n.
eagle-eyed
seeing 438 adj.
ear
ear 415 n.
earl
person of rank
868 n.
early
past 125 adj.
primal 127 adj.
early 135 adj.
earmark
mark 547 vb.
select 605 vb.
intend 617 vb.
earn
acquire 771 vb.
deserve 915 vb.
earned
just 913 adj.
due 915 adj.
earner
worker 686 n.

earnest
resolute 599 adj.
security 767 n.
fervent 818 adj.
seriousness 834 n.
earnings
earnings 771 n.
receiving 782 n.
reward 962 n.
earphones
hearing aid 415 n.
ear plugs
silencer 401 n.
earring
hanging object
217 n.
jewellery 844 n.
earshot
short distance 200 n.
hearing 415 n.
ear-splitting
loud 400 adj.
strident 407 adj.
earth
electricity 160 n.
dwelling 192 n.
world 321 n.
land 344 n.
refuge 662 n.
—up
obstruct 702 vb.
earthenware
pottery 381 n.
earthling
humankind 371 n.
earthly
telluric 321 adj.
earthquake
destroyer 168 n.
oscillation 317 n.
earth sciences
earth sciences 321 n.
earth-shaking
influential 178 adj.
important 638 adj.
earthwork
earthwork 253 n.
defences 713 n.
earthy
sensual 944 adj.
ease
assuage 177 vb.
euphoria 376 n.
repose 683 n.
facility 701 n.
facilitate 701 vb.
relieve 831 vb.

—off/up
decelerate 278 vb.
—oneself
excrete 302 vb.
—out
depose 752 vb.
not retain 779 vb.
easel
art equipment 553 n.
ease of mind
content 828 n.
east
laterality 239 n.
compass point
281 n.
easy
comfortable
376 adj.
intelligible 516 adj.
easy 701 adj.
lenient 736 adj.
sociable 882 adj.
easy-going
inexcitable 823 adj.
indifferent 860 adj.
easy terms
cheapness 812 n.
eat
eat 301 vb.
—away
abate 37 vb.
encroach 306 vb.
—one's words
recant 603 vb.
eatable
edible 301 adj.
eatables
food 301 n.
eaten up with
misjudging 481 adj.
crazy 503 adj.
with affections
817 adj.
eating and drinking
feasting 301 n.
sociability 882 n.
sensualism 944 n.
eating-house
café 192 n.
eaves
roof 226 n.
projection 254 n.
eavesdrop
hear 415 vb.
be curious 453 vb.
eavesdropper
listener 415 n.

inquisitive person
453 n.
ebb
decrease 37 n.vb.
recede 290 vb.
flow 350 vb.
deterioration 655 n.
ebb and flow
fluctuation 317 n.
current 350 n.
ebony
black thing 428 n.
ebullience
excitation 821 n.
ebullient
merry 833 adj.
ebullition
outbreak 176 n.
bubble 355 n.
eccentric
misfit 25 n.
unconformable
84 adj.
crank 504 n.
laughingstock
851 n.
eccentricity
originality 21 n.
speciality 80 n.
eccentricity 503 n.
ecclesiastic
cleric 986 n.
ecclesiastical
985 adj.
echelon
series 71 n.
echo
do likewise 20 vb.
conform 83 vb.
repetition 106 n.
resound 404 vb.
assent 488 vb.
éclat
vigorousness 174 n.
prestige 866 n.
eclectic
mixed 43 adj.
choosing 605 adj.
eclecticism
philosophy 449 n.
eclipse
be superior 34 vb.
obscuration 418 n.
conceal 525 vb.
ecologist
biology 358 n.
economy 814 n.

ecology
relation 9 n.
biology 358 n.
economical
cheap 812 adj.
economical 814 adj.
economics
business 622 n.
management 689 n.
economize
economize 814 vb.
economy
provision 633 n.
economy 814 n.
ecosystem
organism 358 n.
association 706 n.
ecstasy
frenzy 503 n.
excitable state 822 n.
joy 824 n.
ecstatic
rejoicing 835 adj.
ectomorphic
lean 206 adj.
ectoplasm
spiritualism 984 n.
ecumenical
universal 79 adj.
orthodox 976 adj.
eczema
skin disease 651 n.
eddy
vortex 315 n.
rotate 315 vb.
current 350 n.
Eden
mythic heaven 971 n.
edge
advantage 34 n.
nearness 200 n.
edge 234 n.
sharpen 256 vb.
pungency 388 n.
edging
edging 234 n.
edgy
excitable 822 adj.
irascible 892 adj.
edible
edible 301 adj.
edict
decree 737 n.
edification
teaching 534 n.
benefit 615 n.

edifice
edifice 164 n.
edify
educate 534 vb.
make pious 979 vb.
edit
interpret 520 vb.
publish 528 vb.
rectify 654 vb.
edition
edition 589 n.
editor
interpreter 520 n.
bookperson 589 n.
editorial
article 591 n.
educate
inform 524 vb.
educate 534 vb.
educated
instructed 490 adj.
education
culture 490 n.
teaching 534 n.
educational
educational 534 adj.
pedagogic 537 adj.
educator
teacher 537 n.
educe
reason 475 vb.
eel
fish food 301 n.
eerie
frightening 854 adj.
spooky 970 adj.
efface
destroy 165 vb.
obliterate 550 vb.
—oneself
be modest 874 vb.
effect
sequel 67 n.
event 154 n.
cause 156 vb.
effect 157 n.
product 164 n.
spectacle 445 n.
meaning 514 n.
carry out 725 vb.
effective
causal 156 adj.
forceful 571 adj.
instrumental 628 adj.
advisable 642 adj.
successful 727 adj.

effects
property 777 n.
effectual
powerful 160 adj.
operative 173 adj.
effectuate
cause 156 vb.
carry out 725 vb.
effeminate
weak 163 adj.
female 373 adj.
effervesce
be agitated 318 vb.
bubble 355 vb.
be excited 821 vb.
effervescence
bubble 355 n.
effervescent
gaseous 336 adj.
lively 819 adj.
effete
impotent 161 adj.
deteriorated 655 adj.
efficacious
useful 640 adj.
successful 727 adj.
efficacy
ability 160 n.
efficiency
ability 160 n.
efficient
operative 173 adj.
businesslike 622 adj.
instrumental 628 adj.
skilful 694 adj.
effigy
copy 22 n.
image 551 n.
effluence
outflow 298 n.
effluent
dirt 649 n.
effluvium
gas 336 n.
odour 394 n.
efflux
outflow 298 n.
effort
attempt 671 n.
action 676 n.
exertion 682 n.
effortless
easy 701 adj.
effort-wasting
useless 641 adj.

effrontery
insolence 878 n.
effulgence
light 417 n.
effusion
outflow 298 n.
effusive
loquacious 581 adj.
feeling 818 adj.
e.g.
namely 80 adv.
egalitarian
just 913 adj.
egg
source 156 n.
genitalia 167 n.
egghead
intellectual 492 n.
egg on
incite 612 vb.
egg on one's face, get
be clumsy 695 vb.
egg-shaped
round 250 adj.
eggshell
brittleness 330 n.
ego
intrinsicality 5 n.
self 80 n.
spirit 447 n.
egocentric
vain 873 adj.
selfish 932 adj.
egoism
selfishness 932 n.
egotism
vanity 873 n.
selfishness 932 n.
ego trip
selfishness 932 n.
egress
egress 298 n.
eiderdown
coverlet 226 n.
eidetic
lifelike 18 adj.
imaginative 513 adj.
eisteddfod
assembly 74 n.
music 412 n.
either . . . or
optionally 605 adv.
ejaculation
cry 408 n.
eject
eject 300 vb.
depose 752 vb.

make unwelcome
883 vb.
ejection
repulsion 292 n.
eke out
make complete
54 vb.
elaborate
complex 61 adj.
mature 669 vb.
laborious 682 adj.
ornamental 844 adj.
elaboration
improvement 654 n.
élan
vigorousness 174 n.
elapse
elapse 111 vb.
elapsed
past 125 adj.
elastic
flexible 327 adj.
elastic 328 adj.
elasticity
recoil 280 n.
softness 327 n.
elasticity 328 n.
elated
jubilant 833 adj.
elation
excitable state 822 n.
elbow
joint 45 n.
angularity 247 n.
impel 279 vb.
—aside
deflect 282 vb.
elbow grease
friction 333 n.
exertion 682 n.
elbow room
room 183 n.
scope 744 n.
elder
superior 34 n.
prior 119 adj.
older 131 adj.
church officer 986 n.
elderly
ageing 131 adj.
elders
seniority 131 n.
elder
   statesman/
   stateswoman
sage 500 n.
El Dorado

fantasy 513 n.
elect
fated 596 adj.
chosen 605 adj.
vote 605 vb.
commission 751 vb.
election
vote 605 n.
elector
electorate 605 n.
electorate
electorate 605 n.
electric
dynamic 160 adj.
excitable 822 adj.
electrical engineering
electronics 160 n.
mechanics 630 n.
electric chair
means of execution
964 n.
electric eye
camera 442 n.
electrician
stagehand 594 n.
artisan 686 n.
electricity
electricity 160 n.
electrify
empower 160 vb.
invigorate 174 vb.
excite 821 vb.
electrocute
kill 362 vb.
electrode
electricity 160 n.
electrolysis
decomposition 51 n.
electron
minuteness 196 n.
element 319 n.
electronics
electronics 160 n.
microelectronics
196 n.
electroplate
coat 226 vb.
electrum
bullion 797 n.
eleemosynary
benevolent 897 adj.
elegance
elegance 575 n.
elegant
stylistic 566 adj.
elegant 575 adj.
personable 841 adj.

tasteful 846 adj.
fashionable 848 adj.
elegiac
poetic 593 adj.
elegy
poem 593 n.
lament 836 n.
element
component 58 n.
source 156 n.
filament 208 n.
element 319 n.
elemental
simple 44 adj.
elementary
simple 44 adj.
beginning 68 adj.
elements, the
weather 340 n.
elephant
giant 195 n.
mammal 365 n.
elevate
make higher 209 vb.
elevate 310 vb.
delight 826 vb.
dignify 866 vb.
(*see* **elevation**)
elevation
height 209 n.
elevation 310 n.
warm feeling 818 n.
cheerfulness 833 n.
dignification 866 n.
elevator
lifter 310 n.
elevenses
meal 301 n.
eleventh hour
lateness 136 n.
elf
elf 970 n.
elfin
little 196 adj.
fairylike 970 adj.
elicit
extract 304 vb.
discover 484 vb.
manifest 522 vb.
eligible
included 78 adj.
eliminate
eliminate 44 vb.
empty 300 vb.
reject 607 vb.
exempt 919 vb.
elimination

destruction 165 n.
elision
contraction 198 n.
elite
elite 644 n.
beau monde 848 n.
upper class 868 n.
elitism
government 733 n.
elixir
remedy 658 n.
ellipse
arc 250 n.
ellipsis
conciseness 569 n.
elocution
pronunciation
577 n.
elongate
lengthen 203 vb.
elope
decamp 296 vb.
wed 894 vb.
eloquence
eloquence 579 n.
inducement 612 n.
eloquent
forceful 571 adj.
eloquent 579 adj.
elucidate
interpret 520 vb.
elude
avoid 620 vb.
elude 667 vb.
elusive
puzzling 517 adj.
avoiding 620 adj.
escaped 667 adj.
elvish
fairylike 970 adj.
emaciated
lean 206 adj.
unhealthy 651 adj.
emanate
emerge 298 vb.
be visible 443 vb.
emancipation
freedom 744 n.
liberation 746 n.
emasculate
unman 161 vb.
emasculated
feeble 572 adj.
embalm
inter 364 vb.
be fragrant 396 vb.
preserve 666 vb.

embankment
  earthwork 253 n.
  safeguard 662 n.
embargo
  prohibition 757 n.
embarkation
  departure 296 n.
embark on
  begin 68 vb.
  undertake 672 vb.
embarrass
  trouble 827 vb.
embarrassed
  modest 874 adj.
embarrassment
  predicament 700 n.
embassy
  message 529 n.
  envoy 754 n.
embed
  implant 303 vb.
embellish
  make better 654 vb.
  decorate 844 vb.
embellishment
  ornament 574 n.
  ornamentation
    844 n.
ember
  ash 381 n.
embezzlement
  peculation 788 n.
embezzler
  defrauder 789 n.
embitter
  impair 655 vb.
  cause discontent
    829 vb.
  aggravate 832 vb.
  enrage 891 vb.
embittered
  resentful 891 adj.
emblazon
  colour 425 vb.
  mark 547 vb.
  represent 551 vb.
  decorate 844 vb.
emblazoned
  heraldic 547 adj.
emblem
  badge 547 n.
emblematic
  representing
    551 adj.
embody
  comprise 78 vb.
  materialize 319 vb.

represent 551 vb.
embolden
  give courage 855 vb.
emboss
  sculpt 554 vb.
  decorate 844 vb.
embouchure
  orifice 263 n.
  flute 414 n.
embrace
  unite with 45 vb.
  comprise 78 vb.
  enclose 235 vb.
  choose 605 vb.
  endearment 889 n.
embrasure
  window 263 n.
  fortification 713 n.
embrocation
  unguent 357 n.
  balm 658 n.
embroider
  variegate 437 vb.
  exaggerate 546 vb.
  decorate 844 vb.
embroidery
  ornament 574 n.
  needlework 844 n.
embroil
  make quarrels
    709 vb.
embroilment
  complexity 61 n.
embryo
  source 156 n.
  undevelopment
    670 n.
embryonic
  beginning 68 adj.
  immature 670 adj.
emendation
  amendment 654 n.
emerald
  greenness 434 n.
  gem 844 n.
emerge
  emerge 298 vb.
  be disclosed 526 vb.
emergency
  crisis 137 n.
  needfulness 627 n.
  predicament 700 n.
emetic
  purgative 658 n.
  remedial 658 adj.
emigrant
  foreigner 59 n.

emigration
  departure 296 n.
  egress 298 n.
eminence
  greatness 32 n.
  superiority 34 n.
  height 209 n.
  importance 638 n.
  prestige 866 n.
emissary
  messenger 529 n.
  envoy 754 n.
emit
  flow out 298 vb.
  emit 300 vb.
  speak 579 vb.
emollient
  lenitive 177 adj.
  soft 327 adj.
  lubricant 334 n.
  balm 658 n.
  remedial 658 adj.
emolument
  earnings 771 n.
  pay 804 n.
  reward 962 n.
emotion
  warm feeling 818 n.
emotional
  feeling 818 adj.
  impressible 819 adj.
  excitable 822 adj.
emotions
  affections 817 n.
emotive
  descriptive 590 adj.
  felt 818 adj.
empanel
  list 87 vb.
empathize
  imagine 513 vb.
empathy
  imagination 513 n.
  feeling 818 n.
emperor, empress
  sovereign 741 n.
emphasis
  pronunciation
    577 n.
emphasize
  emphasize 532 vb.
  make important
    638 vb.
emphatic
  strong 162 adj.
  assertive 532 adj.
  forceful 571 adj.

empire
  territory 184 n.
  governance 733 n.
  political
    organization
    733 n.
empirical
  experimental
    461 adj.
empiricism
  empiricism 461 n.
emplacement
  location 187 n.
  fortification 713 n.
employ
  employ 622 vb.
  use 673 vb.
employed
  busy 678 adj.
employee
  worker 686 n.
  servant 742 n.
employer
  director 690 n.
  master 741 n.
employment
  job 622 n.
  use 673 n.
  service 745 n.
emporium
  emporium 796 n.
empower
  empower 160 vb.
  permit 756 vb.
empowered
  authoritative
    733 adj.
emptiness
  insubstantiality
    4 n.
  emptiness 190 n.
empty
  empty 190 adj.
  empty 300 vb.
  make flow 350 vb.
  unthinking 450 adj.
  meaningless
    515 adj.
  untrue 543 adj.
  unprovided 636 adj.
  unpossessed
    774 adj.
  hungry 859 adj.
empty-handed
  unprovided 636 adj.
  unsuccessful
    728 adj.

539

empty talk
empty talk 515 n.
empurple
empurple 436 vb.
emulate
do likewise 20 vb.
emulation
jealousy 911 n.
emulsify
thicken 354 vb.
emulsion
facing 226 n.
enable
empower 160 vb.
facilitate 701 vb.
permit 756 vb.
enact
represent 551 vb.
act 594 vb.
carry out 725 vb.
decree 737 vb.
enamel
facing 226 n.
colour 425 vb.
enamour
excite love 887 vb.
encamp
place oneself
  187 vb.
dwell 192 vb.
encampment
abode 192 n.
encapsulate
comprise 78 vb.
abstract 592 vb.
encase
cover 226 vb.
insert 303 vb.
encash
receive 782 vb.
enchain
fetter 747 vb.
enchant
delight 826 vb.
be wonderful
  864 vb.
bewitch 983 vb.
enchanter
sorcerer 983 n.
enchanting
lovable 887 adj.
enchantment
spell 983 n.
encircle
circumscribe
  232 vb.
circuit 626 vb.

enclave
region 184 n.
enclose
circumscribe
  232 vb.
enclose 235 vb.
enclosed
monastic 986 adj.
enclosure
place 185 n.
contents 193 n.
enclosure 235 n.
encode
translate 520 vb.
encomium
praise 923 n.
encompass
surround 230 vb.
encore
repetition 106 n.
applause 923 n.
encounter
meet with 154 vb.
collision 279 n.
meet 295 vb.
fight 716 n.
encourage
conduce 156 vb.
incite 612 vb.
aid 703 vb.
cheer 833 vb.
give courage 855 vb.
encouraging
promising 852 adj.
encroach
encroach 306 vb.
encroachment
overstepping 306 n.
attack 712 n.
encrust
coat 226 vb.
encumber
hinder 702 vb.
encumbrance
encumbrance 702 n.
debt 803 n.
encyclical
publication 528 n.
decree 737 n.
encyclopedia
reference book
  589 n.
encyclopedic
general 79 adj.
knowing 490 adj.
end
end 69 n.vb.

extremity 69 n.
cease 145 vb.
event 154 n.
limit 236 n.
decease 361 n.
objective 617 n.
completion 725 n.
endanger
endanger 661 vb.
endangered species
animal 365 n.
endearing
lovable 887 adj.
endearment
endearment 889 n.
endeavour
attempt 671 n.vb.
endemic
interior 224 adj.
infectious 653 adj.
endless
infinite 107 adj.
perpetual 115 adj.
end of one's tether
limit 236 n.
endomorphic
thick 205 adj.
endorse
endorse 488 vb.
sign 547 vb.
approve 923 vb.
endow
dower 777 vb.
endowed (with)
gifted 694 adj.
possessing 773 adj.
endurance
durability 113 n.
perseverance 600 n.
patience 823 n.
endure
be 1 vb.
last 113 vb.
go on 146 vb.
persevere 600 vb.
feel 818 vb.
be patient 823 vb.
suffer 825 vb.
be courageous
  855 vb.
enduring
permanent 144 adj.
endwise
vertically 215 adv.
enema
purgative 658 n.
enemy

opponent 705 n.
enemy 881 n.
energetic
dynamic 160 adj.
vigorous 174 adj.
forceful 571 adj.
active 678 adj.
energize
invigorate 174 vb.
energy
energy 160 n.
strength 162 n.
vigorousness 174 n.
restlessness 678 n.
energy-consuming
wasteful 634 adj.
energy-saving
economical 814 adj.
enervate
weaken 163 vb.
fatigue 684 vb.
enfeeble
weaken 163 vb.
enfilade
bombardment
  712 n.
enfold
circumscribe
  232 vb.
caress 889 vb.
enforce
compel 740 vb.
enfranchise
liberate 746 vb.
engage
join 45 vb.
employ 622 vb.
commission 751 vb.
—in
do business 622 vb.
undertake 672 vb.
engagement
undertaking 672 n.
battle 718 n.
promise 764 n.
social round 882 n.
love affair 887 n.
duty 917 n.
engender
generate 167 vb.
engine
machine 630 n.
engineer
cause 156 vb.
plan 623 vb.
machinist 630 n.
artisan 686 n.

engineering
　production 164 n.
　mechanics 630 n.
engraft
　add 38 vb.
engrave
　cut 46 vb.
　groove 262 vb.
　engrave 555 vb.
engraving
　picture 553 n.
　engraving 555 n.
engross
　absorb 299 vb.
　engross 449 vb.
engrossed
　obsessed 455 adj.
　possessed 773 adj.
engulf
　destroy 165 vb.
　absorb 299 vb.
enhance
　make important
　　638 vb.
　beautify 841 vb.
enhancement
　improvement 654 n.
　dignification 866 n.
enigma
　question 459 n.
　unknown thing
　　491 n.
　enigma 530 n.
enigmatic
　aphoristic 496 adj.
　unclear 568 adj.
enjoin
　command 737 vb.
enjoy
　enjoy 376 vb.
　dispose of 673 vb.
　possess 773 vb.
　be content 828 vb.
—oneself
　amuse oneself
　　837 vb.
enjoyable
　pleasant 376 adj.
enjoyment
　enjoyment 824 n.
enkindle
　excite 821 vb.
enlace
　enlace 222 vb.
enlarge
　augment 36 vb.
　enlarge 197 vb.

　photograph 551 vb.
—upon
　be diffuse 570 vb.
enlighten
　inform 524 vb.
　educate 534 vb.
enlightened
　wise 498 adj.
　philanthropic
　　901 adj.
enlightenment
　knowledge 490 n.
　wisdom 498 n.
　sanctity 979 m
enlist
　list 87 vb.
　register 548 vb.
　employ 622 vb.
　join a party 708 vb.
　go to war 718 vb.
enliven
　invigorate 174 vb.
　animate 821 vb.
　amuse 837 vb.
enmesh
　ensnare 542 vb.
enmity
　enmity 881 n.
ennoble
　dignify 866 vb.
ennui
　tedium 838 n.
enormity
　greatness 32 n.
　hugeness 195 n.
　wickedness 934 n.
　guilty act 936 n.
enormous
　enormous 32 adj.
enough
　sufficiency 635 n.
enquire
　(see **inquire***)*
enrage
　enrage 891 vb.
enrapture
　delight 826 vb.
　excite love 887 vb.
enrich
　make better
　　654 vb.
　decorate 844 vb.
enrol, enroll
　list 87 vb.
　admit 299 vb.
　register 548 vb.
　join a party 708 vb.

ensconce
　place 187 vb.
　conceal 525 vb.
ensemble
　all 52 n.
　whole 52 n.
enshrine
　sanctify 979 vb.
ensign
　flag 547 n.
　army officer 741 n.
enslave
　oppress 735 vb.
　subjugate 745 vb.
ensnare
　ensnare 542 vb.
　tempt 612 vb.
ensue
　ensue 120 vb.
ensure
　make certain
　　473 vb.
entail
　conduce 156 vb.
entangle
　bedevil 63 vb.
　enlace 222 vb.
　ensnare 542 vb.
entente
　concord 710 n.
enter
　enter 297 vb.
　register 548 vb.
　join a party 708 vb.
　contend 716 vb.
—into
　imagine 513 vb.
　describe 590 vb.
　cooperate 706 vb.
—upon
　begin 68 vb.
enterprise
　vigorousness 174 n.
　undertaking 672 n.
　courage 855 n.
enterprising
　speculative 618 adj.
　enterprising
　　672 adj.
entertain
　amuse 837 vb.
　be hospitable
　　882 vb.
entertainer
　entertainer 594 n.
entertainment
　amusement 837 n.

　social gathering
　　882 n.
enthral, enthrall
　subjugate 745 vb.
　excite love 887 vb.
enthralling
　exciting 821 adj.
enthrone
　dignify 866 vb.
enthuse
　show feeling 818 vb.
enthusiasm
　vigorousness
　　174 n.
　willingness 597 n.
　warm feeling
　　818 n.
enthusiast
　enthusiast 504 n.
　visionary 513 n.
enthusiastic
　optimistic 482 adj.
　fervent 818 adj.
entice
　ensnare 542 vb.
　tempt 612 vb.
enticing
　pleasurable 826 adj.
entire
　whole 52 adj.
　perfect 646 adj.
entitle
　permit 756 vb.
entitlement
　dueness 915 n.
entity
　unit 88 n.
entomologist
　zoologist 367 n.
entourage
　concomitant 89 n.
entrails
　insides 224 n.
entrance
　doorway 263 n.
　arrival 295 n.
　delight 826 vb.
entrancing
　personable 841 adj.
entrant
　incomer 297 n.
　testee 461 n.
　contender 716 n.
entrap
　ensnare 542 vb.
entreat
　entreat 761 vb.

entrée
reception 299 n.
dish 301 n.
entrench, intrench
safeguard 660 vb.
place oneself
187 vb.
—upon
encroach 306 vb.
entrepreneur
gambler 618 n.
merchant 794 n.
entropy
decomposition 51 n.
entrust
commission 751 vb.
give 781 vb.
entry
doorway 263 n.
ingress 297 n.
entwine
enlace 222 vb.
enumerate
specify 80 vb.
number 86 vb.
list 87 vb.
enunciate
affirm 532 vb.
voice 755 vb.
envelop
cover 226 vb.
circumscribe
232 vb.
envelope
receptacle 194 n.
covering 226 n.
correspondence
588 n.
envenom
aggravate 832 vb.
excite hate 888 vb.
enviable
desired 859 adj.
envious
envious 912 adj.
environment
circumstance 8 n.
relation 9 n.
locality 187 n.
surroundings 230 n.
environmentalist
preserver 666 n.
environs
near place 200 n.
envisage
imagine 513 vb.
envoy

messenger 529 n.
envoy 754 n.
envy
be discontented
829 vb.
desire 859 vb.
envy 912 n.vb.
enwrap
fold 261 vb.
enzyme
alterer 143 n.
leaven 323 n.
epaulette
livery 547 n.
badge of rank 743 n.
ephemeral
ephemeral 114 adj.
ephemeris
chronology 117 n.
epic
descriptive 590 adj.
poem 593 n.
epicene
abnormal 84 adj.
epicentre
centre 225 n.
epicure
eater 301 n.
gastronomy 301 n.
people of taste
846 n.
epicurean
sensuous 376 adj.
sensualist 944 n.
epidemic
universal 79 adj.
plague 651 n.
infectious 653 adj.
epidermis
skin 226 n.
epigram
maxim 496 n.
conciseness 569 n.
witticism 839 n.
epilepsy
nervous disorders
651 n.
epilogue
sequel 67 n.
epiphany
revelation 975 n.
episcopacy
church office 985 n.
episcopal
ecclesiastical
985 adj.
episcopate

church office 985 n.
episode
event 154 n.
narrative 590 n.
episodic
discontinuous
72 adj.
epistemology
knowledge 490 n.
epistle
correspondence
588 n.
epitaph
obsequies 364 n.
epithet
name 561 n.
epitome
image 551 n.
conciseness 569 n.
epoch
era 110 n.
epoch-making
notable 638 adj.
eponymous
named 561 adj.
equable
inexcitable 823 adj.
equal
compeer 28 n.
equal 28 adj.
equality
identity 13 n.
equality 28 n.
justice 913 n.
equalize
equalize 28 vb.
average out 30 vb.
equal rights
freedom 744 n.
equal to
sufficient 635 adj.
equanimity
inexcitability 823 n.
equate
identify 13 vb.
equalize 28 vb.
equation
numerical result
85 n.
equator
middle 70 n.
dividing line 92 n.
equatorial
telluric 321 adj.
warm 379 adj.
equestrian,
equestrienne

rider 268 n.
equidistant
middle 70 adj.
parallel 219 adj.
equilateral
symmetrical
245 adj.
equilibrium
equilibrium 28 n.
equine
animal 365 adj.
equinoctial
vernal 128 adj.
autumnal 129 adj.
equip
dress 228 vb.
find means 629 vb.
provide 633 vb.
make ready 669 vb.
equipage
carriage 274 n.
equipment
equipment 630 n.
provision 633 n.
fitting out 669 n.
equipoise
equilibrium 28 n.
equitable
just 913 adj.
honourable 929 adj.
equitation
equitation 267 n.
equity
justice 913 n.
equivalent
analogue 18 n.
equivalent 28 adj.
quid pro quo
150 n.
equivocal
equivocal 518 adj.
unclear 568 adj.
equivocation
sophistry 477 n.
equivocalness
518 n.
falsehood 541 n.
era
era 110 n.
chronology 117 n.
eradicate
destroy 165 vb.
eject 300 vb.
extract 304 vb.
erase
obliterate 550 vb.
clean 648 vb.

ERE

erect
place 187 vb.
make vertical
215 vb.
elevate 310 vb.

ergonomics
exertion 682 n.

eristic
reasoner 475 n.
arguing 475 adj.

ermine
heraldry 547 n.
regalia 743 n.

erode
abate 37 vb.
rub 333 vb.
impair 655 vb.

erogenous
erotic 887 adj.

Eros
libido 859 n.
love 887 n.

erotic
erotic 887 adj.

err
stray 282 vb.
err 495 vb.
be wicked 934 vb.

errand
message 529 n.
mandate 751 n.

errandboy/-girl
courier 529 n.

errant
deviating 282 adj.

erratic
fitful 142 adj.
deviating 282 adj.
inexact 495 adj.
crazy 503 adj.

erratum
mistake 495 n.

erroneous
erroneous 495 adj.

error
deviation 282 n.
misjudgement
481 n.
error 495 n.

ersatz
imitative 20 adj.
spurious 542 adj.

eructation
respiration 352 n.

erudition
erudition 490 n.
learning 536 n.

ESP

erupt
be violent 176 vb.
attack 712 vb.

eruption
outbreak 176 n.
egress 298 n.
voidance 300 n.
skin disease 651 n.

escalade
ascent 308 n.
attack 712 n.

escalate
grow 36 vb.
be dear 811 vb.

escalator
lifter 310 n.

escapade
foolery 497 n.
revel 837 n.

escape
flow out 298 vb.
run away 620 vb.
seek safety 660 vb.
escape 667 n.vb.
be exempt 919 vb.

escape clause
qualification
468 n.
conditions 766 n.

escape hatch
means of escape
667 n.

escapism
fantasy 513 n.

escarpment
high land 209 n.

eschatology
finality 69 n.
theology 973 n.

eschew
avoid 620 vb.

escort
concomitant 89 n.
accompany 89 vb.
look after 457 vb.
keeper 749 n.
court 889 vb.

esoteric
occult 523 adj.
cabbalistic 984 adj.

espalier
frame 218 n.
fence 235 n.

especially
specially 80 adv.

espionage
secret service 459 n.

EST

esplanade
path 624 n.

espouse
choose 605 vb.
wed 894 vb.

esprit
wit 839 n.

esprit de corps
cooperation 706 n.

espy
see 438 vb.

esquire
title 870 n.

essay
article 591 n.

essayist
author 589 n.

essence
essence 1 n.
essential part 5 n.
extraction 304 n.
meaning 514 n.
goodness 644 n.
cosmetic 843 n.

essential
real 1 adj.
requirement 627 n.
chief thing 638 n.

establish
auspicate 68 vb.
stabilize 153 vb.
place 187 vb.
demonstrate 478 vb.

established
permanent 144 adj.
usual 610 adj.

establishment
location 187 n.
corporation 708 n.
(see **establish**)

Establishment, the
authority 733 n.
master 741 n.

estate
territory 184 n.
estate 777 n.

estate duty
tax 809 n.

esteem
repute 866 n.
respect 920 n.vb.

estimable
excellent 644 adj.
approvable 923 adj.

estimate
do sums 86 vb.
measurement 465 n.

EUH

estimate 480 n.vb.

estimation
prestige 866 n.

estrange
set apart 46 vb.
make enemies
881 vb.

estuary
gulf 345 n.

etch
outline 233 vb.
engrave 555 vb.

etching
representation
551 n.

eternal
infinite 107 adj.
perpetual 115 adj.
godlike 965 adj.

eternal triangle
jealousy 911 n.

eternity
infinity 107 n.
perpetuity 115 n.
heaven 971 n.

ether, aether
heavens 321 n.
gas 336 n.
anaesthetic 375 n.

ethereal
celestial 321 adj.

ethical
ethical 917 adj.

ethics
philosophy 449 n.
morals 917 n.

ethnic
ethnic 11 adj.
human 371 adj.

ethology
zoology 367 n.
morals 917 n.

ethos
character 5 n.
conduct 688 n.

etiquette
etiquette 848 n.
formality 875 n.

etymology
linguistics 557 n.

Eucharist
Christian rite 988 n.

eugenics
biology 358 n.

euhemeristic
rational 475 adj.
irreligious 974 adj.

eulogy
praise 923 n.

eunuch
eunuch 161 n.

euphemism
good taste 846 n.
affectation 850 n.

euphony
melody 410 n.

euphoria
euphoria 376 n.
content 828 n.

euphuism
ornament 574 n.

eurhythmic
symmetrical
  245 adj.

eurhythmics
exercise 682 n.

Eurocrat
official 690 n.

euthanasia
killing 362 n.

evacuate
decamp 296 vb.

evacuation
defecation 302 n.
relinquishment
  621 n.

evacuee
outcast 883 n.

evade
avoid 620 vb.
elude 667 vb.

evaginate
invert 221 vb.

evaluate
appraise 465 vb.
estimate 480 vb.

evanescent
transient 114 adj.
disappearing
  446 adj.

evangelical
revelational 975 adj.
orthodox 976 adj.
pietistic 979 adj.

evangelist
preacher 537 n.
religious teacher
  973 n.

evangelize
convert 147 vb.
convince 485 vb.

evaporate
be dispersed 75 vb.
vaporize 338 vb.

disappear 446 vb.

evaporation
loss 77 n.

evasion
sophistry 477 n.
mental dishonesty
  543 n.
avoidance 620 n.
stratagem 698 n.

evasive
equivocal 518 adj.

eve
priority 119 n.
evening 129 n.

Eve
woman 373 n.

even
uniform 16 adj.
equal 28 adj.
regular 81 adj.
flatten 216 vb.
symmetrical
  245 adj.
straight 249 adj.
smooth 258 adj. vb.
inexcitable 823 adj.

even-handed
just 913 adj.

evening
end 69 n.
evening 129 n.

evening dress
formal dress
  228 n.

evensong
church service
  988 n.

event
event 154 n.
contest 716 n.

even tenor
uniformity 16 n.
order 60 n.

eventful
eventful 154 adj.
busy 678 adj.

eventual
future 124 adj.

eventuality
juncture 8 n.
event 154 n.
possibility 469 n.

eventuate
happen 154 vb.

evergreen
perpetual 115 adj.
young 130 adj.

unchangeable
  153 adj.

everlasting
perpetual 115 adj.

eversion
inversion 221 n.

everybody
all 52 n.
everyman 79 n.

everyday
typical 83 adj.
plain 573 adj.
usual 610 adj.

everyman,
  everywoman
everyman 79 n.
commoner 869 n.

everyone
everyman 79 n.

everywhere
widely 183 adv.

evict
eject 300 vb.
deprive 786 vb.

evidence
evidence 466 n.vb.
manifestation 522 n.
indication 547 n.
trace 548 n.

evident
visible 443 adj.
demonstrated
  478 adj.
manifest 522 adj.

evidential
evidential 466 adj.

evil
evil 616 n.adj.
harmful 645 adj.
bane 659 n.
adversity 731 n.
wicked 934 adj.

evildoer
evildoer 904 n.

evil eye
malediction 899 n.
spell 983 n.

evince
evidence 466 vb.
manifest 522 vb.

eviscerate
empty 300 vb.
impair 655 vb.

evocation
remembrance 505 n.
representation
  551 n.

evocative
descriptive 590 adj.

evolution
conversion 147 n.
motion 265 n.
progression 285 n.
biology 358 n.

evolve
become 1 vb.
result 157 vb.
produce 164 vb.
evolve 316 vb.

ewe
sheep 365 n.

ewer
vessel 194 n.

ex-
prior 119 adj.
former 125 adj.

exacerbate
augment 36 vb.
aggravate 832 vb.

exact
careful 457 adj.
accurate 494 adj.
perspicuous
  567 adj.
demand 737 vb.
levy 786 vb.

exacting
difficult 700 adj.
oppressive 735 adj.
fastidious 862 adj.

exactitude
accuracy 494 n.

exaggerate
overrate 482 vb.
exaggerate 546 vb.
boast 877 vb.

exalt
elevate 310 vb.
dignify 866 vb.
praise 923 vb.

exaltation
joy 824 n.

exalted
great 32 adj.
noble 868 adj.

examination, exam
inspection 438 n.
exam 459 n.

examine
scan 438 vb.
interrogate 459 vb.

examinee
respondent 460 n.
testee 461 n.

examiner
  inquirer 459 n.
  interlocutor 584 n.
example
  relevance 9 n.
  prototype 23 n.
  example 83 n.
  warning 664 n.
exasperate
  aggravate 832 vb.
  enrage 891 vb.
excavation
  excavation 255 n.
  descent 309 n.
exceed
  be superior 34 vb.
  overstep 306 vb.
  be intemperate
    943 vb.
excel
  be superior 34 vb.
  be skilful 694 vb.
  (see **excellent***)*
Excellency
  sovereign 741 n.
  title 870 n.
excellent
  great 32 adj.
  supreme 34 adj.
  excellent 644 adj.
  splendid 841 adj.
  renowned 866 adj.
exceller
  exceller 644 n.
exception
  exclusion 57 n.
  nonconformity
    84 n.
  qualification 468 n.
  rejection 607 n.
  conditions 766 n.
  disapprobation
    924 n.
exceptionable
  blameworthy
    924 adj.
exceptional
  abnormal 84 adj.
  wonderful 864 adj.
excerpt
  part 53 n.
  select 605 vb.
excess
  remainder 41 n.
  superfluity 637 n.
  cruel act 898 n.
  intemperance 943 n.

excessive
  exorbitant 32 adj.
  exaggerated
    546 adj.
  superfluous 637 adj.
  dear 811 adj.
  unwarranted
    916 adj.
exchange
  equivalence 28 n.
  substitution 150 n.
  interchange
    151 n.vb.
  barter 791 n.
  trade 791 vb.
  market 796 n.
  finance 797 n.
exchequer
  treasury 799 n.
excise
  subtract 39 vb.
  tax 809 n.
excitable
  impressible 819 adj.
  excitable 822 adj.
  irascible 892 adj.
excitant
  excitant 821 n.
excite
  cause 156 vb.
  invigorate 174 vb.
  incite 612 vb.
  excite 821 vb.
  delight 826 vb.
excitement
  excitation 821 n.
exciting
  eloquent 579 adj.
  dramatic 594 adj.
exclaim
  cry 408 vb.
  voice 577 vb.
  disapprove 924 vb.
exclamation
  wonder 864 n.
exclude
  exclude 57 vb.
  make unwelcome
    883 vb.
  exempt 919 vb.
exclusion
  exclusion 57 n.
  rejection 607 n.
exclusive
  sectional 708 adj.
  sectarian 978 adj.
excommunicate

exclude 57 vb.
  curse 899 vb.
excoriate
  uncover 229 vb.
  reprobate 924 vb.
excrement
  excrement 302 n.
excrescence
  swelling 253 n.
excrete
  excrete 302 vb.
excruciating
  painful 377 adj.
  paining 827 adj.
exculpate
  justify 927 vb.
excursion
  land travel 267 n.
  amusement 837 n.
excursive
  deviating 282 adj.
  prolix 570 adj.
excuse
  pretext 614 n.
  stratagem 698 n.
  forgive 909 vb.
  exempt 919 vb.
  vindication 927 vb.
execrable
  damnable 645 adj.
execrate
  hate 888 vb.
  curse 899 vb.
executant
  musician 413 n.
  doer 676 n.
execute
  kill 362 vb.
  do 676 vb.
  carry out 725 vb.
execution
  capital punishment
    963 n.
executioner
  killer 362 n.
executive
  agent 686 n.
  manager 690 n.
executor
  consignee 754 n.
exegesis
  interpretation 520 n.
exemplar
  prototype 23 n.
  example 83 n.
exemplary
  excellent 644 adj.

exemplify
  exemplify 83 vb.
  manifest 522 vb.
exempt
  exempt 919 vb.
exemption
  permission 756 n.
exercise
  train 534 vb.
  prepare oneself
    669 vb.
  use 673 n.vb.
  exercise 682 n.
exert
  use 673 vb.
—oneself
  exert oneself 682 vb.
exertion
  vigorousness 174 n.
  attempt 671 n.
  exertion 682 n.
exhalation
  respiration 352 n.
  odour 394 n.
exhale
  emit 300 vb.
exhaust
  outlet 298 n.
  waste 634 vb.
  make insufficient
    636 vb.
  fatigue 684 vb.
exhaustion
  helplessness 161 n.
exhaustive
  complete 54 adj.
exhibit
  evidence 466 n.
  show 522 vb.
  indicate 547 vb.
exhibition
  spectacle 445 n.
  exhibit 522 n.
exhibitionism
  ostentation 875 n.
exhibitor
  guide 520 n.
  exhibitor 522 n.
exhilarate
  excite 821 vb.
  delight 826 vb.
exhilaration
  excitable state
    822 n.
exhort
  incite 612 vb.
  advise 691 vb.

exhortation
oration 579 n.
exhume
exhume 364 vb.
exigence, exigency
juncture 8 n.
needfulness 627 n.
exigent
demanding 627 adj.
exiguous
exiguous 196 adj.
exile
exclusion 57 n.
foreigner 59 n.
displacement 188 n.
eject 300 vb.
outcast 883 n.
exist
be 1 vb.
be present 189 vb.
live 360 vb.
existence
existence 1 n.
presence 189 n.
life 360 n.
existentialism
existence 1 n.
exit
doorway 263 n.
departure 296 n.
egress 298 n.
outlet 298 n.
exodus
departure 296 n.
ex officio
authoritative
733 adj.
exonerate
forgive 909 vb.
acquit 960 vb.
exorbitant
exorbitant 32 adj.
exaggerated
546 adj.
dear 811 adj.
exorcism
Christian rite 988 n.
exordium
prelude 66 n.
exoteric
undisguised
522 adj.
exotic
extraneous 59 adj.
unconformable
84 adj.
expand

grow 36 vb.
expand 197 vb.
be broad 205 vb.
expanse
space 183 n.
expansion
expansion 197 n.
diffuseness 570 n.
(*see* **expand**)
expansionism
overstepping 306 n.
bellicosity 718 n.
expansive
spacious 183 adj.
broad 205 adj.
expatiate
be diffuse 570 vb.
be loquacious
581 vb.
expatriate
foreigner 59 n.
egress 298 n.
expect
expect 507 vb.
foresee 510 vb.
not wonder 865 vb.
impose a duty
917 vb.
expectant
attentive 455 adj.
expectant 507 adj.
expectation
probability 471 n.
expectation 507 n.
hope 852 n.
expectorate
eruct 300 vb.
expedience,
  expediency
good policy 642 n.
expedient
contrivance 623 n.
advisable 642 adj.
expedite
hasten 680 vb.
facilitate 701 vb.
expedition
land travel 267 n.
haste 680 n.
warfare 718 n.
expel
eject 300 vb.
reject 607 vb.
expend
waste 634 vb.
expend 806 vb.
expendable

superfluous 637 adj.
unimportant
639 adj.
expenditure
expenditure 806 n.
expense
expenditure 806 n.
expense account
subvention 703 n.
expensive
dear 811 adj.
experience
meet with 154 vb.
knowledge 490 n.
wisdom 498 n.
skill 694 n.
feel 818 vb.
experienced
wise 498 adj.
matured 669 adj.
expert 694 adj.
experiment
experiment
461 n.vb.
experimental
experimental
461 adj.
speculative 618 adj.
attempting 671 adj.
experimenter
experimenter 461 n.
learner 538 n.
expert
instructed 490 adj.
expert 694 adj.
expert 696 n.
proficient person
696 n.
expertise
knowledge 490 n.
skill 694 n.
expiate
atone 941 vb.
expiration
respiration 352 n.
expire
elapse 111 vb.
die 361 vb.
explain
account for 158 vb.
interpret 520 vb.
facilitate 701 vb.
—away
confute 479 vb.
disbelieve 486 vb.
explanation
answer 460 n.

interpretation 520 n.
expletive
scurrility 899 n.
explicable
intelligible 516 adj.
explicit
meaningful 514 adj.
intelligible 516 adj.
undisguised
522 adj.
explode
break 46 vb.
be violent 176 vb.
bang 402 vb.
confute 479 vb.
get angry 891 vb.
exploit
use 673 vb.
misuse 675 vb.
deed 676 n.
be skilful 694 vb.
prowess 855 n.
exploration
land travel 267 n.
inquiry 459 n.
search 459 n.
discovery 484 n.
exploratory
precursory 66 adj.
experimental
461 adj.
explore
travel 267 vb.
(*see* **exploration**)
explorer
traveller 268 n.
inquisitive person
453 n.
explosion
havoc 165 n.
outbreak 176 n.
loudness 400 n.
explosive
combustible
385 adj.
dangerous 661 adj.
explosive 723 n.
excitable 822 adj.
(*see* **explode**)
exponent
numerical element
85 n.
interpreter 520 n.
export
transference 272 n.
egress 298 n.
trade 791 vb.

exporter
  transferrer 272 n.
  merchant 794 n.
expose
  uncover 229 vb.
  show 522 vb.
  disclose 526 vb.
  satirize 851 vb.
  shame 867 vb.
  accuse 928 vb.
  —oneself
  face danger 661 vb.
exposed
  defenceless 161 adj.
  windy 352 adj.
  vulnerable 661 adj.
  unprepared 670 adj.
  (*see* **expose**)
exposed nerve
  sensibility 374 n.
exposed to
  liable 180 adj.
  subject 745 adj.
exposition
  interpretation 520 n.
  dissertation 591 n.
expostulate
  reprove 924 vb.
expostulation
  dissuasion 613 n.
  deprecation 762 n.
exposure
  uncovering 229 n.
  visibility 443 n.
  discovery 484 n.
  disclosure 526 n.
  photography 551 n.
  vulnerability 661 n.
expound
  interpret 520 vb.
  teach 534 vb.
express
  definite 80 adj.
  speeder 277 n.
  mean 514 vb.
  courier 529 n.
  affirm 532 vb.
  phrase 563 vb.
  voice 577 vb.
expression
  number 85 n.
  form 243 n.
  mien 445 n.
  meaning 514 n.
  manifestation 522 n.
  affirmation 532 n.
  word 559 n.

  phrase 563 n.
  feeling 818 n.
expressionless
  impassive 820 adj.
expressive
  meaningful 514 adj.
  expressive 516 adj.
  elegant 575 adj.
expropriate
  deprive 786 vb.
expulsion
  displacement 188 n.
  ejection 300 n.
  penalty 963 n.
  (*see* **expel**)
expulsive
  propulsive 287 adj.
  expulsive 300 adj.
expunge
  obliterate 550 vb.
expurgate
  purify 648 vb.
exquisite
  painful 377 adj.
  savoury 390 adj.
  excellent 644 adj.
  pleasurable 826 adj.
  beautiful 841 adj.
  tasteful 846 adj.
extant
  existing 1 adj.
  recorded 548 adj.
extempore
  instantaneously
    116 adj.
  extempore 609 adv.
extemporize
  compose music
    413 vb.
  improvise 609 vb.
extend
  extend 183 vb.
  enlarge 197 vb.
  lengthen 203 vb.
extensibility
  elasticity 328 n.
extension
  increase 36 n.
  adjunct 40 n.
  protraction 113 n.
  lengthening 203 n.
extensive
  extensive 32 adj.
  spacious 183 adj.
extent
  quantity 26 n.
  degree 27 n.

  greatness 32 n.
  space 183 n.
  length 203 n.
extenuate
  moderate 177 vb.
  qualify 468 vb.
  extenuate 927 vb.
exterior
  extrinsic 6 adj.
  exteriority 223 n.
exterminate
  destroy 165 vb.
  slaughter 362 vb.
external
  exterior 223 adj.n.
externalize
  externalize 223 vb.
  materialize 319 vb.
extinct
  extinct 2 adj.
  past 125 adj.
  nonactive 677 adj.
extinguish
  suppress 165 vb.
  extinguish 382 vb.
extinguisher
  extinguisher
    382 n.
extirpate
  destroy 165 vb.
extol
  praise 923 vb.
  worship 981 vb.
extort
  extract 304 vb.
  levy 786 vb.
extortionate
  dear 811 adj.
  greedy 859 adj.
extra
  additional 38 adj.
  extra 40 n.
  superfluity 637 n.
extract
  part 53 n.
  extract 304 vb.
  deliver 668 vb.
  take 786 vb.
extraction
  genealogy 169 n.
extracurricular
  educational 534 adj.
extradition
  transference 272 n.
extramarital
  extramarital
    951 adj.

extramural
  educational 534 adj.
extraneous
  separate 46 adj.
  extraneous 59 adj.
extraordinary
  unusual 84 adj.
  wonderful 864 adj.
extrasensory
  perception
  psychics 984 n.
extraterrestrial
  extraneous 59 adj.
extravagance
  magniloquence
    574 n.
  prodigality 815 n.
extravagant
  exaggerated
    546 adj.
  wasteful 634 adj.
  dear 811 adj.
  prodigal 815 adj.
  ridiculous 849 adj.
extravaganza
  spectacle 445 n.
  ideality 513 n.
extravasation
  haemorrhage 302 n.
extreme
  exorbitant 32 adj.
  ending 69 adj.
  violent 176 adj.
  limit 236 n.
  severe 735 adj.
extremes
  cruel act 898 n.
extremist
  crank 504 n.
  reformer 654 n.
  revolter 738 n.
extremity,
  extremities
  end 69 n.
  extremity 69 n.
  crisis 137 n.
  vertex 213 n.
  adversity 731 n.
extricate
  extract 304 vb.
  deliver 668 vb.
  disencumber
    701 vb.
  liberate 746 vb.
extrinsic
  extrinsic 6 adj.
  unrelated 10 adj.

extrovert, extravert
extrinsicality 6 n.
sociable 882 adj.
extrude
eject 300 vb.
exuberance
productiveness
171 n.
diffuseness 570 n.
exuberant
fervent 818 adj.
exude
exude 298 vb.
be wet 341 vb.
exult
rejoice 835 vb.
boast 877 vb.
exultant
jubilant 833 adj.
ex voto
devotional 981 adj.
eye
centre 225 n.
eye 438 n.
watch 441 vb.
surveillance 457 n.
court 889 vb.
eyeball to eyeball
near 200 adv.
opposing 704 adj.
eye-catching
manifest 522 adj.
eye for an eye
retaliation 714 n.
eyeful
spectacle 445 n.
a beauty 841 n.
eyeglass
eyeglass 442 n.
eyeless
blind 439 adj.
eyelet
fastening 47 n.
orifice 263 n.
eyelid
shade 226 n.
eyeliner
cosmetic 843 n.
eye-opener
discovery 484 n.
lack of expectation
508 n.
eyesight
vision 438 n.
eyesore
eyesore 842 n.
eyewitness

spectator 441 n.
witness 466 n.
eyrie, eyry
nest 192 n.

F

fab
super 644 adj.
Fabian
reformer 654 n.
fable
fantasy 513 n.
fable 543 n.
narrative 590 n.
fabled
imaginary 513 adj.
renowned 866 adj.
fabric
textile 222 n.
structure 331 n.
materials 631 n.
fabricate
compose 56 vb.
imagine 513 vb.
fake 541 vb.
fabrication
falsehood 541 n.
fabulous
prodigious 32 adj.
imaginary 513 adj.
super 644 adj.
façade, facade
exteriority 223 n.
face 237 n.
duplicity 541 n.
face
coat 226 vb.
line 227 vb.
face 237 n.
be in front 237 vb.
orientate 281 vb.
mien 445 n.
withstand 704 vb.
be courageous
855 vb.
prestige 866 n.
insolence 878 n.
—about
revert 148 vb.
—both ways
tergiversate 603 vb.
face down
inversely 221 adv.
faceless
uniform 16 adj.
anonymous 562 adj.

face-lift
revival 656 n.
beautification 843 n.
face powder
cosmetic 843 n.
facet
exteriority 223 n.
appearance 445 n.
facetious
witty 839 adj.
face to face
opposing 704 adj.
face value
appearance 445 n.
price 809 n.
facial
beautification 843 n.
facile
easy 701 adj.
facilitate
facilitate 701 vb.
give scope 744 vb.
facilities
means 629 n.
facility 701 n.
scope 744 n.
facility
skill 694 n.
facing
near 200 adj.
facing 226 n.
lining 227 n.
opposite 240 adj.
facsimile
copy 22 n.
fact
reality 1 n.
certainty 473 n.
fact-finding
inquiring 459 adj.
faction
dissentient 489 n.
description 590 n.
party 708 n.
dissension 709 n.
sect 978 n.
factiousness
quarrelsomeness
709 n.
sectarianism 978 n.
factitious
untrue 543 adj.
factor
component 58 n.
numerical element
85 n.
cause 156 n.

influence 178 n.
manager 690 n.
factor (in), be a
be related 9 vb.
factorize
simplify 44 vb.
factory
production 164 n.
workshop 687 n.
factory farming
agriculture 370 n.
factotum
servant 742 n.
facts
evidence 466 n.
information 524 n.
facts of life
propagation 167 n.
factual
real 1 adj.
veracious 540 adj.
descriptive 590 adj.
faculty
ability 160 n.
teacher 537 n.
aptitude 694 n.
fad
whim 604 n.
fashion 848 n.
faddist
narrow mind 481 n.
crank 504 n.
fade
shade off 27 vb.
be transient 114 vb.
be dim 419 vb.
lose colour 426 vb.
deteriorate 655 vb.
—away
cease 145 vb.
sound faint 401 vb.
disappear 446 vb.
faeces
excrement 302 n.
faerie
fairy 970 n.
fag
tobacco 388 n.
labour 682 n.
servant 742 n.
fagged out
fatigued 684 adj.
faggot
bunch 74 n.
fuel 385 n.
fail
fall short 307 vb.

not suffice 636 vb.
deteriorate 655 vb.
fail 728 vb.
not observe 769 vb.
disapprove 924 vb.
—one
disappoint 509 vb.
failing
vice 934 n.
fail-safe
tutelary 660 adj.
failure
inferiority 35 n.
stop 145 n.
mistake 495 n.
lost labour 641 n.
bungler 697 n.
failure 728 n.
loser 728 n.
insolvency 805 n.
fain
willingly 597 adv.
faint
weak 163 adj.
be insensible
  375 vb.
muted 401 adj.
dim 419 adj.
indistinct 444 adj.
fatigued 684 adj.
faint-hearted
irresolute 601 adj.
cowardly 856 adj.
faintly
slightly 33 adv.
faint praise
detraction 926 n.
fair
warm 379 adj.
whitish 427 adj.
not bad 644 adj.
palmy 730 adj.
middling 732 adj.
market 796 n.
pleasure ground
  837 n.
beautiful 841 adj.
promising 852 adj.
just 913 adj.
honourable 929 adj.
fair chance
fair chance 159 n.
possibility 469 n.
fair deal
justice 913 n.
fair game
dupe 544 n.

fairground
place of amusement
  837 n.
fair-haired
yellow 433 adj.
fairly
slightly 33 adv.
fair-minded
wise 498 adj.
just 913 adj.
fair play
justice 913 n.
fair shares
participation 775 n.
apportionment
  783 n.
fairway
access 624 n.
route 624 n.
fairy
fairy 970 n.
fairy godmother
protector 660 n.
benefactor 903 n.
fairyland
fantasy 513 n.
prodigy 864 n.
fairy tale
ideality 513 n.
fable 543 n.
fait accompli
reality 1 n.
completion 725 n.
faith
belief 485 n.
probity 929 n.
religious faith 973 n.
piety 979 n.
faithful
lifelike 18 adj.
accurate 494 adj.
true 494 adj.
obedient 739 adj.
observant 768 adj.
trustworthy 929 adj.
pious 979 adj.
faithful, the
church member
  976 n.
faithfulness
loyalty 739 n.
faith healer
doctor 658 n.
faithless
perfidious 930 adj.
irreligious 974 adj.
fake

imitation 20 n.
fake 541 vb.
sham 542 n.
spurious 542 adj.
fall
decrease 37 n.vb.
autumn 129 n.
be destroyed 165 vb.
descent 309 n.
perish 361 vb.
relapse 657 n.
fail 728 vb.
—apart
separate 46 vb.
deteriorate 655 vb.
—away
apostatize 603 vb.
—back on
avail oneself of
  673 vb.
—below
be inferior 35 vb.
not suffice 636 vb.
—down on
not complete
  726 vb.
—for
be credulous 487 vb.
be in love 887 vb.
—foul of
have trouble 731 vb.
—from grace
be wicked 934 vb.
—in love
be in love 887 vb.
—in with
conform 83 vb.
consent 758 vb.
—off
tumble 309 vb.
deteriorate 655 vb.
—out
be dispersed 75 vb.
quarrel 709 vb.
—short
fall short 307 vb.
—upon
attack 712 vb.
fallacy
sophism 477 n.
error 495 n.
fallen, the
death roll 361 n.
fallen woman
prostitute 952 n.
fall guy
dupe 544 n.

fallible
unreliable 474 adj.
illogical 477 adj.
misjudging 481 adj.
foolish 499 adj.
falling off
decrease 37 n.
deterioration 655 n.
fallout
sequel 67 n.
nucleonics 160 n.
radiation 417 n.
poison 659 n.
fallout shelter
refuge 662 n.
fallow
unproductive
  172 adj.
falls
waterfall 350 n.
false
erroneous 495 adj.
false 541 adj.
spurious 542 adj.
perfidious 930 adj.
false alarm
false alarm 665 n.
falsehood
falsehood 541 n.
misrepresentation
  552 n.
false light
misrepresentation
  552 n.
false modesty
prudery 950 n.
false name
misnomer 562 n.
false note
misfit 25 n.
false position
predicament 700 n.
false pretences
deception 542 n.
falsetto
stridor 407 n.
falsify
misinterpret 521 vb.
be false 541 vb.
falsity
falsehood 541 n.
(see false)
falter
stammer 580 vb.
be irresolute 601 vb.
fame
remembrance 505 n.

FAM

publicity 528 n.
famousness 866 n.
familiar
known 490 adj.
usual 610 adj.
impertinent 878 adj.
disrespectful
921 adj.
demon 970 n.
familiarity
knowledge 490 n.
habit 610 n.
friendship 880 n.
family
family 11 n.
breed 77 n.
parental 169 adj.
posterity 170 n.
social group 371 n.
community 708 n.
family planning
unproductiveness
172 n.
family tree
genealogy 169 n.
famine
scarcity 636 n.
hunger 859 n.
famished
underfed 636 adj.
hungry 859 adj.
famous
well-known 528 adj.
renowned 866 adj.
fan
bunch 74 n.
ventilation 352 n.
refrigerate 382 vb.
enthusiast 504 n.
refresh 685 vb.
patron 707 n.
animate 821 vb.
—out
be dispersed 75 vb.
open 263 vb.
fanatic
doctrinaire 473 n.
narrow mind 481 n.
crank 504 n.
zealot 979 n.
fanatical
positive 473 adj.
fancier
breeder 369 n.
enthusiast 504 n.
fanciful
absurd 497 adj.

FAR

imaginary 513 adj.
fan club
lover 887 n.
commender 923 n.
fancy
think 449 vb.
idea 451 n.
suppose 512 vb.
ideality 513 n.
imagine 513 vb.
whim 604 n.
choice 605 n.
ornamental 844 adj.
liking 859 n.
fancy dress
disguise 527 n.
fancy man
libertine 952 n.
fanfare
loudness 400 n.
celebration 876 n.
fang(s)
tooth 256 n.
fanlight
window 263 n.
fantasize
imagine 513 vb.
fantastic
absurd 497 adj.
super 644 adj.
ridiculous 849 adj.
wonderful 864 adj.
fantasy
insubstantiality 4 n.
fantasy 513 n.
imagination 513 n.
aspiration 852 n.
far
distant 199 adj.
farce
foolery 497 n.
stage play 594 n.
farcical
funny 849 adj.
fare
be in a state of
7 vb.
meal 301 n.
price 809 n.
farewell
valediction 296 n.
far-fetched
unbelieved 486 adj.
far-flung
unassembled 75 adj.
farinaceous
powdery 332 adj.

FAS

farm
farm 370 n.
cultivate 370 vb.
—out
lease 784 vb.
farmer
farmer 370 n.
farming
agriculture 370 n.
farrago
medley 43 n.
confusion 61 n.
far-reaching
extensive 32 adj.
farrier
animal husbandry
369 n.
farrow
reproduce itself
167 vb.
far-sighted
intelligent 498 adj.
foreseeing 510 adj.
farthest point
extremity 69 n.
fascia, facia
strip 208 n.
fascinate
engross 449 vb.
motivate 612 vb.
excite love 887 vb.
bewitch 983 vb.
fascination
pleasurableness
826 n.
liking 859 n.
wonder 864 n.
Fascism
government 733 n.
brute force 735 n.
fashion
modality 7 n.
conformity 83 n.
modernism 126 n.
dressing 228 n.
form 243 n.vb.
feature 445 n.
style 566 n.
practice 610 n.
fashion 848 n.
fashionable
fashionable 848 adj.
fast
firm 45 adj.
fixed 153 adj.
speedy 277 adj.
coloured 425 adj.

FAT

retained 778 adj.
fast 946 n.
unchaste 951 adj.
fast breeder reactor
nucleonics 160 n.
fast day
holy day 988 n.
fasten
affix 45 vb.
close 264 vb.
fastener
fastening 47 n.
fastidious
discriminating
463 adj.
clean 648 adj.
fastidious 862 adj.
fastness
fort 713 n.
fast one
trickery 542 n.
fat
fleshy 195 adj.
fat 357 n.
prosperous 730 adj.
fatal
deadly 362 adj.
harmful 645 adj.
fatalism
necessity 596 n.
submission 721 n.
fatality
death roll 361 n.
fate
destiny 155 n.
chance 159 n.
fate 596 n.
nondesign 618 n.
fated
fated 596 adj.
predetermined
608 adj.
fateful
important 638 adj.
fathead
dunce 501 n.
father
kinsman 11 n.
generate 167 vb.
cleric 986 n.
fatherhood
paternity 169 n.
fatherland
home 192 n.
fatherly
parental 169 adj.
benevolent 897 adj.

fathom
long measure 203 n.
plunge 313 vb.
understand 516 vb.
fathomless
deep 211 adj.
fatigue
sleepiness 679 n.
fatigue 684 n.vb.
oppress 735 vb.
be tedious 838 vb.
fatigues
uniform 228 n.
fat of the land
plenty 635 n.
prosperity 730 n.
fatten
grow 36 vb.
enlarge 197 vb.
feed 301 vb.
breed stock 369 vb.
fatuity
absurdity 497 n.
folly 499 n.
fatuous
meaningless
515 adj.
faucet
stopper 264 n.
fault
weakness 163 n.
gap 201 n.
blunder 495 vb.
defect 647 n.
dispraise 924 vb.
vice 934 n.
faultfinder
malcontent 829 n.
detractor 926 n.
faultless
perfect 646 adj.
guiltless 935 adj.
faulty
inexact 495 adj.
ungrammatical
565 adj.
imperfect 647 adj.
faun
mythical being
970 n.
fauna
animality 365 n.
faux pas
mistake 495 n.
favour
advantage 34 n.
influence 178 n.

promote 285 vb.
badge 547 n.
choose 605 vb.
benefit 615 n.vb.
patronize 703 vb.
be auspicious
730 vb.
liking 859 n.
honours 866 n.
kind act 897 n.
injustice 914 n.
approbation 923 n.
favourable
opportune 137 adj.
promising 852 adj.
approving 923 adj.
favourite
chosen 605 adj.
contender 716 n.
loved one 887 n.
favourite 890 n.
favouritism
prejudice 481 n.
fawn
young creature
132 n.
brown 430 adj.
be servile 879 vb.
caress 889 vb.
fealty
loyalty 739 n.
fear
fear 854 n.vb.
respect 920 n.vb.
fearful
nervous 854 adj.
fearlessness
courage 855 n.
feasible
possible 469 adj.
feast
feasting 301 n.
feed 301 vb.
revel 837 vb.
social gathering
882 n.
feast day
festivity 837 n.
holy day 988 n.
feat
deed 676 n.
prowess 855 n.
feather
sort 77 n.
lightness 323 n.
—one's nest
get rich 800 vb.

be selfish 932 vb.
featherbrained
light-minded
456 adj.
foolish 499 adj.
feathered
downy 259 adj.
flying 271 adj.
feather in one's cap
honours 866 n.
feathers
plumage 259 n.
featherweight
-light 323 adj.
pugilist 722 n.
feathery
downy 259 adj.
light 323 adj.
feature(s)
character 5 n.
component 58 n.
speciality 80 n.
face 237 n.
form 243 n.
feature 445 n.
show 522 vb.
broadcast 531 n.
identification 547 n.
dramatize 594 vb.
featureless
uniform 16 adj.
amorphous
244 adj.
febrifuge
antidote 658 n.
febrile
hot 379 adj.
excitable 822 adj.
feckless
useless 641 adj.
fecund
prolific 171 adj.
federal
corporate 708 adj.
federalism
government 733 n.
federation
association 706 n.
political
organization
733 n.
fed up
discontented
829 adj.
bored 838 adj.
fee
estate 777 n.

pay 804 n.
reward 962 n.
feeble
inferior 35 adj.
weak 163 adj.
muted 401 adj.
poorly reasoned
477 adj.
feeble 572 adj.
lax 734 adj.
feeble-minded
unintelligent
499 adj.
feed
feed 301 vb.
provide 633 vb.
refresh 685 vb.
feedback
data processing
86 n.
answer 460 n.
feel
texture 331 n.
have feeling 374 vb.
touch 378 vb.
feel 818 vb.
suffer 825 vb.
resent 891 vb.
—for
pity 905 vb.
—in one's bones
intuit 476 vb.
foresee 510 vb.
—one's way
move slowly 278 vb.
be tentative 461 vb.
—the pinch
be in difficulty
700 vb.
have trouble 731 vb.
feeler
feeler 378 n.
empiricism 461 n.
offer 759 n.
feeling
sense 374 n.
touch 378 n.
intuition 476 n.
opinion 485 n.
vigour 571 n.
feeling 818 n.adj.
feelings
affections 817 n.
feet
foot 214 n.
feet of clay
defect 647 n.

feign
dissemble 541 vb.
feint
trickery 542 n.
stratagem 698 n.
felicitate
congratulate 886 vb.
felicitous
apt 24 adj.
elegant 575 adj.
felicity
happiness 824 n.
feline
cat 365 n.
fell
demolish 165 vb.
high land 209 n.
strike 279 vb.
fell 311 vb.
evil 616 adj.
cruel 898 adj.
fellow
analogue 18 n.
compeer 28 n.
concomitant 89 n.
male 372 n.
colleague 707 n.
fellow citizen
native 191 n.
fellow creature
person 371 n.
fellow feeling
benevolence 897 n.
fellowship
association 706 n.
community 708 n.
friendship 880 n.
fellow traveller
collaborator 707 n.
felon
offender 904 n.
felony
lawbreaking 954 n.
felt
textile 222 n.
female
female 373 n.adj.
feminine
generic 77 adj.
female 373 adj.
feminist
woman 373 n.
reformist 654 n.
femme fatale
motivator 612 n.
a beauty 841 n.
fen

marsh 347 n.
fence
fence 235 n.
obstacle 702 n.
defences 713 n.
parry 713 vb.
thief 789 n.
fencing
duel 716 n.
fender
furnace 383 n.
shelter 662 n.
feral
animal 365 adj.
ferment
turmoil 61 n.
stimulation 174 n.
commotion 318 n.
leaven 323 n.
excitable state 822 n.
fern
plant 366 n.
ferocious
cruel 898 adj.
ferret
mammal 365 n.
ferret out
discover 484 vb.
ferry
carry 273 vb.
boat 275 n.
fertile
imaginative 513 adj.
profitable 640 adj.
(see **fertility***)*
fertility
productiveness
171 n.
fertility drug
propagation 167 n.
fertilizer 171 n.
fertilize
make fruitful
171 vb.
cultivate 370 vb.
fertilizer
fertilizer 171 n.
fervent
hot 379 adj.
fervent 818 adj.
loving 887 adj.
pietistic 979 adj.
fervour
vigorousness 174 n.
warm feeling 818 n.
fester
be unclean 649 vb.

deteriorate 655 vb.
festival
festivity 837 n.
holy day 988 n.
festive
celebratory 876 adj.
sociable 882 adj.
festivity
festivity 837 n.
festoon
curve 248 n.
decorate 844 vb.
fetch
carry 273 vb.
cost 809 vb.
ghost 970 n.
fetching
personable 841 adj.
fête
amusement 837 n.
pageant 875 n.
celebration 876 n.
fetid
fetid 397 adj.
bad 645 adj.
fetish
idol 982 n.
fetlock
foot 214 n.
fetter
tie 45 vb.
hinder 702 vb.
fetter 748 n.
fettered
imprisoned 747 adj.
feud
quarrel 709 n.
revenge 910 n.
feudal
olden 127 adj.
governmental
733 adj.
feudalism
service 745 n.
fever
heat 379 n.
illness 651 n.
excitable state 822 n.
fevered
frenzied 503 adj.
feverish
sick 651 adj.
hasty 680 adj.
excited 821 adj.
few
few 105 adj.
infrequent 140 adj.

scarce 636 adj.
few and far between
discontinuous
72 adj.
few 105 adj.
seldom 140 adv.
fey
bewitched 983 adj.
psychical 984 adj.
fiancé(e)
loved one 887 n.
fiasco
failure 728 n.
fiat
decree 737 n.
fib
untruth 543 n.
fibber
liar 545 n.
fibre
essential part 5 n.
fibre 208 n.
texture 331 n.
fibreglass
textile 222 n.
fibrous
tough 329 adj.
(see **fibre***)*
fickle
changeful 152 adj.
unreliable 474 adj.
capricious 604 adj.
fiction
ideality 513 n.
falsehood 541 n.
novel 590 n.
fictitious
unreal 2 adj.
imaginary 513 adj.
untrue 543 adj.
fiddle
viol 414 n.
contrivance 623 n.
defraud 788 vb.
be dishonest 930 vb.
—with
touch 378 vb.
fiddler
instrumentalist
413 n.
fiddling
trivial 639 adj.
laborious 682 adj.
fidelity
accuracy 494 n.
loyalty 739 n.
probity 929 n.

fidget
  agitation 318 n.
  restlessness 678 n.
  excitability 822 n.
fief
  lands 777 n.
field
  range 183 n.
  enclosure 235 n.
  grassland 348 n.
  function 622 n.
  arena 724 n.
  scope 744 n.
field day
  special day 876 n.
fielder
  player 837 n.
field glasses
  telescope 442 n.
field marshal
  army officer 741 n.
field sports
  sport 837 n.
fiend
  enthusiast 504 n.
  monster 938 n.
  devil 969 n.
fiendish
  wicked 934 adj.
fierce
  furious 176 adj.
  active 678 adj.
  warlike 718 adj.
  irascible 892 adj.
  cruel 898 adj.
fiery
  fiery 379 adj.
  luminous 417 adj.
  fervent 818 adj.
  excitable 822 adj.
fiesta
  festivity 837 n.
fifth column
  perfidy 930 n.
fifty-fifty
  equal 28 adj.
fight
  fight 716 n.vb.
  go to war 718 vb.
—off
  parry 713 vb.
  resist 715 vb.
—shy
  be unwilling 598 vb.
  avoid 620 vb.
fighter
  trier 671 n.

combatant 722 n.
fig leaf
  loincloth 228 n.
  concealment 525 n.
figment
  insubstantial thing 4 n.
  ideality 513 n.
figurative
  semantic 514 adj.
  figurative 519 adj.
  representing 551 adj.
  ornate 574 adj.
figure
  number 85 n.
  do sums 86 vb.
  outline 233 n.
  form 243 n.vb.
  feature 445 n.
  image 551 n.
  represent 551 vb.
  price 809 n.
  person of repute 866 n.
—out
  reason 475 vb.
figurehead
  insubstantial thing 4 n.
  prow 237 n.
  nonentity 639 n.
figure of fun
  laughingstock 851 n.
figure of speech
  trope 519 n.
filament
  filament 208 n.
filch
  steal 788 vb.
file
  class 62 vb.
  procession 71 n.
  receptacle 194 n.
  sharpener 256 n.
  smoother 258 n.
  walk 267 vb.
  rub 333 vb.
  record 548 n.vb.
  formation 722 n.
filial
  filial 170 adj.
  obedient 739 adj.
filibuster
  delay 136 n.
  hinderer 702 n.

filigree
  network 222 n.
  ornamental art 844 n.
fill
  fill 54 vb.
  load 193 vb.
  replenish 633 vb.
  sate 863 vb.
fillet
  strip 208 n.
  cook 301 vb.
filling
  contents 193 n.
  lining 227 n.
fillip
  stimulant 174 n.
  excitant 821 n.
filly
  young creature 132 n.
  horse 273 n.
film
  layer 207 n.
  covering 226 n.
  opacity 423 n.
  film 445 n.
  photograph 551 vb.
filmgoer
  spectator 441 n.
  cinema 445 n.
filmy
  textural 331 adj.
  opaque 423 adj.
filter
  screen 421 n.
  purify 648 vb.
filth
  dirt 649 n.
  impurity 951 n.
filthy
  not nice 645 adj.
final
  ending 69 adj.
  completive 725 adj.
finale
  end 69 n.
finalist
  contender 716 n.
finals
  exam 459 n.
finance
  find means 629 vb.
  finance 797 n.
financial
  businesslike 622 adj.

monetary 797 adj.
financier
  lender 784 n.
  treasurer 798 n.
find
  meet with 154 vb.
  judge 480 vb.
  discover 484 vb.
  provide 633 vb.
  acquire 771 vb.
—fault
  dispraise 924 vb.
—means
  find means 629 vb.
—out
  discover 484 vb.
finder
  telescope 442 n.
  detector 484 n.
finding
  judgement 480 n.
  legal trial 959 n.
fine
  small 33 adj.
  narrow 206 adj.
  rare 325 adj.
  textural 331 adj.
  dry 342 adj.
  transparent 422 adj.
  discriminating 463 adj.
  accurate 494 adj.
  excellent 644 adj.
  splendid 841 adj.
  penalty 963 n.
fine gentleman/lady
  fop 848 n.
  proud person 871 n.
finer feelings
  moral sensibility 819 n.
finery
  clothing 228 n.
  finery 844 n.
fine-spun
  narrow 206 adj.
  textural 331 adj.
finesse
  cunning 698 n.
finger
  piece 53 n.
  finger 378 n.
  indicator 547 n.
  nippers 778 n.
fingerprint(s)
  evidence 466 n.

identification 547 n.
trace 548 n.
finial
vertex 213 n.
finicky
fastidious 862 adj.
finish
completeness 54 n.
end 69 n.vb.
cease 145 vb.
elegance 575 n.
perfection 646 n.
completion 725 n.
—off
murder 362 vb.
finishing school
academy 539 n.
finite
limited 236 adj.
fire
shoot 287 vb.
dismiss 300 vb.
fire 379 n.
kindle 381 vb.
luminary 420 n.
signal 547 n.
vigour 571 n.
bombardment 712 n.
warm feeling 818 n.
—at
fire at 712 vb.
fire alarm
danger signal 665 n.
firearm
firearm 723 n.
firebrand
incendiarism 381 n.
troublemaker 663 n.
agitator 738 n.
firebreak
gap 201 n.
fire brigade
extinguisher 382 n.
fire-eater
desperado 857 n.
fire engine
extinguisher 382 n.
fire escape
means of escape 667 n.
firefighter
extinguisher 382 n.
protector 660 n.
firefly
insect 365 n.
glow-worm 420 n.

firelight
glimmer 419 n.
fireplace
furnace 383 n.
fireproof
incombustible 382 adj.
fire-raising
incendiarism 381 n.
fireside
focus 76 n.
home 192 n.
firewood
fuel 385 n.
fireworks
fireworks 420 n.
celebration 876 n.
firing line
front 237 n.
battleground 724 n.
firm
firm 45 adj.
fixed 153 adj.
dense 324 adj.
rigid 326 adj.
resolute 599 adj.
merchant 794 n.
firmament
heavens 321 n.
first
supreme 34 adj.
first 68 adj.
prior 119 adj.
foremost 283 adj.
best 644 adj.
first aid
therapy 658 n.
firstborn
precursor 66 n.
first choice
choice 605 n.
favourite 890 n.
first-class
supreme 34 adj.
first draft
plan 623 n.
firsthand
original 21 adj.
evidential 466 adj.
first-rate
best 644 adj.
first steps
debut 68 n.
learning 536 n.
firth
gulf 345 n.

fiscal
monetary 797 adj.
fish
fish food 301 n.
fish 365 n.
hunt 619 vb.
—for
search 459 vb.
fisher
hunter 619 n.
fishnet
network 222 n.
fish out of water
misfit 25 n.
fishpond
stock farm 369 n.
fishy
animal 365 adj.
dishonest 930 adj.
fissile
brittle 330 adj.
fission
separation 46 n.
decomposition 51 n.
nucleonics 160 n.
fissure
gap 201 n.
fist
finger 378 n.
nippers 778 n.
fisticuffs
pugilism 716 n.
fit
adjust 24 vb.
cohere 48 vb.
spasm 318 n.
frenzy 503 n.
advisable 642 adj.
healthy 650 adj.
right 913 adj.
—in
conform 83 vb.
—out
provide 633 vb.
make ready 669 vb.
—together
combine 50 vb.
fit for
useful 640 adj.
fit for nothing
useless 641 adj.
fitful
discontinuous 72 adj.
fitful 142 adj.
fitness
relevance 9 n.

fitness 24 n.
preparedness 669 n.
aptitude 694 n.
fits and starts
fitfulness 142 n.
fitter
machinist 630 n.
fitting
fit 24 adj.
advisable 642 adj.
right 913 adj.
fittings
equipment 630 n.
fix
affix 45 vb.
stabilize 153 vb.
murder 362 vb.
predetermine 608 vb.
repair 656 vb.
predicament 700 n.
drug-taking 949 n.
fixation
eccentricity 503 n.
fixative
adhesive 47 n.
fixed
fixed 153 adj.
still 266 adj.
habitual 610 adj.
fixer
trickster 545 n.
mender 656 n.
fixity
resolution 599 n.
obstinacy 602 n.
fixture
adjunct 40 n.
fixture 153 n.
equipment 630 n.
fixtures
property 777 n.
fizz
vigorousness 174 n.
soft drink 301 n.
bubble 355 n.vb.
fizzle
hiss 406 vb.
—out
miscarry 728 vb.
fizzy
windy 352 adj.
bubbly 355 adj.
flabbergasted
fearing 854 adj.
wondering 864 adj.

flabby
　soft 327 adj.
　pulpy 356 adj.
flaccid
　weak 163 adj.
　feeble 572 adj.
flag
　be weak 163 vb.
　paving 226 n.
　flag 547 n.
　be fatigued 684 vb.
—down
　signal 547 vb.
flag day
　request 761 n.
flagellation
　penance 941 n.
　asceticism 945 n.
flagon
　vessel 194 n.
flagrancy
　publicity 528 n.
　ostentation 875 n.
flagrant
　heinous 934 adj.
flagship
　warship 722 n.
flagstaff
　prop 218 n.
flail
　strike 279 vb.
　farm tool 370 n.
flair
　discrimination
　　463 n.
　aptitude 694 n.
　good taste 846 n.
flak
　bombardment
　　712 n.
flake
　small thing 33 n.
　lamina 207 n.
　powder 332 n.
flaky
　brittle 330 adj.
flamboyant
　ornate 574 adj.
flame
　fire 379 n.
　shine 417 vb.
　luminary 420 n.
　redness 431 n.
flameproof
　incombustible
　　382 adj.
flamethrower

gun 723 n.
flaming
　fiery 379 adj.
　fervent 818 adj.
flan
　pastries 301 n.
flange
　edge 234 n.
flank
　laterality 239 n.
flannel
　textile 222 n.
　empty talk 515 n.
　cleaning cloth 648 n.
flap
　come unstuck 49 vb.
　hanging object
　　217 n.
　covering 226 n.
　agitation 318 n.
flare
　be broad 205 vb.
　be hot 379 vb.
　shine 417 vb.
　torch 420 n.
—up
　be excited 821 vb.
　get angry 891 vb.
flash
　instant 116 n.
　move fast 277 vb.
　flash 417 n.
　communicate
　　524 vb.
　signal 547 n.
flashback
　remembrance 505 n.
flasher
　stripper 229 n.
flash in the pan
　insubstantial thing
　　4 n.
　brief span 114 n.
flashlight
　lamp 420 n.
flash point
　casus belli 709 n.
flashy
　florid 425 adj.
　ornate 574 adj.
　vulgar 847 adj.
　showy 875 adj.
flask
　vessel 194 n.
flat
　uniform 16 adj.
　flat 192 n.

low 210 adj.
　flat 216 adj.
　unsharpened
　　257 adj.
　still 266 adj.
　tasteless 387 adj.
　discordant 411 adj.
　assertive 532 adj.
　feeble 572 adj.
　deteriorated
　　655 adj.
　tedious 838 adj.
flats
　marsh 347 n.
flatten
　flatten 216 vb.
　fell 311 vb.
flatter
　misrepresent
　　552 vb.
　beautify 841 vb.
　flatter 925 vb.
—oneself
　expect 507 vb.
　be vain 873 vb.
flatterer
　toady 879 n.
　flatterer 925 n.
flattery
　empty talk 515 n.
　flattery 925 n.
flatulence
　gaseousness 336 n.
　magniloquence
　　574 n.
flaunt
　show 522 vb.
　be ostentatious
　　875 vb.
flautist
　instrumentalist
　　413 n.
flavour
　taste 386 n.
　season 388 vb.
flavourless
　tasteless 387 adj.
flaw
　weakness 163 n.
　defect 647 n.
　blemish 845 n.vb.
flawless
　perfect 646 adj.
flax
　fibre 208 n.
flay
　uncover 229 vb.

dispraise 924 vb.
　flog 963 vb.
flea
　jumper 312 n.
　insect 365 n.
fleabag
　dirty person 649 n.
fleabite
　trifle 639 n.
fleck
　small thing 33 n.
　maculation 437 n.
fledgeling
　young creature
　　132 n.
　bird 365 n.
flee
　run away 620 vb.
fleece
　skin 226 n.
　hair 259 n.
　fleece 786 vb.
fleecy
　soft 327 adj.
fleet
　shipping 275 n.
　speedy 277 adj.
　navy 722 n.
fleeting
　transient 114 adj.
flesh
　meat 301 n.
　matter 319 n.
　humankind 371 n.
　sensualism 944 n.
flesh and blood
　substance 3 n.
　animality 365 n.
fleshy
　fleshy 195 adj.
　pulpy 356 adj.
flexed
　curved 248 adj.
flexible
　conformable
　　83 adj.
　flexible 327 adj.
　tractable 701 adj.
flexion
　curvature 248 n.
　deviation 282 n.
flick
　knock 279 n.
　propel 287 vb.
　touch 378 n.vb.
—the switch
　operate 173 vb.

flicker
  be transient 114 vb.
  oscillate 317 vb.
  flash 417 n.
  be dim 419 vb.
flickering
  fitful 142 adj.
flight
  group 74 n.
  aeronautics 271 n.
  departure 296 n.
  avoidance 620 n.
  escape 667 n.
  air force 722 n.
  defeat 728 n.
flight of fancy
  ideality 513 n.
flighty
  light-minded 456 adj.
flimsy
  insubstantial 4 adj.
  flimsy 163 adj.
  poorly reasoned 477 adj.
flinch
  recoil 280 vb.
  feel pain 377 vb.
  avoid 620 vb.
  quake 854 vb.
fling
  propel 287 vb.
  scope 744 n.
  dance 837 n.
flint
  hardness 326 n.
  lighter 385 n.
  tool 630 n.
flinty
  cruel 898 adj.
flip
  strike 279 vb.
  touch 378 n.vb.
  impertinent 878 adj.
—through
  be attentive 455 vb.
flippant
  light-minded 456 adj.
  witty 839 adj.
flipper
  feeler 378 n.
flirt
  affecter 850 n.
  excite love 887 vb.
flirtation
  whim 604 n.

  love affair 887 n.
flit
  be transient 114 vb.
  be in motion 265 vb.
  fly 271 vb.
  decamp 296 vb.
float
  hang 217 vb.
  swim 269 vb.
  fly 271 vb.
  pushcart 274 n.
  raft 275 n.
  be light 323 vb.
floating vote
  dubiety 474 n.
  no choice 606 n.
flock
  group 74 n.
  hair 259 n.
  animal 365 n.
  laity 987 n.
flock together
  congregate 74 vb.
floe
  ice 380 n.
flog
  incite 612 vb.
  fatigue 684 vb.
  sell 793 vb.
  flog 963 vb.
—a dead horse
  waste effort 641 vb.
flood
  be many 104 vb.
  burst in 297 vb.
  flow 350 vb.
  superabound 637 vb.
floodgate
  outlet 298 n.
  conduit 351 n.
floodlight
  lamp 420 n.
  theatre 594 n.
floor
  layer 207 n.
  base 214 n.
  paving 226 n.
  overlay 226 vb.
  fell 311 vb.
  confute 479 vb.
  arena 724 n.
floor show
  stage show 594 n.
flop
  descend 309 vb.
  failure 728 n.

  miscarry 728 vb.
floppy
  nonadhesive 49 adj.
  soft 327 adj.
flora
  vegetable life 366 n.
  organism 358 n.
florescence
  maturation 669 n.
florid
  florid 425 adj.
  ornate 574 adj.
floss
  hair 259 n.
flotilla
  shipping 275 n.
flotsam
  derelict 779 n.
flounce
  trimming 844 n.
  be angry 891 vb.
flounder
  be uncertain 474 vb.
  be clumsy 695 vb.
  be in difficulty 700 vb.
flour
  cereals 301 n.
  powder 332 n.
flourish
  be fruitful 171 vb.
  brandish 317 vb.
  show 522 vb.
  call 547 n.
  ornament 574 n.
  lettering 586 n.
  flourish 615 vb.
  be healthy 650 vb.
  prosper 730 vb.
  pattern 844 n.
  be ostentatious 875 vb.
flout
  not respect 921 vb.
flow
  continuity 71 n.
  elapse 111 vb.
  current 350 n.
  flow 350 vb.
flow chart
  statistics 86 n.
flower
  grow 36 vb.
  reproduce itself 167 vb.
  flower 366 n.
  elite 644 n.

flowerpot
  vessel 194 n.
  garden 370 n.
flowery
  vegetal 366 adj.
  figurative 519 adj.
  ornate 574 adj.
flowing
  fluid 335 adj.
flown
  absent 190 adj.
  escaped 667 adj.
flu
  infection 651 n.
fluctuate
  be periodic 141 vb.
  vary 152 vb.
fluctuation
  irresolution 601 n.
flue
  chimney 263 n.
  furnace 383 n.
fluency
  eloquence 579 n.
  loquacity 581 n.
fluent
  flowing 350 adj.
  speaking 579 adj.
  loquacious 581 adj.
fluff
  hair 259 n.
  softness 327 n.
  mistake 495 n.
fluffy
  downy 259 adj.
  light 323 adj.
fluid
  unstable 152 adj.
  amorphous 244 adj.
  fluid 335 n.adj.
fluke
  chance 159 n.
  nondesign 618 n.
  success 727 n.
flummox
  puzzle 474 vb.
flunk
  fail 728 vb.
flunkey, flunky
  domestic 742 n.
  toady 879 n.
fluorescent
  luminous 417 adj.
flurry
  derange 63 vb.
  commotion 318 n.
  rain 350 n.

gale 352 n.
distract 456 vb.
activity 678 n.
flush
equal 28 adj.
flat 216 adj.
be hot 379 vb.
glow 417 n.
hunt 619 vb.
clean 648 vb.
moneyed 800 adj.
show feeling 818 vb.
flushed
red 431 adj.
excited 821 adj.
fluster
derange 63 vb.
flustered
agitated 318 adj.
flute
groove 262 vb.
shrill 407 vb.
flute 414 n.
flutter
fly 271 vb.
agitation 318 n.
gambling 618 n.
feeling 818 n.
frighten 854 vb.
flux
motion 265 n.
current 350 n.
fly
elapse 111 vb.
garment 228 n.
fly 271 vb.
move fast 277 vb.
insect 365 n.
intelligent 498 adj.
run away 620 vb.
cunning 698 adj.
—a kite
be tentative 461 vb.
—in the face of
oppose 704 vb.
disobey 738 vb.
flyblown
blemished 845 adj.
flyby
space travel 271 n.
fly-by-night
avoiding 620 adj.
flyer, flier
aeronaut 271 n.
flying
aeronautics 271 n.
aviational 276 adj.

flying colours
trophy 729 n.
flying saucer
spaceship 276 n.
fly in the ointment
hitch 702 n.
flyover
bridge 624 n.
flypaper
trap 542 n.
flypast
pageant 875 n.
fly sheet
canopy 226 n.
flyweight
pugilist 722 n.
flywheel
rotator 315 n.
foal
young creature
132 n.
horse 273 n.
foam
be violent 176 vb.
bubble 355 n.vb.
—at the mouth
go mad 503 vb.
get angry 891 vb.
foamy
light 323 adj.
bubbly 355 adj.
fob off
not observe 769 vb.
—off with
deceive 542 vb.
focal
central 225 adj.
focus
adjust 24 vb.
focus 76 n.vb.
centre 225 n.
converge 293 vb.
gaze 438 vb.
objective 617 n.
—the attention
attract notice
455 vb.
fodder
provender 301 n.
foe
enemy 881 n.
foetus
young creature
132 n.
fog
cloud 355 n.
opacity 423 n.

blur 440 vb.
foggy
dense 324 adj.
cloudy 355 adj.
dim 419 adj.
foghorn
danger signal 665 n.
foible
speciality 80 n.
defect 647 n.
foil
lamina 207 n.
disappoint 509 vb.
be obstructive
702 vb.
sidearms 723 n.
foist
compel 740 vb.
fold
stable 192 n.
enclosure 235 n.
fold 261 n.vb.
—up
cease 145 vb.
folder
receptacle 194 n.
foliage
foliage 366 n.
folio
edition 589 n.
folk
social group 371 n.
folklore
tradition 127 n.
anthropology 371 n.
knowledge 490 n.
follow
do likewise 20 vb.
come after 65 vb.
ensue 120 vb.
result 157 vb.
follow 284 vb.
understand 516 vb.
pursue 619 vb.
serve 742 vb.
observe 768 vb.
—suit
conform 83 vb.
—through
sustain 146 vb.
carry through
725 vb.
follower
concomitant 89 n.
follower 284 n.
dependant 742 n.
sectarian 978 n.

follow-up
sequel 67 n.
folly
folly 499 n.
rashness 857 n.
foment
heat 381 vb.
animate 821 vb.
fond
foolish 499 adj.
crazy 503 adj.
loving 887 adj.
fondle
caress 889 vb.
fondness
liking 859 n.
font
church interior
990 n.
food
food 301 n.
provision 633 n.
food poisoning
digestive disorders
651 n.
foodstuffs
food 301 n.
fool
fool 501 n.
befool 542 vb.
dupe 544 n.
humorist 839 n.
laughingstock
851 n.
foolery
foolery 497 n.
revel 837 n.
foolhardy
rash 857 adj.
foolish
mindless 448 adj.
absurd 497 adj.
foolish 499 adj.
crazy 503 adj.
trivial 639 adj.
foolproof
certain 473 adj.
easy 701 adj.
fool's errand
lost labour
641 n.
fool's paradise
insubstantial thing
4 n.
disappointment
509 n.
aspiration 852 n.

557

foot
base 214 n.
foot 214 n.
prosody 593 n.
infantry 722 n.
football
ball game 837 n.
footfall
gait 265 n.
foothill
high land 209 n.
foothold
support 218 n.
retention 778 n.
footing
state 7 n.
serial place 73 n.
influence 178 n.
basis 218 n.
prestige 866 n.
footlights
theatre 594 n.
footling
trivial 639 adj.
footloose
travelling 267 adj.
free 744 adj.
footman
domestic 742 n.
footmark
trace 548 n.
footnote
commentary 520 n.
footprint
concavity 255 n.
trace 548 n.
footslogger
pedestrian 268 n.
infantry 722 n.
footsore
fatigued 684 adj.
footwear
footwear 228 n.
footwork
motion 265 n.
foozle
be clumsy 695 vb.
fop
fop 848 n.
foppish
affected 850 adj.
for
purposely 617 adv.
forage
provender 301 n.
search 459 vb.
provide 633 vb.

foray
attack 712 n.vb.
brigandage 788 n.
forbear
be lenient 736 vb.
show mercy 905 vb.
forbid
prohibit 757 vb.
forbidding
cheerless 834 adj.
sullen 893 adj.
force
band 74 n.
energy 160 n.
strength 162 n.
vigorousness 174 n.
force 176 vb.
cultivate 370 vb.
meaning 514 n.
vigour 571 n.
misuse 675 n.vb.
exertion 682 n.
personnel 686 n.
compulsion 740 n.
—oneself
be unwilling 598 vb.
forced
horticultural
  370 adj.
inelegant 576 adj.
unwilling 598 adj.
forced, be
be forced 596 vb.
have no choice
  606 vb.
forced labour
labour 682 n.
forced march
marching 267 n.
haste 680 n.
force-feeding
eating 301 n.
compulsion 740 n.
forceful
strong 162 adj.
vigorous 174 adj.
assertive 532 adj.
forceful 571 adj.
compelling 740 adj.
impressive 821 adj.
force of
  circumstances
necessity 596 n.
forceps
extractor 304 n.
nippers 778 n.
forces

armed force 722 n.
forcible
violent 176 adj.
compelling 740 adj.
ford
pass 305 vb.
bridge 624 n.
fore
frontal 237 adj.
forearmed
prepared 669 adj.
forebear(s)
precursor 66 n.
paternity 169 n.
foreboding
foresight 510 n.
prediction 511 n.
warning 664 n.
forecast
predict 511 vb.
foreclosure
expropriation 786 n.
debt 803 n.
forecourt
front 237 n.
forefather(s)
paternity 169 n.
forefinger
finger 378 n.
forefront
front 237 n.
foregoing
preceding 64 adj.
prior 119 adj.
foregone conclusion
predetermination
  608 n.
foreground
nearness 200 n.
front 237 n.
forehead
head 213 n.
face 237 n.
foreign
unrelated 10 adj.
extraneous 59 adj.
foreigner
foreigner 59 n.
foreknow
foresee 510 vb.
foreland
projection 254 n.
forelock
hair 259 n.
foreman, forewoman
manager 690 n.
jury 957 n.

foremost
supreme 34 adj.
foremost 283 adj.
important 638 adj.
forensic
jurisprudential
  958 adj.
forerunner
precursor 66 n.
foresee
foresee 501 vb.
foreseeable
future 124 adj.
expected 507 adj.
foreshadow
predestine 155 vb.
foreshow
predict 511 vb.
foresight
anticipation 135 n.
sagacity 498 n.
foresight 510 n.
forest
multitude 104 n.
wood 366 n.
forestall
be early 135 vb.
foresee 510 vb.
forestry
forestry 366 n.
foretaste
precursor 66 n.
foresight 510 n.
foretell
predict 511 vb.
forethought
sagacity 498 n.
foresight 510 n.
preparation 669 n.
foretoken
predict 511 vb.
forewarn
predict 511 vb.
warn 664 vb.
foreword
prelude 66 n.
forfeit
lose 772 vb.
disentitle 916 vb.
penalty 963 n.
forgather
congregate 74 vb.
forge
form 243 vb.
furnace 383 n.
fake 541 vb.
workshop 687 n.

—ahead
progress 285 vb.
forger
imitator 20 n.
deceiver 545 n.
forgery
sham 542 n.
forget
forget 506 vb.
forgetful
negligent 458 adj.
forgetful 506 adj.
forgettable
trivial 639 adj.
forgivable
forgiven 909 adj.
vindicable
927 adj.
forgive
be lenient 736 vb.
forgive 909 vb.
forgiveness
amnesty 506 n.
forgiveness 909 n.
forgo
relinquish 621 vb.
not retain 779 vb.
fork
bifurcation 92 n.
diverge 294 vb.
farm tool 370 n.
—out
pay 804 vb.
forlorn
friendless 883 adj.
form
modality 7 n.
constitute 56 vb.
form 243 n.vb.
structure 331 n.
appearance 445 n.
educate 534 vb.
class 538 n.
record 548 n.
sculpt 554 n.
practice 610 n.
fashion 848 n.
formality 875 n.
formal
formal 875 adj.
courteous 884 adj.
formalism
ritualism 988 n.
formality
etiquette 848 n.
formality 875 n.
ritual 988 n.

format
form 243 n.
edition 589 n.
formation
composition 56 n.
production 164 n.
form 243 n.
formation 722 n.
formative
formative 243 adj.
forme
press 587 n.
former
former 125 adj.
formication
formication 378 n.
formidable
notable 638 adj.
difficult 700 adj.
frightening 854 adj.
formless
amorphous 244 adj.
formula
rule 81 n.
phrase 563 n.
policy 623 n.
remedy 658 n.
precept 693 n.
formulary
office-book 988 n.
formulate
arrange 62 vb.
affirm 532 vb.
phrase 563 vb.
fornication
unchastity 951 n.
forsake
relinquish 621 vb.
forsaken
alone 88 adj.
relinquished
621 adj.
for sale
offering 759 adj.
not retained 779 adj.
forswear
recant 603 vb.
relinquish 621 vb.
fort
fort 713 n.
forte
skill 694 n.
forth
forward 285 adv.
forthcoming
impending 155 adj.
veracious 540 adj.

forthright
undisguised
522 adj.
veracious 540 adj.
fortification
fortification 713 n.
fortified
strong 162 adj.
defended 713 adj.
fortify
strengthen 162 vb.
safeguard 660 vb.
defend 713 vb.
fortitude
courage 855 n.
fortnight
period 110 n.
fortress
fort 713 n.
fortuitous
casual 159 adj.
unintentional
618 adj.
fortunate
opportune 137 adj.
presageful 511 adj.
prosperous 730 adj.
happy 824 adj.
fortune
chance 159 n.
prediction 511 n.
fate 596 n.
good 615 n.
fortune-teller
diviner 511 n.
occultist 984 n.
forum
conference 584 n.
arena 724 n.
market 796 n.
tribunal 956 n.
forward
early 135 adj.
send 272 vb.
intelligent 498 adj.
be expedient 642 vb.
impertinent 878 adj.
forward-looking
progressive 285 adj.
fossil
antiquity 125 n.
fossilization
hardening 326 n.
foster
conduce 156 vb.
look after 457 vb.
safeguard 660 vb.

patronize 703 vb.
foster child
family 11 n.
foster parent
substitute 150 n.
keeper 749 n.
foul
collide 279 vb.
windy 352 adj.
fetid 397 adj.
bad 645 adj.
unclean 649 adj.
insalubrious
653 adj.
disliked 861 adj.
foul play 930 n.
foul-mouthed
ungracious 885 adj.
cursing 899 adj.
foul play
injustice 914 n.
foul play 930 n.
found
initiate 68 vb.
cause 156 vb.
restored 656 adj.
foundation(s)
beginning 68 n.
source 156 n.
basis 218 n.
founder, foundress
producer 164 n.
patron 707 n.
founder
founder 313 vb.
perish 361 vb.
fail 728 vb.
foundling
derelict 779 n.
foundry
workshop 687 n.
fount
origin 68 n.
source 156 n.
store 632 n.
print-type 587 n.
fountain
outflow 298 n.
stream 350 n.
fourfold
fourfold 97 adj.
four-letter word
word 559 n.
plainness 573 n.
foursome
quarternity 96 n.
dance 837 n.

foursquare
fixed 153 adj.

fourth dimension
time 108 n.

fourth estate
the press 528 n.

fowl
bird 365 n.
poultry 365 n.

fowler
hunter 619 n.

fox
mammal 365 n.
puzzle 474 vb.
slyboots 698 n.

foxhole
tunnel 263 n.
refuge 662 n.

foxtrot
dance 837 n.vb.

foxy
fetid 397 adj.
brown 430 adj.
cunning 698 adj.

foyer
lobby 194 n.
theatre 594 n.

fracas
turmoil 61 n.
fight 716 n.

fraction
part 53 n.
numerical element 85 n.
fraction 102 n.

fractious
unwilling 598 adj.
irascible 892 adj.

fracture
break 46 vb.
gap 201 n.
be brittle 330 vb.
wound 655 n.

fragile
insubstantial 4 adj.
flimsy 163 adj.
brittle 330 adj.

fragment
small thing 33 n.
break 46 vb.
piece 53 n.
fraction 102 n.
pulverize 332 vb.

fragmentary
incomplete 55 adj.
uncompleted 726 adj.

fragrance
fragrance 396 n.

frail
ephemeral 114 adj.
flimsy 163 adj.
brittle 330 adj.

frailty
vice 934 n.

frame
mould 23 n.
receptacle 194 n.
frame 218 n.
outline 233 n.vb.
enclose 235 vb.
form 243 n.vb.
structure 331 n.
garden 370 n.
predetermine 608 vb.
plot 623 vb.

frame of mind
affections 817 n.

frame of reference
referral 9 n.

frame-up
trap 542 n.
false charge 928 n.

framework
frame 218 n.
structure 331 n.

franchise
vote 605 n.
dueness 915 n.

frangible
brittle 330 adj.

franglais
dialect 560 n.

frank
undisguised 522 adj.
artless 699 adj.

frankness
veracity 540 n.
plainness 573 n.

frantic
frenzied 503 adj.
active 678 adj.
excitable 822 adj.

fraternal
akin 11 adj.
corporate 708 adj.
friendly 880 adj.

fraternity
family 11 n.
community 708 n.

fraternize
be sociable 882 vb.

fraud
duplicity 541 n.
trickery 542 n.
impostor 545 n.
peculation 788 n.

fraudulent
deceiving 542 adj.
dishonest 930 adj.

fray
rend 46 vb.
rub 333 vb.
exertion 682 n.
fight 716 n.

frayed
dilapidated 655 adj.

freak
variant 15 n.
nonconformist 84 n.
enthusiast 504 n.
whim 604 n.

freaked out
drugged 949 adj.

freakish
unexpected 508 adj.

freckle
maculation 437 n.
blemish 845 n.

free
unstick 49 vb.
escaped 667 adj.
deliver 668 vb.
disencumber 701 vb.
free 744 adj.
liberate 746 vb.
uncharged 812 adj.

free-and-easy
lax 734 adj.
free 744 adj.
sociable 882 adj.

freebooter
robber 789 n.

free choice
will 595 n.

freedom
opportunity 137 n.
freedom 744 n.

freedom of action
independence 744 n.

free enterprise
scope 744 n.
trade 791 n.

free-for-all
turmoil 61 n.
scope 744 n.

free hand
facility 701 n.

scope 744 n.
permit 756 n.
liberality 813 n.

freehold
proprietary 777 adj.

freeholder
possessor 776 n.

freelance
businesslike 622 adj.
worker 686 n.

freeloader
idler 679 n.

freemasonry
friendship 880 n.

Freemasonry
latency 523 n.
society 708 n.

free play
scope 744 n.

free range
stock farm 369 n.

freethinker
irreligionist 974 n.

free time
leisure 681 n.

free trade
trade 791 n.

freewheel
go smoothly 258 vb.
not act 677 vb.

freewheeling
unconfined 744 adj.

free will
will 595 n.

freeze
halt 145 vb.
harden 326 vb.
render insensible 375 vb.
refrigerate 382 vb.
preserve 666 vb.
restriction 747 n.

freezer
refrigerator 384 n.

freight
contents 193 n.
thing transferred 272 n.
merchandise 795 n.

freighter
carrier 273 n.

French leave
absence 190 n.

frenetic
frenzied 503 adj.

frenzied
frenzied 503 adj.
active 678 adj.
excited 821 adj.

frenzy
turmoil 61 n.
violence 176 n.
commotion 318 n.
frenzy 503 n.
restlessness 678 n.
excitable state 822 n.

frequency
degree 27 n.
frequency 139 n.
periodicity 141 n.
oscillation 317 n.

frequent
repeated 106 adj.
frequent 139 adj.
usual 610 adj.
be wont 610 vb.

fresco
picture 553 n.

fresh
original 21 adj.
new 126 adj.
airy 340 adj.
cold 380 adj.
clean 648 adj.
salubrious 652 adj.
impertinent 878 adj.

freshen
invigorate 174 vb.
blow 352 vb.
purify 648 vb.
sanitate 652 vb.
refresh 685 vb.

fresher, freshman
student 538 n.

fret
rend 46 vb.
rub 333 vb.
cry 408 vb.
worry 825 n.
torment 827 vb.
decorate 844 vb.

fretful
lamenting 836 adj.
irascible 892 adj.

fretwork
network 222 n.

friable
brittle 330 adj.
powdery 332 adj.

friar
monk 986 n.

friary
monastery 986 n.

fricative
speech sound 398 n.

friction
collision 279 n.
friction 333 n.
dissension 709 n.

frictionless
easy 701 adj.
pleasurable 826 adj.

fridge
refrigerator 384 n.

friend
friend 880 n.
kind person 897 n.

Friend
sect 978 n.

friend at court
patron 707 n.

friend in need
aider 703 n.

friendless
friendless 883 adj.

friendly
friendly 880 adj.
sociable 882 adj.
amiable 884 adj.

friendship
friendship 880 n.
love 887 n.

frieze
trimming 844 n.

frigate
warship 722 n.

fright
eyesore 842 n.
fear 854 n.

frighten
frighten 854 vb.
threaten 900 vb.

frigid
cold 380 adj.
impassive 820 adj.
inexcitable 823 adj.
inimical 881 adj.

frill
edging 234 n.
trimming 844 n.

frills
ornament 574 n.
superfluity 637 n.

fringe
edging 234 n.
unimportant
 639 adj.
hairdressing 843 n.
trimming 844 n.

fringe benefits
earnings 771 n.

frippery
bauble 639 n.
finery 844 n.

frisk
leap 312 vb.
search 459 vb.
be cheerful 833 vb.

frisky
active 678 adj.

fritter away
waste 634 vb.
be prodigal 815 vb.

frivolity
folly 499 n.
merriment 833 n.

frivolous
light-minded
 456 adj.
capricious 604 adj.

frizzle
be hot 379 vb.

frizzy
undulatory 251 adj.
hairy 259 adj.

frock
dress 228 n.
canonicals 989 n.

frog
fastening 47 n.
amphibian 365 n.

frogman
diver 313 n.

frogmarch
impel 279 vb.

frolic
leap 312 n.
revel 837 n.

from head to foot
throughout 54 adv.

frond
foliage 366 n.

front
exteriority 223 n.
edge 234 n.
front 237 n.
orientate 281 vb.
preceding 283 n.
appearance 445 n.
duplicity 541 n.
battleground
 724 n.

frontage
face 237 n.
contraposition
 240 n.

frontier
extremity 69 n.
contiguity 202 n.
limit 236 n.

frontispiece
front 237 n.

front line
armed force 722 n.

front man
broadcaster 531 n.
impostor 545 n.

front runner
contender 716 n.
favourite 890 n.

frost
wintriness 380 n.
whiten 427 vb.
blight 659 n.

frosting
covering 226 n.
powderiness 332 n.

frosty
cold 380 adj.
unsociable 883 adj.

froth
moisture 341 n.
bubble 355 n.vb.
be excitable 822 vb.

frothy
light 323 adj.
bubbly 355 adj.
ornate 574 adj.

frown
gesture 547 n.
discontent 829 n.
be sullen 893 vb.

—on
prohibit 757 vb.

frowzy
fetid 397 adj.
dirty 649 adj.

frozen
fixed 153 adj.
still 266 adj.
hard 326 adj.
insensible 375 adj.
chilly 380 adj.
preserved 666 adj.
impassive 820 adj.

fructify
be fruitful 171 vb.

frugal
economical 814 adj.
fasting 946 adj.

fruit
product 164 n.
fruit 301 n.

fruitful
prolific 171 adj.
successful 727 adj.
fruition
maturation 669 n.
completion 725 n.
fruitless
wasted 634 adj.
profitless 641 adj.
unsuccessful
728 adj.
fruit machine
gambling 618 n.
fruity
tasty 386 adj.
resonant 404 adj.
witty 839 adj.
frump
eyesore 842 n.
bad taste 847 n.
frustrate
disappoint 509 vb.
be obstructive
702 vb.
frustration
psychopathy 503 n.
disappointment
509 n.
failure 728 n.
fry
young creature
132 n.
cook 301 vb.
heat 381 vb.
fuddled
foolish 499 adj.
tipsy 949 adj.
fuddy-duddy
archaism 127 n.
fudge
sweet thing 392 n.
be equivocal 518 vb.
fuel
sources of energy
160 n.
propellant 287 n.
fuel 385 n.
provide 633 vb.
animate 821 vb.
fug
stench 397 n.
fugitive
transient 114 adj.
wanderer 268 n.
avoider 620 n.
fugue
musical piece 412 n.

führer, fuehrer
leader 690 n.
autocrat 741 n.
fulcrum
pivot 218 n.
fulfil
do 676 vb.
carry out 725 vb.
observe 768 vb.
fulfilment
completion 725 n.
enjoyment 824 n.
full
whole 52 adj.
full 54 adj.
multitudinous
104 adj.
fleshy 195 adj.
broad 205 adj.
descriptive 590 adj.
full blast
loudness 400 n.
full-blooded
vigorous 174 adj.
full-blown
expanded 197 adj.
completed 725 adj.
full-bodied
tasty 386 adj.
odorous 394 adj.
full circle
revolution 149 n.
circuition 314 n.
full dress
formal dress 228 n.
formality 875 n.
full-fledged
matured 669 adj.
full-grown
grown-up 134 adj.
full heart
warm feeling 818 n.
full house
plenitude 54 n.
crowd 74 n.
full-length
comprehensive
52 adj.
long 203 adj.
full measure
plenitude 54 n.
sufficiency 635 n.
fullness
greatness 32 n.
plenitude 54 n.
plenty 635 n.
satiety 863 n.

full of beans
active 678 adj.
cheerful 833 adj.
full of oneself
vain 873 adj.
full play
facility 701 n.
scope 744 n.
full-scale
extensive 32 adj.
complete 54 adj.
full-size
great 32 adj.
full stop
quiescence 266 n.
punctuation 547 n.
fulminate
be violent 176 vb.
curse 899 vb.
threaten 900 vb.
fulsome
exaggerated
546 adj.
affected 850 adj.
flattering 925 adj.
fumble
be tentative 461 vb.
be clumsy 695 vb.
fume
emit 300 vb.
vaporize 338 vb.
be hot 379 vb.
be angry 891 vb.
fumes
gas 336 n.
stench 397 n.
fumigate
purify 648 vb.
fun
pleasurableness
826 n.
merriment 833 n.
amusement 837 n.
function
number 85 n.
operate 173 vb.
function 622 n.vb.
do 676 vb.
celebration 876 n.
functional
correlative 12 adj.
instrumental
628 adj.
useful 640 adj.
functionary
official 690 n.
consignee 754 n.

fund
store 632 n.vb.
treasury 799 n.
fundamental
intrinsic 5 adj.
fundamental
156 adj.
undermost 214 a
supporting 218 a
important 638 a
fundamentalism
scripture 975 n
fundamentalist
zealot 979 n.
fundamentals
reality 1 n.
chief thing 68 n.
funeral
obsequies 364 n.
funerary
funereal 364 adj.
funereal
dark 418 adj.
black 428 adj.
cheerless 834 adj.
funfair
place of amusement
837 n.
fungicide
poison 659 n.
fungus
plant 366 n.
blight 659 n.
funk
avoid 620 vb.
be cowardly
856 vb.
funnel
chimney 263 n.
conduit 351 n.
direct 689 vb.
funnel-shaped
concave 255 adj.
funny
unusual 84 adj.
amusing 837 adj.
funny 849 adj.
fur
skin 226 n.
hair 259 n.
furbish
decorate 844 vb.
furious
destructive 165 adj.
furious 176 adj.
frenzied 503 adj.
angry 891 adj.

furl
  fold 261 vb.
furlough
  leisure 681 n.
furnace
  furnace 383 n.
  workshop 687 n.
furnish
  find means 629 vb.
  provide 633 vb.
  make ready 669 vb.
furnishing(s)
  contents 193 n.
  equipment 630 n.
furniture
  equipment 630 n.
  property 777 n.
furore
  commotion 318 n.
furrier
  stripper 229 n.
furrow
  furrow 262 n.
furry
  hairy 259 adj.
further
  additional 38 adj.
  promote 285 vb.
  aid 703 vb.
furtherance
  improvement 654 n.
  aid 703 n.
furthest
  distant 199 adj.
furtive
  stealthy 525 adj.
fury
  excitable state 822 n.
  anger 891 n.
  shrew 892 n.
  demon 970 n.
fuse
  combine 50 vb.
  heat 381 vb.
  lighter 385 n.
  safeguard 662 n.
  explosive 723 n.
fuselage
  frame 218 n.
fusilier
  soldiery 722 n.
fusillade
  bombardment 712 n.
fusion
  combination 50 n.
  nucleonics 160 n.

liquefaction 337 n.
  association 706 n.
fuss
  commotion 318 n.
  exaggeration 546 n.
  be busy 678 vb.
  excitation 821 n.
fusspot
  meddler 678 n.
  perfectionist 862 n.
fussy
  fastidious 862 adj.
fusty
  antiquated 127 adj.
  sealed off 264 adj.
  fetid 397 adj.
  dirty 649 adj.
futile
  absurd 497 adj.
  useless 641 adj.
futility
  ineffectuality 161 n.
future
  subsequent 120 adj.
  future 124 adj.
  impending 155 adj.
future generations
  successor 67 n.
  futurity 124 n.
futures
  gambling 618 n.
futurist
  modernist 126 n.
futuristic
  modern 126 adj.
futurity
  futurity 124 n.
futurologist
  oracle 511 n.
fuzz
  hair 259 n.
fuzzy
  amorphous 244 adj.
  hairy 259 adj.
  indistinct 444 adj.

G

gab
  loquacity 581 n.
gabardine
  overcoat 228 n.
gabble
  ululate 409 vb.
  empty talk 515 n.
  be loquacious 581 vb.

gable
  vertex 213 n.
gad about
  wander 267 vb.
gadfly
  insect 365 n.
  excitant 821 n.
gadget
  contrivance 623 n.
  tool 630 n.
gaff
  spear 723 n.
gaffe
  mistake 495 n.
gaffer
  old man 133 n.
  manager 690 n.
gag
  stopper 264 n.
  vomit 300 vb.
  make mute 578 vb.
  restrain 747 vb.
  witticism 839 n.
gaga
  foolish 499 adj.
gage
  defiance 711 n.
  security 767 n.
gaggle
  group 74 n.
gagster, gagman
  dramatist 594 n.
  humorist 839 n.
gaiety
  merriment 833 n.
  sociability 882 n.
gain
  increment 36 n.
  progression 285 n.
  benefit 615 n.
  gain 771 n.vb.
—on
  outstrip 277 vb.
  approach 289 vb.
gainful
  profitable 640 adj.
  gainful 771 adj.
gaining
  anachronistic 118 adj.
  inexact 495 adj.
gainsay
  negate 533 vb.
gait
  gait 265 n.
  equitation 267 n.
gaiters

legwear 228 n.
  canonicals 989 n.
gala
  festivity 837 n.
  pageant 875 n.
galactic
  cosmic 321 adj.
galaxy
  group 74 n.
  star 321 n.
  person of repute 866 n.
gale
  gale 352 n.
gall
  swelling 253 n.
  rub 333 vb.
  give pain 377 vb.
  sourness 393 n.
  torment 827 n.
  malevolence 898 n.
gallant
  courageous 855 adj.
  courteous 884 adj.
  lover 887 n.
galleon
  merchant ship 275 n.
gallery
  lobby 194 n.
  excavation 255 n.
  onlookers 441 n.
  exhibit 522 n.
  theatre 594 n.
  collection 632 n.
galley
  chamber 194 n.
  galley 275 n.
  press 587 n.
gallivant
  wander 267 vb.
  court 889 vb.
gallon
  metrology 465 n.
gallop
  ride 267 vb.
  move fast 277 vb.
gallows
  means of execution 964 n.
gallstones
  digestive disorders 651 n.
galore
  many 104 adj.
  plenty 635 n.
galumph
  be clumsy 695 vb.

563

galvanize
invigorate 174 vb.
incite 612 vb.
excite 821 vb.
gambit
tactics 688 n.
gamble
uncertainty 474 n.
gamble 618 vb.
speculate 791 vb.
—on
be certain 473 vb.
gambler
gambler 618 n.
player 837 n.
gambling
gambling 618 n.
gambol
leap 312 n.vb.
amuse oneself
837 vb.
game
meat 301 n.
animal 365 n.
resolute 599 adj.
gamble 618 vb.
chase 619 n.
stratagem 698 n.
contest 716 n.
amusement 837 n.
gamekeeper
keeper 749 n.
game reserve
zoo 369 n.
preservation 666 n.
games
contest 716 n.
sport 837 n.
gamesmanship
tactics 688 n.
cunning 698 n.
gamesome
lively 819 adj.
merry 833 adj.
gamma ray
radiation 417 n.
gammon
meat 301 n.
gamut
series 71 n.
musical note 410 n.
gamy
pungent 388 adj.
savoury 390 adj.
gang
band 74 n.
party 708 n.

ganger
worker 686 n.
manager 690 n.
gangling
unwieldy 195 adj.
gangplank
bridge 624 n.
gangrene
decay 51 n.
infection 651 n.
gangster
murderer 362 n.
offender 904 n.
gangway
access 624 n.
bridge 624 n.
gantry
stand 218 n.
gaol, jail
gaol 748 n.
gaoler, jailer
gaoler 749 n.
gap
disunion 46 n.
discontinuity 72 n.
gap 201 n.
opening 263 n.
requirement 627 n.
gape
space 201 vb.
open 263 vb.
gaze 438 vb.
wonder 864 vb.
gaping
expanded 197 adj.
garage
stable 192 n.
garb
dressing 228 n.
garbage
dirt 649 n.
garble
misinterpret 521 vb.
garden
garden 370 n.
gardener
gardener 370 n.
garden party
social gathering
882 n.
gardens
pleasure ground
837 n.
gargantuan
huge 195 adj.
gargle
cleanser 648 n.

gargoyle
drain 351 n.
eyesore 842 n.
garish
florid 425 adj.
vulgar 847 adj.
showy 875 adj.
garland
loop 250 n.
honours 886 n.
garlic
condiment 389 n.
garment(s)
garment 228 n.
clothing 228 n.
garner
store 632 vb.
garnish
adjunct 40 n.
condiment 389 n.
decorate 844 vb.
garret
attic 194 n.
garrison
resident 191 n.
defender 713 n.
armed force 722 n.
garrotte
kill 362 vb.
execute 963 vb.
garrulous
loquacious 581 adj.
garter
legwear 228 n.
badge of rank 743 n.
gas
gas 336 n.
render insensible
375 vb.
fuel 385 n.
empty talk 515 n.
weapon 723 n.
execute 963 vb.
gasbag
chatterer 581 n.
gas chamber
slaughterhouse
362 n.
gaseous
gaseous 336 adj.
gash
cut 46 vb.
wound 655 n.vb.
gas mask
safeguard 662 n.
gasoline
fuel 385 n.

gasp
breathe 352 vb.
rasp 407 vb.
be fatigued 684 vb.
wonder 864 vb.
gassy
gaseous 336 adj.
gastronomic
culinary 301 adj.
gluttonous 947 adj.
gate
barrier 235 n.
doorway 263 n.
onlookers 441 n.
receipt 807 n.
gatecrash
intrude 297 vb.
be sociable 882 vb.
gatekeeper
doorkeeper 264 n.
gather
congregate 74 vb.
expand 197 vb.
fold 261 n.vb.
store 632 vb.
acquire 771 vb.
gathering
assembly 74 n.
gating
penalty 963 n.
gauche
clumsy 695 adj.
ill-bred 847 adj.
gaucho
herdsman 369 n.
gaudy
florid 425 adj.
showy 875 adj.
gauge
breadth 205 n.
gauge 465 n.vb.
estimate 480 vb.
gauleiter
tyrant 735 n.
gaunt
lean 206 adj.
gauntlet
glove 228 n.
defiance 711 n.
gauze
textile 222 n.
transparency 422 n.
gavel
badge of rule 743 n.
gawk
gaze 438 vb.
wonder 864 vb.

gawky
foolish 499 adj.
gay
nonconformist 84 n.
luminescent
420 adj.
florid 425 adj.
merry 833 adj.
gaze
gaze 438 vb.
be attentive 455 vb.
gazebo
arbour 194 n.
gazelle
speeder 277 n.
mammal 365 n.
gazette
journal 528 n.
gazetteer
directory 87 n.
guidebook 524 n.
gear
clothing 228 n.
equipment 630 n.
gears
machine 630 n.
gear to
relate 9 vb.
geezer
laughingstock
851 n.
Geiger counter
radiation 417 n.
detector 484 n.
geisha girl
entertainer 594 n.
gelatine
condensation 324 n.
thickening 354 n.
gelatinous
semiliquid 354 adj.
geld
make sterile 172 vb.
gelding
horse 273 n.
gelignite
explosive 723 n.
gem
exceller 644 n.
gem 844 n.
gen
information 524 n.
gender
classification 77 n.
grammar 564 n.
gene
heredity 5 n.

organism 358 n.
genealogy
genealogy 169 n.
general
comprehensive
52 adj.
general 79 adj.
typical 83 adj.
usual 610 adj.
army officer 741 n.
generalissimo
army officer 741 n.
generality
generality 79 n.
inexactness 495 n.
(*see* **general**)
generalize
generalize 79 vb.
general knowledge
erudition 490 n.
general practitioner
doctor 658 n.
general public
commonalty 869 n.
generalship
tactics 688 n.
art of war 718 n.
generate
cause 156 vb.
generate 167 vb.
vitalize 360 vb.
generation
era 110 n.
propagation 167 n.
generator
sources of energy
160 n.
generic
generic 77 adj.
generous
plenteous 635 adj.
giving 781 adj.
liberal 813 adj.
benevolent 897 adj.
disinterested
931 adj.
rewarding 962 adj.
genesis
origin 68 n.
source 156 n.
genetic
genetic 5 adj.
genetics
heredity 5 n.
biology 358 n.
genial
pleasant 376 adj.

warm 379 adj.
cheerful 833 adj.
benevolent 897 adj.
genie
mythical being
970 n.
genital
generative 167 adj.
genitals
genitalia 167 n.
genius
intellect 447 n.
spirit 447 n.
intelligence 498 n.
sage 500 n.
exceller 644 n.
aptitude 694 n.
prodigy 864 n.
genocide
slaughter 362 n.
genre
sort 77 n.
genteel
well-bred 848 adj.
genteel 868 adj.
gentile
heathen 974 n.
profane 980 adj.
gentle
moderate 177 adj.
sloping 220 adj.
lenient 736 adj.
courteous 884 adj.
benevolent 897 adj.
gentle birth
nobility 868 n.
gentleman
male 372 n.
gentlemanly
courteous 884 adj.
honourable 929 adj.
**gentleman's
agreement**
promise 764 n.
compact 765 n.
gentry
aristocracy 868 n.
genuflexion
ritual act 988 n.
genuine
certain 473 adj.
genuine 494 adj.
genus
group 74 n.
breed 77 n.
geocentric
celestial 321 adj.

geodesic, geodetic
geographic 321 adj.
metrical 465 adj.
geographer
earth sciences 321 n.
geography
situation 186 n.
earth sciences 321 n.
geological
primal 127 adj.
geology
earth sciences
321 n.
mineralogy 359 n.
geometry
mathematics 86 n.
geometry 465 n.
geomorphology
earth sciences 321 n.
geoponics
agriculture 370 n.
geosphere
world 321 n.
geostationary
circuitous 314 adj.
rotary 315 adj.
geothermal power
sources of energy
160 n.
geriatric
ageing 131 adj.
geriatrician
doctor 658 n.
germ
source 156 n.
microorganism
196 n.
infection 651 n.
germane
apt 24 adj.
germicide
poison 659 n.
germinal
causal 156 adj.
generative 167 adj.
germinate
reproduce itself
167 vb.
be fruitful 171 vb.
germ-laden
toxic 653 adj.
germ warfare
warfare 718 n.
gerontocracy
government 733 n.
gerontology
gerontology 131 n.

gerrymander
be dishonest 930 vb.
gestation
maturation 669 n.
gesticulate
gesticulate 547 vb.
gesture
motion 265 n.
gesture 547 n.
gesticulate 547 vb.
conduct 688 n.
get
be turned to 147 vb.
understand 516 vb.
acquire 771 vb.
receive 782 vb.
—above oneself
be insolent 878 vb.
—across
communicate
524 vb.
huff 891 vb.
—ahead (of)
precede 283 vb.
—around
travel 267 vb.
be sociable 882 vb.
—away
escape 667 vb.
—back
recoup 31 vb.
—better
get better 654 vb.
be restored 656 vb.
—cracking
move fast 277 vb.
—down to (it)
attempt 671 vb.
work 682 vb.
—even with
retaliate 714 vb.
—in the way
be clumsy 695 vb.
hinder 702 vb.
—in touch
communicate
524 vb.
—involved
undertake 672 vb.
—off
descend 309 vb.
escape 667 vb.
—off with
court 889 vb.
—on
progress 285 vb.
prosper 730 vb.

—one's deserts
be rightly served
714 vb.
—one's own back
retaliate 714 vb.
—on one's nerves
displease 827 vb.
enrage 891 vb.
—on with
accord 24 vb.
be friendly 880 vb.
—rid of
destroy 165 vb.
eject 300 vb.
not retain 779 vb.
—round
befool 542 vb.
avoid 620 vb.
—the better of
defeat 727 vb.
—the hang of
understand 516 vb.
habituate 610 vb.
—to grips with
attempt 671 vb.
—to the bottom of
inquire 459 vb.
understand 516 vb.
—up
ascend 308 vb.
fake 541 vb.
—wind of
discover 484 vb.
—with it
modernize 126 vb.
be in fashion
848 vb.
—worse
deteriorate 655 vb.
get-at-able
accessible 289 adj.
get-together
social gathering
882 n.
getup
form 243 n.
gewgaw
bauble 639 n.
finery 844 n.
geyser
stream 350 n.
heater 383 n.
ghastly
colourless 426 adj.
distressing 827 adj.
unsightly 842 adj.
frightening 854 adj.

ghee, ghi
cookery 301 n.
fat 357 n.
ghetto
exclusion 57 n.
seclusion 883 n.
ghost
insubstantial thing
4 n.
immateriality 320 n.
visual fallacy 440 n.
ghost 970 n.
ghostly
shadowy 419 adj.
spooky 970 adj.
ghoul
monster 938 n.
demon 970 n.
ghoulish
inquisitive 453 adj.
spooky 970 adj.
giant
enormous 32 adj.
giant 195 n.
tall creature 209 n.
gibber
mean nothing
515 vb.
gibberish
absurdity 497 n.
unintelligibility
517 n.
gibbet
means of execution
964 n.
gibbous
convex 253 adj.
gibe, jibe
satirize 851 vb.
indignity 921 n.
giddiness
weakness 163 n.
giddy
light-minded
456 adj.
capricious 604 adj.
rash 857 adj.
gift
aptitude 694 n.
acquisition 771 n.
gift 781 n.
gifted
intelligent 498 adj.
gifted 694 adj.
gift of the gab
eloquence 579 n.
loquacity 581 n.

gig
carriage 274 n.
boat 275 n.
music 412 n.
gigantic
huge 195 adj.
tall 209 adj.
giggle
laugh 835 vb.
gigolo
lover 887 n.
gild
gild 433 vb.
decorate 844 vb.
—the lily
be superfluous
637 vb.
—the pill
please 826 vb.
flatter 925 vb.
gilding
ornamental art
884 n.
gill
stream 350 n.
metrology 465 n.
gillie
retainer 742 n.
gills
respiration 352 n.
gilt
yellow 433 adj.
ornamented
844 adj.
gilt-edged
valuable 644 adj.
gimcrack
bauble 639 n.
gimlet
perforator 263 n.
gimmick
contrivance 623 n.
skill 694 n.
gin
alcoholic drink
301 n.
trap 542 n.
ginger
vigorousness
174 n.
condiment 389 n.
orange 432 adj.
animate 821 vb.
ginger beer
soft drink 301 n.
gingerbread
pastries 301 n.

ginger group
motivator 612 n.
ginger-haired
red 431 adj.
gingerly
carefully 457 adv.
gingery
pungent 388 adj.
gingham
textile 222 n.
ginseng
tonic 658 n.
gin-sodden
drunken 949 adj.
gipsy, gypsy
nonconformist 84 n.
wanderer 268 n.
diviner 511 n.
gird
tie 45 vb.
—oneself
prepare oneself
669 vb.
girder
beam 218 n.
girdle
belt 228 n.
underwear 228 n.
surround 230 vb.
girl
youngster 132 n.
woman 373 n.
girl Friday
worker 686 n.
aider 703 n.
girlfriend
friend 880 n.
loved one 887 n.
girlhood
youth 130 n.
girlish
young 130 adj.
female 373 adj.
immature 670 adj.
giro
treasurer 798 n.
girth
size 195 n.
gist
essential part 5 n.
chief part 52 n.
meaning 514 n.
chief thing 638 n.
give
elasticity 328 n.
give 781 vb.
be liberal 813 vb.

reward 962 vb.
—as good as one gets
interchange 151 vb.
retaliate 714 vb.
—away
disclose 526 vb.
—back
restitute 787 vb.
—birth
reproduce itself
167 vb.
—grounds for
justify 927 vb.
—in
relinquish 621 vb.
submit 721 vb.
—notice
warn 664 vb.
—off
emit 300 vb.
—oneself airs
be affected 850 vb.
be vain 873 vb.
—oneself up
submit 721 vb.
—one's mind to
be attentive 455 vb.
—one's word
testify 466 vb.
promise 764 vb.
—one the slip
elude 667 vb.
—out
publish 528 vb.
—rise to
conduce 156 vb.
—the game away
divulge 526 vb.
—up
cease 145 vb.
disaccustom
611 vb.
relinquish 621 vb.
submit 721 vb.
not complete
726 vb.
not retain 779 vb.
—way
be weak 163 vb.
be irresolute 601 vb.
consent 758 vb.
give-and-take
interchange 151 n.
cooperation 706 n.
compromise 770 n.
giveaway
disclosure 526 n.

given
existing 1 adj.
supposed 512 adj.
given to
habituated 610 adj.
giver
giver 781 n.
benefactor 903 n.
gizzard
maw 194 n.
glacé
cooled 382 adj.
glacial
cold 380 adj.
glaciation
condensation 324 n.
ice 380 n.
glacier
ice 380 n.
glad
willing 597 adj.
pleased 824 adj.
gladden
please 826 vb.
cheer 833 vb.
glade
open space 263 n.
wood 366 n.
glad eye
wooing 889 n.
gladiator
contender 716 n.
glad rags
clothing 228 n.
finery 844 n.
glamorous
personable 841 adj.
glamour
beauty 841 n.
prestige 866 n.
glance
deviate 282 vb.
shine 417 vb.
look 438 n.
gesture 547 n.
glancing
lateral 239 adj.
gland
insides 224 n.
glare
light 417 n.
gaze 438 vb.
be angry 891 vb.
glaring
obvious 443 adj.
glass
cup 194 n.

smoothness 258 n.
draught 301 n.
brittleness 330 n.
weather 340 n.
transparency 422 n.
mirror 442 n.
glassblower
artisan 686 n.
glasses
eyeglass 442 n.
glassy
smooth 258 adj.
tranquil 266 adj.
undimmed 417 adj.
transparent 422 adj.
glaucoma
dim sight 440 n.
glaze
coat 226 vb.
viscidity 354 n.
gleam
flash 417 n.
glean
cultivate 370 vb.
select 605 vb.
acquire 771 vb.
gleanings
anthology 592 n.
glebe
benefice 985 n.
glee
vocal music 412 n.
merriment 833 n.
glen
valley 255 n.
glib
deceiving 542 adj.
loquacious 581 adj.
glide
go smoothly 258 vb.
fly 271 vb.
flow 350 vb.
glider
aeronaut 271 n.
aircraft 276 n.
glimmer
glimmer 419 n.
hint 524 n.
glimmering
sciolism 491 n.
glimpse
see 438 vb.
knowledge 490 n.
glint
flash 417 n.
glisten
shine 417 vb.

glitter
flash 417 n.
ostentation 875 n.

glittering
rich 800 adj.
ornamented
844 adj.
showy 875 adj.

gloaming
half-light 419 n.

gloat
be pleased 824 vb.
rejoice 835 vb.
be malevolent
898 vb.

global
inclusive 78 adj.
universal 79 adj.
telluric 321 adj.

globe
sphere 252 n.
world 321 n.
map 551 n.

globe-trotter
traveller 268 n.

globular
rotund 252 adj.

gloom
darkness 418 n.
dimness 419 n.
sorrow 825 n.
dejection 834 n.

Gloria
praise 923 n.
hymn 981 n.

glorify
make important
638 vb.
praise 923 vb.
worship 981 vb.

glorious
great 32 adj.
excellent 644 adj.
splendid 841 adj.
renowned 866 adj.

glory
light 417 n.
famousness 866 n.
prestige 866 n.

glory in
boast 877 vb.

gloss
smoothness 258 n.
light 417 n.
commentary 520 n.
sham 542 n.
—**over**

conceal 525 vb.

glossary
commentary 520 n.
dictionary 559 n.

glossy
luminous 417 adj.
splendid 841 adj.
journal 528 n.

glove
glove 228 n.

glow
be hot 379 vb.
glow 417 n.
redness 431 n.
warm feeling 818 n.

glower
gaze 438 vb.
be angry 891 vb.

glow-worm
glimmer 419 n.
glow-worm 420 n.

glucose
sweet thing 392 n.

glue
adhesive 47 n.
agglutinate 48 vb.

glued
firm 45 adj.

glue-sniffing
drug-taking 949 n.

gluey
viscid 354 adj.

glum
melancholic
834 adj.

glut
superfluity 637 n.
satiety 863 n.

glutinous
viscid 354 adj.

glut oneself
gluttonize 947 vb.

glutton
sensualist 944 n.
glutton 947 n.

gluttonous
greedy 859 adj.

gluttony
gluttony 947 n.

glycerine
lubricant 334 n.

glyptic
glyptic 554 adj.

gnarled
distorted 246 adj.
rough 259 adj.

gnash one's teeth

be impotent 161 vb.
be angry 891 vb.

gnat
insect 365 n.

gnaw
rend 46 vb.
chew 301 vb.
give pain 377 vb.

gnome
elf 970 n.

gnomic
aphoristic 496 adj.

gnosticism
deism 973 n.

GNP
product 164 n.

go
operate 173 vb.
vigorousness 174 n.
be in motion 265 vb.
travel 267 vb.
walk 267 vb.
recede 290 vb.
disappear 446 vb.
function 622 vb.
—**against**
counteract 182 vb.
oppose 704 vb.
—**against the grain**
displease 827 vb.
cause dislike 861 vb.
—**along with**
concur 181 vb.
assent 488 vb.
—**away**
go away 190 vb.
depart 296 vb.
—**back**
turn round 282 vb.
turn back 286 vb.
—**back on**
recant 603 vb.
not observe 769 vb.
—**by**
elapse 111 vb.
—**down**
descend 309 vb.
founder 313 vb.
—**Dutch**
participate 775 vb.
be sociable 882 vb.
—**easy (on)**
be lenient 736 vb.
show mercy 905 vb.
—**for**
aim at 617 vb.
attack 712 vb.

—**in for**
be wont 610 vb.
undertake 672 vb.
—**into**
inquire 459 vb.
—**it alone**
be free 744 vb.
be unsociable
883 vb.
—**off**
happen 154 vb.
be violent 176 vb.
be loud 400 vb.
deteriorate 655 vb.
—**on**
last 113 vb.
go on 146 vb.
progress 285 vb.
persevere 600 vb.
—**one better**
be superior 34 vb.
outdo 306 vb.
—**one's own way**
dissent 489 vb.
be obstinate 602 vb.
be free 744 vb.
—**out**
emerge 298 vb.
extinguish 382 vb.
—**out of one's way**
(to)
deviate 282 vb.
be willing 597 vb.
—**over**
repeat 106 vb.
search 459 vb.
study 536 vb.
—**round**
circle 314 vb.
circuit 626 vb.
—**straight**
get better 654 vb.
be honourable
929 vb.
—**through**
infiltrate 297 vb.
pass 305 vb.
search 459 vb.
suffer 825 vb.
—**to earth**
be stealthy 525 vb.
—**together**
accompany 89 vb.
—**too far**
overstep 306 vb.
—**to one's head**
inebriate 949 vb.

—to pieces
decompose 51 vb.
deteriorate 655 vb.
—to the wall
perish 361 vb.
—under
be destroyed 165 vb.
—with
accord 24 vb.
accompany 89 vb.
—without
refuse 760 vb.
—wrong
err 495 vb.
miscarry 728 vb.
goad
stimulant 174 n.
impel 279 vb.
animate 821 vb.
enrage 891 vb.
go-ahead
vigorous 174 adj.
enterprising 672 adj.
permit 756 n.
goal
extremity 69 n.
limit 236 n.
goal 295 n.
objective 617 n.
desired object 859 n.
goat
cattle 365 n.
goat-keeping
animal husbandry 369 n.
gobble
ululate 409 vb.
gluttonize 947 vb.
gobbledygook
lack of meaning 515 n.
go-between
intermediary 231 n.
goblet
cup 194 n.
goblin
elf 970 n.
go-cart
pushcart 274 n.
god, goddess
deity 966 n.
idol 982 n.
God
the Deity 965 n.
God-fearing
pious 979 adj.

godforsaken
secluded 883 adj.
wicked 934 adj.
godhead
divineness 965 n.
godless
irreligious 974 adj.
impious 980 adj.
godlike
godlike 965 adj.
godly
pious 979 adj.
godown
storage 632 n.
godparent
parentage 169 n.
gods
onlookers 441 n.
theatre 594 n.
godsend
benefit 615 n.
goer
thoroughbred 273 n.
goffer
groove 262 vb.
go-getter
busy person 678 n.
goggle
gaze 438 vb.
wonder 864 vb.
goggles
eyeglass 442 n.
shelter 662 n.
gogo dancer
entertainer 594 n.
going begging
superfluous 637 adj.
going rate
price 809 n.
goitre
swelling 253 n.
gold
yellowness 433 n.
exceller 644 n.
bullion 797 n.
gold dust, like
infrequent 140 adj.
of price 811 adj.
golden
yellow 433 adj.
valuable 644 adj.
palmy 730 adj.
Golden Age
palmy days 730 n.
happiness 824 n.
golden handshake

reward 962 n.
golden mean
moderation 177 n.
golden rule
precept 693 n.
gold-medallist
proficient person 696 n.
goldmine
store 632 n.
wealth 800 n.
goldsmith
artisan 686 n.
gold standard
finance 797 n.
golf
ball game 837 n.
gondola
rowing boat 275 n.
airship 276 n.
gondolier
boatman 270 n.
gone
past 125 adj.
lost 772 adj.
gong
timekeeper 117 n.
gong 414 n.
decoration 729 n.
goo
viscidity 354 n.
good
good 615 n.adj.
excellent 644 adj.
skilful 694 adj.
obedient 739 adj.
benevolent 897 adj.
honourable 929 adj.
virtuous 933 adj.
good behaviour
conduct 688 n.
virtue 933 n.
good books
approbation 923 n.
good breeding
etiquette 848 n.
goodbye!
296 int.
good cause
philanthropy 901 n.
good chance
probability 471 n.
good character
repute 866 n.
probity 929 n.
good cheer
merriment 833 n.

good company
sociable person 882 n.
good deed
kind act 897 n.
good faith
probity 929 n.
good form
etiquette 848 n.
good-for-nothing
profitless 641 adj.
idler 679 n.
bad person 938 n.
good fortune
prosperity 730 n.
good graces
approbation 923 n.
good humour
cheerfulness 833 n.
good living
gastronomy 301 n.
gluttony 947 n.
good looks
beauty 841 n.
good luck
prosperity 730 n.
goodly
good 615 adj.
good manners
courtesy 884 n.
good name
repute 866 n.
good-natured
benevolent 897 adj.
good neighbour
kind person 897 n.
good offices
aid 703 n.
mediation 720 n.
good policy
good policy 642 n.
good riddance
rubbish 641 n.
liberation 746 n.
relief 831 n.
goods
thing transferred 272 n.
property 777 n.
merchandise 795 n.
good Samaritan
kind person 897 n.
good sense
intelligence 498 n.
good sport
honourable person 929 n.

GOO

good taste
good taste 846 n.
good-tempered
amiable 884 adj.
good turn
kind act 897 n.
goodwill
willingness 597 n.
friendliness 880 n.
benevolence 897 n.
good wishes
congratulation
886 n.
good works
philanthropy 901 n.
sociology 901 n.
goody-goody
affecter 850 n.
pietistic 979 adj.
gooey
viscid 354 adj.
retentive 778 adj.
goof
mistake 495 n.
ninny 501 n.
goofy
foolish 499 adj.
googly
deviation 282 n.
goose
table bird 365 n.
fool 501 n.
gooseberry
three 93 n.
fruit 301 n.
gooseflesh
formication 378 n.
nervousness 854 n.
goosestep
gait 265 n.
Gordian knot
ligature 47 n.
complexity 61 n.
gore
garment 228 n.
pierce 263 vb.
blood 335 n.
gorge
valley 255 n.
sate 863 vb.
gluttonize 947 vb.
gorgeous
florid 425 adj.
super 644 adj.
splendid 841 adj.
showy 875 adj.
Gorgon

GOV

rara avis 84 n.
intimidation 854 n.
gorilla
mammal 365 n.
monster 938 n.
gormandize
eat 301 vb.
gluttonize 947 vb.
(*see* **gourmand**)
gormless
foolish 499 adj.
gory
sanguineous
335 adj.
murderous 362 adj.
bloodstained
431 adj.
gospel
certainty 473 n.
truth 494 n.
revelation 975 n.
scripture 975 n.
gossamer
flimsy 163 adj.
filament 208 n.
lightness 323 n.
gossip
informer 524 n.
news reporter 529 n.
rumour 529 n.
chat 584 n.
Gothic
literal 558 adj.
churchlike 990 adj.
gouache
art equipment 553 n.
gouge out
make concave
255 vb.
extract 304 vb.
gourd
vessel 194 n.
gourmand
eater 301 n.
sensualist 944 n.
glutton 947 n.
gourmandise
gastronomy 301 n.
gourmet
gastronomy 301 n.
people of taste
846 n.
sensualist 944 n.
gout
rheumatism 651 n.
govern
manage 689 vb.

GRA

rule 733 vb.
governance
power 160 n.
governance 733 n.
governess
teacher 537 n.
keeper 749 n.
governing body
director 690 n.
government
management 689 n.
government 733 n.
government post
position of authority
733 n.
government servant
official 690 n.
governor
teacher 537 n.
director 690 n.
governor 741 n.
gown
dress 228 n.
robe 228 n.
canonicals 989 n.
grab
take 786 vb.
grace
elegance 575 n.
gift 781 n.
beauty 841 n.
decorate 844 vb.
good taste 846 n.
mercy 905 n.
prayers 981 n.
retreat 192 n.
graceful
elegant 575 adj.
shapely 841 adj.
tasteful 846 adj.
graceless
inelegant 576 adj.
clumsy 695 adj.
graceless 842 adj.
gracious
tasteful 846 adj.
courteous 884 adj.
benevolent 897 adj.
gradation
degree 27 n.
order 60 n.
arrangement 62 n.
grade
degree 27 n.
graduate 27 vb.
arrange 62 vb.
class 62 vb.

GRA

sort 77 n.
gauge 465 vb.
class 538 n.
gradient
incline 220 n.
gradual
gradational 27 adj.
slow 278 adj.
gradualism
slowness 278 n.
reformism 654 n.
graduand
student 538 n.
graduate
graduate 27 vb.
scholar 492 n.
proficient person
696 n.
succeed 727 vb.
graffiti
script 586 n.
blemish 845 n.
graft
implant 303 vb.
improbity 930 n.
grain
temperament 5 n.
small thing 33 n.
tendency 179 n.
cereals 301 n.
weighing 322 n.
texture 331 n.
grass 366 n.
gram
weighing 322 n.
grammar
grammar 564 n.
grammarian
linguist 557 n.
gramophone
gramophone 414 n.
granary
storage 632 n.
grand
important 638 adj.
super 644 adj.
splendid 841 adj.
worshipful 866 adj.
proud 871 adj.
grandchildren
posterity 170 n.
grandee
aristocrat 868 n.
grandeur
greatness 32 n.
prestige 866 n.
ostentation 875 n.

GRA

grandfather
old man 133 n.
paternity 169 n.
grandiloquence
magniloquence
574 n.
grandiose
huge 195 adj.
ostentatious
875 adj.
grandmother
old woman 133 n.
maternity 169 n.
grandstand
view 438 n.
onlookers 441 n.
grange
farm 370 n.
granite
hardness 326 n.
rock 344 n.
grant
subvention 703 n.
permit 756 vb.
consent 758 n.vb.
give 781 vb.
granted
supposed 512 adj.
granular
powdery 332 adj.
granulation
texture 331 n.
grapeshot
ammunition 723 n.
grapevine
informant 524 n.
rumour 529 n.
graphic
expressive 516 adj.
representing
551 adj.
painted 553 adj.
descriptive 590 adj.
graphics
representation
551 n.
graphite
lubricant 334 n.
graphology
hermeneutics 520 n.
graphs
mathematics 86 n.
grapnel
safeguard 662 n.
grapple
unite with 45 vb.
wrestling 716 n.

GRA

retain 778 vb.
—with
contend 716 vb.
grasp
ability 160 n.
range 183 n.
be wise 498 vb.
understand 516 vb.
possession 773 n.
retention 778 n.
grasping
avaricious 816 adj.
greedy 859 adj.
grass
grass 366 n.
greenness 434 n.
informer 524 n.
grasshopper
jumper 312 n.
insect 365 n.
grasshopper mind
changeable thing
152 n.
inattention 456 n.
grassland(s)
grassland 348 n.
plain 348 n.
grass roots
commonalty 869 n.
grate
pulverize 332 vb.
rub 333 vb.
give pain 377 vb.
furnace 383 n.
rasp 407 vb.
discord 411 vb.
cause dislike 861 vb.
grateful
grateful 907 adj.
gratification
pleasure 376 n.
enjoyment 824 n.
gratify
please 826 vb.
grating
network 222 n.
gratis
uncharged 812 adj.
gratitude
gratitude 907 n.
gratuitous
voluntary 597 adj.
uncharged 812 adj.
undue 916 adj.
gratuity
extra 40 n.
gift 781 n.

GRE

reward 962 n.
grave
great 32 adj.
death 361 n.
tomb 364 n.
engrave 555 vb.
inexcitable 823 adj.
serious 834 adj.
heinous 934 adj.
grave-digger
excavator 255 n.
gravel
paving 226 n.
soil 344 n.
graveyard
cemetery 364 n.
gravitate
descend 309 vb.
weigh 322 vb.
—towards
tend 179 vb.
gravity
attraction 291 n.
gravity 322 n.
importance 638 n.
seriousness 834 n.
gravy
sauce 389 n.
good 615 n.
graze
be contiguous
202 vb.
collide 279 vb.
graze 301 vb.
rub 333 vb.
touch 378 n.vb.
wound 655 vb.
grazing
grassland 348 n.
stock farm 369 n.
grease
smoother 258 n.
lubricant 334 n.
grease 357 n.
facilitate 701 vb.
—the palm
bribe 612 vb.
greasepaint
stage set 594 n.
cosmetic 843 n.
greaseproof
dry 342 adj.
greasy
unctuous 357 adj.
dirty 649 adj.
great
great 32 adj.

GRE

superior 34 adj.
powerful 160 adj.
strong 162 adj.
influential 178 adj.
large 195 adj.
important 638 adj.
excellent 644 adj.
super 644 n.
renowned 866 adj.
proud 871 adj.
greatest
supreme 34 adj.
exceller 644 n.
great-hearted
disinterested
931 adj.
great man/woman
bigwig 638 n.
person of repute
866 n.
greatness
greatness 32 n.
(see **great***)*
great thing
chief thing 638 n.
greed
rapacity 786 n.
avarice 816 n.
selfishness 932 n.
gluttony 947 n.
green
new 126 adj.
young 130 adj.
vomiting 300 adj.
vegetal 366 adj.
sour 393 adj.
green 434 adj.
credulous 487 adj.
ignorant 491 adj.
immature 670 adj.
pleasure ground
837 n.
innocent 935 adj.
green belt
surroundings
230 n.
greenery
foliage 366 n.
green-eyed
jealous 911 adj.
green fingers
agriculture 370 n.
greenhorn
ignoramus 493 n.
beginner 538 n.
greenhouse
garden 370 n.

green light
signal light 420 n.
assent 488 n.
greenroom
theatre 594 n.
greens
vegetable 301 n.
greet
speak to 583 vb.
greet 884 vb.
greetings
respects 920 n.
gregarious
sociable 882 adj.
gremlin
hinderer 702 n.
elf 970 n.
grenade
bomb 723 n.
grenadier
soldiery 722 n.
grey
dim 419 adj.
greyness 429 n.
grey 429 adj.
neutral 625 adj.
cheerless 834 adj.
Grey Eminence
influence 178 n.
greyhound
speeder 277 n.
dog 365 n.
grey matter
intellect 447 n.
grid
correlation 12 n.
electronics 160 n.
network 222 n.
gridiron
network 222 n.
heater 383 n.
grief
sorrow 825 n.
grievance
discontent 829 n.
wrong 914 n.
grieve
suffer 825 vb.
sadden 834 vb.
lament 836 vb.
grievous
distressing 827 adj.
griffin
rara avis 84 n.
grill
cook 301 vb.
heat 381 vb.

interrogate 459 vb.
grille
network 222 n.
window 263 n.
grill room
café 192 n.
grim
serious 834 adj.
frightening 854 adj.
ungracious 885 adj.
sullen 893 adj.
grimace
distortion 246 n.
gesticulate 547 vb.
discontent 829 n.
grime
dirt 649 n.
grimy
dirty 649 adj.
grin
smile 835 vb.
—and bear it
be patient 823 vb.
be cheerful 833 vb.
grind
rend 46 vb.
sharpen 256 vb.
pulverize 332 vb.
rub 333 vb.
rasp 407 vb.
labour 682 n.
oppress 735 vb.
grinder
pulverizer 332 n.
grindstone
sharpener 256 n.
pulverizer 332 n.
grip
tie 45 vb.
cohere 48 vb.
influence 178 n.
handle 218 n.
possession 773 n.
retention 778 n.
impress 821 vb.
gripe
give pain 377 vb.
discontent 829 n.
gripping
exciting 821 adj.
grisly
frightening 854 adj.
gristle
solid body 324 n.
toughness 329 n.
grist (to the mill)
materials 631 n.

provision 633 n.
grit
strength 162 n.
texture 331 n.
powder 332 n.
stamina 600 n.
grizzle
weep 836 vb.
grizzled
grey 429 adj.
groan
cry 408 vb.
be discontented
829 vb.
lamentation 836 n.
grocer
provider 633 n.
tradespeople 794 n.
groceries
provisions 301 n.
grog
alcoholic drink
301 n.
groggy
oscillating 317 adj.
sick 651 adj.
groin
angularity 247 n.
groom
groom 369 vb.
clean 648 vb.
train 534 vb.
make ready 669 vb.
domestic 742 n.
grooming
beautification 843 n.
groove
cut 46 vb.
place 185 n.
furrow 262 n.
habit 610 n.
grope
be tentative 461 vb.
be uncertain 474 vb.
be clumsy 695 vb.
—for
search 459 vb.
gross
whole 52 adj.
unintelligent
499 adj.
manifest 522 adj.
bad 645 adj.
receive 782 vb.
vulgar 847 adj.
heinous 934 adj.
sensual 944 adj.

grotesque
distorted 246 adj.
absurd 497 adj.
imaginative
513 adj.
unsightly 842 adj.
grotto
arbour 194 n.
grotty
bad 645 adj.
grouch
malcontent 829 n.
be sullen 893 vb.
ground
situation 186 n.
base 214 n.
flatten 216 vb.
basis 218 n.
navigate 269 vb.
powdery 332 adj.
land 344 n.
educate 534 vb.
arena 724 n.
grounded
in difficulties
700 adj.
groundless
unreal 2 adj.
insubstantial
4 adj.
illogical 477 adj.
ground plan
map 551 n.
grounds
evidence 466 n.
motive 612 n.
lands 777 n.
groundwork
preparation 669 n.
group
combine 50 vb.
subdivision 53 n.
class 62 vb.
group 74 n.
classification 77 n.
party 708 n.
groupie
youngster 132 n.
grouse
table bird 365 n.
be discontented
829 vb.
grouser
dissentient 489 n.
malcontent 829 n.
grove
wood 366 n.

GRO

grovel
knuckle under
721 vb.
be servile 879 vb.
grow
become 1 vb.
grow 36 vb.
be turned to 147 vb.
expand 197 vb.
cultivate 370 vb.
mature 669 vb.
—up
come of age 134 vb.
grower
producer 164 n.
growing pains
beginning 68 n.
youth 130 n.
growl
ululate 409 vb.
be sullen 893 vb.
threaten 900 vb.
grown-up
adult 134 n.
grown-up 134 adj.
growth
increase 36 n.
swelling 253 n.
agriculture 370 n.
cancer 651 n.
groyne
projection 254 n.
grub
young creature
132 n.
food 301 n.
creepy-crawly
365 n.
grubby
unclean 649 adj.
Grub Street
writing 586 n.
grub up
extract 304 vb.
grudge
be unwilling 598 vb.
be parsimonious
816 vb.
resentment 891 n.
gruel
cereals 301 n.
gruelling
laborious 682 adj.
fatiguing 684 adj.
gruesome
not nice 645 adj.
unsightly 842 adj.

GUE

gruff
hoarse 407 adj.
ungracious 885 adj.
irascible 892 adj.
grumble
be discontented
829 vb.
grumpy
irascible 892 adj.
sullen 893 adj.
Grundyism
prudery 950 n.
grunt
cry 408 n.vb.
ululate 409 vb.
grunting
ungracious 885 adj.
G-string
loincloth 228 n.
guarantee
make certain
473 vb.
safeguard 660 vb.
security 767 n.
guarantor
patron 707 n.
guard
driver 268 n.
surveillance 457 n.
protector 660 n.
defender 713 n.
guarded
cautious 858 adj.
guardian
parentage 169 n.
protector 660 n.
keeper 749 n.
guardian angel
patron 707 n.
benefactor 903 n.
guard of honour
respects 920 n.
guardroom
lockup 748 n.
guards
armed force 722 n.
gudgeon
pivot 218 n.
guerrilla, guerilla
soldier 722 n.
revolter 738 n.
guess
intuit 476 vb.
not know 491 vb.
conjecture 512 n.
guesswork
empiricism 461 n.

GUI

uncertainty 474 n.
conjecture 512 n.
guest
resident 191 n.
friend 880 n.
guff
empty talk 515 n.
guffaw
laughter 835 n.
guidance
directorship 689 n.
advice 691 n.
guide
prototype 23 n.
rule 81 n.
itinerary 267 n.
guide 520 n.
indication 547 n.
direct 689 vb.
adviser 691 n.
guidebook
guidebook 524 n.
guided missile
missile weapon
723 n.
guidelines
precept 693 n.
guild
business 622 n.
corporation 708 n.
merchant 794 n.
guile
cunning 698 n.
guileful
deceiving 542 adj.
perfidious 930 adj.
guileless
artless 699 adj.
honourable 929 adj.
guillotine
stop 145 n.
execute 963 vb.
guilt
wickedness 934 n.
guilt 936 n.
guiltless
guiltless 935 adj.
guilty
guilty 936 adj.
guilty person
offender 904 n.
guinea
coinage 797 n.
guinea pig
animal 365 n.
testee 461 n.
guise

GUN

modality 7 n.
appearance 445 n.
guitar
harp 414 n.
Gulag
prison camp 748 n.
gulf
gap 201 n.
gulf 345 n.
gull
bird 365 n.
befool 542 vb.
defraud 788 vb.
gullet
maw 194 n.
gullible
credulous 487 adj.
gullible 544 adj.
gully
valley 255 n.
conduit 351 n.
gulp
absorb 299 vb.
draught 301 n.
breathe 352 vb.
—down
eat 301 vb.
gum
adhesive 47 n.
agglutinate 48 vb.
elasticity 328 n.
resin 357 n.
gumption
intelligence 498 n.
gun
hunter 619 n.
gun 723 n.
gunboat
warship 722 n.
gun carriage
war chariot 274 n.
gunfire
loudness 400 n.
bombardment
712 n.
gunman
shooter 287 n.
murderer 362 n.
desperado 857 n.
gunner
soldiery 722 n.
gunpowder
explosive 723 n.
gunroom
arsenal 723 n.
gunrunner
thief 789 n.

gunshot
  short distance 200 n.
gunwale, gunnel
  edge 234 n.
gurgle
  flow 350 vb.
  laughter 835 n.
guru
  sage 500 n.
  religious teacher
  973 n.
gush
  flow out 298 vb.
  flow 350 vb.
  diffuseness 570 n.
gushing
  hypocritical
  541 adj.
  affected 850 adj.
gusset
  garment 228 n.
gust
  breeze 352 n.
gusto
  vigorousness 174 n.
  pleasure 376 n.
  enjoyment 824 n.
gut
  empty 300 vb.
  extract 304 vb.
  burn 381 vb.
gutless
  weak 163 adj.
  irresolute 601 adj.
gut reaction
  absence of thought
  450 n.
guts
  vigorousness 174 n.
  insides 224 n.
  resolution 599 n.
  courage 855 n.
gutter
  drain 351 n.
  sink 649 n.
  vulgar 847 adj.
guttersnipe
  low fellow 869 n.
guttural
  speech sound 398 n.
  hoarse 407 adj.
  vocal 577 adj.
guy
  tackling 47 n.
  male 372 n.
  misrepresent
  552 vb.

  satirize 851 vb.
guzzle
  gluttonize 947 vb.
gymkhana
  contest 716 n.
gymnasium
  arena 724 n.
gymnast
  athlete 162 n.
gymnastics
  athletics 162 n.
  exercise 682 n.
  sport 837 n.
gynaecology
  medical art 658 n.
gyrate
  rotate 315 vb.
gyrocompass
  sailing aid 269 n.
gyropilot
  directorship 689 n.
gyroscope
  rotator 315 n.

H

habeas corpus
  legal process 959 n.
haberdasher
  clothier 228 n.
habit
  temperament 5 n.
  regularity 81 n.
  tradition 127 n.
  habit 610 n.
habitat
  locality 187 n.
  abode 192 n.
habitation
  abode 192 n.
habit-forming
  habitual 610 adj.
  inducing 612 adj.
habitual
  repeated 106 adj.
  frequent 139 adj.
  habitual 610 adj.
habituate
  habituate 610 vb.
habitué
  habitué 610 n.
  sociable person
  882 n.
hack
  cut 46 vb.
  ride 267 vb.
  saddle horse 273 n.

  author 589 n.
  worker 686 n.
hackle
  plumage 259 n.
hackneyed
  known 490 adj.
  feeble 572 adj.
  usual 610 adj.
Hades
  mythic hell 972 n.
haemoglobin
  blood 335 n.
haemophilia
  blood disease 651 n.
haemorrhage
  haemorrhage 302 n.
haemorrhoids
  swelling 253 n.
haft
  handle 218 n.
hag
  sorceress 983 n.
haggard
  lean 206 adj.
  fatigued 684 adj.
  suffering 825 adj.
haggis
  meat 301 n.
haggle
  make terms 766 vb.
  bargain 791 vb.
hagiography
  theology 973 n.
hagridden
  bewitched 983 adj.
haiku
  verse form 593 n.
hail
  wintriness 380 n.
  cry 408 n.vb.
  call 547 n.
  greet 884 vb.
  applaud 923 vb.
hail-fellow-well-met
  sociable 882 adj.
hair
  filament 208 n.
  hair 259 n.
haircut, hairdo
  hairdressing 843 n.
hairdresser
  beautician 843 n.
hairless
  hairless 229 adj.
  smooth 258 adj.
hairpiece
  hairdressing 843 n.

hair-raising
  exciting 821 adj.
  frightening 854 adj.
hair's breadth
  short distance 200 n.
hair shirt
  asceticism 945 n.
hair-splitting
  sophistry 477 n.
hair style
  hairdressing 843 n.
hairy
  fibrous 208 adj.
  hairy 259 adj.
  frightening 854 adj.
hakim
  doctor 658 n.
  officer 741 n.
halberd
  axe 723 n.
halcyon days
  palmy days 730 n.
hale
  healthy 650 adj.
half
  incompleteness
  55 n.
  bisection 92 n.
half-and-half
  equal 28 adj.
  mixed 43 adj.
  neutral 625 adj.
half-baked
  immature 670 adj.
  bungled 695 adj.
half-breed
  hybrid 43 n.
half-caste
  hybrid 43 n.
half-done
  neglected 458 adj.
  uncompleted
  726 adj.
half-hearted
  unwilling 598 adj.
  irresolute 601 adj.
  apathetic 820 adj.
half-life
  radiation 417 n.
half-light
  evening 129 n.
  half-light 419 n.
half mast, at
  lamenting 836 adj.
half measures
  shortfall 307 n.
  irresolution 601 n.

insufficiency 636 n.
bungling 695 n.
half-moon
arc 250 n.
half-price
cheap 812 adj.
half-ripe
immature 670 adj.
half-starved
underfed 636 adj.
fasting 946 adj.
half-truth
mental dishonesty
543 n.
halfway
midway 70 adv.
compromise 770 n.
halfway house
retreat 192 n.
half-wit
fool 501 n.
halitosis
stench 397 n.
hall
house 192 n.
chamber 194 n.
lobby 194 n.
hallelujah
rejoicing 835 n.
hymn 981 n.
halliard, halyard
tackling 47 n.
hallmark
label 547 n.
halloo
cry 408 n.
hallow
sanctify 979 vb.
Hallowe'en
sorcery 983 n.
hallucination(s)
insubstantiality 4 n.
error 495 n.
psychopathy 503 n.
fantasy 513 n.
deception 542 n.
hallucinatory
intoxicating 949 adj.
halo
light 417 n.
honours 866 n.
halt
stop 145 n.
halt 145 vb.
come to rest 266 vb.
be obstructive
702 vb.

halter
halter 47 n.
fetter 748 n.
means of execution
964 n.
halting
fitful 142 adj.
slow 278 adj.
halve
bisect 92 vb.
apportion 783 vb.
ham
leg 267 n.
meat 301 n.
act 594 vb.
be affected 850 vb.
—**up**
be witty 839 vb.
hamburger
meat 301 n.
ham-handed
clumsy 695 adj.
hamlet
housing 192 n.
hammer
hammer 279 n.
strike 279 vb.
club 723 n.
—**away at**
persevere 600 vb.
—**out**
form 243 vb.
hammock
hanging object
217 n.
bed 218 n.
hamper
basket 194 n.
hinder 702 vb.
hams
buttocks 238 n.
hamstring
disable 161 vb.
hand
feeler 378 n.
finger 378 n.
indicator 547 n.
lettering 586 n.
instrument 628 n.
worker 686 n.
servant 742 n.
nippers 778 n.
—**down**
transfer 272 vb.
—**out**
provide 633 vb.
—**over**

transfer 272 vb.
relinquish 621 vb.
handbill
advertisement
528 n.
handbook
guidebook 524 n.
textbook 589 n.
handcuff
arrest 747 vb.
handful
small quantity 33 n.
bunch 74 n.
fewness 105 n.
hard task 700 n.
revolter 738 n.
handhold
support 218 n.
retention 778 n.
handicap
equalize 28 vb.
advantage 34 n.
inferiority 35 n.
illness 651 n.
hinder 702 vb.
contest 716 n.
handicraft
business 622 n.
ornamental art
844 n.
hand in glove
in league 708 adv.
hand in hand
joined 45 adj.
handiwork
product 164 n.
deed 676 n.
ornamental art
844 n.
handkerchief
cleaning cloth 648 n.
handle
opportunity 137 n.
operate 173 vb.
handle 218 n.
touch 378 vb.
name 561 n.
tool 630 n.
use 673 vb.
manage 689 vb.
trade 791 vb.
title 870 n.
handling
action 676 n.
conduct 688 n.
management 689 n.
hand-made

nonuniform 17 adj.
produced 164 adj.
handmaid
instrument 628 n.
auxiliary 707 n.
handout
report 524 n.
advertisement
528 n.
gift 781 n.
hand-picked
chosen 605 adj.
excellent 644 adj.
handrail
handle 218 n.
hands
personnel 686 n.
handshake
courteous act 884 n.
handsome
liberal 813 adj.
beautiful 841 adj.
hand's turn
labour 682 n.
hand-to-hand
contending 716 adj.
handwriting
writing 586 n.
handy
little 196 adj.
near 200 adj.
light 323 adj.
useful 640 adj.
skilful 694 adj.
tractable 701 adj.
handyman
mender 656 n.
proficient person
696 n.
hang
come unstuck 49 vb.
hang 217 vb.
show 522 vb.
execute 963 vb.
—**back**
be unwilling 598 vb.
avoid 620 vb.
—**on**
wait 136 vb.
persevere 600 vb.
—**on to**
retain 778 vb.
—**over**
impend 155 vb.
be high 209 vb.
—**together**
accord 24 vb.

be reasonable
475.vb.
—up
cease 145 vb.
hang 217 vb.
—upon
depend 157 vb.
hangar
stable 192 n.
hanger
hanger 217 n.
hanger-on
dependant 742 n.
toady 879 n.
hang gliding
aeronautics 271 n.
sport 837 n.
hangings
hanging object
217 n.
hangman
punisher 963 n.
hangout
abode 192 n.
hangover
sequel 67 n.
crapulence 949 n.
hangup
eccentricity 503 n.
worry 825 n.
hank
bunch 74 n.
hanker after
regret 830 vb.
desire 859 vb.
haphazard
casual 159 adj.
indiscriminate
464 adj.
designless 618 adj.
hapless
unfortunate 731 adj.
happen
be 1 vb.
happen 154 vb.
chance 159 vb.
happening
event 154 n.
amusement 837 n.
happy
opportune 137 adj.
good 615 adj.
successful 727 adj.
happy 824 adj.
pleasurable 826 adj.
cheerful 833 adj.
happy-go-lucky

lax 734 adj.
cheerful 833 adj.
happy returns
congratulation
886 n.
hara-kiri
suicide 362 n.
harangue
orate 579 vb.
dissertation 591 n.
harass
oppress 735 vb.
torment 827 vb.
harbinger
precursor 66 n.
omen 511 n.
messenger 529 n.
harbour
goal 295 n.
shelter 662 n.
hard
vigorously 174 adv.
hard 326 adj.
unclear 568 adj.
laborious 682 adj.
difficult 700 adj.
adverse 731 adj.
thick-skinned
820 adj.
unkind 898 adj.
pitiless 906 adj.
intoxicating 949 adj.
hardback
book 589 n.
hardboard
paper 631 n.
hardboiled
tough 329 adj.
thick-skinned
820 adj.
hard core
solid body 324 n.
obstinate person
602 n.
building material
631 n.
harden
harden 326 vb.
habituate 610 vb.
make insensitive
820 vb.
hard feelings
resentment 891 n.
hard-headed
intelligent 498 adj.
hard-hearted
pitiless 906 adj.

hard-hitting
disapproving
924 adj.
hard life
adversity 731 n.
hard-liner
obstinate person
602 n.
tyrant 735 n.
hard-mouthed
obstinate 602 adj.
hard of hearing
deaf 416 adj.
hard on
oppressive 735 adj.
unjust 914 adj.
hardpan
solid body 324 n.
hard-pressed
in difficulties
700 adj.
hard sell
inducement 612 n.
sale 793 n.
hardship
adversity 731 n.
hard stuff
alcoholic drink
301 n.
hard taskmaster
tyrant 735 n.
perfectionist 862 n.
hard times
adversity 731 n.
hard to please
discontented
829 adj.
fastidious 862 adj.
hard up
poor 801 adj.
hardware
data processing
86 n.
product 164 n.
hard way, the
laboriously 682 adv.
with difficulty
700 adv.
hard words
reproach 924 n.
hardy
stalwart 162 adj.
healthy 650 adj.
courageous 855 adj.
hare
move fast 277 vb.
mammal 365 n.

harebrained
light-minded
456 adj.
foolish 499 adj.
harelip
blemish 845 n.
harem
seclusion 883 n.
harijan
outcast 883 n.
hark back
retrospect 505 vb.
harlequin
variegation 437 n.
fool 501 n.
harlot
prostitute 952 n.
harm
harm 645 n.
impair 655 vb.
harmful
destructive 165 adj.
evil 616 adj.
inexpedient
643 adj.
harmful 645 adj.
baneful 659 adj.
malevolent 898 adj.
harmless
weak 163 adj.
beneficial 644 adj.
safe 660 adj.
innocent 935 adj.
harmonic
musical note 410 n.
harmonica
organ 414 n.
harmonious
melodious 410 adj.
(*see* **harmony**)
harmonium
organ 414 n.
harmonize
compose music
413 vb.
harmony
agreement 24 n.
symmetry 245 n.
melody 410 n.
consensus 488 n.
elegance 575 n.
concord 710 n.
harness
tackling 47 n.
break in 369 vb.
equipment 630 n.
use 673 vb.

harp
harp 414 n.

harp on
repeat oneself
106 vb.

harpoon
spear 723 n.

harpsichord
piano 414 n.

harpy
hellhag 904 n.

harridan
eyesore 842 n.
shrew 892 n.

harrow
farm tool 370 n.
frighten 854 vb.

harrowing
distressing 827 adj.

harry
attack 712 vb.
torment 827 vb.

harsh
strident 407 adj.
discordant 411 adj.
oppressive 735 adj.
paining 827 adj.
unkind 898 adj.

harum-scarum
light-minded
456 adj.
rash 857 adj.

harvest
product 164 n.
abundance 171 n.
agriculture 370 n.
store 632 n.vb.
acquire 771 vb.

harvester
farmer 370 n.

has-been
archaism 127 n.
loser 728 n.

hash
a mixture 43 n.
drug-taking 949 n.

hasp
fastening 47 n.

hassle
quarrel 709 n.

hassock
cushion 218 n.

haste
haste 680 n.

hasten
be early 135 vb.
accelerate 277 vb.

hasten 680 vb.

hasty
negligent 458 adj.
unprepared 670 adj.
hasty 680 adj.
rash 857 adj.
irascible 892 adj.

hat
headgear 228 n.

hatch
group 74 n.
reproduce itself
167 vb.
doorway 263 n.
plan 623 vb.
mature 669 vb.

hatchback
automobile 274 n.

hatchery
stock farm 369 n.

hatchet
axe 723 n.

hatchet job
detraction 926 n.

hatchet man
destroyer 168 n.

hatchment
heraldry 547 n.

hatchway
doorway 263 n.

hate
hate 888 vb.
(*see* **hatred**)

hateful
not nice 645 adj.
disliked 861 adj.
hateful 888 adj.

hatless
uncovered 229 adj.

hatred
phobia 854 n.
enmity 881 n.
hatred 888 n.

hatred of mankind
misanthropy 902 n.

hat trick
triplication 94 n.
success 727 n.

haughty
proud 871 adj.
insolent 878 adj.

haul
draw 288 vb.
booty 790 n.

haulage
transport 272 n.
traction 288 n.

haulier
carrier 273 n.

haunches
buttocks 238 n.

haunt
focus 76 n.
locality 187 n.
home 192 n.
engross 449 vb.
be remembered
505 vb.
be wont 610 vb.
torment 827 vb.
frighten 854 vb.
haunt 970 vb.

haunted
spooky 970 adj.
obsessed 455 adj.

hauteur
pride 871 n.

have
comprise 78 vb.
befool 542 vb.
possess 733 vb.

—**a go**
attempt 671 vb.

—**a hand in**
cause 156 vb.
be instrumental
628 vb.

—**a hold on**
influence 178 vb.

—**an eye to**
intend 617 vb.

—**at**
attack 712 vb.

—**everything**
be complete 54 vb.

—**had enough**
submit 721 vb.

—**had it**
be destroyed 165 vb.
die 361 vb.

—**it in for**
hate 888 vb.
be malevolent
898 vb.

—**nothing to do with**
be unrelated 10 vb.
avoid 620 vb.
make unwelcome
883 vb.

—**no time for**
disregard 458 vb.
dislike 861 vb.
despise 922 vb.

—**on**

wear 228 vb.
befool 542 vb.

—**one's cake and eat
it**
*attempt the
impossible* 470 vb.

—**one's say**
affirm 532 vb.

—**one's way**
will 595 vb.

—**over a barrel**
dominate 733 vb.

—**the best of it**
succeed 727 vb.

—**the makings of**
be likely 471 vb.
give hope 852 vb.

haven
goal 295 n.
shelter 662 n.

have-nots, the
poor person 801 n.
lower classes 869 n.

haversack
bag 194 n.

haves, the
rich person 800 n.
upper class 868 n.

havoc
disorder 61 n.
havoc 165 n.
spoliation 788 n.

hawk
eruct 300 vb.
bird 365 n.
hunt 619 vb.
militarist 722 n.
sell 793 vb.

hawker
traveller 268 n.
pedlar 794 n.

hawser
cable 47 n.

hay
provender 301 n.
grass 366 n.

hay fever
ill health 651 n.

hayloft
attic 194 n.

haystack
store 632 n.

haywire
orderless 61 adj.

hazard
chance 159 n.
gamble 618 vb.

HAZ

danger 661 n.
obstacle 702 n.
hazardous
dangerous 661 adj.
haze
cloud 355 n.
uncertainty 474 n.
hazel
brown 430 adj.
hazy
cloudy 355 adj.
indistinct 444 adj.
uncertain 474 adj.
he
male 372 n.
head
classification 77 n.
energy 160 n.
head 213 n.
vertex 213 n.
face 237 n.
be in front 237 vb.
dome 253 n.
strike 279 vb.
precede 283 vb.
topic 452 n.
intelligence 498 n.
teacher 537 n.
director 690 n.
drug-taking 949 n.
—off
repel 292 vb.
dissuade 613 vb.
headache
pang 377 n.
worry 825 n.
headband
headgear 228 n.
head-count
numeration 86 n.
headdress
headgear 228 n.
header
plunge 313 n.
headgear
headgear 228 n.
head-hunter
killer 362 n.
heading
classification 77 n.
label 547 n.
head in the sand
avoider 620 n.
inaction 677 n.
headland
projection 254 n.
headlight, headlamp

HEA

lamp 420 n.
headline
edition 589 n.
make important
   638 vb.
headlong
violently 176 adv.
hasty 680 adj.
headman
director 690 n.
potentate 741 n.
headmaster,
   headmistress
teacher 537 n.
head-on
frontal 237 adj.
head over heels
inverted 221 adj.
headphones, headset
hearing aid 415 n.
telecommunication
   531 n.
headquarters
focus 76 n.
headrest
prop 218 n.
headroom
room 183 n.
heads or tails
equal chance 159 n.
head start
advantage 34 n.
headstone
obsequies 364 n.
headstrong
wilful 602 adj.
rash 857 adj.
headwaters
stream 350 n.
headway
water travel 269 n.
progression 285 n.
headwind
obstacle 702 n.
heady
strong 162 adj.
exciting 821 adj.
intoxicating 949 adj.
heal
cure 656 vb.
remedy 658 vb.
healer
doctor 658 n.
health
vitality 162 n.
health 650 n.
salubrity 652 n.

HEA

celebration 876 n.
health-giving
salubrious 652 adj.
healthy
vigorous 174 adj.
beneficial 644 adj.
healthy 650 adj.
heap
accumulation 74 n.
small hill 209 n.
store 632 n.vb.
heaps
great quantity 32 n.
multitude 104 n.
hear
hear 415 vb.
try a case 959 vb.
heard
sounding 398 adj.
loud 400 adj.
hearer
listener 415 n.
hearing
hearing 415 n.
legal trial 959 n.
hearing aid
hearing aid 415 n.
hearken
hear 415 vb.
obey 739 vb.
hearsay
evidence 466 n.
rumour 529 n.
hearse
vehicle 274 n.
heart
essence 1 n.
essential part 5 n.
interiority 224 n.
centre 225 n.
life 360 n.
spirit 447 n.
chief thing 638 n.
affections 817 n.
courage 855 n.
heartache
suffering 825 n.
heart and soul
completely 54 adv.
heartburn
digestive disorders
   651 n.
heart-burning
regret 830 n.
resentment 891 n.
heart condition
cardiovascular

HEA

disease 651 n.
hearten
invigorate 174 vb.
give courage
   855 vb.
heartfelt
felt 818 adj.
hearth
home 192 n.
furnace 383 n.
heartland
district 184 n.
interiority 224 n.
heartless
cruel 898 adj.
pitiless 906 adj.
heart-rending
distressing 827 adj.
heart's blood
life 360 n.
heart's desire
objective 617 n.
aspiration 852 n.
heart-shaped
curved 248 adj.
rotund 252 adj.
heartthrob
a beauty 841 n.
loved one 887 n.
heart trouble
cardiovascular
   disease 651 n.
heart-warming
felt 818 adj.
pleasurable 826 adj.
heart-whole
free 744 adj.
indifferent 860 adj.
hearty
vigorous 174 adj.
healthy 650 adj.
felt 818 adj.
cheerful 833 adj.
sociable 882 adj.
heat
dryness 342 n.
heat 379 n.
contest 716 n.
excite 821 vb.
libido 859 n.
anger 891 n.
heater
heater 383 n.
heath
plain 348 n.
heathen
heathen 974 n.

Heath Robinson
imaginative 513 adj.
heave
carry 273 vb.
impel 279 vb.
draw 288 vb.
vomit 300 vb.
oscillate 317 vb.
breathe 352 vb.
exertion 682 n.
—to
bring to rest 266 vb.
heaven
heaven 971 n.
heavenly
celestial 321 adj.
pleasurable 826 adj.
splendid 841 adj.
paradisiac 971 adj.
heavens
heavens 321 n.
heaven-sent
opportune 137 adj.
heavy
inert 175 adj.
weighty 322 adj.
dense 324 adj.
odorous 394 adj.
unintelligent
499 adj.
laborious 682 adj.
severe 735 adj.
serious 834 adj.
tedious 838 adj.
heavy-handed
oppressive 735 adj.
heavy-hearted
melancholic
834 adj.
heavyweight
bigwig 638 n.
pugilist 722 n.
heavy with
impending 155 adj.
prolific 171 adj.
hecatomb
oblation 981 n.
heckle
be obstructive
702 vb.
torment 827 vb.
heckler
dissentient 489 n.
hectic
fervent 818 adj.
excited 821 adj.
hector

threaten 900 vb.
hedge
set off 31 vb.
fence 235 n.
wood 366 n.
avoid 620 vb.
be cautious 858 vb.
hedgehog
prickle 256 n.
hedge-hop
fly 271 vb.
hedonism
pleasure 376 n.
sensualism 944 n.
heed
carefulness 457 n.
observe 768 vb.
heedless
inattentive 456 adj.
rash 857 adj.
heel
foot 214 n.
be oblique 220 vb.
rear 238 n.
kick 279 vb.
cad 938 n.
—over
be inverted 221 vb.
hefty
whopping 32 adj.
stalwart 162 adj.
hegemony
influence 178 n.
authority 733 n.
prestige 866 n.
heifer
cattle 365 n.
height
height 209 n.
elevation 310 n.
metrology 465 n.
heighten
augment 36 vb.
elevate 310 vb.
exaggerate 546 vb.
heinous
heinous 934 adj.
heir, heiress
successor 67 n.
descendant 170 n.
beneficiary 776 n.
rich person 800 n.
heirloom
archaism 127 n.
dower 777 n.
helicopter
aircraft 276 n.

heliocentric
celestial 321 adj.
heliograph
signal 547 n.vb.
helium
lifter 310 n.
lightness 323 n.
helix
coil 251 n.
hell
depth 211 n.
suffering 825 n.
hell 972 n.
hell-bent
intending 617 adj.
rash 857 adj.
hellcat
hellhag 904 n.
hellfire
hell 972 n.
hellish
damnable 645 adj.
infernal 972 adj.
Hell's Angel
ruffian 904 n.
helm
sailing aid 269 n.
directorship 689 n.
helmet
armour 713 n.
helmsman
navigator 270 n.
director 690 n.
helot
slave 742 n.
help
benefit 615 vb.
be expedient 642 vb.
facilitate 701 vb.
aid 703 n.vb.
aider 703 n.
helper
auxiliary 707 n.
servant 742 n.
helpful
willing 597 adj.
cooperative 706 adj.
helping
portion 783 n.
helpless
impotent 161 adj.
weak 163 adj.
hem
edging 234 n.
flank 239 vb.
fold 261 n.vb.
—in

circumscribe
232 vb.
restrain 747 vb.
he-man
violent creature
176 n.
male 372 n.
hemi-
bisected 92 adj.
hemiplegia
nervous disorders
651 n.
hemisphere
region 184 n.
sphere 252 n.
hemistich
verse form 593 n.
hemline
garment 228 n.
hemp
fibre 208 n.
drug-taking 949 n.
hen
poultry 365 n.
henchman
auxiliary 707 n.
retainer 742 n.
hencoop, henhouse
cattle pen 369 n.
henna
orange 432 n.
henpecked
subjected 745 adj.
hepatitis
digestive disorders
651 n.
herald
precursor 66 n.
precede 283 vb.
omen 511 n.
proclaim 528 vb.
messenger 529 n.
heraldry
heraldry 547 n.
herb
potherb 301 n.
medicine 658 n.
herbaceous
vegetal 366 adj.
herbage
grass 366 n.
herbalist
botany 368 n.
doctor 658 n.
herbivore
eater 301 n.
animal 365 n.

herbivorous
feeding 301 adj.
herb tea
soft drink 301 n.
tonic 658 n.
Herculean
stalwart 162 adj.
laborious 682 adj.
Herculean task
hard task 700 n.
herd
group 74 n.
animal 365 n.
imprison 747 vb.
herd instinct
crowd 74 n.
herdsman
herdsman 369 n.
here
here 189 adv.
hereafter
future state 124 n.
here and there
sporadically 75 adv.
hereditary
genetic 5 adj.
filial 170 adj.
proprietary 777 adj.
heredity
heredity 5 n.
heresy
unbelief 486 n.
heterodoxy 977 n.
heretic
nonconformist 84 n.
unbeliever 486 n.
heretical
erroneous 495 adj.
heritable
genetic 5 adj.
heritage
posterity 170 n.
dower 777 n.
hermaphrodite
eunuch 161 n.
hermeneutics
hermeneutics 520 n.
hermetic, hermetical
cabbalistic 984 adj.
hermit
solitary 883 n.
ascetic 945 n.
pietist 979 n.
hermitage
retreat 192 n.
monastery 986 n.
hero, heroine

acting 594 n.
brave person 855 n.
prodigy 864 n.
favourite 890 n.
heroic
laborious 682 adj.
courageous 855 adj.
worshipful 866 adj.
heroin
drug-taking 949 n.
hero worship
praise 923 n.
deification 982 n.
herringbone
pattern 844 n.
hesitant
unwilling 598 adj.
hesitate
pause 145 vb.
be uncertain 474 vb.
hesitation
doubt 486 n.
unwillingness 598 n.
nervousness 854 n.
caution 858 n.
hessian
textile 222 n.
heterodox
unconformable
84 adj.
heterodox 977 adj.
heterogeneous
nonuniform 17 adj.
multiform 82 adj.
heterosexual
typical 83 adj.
heuristic
inquiring 459 adj.
demonstrating
478 adj.
hew
cut 46 vb.
form 243 vb.
fell 311 vb.
hex
spell 983 n.
hexagon
angular figure
247 n.
heyday
palmy days 730 n.
hiatus
interval 201 n.
opening 263 n.
hibernation
winter 129 n.
sleep 679 n.

hiccup, hiccough
eruct 300 vb.
hidden
concealed 525 adj.
secluded 883 adj.
hidden hand
influence 178 n.
troublemaker 663 n.
hide
skin 226 n.
lurk 523 vb.
conceal 525 vb.
safeguard 660 vb.
be cowardly 856 vb.
hideaway, hideout
hiding-place 527 n.
hidebound
narrow-minded
481 adj.
obstinate 602 adj.
hideous
ugly 842 adj.
hiding
defeat 728 n.
corporal
punishment 963 n.
hiding-place
hiding-place 527 n.
hierarchy
degree 27 n.
series 71 n.
hieratic
priestly 985 adj.
hieroglyphics
enigma 530 n.
writing 586 n.
hierophant
religious teacher
973 n.
high
great 32 adj.
high 209 adj.
topmost 213 adj.
elevated 310 adj.
pungent 388 adj.
strident 407 adj.
important 638 adj.
excitable state 822 n.
noble 868 adj.
drugged 949 adj.
high and mighty
prideful 871 adj.
insolent 878 adj.
highbrow
intellectual 492 n.
high-caste
worshipful 866 adj.

high-class
genteel 868 adj.
high-coloured
florid 425 adj.
High Command
master 741 n.
High Commissioner
governor 741 n.
envoy 754 n.
high day
holy day 988 n.
high-density
assembled 74 adj.
housing 192 n.
highest
supreme 34 adj.
topmost 213 adj.
highfalutin
rhetorical 574 adj.
ostentatious
875 adj.
high fidelity
accuracy 494 n.
gramophone 414 n.
high-flown
imaginative 513 adj.
rhetorical 574 adj.
high frequency
radiation 417 n.
high-handed
oppressive 735 adj.
proud 871 adj.
high-hat
prideful 871 adj.
highland
high land 209 n.
high-level
important 638 adj.
directing 689 adj.
high-life
festivity 837 n.
upper class 868 n.
highlight
publish 528 vb.
emphasize 532 vb.
indicate 547 vb.
high living
intemperance 943 n.
highly coloured
expressive 516 adj.
highly-strung
lively 819 adj.
excitable 822 adj.
high-minded
honourable 929 adj.
disinterested
931 adj.

Highness
sovereign 741 n.
high-pitched
strident 407 adj.
high pressure
vigorousness 174 n.
high-priority
important 638 adj.
high society
beau monde 848 n.
high-sounding
affected 850 adj.
high-spirited
lively 819 adj.
high spirits
cheerfulness 833 n.
merriment 833 n.
high-tension
dynamic 160 adj.
high time
lateness 136 n.
high treason
perfidy 930 n.
highway
road 624 n.
highway code
traffic control 305 n.
highwayman
robber 789 n.
hijack
steal 788 vb.
hike
walk 267 vb.
hiker
pedestrian 268 n.
hilarious
funny 849 adj.
hilarity
merriment 833 n.
hill
high land 209 n.
incline 220 n.
hillock
small hill 209 n.
hillside
incline 220 n.
hilly
alpine 209 adj.
hilt
handle 218 n.
hind
back 238 adj.
hinder
disable 161 vb.
back 238 adj.
retard 278 vb.
hinder 702 vb.

(*see* **hindrance**)
hindmost
ending 69 adj.
back 238 adj.
hindquarters
buttocks 238 n.
hindrance
delay 136 n.
hindrance 702 n.
obstacle 702 n.
restraint 747 n.
hindsight
remembrance 505 n.
Hinduism
religious faith 973 n.
hinge
joint 45 n.
fastening 47 n.
pivot 218 n.
hinge on
depend 157 vb.
hint
tincture 43 n.
hint 524 n.vb.
indication 547 n.
advice 691 n.
hinterland
interiority 224 n.
hippie, hippy
nonconformist 84 n.
hippodrome
arena 724 n.
hips
buttocks 238 n.
hipster
beau monde 848 n.
hire
employ 622 vb.
lease 784 vb.
hire 785 vb.
hireling
servant 742 n.
hire purchase
borrowing 785 n.
hirer
lender 784 n.
hirsute
hairy 259 adj.
hiss
hiss 406 vb.
disapprobation
924 n.
histogram
statistics 86 n.
historian
antiquarian 125 n.
chronicler 549 n.

narrator 590 n.
historic
renowned 866 adj.
historical
past 125 adj.
olden 127 adj.
true 494 adj.
history
past time 125 n.
record 548 n.
narrative 590 n.
histrionics
exaggeration 546 n.
acting 594 n.
affectation 850 n.
hit
strike 279 vb.
discover 484 vb.
exceller 644 n.
success 727 n.
—it off
befriend 880 vb.
hitch
tie 45 vb.
ligature 47 n.
hitch 702 n.
hitchhike
ride 267 vb.
hit or miss
negligent 458 adj.
inexact 495 adj.
hive
stock farm 369 n.
storage 632 n.
activity 678 n.
hive off
take away 786 vb.
hoard
store 632 n.vb.
safeguard 660 vb.
be parsimonious
816 vb.
hoarding
advertisement
528 n.
hoarfrost
wintriness 380 n.
hoarse
hoarse 407 adj.
voiceless 578 adj.
hoary
ageing 131 adj.
whitish 427 adj.
hoax
trickery 542 n.
false alarm 665 n.
hob

stand 218 n.
hobble
disable 161 vb.
move slowly 278 vb.
fetter 748 n.
hobby
business 622 n.
amusement 837 n.
hobbyhorse
eccentricity 503 n.
hobgoblin
elf 970 n.
hobnob
be sociable 882 vb.
Hobson's choice
no choice 606 n.
hock
wine 301 n.
give security 767 vb.
hocus-pocus
sleight 542 n.
hod
vessel 194 n.
hoe
farm tool 370 n.
hog
pig 365 n.
appropriate 786 vb.
be selfish 932 vb.
glutton 947 n.
hoi polloi
commonalty 869 n.
hoist
lifter 310 n.
flag 547 n.
hokum
empty talk 515 n.
hold
cohere 48 vb.
comprise 78 vb.
go on 146 vb.
influence 178 n.
cellar 194 n.
base 214 n.
handle 218 n.
support 218 n.vb.
opine 485 vb.
affirm 532 vb.
storage 632 n.
wrestling 716 n.
imprison 747 vb.
possession 773 n.
retention 778 n.
—back
pause 145 vb.
be unwilling 598 vb.
restrain 747 vb.

—down
dominate 733 vb.
subjugate 745 vb.
—fast
cohere 48 vb.
stand firm 599 vb.
—good
be true 494 vb.
—off
parry 713 vb.
—office
function 622 vb.
rule 733 vb.
—on
wait 136 vb.
retain 778 vb.
—one's own
be equal 28 vb.
withstand 704 vb.
—out
stand firm 599 vb.
—tight
unite with 45 vb.
retain 778 vb.
—together
accord 24 vb.
cooperate 706 vb.
—up
put off 136 vb.
support 218 vb.
hinder 702 vb.
rob 788 vb.
—water
be reasonable
　475 vb.
holdall
bag 194 n.
holder
receptacle 194 n.
handle 218 n.
possessor 776 n.
holding
farm 370 n.
lands 777 n.
holdup
delay 136 n.
hitch 702 n.
hole
cavity 255 n.
orifice 263 n.
hiding-place 527 n.
predicament 700 n.
hole-and-corner
stealthy 525 adj.
holiday
leisure 681 n.
amusement 837 n.

holier than thou
affected 850 adj.
pietistic 979 adj.
holism
philosophy 449 n.
hollow
insubstantial 4 adj.
empty 190 adj.
cavity 255 n.
furrow 262 n.
resonant 404 adj.
sophistical 477 adj.
hypocritical
　541 adj.
Hollywood
cinema 445 n.
holocaust
slaughter 362 n.
burning 381 n.
hologram
image 551 n.
holograph
script 586 n.
holster
case 194 n.
arsenal 723 n.
holt
wood 366 n.
holy
divine 965 adj.
godlike 965 adj.
sanctified 979 adj.
devotional 981 adj.
Holy Bible
scripture 975 n.
Holy Communion
Christian rite 988 n.
holy day
holy day 988 n.
Holy Ghost
Holy Ghost 965 n.
Holy of Holies
holy place 990 n.
holy terror
bane 659 n.
bad person 938 n.
Holy Week
holy day 988 n.
homage
submission 721 n.
loyalty 739 n.
respects 920 n.
home
native 191 adj.
home 192 n.
house 192 n.
homecoming

return 286 n.
home economics
cookery 301 n.
home help
cleaner 648 n.
homeland
territory 184 n.
home 192 n.
homeless
displaced 188 adj.
travelling 267 adj.
poor 801 adj.
homeless person
wanderer 268 n.
outcast 883 n.
homely
comfortable
　376 adj.
plain 573 adj.
homemade
produced 164 adj.
artless 699 adj.
home rule
independence 744 n.
homesickness
suffering 825 n.
desire 859 n.
homespun
produced 164 adj.
plain 573 adj.
artless 699 adj.
homestead
home 192 n.
home truth
veracity 540 n.
plainness 573 n.
homework
study 536 n.
preparation 669 n.
homicidal maniac
violent creature
　176 n.
killer 362 n.
homicide
homicide 362 n.
homiletics
teaching 534 n.
homily
lecture 534 n.
oration 579 n.
hominid
humankind 371 n.
hominoid
human 371 adj.
homoeopathic,
　homeopathic
small 33 adj.

medical 658 adj.
homoeopathy,
　homeopathy
medical art 658 n.
homogeneous
uniform 16 adj.
homologous
relative 9 adj.
homonym
word 559 n.
homo sapiens
humankind 371 n.
homosexual
nonconformist 84 n.
homunculus
dwarf 196 n.
hone
sharpen 256 vb.
honest
genuine 494 adj.
veracious 540 adj.
ethical 917 adj.
honourable 929 adj.
honey
sweet thing 392 n.
yellowness 433 n.
darling 890 n.
honeycomb
network 222 n.
cavity 255 n.
porosity 263 n.
sweet thing 392 n.
honeycombed
cellular 194 adj.
honeyed words
inducement 612 n.
flattery 925 n.
honeymoon
concord 710 n.
wedding 894 n.
honeypot
focus 76 n.
honk
loudness 400 n.
danger signal 665 n.
honorarium
reward 962 n.
honorary
voluntary 597 adj.
uncharged 812 adj.
honorific
title 870 n.
celebratory 876 adj.
honour
decoration 729 n.
prestige 866 n.
honour 866 vb.

HON

title 870 n.
celebrate 876 vb.
pay one's respects 884 vb.
grant claims 915 vb.
respect 920 n.vb.
probity 929 n.
purity 950 n.
worship 981 n.vb.
honourable
  honourable 929 adj.
honours
  honours 866 n.
hood
  headgear 228 n.
  screen 421 n.vb.
hooded
  covered 226 adj.
  concealed 525 adj.
hoodlum
  ruffian 904 n.
hoodwink
  deceive 542 vb.
hooey
  empty talk 515 n.
hoof
  foot 214 n.
hoofer
  entertainer 594 n.
hook
  hanger 217 n.
  angularity 247 n.
  knock 279 n.
  trap 542 n.
  nippers 778 n.
  take 786 vb.
hook and eye
  fastening 47 n.
hooked on
  obsessed 455 adj.
  enamoured 887 adj.
  drugged 949 adj.
hookup
  union 45 n.
  association 706 n.
hooligan
  ruffian 904 n.
hoop
  circle 250 n.
  plaything 837 n.
hoot
  cry 408 n.vb.
  laugh 835 vb.
  disapprove 924 vb.
hooter
  megaphone 400 n.
  signal 547 n.

HOR

hop
  leap 312 n.vb.
  be agitated 318 vb.
  dancing 837 n.
  social gathering 882 n.
—it
  decamp 296 vb.
hope
  hope 852 n.vb.
hopeful
  probable 471 adj.
  expectant 507 adj.
  hoper 852 n.
  promising 852 adj.
hopeless
  impossible 470 adj.
  useless 641 adj.
  hopeless 853 adj.
  unpromising 853 adj.
hopper
  vat 194 n.
hops
  potherb 301 n.
horde
  multitude 104 n.
  army 722 n.
  rabble 869 n.
horizon
  distance 199 n.
  limit 236 n.
  visibility 443 n.
horizontal
  flat 216 adj.
hormone
  drug 658 n.
horn
  cup 194 n.
  protuberance 254 n.
  horn 414 n.
hornet
  noxious animal 904 n.
hornet's nest
  bane 659 n.
  pitfall 663 n.
horny
  hard 326 adj.
horny-handed
  labouring 682 adj.
horology
  chronometry 117 n.
horoscope
  prediction 511 n.
horrible
  unpleasant 827 adj.

HOS

frightening 854 adj.
horrid
  not nice 645 adj.
  hateful 888 adj.
horrific
  frightening 854 adj.
horrify
  displease 827 vb.
  frighten 854 vb.
  excite hate 888 vb.
horror
  eyesore 842 n.
  fear 854 n.
  monster 938 n.
hors de combat
  useless 641 adj.
hors-d'oeuvres
  hors-d'oeuvres 301 n.
horse
  horse 273 n.
  cavalry 722 n.
horse-breeding
  animal husbandry 369 n.
horse-drawn
  vehicular 274 adj.
horseman,
  horsewoman
  rider 268 n.
  cavalry 722 n.
horsemanship
  equitation 267 n.
horseplay
  revel 837 n.
horsepower
  energy 160 n.
horse sense
  intelligence 498 n.
horseshoe
  curve 248 n.
  talisman 983 n.
horse-trading
  conditions 766 n.
  barter 791 n.
horsewhip
  flog 963 vb.
hortative, hortatory
  inducing 612 adj.
  advising 691 adj.
horticulture
  flower 366 n.
  agriculture 370 n.
hosanna
  rejoicing 835 n.
  hymn 981 n.

HOT

hose
  conduit 351 n.
  extinguisher 382 n.
hosiery
  legwear 228 n.
hospice
  retreat 192 n.
hospitable
  (*see* **hospitality**)
hospital
  hospital 658 n.
hospitality
  liberality 813 n.
  friendliness 880 n.
  sociability 882 n.
host
  multitude 104 n.
  infection 651 n.
  army 722 n.
  sociable person 882 n.
hostage
  prisoner 750 n.
  security 767 n.
hostel
  quarters 192 n.
hostess
  sociable person 882 n.
hostile
  attacking 712 adj.
  adverse 731 adj.
  inimical 881 adj.
  disapproving 924 adj.
hostilities
  belligerency 718 n.
hostility
  hindrance 702 n.
  dissension 709 n.
  (*see* **hostile**)
hot
  hot 379 adj.
  pungent 388 adj.
  fervent 818 adj.
  angry 891 adj.
  illegal 954 adj.
hot air
  empty talk 515 n.
hotbed
  seedbed 156 n.
  infection 651 n.
hot-blooded
  violent 176 adj.
hotchpotch,
  hodgepodge
  medley 43 n.

hotel
inn 192 n.
hotelier
caterer 633 n.
hot gospeller
preacher 537 n.
zealot 979 n.
hothead
desperado 857 n.
hothouse
extraneous 59 adj.
seedbed 156 n.
hot line
telecommunication
531 n.
hotplate
heater 383 n.
hotpot
dish 301 n.
hot potato
difficulty 700 n.
hot seat
predicament 700 n.
hot under the collar
excited 821 adj.
angry 891 adj.
hot up
heat 381 vb.
endanger 661 vb.
hot water
predicament 700 n.
hound
dog 365 n.
be malevolent
898 vb.
cad 938 n.
hounding
pursuit 619 n.
hour
juncture 8 n.
period 110 n.
clock time 117 n.
hourglass
timekeeper 117 n.
narrowing 206 n.
hour hand
indicator 547 n.
hourly
periodic 110 adj.
house
race 11 n.
edifice 164 n.
house 192 n.
playgoer 594 n.
corporation 708 n.
house arrest
detention 747 n.

houseboat
small house 192 n.
boat 275 n.
housebound
quiescent 266 adj.
house-breaker
thief 789 n.
household
family 11 n.
inhabitants 191 n.
householder
resident 191 n.
household name
famousness 866 n.
housekeeper
caterer 633 n.
manager 690 n.
housekeeping
management 689 n.
houseman
doctor 658 n.
house of cards
weak thing 163 n.
house party
social gathering
882 n.
housetop
vertex 213 n.
roof 226 n.
house-trained
well-bred 848 adj.
house-warming
social gathering
882 n.
housewife
caterer 633 n.
manager 690 n.
housework
labour 682 n.
housing
housing 192 n.
frame 218 n.
hovel
small house 192 n.
hover
impend 155 vb.
hang 217 vb.
fly 271 vb.
be irresolute 601 vb.
hovercraft
ship 275 n.
aircraft 276 n.
howl
cry 408 n.vb.
ululate 409 vb.
weep 836 vb.
howler

mistake 495 n.
hoyden
youngster 132 n.
hub
focus 76 n.
centre 225 n.
chief thing 638 n.
hubbub
commotion 318 n.
loudness 400 n.
hubris
pride 871 n.
huckster
pedlar 794 n.
huddle
crowd 74 n.
make smaller
198 vb.
conference 584 n.
hue
hue 425 n.
hue and cry
chase 619 n.
huff
resentment 891 n.
hug
cohere 48 vb.
be near 200 vb.
gesture 547 n.
endearment 889 n.
—**oneself**
be pleased 824 vb.
huge
enormous 32 adj.
huge 195 adj.
hulk
bulk 195 n.
ship 275 n.
hull
ship 275 n.
hullabaloo
turmoil 61 n.
loudness 400 n.
hum
stink 397 vb.
faintness 401 n.
roll 403 n.vb.
sing 413 vb.
activity 678 n.
—**and haw**
stammer 580 vb.
be irresolute 601 vb.
human
human 371 adj.
frail 934 adj.
human being
humankind 371 n.

person 371 n.
humane
benevolent 897 adj.
human error
vulnerability 661 n.
humanism
philosophy 449 n.
philanthropy 901 n.
humanist
scholar 492 n.
humanitarian
philanthropist
901 n.
humanities
culture 490 n.
literature 557 n.
humanity
humankind 371 n.
benevolence 897 n.
pity 905 n.
human nature
humankind 371 n.
human rights
dueness 915 n.
humble
inconsiderable
33 adj.
inferior 35 adj.
impress 821 vb.
plebeian 869 adj.
humble 872 adj.
modest 874 adj.
respectful 920 adj.
humbug
empty talk 515 n.
falsehood 541 n.
impostor 545 n.
affecter 850 n.
humdrum
plain 573 adj.
tedious 838 adj.
humid
humid 341 adj.
humidifier
air 340 n.
humidity
moisture 341 n.
humiliate
shame 867 vb.
humiliate 872 vb.
humility
humility 872 n.
disinterestedness
931 n.
piety 979 n.
hummock
small hill 209 n.

humorist
  entertainer 594 n.
  humorist 839 n.
humorous
  witty 839 adj.
  funny 849 adj.
humour
  temperament 5 n.
  whim 604 n.
  be lenient 736 vb.
  affections 817 n.
  laughter 835 n.
  wit 839 n.
  flatter 925 vb.
humourless
  serious 834 adj.
  dull 840 adj.
hump
  small hill 209 n.
  carry 273 vb.
humpy
  convex 253 adj.
humus
  soil 344 n.
hunch
  intuition 476 n.
  supposition 512 n.
hunchbacked
  deformed 246 adj.
  blemished 845 adj.
hundred percent, one
  perfect 646 adj.
hunger
  rapacity 786 n.
  desire 859 n.
  be hungry 859 vb.
hunger strike
  fast 946 n.
hungry
  hungry 859 adj.
hungry for
  inquisitive 453 adj.
  desiring 859 adj.
hunk
  piece 53 n.
  bulk 195 n.
hunt
  oscillate 317 vb.
  search 459 n.
  hunt 619 vb.
hunter
  thoroughbred
    273 n.
  hunter 619 n.
hunting
  pursuit 619 n.
  sport 837 n.

hurdle
  fence 235 n.
  obstacle 702 n.
hurdler
  thoroughbred
    273 n.
  jumper 312 n.
hurl
  propel 287 vb.
hurly-burly
  turmoil 61 n.
  commotion 318 n.
hurrah, hurray,
  hooray
  rejoicing 835 n.
hurricane
  storm 176 n.
  gale 352 n.
hurried
  brief 114 adj.
  negligent 458 adj.
  hasty 680 adj.
hurry
  move fast 277 vb.
  hasten 680 vb.
hurt
  give pain 377 vb.
  impair 655 vb.
  hurt 827 vb.
  resentful 891 adj.
hurtful
  paining 827 adj.
  maleficent 898 adj.
hurtle
  be violent 176 vb.
  move fast 277 vb.
husband
  store 632 vb.
  spouse 894 n.
husbandry
  agriculture 370 n.
  management
    689 n.
  economy 814 n.
hush
  quietude 266 n.
  silence 399 n.vb.
—up
  keep secret 525 vb.
hush-hush
  concealed 525 adj.
hush money
  incentive 612 n.
  reward 962 n.
husk
  skin 226 n.
  grass 366 n.

  rubbish 641 n.
husky
  stalwart 162 adj.
  dog 365 n.
  hoarse 407 adj.
hussy
  insolent person
    878 n.
hustings
  rostrum 539 n.
  vote 605 n.
hustle
  activity 678 n.
  hasten 680 vb.
hut
  small house 192 n.
hutch
  stable 192 n.
hybrid
  hybrid 43 n.
hydra
  rara avis 84 n.
hydra-headed
  multiform 82 adj.
hydrant
  conduit 351 n.
hydrate
  add water 339 vb.
hydroelectricity
  sources of energy
    160 n.
hydrogenate
  gasify 336 vb.
hydrography
  earth sciences 321 n.
hydrology
  earth sciences 321 n.
  fluidity 335 n.
hydrometry
  fluidity 335 n.
hydrophobia
  infection 651 n.
hydroponics
  agriculture 370 n.
hydrotherapy
  therapy 658 n.
hygiene
  health 650 n.
  hygiene 652 n.
hygienic
  safe 660 adj.
hygrometer
  meter 465 n.
hymn
  praise 923 n.
  hymn 981 n.
hype (up)

  advertisement
    528 n.
  praise 923 vb.
hyped up
  excited 821 adj.
hyperbola
  curve 248 n.
hyperbole
  trope 519 n.
  exaggeration 546 n.
hypercritical
  fastidious 862 adj.
  disapproving
    924 adj.
hypermarket
  shop 796 n.
hypersensitive
  sensitive 819 adj.
hypersonic
  speedy 277 adj.
hypertension
  cardiovascular
    disease 651 n.
hyphenation
  punctuation 547 n.
hypnosis
  insensibility 375 n.
  sleep 679 n.
hypnotic
  influential 178 adj.
  inducing 612 adj.
  soporific 679 adj.
hypnotist
  motivator 612 n.
  psychic 984 n.
hypnotize
  render insensible
    375 vb.
hypochondriac
  madman 504 n.
  sick person 651 n.
  moper 834 n.
hypocrisy
  duplicity 541 n.
  deception 542 n.
hypocrite
  affecter 850 n.
hypothecate
  give security 767 vb.
hypothermia
  coldness 380 n.
hypothesis
  opinion 485 n.
hypothetical
  suppositional
    512 adj.
  imaginary 513 adj.

hysteria
psychopathy 503 n.
hysterical
excited 821 adj.
hysterics
excitable state 822 n.

I

I
self 80 n.
iatrogenic
diseased 651 adj.
ice
smoothness 258 n.
ice 380 n.
refrigeration 382 n.
sweeten 392 vb.
iceberg
ice 380 n.
icebox
refrigerator 384 n.
ice cream
dessert 301 n.
ice rink
arena 724 n.
pleasure ground
837 n.
ice skating
sport 837 n.
icicle
ice 380 n.
unfeeling person
820 n.
icing
covering 226 n.
sweet thing 392 n.
icon
image 551 n.
iconoclast
destroyer 168 n.
zealot 979 n.
iconoclastic
impious 980 adj.
iconography
art style 553 n.
icy
cold 380 adj.
impassive 820 adj.
unsociable 883 adj.
id
self 80 n.
spirit 447 n.
idea
idea 451 n.
opinion 485 n.
ideality 513 n.

ideal
prototype 23 n.
ideational 451 adj.
imaginary 513 adj.
perfection 646 n.
desired object 859 n.
idealism
immateriality 320 n.
philosophy 449 n.
fantasy 513 n.
disinterestedness
931 n.
idealist
visionary 513 n.
perfectionist 862 n.
philanthropist
901 n.
ideality
ideality 513 n.
idealize
overrate 482 vb.
imagine 513 vb.
ideals
morals 917 n.
disinterestedness
931 n.
ideate
think 449 vb.
imagine 513 vb.
identical
identical 13 adj.
one 88 adj.
identification
identification 547 n.
identify
discover 484 vb.
identity
identity 13 n.
self 80 n.
authenticity 494 n.
ideological
philosophic 449 adj.
ideology
philosophy 449 n.
creed 485 n.
idiocy
folly 499 n.
insanity 503 n.
idiom
speciality 80 n.
connotation 514 n.
dialect 560 n.
phrase 563 n.
style 566 n.
idiomatic
semantic 514 adj.
linguistic 557 adj.

idiosyncrasy
temperament 5 n.
speciality 80 n.
habit 610 n.
idiot
fool 501 n.
idiotic
foolish 499 adj.
crazy 503 adj.
idle
profitless 641 adj.
unused 674 adj.
lazy 679 adj.
idleness
unproductiveness
172 n.
leisure 681 n.
idler
idler 679 n.
idol
image 551 n.
person of repute
866 n.
favourite 890 n.
idol 982 n.
idolater, idolatress
idolater 982 n.
idolatry
love 887 n.
cult 981 n.
idolatry 982 n.
idolize
love 887 vb.
respect 920 vb.
idolatrize 982 vb.
idyllic
pleasurable 826 adj.
if
if 8 adv.
igloo
dwelling 192 n.
ignite
kindle 381 vb.
igniter
lighter 385 n.
ignoble
discreditable
867 adj.
ignominious
degrading 867 adj.
ignoramus
ignoramus 493 n.
ignorance
ignorance 491 n.
ignorant
ignorant 491 adj.
ill-bred 847 adj.

ignore
be blind 439 vb.
be inattentive
456 vb.
disregard 458 vb.
be rude 885 vb.
ill
evil 616 n.
sick 651 adj.
ill-advised
unwise 499 adj.
inexpedient 643 adj.
ill-assorted
disagreeing 25 adj.
ill at ease
suffering 825 adj.
ill-bred
ill-bred 847 adj.
ill-considered
(*see ill-advised*)
ill-defined
amorphous 244 adj.
indistinct 444 adj.
ill-disposed
malevolent 898 adj.
illegal
prohibited 757 adj.
dishonest 930 adj.
illegal 954 adj.
illegible
unintelligible
517 adj.
illegitimacy
bastardy 954 n.
illegality 954 n.
ill-fated
unfortunate 731 adj.
ill feeling
enmity 881 n.
ill-gotten
acquired 771 adj.
illiberal
biased 481 adj.
parsimonious
816 adj.
illicit
illegal 954 adj.
illimitable
infinite 107 adj.
ill-informed
mistaken 495 adj.
illiterate
uninstructed
491 adj.
ill-judged
ill-timed 138 adj.
unwise 499 adj.

ill-mannered
 ill-bred 847 adj.
 discourteous
  885 adj.
ill-natured
 malevolent 898 adj.
illness
 illness 651 n.
illogical
 illogical 477 adj.
 erroneous 495 adj.
ill-omened
 inopportune
  138 adj.
 unpromising
  853 adj.
ill-spent
 wasted 634 adj.
 profitless 641 adj.
ill-starred
 unfortunate 731 adj.
ill-tempered
 sullen 893 adj.
ill-treat
 ill-treat 645 vb.
 misuse 675 vb.
illuminate
 illuminate 420 vb.
 colour 425 vb.
 interpret 520 vb.
 decorate 844 vb.
illuminati
 intellectual 492 n.
illumination
 light 417 n.
 knowledge 490 n.
 revelation 975 n.
illuminations
 fireworks 420 n.
illuminator
 artist 556 n.
ill-use
 ill-treat 645 vb.
illusion
 visual fallacy 440 n.
 error 495 n.
 sleight 542 n.
illusionist
 conjuror 545 n.
illusory
 deceiving 542 adj.
illustrate
 exemplify 83 vb.
 represent 551 vb.
 decorate 844 vb.
illustration
 example 83 n.

 picture 553 n.
illustrative
 typical 83 adj.
illustrator
 artist 556 n.
illustrious
 renowned 866 adj.
ill will
 malevolence 898 n.
ill wind
 adversity 731 n.
ill-wisher
 troublemaker 663 n.
image
 copy 22 n.
 reflection 417 n.
 appearance 445 n.
 ideality 513 n.
 trope 519 n.
 image 551 n.
 idol 982 n.
imagery
 metaphor 519 n.
imaginary
 unreal 2 adj.
 insubstantial 4 adj.
 imaginary 513 adj.
imagination
 vision 438 n.
 imagination 513 n.
imaginative
 original 21 adj.
 imaginative 513 adj.
 descriptive 590 adj.
imagine
 suppose 512 vb.
 imagine 513 vb.
imam
 governor 741 n.
 priest 986 n.
imbalance
 inequality 29 n.
 distortion 246 n.
imbecile
 fool 501 n.
 insane 503 adj.
imbibe
 absorb 299 vb.
 drink 301 vb.
imbroglio
 confusion 61 n.
imbue
 pervade 189 vb.
 infuse 303 vb.
imitate
 liken 18 vb.
 imitate 20 vb.

 represent 551 vb.
imitation
 imitation 20 n.
 sham 542 n.
imitative
 simulating 18 adj.
 imitative 20 adj.
 unthinking 450 adj.
immaculate
 perfect 646 adj.
 clean 648 adj.
 pure 950 adj.
immanent
 intrinsic 5 adj.
immaterial
 irrelevant 10 adj.
 immaterial 320 adj.
immature
 young 130 adj.
 immature 670 adj.
immeasurable
 infinite 107 adj.
immediate
 instantaneous
  116 adj.
immemorial
 immemorial
  127 adj.
immense
 enormous 32 adj.
 huge 195 adj.
immensity
 space 183 n.
immerse
 plunge 313 vb.
 drench 341 vb.
immersion
 Christian rite 988 n.
immigrant
 settler 191 n.
 incomer 297 n.
imminent
 impending 155 adj.
immiscible
 nonadhesive
  49 adj.
immobile
 still 266 adj.
immobility
 stability 153 n.
 inaction 677 n.
immobilize
 bring to rest 266 vb.
 make inactive
  679 vb.
immoderate
 violent 176 adj.

 exaggerated
  546 adj.
 intemperate
  943 adj.
immodest
 unchaste 951 adj.
immolate
 kill 362 vb.
immoral
 dishonest 930 adj.
immorality
 wrong 914 n.
 wickedness 934 n.
 unchastity 951 n.
immortal
 perpetual 115 adj.
 renowned 866 adj.
Immortal(s)
 deity 966 n.
immortalize
 perpetuate 115 vb.
 honour 866 vb.
immovable
 fixed 153 adj.
 resolute 599 adj.
immune
 invulnerable
  660 adj.
immunity
 nonliability 919 n.
immunization
 hygiene 652 n.
 protection 660 n.
immure
 imprison 747 vb.
—oneself
 be unsociable
  883 vb.
immutable
 unchangeable
  153 adj.
imp
 child 132 n.
 demon 970 n.
 elf 970 n.
impact
 influence 178 n.
 collision 279 n.
 excitation 821 n.
impair
 weaken 163 vb.
 harm 645 vb.
 impair 655 vb.
impale
 pierce 263 vb.
impart
 inform 524 vb.

impartial
neutral 625 adj.
just 913 adj.
impassable
closed 264 adj.
impracticable
470 adj.
impasse
difficulty 700 n.
impassioned
forceful 571 adj.
fervent 818 adj.
impassive
impassive 820 adj.
unastonished
865 adj.
impatience
haste 680 n.
excitability 822 n.
irascibility 892 n.
impeach
indict 928 vb.
impeccable
perfect 646 adj.
impecunious
poor 801 adj.
impede
hinder 702 vb.
impediment
obstacle 702 n.
impedimenta
equipment 630 n.
encumbrance 702 n.
impel
impel 279 vb.
motivate 612 vb.
impending
impending 155 adj.
approaching
289 adj.
impenetrable
closed 264 adj.
dense 324 adj.
unintelligible
517 adj.
thick-skinned
820 adj.
impenitence
impenitence 940 n.
imperative
necessary 596 adj.
commanding
737 adj.
compelling 740 adj.
imperceptible
minute 196 adj.
invisible 444 adj.

imperceptive
indiscriminating
464 adj.
imperfect
inferior 35 adj.
deficient 307 adj.
imperfect 647 adj.
uncompleted
726 adj.
blemished 845 adj.
imperfection
imperfection 647 n.
blemish 845 n.
imperial
ruling 733 adj.
imperialism
governance 733 n.
imperil
endanger 661 vb.
imperious
authoritative
733 adj.
insolent 878 adj.
imperishable
perpetual 115 adj.
renowned 866 adj.
impermanence
transience 114 n.
changeableness
152 n.
impermeable
closed 264 adj.
impersonal
impassive 820 adj.
indifferent 860 adj.
just 913 adj.
impersonate
represent 551 vb.
act 594 vb.
impersonator
entertainer 594 n.
imperspicuity
imperspicuity 568 n.
impertinence
sauciness 878 n.
rudeness 885 n.
impertinent
disrespectful
921 adj.
imperturbability
inexcitability 823 n.
lack of wonder
865 n.
impervious
dense 324 adj.
unintelligent
499 adj.

thick-skinned
820 adj.
impetrate
entreat 761 vb.
impetuosity
vigorousness 174 n.
rashness 857 n.
impetuous
hasty 680 adj.
excitable 822 adj.
impetus
spurt 277 n.
impulse 279 n.
motive 612 n.
impiety
impiety 980 n.
impinge
encroach 306 vb.
impious
impious 980 adj.
impish
fairylike 970 adj.
implacable
resolute 599 adj.
pitiless 906 adj.
revengeful 910 adj.
implant
implant 303 vb.
educate 534 vb.
habituate 610 vb.
implausible
improbable 472 adj.
implement
tool 630 n.
carry out 725 vb.
implicate
accuse 928 vb.
implication
relation 9 n.
meaning 514 n.
implicit
intrinsic 5 adj.
tacit 523 adj.
implore
entreat 761 vb.
imply
evidence 466 vb.
mean 514 vb.
imply 523 vb.
impolite
discourteous
885 adj.
impolitic
inexpedient
643 adj.
imponderable
light 323 adj.

import
transference 272 n.
admit 299 vb.
meaning 514 n.
importance
importance 638 n.
important
crucial 137 adj.
fundamental
156 adj.
importer
merchant 794 n.
importunate
requesting 761 adj.
annoying 827 adj.
importune
torment 827 vb.
impose
command 737 vb.
command respect
920 vb.
—on
deceive 542 vb.
imposing
impressive 821 adj.
imposition
bane 659 n.
injustice 914 n.
penalty 963 n.
impossibility
impossibility 470 n.
impossible
impossible 470 adj.
difficult 700 adj.
intolerable 827 adj.
impost
tax 809 n.
impostor
impostor 545 n.
usurper 916 n.
impotence
impotence 161 n.
unproductiveness
172 n.
impound
imprison 747 vb.
impoverish
impoverish 801 vb.
impracticable
impracticable
470 adj.
impractical
irrelevant 10 adj.
imaginative 513 adj.
imprecation
entreaty 761 n.
malediction 899 n.

imprecise
inexact 495 adj.
unclear 568 adj.
imprecision
generality 79 n.
impregnable
invulnerable
660 adj.
impregnate
make fruitful
171 vb.
infuse 303 vb.
impresario
stage manager
594 adj.
impress
influence 178 vb.
attract notice
455 vb.
motivate 612 vb.
impress 821 vb.
command respect
920 vb.
—on
emphasize 532 vb.
impressible
impressible 819 adj.
impression
appearance 445 n.
idea 451 n.
intuition 476 n.
opinion 485 n.
indication 547 n.
representation
551 n.
edition 589 n.
acting 594 n.
feeling 818 n.
impressionable
impressible 819 adj.
excitable 822 adj.
impressionistic
representing
551 adj.
descriptive 590 adj.
impressive
influential 178 adj.
forceful 571 adj.
notable 638 adj.
impressive 821 adj.
wonderful 864 adj.
respected 920 adj.
imprimatur
permit 756 n.
imprint
identification 547 n.
label 547 n.

letterpress 587 n.
imprison
imprison 747 vb.
improbability
improbability 472 n.
improbable
improbable 472 adj.
unexpected 508 adj.
improbity
improbity 930 n.
impromptu
spontaneous
609 adj.
unprepared 670 adj.
improper
unapt 25 adj.
vulgar 847 adj.
disreputable
867 adj.
impropriety
inaptitude 25 n.
solecism 565 n.
bad taste 847 n.
undueness 916 n.
improve
get better 654 vb.
make better 654 vb.
improvement
progression 285 n.
improvement 654 n.
improver
reformer 654 n.
improvidence
waste 634 n.
improvident
prodigal 815 adj.
improvise
compose music
413 vb.
improvise 609 vb.
be unprepared
670 vb.
imprudence
folly 499 n.
impudent
impertinent 878 adj.
impugn
cause doubt 486 vb.
negate 533 vb.
impulse
energy 160 n.
impulse 279 n.
whim 604 n.
spontaneity 609 n.
motive 612 n.
feeling 818 n.
desire 859 n.

impulsive
hasty 680 adj.
rash 857 adj.
impunity
nonliability 919 n.
impure
not nice 645 adj.
unclean 649 adj.
vulgar 847 adj.
impure 951 adj.
impurity
wickedness 934 n.
imputation
slur 867 n.
impute
attribute 158 vb.
blame 924 vb.
inability
impotence 161 n.
unskilfulness 695 n.
inaccessible
removed 199 adj.
inaccuracy
inexactness 495 n.
inaction
inaction 677 n.
inactive
inert 175 adj.
inactive 679 adj.
apathetic 820 adj.
inactivity
quiescence 266 n.
nonuse 674 n.
inactivity 679 n.
leisure 681 n.
inadequate
insufficient 636 adj.
unskilful 695 adj.
inadmissible
excluded 57 adj.
wrong 914 adj.
inadvertent
unintentional
618 adj.
inadvisable
inexpedient 643 adj.
inalienable
retained 778 adj.
due 915 adj.
inane
foolish 499 adj.
meaningless
515 adj.
inanimate
inorganic 359 adj.
dead 361 adj.
mindless 448 adj.

inanition
weakness 163 n.
in a nutshell
concisely 569 adv.
inappeasable
greedy 859 adj.
inapplicable
irrelevant 10 adj.
inappreciable
minute 196 adj.
unimportant 639 adj.
inapprehensible
unintelligible
517 adj.
inappropriate
unapt 25 adj.
inexpedient 643 adj.
in arrears
nonpaying 805 adj.
inarticulate
stammering 580 adj.
taciturn 582 adj.
artless 699 adj.
inartistic
graceless 842 adj.
inattention
inattention 456 n.
inattentive
unthinking 450 adj.
inattentive 456 adj.
inaudible
silent 399 adj.
muted 401 adj.
inaugural
beginning 68 adj.
inaugurate
auspicate 68 vb.
inauguration
debut 68 n.
inauspicious
inopportune
138 adj.
in black and white
recorded 548 adj.
written 586 adj.
inborn
genetic 5 adj.
inbred
genetic 5 adj.
with affections
817 adj.
incalculable
infinite 107 adj.
casual 159 adj.
incandescent
fiery 379 adj.
luminous 417 adj.

incantation
spell 983 n.
incapable
powerless 161 adj.
unskilful 695 adj.
incapacitate
disable 161 vb.
incapacity
impotence 161 n.
unintelligence
499 n.
incarcerate
imprison 747 vb.
incarnate
alive 360 adj.
manifest 522 vb.
incarnation
materiality 319 n.
theophany 965 n.
incautious
unwise 499 adj.
rash 857 adj.
incendiary
incendiarism 381 n.
bomb 723 n.
incense
scent 396 n.
enrage 891 vb.
oblation 981 n.
incentive
incentive 612 n.
inception
beginning 68 n.
incertitude
uncertainty 474 n.
incessant
frequent 139 adj.
unceasing 146 adj.
incest
illicit love 951 n.
inch
long measure 203 n.
move slowly 278 vb.
in charge
in control 689 adv.
inchoate
amorphous 244 adj.
incident
event 154 n.
incidental
extrinsic 6 adj.
accompanying
89 adj.
happening 154 adj.
casual 159 adj.
incinerate
burn 381 vb.

incinerator
furnace 383 n.
incipient
beginning 68 adj.
in circulation
published 528 adj.
incise
cut 46 vb.
groove 262 vb.
incision
wound 655 n.
incisive
keen 174 adj.
assertive 532 adj.
forceful 571 adj.
incite
make violent
176 vb.
incite 612 vb.
incivility
disrespect 921 n.
inclemency
wintriness 380 n.
inclination
tendency 179 n.
willingness 597 n.
liking 859 n.
inclinations
affections 817 n.
incline
tend 179 vb.
incline 220 n.
make oblique
220 vb.
motivate 612 vb.
include
add 38 vb.
comprise 78 vb.
inclusion
inclusion 78 n.
participation 775 n.
inclusive
comprehensive
52 adj.
inclusive 78 adj.
incognito
anonymous 562 adj.
incoherent
frenzied 503 adj.
meaningless
515 adj.
incombustible
incombustible
382 adj.
income
earnings 771 n.
receipt 807 n.

incomer
upstart 126 n.
incomer 297 n.
incommensurable
disagreeing 25 adj.
incommode
trouble 827 vb.
incommunicable
inexpressible
517 adj.
incommunicado
imprisoned 747 adj.
incommunicative
taciturn 582 adj.
incomparable
inimitable 21 adj.
supreme 34 adj.
incompatible
disagreeing 25 adj.
inimical 881 adj.
**incompetence,
  incompetency**
unskilfulness 695 n.
incompetent
fool 501 n.
bungler 697 n.
incomplete
incomplete 55 adj.
deficient 307 adj.
uncompleted
726 adj.
incomprehensible
unintelligible
517 adj.
incompressible
dense 324 adj.
inconceivable
impossible 470 adj.
unbelieved 486 adj.
incongruous
disagreeing 25 adj.
unconformable
84 adj.
inconsequential
irrelevant 10 adj.
illogical 477 adj.
unimportant
639 adj.
inconsiderable
inconsiderable
33 adj.
unimportant
639 adj.
inconsiderate
inattentive 456 adj.
discourteous
885 adj.

inconsistency
changeableness
152 n.
inconsistent
disagreeing 25 adj.
capricious 604 adj.
inconsolable
regretting 830 adj.
inconspicuous
indistinct 444 adj.
inconstant
light-minded
456 adj.
capricious 604 adj.
incontestable
undisputed 473 adj.
incontinence
helplessness 161 n.
intemperance 943 n.
incontrovertible
undisputed 473 adj.
inconvenience
suffering 825 n.
inconvenient
ill-timed 138 adj.
hindering 702 adj.
incorporate
join 45 vb.
combine 50 vb.
absorb 299 vb.
incorporation
inclusion 78 n.
incorporeal
immaterial 320 adj.
incorrect
inexact 495 adj.
incorrectness
ill-breeding 847 n.
incorrigible
obstinate 602 adj.
impenitent 940 adj.
incorruptible
honourable 929 adj.
increase
increase 36 n.
propagation 167 n.
gain 771 n.
incredible
unbelieved 486 adj.
wonderful 864 adj.
incredulous
unbelieving 486 adj.
increment
increment 36 n.
incriminate
blame 924 vb.
accuse 928 vb.

incubate
breed stock 369 vb.
mature 669 vb.
incubator
seedbed 156 n.
preserver 666 n.
incubus
encumbrance 702 n.
demon 970 n.
inculcate
educate 534 vb.
inculpate
blame 924 vb.
accuse 928 vb.
incumbency
job 622 n.
benefice 985 n.
incumbent
resident 191 n.
beneficiary 776 n.
obligatory 917 adj.
cleric 986 n.
incur
meet with 154 vb.
be liable 180 vb.
acquire 771 vb.
incurable
deadly 362 adj.
obstinate 602 adj.
sick 651 adj.
incuriosity
incuriosity 454 n.
incurious
incurious 454 adj.
apathetic 820 adj.
indifferent 860 adj.
incursion
ingress 297 n.
attack 712 n.
in custody
imprisoned 747 adj.
indebted
indebted 803 adj.
grateful 907 adj.
indecent
disreputable
867 adj.
impure 951 adj.
indecision
dubiety 474 n.
irresolution 601 n.
indecorum
ill-breeding 847 n.
indefatigable
persevering 600 adj.
industrious 678 adj.
indefeasible

established 153 adj.
undisputed 473 adj.
indefensible
heinous 934 adj.
indefinable
inexpressible
517 adj.
indefinite
general 79 adj.
indistinct 444 adj.
indefiniteness
uncertainty 474 n.
indelible
fixed 153 adj.
remembered
505 adj.
indelicate
vulgar 847 adj.
impure 951 adj.
in demand
required 627 adj.
indemnification
restitution 787 n.
indemnity
offset 31 n.
security 767 n.
restitution 787 n.
payment 804 n.
indent
crinkle 251 vb.
notch 260 n.vb.
demand 737 vb.
indentation
notch 260 n.
indenture
compact 765 n.
independence
unrelatedness 10 n.
nonconformity
84 n.
independence 744 n.
independent
free person 744 n.
sectarian 978 n.adj.
indescribable
wonderful 864 adj.
indestructible
unyielding 162 adj.
indeterminate
causeless 159 adj.
uncertain 474 adj.
indetermination
nondesign 618 n.
index
relate 9 vb.
class 62 vb.
list 87 n.vb.

finger 378 n.
indicator 547 n.
record 548 n.vb.
edition 589 n.
Index
prohibition 757 n.
Indian file
procession 71 n.
Indian summer
revival 656 n.
palmy days 730 n.
indicate
show 522 vb.
indicate 547 vb.
indication
evidence 466 n.
hint 524 n.
indication 547 n.
indicative
evidential 466 adj.
disclosing 526 adj.
indict
indict 928 vb.
indictable
punishable 963 adj.
indifference
indifference 860 n.
indifferent
unrelated 10 adj.
incurious 454 adj.
choiceless 606 adj.
apathetic 820 adj.
indifferent 860 adj.
indigenous
intrinsic 5 adj.
native 191 adj.
indigent
poor 801 adj.
indigestible
tough 329 adj.
uncooked 670 adj.
indigestion
digestive disorders
651 n.
indignant
resentful 891 adj.
indignation meeting
deprecation
762 n.
malcontent 829 n.
indignity
indignity 921 n.
indigo
blue 435 adj.
indirect
oblique 220 adj.
deviating 282 adj.

roundabout
626 adj.
indiscernible
invisible 444 adj.
indiscerptible
indivisible 52 adj.
indiscipline
anarchy 734 n.
disobedience 738 n.
indiscreet
unwise 499 adj.
disclosing 526 adj.
indiscretion
guilty act 936 n.
indiscriminate
indiscriminate
464 adj.
designless 618 adj.
indiscrimination
generality 79 n.
indiscrimination
464 n.
indispensable
necessary 596 adj.
important 638 adj.
indisposed
unwilling 598 adj.
sick 651 adj.
indisputability
certainty 473 n.
indissoluble
indivisible 52 adj.
indistinct
shadowy 419 adj.
indistinct 444 adj.
indistinctness
faintness 401 n.
indistinguishable
identical 13 adj.
indite *write* 586 vb.
individual
original 21 adj.
special 80 adj.
unit 88 n.
person 371 n.
individualism
particularism 80 n.
selfishness 932 n.
individualist
free person 744 n.
egotist 932 n.
individuality
speciality 80 n.
nonconformity
84 n.
(*see* **individual**)

indivisible
simple 44 adj.
indivisible 52 adj.
one 88 adj.
indocility
obstinacy 602 n.
indoctrinate
convince 485 vb.
teach 534 vb.
indolence
sluggishness 679 n.
indomitable
persevering 600 adj.
courageous 855 adj.
indoor
interior 224 adj.
in dribs and drabs
piecemeal 53 adv.
indubitable
undisputed 473 adj.
induce
induce 612 vb.
inducement
attraction 291 n.
inducement 612 n.
induct
auspicate 68 vb.
induction
reasoning 475 n.
indulge
smoke 388 vb.
please 826 vb.
(*see* indulgence)
—oneself
be selfish 932 vb.
indulgence
laxity 734 n.
forgiveness 909 n.
intemperance
943 n.
indulgent
benevolent 897 adj.
induration
hardening 326 n.
impenitence 940 n.
industrial
productive 164 adj.
businesslike
622 adj.
industrialist
producer 164 n.
industrious
studious 536 adj.
industrious 678 adj.
industry
production 164 n.
business 622 n.

labour 682 n.
inebriation
drunkenness 949 n.
inedible
tough 329 adj.
unsavoury 391 adj.
ineffable
inexpressible
517 adj.
wonderful 864 adj.
ineffaceable
remembered
505 adj.
ineffective
powerless 161 adj.
feeble 572 adj.
unsuccessful
728 adj.
ineffectual
useless 641 adj.
unskilful 695 adj.
inefficient
useless 641 adj.
bad 645 adj.
unskilful 695 adj.
inelastic
rigid 326 adj.
inelegant
inelegant 576 adj.
graceless 842 adj.
ineligible
rejected 607 adj.
ineluctable
certain 473 adj.
inept
absurd 497 adj.
unskilful 695 adj.
inequality
dissimilarity 19 n.
inequality 29 n.
injustice 914 n.
inequitable
unjust 914 adj.
ineradicable
fixed 153 adj.
inert
inert 175 adj.
insensible 375 adj.
nonactive 677 adj.
inertia
inertness 175 n.
inactivity 679 n.
indifference 860 n.
inescapable
necessary 596 adj.
inessential
extrinsic 6 adj.

trifle 639 n.
inestimable
valuable 644 adj.
of price 811 adj.
inevitable
impending 155 adj.
necessary 596 adj.
inexact
general 79 adj.
inexact 495 adj.
inexcitable
inexcitable 823 adj.
inexcusable
wrong 914 adj.
inexhaustible
unceasing 146 adj.
plenteous 635 adj.
inexorable
necessary 596 adj.
pitiless 906 adj.
inexpectant
inexpectant 508 adj.
unprepared 670 adj.
inexpedient
ill-timed 138 adj.
inexpedient 643 adj.
inexpensive
cheap 812 adj.
inexperience
ignorance 491 n.
unskilfulness 695 n.
inexpert
unskilled 695 adj.
inexplicable
causeless 159 adj.
unintelligible
517 adj.
inexpressible
inexpressible
517 adj.
wonderful 864 adj.
inextinguishable
unyielding 162 adj.
inextricable
firm 45 adj.
cohesive 48 adj.
difficult 700 adj.
infallibility
perfection 646 n.
infallible
certain 473 adj.
accurate 494 adj.
veracious 540 adj.
infamous
disreputable
867 adj.
heinous 934 adj.

infamy
wickedness 934 n.
infancy
nonage 130 n.
youth 130 n.
infant
beginning 68 adj.
child 132 n.
infanticide
homicide 362 n.
infantile
infantine 132 adj.
foolish 499 adj.
infantry
pedestrian 268 n.
infantry 722 n.
infatuated
misjudging 481 adj.
crazy 503 adj.
enamoured
887 adj.
infatuation
folly 499 n.
infect
influence 178 vb.
transfer 272 vb.
make unclean
649 vb.
excite 821 vb.
infection
infection 651 n.
poison 659 n.
infectious
transferable
272 adj.
infectious 653 adj.
infelicitous
inexpedient 643 adj.
infer
reason 475 vb.
imply 523 vb.
inferable
attributed 158 adj.
inferior
inferior 35 n.adj.
back 238 adj.
nonentity 639 n.
bad 645 adj.
middling 732 adj.
commoner 869 n.
inferiority
inferiority 35 n.
inferiority complex
eccentricity 503 n.
infernal
damnable 645 adj.
infernal 972 adj.

inferno
hell 972 n.
inferred
attributed 158 adj.
tacit 523 adj.
infertile
unproductive
172 adj.
infest
be many 104 vb.
trouble 827 vb.
infestation
bane 659 n.
infidel
unbeliever 486 n.
infidelity
illicit love 951 n.
in-fighting
dissension 709 n.
infiltrate
pervade 189 vb.
infiltrate 297 vb.
infiltration
mixture 43 n.
sedition 738 n.
infinite
multitudinous
104 adj.
infinite 107 adj.
infinitesimal
minute 196 adj.
infinity
infinity 107 n.
infirm
unhealthy 651 adj.
infirmary
hospital 658 n.
infirmity
weakness 163 n.
irresolution 601 n.
infix
implant 303 vb.
educate 534 vb.
inflame
make violent
176 vb.
heat 381 vb.
excite 821 vb.
aggravate 832 vb.
excite love 887 vb.
inflammable
combustible
385 adj.
inflammation
burning 381 n.
painfulness 827 n.
inflatable

bladder 194 n.
inflate
enlarge 197 vb.
blow up 352 vb.
inflated
exaggerated
546 adj.
rhetorical 574 adj.
inflation
increase 36 n.
finance 797 n.
inflationary
dear 811 adj.
inflexible
rigid 326 adj.
obstinate 602 adj.
pitiless 906 adj.
inflexion, inflection
curvature 248 n.
grammar 564 n.
pronunciation
577 n.
inflict
punish 963 vb.
infliction
adversity 731 n.
suffering 825 n.
inflow
ingress 297 n.
current 350 n.
influence
modify 143 vb.
power 160 n.
influence 178 n.vb.
bias 481 vb.
teach 534 vb.
motivate 612 vb.
authority 733 n.
prestige 866 n.
influential
great 32 adj.
influential 178 adj.
influenza
infection 651 n.
influx
ingress 297 n.
in force
operative 173 adj.
inform
inform 524 vb.
educate 534 vb.
—against
inform 524 vb.
accuse 928 vb.
informal
lax 734 adj.
unconfined 744 adj.

nonobservant
769 adj.
informant
informant 524 n.
news reporter 529 n.
correspondent
588 n.
information
information 524 n.
message 529 n.
news 529 n.
informative
informative 524 adj.
disclosing 526 adj.
loquacious 581 adj.
informer
informer 524 n.
accuser 928 n.
infraction
disobedience 738 n.
infrangible
tough 329 adj.
infrastructure
base 214 n.
infrequency
fewness 105 n.
infrequency 140 n.
infrequent
discontinuous
72 adj.
fitful 142 adj.
infringe
encroach 306 vb.
be undue 916 vb.
infuriate
make violent
176 vb.
make mad 503 vb.
enrage 891 vb.
infuriating
annoying 827 adj.
infuse
infuse 303 vb.
infusion
draught 301 n.
solution 337 n.
ingenue
ingenue 699 n.
ingenuity
skill 694 n.
cunning 698 n.
ingenuous
artless 699 adj.
ingest
absorb 299 vb.
eat 301 vb.
inglorious

unsuccessful
728 adj.
middling 732 adj.
inglorious 867 adj.
ingot
bullion 797 n.
ingrained
intrinsic 5 adj.
habitual 610 adj.
ingratiating
servile 879 adj.
flattering 925 adj.
ingratitude
ingratitude 908 n.
ingredient(s)
component 58 n.
contents 193 n.
ingress
ingress 297 n.
inhabit
be present 189 vb.
dwell 192 vb.
inhabitant
dweller 191 n.
inhabited
occupied 191 adj.
inhale
breathe 352 vb.
smell 394 vb.
inhaler
medicine 658 n.
in hand
stored 632 adj.
inharmonious
disagreeing 25 adj.
discordant 411 adj.
inherent
intrinsic 5 adj.
component 58 adj.
inherit
inherit 771 vb.
inheritance
dower 777 n.
transfer 780 n.
inherited
genetic 5 adj.
acquired 771 adj.
inheritor
successor 67 n.
beneficiary 776 n.
inhibit
counteract 182 vb.
inhibition
eccentricity 503 n.
prohibition 757 n.
inhospitable
unsociable 883 adj.

inhumanity
inhumanity 898 n.
misanthropy 902 n.
pitilessness 906 n.

inimical
opposing 704 adj.
inimical 881 adj.

inimitable
inimitable 21 adj.

iniquitous
unjust 914 adj.

initial
first 68 adj.
sign 547 vb.
initials 558 n.

initiate
initiate 68 vb.
train 534 vb.
learner 538 n.

initiation
debut 68 n.
rite 988 n.

initiative
vigorousness 174 n.

inject
infuse 303 vb.

injection
medicine 658 n.

injudicious
unwise 499 adj.

injunction
precept 693 n.
command 737 n.
legal process 959 n.

injure
harm 645 vb.
hurt 827 vb.
be malevolent
898 vb.

injurious
harmful 645 adj.
insolent 878 adj.
wrong 914 adj.

injury
wound 655 n.

injustice
injustice 914 n.

ink
art equipment 553 n.

inkling
hint 524 n.

inky
dark 418 adj.
black 428 adj.

inlaid
ornamented
844 adj.

inland
inland 344 adj.

in-laws
family 11 n.

inlay
line 227 vb.
insert 303 vb.
variegate 437 vb.

inlet
gulf 345 n.

in limbo
neglected 458 adj.
disused 674 adj.

inmate
resident 191 n.

inmost, innermost
interior 224 adj.

inn
inn 192 n.

innards
insides 224 n.

innate
genetic 5 adj.

inner
interior 224 adj.

inner being
essence 1 n.

inner city
urban 192 adj.

inner man, inner
woman
spirit 447 n.
affections 817 n.

innings
period 110 n.

innkeeper
caterer 633 n.

innocence
innocence 935 n.
acquittal 960 n.

innocent
artless 699 adj.
innocent 935 n.adj.
good person
937 n.
pure 950 adj.

innocuous
beneficial 644 adj.

innovation
newness 126 n.
change 143 n.

innovator
precursor 66 n.

innuendo
latency 523 n.
detraction 926 n.

innumerable

inland
multitudinous
104 adj.

innumerate
uninstructed
491 adj.

inoculate
implant 303 vb.
teach 534 vb.

inoculation
hygiene 652 n.

inoffensive
beneficial 644 adj.
amiable 884 adj.

in on
knowing 490 adj.
informed 524 adj.
sharing 775 adj.

inoperable
deadly 362 adj.
impracticable
470 adj.

inoperative
powerless 161 adj.
nonactive 677 adj.

inopportune
inopportune
138 adj.

in orders
clerical 986 adj.

inordinate
exorbitant 32 adj.

inorganic
inorganic 359 adj.

inorganic chemistry
physics 319 n.

in play
unceasing 146 adj.
operative 173 adj.

in preparation
in preparation
669 adv.

input
data processing
86 n.
requirement 627 n.

inquest
inquest 364 n.
inquiry 459 n.
legal trial 959 n.

in question
in question
452 adv.
moot 459 adj.

inquietude
worry 825 n.

inquire, enquire
inquire 459 vb.

inquiry
inquiry 459 n.

inquisition
inquiry 459 n.
interrogation 459 n.

inquisitive
inquisitive 453 adj.
inquiring 459 adj.

inquisitive person
inquisitive person
453 n.
questioner 459 n.
meddler 678 n.

inquisitor
questioner 459 n.

in reserve
stored 632 adj.

inroad(s)
ingress 297 n.
arrogation 916 n.

inrush
ingress 297 n.

insalubrious
unclean 649 adj.
insalubrious
653 adj.

ins and outs
particulars 80 n.

insane
insane 503 adj.

insanitary
unclean 649 adj.
insalubrious
653 adj.

insanity
insanity 503 n.

insatiable
greedy 859 adj.

inscape
essential part 5 n.

inscribe
record 548 vb.
write 586 vb.

inscriber
calligrapher 586 n.

inscription
obsequies 364 n.
script 586 n.

inscrutable
impassive 820 adj.

insect
insect 365 n.

insecticide
poison 659 n.

insecurity
vulnerability
661 n.

inseminate
make fruitful
171 vb.
insensate
insensible 375 adj.
unwise 499 adj.
thick-skinned
820 adj.
insensibility
insensibility 375 n.
moral insensibility
820 n.
insensible
insensible 375 adj.
impassive 820 adj.
indifferent 860 adj.
insensibly
slightly 33 adv.
insensitive
thick-skinned
820 adj.
inseparable
firm 45 adj.
cohesive 48 adj.
friendly 880 adj.
insert
load 193 vb.
insert 303 vb.
insertion
adjunct 40 n.
insertion 303 n.
inset
insertion 303 n.
inshore
near 200 adj.
inside
interiority 224 n.
imprisoned 747 adj.
inside agent
secret service 459 n.
inside job
plot 623 n.
inside out
inverted 221 adj.
insides
insides 224 n.
insidious
occult 523 adj.
cunning 698 adj.
insight
intellect 447 n.
discrimination
463 n.
intuition 476 n.
imagination 513 n.
interpretation 520 n.
insignia

badge 547 n.
insignificance
smallness 33 n.
unimportance
639 n.
insincere
unmeant 515 adj.
hypocritical
541 adj.
insinuate
imply 523 vb.
hint 524 vb.
—oneself
enter 297 vb.
flatter 925 vb.
insinuation
latency 523 n.
detraction 926 n.
insipid
tasteless 387 adj.
feeble 572 adj.
dull 840 adj.
insist
emphasize 532 vb.
compel 740 vb.
insistence, insistency
affirmation 532 n.
importance 638 n.
insobriety
drunkenness 949 n.
insolence
insolence 878 n.
insoluble
impracticable
470 adj.
puzzling 517 adj.
insolvency
insolvency 805 n.
insomnia
restlessness 678 n.
insouciance
negligence 458 n.
indifference 860 n.
inspect
scan 438 vb.
inspection
inspection 438 n.
surveillance 457 n.
inquiry 459 n.
inspector
inquirer 459 n.
estimator 480 n.
manager 690 n.
inspiration
causation 156 n.
intuition 476 n.
imagination 513 n.

contrivance 623 n.
excitation 821 n.
revelation 975 n.
inspire
cheer 833 vb.
give courage 855 vb.
(*see* **inspiration**)
inspired
forceful 571 adj.
excited 821 adj.
revelational 975 adj.
inspirit
animate 821 vb.
cheer 833 vb.
in spite of
although 182 adv.
instability
changeableness
152 n.
vulnerability 661 n.
excitability 822 n.
install
auspicate 68 vb.
commission 751 vb.
installation
location 187 n.
workshop 687 n.
instalment
part 53 n.
reading matter
589 n.
instance
example 83 n.
instant
brief span 114 n.
instant 116 n.
ready-made
669 adj.
requesting 761 adj.
instantaneous
instantaneous
116 adj.
instead
instead 150 adv.
instigate
induce 612 vb.
instigator
motivator 612 n.
instil
infuse 303 vb.
educate 534 vb.
instinct
tendency 179 n.
absence of intellect
448 n.
absence of thought
450 n.

intuition 476 n.
habit 610 n.
nondesign 618 n.
instinctive
involuntary 596 adj.
spontaneous 609 adj.
instincts
affections 817 n.
institute
auspicate 68 vb.
cause 156 vb.
academy 539 n.
institution
academy 539 n.
practice 610 n.
rite 988 n.
institutionalize
make uniform 16 vb.
in stock
stored 632 adj.
instruct
inform 524 vb.
educate 534 vb.
command 737 vb.
instruction
information 524 n.
teaching 534 n.
command 737 n.
instructive
informative 524 adj.
educational 534 adj.
instructor
teacher 537 n.
trainer 537 n.
instrument
instrument 628 n.
means 629 n.
tool 630 n.
agent 686 n.
instrumental
musical 412 adj.
instrumental
628 adj.
mechanical 630 adj.
used 673 adj.
instrumentalist
instrumentalist
413 n.
instrumentality
agency 173 n.
instrumentality
628 n.
instrumentation
melody 410 n.
insubordinate
anarchic 734 adj.
disobedient 738 adj.

insubstantial
unreal 2 adj.
insubstantial 4 adj.
immaterial 320 adj.
insufferable
intolerable 827 adj.
disliked 861 adj.
insufficiency
shortfall 307 n.
insufficiency 636 n.
insular
alone 88 adj.
insular 349 adj.
insularity
narrow mind 481 n.
insulate
set apart 46 vb.
insulation
lining 227 n.
preservation 666 n.
insulator
electricity 160 n.
insulin
drug 658 n.
insult
rudeness 885 n.
not respect 921 vb.
insuperable
impracticable
   470 adj.
difficult 700 adj.
insupportable
intolerable 827 adj.
insurance
security 767 n.
caution 858 n.
insure
give security 767 vb.
insurgent
revolter 738 n.
insurmountable
impracticable
   470 adj.
insurrection
revolt 738 n.
intact
intact 52 adj.
undamaged 646 adj.
safe 660 adj.
intaglio
sculpture 554 n.
intake
reception 299 n.
requirement 627 n.
waste 634 n.
intangible
immaterial 320 adj.

integer
number 85 n.
unit 88 n.
integral
whole 52 adj.
integral part
component 58 n.
integrate
combine 50 vb.
make complete
   54 vb.
integration
inclusion 78 n.
unity 88 n.
integrity
probity 929 n.
virtue 933 n.
integument
skin 226 n.
intellect
intellect 447 n.
intellectual
mental 447 adj.
intellectual 492 n.
intelligence
secret service 459 n.
intelligence 498 n.
news 529 n.
intelligent
intelligent 498 adj.
intelligentsia
intellectual 492 n.
intelligible
intelligible 516 adj.
perspicuous
   567 adj.
intemperance
intemperance 943 n.
intemperate
violent 176 adj.
intend
predestine 155 vb.
mean 514 vb.
will 595 vb.
predetermine
   608 vb.
intend 617 vb.
desire 859 vb.
intense
great 32 adj.
vigorous 174 adj.
fervent 818 adj.
intensify
augment 36 vb.
aggravate 832 vb.
intensity
degree 27 n.

greatness 32 n.
intent
attentive 455 adj.
intention
connotation 514 n.
will 595 n.
intention 617 n.
plan 623 n.
intentional
volitional 595 adj.
intended 617 adj.
inter
inter 364 vb.
interaction
correlation 12 n.
agency 173 n.
interbred
ethnic 11 adj.
mixed 43 adj.
intercalary
interjacent 231 adj.
intercede
mediate 720 vb.
intercept
converge 293 vb.
be curious 453 vb.
hinder 702 vb.
interceptor
air force 722 n.
intercession
aid 703 n.
prayers 981 n.
intercessor
mediator 720 n.
interchange
correlation 12 n.
substitute 150 vb.
interchange
   151 n.vb.
interchangeable
identical 13 adj.
equivalent 28 adj.
intercom
telecommunication
   531 n.
intercommunicate
connect 45 vb.
be contiguous
   202 vb.
intercommunication
information 524 n.
intercommunion
interlocution 584 n.
intercommunity
sociality 882 n.
interconnect
correlate 12 vb.

connect 45 vb.
intercontinental
   ballistic missile
missile weapon
   723 n.
intercourse
union 45 n.
coition 45 n.
interdependence
correlation 12 n.
interdict
prohibition
   757 n.
interdictor
air force 722 n.
interest
relation 9 n.
increment 36 n.
influence 178 n.
curiosity 453 n
attract notice
   455 vb.
importance
   638 n.
gain 771 n.
interest 803 n.
impress 821 vb.
amusement
   837 n.
—oneself in
be active 678 vb.
interests
affairs 154 n.
business 622 n.
interface
contiguity 202 n.
partition 231 n.
interfere
counteract 182 vb.
meddle 678 vb.
obstruct 702 vb.
—with
debauch 951 vb.
interference
radiation 417 n.
interferer
meddler 678 n.
hinderer 702 n.
interferon
antidote 658 n.
interim
lull 145 n.
interior
intrinsic 5 adj.
interiority 224 n.
interior 224 adj.
land 344 n.

interior decoration
ornamental art
844 n.
interjacency
interjacency 231 n.
interject
put between 231 vb.
interjection
interjection 231 n.
speech 579 n.
interlace
enlace 222 vb.
interleave
put between 231 vb.
interlock
join 45 vb.
enlace 222 vb.
interlocutor
questioner 459 n.
interlocutor 584 n.
interloper
intruder 59 n.
interlude
lull 145 n.
intermarry
wed 894 vb.
intermediary
intermediary 231 n.
mediator 720 n.
intermediate
middle 70 adj.
interjacent 231 adj.
**intermediate
technology**
smallness 33 n.
middle way 625 n.
interment
interment 364 n.
intermezzo
musical piece 412 n.
interminable
infinite 107 adj.
intermingle
mix 43 vb.
intermit
be discontinuous
72 vb.
intermittent
discontinuous
72 adj.
fitful 142 adj.
intern
doctor 658 n.
imprison 747 vb.
internal
interior 224 adj.
internalize

absorb 299 vb.
international
comprehensive
52 adj.
national 371 adj.
unpossessed
774 adj.
internationalist
philanthropist
901 n.
internationalize
communalize
775 vb.
internecine
destructive 165 adj.
internment
detention 747 n.
interpellate
interrogate 459 vb.
interplanetary
cosmic 321 adj.
interplay
correlation 12 n.
interpolate
put between 231 vb.
interpolation
insertion 303 n.
interpose
put between 231 vb.
meddle 678 vb.
interpret
interpret 520 vb.
interpretation
connotation 514 n.
interpretation 520 n.
acting 594 n.
interpreter
interpreter 520 n.
interracial
ethnic 11 adj.
correlative 12 adj.
interregnum
government 733 n.
interrelate
correlate 12 vb.
interrogate
interrogate 459 vb.
interrogator
inquisitive person
453 n.
questioner 459 n.
interrupt
intrude 297 vb.
be rude 885 vb.
interruption
untimeliness 138 n.
interval 201 n.

interjection 231 n.
hindrance 702 n.
intersection
crossing 222 n.
road 624 n.
interspace
interval 201 n.
intersperse
put between 231 vb.
interstice
gap 201 n.
interstitial
interior 224 adj.
intertwine
enlace 222 vb.
interval
disunion 46 n.
period 110 n.
lull 145 n.
interval 201 n.
intervene
meddle 678 vb.
mediate 720 vb.
intervention
instrumentality
628 n.
mediation 720 n.
interview
exam 459 n.
interrogate 459 vb.
interviewer
questioner 459 n.
interlocutor 584 n.
interwar
peaceful 717 adj.
interweave
enlace 222 vb.
interwoven
crossed 222 adj.
intestine(s)
insides 224 n.
in the clear
safe 660 adj.
acquitted 960 adj.
in the flesh
alive 360 adj.
in the red
indebted 803 adj.
in the running
contending 716 adj.
in the same boat
sharing 775 adj.
in the teeth of
with difficulty
700 adv.
in opposition
704 adv.

in the thick of
in the act 676 adv.
in the way
hindering 702 adj.
in the wings
prospectively
124 adv.
intimacy
coition 45 n.
friendship 880 n.
love 887 n.
intimate
hint 524 vb.
indicate 547 vb.
close friend 880 n.
intimation
hint 524 n.
intimidate
frighten 854 vb.
threaten 900 vb.
intimidation
terror tactics 712 n.
intimidation 854 n.
intolerable
intolerable 827 adj.
intolerance
narrow mind 481 n.
intolerant
biased 481 adj.
severe 735 adj.
pitiless 906 adj.
orthodox 976 adj.
intonation
sound 398 n.
voice 577 n.
intone
sing 413 vb.
intoxicant
drug-taking 949 n.
intoxicate
excite 821 vb.
delight 826 vb.
intoxicating
strong 162 adj.
intoxicating 949 adj.
intoxication
drunkenness 949 n.
intractable
wilful 602 adj.
difficult 700 adj.
disobedient 738 adj.
intramural
educational 534 adj.
intransigent
obstinate 602 adj.
in transit
in transit 272 adv.

intrepid
  unfearing 855 adj.
intricacy
  convolution 251 n.
intricate
  complex 61 adj.
  difficult 700 adj.
  ornamental 844 adj.
intrigue
  motivate 612 vb.
  plot 623 n.vb.
  impress 821 vb.
  love affair 887 n.
intrinsic
  intrinsic 5 adj.
introduce
  initiate 68 vb.
  precede 283 vb.
  insert 303 vb.
  befriend 880 vb.
introduction
  prelude 66 n.
  teaching 534 n.
  courteous act 884 n.
introductory
  precursory 66 adj.
introspection
  meditation 449 n.
introverted
  intrinsic 5 adj.
  unsociable 883 adj.
intrude
  intrude 297 vb.
  meddle 678 vb.
intruder
  misfit 25 n.
  intruder 59 n.
  incomer 297 n.
  offender 904 n.
intrusive
  unrelated 10 adj.
  extraneous 59 adj.
intuit
  intuit 476 vb.
intuition
  absence of thought
    450 n.
  intuition 476 n.
  feeling 818 n.
  psychics 984 n.
intuitive
  intuitive 476 adj.
inundate
  drench 341 vb.
  flow 350 vb.
  superabound
    637 vb.

inure
  train 534 vb.
  habituate 610 vb.
inured
  thick-skinned
    820 adj.
inutility
  inutility 641 n.
  nonuse 674 n.
invade
  burst in 297 vb.
  encroach 306 vb.
  wage war 718 vb.
invader
  intruder 59 n.
  incomer 297 n.
  attacker 712 n.
invaginate
  invert 221 vb.
in vain
  wasted 634 adj.
  profitless 641 adj.
invalid
  powerless 161 adj.
  weakling 163 n.
  sick person 651 n.
  unwarranted
    916 adj.
invalidate
  negate 533 vb.
  abrogate 752 vb.
invaluable
  valuable 644 adj.
  of price 811 adj.
invariable
  uniform 16 adj.
  unchangeable
    153 adj.
  usual 610 adj.
invasion
  ingress 297 n.
  attack 712 n.
invective
  oratory 579 n.
  scurrility 899 n.
inveigh (against)
  reprobate 924 vb.
inveigle
  ensnare 542 vb.
  tempt 612 vb.
invent
  produce 164 vb.
  imagine 513 vb.
invention
  discovery 484 n.
  fable 543 n.
  contrivance 623 n.

inventive
  original 21 adj.
  imaginative 513 adj.
inventor
  producer 164 n.
  detector 484 n.
inventory
  list 87 n.vb.
  account 808 vb.
inversion
  inversion 221 n.
invert
  nonconformist 84 n.
  invert 221 vb.
invertebrate
  animal 365 n.adj.
  coward 856 n.
invest
  surround 230 vb.
  besiege 712 vb.
  commission 751 vb.
  speculate 791 vb.
—in
  purchase 792 vb.
investigate
  inquire 459 vb.
  estimate 480 vb.
investigation
  inquiry 459 n.
  study 536 n.
investigator
  detective 459 n.
  inquirer 459 n.
investiture
  mandate 751 n.
investment
  estate 777 n.
  expenditure 806 n.
investor
  lender 784 n.
inveterate
  immemorial
    127 adj.
  habitual 610 adj.
invidious
  unpleasant 827 adj.
invigilate
  invigilate 457 vb.
invigilator
  keeper 749 n.
invigorate
  invigorate 174 vb.
  refresh 685 vb.
  animate 821 vb.
  cheer 833 vb.
invigorating
  salubrious 652 adj.

invincible
  unyielding 162 adj.
  unbeaten 727 adj.
inviolable
  due 915 adj.
inviolate
  concealed 525 adj.
invisible
  invisible 444 adj.
  latent 523 adj.
invitation
  inducement 612 n.
  offer 759 n.
  request 761 n.
invite
  be hospitable
    882 vb.
inviting
  inducing 612 adj.
  pleasurable 826 adj.
invoice
  list 87 n.
  price 809 n.vb.
invoke
  speak to 583 vb.
  entreat 761 vb.
  worship 981 vb.
  practise sorcery
    983 vb.
involucre
  covering 226 n.
involuntary
  involuntary 596 adj.
  compelling 740 adj.
involution
  convolution 251 n.
involve
  conduce 156 vb.
  imply 523 vb.
  accuse 928 vb.
involved
  complex 61 adj.
  unclear 568 adj.
involvement
  relation 9 n.
  participation
    775 n.
  liking 859 n.
invulnerable
  invulnerable
    660 adj.
inward
  interior 224 adj.
  incoming 297 adj.
in writing
  recorded 548 adj.
  written 586 adj.

inwrought
intrinsic 5 adj.
ornamented
844 adj.
ion
element 319 n.
ionosphere
atmosphere 340 n.
iota
small quantity 33 n.
IOU
title deed 767 n.
ipso facto
actually 1 adv.
IQ
intelligence 498 n.
irascible
quarrelling 709 adj.
irascible 892 adj.
irate
angry 891 adj.
irenics
peace offering
719 n.
iridescence
variegation 437 n.
iridescent
changeful 152 adj.
iridescent 437 adj.
iris
eye 438 n.
irk
torment 827 vb.
irksome
annoying 827 adj.
tedious 838 adj.
iron
strength 162 n.
smoother 258 n.
hardness 326 n.
—out
unravel 62 vb.
flatten 216 vb.
facilitate 701 vb.
ironclad
defended 713 adj.
Iron Curtain
exclusion 57 n.
ironic, ironical
figurative 519 adj.
derisive 851 adj.
iron rations
insufficiency 636 n.
irons
fetter 748 n.
irony
wit 839 n.

affectation 850 n.
irradiation
light 417 n.
lighting 420 n.
irrational
illogical 477 adj.
unwise 499 adj.
irreconcilable
unrelated 10 adj.
malcontent 829 n.
regretting 830 adj.
inimical 881 adj.
irrecoverable
past 125 adj.
lost 772 adj.
irredeemable
wicked 934 adj.
irreducible
simple 44 adj.
irrefutable
undisputed 473 adj.
irregular
nonuniform 17 adj.
multiform 82 adj.
unconformable
84 adj.
distorted 246 adj.
illegal 954 adj.
irrelevant
irrelevant 10 adj.
deviating 282 adj.
unimportant
639 adj.
irreligion
irreligion 974 n.
irremediable
unpromising
853 adj.
irremovable
fixed 153 adj.
irreparable
unpromising
853 adj.
irreplaceable
valuable 644 adj.
irrepressible
wilful 602 adj.
independent
744 adj.
lively 819 adj.
irreproachable
virtuous 933 adj.
irresistible
strong 162 adj.
influential 178 adj.
inducing 612 adj.
compelling 740 adj.

irresolute
irresolute 601 adj.
irrespective
unrelated 10 adj.
irresponsible
capricious 604 adj.
undutiful 918 adj.
irretrievable
lost 772 adj.
irreverent
disrespectful
921 adj.
impious 980 adj.
irreversible
unchangeable
153 adj.
unpromising
853 adj.
irrevocable
certain 473 adj.
unpromising
853 adj.
irrigate
make fruitful
171 vb.
moisten 341 vb.
irrigation
agriculture 370 n.
irritable
sensitive 819 adj.
irascible 892 adj.
irritant
excitant 821 n.
irritate
give pain 377 vb.
itch 378 vb.
cause discontent
829 vb.
aggravate 832 vb.
enrage 891 vb.
irritation
worry 825 n.
anger 891 n.
Islam
religious faith 973 n.
island
island 349 n.
ism
creed 485 n.
iso-
equal 28 adj.
isobar
weather 340 n.
isolate
set apart 46 vb.
seclude 883 vb.
isolated

alone 88 adj.
insular 349 adj.
isolation
unrelatedness 10 n.
seclusion 883 n.
isometrics
exercise 682 n.
isotope
element 319 n.
issue
effect 157 n.
posterity 170 n.
outflow 298 n.
emerge 298 vb.
topic 452 n.
publish 528 vb.
edition 589 n.
completion 725 n.
isthmus
narrowing 206 n.
land 344 n.
bridge 624 n.
italic
lettering 586 n.
italicize
emphasize 532 vb.
itch
formication 378 n.
itch 378 vb.
curiosity 453 n.
skin disease 651 n.
desire 859 n.
item
part 53 n.
component 58 n.
object 319 n.
itemize
specify 80 vb.
list 87 vb.
iterate
repeat 106 vb.
itinerant
travelling 267 adj.
itinerary
itinerary 267 n.
guidebook 524 n.
ivory
hardness 326 n.
white thing 427 n.
ivory tower
refuge 662 n.
seclusion 883 n.

J

jab
knock 279 n.

wound 655 n.
medicine 658 n.
attempt 671 n.
jabber
mean nothing
    515 vb.
chatter 581 n.
jack
prop 218 n.
lifter 310 n.
rotator 315 n.
flag 547 n.
jackanapes
insolent person
    878 n.
jackboot
tyrant 735 n.
jacket
wrapping 226 n.
jacket 228 n.
Jack-in-office
official 690 n.
insolent person
    878 n.
Jack-in-the-box
lack of expectation
    508 n.
plaything 837 n.
Jack of all trades
proficient person
    696 n.
bungler 697 n.
jackpot
acquisition 771 n.
jack up
support 218 vb.
elevate 310 vb.
jade
saddle horse 273 n.
woman 373 n.
greenness 434 n.
fatigue 684 vb.
gem 844 n.
sate 863 vb.
jagged
rough 259 adj.
notched 260 adj.
jail
gaol 748 n.
jailer
gaoler 749 n.
jalopy
automobile 274 n.
jam
crowd 74 n.
sweet thing 392 n.
predicament 700 n.

—in
fill 54 vb.
insert 303 vb.
jamb
pillar 218 n.
jamboree
amusement 837 n.
jammy
viscid 354 adj.
super 644 adj.
jam-packed
firm 45 adj.
full 54 adj.
jam session
music 412 n.
jangle
discord 411 vb.
bicker 709 vb.
janitor
doorkeeper 264 n.
japan
coat 226 vb.
blacken 428 vb.
jape
witticism 839 n.
jar
disagree 25 vb.
vessel 194 n.
rasp 407 vb.
discord 411 vb.
dissension 709 n.
displease 827 vb.
jargon
unintelligibility
    517 n.
slang 560 n.
jaundiced
biased 481 adj.
unhealthy 651 adj.
jealous 911 adj.
jaunt
land travel 267 n.
amusement 837 n.
jaunty
cheerful 833 adj.
showy 875 adj.
javelin
missile 287 n.
jaw
protuberance 254 n.
be loquacious
    581 vb.
jaws
maw 194 n.
eater 301 n.
jay walker
inattention 456 n.

jazz
music 412 n.
jazz band
orchestra 413 n.
jazzman
musician 413 n.
jazzy
florid 425 adj.
jealousy
discontent 829 n.
jealousy 911 n.
jeans
informal dress
    228 n.
trousers 228 n.
jeep
automobile 274 n.
jeer
ridicule 851 vb.
not respect 921 vb.
jejune
feeble 572 adj.
insufficient
    636 adj.
Jekyll and Hyde
duality 90 n.
jell
thicken 354 vb.
jelly
dessert 301 n.
jemmy, jimmy
force 176 vb.
tool 630 n.
jeopardize
endanger 661 vb.
jeremiad
lament 836 n.
censure 924 n.
jerk
move 265 vb.
impulse 279 n.
agitation 318 n.
ninny 501 n.
jerkin
jacket 228 n.
jerky
discontinuous
    72 adj.
fitful 142 adj.
jerry-built
flimsy 163 adj.
jersey
textile 222 n.
jersey 228 n.
cattle 365 n.
jest
witticism 839 n.

jester
fool 501 n.
humorist 839 n.
jet
aircraft 276 n.
speeder 277 n.
propellant 287 n.
outflow 298 n.
stream 350 n.
black thing 428 n.
gem 844 n.
jet lag
delay 136 n.
air travel 271 n.
jet-propelled
speedy 277 adj.
jetsam
derelict 779 n.
jet set
beau monde 848 n.
jettison
ejection 300 n.
not retain 779 vb.
jetty
projection 254 n.
shelter 662 n.
jewel
exceller 644 n.
gem 844 n.
jewellery
jewellery 844 n.
Jewish
religious 973 adj.
jib
prow 237 n.
sail 275 n.
deviate 282 vb.
avoid 620 vb.
jibe
(see gibe)
jig
leap 312 n.
dance 837 n.
jiggle
agitate 318 vb.
jigsaw
combination 50 n.
indoor game 837 n.
jilt
disappoint 509 vb.
relinquish 621 vb.
jingle
resound 404 vb.
doggerel 593 n.
jingoism
bellicosity 718 n.
boasting 877 n.

jingoist
  militarist 722 n.
jinn, djinn
  mythical being
    970 n.
jinx
  spell 983 n.
jitters
  agitation 318 n.
  nervousness 854 n.
jive
  dance 837 n.vb.
job
  function 622 n.
  job 622 n.
  undertaking 672 n.
  hard task 700 n.
  foul play 930 n.
jobbery
  improbity 930 n.
jobbing
  barter 791 n.
jobless
  unused 674 adj.
  nonactive 677 adj.
job lot
  medley 43 n.
jockey
  rider 268 n.
  be cunning 698 vb.
jocular
  merry 833 adj.
  witty 839 adj.
jodhpurs
  trousers 228 n.
jog
  gait 265 n.
  agitate 318 vb.
  gesticulate 547 vb.
  incite 612 vb.
jogger
  pedestrian 268 n.
jogging
  exercise 682 n.
joie de vivre
  cheerfulness 833 n.
join
  join 45 vb.
  agglutinate 48 vb.
  bring together
    74 vb.
  meet 295 vb.
  join a party 708 vb.
—forces
  cooperate 706 vb.
—in
  conform 83 vb.

participate 775 vb.
  be sociable 882 vb.
—up
  go to war 718 n.
joiner
  artisan 686 n.
joint
  joint 45 n.
  angularity 247 n.
  meat 301 n.
  corporate 708 adj.
  sharing 775 adj.
  drug-taking 949 n.
jointed
  angular 247 adj.
joist
  beam 218 n.
joke
  trickery 542 n.
  witticism 839 n.
joker
  nonconformist 84 n.
  humorist 839 n.
jollity
  merriment 833 n.
jolly
  merry 833 adj.
  sociable 882 adj.
jolt
  be rough 259 vb.
  move slowly 278 vb.
  impulse 279 n.
  lack of expectation
    508 n.
  animate 821 vb.
josh
  ridicule 851 vb.
joss
  idol 982 n.
joss house
  temple 990 n.
joss stick
  scent 396 n.
jostle
  be contiguous
    202 vb.
  obstruct 702 vb.
jot
  small quantity 33 n.
jot down
  record 548 vb.
journal
  journal 528 n.
  the press 528 n.
  record 548 n.
  biography 590 n.
  account book 808 n.

journalese
  neology 560 n.
journalism
  publicity 528 n.
  writing 586 n.
journalist
  news reporter
    529 n.
  author 589 n.
journey
  travel 267 vb.
journeyman
  artisan 686 n.
joust
  contest 716 n.
jovial
  merry 833 adj.
  sociable 882 adj.
jowl
  laterality 239 n.
joy
  joy 824 n.
joyful
  happy 824 adj.
  merry 833 adj.
joy ride
  stealing 788 n.
jubilant
  jubilant 833 adj.
jubilation
  rejoicing 835 n.
  celebration 876 n.
jubilee
  period 110 n.
  anniversary 141 n.
  rejoicing 835 n.
Judaism
  religious faith 973 n.
judge
  judge 480 vb.
  judge 957 n.
judgement
  discrimination
    463 n.
  judgement 480 n.
  opinion 485 n.
  sagacity 498 n.
  decree 737 n.
  legal trial 959 n.
  punishment 963 n.
judgement seat
  tribunal 956 n.
judicature
  jurisdiction 955 n.
judiciary
  judge 957 n.
judicious

discriminating
    463 adj.
  judicial 480 adj.
  wise 498 adj.
  advisable 642 adj.
judo
  defence 713 n.
  wrestling 716 n.
jug
  vessel 194 n.
juggernaut
  destroyer 168 n.
  lorry 274 n.
juggle
  be cunning 698 vb.
juggler
  conjuror 545 n.
  entertainer 594 n.
juice
  fluid 335 n.
  moisture 341 n.
  fuel 385 n.
juicy
  vernal 128 adj.
  fluid 335 adj.
  humid 341 adj.
  savoury 390 adj.
  impure 951 adj.
juju
  talisman 983 n.
jujube
  sweet thing 392 n.
jukebox
  gramophone 414 n.
jumble
  medley 43 n.
  jumble 63 vb.
  not discriminate
    464 vb.
jumbo
  giant 195 n.
jump
  interval 201 n.
  spurt 277 n.
  leap 312 n.vb.
  agitation 318 n.
—at
  be willing 597 vb.
  desire 859 vb.
—on the bandwagon
  do likewise 20 vb.
  conform 83 vb.
  apostatize 603 vb.
  be in fashion
    848 vb.
—the gun
  be early 135 vb.

—the queue
  precede 283 vb.
—to conclusions
  prejudge 481 vb.
jumper
  jersey 228 n.
  thoroughbred
    273 n.
  jumper 312 n.
jumpy
  agitated 318 adj.
  nervous 854 adj.
junction
  joint 45 n.
  railway 624 n.
  road 624 n.
juncture
  juncture 8 n.
  occasion 137 n.
  event 154 n.
jungle
  confusion 61 n.
  wood 366 n.
junior
  inferior 35 n.adj.
  young 130 adj.
junk
  sailing ship 275 n.
  rubbish 641 n.
junket
  meal 301 n.
  revel 837 n.vb.
junkie, junky
  drug-taking 949 n.
junta
  party 708 n.
juridical
  judicial 480 adj.
  jurisdictional
    955 adj.
jurisconsult
  jurist 958 n.
jurisdiction
  authority 733 n.
  jurisdiction 955 n.
jurisprudence
  law 953 n.
jury
  estimator 480 n.
  jury 957 n.
just
  just 913 adj.
  disinterested
    931 adj.
  legal 953 adj.
just cause
  vindication 927 n.

justice
  justice 913 n.
  probity 929 n.
  judge 957 n.
  reward 962 n.
justiciable
  accusable 928 adj.
  jurisdictional
    955 adj.
justifiable
  vindicable 927 adj.
justification
  pretext 614 n.
  vindication 927 n.
justify
  demonstrate 478 vb.
  justify 927 vb.
jut
  jut 254 vb.
jute
  fibre 208 n.
  textile 222 n.
juvenile
  youngster 132 n.
  infantine 132 adj.
  immature 670 adj.
juvenile delinquent
  offender 904 n.
juxtapose
  juxtapose 202 vb.
  compare 462 vb.

K

kagoule, cagoule
  jacket 228 n.
kaleidoscope
  medley 43 n.
  changeable thing
    152 n.
  variegation 437 n.
  optical device 442 n.
kaleidoscopic
  coloured 425 adj.
kamikaze
  murderer 362 n.
kangaroo
  jumper 312 n.
  mammal 365 n.
kangaroo court
  lawlessness 954 n.
kapok
  fibre 208 n.
kaput
  destroyed 165 adj.
  useless 641 adj.
karate

  wrestling 716 n.
karma
  fate 596 n.
kebabs
  dish 301 n.
kedgeree
  fish food 301 n.
keel
  base 214 n.
  ship 275 n.
keelhaul
  punish 963 vb.
keel over
  be inverted 221 vb.
keen
  keen 174 adj.
  sharp 256 adj.
  cold 380 adj.
  willing 597 adj.
  felt 818 adj.
  lament 836 n.vb.
keen on
  enamoured 887 adj.
keep
  look after 457 vb.
  provide 633 vb.
  refuge 662 n.
  fort 713 n.
  defend 713 vb.
  observe 768 vb.
  retain 778 vb.
  celebrate 876 vb.
—alive
  sustain 146 vb.
  preserve 666 vb.
—a low profile
  keep secret 525 vb.
—an eye
  look after 457 vb.
  safeguard 660 vb.
—at arm's length
  repel 292 vb.
  resist 715 vb.
—back
  keep secret 525 vb.
  restrain 747 vb.
  retain 778 vb.
—down
  suppress 165 vb.
  subjugate 745 vb.
—faith
  keep faith 768 vb.
  be honourable
    929 vb.
—fit
  be healthy 650 vb.
—going

  go on 146 vb.
—in
  imprison 747 vb.
—in step
  conform 83 vb.
—in touch
  correspond 588 vb.
  visit 882 vb.
—off
  avoid 620 vb.
  parry 713 vb.
—on
  sustain 146 vb.
  persevere 600 vb.
—oneself to oneself
  be unsociable
    883 vb.
—one's head
  be courageous
    855 vb.
—order
  safeguard 660 vb.
  manage 689 vb.
—out
  exclude 57 vb.
—time (with)
  time 117 vb.
  synchronize 123 vb.
—track of
  be mindful 455 vb.
—up
  sustain 146 vb.
—up with
  be equal 28 vb.
—up with the
    Joneses
  conform 83 vb.
keeper
  surveillance 457 n.
  protector 660 n.
  keeper 749 n.
keepsake
  reminder 505 n.
keg
  vat 194 n.
kennel
  stable 192 n.
  lockup 748 n.
kepi
  headgear 228 n.
kept woman
  kept woman 952 n.
kerb
  edge 234 n.
  road 624 n.
kerchief
  headgear 228 n.

kerfuffle
commotion 318 n.
kernel
centre 225 n.
chief thing 638 n.
kerosene
fuel 385 n.
ketch
sailing ship 275 n.
ketchup
sauce 389 n.
kettle
cauldron 194 n.
key
crucial 137 adj.
influential 178 adj.
opener 263 n.
key 410 n.
answer 460 n.
interpretation 520 n.
translation 520 n.
important 638 adj.
keyboard
data processing
86 n.
piano 414 n.
keyed up
expectant 507 adj.
excited 821 adj.
keyhole
orifice 263 n.
key man/woman
bigwig 638 n.
manager 690 n.
expert 696 n.
keynote
musical note 410 n.
chief thing 638 n.
keypunch
data processing
86 n.
keystone
summit 213 n.
khaki
uniform 228 n.
brown 430 adj.
kibbutz
farm 370 n.
kick
be violent 176 vb.
kick 279 vb.
recoil 280 n.
propel 287 vb.
pungency 388 n.
gesture 547 n.
resist 715 vb.
disobey 738 vb.

—oneself
regret 830 vb.
—one's heels
be inactive 679 vb.
—out
eject 300 vb.
—the habit
disaccustom 611 vb.
kicked around
subjected 745 adj.
kicks
excitation 821 n.
kid
child 132 n.
young creature
132 n.
skin 226 n.
befool 542 vb.
kid gloves
leniency 736 n.
kidnap
steal 788 vb.
kidney
sort 77 n.
meat 301 n.
kidney donor
good giver 813 n.
kidney failure
digestive disorders
651 n.
kid's stuff
easy thing 701 n.
kill
destroy 165 vb.
kill 362 vb.
—oneself
kill oneself 362 vb.
—time
amuse oneself
837 vb.
killer
killer 362 n.
killjoy
hinderer 702 n.
moper 834 n.
kiln
furnace 383 n.
kilo, kilogram
weighing 322 n.
kilt
skirt 228 n.
kimono
robe 228 n.
kin
kinsman 11 n.
kind
sort 77 n.

beneficial 644 adj.
benevolent 897 adj.
kindergarten
school 539 n.
kind-hearted
benevolent 897 adj.
kindle
cause 156 vb.
kindle 381 vb.
incite 612 vb.
feel 818 vb.
kindling
fuel 385 n.
kindness
love 887 n.
benevolence 897 n.
kindred
kinsman 11 n.
kindred spirit
close friend 880 n.
kinesics
gesture 547 n.
kinetic
dynamic 160 adj.
moving 265 adj.
king
sovereign 741 n.
kingdom
territory 184 n.
political
organization
733 n.
Kingdom of God
heaven 971 n.
kingly
ruling 733 adj.
worshipful 866 adj.
noble 868 adj.
kingpin
bigwig 638 n.
kink
coil 251 n.
eccentricity 503 n.
defect 647 n.
kinky
abnormal 84 adj.
kinsfolk
kinsman 11 n.
kinship
consanguinity 11 n.
similarity 18 n.
kinsman, kinswoman
kinsman 11 n.
kiosk
shop 796 n.
kipper
dry 342 vb.

preserve 666 vb.
kippers
fish food 301 n.
kirk
church 990 n.
kiss
courteous act
884 n.
endearment 889 n.
kissable
personable 841 adj.
lovable 887 adj.
kiss of life
revival 656 n.
kit
accumulation 74 n.
clothing 228 n.
equipment 630 n.
kitbag
bag 194 n.
kitchen
cookery 301 n.
kite
airship 276 n.
kite-flying
empiricism 461 n.
rumour 529 n.
kith and kin
kinsman 11 n.
kit out
provide 633 vb.
make ready 669 vb.
kitsch
bad taste 847 n.
kitten
young creature
132 n.
cat 365 n.
kittenish
infantine 132 adj.
merry 833 adj.
kitty
joint possession
775 n.
kleptomaniac
thief 789 n.
knack
habit 610 n.
aptitude 694 n.
knacker
killer 362 n.
knackered
fatigued 684 adj.
knap
break 46 vb.
knapsack
bag 194 n.

knave
  low fellow 869 n.
  knave 938 n.
knavish
  rascally 930 adj.
knead
  form 243 vb.
  soften 327 vb.
  rub 333 vb.
knee
  angularity 247 n.
  leg 267 n.
  kick 279 vb.
kneecap
  torture 963 vb.
knee-high
  infantine 132 adj.
  dwarfish 196 adj.
knee-jerk response
  absence of thought
  450 n.
kneel
  stoop 311 vb.
  knuckle under
  721 vb.
  pay one's respects
  884 vb.
  worship 981 vb.
kneeler
  cushion 218 n.
knees-up
  revel 837 n.
knell
  ruin 165 n.
  obsequies 364 n.
  lament 836 n.
knickerbockers
  trousers 228 n.
knickers
  underwear 228 n.
knick-knack,
  nicknack
  bauble 639 n.
  plaything 837 n.
  finery 844 n.
knife
  cut 46 vb.
  sharp edge 256 n.
  sidearms 723 n.
knife-edge
  narrowness 206 n.
knight
  rider 268 n.
  cavalry 722 n.
  brave person
  855 n.
  dignify 866 vb.

person of rank
  868 n.
knight errant
  crank 504 n.
  visionary 513 n.
  defender 713 n.
  philanthropist
  901 n.
knighthood
  honours 866 n.
knit
  tie 45 vb.
  weave 222 vb.
knitting
  needlework 844 n.
knob
  handle 218 n.
  swelling 253 n.
knobbly
  rough 259 adj.
knock
  knock 279 n.
  propulsion 287 n.
  detract 926 vb.
  —about
  travel 267 vb.
  misuse 675 vb.
  —down
  demolish 165 vb.
  fell 311 vb.
  —off
  subtract 39 vb.
  cease 145 vb.
  steal 788 vb.
  debauch 951 vb.
  —out
  render insensible
  375 vb.
knockabout
  dramatic 594 adj.
  funny 849 adj.
knocker
  hammer 279 n.
  signal 547 n.
knocking
  loudness 400 n.
  roll 403 n.
knock-kneed
  deformed 246 adj.
knock-on effect
  continuity 71 n.
knockout
  exceller 644 n.
  victory 727 n.
knoll
  small hill 209 n.
knot

tie 45 vb.
  ligature 47 n.
  complexity 61 n.
  crowd 74 n.
  solid body 324 n.
knots
  velocity 277 n.
knotty
  moot 459 adj.
  difficult 700 adj.
know
  know 490 vb.
  memorize 505 vb.
  understand 516 vb.
  befriend 880 vb.
  —one's place
  conform 83 vb.
  show respect 920 vb.
  —one's stuff
  be expert 694 vb.
knowall
  wiseacre 500 n.
know-how
  means 629 n.
  skill 694 n.
knowing
  cunning 698 adj.
knowledge
  knowledge 490 n.
knowledgeable
  instructed 490 adj.
  wise 498 adj.
known as
  named 561 adj.
knuckle
  joint 45 n.
knuckle under
  knuckle under
  721 vb.
knurled
  rough 259 adj.
Koran
  non-Biblical
  scripture 975 n.
kosher
  edible 301 adj.
  ritual 988 adj.
kowtow, kotow
  be servile 879 vb.
  show respect 920 vb.
kraal
  enclosure 235 n.
kudos
  prestige 866 n.
  approbation 923 n.
kung fu
  wrestling 716 n.

kwashiorkor
  tropical disease
  651 n.
kyle
  gulf 345 n.

L

laager
  fort 713 n.
lab
  classroom 539 n.
label
  class 62 vb.
  label 547 n.
labial
  speech sound 398 n.
laboratory
  testing agent 461 n.
  workshop 687 n.
laborious
  industrious 678 adj.
  laborious 682 adj.
labour
  obstetrics 167 n.
  emphasize 532 vb.
  job 622 n.
  labour 682 n.
  personnel 686 n.
  hard task 700 n.
  —in vain
  waste effort 641 vb.
  —the obvious
  waste effort 641 vb.
  —under
  be in a state of 7 vb.
labour camp
  prison camp 748 n.
labour-consuming
  wasteful 634 adj.
laboured
  inelegant 576 adj.
  matured 669 adj.
labourer
  producer 164 n.
  worker 686 n.
labour-intensive
  businesslike
  622 n.
labour of love
  kind act 897 n.
  disinterestedness
  931 n.
labour-saving
  mechanical 630 adj.
  leisurely 681 adj.
  economical 814 adj.

labyrinth
complexity 61 n.
meandering 251 n.

lac
resin 357 n.

lace
mix 43 vb.
tie 45 vb.
network 222 n.
textile 222 n.
needlework 844 n.

lacerate
rend 46 vb.
wound 655 vb.

laches
guilty act 936 n.

lachrymose
lamenting 836 adj.

lack
deficit 55 n.
shortfall 307 n.
require 627 vb.
scarcity 636 n.
imperfection 647 n.

lackadaisical
apathetic 820 adj.
indifferent 860 adj.

lackey
instrument 628 n.
domestic 742 n.

lacking
absent 190 adj.
deficient 307 adj.
lost 722 adj.
(*see* **lack**)

lacklustre
dim 419 adj.
dejected 834 adj.

lack of interest
incuriosity 454 n.
indifference 860 n.

lack of practice
desuetude 611 n.
unskilfulness 695 n.

laconic
taciturn 582 adj.

lacquer
coat 226 vb.
decorate 844 vb.

lactescence
semitransparency 424 n.
whiteness 427 n.

lacuna
gap 201 n.

lacy
flimsy 163 adj.

lad
youngster 132 n.

ladder
series 71 n.
ascent 308 n.
means of escape 667 n.

laden
full 54 adj.
weighty 322 adj.

la-di-da
affected 850 adj.

lading
contents 193 n.
gravity 322 n.

ladle
ladle 194 n.
transpose 272 vb.

lady
lady 373 n.

Lady Bountiful
good giver 813 n.

lady-in-waiting
retainer 742 n.

ladykiller
libertine 952 n.

ladylike
well-bred 848 adj.

lag
be late 136 vb.
cover 226 vb.
move slowly 278 vb.
follow 284 vb.
fall short 307 vb.
offender 904 n.

lager
alcoholic drink 301 n.

laggard
slowcoach 278 n.
lazy 679 adj.

lagging
wrapping 226 n.
lining 227 n.

lagoon
lake 346 n.

laid
born 360 adj.

laid-back
reposeful 683 adj.

laid off
disused 674 adj.
nonactive 677 adj.

laid up
sick 651 adj.

lair
dwelling 192 n.

refuge 662 n.

laird
master 741 n.

laissez faire, laisser faire
freedom 744 n.
trade 791 n.

laity
laity 987 n.

lake
lake 346 n.

lama
priest 986 n.

lamasery
monastery 986 n.

lamb
young creature 132 n.
meat 301 n.
sheep 365 n.
darling 890 n.
innocent 935 n.

lambaste, lambast
strike 279 vb.
reprove 924 vb.

lambency
touch 378 n.
glow 417 n.

lame
disable 161 vb.
crippled 163 adj.
feeble 572 adj.
impair 655 vb.

lame duck
nonpayer 805 n.

lament
cry 408 vb.
regret 830 vb.
lament 836 n.vb.

lamentable
bad 645 adj.
distressing 827 adj.

lamentation
lamentation 836 n.

lamina
lamina 207 n.

lamp
lamp 420 n.
signal 547 n.

lampoon
satire 851 n.

lance
sharp point 256 n.
spear 723 n.

lancer
cavalry 722 n.
soldiery 722 n.

lancet
perforator 263 n.

land
region 184 n.
land 295 vb.
land 344 n.
lands 777 n.

landed
possessing 773 adj.
proprietary 777 adj.

landfall
arrival 295 n.

landing
stand 218 n.
arrival 295 n.
descent 309 n.

landing craft
warship 722 n.

land-line
telecommunication 531 n.

landlord, landlady
caterer 633 n.
owner 776 n.

landmark
projection 254 n.
signpost 547 n.
important matter 638 n.

landmass
region 184 n.

landowner
owner 776 n.

lands
lands 777 n.

landscape
land 344 n.
spectacle 445 n.

landscape gardening
ornamental art 844 n.

landslide
revolution 149 n.
ruin 165 n.
defeat 728 n.

landslip
incline 220 n.

lane
path 624 n.
route 624 n.

language
language 557 n.
speech 579 n.

languid
inert 175 adj.
inactive 679 adj.

languish
be ill 651 vb.
be fatigued 684 vb.
be dejected 834 vb.
be affected 850 vb.

languor
inertness 175 n.

lank
graceless 842 adj.

lanky
narrow 206 adj.
tall 209 adj.

lanolin
unguent 357 n.

lantern
lamp 420 n.

lanyard
cable 47 n.

lap
period 110 n.
seat 218 n.
surround 230 vb.
outstrip 277 vb.
drink 301 vb.
moisten 341 vb.
flow 350 vb.
circuit 626 n.vb.
refuge 662 n.

—up
absorb 299 vb.
hear 415 vb.

laparotomy
surgery 658 n.

lapel
fold 261 n.

lapidary
engraver 556 n.

lapidate
lapidate 712 vb.

lappet
hanging object
217 n.

lapse
elapse 111 vb.
deviation 282 n.
inattention 456 n.
be unpractised
611 vb.
deteriorate 655 vb.
guilty act 936 n.

lapsed
unbelieving 486 adj.
nonobservant
769 adj.

larceny
stealing 788 n.

lard

cookery 301 n.
fat 357 n.

larder
provisions 301 n.
storage 632 n.

large
great 32 adj.
spacious 183 adj.
large 195 adj.

largesse
liberality 813 n.

largo
adagio 412 adv.

lariat
halter 47 n.

lark
climber 308 n.
vocalist 413 n.
revel 837 n.

lark about/around
be absurd 497 vb.
amuse oneself
837 vb.

larva
young creature
132 n.
insect 365 n.

larynx
air pipe 353 n.
voice 577 n.

lascivious
lecherous 951 adj.

laser
electronics 160 n.
weapon 723 n.

lash
tie 45 vb.
strike 279 vb.
incentive 612 n.
animate 821 vb.
reprobate 924 vb.
flog 963 vb.

—out
be violent 176 vb.

lashings
great quantity 32 n.
plenty 635 n.

lass
youngster 132 n.

lassitude
sleepiness 679 n.
fatigue 684 n.

lasso
halter 47 n.

last
mould 23 n.
ending 69 adj.

last 113 vb.
stay 144 vb.
completive 725 adj.

lasting
lasting 113 adj.
permanent 144 adj.
unyielding 162 adj.

last minute
lateness 136 n.
crisis 137 n.

last post
obsequies 364 n.

last resort
necessity 596 n.

last rites
obsequies 364 n.

last straw
completion 725 n.
annoyance 827 n.

last throw
gambling 618 n.

last word in
modernism 126 n.

last words
valediction 296 n.

latch
fastening 47 n.

late
former 125 adj.
modern 126 adj.
vespertine 129 adj.
late 136 adj.adv.
ill-timed 138 adj.
slow 278 adj.
dead 361 adj.

latecomer
posteriority 120 n.

late developer
learner 538 n.

latency
latency 523 n.

latent
latent 523 adj.
concealed 525 adj.

later
after 65 adv.
subsequent 120 adj.
not now 122 adv.

lateral
lateral 239 adj.

lateral thinking
meditation 449 n.

latest, the
fashion 848 n.

lath
lamina 207 n.
strip 208 n.

last 113 vb.
stay 144 vb.
completive 725 adj.

lasting
lasting 113 adj.
permanent 144 adj.
unyielding 162 adj.

latitude
region 184 n.
breadth 205 n.
scope 744 n.

latitude and
longitude
situation 186 n.
coordinate 465 n.

latitudinarianism
heterodoxy 977 n.

latrine
latrine 649 n.

latter-day
modern 126 adj.

lattice
network 222 n.
window 263 n.

laudable
approvable 923 adj.

laugh
be cheerful 833 vb.
laugh 835 vb.

—at
ridicule 851 vb.
hold cheap 922 vb.

—off
disregard 458 vb.

laughable
absurd 497 adj.
foolish 499 adj.
amusing 837 adj.
ridiculous 849 adj.

laughingstock
laughingstock
851 n.

laughter
merriment 833 n.
laughter 835 n.

launch
initiate 68 vb.
navigate 269 vb.
ship 275 n.
propel 287 vb.

—out
be loquacious
581 vb.

—out at
attack 712 vb.

launching pad
space travel 271 n.

launder
clean 648 vb.

lathe
rotator 315 n.

lather
bubble 355 n.
clean 648 vb.

launderette
ablutions 648 n.

laundry
ablutions 648 n.

laurels
trophy 729 n.
honours 866 n.

lavatory
latrine 649 n.

lavender
purple 436 adj.
preserver 666 n.

lavish
liberal 813 adj.
prodigal 815 adj.

law
rule 81 n.
necessity 596 n.
habit 610 n.
precept 693 n.
decree 737 n.
law 953 n.

law-abiding
peaceful 717 adj.
obedient 739 adj.

law and order
peace 717 n.

law-breaker
offender 904 n.

lawcourt
lawcourt 956 n.

lawful
due 915 adj.
legal 953 adj.

lawless
anarchic 734 adj.
lawless 954 adj.

lawn
textile 222 n.
garden 370 n.

laws
political
organization
733 n.

lawsuit
litigation 959 n.

lawyer
lawyer 958 n.

lax
negligent 458 adj.
lax 734 adj.
lenient 736 adj.
nonobservant
769 adj.

laxative
excretory 302 adj.
purgative 658 n.

laxity
scope 744 n.
(*see* **lax**)

lay
reproduce itself
167 vb.
place 187 vb.
vocal music 412 n.
gamble 618 vb.
unskilled 695 adj.
debauch 951 vb.
laical 987 adj.

—aside
stop using 674 vb.

—at one's door
attribute 158 vb.
accuse 928 vb.

—bare
disclose 526 vb.

—by
store 632 vb.

—down
let fall 311 vb.
suppose 512 vb.

—down the law
dogmatize 473 vb.
decree 737 vb.

—in
store 632 vb.

—off
dismiss 300 vb.
stop using 674 vb.

—out
arrange 62 vb.
flatten 216 vb.
inter 364 vb.
expend 806 vb.

—up
store 632 vb.
stop using 674 vb.

—waste
lay waste 165 vb.

layabout
idler 679 n.

lay-by
traffic control
305 n.

layer
layer 207 n.

layette
clothing 228 n.

lay figure
image 551 n.

laying on of hands
medical art 658 n.
Christian rite
988 n.

layman, laywoman
lay person 987 n.

layout
arrangement 62 n.

laze
be inactive 679 vb.
repose 683 vb.

lazy
negligent 458 adj.
lazy 679 adj.

lea
shore 344 n.
grassland 348 n.

leach
drench 341 vb.
purify 648 vb.

lead
advantage 34 n.
halter 47 n.
precedence 64 n.
sailing aid 269 n.
precede 283 vb.
gauge 465 n.
hint 524 n.
print-type 587 n.
actor 594 n.
direct 689 vb.

—astray
mislead 495 vb.

—on
excite love 887 vb.

—to
conduce 156 vb.
tend 179 vb.

—up to
prepare 669 vb.

leaden
weighty 322 adj.
grey 429 adj.
tedious 838 adj.

leader
superior 34 n.
precursor 66 n.
article 591 n.
leader 690 n.

leadership
directorship 689 n.
authority 733 n.

leading
supreme 34 adj.
influential 178 adj.
foremost 283 adj.
important 638 adj.
directing 689 adj.

leading light
sage 500 n.
bigwig 638 n.

leading strings
nonage 130 n.

leads
roof 226 n.

leaf
lamina 207 n.
foliage 366 n.

leafless
wintry 129 adj.
uncovered 229 adj.

leaflet
foliage 366 n.
the press 528 n.

leaf through
scan 438 vb.

league
long measure 203 n.
association 706 n.

leak
outflow 298 n.
be wet 341 vb.
divulge 526 vb.
waste 634 vb.
not retain 779 vb.

leakage
decrease 37 n.
loss 772 n.

leaky
porous 263 adj.
imperfect 647 adj.
unsafe 661 adj.

lean
tend 179 vb.
lean 206 adj.
be oblique 220 vb.
be biased 481 vb.

—on
be supported
218 vb.
compel 740 vb.

—over backwards
compensate 31 vb.
be willing 597 vb.

leaning
willingness 597 n.
liking 859 n.

lean-to
small house 192 n.

leap
spurt 277 n.
leap 312 n.vb.
dance 837 vb.

—at
be willing 597 vb.

leapfrog
children's games
837 n.

leap in the dark
uncertainty 474 n.
gambling 618 n.

leaps and bounds
progression 285 n.

learn
memorize 505 vb.
understand 516 vb.
learn 536 vb.

learned
instructed 490 adj.
studious 536 adj.

learner
scholar 492 n.
learner 538 n.

learning
knowledge 490 n.
learning 536 n.

lease
lease 784 vb.
hire 785 vb.

leasehold
proprietary 777 adj.

leash
halter 47 n.

least
lesser 35 adj.

least one can do
dueness 915 n.

leather
skin 226 n.
materials 631 n.
spank 963 vb.

leathery
tough 329 adj.
unsavoury 391 adj.

leave
depart 296 vb.
relinquish 621 vb.
leisure 681 n.
permission 756 n.
bequeath 780 vb.

—behind
outstrip 277 vb.
outdo 306 vb.

—off
cease 145 vb.

—one cold
be indifferent 860 vb.

—one in the lurch
deceive 542 vb.
fail in duty 918 vb.

—out
exclude 57 vb.

—undone
neglect 458 vb.

not complete
726 vb.

leaven
alterer 143 n.
influence 178 n.
leaven 323 n.
make better 654 vb.

leave-taking
valediction 296 n.

leavings
leavings 41 n.

lecher
libertine 952 n.

lecherous
lecherous 951 adj.

lectern
rostrum 539 n.

lecture
lecture 534 n.
dissertation 591 n.
reprimand 924 n.

lecturer
lecture 534 n.
speaker 579 n.

ledge
shelf 218 n.
projection 254 n.

ledger
account book 808 n.

lee
laterality 239 n.
shelter 662 n.

leech
coherence 48 n.
taker 786 n.

leer
look 438 n.
court 889 vb.

leeway
room 183 n.
deviation 282 n.

left
remaining 41 adj.
sinistral 242 adj.
political party 708 n.

left-handed
sinistral 242 adj.
clumsy 695 adj.

left in the lurch
in difficulties 700 adj.

leftovers
leavings 41 n.
dish 301 n.

left-winger
political party 708 n.

leg

stand 218 n.
leg 267 n.

legacy
sequel 67 n.
dower 777 n.

legal
legal 953 adj.

legal adviser
law agent 958 n.

legalist
narrow mind 481 n.

legality
legality 953 n.

legalize
permit 756 vb.
make legal 953 vb.

legal profession
bar 958 n.

legate
envoy 754 n.

legatee
beneficiary 776 n.

legation
envoy 754 n.

legend
commentary 520 n.
phrase 563 n.
narrative 590 n.

legendary
imaginary 513 adj.
renowned 866 adj.

legerdemain
sleight 542 n.

leggings
legwear 228 n.

leggy
legged 267 adj.

legible
intelligible 516 adj.

legion
army 722 n.
formation 722 n.

legionary
soldier 722 n.

legislate
decree 737 vb.
make legal 953 vb.

legislation
legislation 953 n.

legislative
legal 953 adj.

legislative assembly
parliament 692 n.

legislator
director 690 n.

legitimate
genuine 494 adj.

legal 953 adj.

legitimize
make legal 953 vb.

legman
news reporter 529 n.

leg-pull
trickery 542 n.

leg to stand on
pretext 614 n.

leguminous
vegetal 366 adj.

let-up
progression 285 n.
elevation 310 n.

legwork
labour 682 n.

leisure
leisure 681 n.
amusement 837 n.

leisurely
slow 278 adj.
leisurely 681 adj.

leitmotiv, leitmotif
melody 410 n.
topic 452 n.

lemma
argumentation 475 n.

lemmings
suicide 362 n.

lemon
sourness 393 n.
yellowness 433 n.
loser 728 n.

lemonade
soft drink 301 n.

lend
provide 633 vb.
lend 784 vb.
credit 802 vb.

—a hand
aid 703 vb.

—colour to
evidence 466 vb.

lender
lender 784 n.

length
quantity 26 n.
size 195 n.
distance 199 n.
interval 201 n.
length 203 n.

lengthen
augment 36 vb.
continue 71 vb.
lengthen 203 vb.

lengthy
  prolix 570 adj.
lenient
  lenient 736 adj.
lenitive
  moderator 177 n.
  lenitive 177 adj.
lens
  optical device 442 n.
  photography 551 n.
Lent
  fast 946 n.
leopard
  cat 365 n.
  maculation 437 n.
leotard
  suit 228 n.
leper
  outcast 883 n.
lepidopterist
  zoologist 367 n.
leprechaun
  elf 970 n.
leprosy
  skin disease 651 n.
lesbian
  nonconformist 84 n.
lesion
  wound 655 n.
lessee
  possessor 776 n.
lessen
  abate 37 vb.
  moderate 177 vb.
lesser
  lesser 35 adj.
lesson
  lecture 534 n.
  study 536 n.
  warning 664 n.
let
  permit 756 vb.
  lease 784 vb.
—alone
  avoid 620 vb.
  give scope 744 vb.
—down
  lower 311 vb.
—fall
  let fall 311 vb.
  hint 524 vb.
—fly
  be violent 176 vb.
  strike 279 vb.
—go
  let fall 311 vb.
  not retain 779 vb.

—in
  admit 299 vb.
—off
  shoot 287 vb.
  acquit 960 vb.
—off steam
  revel 837 vb.
—one down
  disappoint 509 vb.
  fail in duty 918 vb.
—oneself go
  deteriorate 655 vb.
  revel 837 vb.
—oneself in for
  undertake 672 vb.
—out
  enlarge 197 vb.
  lengthen 203 vb.
  divulge 526 vb.
—up
  cease 145 vb.
—well alone
  not act 677 vb.
  be cautious 858 vb.
letdown
  disappointment 509 n.
lethal
  deadly 362 adj.
  toxic 653 adj.
lethargic
  inactive 679 adj.
lethargy
  fatigue 684 n.
  moral insensibility 820 n.
Lethe
  oblivion 506 n.
  mythic hell 972 n.
let off
  forgiven 909 adj.
  acquittal 960 n.
let-out
  pretext 614 n.
  means of escape 667 n.
letter
  letter 558 n.
  correspondence 588 n.
lettered
  instructed 490 adj.
lettering
  lettering 586 n.
  ornamental art 844 n.
letter of the law

severity 735 n.
letterpress
  letterpress 587 n.
letters
  erudition 490 n.
  literature 557 n.
  correspondence 588 n.
letup
  lull 145 n.
leukaemia
  blood disease 651 n.
levee
  earthwork 253 n.
  social gathering 882 n.
level
  degree 27 n.
  equality 28 n.
  serial place 73 n.
  demolish 165 vb.
  layer 207 n.
  flat 216 adj.
  smooth 258 adj.vb.
  fell 311 vb.
  inexcitable 823 adj.
—at
  aim 281 vb.
—off
  decrease 37 vb.
—up or down
  make uniform 16 vb.
level crossing
  railway 624 n.
level-headed
  wise 498 adj.
levels
  lowness 210 n.
  plain 348 n.
lever
  handle 218 n.
  pivot 218 n.
  lifter 310 n.
  tool 630 n.
leverage
  influence 178 n.
  scope 744 n.
levitate
  ascend 308 vb.
  be light 323 vb.
Levite
  priest 986 n.
levity
  folly 499 n.
  merriment 833 n.
levy

armed force 722 n.
  levy 786 vb.
  tax 809 n.vb.
lewd
  impure 951 adj.
  lecherous 951 adj.
lexical
  verbal 559 adj.
lexicography
  linguistics 557 n.
lexicon
  dictionary 559 n.
  reference book 589 n.
liability
  tendency 179 n.
  liability 180 n.
  vulnerability 661 n.
  duty 917 n.
liable
  subject 745 adj.
liaison
  bond 47 n.
  love affair 887 n.
liar
  liar 545 n.
libation
  drinking 301 n.
libel
  calumny 926 n.
  false charge 928 n.
liberal
  plenteous 635 adj.
  reformer 654 n.
  leniency 736 n.
  liberal 813 adj.
liberality
  liberality 813 n.
  benevolence 897 n.
liberalize
  liberate 746 vb.
liberal studies
  curriculum 534 n.
liberate
  deliver 668 vb.
  disencumber 701 vb.
  liberate 746 vb.
liberation
  freedom 744 n.
libertarian
  free person 744 n.
libertine
  libertine 952 n.
liberty
  freedom 744 n.

LIB

scope 744 n.
permission 756 n.
libidinous
lecherous 951 adj.
libido
libido 859 n.
librarian
bookperson 589 n.
library
library 589 n.
librettist
author 589 n.
libretto
vocal music 412 n.
licence
laxity 734 n.
permit 756 n.
license
commission 751 vb.
permit 756 vb.
licensee
consignee 754 n.
licentious
sensual 944 adj.
lecherous 951 adj.
lichen
plant 366 n.
licit
legal 953 adj.
lick
eat 301 vb.
moisten 341 vb.
touch 378 vb.
taste 386 vb.
defeat 727 vb.
caress 889 vb.
—**into shape**
form 243 vb.
educate 534 vb.
—**one's lips**
enjoy 376 vb.
gluttonize 947 vb.
licking
defeat 728 n.
lickspittle
toady 879 n.
lid
covering 226 n.
stopper 264 n.
lido
pleasure ground 837 n.
lie
be situated 186 vb.
be horizontal 216 vb.
be false 541 vb.

LIF

untruth 543 n.
—**down**
be horizontal 216 vb.
repose 683 vb.
—**in wait**
ambush 527 vb.
—**low**
disappear 446 vb.
lurk 523 vb.
liege
master 741 n.
lie of the land
circumstance 8 n.
direction 281 n.
lieutenant
auxiliary 707 n.
army officer 741 n.
naval officer 741 n.
life
existence 1 n.
vitality 162 n.
life 360 n.
biography 590 n.
vocation 622 n.
life belt
safeguard 662 n.
lifeblood
essential part 5 n.
life 360 n.
lifeboat
safeguard 662 n.
life cycle
regular return 141 n.
life-giving
generative 167 adj.
lifeguard
protector 660 n.
defender 713 n.
life jacket
safeguard 662 n.
lifeless
inert 175 adj.
dead 361 adj.
lifelike
lifelike 18 adj.
lifeline
safeguard 662 n.
lifelong
lasting 113 adj.
life-saver
preserver 666 n.
life sentence
long duration 113 n.
life-size
large 195 adj.
life story

LIG

biography 590 n.
life-style
habit 610 n.
way 624 n.
life-support system
preserver 666 n.
lifetime
period 110 n.
long duration 113 n.
lift
carry 273 vb.
lifter 310 n.
elevate 310 vb.
steal 788 vb.
relieve 831 vb.
lift-off
space travel 271 n.
ligament
ligature 47 n.
ligature
ligature 47 n.
light
light 323 adj.
kindle 381 vb.
light 417 n.
luminary 420 n.
illuminate 420 vb.
soft-hued 425 adj.
truth 494 n.
trivial 639 adj.
easy 701 adj.
unchaste 951 adj.
revelation 975 n.
lighten
lighten 323 vb.
make bright 417 vb.
disencumber 701 vb.
lighter
boat 275 n.
lighter 385 n.
light-fingered
thieving 788 adj.
light-headed
light-minded 456 adj.
light-hearted
cheerful 833 adj.
lighthouse
signal light 420 n.
signpost 547 n.
lighting
lighting 420 n.
light-minded
light-minded 456 adj.
capricious 604 adj.

LIL

lightning
electricity 160 n.
velocity 277 n.
flash 417 n.
light of nature
intuition 476 n.
light rein
leniency 736 n.
light relief
ridiculousness 849 n.
lights
knowledge 490 n.
intelligence 498 n.
lightship
sailing aid 269 n.
light-skinned
colourless 426 adj.
lights out
obscuration 418 n.
lightweight
light 323 adj.
nonentity 639 n.
trivial 639 adj.
light year
distance 199 n.
lignite
fuel 385 n.
likeable
lovable 887 adj.
like
similar 18 adj.
enjoy 376 vb.
be friendly 880 vb.
love 887 vb.
likelihood
probability 471 n.
likely
probable 471 adj.
credible 485 adj.
promising 852 adj.
like-minded
assenting 488 adj.
liken
liken 18 vb.
compare 462 vb.
likeness
similarity 18 n.
copy 22 n.
metaphor 519 n.
representation 551 n.
liking
liking 859 n.
lilac
purple 436 adj.
lilliputian
little 196 adj.

lilt
sing 413 vb.

lily
white thing 427 n.
a beauty 841 n.

limb
piece 53 n.
leg 267 n.
tree 366 n.

limber
flexible 327 adj.
gun 723 n.

limber up
prepare oneself
669 vb.

limbo
prison 748 n.
hell 972 n.

lime
fertilizer 171 n.
bleacher 426 n.
greenness 434 n.
ensnare 542 vb.

limelight
publicity 528 n.

limerick
doggerel 593 n.

limit
finite quantity 26 n.
extremity 69 n.
edge 234 n.
limit 236 n.vb.
restrain 747 vb.

limitation
limit 236 n.
qualification 468 n.
defect 647 n.
restriction 747 n.

limitless
infinite 107 adj.
huge 195 adj.

limn
represent 551 vb.

limousine
automobile 274 n.

limp
inert 175 adj.
move slowly 278 vb.
soft 327 adj.
feeble 572 adj.

limpet
coherence 48 n.
bomb 723 n.

limpid
transparent 422 adj.
perspicuous
567 adj.

linage
letterpress 587 n.

linchpin
chief thing 638 n.

linctus
medicine 658 n.

line
race 11 n.
cable 47 n.
continuity 71 n.
breed 77 n.
genealogy 169 n.
line 203 n.
line 227 vb.
straightness 249 n.
direction 281 n.
stripe 437 n.
telecommunication
531 n.
vocation 622 n.
policy 623 n.
railway 624 n.
tactics 688 n.
formation 722 n.
merchandise 795 n.

—up
be in order 60 vb.

lineage
genealogy 169 n.
nobility 868 n.

lineament(s)
outline 233 n.
feature 445 n.

linear
straight 249 adj.
metrical 465 adj.

lined
ageing 131 adj.
furrowed 262 adj.

linen
textile 222 n.
underwear 228 n.

liner
lining 227 n.
ship 275 n.

lines
form 243 n.
feature 445 n.
poem 593 n.
defences 713 n.

lineup
assemblage 74 n.

linger
be late 136 vb.
go on 146 vb.

lingerie
underwear 228 n.

lingo
language 557 n.
dialect 560 n.

lingua franca
language 557 n.

linguist
interpreter 520 n.
linguist 557 n.

linguistics
linguistics 557 n.

liniment
unguent 357 n.
balm 658 n.

lining
lining 227 n.

link
relation 9 n.
connect 45 vb.
bond 47 n.
intermediary 231 n.

links
pleasure ground
837 n.

linkup
union 45 n.

linotype
print 587 n.

lint
surgical dressing
658 n.

lintel
beam 218 n.
doorway 263 n.

lion
cat 365 n.
bigwig 638 n.
person of repute
866 n.

lion-hearted
courageous 855 adj.

lionize
honour 866 vb.
praise 923 vb.

lion's share
chief part 52 n.

lion-tamer
trainer 537 n.

lip
edge 234 n.
projection 254 n.
sauciness 878 n.

lip-read
translate 520 vb.

lip service
sham 542 n.

lipstick
cosmetic 843 n.

lingo
liquefy
liquefy 337 vb.

liquescent
fluid 335 adj.

liqueur
alcoholic drink
301 n.

liquid
fluid 335 n.adj.
speech sound 398 n.

liquidate
destroy 165 vb.
slaughter 362 vb.
pay 804 vb.

liquidator
receiver 782 n.

liquidity
funds 797 n.

liquidize
cook 301 vb.

liquor
stimulant 174 n.
drunkenness 949 n.

liquorice, licorice
sweets 301 n.

lisp
speech defect 580 n.

lissom
shapely 841 adj.

list
list 87 n.vb.
obliquity 220 n.

listed
included 78 adj.

listen
hear 415 vb.
be attentive 455 vb.

listener
listener 415 n.
broadcasting 531 n.

listless
weakly 163 adj.
incurious 454 adj.
dejected 834 adj.

lists
arena 724 n.

litany
prayers 981 n.

literacy
culture 490 n.

literal
narrow-minded
481 adj.
accurate 494 adj.
semantic 514 adj.
interpretive 520 adj.
literal 558 adj.

literary
stylistic 566 adj.
literary criticism
interpretation 520 n.
literature 557 n.
literary person
author 589 n.
bookperson 589 n.
literate
instructed 490 adj.
literati
intellectual 492 n.
literature
literature 557 n.
reading matter
589 n.
lithe
flexible 327 adj.
lithic
hard 326 adj.
lithograph
print 587 vb.
litigant
litigant 959 n.
litigate
litigate 959 vb.
litigious
quarrelling 709 adj.
litmus paper
testing agent 461 n.
litotes
trope 519 n.
litre
metrology 465 n.
litter
confusion 61 n.
young creature
132 n.
bed 218 n.
rubbish 641 n.
dirt 649 n.
litterlout
dirty person 649 n.
little
small 33 adj.
seldom 140 adv.
little 196 adj.
little people
fairy 970 n.
littoral
coastal 344 adj.
liturgy
ritual 988 n.
live
be 1 vb.
dynamic 160 adj.
dwell 192 vb.

alive 360 adj.
live 360 vb.
—and let live
not act 677 vb.
—it up
revel 837 vb.
—with
wed 894 vb.
lived in
occupied 191 adj.
livelihood
vocation 622 n.
liveliness
vitality 162 n.
livelong
lasting 113 adj.
lively
active 678 adj.
lively 819 adj.
cheerful 833 adj.
liven up
vitalize 360 vb.
be cheerful 833 vb.
liver
insides 224 n.
meat 301 n.
liverish
irascible 892 adj.
livery
uniform 228 n.
livery 547 n.
livestock
cattle 365 n.
live wire
electricity 160 n.
busy person
678 n.
livid
blackish 428 adj.
purple 436 adj.
angry 891 adj.
living
vocation 622 n.
benefice 985 n.
living matter
organism 358 n.
life 360 n.
living room
chamber 194 n.
living soul
person 371 n.
lizard
reptile 365 n.
load
fill 54 vb.
stow 187 vb.
contents 193 n.

thing transferred
272 n.
encumbrance
702 n.
loadstone, lodestone
magnet 291 n.
loaf
head 213 n.
cereals 301 n.
intelligence 498 n.
be inactive 679 vb.
loafer
idler 679 n.
loam
soil 344 n.
loan
lending 784 n.
loath, loth
unwilling 598 adj.
loathe
dislike 861 vb.
hate 888 vb.
loathsome
not nice 645 adj.
hateful 888 adj.
lob
propel 287 vb.
lobby
influence 178 n.vb.
lobby 194 n.
motivator 612 n.
petitioner 763 n.
—against
deprecate 762 vb.
lobe
ear 415 n.
lobster
fish food 301 n.
local
regional 184 adj.
native 191 n.
tavern 192 n.
provincial 192 adj.
near 200 adj.
local colour
description 590 n.
locale
situation 186 n.
locality
district 184 n.
locality 187 n.
localize
place 187 vb.
restrain 747 vb.
locate
place 187 vb.
discover 484 vb.

location
location 187 n.
loch
lake 346 n.
lock
fastening 47 n.
hair 259 n.
close 264 vb.
conduit 351 n.
safeguard 662 n.
—up
imprison 747 vb.
locker
compartment 194 n.
locket
jewellery 844 n.
lockout
exclusion 57 n.
locksmith
artisan 686 n.
lock, stock and
barrel
all 52 n.
lockup
lockup 748 n.
locomotion
motion 265 n.
locomotive
locomotive 274 n.
vehicular 274 adj.
locum, locum tenens
substitute 150 n.
doctor 658 n.
locust
destroyer 168 n.
bane 659 n.
locution
phrase 563 n.
lodestar, loadstar
motive 612 n.
lodge
small house 192 n.
dwell 192 vb.
be quiescent 266 vb.
lodger
resident 191 n.
lodgings
quarters 192 n.
loft
attic 194 n.
propel 287 vb.
lofty
high 209 adj.
worshipful 866 adj.
proud 871 adj.
disinterested
931 adj.

log
  sailing aid 269 n.
  fuel 385 n.
  gauge 465 n.
  record 548 n.
logarithm
  numerical element
    85 n.
logbook
  chronology 117 n.
logic
  reasoning 475 n.
logical
  relevant 9 adj.
  philosophic 449 adj.
  rational 475 adj.
  necessary 596 adj.
logic-chopping
  sophistry 477 n.
logician
  reasoner 475 n.
logistics
  provision 633 n.
  fitting out 669 n.
logophile
  linguist 557 n.
logotype, logo
  label 547 n.
  print-type 587 n.
logrolling
  cooperation 706 n.
loin
  buttocks 238 n.
loincloth
  loincloth 228 n.
loins
  genitalia 167 n.
loiter
  be stealthy 525 vb.
  be inactive 679 vb.
loiterer
  slowcoach 278 n.
loll
  be horizontal
    216 vb.
  be inactive 679 vb.
  repose 683 vb.
lollipop
  sweet thing 392 n.
lone
  one 88 adj.
  unsociable 883 adj.
lonely
  alone 88 adj.
  empty 190 adj.
  friendless 883 adj.
  secluded 883 adj.

loner
  nonconformist 84 n.
  solitary 883 n.
long
  lasting 113 adj.
  long 203 adj.
  prolix 570 adj.
  desire 859 vb.
—for
  desire 859 vb.
longevity
  long duration 113 n.
  old age 131 n.
longhand
  writing 586 n.
longing
  desire 859 n.
longitude
  length 203 n.
longlasting
  perpetual 115 adj.
long-legged
  tall 209 adj.
long odds
  improbability 472 n.
long-range
  distant 199 adj.
long run
  futurity 124 n.
longshore
  seafaring 269 adj.
long shot
  improbability 472 n.
longstanding
  lasting 113 adj.
  immemorial
    127 adj.
longsuffering
  patient 823 adj.
long-term
  lasting 113 adj.
longwinded
  prolix 570 adj.
long words
  magniloquence
    574 n.
loo
  latrine 649 n.
look
  form 243 n.
  look 438 n.
  appearance 445 n.
  mien 445 n.
  be curious 453 vb.
—after
  look after 457 vb.
  safeguard 660 vb.

—ahead
  foresee 510 vb.
—askance (at)
  disapprove 924 vb.
—at
  gaze 438 vb.
  watch 441 vb.
—back
  retrospect 505 vb.
  regret 830 vb.
—down on
  despise 922 vb.
—for
  search 459 vb.
—forward (to)
  expect 507 vb.
  hope 852 vb.
—into
  inquire 459 vb.
—like
  resemble 18 vb.
—on
  be present 189 vb.
  not act 677 vb.
—out
  invigilate 457 vb.
  be cautious 858 vb.
—through
  be rude 885 vb.
—up to
  honour 866 vb.
  respect 920 vb.
lookalike
  analogue 18 n.
  actor 594 n.
looker-on
  spectator 441 n.
look-in
  opportunity 137 n.
looking glass
  mirror 442 n.
looking up
  improved 654 adj.
lookout
  view 438 n.
  surveillance 457 n.
  expectation 507 n.
  warner 664 n.
loom
  impend 155 vb.
  weaving 222 n.
  be dim 419 vb.
  be visible 443 vb.
loony
  crazy 503 adj.
  madman 504 n.
loop

loop 250 n.
  circuit 626 n.
loophole
  window 263 n.
  contrivance 623 n.
  means of escape
    667 n.
loose
  disunite 46 vb.
  nonadhesive 49 adj.
  hanging 217 adj.
  lax 734 adj.
  liberate 746 vb.
  unchaste 951 adj.
—off at
  shoot 287 vb.
loosebox
  cart 274 n.
loose ends
  noncompletion
    726 n.
loose-limbed
  flexible 327 adj.
loose morals
  wickedness 934 n.
loosen
  (*see* **loose**)
looseness
  inexactness 495 n.
loot
  booty 790 n.
looter
  taker 786 n.
lop
  cut 46 vb.
lope
  gait 265 n.
  move fast 277 vb.
lop-eared
  hanging 217 adj.
lopsided
  unequal 29 adj.
lopsidedness
  distortion 246 n.
loquacious
  loquacious 581 adj.
lord, lady
  bigwig 638 n.
  master 741 n.
  owner 776 n.
  person of rank
    868 n.
Lord
  God the Son 965 n.
lord it (over)
  oppress 735 vb.
  be proud 871 vb.

lordly
authoritarian
735 adj.
Lord's day
holy day 988 n.
lordship
position of authority
733 n.
title 870 n.
Lord's Supper, the
church service
988 n.
lore
tradition 127 n.
erudition 490 n.
learning 536 n.
lorgnette
eyeglass 442 n.
lorry
lorry 274 n.
lose
misplace 188 vb.
be defeated 728 vb.
lose 772 vb.
—colour
lose colour 426 vb.
—control
be lax 734 vb.
—face
lose repute 867 vb.
—ground
regress 286 vb.
—heart
despair 853 vb.
—one's nerve
be cowardly 856 vb.
—sight of
neglect 458 vb.
—the scent
be uncertain 474 vb.
—the thread
be unrelated 10 vb.
be inattentive
456 vb.
—the way
stray 282 vb.
—track of
misplace 188 vb.
be inattentive
456 vb.
—weight
lighten 323 vb.
loser
loser 728 n.
losing
profitless 641 adj.
loss

decrement 42 n.
disappearance
446 n.
waste 634 n.
loss 772 n.
loss-making
profitless 641 adj.
lost
destroyed 165 adj.
misplaced 188 adj.
lost 772 adj.
lost cause
defeat 728 n.
lost labour
lost labour 641 n.
lost sheep
bad person 938 n.
lot
all 52 n.
bunch 74 n.
territory 184 n.
fate 596 n.
portion 783 n.
loth
(*see* **loath**)
lotion
cleanser 648 n.
lots
great quantity 32 n.
plenty 635 n.
lottery
equal chance 159 n.
gambling 618 n.
louche
disreputable
867 adj.
loud
loud 400 adj.
resonant 404 adj.
florid 425 adj.
vulgar 847 adj.
loudhailer
megaphone 400 n.
loudmouth
rude person 885 n.
loudspeaker
megaphone 400 n.
hearing aid 415 n.
lounge
chamber 194 n.
be inactive 679 vb.
repose 683 vb.
lounger
seat 218 n.
idler 679 n.
lour, lower
hang 217 vb.

be sullen 893 vb.
threaten 900 vb.
louse
insect 365 n.
cad 938 n.
lousy
not nice 645 adj.
unclean 649 adj.
lout
rude person 885 n.
ruffian 904 n.
loutish
ill-bred 847 adj.
louvre
air pipe 353 n.
lovable
personable 841 adj.
lovable 887 adj.
love
zero 103 n.
liking 859 n.
love 887 n.vb.
loved one 887 n.
lover 887 n.
caress 889 vb.
pet 889 vb.
darling 890 n.
disinterestedness
931 n.
love affair
love affair 887 n.
love all
draw 28 n.
love and peace
concord 710 n.
love child
bastardy 954 n.
loved one
loved one 887 n.
love feast
public worship
981 n.
love-hate
contrary 14 adj.
loveless
indifferent 860 adj.
unwanted 860 adj.
love letter
wooing 889 n.
lovely
super 644 adj.
pleasurable
826 adj.
a beauty 841 n.
lovable 887 adj.
love-making
wooing 889 n.

love-match
type of marriage
894 n.
love philtre
stimulant 174 n.
lover
lover 887 n.
lovesick
loving 887 adj.
love story
novel 590 n.
loving cup
sociability 882 n.
loving-kindness
benevolence 897 n.
loving words
endearment 889 n.
low
inferior 35 adj.
low 210 adj.
muted 401 adj.
ululate 409 vb.
dejected 834 adj.
vulgar 847 adj.
disreputable
867 adj.
humble 872 adj.
rascally 930 adj.
lowborn
plebeian 869 adj.
lowbrow
uninstructed
491 adj.
ignoramus 493 n.
low-budget
cheap 812 adj.
low-caste
inferior 35 adj.
plebeian 869 adj.
low-density
few 105 adj.
lowdown
information 524 n.
lower
(*see* **lour**)
lower
inferior 35 adj.
lower 311 vb.
vulgarize 847 vb.
humiliate 872 vb.
—oneself
demean onself
867 vb.
lower classes
lower classes 869 n.
low-grade
inferior 35 adj.

low-key
 moderate 177 adj.
lowlander
 dweller 191 n.
lowlands
 lowness 210 n.
 plain 348 n.
low-level
 unimportant
  639 adj.
low-life
 wickedness 934 n.
lowly
 plebeian 869 adj.
 humble 872 adj.
low opinion
 disapprobation
  924 n.
lowpaid
 poor 801 adj.
low profile
 secrecy 525 n.
low turnout
 fewness 105 n.
low voice
 voicelessness 578 n.
low water
 poverty 801 n.
loyal
 obedient 739 adj.
 observant 768 adj.
 patriotic 901 adj.
 trustworthy 929 adj.
 disinterested
  931 adj.
loyalist
 defender 713 n.
loyalty
 loyalty 739 n.
lozenge
 angular figure
  247 n.
 medicine 658 n.
lubber
 bungler 697 n.
lubricant
 lubricant 334 n.
lubricate
 smooth 258 vb.
 lubricate 334 vb.
lubricious
 smooth 258 adj.
 impure 951 adj.
lucid
 sane 502 adj.
 perspicuous
  567 adj.

luck
 chance 159 n.
 nondesign 618 n.
 prosperity 730 n.
luck-bringer
 talisman 983 n.
luckless
 unfortunate 731 adj.
lucky
 opportune 137 adj.
 prosperous 730 adj.
 happy 824 adj.
lucky charm
 talisman 983 n.
lucky dip
 medley 43 n.
lucrative
 gainful 771 adj.
lucre
 money 797 n.
Luddite
 destroyer 168 n.
ludicrous
 absurd 497 adj.
 ridiculous 849 adj.
lug
 handle 218 n.
 draw 288 vb.
luggage
 thing transferred
  272 n.
lugger
 merchant ship
  275 n.
lugubrious
 cheerless 834 adj.
lukewarm
 neutral 625 adj.
 indifferent 860 adj.
lull
 discontinuity 72 n.
 lull 145 n.
 assuage 177 vb.
 quiescence 266 n.
 inactivity 679 n.
 repose 683 n.
 peace 717 n.
 relieve 831 vb.
lullaby
 soporific 679 n.
lumbago
 rheumatism 651 n.
lumbar
 back 238 adj.
lumber
 leavings 41 n.
 move slowly 278 vb.

 wood 366 n.
 rubbish 641 n.
lumbering
 unwieldy 195 adj.
 clumsy 695 adj.
lumberjack
 forestry 366 n.
luminary
 star 321 n.
 luminary 420 n.
 sage 500 n.
luminescent
 luminescent
  420 adj.
luminous
 luminous 417 adj.
lump
 bulk 195 n.
 swelling 253 n.
 solid body 324 n.
—together
 not discriminate
  464 vb.
lump in one's throat
 feeling 818 n.
lumpish
 inert 175 adj.
 inactive 679 adj.
lumpy
 rough 259 adj.
 semiliquid 354 adj.
lunacy
 folly 499 n.
 insanity 503 n.
lunar
 celestial 321 adj.
lunar module
 spaceship 276 n.
lunatic
 madman 504 n.
lunatic asylum
 lunatic asylum
  503 n.
lunatic fringe
 crank 504 n.
lunch
 meal 301 n.
lung(s)
 insides 224 n.
 respiration 352 n.
 voice 577 n.
lunge
 lunge 712 n.
lurch
 walk 267 vb.
 oscillate 317 vb.
 be drunk 949 vb.

lure
 tempt 612 vb.
 desired object 859 n.
lurid
 florid 425 adj.
 frightening 854 adj.
lurk
 be unseen 444 vb.
 lurk 523 vb.
luscious
 savoury 390 adj.
 pleasurable 826 adj.
lush
 prolific 171 adj.
 vegetal 366 adj.
lust
 libido 859 n.
 unchastity 951 n.
lustrate
 perform ritual
  988 vb.
lustre
 light 417 n.
lustreless
 dim 419 adj.
lustrous
 luminous 417 adj.
 noteworthy 866 adj.
lusty
 strong 162 adj.
 vigorous 174 adj.
lute
 harp 414 n.
luxuriant
 prolific 171 adj.
 plenteous 635 adj.
luxuriate in
 enjoy 376 vb.
 be intemperate
  943 vb.
luxurious
 comfortable
  376 adj.
 pleasurable 826 adj.
luxury
 superfluity 637 n.
 wealth 800 n.
luxury-lover
 sensualist 944 n.
lye
 solution 337 n.
lying
 false 541 adj.
 untrue 543 adj.
lying down
 supine 216 adj.
 submitting 721 adj.

lymph
fluid 335 n.
lynch
kill 362 vb.
lynch law
anarchy 734 n.
lynx-eyed
seeing 438 adj.
lyophilize
refrigerate 382 vb.
lyre
harp 414 n.
lyric
vocal music 412 n.
poetic 593 adj.
lyrical
poetic 593 adj.
excited 821 adj.
rejoicing 835 adj.
approving 923 adj.

M

macabre
frightening 854 adj.
spooky 970 adj.
macaroni
dish 301 n.
mace
condiment 389 n.
club 723 n.
badge of rule 743 n.
macerate
drench 341 vb.
machete, machet
sharp edge 256 n.
machiavellian
cunning 698 adj.
perfidious 930 adj.
machicolation
fortification 713 n.
machination
plot 623 n.
stratagem 698 n.
machine
produce 164 vb.
machine 630 n.
machinelike
involuntary 596 adj.
machine-made
produced 164 adj.
machinery
machine 630 n.
machinist
machinist 630 n.
artisan 686 n.
machismo
male 372 n.

mackerel
fish food 301 n.
mackintosh
overcoat 228 n.
macramé
network 222 n.
macrocosm
generality 79 n.
macroscopic
large 195 adj.
visible 443 adj.
mad
furious 176 adj.
absurd 497 adj.
insane 503 adj.
angry 891 adj.
madam
lady 373 n.
bawd 952 n.
madcap
foolish 499 adj.
desperado 857 n.
madden
make mad 503 vb.
enrage 891 vb.
made man
prosperous person 730 n.
made to measure
tailored 228 adj.
madhouse
lunatic asylum 503 n.
madman, madwoman
madman 504 n.
madness
insanity 503 n.
Madonna
Madonna 968 n.
madrigal
vocal music 412 n.
maelstrom
vortex 315 n.
pitfall 663 n.
maenad
drunkard 949 n.
maestro
orchestra 413 n.
proficient person 696 n.
Mafia
offender 904 n.
magazine
journal 528 n.
reading matter 589 n.

arsenal 723 n.
firearm 723 n.
maggot
creepy-crawly 365 n.
whim 604 n.
maggoty
unclean 649 adj.
Magi
sage 500 n.
sorcerer 983 n.
magic
influence 178 n.
wonderful 864 adj.
fairylike 970 adj.
sorcery 983 n.
magical
magical 983 adj.
magician
conjuror 545 n.
sorcerer 983 n.
magic instrument
magic instrument 983 n.
magic lantern
optical device 442 n.
magisterial
skilful 694 adj.
ruling 733 adj.
magistracy
magistracy 957 n.
magistrate
judge 957 n.
magnanimity
benevolence 897 n.
magnanimous
forgiving 909 adj.
magnate
bigwig 638 n.
aristocrat 868 n.
magnet
magnet 291 n.
incentive 612 n.
magnetic
dynamic 160 adj.
attracting 291 adj.
magnetic field
energy 160 n.
magnetic needle
sailing aid 269 n.
magnetic tape
data processing 86 n.
hearing-aid 415 n.
magnetism
attraction 291 n.
magnificent

excellent 644 adj.
splendid 841 adj.
ostentatious 875 adj.
magnify
enlarge 197 vb.
exaggerate 546 vb.
make important 638 vb.
worship 981 vb.
magnifying glass
eyeglass 442 n.
magniloquence
magniloquence 574 n.
magnitude
greatness 32 n.
size 195 n.
light 417 n.
importance 638 n.
magnum
vessel 194 n.
magnum opus
masterpiece 694 n.
maharaja
potentate 741 n.
maharishi
religious teacher 973 n.
mahatma
sage 500 n.
mah-jong
indoor game 837 n.
mahogany
tree 366 n.
brownness 430 n.
mahout
rider 268 n.
maid
youngster 132 n.
domestic 742 n.
spinster 895 n.
maiden
first 68 adj.
woman 373 n.
virgin 950 n.
maiden speech
debut 68 n.
maieutic
inquiring 459 adj.
rational 475 adj.
mail
covering 226 n.
send 272 vb.
postal communications 531 n.

armour 713 n.
mailed fist
brute force 735 n.
mailing list
correspondence
588 n.
maim
disable 161 vb.
impair 655 vb.
main
great 32 adj.
supreme 34 adj.
conduit 351 n.
important 638 adj.
main chance
gain 771 n.
main force
compulsion 740 n.
mainframe
counting instrument
86 n.
mainland
inland 344 adj.
mainline
drug oneself 949 vb.
mainmast
sail 275 n.
main part
main part 32 n.
chief thing 638 n.
mainspring
cause 156 n.
motive 612 n.
mainstay
prop 218 n.
chief thing 638 n.
mainstream
greater number
104 n.
tendency 179 n.
Main Street
averageness 732 n.
maintain
sustain 146 vb.
support 218 vb.
affirm 532 vb.
provide 633 vb.
preserve 666 vb.
maintenance
subvention 703 n.
maisonette
flat 192 n.
maize
cereals 301 n.
majestic
impressive 821 adj.
proud 871 adj.

formal 875 adj.
majesty
greatness 32 n.
authority 733 n.
sovereign 741 n.
prestige 866 n.
nobility 868 n.
major
superior 34 adj.
older 131 adj.
important 638 adj.
army officer 741 n.
majority
main part 32 n.
greater number
104 n.
adultness 134 n.
make
composition 56 n.
constitute 56 vb.
sort 77 n.
cause 156 vb.
produce 164 vb.
form 243 vb.
estimate 480 vb.
compel 740 vb.
gain 771 vb.
—**a clean sweep (of)**
revolutionize
149 vb.
—**a comeback**
be restored 656 vb.
—**a fool of oneself**
act foolishly 695 vb.
—**amends**
restitute 787 vb.
atone 941 vb.
—**a show of**
dissemble 541 vb.
be affected 850 vb.
—**away with**
destroy 165 vb.
steal 788 vb.
—**better**
transform 147 vb.
make better 654 vb.
—**capital out of**
use 673 vb.
—**certain**
make certain
473 vb.
—**do with**
substitute 150 vb.
avail oneself of
673 vb.
—**eyes at**
court 889 vb.

—**fast**
tighten 45 vb.
stabilize 153 vb.
—**for**
steer for 281 vb.
—**free with**
appropriate 786 vb.
be insolent 878 vb.
—**fun of**
befool 542 vb.
ridicule 851 vb.
—**good**
succeed 727 vb.
—**hay while the sun
shines**
profit by 137 vb.
—**headway**
progress 285 vb.
get better 654 vb.
—**inroads on**
encroach 306 vb.
waste 634 vb.
—**into**
convert 147 vb.
—**it**
triumph 727 vb.
prosper 730 vb.
—**it up**
make peace 719 vb.
—**light of**
underestimate
483 vb.
do easily 701 vb.
—**love**
unite with 45 vb.
love 887 vb.
—**merry**
rejoice 835 vb.
revel 837 vb.
—**money**
get rich 800 vb.
—**much of**
advertise 528 vb.
make important
638 vb.
honour 866 vb.
pet 889 vb.
—**off with**
steal 788 vb.
—**one jump**
surprise 508 vb.
frighten 854 vb.
—**one of**
be included 78 vb.
—**oneself**
be unwilling 598 vb.
—**out**

see 438 vb.
decipher 520 vb.
succeed 727 vb.
—**over**
transfer 272 vb.
assign 780 vb.
—**overtures**
approach 289 vb.
befriend 880 vb.
—**sense**
be intelligible
516 vb.
—**shift with**
substitute 150 vb.
avail oneself of
673 vb.
—**short work of**
destroy 165 vb.
do easily 701 vb.
—**sure**
make certain
473 vb.
—**terms**
make terms 766 vb.
—**the best of**
compromise 770 vb.
be content 828 vb.
—**the grade**
suffice 635 vb.
—**the most of**
make better 654 vb.
use 673 vb.
—**the running**
outstrip 277 vb.
outdo 306 vb.
—**things worse**
deteriorate 655 vb.
aggravate 832 vb.
—**too much of**
overrate 482 vb.
exaggerate 546 vb.
—**unwelcome**
exclude 57 vb.
make unwelcome
883 vb.
—**up**
constitute 56 vb.
produce 164 vb.
imagine 513 vb.
—**up for**
atone 941 vb.
—**up to**
be servile 879 vb.
flatter 925 vb.
—**way for**
deviate 282 vb.
resign 753 vb.

—worse
aggravate 832 vb.
make-believe
fantasy 513 n.
maker
producer 164 n.
the Deity 965 n.
makeshift
substitute 150 n.
imperfect 647 adj.
unprepared 670 adj.
make-up
character 5 n.
composition 56 n.
structure 331 n.
cosmetic 843 n.
makeweight
offset 31 n.
maladjusted
unapt 25 adj.
insane 503 adj.
maladjustment
discontent 829 n.
maladministration
misuse 675 n.
bungling 695 n.
maladroit
clumsy 695 adj.
malady
disease 651 n.
malaise
suffering 825 n.
malapropism
misnomer 562 n.
solecism 565 n.
malapropos
unapt 25 adj.
ill-timed 138 adj.
malaria
tropical disease
651 n.
malarkey
empty talk 515 n.
malcontent
dissentient 489 n.
malcontent 829 n.
male
male 372 n.adj.
malediction
malediction 899 n.
malefactor
evildoer 904 n.
offender 904 n.
maleficent
maleficent 898 adj.
wicked 934 adj.
malevolence

malevolence 898 n.
malevolent
harmful 645 adj.
malevolent 898 adj.
diabolic 969 adj.
malformation
deformity 246 n.
malfunction
fail 728 vb.
malice
joy 824 n.
malevolence 898 n.
malicious
harmful 645 adj.
malign
harmful 645 adj.
malevolent 898 adj.
defame 926 vb.
malignant
deadly 362 adj.
malevolent 898 adj.
malinger
dissemble 541 vb.
fail in duty 918 vb.
malingerer
impostor 545 n.
malleable
flexible 327 adj.
tractable 701 adj.
impressible 819 adj.
mallet
hammer 279 n.
malnutrition
insufficiency 636 n.
disease 651 n.
malodorous
fetid 397 adj.
malpractice
guilty act 936 n.
maltings
workshop 687 n.
maltreat
ill-treat 645 vb.
misuse 675 vb.
torment 827 vb.
malversation
peculation 788 n.
mammal
mammal 365 n.
Mammon
money 797 n.
devil 969 n.
mammoth
giant 195 n.
animal 365 n.
man
adult 134 n.

operate 173 vb.
humankind 371 n.
male 372 n.
defend 713 vb.
domestic 742 n.
mana
power 160 n.
divineness 965 n.
man/woman about
town
expert 696 n.
beau monde 848 n.
manacle
fetter 747 vb.
manage
be able 160 vb.
look after 457 vb.
undertake 672 vb.
manage 689 vb.
be successful
727 vb.
manageable
tractable 701 adj.
obedient 739 adj.
management
management 689 n.
manager
doer 676 n.
director 690 n.
manager 690 n.
consignee 754 n.
managerial
directing 689 adj.
mañana
inactivity 679 n.
man-at-arms
soldier 722 n.
mandamus
warrant 737 n.
mandarin
fruit 301 n.
official 690 n.
mandate
mandate 751 n.
mandatory
commanding
737 adj.
obligatory 917 adj.
mandibles
eater 301 n.
mane
hair 259 n.
man-eater
noxious animal
904 n.
manège
equitation 267 n.

man Friday
aider 703 n.
manful
courageous 855 adj.
mange
animal disease
651 n.
mangle
distort 246 vb.
extractor 304 n.
drier 342 n.
wound 655 vb.
mangled
incomplete 55 adj.
inexact 495 adj.
mangy
hairless 229 adj.
manhandle
move 265 vb.
man-hater
misanthrope 902 n.
manhole
orifice 263 n.
manhood,
womanhood
adultness 134 n.
manhour(s)
job 622 n.
labour 682 n.
manhunt
chase 619 n.
mania
mania 503 n.
maniac
madman 504 n.
manic
insane 503 adj.
manic depression
psychopathy 503 n.
manicure
beautification 843 n.
manifest
appearing 445 adj.
manifest
522 adj.vb.
show feeling 818 vb.
manifestation
appearance 445 n.
manifestation 522 n.
manifesto
publication 528 n.
manifold
multiform 82 adj.
manikin, mannikin
dwarf 196 n.
manila, manilla
fibre 208 n.

**man/woman in the
    street**
  everyman 79 n.
manipulate
  operate 173 vb.
  touch 378 vb.
  fake 541 vb.
  motivate 612 vb.
  misuse 675 vb.
  manage 689 vb.
manipulator
  motivator 612 n.
mankind
  humankind 371 n.
manly
  grown-up 134 adj.
  strong 162 adj.
  male 372 adj.
  courageous 855 adj.
man-made
  produced 164 adj.
manna
  food 301 n.
manner
  sort 77 n.
  way 624 n.
  conduct 688 n.
mannered
  affected 850 adj.
mannerism
  speciality 80 n.
  style 566 n.
  habit 610 n.
mannerless
  discourteous
    885 adj.
mannerly
  courteous 884 adj.
manners
  etiquette 848 n.
  courtesy 884 n.
mannish
  male 372 adj.
manoeuvrable
  tractable 701 adj.
manoeuvre
  deed 676 n.
  tactics 688 n.
  be cunning 698 vb.
manoeuvrer
  slyboots 698 n.
manoeuvres
  marching 267 n.
  art of war 718 n.
man/woman of action
  doer 676 n.
  busy person 678 n.

**man/woman of
    business**
  merchant 794 n.
**man/woman of
    honour**
  person of repute
    866 n.
**man/woman of
    letters**
  scholar 492 n.
  bookperson 589 n.
**man/woman of
    means**
  rich person 800 n.
**man/woman of
    property**
  prosperous person
    730 n.
  owner 776 n.
man of straw
  insubstantial thing
    4 n.
  nonentity 639 n.
**man/woman of the
    hour**
  person of repute
    866 n.
  favourite 890 n.
**man/woman of the
    people**
  commoner 869 n.
**man/woman of the
    world**
  expert 696 n.
  beau monde 848 n.
**man/woman on the
    spot**
  presence 189 n.
  delegate 754 n.
manor
  house 192 n.
  lands 777 n.
man-o'-war
  warship 722 n.
manpower
  means 629 n.
  personnel 686 n.
manqué
  unsuccessful
    728 adj.
manse
  parsonage 986 n.
mansion
  house 192 n.
manslaughter
  homicide 362 n.
mantelpiece

  shelf 218 n.
mantilla
  headgear 228 n.
mantle
  cover 226 vb.
  cloak 228 n.
  lamp 420 n.
  show feeling 818 vb.
mantra
  maxim 496 n.
mantrap
  trap 542 n.
manual
  textbook 589 n.
  instrumental
    628 adj.
manufacture
  production 164 n.
  produce 164 vb.
  business 622 n.
manufacturer
  producer 164 n.
manure
  fertilizer 171 n.
manuscript
  script 586 n.
  book 589 n.
many
  many 104 adj.
many-sided
  multiform 82 adj.
  skilful 694 adj.
map
  itinerary 267 n.
  map 551 n.
maquette
  sculpture 554 n.
mar
  impair 655 vb.
  blemish 845 vb.
marathon
  distance 199 n.
  contest 716 n.
marauder
  robber 789 n.
marble
  smoothness 258 n.
  white thing 427 n.
  variegate 437 vb.
  unfeeling person
    820 n.
  plaything 837 n.
marcasite
  finery 844 n.
march
  gait 265 n.
  marching 267 n.

  progression 285 n.
  route 624 n.
—against
  charge 712 vb.
marcher
  pedestrian 268 n.
  agitator 738 n.
marches
  limit 236 n.
march-past
  pageant 875 n.
mare
  horse 273 n.
mare's nest
  fable 543 n.
margin
  remainder 41 n.
  room 183 n.
  edge 234 n.
  edition 589 n.
  superfluity 637 n.
marginal
  inconsiderable
    33 adj.
  marginal 234 adj.
**marijuana,
    marihuana**
  drug-taking 949 n.
marina
  stable 192 n.
  shelter 662 n.
marinade, marinate
  preserve 666 vb.
marine
  seafaring 269 adj.
  shipping 275 n.
  naval man 722 n.
mariner
  mariner 270 n.
marionette
  image 551 n.
  plaything 837 n.
marital
  matrimonial
    894 adj.
maritime
  marine 275 adj.
  oceanic 343 adj.
marjoram
  potherb 301 n.
mark
  sort 77 n.
  speciality 80 n.
  feature 445 n.
  identification 547 n.
  mark 547 vb.
  trace 548 n.

importance 638 n.
blemish 845 n.vb.
—**down**
cheapen 812 vb.
—**out**
set apart 46 vb.
indicate 547 vb.
—**time**
time 117 vb.
be quiescent 266 vb.
await 507 vb.
—**up**
overcharge 811 vb.
marker
indication 547 n.
market
sell 793 vb.
market 796 n.
market garden
farm 370 n.
marketplace
focus 76 n.
market 796 n.
market research
inquiry 459 n.
markings
identification 547 n.
marksman,
   markswoman
shooter 287 n.
marksmanship
skill 694 n.
marl
soil 344 n.
marmalade
sweet thing 392 n.
marmoreal
glyptic 554 adj.
maroon
red 431 adj.
signal 547 n.
solitary 883 n.
marquee
canopy 226 n.
marquetry
ornamental art
  844 n.
marriage
union 45 n.
marriage 894 n.
marriageable
grown-up 134 adj.
marriage broker
intermediary
  231 n.
marriage of
  convenience

type of marriage
  894 n.
marrow
substance 3 n.
essential part 5 n.
vegetable 301 n.
marry
marry 894 vb.
wed 894 vb.
marsh
marsh 347 n.
marshal
arrange 62 vb.
official 690 n.
marshy
marshy 347 adj.
semiliquid 354 adj.
dirty 649 adj.
marsupial
mammal 365 n.
martial
warlike 718 adj.
courageous 855 adj.
martial law
brute force 735 n.
Martian
foreigner 59 n.
planetary 321 adj.
martinet
tyrant 735 n.
martyr
kill 362 vb.
torment 827 vb.
pietist 979 n.
martyrdom
death 361 n.
pain 377 n.
suffering 825 n.
honours 866 n.
marvel
prodigy 864 n.
wonder 864 vb.
marvellous
prodigious 32 adj.
excellent 644 adj.
pleasurable 826 adj.
wonderful 864 adj.
Marxism
philosophy 449 n.
Marxist
revolutionist 149 n.
political party 708 n.
marzipan
sweet thing 392 n.
mascara
cosmetic 843 n.
mascot

talisman 983 n.
masculine
generic 77 adj.
male 372 adj.
mash
soften 327 vb.
pulverize 332 vb.
pulpiness 356 n.
mask
screen 421 n.vb.
conceal 525 n.
disguise 527 n.
masochist
nonconformist 84 n.
sensualist 944 n.
mason
artisan 686 n.
Masonic
sectional 708 adj.
masonry
building material
  631 n.
masque
stage play 594 n.
masquerade
disguise 527 n.
masquerader
impostor 545 n.
mass
quantity 26 n.
main part 32 n.
chief part 52 n.
accumulation 74 n.
crowd 74 n.
general 79 adj.
greater number
  104 n.
bulk 195 n.
size 195 n.
matter 319 n.
gravity 322 n.
solid body 324 n.
public worship
  981 n.
massacre
slaughter 362 n.vb.
massage
friction 333 n.
touch 378 n.vb.
surgery 658 n.
beautification 843 n.
massed
multitudinous
  104 adj.
dense 324 adj.
masses, the
commonalty 869 n.

masseur, masseuse
doctor 658 n.
massive
great 32 adj.
large 195 adj.
weighty 322 adj.
mass media
information 524 n.
mass meeting
assembly 74 n.
mass production
uniformity 16 n.
production 164 n.
productiveness 171 n.
mast
prop 218 n.
sail 275 n.
mastectomy
surgery 658 n.
master
sage 500 n.
understand 516 vb.
teacher 537 n.
proficient person
  696 n.
victor 727 n.
master 741 n.
—**one's feelings**
keep calm 823 vb.
masterful
skilful 694 adj.
authoritative
  733 adj.
master key
instrument 628 n.
masterless
independent
  744 adj.
masterly
skilful 694 adj.
mastermind
intellectual 492 n.
planner 623 n.
direct 689 vb.
master of ceremonies
leader 690 n.
reveller 837 n.
masterpiece
exceller 644 n.
masterpiece 694 n.
master plan
plan 623 n.
master spirit
sage 500 n.
masterstroke
contrivance 623 n.
masterpiece 694 n.

mastery
  knowledge 490 n.
  skill 694 n.
  victory 727 n.
mastic
  resin 357 n.
masticate
  chew 301 vb.
mastiff
  dog 365 n.
mat
  enlace 222 vb.
  floor-cover 226 n.
matador
  killer 362 n.
match
  analogue 18 n.
  resemble 18 vb.
  compeer 28 n.
  pair 90 vb.
  lighter 385 n.
  compare 462 vb.
  contest 716 n.
  marriage 894 n.
—against
  oppose 704 vb.
matchless
  supreme 34 adj.
  best 644 adj.
matchlock
  firearm 723 n.
matchmaker
  intermediary 231 n.
matchwood
  weak thing 163 n.
mate
  analogue 18 n.
  unite with 45 vb.
  pair 90 vb.
  mariner 270 n.
  colleague 707 n.
  chum 880 n.
  spouse 894 n.
material
  real 1 adj.
  substantiality 3 n.
  textile 222 n.
  matter 319 n.
  information 524 n.
  materials 631 n.
  important 638 adj.
materialism
  materiality 319 n.
materialistic
  selfish 932 adj.
materialize
  happen 154 vb.

materialize 319 vb.
  appear 445 vb.
materials
  means 629 n.
  materials 631 n.
maternal
  parental 169 adj.
  benevolent
    897 adj.
maternity
  maternity 169 n.
matey
  friendly 880 adj.
mathematical
  statistical 86 adj.
  accurate 494 adj.
mathematician
  enumerator 86 n.
mathematics
  mathematics 86 n.
matinée
  dramaturgy
    594 n.
matins
  church service
    988 n.
matriarch
  maternity 169 n.
  master 741 n.
matriculation
  exam 459 n.
matrimony
  marriage 894 n.
matrix
  mould 23 n.
  number 85 n.
matron
  woman 373 n.
  nurse 658 n.
  manager 690 n.
  spouse 894 n.
matronly
  grown-up 134 adj.
matt, mat
  soft-hued 425 adj.
matted
  hairy 259 adj.
  dense 324 adj.
matter
  substantiality 3 n.
  matter 319 n.
  solid body 324 n.
  topic 452 n.
  be important
    638 vb.
  ulcer 651 n.
matter of course

  lack of wonder
    865 n.
matter of fact
  reality 1 n.
  prosaic 593 adj.
matters
  affairs 154 n.
matting
  floor-cover 226 n.
mattress
  cushion 218 n.
mature
  grown-up 134 adj.
  perfect 646 vb.
  matured 669 adj.
  mature 669 vb.
maturity
  adultness 134 n.
  completion 725 n.
matutinal
  matinal 128 adj.
maudlin
  feeling 818 adj.
  tipsy 949 adj.
maul
  ill-treat 645 vb.
  wound 655 vb.
  dispraise 924 vb.
maunder
  move slowly 278 vb.
  be diffuse 570 vb.
mausoleum
  tomb 364 n.
mauve
  purple 436 adj.
maverick
  nonconformist 84 n.
  nonobservant
    769 adj.
maw
  maw 194 n.
mawkish
  feeling 818 adj.
maxim
  maxim 496 n.
maximize
  exaggerate 546 vb.
maximum
  superiority 34 n.
  plenitude 54 n.
  size 195 n.
may
  be possible 469 vb.
maya
  insubstantiality 4 n.
mayhem
  disorder 61 n.

mayonnaise
  sauce 389 n.
mayor
  councillor 692 n.
maze
  complexity 61 n.
  meandering 251 n.
  enigma 530 n.
mazurka
  dance 837 n.
McCarthyism
  phobia 854 n.
me
  subjectivity 320 n.
mead
  alcoholic drink
    301 n.
meadow(s)
  grassland 348 n.
meagre
  small 33 adj.
  lean 206 adj.
  economical 814 adj.
meagreness
  scarcity 636 n.
meal
  cereals 301 n.
  meal 301 n.
mealy-mouthed
  hypocritical
    541 adj.
mean
  average 30 n.
  middle 70 n.
  statistics 86 n.
  mean 514 vb.
  represent 551 vb.
  bad 645 adj.
  parsimonious
    816 adj.
  disreputable
    867 adj.
  plebeian 869 adj.
  unkind 898 adj.
—to
  intend 617 vb.
—well
  be benevolent
    897 vb.
meander
  meander 251 vb.
meanie
  niggard 816 n.
meaning
  meaning 514 n.
  interpretation
    520 n.

MEA

meaningful
meaningful 514 adj.
intelligible 516 adj.
meaningless
meaningless 515 adj.
mean-minded
selfish 932 adj.
meanness
parsimony 816 n.
means
contrivance 623 n.
instrumentality
628 n.
means 629 n.
funds 797 n.
mean-spirited
cowardly 856 adj.
servile 879 adj.
means test
inquiry 459 n.
meanwhile
while 108 adv.
measles
infection 651 n.
measly
unimportant
639 adj.
bad 645 adj.
measure
finite quantity 26 n.
moderation 177 n.
measure 183 n.
size 195 n.
tempo 410 n.
gauge 465 n.
measure 465 vb.
estimate 480 vb.
prosody 593 n.
deed 676 n.
portion 783 n.
—up to
be able 160 vb.
measured
periodical 141 adj.
moderate 177 adj.
measureless
infinite 107 adj.
measurement
size 195 n.
measurement 465 n.
(*see* **measure**)
measures
policy 623 n.
action 676 n.
meat
food 301 n.
meat 301 n.

MED

Mecca
focus 76 n.
mechanic
machinist 630 n.
mechanical
involuntary 596 adj.
mechanical 630 adj.
mechanics
mechanics 630 n.
mechanism
machine 630 n.
mechanize
produce 164 vb.
medal
badge 547 n.
decoration 729 n.
medallion
jewellery 844 n.
medallist
victor 727 n.
meddle
be curious 453 vb.
meddle 678 vb.
obstruct 702 vb.
mediate 720 vb.
meddler
meddler 678 n.
media, the
publication 528 n.
broadcasting 531 n.
medial
middle 70 adj.
median
average 30 n.
media personality
broadcaster 531 n.
favourite 890 n.
mediate
mediate 720 vb.
mediation
mediation 720 n.
mediator
intermediary 231 n.
mediator 720 n.
medicable
restored 656 adj.
medical
inquiry 459 n.
medical 658 adj.
medical care
therapy 658 n.
medical officer
sanitarian 652 n.
doctor 658 n.
medical practitioner
doctor 658 n.
medicament

MEE

medicine 658 n.
medicate
cure 656 vb.
doctor 658 vb.
medication
medicine 658 n.
medicinal
remedial 658 adj.
medicine
medical art 658 n.
medicine 658 n.
medicine man
sorcerer 983 n.
medieval, mediaeval
olden 127 adj.
**medievalist,
mediaevalist**
antiquarian 125 n.
mediocre
inferior 35 adj.
middling 732 adj.
mediocrity
nonentity 639 n.
meditate
meditate 449 vb.
intend 617 vb.
meditation
meditation 449 n.
prayers 981 n.
medium
average 30 n.
instrumentality
628 n.
psychic 984 n.
medley
medley 43 n.
confusion 61 n.
meek
obedient 739 adj.
humble 872 adj.
meet
fit 24 adj.
congregate 74 vb.
meet with 154 vb.
converge 293 vb.
meet 295 vb.
—an obligation
grant claims 915 vb.
—halfway
pacify 719 vb.
meeting
assembly 74 n.
collision 279 n.
convergence 293 n.
conference 584 n.
social gathering
882 n.

MEL

meeting place
focus 76 n.
meeting place
192 n.
megalith
antiquity 125 n.
megalithic
huge 195 adj.
megalomania
mania 503 n.
vanity 873 n.
megalopolis
city 184 n.
megaphone
megaphone 400 n.
megaton
weighing 322 n.
melancholic
madman 504 n.
melancholy
psychopathy 503 n.
unhappy 825 adj.
melancholy 834 n.
melanin
black pigment
428 n.
mêlée, melee
turmoil 61 n.
fight 716 n.
meliorate
make better 654 vb.
mellifluous
melodious 410 adj.
mellow
soften 327 vb.
soft-hued 425 adj.
get better 654 vb.
mature 669 vb.
drunk 949 adj.
melodic
melodious 410 adj.
melodious
melodious 410 adj.
pleasurable 826 adj.
melodrama
stage play 594 n.
melodramatic
exaggerated
546 adj.
exciting 821 adj.
melody
melody 410 n.
melt
be dispersed 75 vb.
liquefy 337 vb.
heat 381 vb.
pity 905 vb.

—away
decrease 37 vb.
disappear 446 vb.
waste 634 vb.
meltdown
ruin 165 n.
melting pot
mixture 43 n.
member
part 53 n.
component 58 n.
society 708 n.
participator 775 n.
membership
inclusion 78 n.
association 706 n.
participation 775 n.
membrane
skin 226 n.
memento
reminder 505 n.
memo
reminder 505 n.
memoir(s)
record 548 n.
biography 590 n.
memorabilia
remembrance 505 n.
record 548 n.
memorable
remembered
505 adj.
notable 638 adj.
memorandum
reminder 505 n.
record 548 n.
memorial
monument 548 n.
trophy 729 n.
memorize
memorize 505 vb.
learn 536 vb.
memory
memory 505 n.
storage 632 n.
famousness 866 n.
menace
danger 661 n.
threat 900 n.
ménage à trois
type of marriage
894 n.
menagerie
zoo 369 n.
collection 632 n.
mend
get better 654 vb.

repair 656 vb.
—one's ways
get better 654 vb.
mendacity
falsehood 541 n.
mendicant
beggar 763 n.
menial
inferior 35 adj.
servant 742 n.
meniscus
optical device 442 n.
menopause
middle age 131 n.
menses
haemorrhage 302 n.
menstrual
seasonal 141 adj.
excretory 302 adj.
mensurable
numerable 86 adj.
measured 465 adj.
mensuration
measurement 465 n.
mental
mental 447 adj.
insane 503 adj.
mental block
oblivion 506 n.
mental capacity
intellect 447 n.
intelligence 498 n.
mental deficiency
unintelligence
499 n.
mental dishonesty
mental dishonesty
543 n.
mental hospital
lunatic asylum
503 n.
mental illness
insanity 503 n.
mentality
intellect 447 n.
affections 817 n.
mentally
   handicapped
unintelligent
499 adj.
mental reservation
mental dishonesty
543 n.
mention
referral 9 n.
notice 455 vb.
hint 524 vb.

speak 579 vb.
mentor
teacher 537 n.
adviser 691 n.
menu
meal 301 n.
mephitis
stench 397 n.
insalubrity 653 n.
mercantile
businesslike
622 adj.
trading 791 adj.
mercenary
militarist 722 n.
avaricious
816 adj.
venal 930 adj.
selfish 932 adj.
mercerize
be tough 329 vb.
merchandise
merchandise
795 n.
merchant
merchant 794 n.
merciful
lenient 736 adj.
pitying 905 adj.
merciless
severe 735 adj.
pitiless 906 adj.
mercurial
changeful 152 adj.
unstable 152 adj.
speedy 277 adj.
light-minded
456 adj.
irresolute 601 adj.
capricious 604 adj.
mercy
mercy 905 n.
mere
inconsiderable
33 adj.
lake 346 n.
meretricious
spurious 542 adj.
ornate 574 adj.
vulgar 847 adj.
merge
mix 43 vb.
combine 50 vb.
be included 78 vb.
cooperate 706 vb.
—into
be turned to 147 vb.

merger
union 45 n.
association 706 n.
meridian
noon 128 n.
summit 213 n.
merit
goodness 644 n.
deserve 915 vb.
virtues 933 n.
meritocracy
elite 644 n.
meritorious
deserving 915 adj.
approvable 923 adj.
mermaid
mythical being
970 n.
merry
merry 833 adj.
amusing 837 adj.
merry-go-round
rotator 315 n.
merry-maker
reveller 837 n.
mescalin, mescaline
drug-taking 949 n.
mesh(es)
unite with 45 vb.
gap 201 n.
network 222 n.
trap 542 n.
mesmerize
render insensible
375 vb.
frighten 854 vb.
mesomorphic
stalwart 162 adj.
meson
element 319 n.
mess
confusion 61 n.
predicament
700 n.
message
message 529 n.
messenger
messenger 529 n.
messiah
leader 690 n.
religious teacher
973 n.
mess kit
uniform 228 n.
messmate
eater 301 n.
chum 880 n.

messy
  orderless
    61 adj.
  dirty 649 adj.
metal
  hardness 326 n.
  mineral 359 n.
metal detector
  detector 484 n.
metalled
  communicating
    624 adj.
metallic
  inorganic 359 adj.
  strident 407 adj.
metallurgy
  mineralogy 359 n.
metalwork
  ornamental art
    844 n.
metamorphose
  transform 147 vb.
metaphor
  metaphor 519 n.
  ornament 574 n.
metaphorical
  semantic 514 adj.
  figurative 519 adj.
metaphysics
  existence 1 n.
  philosophy 449 n.
metastasis
  transference 272 n.
metathesis
  transference 272 n.
  trope 519 n.
metempsychosis
  transformation
    143 n.
meteor
  meteor 321 n.
meteoric
  brief 114 adj.
  speedy 277 adj.
meteorite
  meteor 321 n.
meteorologist
  weather 340 n.
  oracle 511 n.
mete out
  apportion 783 vb.
meter
  gauge 465 vb.
  detector 484 n.
methane
  gas 336 n.
method

  order 60 n.
  regularity 81 n.
  way 624 n.
methodical
  orderly 60 adj.
  regular 81 adj.
methodological
  rational 475 adj.
Methuselah
  old person 133 n.
meticulous
  careful 457 adj.
  accurate 494 adj.
  fastidious 862 adj.
metre
  prosody 593 n.
metric
  metrical 465 adj.
metrology
  metrology 465 n.
metronome
  timekeeper 117 n.
metropolis
  city 184 n.
metropolitan
  dweller 191 n.
  central 225 adj.
  ecclesiarch 986 n.
mettle
  vigorousness 174 n.
  resolution 599 n.
mettlesome
  vigorous 174 adj.
  lively 819 adj.
  courageous 855 adj.
mewl
  cry 408 vb.
  ululate 409 vb.
mews
  flat 192 n.
  stable 192 n.
mezzanine
  layer 207 n.
mezzotint
  engraving 555 n.
miaow
  ululate 409 vb.
miasma
  stench 397 n.
  insalubrity 653 n.
  poison 659 n.
micro-
  minute 196 adj.
microbe
  microorganism
    196 n.
microbiology

  biology 358 n.
microchip
  microelectronics
    196 n.
microcosm
  miniature 196 n.
  universe 321 n.
microelectronics
  counting instrument
    86 n.
  electronics 160 n.
  microelectronics
    196 n.
microfiche,
  microfilm
  record 548 n.
micrometry
  measurement 465 n.
  accuracy 494 n.
microorganism
  microorganism
    196 n.
microphone
  megaphone 400 n.
  hearing aid 415 n.
  telecommunication
    531 n.
microprocessor
  counting instrument
    86 n.
  microelectronics
    196 n.
microscope
  microscopy 196 n.
  microscope 442 n.
microscopic
  minute 196 adj.
microwave
  radiation 417 n.
mid
  middle 70 adj.
  between 231 adv.
Midas touch
  prosperity 730 n.
  wealth 800 n.
midday
  noon 128 n.
midden
  rubbish 641 n.
middle
  middle 70 n.adj.
  centre 225 n.
  interjacent 231 adj.
middle age
  middle age 131 n.
Middle Ages
  antiquity 125 n.

middlebrow
  median 30 adj.
middle classes
  middle classes
    869 n.
middleman
  intermediary
    231 n.
  agent 686 n.
middle-of-the-road
  neutral 625 adj.
middling
  not bad 644 adj.
  middling 732 adj.
midge
  insect 365 n.
midget
  dwarf 196 n.
midnight
  midnight 129 n.
midriff
  partition 231 n.
midst
  middle 70 n.
  between 231 adv.
midstream
  middle way 625 n.
midsummer
  summer 128 n.
midway
  midway 70 adv.
midwife
  obstetrics 167 n.
  instrument 628 n.
  doctor 658 n.
midwinter
  winter 129 n.
mien
  mien 445 n.
  conduct 688 n.
might
  power 160 n.
  strength 162 n.
  be possible 469 vb.
might and main
  exertion 682 n.
mighty
  great 32 adj.
  powerful 160 adj.
  strong 162 adj.
  influential 178 adj.
  worshipful 866 adj.
migraine
  pang 377 n.
migrant
  wanderer 268 n.
  bird 365 n.

migration
  departure 296 n.
migratory
  travelling 267 adj.
milch cow
  abundance 171 n.
mild
  moderate 177 adj.
  warm 379 adj.
  amiable 884 adj.
mildew
  blight 659 n.
mileage
  distance 199 n.
  length 203 n.
  utility 640 n.
milepost
  signpost 547 n.
milestone
  degree 27 n.
  serial place 73 n.
  event 154 n.
  signpost 547 n.
milieu
  circumstance 8 n.
  surroundings 230 n.
militant
  busy person 678 n.
  opposing 704 adj.
  attacking 712 adj.
militarism
  bellicosity 718 n.
military
  warlike 718 adj.
militate against
  counteract 182 vb.
militia
  defender 713 n.
  army 722 n.
milk
  milk 301 n.
  extract 304 vb.
  take 786 vb.
—dry
  waste 634 vb.
milk and water
  insipidity 387 n.
milkmaid
  herdsman 369 n.
milksop
  weakling 163 n.
  ninny 501 n.
milky
  semitransparent
    424 adj.
  whitish 427 adj.
mill

notch 260 vb.
  pulverizer 332 n.
  workshop 687 n.
—around
  congregate 74 vb.
  be agitated 318 vb.
millennium
  future state 124 n.
  aspiration 852 n.
millet
  cereals 301 n.
millinery
  headgear 228 n.
million
  over one hundred
    99 n.
  multitude 104 n.
millionaire,
  millionairess
  rich person 800 n.
millstone
  pulverizer 332 n.
  encumbrance 702 n.
mime
  mimicry 20 n.
  gesticulate 547 vb.
  act 594 vb.
mimesis
  representation
    551 n.
mimic
  imitator 20 n.
  actor 594 n.
  satirize 851 vb.
minaret
  high structure 209 n.
minatory
  threatening 900 adj.
mince
  rend 46 vb.
  meat 301 n.
  pulverize 332 vb.
  be affected 850 vb.
—matters
  be fastidious 862 vb.
mind
  intellect 447 n.
  spirit 447 n.
  be careful 457 vb.
  look after 457 vb.
  opinion 485 n.
  intention 617 n.
  resent 891 vb.
mind-bending,
  mind-blowing
  intoxicating 949 adj.
mind-boggling

wonderful 864 adj.
minder
  machinist 630 n.
mindful
  attentive 455 adj.
  remembering
    505 adj.
mindless
  mindless 448 adj.
  unthinking 450 adj.
mind of one's own
  obstinacy 602 n.
mind reader
  psychic 984 n.
mind's eye
  imagination 513 n.
mine
  great quantity 32 n.
  demolish 165 vb.
  excavation 255 n.
  extract 304 vb.
  store 632 n.
  bomb 723 n.
minefield
  pitfall 663 n.
  defences 713 n.
miner
  excavator 255 n.
  extractor 304 n.
mineral
  mineral 359 n.
mineralogy
  mineralogy 359 n.
mineral water
  soft drink 301 n.
minesweeper
  warship 722 n.
mingle
  mix 43 vb.
mingy
  parsimonious
    816 adj.
mini-
  little 196 adj.
miniature
  little 196 adj.
  picture 553 n.
minibus
  bus 274 n.
minikin
  dwarf 196 n.
minim
  notation 410 n.
minimal
  small 33 adj.
  lesser 35 adj.
minimize

abate 37 vb.
  underestimate
    483 vb.
  detract 926 vb.
minimum
  small quantity 33 n.
  sufficiency 635 n.
minion
  dependant 742 n.
minister
  agent 686 n.
  envoy 754 n.
  pastor 986 n.
—to
  minister to 703 vb.
ministerial
  governmental
    733 adj.
ministration
  ministration 988 n.
ministry
  vocation 622 n.
  management 689 n.
  clergy 986 n.
mink
  skin 226 n.
minor
  inconsiderable
    33 adj.
  lesser 35 adj.
  youth 130 n.
  unimportant
    639 adj.
minority
  fewness 105 n.
  nonage 130 n.
minstrel
  musician 413 n.
  entertainer 594 n.
mint
  mould 23 n.
  potherb 301 n.
  workshop 687 n.
  mint 797 vb.
mint condition
  perfection 646 n.
minuet
  dance 837 n.
minus
  nonexistent 2 adj.
  deficient 307 adj.
  losing 772 adj.
minute
  period 110 n.
  minute 196 adj.
  careful 457 adj.
  record 548 vb.

minutiae
particulars 80 n.
trifle 639 n.
minx
insolent person
878 n.
miracle
prodigy 864 n.
miraculous
unusual 84 adj.
wonderful 864 adj.
mirage
insubstantial thing
4 n.
visual fallacy 440 n.
deception 542 n.
mire
marsh 347 n.
mirror
resemble 18 vb.
mirror 442 n.
show 522 vb.
mirror image
reflection 417 n.
mirth
merriment 833 n.
misadventure
misfortune 731 n.
misalliance
type of marriage
894 n.
misanthropist
misanthrope 902 n.
misapplication
misuse 675 n.
misapprehend
err 495 vb.
misapprehension
misinterpretation
521 n.
misappropriation
misuse 675 n.
peculation 788 n.
misbegotten
contemptible
922 adj.
bastard 954 adj.
misbehave
be foolish 499 vb.
behave 688 vb.
disobey 738 vb.
miscalculation
misjudgement
481 n.
mistake 495 n.
miscall
misname 562 vb.

miscarriage
failure 728 n.
miscarry
miscarry 728 vb.
miscegenation
type of marriage
894 n.
miscellaneous
nonuniform 17 adj.
mixed 43 adj.
miscellany
accumulation 74 n.
anthology 592 n.
mischance
misfortune 731 n.
mischief
evil 616 n.
impairment 655 n.
mischiefmaker
troublemaker 663 n.
agitator 738 n.
mischievous
destructive 165 adj.
harmful 645 adj.
disobedient 738 adj.
malevolent 898 adj.
misconceive
misjudge 481 vb.
misinterpret 521 vb.
misconduct
be unskilful 695 vb.
guilty act 936 n.
misconstrue
misinterpret 521 vb.
miscreant
knave 938 n.
misdeed
guilty act 936 n.
misdemeanour
guilty act 936 n.
lawbreaking 954 n.
misdirect
mislead 495 vb.
misdoing
wrong 914 n.
guilty act 936 n.
mise-en-scène
stage set 594 n.
miser
niggard 816 n.
miserable
unimportant
639 adj.
unfortunate 731 adj.
unhappy 825 adj.
misery
adversity 731 n.

sorrow 825 n.
moper 834 n.
misfeasance
lawbreaking 954 n.
misfire
bungling 695 n.
misfit
unrelatedness 10 n.
misfit 25 n.
displacement 188 n.
misfortune
misfortune 731 n.
misgiving(s)
doubt 486 n.
misguided
misjudging 481 adj.
mistaken 495 adj.
mishandle
ill-treat 645 vb.
be unskilful 695 vb.
mishap
misfortune 731 n.
mishit
be clumsy 695 vb.
mishmash
medley 43 n.
misinform
mislead 495 vb.
be false 541 vb.
misinterpret
misjudge 481 vb.
blunder 495 vb.
misinterpret 521 vb.
misjudge
mistime 138 vb.
misjudge 481 vb.
misinterpret 521 vb.
misjudgement
misjudgement
481 n.
mistake 495 n.
mislaid
misplaced 188 adj.
mislay
derange 63 vb.
lose 772 vb.
mislead
mislead 495 vb.
befool 542 vb.
mismanage
misuse 675 vb.
be unskilful 695 vb.
mismatched
disagreeing 25 adj.
misnomer
misnomer 562 n.
misogyny

celibacy 895 n.
misanthropy 902 n.
misplace
misplace 188 vb.
misplaced
irrelevant 10 adj.
unapt 25 adj.
misplaced 188 adj.
misprint
mistake 495 n.
misprize
underestimate
483 vb.
mispronounce
be ungrammatical
565 vb.
misproportion
distortion 246 n.
misquote
blunder 495 vb.
misread
misinterpret 521 vb.
misrepresent
distort 246 vb.
misinterpret 521 vb.
satirize 851 vb.
misrepresentation
untruth 543 n.
misrepresentation
552 n.
miss
youngster 132 n.
fall short 307 vb.
blunder 495 vb.
fail 728 vb.
lose 772 vb.
regret 830 vb.
—out
exclude 57 vb.
—the boat/bus
lose a chance
138 vb.
missal
office-book 988 n.
misshape
distort 246 vb.
missile
missile 287 n.
missile weapon
rocket 276 n.
missile weapon
723 n.
missing
nonexistent 2 adj.
absent 190 adj.
required 627 adj.
lost 772 adj.

missing link
  discontinuity 72 n.
mission
  vocation 622 n.
  mandate 751 n.
  envoy 754 n.
  philanthropy 901 n.
  church ministry
    985 n.
missionary
  preacher 537 n.
  religious teacher
    973 n.
missive
  correspondence
    588 n.
misspell
  be ungrammatical
    565 vb.
misstatement
  untruth 543 n.
mist
  cloud 355 n.
  opacity 423 n.
  blur 440 vb.
  invisibility 444 n.
  uncertainty 474 n.
mistake
  mistake 495 n.
  solecism 565 n.
mistaken
  misjudging 481 adj.
misteach
  misteach 535 vb.
mistime
  mistime 138 vb.
mistreatment
  misuse 675 n.
mistress
  lady 373 n.
  master 741 n.
  owner 776 n.
  loved one 887 n.
mistrust
  doubt 486 n.vb.
misty
  cloudy 355 adj.
  dim 419 adj.
  opaque 423 adj.
  indistinct 444 adj.
misunderstand
  err 495 vb.
  misinterpret 521 vb.
misunderstanding
  dissension 709 n.
misuse
  waste 634 n.vb.

misuse 675 n.vb.
mite
  small quantity
    33 n.
  child 132 n.
  insect 365 n.
mitigate
  moderate 177 vb.
  qualify 468 vb.
  relieve 831 vb.
  extenuate 927 vb.
mitre
  joint 45 n.
  vestments 989 n.
mitt
  glove 228 n.
  feeler 378 n.
mix
  mix 43 vb.
  jumble 63 vb.
mixed-ability
  educational 534 adj.
mixed bag
  medley 43 n.
mixed blessing
  inexpedience 643 n.
mixture
  mixture 43 n.
  composition 56 n.
  medicine 658 n.
mix-up
  confusion 61 n.
mnemonic
  reminder 505 n.
moan
  cry 408 vb.
  be discontented
    829 vb.
moat
  fence 235 n.
  conduit 351 n.
  defences 713 n.
mob
  rampage 61 vb.
  crowd 74 n.
  multitude 104 n.
  pursue 619 vb.
  charge 712 vb.
  rabble 869 n.
  congratulate 886 vb.
mobile
  moving 265 adj.
  sculpture 554 n.
mobility
  changeableness
    152 n.
mobilize

bring together
    74 vb.
  make ready 669 vb.
mob law
  anarchy 734 n.
mobster
  offender 904 n.
mock
  simulating 18 adj.
  spurious 542 adj.
  ridicule 851 n.vb.
  not respect 921 vb.
mocker
  detractor 926 n.
mockery
  insubstantial thing
    4 n.
  mimicry 20 n.
mock-heroic
  derisive 851 adj.
mock modesty
  affectation 850 n.
mock-up
  exhibit 522 n.
mod
  youngster 132 n.
  fop 848 n.
modal
  such 7 adj.
  circumstantial 8 adj.
mode
  modality 7 n.
  statistics 86 n.
  key 410 n.
  way 624 n.
  fashion 848 n.
model
  copy 22 n.
  prototype 23 n.
  little 196 adj.
  form 243 vb.
  image 551 n.
  sculpt 554 vb.
  plan 623 n.
  paragon 646 n.
  perfect 646 adj.
moderate
  median 30 adj.
  moderate
    177 adj.vb.
  qualify 468 vb.
  moderate 625 n.
  political party 708 n.
  relieve 831 vb.
moderation
  moderation 177 n.
  pacification 719 n.

temperance 942 n.
moderator
  moderator 177 n.
  ecclesiarch 986 n.
modern
  modern 126 adj.
  fashionable 848 adj.
modernism
  modernism 126 n.
modernize
  modernize 126 vb.
  modify 143 vb.
  revolutionize
    149 vb.
  restore 656 vb.
modest
  inconsiderable
    33 adj.
  middling 732 adj.
  modest 874 adj.
modesty
  modesty 874 n.
modicum
  small quantity 33 n.
  portion 783 n.
modification
  change 143 n.
  qualification 468 n.
modify
  modify 143 vb.
modish
  fashionable 848 adj.
modiste
  clothier 228 n.
modular
  metrical 465 adj.
modulate
  adjust 24 vb.
modulation
  change 143 n.
  key 410 n.
  voice 577 n.
module
  prototype 23 n.
  component 58 n.
modus operandi
  way 624 n.
modus vivendi
  way 624 n.
  compromise 770 n.
mogul
  bigwig 638 n.
  sovereign 741 n.
mohair
  textile 222 n.
Mohammedanism
  religious faith 973 n.

moiety
bisection 92 n.
portion 783 n.

moiré
iridescent 437 adj.

moist
humid 341 adj.

moisten
moisten 341 vb.

moisture
moisture 341 n.

molar
tooth 256 n.

molasses
sweet thing 392 n.

mole
projection 254 n.
mammal 365 n.
latency 523 n.
informer 524 n.
safeguard 662 n.
blemish 845 n.

molecule
element 319 n.

molehill
small hill 209 n.

molest
torment 827 vb.
debauch 951 vb.

moll
kept woman 952 n.

mollify
pacify 719 vb.

mollusc
marine life 365 n.

mollycoddle
weakling 163 n.
ninny 501 n.

molten
liquefied 337 adj.
fiery 379 adj.

moment
brief span 114 n.
instant 116 n.
occasion 137 n.
cause 156 n.
importance 638 n.

momentary
brief 114 adj.

momentous
crucial 137 adj.
eventful 154 adj.
influential 178 adj.
important 638 adj.

momentum
impulse 279 n.

monarch

sovereign 741 n.

monarchy
government 733 n.

monasticism
seclusion 883 n.
celibacy 895 n.
monasticism 985 n.

monaural
sounding 398 adj.

monetarist
economy 814 n.

monetary
monetary 797 adj.

money
money 797 n.

moneybox
treasury 799 n.

money-changer
minter 797 n.

money for jam/old rope
easy thing 701 n.

money-grubber
niggard 816 n.

moneylender
lender 784 n.

money-making
gainful 771 adj.
wealth 800 n.

money-saving
economical 814 adj.

mongolism
unintelligence 499 n.

mongrel
hybrid 43 n.
dog 365 n.

monitor
listener 415 n.
inquire 459 vb.
adviser 691 n.

monitory
cautionary 664 adj.

monk
monk 986 n.

monkey
mammal 365 n.
bad person 938 n.

monkey tricks
foolery 497 n.
disobedience 738 n.

monkish
unwedded 895 adj.
monastic 986 adj.

mono
one 88 adj.
sounding 398 adj.

monochrome

uniform 16 adj.
achromatism 426 n.

monocle
eyeglass 442 n.

monogamy
type of marriage 894 n.

monogram
label 547 n.
initials 558 n.

monograph
dissertation 591 n.

monolith
monument 548 n.

monolithic
uniform 16 adj.
one 88 adj.

monologue
soliloquy 585 n.

monomania
eccentricity 503 n.

monomaniac
madman 504 n.

monopolist
restriction 747 n.
egotist 932 n.

monopolistic
restraining 747 adj.
avaricious 816 adj.

monopolize
engross 449 vb.
appropriate 786 vb.

monopoly
exclusion 57 n.
corporation 708 n.
restriction 747 n.
possession 773 n.

monosyllabic
concise 569 adj.
taciturn 582 adj.

monotheism
deism 973 n.

monotone
musical note 410 n.

monotonous
uniform 16 adj.
repeated 106 adj.
feeble 572 adj.

monotony
tedium 838 n.

monsoon
rain 350 n.
wind 352 n.

monster
eyesore 842 n.
prodigy 864 n.
monster 938 n.

monstrosity
abnormality 84 n.
deformity 246 n.

monstrous
exorbitant 32 adj.
huge 195 adj.
ugly 842 adj.
wonderful 864 adj.
heinous 934 adj.

montage
cinema 445 n.
picture 553 n.

month
period 110 n.

monthly
seasonal 141 adj.
journal 528 n.
usual 610 adj.

monument
antiquity 125 n.
reminder 505 n.
monument 548 n.
trophy 729 n.

monumental
enormous 32 adj.

moo
ululate 409 vb.

mooch about
be inactive 679 vb.

mood
temperament 5 n.
grammar 564 n.
affections 817 n.

moody
capricious 604 adj.
melancholic 834 adj.
sullen 893 adj.

moon
changeable thing 152 n.
moon 321 n.
luminary 420 n.
be inattentive 456 vb.

moon, the
impossibility 470 n.

moonless
unlit 418 adj.

moonlight
glimmer 419 n.
work 682 vb.

moonlight flit
departure 296 n.

moonshine
alcoholic drink 301 n.

empty talk 515 n.
moor
tie 45 vb.
place 187 vb.
plain 348 n.
moored
quiescent 266 adj.
mooring(s)
cable 47 n.
moorland
space 183 n.
high land 209 n.
moot
moot 459 adj.
uncertain 474 adj.
propound 512 vb.
moot point
topic 452 n.
mop
cleaning utensil
648 n.
—and mow
haunt 970 vb.
—up
destroy 165 vb.
absorb 299 vb.
carry through
725 vb.
mope
be dejected 834 vb.
moped
bicycle 274 n.
moper
moper 834 n.
moraine
thing transferred
272 n.
moral
maxim 496 n.
precept 693 n.
ethical 917 adj.
morale
state 7 n.
morale-boosting
aiding 703 adj.
morality
right 913 n.
morals 917 n.
moralize
judge 480 vb.
teach 534 vb.
morals
conduct 688 n.
morals 917 n.
virtue 933 n.
moral support
aid 703 n.

moral training
education 534 n.
moral turpitude
wickedness 934 n.
morass
marsh 347 n.
moratorium
delay 136 n.
nonpayment 805 n.
morbid
abnormal 84 adj.
diseased 651 adj.
mordant
keen 174 adj.
pungent 388 adj.
forceful 571 adj.
disapproving
924 adj.
more
beyond 34 adv.
in addition 38 adv.
mores
practice 610 n.
morganatic
matrimonial
894 adj.
morgue
interment 364 n.
moribund
sick 651 adj.
dying 361 adj.
morning
morning 128 n.
morning after
sequel 67 n.
morocco
skin 226 n.
moron
fool 501 n.
moronic
unintelligent
499 adj.
morose
melancholic
834 adj.
moroseness
unsociability
883 n.
morphine, morphia
anaesthetic 375 n.
drug 658 n.
morphology
form 243 n.
linguistics 557 n.
morrow
futurity 124 n.
morse

telecommunication
531 n.
signal 547 n.
morsel
small quantity 33 n.
piece 53 n.
mouthful 301 n.
mortal
ephemeral 114 adj.
deadly 362 adj.
person 371 n.
human 371 adj.
mortality
transience 114 n.
death 361 n.
death roll 361 n.
mortar
adhesive 47 n.
gun 723 n.
mortgage
security 767 n.
debt 803 n.
mortician
interment 364 n.
mortification
decay 51 n.
annoyance 827 n.
regret 830 n.
humiliation 872 n.
asceticism 945 n.
mortify
hurt 827 vb.
humiliate 872 vb.
mortise, mortice
join 45 vb.
mortise lock
fastening 47 n.
mortuary
interment 364 n.
mosaic
medley 43 n.
chequer 437 n.
ornamental art
844 n.
Moslem
(*see* **Muslim**)
mosque
temple 990 n.
mosquito
insect 365 n.
moss
marsh 347 n.
plant 366 n.
mossy
vegetal 366 adj.
mot
witticism 839 n.

motel
inn 192 n.
motet
hymn 981 n.
moth
insect 365 n.
blight 659 n.
mothball
preserver 666 n.
mothballed
disused 674 adj.
moth-eaten
dilapidated 655 adj.
mother
maternity 169 n.
pet 889 vb.
nun 986 n.
mother figure
substitute 150 n.
motherhood
maternity 169 n.
motherland
home 192 n.
motherly
parental 169 adj.
loving 887 adj.
mother-of-pearl
variegation 437 n.
gem 844 n.
mother tongue
language 557 n.
motif, motive
musical piece
412 n.
topic 452 n.
pattern 844 n.
motion
motion 265 n.
defecation 302 n.
topic 452 n.
gesticulate 547 vb.
activity 678 n.
motionless
still 266 adj.
motivate
motivate 612 vb.
motive
moving 265 adj.
motive 612 n.
motiveless
designless 618 adj.
motive power
energy 160 n.
motley
nonuniformity 17 n.
multiform 82 adj.
variegated 437 adj.

motocross
racing 716 n.
motor
sources of energy
160 n.
automobile 274 n.
machine 630 n.
motorcar
automobile 274 n.
motoring
land travel 267 n.
motorist
driver 268 n.
motorized
vehicular 274 adj.
mechanical 630 adj.
motorway
road 624 n.
mottled
mottled 437 adj.
motto
maxim 496 n.
heraldry 547 n.
moue
gesture 547 n.
mould
modality 7 n.
mould 23 n.
decay 51 n.
form 243 n.vb.
soil 344 n.
plant 366 n.
educate 534 vb.
sculpt 554 vb.
dirt 649 n.
blight 659 n.
decorate 844 vb.
—oneself on
do likewise 20 vb.
moulder
decompose 51 vb.
deteriorate 655 vb.
moulding
ornamental art
844 n.
moulting
uncovering 229 n.
mound
small hill 209 n.
dome 253 n.
mount
support 218 vb.
ride 267 vb.
saddle horse 273 n.
ascend 308 vb.
dramatize 594 vb.
mountain

bulk 195 n.
high land 209 n.
mountaineer
climber 308 n.
mountainous
huge 195 adj.
alpine 209 adj.
mountebank
impostor 545 n.
mounted troops
cavalry 722 n.
mourn
lament 836 vb.
mourner
obsequies 364 n.
weeper 836 n.
mournful
melancholic
834 adj.
mourning
formal dress 228 n.
obsequies 364 n.
mouse
mammal 365 n.
coward 856 n.
mousse
dessert 301 n.
bubble 355 n.
moustache
hair 259 n.
mousy
grey 429 adj.
graceless 842 adj.
mouth
maw 194 n.
orifice 263 n.
chew 301 vb.
voice 577 vb.
sauciness 878 n.
mouthful
mouthful 301 n.
mouthorgan
organ 414 n.
mouthpiece
air pipe 353 n.
interpreter 520 n.
informant 524 n.
deputy 755 n.
mouthwash
cleanser 648 n.
mouth-watering
tasty 386 adj.
movable
moving 265 adj.
property 777 n.
move
operate 173 vb.

move 265 vb.
transpose 272 vb.
propound 512 vb.
gesture 547 n.
motivate 612 vb.
attempt 671 n.
deed 676 n.
tactics 688 n.
stratagem 698 n.
excite 821 vb.
—with the times
modernize 126 vb.
moved
impressible 819 adj.
movement
motion 265 n.
musical piece 412 n.
activity 678 n.
party 708 n.
mover
motivator 612 n.
adviser 691 n.
movies
film 445 n.
moving
exciting 821 adj.
distressing 827 adj.
mow
cut 46 vb.
cultivate 370 vb.
—down
slaughter 362 vb.
Mr/Miss Right
favourite 890 n.
Mrs Grundy
prude 950 n.
Mr/Miss X
unknown thing
491 n.
much
great quantity 32 n.
many 104 adj.
mucilage
semiliquidity 354 n.
muck
rubbish 641 n.
dirt 649 n.
muck about
be absurd 497 vb.
—up
impair 655 vb.
muckraker
news reporter 529 n.
defamer 926 n.
mucky
dirty 649 adj.
mucus

excrement 302 n.
semiliquidity
354 n.
mud
marsh 347 n.
dirt 649 n.
muddle
confusion 61 n.
derange 63 vb.
not discriminate
464 vb.
muddled
unclear 568 adj.
muddle-headed
poorly reasoned
477 adj.
unintelligent
499 adj.
muddy
agitate 318 vb.
marshy 347 adj.
dirty 649 adj.
make unclean
649 vb.
mud-slinging
detraction 926 n.
muff
glove 228 n.
be clumsy 695 vb.
bungler 697 n.
muffin
cereals 301 n.
muffle
cover 226 vb.
mute 401 vb.
conceal 525 vb.
muffled
nonresonant
405 adj.
muffler
neckwear 228 n.
mufti
informal dress
228 n.
theologian 973 n.
mug
cup 194 n.
face 237 n.
strike 279 vb.
ninny 501 n.
study 536 vb.
dupe 544 n.
rob 788 vb.
mugger
violent creature
176 n.
robber 789 n.

muggy
  sealed off 264 adj.
  humid 341 adj.
mulatto
  hybrid 43 n.
mulch
  fertilizer 171 n.
  cultivate 370 vb.
mulct
  fleece 786 vb.
  punish 963 vb.
mule
  hybrid 43 n.
  footwear 228 n.
muleteer
  driver 268 n.
mulish
  obstinate 602 adj.
mull
  sweeten 392 vb.
—over
  think 449 vb.
mullah
  theologian 973 n.
mullion
  pillar 218 n.
  window 263 n.
multi-
  plural 101 adj.
multicoloured
  variegated 437 adj.
multifarious
  multiform 82 adj.
multiform
  multiform 82 adj.
multilateral
  lateral 239 adj.
  contractual 765 adj.
multinational
  company
  corporation 708 n.
multipartite
  disunited 46 adj.
  multifid 100 adj.
multiple
  numerical element
    85 n.
  plural 101 adj.
  many 104 adj.
multiplication
  numerical operation
    86 n.
  propagation 167 n.
multiplicity
  plurality 101 n.
  multitude 104 n.
multiply

do sums 86 vb.
  reproduce 166 vb.
  reproduce itself
    167 vb.
multipurpose
  general 79 adj.
  useful 640 adj.
multiracial
  mixed 43 adj.
multitude
  crowd 74 n.
  multitude 104 n.
mum
  voiceless 578 adj.
  taciturn 582 adj.
mumble
  chew 301 vb.
  stammer 580 vb.
mumbo jumbo
  lack of meaning
    515 n.
  idolatry 982 n.
mummery
  sham 542 n.
  ostentation 875 n.
mummify
  preserve 666 vb.
mummy
  maternity 169 n.
  corpse 363 n.
mumps
  infection 651 n.
munch
  chew 301 vb.
mundane
  tedious 838 adj.
municipal
  regional 184 adj.
municipality
  district 184 n.
  jurisdiction 955 n.
munificent
  liberal 813 adj.
muniment(s)
  record 548 n.
  title deeds 767 n.
munitions
  arms 723 n.
mural
  picture 553 n.
murder
  homicide 362 n.
  murder 362 vb.
murderer
  murderer 362 n.
murderous
  murderous 362 adj.

murk
  darkness 418 n.
murky
  dark 418 adj.
  opaque 423 adj.
  latent 523 adj.
murmur
  faintness 401 n.
  be discontented
    829 vb.
muscle
  ligature 47 n.
  power 160 n.
  exertion 682 n.
muscle-bound
  rigid 326 adj.
muscle in
  intrude 297 vb.
muscle man
  athlete 162 n.
  bulk 195 n.
muscular
  stalwart 162 adj.
muse
  meditate 449 vb.
Muses, the
  musician 413 n.
  literature 557 n.
  poetry 593 n.
museum
  antiquity 125 n.
  collection 632 n.
museum piece
  archaism 127 n.
mush
  pulpiness 356 n.
mushroom
  grow 36 vb.
  be fruitful 171 vb.
  dome 253 n.
  vegetable 301 n.
mushroom cloud
  radiation 417 n.
mushy
  pulpy 356 adj.
music
  melody 410 n.
  music 412 n.
musical
  melodious 410 adj.
  musical 412 adj.
musical box
  gramophone 414 n.
musical chairs
  indoor game 837 n.
musical comedy
  stage play 594 n.

musical instrument
  musical instrument
    414 n.
music centre
  gramophone 414 n.
music critic
  musician 413 n.
music hall
  place of amusement
    837 n.
musician
  musician 413 n.
musicianship
  musical skill 413 n.
music lover
  musician 413 n.
musk
  scent 396 n.
musket
  firearm 723 n.
musketeer
  shooter 287 n.
Muslim, Moslem
  religious 973 adj.
muslin
  textile 222 n.
mussel
  fish food 301 n.
must, a
  necessity 596 n.
  requirement 627 n.
mustard
  condiment 389 n.
  yellowness 433 n.
mustard gas
  poison 659 n.
muster
  bring together
    74 vb.
  number 86 vb.
musty
  fetid 397 adj.
  dirty 649 adj.
mutable
  changeable 143 adj.
  changeful 152 adj.
mutation
  abnormality
    84 n.
  change 143 n.
mute
  silent 399 adj.
  silencer 401 n.
  voiceless 578 adj.
  taciturn 582 adj.
muted
  muted 401 adj.

nonresonant
405 adj.
soft-hued 425 adj.
mutilate
impair 655 vb.
make ugly 842 vb.
torture 963 vb.
mutineer
revolter 738 n.
mutinous
defiant 711 adj.
disobedient 738 adj.
undutiful 918 adj.
mutiny
revolt 738 n.vb.
mutt
dunce 501 n.
mutter
sound faint 401 vb.
stammer 580 vb.
be discontented
829 vb.
mutton
meat 301 n.
mutual
correlative 12 adj.
interchanged
151 adj.
mutual assistance
cooperation 706 n.
mutualist
participator 775 n.
muzak
music 412 n.
muzzle
protuberance 254 n.
make mute 578 vb.
hinder 702 vb.
firearm 723 n.
restrain 747 vb.
muzzy
tipsy 949 adj.
mycology
botany 368 n.
myopic
dim-sighted 440 adj.
myriad
many 104 adj.
myrrh
resin 357 n.
scent 396 n.
myself
self 80 n.
subjectivity 320 n.
mystagogue
teacher 537 n.
leader 690 n.

mysteries
religion 973 n.
rite 988 n.
mysterious
unusual 84 adj.
puzzling 517 adj.
occult 523 adj.
mystery
unknown thing
491 n.
enigma 530 n.
secret 530 n.
rite 988 n.
mystic
inexpressible
517 adj.
religious 973 adj.
pietist 979 n.
cabbalistic 984 adj.
mystical
divine 965 adj.
devotional 981 adj.
mysticism
meditation 449 n.
religion 973 n.
mystification
sophistry 447 n.
unintelligibility
517 n.
concealment 525 n.
mystify
puzzle 474 vb.
mystique
prestige 886 n.
cult 981 n.
myth
fantasy 513 n.
fable 543 n.
mythical, mythic
insubstantial 4 adj.
imaginary 513 adj.
mythological
966 adj.
fairylike 970 adj.
mythical beast
rara avis 84 n.
mythical being
rara avis 84 n.
mythical being
970 n.
mythological
mythological
966 adj.
mythology
tradition 127 n.
anthropology 371 n.
fable 543 n.

N

nab
arrest 747 vb.
take 786 vb.
nacelle
airship 276 n.
nacre
variegation 437 n.
nadir
zero 103 n.
depth 211 n.
nag
saddle horse 273 n.
incite 612 vb.
bicker 709 vb.
torment 827 vb.
naiad
nymph 967 n.
nail
affix 45 vb.
fastening 47 n.
hanger 217 n.
perforator 263 n.
nail file
smoother 258 n.
nails
hardness 326 n.
nippers 778 n.
naive, naïve
foolish 499 adj.
artless 699 adj.
naked
uncovered 229 adj.
undisguised
522 adj.
vulnerable 661 adj.
namby-pamby
weakling 163 n.
name
name 561 n.vb.
repute 886 n.
accuse 928 vb.
nameless
anonymous 562 adj.
inglorious 867 adj.
namely
namely 80 adv.
nameplate
label 547 n.
namer
nomenclator 561 n.
namesake
name 561 n.
nanny
protector 660 n.
retainer 742 n.
keeper 749 n.

nap
hair 259 n.
texture 331 n.
sleep 679 n.
nape
rear 238 n.
napkin
cleaning cloth
648 n.
nappy
loincloth 228 n.
narcissism
vanity 873 n.
narcosis
insensibility 375 n.
narcotic
anaesthetic 375 n.
drug 658 n.
drug-taking 949 n.
nark
informer 524 n.
narrate
describe 590 vb.
narrative
narrative 590 n.
narrator
narrator 590 n.
narrow
make smaller
198 vb.
narrow 206 adj.
narrow-minded
481 adj.
restraining 747 adj.
—down
simplify 44 vb.
narrowboat
boat 275 n.
narrow-minded
narrow-minded
481 adj.
narrow squeak
escape 667 n.
nasal
speech sound 398 n.
dialectal 560 adj.
nascent
beginning 68 adj.
nasty
unsavoury 391 adj.
fetid 397 adj.
not nice 645 adj.
unclean 649 adj.
unpleasant 827 adj.
malevolent 898 adj.
natal
first 68 adj.

natality
　propagation 167 n.
natatory
　swimming 269 adj.
nation
　nation 371 n.
national
　ethnic 11 adj.
　native 191 n.adj.
　national 371 adj.
　subject 742 n.
national dress
　clothing 228 n.
　livery 547 n.
nationalism
　particularism 80 n.
　patriotism 901 n.
nationalistic
　biased 481 adj.
nationality
　nation 371 n.
nationalize
　communalize
　　775 vb.
national park
　pleasure ground
　　837 n.
nationhood
　independence 744 n.
　political
　　organization
　　733 n.
nationwide
　universal 79 adj.
native
　genetic 5 adj.
　intrinsic 5 adj.
　native 191 n.adj.
native land
　home 192 n.
native state
　undevelopment
　　670 n.
nativity
　origin 68 n.
　propagation 167 n.
natter
　chat 584 n.
natty
　clean 648 adj.
　personable 841 adj.
natural
　real 1 adj.
　lifelike 18 adj.
　material 319 adj.
　probable 471 adj.
　true 494 adj.

　fool 501 n.
　plain 573 adj.
　spontaneous
　　609 adj.
　usual 610 adj.
　artless 699 adj.
natural bent
　aptitude 694 n.
natural child
　bastardy 954 n.
natural history
　biology 358 n.
naturalism
　accuracy 494 n.
　description 590 n.
naturalist
　biology 358 n.
naturalistic
　representing
　　551 adj.
　descriptive 590 adj.
naturalization
　location 187 n.
naturalize
　make conform
　　83 vb.
　transform 147 vb.
　admit 299 vb.
naturalized
　native 191 adj.
natural philosophy
　physics 319 n.
natural resources
　means 629 n.
　store 632 n.
natural selection
　biology 358 n.
nature
　character 5 n.
　sort 77 n.
　affections 817 n.
Nature
　producer 164 n.
　matter 319 n.
nature cure
　medical art 658 n.
nature reserve
　preservation 666 n.
naturist
　stripper 229 n.
　sanitarian 652 n.
naturopath
　doctor 658 n.
naught
　insubstantiality 4 n.
　(*see* **nought**)
naughty

　disobedient 738 adj.
　impure 951 adj.
nausea
　voidance 300 n.
　dislike 861 n.
nauseate
　be unpalatable
　　391 vb.
　cause dislike 861 vb.
nauseated
　vomiting 300 adj.
　sick 651 adj.
nauseous
　unpleasant 827 adj.
nautical
　seafaring 269 adj.
　seamanlike 270 adj.
　marine 275 adj.
naval
　seafaring 269 adj.
　warlike 718 adj.
nave
　church interior
　　990 n.
navel
　centre 225 n.
navigable
　deep 211 adj.
　seafaring 269 adj.
navigate
　navigate 269 vb.
navigation
　navigation 269 n.
navigator
　navigator 270 n.
　director 690 n.
navvy
　worker 686 n.
navy
　blue 435 adj.
　navy 722 n.
nay
　negation 533 n.
　refusal 760 n.
neap tide
　lowness 210 n.
near
　akin 11 adj.
　near 200 adj.adv.
　approach 289 vb.
nearly
　almost 33 adv.
near side
　laterality 239 n.
　sinistrality 242 n.
near-sighted
　dim-sighted 440 adj.

near the knuckle
　impure 951 adj.
near thing
　escape 667 n.
neat
　unmixed 44 adj.
　orderly 60 adj.
　elegant 575 adj.
　clean 648 adj.
　skilful 694 adj.
　personable 841 adj.
　intoxicating
　　949 adj.
neaten
　unravel 62 vb.
　make better 654 vb.
nebula
　star 321 n.
nebulous
　amorphous 244 adj.
　celestial 321 adj.
　dim 419 adj.
necessary
　necessary 596 adj.
necessary, a
　necessity 596 n.
　requirement 627 n.
necessitate
　necessitate 596 vb.
　compel 740 vb.
necessitous
　poor 801 adj.
necessity
　destiny 155 n.
　necessity 596 n.
　no choice 606 n.
　requirement 627 n.
　compulsion 740 n.
neck
　narrowness 206 n.
　pillar 218 n.
neck and neck
　equal 28 adj.
　synchronous
　　123 adj.
necking
　endearment 889 n.
necklace
　neckwear 228 n.
　jewellery 844 n.
neckwear
　neckwear 228 n.
necrology
　death roll 361 n.
necromancy
　divination 511 n.
　sorcery 983 n.

necrophilia
abnormality 84 n.
necropolis
cemetery 364 n.
necrosis
decay 51 n.
nectar
sweet thing 392 n.
need
shortfall 307 n.
requirement 627 n.
poverty 801 n.
needful
required 627 adj.
needle
sharp point 256 n.
perforator 263 n.
indicator 547 n.
incite 612 vb.
torment 827 vb.
needlecord
textile 222 n.
needless
superfluous 637 adj.
needlework
needlework 844 n.
needy
poor 801 adj.
ne'er-do-well
idler 679 n.
bad person 938 n.
nefarious
disreputable
  867 adj.
heinous 934 adj.
negate
be contrary 14 vb.
tell against 467 vb.
negate 533 vb.
reject 607 vb.
negation
negation 533 n.
negative
negative 533 adj.
negate 533 vb.
photography 551 n.
unsuccessful
  728 adj.
refuse 760 vb.
neglect
negligence 458 n.
neglect 458 vb.
dilapidation 655 n.
not use 674 vb.
not observe 769 vb.
fail in duty 918 vb.
neglected

neglected 458 adj.
forgotten 506 adj.
neglectful
negligent 458 adj.
negligee
nightwear 228 n.
negligence
negligence 458 n.
laxity 734 n.
indifference 860 n.
undutifulness 918 n.
negligent
negligent 458 adj.
forgetful 506 adj.
negligible
inconsiderable
  33 adj.
unimportant
  639 adj.
negotiable
transferable
  272 adj.
possible 469 adj.
transferred 780 adj.
negotiate
cooperate 706 vb.
make terms 766 vb.
bargain 791 vb.
negotiations
conference 584 n.
negotiator
mediator 720 n.
envoy 754 n.
Negritude
nation 371 n.
civilization 654 n.
neigh
ululate 409 vb.
neighbour
be near 200 vb.
friend 880 n.
neighbourhood
locality 187 n.
near place 200 n.
surroundings 230 n.
neighbourly
sociable 882 adj.
neither
neither 606 adv.
nekton
marine life 365 n.
Nemesis
avenger 910 n.
justice 913 n.
neoclassical
architectural
  192 adj.

neocolonialism
governance 733 n.
neolithic
secular 110 adj.
primal 127 adj.
barbaric 869 adj.
neological
neological 560 adj.
neologism
neology 560 n.
neology
neology 560 n.
neophyte
beginner 538 n.
neoteric
modern 126 adj.
nephew
kinsman 11 n.
ne plus ultra
superiority 34 n.
extremity 69 n.
perfection 646 n.
nepotism
injustice 914 n.
improbity 930 n.
nereid
nymph 967 n.
nerve
strengthen 162 vb.
courage 855 n.
sauciness 878 n.
nerve centre
focus 76 n.
nerve gas
weapon 723 n.
nerveless
impotent 161 adj.
irresolute 601 adj.
nerve-racking
distressing 827 adj.
frightening 854 adj.
nerves
psychopathy 503 n.
excitability 822 n.
nervousness 854 n.
nervous
agitated 318 adj.
irresolute 601 adj.
nervous 854 adj.
nervous breakdown
nervous disorders
  651 n.
nervous system
sense 374 n.
nervy
excitable 822 adj.
nest

group 74 n.
nest 192 n.
dwell 192 vb.
refuge 662 n.
nest egg
store 632 n.
wealth 800 n.
nestle
caress 889 vb.
nestled
located 187 adj.
nestling
young creature
  132 n.
Nestor
sage 500 n.
net
remaining 41 adj.
bring together
  74 vb.
receptacle 194 n.
network 222 n.
enclosure 235 n.
semitransparency
  424 n.
trap 542 n.
acquire 771 vb.
nether
low 210 adj.
netherworld
hell 972 n.
net profit
gain 771 n.
netting
network 222 n.
nettle
prickle 256 n.
bane 659 n.
huff 891 vb.
network
correlation 12 n.
gap 201 n.
network 222 n.
broadcasting 531 n.
networking
cooperation 706 n.
neuralgia
pang 377 n.
neurasthenia
psychopathy 503 n.
melancholy 834 n.
neurologist
doctor 658 n.
neurosis
psychopathy 503 n.
neurotic
insane 503 adj.

madman 504 n.
neuter
generic 77 adj.
eunuch 161 n.
unman 161 vb.
neutral
median 30 adj.
grey 429 adj.
choiceless 606 adj.
neutral 625 adj.
pacifist 717 n.
independent
744 adj.
indifferent 860 adj.
neutralize
disable 161 vb.
counteract 182 vb.
remedy 658 vb.
neutron
element 319 n.
never
never 109 adv.
never-ending
perpetual 115 adj.
uncompleted
726 adj.
never-failing
successful 727 adj.
new
first 68 adj.
new 126 n.
unhabituated
611 adj.
new birth
life 360 n.
revival 656 n.
newborn
infantine 132 adj.
new broom
busy person 678 n.
newcomer
incomer 297 n.
newfangled
modern 126 adj.
neological 560 adj.
new leaf
improvement 654 n.
new look
modernism 126 n.
repair 656 n.
newlywed ▸
spouse 894 n.
new man/woman
changed person
147 n.
newness
originality 21 n.

newness 126 n.
news
information 524 n.
news 529 n.
newscaster
broadcaster 531 n.
news flash
broadcast 531 n.
newsletter
publicity 528 n.
newspaper
the press 528 n.
newspaperman,
newspaperwoman
news reporter
529 n.
newspeak
neology 560 n.
newsprint
script 586 n.
paper 631 n.
newsreader
broadcaster 531 n.
newsreel
film 445 n.
news reporter
news reporter 529 n.
newssheet
the press 528 n.
newsworthy
notable 638 adj.
newsy
informative 524 adj.
loquacious 581 adj.
newt
amphibian 365 n.
New Testament
scripture 975 n.
new town
district 184 n.
new wave
music 412 n.
film 445 n.
New World
region 184 n.
next
sequential 65 adj.
subsequent 120 adj.
next door
near 200 adj.
next of kin
kinsman 11 n.
beneficiary 776 n.
next step
progression 285 n.
next world
the dead 361 n.

nexus
bond 47 n.
nib
stationery 586 n.
nibble
mouthful 301 n.
eat 301 vb.
nice
pleasant 376 adj.
savoury 390 adj.
discriminating
463 adj.
clean 648 adj.
pleasurable 826 adj.
tasteful 846 adj.
fastidious 862 adj.
amiable 884 adj.
nicety
differentiation 15 n.
discrimination
463 n.
niche
place 185 n.
compartment 194 n.
cavity 255 n.
honours 866 n.
nick
notch 260 n.vb.
mark 547 vb.
lockup 748 n.
steal 788 vb.
nickname
name 561 n.vb.
nick of time
occasion 137 n.
nicotine
tobacco 388 n.
poison 659 n.
niece
kinsman 11 n.
nifty
speedy 277 adj.
niggard
niggard 816 n.
niggardly
insufficient 636 adj.
niggle
cause discontent
829 vb.
dispraise 924 vb.
niggling
trivial 639 adj.
night
darkness 418 n.
nightcap
draught 301 n.
soporific 679 n.

nightclothes
nightwear 228 n.
night club
place of amusement
837 n.
nightfall
evening 129 n.
darkness 418 n.
nightingale
vocalist 413 n.
night life
festivity 837 n.
nightmare
fantasy 513 n.
suffering 825 n.
nightmarish
frightening
854 adj.
spooky 970 adj.
night out
revel 837 n.
night safe
storage 632 n.
night sky
heavens 321 n.
nighttime
evening 129 n.
night watchman
protector 660 n.
keeper 749 n.
nihilism
anarchy 734 n.
sedition 738 n.
nihilist
revolter 738 n.
nihilistic
anarchic 734 adj.
irreligious 974 adj.
nil
zero 103 n.
nimble
speedy 277 adj.
skilful 694 adj.
nimble-witted
intelligent 498 adj.
nimbus
cloud 355 n.
light 417 n.
nincompoop
ninny 501 n.
nine days' wonder
insubstantial thing
4 n.
brief span 114 n.
prodigy 864 n.
ninny
ninny 501 n.

nip
make smaller
198 vb.
shorten 204 vb.
move fast 277 vb.
draught 301 n.
pang 377 n.
—**in the bud**
suppress 165 vb.
nipper
youngster 132 n.
nippers
extractor 304 n.
nippers 778 n.
nipple
bosom 253 n.
nippy
cold 380 adj.
active 678 adj.
nirvana
extinction 2 n.
heaven 971 n.
nit
insect 365 n.
dirt 649 n.
nit-picking
trivial 639 adj.
fastidiousness
862 n.
nitrates
fertilizer 171 n.
nitroglycerine
explosive 723 n.
nitwit
dunce 501 n.
nix
zero 103 n.
mythical being
970 n.
no
refusal 760 n.
no alternative
no choice 606 n.
nob
head 213 n.
aristocrat 868 n.
nobble
disable 161 vb.
steal 788 vb.
nobbly
projecting 254 adj.
nobility
aristocracy 868 n.
nobility 868 n.
noble
impressive 821 adj.
splendid 841 adj.

well-bred 848 adj.
worshipful 866 adj.
person of rank
868 n.
proud 871 adj.
disinterested
931 adj.
nobleman,
noblewoman
person of rank
868 n.
noble savage
ingenue 699 n.
nobody
nobody 190 n.
nonentity 639 n.
no case to answer
acquittal 960 n.
no chance
impossibility 470 n.
no change
identity 13 n.
permanence 144 n.
no charge
no charge 812 n.
no choice
no choice 606 n.
no concern of
unrelatedness 10 n.
nocturnal
vespertine 129 adj.
dark 418 adj.
nocturne
musical piece
412 n.
nod
oscillate 317 vb.
be inattentive
456 vb.
assent 488 n.vb.
hint 524 n.
gesture 547 n.
sleep 679 vb.
consent 758 vb.
node
joint 45 n.
swelling 253 n.
nodule
swelling 253 n.
no entry
exclusion 57 n.
no escape
necessity 596 n.
noes, the
dissentient 489 n.
no exception
inclusion 78 n.

no feelings
moral insensibility
820 n.
noggin
draught 301 n.
no go
impossibility 470 n.
failure 728 n.
no-go area
battleground 724 n.
restriction 747 n.
no holds barred
wrestling 716 n.
unconditional
744 adj.
noise
sound 398 n.
loudness 400 n.
rumour 529 n.
noiseless
silent 399 adj.
noisome
fetid 397 adj.
unclean 649 adj.
noisy
loud 400 adj.
no joke
reality 1 n.
important matter
638 n.
no kidding
veracity 540 n.
nomad
wanderer 268 n.
no manners
ill-breeding 847 n.
discourtesy 885 n.
no-man's-land
territory 184 n.
emptiness 190 n.
nonownership
774 n.
nom de plume
misnomer 562 n.
nomenclature
identification 547 n.
nomenclature 561 n.
nominal
insubstantial 4 adj.
named 561 adj.
trivial 639 adj.
nominate
select 605 vb.
commission 751 vb.
nominee
delegate 754 n.
nonacceptance

rejection 607 n.
refusal 760 n.
nonadherence
nonobservance
769 n.
nonadhesive
nonadhesive 49 adj.
nonage
nonage 130 n.
nonaggression pact
pacification 719 n.
treaty 765 n.
nonalcoholic
beverage
soft drink 301 n.
nonalignment
no choice 606 n.
freedom 744 n.
no name
no name 562 n.
nonappearance
absence 190 n.
invisibility 444 n.
nonattendance
absence 190 n.
nonavailability
nonuse 674 n.
nonbiodegradable
unyielding 162 adj.
nonce word
neology 560 n.
nonchalance
negligence 458 n.
inexcitability 823 n.
indifference 860 n.
noncombatant
pacifist 717 n.
noncommissioned
officer
army officer 741 n.
noncommittal
reticent 525 adj.
cautious 858 adj.
nonconformist
nonconformist 84 n.
dissentient 489 n.
nonobservant
769 adj.
schismatic 978 n.
nonconformity
nonconformity
84 n.
sectarianism 978 n.
noncooperation
unwillingness 598 n.
resistance 715 n.
disobedience 738 n.

nondescript
trivial 639 adj.
nondiscriminatory
inclusive 78 adj.
nondrinker
avoider 620 n.
none
zero 103 n.
nonentity
nonentity 639 n.
object of scorn
867 n.
nonessential
unimportant
639 adj.
none the worse
restored 656 adj.
non-event
failure 728 n.
nonexistence
nonexistence 2 n.
nonfiction
literature 557 n.
description 590 n.
nonfigurative
representing
551 adj.
nonfulfilment
shortfall 307 n.
noncompletion
726 n.
nonfunctional
useless 641 adj.
ornamental
844 adj.
noninflammable
incombustible
382 adj.
nonintervention
inaction 677 n.
noninvolvement
avoidance 620 n.
peace 717 n.
nonliable
nonliable 919 adj.
nonobservance
negligence 458 n.
nonobservance
769 n.
no-nonsense
undisguised
522 adj.
artless 699 adj.
nonpareil
exceller 644 n.
paragon 646 n.
nonpartisan

independent
744 adj.
nonpayment
nonpayment 805 n.
nonplussed
doubting 474 adj.
puzzled 517 adj.
in difficulties
700 adj.
nonpractising
nonobservant
769 adj.
irreligious 974 adj.
nonprofessional
unskilled 695 adj.
non-profitmaking
disinterested
931 adj.
nonproliferation
pacification 719 n.
nonresidence
absence 190 n.
nonsense
absurdity 497 n.
silly talk 515 n.
nonsense verse
doggerel 593 n.
nonsensical
absurd 497 adj.
foolish 499 adj.
meaningless
515 adj.
nonsequitur
irrelevance 10 n.
sophism 477 n.
nonskid
dry 342 adj.
nonsmoker
abstainer 942 n.
nonstandard
dialectal 560 adj.
nonstarter
difficulty 700 n.
loser 728 n.
nonstop
continuous 71 adj.
unceasing 146 adj.
non-U
ill-bred 847 adj.
plebeian 869 adj.
nonviolence
moderation 177 n.
peace 717 n.
nonvoter
disapprover 924 n.
nonvoting
choiceless 606 adj.

noodles
dish 301 n.
nook
compartment 194 n.
hiding-place 527 n.
noon
noon 128 n.
no one
nobody 190 n.
no option
necessity 596 n.
noose
halter 47 n.
means of execution
964 n.
no picnic
hard task 700 n.
no quarter
pitilessness 906 n.
norm
prototype 23 n.
average 30 n.
rule 81 n.
normal
median 30 adj.
typical 83 adj.
normality
sanity 502 n.
normalize
make conform
83 vb.
normative
regular 81 adj.
educational 534 adj.
north
compass point
281 n.
northern
opposite 240 adj.
directed 281 adj.
northern lights
glow 417 n.
North Pole
summit 213 n.
coldness 380 n.
nor'wester
gale 352 n.
nose
face 237 n.
prow 237 n.
protuberance 254 n.
odour 394 n.
detect 484 vb.
—around
inquire 459 vb.
be curious 453 vb.
nose cone

rocket 276 n.
nose dive
aeronautics 271 n.
descent 309 n.
nosegay
bunch 74 n.
fragrance 396 n.
nose to tail
continuously
71 adv.
nosey, nosy
inquisitive 453 adj.
inquiring 459 adj.
nosology
pathology 651 n.
nostalgia
regret 830 n.
melancholy 834 n.
no stomach for
unwillingness 598 n.
dislike 861 n.
nostril
orifice 263 n.
air pipe 353 n.
no strings attached
unconditional
744 adj.
nostrum
contrivance 623 n.
remedy 658 n.
no such thing
nonexistence 2 n.
notable
bigwig 638 n.
notable 638 adj.
person of repute
866 n.
noteworthy 866 adj.
notary
notary 958 n.
not at all
in no way 33 adv.
notation
numerical operation
86 n.
notation 410 n.
not beat about the
bush
speak plainly
573 vb.
not catch on
be unpractised
611 vb.
notch
cut 46 vb.
gap 201 n.
notch 260 n.vb.

—up
number 86 vb.
register 548 vb.
not count
be unimportant
639 vb.
not counting
exclusive of 57 adv.
not cricket
injustice 914 n.
not done
unconformable
84 adj.
unwonted 611 adj.
note
musical note 410 n.
cognize 447 vb.
notice 455 vb.
record 548 vb.
write 586 vb.
correspondence
588 n.
paper money 797 n.
famousness 866 n.
notebook
reminder 505 n.
record 548 n.
stationery 586 n.
not enough
insufficiency 636 n.
note of hand
paper money 797 n.
notepaper
stationery 586 n.
paper 631 n.
notes
commentary 520 n.
record 548 n.
noteworthy
notable 638 adj.
noteworthy 866 adj.
not far
near 200 adj.adv.
**not give a straight
answer**
be equivocal 518 vb.
dissemble 541 vb.
not guilty
guiltless 935 adj.
acquitted 960 adj.
nothing
nonexistence 2 n.
zero 103 n.
trifle 639 n.
notice
period 110 n.
see 438 vb.

notice 455 vb.
detect 484 vb.
advertisement
528 n.
article 591 n.
warning 664 n.
noticeable
visible 443 adj.
manifest 522 adj.
notification
information 524 n.
publication 528 n.
notify
communicate
524 vb.
proclaim 528 vb.
notion
idea 451 n.
supposition 512 n.
notional
ideational 451 adj.
suppositional
512 adj.
not mind
acquiesce 488 vb.
be indifferent
860 vb.
not of this world
extraneous 59 adj.
divine 965 adj.
not one's type
dislike 861 n.
hateful object 888 n.
notorious
well-known 528 adj.
disreputable 867 adj.
not out
unceasing 146 adj.
not required
unused 674 adj.
not responsible
nonliable 919 n.
guiltless 935 adj.
not the thing
desuetude 611 n.
undueness 916 n.
not to be trusted
dishonest 930 adj.
not turn a hair
keep calm 823 vb.
not working
orderless 61 adj.
not worthwhile
trivial 639 adj.
profitless 641 adj.
nought
zero 103 n.

noumenal
insubstantial 4 adj.
intuitive 476 adj.
noun
part of speech 564 n.
nourish
feed 301 vb.
aid 703 vb.
nourishing
nourishing 301 adj.
nous
intelligence 498 n.
nouveau riche
upstart 126 n.
vulgarian 847 n.
nova
star 321 n.
novel
new 126 adj.
novel 590 n.
novelettish
feeble 572 adj.
vulgar 847 adj.
novelist
author 589 n.
novelty
bauble 639 n.
pleasurableness
826 n.
(*see* **novel**)
novice
ignoramus 493 n.
beginner 538 n.
bungler 697 n.
monk 986 n.
nun 986 n.
novitiate
learning 536 n.
preparation 669 n.
nowadays
present time 121 n.
now and again/then
sometimes 139 adv.
fitfully 142 adv.
nowhere
nonexistent 2 adj.
not here 190 adv.
no wiser
uninstructed
491 adj.
noxious
harmful 645 adj.
insalubrious
653 adj.
noxious animal
creepy-crawly
365 n.

noxious animal
904 n.
nozzle
orifice 263 n.
outlet 298 n.
nuance
differentiation
15 n.
small quantity 33 n.
discrimination
463 n.
nub
essential part 5 n.
centre 225 n.
chief thing 638 n.
nubbly
convex 253 adj.
rough 259 adj.
nubile
grown-up 134 adj.
nuclear
dynamic 160 adj.
nuclear blast
havoc 165 n.
nuclear deterrent
arms 723 n.
nuclear disarmament
pacification 719 n.
nuclear physics
nucleonics 160 n.
nuclear power
sources of energy
160 n.
nucleate
be dense 324 vb.
nucleolus
organism 358 n.
nucleonics
nucleonics 160 n.
nucleus
centre 225 n.
element 319 n.
solid body 324 n.
nude
uncovered 229 adj.
art subject 553 n.
nudge
knock 279 n.
hint 524 n.vb.
nudist
stripper 229 n.
sanitarian 652 n.
nudity
bareness 229 n.
nugatory
unimportant
639 adj.

nugget
  solid body 324 n.
  bullion 797 n.
nuisance
  meddler 678 n.
  annoyance 827 n.
null
  nonexistent 2 adj.
  meaningless
    515 adj.
null and void
  powerless 161 adj.
  abrogated 752 adj.
nullify
  nullify 2 vb.
  abrogate 752 vb.
numb
  insensible 375 adj.
number
  quantity 26 n.
  number 85 n.
  plurality 101 n.
  —**with**
  number with 78 vb.
numbered
  statistical 86 adj.
numberless
  infinite 107 adj.
number one
  self 80 n.
numen
  divineness 965 n.
numerable
  numerable 86 adj.
numeracy
  numeration 86 n.
numeral
  number 85 n.
numerate
  instructed 490 adj.
numeration
  numeration 86 n.
numerical
  numerical 85 adj.
numerous
  many 104 adj.
numinous
  frightening 854 adj.
  divine 965 adj.
numismatics
  coinage 797 n.
numskull, numbskull
  dunce 501 n.
nun
  nun 986 n.
nuncio
  envoy 754 n.

nunnery
  monastery 986 n.
nuptial
  matrimonial
    894 adj.
nurse
  look after 457 vb.
  nurse 658 n.
  doctor 658 vb.
  preserve 666 vb.
  minister to 703 vb.
  domestic 742 n.
  keeper 749 n.
  pet 889 vb.
nursemaid
  keeper 749 n.
nursery
  nonage 130 n.
  seedbed 156 n.
  training school
    539 n.
nurseryman,
  nurserywoman
  gardener 370 n.
nursery rhyme
  doggerel 593 n.
nursing home
  hospital 658 n.
nursling
  child 132 n.
nurture
  food 301 n.
  educate 534 vb.
nut
  fastening 47 n.
  fruit 301 n.
  crank 504 n.
  enthusiast 504 n.
nutrition
  eating 301 n.
  food 301 n.
nutritional
  nourishing 301 adj.
  remedial 658 adj.
nutritionist
  dieting 301 n.
nutritious
  nourishing 301 adj.
  salubrious 652 adj.
nuts and bolts
  component 58 n.
  means 629 n.
  machine 630 n.
nutshell
  conciseness 569 n.
nutty
  pungent 388 adj.

  crazy 503 adj.
nuzzle
  caress 889 vb.
nylon
  textile 222 n.
nymph
  nymph 967 n.
nymphet
  youngster 132 n.
  loose woman 952 n.
nymphomania
  libido 859 n.

O

oaf
  dunce 501 n.
  bungler 697 n.
oak
  strength 162 n.
  tree 366 n.
oar
  propellant 287 n.
  boatman 270 n.
oasis
  land 344 n.
oath
  testimony 466 n.
  oath 532 n.
  promise 764 n.
  scurrility 899 n.
oatmeal
  cereals 301 n.
  brown 430 adj.
oats
  provender 301 n.
  grass 366 n.
obdurate
  obstinate 602 adj.
  severe 735 adj.
obedience
  obedience 739 n.
obedient
  willing 597 adj.
  obedient 739 adj.
  observant 768 adj.
  (*see* **obey**)
obeisance
  submission 721 n.
obelisk
  monument 548 n.
obese
  fleshy 195 adj.
obesity
  disease 651 n.
obey
  conform 83 vb.
  obey 739 vb.

  be subject 745 vb.
obfuscate
  conceal 525 vb.
obituary
  obsequies 364 n.
object
  substance 3 n.
  object 319 n.
  objective 617 n.
  (*see* **objection**)
objectify
  make extrinsic 6 vb.
  materialize 319 vb.
objection
  qualification 468 n.
  dissent 489 n.
  resistance 715 n.
objectionable
  unpleasant 827 adj.
  wrong 914 adj.
objective
  goal 295 n.
  true 494 adj.
  objective 617 n.
  aspiration 852 n.
object lesson
  example 83 n.
objector
  dissentient 489 n.
objet d'art
  masterpiece 694 n.
objet trouvé
  sculpture 554 n.
oblation
  oblation 981 n.
obligation
  necessity 596 n.
  needfulness 627 n.
  duty 917 n.
obligatory
  necessary 596 adj.
  compelling 740 adj.
  obligatory 917 adj.
oblige
  necessitate 596 vb.
  compel 740 vb.
obliged
  indebted 803 adj.
  grateful 907 adj.
obliging
  courteous 884 adj.
  benevolent 897 adj.
oblique
  oblique 220 adj.
obliterate
  destroy 165 vb.
  obliterate 550 vb.

obliteration
extinction 2 n.
obliteration 550 n.
oblivion
oblivion 506 n.
oblivious
inattentive 456 adj.
forgetful 506 adj.
oblong
longitudinal
203 adj.
obloquy
slur 867 n.
detraction 926 n.
obnoxious
hateful 888 adj.
oboe
flute 414 n.
obscene
impure 951 adj.
obscurantism
misteaching 535 n.
obscure
darken 418 vb.
shadowy 419 adj.
unknown 491 adj.
puzzling 517 adj.
latent 523 adj.
conceal 525 vb.
inglorious 867 adj.
obscurity
darkness 418 n.
obsequies
obsequies 364 n.
obsequious
servile 879 adj.
observance
observance 768 n.
celebration 876 n.
rite 988 n.
observant
vigilant 457 adj.
observation
inspection 438 n.
attention 455 n.
maxim 496 n.
affirmation 532 n.
observatory
astronomy 321 n.
view 438 n.
observe
see 438 vb.
watch 441 vb.
affirm 532 vb.
observe 768 vb.
observer
spectator 441 n.

obsess
engross 449 vb.
make mad 503 vb.
obsessed
obsessed 455 adj.
obsession
folly 499 n.
eccentricity 503 n.
opinionatedness
602 n.
obsessive
habitual 610 adj.
obsolete
extinct 2 adj.
antiquated
127 adj.
disused 674 adj.
obstacle
barrier 235 n.
obstacle 702 n.
obstetrician
obstetrics 167 n.
doctor 658 n.
obstinate
unyielding 162 adj.
volitional 595 adj.
obstinate 602 adj.
disobedient
738 adj.
obstreperous
violent 176 adj.
obstruct
obstruct 702 vb.
resist 715 vb.
obstruction
closure 264 n.
hindrance 702 n.
obstructionist
hinderer 702 n.
opponent 705 n.
obstructive
hindering 702 adj.
obtain
be general 79 vb.
be wont 610 vb.
acquire 771 vb.
obtainable
accessible 289 adj.
obtuse
unintelligent
499 adj.
thick-skinned
820 adj.
obverse
face 237 n.
obviate
avoid 620 vb.

disencumber
701 vb.
obvious
obvious 443 adj.
intelligible 516 adj.
manifest 522 adj.
occasion
juncture 8 n.
occasion 137 n.
event 154 n.
cause 156 vb.
celebration 876 n.
occasional
opportune 137 adj.
infrequent 140 adj.
celebratory 876 adj.
occidental
lateral 239 adj.
occlude
close 264 vb.
occult
occult 523 adj.
cabbalistic 984 adj.
occultism
occultism 984 n.
occupant
resident 191 n.
occupation
presence 189 n.
business 622 n.
job 622 n.
action 676 n.
occupational
habitual 610 adj.
businesslike
622 n.
occupational therapy
therapy 658 n.
occupied
busy 678 adj.
occupier
resident 191 n.
possessor 776 n.
occupy
fill 54 vb.
dwell 192 vb.
attract notice
455 vb.
employ 622 vb.
possess 773 vb.
appropriate 786 vb.
occur
happen 154 vb.
—to
dawn upon 449 vb.
occurrence
event 154 n.

ocean
ocean 343 n.
ocean-going
seafaring 269 adj.
marine 275 adj.
oceanic
oceanic 343 adj.
oceanography
oceanography
343 n.
ochre
brown pigment
430 n.
octagon
angular figure
247 n.
octave
musical note 410 n.
octavo
edition 589 n.
octet
duet 412 n.
octogenarian
old person 133 n.
octopus
marine life 365 n.
ocular
seeing 438 adj.
oculist
doctor 658 n.
odalisque
slave 742 n.
odd
unequal 29 adj.
remaining 41 adj.
unusual 84 adj.
numerical 85 adj.
crazy 503 adj.
puzzling 517 adj.
oddity
misfit 25 n.
nonconformist
84 n.
crank 504 n.
odd man out
misfit 25 n.
dissentient 489 n.
oddment(s)
extra 40 n.
medley 43 n.
odds
advantage 34 n.
fair chance 159 n.
dissension 709 n.
odds and ends
leavings 41 n.
medley 43 n.

ode
poem 593 n.
odious
hateful 888 adj.
odium
odium 888 n.
odorous
odorous 394 adj.
odour
odour 394 n.
odourless
odourless 395 adj.
odyssey
land travel 267 n.
Oedipus complex
eccentricity 503 n.
of age
grown-up 134 adj.
of course
certainly 473 adv.
off
decomposed 51 adj.
pungent 388 adj.
offal
insides 224 n.
meat 301 n.
offbeat
unconformable
84 adj.
off-chance
possibility 469 n.
off colour
sick 651 adj.
off-course
deviating 282 adj.
off day
untimeliness 138 n.
off duty
leisurely 681 adj.
offence
resentment 891 n.
lawbreaking 954 n.
offend
displease 827 vb.
huff 891 vb.
offender
offender 904 n.
offensive
fetid 397 adj.
attack 712 n.
unpleasant 827 adj.
impertinent 878 adj.
impure 951 adj.
offensive remark
calumny 926 n.
offer
incentive 612 n.

provide 633 vb.
offer 759 n.vb.
make terms 766 vb.
offering
offering 781 n.
offertory
oblation 981 n.
off form
clumsy 695 adj.
off guard
negligent 458 adj.
inexpectant
508 adj.
offhand, offhanded
negligent 458 adj.
spontaneous
609 adj.
discourteous
885 adj.
office
function 622 n.
workshop 687 n.
position of authority
733 n.
duty 917 n.
jurisdiction 955 n.
church service
988 n.
office-bearer
official 690 n.
officer
officer 741 n.
official
genuine 494 adj.
businesslike
622 adj.
official 690 n.
authoritative
733 adj.
governmental
733 adj.
officer 741 n.
formal 875 adj.
officiate
function 622 vb.
perform ritual
988 vb.
officious
inquisitive 453 adj.
meddling 678 adj.
off key
discordant 411 adj.
off-line
computerized
86 adj.
off-load
displace 188 vb.

offprint
letterpress 587 n.
off-putting
repellent 292 adj.
hindering 702 adj.
off-season
cheap 812 adj.
offset
offset 31 n.
remainder 41 n.
qualification 468 n.
offshoot
adjunct 40 n.
descendant 170 n.
sect 978 n.
offside
laterality 239 n.
dextral 241 adj.
wrong 914 adj.
offspring
kinsman 11 n.
effect 157 n.
posterity 170 n.
off the beaten track
secluded 883 adj.
off the cuff
extempore 609 adv.
off-the-peg
tailored 228 adj.
off the point
irrelevant 10 adj.
off the record
occult 523 adj.
off-white
whitish 427 adj.
of one's own accord
voluntary 597 adj.
often
often 139 adv.
ogee
convolution 251 n.
ogle
look 438 n.
court 889 vb.
ogre, ogress
giant 195 n.
intimidation 854 n.
monster 938 n.
oil
lubricant 334 n.
oil 357 n.
fuel 385 n.
balm 658 n.
facilitate 701 vb.
**oil on troubled
waters**
moderator 177 n.

oils
art equipment
553 n.
oilskins
overcoat 228 n.
shelter 662 n.
oil well
store 632 n.
oily
smooth 258 adj.
unctuous 357 adj.
flattering 925 adj.
ointment
unguent 357 n.
balm 658 n.
OK, okay
in order 60 adv.
assent 488 n.
not bad 644 adj.
old
olden 127 adj.
ageing 131 adj.
old age
old age 131 n.
old-boy network
latency 523 n.
olden days
past time 125 n.
old-fashioned
antiquated 127 adj.
unwonted 611 adj.
old flame
loved one 887 n.
old fogey
archaism 127 n.
laughingstock
851 n.
old hand
expert 696 n.
oldie
archaism 127 n.
old lag
prisoner 750 n.
old maid
spinster 895 n.
old master
picture 553 n.
artist 556 n.
old people's home
shelter 662 n.
old-school
antiquated 127 adj.
opinionatedness
602 n.
old school tie
livery 547 n.

remedy 658 n.

old-stager
expert 696 n.

Old Testament
scripture 975 n.

old-timer
archaism 127 n.
old man 133 n.

old wives' tales
fable 543 n.

old-world
antiquated 127 adj.
courteous 884 adj.

oligarchy
government 733 n.

olive branch
peace offering
719 n.

Olympian
aristocrat 868 n.
genteel 868 adj.
Olympian deity
967 n.

Olympic Games
contest 716 n.

Olympus
mythic heaven
971 n.

ombudsman
inquirer 459 n.
estimator 480 n.

omelette
dish 301 n.

omen
omen 511 n.
warning 664 n.

ominous
presageful 511 adj.
cautionary 664 adj.
unpromising
853 adj.
threatening 900 adj.

omission
exclusion 57 n.
negligence 458 n.
nonobservance
769 n.

omit
be taciturn 582 vb.
(*see* **omission**)

omnibus
comprehensive
52 adj.
bus 274 n.

omnifarious
multiform 82 adj.

omnipotence
power 160 n.

omniscient
knowing 490 adj.

omnivorous
greedy 859 adj.

on and off
by turns 141 adv.
changeably 152 adv.

on approval
chosen 605 adj.

on a shoestring
parsimonious
816 adj.

on call
expectant 507 adj.
prepared 669 adj.

once
singly 88 adv.
not now 122 adv.

once bitten, twice shy
cautious 858 adj.

once more
twice 91 adv.
again 106 adv.

once-over
inspection 438 n.

once upon a time
formerly 125 adv.

oncoming
approaching
289 adj.

one
simple 44 adj.
unit 88 n.
person 371 n.

one and all
all 52 n.
everyman 79 n.

one and only
inimitable 21 adj.

one another
correlatively 12 adv.

on edge, be
be excitable 822 vb.
be nervous 854 vb.

one-horse
trivial 639 adj.

one in a thousand
exceller 644 n.

one in the eye for
disappointment
509 n.

oneiromancy
divination 511 n.

on end
vertical 215 n.

oneness
identity 13 n.

simpleness 44 n.
unity 88 n.

one-night stand
music 412 n.
dramaturgy 594 n.

one of
component 58 n.

one-off
one 88 adj.

one or two
plurality 101 n.

onerous
hindering 702 adj.
annoying 827 adj.

one's betters
superior 34 n.

one-sided
biased 481 adj.
unjust 914 adj.

one's own devices
scope 744 n.

one's own man/woman, be
will 595 vb.
be free 744 vb.

one's stars
destiny 155 n.

one thing after another
continuity 71 n.

onetime
prior 119 adj.

one-track mind
narrow mind
481 n.

one up
superior 34 adj.

oneupmanship
sagacity 498 n.
tactics 688 n.

one-way
directed 281 adj.

on foot
on foot 267 adv.
preparatory
669 adj.

ongoing
continuous 71 adj.

on guard
vigilant 457 adj.

onion
vegetable 301 n.

on-line
computerized
86 adj.

onlooker
spectator 441 n.

only
slightly 33 adv.
one 88 adj.

on-off
discontinuous
72 adj.
fitful 142 adj.

onomastic
naming 561 adj.

onomatopoeia
mimicry 20 n.

on one's hands
superfluous 637 adj.

on one's toes
vigilant 457 adj.

onset
beginning 68 n.
approach 289 n.
attack 712 n.

onshore
coastal 344 adj.

onside
laterality 239 n.
sinistrality 242 n.

onslaught
attack 712 n.
censure 924 n.

on spec
experimentally
461 adv.

on tap
provisioning
633 adj.

on tenterhooks
expectant 507 adj.

on the ball
attentive 455 adj.
intelligent 498 adj.

on the cards
probable 471 adj.

on the contrary
contrarily 14 adv.

on the dole
nonactive 677 adj.

on the face of it
apparently
445 adv.

on the level
artless 699 adj.
honourable 929 adj.

on the make
acquiring 771 adj.

on the map
renowned 866 adj.

on the nod
unanimously
488 adv.

on the rocks
cooled 382 adj.
grounded 728 adj.
on the run
on the move
  265 adv.
endangered 661 adj.
on the shelf
unwanted 860 adj.
unwedded 895 adj.
on the spot
on the spot 189 adj.
on the up and up
prosperous 730 adj.
honourable 929 adj.
on the way
in transit 272 adv.
en passant 305 adv.
on time
early 135 adj.
timely 137 adj.
on tiptoe
aloft 209 adv.
stealthy 525 adj.
ontology
existence 1 n.
philosophy 449 n.
onus
demonstration
  478 n.
encumbrance 702 n.
onward
forward 285 adv.
ooze
move slowly 278 vb.
exude 298 vb.
be wet 341 vb.
marsh 347 n.
flow 350 vb.
—out
be disclosed 526 vb.
oozing
full 54 adj.
oozy
marshy 347 adj.
flowing 350 adj.
opacity
opacity 423 n.
imperspicuity 568 n.
opalescent
semitransparent
  424 adj.
iridescent 437 adj.
opaque
opaque 423 adj.
open
cut 46 vb.

disunite 46 vb.
begin 68 vb.
expand 197 vb.
uncover 229 vb.
open 263 adj.vb.
visible 443 adj.
uncertain 474 adj.
manifest 522 adj.
artless 699 adj.
—fire
fire at 712 vb.
—up
initiate 68 vb.
manifest 522 vb.
facilitate 701 vb.
open air
exteriority 223 n.
salubrity 652 n.
open arms
friendliness 880 n.
open country
space 183 n.
plain 348 n.
opener
opener 263 n.
open-eyed
attentive 455 adj.
open-handed
liberal 813 adj.
open house
liberality 813 n.
sociability 882 n.
opening
prelude 66 n.
debut 68 n.
opportunity 137 n.
opening 263 n.
open letter
publicity 528 n.
open-minded
choiceless 606 adj.
open question
uncertainty 474 n.
open sesame
opener 263 n.
spell 983 n.
open to
liable 180 adj.
vulnerable 661 adj.
opera
vocal music 412 n.
operable
possible 469 adj.
medical 658 adj.
opera glasses
telescope 442 n.
opera house

theatre 594 n.
opera singer
vocalist 413 n.
operate
operate 173 vb.
function 622 vb.
use 673 vb.
operatic
musical 412 adj.
operation
instrumentality
  628 n.
surgery 658 n.
undertaking 672 n.
labour 682 n.
operational
operative 173 adj.
prepared 669 adj.
operational research
policy 623 n.
management 689 n.
operations
warfare 718 n.
operative
powerful 160 adj.
operative 173 adj.
worker 686 n.
operator
machinist 630 n.
doer 676 n.
ophthalmic
seeing 438 adj.
opiate
moderator 177 n.
soporific 679 n.
opine
opine 485 vb.
opinion
idea 451 n.
opinion 485 n.
supposition 512 n.
opinionated
positive 473 adj.
narrow-minded
  481 adj.
opinion poll
vote 605 n.
opium
drug 658 n.
soporific 679 n.
opponent
opponent 705 n.
opportune
apt 24 adj.
opportune 137 adj.
opportunism
good policy 642 n.

improbity 930 n.
opportunist
enterprising
  672 adj.
egotist 932 n.
opportunity
opportunity 137 n.
scope 744 n.
oppose
oppose 704 vb.
deprecate 762 vb.
(see opposition)
opposite
contrary 14 adj.
opposite 240 adj.
opposite number
correlation 12 n.
compeer 28 n.
opposites
polarity 14 n.
opposites 704 n.
opposition
counteraction 182 n.
opposition 704 n.
resistance 715 n.
opposition, the
dissentient 489 n.
oppress
oppress 735 vb.
torment 827 vb.
oppression
severity 735 n.
dejection 834 n.
oppressive
warm 379 adj.
oppressive 735 adj.
oppressor
tyrant 735 n.
opprobrious
degrading 867 adj.
opt (for)
choose 605 vb.
optical
seeing 438 adj.
optical device
optical device 442 n.
optical illusion
visual fallacy 440 n.
optician
doctor 658 n.
optics
optics 417 n.
optimism
cheerfulness 833 n.
hope 852 n.
optimistic
optimistic 482 adj.

optimum
  best 644 adj.
option
  choice 605 n.
optional
  voluntary 597 adj.
  choosing 605 adj.
opulence
  wealth 800 n.
opus
  product 164 n.
  musical piece
    412 n.
oracle
  sage 500 n.
  oracle 511 n.
oracular
  uncertain 474 adj.
  aphoristic 496 adj.
  wise 498 adj.
  predicting 511 adj.
  equivocal 518 adj.
  unclear 568 adj.
oral
  vocal 577 adj.
  speaking 579 adj.
orange
  fruit 301 n.
  orange 432 n.adj.
orangery
  garden 370 n.
oration
  oration 579 n.
orator
  speaker 579 n.
oratorical
  figurative 519 adj.
  rhetorical 574 adj.
  eloquent 579 adj.
oratorio
  vocal music 412 n.
oratory
  church 990 n.
orb
  sphere 252 n.
  regalia 743 n.
orbit
  influence 178 n.
  space travel 271 n.
  circle 314 vb.
  function 622 n.
orchard
  garden 370 n.
orchestra
  orchestra 413 n.
orchestrate
  compose 56 vb.

compose music
  413 vb.
ordain
  decree 737 vb.
  be ecclesiastical
    985 vb.
ordained
  fated 596 adj.
  clerical 986 adj.
ordeal
  experiment 461 n.
  suffering 825 n.
order
  order 60 n. .
  sort 77 n.
  require 627 vb.
  community 708 n.
  decoration 729 n.
  command 737 n.vb.
  title 870 n.
  monk 986 n.
orderless
  orderless 61 adj.
  amorphous 244 adj.
orderly
  orderly 60 adj.
  regular 81 adj.
  businesslike
    622 adj.
  servant 742 n.
order of service
  Christian rite 988 n.
order of the day
  affairs 154 n.
  policy 623 n.
order paper
  topic 452 n.
ordinal
  numerical 85 adj.
ordinance
  precept 693 n.
  legislation 953 n.
  rite 988 n.
ordinand
  cleric 986 n.
ordinary
  median 30 adj.
  typical 83 adj.
  usual 610 adj.
  middling 732 adj.
  unastonishing
    865 adj.
ordination
  mandate 751 n.
ordnance
  gun 723 n.
ordure

excrement 302 n.
ore
  mineral 359 n.
organ
  part 53 n.
  organ 414 n.
  the press 528 n.
  instrument 628 n.
organic
  structural 331 adj.
  organic 358 adj.
organism
  organism 358 n.
  life 360 n.
organist
  instrumentalist
    413 n.
organization
  arrangement 62 n.
  structure 331 n.
  management 689 n.
  corporation 708 n.
  (*see* **organize**)
organize
  compose 56 vb.
  plan 623 vb.
organizer
  planner 623 n.
orgasm
  spasm 318 n.
  excitation 821 n.
orgiastic
  sensual 944 adj.
orgy
  feasting 301 n.
  plenty 635 n.
  sensualism 944 n.
oriental
  lateral 239 adj.
  directed 281 adj.
orientate
  orientate 281 vb.
orientation
  situation 186 n.
  direction 281 n.
orienteering
  land travel 267 n.
orifice
  orifice 263 n.
origami
  sculpture 554 n.
origin
  origin 68 n.
  source 156 n.
  genealogy 169 n.
original
  original 21 adj.

prototype 23 n.
  first 68 adj.
  nonconformist 84 n.
  new 126 adj.
originality
  originality 21 n.
  imagination 513 n.
original sin
  heredity 5 n.
  guilt 936 n.
originate
  initiate 68 vb.
  produce 164 vb.
originator
  producer 164 n.
  planner 623 n.
orisons
  prayers 981 n.
ormolu
  ornamental art
    844 n.
ornament
  ornament 574 n.
  ornamentation
    844 n.
ornamental
  useless 641 adj.
  ornamental 844 adj.
ornamentation
  ornamentation
    844 n.
ornate
  ornate 574 adj.
  splendid 841 adj.
  ornamented
    844 adj.
ornithology
  zoology 367 n.
orphan
  survivor 41 n.
  derelict 779 n.
orphanage
  retreat 192 n.
orthodontist
  doctor 658 n.
orthodox
  conformable 83 adj.
  creedal 485 adj.
  orthodox 976 adj.
orthography
  letter 558 n.
orthopaedics
  therapy 658 n.
oscillate
  oscillate 317 vb.
  be irresolute
    601 vb.

oscillation
periodicity 141 n.
changeableness
152 n.
oscillation 317 n.

osmosis
ingress 297 n.

ossified
antiquated 127 adj.

ossify
harden 326 vb.

ostensible
appearing 445 adj.
ostensible 614 adj.

ostentation
affectation 850 n.
vanity 873 n.
ostentation 875 n.

osteopath
doctor 658 n.

ostler
animal husbandry
369 n.

ostracism
exclusion 57 n.

ostracize
make unwelcome
883 vb.

ostrich
avoider 620 n.

other
extrinsicality 6 n.
different 15 adj.

other ranks
inferior 35 n.
nonentity 639 n.

other side
opposition 704 n.
enemy 881 n.

otherworldly
immaterial 320 adj.
psychic 447 adj.
pious 979 adj.

otiose
unproductive
172 adj.

ought
be due 915 vb.

ounce
small quantity 33 n.

oust
eject 300 vb.
depose 752 vb.
deprive 786 vb.

out
absent 190 adj.
eject 300 vb.

inexact 495 adj.
matured 669 adj.
disapproved
924 adj.

outback
district 184 n.

outbid
bargain 791 vb.

outbreak
outbreak 176 n.
egress 298 n.
excitable state 822 n.

outbuilding
small house 192 n.

outburst
excitable state 822 n.

outcast
derelict 779 n.
outcast 883 n.

outcaste
commoner 869 n.

outclass
be superior 34 vb.
outdo 306 vb.

out cold
insensible 375 adj.

outcome
event 154 n.
effect 157 n.

outcrop
projection 254 n.

outcry
cry 408 n.
disapprobation
924 n.

outdated
antiquated 127 adj.

outdistance
outstrip 277 vb.

outdo
outdo 306 vb.

outdoor(s)
exterior 223 adj.

outer space
exteriority 223 n.
universe 321 n.

outface
be resolute 599 vb.
be insolent 878 vb.

outfall
outflow 298 n.

outfit
all 52 n.
component 58 n.
clothing 228 n.
equipment 630 n.
party 708 n.

outfitter
clothier 228 n.

outflank
defeat 727 vb.

outflow
outflow 298 n.

outgoing
outgoing 298 adj.
resigning 753 adj.
sociable 882 adj.

outgoings
expenditure 806 n.

outgrow
disaccustom 611 vb.
stop using 674 vb.

outhouse
small house 192 n.

outing
land travel 267 n.
amusement 837 n.

outlandish
unconformable
84 adj.
ridiculous 849 adj.

outlast
outlast 113 vb.

outlaw
exclude 57 vb.
robber 789 n.
outcast 883 n.
offender 904 n.
make illegal 954 vb.

outlawry
brigandage 788 n.
lawlessness 954 n.

outlay
expenditure 806 n.

outlet
outlet 298 n.

outline
outline 233 n.vb.
form 243 n.vb.
appearance 445 n.
describe 590 vb.

outlive
outlast 113 vb.

outlook
futurity 124 n.
destiny 155 n.
view 438 n.
expectation 507 n.

outlying
distant 199 adj.
exterior 223 adj.

outmanoeuvre
defeat 727 vb.

outmoded

antiquated 127 adj.

outnumber
be many 104 vb.

out of
akin 11 adj.

out of commission
disused 674 adj.
inactive 679 adj.

out of control
riotous 738 adj.
excited 821 adj.

out of date
anachronistic
118 adj.
antiquated 127 adj.

out of doors
exteriority 223 n.
salubrity 652 n.

out of fashion
antiquated 127 adj.

out of favour
disliked 861 adj.

out of keeping
unapt 25 adj.

out of line
disorderly 61 adj.
unconformable
84 adj.

out of one's depth
in difficulties
700 adj.

out of order
orderless 61 adj.
useless 641 adj.

out of place
misplaced 188 adj.

out of pocket
losing 772 adj.

out of practice
clumsy 695 adj.

out of proportion
disagreeing 25 adj.

out of reach
too far 199 adv.

out of sorts
sick 651 adj.
dejected 834 adj.

out of step
nonuniform 17 adj.
unconformable
84 adj.

out of the question
impossible 470 adj.
rejected 607 adj.

out of the way
unusual 84 adj.
secluded 883 adj.

out of touch
  ignorant 491 adj.
out of tune
  discordant 411 adj.
out of turn
  ill-timed 138 adj.
outpace
  outstrip 277 vb.
out-patient
  sick person 651 n.
outplay
  defeat 727 vb.
outpost
  farness 199 n.
outpouring
  outflow 298 n.
  diffuseness 570 n.
output
  data processing
    86 n.
  product 164 n.
outrage
  shame 867 vb.
  huff 891 vb.
  cruel act 898 n.
  not respect 921 vb.
  guilty act 936 n.
outrageous
  exorbitant 32 adj.
  heinous 934 adj.
outrank
  be superior 34 vb.
outright
  completely 54 adv.
outrival
  be superior 34 vb.
outset
  start 68 n.
  departure 296 n.
outshine
  be superior 34 vb.
  have a reputation
    866 vb.
outside
  exteriority 223 n.
  appearance 445 n.
outsider
  misfit 25 n.
  intruder 59 n.
  nonconformist
    84 n.
  outcast 883 n.
outsize
  huge 195 adj.
outskirts
  surroundings 230 n.
outspoken

  undisguised
    522 adj.
  assertive 532 adj.
  veracious 540 adj.
outstanding
  superior 34 adj.
  notable 638 adj.
  owed 803 adj.
outstay
  outlast 113 vb.
—one's welcome
  intrude 297 vb.
outstrip
  outstrip 277 vb.
out to
  intending 617 adj.
outvote
  reject 607 vb.
outward
  extrinsic 6 adj.
  exterior 223 adj.
outward bound
  outgoing 298 adj.
outweigh
  compensate 31 vb.
  prevail 178 vb.
outwit
  be superior 34 vb.
  befool 542 vb.
outworn
  antiquated 127 adj.
oval
  arc 250 n.
ovary
  genitalia 167 n.
ovate
  round 250 adj.
ovation
  applause 923 n.
oven
  cookery 301 n.
  furnace 383 n.
over
  beyond 34 adv.
  remaining 41 adj.
  past 125 adj.
overact
  act 594 vb.
  be affected 850 vb.
overactivity
  overactivity 678 n.
overall
  inclusive 78 adj.
overalls
  suit, apron 228 n.
  shelter 662 n.
overambitious

  enterprising
    672 adj.
over and above
  in addition 38 adv.
over and done with
  past 125 adj.
  forgotten 506 adj.
over and over
  repeatedly 106 adv.
overawe
  dominate 733 vb.
  command respect
    920 vb.
overbalance
  tumble 309 vb.
overbearing
  oppressive 735 adj.
  proud 871 adj.
overbid
  bargain 791 vb.
overblown
  expanded 197 adj.
overburden
  make heavy 322 vb.
  ill-treat 645 vb.
overcast
  cloudy 355 adj.
  sullen 893 adj.
overcharge
  overcharge 811 vb.
overcoat
  overcoat 228 n.
overcome
  overmaster 727 vb.
  sadden 834 vb.
overcompensate
  exaggerate 546 vb.
overconfidence
  overestimation
    482 n.
overcropping
  misuse 675 n.
overcrowded
  assembled 74 adj.
overdo
  exaggerate
    546 vb.
overdone
  tough 329 adj.
  exaggerated
    546 adj.
  affected 850 adj.
overdose
  poison 659 n.
  satiety 863 n.
overdraft
  insolvency 805 n.

overdraw
  be in debt 803 vb.
overdressed
  vulgar 847 adj.
overdrive
  power 160 n.
overdue
  late 136 adj.
overeating
  eating 301 n.
  gluttony 947 n.
overegg the pudding
  superabound
    637 vb.
overemphasize
  exaggerate 546 vb.
overestimate
  overrate 482 vb.
overexertion
  overactivity 678 n.
  fatigue 684 n.
overexposed
  colourless 426 adj.
overfamiliar
  impertinent
    878 adj.
overfill
  fill 54 vb.
overfishing
  unproductiveness
    172 n.
  misuse 675 n.
overflow
  be complete 54 vb.
  flow out 298 vb.
  waterfall 350 n.
  drain 351 n.
  redundance 637 n.
overgraze
  make sterile
    172 vb.
overgrown
  expanded 197 adj.
overhang
  hang 217 vb.
  overlie 226 vb.
  jut 254 vb.
overhaul
  outstrip 277 vb.
  search 459 vb.
  repair 656 vb.
overhead
  aloft 209 adv.
overheads
  cost 809 n.
overhear
  hear 415 vb.

overheated
hot 379 adj.
excited 821 adj.
overindulgence
intemperance 943 n.
overjoyed
pleased 824 adj.
jubilant 833 adj.
overkill
superfluity 637 n.
overlap
overlie 226 vb.
encroach 306 vb.
overlie
overlie 226 vb.
overload
make heavy 322 vb.
overlook
be high 209 vb.
disregard 458 vb.
not use 674 vb.
forgive 909 vb.
overlord
master 741 n.
overmanning
superfluity 637 n.
overmaster
overmaster 727 vb.
dominate 733 vb.
overmighty
proud 871 adj.
overnight
newly 126 adv.
overoptimism
overestimation 482 n.
overpaid
rich 800 adj.
overpaint
coat 226 vb.
obliterate 550 vb.
overparticular
fastidious 862 adj.
overplay one's hand
misjudge 481 vb.
overplus
superfluity 637 n.
overpopulate
superabound 637 vb.
overpower
be strong 162 vb.
overmaster 727 vb.
overpowering
impressive 821 adj.
overpraise
overrate 482 vb.

praise 923 n.vb.
overpriced
dear 811 adj.
overprint
obliterate 550 vb.
overproof
intoxicating 949 adj.
overrate
overrate 482 vb.
overrated
unimportant 639 adj.
overreach
deceive 542 vb.
be cunning 698 vb.
—oneself
fail 728 vb.
override
prevail 178 vb.
overmaster 727 vb.
overriding
supreme 34 adj.
compelling 740 adj.
overripe
imperfect 647 adj.
matured 669 adj.
overrule
dominate 733 vb.
abrogate 752 vb.
overruling
supreme 34 adj.
authoritative 733 adj.
overrun
encroach 306 vb.
appropriate 786 vb.
overseas
abroad 59 adv.
removed 199 adj.
overseer
manager 690 n.
oversensitive
sensitive 819 adj.
oversexed
lecherous 951 adj.
overshadow
be superior 34 vb.
darken 418 vb.
oversight
negligence 458 n.
mistake 495 n.
management 689 n.
oversize
huge 195 adj.
oversleep
be late 136 vb.

overspill
redundance 637 n.
overstated
exaggerated 546 adj.
overstep
overstep 306 vb.
overstrung
lively 819 adj.
overt
undisguised 522 adj.
overtake
outstrip 277 vb.
overtax
fatigue 684 vb.
oppress 735 vb.
overthrow
revolution 149 n.
fell 311 vb.
overmaster 727 vb.
unthrone 734 vb.
overtime
exertion 682 n.
overtone
latency 523 n.
overtop
crown 213 vb.
overtrump
overmaster 727 vb.
overtrustful
credulous 487 adj.
overture(s)
prelude 66 n.
approach 289 n.
peace offering 719 n.
overturn
revolutionize 149 vb.
invert 221 vb.
overuse
misuse 675 n.
overweening
proud 871 adj.
insolent 878 adj.
overweight
fleshy 195 adj.
make heavy 322 vb.
overwhelm
destroy 165 vb.
superabound 637 vb.
defeat 727 vb.
impress 821 vb.
overwhelming
felt 818 adj.

impressive 821 adj.
wonderful 864 adj.
overwork
misuse 675 vb.
work 682 vb.
overwrought
fervent 818 adj.
excited 821 adj.
ovoid
round 250 adj.
ovum
genitalia 167 n.
owe
be in debt 803 vb.
owing to
caused 157 adj.
attributed 158 adj.
owl
bird 365 n.
omen 511 n.
owlish
unintelligent 499 adj.
own
confess 526 vb.
possess 773 vb.
owner
owner 776 n.
ownership
possession 773 n.
ox
beast of burden 273 n.
Oxbridge
educational 534 adj.
oxygen
air 340 n.
oyster
fish food 301 n.
taciturnity 582 n.
ozone
salubrity 652 n.

P

pabulum
food 301 n.
pace
synchronize 123 vb.
gait 265 n.
walk 267 vb.
velocity 277 n.
pacemaker
substitute 150 n.
leader 690 n.
pacific
peaceful 717 adj.

PAC   PAI   PAL   PAL

pacification
  pacification 719 n.
pacifier
  mediator 720 n.
pacifist
  pacifist 717 n.
pacify
  assuage 177 vb.
  pacify 719 vb.
pack
  fill 54 vb.
  group 74 n.
  load 193 vb.
  line 227 vb.
  be dense 324 vb.
  hunter 619 n.
  store 632 vb.
  encumbrance 702 n.
—**the jury**
  predetermine
    608 vb.
—**up**
  fail 728 vb.
package
  bunch 74 n.
package deal
  inclusion 78 n.
packaging
  receptacle 194 n.
  wrapping 226 n.
packet
  bunch 74 n.
  small box 194 n.
packhorse
  beast of burden
    273 n.
packing
  lining 227 n.
  storage 632 n.
pact
  compact 765 n.
pad
  abode 192 n.
  foot 214 n.
  line 227 vb.
  walk 267 vb.
  stationery 586 n.
—**out**
  be diffuse 570 vb.
padding
  lining 227 n.
  softness 327 n.
  pleonasm 570 n.
paddle
  walk 267 vb.
  row, swim 269 vb.
  propellant 287 n.

—**one's own canoe**
  be free 744 vb.
paddling
  aquatics 269 n.
paddock
  enclosure 235 n.
padlock
  fastening 47 n.
padre
  cleric 986 n.
paean
  applause 923 n.
  hymn 981 n.
paediatrician
  doctor 658 n.
paediatrics
  medical art 658 n.
pagan
  heathen 974 n.
  profane 980 adj.
  idolater 982 n.
page
  courier 529 n.
  edition 589 n.
  retainer 742 n.
pageant
  pageant 875 n.
pagination
  numeration 86 n.
pagoda
  temple 990 n.
pail
  vessel 194 n.
pain
  pain 377 n.
  suffering 825 n.
  painfulness 827 n.
painful
  painful 377 adj.
  laborious 682 adj.
pain in the neck
  annoyance 827 n.
  bore 838 n.
painkiller
  anaesthetic 375 n.
  antidote 658 n.
pain-killing
  lenitive 177 adj.
  relieving 831 adj.
painless
  comfortable
    376 adj.
  easy 701 adj.
pains
  attention 455 n.
  carefulness 457 n.
painstaking

laborious 682 adj.
  fastidious 862 adj.
paint
  coat 226 vb.
  pigment 425 n.
  paint 553 vb.
  describe 590 vb.
  cosmetic 843 n.
  decorate 844 vb.
paintbox
  art equipment 553 n.
painted
  coloured 425 adj.
  false 541 adj.
painter
  cable 47 n.
  artist 556 n.
painting
  representation
    551 n.
  painting 553 n.
paints
  art equipment 553 n.
pair
  analogue 18 n.
  unite with 45 vb.
  duality 90 n.
pal
  chum 880 n.
palace
  house 192 n.
paladin
  combatant 722 n.
  brave person 855 n.
palaeography
  palaeology 125 n.
palaeolithic
  primal 127 adj.
palanquin
  vehicle 274 n.
palatable
  edible 301 adj.
  tasty 386 adj.
palate
  taste 386 n.
palatial
  architectural
    192 adj.
palaver
  chatter 581 n.
  confer 584 vb.
pale
  fence 235 n.
  soft-hued 425 adj.
  colourless 426 adj.
  whitish 427 adj.
  quake 854 vb.

palette
  art equipment
    553 n.
palimpsest
  script 586 n.
  use 673 n.
palindrome
  inversion 221 n.
paling
  fence 235 n.
palisade
  defences 713 n.
pall
  coverlet 226 n.
  be tedious 838 vb.
  sate 863 vb.
pallet
  bed 218 n.
  carrier 273 n.
palletize
  load 193 vb.
palliate
  moderate 177 vb.
  qualify 468 vb.
  extenuate 927 vb.
palliative
  moderator 177 n.
pallid
  colourless 426 adj.
pallor
  achromatism 426 n.
pally
  friendly 880 adj.
palm
  tree 366 n.
  feeler 378 n.
  oracle 511 n.
  trophy 729 n.
—**off**
  deceive 542 vb.
palmate
  notched 260 adj.
palmer
  traveller 268 n.
  pietist 979 n.
palmistry
  divination 511 n.
palmy days
  palmy days 730 n.
palp
  feeler 378 n.
palpable
  substantial 3 adj.
  material 319 adj.
  tactual 378 adj.
palpate
  touch 378 vb.

648

palpitation
agitation 318 n.
feeling 818 n.
nervousness 854 n.
palsy
insensibility 375 n.
nervous disorders
651 n.
palter
be irresolute 601 vb.
paltry
inconsiderable
33 adj.
unimportant
639 adj.
pamper
pet 889 vb.
pampered
comfortable
376 adj.
sensual 944 adj.
pamphlet
the press 528 n.
book 589 n.
pamphleteer
argue 475 vb.
publish 528 vb.
dissertator 591 n.
pan
eliminate 44 vb.
cauldron 194 n.
scales 322 n.
photography 551 n.
dispraise 924 vb.
—out
happen 154 vb.
panacea
remedy 658 n.
panache
plumage 259 n.
ostentation 875 n.
pancake
fly 271 vb.
dish 301 n.
pandemic
universal 79 adj.
infectious 653 adj.
pandemonium
turmoil 61 n.
loudness 400 n.
pander
bawd 952 n.
pander (to)
minister to 703 vb.
pane
transparency 422 n.
panegyric

praise 923 n.
panel
band 74 n.
list 87 n.
lamina 207 n.
council 692 n.
tribunal 956 n.
panel game
indoor game 837 n.
panelling •
ornamental art
844 n.
pang
pang 377 n.
panic
fear 854 n.
be cowardly 856 vb.
pannier
bag 194 n.
basket 194 n.
panoply
armour 713 n.
panorama
generality 79 n.
view 438 n.
pant
breathe 352 vb.
be fatigued 684 vb.
—for
desire 859 vb.
pantaloons
trousers 228 n.
pantheism
deism 973 n.
pantheon
temple 990 n.
panties
underwear 228 n.
pantomime
mimicry 20 n.
gesture 547 n.
stage play 594 n.
pantry
chamber 194 n.
provisions 301 n.
pants
underwear 228 n.
pap
pulpiness 356 n.
insipidity 387 n.
papacy
the church 985 n.
papal
ecclesiastical
985 adj.
paper
insubstantial 4 adj.

thinness 206 n.
line 227 vb.
report 524 n.
the press 528 n.
stationery 586 n.
dissertation 591 n.
paper 631 n.
—over the cracks
conceal 525 vb.
paperback
book 589 n.
paper modelling
sculpture 554 n.
papers
record 548 n.
paper tiger
sham 542 n.
paperwork
writing 586 n.
papery
brittle 330 adj.
papier-mâché
pulpiness 356 n.
sculpture 554 n.
par
equivalence 28 n.
parable
metaphor 519 n.
narrative 590 n.
parabola
curve 248 n.
parachute
fly 271 vb.
safeguard 662 n.
parachutist
aeronaut 271 n.
parade
marching 267 n.
show 522 vb.
pageant 875 n.
parade ground
arena 724 n.
paradigm
prototype 23 n.
grammar 564 n.
Paradise
happiness 824 n.
heaven 971 n.
paradox
argumentation
475 n.
lack of expectation
508 n.
paraffin
fuel 385 n.
paragon
paragon 646 n.

prodigy 864 n.
paragraph
phrase 563 n.
parallel
analogue 18 n.
parallel 219 adj.
compare 462 vb.
paralyse
disable 161 vb.
render insensible
375 vb.
paralysed
still 266 adj.
paralysis
inertness 175 n.
insensibility 375 n.
paramedic
doctor 658 n.
parameter
numerical element
85 n.
paramilitary
warlike 718 adj.
paramount
supreme 34 adj.
authoritative
733 adj.
paramour
lover 887 n.
paranoia
psychopathy
503 n.
paranoid
insane 503 adj.
paranormal
paranormal
984 adj.
parapet
fortification 713 n.
paraphernalia
medley 43 n.
equipment 630 n.
property 777 n.
paraphrase
translation 520 n.
paraplegia
nervous disorders
651 n.
parapsychology
psychics 984 n.
parasite
idler 679 n.
dependant 742 n.
beggar 763 n.
toady 879 n.
parasol
shade 226 n.

paratrooper
aeronaut 271 n.
armed force
722 n.
parboil
cook 301 vb.
parcel
piece 53 n.
bunch 74 n.
apportion 783 vb.
parched
dry 342 adj.
hungry 859 adj.
parchment
stationery 586 n.
pardon
amnesty 506 n.
forgive 909 vb.
pardonable
vindicable 927 adj.
pare
abate 37 vb.
cut 46 vb.
laminate 207 vb.
parent
parentage 169 n.
parentage
consanguinity 11 n.
attribution 158 n.
parental
parental 169 adj.
parenthesis
discontinuity 72 n.
interjection 231 n.
parenthood
parentage 169 n.
pariah
dog 365 n.
outcast 883 n.
parish
parish 985 n.
parishioner
native 191 n.
lay person 987 n.
parish priest
pastor 986 n.
parity
similarity 18 n.
equality 28 n.
park
place 187 vb.
enclosure 235 n.
grassland 348 n.
pleasure ground
837 n.
parka
jacket 228 n.

Parkinson's law
expansion 197 n.
parlance
style 566 n.
speech 579 n.
parley
confer 584 vb.
make terms 766 vb.
parliament
parliament 692 n.
parliamentarian
councillor 692 n.
parlour
chamber 194 n.
parlour game
indoor game 837 n.
domestic 742 n.
parochial
regional 184 adj.
provincial 192 adj.
narrow-minded
481 adj.
parodist
humorist 839 n.
parody
imitate 20 vb.
misrepresent
552 vb.
satire 851 n.
parole
permit 756 n.
paronomasia
equivocalness
518 n.
trope 519 n.
paroxysm
spasm 318 n.
frenzy 503 n.
parricide
murderer 362 n.
parrot
imitator 20 n.
repeat 106 vb.
chatterer 581 n.
parry
repel 292 vb.
parry 713 vb.
resist 715 vb.
parse
parse 564 vb.
parsimonious
parsimonious
816 adj.
parsley
potherb 301 n.
parson
cleric 986 n.

parsonage
parsonage 986 n.
part
disunite 46 vb.
part 53 n.
incompleteness
55 n.
component 58 n.
diverge 294 vb.
acting 594 n.
function 622 n.
portion 783 n.
—with
not retain 779 vb.
partake
participate 775 vb.
Parthian shot
valediction 296 n.
partial
incomplete 55 adj.
fractional 102 adj.
partiality
prejudice 481 n.
liking 859 n.
injustice 914 n.
participate
cooperate 706 vb.
participate 775 vb.
participation
association 706 n.
participation 775 n.
participator
participator 775 n.
particle
small thing 33 n.
minuteness 196 n.
parti-coloured
variegated 437 adj.
particular
special 80 adj.
careful 457 adj.
fastidious 862 adj.
particularism
sectarianism 978 n.
particularize
specify 80 vb.
particulars
particulars 80 n.
description 590 n.
parting
separation 46 n.
dividing line 92 n.
departure 296 n.
partisan
biased 481 adj.
patron 707 n.
sectional 708 adj.

revolter 738 n.
sectarian 978 adj.
partition
separation 46 n.
dividing line 92 n.
partition 231 n.
apportionment
783 n.
partner
accompany 89 vb.
colleague 707 n.
participator 775 n.
spouse 894 n.
partnership
corporation 708 n.
participation 775 n.
part of speech
part of speech 564 n.
parts
region 184 n.
contents 193 n.
parturition
obstetrics 167 n.
party
band 74 n.
party 708 n.
signatory 765 n.
social gathering
882 n.
litigant 959 n.
party-goer
reveller 837 n.
party line
policy 623 n.
tactics 688 n.
party member
political party
708 n.
party to
assenting 488 adj.
party wall
partition 231 n.
parvenu
upstart 126 n.
pass
elapse 111 vb.
be past 125 vb.
gap 201 n.
opener 263 n.
excrete 302 vb.
pass 305 vb.
overstep 306 vb.
access 624 n.
suffice 635 vb.
predicament 700 n.
lunge 712 n.
permit 756 n.vb.

approve 923 vb.
make legal 953 vb.
—away
pass away 2 vb.
die 361 vb.
—for
resemble 18 vb.
—muster
suffice 635 vb.
be good 644 vb.
—off
happen 154 vb.
dissemble 541 vb.
—on
transfer 272 vb.
progress 285 vb.
communicate
　524 vb.
—out
be insensible 375 vb.
—over
disregard 458 vb.
reject 607 vb.
—the buck
avoid 620 vb.
not act 677 vb.
—the time
pass time 108 vb.
amuse oneself
　837 vb.
passable
not bad 644 adj.
middling 732 adj.
passage
lobby 194 n.
motion 265 n.
land travel 267 n.
water travel 269 n.
passage 305 n.
edition 589 n.
access 624 n.
passbook
permit 756 n.
account book 808 n.
passenger
rider 268 n.
passerby
spectator 441 n.
passim
sporadically 75 adv.
passion
vigour 571 n.
warm feeling 818 n.
desire 859 n.
love 887 n.
anger 891 n.
passionate

fervent 818 adj.
excitable 822 adj.
loving 887 adj.
passionless
impassive 820 adj.
indifferent 860 adj.
passive
inert 175 adj.
inexcitable 823 adj.
passive resistance
resistance 715 n.
disobedience 738 n.
passport
opener 263 n.
credential 466 n.
permit 756 n.
password
opener 263 n.
identification 547 n.
permit 756 n.
past
past 125 adj.
antiquated 127 adj.
disrepute 867 adj.
pasta
dish 301 n.
paste
adhesive 47 n.
softness 327 n.
sham 542 n.
finery 844 n.
pasteboard
paper 631 n.
pastel
soft-hued 425 adj.
art equipment 553 n.
pasteurize
sanitate 652 vb.
pastiche
art style 553 n.
pastille
sweet thing 392 n.
pastime
amusement 837 n.
pasting
knock 279 n.
past it
ageing 131 adj.
useless 641 adj.
past master
proficient person
　696 n.
pastor
pastor 986 n.
pastoral
agrarian 370 adj.
priestly 985 adj.

pastoral care
ministration 988 n.
pastry
pastries 301 n.
past tense
past time 125 n.
pasturage
grassland 348 n.
pasture
feed 301 vb.
graze 301 vb.
grassland 348 n.
pasty
pastries 301 n.
pulpy 356 adj.
colourless 426 adj.
pat
apt 24 adj.
touch 378 n.vb.
caress 889 vb.
—on the back
applaud 923 vb.
patch
adjunct 40 n.
piece 53 n.
variegate 437 vb.
repair 656 n.vb.
surgical dressing
　658 n.
—up
repair 656 vb.
make peace 719 vb.
patchwork
variegation 437 n.
needlework 844 n.
patchy
nonuniform 17 adj.
discontinuous
　72 adj.
imperfect 647 adj.
patent
manifest 522 adj.
permit 756 n.vb.
patented
proprietary 777 adj.
paterfamilias
paternity 169 n.
paternal
parental 169 adj.
benevolent 897 adj.
paternalism
governance 733 n.
paternity
paternity 169 n.
path
passage 305 n.
trace 548 n.

path 624 n.
pathetic
bad 645 adj.
felt 818 adj.
distressing 827 adj.
pathfinder
precursor 66 n.
traveller 268 n.
pathogen
infection 651 n.
pathology
pathology 651 n.
medical art 658 n.
pathos
painfulness 827 n.
pathway
path 624 n.
patience
perseverance 600 n.
patience 823 n.
patient
sick person 651 n.
patina
greenness 434 n.
impairment 655 n.
patio
lobby 194 n.
patois
dialect 560 n.
patrial
native 191 n.
patriarch
old man 133 n.
paternity 169 n.
ecclesiarch 986 n.
patriarchy
government 733 n.
patrician
aristocrat 868 n.
patricide
homicide 362 n.
patrilinear
akin 11 adj.
patrimony
possession 773 n.
dower 777 n.
patriot
defender 713 n.
patriot 901 n.
patriotism
patriotism 901 n.
patrol
safeguard 660 vb.
armed force 722 n.
restrain 747 vb.
patron, patroness
enthusiast 504 n.

PAT

protector 660 n.
patron 707 n.
defender 713 n.
purchaser 792 n.
friend 880 n.
benefactor 903 n.
patronage
influence 178 n.
protection 660 n.
approbation 923 n.
patronize
choose 605 vb.
patronize 703 vb.
be proud 871 vb.
befriend 880 vb.
patter
faintness 401 n.
empty talk 515 n.
slang 560 n.
loquacity 581 n.
pattern
prototype 23 n.
composition 56 n.
example 83 n.
form 243 n.vb.
structure 331 n.
paragon 646 n.
pattern 844 n.
patty
pastries 301 n.
paucity
scarcity 636 n.
paunch
swelling 253 n.
pauper
poor person 801 n.
pause
delay 136 n.
lull 145 n.
interval 201 n.
doubt 486 n.
not act 677 vb.
pave
overlay 226 vb.
smooth 258 vb.
—the way
facilitate 701 vb.
pavement
path 624 n.
pavilion
canopy 226 n.
paving
paving 226 n.
paw
foot 214 n.
feeler 378 n.
caress 889 vb.

PEA

pawn
dupe 544 n.
instrument 628 n.
slave 742 n.
security 767 n.
borrow 785 vb.
pawnbroker
lender 784 n.
pay
be profitable 771 vb.
pay 804 n.vb.
reward 962 n.vb.
—dividends
be successful
727 vb.
—for
defray 804 vb.
be punished 963 vb.
—off
make inactive
679 vb.
—one out
retaliate 714 vb.
—one's respects to
pay one's respects
884 vb.
—out
lengthen 203 vb.
payable
owed 803 adj.
payee
recipient 782 n.
payload
contents 193 n.
paymaster
treasurer 798 n.
payment
payment 804 n.
payoff
completion 725 n.
payroll
personnel 686 n.
peace
quietude 266 n.
peace 717 n.
pleasurableness
826 n.
peaceable
amiable 884 adj.
peace and quiet
repose 683 n.
seclusion 883 n.
peaceful
tranquil 266 adj.
peaceful 717 adj.
peace-lover
pacifist 717 n.

PEC

peacemaker
mediator 720 n.
peacemaking
pacification 719 n.
peace offering
peace offering
719 n.
peace of mind
content 828 n.
peach
a beauty 841 n.
peach (on)
divulge 526 vb.
peacock
fop 848 n.
be ostentatious
875 vb.
peak
summit 213 n.
shade 226 n.
perfection 646 n.
peaky
lean 206 adj.
unhealthy 651 adj.
peal
loudness 400 n.
resonance 404 n.
campanology 412 n.
gong 414 n.
peanuts
trifle 639 n.
money 797 n.
pearl
white thing 427 n.
a beauty 841 n.
gem 844 n.
pearly
soft-hued 425 adj.
whitish 427 adj.
iridescent 437 adj.
pear-shaped
round 250 adj.
peasant
farmer 370 n.
country-dweller
869 n.
pea-shooter
propellant 287 n.
peat
fuel 385 n.
marsh 347 n.
pebble
hardness 326 n.
soil 344 n.
peccadillo
guilty act 936 n.
peccant

PED

diseased 651 adj.
wicked 934 adj.
peck
eat 301 vb.
peckish
hungry 859 adj.
pectoral
vestments 989 n.
peculate
defraud 788 vb.
peculiar
unusual 84 adj.
peculiarity
temperament 5 n.
speciality 80 n.
pecuniary
monetary 797 adj.
pedagogic
educational 534 adj.
pedagogue
scholar 492 n.
teacher 537 n.
pedal
propellant 287 n.
play music 413 vb.
tool 630 n.
pedal power
energy 160 n.
vehicle 274 n.
pedant
narrow mind 481 n.
scholar 492 n.
perfectionist 862 n.
pedantic
accurate 494 adj.
peddle
sell 793 vb.
pederast
libertine 952 n.
pedestal
stand 218 n.
pedestrian
pedestrian 268 n.
feeble 572 adj.
dull 840 adj.
pedestrian crossing
traffic control 305 n.
pedicure
beautification
843 n.
pedigree
genealogy 169 n.
nobility 868 n.
pediment
summit 213 n.
pedlar
pedlar 794 n.

peek
look 438 n.
be curious 453 vb.

peel
leavings 41 n.
skin 226 n.
uncover 229 vb.

—off
unstick 49 vb.

peep
look 438 n.
be curious 453 vb.

peephole
window 263 n.

peeping Tom
inquisitive person
453 n.

peep show
spectacle 455 n.

peer
compeer 28 n.
scan 438 vb.
be dim-sighted
440 vb.
person of rank
868 n.

peerage
honours 866 n.

peerless
best 644 adj.

peeve
enrage 891 vb.

peevish
irascible 892 adj.
sullen 893 adj.

peg
fastening 47 n.
hanger 217 n.
stopper 264 n.
pretext 614 n.

peg away
persevere 600 vb.

pejorative
depreciating 483 adj.
word 559 n.
detracting 926 adj.

pellet
sphere 252 n.
missile 287 n.

pellicle
skin 226 n.

pellucid
transparent 422 adj.
intelligible 516 adj.

pelt
skin 226 n.
move fast 277 vb.

rain 350 vb.
lapidate 712 vb.

pen
enclosure 235 n.
stationery 586 n.
write 586 vb.
imprison 747 vb.
lockup 748 n.

penal
punitive 963 adj.

penal code
law 953 n.
penalty 963 n.

penalize
make illegal 945 vb.
punish 963 vb.

penal servitude
penalty 963 n.

penal settlement
prison camp 748 n.

penalty
penalty 963 n.

penance
penance 941 n.
asceticism 945 n.

penchant
tendency 179 n.

pencil
art equipment 553 n.
stationery 586 n.

pendant
analogue 18 n.
hanging object
217 n.
jewellery 844 n.

pendent
hanging 217 adj.

pending
while 108 adv.

pendulous
nonadhesive 49 adj.

pendulum
timekeeper 117 n.
hanging object
217 n.
oscillation 317 n.

penetrate
pierce 263 vb.
infiltrate 297 vb.
impress 821 vb.

penetrating
strident 407 adj.
felt 818 adj.

penetration
ingress 297 n.
passage 305 n.
sagacity 498 n.

penfriend
correspondent
588 n.

penicillin
drug 658 n.

peninsula
projection 254 n.

penis
genitalia 167 n.

penitent
penitent 939 n.
ascetic 945 n.

penitential
repentant 939 adj.
atoning 941 adj.

penitentiary
prison 748 n.

penknife
sharp edge 256 n.

penman, penwoman
calligrapher 586 n.

pen name
misnomer 562 n.

pennant
flag 547 n.

penniless
poor 801 adj.

penny-wise
parsimonious
816 adj.

penology
punishment 963 n.

penpusher
recorder 549 n.

pension
quarters 192 n.
resignation 753 n.
pay 804 n.

pensioner
old person 133 n.

pension off
stop using 674 vb.
not retain 779 vb.

pensive
thoughtful 449 adj.

pentagon
angular figure
247 n.

pentagram
talisman 983 n.

penthouse
flat 192 n.
attic 194 n.

pent up
restrained 747 adj.

penultimate
ending 69 adj.

penumbra
half-light 419 n.

penurious
poor 801 adj.

people
place oneself
187 vb.
native 191 n.
nation 371 n.
subject 742 n.
commonalty 869 n.

pep
vigorousness 174 n.

pepper
pierce 263 vb.
shoot 287 vb.
condiment 389 n.
wound 655 vb.

peppery
pungent 388 adj.
irascible 892 adj.

pep pill
stimulant 174 n.
drug-taking 949 n.

pep talk
inducement 612 n.

peptic
remedial 658 adj.

pep up
invigorate 174 vb.
make appetizing
390 vb.

perambulate
walk 267 vb.

perambulator
pushcart 274 n.

perceive
cognize 447 vb.

percentage
part 53 n.
ratio 85 n.
discount 810 n.

perception
vision 438 n.
sagacity 498 n.

perch
place oneself
187 vb.
nest 192 n.
sit down 311 vb.
repose 683 vb.

percipience
intellect 447 n.

percolate
infiltrate 297 vb.
pass 305 vb.
flow 350 vb.

percolator
cauldron 194 n.

percussion
impulse 279 n.
musical instrument
414 n.

perdition
ruin 165 n.
hell 972 n.

peremptory
assertive 532 adj.
commanding
737 adj.
obligatory 917 adj.

perennial
perpetual 115 adj.

perfect
perfect 646 adj.vb.
mature 669 vb.
carry through
725 vb.

perfection
perfection 646 n.
beauty 841 n.

perfectionist
trier 671 n.
perfectionist 862 n.

perfidious
deceiving 542 adj.
perfidious 930 adj.

perforate
pierce 263 vb.

perforation
perforation 263 n.

perform
act 594 vb.
be instrumental
628 vb.
do 676 vb.
observe 768 vb.

performance
production 164 n.
musical skill 413 n.
dramaturgy 594 n.
effectuation 725 n.

performer
musician 413 n.
entertainer 594 n.

perfume
odour 394 n.
scent 396 n.
cosmetic 843 n.

perfunctory
deficient 307 adj.
negligent 458 adj.
uncompleted
726 adj.

pergola
arbour 194 n.

perhaps
possibly 469 adv.

perigee
short distance 200 n.

peril
danger 661 n.

perimeter
outline 233 n.

period
end 69 n.
period 110 n.
limit 236 n.
haemorrhage 302 n.
phrase 563 n.

periodic, periodical
periodic 110 adj.

periodical
journal 528 n.

periodicity
recurrence 106 n.
periodicity 141 n.

peripatetic
travelling 267 adj.

peripeteia
event 154 n.

peripheral
unimportant
639 adj.

periphery
surroundings 230 n.

periphrasis
pleonasm 570 n.

periscope
telescope 442 n.

perish
decompose 51 vb.
perish 361 vb.

perishable
ephemeral 114 adj.

perjurer
liar 545 n.

perjury
untruth 543 n.

perk, perquisite
reward 962 n.

perk up
be refreshed 685 vb.
be cheerful 833 vb.

perky
cheerful 833 adj.
impertinent 878 adj.

perm
hairdressing 843 n.

permanence
permanence 144 n.

stability 153 n.

permeable
porous 263 adj.

permeate
pervade 189 vb.
infiltrate 297 vb.
pass 305 vb.

permissible
permitted 756 adj.
legal 953 adj.

permission
permission 756 n.

permissive
lax 734 adj.

permissive society
scope 744 n.
unchastity 951 n.

permit
be lax 734 vb.
permit 756 n.vb.

permutation
change 143 n.

pernicious
harmful 645 adj.

pernickety
fastidious 862 adj.

peroration
oration 579 n.

peroxide
bleacher 426 n.

perpendicular
vertical 215 adj.

perpetrate
do 676 vb.
do wrong 914 vb.

perpetrator
doer 676 n.
agent 686 n.

perpetual
existing 1 adj.
continuous 71 adj.
perpetual 115 adj.
frequent 139 adj.

perpetuate
perpetuate 115 vb.

perpetuity
perpetuity 115 n.

perplex
puzzle 474 vb.
trouble 827 vb.

perplexity
difficulty 700 n.

perquisite
(*see* **perk**)

persecute
pursue 619 vb.
be severe 735 vb.

torment 827 vb.
be malevolent
898 vb.

persecutor
tyrant 735 n.

perseverance
perseverance 600 n.

persevere
stay 144 vb.
persevere 600 vb.
exert oneself 682 vb.

persiflage
witticism 839 n.
ridicule 851 n.

persist
go on 146 vb.
persevere 600 vb.

persistent
lasting 113 adj.
unyielding 162 adj.
obstinate 602 adj.

person
self 80 n.
object 319 n.
person 371 n.

personable
personable 841 adj.

personage
acting 594 n.
bigwig 638 n.

persona grata
favourite 890 n.

personal
intrinsic 5 adj.
special 80 adj.
human 371 adj.
proprietary 777 adj.
impertinent 878 adj.

personal effects
property 777 n.

personalities
calumny 926 n.

personality
self 80 n.
speciality 80 n.
spirit 447 n.
bigwig 638 n.
affections 817 n.

personalize
specify 80 vb.

personal reasons
motive 612 n.

personal remarks
scurrility 899 n.
calumny 926 n.

personate
act 594 vb.

personification
  metaphor 519 n.
personify
  materialize 319 vb.
  manifest 522 vb.
personnel
  personnel 686 n.
perspective
  relativeness 9 n.
  range 183 n.
  length 203 n.
  convergence 293 n.
  view 438 n.
perspicacious
  seeing 438 adj.
  intelligent 498 adj.
perspicuous
  intelligible 516 adj.
  perspicuous
    567 adj.
perspiration
  excretion 302 n.
perspire
  be hot 379 vb.
persuadability
  persuadability 612 n.
persuade
  convince 485 vb.
  induce 612 vb.
—against
  dissuade 613 vb.
persuader
  motivator 612 n.
persuasible
  credulous 487 adj.
  impressible 819 adj.
persuasion
  belief 485 n.
persuasion
  belief 485 n.
  inducement 612 n.
persuasive
  influential 178 adj.
  plausible 471 adj.
  inducing 612 adj.
pert
  cheerful 833 adj.
  impertinent 878 adj.
pertain
  be related 9 vb.
  be included 78 vb.
pertinacity
  perseverance 600 n.
pertinent
  relevant 9 adj.
perturbation
  agitation 318 n.

  excitation 821 n.
peruse
  study 536 vb.
pervade
  pervade 189 vb.
pervasive
  ubiquitous 189 adj.
perverse
  wilful 602 adj.
  disobedient 738 adj.
perversion
  misteaching 535 n.
  falsehood 541 n.
  misuse 675 n.
pervert
  nonconformist 84 n.
  distort 246 vb.
  mislead 495 vb.
  pervert 655 vb.
  make wicked
    934 vb.
  libertine 952 n.
perverted
  vicious 934 adj.
pesky
  annoying 827 adj.
pessary
  surgical dressing
    658 n.
pessimism
  underestimation
    483 n.
  hopelessness 853 n.
pessimist
  moper 834 n.
  alarmist 854 n.
pest
  plague 651 n.
  bane 659 n.
  annoyance 827 n.
  hateful object 888 n.
pester
  torment 827 vb.
pesticide
  poison 659 n.
pestilence
  plague 651 n.
pestilent, pestilential
  toxic 653 adj.
  baneful 659 adj.
pet
  animal 365 n.
  caress, pet 889 vb.
  darling 890 n.
petal
  flower 366 n.
pet aversion

  hateful object 888 n.
peter out
  decrease 37 vb.
  cease 145 vb.
petition
  request 761 n.vb.
—against
  deprecate 762 vb.
petitioner
  petitioner 763 n.
  litigant 959 n.
  worshipper 981 n.
petrified
  fearing 854 adj.
petrify
  harden 326 vb.
  frighten 854 vb.
petrol, petroleum
  oil 357 n.
  fuel 385 n.
petrology
  mineralogy 359 n.
petticoat
  underwear 228 n.
pettifogger
  trickster 545 n.
  lawyer 958 n.
pettifogging
  sophistical 477 adj.
  rascally 930 adj.
pettish
  irascible 892 adj.
petty
  inconsiderable
    33 adj.
  narrow-minded
    481 adj.
  unimportant
    639 adj.
  contemptible
    922 adj.
petulant
  discontented
    829 adj.
pew
  church interior
    990 n.
phalanx
  solid body 324 n.
  formation 722 n.
phallic
  generative 167 adj.
phantasm
  ghost 970 n.
phantasmagoria
  visual fallacy 440 n.
  spectacle 445 n.

phantom
  insubstantial thing
    4 n.
  visual fallacy 440 n.
  ghost 970 n.
pharisaic,
  pharisaical
  hypocritical
    541 adj.
  pietistic 979 adj.
pharmacology
  medical art 658 n.
pharmacopoeia
  medicine 658 n.
pharmacy
  druggist 658 n.
phase
  modality 7 n.
  regularize 62 vb.
  synchronize 123 vb.
  appearance 445 n.
pheasant
  table bird 365 n.
phenomenal
  appearing 445 adj.
  wonderful 864 adj.
phenomenon
  event 154 n.
  appearance 445 n.
  prodigy 864 n.
phial
  vessel 194 n.
philanderer
  lover 887 n.
philanthropist
  philanthropist
    901 n.
philanthropy
  benevolence 897 n.
  philanthropy 901 n.
philatelist
  enthusiast 504 n.
philippic
  censure 924 n.
philistine
  ignoramus 493 n.
  vulgarian 847 n.
philologist
  linguist 557 n.
philology
  linguistics 557 n.
philosopher
  philosophy 449 n.
  sage 500 n.
philosophical,
  philosophic
  philosophic 449 adj.

inexcitable 823 adj.
patient 823 adj.
philosophize
meditate 449 vb.
reason 475 vb.
philosophy
philosophy 449 n.
philtre
magic instrument
983 n.
spell 983 n.
phlegm
excrement 302 n.
phlegmatic
impassive 820 adj.
phobia
psychopathy 503 n.
phobia 854 n.
hatred 888 n.
phoenix
mythical being
970 n.
phone
hearing aid 415 n.
communicate
524 vb.
phoneme
word 559 n.
phone-tapper
inquisitive person
453 n.
phonetic
sounding 398 adj.
vocal 577 adj.
phonetician
linguist 557 n.
phonetics
acoustics 398 n.
phoney, phony
spurious 542 adj.
impostor 545 n.
affected 850 adj.
phosphates
fertilizer 171 n.
phosphorescent
luminous 417 adj.
photo
photography 551 n.
photocomposition
print 587 n.
photocopier
recording
instrument 549 n.
photocopy
copy 20 vb.
photo finish
draw 28 n.

photogenic
beautiful 841 adj.
photograph
record 548 n.vb.
photograph 551 vb.
photographer
photography 551 n.
photographic
lifelike 18 adj.
accurate 494 adj.
photography
camera 442 n.
photography 551 n.
photon
element 319 n.
radiation 417 n.
photoplay
cinema 445 n.
photosensitive
luminous 417 adj.
photosetting
print 587 n.
phrase
phrase 563 n.vb.
phrasemonger
phrasemonger
574 n.
phraseology
phrase 563 n.
style 566 n.
phrasing
musical skill 413 n.
phrenology
head 213 n.
phylactery
maxim 496 n.
talisman 983 n.
phylogeny
biology 358 n.
physic
medicine 658 n.
physical
substantial 3 adj.
material 319 n.
sensuous 376 adj.
physical education
exercise 682 n.
physical wreck
dilapidation 655 n.
physician
doctor 658 n.
physics
physics 319 n.
physiognomy
face 237 n.
feature 445 n.
physiological

biological 358 adj.
physiology
structure 331 n.
biology 358 n.
physiotherapist
doctor 658 n.
physique
vitality 162 n.
structure 331 n.
pianist
instrumentalist
413 n.
piano
muted 401 adj.
piano 414 n.
dejected 834 adj.
pianola
piano 414 n.
piazza
meeting place 192 n.
lobby 194 n.
picador
athlete 162 n.
picaresque
descriptive 590 adj.
rascally 930 adj.
piccolo
flute 414 n.
pick
sharp point 256 n.
extractor 304 n.
choice 605 n.
elite 644 n.
take 786 vb.
—and choose
be capricious
604 vb.
be fastidious 862 vb.
—holes
dispraise 924 vb.
—off
kill 362 vb.
—on
blame 924 vb.
—out
set apart 46 vb.
extract 304 vb.
see 438 vb.
select 605 vb.
—over
search 459 vb.
—to pieces
demolish 165 vb.
—up
elevate 310 vb.
detect 484 vb.
be restored 656 vb.

arrest 747 vb.
acquire 771 vb.
pickaxe
perforator 263 n.
extractor 304 n.
picker
farmer 370 n.
picket
tie 45 vb.
be obstructive
702 vb.
picket line
exclusion 57 n.
pickings
earnings 771 n.
booty 790 n.
pickle
sauce 389 n.
preserve 666 vb.
predicament
700 n.
pick-me-up
tonic 658 n.
pickpocket
thief 789 n.
pick-up
gramophone 414 n.
loose woman 952 n.
picnic
meal 301 n.
easy thing 701 n.
amusement 837 n.
pictorial
representing
551 adj.
painted 553 adj.
picture
imagine 513 vb.
spectacle 445 n.
represent 551 vb.
picture 553 n.
a beauty 841 n.
picture house
cinema 445 n.
pictures
film 445 n.
picturesque
descriptive 590 adj.
pleasurable 826 adj.
ornamental 844 adj.
pidgin
language 557 n.
dialect 560 n.
pie
dish 301 n.
pastries 301 n.
print-type 587 n.

piece
piece 53 n.
unit 88 n.
musical piece 412 n.
reading matter 589 n.
portion 783 n.
pièce de résistance
dish 301 n.
masterpiece 694 n.
piecemeal
piecemeal 53 adv.
piece of cake
easy thing 701 n.
piece together
join 45 vb.
decipher 520 vb.
piecework
labour 682 n.
pied
pied 437 adj.
pier
prop 218 n.
projection 254 n.
pierce
pierce 263 vb.
hurt 827 vb.
piercing
loud 400 adj.
strident 407 adj.
pierrot, pierrette
entertainer 594 n.
pietism
pietism 979 n.
piety
piety 979 n.
piffle
silly talk 515 n.
pig
pig 365 n.
dirty person 649 n.
glutton 947 n.
pigeon
bird 365 n.
pigeon-chested
deformed 246 adj.
pigeonhole
classification 77 n.
put off 136 vb.
compartment 194 n.
pigeon post
postal communications 531 n.
pig farm, piggery
stock farm 369 n.
piggybank

treasury 799 n.
pig-headed
obstinate 602 adj.
pig in a poke
uncertainty 474 n.
gambling 618 n.
pigment
pigment 425 n.
pigmentation
hue 425 n.
blackness 428 n.
pigmy
dwarf 196 n.
pigskin
skin 226 n.
pigsty
cattle pen 369 n.
sink 649 n.
pigtail
hair 259 n.
pike
fish 365 n.
spear 723 n.
pilaster
pillar 218 n.
pile
accumulation 74 n.
edifice 164 n.
pillar 218 n.
texture 331 n.
store 632 vb.
wealth 800 n.
—it on
exaggerate 546 vb.
—up
bring together 74 vb.
acquire 771 vb.
pile driver
ram 279 n.
piles
swelling 253 n.
pileup
collision 279 n.
pilfer
steal 788 vb.
pilgrim
traveller 268 n.
pilgrimage
act of worship 981 n.
pill
medicine 658 n.
pillage
rob 788 vb.
pillar
pillar 218 n.

refuge 662 n.
person of repute 866 n.
pillbox
small box 194 n.
fort 713 n.
pillion
seat 218 n.
rider 268 n.
pillory
lockup 748 n.
satirize 851 vb.
pillory 964 n.
pillow
cushion 218 n.
soften 327 vb.
sleep 679 n.
pilot
navigator 270 n.
aeronaut 271 n.
direct 689 vb.
pilot scheme
experiment 461 n.
pimp
bawd 952 n.
pimple
swelling 253 n.
skin disease 651 n.
pin
join 45 vb.
fastening 47 n.
sharp point 256 n.
perforator 263 n.
restrain 747 vb.
—down
retain 778 vb.
—on
accuse 928 vb.
pinafore
apron 228 n.
pinball
ball game 837 n.
pince-nez
eyeglass 442 n.
pincers
nippers 778 n.
pinch
small quantity 33 n.
crisis 137 n.
make smaller 198 vb.
give pain 377 vb.
predicament 700 n.
adversity 731 n.
steal 788 vb.
economize 814 vb.

pine
tree 366 n.
be ill 651 vb.
—for
desire 859 vb.
ping
resound 404 vb.
pingpong
ball game 837 n.
pinguid
fatty 357 adj.
pinhead
minuteness 196 n.
dunce 501 n.
pin hole
perforation 263 n.
pinion
wing 271 n.
fetter 747 vb.
pink
notch 260 n.
pierce 263 vb.
red 431 adj.
sectional 708 adj.
pink of condition
health 650 n.
pinnace
boat 275 n.
pinnacle
summit 213 n.
pinpoint
specify 80 vb.
minuteness 196 n.
orientate 281 vb.
pinprick
trifle 639 n.
annoyance 827 n.
pins and needles
pang 377 n.
pint
metrology 465 n.
draught 301 n.
pin-up
a beauty 841 n.
favourite 890 n.
pioneer
precursor 66 n.
initiate 68 vb.
settler 191 n.
traveller 268 n.
pious
pious 979 adj.
pip
flower 366 n.
signal 547 n.
pipe
tube 263 n.

conduit 351 n.
air pipe 353 n.
tobacco 388 n.
shrill 407 vb.
play music 413 vb.
flute 414 n.
—down
cease 145 vb.
be quiescent 266 vb.
—up
speak 579 vb.
pipe dream
fantasy 513 n.
aspiration 852 n.
pipeline
store 632 n.
provision 633 n.
piper
instrumentalist
413 n.
piping
tube 263 n.
trimming 844 n.
pips
broadcast 531 n.
badge of rank 743 n.
pipsqueak
nonentity 639 n.
piquant
pungent 388 adj.
exciting 821 adj.
pique
hurt 827 vb.
resentment 891 n.
piracy
brigandage 788 n.
pirate
mariner 270 n.
robber 789 n.
piratical
thieving 788 adj.
pirouette
rotate 315 vb.
pis aller
substitute 150 n.
compromise 770 n.
piscina
church utensil
990 n.
pissed
tipsy 949 adj.
pissed off
dejected 834 adj.
pistol
pistol 723 n.
piston
periodicity 141 n.

pit
excavation 255 n.
tunnel 263 n.
trap 542 n.
playgoer 594 n.
—against
oppose 704 vb.
pit-a-pat
agitation 318 n.
faintness 401 n.
pitch
degree 27 n.
serial place 73 n.
territory 184 n.
summit 213 n.
obliquity 220 n.
propel 287 vb.
tumble 309 vb.
oscillate 317 vb.
resin 357 n.
sound 398 n.
musical note 410 n.
arena 724 n.
—into
attack 712 vb.
dispraise 924 vb.
pitcher
vessel 194 n.
pitchfork
propel 287 vb.
farm tool 370 n.
pitchy
resinous 357 adj.
dark 418 adj.
piteous
pitiable 905 adj.
pitfall
trap 542 n.
pitfall 663 n.
pith
substance 3 n.
interiority 224 n.
pulpiness 356 n.
pithy
aphoristic 496 adj.
meaningful 514 adj.
pitiable
unimportant
639 adj.
pitiable 905 adj.
contemptible
922 adj.
pitiful
unimportant
639 adj.
distressing 827 adj.
pitiless

pitiless 906 adj.
pittance
small quantity 33 n.
portion 783 n.
pitted
rough 259 adj.
blemished 845 adj.
pitter-patter
faintness 401 n.
pity
pity 905 n.vb.
pivot
influence 178 n.
pivot 218 n.
chief thing 638 n.
pivot on
depend 157 vb.
pixie, pixy
elf 970 n.
pizza
dish 301 n.
placable
forgiving 909 adj.
placard
advertisement
528 n.
placate
pacify 719 vb.
placatory
pacificatory 719 adj.
place
arrange 62 vb.
serial place 73 n.
place 185 n.
situation 186 n.
place 187 vb.
aim 281 vb.
placebo
medicine 658 n.
placement
location 187 n.
place of amusement
place of amusement
837 n.
place of residence
abode 192 n.
place of worship
temple 990 n.
placid
inexcitable 823 adj.
placket
opening 263 n.
plagiarism
imitation 20 n.
stealing 788 n.
plagiarize
fake 541 vb.

borrow 785 vb.
plague
plague 651 n.
bane 659 n.
torment 827 vb.
plague spot
infection 651 n.
plague-stricken
diseased 651 adj.
plaguey, plaguy
annoying 827 adj.
plaid
cloak 228 n.
variegated 437 adj.
plain
simple 44 adj.
horizontality 216 n.
plain 348 n.
obvious 443 adj.
intelligible 516 adj.
undisguised
522 adj.
assertive 532 adj.
veracious 540 adj.
plain 573 n.
artless 699 adj.
ugly 842 adj.
plain-clothes man
detective 459 n.
plain living
temperance 942 n.
plain sailing
easy thing 701 n.
plainsong
vocal music 412 n.
plaint
lament 836 n.
plaintiff
accuser 928 n.
plaintive
lamenting 836 adj.
plait
weave 222 vb.
hair 259 n.
plan
structure 331 n.
map 551 n.
intention 617 n.
plan 623 n.vb.
tactics 688 n.
—ahead
foresee 510 vb.
planchette
spiritualism 984 n.
plane
horizontality 216 n.
sharp edge 256 n.

smoother 258 n.
aircraft 276 n.
planet
planet 321 n.
planetarium
astronomy 321 n.
planetary
planetary 321 adj.
plangent
resonant 404 adj.
lamenting 836 adj.
plank
lamina 207 n.
shelf 218 n.
policy 623 n.
materials 631 n.
plankton
microorganism
   196 n.
planner
theorist 512 n.
motivator 612 n.
planner 623 n.
plant
young plant 132 n.
place 187 vb.
implant 303 vb.
plant 366 n.
cultivate 370 vb.
trap 542 n.
equipment 630 n.
workshop 687 n.
false charge 928 n.
plantation
wood 366 n.
planted
firm 45 adj.
agrarian 370 adj.
planter
settler 191 n.
gardener 370 n.
plaque
dirt 649 n.
honours 866 n.
plash
flow 350 vb.
plasma
blood 335 n.
plasmic
organic 358 adj.
plaster
adhesive 47 n.
facing 226 n.
surgical dressing
   658 n.
—down
flatten 216 vb.

smooth 258 vb.
plasterboard
paper 631 n.
plastered
tipsy 949 adj.
plasterer
artisan 686 n.
plaster saint
paragon 646 n.
plastic
formative 243 adj.
flexible 327 adj.
spurious 542 adj.
materials 631 n.
plastic arts
sculpture 554 n.
plasticity
changeableness
   152 n.
softness 327 n.
plastics
resin 357 n.
plastic surgery
beautification 843 n.
plate
mould 23 n.
plate 194 n.
coat 226 vb.
label 547 n.
photography 551 n.
trophy 729 n.
plateau
high land 209 n.
plain 348 n.
platform
stand 218 n.
rostrum 539 n.
policy 623 n.
arena 724 n.
platitude
lack of meaning
   515 n.
platitudinous
aphoristic 496 adj.
Platonic
pure 950 adj.
Platonism
philosophy 449 n.
platoon
formation 722 n.
platter
plate 194 n.
plaudits
applause 923 n.
plausible
plausible 471 adj.
credible 485 adj.

hypocritical
   541 adj.
ostensible 614 adj.
vindicable 927 adj.
play
agency 173 n.
flow 350 vb.
play music 413 vb.
stage play 594 n.
act 594 vb.
gamble 618 vb.
action 676 n.
scope 744 n.
amuse oneself
   837 vb.
—ball
cooperate 706 vb.
—down
underestimate
   483 vb.
—fair
be honourable
   929 vb.
—for time
be obstructive
   702 vb.
—havoc with
jumble 63 vb.
impair 655 vb.
—into one's hands
blunder 495 vb.
—it by ear
intuit 476 vb.
be cautious 858 vb.
—on
use 673 vb.
—safe
be cautious 858 vb.
—second fiddle
be inferior 35 vb.
—the fool
be absurd 497 vb.
—the game
be honourable
   929 vb.
—the market
speculate 791 vb.
—to the gallery
act 594 vb.
be affected 850 vb.
—tricks on
befool 542 vb.
—up
overrate 482 vb.
disobey 738 vb.
play-acting
duplicity 541 n.

acting 594 n.
playback
repetition 106 n.
playboy
reveller 837 n.
beau monde 848 n.
player
instrumentalist
   413 n.
actor 594 n.
gambler 618 n.
player 837 n.
playful
merry 833 adj.
amused 837 adj.
playgoer
playgoer 594 n.
playground
arena 724 n.
pleasure ground
   837 n.
playgroup
school 539 n.
playhouse
theatre 594 n.
playing field
arena 724 n.
playmate
chum 880 n.
play on words
equivocalness
   518 n.
wit 839 n.
plaything
bauble 639 n.
plaything 837 n.
playwright
dramatist 594 n.
plea
argument 475 n.
pretext 614 n.
request 761 n.
litigation 959 n.
plead
argue 475 vb.
plead 614 vb.
justify 927 vb.
pleader
reasoner 475 n.
law agent 958 n.
pleasance
pleasure ground
   837 n.
pleasant
pleasant 376 adj.
pleasurable
   826 adj.

pleasantry
 wit 839 n.
please
 please 826 vb.
 amuse 837 vb.
—oneself
 please oneself
  734 vb.
pleased
 willing 597 adj.
pleased with oneself
 vain 873 adj.
pleasurable
 pleasant 376 adj.
 pleasurable 826 adj.
pleasure
 pleasure 376 n.
 joy 824 n.
pleasure ground
 pleasure ground
  837 n.
pleasure-loving
 sensuous 376 adj.
 sensual 944 adj.
pleasure-seeker
 reveller 837 n.
pleat
 fold 261 n.
plebeian
 commoner 869 n.
 plebeian 869 adj.
plebiscite
 vote 605 n.
pledge
 thing transferred
  272 n.
 oath 532 n.
 promise 764 n.vb.
 security 767 n.
 toast 876 vb.
plenary
 complete 54 adj.
plenipotentiary
 powerful 160 adj.
 delegate 754 n.
plenitude
 plenitude 54 n.
plentiful
 plenteous 635 adj.
plenty
 great quantity
  32 n.
 store 632 n.
 plenty 635 n.
 prosperity 730 n.
pleonasm
 pleonasm 570 n.

plethora
 redundance 637 n.
plexus
 network 222 n.
pliability
 persuadability
  612 n.
pliable
 flexible 327 adj.
pliant
 conformable 83 adj.
 flexible 327 adj.
 tractable 701 adj.
pliers
 tool 630 n.
 nippers 778 n.
plight
 circumstance 8 n.
 adversity 731 n.
plimsolls
 footwear 228 n.
plinth
 base 214 n.
 stand 218 n.
plod
 move slowly 278 vb.
 persevere 600 vb.
plonk
 wine 301 n.
 nonresonance
  405 n.
plop
 plunge 313 vb.
 sound faint 401 vb.
plosive
 speech sound 398 n.
plot
 garden 370 n.
 topic 452 n.
 narrative 590 n.
 dramaturgy 594 n.
 plot 623 n.vb.
 stratagem 698 n.
 compact 765 n.
plotted
 measured 465 adj.
plotter
 planner 623 n.
 slyboots 698 n.
plough
 farm tool 370 n.
 cultivate 370 vb.
—back
 economize 814 vb.
ploughed
 unsuccessful
  728 adj.

ploughman
 farmer 370 n.
 country-dweller
  869 n.
ploy
 contrivance 623 n.
 stratagem 698 n.
pluck
 uncover 229 vb.
 draw 288 vb.
 extract 304 vb.
 agitate 318 vb.
 cultivate 370 vb.
 play music 413 vb.
 fleece 786 vb.
 courage 855 n.
—to pieces
 rend 46 vb.
plucky
 courageous 855 adj.
plug
 stopper 264 n.
 staunch 350 vb.
 tobacco 388 n.
 advertise 528 vb.
 emphasize 532 vb.
—away at
 persevere 600 vb.
—in
 connect 45 vb.
plum
 fruit 301 n.
 purpleness 436 n.
 desired object 859 n.
plumage
 plumage 259 n.
plumb
 be deep 211 vb.
 vertical 215 adj.
 measure 465 vb.
plumber
 mender 656 n.
plumbing
 conduit 351 n.
 cleansing 648 n.
plume
 plumage 259 n.
plume oneself (on)
 be vain 873 vb.
plummet
 founder 313 vb.
 gravity 322 n.
plummy
 speaking 579 adj.
 super 644 adj.
plumose
 downy 259 adj.

plump
 fleshy 195 adj.
—for
 choose 605 vb.
plunder
 rob 788 vb.
 booty 790 n.
plunge
 aquatics 269 n.
 enter 297 vb.
 descend 309 vb.
 plunge 313 n.vb.
 drench 341 vb.
 gambling 618 n.
 ablutions 648 n.
 be rash 857 vb.
plural
 plural 101 adj.
 grammatical
  564 adj.
pluralism
 government 733 n.
plurality
 greater number
  104 n.
plus
 in addition 38 adv.
plush
 softness 327 n.
plushy
 rich 800 adj.
 ostentatious
  875 adj.
plutocrat
 master 741 n.
 rich person 800 n.
plutonium
 fuel 385 n.
 poison 659 n.
ply
 be periodic 141 vb.
 layer 207 n.
 use 673 vb.
 do 676 vb.
 request 761 vb.
pneumatic
 gaseous 336 adj.
 airy 340 adj.
pneumonia
 respiratory disease
  651 n.
poach
 cook 301 vb.
 steal 788 vb.
poacher
 hunter 619 n.
 thief 789 n.

pocket
  stow 187 vb.
  pocket 194 n.
  little 196 adj.
  garment 228 n.
  insert 303 vb.
  take 786 vb.
pockmark
  blemish 845 n.vb.
pococurante
  apathetic 820 adj.
  indifferent 860 adj.
pod
  receptacle 194 n.
podgy
  fleshy 195 adj.
podium
  stand 218 n.
  rostrum 539 n.
poem
  poem 593 n.
poet
  poet 593 n.
poetic
  imaginative 513 adj.
  poetic 593 adj.
poetic justice
  punishment 963 n.
poetics
  poetry 593 n.
poetry
  poetry 593 n.
po-faced
  serious 834 adj.
pogrom
  slaughter 362 n.
poignant
  painful 377 adj.
  felt 818 adj.
point
  juncture 8 n.
  relevance 9 n.
  degree 27 n.
  place 185 n.
  minuteness 196 n.
  sharp point 256 n.
  aim 281 vb.
  topic 452 n.
  gesticulate 547 vb.
  lettering 586 n.
  use 673 n.
  —out
  show 522 vb.
  inform 524 vb.
  —to
  attribute 158 vb.
  predict 511 vb.

  indicate 547 vb.
point at issue
  question 459 n.
point duty
  traffic control 305 n.
pointed
  sharp 256 adj.
  convergent 293 adj.
  meaningful 514 adj.
pointer
  dog 365 n.
  indicator 547 n.
pointless
  irrelevant 10 adj.
  useless 641 adj.
point of view
  opinion 485 n.
point-to-point
  equitation 267 n.
poise
  conduct 688 n.
  inexcitability 823 n.
poison
  murder 362 vb.
  make unclean
    649 vb.
  poison 659 n.
  excite hate 888 vb.
poisoner
  murderer 362 n.
poison gas
  weapon 723 n.
poisonous
  deadly 362 adj.
  harmful 645 adj.
  toxic 653 adj.
poison pen
  defamer 926 n.
poke
  pierce 263 vb.
  gesticulate 547 vb.
  —one's nose in
  be curious 453 vb.
  meddle 678 vb.
  —out
  jut 254 vb.
poker
  card game 837 n.
poker-faced
  serious 834 adj.
poky
  little 196 adj.
polar
  opposite 240 adj.
  telluric 321 adj.
  cold 380 adj.
polarity

  polarity 14 n.
polarization
  reflection 417 n.
pole
  extremity 69 n.
  farness 199 n.
  pillar 218 n.
  impel 279 vb.
polemic
  argument 475 n.
polemics
  argument 475 n.
  contention 716 n.
pole star
  star 321 n.
  signpost 547 n.
pole vault
  leap 312 vb.
police
  safeguard 660 vb.
  restrain 747 vb.
  police 955 n.
police court
  lawcourt 956 n.
police state
  despotism 733 n.
police station
  lockup 748 n.
policy
  sagacity 498 n.
  policy 623 n.
  tactics 688 n.
  management 689 n.
  title deed 767 n.
poliomyelitis, polio
  nervous disorders
    651 n.
polish
  smoothness 258 n.
  friction 333 n.
  make bright 417 vb.
  elegance 575 n.
  cleanser 648 n.
  make better 654 vb.
  good taste 846 n.
  —off
  carry through
    725 vb.
politburo
  party 708 n.
polite
  elegant 575 adj.
  courteous 884 adj.
  respectful 920 adj.
politic
  wise 498 adj.
  advisable 642 adj.

political
  directing 689 adj.
  governmental
    733 adj.
political economy
  management 689 n.
political organization
  *political
    organization*
    733 n.
political party
  political party 708 n.
politician
  manager 690 n.
  political party 708 n.
politics
  tactics 688 n.
  government 733 n.
polka
  dance 837 n.
poll
  numeration 86 n.
  inquiry 459 n.
  vote 605 n.vb.
pollard
  make smaller 198 vb.
pollen
  powder 332 n.
  flower 366 n.
pollination
  propagation 167 n.
pollster
  enumerator 86 n.
  inquirer 459 n.
pollute
  impair 655 vb.
  misuse 675 vb.
pollution
  uncleanness 649 n.
  insalubrity 653 n.
polo
  ball game 837 n.
polo-neck
  jersey 228 n.
poltergeist
  ghost 970 n.
poltroon
  coward 856 n.
poly-
  plural 101 adj.
polychromatic
  variegated 437 adj.
polyester
  textile 222 n.
polygamy
  type of marriage
    894 n.

polyglot
speaking 579 adj.

polygon
angular figure
247 n.

polymath
scholar 492 n.

polyp
swelling 253 n.

polysyllable
word 559 n.

polytechnic
academy 539 n.

polytheism
deism 973 n.

polythene
wrapping 226 n.
materials 631 n.

pomander
scent 396 n.

pommel
handle 218 n.
sphere 252 n.

pomp
ostentation 875 n.

pompom
trimming 844 n.

pompous
rhetorical 574 adj.
ostentatious
875 adj.

ponce
bawd 952 n.

ponce about
be affected 850 vb.

poncho
cloak 228 n.

pond
lake 346 n.

ponder
meditate 449 vb.

ponderous
weighty 322 adj.
inelegant 576 adj.
clumsy 695 adj.

pong
stench 397 n.

poniard
sidearms 723 n.

pontiff
priest 986 n.

pontifical
positive 473 adj.
ecclesiastical
985 adj.

pontificals
vestments 989 n.

pontificate
dogmatize 473 vb.

pontoon
raft 275 n.

pony
saddle horse 273 n.

ponytail
hair 259 n.

pony-trekking
sport 837 n.

poodle
dog 365 n.
toady 879 n.

pooh-pooh
hold cheap 922 vb.

pool
lake 346 n.
store 632 n.vb.
joint possession
775 n.
ball game 837 n.

pool room
gaming-house
618 n.
place of amusement
837 n.

pools
gambling 618 n.

poop
poop 238 n.

poor
unproductive
172 adj.
feeble 572 adj.
unimportant
639 adj.
bad 645 adj.
unfortunate 731 adj.
poor 801 adj.
unhappy 825 adj.

poor, the
poor person 801 n.

poor hand
bungler 697 n.

poorhouse
retreat 192 n.

poorly
weakly 163 adj.
sick 651 adj.

poor relation
inferior 35 n.

poor relief
sociology 901 n.

pop
soft drink 301 n.
bang 402 n.
music 412 n.

borrow 785 vb.

—out
jut 254 vb.
emerge 298 vb.

—up
appear 445 vb.

pope
ecclesiarch 986 n.

pop-eyed
wondering 864 adj.

pop group
band 74 n.

popgun
plaything 837 n.

popper
fastening 47 n.

poppet
darling 890 n.

poppycock
empty talk 515 n.

pop singer
vocalist 413 n.
entertainer 594 n.

populace
inhabitants 191 n.
commonalty 869 n.

popular
general 79 adj.
native 191 adj.
approved 923 adj.

popularity
repute 866 n.
sociability 882 n.
lovableness 887 n.

popularize
interpret 520 vb.
facilitate 701 vb.
vulgarize 847 vb.

populate
be fruitful 171 vb.
dwell 192 vb.

population
inhabitants 191 n.

populist
political party
708 n.
philanthropist
901 n.

populous
multitudinous
104 adj.

porcelain
brittleness 330 n.
pottery 381 n.

porch
lobby 194 n.
doorway 263 n.

pore
orifice 263 n.
scan 438 vb.
study 536 vb.

pork
meat 301 n.

pork barrel
incentive 612 n.

pornographic
erotic 887 adj.

pornography
impurity 951 n.

porous
porous 263 adj.

porridge
cereals 301 n.
pulpiness 356 n.

port
stopping place
145 n.
sinistrality 242 n.
goal 295 n.
wine 301 n.
redness 431 n.
conduct 688 n.

portable
transferable
272 adj.
broadcasting
531 n.

portage
transport 272 n.

portal
doorway 263 n.

portcullis
obstacle 702 n.
fort 713 n.

portend
predict 511 vb.

portent
omen 511 n.

portentous
presageful 511 adj.
frightening 854 adj.

porter
doorkeeper 264 n.
bearer 273 n.
servant 742 n.

porterage
transport 272 n.

portfolio
case 194 n.
collection 632 n.
authority 733 n.
title deed 767 n.

porthole
window 263 n.

porfico
lobby 194 n.

portion
part 53 n.
meal 301 n.
participation 775 n.
portion 783 n.

portly
fleshy 195 adj.

portmanteau
box 194 n.

portrait
picture 553 n.
description 590 n.

portraiture
representation
551 n.

portray
represent 551 vb.

pose
be an example
23 vb.
appearance 445 n.
interrogate 459 vb.
conduct 688 n.
be affected 850 vb.

poser
question 459 n.
difficulty 700 n.

poseur, poseuse
imitator 20 n.
affecter 850 n.

posh
genteel 868 adj.
ostentatious
875 adj.

posit
suppose 512 vb.

position
state 7 n.
arrange 62 vb.
serial place 73 n.
place 187 vb.
opinion 485 n.
job 622 n.
prestige 866 n.

positive
real 1 adj.
positive 473 adj.
believing 485 adj.
affirmative
532 adj.

positivism
materiality 319 n.
philosophy 449 n.

posology *medical art*
658 n.

posse
band 74 n.

possess
possess 773 vb.
excite 821 vb.

possessed
obsessed 455 adj.
frenzied 503 adj.

possession
possession 773 n.
property 777 n.

possessive
greedy 859 adj.
jealous 911 adj.
selfish 932 adj.

possessor
master 741 n.
possessor 776 n.

possibility
opportunity 137 n.
possibility 469 n.

possible
possible 469 adj.
credible 485 adj.

post
subsequent 120 adj.
situation 186 n.
place 187 vb.
pillar 218 n.
send 272 vb.
postal
communications
531 n.
register 548 vb.
correspondence
588 n.
job 622 n.
position of authority
733 n.
account 808 vb.

postal
epistolary 588 adj.

postbag
correspondence
588 n.

postdate
misdate 118 vb.

poster
advertisement
528 n.

posterior
subsequent 120 adj.
buttocks 238 n.

posterity
posteriority
120 n.
posterity 170 n.

postern
doorway 263 n.

postgraduate
student 538 n.

posthaste
swiftly 277 adv.

posthumous
subsequent 120 adj.
late 136 adj.

postilion, postillion
rider 268 n.

posting
location 187 n.
mandate 751 n.

postman, postwoman
courier 529 n.

postmortem
inquest 364 n.

post office
postal
communications
531 n.

postpone
put off 136 vb.
not complete
726 vb.

postscript
adjunct 40 n.
sequel 67 n.

postulant
petitioner 763 n.
lay person 987 n.

postulate
axiom 496 n.
supposition 512 n.

posture
form 243 n.
mien 445 n.
conduct 688 n.
be affected 850 vb.

postwar
peaceful 717 adj.

posy
bunch 74 n.

pot
vessel 194 n.
pottery 381 n.
abstract 592 vb.
preserve 666 vb.
trophy 729 n.
drug-taking 949 n.
—at
shoot 287 vb.

potable
edible 301 adj.

potash
fertilizer 171 n.

potation(s)
drinking 301 n.

potato
vegetable 301 n.

pot-bellied
fleshy 195 adj.

potboiler
novel 590 n.

potency
power 160 n.

potent
powerful 160 adj.
strong 162 adj.
influential 178 adj.
intoxicating
949 adj.

potentate
potentate 741 n.

potential
unreal 2 adj.
energy 160 n.
possible 469 adj.

potentiality
ability 160 n.

pother
excitable state
822 n.

potherb
potherb 301 n.

pothole
cavity 255 n.
orifice 263 n.

pot-holing
descent 309 n.

potion
draught 301 n.
medicine 658 n.

potluck
chance 159 n.
nonpreparation
670 n.

potpourri
medley 43 n.
scent 396 n.

potted
compendious
592 adj.
preserved 666 adj.

potter
be inactive 679 vb.
artisan 686 n.

pottery
pottery 381 n.

potty
crazy 503 adj.
unimportant
639 adj.

pot-valiant
drunk 949 adj.
pouch
pocket 194 n.
pouchy
expanded 197 adj.
poultice
surgical dressing
658 n.
poultry
poultry 365 n.
poultry farming
animal husbandry
369 n.
pounce
move fast 277 vb.
descent 309 n.
leap 312 vb.
—on
surprise 508 vb.
attack 712 vb.
pound
enclosure 235 n.
pulverize 332 vb.
lockup 748 n.
funds 797 n.
poundage
discount 810 n.
pour
let fall 311 vb.
flow 350 vb.
rain 350 vb.
—in
burst in 297 vb.
—out
empty 300 vb.
pout
jut 254 vb.
gesture 547 n.
be sullen 893 vb.
poverty
scarcity 636 n.
poverty 801 n.
powder
overlay 226 n.
powder 332 n.
pulverize 332 vb.
explosive 723 n.
cosmetic 843 n.
powdery
powdery 332 adj.
power
power 160 n.
empower 160 vb.
strength 162 n.
operate 173 vb.
vigour 571 n.

instrumentality
628 n.
authority 733 n.
power behind the
throne
influence 178 n.
latency 523 n.
powered
dynamic 160 adj.
mechanical 630 adj.
powerful
powerful 160 adj.
vigorous 174 adj.
(see power)
powerhouse
sources of energy
160 n.
busy person 678 n.
powerless
powerless 161 adj.
weak 163 adj.
unimportant
639 adj.
power station
sources of energy
160 n.
powers that be
master 741 n.
power vacuum
anarchy 734 n.
powwow
conference 584 n.
pox
venereal disease
651 n.
PR
publicity 528 n.
practicable
possible 469 adj.
advisable 642 adj.
practical
intelligent 498 adj.
advisable 642 adj.
used 673 adj.
practical ability
skill 694 n.
practical joke
foolery 497 n.
practical joker
humorist 839 n.
practice
practice 610 n.
medical art 658 n.
preparation 669 n.
use 673 n.
exercise 682 n.
observance 768 n.

etiquette 848 n.
practise
play music 413 vb.
learn 536 vb.
habituate 610 vb.
(see practice)
practised
knowing 490 adj.
expert 694 adj.
practising
orthodox 976 adj.
practitioner
doer 676 n.
expert 696 n.
pragmatic
useful 640 adj.
advisable 642 adj.
pragmatism
philosophy 449 n.
prairie
plain 348 n.
praise
praise 923 n.vb.
praiseworthy
excellent 644 adj.
approvable 923 adj.
pram
pushcart 274 n.
prance
ride 267 vb.
leap 312 vb.
prandial
culinary 301 adj.
prank
revel 837 n.
prate
mean nothing
515 vb.
be loquacious
581 vb.
prattle
empty talk 515 n.
pray
entreat 761 vb.
worship 981 vb.
—for
patronize 703 vb.
desire 859 vb.
prayer
prayers 981 n.
prayer book
office-book 988 n.
prayer meeting
public worship
981 n.
prayers
prayers 981 n.

pre-
prior 119 adj.
preach
teach 534 vb.
orate 579 vb.
—to the converted
waste effort 641 vb.
preacher
preacher 537 n.
preachify
orate 579 vb.
be pious 979 vb.
preamble
prelude 66 n.
prearrange
predetermine
608 vb.
prebendary
ecclesiarch 986 n.
precarious
unsafe 661 adj.
precaution
caution 858 n.
precautionary
preparatory
669 adj.
precede
come before 64 vb.
precede 283 vb.
precedence
precedence 64 n.
seniority 131 n.
importance 638 n.
precedent
originality 21 n.
prototype 23 n.
precursor 66 n.
example 83 n.
guide 520 n.
precept 693 n.
precentor
choir 413 n.
precept
maxim 496 n.
advice 691 n.
precept 693 n.
preceptor
teacher 537 n.
precinct(s)
place 185 n.
surroundings 230 n.
preciosity
ornament 574 n.
affectation 850 n.
precious
valuable 644 adj.
of price 811 adj.

precipice
incline 220 n.
precipitate
leavings 41 n.
cause 156 vb.
eject 300 vb.
let fall 311 vb.
hasty 680 adj.
rash 857 adj.
precipitation
condensation 324 n.
rain 350 n.
precipitous
vertical 215 adj.
précis
conciseness 569 n.
precise
definite 80 adj.
accurate 494 adj.
fastidious 862 adj.
precisian
perfectionist 862 n.
zealot 979 n.
precision
accuracy 494 n.
preclude
exclude 57 vb.
precocious
early 135 adj.
immature 670 adj.
precognition
foresight 510 n.
psychics 984 n.
preconception
prejudgement
481 n.
precondemn
prejudge 481 vb.
precursor
precursor 66 n.
priority 119 n.
precursory
precursory 66 adj.
predator
tyrant 735 n.
noxious animal
904 n.
predecessor
precursor 66 n.
predestination
destiny 155 n.
fate 596 n.
predetermination
608 n.
predestine
predestine 155 vb.
intend 617 vb.

predetermination
necessity 596 n.
predetermination
608 n.
predetermine
predestine 155 vb.
predetermine
608 vb.
plan 623 vb.
predicament
predicament 700 n.
predicate
affirm 532 vb.
predict
predict 511 vb.
predictable
unchangeable
153 adj.
predigested
edible 301 adj.
ready-made
669 adj.
predilection
tendency 179 n.
liking 859 n.
predispose
influence 178 vb.
motivate 612 vb.
predisposition
tendency 179 n.
predominance
power 160 n.
authority 733 n.
predominate
predominate 34 vb.
overmaster 727 vb.
preeminent
supreme 34 adj.
noteworthy 866 adj.
preempt
exclude 57 vb.
be early 135 vb.
acquire 771 vb.
preen
primp 843 vb.
be vain 873 vb.
prefabricate
produce 164 vb.
prefabricated
ready-made
669 adj.
preface
put in front 64 vb.
prelude 66 n.
prefatory
precursory
66 adj.

prefect
officer 741 n.
prefer
promote 285 vb.
choose 605 vb.
preferable
superior 34 adj.
chosen 605 adj.
preference
choice 605 n.
preferment
progression 285 n.
improvement 654 n.
prefigure
predict 511 vb.
prefix
put in front 64 vb.
precursor 66 n.
pregnable
defenceless 161 adj.
pregnant
fertilized 167 adj.
prolific 171 adj.
meaningful 514 adj.
prehensile
tactual 378 adj.
retentive 778 adj.
prehistoric
past 125 n.
olden 127 adj.
prehistory
antiquity 125 n.
prejudge
prejudge 481 vb.
prejudice
prejudice 481 n.
hatred 888 n.
injustice 914 n.
prejudicial
harmful 645 adj.
prelate
ecclesiarch 986 n.
preliminaries
beginning 68 n.
preliminary
prelude 66 n.
precursory 66 adj.
preparatory
669 adj.
prelude
prelude 66 n.
premarital
matrimonial
894 adj.
premature
ill-timed 138 adj.
immature 670 adj.

premeditate
intend 617 vb.
premeditation
predetermination
608 n.
premenstrual tension
worry 825 n.
premier
director 690 n.
premiere, première
debut 68 n.
dramaturgy 594 n.
premiership
directorship 689 n.
premise
supposition 512 n.
premises
place 185 n.
shop 796 n.
premium
receipt 807 n.
premium bond
gambling 618 n.
premonition
foresight 510 n.
warning 664 n.
preoccupation
abstractedness
456 n.
preoccupy
engross 449 vb.
preordination
fate 596 n.
predetermination
608 n.
prep
study 536 n.
preparation
provision 633 n.
preparation 669 n.
preparatory
preparatory
669 adj.
prepare
train 534 vb.
plan 623 vb.
prepare 669 vb.
prepared
vigilant 457 adj.
expectant 507 adj.
prepense
volitional 595 adj.
preponderance
inequality 29 n.
superiority 34 n.
preposition
part of speech 564 n.

prepossessing
personable 841 adj.
preposterous
absurd 497 adj.
ridiculous 849 adj.
prerequisite
requirement 627 n.
prerogative
advantage 34 n.
freedom 744 n.
dueness 915 n.
presage
omen 511 n.
indicate 547 vb.
presageful
presageful 511 adj.
presbyter
ecclesiarch 986 n.
presbytery
synod 985 n.
parsonage 986 n.
preschool
young 130 adj.
prescient
foreseeing 510 adj.
prescribe
doctor 658 vb.
advise 691 vb.
prescript
decree 737 n.
prescription
remedy 658 n.
prescriptive
established 153 adj.
habitual 610 adj.
presence
presence 189 n.
mien 445 n.
present
present 121 adj.
synchronous 123 adj.
modern 126 adj.
on the spot 189 adj.
show 522 vb.
represent 551 vb.
dramatize 594 vb.
offer 759 n.vb.
gift 781 n.
presentable
personable 841 adj.
presentation
manifestation 522 n.
giving 781 n.
reward 962 n.
presenter
broadcaster 531 n.

presentiment
intuition 476 n.
foresight 510 n.
preservation
protection 660 n.
preservation 666 n.
preservative
preserving 666 adj.
preserve
record 548 vb.
store 632 vb.
preserve 666 vb.
preserver
preserver 666 n.
preside
direct 689 vb.
presidency
position of authority 733 n.
president
director 690 n.
officer 741 n.
press
crowd 74 n.
smooth 258 vb.
the press 528 n.
press 587 n.
incite 612 vb.
request 761 vb.
caress 889 vb.
—**the button**
operate 173 vb.
wage war 718 vb.
press conference
publication 528 n.
pressgang
compulsion 740 n.
pressing
record 548 n.
compelling 740 adj.
**pressman,
presswoman**
news reporter 529 n.
press release
publication 528 n.
press-stud
fastening 47 n.
pressure
energy 160 n.
compression 198 n.
impulse 279 n.
touch 378 n.
inducement 612 n.
restriction 747 n.
pressure group
influence 178 n.
motivator 612 n.

pressurize
motivate 612 vb.
prestige
influence 178 n.
importance 638 n.
prestige 866 n.
presume
expect 507 vb.
suppose 512 vb.
be undue 916 vb.
—**on**
avail oneself of 673 vb.
presumptive
evidential 466 adj.
probable 471 adj.
presumptuous
insolent 878 adj.
unwarranted 916 adj.
presuppose
suppose 512 vb.
pretence
duplicity 541 n.
sham 542 n.
pretext 614 n.
ostentation 875 n.
pretend
imagine 513 vb.
dissemble 541 vb.
pretender
impostor 545 n.
usurper 916 n.
pretentious
affected 850 adj.
ostentatious 875 adj.
preternatural
paranormal 984 adj.
pretext
pretext 614 n.
prettify
decorate 844 vb.
pretty
beautiful 841 adj.
pretty pass
predicament 700 n.
prevail
be general 79 vb.
prevail 178 vb.
overmaster 727 vb.
—**upon**
influence 178 vb.
induce 612 vb.
prevalent
extensive 32 adj.

universal 79 adj.
usual 610 adj.
prevaricate
be equivocal 518 vb.
dissemble 541 vb.
prevenience
anticipation 135 n.
prevent
counteract 182 vb.
avoid 620 vb.
prevention
hindrance 702 n.
preventive
preserving 666 adj.
preview
priority 119 n.
manifestation 522 n.
previous
prior 119 adj.
early 135 adj.
prewar
antiquated 127 adj.
prey
chase 619 n.
unlucky person 731 n.
—**on**
eat 301 vb.
ill-treat 645 vb.
—**on one's mind**
trouble 827 vb.
prey to
liable 180 adj.
price
price 809 n.vb.
penalty 963 n.
priceless
valuable 644 adj.
of price 811 adj.
price ring
restriction 747 n.
prick
pierce 263 vb.
itch 378 vb.
mark 547 vb.
incite 612 vb.
wound 655 vb.
—**up**
jut 254 vb.
elevate 310 vb.
—**up one's ears**
be curious 453 vb.
prickle
prickle 256 n.

prickliness
  quarrelsomeness
  709 n.
  irascibility 892 n.
pricy
  dear 811 adj.
pride
  pride 871 n.
  ostentation 875 n.
pride of place
  precedence 64 n.
priest, priestess
  priest 986 n.
priesthole
  hiding-place 527 n.
priesthood
  clergy 986 n.
prig
  affecter 850 n.
  prude 950 n.
prim
  serious 834 adj.
  prudish 950 adj.
primacy
  superiority 34 n.
  prestige 866 n.
prima donna
  vocalist 413 n.
  proud person 871 n.
prima facie
  evidential 466 adj.
primal
  primal 127 adj.
primary
  simple 44 adj.
  fundamental
  156 adj.
  important 638 adj.
primate
  mammal 365 n.
  ecclesiarch 986 n.
prime
  morning 128 n.
  adultness 134 n.
  important 638 adj.
  excellent 644 adj.
  make ready 669 vb.
  palmy days 730 n.
primed
  instructed 490 adj.
  prepared 669 adj.
prime minister
  director 690 n.
prime mover
  cause 156 n.
primer
  textbook 589 n.

primeval, primaeval
  primal 127 adj.
priming
  explosive 723 n.
primitive
  primal 127 adj.
  artist 556 n.
  artless 699 adj.
primogeniture
  seniority 131 n.
  sonship 170 n.
primordial
  beginning 68 adj.
primp
  primp 843 vb.
primrose path
  wickedness 934 n.
prince, princess
  potentate 741 n.
  aristocrat 868 n.
princely
  ruling 733 adj.
  liberal 813 adj.
  noble 868 adj.
principal
  supreme 34 adj.
  teacher 537 n.
  director 690 n.
principality
  political
    organization
    733 n.
principle
  essential part 5 n.
  rule 81 n.
  element 319 n.
  idea 451 n.
  opinion 485 n.
  axiom 496 n.
  precept 693 n.
principled
  honourable 929 adj.
prink
  primp 843 vb.
print
  publish 528 vb.
  photography 551 n.
  printing 555 n.
  print 587 n.vb.
printer
  printer 587 n.
printing
  printing 555 n.
  lettering 586 n.
printing press
  publicity 528 n.
  press 587 n.

printout
  data processing 86 n.
  product 164 n.
  letterpress 587 n.
print-type
  print-type 587 n.
prior
  prior 119 adj.
  monk 986 n.
prioress
  nun 986 n.
priority
  precedence 64 n.
  priority 119 n.
  seniority 131 n.
  chief thing 638 n.
priory
  monastery 986 n.
prism
  chromatics 425 n.
  optical device 442 n.
prismatic
  variegated 437 adj.
prison
  prison 748 n.
prison-breaker
  escaper 667 n.
prisoner
  prisoner 750 n.
prison officer
  gaoler 749 n.
privacy
  seclusion 883 n.
private
  occult 523 adj.
  soldiery 722 n.
  possessed 773 adj.
privateer
  warship 722 n.
  robber 789 n.
private eye
  detective 459 n.
private parts
  genitalia 167 n.
privation
  loss 772 n.
  poverty 801 n.
privatization
  transfer 780 n.
privilege
  permit 756 vb.
  dueness 915 n.
  nonliability 919 n.
privy
  knowing 490 adj.
  latrine 649 n.
privy seal

  badge of rule 743 n.
prize
  trophy 729 n.
  booty 790 n.
  desired object 859 n.
  honour 866 vb.
  approve 923 vb.
  reward 962 n.
—open
  force 176 vb.
prizefight
  pugilism 716 n.
prizewinner
  proficient person
  696 n.
  victor 727 n.
prizewinning
  successful 727 adj.
pro
  expert 696 n.
  deputizing 755 adj.
PRO
  publicizer 528 n.
probability
  fair chance 159 n.
  probability 471 n.
probable
  probable 471 adj.
  credible 485 adj.
probation
  experiment 461 n.
probationer
  beginner 538 n.
  offender 904 n.
probation officer
  keeper 749 n.
probative
  evidential 466 adj.
  demonstrating
  478 adj.
probe
  inquiry 459 n.
  be tentative 461 vb.
  detector 484 n.
probity
  morals 917 n.
  probity 929 n.
problem
  topic 452 n.
  question 59 n.
  enigma 530 n.
  difficulty 700 n.
  worry 825 n.
problematic,
  problematical
  uncertain 474 adj.
  difficult 700 adj.

proboscis
protuberance 254 n.
procedure
policy 623 n.
way 624 n.
ritual 988 n.
proceed
travel 267 vb.
progress 285 vb.
proceeding(s)
deed 676 n.
legal process 959 n.
proceeds
earnings 771 n.
receipt 807 n.
process
computerize 86 vb.
convert 147 vb.
operate 173 vb.
processed
produced 164 adj.
ready-made
669 adj.
procession
retinue 67 n.
procession 71 n.
ritual act 988 n.
processor
data processing
86 n.
process-server
law officer 955 n.
proclaim
proclaim 528 vb.
decree 737 vb.
proclamation
publication 528 n.
call 547 n.
proclivity
tendency 179 n.
procrastinate
put off 136 vb.
not act 677 vb.
procreate
generate 167 vb.
proctor
law agent 958 n.
procumbent
supine 216 adj.
procurator
law agent 958 n.
procure
cause 156 vb.
acquire 771 vb.
procurer
provider 633 n.
bawd 952 n.

prod
impel 279 vb.
gesticulate 547 vb.
incite 612 vb.
prodigal
wasteful 634 adj.
prodigal 815 adj.
prodigal son
penitent 939 n.
prodigious
prodigious 32 adj.
wonderful 864 adj.
prodigy
exceller 644 n.
prodigy 864 n.
produce
cause 156 vb.
produce 164 vb.
manifest 522 vb.
dramatize 594 vb.
provision 633 n.
producer
producer 164 n.
stage manager
594 n.
product
product 164 n.
production
production 164 n.
dramaturgy 594 n.
productive
productive 164 adj.
profitable 640 adj.
gainful 771 adj.
productivity
productiveness
171 n.
profanation
misuse 675 n.
impiety 980 n.
profane
not respect 921 vb.
wicked 934 adj.
irreligious 974 adj.
profane 980 adj.
profanity
scurrility 899 n.
profess
believe 485 vb.
affirm 532 vb.
plead 614 vb.
profession
creed 485 n.
affirmation 532 n.
vocation 622 n.
professional
instructed 490 adj.

businesslike
622 adj.
expert 696 n.
professionalism
skill 694 n.
professor
scholar 492 n.
teacher 537 n.
proffer
offer 759 n.vb.
proficiency
skill 694 n.
proficient person
proficient person
696 n.
profile
outline 233 n.vb.
laterality 239 n.
feature 445 n.
description 590 n.
profit
increment 36 n.
benefit 615 n.vb.
gain 771 n.
—**by**
profit by 137 vb.
use 673 vb.
profitable
prolific 171 adj.
profitable 640 adj.
profiteer
overcharge 811 vb.
profitless
wasted 634 adj.
profitless 641 adj.
losing 772 n.
profligate
vicious 934 adj.
profound
great 32 adj.
deep 211 adj.
wise 498 adj.
felt 818 adj.
profuse
diffuse 570 adj.
liberal 813 adj.
profusion
great quantity 32 n.
plenty 635 n.
redundance 637 n.
progenitor,
  progenitrix
source 156 n.
progeny
posterity 170 n.
prognosis
prediction 511 n.

medical art 658 n.
prognostic
omen 511 n.
program
data processing
86 n.
computerize 86 vb.
programme
broadcast 531 n.
plan 623 n.vb.
policy 623 n.
programmed
  learning
teaching 534 n.
programmer
enumerator 86 n.
progress
increase 36 n.
motion 265 n.
travel 267 vb.
progression 285 n.
improvement 654 n.
progression
series 71 n.
ratio 85 n.
progressive
progressive 285 adj.
reformer 654 n.
prohibit
restrain 747 vb.
prohibit 757 vb.
prohibition
prohibition 757 n.
temperance 942 n.
prohibitive
hindering 702 adj.
dear 811 adj.
project
externalize 223 vb.
jut 254 vb.
plan 623 n.vb.
undertaking 672 n.
—**an image**
impress 821 vb.
projectile
missile 287 n.
ammunition 723 n.
projection
projection 254 n.
cinema 445 n.
image 551 n.
map 551 n.
projector
optical device 442 n.
prolegomena
prelude 66 n.
dissertation 591 n.

proletarian
vulgarian 847 n.
commoner 869 n.
proletariat
lower classes 869 n.
proliferate
be fruitful 171 vb.
abound 635 vb.
prolific
productive 164 adj.
prolific 171 adj.
prolix
prolix 570 adj.
prologue
prelude 66 n.
oration 579 n.
actor 594 n.
prolong
spin out 113 vb.
prolongation
lengthening 203 n.
prom
music 412 n.
promenade
pedestrianism
    267 n.
path 624 n.
be ostentatious
    875 vb.
prominence
prominence 254 n.
elevation 310 n.
importance 638 n.
prestige 866 n.
prominent
projecting 254 adj.
obvious 443 adj.
promiscuity
indiscrimination
    464 n.
unchastity 951 n.
promise
oath 532 n.
be auspicious
    730 vb.
promise 764 n.vb.
compact 765 n.
promised land
objective 617 n.
aspiration 852 n.
promising
promising 852 adj.
promissory
promissory 764 adj.
promontory
projection 254 n.
land 344 n.

promote
tend 179 vb.
promote 285 vb.
advertise 528 vb.
be instrumental
    628 vb.
be expedient 642 vb.
make better 654 vb.
aid 703 vb.
dignify 866 vb.
promoter
publicizer 528 n.
planner 623 n.
prompt
early 135 adj.
speedy 277 adj.
remind 505 vb.
hint 524 n.vb.
incite 612 vb.
advise 691 vb.
prompter
stagehand 594 n.
promulgate
proclaim 528 vb.
decree 737 vb.
prone
supine 216 adj.
prone to
tending 179 adj.
prong
sharp point 256 n.
pronounce
proclaim 528 vb.
affirm 532 vb.
speak 579 vb.
pronounced
obvious 443 adj.
vocal 577 adj.
pronouncement
judgement 480 n.
publication 528 n.
pronunciation
pronunciation
    577 n.
proof
sealed off 264 adj.
demonstration
    478 n.
letterpress 587 n.
invulnerable
    660 adj.
resisting 715 adj.
impassive 820 adj.
prop
prop 218 n.
support 218 vb.
stage set 594 n.

—up
preserve 666 vb.
aid 703 vb.
propaganda
publicity 528 n.
misteaching 535 n.
propagandist
publicizer 528 n.
preacher 537 n.
motivator 612 n.
propagate
generate 167 vb.
publish 528 vb.
propel
propel 287 vb.
propellant
propellant 287 n.
explosive 723 n.
propeller
propellant 287 n.
rotator 315 n.
propensity
tendency 179 n.
liking 859 n.
proper
characteristic 5 adj.
relevant 9 adj.
advisable 642 adj.
possessed 773 adj.
well-bred 848 adj.
right 913 adj.
virtuous 933 adj.
property
ability 160 n.
stage set 594 n.
property 777 n.
prophecy
prediction 511 n.
revelation 975 n.
prophesy
predict 511 vb.
prophet, prophetess
sage 500 n.
oracle 511 n.
preacher 537 n.
warner 664 n.
religious teacher
    973 n.
prophetic
predicting 511 adj.
revelational 975 adj.
prophylaxis
hygiene 652 n.
protection 660 n.
propinquity
nearness 200 n.
propitiate

pacify 719 vb.
atone 941 vb.
propitious
opportune 137 adj.
aiding 703 adj.
promising 852 adj.
proportion
correlation 12 n.
ratio 85 n.
symmetry 245 n.
portion 783 n.
proportionate
correlative 12 adj.
proportions
size 195 n.
proposal
intention 617 n.
plan 623 n.
advice 691 n.
offer 759 n.
wooing 889 n.
propose
propound 512 vb.
intend 617 vb.
advise 691 vb.
proposition
topic 452 n.
supposition 512 n.
debauch 951 vb.
propound
propound 512 vb.
offer 759 vb.
proprietary
proprietary 777 adj.
proprietor,
    proprietress
owner 776 n.
propriety
fitness 24 n.
good taste 846 n.
propulsion
propulsion 287 n.
prorogation
delay 136 n.
prosaic
prosaic 593 adj.
dull 840 adj.
proscenium
stage set 594 n.
proscribe
prohibit 757 vb.
condemn 961 vb.
proscribed person
outcast 883 n.
proscription
penalty 963 n.
(see **proscribe***)*

prose
plainness 573 n.
prose 593 n.
prosecute
do 676 vb.
indict 928 vb.
prosecution
accusation 928 n.
litigation 959 n.
prosecutor
accuser 928 n.
proselyte
learner 538 n.
proselytize
convert 147 vb.
teach 534 vb.
prosing
prolix 570 adj.
loquacious 581 adj.
prosody
prosody 593 n.
prosopography
description 590 n.
prospect
futurity 124 n.
view 438 n.
search 459 vb.
probability 471 n.
prediction 511 n.
prospective
future 124 adj.
expected 507 adj.
prospector
inquirer 459 n.
prospectus
list 87 n.
policy 623 n.
prosper
flourish 615 vb.
prosper 730 vb.
prosperous
successful 727 adj.
prosperous 730 adj.
rich 800 adj.
happy 824 adj.
prosthetics
surgery 658 n.
prostitute
pervert 655 vb.
prostitute 952 n.
prostitution
misuse 675 n.
social evil 951 n.
prostrate
supine 216 adj.
flatten 216 vb.
fatigued 684 adj.

—oneself
stoop 311 vb.
show respect 920 vb.
prostration
helplessness 161 n.
sorrow 825 n.
(*see* prostrate)
prosy
prolix 570 adj.
tedious 838 adj.
protagonist
actor 594 n.
protean
multiform 82 adj.
changeful 152 adj.
protect
screen 421 vb.
safeguard 660 vb.
patronize 703 vb.
befriend 880 vb.
protection
surveillance 457 n.
protection 660 n.
safeguard 662 n.
preservation 666 n.
protectionism
restriction 747 n.
protection racket
peculation 788 n.
protective clothing
shelter 662 n.
armour 713 n.
protector
protector 660 n.
defender 713 n.
protectorate
*political
organization*
733 n.
protégé(e)
dependant 742 n.
protest
oppose 704 vb.
resistance 715 n.
deprecation 762 n.
disapprobation
924 n.
Protestantism
Protestantism 976 n.
protester
dissentient 489 n.
agitator 738 n.
protocol
etiquette 848 n.
formality 875 n.
proton
element 319 n.

protoplasm
organism 358 n.
prototype
prototype 23 n.
protozoan
microorganism
196 n.
protract
spin out 113 vb.
lengthen 203 vb.
protractor
angular measure
247 n.
protrude
jut 254 vb.
protuberance
protuberance 254 n.
proud
proud 871 adj.
insolent 878 adj.
prove
demonstrate 478 vb.
proven
trustworthy 929 adj.
provenance
origin 68 n.
provender
provender 301 n.
provision 633 n.
proverb
maxim 496 n.
proverbial
known 490 adj.
aphoristic 496 adj.
provide
store 632 vb.
provide 633 vb.
give 781 vb.
providence
foresight 510 n.
Providence
divineness 965 n.
provident
foreseeing 510 adj.
providential
opportune 137 adj.
divine 965 adj.
province
district 184 n.
function 622 n.
provincial
provincial 192 adj.
country-dweller
869 n.
proving ground
testing agent 461 n.
provision

means 629 n.
provision 633 n.
fitting out 669 n.
conditions 766 n.
provisional
substituted 150 adj.
experimental
461 adj.
conditional 766 adj.
provisions
provisions 301 n.
proviso
qualification 468 n.
conditions 766 n.
provocation
inducement 612 n.
annoyance 827 n.
provocative
impertinent 878 adj.
impure 951 adj.
provoke
cause 156 vb.
incite 612 vb.
torment 827 vb.
prow
prow 237 n.
prowess
skill 694 n.
prowess 855 n.
prowl
be stealthy 525 vb.
proximate
near 200 adj.
proximity
nearness 200 n.
proxy
substitute 150 n.
consignee 754 n.
prude
prude 950 n.
prudence
sagacity 498 n.
foresight 510 n.
caution 858 n.
prudish
prudish 950 adj.
prune
subtract 39 vb.
shorten 204 vb.
prurient
inquisitive 453 adj.
impure 951 adj.
pry
be curious 453 vb.
inquire 459 vb.
psalm
hymn 981 n.

psalmbook
hymnal 988 n.
psalmist
theologian 973 n.
psalter
hymnal 988 n.
psephology
vote 605 n.
pseud, pseudo
impostor 545 n.
pseudo-
spurious 542 adj.
pseudonym
misnomer 562 n.
psi faculty
intuition 476 n.
psychics 984 n.
psyche
intellect 447 n.
spirit 447 n.
psychedelic
intoxicating 949 adj.
psyched up
prepared 669 adj.
psychiatric hospital
lunatic asylum
503 n.
psychiatrist
psychologist 447 n.
doctor 658 n.
psychiatry
psychology 447 n.
therapy 658 n.
psychic
psychic 447 adj.
psychic 984 n.
psychical 984 adj.
psychic profile
description 590 n.
psychics
psychics 984 n.
psychoanalysis
therapy 658 n.
psychograph
spiritualism 984 n.
psychokinesis
psychics 984 n.
psychological
psychic 447 adj.
behaving 688 adj.
**psychological
moment**
crisis 137 n.
psychologist
psychologist 447 n.
psychology
psychology 447 n.

affections 817 n.
psychopath
madman 504 n.
psychopathic
insane 503 adj.
psychopathology
medical art 658 n.
psychopathy
psychopathy 503 n.
psychosis
psychopathy 503 n.
psychosomatic
psychic 447 adj.
diseased 651 adj.
psychotherapy
therapy 658 n.
psychotic
insane 503 adj.
madman 504 n.
psychotropic
intoxicating 949 adj.
pub
tavern 192 n.
pub-crawl
drunkenness 949 n.
puberty
preparedness 669 n.
pubescence
youth 130 n.
hair 259 n.
public
social group 371 n.
national 371 adj.
known 490 adj.
manifest 522 adj.
formal 875 adj.
publican
caterer 633 n.
publication
publication 528 n.
book 589 n.
public convenience
latrine 649 n.
public figure
person of repute
866 n.
public house
tavern 192 n.
publicist
publicizer 528 n.
publicity
knowledge 490 n.
publicity 528 n.
publicize
advertise 528 vb.
public opinion
consensus 488 n.

public ownership
joint possession
775 n.
public relations
publicity 528 n.
public speaking
oratory 579 n.
public-spirited
patriotic 901 adj.
publish
publish 528 vb.
print 587 vb.
publisher
publicizer 528 n.
bookperson 589 n.
puce
brown 430 adj.
purple 436 adj.
pucker
fold 261 n.vb.
puckish
harmful 645 adj.
pudding
dessert 301 n.
puddle
shallowness 212 n.
lake 346 n.
puddled
opaque 423 adj.
pudency
modesty 874 n.
pudgy
fleshy 195 adj.
puerile
foolish 499 adj.
puff
breeze 352 n.
blow 352 vb.
breathe 352 vb.
smoke 388 vb.
advertisement
528 n.
boast 877 n.vb.
—up
enlarge 197 vb.
puffed up
overrated 482 adj.
prideful 871 adj.
puffy
fleshy 195 adj.
pug
dog 365 n.
trace 548 n.
pugilism
pugilism 716 n.
pugilist
pugilist 722 n.

pugnacious
quarrelling 709 adj.
contending 716 adj.
puissant
powerful 160 adj.
puke
vomit 300 vb.
pukka
genuine 494 adj.
pule
cry 408 vb.
weep 836 vb.
pull
influence 178 n.
draw 288 vb.
attraction 291 n.
extract 304 vb.
—a fast one
be cunning 698 vb.
—down
demolish 165 vb.
fell 311 vb.
—it off
succeed 727 vb.
—oneself together
be relieved 831 vb.
—one's leg
befool 542 vb.
—one's punches
be lenient 736 vb.
—out
lengthen 203 vb.
open 263 vb.
decamp 296 vb.
extract 304 vb.
—strings
influence 178 vb.
—through
be restored 656 vb.
—together
cooperate 706 vb.
—to pieces
demolish 165 vb.
detract 926 vb.
—up
come to rest
266 vb.
extract 304 vb.
pulley
tool 630 n.
pull-in
café 192 n.
pullover
jersey 228 n.
pullulate
be many 104 vb.
be fruitful 171 vb.

pulp
  demolish 165 vb.
  soften 327 vb.
  pulpiness 356 n.
pulpit
  rostrum 539 n.
  church interior
    990 n.
pulsar
  star 321 n.
pulsate
  be periodic 141 vb.
  oscillate 317 vb.
pulse
  be periodic 141 vb.
  be agitated 318 vb.
pulses
  vegetable 301 n.
pulverize
  pulverize 332 vb.
pumice stone
  cleanser 648 n.
pummel
  strike 279 vb.
pump
  extract 304 vb.
  brandish 317 vb.
  interrogate 459 vb.
—out
  empty 300 vb.
  make flow 350 vb.
—up
  blow up 352 vb.
pump rooms
  place of amusement
    837 n.
pumps
  footwear 228 n.
pun
  equivocalness
    518 n.
  be witty 839 vb.
punch
  mould 23 n.
  vigorousness 174 n.
  perforator 263 n.
  strike 279 vb.
  alcoholic drink
    301 n.
  printing 555 n.
  vigour 571 n.
Punch and Judy
  stage play 594 n.
punch-drunk
  insensible 375 adj.
punch line
  witticism 839 n.

punch-up
  fight 716 n.
punctilio
  etiquette 848 n.
  formality 875 n.
punctilious
  observant 768 adj. ·
  formal 875 adj.
  trustworthy 929 adj.
punctual
  early 135 adj.
  accurate 494 adj.
punctuate
  variegate 437 vb.
  mark 547 vb.
punctuation
  punctuation 547 n.
puncture
  perforation 263 n.
pundit
  sage 500 n.
  expert 696 n.
pungency
  sourness 393 n.
  vigour 571 n.
pungent
  pungent 388 adj.
  odorous 394 adj.
  felt 818 adj.
  witty 839 adj.
punish
  punish 963 vb.
punishing
  laborious 682 adj.
  fatiguing 684 adj.
punishment
  punishment 963 n.
punitive
  retaliatory 714 adj.
  severe 735 adj.
punk
  nonconformist 84 n.
  bad 645 adj.
  ruffian 904 n.
punt
  rowing boat 275 n.
punter
  boatman 270 n.
  gambler 618 n.
puny
  weak 163 adj.
  little 196 adj.
  unimportant
    639 adj.
pup
  reproduce itself
    167 vb.

(see **puppy***)*
pupil
  eye 438 n.
  learner 538 n.
pupillage
  nonage 130 n.
puppet
  image 551 n.
  instrument 628 n.
  nonentity 639 n.
  dependant 742 n.
  plaything 837 n.
puppy
  young creature
    132 n.
  fop 848 n.
purchasable
  venal 930 adj.
purchase
  purchase 792 n.vb.
purchaser
  purchaser 792 n.
purdah
  seclusion 883 n.
pure
  unmixed 44 adj.
  genuine 494 adj.
  clean 648 adj.
  salubrious 652 adj.
  disinterested
    931 adj.
  innocent 935 adj.
  pure 950 adj.
purebred
  thoroughbred
    273 n.
puree
  pulpiness 356 n.
purgation
  penance 941 n.
purgative
  excretory 302 adj.
  purgative 658 n.
purgatory
  suffering 825 n.
  hell 972 n.
purge
  slaughter 362 n.vb.
  purify 648 vb.
  purgative 658 n.
purification
  ritual act 988 n.
purify
  purify 648 vb.
  sanitate 652 vb.
purist
  perfectionist 862 n.

puritan
  prudish 950 adj.
puritanical
  severe 735 adj.
  serious 834 adj.
  ascetic 945 adj.
purity
  simpleness 44 n.
  good taste 846 n.
  modesty 874 n.
  virtue 933 n.
  purity 950 n.
  sanctity 979 n.
purlieus
  district 184 n.
  surroundings 230 n.
purloin
  steal 788 vb.
purple
  purple 436 adj.
purple passage
  ornament 574 n.
purport
  meaning 514 n.
purpose
  will 595 n.vb.
  intention 617 n.
purposeful
  resolute 599 adj.
purposeless
  designless 618 adj.
  useless 641 adj.
purr
  ululate 409 vb.
  be pleased 824 vb.
purse
  pocket 194 n.
  fold 261 vb.
  treasury 799 n.
purser
  provider 633 n.
purse strings
  authority 733 n.
  treasury 799 n.
pursue
  follow 284 vb.
  pursue 619 vb.
  court 889 vb.
pursuit
  pursuit 619 n.
  business 622 n.
purulent
  diseased 651 adj.
purvey
  provide 633 vb.
purveyor
  caterer 633 n.

purview
range 183 n.
pus
ulcer 651 n.
push
crisis 137 n.
impulse 279 n.
propulsion 287 n.
propel 287 vb.
ejection 300 n.
motivate 612 vb.
be active 678 vb.
—around
despise 922 vb.
—in
intrude 297 vb.
—off
start out 296 vb.
decamp 296 vb.
—on
progress 285 vb.
—one's luck
gamble 618 vb.
be rash 857 vb.
push-button
instrumental
628 adj.
pushchair
pushcart 274 n.
pusher
busy person 678 n.
drug-taking 949 n.
pushful, pushing
vigorous 174 adj.
assertive 532 adj.
active 678 adj.
pushover
easy thing 701 n.
victory 727 n.
pushy
meddling 678 adj.
pusillanimous
cowardly 856 adj.
pussyfoot
be stealthy 525 vb.
put
firm 45 adj.
place 187 vb.
—across
convince 485 vb.
—aside
set apart 46 vb.
—back
replace 187 vb.
—by
store 632 vb.
—down

destroy 165 vb.
kill 362 vb.
—forward
promote 285 vb.
—into practice
use 673 vb.
do 676 vb.
—off
put off 136 vb.
be neglectful
458 vb.
dissuade 613 vb.
cause dislike
861 vb.
—on
wear 228 vb.
dissemble 541 vb.
—on airs
be affected 850 vb.
—one's back up
huff 891 vb.
—oneself out
exert oneself 682 vb.
—one's finger on
detect 484 vb.
—one's foot down
accelerate 277 vb.
prohibit 757 vb.
—one's foot in it
be clumsy 695 vb.
—out
extinguish 382 vb.
publish 528 vb.
—out of commission
disable 161 vb.
stop using 674 vb.
—over
convince 485 vb.
communicate
524 vb.
**—the cart before the
horse**
act foolishly 695 vb.
—together
combine 50 vb.
—to music
compose music
413 vb.
—to rights
regularize 62 vb.
—up to
incite 612 vb.
—up with
be patient 823 vb.
suffer 825 vb.
putative
attributed 158 adj.

supposed 512 adj.
put off
distracted 456 adj.
put on
hypocritical
541 adj.
put out
discontented
829 adj.
putrefaction
decay 51 n.
putrefy
decompose 51 vb.
putrid
fetid 397 adj.
not nice 645 adj.
putsch
revolt 738 n.
putt
propel 287 vb.
puttees
legwear 228 n.
put to it, be
be in difficulty
700 vb.
putty
adhesive 47 n.
put-up job
predetermination
608 n.
false charge 928 n.
puzzle
puzzle 474 vb.
enigma 530 n.
pyjamas
nightwear 228 n.
pylon
electronics 160 n.
pyramid
series 71 n.
edifice 164 n.
high structure
209 n.
pyramidal
tapering 256 adj.
pyre
interment 364 n.
pyromaniac
destroyer 168 n.
pyrotechnics
fireworks 420 n.
Pyrrhonism
doubt 486 n.
python
compressor 198 n.
reptile 365 n.
oracle 511 n.

Q

QC
lawyer 958 n.
QED
argumentation
475 n.
quack
impostor 545 n.
unskilled 695 adj.
quad
quaternity 96 n.
quadrangle
place 185 n.
quadrant
angular measure
247 n.
quadrennial
seasonal 141 adj.
quadrilateral
angular figure 247 n.
quadrille
dance 837 n.
quadruped
animal 365 n.
quadruple
fourfold 97 adj.
quaff
drink 301 vb.
revel 837 vb.
quagmire
marsh 347 n.
difficulty 700 n.
quail
table bird 365 n.
quake 854 vb.
quaint
ornamental 844 adj.
ridiculous 849 adj.
quake
quake 854 vb.
Quakers
sect 978 n.
qualification(s)
fitness 24 n.
ability 160 n.
qualification 468 n.
aptitude 694 n.
(see qualify)
qualified
prepared 669 adj.
expert 694 adj.
qualify
moderate 177 vb.
discriminate 463 vb.
qualify 468 vb.
suffice 635 vb.

qualities
affections 817 n.
virtues 933 n.
quality
character 5 n.
superiority 34 n.
goodness 644 n.
qualms
doubt 486 n.
nervousness 854 n.
quandary
predicament 700 n.
quango
council 692 n.
quantify
quantify 26 vb.
measure 465 vb.
quantitative
quantitative 26 adj.
quantity
quantity 26 n.
number 85 n.
multitude 104 n.
quantum
element 319 n.
quarantine
hygiene 652 n.
protection 660 n.
seclusion 883 n.
quark
element 319 n.
quarrel
quarrel 709 n.vb.
quarrelsome
quarrelling 709 adj.
sullen 893 adj.
quarry
source 156 n.
excavation 255 n.
extract 304 vb.
objective 617 n.
store 632 n.
quarter
sunder 46 vb.
quadrisection 98 n.
district 184 n.
place 187 vb.
compass point
281 n.
mercy 905 n.
quarterdeck
vertex 213 n.
quartering
heraldry 547 n.
quarterly
three 93 adj.
journal 528 n.

quartermaster
provider 633 n.
quarters
quarters 192 n.
quartet
orchestra 413 n.
quarto
edition 589 n.
quasar
star 321 n.
quash
abrogate 752 vb.
quasi
similar 18 adj.
misnamed 562 adj.
quaternity
quaternity 96 n.
quatrain
verse form 593 n.
quaver
notation 410 n.
stammer 580 vb.
quake 854 vb.
quay
edge 234 n.
shelter 662 n.
queasy
sick 651 adj.
disliking 861 adj.
queen
nonconformist
84 n.
sovereign 741 n.
queenly
impressive 821 adj.
worshipful 866 adj.
queer
nonconformist 84 n.
abnormal 84 adj.
unusual 84 adj.
crazy 503 adj.
sick 651 adj.
queer one's pitch
harm 645 vb.
quell
suppress 165 vb.
subjugate 745 vb.
quench
suppress 165 vb.
snuff out 418 vb.
sate 863 vb.
quern
pulverizer 332 n.
querulous
discontented
829 adj.
irascible 892 adj.

query
question 459 n.
quest
pursuit 619 n.
undertaking 672 n.
question
topic 452 n.
question 459 n.
interrogate 459 vb.
doubt 486 vb.
questionable
moot 459 adj.
disreputable
867 adj.
questioner
listener 415 n.
questioner 459 n.
question mark
uncertainty 474 n.
punctuation 547 n.
question master
broadcaster 531 n.
questionnaire
list 87 n.
question 459 n.
queue
procession 71 n.
await 507 vb.
quibble
argue 475 vb.
sophisticate 477 vb.
pretext 614 n.
quick
speedy 277 adj.
intelligent 498 adj.
active 678 adj.
witty 839 adj.
quick-change artist
entertainer 594 n.
quicken
accelerate 277 vb.
animate 821 vb.
quicksand
marsh 347 n.
pitfall 663 n.
quicksilver
changeable thing
152 n.
quick-tempered
irascible 892 adj.
quick-witted
intelligent 498 adj.
quid
tobacco 388 n.
funds 797 n.
quiddity
essence 1 n.

quid pro quo
quid pro quo 150 n.
retaliation 714 n.
quiescence
quiescence 266 n.
peace 717 n.
quiescent
quiescent 266 adj.
inexcitable 823 adj.
quiet
assuage 177 vb.
quietude 266 n.
silent 399 n.
soft-hued 425 adj.
peaceful 717 adj.
inexcitable 823 adj.
secluded 883 n.
quieten
silence 399 vb.
quietude
(*see* quiet)
quietus
killing 362 n.
quiff
hair 259 n.
quill
plumage 259 n.
stationery 586 n.
quilt
coverlet 226 n.
quin
five 99 n.
quincunx
crossing 222 n.
quinine
antidote 658 n.
quinquennial
seasonal 141 adj.
quintessence
essential part 5 n.
quintet
orchestra 413 n.
quip
witticism 839 n.
quire
paper 631 n.
quirk
whim 604 n.
quisling
turncoat 603 n.
quit
depart 296 vb.
resign 753 vb.
fail in duty 918 vb.
quite
slightly 33 adv.
completely 54 adv.

quits
  equivalence 28 n.
quits, be
  retaliate 714 vb.
quittance
  payment 804 n.
quitter
  turncoat 603 n.
  resignation 753 n.
quiver
  be agitated 318 vb.
  arsenal 723 n.
  be excited 821 vb.
  quake 854 vb.
quixotic
  imaginative 513 adj.
  disinterested
    931 adj.
quiz
  interrogate 459 vb.
  indoor game 837 n.
quizzical
  inquiring 459 adj.
  derisive 851 adj.
quoin
  angularity 247 n.
  press 587 n.
quoit(s)
  missile 287 n.
  ball game 837 n.
quondam
  former 125 adj.
quorum
  electorate 605 n.
  sufficiency 635 n.
quota
  finite quantity 26 n.
  portion 783 n.
quotation
  referral 9 n.
  price 809 n.
quote
  exemplify 83 vb.
  repeat 106 vb.
quotidian
  seasonal 141 adj.
quotient
  numerical element
    85 n.

R

rabbi
  theologian 973 n.
rabbit
  mammal 365 n.

  bungler 697 n.
  coward 856 n.
rabbiting
  chase 619 n.
rabbit on
  be loquacious
    581 vb.
rabble
  rabble 869 n.
rabble-rouser
  agitator 738 n.
Rabelaisian
  impure 951 adj.
rabid
  frenzied 503 adj.
  angry 891 adj.
rabies
  animal disease
    651 n.
race
  race 11 n.
  genealogy 169 n.
  speeding 277 n.
  current 350 n.
  hasten 680 vb.
  racing 716 n.
racecourse
  arena 724 n.
racehorse
  thoroughbred
    273 n.
  speeder 277 n.
race relations
  sociality 882 n.
racial
  ethnic 11 adj.
  human 371 adj.
racialism
  prejudice 481 n.
  hatred 888 n.
racing
  racing 716 n.
  sport 837 n.
racism
  prejudice 481 n.
rack
  shelf 218 n.
  purify 648 vb.
  torment 827 vb.
  instrument of
    torture 964 n.
racket
  turmoil 61 n.
  loudness 400 n.
  foul play 930 n.
racketeer
  offender 904 n.

rackety
  riotous 738 adj.
  merry 833 adj.
rack rents
  dearness 811 n.
raconteur,
  raconteuse
  narrator 590 n.
  humorist 839 n.
racy
  vigorous 174 adj.
  savoury 390 adj.
  lively 819 adj.
  witty 839 adj.
radar
  detector 484 n.
  telecommunication
    531 n.
radiance
  glow, light 417 n.
radiant
  radiating 417 adj.
  luminescent
    420 adj.
  happy 824 adj.
  beautiful 841 adj.
radiate
  be dispersed 75 vb.
  emit 300 vb.
radiation
  nucleonics 160 n.
  radiation 417 n.
  poison 659 n.
radiator
  heater 383 n.
radical
  intrinsic 5 adj.
  complete 54 adj.
  revolutionary
    149 adj.
  fundamental
    156 adj.
  important 638 adj.
  reformer 654 n.
  sectional 708 adj.
radio
  broadcasting 531 n.
radioactive
  dangerous 661 adj.
radioactivity
  nucleonics 160 n.
  radiation 417 n.
radiogram
  gramophone 414 n.
radiography
  photography 551 n.
  medical art 658 n.

radio ham
  listener 415 n.
  enthusiast 504 n.
radiophonic
  sounding 398 adj.
radioscopy
  optics 417 n.
radiotelegraphy
  telecommunication
    531 n.
radiotherapy
  medical art 658 n.
radio wave(s)
  radiation 417 n.
  broadcasting 531 n.
radius
  range 183 n.
  breadth 205 n.
raffia
  fibre 208 n.
raffish
  vulgar 847 adj.
raffle
  gambling 618 n.
raft
  raft 275 n.
rafter
  beam 218 n.
  roof 226 n.
rag
  the press 528 n.
  trickery 542 n.
  torment 827 vb.
  revel 837 n.
  ridicule 851 vb.
raga
  musical piece 412 n.
ragamuffin
  low fellow 869 n.
ragbag
  medley 43 n.
rage
  violence 176 n.
  excitable state 822 n.
  fashion 848 n.
  desire 859 n.
  anger 891 n.
ragged
  uncovered 229 adj.
  undulatory 251 adj.
raggedness
  nonuniformity
    17 n.
  poverty 801 n.
rags
  piece 53 n.
  clothing 228 n.

ragtime
 music 412 n.

raid
 burst in 297 vb.
 attack 712 n.vb.
 brigandage 788 n.

raider
 attacker 712 n.
 robber 789 n.

rail
 handle 218 n.
 transport 272 n.
 reprobate 924 vb.

railing
 fence 235 n.
 safeguard 662 n.

raillery
 ridicule 851 n.

railroad
 compel 740 vb.

railway
 railway 624 n.

raiment
 clothing 228 n.

rain
 rain 350 n.vb.
 abound 635 vb.

rainbow
 arc 250 n.
 variegation 437 n.

raincoat
 overcoat 228 n.

rainfall
 rain 350 n.

rain gauge
 weather 340 n.

rainproof
 dry 342 adj.

rainy
 rainy 350 adj.

rainy day
 adversity 731 n.

raise
 augment 36 vb.
 make higher 209 vb.
 elevate 310 vb.
 breed stock 369 vb.
 improvement
  654 n.

—one's sights
 aim at 617 vb.

—one's voice
 emphasize 532 vb.
 speak 579 vb.

—spirits
 practise sorcery
  983 vb.

—the alarm
 raise the alarm
  665 vb.

—the money
 find means 629 vb.

raison d'être
 reason why 156 n.

raj
 governance 733 n.

rake
 obliquity 220 n.
 farm tool 370 n.
 fire at 712 vb.
 libertine 952 n.

—in
 bring together
  74 vb.
 gain 771 vb.

—over
 search 459 vb.

—together
 acquire 771 vb.

—up
 retrospect 505 vb.

rake-off
 discount 810 n.
 reward 962 n.

rakish
 oblique 220 adj.
 showy 875 adj.

rally
 assemblage 74 n.
 continuance 146 n.
 call 547 n.
 incite 612 vb.
 be restored 656 vb.
 contest 716 n.
 ridicule 851 vb.
 give courage 855 vb.

rallying point
 focus 76 n.

ram
 ram 279 n.
 collide 279 vb.
 sheep 365 n.
 charge 712 vb.

ramble
 wander 267 vb.
 be diffuse 570 vb.

rambler
 wanderer 268 n.

rambling
 orderless 61 adj.
 deviating 282 adj.
 sport 837 n.

ramekin
 bowl 194 n.

ramification
 branch 53 n.
 divergence 294 n.

ramp
 obliquity 220 n.
 ascent 308 n.
 trickery 542 n.
 get angry 891 vb.

rampage
 rampage 61 vb.
 be violent 176 vb.
 excitable state 822 n.

rampant
 furious 176 adj.
 vertical 215 adj.
 heraldic 547 adj.
 plenteous 635 adj.

rampart
 fortification 713 n.

ramshackle
 dilapidated 655 adj.

ranch
 stock farm 369 n.

rancher
 herdsman 369 n.

rancid
 unsavoury 391 adj.

rancour
 resentment 891 n.
 malevolence 898 n.

random
 orderless 61 adj.
 casual 159 adj.
 indiscriminate
  464 adj.
 designless 618 adj.

randy
 lecherous 951 adj.

range
 arrange 62 vb.
 series 71 n.
 range 183 n.
 plain 348 n.
 furnace 383 n.
 arena 724 n.
 scope 744 n.
 merchandise 795 n.

—oneself with
 join a party 708 vb.

range finder
 direction 281 n.
 telescope 442 n.

ranger
 keeper 749 n.

rangy
 narrow 206 adj.
 tall 209 adj.

rank
 graduate 27 vb.
 class 62 vb.
 serial place 73 n.
 vegetal 366 adj.
 fetid 397 adj.
 estimate 480 vb.
 plenteous 635 adj.
 importance 638 n.
 nobility 868 n.
 heinous 934 adj.

rank and file
 commonalty 869 n.

rankle
 hurt 827 vb.

ranks, the
 soldiery 722 n.

ransack
 lay waste 165 vb.
 search 459 vb.

ransom
 deliverance 668 n.
 purchase 792 n.vb.
 price 809 n.

rant
 empty talk 515 n.
 magniloquence
  574 n.
 boast 877 vb.

rap
 knock 279 n.
 bang 402 n.

—over the knuckles
 reprove 924 vb.
 spank 963 vb.

rapacious
 avaricious 816 adj.

rapacity
 rapacity 786 n.

rape
 taking 786 n.
 rape 951 n.

rapid
 speedy 277 adj.

rapids
 waterfall 350 n.

rapier
 sidearms 723 n.

rapine
 spoliation 788 n.

rapist
 libertine 952 n.

rapport
 relation 9 n.
 concord 710 n.

rapprochement
 pacification 719 n.

rapscallion
knave 938 n.
rapt
attentive 455 adj.
abstracted 456 adj.
wondering 864 adj.
raptorial
taking 786 adj.
rapture(s)
joy 824 n.
rejoicing 835 n.
rapturous
felt 818 adj.
pleased 824 adj.
rare
few 105 adj.
infrequent 140 adj.
culinary 301 adj.
rare 325 adj.
scarce 636 adj.
excellent 644 adj.
wonderful 864 adj.
rarefy
rarefy 325 vb.
rarity
paragon 646 n.
(see **rare***)*
rascal
knave 938 n.
rascally
disreputable
867 adj.
rascally 930 adj.
rash
skin disease 651 n.
hasty 680 adj.
rash 857 adj.
rasher
piece 53 n.
rasp
rub 333 vb.
breathe 352 vb.
rasp 407 vb.
discord 411 vb.
raspberry
fruit 301 n.
gesture 547 n.
reprimand 924 n.
Rastafarianism
religious faith
973 n.
rat
mammal 365 n.
inform 524 vb.
deceiver 545 n.
turncoat 603 n.
apostatize 603 vb.

noxious animal
904 n.
knave 938 n.
rat catcher
hunter 619 n.
ratchet
tooth 256 n.
rate
degree 27 n.
class 62 vb.
velocity 277 n.
estimate 480 vb.
price 809 n.vb.
ratepayer
resident 191 n.
ratify
endorse 488 vb.
sign 547 vb.
make legal 953 vb.
rating
naval man 722 n.
tax 809 n.
ratio
relativeness 9 n.
ratio 85 n.
ratiocinate
reason 475 vb.
ration
make insufficient
636 vb.
portion 783 n.
rational
mental 447 adj.
philosophic 449 adj.
rational 475 adj.
sane 502 adj.
rationale
attribution 158 n.
rationalism
philosophy 449 n.
reasoning 475 n.
rationalist
irreligionist 974 n.
rationalize
reason 475 vb.
plan 623 vb.
rationing
restriction 747 n.
rations
provision 633 n.
ratlines
tackling 47 n.
rat race
rotation 315 n.
activity 678 n.
rat-tat, rat-a-tat
bang 402 n.

rattle
derange 63 vb.
oscillate 317 vb.
crackle 402 vb.
gong 414 n.
be loquacious
581 vb.
plaything 837 n.
frighten 854 vb.
rattled
distracted 456 adj.
angry 891 adj.
ratty
angry 891 adj.
raucous
hoarse 407 adj.
discordant 411 adj.
ravage
lay waste 165 vb.
ravaged
unsightly 842 adj.
rave
be insane 503 vb.
mean nothing
515 vb.
be pleased 824 vb.
ravel
complexity 61 n.
raven
eat 301 vb.
omen 511 n.
—for
desire 859 vb.
ravenous
hungry 859 adj.
rave-up
revel 837 n.
ravine
gap 201 n.
valley 255 n.
raving
frenzied 503 adj.
excited 821 adj.
raving beauty
a beauty 841 n.
raving lunatic
madman 504 n.
ravioli
dish 301 n.
ravish
take away 786 vb.
delight 826 vb.
debauch 951 vb.
ravishing
splendid 841 adj.
raw
new 126 adj.

young 130 adj.
uncovered 229 adj.
culinary 301 adj.
sentient 374 adj.
painful 377 adj.
cold 380 adj.
ignorant 491 adj.
immature 670 adj.
unskilled 695 adj.
sensitive 819 adj.
raw deal
misfortune 731 n.
rawhide
skin 226 n.
raw material(s)
source 156 n.
means 629 n.
materials 631 n.
ray
flash 417 n.
rayon
textile 222 n.
raze
demolish 165 vb.
fell 311 vb.
razor
sharp edge 256 n.
razor's edge
danger 661 n.
re
concerning 9 adv.
reach
ability 160 n.
range 183 n.
distance 199 n.
arrive 295 vb.
suffice 635 vb.
react
be active 678 vb.
—against
dislike 861 vb.
reaction
effect 157 n.
recoil 280 n.
sense 374 n.
answer 460 n.
retaliation 714 n.
feeling 818 n.
reactionary
regressive 286 adj.
opponent 705 n.
reactivation
revival 656 n.
read
gauge 465 vb.
decipher 520 vb.
study 536 vb.

—off
  gauge 465 vb.
readable
  intelligible 516 adj.
reader
  scholar 492 n.
  bookperson 589 n.
  textbook 589 n.
readership
  publicity 528 n.
readiness
  tendency 179 n.
  willingness 597 n.
  completion 725 n.
reading
  measurement 465 n.
  erudition 490 n.
  interpretation 520 n.
  study 536 n.
reading matter
  reading matter
    589 n.
readjustment
  restoration 656 n.
ready
  on the spot 189 adj.
  intelligent 498 adj.
  expectant 507 adj.
  loquacious 581 adj.
  willing 597 adj.
  prepared 669 adj.
  obedient 739 adj.
  consenting 758 adj.
ready-made
  ready-made
    669 adj.
ready-to-wear
  tailored 228 adj.
reagent
  testing agent 461 n.
real
  real 1 adj.
  substantial 3 adj.
  material 319 adj.
  true 494 adj.
real estate
  lands 777 n.
realism
  accuracy 494 n.
  veracity 540 n.
  representation
    551 n.
realist
  materiality 319 n.
realistic
  lifelike 18 adj.
  wise 498 adj.

  descriptive 590 adj.
reality
  reality 1 n.
  truth 494 n.
realizable
  possible 469 adj.
realization
  event 154 n.
  discovery 484 n.
  representation
    551 n.
  effectuation 725 n.
  feeling 818 n.
realize
  cognize 447 vb.
  imagine 513 vb.
  understand 516 vb.
  acquire 771 vb.
realm
  territory 184 n.
  function 622 n.
  political organ-
    ization 733 n.
realpolitik
  tactics 688 n.
real thing, the
  reality 1 n.
  no imitation 21 n.
  authenticity 494 n.
realty
  lands 777 n.
ream
  paper 631 n.
reamer
  perforator 263 n.
  cleaning utensil
    648 n.
reams
  great quantity 32 n.
reanimate
  vitalize 360 vb.
  refresh 685 vb.
reap
  cultivate 370 vb.
  acquire 771 vb.
reappear
  reoccur 106 vb.
  be restored 656 vb.
rear
  sequel 67 n.
  make vertical
    215 vb.
  buttocks 238 n.
  rear 238 n.
  leap 312 vb.
  breed stock 369 vb.
  educate 534 vb.

rearrange
  modify 143 vb.
reason
  reason why 156 n.
  intellect 447 n.
  reasoning 475 n.
  sanity 502 n.
—badly
  reason badly
    477 vb.
reasonable
  moderate 177 adj.
  plausible 471 adj.
  rational 475 adj.
  wise 498 adj.
  sane 502 adj.
  cheap 812 adj.
  just 913 adj.
reasoning
  reasoning 475 n.
reassemble
  repair 656 vb.
reassure
  give courage 855 vb.
reawakening
  revival 656 n.
rebarbative
  disliked 861 adj.
rebate
  discount 810 n.
rebel
  nonconformist
    84 n.
  revolter 738 n.
rebellion
  revolt 738 n.
rebellious
  defiant 711 adj.
  disobedient 738 adj.
  undutiful 918 adj.
rebirth
  revival 656 n.
reborn
  converted 147 adj.
rebound
  recoil 280 n.vb.
rebuff
  repulsion 292 n.
  rejection 607 n.
  resistance 715 n.
  defeat 728 n.
  refusal 760 n.
  rudeness 885 n.
rebuild
  reproduce 166 vb.
rebuke
  reprove 924 vb.

rebus
  enigma 530 n.
rebut
  confute 479 vb.
rebuttal
  rejoinder 460 n.
  confutation 479 n.
  negation 533 n.
recalcitrance,
  recalcitrancy
  resistance 715 n.
recalcitrant
  unwilling 598 adj.
  disobedient 738 adj.
recall
  retrospect 505 vb.
  depose 752 vb.
recant
  recant 603 vb.
  be penitent 939 vb.
recapitulate
  repeat 106 vb.
recapture
  retrospect 505 vb.
  retrieve 656 vb.
recast
  modify 143 vb.
  rectify 654 vb.
recede
  regress 286 vb.
  recede 290 vb.
receipt
  receipt 807 n.
receipts
  earnings 771 n.
receive
  admit 299 vb.
  receive 782 vb.
  greet 884 vb.
received
  usual 610 adj.
receiver
  hearing aid 415 n.
  recipient 782 n.
  thief 789 n.
recension
  amendment 654 n.
recent
  new 126 adj.
receptacle
  receptacle 194 n.
reception
  reception 299 n.
  hearing 415 n.
  receiving 782 n.
  social gathering
    882 n.

receptionist
recorder 549 n.
receptive
studious 536 adj.
willing 597 adj.
receiving 782 adj.
recess
compartment 194 n.
repose 683 n.
recesses
interiority 224 n.
recession
decrease 37 n.
recession 290 n.
deterioration 655 n.
recessional
hymn 981 n.
recessive
reverted 148 adj.
recherché
excellent 644 adj.
recidivism
reversion 148 n.
relapse 657 n.
recidivist
offender 904 n.
recipe
cookery 301 n.
precept 693 n.
recipient
recipient 782 n.
reciprocal
correlative 12 adj.
reciprocate
correlate 12 vb.
be periodic 141 vb.
cooperate 706 vb.
reciprocation
interchange 151 n.
reciprocity
correlation 12 n.
cooperation 706 n.
recital
music 412 n.
recitation
oration 579 n.
recite
repeat 106 vb.
speak 579 vb.
reckless
rash 857 adj.
reckon
do sums 86 vb.
measure 465 vb.
expect 507 vb.
reckoning
numeration 86 n.

accounts 808 n.
punishment 963 n.
reclaim
make better 654 vb.
restore 656 vb.
claim 915 vb.
recline
be horizontal 216 vb.
repose 683 vb.
recluse
solitary 883 n.
recognition
knowledge 490 n.
thanks 907 n.
dueness 915 n.
approbation 923 n.
recognizable
visible 443 adj.
intelligible 516 adj.
manifest 522 adj.
recognizance
security 767 n.
recognize
see 438 vb.
know 490 vb.
remember 505 vb.
grant claims 915 vb.
recoil
recoil 280 n.vb.
elasticity 328 n.
dislike 861 vb.
recollect
remember 505 vb.
retrospect 505 vb.
recommend
incite 612 vb.
patronize 703 vb.
recommendation
credential 466 n.
advice 691 n.
recompense
reward 962 n.vb.
reconcile
pacify 719 vb.
content 828 vb.
reconciliation
concord 710 n.
propitiation 941 n.
recondite
puzzling 517 adj.
concealed 525 adj.
recondition
repair 656 vb.
reconnaissance
inspection 438 n.
reconnoitre

scan 438 vb.
reconsider
rectify 654 vb.
reconstitute
restore 656 vb.
reconstruct
restore 656 vb.
reconstruction
conjecture 512 n.
record
superiority 34 n.
record 548 n.vb.
*recording
instrument* 549 n.
write 586 vb.
describe 590 vb.
best 644 adj.
conduct 688 n.
record-breaking
enormous 32 adj.
best 644 adj.
recorder
flute 414 n.
recorder 549 n.
recording
gramophone 414 n.
broadcast 531 n.
record 548 n.
recording instrument
*recording
instrument* 549 n.
record-keeping
registration 548 n.
record player
gramophone 414 n.
recount
communicate
524 vb.
describe 590 vb.
recoup
recoup 31 vb.
recourse
contrivance 623 n.
recover
recoup 31 vb.
be restored 656 vb.
recovery
recuperation 656 n.
revival 656 n.
recreant
turncoat 603 n.
knave 938 n.
recreation
refreshment 685 n.
amusement 837 n.
recrimination(s)
dissension 709 n.

reproach 924 n.
recrudescence
relapse 657 n.
recruit
augment 36 vb.
beginner 538 n.
employ 622 vb.
auxiliary 707 n.
soldier 722 n.
rectangle
angular figure
247 n.
rectify
regularize 62 vb.
rectify 654 vb.
rectilineal
straight 249 adj.
rectitude
probity 929 n.
recto
dextrality 241 n.
rector
pastor 986 n.
rectory
parsonage 986 n.
rectum
insides 224 n.
recumbent
supine 216 adj.
recuperate
be restored 656 vb.
recur
recur 139 vb.
recurrence
recurrence 106 n.
periodicity 141 n.
relapse 657 n.
recurrent
frequent 139 adj.
recusant
disobedient 738 adj.
schismatic 978 n.
recyclable
decomposable
51 adj.
recycle
restore 656 vb.
use 673 vb.
economize 814 vb.
red
fiery 379 adj.
red 431 adj.
Red
revolutionist 149 n.
political party
708 n.
revolter 738 n.

redact
rectify 654 vb.

redactor
bookperson 589 n.

red alert
danger signal 665 n.

red-blooded
courageous
855 adj.

redbrick
educational 534 adj.

red carpet
formality 875 n.

Red Cross
doctor 658 n.

redden
redden 431 vb.

redeem
compensate 31 vb.
deliver 668 vb.
purchase 792 vb.
atone 941 vb.

redemption
liberation 746 n.
divine function
965 n.

red flag
danger signal 665 n.

redhanded
in the act 676 adv.
guilty 936 adj.

red herring
irrelevance 10 n.

red-hot
hot 379 adj.
fervent 818 adj.

redintegrate
restore 656 vb.

redirect
send 272 vb.

red-letter day
special day 876 n.

red light
danger signal 665 n.

red-light district
brothel 951 n.

redo
restore 656 vb.

redolent
odorous 394 adj.

redouble
double 91 vb.
invigorate 174 vb.

redoubtable
frightening 854 adj.

redound to
tend 179 vb.

redress
remedy 658 n.
justice 913 n.
equalize 28 vb.

red tape
delay 136 n.
governance 733 n.

reduce
abate 37 vb.
decompose 51 vb.
render few 105 vb.
make smaller
198 vb.
abstract 592 vb.
subjugate 745 vb.
—to
convert 147 vb.
—weight
lighten 323 vb.

reduction
discount 810 n.

redundancy,
redundance
plenty 635 n.
redundance 637 n.

redundant
redundant 637 adj.
unused 674 adj.

reduplicate
repeat 106 vb.

reecho
resound 404 vb.

reed
weak thing 163 n.
grass 366 n.
flute 414 n.

re-education camp
prison camp 748 n.

reedy
strident 407 adj.

reef
fold 261 vb.
rock 344 n.
pitfall 663 n.

reefer
jacket 228 n.
drug-taking 949 n.

reek
stench 397 n.

reel
rotator 315 n.
oscillate 317 vb.
dance 837 n.
—off
be loquacious
581 vb.

reentry

return 286 n.

reestablish
restore 656 vb.

reface
repair 656 vb.

refection
meal 301 n.
refreshment 685 n.

refer
indicate 547 vb.
—to
relate 9 vb.
mean 514 vb.
consult 691 vb.

referee
estimator 480 n.
mediator 720 n.

reference
referral 9 n.
relation 9 n.
credential 466 n.
connotation 514 n.

reference book
reference book
589 n.

referendum
vote 605 n.

refill
replenish 633 vb.

refine
purify 648 vb.

refined
tasteful 846 adj.
pure 950 adj.

refinement
discrimination
463 n.
fastidiousness
862 n.

refinery
workshop 687 n.

refit
repair 656 vb.

reflation
dilation 197 n.
finance 797 n.

reflect
resemble 18 vb.
shine 417 vb.
meditate 449 vb.
show 522 vb.
represent 551 vb.
—on
shame 867 vb.

reflection
copy 22 n.
reflection 417 n.

meditation 449 n.
image 551 n.
slur 867 n.

reflector
mirror 442 n.
telescope 442 n.

reflex
recoil 280 n.
involuntary 596 adj.
habituation 610 n.

reflexive
reverted 148 adj.

reflux
return 286 n.
current 350 n.

reforest
restore 656 vb.

reform
transform 147 vb.
make better 654 vb.
philanthropize
897 vb.
be penitent 939 vb.

reformatory
prison 748 n.

reformer
reformer 654 n.

refract
radiate 417 vb.

refractory
wilful 602 adj.
disobedient 738 adj.

refrain
repetition 106 n.
tune 412 n.
verse form 593 n.
avoid 620 vb.
not act 677 vb.
be temperate
942 vb.

refresh
invigorate 174 vb.
revive 656 vb.
refresh 685 vb.

refresher
tonic 658 n.
refreshment 685 n.

refreshing
refreshing 685 adj.
pleasurable
826 adj.

refreshment
meal 301 n.
repose 683 n.
refreshment 685 n.
amusement 837 n.
(see **refresh**)

refrigerate
refrigerate 382 vb.
preserve 666 vb.

refuel
store 632 vb.
replenish 633 vb.

refuge
retreat 192 n.
refuge 662 n.

refugee
foreigner 59 n.
wanderer 268 n.
outcast 883 n.

refund
decrement 42 n.

refurbish
repair 656 vb.

refusal
rejection 607 n.
refusal 760 n.

refuse
rubbish 641 n.
dirt 649 n.
refuse 760 vb.

refutation
confutation 479 n.

regain
acquire 771 vb.

regal
ruling 733 adj.
impressive 821 adj.
noble 868 adj.

regale (with)
feed 301 vb.
delight 826 vb.
be hospitable
  882 vb.

regalia
regalia 743 n.

regard
be related 9 vb.
look 438 n.
attention 455 n.
repute 866 n.
love 887 n.vb.
respect 920 n.vb.

regardless
inattentive 456 adj.
rash 857 adj.

regards
respects 920 n.

regatta
racing 716 n.

regency
governance 733 n.

regenerate
converted 147 adj.

repentant 939 adj.

regeneration
revival 656 n.

regent
potentate 741 n.

reggae
music 412 n.

regicide
revolter 738 n.

regime
management 689 n.
governance 733 n.

regimen
dieting 301 n.
therapy 658 n.

regiment
formation 722 n.
dominate 733 vb.

regimentals
uniform 228 n.

regimentation
uniformity 16 n.
compulsion 740 n.

region
region 184 n.

regional
regional 184 adj.
provincial 192 adj.

register
class 62 vb.
list 87 n.
notice 455 vb.
indicate 547 vb.
register 548 vb.
account book 808 n.

registrar
recorder 549 n.
doctor 658 n.

registration
registration 548 n.

registry
registration 548 n.

regnant
ruling 733 adj.

regress
regress 286 vb.
relapse 657 vb.

regression
change 143 n.
reversion 148 n.
deterioration 655 n.

regressive
regressive 286 adj.

regret
disappointment
  509 n.
sorrow 825 n.

regret 830 n.vb.
disapprove 924 vb.

regretful
unhappy 825 adj.
repentant 939 adj.

regrettable
regretted 830 adj.

regular
regular 81 adj.
frequent 139 adj.
symmetrical
  245 adj.
habitué 610 n.
soldier 722 n.

regularity
uniformity 16 n.
periodicity 141 n.

regularize
regularize 62 vb.
make conform
  83 vb.

regulate
regularize 62 vb.

regulation
rule 81 n.
legislation 953 n.

regurgitation
return 286 n.
voidance 300 n.

rehabilitate
restore 656 vb.
vindicate 927 vb.

rehash
repetition 106 n.

rehearsal
dramaturgy 594 n.

rehearse
repeat 106 vb.
describe 590 vb.
prepare oneself
  669 vb.

reign
date 108 n.
governance 733 n.
rule 733 vb.

reign of terror
intimidation 854 n.

reimburse
restitute 787 vb.
pay 804 vb.

rein(s)
halter 47 n.
moderator 177 n.
management 689 n.

reincarnation
transformation
  143 n.

reinforce
augment 36 vb.
strengthen 162 vb.
support 218 vb.
aid 703 vb.

reinforcement(s)
auxiliary 707 n.

rein in
retard 278 vb.
restrain 747 vb.

reinstatement
reversion 148 n.
restitution 787 n.

reissue
edition 589 n.

reiterate
repeat 106 vb.

reject
inferior 35 n.
reject 607 vb.
rubbish 641 n.
not use 674 vb.
disapprove 924 vb.

rejection
rejection 607 n.
refusal 760 n.

rejoice
be pleased 824 vb.
rejoice 835 vb.
revel 837 vb.

rejoicing
celebration 876 n.

rejoin
meet 295 vb.

rejoinder
rejoinder 460 n.
sauciness 878 n.

rejuvenate
revive 656 vb.

rekindle
revive 656 vb.
animate 821 vb.

relapse
reversion 148 n.
relapse 657 n.vb.

relate
relate 9 vb.
attribute 158 vb.
describe 590 vb.

related
akin 11 adj.

relation
relation 9 n.
kinsman 11 n.
correlation 12 n.

relationship
relation 9 n.

consanguinity 11 n.
friendship 880 n.

relative
relative 9 adj.
comparative 27 adj.

relativism
philosophy 449 n.

relativity
relativeness 9 n.

relax
repose 683 vb.
be lenient 736 vb.
relieve 831 vb.

relaxation
repose 683 n.
liberation 746 n.
amusement 837 n.

relaxed
reposeful 683 adj.

relay
publish 528 vb.
broadcast 531 n.
auxiliary 707 n.

release
show 522 vb.
deliver 668 vb.
liberation 746 n.
nonretention 779 n.

relegate
displace 188 vb.
transpose 272 vb.

relegation
ejection 300 n.

relent
be moderate 177 vb.
show mercy 905 vb.
forgive 909 vb.

relentless
severe 735 adj.
pitiless 906 adj.

relevance, relevancy
relevance 9 n.
fitness 24 n.
meaning 514 n.

relevant
relevant 9 adj.
important 638 adj.

reliability
credit 802 n.

reliable
unchangeable
153 adj.
probable 471 adj.
certain 473 adj.
credible 485 adj.
genuine 494 adj.
safe 660 adj.

observant 768 adj.
trustworthy 929 adj.

reliance
belief 485 n.
expectation 507 n.

relic
archaism 127 n.
reminder 505 n.
trace 548 n.
talisman 983 n.

relict
widowhood 896 n.

relief
contrariety 14 n.
substitute 150 n.
moderation 177 n.
outline 233 n.
form 243 n.
feature 445 n.
sculpture 554 n.
deliverance 668 n.
refreshment 685 n.
aid 703 n.
relief 831 n.

relieve
come after 65 vb.
assuage 177 vb.
remedy 658 vb.
disencumber
701 vb.
liberate 746 vb.
relieve 831 vb.
—of
take away 786 vb.
—oneself
excrete 302 vb.

religion
religion 973 n.
piety 979 n.
public worship
981 n.

religiose
pietistic 979 adj.

religious
observant 768 adj.
religious 973 adj.
pious 979 adj.

religious faith
religious faith 973 n.

religious teacher
religious teacher
973 n.

religious truth
orthodoxy 976 n.

reline
repair 656 vb.

relinquish

cease 145 vb.
be irresolute 601 vb.
relinquish 621 vb.
stop using 674 vb.
abrogate 752 vb.
resign 753 vb.
not retain 779 vb.

relish
pleasure 376 n.
taste 386 n.
condiment 389 n.
enjoyment 824 n.
liking 859 n.

reload
replenish 633 vb.

reluctance
slowness 278 n.
unwillingness 598 n.

rely (on)
believe 485 vb.
hope 852 vb.

rem
radiation 417 n.

remain
be left 41 vb.
last 113 vb.
stay 144 vb.
go on 146 vb.

remainder
difference 15 n.
remainder 41 n.
book 589 n.
superfluity 637 n.
sell 793 vb.

remains
remainder 41 n.
trace 548 n.

remake
reproduce 166 vb.
film 445 n.

remand
detention 747 n.

remanded
captive 750 adj.
accused 928 adj.

remark
affirm 532 vb.
speech 579 n.
—on
notice 455 vb.

remarkable
unusual 84 adj.
notable 638 adj.
wonderful 864 adj.

remedial
lenitive 177 adj.
remedial 658 adj.

remedy
answer 460 n.
means 629 n.
remedy 658 n.vb.
be just 913 vb.

remember
remember 505 vb.

remembrance
remembrance 505 n.
celebration 876 n.

remind
remind 505 vb.
hint 524 vb.

reminder
reminder 505 n.
monument 548 n.
record 548 n.

reminisce
remember 505 vb.

remiss
negligent 458 adj.
lax 734 adj.

remission
lull 145 n.
forgiveness 909 n.

remit
abate 37 vb.
send 272 vb.

remittance
transference 272 n.
payment 804 n.

remittent
periodical 141 adj.

remnant
remainder 41 n.
fewness 105 n.

remodel
transform 147 vb.
revolutionize
149 vb.

remonstrance
report 524 n.

remonstrate
deprecate 762 vb.
disapprove 924 vb.

remorse
regret 830 n.
pity 905 n.
penitence 939 n.

remorseless
pitiless 906 adj.

remote
distant 199 adj.
secluded 883 adj.

removal
displacement 188 n.
transference 272 n.

departure 296 n.
extraction 304 n.
deposal 752 n.
remove
degree 27 n.
take away 786 vb.
remunerate
reward 962 vb.
remuneration
earnings 771 n.
remunerative
profitable 640 adj.
renaissance
revival 656 n.
rend
rend 46 vb.
wound 655 vb.
render
liquefy 337 vb.
play music 413 vb.
give 781 vb.
rendering
facing 226 n.
translation 520 n.
rendezvous
focus 76 n.
meet 295 vb.
social round 882 n.
renegade
turncoat 603 n.
knave 938 n.
renege on
not observe 769 vb.
renew
reproduce 166 vb.
make better 654 vb.
renewal
repetition 106 n.
repair 656 n.
revival 656 n.
renounce
recant 603 vb.
relinquish 621 vb.
not retain 779 vb.
renovate
repair 656 vb.
restore 656 vb.
renown
famousness 866 n.
renowned
known 490 adj.
rent
gap 201 n.
hire 785 vb.
receipt 807 n.
rent collector
receiver 782 n.

renunciation
recantation 603 n.
relinquishment
621 n.
temperance 942 n.
reoccur
reoccur 106 vb.
recur 139 vb.
reorganize
transform 147 vb.
rectify 654 vb.
rep
drama 594 n.
seller 793 n.
repair
repair 656 n.vb.
reparation
restitution 787 n.
atonement 941 n.
repartee
answer 460 n.
witticism 839 n.
repast
meal 301 n.
repatriate
displace 188 vb.
repay
be profitable
771 vb.
restitute 787 vb.
avenge 910 vb.
reward 962 vb.
repeal
abrogate 752 vb.
repeat
do likewise 20 vb.
repeat 106 vb.
memorize 505 vb.
emphasize 532 vb.
—oneself
repeat oneself
106 vb.
be diffuse 570 vb.
repeated
frequent 139 adj.
repeater
timekeeper 117 n.
pistol 723 n.
repel
repel 292 vb.
parry 713 vb.
cause dislike 861 vb.
repellent
repellent 292 adj.
unpleasant 827 adj.
ugly 842 adj.
repent

become pious
979 vb.
repentance
regret 830 n.
penitence 939 n.
repercussion
effect 157 n.
recoil 280 n.
repertoire
acting 594 n.
collection 632 n.
repetition
repetition 106 n.
reproduction
166 n.
repetitive
tedious 838 adj.
rephrase
phrase 563 vb.
repine
be discontented
829 vb.
regret 830 vb.
replace
substitute 150 vb.
replace 187 vb.
restore 656 vb.
replacement
successor 67 n.
replanting
restoration 656 n.
replay
repetition 106 n.
replenish
fill 54 vb.
replenish 633 vb.
replete
full 54 adj.
sated 863 adj.
repletion
sufficiency 635 n.
replica
copy 22 n.
reply
answer 460 n.vb.
rejoinder 460 n.
report
loudness 400 n.
bang 402 n.
report 524 n.
communicate
524 vb.
news 529 n.
record 548 n.
describe 590 vb.
reportage
description 590 n.

reporter
informant 524 n.
publicizer 528 n.
news reporter 529 n.
repose
leisure 681 n.
repose 683 n.vb.
reposeful
tranquil 266 adj.
comfortable
376 adj.
reposeful 683 adj.
repository
receptacle 194 n.
repossess
appropriate 786 vb.
repoussé
projecting 254 adj.
reprehensible
wrong 914 adj.
blameworthy
924 adj.
represent
imagine 513 vb.
represent 551 vb.
describe 590 vb.
deputize 755 vb.
representation
manifestation 522 n.
report 524 n.
representation
551 n.
drama 594 n.
vote 605 n.
commission 751 n.
representative
typical 83 adj.
agent 686 n.
consignee 754 n.
delegate 754 n.
repress
subjugate 745 vb.
restrain 747 vb.
repression
eccentricity 503 n.
restraint 747 n.
prohibition 757 n.
moral insensibility
820 n.
reprieve
escape 667 n.
deliverance 668 n.
acquittal 960 n.
reprimand
reprimand 924 n.
reprint
copy 20 vb.

REP

duplicate 22 n.
edition 589 n.
reprisal
retaliation 714 n.
reprise
tune 412 n.
reproach
object of scorn
867 n.
slur 867 n.
reproach 924 n.
accusation 928 n.
reproachful
resentful 891 adj.
disapproving
924 adj.
reproach oneself
be penitent 939 vb.
reprobate
reprobate 924 vb.
bad person 938 n.
reprocess
repeat 106 vb.
reproduce
copy 20 vb.
reproduce 166 vb.
—itself
reproduce itself
167 vb.
reproduction
copy 22 n.
reproduction 166 n.
propagation 167 n.
representation
551 n.
reproductive
generative 167 adj.
reproof
reprimand 924 n.
reprove
reprove 924 vb.
reptile
reptile 365 n.
knave 938 n.
republic
political
organization
733 n.
republican
governmental
733 adj.
political party
708 n.
repudiate
dissent 489 vb.
recant 603 vb.
reject 607 vb.

RES

repudiation
nonobservance
769 n.
repugnance
resistance 715 n.
dislike 861 n.
repulse
repulsion 292 n.
reject 607 vb.
defeat 727 vb.
refusal 760 n.
repulsion
repulsion 292 n.
dislike 861 n.
repulsive
repellent 292 adj.
ugly 842 adj.
hateful 888 adj.
reputable
reputable 866 adj.
respected 920 adj.
honourable 929 adj.
reputation
repute 866 n.
repute
importance 638 n.
credit 802 n.
repute 866 n.
request
request 761 n.vb.
requiem
obsequies 364 n.
lament 836 n.
require
fall short 307 vb.
necessitate 596 vb.
require 627 vb.
requirement
qualification 468 n.
requirement 627 n.
conditions 766 n.
requisite
necessary 596 adj.
required 627 adj.
requisition
demand 737 n.vb.
appropriate 786 vb.
requital
retaliation 714 n.
thanks 907 n.
punishment 963 n.
requite
reward 962 vb.
rerun
repeat 106 vb.
rescind
abrogate 752 vb.

RES

rescript
answer 460 n.
decree 737 n.
rescue
deliverance 668 n.
defend 713 vb.
rescuer
preserver 666 n.
defender 713 n.
benefactor 903 n.
research
be curious 453 vb.
inquiry 459 n.
experiment 461 vb.
study 536 n.
resemblance
similarity 18 n.
resent
be discontented
829 vb.
resent 891 vb.
resentful
resentful 891 adj.
resentment
resentment 891 n.
jealousy 911 n.
reservation
qualification 468 n.
doubt 486 n.
registration 548 n.
preservation 666 n.
reserve
be early 135 vb.
substitute 150 n.
enclosure 235 n.
taciturnity 582 n.
store 632 vb.
modesty 874 n.
seclusion 883 n.
—for
intend 617 vb.
reserved
reticent 525 adj.
reserves
extra 40 n.
armed force 722 n.
funds 797 n.
reservist
substitute 150 n.
soldier 722 n.
reservoir
lake 346 n.
storage 632 n.
resettle
eject 300 vb.
reshape
modify 143 vb.

RES

reside (in)
dwell 192 vb.
residence
abode 192 n.
house 192 n.
resident
on the spot 189 adj.
resident 191 n.
resident alien
foreigner 59 n.
settler 191 n.
residual
remaining 41 adj.
residue
remainder 41 n.
resign
resign 753 vb.
resignation
relinquishment
621 n.
submission 721 n.
resignation 753 n.
patience 823 n.
resigning
former 125 adj.
resilience
strength 162 n.
elasticity 328 n.
resilient
cheerful 833 adj.
resin
resin 357 n.
resist
resist 715 vb.
resistance
electricity 160 n.
obstinacy 602 n.
opposition 704 n.
resistance 715 n.
resolute
resolute 599 adj.
courageous 855 adj.
resolution
decomposition 51 n.
vigorousness 174 n.
resolution 599 n.
intention 617 n.
resolve
decipher 520 vb.
be resolute 599 vb.
intend 617 vb.
resonance
roll 403 n.
resonance 404 n.
resonant
sounding 398 adj.
speaking 579 adj.

resort
focus 76 n.
contrivance 623 n.
resort to
congregate 74 vb.
avail oneself of
673 vb.
resound
resound 404 vb.
resource
contrivance 623 n.
resourceful
imaginative 513 adj.
skilful 694 adj.
resources
means 629 n.
wealth 800 n.
respect
relation 9 n.
observe 768 vb.
fear 854 n.vb.
respect 920 n.vb.
respectable
not bad 644 adj.
reputable 866 adj.
honourable 929 adj.
respectful
respectful 920 adj.
respective
relative 9 adj.
respectively
pro rata 783 adv.
respects
respects 920 n.
respiration
respiration 352 n.
respirator
hospital 658 n.
preserver 666 n.
respiratory disease
respiratory disease
651 n.
respite
delay 136 n.
lull 145 n.
deliverance 668 n.
resplendent
splendid 841 adj.
respond
answer 460 vb.
cooperate 706 vb.
feel 818 vb.
respondent
respondent 460 n.
litigant 959 n.
response
effect 157 n.

answer 460 n.
feeling 818 n.
responsibility
function 622 n.
mandate 751 n.
duty 917 n.
responsible
causal 156 adj.
observant 768 adj.
obliged 917 adj.
trustworthy 929 adj.
guilty 936 adj.
responsive
sentient 374 adj.
impressible 819 adj.
rest
remainder 41 n.
stay 144 vb.
pause 145 vb.
prop 218 n.
repose 683 n.vb.
restaurant
café 192 n.
restaurateur
caterer 633 n.
restful
reposeful 683 adj.
rest home
retreat 192 n.
hospital 658 n.
resting
unused 674 adj.
restitution
restitution 787 n.
dueness 915 n.
vindication 927 n.
restive
wilful 602 adj.
discontented
829 adj.
restless
active 678 adj.
excitable 822 adj.
restoration
improvement 654 n.
restoration 656 n.
restitution 787 n.
restorative
restorative 656 adj.
tonic 658 n.
restore
make complete
54 vb.
replace 187 vb.
remedy 658 vb.
(*see* **restoration**)
restrain

dissuade 613 vb.
hinder 702 vb.
restrain 747 vb.
restrained
plain 573 adj.
restraint
moderation 177 n.
restraint 747 n.
temperance 942 n.
restrict
limit 236 vb.
restriction
qualification 468 n.
hindrance 702 n.
restriction 747 n.
result
sequel 67 n.
result 157 vb.
product 164 n.
answer 460 n.
completion 725 n.
resultant
caused 157 adj.
resume
begin 68 vb.
repeat 106 vb.
be concise 569 vb.
appropriate 786 vb.
resumé
compendium 592 n.
resurgence
revival 656 n.
resurrection
revival 656 n.
resuscitate
revive 656 vb.
animate 821 vb.
retail
communicate
524 vb.
sell 793 vb.
retailer
provider 633 n.
tradespeople 794 n.
retain
tie 45 vb.
remember 505 vb.
preserve 666 vb.
retain 778 vb.
retainer
retainer 742 n.
reward 962 n.
retaliate
retaliate 714 vb.
retaliatory
retaliatory 714 adj.
revengeful 910 adj.

retard
retard 278 vb.
retarded
unintelligent
499 adj.
retch
vomit 300 vb.
retention
retention 778 n.
(*see* **retain**)
retentive
retentive 778 adj.
reticent
reticent 525 n.
reticulated
mottled 437 adj.
reticulation
network 222 n.
reticule
bag 194 n.
retina
eye 438 n.
retinue
retinue 67 n.
procession 71 n.
retire
recede 290 vb.
depart 296 vb.
resign 753 vb.
retired
former 125 adj.
leisurely 681 adj.
resigning 753 adj.
retirement
relinquishment
621 n.
resignation 753 n.
retiring
modest 874 adj.
unsociable 883 adj.
retort
vessel 194 n.
answer 460 n.vb.
testing agent
461 n.
witticism 839 n.
retouch
repair 656 vb.
retrace
revert 148 vb.
retrospect 505 vb.
—one's steps
turn back 286 vb.
retract
recant 603 vb.
retractable
drawing 288 adj.

retreat
  retreat 192 n.
  regression 286 n.
  refuge 662 n.
  be defeated 728 vb.
  seclusion 883 n.
retrench
  economize 814 vb.
retrenchment
  diminution 37 n.
retribution
  retaliation 714 n.
  punishment 963 n.
retrieval
  data processing
    86 n.
  taking 786 n.
retrieve
  recoup 31 vb.
  restitute 787 vb.
retro-
  rearward 238 adv.
retroactive
  retrospective
    125 adj.
  recoiling 280 adj.
retroflex
  curved 248 adj.
retrograde
  regressive 286 adj.
  deteriorated
    655 adj.
retrogression
  relapse 657 n.
retrospection
  remembrance 505 n.
retrospective
  retrospective
    125 adj.
retroussé
  curved 248 adj.
retroversion
  inversion 221 n.
return
  recurrence 106 n.
  revert 148 vb.
  recoil 280 n.vb.
  return 286 n.
  answer 460 n.
  vote 605 n.vb.
  reject 607 vb.
  retaliate 714 vb.
  restitute 787 vb.
  reward 962 n.
returns
  record 548 n.
  receipt 807 n.

reunion
  concord 710 n.
  social gathering
    882 n.
reusable
  useful 640 adj.
reuse
  economize 814 vb.
revamp
  repair 656 vb.
revanchist
  avenger 910 n.
reveal
  disclose 526 vb.
  publish 528 vb.
revealed
  revelational 975 adj.
revealing
  transparent 422 adj.
reveille
  call 547 n.
revel
  revel 837 n.vb.
  celebrate 876 vb.
  be intemperate
    943 vb.
—in
  enjoy 376 vb.
revelation
  discovery 484 n.
  truth 494 n.
  lack of expectation
    508 n.
  prediction 511 n.
  disclosure 526 n.
  revelation 975 n.
reveller
  reveller 837 n.
revendication
  dueness 915 n.
revenge
  revenge 910 n.
—oneself
  avenge 910 vb.
  punish 963 vb.
revengeful
  malevolent 898 adj.
  revengeful 910 adj.
revenue
  receipt 807 n.
reverberant
  resonant 404 adj.
reverberate
  recoil 280 vb.
revere
  honour 866 vb.
  respect 920 vb.

  worship 981 vb.
reverence
  respect 920 n.vb.
  worship 981 n.
reverend
  worshipful 866 adj.
  cleric 986 n.
reverent
  pious 979 adj.
reverie
  thought 449 n.
  abstractedness
    456 n.
  fantasy 513 n.
reversal
  reversion 148 n.
  lack of expectation
    508 n.
  abrogation 752 n.
reverse
  contrariety 14 n.
  revert 148 vb.
  back 238 adj.
  contraposition
    240 n.
  regress 286 vb.
  defeat 728 n.
reversion
  reversion 148 n.
  regression 286 n.
  transfer 780 n.
revert
  revert 148 vb.
revetment
  facing 226 n.
revictual
  replenish 633 vb.
review
  assemblage 74 n.
  inspection 438 n.
  meditate 449 vb.
  estimate 480 n.vb.
  retrospect 505 vb.
  report 524 n.
  journal 528 n.
  article 591 n.
  rectify 654 vb.
  pageant 875 n.
reviewer
  interpreter 520 n.
  bookperson 589 n.
  dissertator 591 n.
revile
  curse 899 vb.
  reprobate 924 vb.
revise
  modify 143 vb.

  rectify 654 vb.
revised
  improved 654 adj.
reviser
  alterer 143 n.
  author 589 n.
revision
  study 536 n.
  amendment 654 n.
revitalize
  revive 656 vb.
revival
  strengthening 162 n.
  revival 656 n.
  (see **revive**)
revivalist
  zealot 979 n.
  worshipper 981 n.
revive
  vitalize 360 vb.
  be restored 656 vb.
  revive 656 vb.
  be refreshed 685 vb.
  animate 821 vb.
reviver
  tonic 658 n.
  refreshment 685 n.
revocation
  recantation 603 n.
revoke
  abrogate 752 vb.
  not retain 779 vb.
revolt
  revolt 738 n.vb.
  cause dislike 861 vb.
revolter
  revolter 738 n.
revolting
  not nice 645 adj.
  disliked 861 adj.
revolution
  regular return
    141 n.
  revolution 149 n.
  rotation 315 n.
  revolt 738 n.
revolutionary
  modern 126 adj.
  revolutionist
    149 n.
  revolutionary
    149 adj.
  reformer 654 n.
  revolter 738 n.
revolutionize
  revolutionize
    149 vb.

REV

revolve
  rotate 315 vb.
  meditate 449 vb.
revolver
  pistol 723 n.
revue
  stage show 594 n.
revulsion
  recoil 280 n.
  hatred 888 n.
reward
  incentive 612 n.
  trophy 729 n.
  honours 866 n.
  thanks 907 n.
  reward 962 n.vb.
reword
  translate 520 vb.
rewrite
  rectify 654 vb.
rhapsodical
  imaginative 513 adj.
rhapsodist
  poet 593 n.
rhapsodize
  imagine 513 vb.
rhapsody
  musical piece
    412 n.
rhetoric
  oratory 579 n.
  ostentation 875 n.
rhetorical
  figurative 519 adj.
  exaggerated
    546 adj.
  rhetorical 574 adj.
rhetorician
  speaker 579 n.
rheumatic
  crippled 163 adj.
rheumatism
  rheumatism 651 n.
rhinestone
  finery 844 n.
rhizome
  plant 366 n.
rhomboid
  angular
    figure 247 n.
rhumb
  compass point
    281 n.
rhyme
  poetry 593 n.
rhymer
  poet 593 n.

RIC

rhyming
  similar 18 adj.
  poetic 593 adj.
rhythm
  recurrence 106 n.
  periodicity 141 n.
  tempo 410 n.
  prosody 593 n.
rhythmic,
  rhythmical
  periodical 141 adj.
  oscillating 317 adj.
rib
  ridicule 851 vb.
ribald
  vulgar 847 adj.
  derisive 851 adj.
  impure 951 adj.
ribband
  (*see* ribbon)
ribbed
  textural 331 adj.
ribbon
  ligature 47 n.
  strip 208 n.
  decoration 729 n.
  trimming 844 n.
ribbon development
  expansion 197 n.
  overstepping 306 n.
ribs
  frame 218 n.
  laterality 239 n.
rice
  cereals 301 n.
rich
  prolific 171 adj.
  nourishing 301 adj.
  fatty 357 adj.
  savoury 390 adj.
  florid 425 adj.
  ornate 574 adj.
  rich 800 adj.
  ornamented
    844 adj.
riches
  wealth 800 n.
rick
  disable 161 vb.
rickets
  deformity 246 n.
  disease 651 n.
rickety
  flimsy 163 adj.
  dilapidated 655 adj.
rickshaw
  cab 274 n.

RIG

ricochet
  recoil 280 n.vb.
riddance
  deliverance 668 n.
  liberation 746 n.
riddle
  pierce 263 vb.
  enigma 530 n.
ride
  ride 267 vb.
  path 624 n.
—down
  pursue 619 vb.
  charge 712 vb.
—roughshod over
  oppress 735 vb.
rider
  adjunct 40 n.
  rider 268 n.
  cavalry 722 n.
ridge
  high land 209 n.
ridged
  rough 259 adj.
ridicule
  laughter 835 n.
  ridicule 851 vb.
  not respect 921 vb.
ridiculous
  absurd 497 adj.
  amusing 837 adj.
  ridiculous 849 adj.
riding
  equitation 267 n.
  sport 837 n.
rife, be
  prevail 178 vb.
riffraff
  rabble 869 n.
rifle
  firearm 723 n.
  steal 788 vb.
—through
  search 459 vb.
rifleman
  soldiery 722 n.
rift
  gap 201 n.
  dissension 709 n.
rig
  tackling 47 n.
  dressing 228 n.
  fake 541 vb.
—out
  dress 228 vb.
  make ready
    669 vb.

RIG

rigging
  tackling 47 n.
right
  dextrality 241 n.
  true 494 adj.
  advisable 642 adj.
  repair 656 vb.
  political party
    708 n.
  right 913 n.adj.
  dueness 915 n.
—oneself
  equalize 28 vb.
righteous
  just 913 adj.
  virtuous 933 adj.
rightful
  right 913 adj.
  due 915 adj.
right-handed
  dextral 241 adj.
right-hand man
  auxiliary 707 n.
right of way
  passage 305 n.
  access 624 n.
rights
  freedom 744 n.
  dueness 915 n.
right side
  face 237 n.
right thing, the
  duty 917 n.
right time
  occasion 137 n.
right wing
  dextrality 241 n.
  sectional 708 adj.
rigid
  unyielding 162 adj.
  rigid 326 adj.
  obstinate 602 adj.
rigmarole
  lack of meaning
    515 n.
rigorist
  tyrant 735 n.
  perfectionist 862 n.
rigorous
  severe 735 adj.
  fastidious 862 adj.
  pitiless 906 adj.
rigour
  accuracy 494 n.
  severity 735 n.
rig-out
  dressing 228 n.

rile
  torment 827 vb.
  enrage 891 vb.
rill
  stream 350 n.
rim
  edge 234 n.
rime
  wintriness 380 n.
rind
  skin 226 n.
ring
  outline 233 n.
  circle 250 n.
  be loud 400 vb.
  resound 404 vb.
  play music 413 vb.
  communicate
    524 vb.
  association 706 n.
  arena 724 n.
  badge of rule 743 n.
  restriction 747 n.
  jewellery 844 n.
  love token 889 n.
—a bell
  be remembered
    505 vb.
—in
  initiate 68 vb.
—off
  cease 145 vb.
  be mute 578 vb.
ring, the
  pugilism 716 n.
ringer
  analogue 18 n.
  campanology 412 n.
ringing
  resonant 404 adj.
  melodious 410 adj.
ringleader
  motivator 612 n.
  leader 690 n.
  agitator 738 n.
ringlet
  coil 251 n.
  hair 259 n.
ringmaster
  manager 690 n.
ringside seat
  near place 200 n.
  view 438 n.
rink
  arena 724 n.
  pleasure ground
    837 n.

rinse
  drench 341 vb.
  clean 648 vb.
riot
  rampage 61 vb.
  abound 635 vb.
  revolt 738 vb.
  lawlessness 954 n.
rioter
  rioter 738 n.
riotous
  disorderly 61 adj.
  anarchic 734 adj.
  riotous 738 adj.
rip
  rend 46 vb.
  move fast 277 vb.
  wave 350 n.
  libertine 952 n.
—off
  defraud 788 vb.
  overcharge 811 vb.
—out
  extract 304 vb.
RIP
  in memoriam
    364 adv.
riparian
  marginal 234 adj.
  coastal 344 adj.
ripcord
  fastening 47 n.
ripe
  matured 669 adj.
ripen
  perfect 646 vb.
  mature 669 vb.
  carry through
    725 vb.
ripeness
  occasion 137 n.
riper years
  middle age 131 n.
rip-off
  expropriation 786 n.
riposte
  answer 460 n.vb.
ripple
  shallowness 212 n.
  crinkle 251 vb.
  wave 350 n.
rip-roaring
  merry 833 adj.
rise
  increase 36 n.
  beginning 68 n.
  high land 209 n.

  be oblique 220 vb.
  ascend 308 vb.
  revolt 738 vb.
—above
  be disinterested
    931 vb.
—in the world
  prosper 730 vb.
—to one's feet
  be vertical 215 vb.
  show respect 920 vb.
—to the occasion
  improvise 609 vb.
  succeed 727 vb.
rishi
  religious teacher
    973 n.
risible
  ridiculous 849 adj.
rising
  influential 178 adj.
  prosperous 730 adj.
  revolt 738 n.
  dear 811 adj.
rising generation
  youth 130 n.
risk
  gambling 618 n.
  danger 661 n.
  speculate 791 vb.
  be rash 857 vb.
risk of
  possibility 469 n.
risk-taker
  gambler 618 n.
  brave person
    855 n.
risk-taking
  calculation of
    chance 159 n.
risky
  speculative 618 adj.
  dangerous 661 adj.
risqué
  witty 839 adj.
  impure 951 adj.
rissoles
  meat 301 n.
rite
  rite 988 n.
ritual
  formality 875 n.
  ritual 988 n.adj.
ritualistic
  formal 875 adj.
  pietistic 979 adj.
  ritualistic 988 adj.

ritzy
  rich 800 adj.
  ostentatious
    875 adj.
rival
  compeer 28 n.
  be good 644 vb.
  contender 716 n.
rivalry
  contention
    716 n.
  jealousy 911 n.
river
  stream 350 n.
riverside
  edge 234 n.
  shore 344 n.
rivet
  affix 45 vb.
  fastening 47 n.
—the attention
  attract notice
    455 vb.
  impress 821 vb.
riviera
  pleasure ground
    837 n.
rivulet
  stream 350 n.
road
  housing 192 n.
  transport 272 n.
  road 624 n.
road block
  obstacle 702 n.
roadhog
  driver 268 n.
  egotist 932 n.
roadhouse
  inn 192 n.
road map
  itinerary 267 n.
  map 551 n.
roads, roadstead
  stable 192 n.
  gulf 345 n.
road show
  dramaturgy
    594 n.
roadside
  edge 234 n.
  marginal 234 adj.
roadworthy
  transferable
    272 adj.
roam
  wander 267 vb.

ROA

roan
horse 273 n.
brown 430 adj.
pied 437 adj.

roar
be violent 176 vb.
vociferate 408 vb.
be angry 891 vb.

roaring trade
prosperity 730 n.

roast
cook 301 vb.
heat 381 vb.
reprove 924 vb.

rob
rob 788 vb.

robber
robber 789 n.

robe
robe 228 n.
canonicals 989 n.

robot
machine 630 n.
slave 742 n.

robot-like
mechanical 630 adj.

robust
stalwart 162 adj.
healthy 650 adj.

rock
be unequal 29 vb.
fixture 153 n.
assuage 177 vb.
oscillate 317 vb.
solid body 324 n.
rock 344 n.
refuge 662 n.
pet 889 vb.

rock bottom
inferiority 35 n.
base 214 n.

rock-climbing
sport 837 n.

rocker
youngster 132 n.

rocket
grow 36 vb.
rocket 276 n.
signal light 420 n.
missile weapon
723 n.
reprimand 924 n.

rocketry
aeronautics 271 n.

rock 'n' roll
music 412 n.
dance 837 n.

ROL

rocky
unstable 152 adj.
hard 326 adj.
territorial 344 adj.

rococo
ornamentation
844 n.

rod
prop 218 n.
gauge 465 n.
incentive 612 n.
scourge 964 n.

rod and line
chase 619 n.

rodent
mammal 365 n.

rodeo
contest 716 n.

rod of iron
severity 735 n.

rodomontade
magniloquence
574 n.

roe
fish food 301 n.

roentgen, röntgen
radiation 417 n.

rogation
prayers 981 n.

rogue
trickster 545 n.
knave 938 n.

rogue elephant
solitary 883 n.
noxious animal
904 n.

roguish
merry 833 adj.
witty 839 adj.

roister
rampage 61 vb.
revel 837 vb.

role
acting 594 n.
function 622 n.

role-playing
representation
551 n.
conduct 688 n.

roll
bunch 74 n.
list 87 n.
textile 222 n.
twine 251 vb.
cylinder 252 n.
go smoothly 258 vb.
fold 261 vb.

ROM

be in motion 265 vb.
propel 287 vb.
rotation 315 n.
roll 403 n.vb.
record 548 n.
—back
evolve 316 vb.
—in
burst in 297 vb.
be received 782 vb.
—on
go on 146 vb.
—out
flatten 216 vb.
—up
congregate 74 vb.
fold 261 vb.
arrive 295 vb.

roll call
statistics 86 n.
nomenclature 561 n.

roller
cylinder 252 n.
smoother 258 n.
rotator 315 n.
hairdressing 843 n.

rollick
be cheerful 833 vb.
amuse oneself
837 vb.

rolling
alpine 209 adj.
undulatory 251 adj.
fluctuation 317 n.

rolling stock
train 274 n.

rolling stone
wanderer 268 n.

roly-poly
fleshy 195 adj.
dessert 301 n.

roman
written 586 adj.
print-type 587 n.

Roman candle
fireworks 420 n.

Roman Catholicism
Catholicism 976 n.

romance
ideality 513 n.
fable 543 n.
novel 590 n.
love affair 887 n.

romancer
visionary 513 n.

romantic
imaginative 513 adj.

ROO

feeling 818 adj.
impressible
819 adj.
loving 887 adj.

Romany
wanderer 268 n.

romp
leap 312 vb.
amuse oneself
837 vb.

rompers
trousers 228 n.

rondo
musical piece
412 n.

rood
cross 222 n.
church interior
990 n.

roof
dwelling 192 n.
roof 226 n.
shelter 662 n.

roofless
displaced 188 adj.

rook
bird 365 n.
deceive 542 vb.
trickster 545 n.

rookery
nest 192 n.

rookie
beginner 538 n.

room
room 183 n.
chamber 194 n.
scope 744 n.

rooms
quarters 192 n.

roomy
spacious
183 adj.

roost
nest 192 n.
dwell 192 vb.
sit down 311 vb.
sleep 679 vb.

root
numerical element
85 n.
stabilize 153 vb.
base 214 n.
plant 366 n.
—out
eject 300 vb.
—up
extract 304 vb.

root and branch
completely 54 adv.
revolutionary
149 adj.
rooted
firm 45 adj.
fixed 153 adj.
still 266 adj.
habitual 610 adj.
rootless
unstable 152 adj.
displaced 188 adj.
travelling 267 adj.
roots
source 156 n.
rope
tie 45 vb.
cable 47 n.
scope 744 n.
fetter 748 n.
means of execution
964 n.
ropy, ropey
fibrous 208 adj.
semiliquid 354 adj.
bad 645 adj.
rosary
prayers 981 n.
rose
fragrance 396 n.
redness 431 n.
a beauty 841 n.
rose-coloured
promising 852 adj.
rosette
badge 547 n.
rosewater
scent 396 n.
rosin
resin 357 n.
roster
list 87 n.
rostrate
angular 247 adj.
curved 248 adj.
rostrum
stand 218 n.
rostrum 539 n.
rosy
red 431 adj.
promising 852 adj.
rosy-cheeked
healthy 650 adj.
personable 841 adj.
rot
decay 51 n.
silly talk 515 n.

blight 659 n.
rota
list 87 n.
regular return 141 n.
rotary
rotary 315 adj.
rotate
twine 251 vb.
rotate 315 vb.
rotation
continuity 71 n.
motion 265 n.
(*see* **rotate**)
rotator
rotator 315 n.
rotor
rotator 315 n.
rotten
not nice 645 adj.
diseased 651 adj.
dilapidated 655 adj.
vicious 934 adj.
rotter
cad 938 n.
rotund
fleshy 195 adj.
rotund 252 adj.
roué
libertine 952 n.
rouge
redden 431 vb.
cosmetic 843 n.
rough
nonuniform 17 adj.
violent 176 adj.
amorphous 244 adj.
rough 259 adj.
hoarse 407 adj.
difficult 700 adj.
graceless 842 adj.
roughage
food 301 n.
rough and ready
imperfect 647 adj.
rough and tumble
turmoil 61 n.
roughcast
facing 226 n.
rough diamond
undevelopment
670 n.
rough draft
incompleteness
55 n.
rough edge of one's
tongue
scurrility 899 n.

reproach 924 n.
roughen
roughen 259 vb.
rough-hew
form 243 vb.
sculpt 554 vb.
roughhouse
turmoil 61 n.
roughness
violence 176 n.
roughness 259 n.
(*see* **rough**)
roulette
gambling 618 n.
round
period 110 n.
fleshy 195 adj.
make curved
248 vb.
round 250 adj.
circle 314 vb.
vocal music 412 n.
habit 610 n.
circuit 626 n.
ammunition 723 n.
—off
make complete
54 vb.
—on
retaliate 714 vb.
—up
bring together
74 vb.
roundabout
circumjacent
230 adj.
deviating 282 adj.
traffic control
305 n.
circuitous 314 adj.
rotator 315 n.
prolix 570 adj.
roundabout
626 adj.
rounded
arched 253 adj.
smooth 258 adj.
roundel
circle 250 n.
rounders
ball game 837 n.
round-eyed
wondering 864 adj.
round robin
deprecation 762 n.
round-shouldered
deformed 246 adj.

roundsman/ -woman
seller 793 n.
round trip
circuition 314 n.
rouse
incite 612 vb.
excite 821 vb.
—oneself
be active 678 vb.
rousing
eloquent 579 adj.
exciting 821 adj.
rout
disperse 75 vb.
defeat 727 vb.
rabble 869 n.
route
itinerary 267 n.
route 624 n.
routine
uniformity 16 n.
order 60 n.
regular return
141 n.
habitual 610 adj.
business 622 n.
conduct 688 n.
formality 875 n.
rover
wanderer 268 n.
roving
unstable 152 adj.
row
turmoil 61 n.
series 71 n.
violence 176 n.
row 269 vb.
loudness 400 n.
bicker 709 vb.
rowdy
riotous 738 adj.
ruffian 904 n.
rowel
sharp point 256 n.
rower
boatman 270 n.
rowing
aquatics 269 n.
sport 837 n.
royal
ruling 733 adj.
noble 868 adj.
royalty
position of authority
733 n.
sovereign 741 n.
receipt 807 n.

rub
be contiguous
202 vb.
rub 333 vb.
give pain 377 vb.
hindrance 702 n.
painfulness 827 n.
—down
smooth 258 vb.
groom 369 vb.
—in
emphasize 532 vb.
aggravate 832 vb.
—out
murder 362 vb.
obliterate 550 vb.
—shoulders with
be contiguous
202 vb.
—up the wrong way
cause dislike 861 vb.
huff 891 vb.
rubber
elasticity 328 n.
obliteration 550 n.
card game 837 n.
rubberstamp
conform 83 vb.
endorse 488 vb.
rubbery
elastic 328 adj.
tough 329 adj.
rubbing
duplicate 22 n.
rubbish
leavings 41 n.
silly talk 515 n.
rubbish 641 n.
rubbish heap
sink 649 n.
rubbishy
trivial 639 adj.
profitless 641 adj.
rubble
piece 53 n.
rubicund
red 431 adj.
rubric
precept 693 n.
ruby
redness 431 n.
gem 844 n.
ruche
fold 261 n.
ruck
generality 79 n.
fold 261 n.vb.

rucksack
bag 194 n.
ructions
turmoil 61 n.
rudder
sailing aid 269 n.
directorship 689 n.
ruddy
florid 425 adj.
red 431 adj.
healthy 650 adj.
rude
violent 176 adj.
inelegant 576 adj.
ill-bred 847 adj.
discourteous
885 adj.
rudimentary
beginning 68 adj.
immature 670 adj.
rue
regret 830 vb.
rueful
melancholic
834 adj.
ruff
neckwear 228 n.
ruffian
ruffian 904 n.
ruffianly
ill-bred 847 adj.
ruffle
roughen 259 vb.
fold 261 n.vb.
agitate 318 vb.
enrage 891 vb.
rug
coverlet 226 n.
floor-cover 226 n.
rugged
stalwart 162 adj.
difficult 700 adj.
ruggedness
roughness 259 n.
ruin
antiquity 125 n.
ruin 165 n.
waste 634 vb.
dilapidation 655 n.
loss 772 n.
impoverish 801 vb.
ruinous
destructive 165 adj.
harmful 645 adj.
dilapidated
655 adj.
adverse 731 adj.

ruins
oldness 127 n.
rule
order 60 n.
rule 81 n.
prevail 178 vb.
line 203 n.
judge 480 vb.
precept 693 n.
rule 733 vb.
—out
exclude 57 vb.
rule of thumb
empiricism 461 n.
intuition 476 n.
ruler
gauge 465 n.
potentate 741 n.
ruling
judgement 480 n.
ruling passion
eccentricity 503 n.
rum
unusual 84 adj.
alcoholic drink
301 n.
rumble
roll 403 vb.
understand 516 vb.
rumbustious
disorderly 61 adj.
excitable 822 adj.
ruminant
animal 365 n.adj.
ruminate
graze 301 vb.
meditate 449 vb.
rummage
search 459 vb.
rumour
rumour 529 n.vb.
rump
remainder 41 n.
buttocks 238 n.
rumple
jumble 63 vb.
fold 261 n.vb.
rumpus
turmoil 61 n.
run
series 71 n.
elapse 111 vb.
continuance 146 n.
pedestrianism
267 n.
move fast 277 vb.
flow out 298 vb.

liquefy 337 vb.
flow 350 vb.
run away 620 vb.
manage 689 vb.
—after
pursue 619 vb.
court 889 vb.
—amok
be violent 176 vb.
go mad 503 vb.
—away
run away 620 vb.
—down
decrease 37 vb.
collide 279 vb.
pursue 619 vb.
dispraise 924 vb.
—into
meet 295 vb.
—off
empty 300 vb.
—on
run on 71 vb.
be loquacious
581 vb.
—out
not suffice 636 vb.
—over
collide 279 vb.
—riot
be violent 176 vb.
exaggerate 546 vb.
superabound
637 vb.
be excitable 822 vb.
—the gauntlet
face danger 661 vb.
—through
kill 362 vb.
wound 655 vb.
expend 806 vb.
—to seed
deteriorate 655 vb.
—up
produce 164 vb.
be in debt 803 vb.
—wild
be violent 176 vb.
runaway
avoider 620 n.
escaper 667 n.
run-down
compendium 592 n.
sick 651 adj.
dilapidated
655 adj.
disused 674 adj.

RUN

rune(s)
lettering 586 n.
spell 983 n.

rung
degree 27 n.
ascent 308 n.

runnel
stream 350 n.
conduit 351 n.

runner
pedestrian 268 n.
speeder 277 n.
courier 529 n.
contender 716 n.

running
continuous 71 adj.
sport 837 n.

runny
nonadhesive 49 adj.
fluid 335 adj.

run of, the
scope 744 n.

run-off
contest 716 n.

run-of-the-mill
median 30 adj.
generality 79 n.

runt
dwarf 196 n.

runway
air travel 271 n.

rupture
separation 46 n.
wound 655 n.
dissension 709 n.

rural
regional 184 adj.
provincial 192 adj.
campestral 348 adj.

ruse
trickery 542 n.
stratagem 698 n.

rush
crowd 74 n.
spurt 277 n.
commotion 318 n.
unprepared 670 adj.
hasten 680 vb.
charge 712 vb.
—about
be excitable 822 vb.

rushed
hasty 680 adj.

russet
brown 430 adj.

rust
decay 51 n.

oldness 127 n.
blunt 257 vb.
desuetude 611 n.
dilapidation 655 n.
blight 659 n.
stop using 674 vb.

rustic
native 191 n.
provincial 192 adj.
agrarian 370 adj.
country-dweller
869 n.

rustication
seclusion 883 n.

rustle
sound faint 401 vb.

rustler
thief 789 n.

rusty
antiquated 127 adj.
unsharpened
257 adj.
strident 407 adj.
red 431 adj.
unhabituated
611 adj.
clumsy 695 adj.

rut
furrow 262 n.
habit 610 n.

ruthless
pitiless 906 adj.

rye
cereals 301 n.

S

Sabbatarian(s)
zealot 979 n.

Sabbath
repose 683 n.
holy day 988 n.

sable
skin 226 n.
blackness 428 n.

sabotage
disable 161 vb.
hindrance 702 n.
revolt 738 n.

saboteur
destroyer 168 n.
rioter 738 n.

sabre
sidearms 723 n.

sabre-rattling
intimidation 854 n.

SAC

saccharine
sweet 392 adj.

sacerdotal
priestly 985 adj.

sachet
scent 396 n.

sack
bag 194 n.
dismiss 300 vb.
deposal 752 n.
spoliation 788 n.

sackcloth
asceticism 945 n.

sackcloth and ashes
penance 941 n.

sacking
textile 222 n.

sacrament
rite 988 n.

sacramental
devotional 981 adj.
ritual 988 adj.

sacred
divine 965 adj.
sanctified 979 adj.

sacrifice
loss 772 n.
propitiation 941 n.
oblation 981 n.
—oneself
offer oneself 759 vb.
suffer 825 vb.
be disinterested
931 vb.

sacrificer
worshipper 981 n.

sacrificial
losing 772 adj.
atoning 941 adj.
devotional 981 adj.

sacrilege
impiety 980 n.

sacrilegious
disrespectful
921 adj.
impious 980 adj.

sacristan
church officer
986 n.

sacristy
church interior
990 n.

sacrosanct
creedal 485 adj.
invulnerable
660 adj.
sanctified 979 adj.

SAF

sad
funereal 364 adj.
melancholic
834 adj.

sadden
sadden 834 vb.

saddle
high land 209 n.
seat 218 n.
start out 296 vb.
break in 369 vb.
—with
attribute 158 vb.
impose a duty
917 vb.

sadism
abnormality 84 n.
inhumanity 898 n.

sadist
monster 938 n.

sadistic
cruel 898 adj.

safari
land travel 267 n.

safari park
pleasance 192 n.
zoo 369 n.

safe
storage 632 n.
safe 660 adj.
treasury 799 n.

safe and sound
undamaged 646 adj.

safe-breaker
thief 789 n.

safe conduct
opener 263 n.
permit 756 n.

safe-deposit
storage 632 n.
treasury 799 n.

safeguard
safeguard 660 vb.
safeguard 662 n.

safekeeping
protection 660 n.
preservation 666 n.

safe place
hiding-place 527 n.
refuge 662 n.

safety
safety 660 n.

safety catch
fastening 47 n.

safety device
safeguard 662 n.
preserver 666 n.

safety first
  caution 858 n.
safety valve
  safeguard 662 n.
  means of escape
    667 n.
sag
  be weak 163 vb.
  hang 217 vb.
  be curved 248 vb.
  be dejected 834 vb.
saga
  narrative 590 n.
sagacious
  intelligent 498 adj.
  foreseeing 510 adj.
sagacity
  skill 694 n.
sage
  potherb 301 n.
  wise 498 adj.
  sage 500 n.
sail
  water travel 269 n.
  sail 275 n.
sailcloth
  textile 222 n.
sailing
  aquatics 269 n.
  sport 837 n.
sailing ship
  sailing ship 275 n.
sailor
  mariner 270 n.
  naval man 722 n.
saint
  saint 968 n.
  pietist 979 n.
sainthood
  sanctity 979 n.
saintly
  virtuous 933 adj.
  angelic 968 adj.
saint's day
  holy day 988 n.
salaam
  courteous act 884 n.
salable
  salable 793 adj.
salacious
  impure 951 adj.
salad
  dish 301 n.
  vegetable 301 n.
salamander
  rara avis 84 n.
salary

  earnings 771 n.
sale
  sale 793 n.
salesman,
  saleswoman
  seller 793 n.
salesmanship
  publicity 528 n.
  inducement 612 n.
  sale 793 n.
salient
  region 184 n.
  projecting 254 adj.
  obvious 443 adj.
  battleground 724 n.
saline
  salty 388 adj.
saliva
  excrement 302 n.
  lubricant 334 n.
salivate
  exude 298 vb.
sallow
  colourless 426 adj.
  unhealthy 651 adj.
sally
  attack 712 n.
  witticism 839 n.
sally forth
  emerge 298 vb.
salmon
  fish food 301 n.
salmonella
  poison 659 n.
salon
  chamber 194 n.
  beau monde 848 n.
saloon
  tavern 192 n.
salt
  salty 388 adj.
  condiment 389 n.
  chief thing 638 n.
  preserve 666 vb.
  wit 839 n.
—away
  store 632 vb.
salt flat
  marsh 347 n.
salt of the earth
  elite 644 n.
  good person 937 n.
saltpetre
  explosive 723 n.
salty
  witty 839 adj.
salubrious

  salubrious 652 adj.
salutary
  beneficial 644 adj.
salutation
  allocution 583 n.
  courteous act 884 n.
salute
  signal 547 vb.
  speak to 583 vb.
  greet 884 vb.
  congratulation
    886 n.
  show respect 920 vb.
  praise 923 vb.
salvage
  restore 656 vb.
  deliverance 668 n.
salvation
  preservation 666 n.
  deliverance 668 n.
salve
  unguent 357 n.
  balm 658 n.
salve one's
  conscience
  justify 927 vb.
  atone 941 vb.
salver
  church utensil
    990 n.
salvo
  bang 402 n.
  bombardment
    712 n.
  applause 923 n.
sal volatile
  tonic 658 n.
same
  identical 13 adj.
  uniform 16 adj.
  equal 28 adj.
  indiscriminate
    464 adj.
sameness
  tedium 838 n.
same time
  synchronism 123 n.
same wavelength
  consensus 488 n.
  friendliness 880 n.
samovar
  cauldron 194 n.
sample
  part 53 n.
  example 83 n.
  taste 386 vb.
  experiment 461 vb.

  exhibit 522 n.
sampler
  needlework 844 n.
samurai
  militarist 722 n.
sanative
  restorative 656 adj.
sanatorium
  hospital 658 n.
sanctify
  sanctify 979 vb.
  idolatrize 982 vb.
sanctimonious
  hypocritical
    541 adj.
  pietistic 979 adj.
sanction
  endorse 488 vb.
  compulsion 740 n.
  approve 923 vb.
sanctioned
  reputable 866 adj.
  due 915 adj.
sanctity
  sanctity 979 n.
sanctuary
  retreat 192 n.
  refuge 662 n.
  holy place 990 n.
sanctum
  holy place 990 n.
sand
  powder 332 n.
  soil 344 n.
sandals
  footwear 228 n.
sandbag(s)
  defences 713 n.
sandbank
  island 349 n.
  pitfall 663 n.
sandblast
  engrave 555 vb.
  clean 648 vb.
sandcastle
  weak thing 163 n.
sandpaper
  smoother 258 n.
  roughness 259 n.
sands
  dryness 342 n.
sandwich
  put between 231 vb.
  mouthful 301 n.
sandwich board
  advertisement
    528 n.

sandy
  powdery 332 adj.
  dry 342 adj.
  yellow 433 adj.
sane
  sane 502 adj.
sangfroid
  inexcitability 823 n.
sanguinary
  sanguineous
    335 adj.
  murderous 362 adj.
sanguine
  red 431 adj.
  optimistic 482 adj.
  cheerful 833 adj.
sanitary
  cleansing 648 adj.
  salubrious 652 adj.
sanitary engineer
  sanitarian 652 n.
sanitation
  hygiene 652 n.
sanserif
  print-type 587 n.
Santa Claus
  good giver 813 n.
sap
  essential part 5 n.
  weaken 163 vb.
  fluid 335 n.
  impair 655 vb.
  besiege 712 vb.
—the foundations
  demolish 165 vb.
sapient
  wise 498 adj.
sapling
  young plant 132 n.
sapper
  excavator 255 n.
  soldiery 722 n.
Sapphic
  poetic 593 adj.
sapphire
  blueness 435 n.
  gem 844 n.
sappy
  vernal 128 adj.
  fluid 335 adj.
sarcasm
  ridicule 851 n.
  reproach 924 n.
sarcastic
  witty 839 adj.
  derisive 851 adj.
sarcophagus

  interment 364 n.
sardine
  fish food 301 n.
sardonic
  derisive 851 adj.
sari
  robe 228 n.
sarong
  loincloth 228 n.
  skirt 228 n.
sartorial
  tailored 228 adj.
sash
  belt 228 n.
  window 263 n.
  decoration 729 n.
Sassenach
  foreigner 59 n.
Satan
  Satan 969 n.
satanic
  cruel 898 adj.
  wicked 934 adj.
  diabolic 969 adj.
Satanism
  diabolism 969 n.
satchel
  bag 194 n.
satchet
  bag 194 n.
sate
  be tedious 838 vb.
  sate 863 vb.
satellite
  concomitant 89 n.
  spaceship 276 n.
  follower 284 n.
  satellite 321 n.
  auxiliary 707 n.
  dependant 742 n.
satiate
  suffice 635 vb.
  (*see* **sate**)
satiety
  sufficiency 635 n.
  superfluity 637 n.
  satiety 863 n.
satin
  textile 222 n.
  smoothness 258 n.
satire
  satire 851 n.
satirical
  derisive 851 adj.
  disrespectful
    921 adj.
satirist

  humorist 839 n.
  detractor 926 n.
satisfaction
  sufficiency 635 n.
  content 828 n.
  approbation 923 n.
  atonement 941 n.
satisfactory
  sufficient 635 adj.
  not bad 644 adj.
satisfy
  fill 54 vb.
  convince 485 vb.
  suffice 635 vb.
  content 828 vb.
—oneself
  be certain 473 vb.
saturate
  drench 341 vb.
  superabound
    637 vb.
saturation point
  plenitude 54 n.
  limit 236 n.
saturnalia
  festivity 837 n.
saturnalian
  disorderly 61 adj.
saturnine
  serious 834 adj.
  sullen 893 adj.
satyr
  mythical being
    970 n.
sauce
  stimulant 174 n.
  sauce 389 n.
  sauciness 878 n.
saucepan
  cauldron 194 n.
saucer
  plate 194 n.
saucy
  impertinent 878 adj.
  disrespectful
    921 adj.
sauna
  ablutions 648 n.
saunter
  wander 267 vb.
  move slowly 278 vb.
sausage
  meat 301 n.
savage
  violent creature
    176 n.
  wound 655 vb.

  ingenue 699 n.
  attack 712 vb.
  severe 735 adj.
  vulgarian 847 n.
  barbaric 869 adj.
  cruel 898 adj.
  dispraise 924 vb.
savagery
  violence 176 n.
  inhumanity 898 n.
savant
  scholar 492 n.
  expert 696 n.
save
  store 632 vb.
  preserve 666 vb.
  deliver 668 vb.
  not use 674 vb.
  retain 778 vb.
  economize 814 vb.
saving clause
  qualification 468 n.
saving grace
  virtues 933 n.
savings
  store 632 n.
  economy 814 n.
savings bank
  treasury 799 n.
saviour
  preserver 666 n.
  benefactor 903 n.
Saviour
  God the Son 965 n.
savoir faire
  skill 694 n.
  etiquette 848 n.
savoir vivre
  sociability 882 n.
savour
  taste 386 n.vb.
  make appetizing
    390 vb.
—of
  resemble 18 vb.
savoury
  dish 301 n.
  savoury 390 adj.
saw
  cut 46 vb.
  notch 260 n.
  play music 413 vb.
  maxim 496 n.
—the air
  gesticulate 547 vb.
sawdust
  powder 332 n.

saxophone
flute 414 n.
say
affirm 532 vb.
speak 579 vb.
—no
negate 533 vb.
refuse 760 vb.
saying
maxim 496 n.
phrase 563 n.
say-so
affirmation 532 n.
scab
nonconformist 84 n.
covering 226 n.
scabbard
case 194 n.
arsenal 723 n.
scabby
rough 259 adj.
unclean 649 adj.
scabrous
impure 951 adj.
scaffold
structure 331 n.
means of execution
964 n.
scaffolding
frame 218 n.
scald
burn 381 vb.
scalding
hot 379 adj.
paining 827 adj.
scale
relativeness 9 n.
series 71 n.
skin 226 n.
climb 308 vb.
scales 322 n.
musical note 410 n.
opacity 423 n.
gauge 465 n.
—down
abate 37 vb.
scallop
edging 234 n.
crinkle 251 vb.
fish food 301 n.
scalp
head 213 n.
trophy 729 n.
scalpel
sharp edge 256 n.
scaly
layered 207 adj.

dermal 226 adj.
scamp
neglect 458 vb.
not complete
726 vb.
bad person 938 n.
scamper
move fast 277 vb.
scan
scan 438 vb.
be attentive 455 vb.
inquire 459 vb.
poetize 593 vb.
scandal
slur 867 n.
calumny 926 n.
scandalize
displease 827 vb.
cause dislike 861 vb.
incur blame 924 vb.
scandalmonger
news reporter 529 n.
defamer 926 n.
scanner
hospital 658 n.
scansion
prosody 593 n.
scant
exiguous 196 adj.
insufficient 636 adj.
scanty
few 105 adj.
insufficient 636 adj.
scapegoat
substitute 150 n.
unlucky person
731 n.
sufferer 825 n.
oblation 981 n.
scapegrace
bad person 938 n.
scar
high land 209 n.
trace 548 n.
blemish 845 n.vb.
scarab
talisman 983 n.
scarce
infrequent 140 adj.
scarce 636 adj.
scarcity
fewness 105 n.
scare
false alarm 665 n.
frighten 854 vb.
scarecrow
thinness 206 n.

eyesore 842 n.
scaremonger
alarmist 854 n.
scarf
neckwear 228 n.
scarify
wound 655 vb.
scarlet
redness 431 n.
scarp
verticality 215 n.
fortification 713 n.
scarper
fail in duty 918 vb.
scathe
impair 655 vb.
scatheless
undamaged 646 adj.
scathing
paining 827 adj.
scatological
impure 951 adj.
scatter
be dispersed 75 vb.
displace 188 vb.
let fall 311 vb.
waste 634 vb.
scatterbrained
light-minded
456 adj.
foolish 499 adj.
scatty
light-minded
456 adj.
crazy 503 adj.
scavenger
cleaner 648 n.
scenario
narrative 590 n.
stage play 594 n.
scene
situation 186 n.
view 438 n.
spectacle 445 n.
exhibit 522 n.
dramaturgy 594 n.
arena 724 n.
excitable state
822 n.
scenery
land 344 n.
beauty 841 n.
(see **scene***)*
scenic
impressive 821 adj.
beautiful 841 adj.
showy 875 adj.

scent
scent 396 n.
detect 484 vb.
foresee 510 vb.
trace 548 n.
cosmetic 843 n.
sceptic
irreligionist 974 n.
sceptical
doubting 474 adj.
unbelieving
486 adj.
dissenting 489 adj.
sceptre
regalia 743 n.
schedule
list 87 n.
plan 623 vb.
schematic
orderly 60 adj.
planned 623 adj.
scheme
plan 623 n.
plot 623 n.vb.
be cunning 698 vb.
schemer
slyboots 698 n.
scheming
dishonest 930 adj.
scherzo
musical piece 412 n.
schism
schism 978 n.
schismatic
quarrelling 709 adj.
schismatic 978 n.
schizoid
insane 503 adj.
schizophrenia
psychopathy 503 n.
schmaltzy
feeling 818 adj.
scholar
scholar 492 n.
learner 538 n.
scholarly
instructed 490 adj.
studious 536 adj.
scholarship
erudition 490 n.
subvention 703 n.
scholastic
intellectual 492 n.
educational 534 adj.
scholastic 539 adj.
scholasticism
theology 973 n.

SCH

school
 educate 534 vb.
 school 539 n.

schoolboy, schoolgirl
 youngster 132 n.
 learner 538 n.

schooling
 teaching 534 n.

schoolmaster,
 schoolmistress
 teacher 537 n.

schooner
 sailing ship 275 n.

sciatica
 rheumatism 651 n.

science
 physics 319 n.
 science 490 n.

science fiction
 ideality 513 n.
 novel 590 n.

scientific
 accurate 494 adj.

scientist
 physics 319 n.
 intellectual 492 n.

scientologist
 sect 978 n.

sci-fi
 (*see* **science fiction**)

scimitar
 sidearms 723 n.

scintillate
 shine 417 vb.
 be witty 839 vb.

sciolistic
 dabbling 491 adj.

scion
 young plant 132 n.
 descendant 170 n.

scission
 scission 46 n.

scissors
 cross 222 n.
 sharp edge 256 n.

sclerosis
 hardening 326 n.

scoff
 ridicule 851 n.vb.
 despise 922 vb.
 gluttonize 947 vb.

scoffer
 unbeliever 486 n.
 detractor 926 n.

scold
 shrew 892 n.
 reprobate 924 vb.

SCO

scone
 cereals 301 n.

scoop
 ladle 194 n.
 extractor 304 n.
 news 529 n.

—out
 make concave
 255 vb.

scoot
 move fast 227 vb.

scooter
 bicycle 274 n.

scope
 range 183 n.
 meaning 514 n.
 function 622 n.
 scope 744 n.

scorch
 move fast 277 vb.
 burn 381 vb.

scorched earth policy
 unproductiveness
 172 n.
 warfare 718 n.

scorcher
 speeder 277 n.
 exceller 644 n.

score
 cut 46 vb.
 numerical result
 85 n.
 list 87 vb.
 groove 262 vb.
 music 412 n.
 register 548 vb.
 wound 655 vb.
 triumph 727 vb.
 accounts 808 n.

—off
 be superior 34 vb.
 humiliate 872 vb.

score, a
 twenty and over
 99 n.

scores
 multitude 104 n.

scorn
 reject 607 vb.
 disrespect 921 n.
 contempt 922 n.

scorpion
 noxious animal
 904 n.

scotch
 wound 655 vb.

scot free

SCR

 nonliable 919 adj.

scoundrel
 knave 938 n.

scour
 move fast 277 vb.
 search 459 vb.
 clean 648 vb.

scourge
 bane 659 n.
 oppress 735 vb.
 scourge 964 n.

scourings
 leavings 41 n.

scout
 precursor 66 n.
 scan 438 vb.
 inquirer 459 n.

scowl
 look 438 n.
 discontent 829 n.
 sullenness 893 n.

scrabble
 search 459 vb.

scraggy
 lean 206 adj.

scram
 decamp 296 vb.

scramble
 mix 43 vb.
 derange 63 vb.
 cook 301 vb.
 climb 308 vb.
 haste 680 n.

scrap
 small quantity 33 n.
 piece 53 n.
 stop using 674 vb.
 fight 716 n.vb.

scrapbook
 reminder 505 n.
 anthology 592 n.

scrape
 collision 279 n.
 rub 333 vb.
 touch 378 vb.
 rasp 407 vb.
 foolery 497 n.
 predicament 700 n.
 be parsimonious
 816 vb.
 guilty act 936 n.

scraperboard
 engraving 555 n.

scrap heap
 rubbish 641 n.

scrap of paper
 ineffectuality 161 n.

SCR

 perfidy 930 n.

scrappy
 incomplete 55 adj.

scraps
 leavings 41 n.
 rubbish 641 n.

scratch
 inferior 35 adj.
 rend 46 vb.
 be violent 176 vb.
 itch 378 vb.
 touch 378 vb.
 trace 548 n.
 relinquish 621 vb.
 trifle 639 n.
 wound 655 n.vb.
 unprepared 670 adj.
 unskilled 695 adj.
 resign 753 vb.

scratchy
 agitated 318 adj.
 strident 407 adj.
 irascible 892 adj.

scrawl
 unintelligibility
 527 n.
 write 586 vb.

scrawny
 lean 206 adj.

scream
 feel pain 377 vb.
 shrill 407 vb.

scree
 incline 220 n.

screech
 stridor 407 n.

screed
 script 586 n.
 dissertation 591 n.

screen
 canopy 226 n.
 partition 231 n.
 porosity 263 n.
 screen 421 n.vb.
 cinema 445 n.
 inquire 459 vb.
 show 522 vb.
 disguise 527 n.
 pretext 614 n.
 shelter 662 n.

screenplay
 cinema 445 n.

screw
 affix 45 vb.
 fastening 47 n.
 distort 246 vb.
 coil 251 n.

SCR

propellant 287 n.
rob 788 vb.
niggard 816 n.
screwdriver
tool 630 n.
screwy
crazy 503 adj.
scribble
lack of meaning
515 n.
write 586 vb.
scribbler
author 589 n.
scribe
mark 547 vb.
recorder 549 n.
calligrapher 586 n.
theologian 973 n.
scrimmage
quarrel 709 n.
scrimshaw
ornamental art
844 n.
script
script 586 n.
stage play 594 n.
scriptural
scriptural 975 adj.
scripturalist
theologian 973 n.
the orthodox 976 n.
scripture
credential 466 n.
scripture 975 n.
script writer
dramatist 594 n.
scrofulous
impure 951 adj.
scroll
coil 251 n.
lettering 586 n.
Scrooge
niggard 816 n.
scrounge
beg 761 vb.
scrounger
idler 679 n.
beggar 763 n.
scrub
rub 333 vb.
wood 366 n.
clean 648 vb.
scrubber
prostitute 952 n.
scrubbing brush
cleaning utensil
648 n.

SCU

scrubby
arboreal 366 adj.
scruff
rear 238 n.
scruffy
unclean 649 adj.
disreputable
867 adj.
scrum
crowd 74 n.
fight 716 n.
scrumptious
savoury 390 adj.
scrunch
chew 301 vb.
pulverize 332 vb.
scruple
weighing 322 n.
doubt 486 n.
scrupulous
careful 457 adj.
fastidious 862 adj.
honourable 929 adj.
scrutineer
inquirer 459 n.
scrutinize
scan 438 vb.
scrutiny
attention 455 n.
inquiry 459 n.
scud
move fast 277 vb.
cloud 355 n.
scuff
rub 333 vb.
scuffle
fight 716 n.
scull
row 269 vb.
scullery
chamber 194 n.
scullion
cleaner 648 n.
domestic 742 n.
sculpt
sculpt 554 vb.
sculptor, sculptress
sculptor 556 n.
sculpture
sculpture 554 n.
scum
leavings 41 n.
layer 207 n.
dirt 649 n.
rabble 869 n.
scumble
coat 226 vb.

SEA

paint 553 vb.
scupper
suppress 165 vb.
slaughter 362 vb.
scurf
dirt 649 n.
scurrilous
cursing 899 adj.
detracting 926 adj.
scurry
move fast 277 vb.
hasten 680 vb.
scurvy
disease 651 n.
scuttle
vessel 194 n.
pierce 263 vb.
decamp 296 vb.
plunge 313 vb.
scythe
cut 46 vb.
farm tool 370 n.
sea
ocean 343 n.
wave 350 n.
sea air
salubrity 652 n.
seaboard
shore 344 n.
seafarer
mariner 270 n.
seafaring
seafaring 269 adj.
marine 275 adj.
seafood
fish food 301 n.
seal
mould 23 n.
close 264 vb.
mammal 365 n.
endorse 488 vb.
label 547 n.
badge of rule 743 n.
—up
imprison 747 vb.
sea lane
route 624 n.
sealed book
unknown thing
491 n.
secret 530 n.
sea legs
equilibrium 28 n.
sea level
lowness 210 n.
sealing wax
adhesive 47 n.

SEA

seam
joint 45 n.
dividing line 92 n.
layer 207 n.
store 632 n.
seaman
mariner 270 n.
seamanship
navigation 269 n.
skill 694 n.
seamless
whole 52 adj.
seamstress
clothier 228 n.
séance
spiritualism 984 n.
seaplane
aircraft 276 n.
sear
dry 342 adj.
make insensitive
820 vb.
search
search 459 n.vb.
searcher
inquirer 459 n.
searching
inquisitive 453 adj.
paining 827 adj.
searchlight
lamp 420 n.
seashore
shore 344 n.
seasick
vomiting 300 adj.
seaside
shore 344 n.
pleasure ground
837 n.
season
time 108 n.
regular return 141 n.
season 388 vb.
habituate 610 vb.
preserve 666 vb.
mature 669 vb.
seasonable
timely 137 adj.
seasonal
seasonal 141 adj.
celebratory 876 adj.
seasoned
expert 694 adj.
seasoning
condiment 389 n.
seat
equilibrium 28 n.

station 187 n.
house 192 n.
seat 218 n.
buttocks 238 n.
seat belt
preserver 666 n.
seated, be
sit down 311 vb.
seating
room 183 n.
seaway
room 183 n.
seaworthy
seafaring 269 adj.
secateurs
sharp edge 256 n.
secede
dissent 489 vb.
schismatize 978 vb.
secessionist
schismatic 978 n.
seclude
seclude 883 vb.
seclusion
farness 199 n.
seclusion 883 n.
second
sequential 65 adj.
double 91 adj.
instant 116 n.
endorse 488 vb.
patronize 703 vb.
deputy 755 n.
secondary
inferior 35 adj.
unimportant
639 adj.
second-best
inferior 35 adj.
substitute 150 n.
second chance
mercy 905 n.
second childhood
old age 131 n.
seconder
assenter 488 n.
patron 707 n.
second fiddle
nonentity 639 n.
second-hand
used 673 adj.
second nature
habit 610 n.
second-rate
inferior 35 adj.
middling 732 adj.
second sight

foresight 510 n.
psychics 984 n.
second thoughts
sequel 67 n.
change of allegiance
603 n.
amendment 654 n.
regret 830 n.
secrecy
secrecy 525 n.
taciturnity 582 n.
secret
unknown thing
491 n.
occult 523 adj.
secret 530 n.
secretariat
workshop 687 n.
management 689 n.
secretary
recorder 549 n.
auxiliary 707 n.
secrete
excrete 302 vb.
conceal 525 vb.
secretive
reticent 525 adj.
secret service
secret service 459 n.
sect
party 708 n.
sect 978 n.
sectarian
biased 481 adj.
sectional 708 adj.
sectarian 978 n.adj.
section
subdivision 53 n.
classification 77 n.
sectional
sectional 708 adj.
sectarian 978 adj.
sector
subdivision 53 n.
arc 250 n.
battleground 724 n.
secular
secular 110 adj.
lasting 113 adj.
laical 987 adj.
secularize
laicize 987 vb.
secure
firm 45 adj.
fixed 153 adj.
safeguard 660 vb.
give security 767 vb.

security
safety 660 n.
security 767 n.
security forces
protector 660 n.
security risk
vulnerability 661 n.
sedate
slow 278 adj.
inexcitable 823 adj.
sedated
tranquil 266 adj.
sedative
moderator 177 n.
drug 658 n.
soporific 679 n.adj.
sedentary
quiescent 266 adj.
sediment
leavings 41 n.
dirt 649 n.
sedimentation
condensation 324 n.
sedition
sedition 738 n.
perfidy 930 n.
seditious
revolutionary
149 adj.
disobedient 738 adj.
seduce
induce 612 vb.
cause desire 859 vb.
debauch 951 vb.
seducer
libertine 952 n.
seductive
attracting 291 adj.
pleasurable 826 adj.
lovable 887 adj.
sedulous
studious 536 adj.
industrious 678 adj.
see
see 438 vb.
watch 441 vb.
cognize 447 vb.
understand 516 vb.
church office 985 n.
—eye to eye
concord 710 vb.
—the light
discover 484 vb.
be penitent 939 vb.
—through
understand 516 vb.
carry out 725 vb.

—to
look after 457 vb.
seed
source 156 n.
reproduce itself
167 vb.
posterity 170 n.
flower 366 n.
seedbed
seedbed 156 n.
seeded player
proficient person
696 n.
seedling
young plant 132 n.
seedy
weakly 163 adj.
sick 651 adj.
dilapidated 655 adj.
beggarly 801 adj.
seeing
vision 438 n.
visibility 443 n.
seek
search 459 vb.
pursue 619 vb.
seeker
inquirer 459 n.
petitioner 763 n.
seem
resemble 18 vb.
appear 445 vb.
seeming
hypocritical
541 adj.
ostensible 614 adj.
seemly
advisable 642 adj.
tasteful 846 adj.
seep
infiltrate 297 vb.
exude 298 vb.
seer
sage 500 n.
oracle 511 n.
visionary 513 n.
sorcerer 983 n.
seersucker
textile 222 n.
seesaw
fluctuation 317 n.
be irresolute 601 vb.
pleasure ground
837 n.
seethe
be hot 379 vb.
be excited 821 vb.

see-through
transparent 422 adj.
segment
part 53 n.
subdivision 53 n.
segmentation
scission 46 n.
segregate
set apart 46 vb.
segregation
exclusion 57 n.
seclusion 883 n.
seisin
possession 773 n.
seismic
violent 176 adj.
oscillating 317 adj.
notable 638 adj.
seismograph
*recording
instrument* 549 n.
seize
arrest 747 vb.
take 786 vb.
—the chance
profit by 137 vb.
—up
halt 145 vb.
fail 728 vb.
seizure
spasm 318 n.
nervous disorders
651 n.
taking 786 n.
seldom
seldom 140 adv.
select
set apart 46 vb.
select 605 vb.
excellent 644 adj.
selection
anthology 592 n.
choice 605 n.
selective
discriminating
463 adj.
self
intrinsicality 5 n.
self 80 n.
self-abasement
humility 872 n.
self-abnegation
disinterestedness
931 n.
self-absorption
selfishness 932 n.
self-advertisement

boasting 877 n.
self-aggrandizement
selfishness 932 n.
self-assertion
insolence 878 n.
self-assurance
vanity 873 n.
self-assured
assertive 532 adj.
self-centred
vain 873 adj.
selfish 932 adj.
self-complacency
vanity 873 n.
self-condemned
repentant 939 adj.
self-confidence
positiveness 473 n.
pride 871 n.
self-conscious
affected 850 adj.
nervous 854 adj.
self-consistent
agreeing 24 adj.
self-contained
complete 54 adj.
independent
744 adj.
self-control
moderation 177 n.
restraint 747 n.
temperance 942 n.
self-correcting
compensatory
31 adj.
self-deception
credulity 487 n.
deception 542 n.
self-defence
resistance 715 n.
vindication 927 n.
self-denial
asceticism 945 n.
self-depreciation
modesty 874 n.
self-determination
independence 744 n.
self-devotion
willingness 597 n.
oblation 981 n.
self-discipline
temperance 942 n.
self-effacing
modest 874 adj.
self-employed
businesslike
622 adj.

self-esteem
pride 871 n.
self-evident
manifest 522 adj.
self-examination
inquiry 459 n.
self-explanatory
intelligible 516 adj.
self-expression
independence 744 n.
self-glorification
vanity 873 n.
self-governing
independent
744 adj.
self-help
aid 703 n.
self-importance
vanity 873 n.
ostentation 875 n.
self-imposed
voluntary 597 adj.
self-indulgence
pleasure 376 n.
selfishness 932 n.
sensualism 944 n.
self-interest
selfishness 932 n.
selfish
selfish 932 adj.
selfless
disinterested
931 adj.
self-made
man/woman
rich person 800 n.
self-motivated
independent
744 adj.
self-opinionated
person
doctrinaire 473 n.
self-pitying
melancholic
834 adj.
self-possession
inexcitability 823 n.
self-preservation
preservation 666 n.
self-regarding
selfish 932 adj.
self-reliant
independent
744 adj.
self-reproach
regret 830 n.
penitence 939 n.

self-respect
pride 871 n.
self-restraint
temperance 942 n.
self-righteous
pietistic 979 adj.
self-rule
independence 744 n.
self-sacrifice
disinterestedness
931 n.
selfsame
identical 13 adj.
self-satisfaction
vanity 873 n.
self-seeking
selfish 932 adj.
self-service
meal 301 n.
self-styled
misnamed 562 adj.
self-sufficiency
sufficiency 635 n.
independence 744 n.
self-supporting
independent
744 adj.
self-surrender
piety 979 n.
self-taught
studious 536 adj.
self-willed
wilful 602 adj.
disobedient 738 adj.
sell
trickery 542 n.
sell 793 vb.
—out
be dishonest 930 vb.
—short
detract 926 vb.
seller
seller 793 n.
seller's market
scarcity 636 n.
sell-out
perfidy 930 n.
selvedge, selvage
edging 234 n.
semantic
semantic 514 adj.
semantics
linguistics 557 n.
semaphore
telecommunication
531 n.
signal 547 n.vb.

semasiology
linguistics 557 n.
semblance
similarity 18 n.
appearance 445 n.
semen
genitalia 167 n.
semester
period 110 n.
semi-
incomplete 55 adj.
bisected 92 adj.
semicircle
arc 250 n.
semicircular
curved 248 adj.
semiconscious
insensible 375 adj.
semidarkness
half-light 419 n.
semidetached
architectural
192 adj.
semifinal
contest 716 n.
semiliquid
semiliquid 354 adj.
seminal
causal 156 adj.
generative 167 adj.
seminar
class 538 n.
conference 584 n.
seminary
training school
539 n.
semiology, semiotics
hermeneutics 520 n.
semiprecious stone
gem 844 n.
semiskilled
unskilled 695 adj.
semitone
musical note 410 n.
senate
parliament 692 n.
senator
councillor 692 n.
send
send 272 vb.
emit 300 vb.
—back
reject 607 vb.
—down
abate 37 vb.
eject 300 vb.
—flying

propel 287 vb.
—for
command 737 vb.
—out
emit 300 vb.
—packing
repel 292 vb.
dismiss 300 vb.
—to Coventry
exclude 57 vb.
make unwelcome
883 vb.
—up
augment 36 vb.
satirize 851 vb.
sender
transferrer 272 n.
send-off
valediction 296 n.
senile
ageing 131 adj.
foolish 499 adj.
senior
superior 34 n.adj.
older 131 adj.
master 741 n.
seniority
seniority 131 n.
authority
733 n.
sensation
sense 374 n.
news 529 n.
feeling 818 n.
prodigy 864 n.
sensational
exciting 821 adj.
wonderful 864 adj.
showy 875 adj.
sensationalism
publicity 528 n.
ostentation 875 n.
sense
sense 374 n.
intuit 476 vb.
detect 484 vb.
intelligence 498 n.
meaning 514 n.
feeling 818 n.
senseless
absurd 497 adj.
sense of humour
wit 839 n.
senses
sanity 502 n.
sensibility
sensibility 374 n.

moral sensibility
819 n.
sensible
material 319 adj.
sentient 374 adj.
wise 498 adj.
sensitive
discriminating
463 adj.
sensitive 819 adj.
sensitivity
moral sensibility
819 n.
sensor
detector 484 n.
sensory
sentient 374 adj.
sensual
sensuous 376 adj.
sensual 944 adj.
sensuality
pleasure 376 n.
sensualism 944 n.
sensuous
sensuous 376 adj.
pleasurable 826 adj.
sentence
period 110 n.
phrase 563 n.
penalty 963 n.
sententious
judicial 480 adj.
aphoristic 496 adj.
sentient
sentient 374 adj.
feeling 818 adj.
sentiment
opinion 485 n.
feeling 818 n.
love 887 n.
sentimental
feeling 818 adj.
impressible 819 adj.
loving 887 adj.
sentimentality
feeling 818 n.
sentry, sentinel
surveillance 457 n.
warner 664 n.
separability
disunion 46 n.
noncoherence 49 n.
separate
unrelated 10 adj.
separate 46 adj.vb.
unassembled 75 adj.
discriminate 463 vb.

divorce 896 vb.
separation
separation 46 n.
gap 201 n.
dissension 709 n.
schism 978 n.
separatist
dissentient 489 n.
schismatic 978 n.
sepia
brown pigment
430 n.
sepsis
infection 651 n.
septet
duet 412 n.
septic
toxic 653 adj.
septicaemia
infection 651 n.
septic tank
sink 649 n.
sepulchral
funereal 364 adj.
resonant 404 adj.
sepulchre
tomb 364 n.
sequel
sequel 67 n.
effect 157 n.
sequence
sequence 65 n.
continuity 71 n.
sequential
subsequent
120 adj.
sequester
set apart 46 vb.
seclude 883 vb.
sequestration
expropriation
786 n.
sequin
finery 844 n.
seraglio
womankind 373 n.
seraphic
virtuous 933 adj.
angelic 968 adj.
sere
continuity 71 n.
serenade
sing 413 vb.
wooing 889 n.
serendipity
chance 159 n.
discovery 484 n.

serene
 tranquil 266 adj.
 inexcitable 823 adj.
serenity
 content 828 n.
serf
 slave 742 n.
sergeant
 army officer 741 n.
serial
 continuous 71 adj.
 recurrence 106 n.
 reading matter
  589 n.
serialization
 sequence 65 n.
serialize
 publish 528 vb.
series
 sequence 65 n.
 series 71 n.
 continuance 146 n.
serious
 great 32 adj.
 intending 617 adj.
 important 638 adj.
 dangerous 661 adj.
 serious 834 adj.
sermon
 lecture 534 n.
 oration 579 n.
sermonize
 be pious 979 vb.
serpent
 reptile 365 n.
 sibilation 406 n.
 slyboots 698 n.
 noxious animal
  904 n.
serpentine
 snaky 251 adj.
serrated
 angular 247 adj.
 toothed 256 adj.
serried
 assembled 74 adj.
 dense 324 adj.
serum
 blood 335 n.
servant
 servant 742 n.
serve
 follow 284 vb.
 function 622 vb.
 suffice 635 vb.
 be expedient 642 vb.
 serve 742 vb.

 apportion 783 vb.
—one right
 be rightly served
  714 vb.
—one's turn
 be useful 640 vb.
server
 church officer
  986 n.
service
 instrumentality
  628 n.
 utility 640 n.
 restore 656 vb.
 service 745 n.
 kind act 897 n.
 church service
  988 n.
serviceable
 instrumental
  628 adj.
 useful 640 adj.
serviceman,
 servicewoman
 soldier 722 n.
servile
 servile 879 adj.
servitor
 domestic 742 n.
 servitude 745 n.
servomotor
 machine 630 n.
sesquicentenary
 fifth and over
  99 adj.
sesquipedalian
 long 203 adj.
 diffuse 570 adj.
session
 council 692 n.
 lawcourt 956 n.
set
 firm 45 adj.
 arrange 62 vb.
 series 71 n.
 accumulation 74 n.
 unit 88 n.
 stabilize 153 vb.
 tendency 179 n.
 place 187 vb.
 pendency 217 n.
 form 243 n.
 be dense 324 vb.
 class 538 n.
 stage set 594 n.
 obstinate 602 adj.
 collection 632 n.

 doctor 658 vb.
 attempt 671 n.
 party 708 n.
 contest 716 n.
 hairdressing 843 n.
—about
 begin 68 vb.
—against
 dissuade 613 vb.
 cause dislike 861 vb.
—an example
 motivate 612 vb.
 behave 688 vb.
—apart
 set apart 46 vb.
—aside
 store 632 vb.
 abrogate 752 vb.
 not observe 769 vb.
—back
 put off 136 vb.
—down
 place 187 vb.
 write 586 vb.
—forth
 start out 296 vb.
—in
 begin 68 vb.
 stay 144 vb.
—in motion
 initiate 68 vb.
—off
 correlate 12 vb.
 initiate 68 vb.
 decorate 844 vb.
—on
 incite 612 vb.
 attack 712 vb.
—one's heart/mind
 on
 be resolute 599 vb.
 desire 859 vb.
—out
 arrange 62 vb.
 start out 296 vb.
 show 522 vb.
—right
 rectify 654 vb.
—sail
 navigate 269 vb.
—to
 undertake 672 vb.
—up
 auspicate 68 vb.
 stabilize 153 vb.
 elevate 310 vb.
 cure 656 vb.

setback
 hitch 702 n.
 adversity 731 n.
set books
 curriculum 534 n.
set fair
 palmy 730 adj.
set in one's ways
 obstinate 602 adj.
set square
 gauge 465 n.
sett
 paving 226 n.
settee
 seat 218 n.
setting
 situation 186 n.
 surroundings
  230 n.
settle
 arrange 62 vb.
 place oneself
  187 vb.
 dwell 192 vb.
 descend 309 vb.
 judge 480 vb.
 pay 804 vb.
—down
 be quiescent 266 vb.
—for
 bargain 791 vb.
settled
 ending 69 adj.
 established 153 adj.
 located 187 adj.
 positive 473 adj.
 usual 610 adj.
settlement
 station 187 n.
 inhabitants 191 n.
 transfer 780 n.
 payment 804 n.
settler
 settler 191 n.
 incomer 297 n.
set-to
 fight 716 n.
set-up
 circumstance 8 n.
 structure 331 n.
set upon
 resolute 599 adj.
 desiring 859 adj.
seventh heaven
 happiness 824 n.
sever
 disunite 46 vb.

severable
severable 46 adj.
several
plurality 101 n.
many 104 adj.
severance
separation 46 n.
severe
violent 176 adj.
plain 573 adj.
severe 735 adj.
paining 827 adj.
serious 834 adj.
pitiless 906 adj.
severity
severity 735 n.
sew
join 45 vb.
sewage
leavings 41 n.
swill 649 n.
sewer
drain 351 n.
sink 649 n.
insalubrity 653 n.
sewerage
cleansing 648 n.
sewn up
completed 725 adj.
sex
coition 45 n.
classification 77 n.
propagation 167 n.
sex appeal
inducement 612 n.
beauty 841 n.
lovableness 887 n.
sex discrimination
injustice 914 n.
sexism
prejudice 481 n.
sex maniac
libertine 952 n.
sexpot
loose woman 952 n.
sextant
sailing aid 269 n.
sextet
duet 412 n.
sexton
church officer 986 n.
sexual
generic 77 adj.
generative 167 adj.
sexual desire
libido 859 n.
sexual intercourse

coition 45 n.
sexual inversion
abnormality 84 n.
sexuality
sensualism 944 n.
sexy
personable 841 adj.
erotic 887 adj.
shabby
dilapidated 655 adj.
beggarly 801 adj.
dishonest 930 adj.
shack
small house 192 n.
shackle
halter 47 n.
fetter 747 vb.
fetter 748 n.
shade
small quantity 33 n.
shade 226 n.
dimness 419 n.
screen 421 n.vb.
hue 425 n.
refresh 685 vb.
ghost 970 n.
—off
shade off 27 vb.
shading
obscuration 418 n.
painting 553 n.
shadow
insubstantial thing
4 n.
analogue 18 n.
concomitant 89 n.
follow 284 vb.
dimness 419 n.
screen 421 vb.
fantasy 513 n.
pursue 619 vb.
close friend 880 n.
shadowy
insubstantial 4 adj.
immaterial 320 adj.
shadowy 419 adj.
uncertain 474 adj.
shady
cold 380 adj.
shadowy 419 adj.
dishonest 930 adj.
shaft
pillar 218 n.
excavation 255 n.
tunnel 263 n.
flash 417 n.
tool 630 n.

missile weapon
723 n.
shaggy
hairy 259 adj.
shake
mix 43 vb.
derange 63 vb.
impulse 279 n.
brandish 317 vb.
be agitated 318 vb.
cause doubt 486 vb.
impress 821 vb.
quake 854 vb.
—hands
make peace 719 vb.
greet 884 vb.
—hands on
contract 765 vb.
—off
unstick 49 vb.
outstrip 277 vb.
—up
agitate 318 vb.
animate 821 vb.
shakedown
bed 218 n.
shaken
agitated 318 adj.
irresolute 601 adj.
shake-up
revolution 149 n.
shaky
flimsy 163 adj.
unsafe 661 adj.
shale
rock 344 n.
shallow
inconsiderable
33 adj.
shallow 212 adj.
dabbling 491 adj.
foolish 499 adj.
trivial 639 adj.
affected 850 adj.
sham
dissemble 541 vb.
sham 542 n.
shaman
sorcerer 983 n.
shamble
move slowly 278 vb.
shambles
confusion 61 n.
havoc 165 n.
bungling 695 n.
shame
slur 867 n.

shame 867 vb.
humiliation 872 n.
shamefaced
guilty 936 adj.
shameful
discreditable
867 adj.
heinous 934 adj.
shameless
thick-skinned
820 adj.
insolent 878 adj.
dishonest 930 adj.
unchaste 951 adj.
shampoo
cleanser 648 n.
shamrock
heraldry 547 n.
shandy
alcoholic drink
301 n.
shanghai
take away 786 vb.
shank
leg 267 n.
Shanks's pony
pedestrianism
267 n.
shanty
small house 192 n.
vocal music 412 n.
shape
sort 77 n.
form 243 n.vb.
structure 331 n.
feature 445 n.
shapeless
amorphous 244 adj.
shapely
shapely 841 adj.
shard, sherd
piece 53 n.
share
part 53 n.
sharp edge 256 n.
participation 775 n.
portion 783 n.
shareholder
receiver 782 n.
share-out
participation 775 n.
portion 783 n.
sharing
equal 28 adj.
shark
fish 365 n.
defrauder 789 n.

sharp
keen 174 adj.
sharp 256 adj.
sour 393 adj.
musical note 410 n.
discordant 411 adj.
intelligent 498 adj.
cunning 698 adj.
paining 827 adj.
ungracious 885 adj.
sharpen
sharpen 256 vb.
sharpener
sharpener 256 n.
sharper
trickster 545 n.
sharp-eyed
attentive 455 adj.
vigilant 457 adj.
sharp point
sharp point 256 n.
perforator 263 n.
sharp practice
trickery 542 n.
sharpshooter
shooter 287 n.
sharp tongue
quarrelsomeness
709 n.
shatter
break 46 vb.
demolish 165 vb.
be brittle 330 vb.
shattering
notable 638 adj.
wonderful 864 adj.
shatterproof
unyielding 162 adj.
invulnerable
660 adj.
shave
cut 46 vb.
be near 200 vb.
shorten 204 vb.
smooth 258 vb.
hairdressing 843 n.
shaven
hairless 229 adj.
shaver
cosmetic 843 n.
shaving(s)
leavings 41 n.
lamina 207 n.
shawl
cloak 228 n.
she
woman 373 n.

sheaf
bunch 74 n.
shear
shorten 204 vb.
distortion 246 n.
groom 369 vb.
shears
sharp edge 256 n.
farm tool 370 n.
sheath
case 194 n.
covering 226 n.
sheathe
cover 226 vb.
insert 303 vb.
shed
decrease 37 vb.
small house 192 n.
doff 229 vb.
emit 300 vb.
let fall 311 vb.
disaccustom 611 vb.
relinquish 621 vb.
—**blood**
kill 362 vb.
sheen
reflection 417 n.
sheep
imitator 20 n.
sheep 365 n.
sheep farmer
breeder 369 n.
sheepfold
enclosure 235 n.
sheepish
modest 874 adj.
guilty 936 adj.
sheep's eyes
wooing 889 n.
sheer
simple 44 adj.
vertical 215 adj.
transparent 422 adj.
sheer off
deviate 282 vb.
sheet
lamina 207 n.
coverlet 226 n.
the press 528 n.
paper 631 n.
sheet anchor
protection 660 n.
sheets
tackling 47 n.
shelf
shelf 218 n.
projection 254 n.

shelf-room
storage 632 n.
shell
mould 23 n.
emptiness 190 n.
exteriority 223 n.
covering 226 n.
skin 226 n.
uncover 229 vb.
hardness 326 n.
structure 331 n.
ammunition 723 n.
seclusion 883 n.
—**out**
give 781 vb.
pay 804 vb.
shellac
resin 357 n.
shellfish
fish food 301 n.
shellshock
psychopathy 503 n.
shelter
dwelling 192 n.
stable 192 n.
hiding-place 527 n.
shelter 662 n.
shelve
put off 136 vb.
be oblique 220 vb.
avoid 620 vb.
shelving
compartment 194 n.
shepherd
herdsman 369 n.
protector 660 n.
direct 689 vb.
leader 690 n.
pastor 986 n.
sherbet
soft drink 301 n.
sheriff
law officer 955 n.
sherry
wine 301 n.
shibboleth
identification 547 n.
shield
screen 421 n.vb.
safeguard 660 vb.
armour 713 n.
defend 713 vb.
shift
period 110 n.
change 143 n.
displacement 188 n.
transpose 272 vb.

labour 682 n.
stratagem 698 n.
take away 786 vb.
—**one's ground**
tergiversate 603 vb.
shifting
transient 114 adj.
unstable 152 adj.
shiftless
unprepared
670 adj.
shifty
cunning 698 adj.
dishonest 930 adj.
shillings and pence
money 797 n.
shilly-shally
be irresolute 601 vb.
shimmer
shine 417 vb.
shin
leg 267 n.
meat 301 n.
shindy, shindig
turmoil 61 n.
fight 716 n.
shine
shine 417 vb.
have a reputation
866 vb.
—**on**
be auspicious
730 vb.
shingle
lamina 207 n.
roof 226 n.
shore 344 n.
building material
631 n.
shining light
sage 500 n.
shiny
smooth 258 adj.
luminous 417 adj.
ship
carry 273 vb.
ship 275 n.
warship 722 n.
shipmates
mariner 270 n.
shipment
thing transferred
272 n.
shipper
carrier 273 n.
shipping
shipping 275 n.

shipshape
  orderly 60 adj.
shipwreck
  ruin 165 n.
shipyard
  workshop 687 n.
shire
  district 184 n.
shirk
  avoid 620 vb.
  fail in duty 918 vb.
shirker
  negligence 458 n.
shirr
  fold 261 vb.
shirt
  shirt 228 n.
shirty
  angry 891 adj.
shiver
  be agitated 318 vb.
  be cold 380 vb.
  quake 854 vb.
shoal
  group 74 n.
  shallow 212 adj.
shock
  bunch 74 n.
  electricity 160 n.
  violence 176 n.
  lack of expectation 508 n.
  illness 651 n.
  suffering 825 n.
  cause discontent 829 vb.
  frighten 854 vb.
  incur blame 924 vb.
shockable
  prudish 950 adj.
shock-headed
  hairy 259 adj.
shocking
  not nice 645 adj.
  distressing 827 adj.
  wonderful 864 adj.
  discreditable 867 adj.
  heinous 934 adj.
shockproof
  tough 329 adj.
shock treatment
  therapy 658 n.
shock troops
  attacker 712 n.
shod
  dressed 228 adj.

shoddy
  bad 645 adj.
  bad taste 847 n.
shoe
  footwear 228 n.
shoo away
  dismiss 300 vb.
shoot
  young plant 132 n.
  move fast 277 vb.
  kick 279 vb.
  shoot 287 vb.
  kill 362 vb.
  vegetate 366 vb.
  photograph 551 vb.
  fire at 712 vb.
—ahead
  progress 285 vb.
  outdo 306 vb.
—a line
  boast 877 vb.
—down
  fell 311 vb.
  confute 479 vb.
—the rapids
  navigate 269 vb.
—up
  grow 36 vb.
  ascend 308 vb.
shooter
  shooter 287 n.
  hunter 619 n.
shooting
  sport 837 n.
shooting pain
  pang 377 n.
shooting range
  arena 724 n.
shooting star
  meteor 321 n.
shooting stick
  prop 218 n.
shoot-out
  fight 716 n.
shop
  topic 452 n.
  inform 524 vb.
  purchase 792 vb.
  shop 796 n.
—around
  choose 605 vb.
shop assistant
  seller 793 n.
shopfloor
  workshop 687 n.
shopkeeper
  tradespeople 794 n.

shoplifter
  thief 789 n.
shopper
  purchaser 792 n.
shopping centre
  emporium 796 n.
shopping list
  requirement 627 n.
shop-soiled
  imperfect 647 adj.
shop steward
  official 690 n.
  delegate 754 n.
shop window
  exhibit 522 n.
  market 796 n.
shore
  shore 344 n.
shore up
  support 218 vb.
shorn
  short 204 adj.
short
  brief 114 adj.
  dwarfish 196 adj.
  short 204 adj.
  deficient 307 adj.
  brittle 330 adj.
  concise 569 adj.
  taciturn 582 adj.
  scarce 636 adj.
  poor 801 adj.
  ungracious 885 adj.
shortage
  shortfall 307 n.
shortbread
  pastries 301 n.
shortchange
  deceive 542 vb.
  overcharge 811 vb.
shortcoming(s)
  shortfall 307 n.
  vice 934 n.
short cut
  straightness 249 n.
short drink
  draught 301 n.
shorten
  shorten 204 vb.
shortfall
  shortfall 307 n.
shorthand
  writing 586 n.
short-lived
  ephemeral 114 adj.
shorts
  trousers 228 n.

short shrift
  pitilessness 906 n.
short-sighted
  dim-sighted 440 adj.
  misjudging 481 adj.
short supply
  scarcity 636 n.
short-tempered
  irascible 892 adj.
short-term
  brief 114 adj.
short work
  easy thing 701 n.
shot
  stimulant 174 n.
  shooter 287 n.
  bang 402 n.
  photography 551 n.
  medicine 658 n.
  ammunition 723 n.
shot across the bows
  warning 664 n.
  terror tactics 712 n.
shot at
  attempt 671 n.
shotgun
  firearm 723 n.
shot in the dark
  empiricism 461 n.
  conjecture 512 n.
shot through
  perforated 263 adj.
  iridescent 437 adj.
shoulder
  prop 218 n.
  carry 273 vb.
  impel 279 vb.
—one's responsibility
  incur a duty 917 vb.
shout
  vociferate 408 vb.
  get angry 891 vb.
—down
  make mute 578 vb.
  be obstructive 702 vb.
shove
  move 265 vb.
  impulse 279 n.
  gesture 547 n.
—aside
  not respect 921 vb.
—off
  decamp 296 vb.

shovel
ladle 194 n.
transpose 272 vb.

show
be visible 443 vb.
spectacle 445 n.
appear 445 vb.
demonstrate 478 vb.
exhibit 522 n.
show 522 vb.
deception 542 n.
indicate 547 vb.
stage show 594 n.
ostentation 875 n.

—fight
defy 711 vb.

—in
admit 299 vb.

—off
be affected 850 vb.
be ostentatious
  875 vb.

—one's face
be present 189 vb.

—one's hand
divulge 526 vb.

—out
dismiss 300 vb.

—signs (of)
evidence 466 vb.
indicate 547 vb.

—the ropes
train 534 vb.

—the way
direct 689 vb.

—up
arrive 295 vb.
confute 479 vb.
shame 867 vb.

show business
drama 594 n.

showcase
exhibit 522 n.

showdown
disclosure 526 n.

shower
descend 309 vb.
let fall 311 vb.
rain 350 n.vb.
abound 635 vb.
ablutions 648 n.
be liberal 813 vb.

showerproof
dry 342 adj.

showing
uncovered 229 adj.
visible 443 adj.

showman
exhibitor 522 n.
stage manager
  594 n.

showmanship
publicity 528 n.

show of hands
vote 605 n.

showpiece
exhibit 522 n.

showy
vulgar 847 adj.
showy 875 adj.

shrapnel
ammunition 723 n.

shred
small thing 33 n.
cut 46 vb.
strip 208 n.

shredded
fragmentary 53 adj.

shrew
quarreller 709 n.
shrew 892 n.

shrewd
intelligent 498 adj.
cunning 698 adj.

shrewd idea
conjecture 512 n.

shrewish
irascible 892 adj.

shriek
feel pain 377 vb.
cry 408 n.
lament 836 n.

shrill
loud 400 adj.
shrill 407 vb.

shrimp
dwarf 196 n.
marine life 365 n.

shrine
temple 990 n.

shrink
decrease 37 vb.
become small
  198 vb.
recoil 280 vb.
avoid 620 vb.

—from
dislike 861 vb.

shrinkage
decrement 42 n.
contraction 198 n.

shrinking
unwilling 598 adj.
modest 874 adj.

shrive
perform ritual
  988 vb.

shrivel
deteriorate 655 vb.

shrivelled
lean 206 adj.
dry 342 adj.

shroud
grave clothes 364 n.
conceal 525 vb.

shrouds
tackling 47 n.

shrub
tree 366 n.

shrubbery
garden 370 n.

shrug
gesture 547 n.
be indifferent
  860 vb.

shrunk
contracted 198 adj.

shudder
agitation 318 n.
quake 854 vb.

—at
dislike 861 vb.

shuffle
mix 43 vb.
jumble 63 vb.
interchange
  151 n.vb.
walk 267 vb.
transpose 272 vb.
move slowly 278 vb.
tergiversate 603 vb.

shun
avoid 620 vb.
dislike 861 vb.

shunt
deflect 282 vb.

shut
close 264 vb.

—down
cease 145 vb.

—in
surround 230 vb.
imprison 747 vb.

—out
exclude 57 vb.

—up
be mute 578 vb.
imprison 747 vb.

shutdown
stop 145 n.

shutter

shrive
covering 226 n.
shade 226 n.

shuttle
weaving 222 n.
oscillate 317 vb.

shuttle service
periodicity 141 n.

shy
propel 287 vb.
unwilling 598 adj.
avoiding 620 adj.
modest 874 adj.
unsociable 883 adj.

sibilant
speech sound 398 n.
sibilant 406 adj.

sibling
kinsman 11 n.

sibyl
oracle 511 n.

sic
truly 494 adv.

sick
vomiting 300 n.
insane 503 adj.
sick 651 adj.
dejected 834 adj.

sickbed
illness 651 n.
hospital 658 n.

sicken
be ill 651 vb.
displease 827 vb.
cause dislike 861 vb.

sickening
unsavoury 391 adj.
not nice 645 adj.

sickle
sharp edge 256 n.
farm tool 370 n.

sick list
sick person 651 n.

sickly
unhealthy 651 adj.

sickness
illness 651 n.

sick of
bored 838 adj.
sated 863 adj.

sickroom
hospital 658 n.

side
race 11 n.
situation 186 n.
laterality 239 n.
party 708 n.
pride 871 n.

—with
patronize 703 vb.
sideboard
·*cabinet* 194 n.
side effect
effect 157 n.
sidekick
auxiliary 707 n.
sidelight
knowledge 490 n.
sideline(s)
exteriority 223 n.
edge 234 n.
business 622 n.
sidelong
obliquely 220 adv.
sideshow
trifle 639 n.
sideslip
deviation 282 n.
sidesman,
    sideswoman
church officer 986 n.
sidesplitting
funny 849 adj.
sidestep
deviate 282 vb.
avoid 620 vb.
sidetrack
deflect 282 vb.
sideways
sideways 239 adv.
siding
railway 624 n.
sidle
be oblique 220 vb.
deviate 282 vb.
siege
circumscription
    232 n.
sierra
high land 209 n.
siesta
sleep 679 n.
sieve
porosity 263 n.
sift
eliminate 44 vb.
class 62 vb.
discriminate 463 vb.
select 605 vb.
purify 648 vb.
sigh
breathe 352 vb.
sound faint 401 vb.
be dejected 834 vb.
lamentation 836 n.

sight
vision 438 n.
spectacle 445 n.
detect 484 vb.
eyesore 842 n.
sightless
blind 439 adj.
sights
direction 281 n.
sightseer
traveller 268 n.
spectator 441 n.
inquisitive person
    453 n.
sign
evidence 466 n.
endorse 488 vb.
omen 511 n.
badge 547 n.
gesture 547 n.
indication 547 n.
label 547 n.
sign 547 vb.
letter 558 n.
contract 765 vb.
prodigy 864 n.
—off
resign 753 vb.
—on
join a party 708 vb.
signal
signal 547 n.vb.
notable 638 adj.
signalize
indicate 547 vb.
celebrate 876 vb.
signalling
telecommunication
    531 n.
signatory
signatory 765 n.
signature
assent 488 n.
identification 547 n.
signboard
label 547 n.
significance
connotation 514 n.
importance 638 n.
significant
evidential 466 adj.
signify
mean 514 vb.
indicate 547 vb.
sign language
gesture 547 n.
sign of the cross

ritual act 988 n.
sign of the times
omen 11 n.
signpost
signpost 547 n.
silage
provender 301 n.
silence
silence 399 n.vb.
confute 479 vb.
make mute 578 vb.
silencer
silencer 401 n.
nonresonance
    405 n.
silent
silent 399 adj.
reticent 525 adj.
voiceless 578 adj.
taciturn 582 adj.
silhouette
outline 233 n.vb.
feature 445 n.
picture 553 n.
silicon chip
microelectronics
    196 n.
silicosis
respiratory disease
    651 n.
silk
textile 222 n.
lawyer 958 n.
silky
smooth 258 adj.
textural 331 adj.
sill
shelf 218 n.
silly
absurd 497 adj.
foolish 499 adj.
silo
storage 632 n.
gun 723 n.
silt
soil 344 n.
silver
bullion 797 n.
money 797 n.
decorate 844 vb.
silverplate
coat 226 vb.
silversmith
artisan 686 n.
silvery
melodious 410 adj.
white 427 adj.

silviculture
forestry 366 n.
similar
similar 18 adj.
simile
analogue 18 n.
comparison 462 n.
metaphor 519 n.
ornament 574 n.
simmer
cook 301 vb.
resent 891 vb.
simony
improbity 930 n.
simper
be affected 850 vb.
simple
simple 44 adj.
credulous 487 adj.
foolish 499 adj.
intelligible 516 adj.
plain 573 adj.
artless 699 adj.
easy 701 adj.
simple life
temperance
    942 n.
asceticism 945 n.
simpleton
ignoramus 493 n.
ninny 501 n.
simplicity
simpleness 44 n.
(*see* **simple**)
simplify
simplify 44 vb.
decompose 51 vb.
interpret 520 vb.
facilitate 701 vb.
simulacrum
sham 542 n.
simulate
imitate 20 vb.
simulator
testing agent 461 n.
simultaneous
instantaneous
    116 adj.
synchronous
    123 adj.
sin
be wicked 934 vb.
guilty act 936 n.
since
subsequently
    120 adv.
hence 158 adv.

sincere
veracious 540 adj.
artless 699 adj.
sincerity
probity 929 n.
sinecure
inaction 677 n.
easy thing 701 n.
sine qua non
concomitant 89 n.
requirement 627 n.
chief thing 638 n.
sinewy
stalwart 162 adj.
tough 329 adj.
sinful
wicked 934 adj.
guilty 936 adj.
sing
sing 413 vb.
—for joy
rejoice 835 vb.
singable
melodious 410 adj.
singe
burn 381 vb.
blacken 428 vb.
singer
vocalist 413 n.
single
simple 44 adj.
one 88 adj.
gramophone 414 n.
unwedded 895 adj.
—out
set apart 46 vb.
single combat
duel 716 n.
single file
procession 71 n.
single-handed
alone 88 adj.
single-minded
obsessed 455 adj.
resolute 599 adj.
singlet
underwear 228 n.
singleton
unit 88 n.
singsong
repeated 106 adj.
social gathering 882 n.
singular
unusual 84 adj.
one 88 adj.
singularity

speciality 80 n.
sinister
evil 616 adj.
adverse 731 adj.
frightening 854 adj.
sink
decrease 37 vb.
suppress 165 vb.
receptacle 194 n.
founder 313 vb.
drain 351 n.
sink 649 n.
deteriorate 655 vb.
—in
infiltrate 297 vb.
impress 821 vb.
sinker
diver 313 n.
gravity 322 n.
sinking heart
dejection 834 n.
sinless
innocent 935 adj.
sinner
offender 904 n.
bad person 938 n.
sin offering
propitiation 941 n.
sinuous
convoluted 251 adj.
sinus
cavity 255 n.
sinusitis
respiratory disease 651 n.
sip
mouthful 301 n.
drink 301 vb.
siphon, syphon
extractor 304 n.
conduit 351 n.
siphon off
transpose 272 vb.
sir
male 372 n.
title 870 n.
sire
generate 167 vb.
siren
vocalist 413 n.
signal 547 n.
danger signal 665 n.
a beauty 841 n.
mythical being 970 n.
sister
kinsman 11 n.

woman 373 n.
nurse 658 n.
friend 880 n.
nun 986 n.
sisterhood
family 11 n.
community 708 n.
Sisyphean
useless 641 adj.
sit
sit down 311 vb.
—about/around
be inactive 679 vb.
—back
not act 677 n.
repose 683 vb.
—down
sit down 311 vb.
—for
represent 551 vb.
deputize 755 vb.
—on
suppress 165 vb.
subjugate 745 vb.
—on the fence
be neutral 606 vb.
not act 677 n.
—out
go on 146 vb.
—tight
be quiescent 266 vb.
—up
be attentive 455 vb.
—up with
look after 457 vb.
sitar
harp 414 n.
site
situation 186 n.
place 187 vb.
sit-in
presence 189 n.
sitter
testee 461 n.
art equipment 553 n.
easy thing 701 n.
sitting
council 692 n.
sitting duck
vulnerability 661 n.
sitting pretty
successful 727 adj.
situate
place 187 vb.
situation
circumstance 8 n.
situation 186 n.

surroundings 230 n.
job 622 n.
predicament 700 n.
sixth sense
intuition 476 n.
occultism 984 n.
sizable
great 32 adj.
large 195 adj.
size
greatness 32 n.
arrange 62 vb.
size 195 n.
coat 226 vb.
importance 638 n.
—up
estimate 480 vb.
sizzle
be hot 379 vb.
hiss 406 vb.
skate
go smoothly 258 vb.
sledge 274 n.
—on thin ice
be in danger 661 vb.
skating
sport 837 n.
skein
bunch 74 n.
skeletal
lean 206 adj.
structural 331 adj.
skeleton
thinness 206 n.
frame 218 n.
outline 233 n.
structure 331 n.
corpse 363 n.
compendium 592 n.
sketch
incompleteness 55 n.
outline 233 n.vb.
represent 551 vb.
picture 553 n.
describe 590 vb.
compendium 592 n.
stage play 594 n.
sketch map
map 551 n.
sketchy
incomplete 55 adj.
skew
statistics 86 n.
oblique 220 adj.
distort 246 vb.

skewer
pierce 263 vb.

ski
sledge 274 n.
amuse oneself
837 vb.

skid
deviate 282 vb.

skiff
rowing boat 275 n.

skiing
sport 837 n.

skilful
skilful 694 adj.

skill
ability 160 n.
skill 694 n.

skilled worker
artisan 686 n.
expert 696 n.

skim
be near 200 vb.
be contiguous
202 vb.
move fast 277 vb.
purify 648 vb.
—off
select 605 vb.
—through
scan 438 vb.

skimp
neglect 458 vb.
be parsimonious
816 vb.

skimpy
short 204 adj.

skin
layer 207 n.
exteriority 223 n.
skin 226 n.
uncover 229 vb.
fleece 786 vb.

skin-and-bone
lean 206 adj.
underfed 636 adj.

skin-deep
shallow 212 adj.

skin disease
skin disease 651 n.

skin diving
sport 837 n.

skinflint
niggard 816 n.

skin game
peculation 788 n.

skinhead
youngster 132 n.

skinny
lean 206 adj.

skintight
cohesive 48 adj.
tailored 228 adj.

skip
vessel 194 n.
decamp 296 vb.
leap 312 n.vb.
neglect 458 vb.
not complete
726 vb.
not observe 769 vb.

skipper
mariner 270 n.
direct 689 vb.

skipping
children's games
837 n.

skirl
stridor 407 n.

skirmish
fight 716 n.vb.

skirt
be near 200 vb.
base 214 n.
skirt 228 n.
edge 234 n.
pass 305 vb.
circuit 626 vb.

skit
satire 851 n.

skittish
capricious
604 adj.
excitable 822 adj.

skittle
fell 311 vb.

skittles
ball game 837 n.

skive
laminate 207 vb.
be inactive 679 vb.

skivvy
domestic 742 n.

**skulduggery,
skullduggery**
improbity 930 n.

skulk
be stealthy 525 vb.

skulker
hider 527 n.

skull
head 213 n.
corpse 363 n.

skull cap
headgear 228 n.

sky
summit 213 n.
heavens 321 n.

sky diver
aeronaut 271 n.

skylab
satellite 321 n.

skylarking
foolery 497 n.

skylight
window 263 n.

skyline
distance 199 n.

skyscraper
high structure 209 n.

slab
lamina 207 n.
shelf 218 n.

slack
nonadhesive 49 adj.
weak 163 adj.
negligent 458 adj.
be unwilling 598 vb.
lazy 679 adj.
lax 734 adj.

slacken
decrease 37 vb.
weaken 163 vb.
moderate 177 vb.
—speed
decelerate 278 vb.

slacks
informal dress
228 n.

slag
ash 381 n.
rubbish 641 n.

slake
drink 301 vb.
sate 863 vb.

slalom
deviation 282 n.

slam
close 264 vb.
strike 279 vb.
bang 402 n.vb.
detract 926 vb.

slander
calumny 926 n.
false charge 928 n.

slanderer
defamer 926 n.

slang
slang 560 n.

slanging match
quarrel 709 n.
scurrility 899 n.

slangy
dialectal 560 adj.

slant
obliquity 220 n.
view 438 n.
bias 481 n.

slap
spank 963 vb.
—down
restrain 747 vb.

slap and tickle
endearment 889 n.

slapdash
negligent 458 adj.
rash 857 adj.

slaphappy
rash 857 adj.

slap in the face
refusal 760 n.
humiliation
872 n.

slapstick
ridiculousness
849 n.

slap-up
liberal 813 adj.

slash
cut, rend 46 vb.
notch 260 vb.
cheapen 812 vb.
dispraise 924 vb.

slashing
forceful 571 adj.

slat
strip 208 n.

slate
lamina 207 n.
policy 623 n.
dispraise 924 vb.

slattern
dirty person 649 n.

slaughter
slaughter 362 n.vb.

slaughterhouse
slaughterhouse
362 n.

slave
busy person 678 n.
worker 686 n.
slave 742 n.
—away
work 682 vb.

slave-driver
tyrant 735 n.

slaver
exude 298 vb.
excrement 302 n.

slavery
servitude 745 n.

slavey
domestic 742 n.

slavish
imitative 20 adj.
servile 879 adj.

slay
kill 362 vb.

slayer
killer 362 n.

sleazy
dirty 649 adj.

sledge, sled
sledge 274 n.

sledge-hammer
hammer 279 n.
compelling 740 adj.

sleek
smooth 258 adj.
prosperous 730 adj.
personable 841 adj.

sleep
be quiescent 266 vb.
insensibility 375 n.
be inattentive
456 vb.
sleep 679 n.vb.

—around
be impure 951 vb.

—it off
be sober 948 vb.

—on it
meditate 449 vb.

—with
unite with 45 vb.

sleeper
railway 624 n.
idler 679 n.

sleep-inducing
soporific 679 adj.

sleeping
latent 523 adj.
inactive 679 adj.
abrogated 752 adj.

sleeping pill/tablet
soporific 679 n.

sleepless
persevering 600 adj.
active 678 adj.

sleepwalker
pedestrian 268 n.

sleepy
sleepy 679 adj.
fatigued 684 adj.

sleet
wintriness 380 n.

sleeve
garment 228 n.

sleigh
sledge 274 n.

sleight of hand
sleight 542 n.

slender
small 33 adj.
narrow 206 adj.
shapely 841 adj.

slender means
poverty 801 n.

sleuth
detective 459 n.

slew
rotate 315 vb.

slice
cut 46 vb.
piece 53 n.
laminate 207 vb.
deflect 282 vb.
propel 287 vb.
portion 783 n.

slick
smooth 258 adj.
deceiving 542 adj.
cunning 698 adj.

slicker
trickster 545 n.

slide
obliquity 220 n.
go smoothly 258 vb.
deviate 282 vb.
descent 309 n.
photography 551 n.
pleasure ground
837 n.

—back
relapse 657 vb.

slide rule
counting instrument
86 n.

slight
inconsiderable
33 adj.
exiguous 196 adj.
disregard 458 vb.
underestimate
483 vb.
trivial 639 adj.
indignity 921 n.
detract 926 vb.

slim
narrow 206 adj.
shapely 841 adj.

slime
semiliquidity 354 n.

dirt 649 n.

slimming
dieting 301 n.

slimy
viscid 354 adj.
servile 879 adj.

sling
hang 217 vb.
propel 287 vb.
surgical dressing
658 n.
lapidate 712 vb.
missile weapon
723 n.

slink
be stealthy 525 vb.

slinky
tailored 228 adj.
shapely 841 adj.

slip
come unstuck
49 vb.
youngster 132 n.
underwear 228 n.
go smoothly 258 vb.
tumble 309 vb.
mistake 495 n.
solecism 565 n.

—back
relapse 657 vb.

—by
elapse 111 vb.

—into
wear 228 vb.

—off
doff 229 vb.

—through
escape 667 vb.

—up
blunder 495 vb.

slipper
footwear 228 n.

slipperiness
changeableness
152 n.
unreliability 474 n.

slippery
nonadhesive 49 adj.
smooth 258 adj.
unctuous 357 adj.
deceiving 542 adj.
unsafe 661 adj.
dishonest 930 adj.

slips
workshop 687 n.

slipshod
negligent 458 adj.

lax 734 adj.

slip stream
wind 352 n.

slip-up
mistake 495 n.

slit
sunder 46 vb.
furrow 262 n.

slither
be in motion
265 vb.

slithery
smooth 258 adj.

sliver
piece 53 n.

slob
cad 938 n.

slobber
exude 298 vb.
excrement 302 n.

slog
propel 287 vb.
work 682 vb.
persevere 600 vb.

slogan
maxim 496 n.
advertisement
528 n.
call 547 n.

slogger
busy person 678 n.
pugilist 722 n.

sloop
sailing ship 275 n.

slop
let fall 311 vb.
waste 634 vb.

—over
flow out 298 vb.

slope
high land 209 n.
be oblique 220 vb.

—off
decamp 296 vb.

sloping
sloping 220 adj.

sloppy
orderless 61 adj.
semiliquid 354 adj.
negligent 458 adj.
feeble 572 adj.
feeling 818 adj.

slops
insipidity 387 n.
swill 649 n.

slosh
flow 350 vb.

slot
serial place 73 n.
gap 201 n.
orifice 263 n.
sloth
sluggishness 679 n.
slot machine
treasury 799 n.
slouch
move slowly 278 vb.
stoop 311 vb.
idler 679 n.
slough
doff 229 vb.
marsh 347 n.
slovenly
orderless 61 adj.
negligent 458 adj.
dirty 649 adj.
slow
late 136 adj.
slow 278 adj.
unintelligent
   499 adj.
leisurely 681 adj.
tedious 838 adj.
—down
decelerate 278 vb.
hinder 702 vb.
slowcoach
slowcoach 278 n.
slub
weave 222 vb.
sludge
semiliquidity 354 n.
dirt 649 n.
slug
strike 279 vb.
draught 301 n.
creepy-crawly
   365 n.
ammunition 723 n.
sluggish
inert 175 adj.
apathetic 820 adj.
sluice
drench 341 vb.
conduit 351 n.
clean 648 vb.
slum
housing 192 n.
dilapidation 655 n.
slumber
sleep 679 n.vb.
slump
decrease 37 n.vb.
deteriorate 655 vb.

adversity 731 n.
slur
slur 867 n.
calumny 926 n.
slush
semiliquidity 354 n.
slushy
feeling 818 adj.
slut
dirty person 649 n.
sly
cunning 698 adj.
smack
tincture 43 n.
sailing ship 275 n.
taste 386 n.
spank 963 vb.
—of
resemble 18 vb.
—one's lips
enjoy 376 vb.
small
small 33 adj.
infantine 132 adj.
little 196 adj.
unimportant
   639 adj.
small arms
firearm 723 n.
small beer
trifle 639 n.
smaller
contracted 198 adj.
small fry
child 132 n.
nonentity 639 n.
smallholder
farmer 370 n.
small hours
morning 128 n.
lateness 136 n.
small talk
chatter 581 n.
small-time
trivial 639 adj.
smarmy
flattering 925 adj.
smart
speedy 277 adj.
feel pain 377 vb.
intelligent 498 adj.
cunning 698 adj.
suffer 825 vb.
witty 839 adj.
fashionable 848 adj.
smart aleck
wiseacre 500 n.

smarten up
beautify 841 vb.
smart set
beau monde 848 n.
smash
break 46 vb.
force 176 vb.
strike 279 vb.
pulverize 332 vb.
smasher
exceller 644 n.
a beauty 841 n.
smattering
sciolism 491 n.
smear
overlay 226 vb.
make unclean
   649 vb.
slur 867 n.
defame 926 vb.
smell
sense 374 n.
smell 394 vb.
stink 397 vb.
—a rat
detect 484 vb.
smelling salts
tonic 658 n.
smelly
fetid 397 adj.
smelt
heat 381 vb.
smile
smile 835 vb.
—on
be auspicious
   730 vb.
smiling
cheerful 833 adj.
smirch
make unclean
   649 vb.
defame 926 vb.
smirk
be affected 850 vb.
smite
strike 279 vb.
smith
artisan 686 n.
smithereens
small thing 33 n.
smitten
enamoured 887 adj.
smock
shirt 228 n.
smog
insalubrity 653 n.

smoke
emit 300 vb.
vaporize 338 vb.
be hot 379 vb.
tobacco 388 n.
smoke 388 vb.
preserve 666 vb.
—out
eject 300 vb.
smoke-filled
insalubrious
   653 adj.
smoke screen
opacity 423 n.
concealment 525 n.
pretext 614 n.
smoky
dim 419 adj.
dirty 649 adj.
(see **smoke***)*
smooch
caress 889 vb.
smooth
orderly 60 adj.
flatten 216 vb.
hairless 229 adj.
smooth 258 adj.vb.
tranquil 266 adj.
facilitate 701 vb.
flattering 925 adj.
smoothie, smoothy
slyboots 698 n.
smooth-running
lubricated 334 adj.
tractable 701 adj.
smooth-tongued
hypocritical
   541 adj.
flattering 925 adj.
smother
suppress 165 vb.
cover 226 vb.
murder 362 vb.
extinguish 382 vb.
conceal 525 vb.
smoulder
be hot 379 vb.
lurk 523 vb.
be inactive 679 vb.
resent 891 vb.
smudge
blacken 428 vb.
blemish 845 n.
smug
vain 873 adj.
smuggle
steal 788 vb.

smuggler
thief 789 n.

smugness
content 828 n.

smut
ash 381 n.
dirt 649 n.

smutty
impure 951 adj.

snack
mouthful 301 n.

snack bar
café 192 n.

snaffle
take 786 vb.
steal 788 vb.

snag
projection 254 n.
hitch 702 n.

snail
slowcoach 278 n.

snake
meander 251 vb.
reptile 365 n.
slyboots 698 n.
noxious animal
   904 n.

snake-charmer
sorcerer 983 n.

snake in the grass
latency 523 n.
troublemaker 663 n.

snap
break 46 vb.
be brittle 330 vb.
crackle 402 vb.
photography 551 n.
spontaneous
   609 adj.
unprepared 670 adj.
card game 837 n.
be irascible 892 vb.
—one's fingers at
defy 711 vb.
—out of it
be restored 656 vb.
be cheerful 833 vb.
—up
take 786 vb.

snappy
speedy 277 adj.
aphoristic 496 adj.
personable 841 adj.

snapshot
photography 551 n.

snare
trap 542 n.

snarl
ululate 409 vb.
be sullen 893 vb.

snarl-up
complexity 61 n.

snatch
take 786 vb.

snatcher
taker 786 n.

snatchy
discontinuous
   72 adj.

snazzy
fashionable 848 adj.

sneak
informer 524 n.
be stealthy 525 vb.
be servile 879 vb.

sneaking
tacit 523 adj.

sneer
contempt 922 n.

sneeze
breathe 352 vb.

snick
cut 46 vb.

snide
detracting 926 adj.

sniff
breathe 352 vb.
smell 394 vb.
be insolent 878 vb.
—at
despise 922 vb.

sniffing
drug-taking 949 n.

sniffly
diseased 651 adj.

sniffy
despising 922 adj.

snifter
draught 301 n.

snigger
laugh 835 vb.

snip
cut 46 vb.
piece 53 n.

snipe
fire at 712 vb.

sniper
shooter 287 n.

sniping
dissension 709 n.

snippet
piece 53 n.

snitch
inform 524 vb.

snivel
weep 836 vb.

snob
proud person 871 n.

snobbish
ill-bred 847 adj.
affected 850 adj.
despising 922 adj.

snob value
prestige 866 n.

snog
caress 889 vb.

snook
sauciness 878 n.

snoop
be curious 453 vb.
be stealthy 525 vb.

snooper
inquisitive person
   453 n.
detective 459 n.

snooty
insolent 878 adj.

snooze
sleep 679 n.vb.

snore
sleep 679 vb.

snort
breathe 352 vb.
rasp 407 vb.
ululate 409 vb.
contempt 922 n.

snout
protuberance 254 n.

snow
snow 380 n.
—under
be many 104 vb.

snowball
grow 36 vb.
accumulation 74 n.
missile 287 n.

snowbound
wintry 129 adj.

snowflake
softness 327 n.
snow 380 n.

snowman
insubstantial thing
   4 n.

snowshoes
sledge 274 n.

snowstorm
wintriness 380 n.

snowy
cold 380 adj.
white 427 adj.

pure 950 adj.

snub
unsharpened
   257 adj.
humiliate 872 vb.
be rude 885 vb.
reprimand 924 n.

snuff
extinguish 382 vb.
tobacco 388 n.
—out
suppress 165 vb.
snuff out 418 vb.

snuffle
breathe 352 vb.

snuffy
irascible 892 adj.
despising 922 adj.

snug
adjusted 24 adj.
comfortable
   376 adj.
content 828 adj.

snuggery
retreat 192 n.

snuggle
caress 889 vb.

so
similarly 18 adv.
hence 158 adv.
true 494 adj.

soak
pervade 189 vb.
drench 341 vb.
overcharge 811 vb.
sate 863 vb.
—through
infiltrate 297 vb.
—up
absorb 299 vb.

so-and-so
no name 562 n.

soap
cleanser 648 n.

soapbox
rostrum 539 n.

soapy
bubbly 355 adj.
servile 879 adj.

soar
be high 209 vb.
fly 271 vb.
ascend 308 vb.

sob
respiration 352 n.
cry 408 n.vb.
weep 836 vb.

sober
moderate 177 adj.
soft-hued 425 adj.
sane 502 adj.
plain 573 adj.
serious 834 adj.
depress 834 vb.
cautious 858 adj.
sober 948 adj.
sobriety
sobriety 948 n.
sobriquet
name 561 n.
sob-stuff
excitation 821 n.
so-called
spurious 542 adj.
misnamed 562 adj.
sociable
friendly 880 adj.
sociable 882 adj.
amiable 884 adj.
social
national 371 adj.
corporate 708 adj.
social gathering
882 n.
social climber
vulgarian 847 n.
social engineering
reformism 654 n.
sociology 901 n.
social group
social group 371 n.
socialism
government 733 n.
joint possession
775 n.
philanthropy 901 n.
socialite
beau monde 848 n.
sociable person
882 n.
socialize
be sociable 882 vb.
social science
anthropology 371 n.
sociology 901 n.
social security
subvention 703 n.
social services
sociology 901 n.
social worker
reformer 654 n.
philanthropist
901 n.
society

society 708 n.
beau monde 848 n.
sociology
sociology 901 n.
sociopath
madman 504 n.
sock
legwear 228 n.
strike 279 vb.
socket
place 185 n.
receptacle 194 n.
cavity 255 n.
sod
soil 344 n.
soda
soft drink 301 n.
cleanser 648 n.
sodality
association 706 n.
sodden
drenched 341 adj.
sodomy
illicit love 951 n.
sofa
seat 218 n.
soft
weak 163 adj.
soft 327 adj.
comfortable
376 adj.
muted 401 adj.
foolish 499 adj.
lenient 736 adj.
soft drink
soft drink 301 n.
soften
soften 327 vb.
extenuate 927 vb.
(see soft*)*
—up
induce 612 vb.
prepare 669 vb.
fire at 712 vb.
soft focus
dimness 419 n.
soft-hearted
impressible 819 adj.
pitying 905 adj.
soft nothings
endearment 889 n.
soft on
enamoured 887 adj.
soft option
easy thing 701 n.
soft-pedal
moderate 177 vb.

soft sell
advertisement
528 n.
inducement 612 n.
soft soap
flattery 925 n.
soft-spoken
speaking 579 adj.
soft spot
moral sensibility
819 n.
soft touch
dupe 544 n.
software
data processing
86 n.
softy, softie
ninny 501 n.
soggy
pulpy 356 adj.
soi-disant
misnamed 562 adj.
soil
soil 344 n.
make unclean
649 vb.
blemish 845 vb.
soirée
social gathering
882 n.
sojourn
dwell 192 vb.
solace
relief 831 n.
solar energy
sources of energy
160 n.
solar system
sun 321 n.
sold
salable 793 adj.
solder
join 45 vb.
adhesive 47 n.
soldier
soldier 722 n.
soldier of fortune
militarist 722 n.
sold on
believing 485 adj.
enamoured 887 adj.
sole
one 88 adj.
foot 214 n.
solecism
solecism 565 n.
solemn

great 32 adj.
serious 834 adj.
formal 875 adj.
solemnity
rite 988 n.
solemnization
celebration 876 n.
sol-fa
vocal music 412 n.
solicitation
inducement 612 n.
request 761 n.
solicitor
law agent 958 n.
solicitous
careful 457 adj.
desiring 859 adj.
solicitude
attention 455 n.
worry 825 n.
solid
substantial 3 adj.
cohesive 48 adj.
material 319 n.
solid body 324 n.
dense 324 adj.
serious 834 adj.
solidarity
cooperation 706 n.
concord 710 n.
solid body
solid body 324 n.
solidify
cohere 48 vb.
be dense 324 vb.
solidity
substantiality 3 n.
materiality 319 n.
opacity 423 n.
soliloquy
soliloquy 585 n.
solitary
nonconformist 84 n.
alone 88 adj.
solitary 883 n.
solitude
seclusion 883 n.
solo
unit 88 n.
duet 412 n.
soloist
musician 413 n.
soluble
fluid 335 adj.
solution
solution 337 n.
answer 460 n.

interpretation 520 n.
completion 725 n.
solve
decipher 520 vb.
solvent
liquefaction 337 n.
moneyed 800 adj.
sombre
funereal 364 adj.
dark 418 adj.
cheerless 834 adj.
some
quantitative 26 adj.
plurality 101 n.
somebody
person 371 n.
bigwig 638 n.
someone
person 371 n.
somersault
overturning 221 n.
something
object 319 n.
something wrong
hitch 702 n.
sometime
not now 122 adv.
sometimes
sometimes 139 adv.
somewhere
somewhere 185 adv.
somewhere else
not here 190 adv.
so minded
volitional 595 adj.
intending 617 adj.
somnambulism
pedestrianism
267 n.
somnolent
sleepy 679 adj.
son
descendant 170 n.
sonant
speech sound 398 n.
vocal 577 adj.
sonar
detector 484 n.
sonata
musical piece 412 n.
song
vocal music 412 n.
songster
bird 365 n.
vocalist 413 n.
sonic
sounding 398 adj.

sonic boom
bang 402 n.
sonnet
verse form 593 n.
sonority
resonance 404 n.
sound 398 n.
sonorous
loud 400 adj.
rhetorical 574 adj.
soon
betimes 135 adv.
soot
ash 381 n.
black thing 428 n.
soothe
assuage 177 vb.
please 826 vb.
soothsayer
oracle 511 n.
sooty
dark 418 adj.
black 428 adj.
sop
mouthful 301 n.
incentive 612 n.
sophism
sophism 477 n.
sophist
sophist 477 n.
sophisticate
impair 655 vb.
people of taste
846 n.
sophistication
culture 490 n.
skill 694 n.
good taste 846 n.
sophistry
sophistry 477 n.
sophomore
student 538 n.
soporific
soporific 679 n.adj.
sopping
drenched 341 adj.
soppy
impressible 819 adj.
soprano
vocalist 413 n.
sorcerer
sorcerer 983 n.
sorcery
sorcery 983 n.
sordid
not nice 645 adj.
vulgar 847 adj.

sore
painful 377 adj.
ulcer 651 n.
sensitive 819 adj.
painfulness 827 n.
resentful 891 adj.
sore point
resentment 891 n.
sorority
community 708 n.
sorrow
sorrow 825 n.
lament 836 vb.
sorrowful
unhappy 825 adj.
sorry
regretting 830 adj.
repentant 939 adj.
sorry for
pitying 905 adj.
sort
class 62 vb.
sort 77 n.
—out
exclude 57 vb.
discriminate 463 vb.
sortie
attack 712 n.
SOS
signal 547 n.
so-so
imperfect 647 adj.
middling 732 adj.
sot
drunkard 949 n.
soteriology
theology 973 n.
sottish
drunken 949 adj.
sotto voce
faintly 401 adv.
soufflé
dish 301 n.
soul
essence 1 n.
interiority 224 n.
life 360 n.
person 371 n.
spirit 447 n.
affections 817 n.
soulful
feeling 818 adj.
soulless
impassive 820 adj.
tedious 838 adj.
soul mate
close friend 880 n.

loved one 887 n.
soul-stirring
exciting 821 adj.
sound
unyielding 162 adj.
plunge 313 vb.
sound 398 n.
be loud 400 vb.
be heard 415 vb.
be tentative 461 vb.
measure 465 vb.
genuine 494 adj.
perfect 646 adj.
healthy 650 adj.
orthodox 976 adj.
—out
interrogate 459 vb.
sound barrier
limit 236 n.
sound character
honourable person
929 n.
sounding board
publicity 528 n.
soundings
depth 211 n.
inquiry 459 n.
soundless
silent 399 adj.
sound mind
sanity 502 n.
soundproofing
lining 227 n.
barrier 235 n.
sound recording
registration 548 n.
sound track
sound 398 n.
cinema 445 n.
sound wave
oscillation 317 n.
soup
hors-d'oeuvres
301 n.
semiliquidity 354 n.
soupçon
small quantity 33 n.
souped-up
dynamic 160 adj.
soup kitchen
subvention 703 n.
sour
unsavoury 391 adj.
sour 393 adj.
amiss 616 adv.
aggravate 832 vb.
sullen 893 adj.

source
origin 68 n.
source 156 n.
informant 524 n.

sour grapes
pretext 614 n.

sourpuss
moper 834 n.

souse
plunge 313 vb.
drench 341 vb.
preserve 666 vb.

south
compass point
281 n.

southern
opposite 240 adj.

southpaw
sinistrality 242 n.

souvenir
reminder 505 n.

sou'wester
headgear 228 n.

sovereign
remedial 658 adj.
sovereign 741 n.
coinage 797 n.

sovereignty
governance 733 n.

soviet
council 692 n.

sow
disperse 75 vb.
produce 164 vb.
pig 365 n.
cultivate 370 vb.
—**one's wild oats**
be intemperate
943 vb.
—**the seeds of**
cause 156 vb.

sower
farmer 370 n.

spa
hospital 658 n.

space
room 183 n.
space 183 n.
distance 199 n.
interval 201 n.
space 201 vb.
opening 263 n.

spaced out
drugged 949 adj.

space flight
space travel
271 n.

spaceman,
 spacewoman
traveller 268 n.
aeronaut 271 n,

spaceship
spaceship 276 n.

space station
satellite 321 n.

space-time
 continuum
universe 321 n.

spacious
spacious 183 adj.

spade
farm tool 370 n.

spadework
preparation 669 n.
labour 682 n.

spaghetti
dish 301 n.

span
connect 45 vb.
bond 47 n.
duality 90 n.
period 110 n.
extend 183 vb.
breadth 205 n.
overlie 226 vb.
measure 465 vb.
bridge 624 n.

spangle
finery 844 n.

spank
spank 963 vb.

spanner
tool 630 n.

spanner in the works
hitch 702 n.

spar
hanger 217 n.
pugilism 716 n.

spare
additional 38 adj.
remaining 41 adj.
lean 206 adj.
plain 573 adj.
superfluous 637 adj.
unused 674 adj.
not retain 779 vb.
show mercy 905 vb.
—**no effort**
exert oneself 682 vb.
—**no expense**
be liberal 813 vb.

spared
safe 660 adj.

spare part(s)

component 58 n.

spare time
leisure 681 n.

sparing
economical 814 adj.
temperate 942 adj.

spark
vigorousness 174 n.
fire 379 n.
flash 417 n.

spark off
initiate 68 vb.
cause 156 vb.

sparkling
luminous 417 adj.
witty 839 adj.

sparse
few 105 adj.
scarce 636 adj.

Spartan
ascetic 945 adj.

spasm
fitfulness 142 n.
spasm 318 n.
pang 377 n.
activity 678 n.

spasmodic
discontinuous
72 adj.

spastic
sick person 651 n.

spat
quarrel 709 n.

spatchcock
put between 231 vb.

spate
great quantity 32 n.
waterfall 350 n.

spatial
spatial 183 adj.

spatiotemporal
material 319 adj.

spats
legwear 228 n.

spatter
make unclean
649 vb.

spatula
ladle 194 n.

spawn
generate 167 vb.

spay
unman 161 vb.

speak
divulge 526 vb.
speak 579 vb.
—**for**

deputize 755 vb.
—**for itself**
evidence 466 vb.
be intelligible
516 vb.
—**one's mind**
be truthful 540 vb.
—**out**
affirm 532 vb.
be courageous
855 vb.
—**plainly**
speak plainly
573 vb.
—**to**
speak to 583 vb.
—**up**
be loud 400 vb.
—**up for**
vindicate 927 vb.

speaker
megaphone 400 n.
speaker 579 n.

spear
pierce 263 vb.
spear 723 n.

spearhead
front 237 n.
leader 690 n.
attacker 712 n.

special
characteristic 5 adj.
special 80 adj.
unconformable
84 adj.
chosen 605 adj.

special case
variant 15 n.

specialism
knowledge 490 n.
skill 694 n.

specialist
scholar 492 n.
expert 696 n.

speciality
speciality 80 n.
(*see* **special**)

specialize
study 536 vb.

special offer
incentive 612 n.
discount 810 n.

species
breed 77 n.

specific
special 80 adj.
remedy 658 n.

specification
classification 77 n.
particulars 80 n.
description 590 n.
specify
specify 80 vb.
name 561 vb.
specimen
prototype 23 n.
example 83 n.
specious
plausible 471 adj.
ostensible 614 adj.
ostentatious
875 adj.
speck
small thing 33 n.
blemish 845 n.
speckled
mottled 437 adj.
spectacle
spectacle 445 n.
stage show 594 n.
spectacles
eyeglass 442 n.
spectacular
showy 875 adj.
spectator
spectator 441 n.
spectral
insubstantial 4 adj.
spooky 970 adj.
spectre
visual fallacy 440 n.
ghost 970 n.
spectroscopy
optics 417 n.
spectrum
series 71 n.
colour 425 n.
variegation 437 n.
speculate
meditate 449 vb.
suppose 512 vb.
speculation
gambling 618 n.
trade 791 n.
speculative
uncertain 474 adj.
speculative 618 adj.
speech
language 557 n.
oration 579 n.
speech 579 n.
speechify
orate 579 vb.
speech impediment

speech defect 580 n.
speechless
voiceless 578 adj.
wondering 864 adj.
speech therapist
doctor 658 n.
speed
motion 265 n.
velocity 277 n.
facilitate 701 vb.
—up
accelerate 277 vb.
promote 285 vb.
speedboat
boat 275 n.
speeder
driver 268 n.
speeder 277 n.
speedometer
*recording
instrument* 549 n.
speed rate
velocity 277 n.
speed trap
traffic control 305 n.
speedway
racing 716 n.
speedy
speedy 277 adj.
speleology
descent 309 n.
sport 837 n.
spell
period 110 n.
influence 178 n.
predict 511 vb.
mean 514 vb.
imply 523 vb.
spell 558 vb.
spell 983 n.
—out
speak plainly
573 vb.
spellbind
motivate 612 vb.
be wonderful
864 vb.
bewitch 983 vb.
spellbinding
eloquent 579 adj.
spellbound
bewitched 983 adj.
spelling
letter 558 n.
spencer
jacket 228 n.
spend

waste 634 vb.
expend 806 vb.
spendthrift
prodigal 815 n.
spent
weakened 163 adj.
fatigued 684 adj.
sperm
genitalia 167 n.
spew
vomit 300 vb.
sphere
circumstance 8 n.
region 184 n.
sphere 252 n.
function 622 n.
spherical
rotund 252 adj.
sphinx
rara avis 84 n.
secret 530 n.
spice
mix 43 vb.
stimulant 174 n.
condiment 389 n.
pleasurableness
826 n.
spick and span
orderly 60 adj.
clean 648 adj.
spicy
pungent 388 adj.
fragrant 396 adj.
impure 951 adj.
(*see* **spice**)
spider
creepy-crawly
365 n.
planner 623 n.
spiderman
lifter 310 n.
spider's web
complexity 61 n.
ambush 527 n.
spidery
written 586 adj.
spiel
empty talk 515 n.
loquacity 581 n.
spike
sharp point 256 n.
pierce 263 vb.
—the guns
disable 161 vb.
spikes
footwear 228 n.
spiky

sharp 256 adj.
spill
overturning 221 n.
flow out 298 vb.
make flow 350 vb.
waste 634 vb.
spillway
waterfall 350 n.
spilt milk
loss 772 n.
spin
weave 222 vb.
land travel 267 n.
rotation 315 n.
—a yarn
be untrue 543 vb.
—out
spin out 113 vb.
spinal
supporting 218 adj.
back 238 adj.
spindle
pivot 218 n.
rotator 315 n.
spindle-shaped
tapering 256 adj.
spindly
lean 206 adj.
spindrift
bubble 355 n.
spine
pillar 218 n.
rear 238 n.
prickle 256 n.
spine-chilling
exciting 821 adj.
spineless
impotent 161 adj.
weak 163 adj.
spinner
weaving 222 n.
planner 623 n.
spinney
wood 366 n.
spin-off
sequel 67 n.
effect 157 n.
spinster
spinster 895 n.
spiny
sharp 256 adj.
spiracle
orifice 263 n.
spiral
coil 251 n.
ascend 308 vb.
rotation 315 n.

SPI

spire
 high structure 209 n.
 church exterior
  990 n.

spirit
 temperament 5 n.
 self 80 n.
 vigorousness 174 n.
 life 360 n.
 spirit 447 n.
 meaning 514 n.
 vigour 571 n.
 affections 817 n.
 courage 855 n.
 ghost 970 n.
 —away
 steal 788 vb.

spirited
 lively 819 adj.
 courageous 855 adj.

spiritless
 apathetic 820 adj.
 cowardly 856 adj.

spirit of place
 locality 187 n.

spirit of the age
 tendency 179 n.

spirits
 state 7 n.
 alcoholic drink
  301 n.
 cheerfulness 833 n.

spiritual
 immaterial 320 adj.
 psychic 447 adj.
 religious 973 adj.

spiritualism
 spiritualism 984 n.

spiritualist
 occultist 984 n.

spiritualistic
 psychic 447 adj.
 psychical 984 adj.

spirituous
 intoxicating 949 adj.

spirt
 (*see* **spurt**)

spiry
 high 209 adj.
 tapering 256 adj.

spit
 projection 254 n.
 pierce 263 vb.
 eruct 300 vb.
 rotator 315 n.
 rain 350 vb.
 hiss 406 vb.

SPL

 —at/on
 not respect 921 vb.
 —out
 eject 300 vb.

spit and polish
 cleanness 648 n.
 formality 875 n.

spite
 resentment 891 n.
 malevolence 898 n.
 detraction 926 n.

spiteful
 malevolent 898 adj.

spit-roast
 cook 301 vb.

spitting image
 analogue 18 n.

spittle
 excrement 302 n.

spittoon
 sink 649 n.

splash
 small quantity 33 n.
 moisten 341 vb.
 flow 350 vb.
 advertise 528 vb.
 make unclean
  649 vb.
 ostentation 875 n.
 —out
 expend 806 vb.

splashdown
 space travel 271 n.

splay
 be broad 205 vb.
 diverge 294 vb.

spleen
 insides 224 n.
 sullenness 893 n.

splendid
 excellent 644 adj.
 splendid 841 adj.
 ostentatious
  875 adj.

splendour
 light 417 n.
 beauty 841 n.
 prestige 866 n.
 ostentation 875 n.

splenetic
 irascible 892 adj.

splice
 tie 45 vb.
 marry 894 vb.

splint
 surgical dressing
  658 n.

SPO

splinter
 break 46 vb.
 piece 53 n.
 be brittle 330 vb.

splinter group
 dissentient 489 n.
 party 708 n.

split
 sunder 46 vb.
 gap 201 n.
 laminate 207 vb.
 be brittle 330 vb.
 inform 524 vb.
 dissension 709 n.
 apportion 783 vb.
 —hairs
 sophisticate 477 vb.
 —off
 diverge 294 vb.
 —the difference
 average out 30 vb.
 —up
 divorce 896 vb.

split personality
 psychopathy
  503 n.

splotch, splodge
 maculation 437 n.

splurge
 prodigality 815 n.

splutter
 hiss 406 vb.
 stammer 580 vb.

spoil
 impair 655 vb.
 hinder 702 vb.
 be lax 734 vb.
 booty 790 n.
 make ugly 842 vb.
 pet 889 vb.
 —one's chances
 act foolishly
  695 vb.

spoiling for
 willing 597 adj.

spoils
 trophy 729 n.
 booty 790 n.

spoilsport
 moper 834 n.
 disapprover 924 n.

spoilt
 deteriorated
  655 adj.

spoke(s)
 line 203 n.
 divergence 294 n.

SPO

**spokesman,
 spokeswoman**
 (*see* **spokesperson**)

spokesperson
 interpreter 520 n.
 messenger 529 n.
 speaker 579 n.
 deputy 755 n.

spondee
 prosody 593 n.

sponge
 porosity 263 n.
 absorb 299 vb.
 drier 342 n.
 clean 648 vb.
 beg 761 vb.

sponger
 idler 679 n.
 beggar 763 n.

spongy
 soft 327 adj.
 marshy 347 adj.

sponsor
 patron 707 n.

sponsorship
 aid 703 n.

spontaneity
 spontaneity 609 n.

spontaneous
 involuntary 596 adj.
 voluntary 597 adj.
 spontaneous
  609 adj.
 unprepared
  670 adj.
 artless 699 adj.

spoof
 satire 851 n.

spooky
 spooky 970 adj.

spool
 rotator 315 n.

spoon
 ladle 194 n.

spoonerism
 inversion 221 n.
 absurdity 497 n.

spoon-feed
 be lenient 736 vb.

spoor
 trace 548 n.

sporadic
 infrequent 140 adj.

spore
 source 156 n.

sport
 nonconformist 84 n.

athletics 162 n.
wear 228 vb.
exercise 682 n.
sport 837 n.
laughingstock
 851 n.
be ostentatious
 875 vb.
honourable person
 929 n.
sporting chance
 fair chance 159 n.
sportive
 merry 833 adj.
 amused 837 adj.
sportsman,
 sportswoman
 hunter 619 n.
 player 837 n.
sportsmanship
 sport 837 n.
 probity 929 n.
spot
 small thing 33 n.
 place 185 n.
 variegate 437 vb.
 detect 484 vb.
 make unclean
 649 vb.
 pattern 844 n.
 blemish 845 n.
 slur 867 n.
spot check
 inquiry 459 n.
spotless
 clean 648 adj.
 pure 950 adj.
spotlight
 lighting 420 n.
 publicity 528 n.
spot on
 accurate 494 adj.
spotted
 mottled 437 adj.
spotty
 diseased 651 adj.
 blemished 845 adj.
spouse
 spouse 894 n.
spout
 outlet 298 n.
 flow 350 vb.
 conduit 351 n.
 be loquacious
 581 vb.
sprain
 disable 161 vb.

distort 246 vb.
sprat
 fish food 301 n.
sprawl
 dispersion 75 n.
 expand 197 vb.
 be horizontal
 216 vb.
spray
 bunch 74 n.
 emit 300 vb.
 vaporizer 338 n.
 bubble 355 n.
 foliage 366 n.
spread
 grow 36 vb.
 disperse 75 vb.
 extend 183 vb.
 expand 197 vb.
 overlay 226 vb.
 feasting 301 n.
—around
 publish 528 vb.
spread-eagle
 fell 311 vb.
spree
 revel 837 n.
sprig
 foliage 366 n.
sprightly
 active 678 adj.
spring
 spring 128 n.
 source 156 n.
 coil 251 n.
 move fast 277 vb.
 recoil 280 n.
 leap 312 n.vb.
 elasticity 328 n.
 stream 350 n.
 motive 612 n.
 machine 630 n.
—up
 begin 68 vb.
 leap 312 vb.
 be visible 443 vb.
springboard
 lifter 310 n.
 aider 703 n.
springe
 trap 542 n.
springlike
 vernal 128 adj.
spring tide
 high water 209 n.
springtime
 spring 128 n.

springy
 soft 327 adj.
 elastic 328 adj.
sprinkle
 emit 300 vb.
 let fall 311 vb.
 moisten 341 vb.
 variegate 437 vb.
sprinkler
 extinguisher 382 n.
sprinkling
 small quantity 33 n.
 tincture 43 n.
sprint
 spurt 277 n.
 racing 716 n.
sprocket
 tooth 256 n.
sprout
 grow 36 vb.
 young plant 132 n.
 reproduce itself
 167 vb.
 expand 197 vb.
spruce
 clean 648 adj.vb.
—up
 make better 654 vb.
spry
 active 678 adj.
 cheerful 833 adj.
spume
 bubble 355 n.vb.
spunk
 vigorousness 174 n.
 courage 855 n.
spur
 branch 53 n.
 projection 254 n.
 sharp point 256 n.
 accelerate 277 vb.
 impel 279 vb.
 incentive 612 n.
 hasten 680 vb.
 excitant 821 n.
spurious
 spurious 542 adj.
spurn
 kick 279 vb.
 reject 607 vb.
 despise 922 vb.
spur of the moment
 spontaneity 609 n.
spurt
 spurt 277 n.
 activity 678 n.
spurt, spirt

flow out 298 vb.
flow 350 vb.
sputnik
 satellite 321 n.
sputter
 sibilation 406 n.
 be dim 419 vb.
 stammer 580 vb.
sputum
 excrement 302 n.
spy
 scan, see 438 vb.
 watch 441 vb.
 inquisitive person
 453 n.
 detective 459 n.
 informer 524 n.
spyglass
 telescope 442 n.
squabble
 bicker 709 vb.
squad
 band 74 n.
 personnel 686 n.
squadron
 formation 722 n.
squalid
 unclean 649 adj.
 beggarly 801 adj.
 disreputable
 867 adj.
squall
 storm 176 n.
 commotion 318 n.
 gale 352 n.
 cry 408 vb.
squalor
 uncleanness 649 n.
squander
 waste 634 vb.
 misuse 675 vb.
 be prodigal 815 vb.
square
 make conform
 83 vb.
 quadruple 97 vb.
 housing 192 n.
 angular figure
 247 n.
 bribe 612 vb.
 bad taste 847 n.
 honourable 929 adj.
—accounts (with)
 pay 804 vb.
 avenge 910 vb.
—with
 accord 24 vb.

square deal
  justice 913 n.
square peg in a round hole
  misfit 25 n.
square root
  numerical element 85 n.
squash
  crowd 74 n.
  suppress 165 vb.
  flatten 216 vb.
  soft drink 301 n.
  confute 479 vb.
  humiliate 872 vb.
squashy
  soft 327 adj.
  pulpy 356 adj.
squat
  place oneself 187 vb.
  quarters 192 n.
  short 204 adj.
  low 210 adj.
  encroach 306 vb.
  sit down 311 vb.
squatter
  intruder 59 n.
  resident 191 n.
  usurper 916 n.
squaw
  spouse 894 n.
squawk
  ululation 409 n.
squeak
  faintness 401 n.
  stridor 407 n.
squeal
  shrill 407 vb.
  ululate 409 vb.
  inform 524 vb.
  deprecate 762 vb.
squealer
  informer 524 n.
squeamish
  disliking 861 adj.
  fastidious 862 adj.
squeeze
  crowd 74 n.
  make smaller 198 vb.
  restriction 747 n.
  endearment 889 n.
  —out/from
  extract 304 vb.
  —in
  fill 54 vb.

stow 187 vb.
—through
  pass 305 vb.
squelch
  be wet 341 vb.
squelchy
  marshy 347 adj.
squib
  bang 402 n.
  satire 851 n.
squidgy
  semiliquid 354 adj.
squiggle
  coil 251 n.
  lettering 586 n.
squint
  obliquity 220 n.
  window 263 n.
  be dim-sighted 440 vb.
squire
  accompany 89 vb.
  retainer 742 n.
  aristocrat 868 n.
  court 889 n.
squirearchy
  aristocracy 868 n.
squirm
  wriggle 251 vb.
  be agitated 318 vb.
  feel pain 377 vb.
  suffer 825 vb.
squirt
  small quantity 33 n.
  emit 300 vb.
  nonentity 639 n.
squishy
  semiliquid 354 adj.
stab
  pierce 263 vb.
  pang 377 n.
  wound 655 n.vb.
stability
  equilibrium 28 n.
  stability 153 n.
stabilize
  stabilize 153 vb.
stab in the back
  foul play 930 n.
stable
  group 74 n.
  fixed 153 adj.
  stable 192 n.
  inexcitable 823 adj.
  (*see* **stability**)
staccato
  adagio 412 adv.

stack
  bring together 74 n.
  store 632 n.vb.
stacked
  predetermined 608 adj.
stadium
  arena 724 n.
staff
  prop 218 n.
  personnel 686 n.
  director 690 n.
  army officer 741 n.
  domestic 742 n.
stag
  male animal 372 n.
  gambler 618 n.
stage
  juncture 8 n.
  degree 27 n.
  situation 186 n.
  stand 218 n.
  show 522 vb.
  rostrum 539 n.
  theatre 594 n.
  dramatize 594 vb.
  arena 724 n.
stagecraft
  dramaturgy 594 n.
stagehand
  stagehand 594 n.
stage-manage
  cause 156 vb.
stage manager
  stage manager 594 n.
stagestruck
  dramatic 594 adj.
stagger
  move slowly 278 vb.
  tumble 309 vb.
  fluctuation 317 n.
  surprise 508 vb.
  impress 821 vb.
staging
  frame 218 n.
  dramaturgy 594 n.
stagnant
  inert 175 adj.
  insalubrious 653 adj.
stagnation
  quiescence 266 n.
  inaction 677 n.
stag party
  male 372 n.

stagy
  dramatic 594 adj.
  affected 850 adj.
  showy 875 adj.
staid
  inexcitable 823 adj.
  serious 834 adj.
stain
  tincture 43 n.
  pigment 425 n.
  mark 547 n.
  blemish 845 n.vb.
  slur 867 n.
stained glass
  ornamental art 844 n.
stainless
  clean 648 adj.
  virtuous 933 adj.
stairs
  ascent 308 n.
stake
  pillar 218 n.
  gambling 618 n.
  endanger 661 vb.
  security 767 n.
  —out
  limit 236 vb.
stake, the
  means of execution 964 n.
stakeholder
  consignee 754 n.
stakes
  contest 716 n.
stale
  antiquated 127 adj.
  unsavoury 391 adj.
  deteriorated 655 adj.
  fatigued 684 adj.
  tedious 838 adj.
stalemate
  draw 28 n.
  stop 145 n.
  obstacle 702 n.
stalk
  prop 218 n.
  walk 267 vb.
  foliage 366 n.
  hunt 619 vb.
stalking horse
  pretext 614 n.
  stratagem 698 n.
stall
  put off 136 vb.
  halt 145 vb.

stable 192 n.
seat 218 n.
be equivocal 518 vb.
shop 796 vb.
stallion
horse 273 n.
stalls
playgoer 594 n.
stalwart
stalwart 162 adj.
stamina
stamina 600 n.
stammer
stammer 580 vb.
stamp
mould 23 n.
sort 77 n.
form 243 n.vb.
make concave
255 vb.
knock 279 n.
endorse 488 vb.
label 547 n.
gesticulate 547 vb.
be angry 891 vb.
applaud 923 vb.
—on
suppress 165 vb.
be severe 735 vb.
—out
suppress 165 vb.
extinguish 382 vb.
stamp collector
enthusiast 504 n.
stampede
move fast 277 n.
frighten 854 vb.
stamping ground
home 192 n.
stance
form 243 n.
stand
be in a state of 7 vb.
be situated 186 vb.
place 187 vb.
be vertical 215 vb.
stand 218 n.
resistance 715 n.
arena 724 n.
offer oneself 759 vb.
expend 806 vb.
be patient 823 vb.
—by
be present 189 vb.
prepare oneself
669 vb.
aid 703 vb.

keep faith 768 vb.
—down
resign 753 vb.
—for
be 1 vb.
substitute 150 vb.
mean 514 vb.
represent 551 vb.
be patient 823 vb.
—off
make inactive
679 vb.
—out
be visible 443 vb.
—out against
resist 715 vb.
—still
be quiescent 266 vb.
—to reason
be reasonable
475 vb.
—up and be counted
be courageous
855 vb.
—up for
patronize 703 vb.
—up to
withstand 704 vb.
defy 711 vb.
standard
uniform 16 adj.
prototype 23 n.
degree 27 n.
median 30 adj.
general 79 adj.
typical 83 adj.
flag 547 n.
standardize
regularize 62 vb.
make conform
83 vb.
standards
morals 917 n.
standby
aider 703 n.
stand-in
substitute 150 n.
deputy 755 n.
standing
state 7 n.
serial place 73 n.
vertical 215 adj.
prestige 866 n.
standoffish
prideful 871 adj.
unsociable 883 adj.
standpipe

conduit 351 n.
standpoint
situation 186 n.
view 438 n.
standstill
lull 145 n.
stop 145 n.
stanza
verse form 593 n.
staple
fastening 47 n.
fibre 208 n.
sharp point 256 n.
texture 331 n.
important 638 adj.
merchandise 795 n.
star
divergence 294 n.
star 321 n.
luminary 420 n.
actor 594 n.
exceller 644 n.
badge of rank 743 n.
favourite 890 n.
starboard
dextrality 241 n.
starch
harden 326 vb.
clean 648 vb.
starchy
rigid 326 adj.
formal 875 adj.
star-crossed
unfortunate 731 adj.
stardom
famousness 866 n.
stare
gaze 438 vb.
wonder 864 vb.
stargazer
astronomy 321 n.
stark
wintry 129 adj.
uncovered 229 adj.
plain 573 adj.
starless
unlit 418 adj.
starlight
glimmer 419 n.
starry-eyed
happy 824 adj.
hoping 852 adj.
stars
influence 178 n.
fate 596 n.
start
advantage 34 n.

start 68 n.
departure 296 n.
agitation 318 n.
—up
initiate 68 vb.
starter
hors-d'oeuvres
301 n.
contender 716 n.
starting point
start 68 n.
departure 296 n.
startle
surprise 508 vb.
frighten 854 vb.
starvation
fasting 946 n.
starve
make thin 206 vb.
be hungry 859 vb.
starve 946 vb.
stasis
stop 145 n.
inertness 175 n.
state
state 7 n.
situation 186 n.
affirm 532 vb.
political
organization
733 n.
affections 817 n.
formality 875 n.
statecraft
management 689 n.
statehood
nation 371 n.
independence
744 n.
stateless person
outcast 883 n.
stately
impressive 821 adj.
proud 871 adj.
formal 875 adj.
statement
list 87 n.
topic 452 n.
report 524 n.
affirmation 532 n.
accounts 808 n.
state of affairs
circumstance 8 n.
affairs 154 n.
state of grace
innocence 935 n.
sanctity 979 n.

state of mind
  affections 817 n.
state ownership
  joint possession
  775 n.
statesman,
  stateswoman
  sage 500 n.
  manager 690 n.
statesmanship
  sagacity 498 n.
  tactics 688 n.
static
  electricity 160 n.
  quiescent 266 adj.
station
  serial place 73 n.
  stopping place
  145 n.
  station 187 n.
  railway 624 n.
  nobility 868 n.
stationary
  quiescent 266 adj.
stationery
  stationery 586 n.
statism
  despotism 733 n.
statistical
  statistical 86 adj.
statistician
  enumerator 86 n.
statistics
  statistics 86 n.
statuary
  sculpture 554 n.
statue
  image 551 n.
  sculpture 554 n.
  honours 866 n.
statuesque
  tall 209 adj.
  beautiful 841 adj.
stature
  height 209 n.
status
  state 7 n.
  circumstance 8 n.
  prestige 866 n.
status quo
  permanence 144 n.
statute
  legislation 953 n.
statutory
  preceptive 693 adj.
  legal 953 adj.
staunch

staunch 350 vb.
resolute 599 adj.
trustworthy 929 adj.
stave
  notation 410 n.
  verse form 593 n.
  club 723 n.
stave in
  make concave
  255 vb.
  pierce 263 vb.
—off
  parry 713 vb.
stay
  tackling 47 n.
  delay 136 n.
  stay 144 vb.
  cease 145 vb.
  dwell 192 vb.
  prop 218 n.
  be quiescent 266 vb.
  visit 882 vb.
—away
  be absent 190 vb.
—put
  be quiescent 266 vb.
  be obstinate 602 vb.
stay-at-home
  quiescent 266 adj.
  solitary 883 n.
staying power
  stamina 600 n.
steadfast
  fixed 153 adj.
  obedient 739 adj.
steady
  uniform 16 adj.
  regular 81 adj.
  fixed 153 adj.
  support 218 vb.
  still 266 adj.
  persevering 600 adj.
  impassive 820 adj.
steak
  meat 301 n.
steal
  be stealthy 525 vb.
  steal 788 vb.
—a march on
  be early 135 vb.
—away
  escape 667 vb.
—upon
  surprise 508 vb.
stealth
  cunning 698 n.
stealthy

stealthy 525 adj.
cunning 698 adj.
steam
  energy 160 n.
  be in motion 265 vb.
  propellant 287 n.
  emit 300 vb.
  cook 301 vb.
  vaporize 338 vb.
  cloud 355 n.
steam engine
  locomotive 274 n.
steamer
  ship 275 n.
steamroller
  demolish 165 vb.
  locomotive 274 n.
  compel 740 vb.
steamy
  vaporific 338 adj.
  heated 381 adj.
steed
  horse 273 n.
steel
  strengthen 162 vb.
  sharp edge 256 n.
  hardness 326 n.
—oneself
  be resolute 599 vb.
steely
  hard 326 adj.
  grey 429 adj.
  cruel 898 adj.
steep
  high 209 adj.
  deep 211 adj.
  vertical 215 adj.
  sloping 220 adj.
  drench 341 vb.
  difficult 700 adj.
steeple
  high structure 209 n.
steeplechase
  racing 716 n.
steeplejack
  climber 308 n.
steer
  cattle 365 n.
  direct 689 vb.
—clear of
  deviate 282 vb.
steerage
  directorship 689 n.
steering committee
  consignee 754 n.
steersman
  navigator 270 n.

stellar
  celestial 321 adj.
stem
  staunch 350 vb.
  foliage 366 n.
  withstand 704 vb.
stench
  stench 397 n.
stencil
  mould 23 n.
  paint 553 vb.
stenographer
  stenographer 586 n.
stentorian
  loud 400 adj.
step
  degree 27 n.
  short distance
  200 n.
  stand 218 n.
  walk 267 vb.
—in
  mediate 720 vb.
—into the shoes of
  come after 65 vb.
—up
  augment 36 vb.
  invigorate 174 vb.
stepbrother,
  stepsister
  kinsman 11 n.
step by step
  by degrees 27 adv.
steppe
  horizontality
  216 n.
  plain 348 n.
stepping-stone
  degree 27 n.
  bridge 624 n.
steps
  series 71 n.
  ascent 308 n.
  policy 623 n.
  action 676 n.
stereo
  gramophone 414 n.
stereophonic
  sounding 398 adj.
stereoscope
  optical device 442 n.
stereoscopic
  seeing 438 adj.
stereotype
  make uniform
  16 vb.
  print 587 vb.

sterile
unproductive
172 adj.
profitless 641 adj.
salubrious 652 adj.

sterility
impotence 161 n.

sterilization
impotence 161 n.
hygiene 652 n.

sterling
genuine 494 adj.
monetary 797 adj.
virtuous 933 adj.

stern
buttocks 238 n.
poop 238 n.
serious 834 adj.
unkind 898 adj.

steroid
drug 658 n.

stertorous
puffing 352 adj.

stethoscope
hearing aid 415 n.

stevedore
bearer 273 n.

stew
a mixture 43 n.
dish 301 n.
cook 301 vb.
mature 669 vb.
predicament 700 n.
excitable state 822 n.

steward, stewardess
provider 633 n.
manager 690 n.
domestic 742 n.
treasurer 798 n.

stewardship
management 689 n.

stick
cohere 48 vb.
halt 145 vb.
prop 218 n.
pierce 263 vb.
club 723 n.
scourge 964 n.
—**at nothing**
be resolute 599 vb.
—**fast**
stand firm 599 vb.
—**in a rut/groove**
be wont 610 vb.
—**in one's throat**
cause dislike 861 vb.
—**it out**

persevere 600 vb.
—**on**
affix 45 vb.
—**one's neck out**
face danger 661 vb.
be rash 857 vb.
—**out**
jut 254 vb.
be visible 443 vb.
—**to one's guns**
persevere 600 vb.
—**up**
be vertical 215 vb.
—**up for**
patronize 703 vb.

sticker
label 547 n.

sticking plaster
substitute 150 n.
surgical dressing
658 n.

stick-in-the-mud
permanence 144 n.
obstinate person
602 n.

stickler
perfectionist 862 n.

sticky
cohesive 48 adj.
viscid 354 adj.
difficult 700 adj.

stiff
rigid 326 adj.
corpse 363 n.
obstinate 602 adj.
fatigued 684 adj.
clumsy 695 adj.
severe 735 adj.
restraining 747 adj.
formal 875 adj.
unsociable 883 adj.

stiffen
harden 326 vb.
make inactive
679 vb.

stiffener
prop 218 n.

stiff-necked
obstinate 602 adj.
proud 871 adj.

stiff upper lip
resolution 599 n.

stifle
suppress 165 vb.
kill 362 vb.
be hot 379 vb.
extinguish 382 vb.

conceal 525 vb.
make mute 578 vb.
prohibit 757 vb.

stigma
slur 867 n.

stigmatize
mark 547 vb.
defame 926 vb.

stile
access 624 n.
obstacle 702 n.

stiletto
sharp point 256 n.
sidearms 723 n.

still
assuage 177 vb.
still 266 adj.
heater 383 n.
silent 399 adj.
inactive 679 adj.

stillborn
dead 361 adj.
unsuccessful
728 adj.

still life
art subject 553 n.

stillroom
storage 632 n.

stilted
ornate 574 adj.
affected 850 adj.

stilts
stand 218 n.
lifter 310 n.

stimulant
stimulant 174 n.
incentive 612 n.
drug 658 n.
excitant 821 n.

stimulate
invigorate 174 vb.
incite 612 vb.
animate 821 vb.

stimulus
stimulant 174 n.

sting
pang 377 n.
pungency 388 n.
wound 655 vb.
overcharge 811 vb.
torment 827 vb.

stingy
insufficient 636 adj.
parsimonious
816 adj.

stink
stink 397 vb.

stinker
cad 938 n.

stint
finite quantity 26 n.
period 110 n.
make insufficient
636 vb.
labour 682 n.
be parsimonious
816 vb.

stipend
subvention 703 n.

stipendiary
receiving 782 adj.

stipple
variegate 437 vb.

stipulation
requirement 627 n.
conditions 766 n.

stir
mix 43 vb.
commotion 318 n.
activity 678 n.
excite 821 vb.

stirrer
troublemaker 663 n.

stirring
eventful 154 adj.
exciting 821 adj.

stitch
pang 377 n.
needlework 844 n.

stochastic
casual 159 adj.

stock
race 11 n.
typical 83 adj.
genealogy 169 n.
animal 365 n.
sauce 389 n.
usual 610 adj.
store 632 n.
merchandise 795 n.

stockade
enclosure 235 n.
defences 713 n.

stock-breeding
animal husbandry
369 n.

stockbroker
merchant 794 n.

stock exchange
market 796 n.

stockholder
participator 775 n.

stocking(s)
legwear 228 n.

stock-in-trade
equipment 630 n.
merchandise 795 n.
stockman
herdsman 369 n.
stockpile
store 632 n.vb.
stockroom
storage 632 n.
stocks
pillory 964 n.
stocks and shares
estate 777 n.
stocky
stalwart 162 adj.
short 204 adj.
stodgy
semiliquid 354 adj.
tedious 838 adj.
stoical, stoic
impassive 820 adj.
stoicism
philosophy 449 n.
inexcitability 823 n.
stoke
fire 385 vb.
stole
neckwear 228 n.
vestments 989 n.
stolid
unintelligent
499 n.
impassive 820 adj.
stomach
maw 194 n.
be patient 823 vb.
stomachache
digestive disorders
651 n.
stone
missile 287 n.
hardness 326 n.
building material
631 n.
lapidate 712 vb.
gem 844 n.
Stone Age
era 110 n.
stoned
dead drunk 949 adj.
drugged 949 adj.
stone's throw
short distance 200 n.
stonewall
be obstructive
702 vb.
stonework

structure 331 n.
stony
unproductive
172 adj.
rough 259 adj.
territorial 344 adj.
impassive 820 adj.
pitiless 906 adj.
stooge
dupe 544 n.
laughingstock
851 n.
stool
seat 218 n.
excrement 302 n.
stoolpigeon
informer 524 n.
stoop
stoop 311 vb.
be humble 872 vb.
—to
demean oneself
867 vb.
stop
end 69 n.vb.
stop 145 n.
punctuation 547 n.
repair 656 vb.
obstruct 702 vb.
restrain 747 vb.
prohibit 757 vb.
—a leak
staunch 350 vb.
stopgap
substitute 150 n.
stop-go
discontinuous
72 adj.
stopover
goal 295 n.
stoppage
strike 145 n.
hitch 702 n.
stopper
stopper 264 n.
stopwatch
timekeeper 117 n.
storage
storage 632 n.
store
great quantity 32 n.
accumulation 74 n.
store 632 n.vb.
shop 796 n.
storehouse
storage 632 n.
storekeeper

provider 633 n.
tradespeople 794 n.
storeroom
storage 632 n.
stores
provisions 301 n.
provision 633 n.
storey
compartment 194 n.
layer 207 n.
storm
turmoil 61 n.
storm 176 n.
commotion 318 n.
gale 352 n.
overmaster 727 vb.
take 786 vb.
be angry 891 vb.
storm in a teacup
trifle 639 n.
storm troops
attacker 712 n.
stormy
violent 176 adj.
windy 352 adj.
story
fable 543 n.
narrative 590 n.
story-teller
liar 545 n.
narrator 590 n.
stout
stalwart 162 adj.
fleshy 195 adj.
alcoholic drink
301 n.
courageous 855 adj.
stove
furnace 383 n.
stow
stow 187 vb.
—away
conceal 525 vb.
stowage
room 183 n.
storage 632 n.
stowaway
intruder 59 n.
hider 527 n.
straddle
be broad 205 vb.
overlie 226 vb.
strafe
bombardment
712 n.
reprobate 924 vb.
straggle

provider 633 n.
be dispersed 75 vb.
stray 282 vb.
straggling
orderless 61 adj.
straight
orderly 60 adj.
continuous 71 adj.
straight 249 adj.
honourable 929 adj.
straighten
straighten 249 vb.
—out
regularize 62 vb.
straight face
seriousness 834 n.
straightforward
veracious 540 adj.
trustworthy
929 adj.
straight from the
shoulder
vigorously 174 adv.
straight man
laughingstock
851 n.
strain
race 11 n.
breed 77 n.
weaken 163 vb.
force 176 vb.
distortion 246 n.
traction 288 n.
pain 377 n.
sound 398 n.
style 566 n.
purify 648 vb.
exertion 682 n.
fatigue 684 n.vb.
worry 825 n.
strainer
sorting 62 n.
porosity 263 n.
strains
poem 593 n.
strait(s)
narrowness 206 n.
gulf 345 n.
predicament 700 n.
straitjacket
compressor 198 n.
fetter 748 n.
straitlaced
prudish 950 adj.
strand
fibre 208 n.
hair 259 n.
shore 344 n.

stranded
 grounded 728 adj.
strange
 unusual 84 adj.
 puzzling 517 adj.
 wonderful 864 adj.
strange behaviour
 eccentricity 503 n.
stranger
 foreigner 59 n.
strangle
 suppress 165 vb.
 kill 362 vb.
stranglehold
 retention 778 n.
strangulation
 compression 198 n.
strap
 tie 45 vb.
strapping
 stalwart 162 adj.
stratagem
 stratagem 698 n.
strategic, strategical
 planned 623 adj.
 cunning 698 adj.
 warlike 718 adj.
strategist
 planner 623 n.
 slyboots 698 n.
strategy
 policy 623 n.
 tactics 688 n.
 art of war 718 n.
stratification
 stratification 207 n.
stratosphere
 atmosphere 340 n.
stratum
 layer 207 n.
straw
 insubstantial thing
  4 n.
 trifle 639 n.
straw-coloured
 yellow 433 adj.
straw in the wind
 indication 547 n.
straw poll
 inquiry 459 n.
stray
 be dispersed 75 vb.
 wanderer 268 n.
 stray 282 vb.
 err 495 vb.
 derelict 779 n.
streak

tincture 43 n.
 line 203 n.
 move fast 277 vb.
 flash 417 n.
 stripe 437 n.
streaker
 stripper 229 n.
stream
 classification 77 n.
 hang 217 vb.
 stream 350 n.
 flow 350 vb.
 class 538 n.
streamer
 flag 547 n.
 trimming 844 n.
streaming
 nonadhesive 49 adj.
 hanging 217 adj.
streamline
 smooth 258 vb.
 rectify 654 vb.
street
 housing 192 n.
 road 624 n.
street furniture
 traffic control 305 n.
streetwalker
 prostitute 952 n.
strength
 strength 162 n.
 stamina 600 n.
strengthen
 strengthen 162 vb.
 corroborate 466 vb.
strength of character
 resolution 599 n.
strenuous
 vigorous 174 adj.
 labouring 682 adj.
stress
 distortion 246 n.
 emphasize 532 vb.
 pronunciation
  577 n.
 prosody 593 n.
 difficulty 700 n.
stretch
 period 110 n.
 range 183 n.
 lengthen 203 vb.
 overstep 306 vb.
 elasticity 328 n.
 exaggerate 546 vb.
—a point
 be lenient 736 vb.
 compromise 770 vb.

stretchable
 elastic 328 adj.
stretched out
 supine 216 adj.
stretcher
 bed 218 n.
stretcher case
 sick person 651 n.
strew
 disperse 75 vb.
striation
 stripe 437 n.
stricken
 suffering 825 adj.
strict
 severe 735 adj.
 orthodox 976 adj.
stricture
 reprimand 924 n.
stride
 gait 265 n.
 walk 267 vb.
strident
 strident 407 adj.
 vocal 577 adj.
strife
 quarrel 709 n.
 contention 716 n.
strike
 strike 145 n.
 cease 145 vb.
 strike 279 vb.
 discover 484 vb.
 impress 821 vb.
—a balance
 average out 30 vb.
—a blow for
 do 676 vb.
—a pose
 be affected 850 vb.
—at
 strike at 712 vb.
—dumb
 be wonderful
  864 vb.
—off
 exclude 57 vb.
 eject 300 vb.
—one
 dawn upon 449 vb.
 attract notice
  455 vb.
—out
 obliterate 550 vb.
—root
 place oneself
  187 vb.

—up
 play music 413 vb.
strike force
 attacker 712 n.
striker
 revolter 738 n.
striking
 impressive 821 adj.
 wonderful 864 adj.
string
 cable 47 n.
 series 71 n.
 band 74 n.
—along
 befool 542 vb.
—along with
 accompany 89 vb.
—out
 disperse 75 vb.
 lengthen 203 vb.
—together
 connect 45 vb.
string course
 layer 207 n.
stringency
 severity 735 n.
strings
 influence 178 n.
 orchestra 413 n.
 musical instrument
  414 n.
 conditions 766 n.
stringy
 fibrous 208 adj.
 tough 329 adj.
strip
 line 203 n.
 lamina 207 n.
 strip 208 n.
 uncover 229 vb.
 clean 648 vb.
 deprive 786 vb.
stripe
 stripe 437 n.
 badge of rank 743 n.
 pattern 844 n.
stripling
 youngster 132 n.
stripper
 stripper 229 n.
strip show
 stage show 594 n.
strive
 exert oneself 682 vb.
 contend 716 vb.
stroboscope
 optical device 442 n.

stroke
instant 116 n.
row 269 vb.
knock 279 n.
spasm 318 n.
touch 378 n.vb.
punctuation 547 n.
lettering 586 n.
*cardiovascular
disease* 651 n.
deed 676 n.
caress 889 vb.

stroll
move slowly 278 vb.

stroller
wanderer 268 n.

strong
strong 162 adj.
vigorous 174 adj.
violent 176 adj.
pungent 388 adj.
florid 425 adj.
assertive 532 adj.
forceful 571 adj.
healthy 650 adj.
invulnerable
660 adj.
fervent 818 adj.
intoxicating 949 adj.

strong-arm tactics
violence 176 n.
compulsion 740 n.

strongbox
treasury 799 n.

stronghold
fort 713 n.

strong language
scurrility 899 n.

strongly worded
forceful 571 adj.
disapproving
924 adj.

strong man
athlete 162 n.

strong-minded
resolute 599 adj.

strong point
skill 694 n.

strongroom
treasury 799 n.

strop
sharpener 256 n.

strophe
verse form 593 n.

stroppy
irascible 892 adj.

struck dumb

wondering 864 adj.

structural
intrinsic 5 adj.
supporting 218 adj.
structural 331 adj.

structuralism
interpretation 520 n.

structure
composition 56 n.
edifice 164 n.
structure 331 n.

struggle
be violent 176 vb.
exert oneself 682 vb.
be in difficulty
700 vb.
contest 716 n.

—against
resist 715 vb.

strum
play music 413 vb.

strung out
unassembled 75 adj.

strung up
excited 821 adj.

strut
prop 218 n.
walk 267 vb.
be proud 871 vb.

stub
remainder 41 n.
label 547 n.

stubble
leavings 41 n.
roughness 259 n.
grass 366 n.

stubborn
unyielding 162 adj.
obstinate 602 adj.

stubby
thick 205 adj.
unsharpened
257 adj.

stub one's toe
collide 279 vb.

—out
extinguish 382 vb.

stucco
facing 226 n.

stuck
firm 45 adj.

stuck fast
retained 778 adj.

stuck-up
prideful 871 adj.

stud
fastening 47 n.

stock farm 369 n.
variegate 437 vb.

student
scholar 492 n.
student 538 n.

studied
intended 617 adj.
affected 850 adj.

studio
art equipment 553 n.
workshop 687 n.

studious
studious 536 adj.

study
musical piece 412 n.
scan 438 vb.
meditation 449 n.
be attentive 455 vb.
study 536 n.vb.
picture 553 n.
dissertation 591 n.
workshop 687 n.

stuff
essential part 5 n.
fill 54 vb.
textile 222 n.
line 227 vb.
matter 319 n.
texture 331 n.
rubbish 641 n.
preserve 666 vb.
merchandise 795 n.

—oneself
gluttonize 947 vb.

stuff and nonsense
absurdity 497 n.
silly talk 515 n.

stuffed shirt
vain person 873 n.

stuffing
contents 193 n.
lining 227 n.

stuffy
sealed off 264 adj.
warm 379 adj.
dull 840 adj.

stumble
tumble 309 vb.
blunder 495 vb.

—on
discover 484 vb.

stumbling block
obstacle 702 n.

stump
remainder 41 n.
projection 254 n.
move slowly 278 vb.

puzzle 474 vb.

stumps
leg 267 n.

stumpy
short 204 adj.

stun
render insensible
375 vb.
deafen 416 vb.
surprise 508 vb.
be wonderful
864 vb.

stung
excited 821 adj.
angry 891 adj.

stunning
super 644 adj.

stunt
shorten 204 vb.
fly 271 vb.
deed 676 n.
pageant 875 n.

stunted
dwarfish 196 adj.

stunt man/woman
athlete 162 n.

stupefy
render insensible
375 vb.
impress 821 vb.

stupendous
wonderful 864 adj.

stupid
unintelligent
499 adj.

stupor
insensibility 375 n.
sluggishness 679 n.

sturdy
stalwart 162 adj.

stutter
speech defect
580 n.

sty
stable 192 n.
swelling 253 n.

Stygian
dark 418 adj.
infernal 972 adj.

style
modality 7 n.
sort 77 n.
name 561 n.vb.
style 566 n.
elegance 575 n.
way 624 n.
fashion 848 n.

styling
hairdressing 843 n.

stylish
elegant 575 adj.
fashionable 848 adj.

stylized
formed 243 adj.

stylus
gramophone 414 n.
stationery 586 n.

stymie
be obstructive
702 vb.

suave
courteous 884 adj.

sub-
inferior 35 adj.

sub
substitute 150 n.

subaltern
army officer 741 n.

subaqua
sport 837 n.

subaudition
interpretation 520 n.

subconscious
spirit 447 n.
intuitive 476 adj.

subdivide
sunder 46 vb.

subdue
overmaster 727 vb.
restrain 747 vb.

subdued
muted 401 adj.
dejected 834 adj.

subedit
publish 528 vb.

subeditor
author 589 n.

subgroup
subdivision 53 n.

subhead
classification 77 n.

subhuman
animal 365 adj.

subject
prototype 23 n.
liable 180 adj.
topic 452 n.
testee 461 n.
subject 742 n.
subject 745 adj.
subjugate 745 vb.

subjection
subjection 745 n.

subjective

intrinsic 5 adj.
mental 447 adj.

subjectivity
subjectivity 320 n.

subject matter
topic 452 n.

subjoin
add 38 vb.

subjugate
subjugate 745 vb.

sublet
lease 784 vb.

subtlety
discrimination
463 n.
fastidiousness
862 n.

sublimate
vaporize 338 vb.
purify 648 vb.

sublime
great 32 adj.
high 209 adj.
impressive 821 adj.
splendid 841 adj.
divine 965 adj.

subliminal
psychic 447 adj.

sublimity
beauty 841 n.
(*see* **sublime**)

submarine
deep 211 adj.
warship 722 n.

submerge
plunge 313 vb.
obliterate 550 vb.

submerged
deep 211 adj.
latent 523 adj.

submission
argument 475 n.
submission 721 n.
resignation 753 n.
entreaty 761 n.
humility 872 n.

submissive
weak 163 adj.
tractable 701 adj.

submit
acquiesce 488 vb.
propound 512 vb.
submit 721 vb.
(*see* **submission**)

subnormal
unintelligent
499 adj.

subordinate
inferior 35 n.adj.
dependant 742 n.
subject 745 adj.

suborn
bribe 612 vb.

subpoena
legal process 959 n.

subscribe
sign 547 vb.
contract 765 vb.

—to
patronize 703 vb.

subscriber
assenter 488 n.
signatory 765 n.
giver 781 n.

subscription
payment 804 n.

subsection
classification 77 n.

subsequent
subsequent 120 adj.

subserve
be instrumental
628 vb.

subservient
aiding 703 adj.
servile 879 adj.

subside
decrease 37 vb.

subsidence
descent 309 n.

subsidiary
inferior 35 n.
additional 38 adj.
unimportant
639 adj.
aiding 703 adj.

subsidize
aid 703 vb.

subsidy
subvention 703 n.

subsist
be 1 vb.
live 360 vb.

subsistence farming
agriculture 370 n.
sufficiency 635 n.

subsoil
soil 344 n.

subspecies
breed 77 n.

substance
substance 3 n.
main part 32 n.
matter 319 n.

meaning 514 n.
chief thing 638 n.
wealth 800 n.

substandard
inferior 35 adj.

substantial
substantial 3 adj.
great 32 adj.

substantiate
demonstrate 478 vb.

substantive
part of speech 564 n.

substitute
substitute 150 n.vb.
deputy 755 n.

substratum
base 214 n.

substructure
base 214 n.

subsume
class 62 vb.

subteenage
young 130 adj.

subterfuge
pretext 614 n.
stratagem 698 n.

subterranean
deep 211 adj.
concealed 525 adj.

subtle
intelligent 498 adj.
cunning 698 adj.

subtlety
sophistry 477 n.
sagacity 498 n.

subtract
subtract 39 vb.

subtraction
numerical operation
86 n.

suburb(s)
district 184 n.
housing 192 n.
surroundings 230 n.

suburban
regional 184 adj.
urban 192 adj.

subvention
subvention 703 n.

subversion
revolt 738 n.

subversive
revolutionary
149 adj.

subvert
revolutionize
149 vb.

SUB

subway
tunnel 263 n.
railway 624 n.
succeed
come after 65 vb.
follow 284 vb.
succeed 727 vb.
prosper 730 vb.
—to
inherit 771 vb.
—to the throne
take authority
733 vb.
success
success 727 n.
famousness 866 n.
successful
completed 725 adj.
successful 727 adj.
successful person
prosperous person
730 n.
succession
sequence 65 n.
series 71 n.
posteriority 120 n.
successive
sequential 65 adj.
successor
successor 67 n.
succinct
concise 569 adj.
succour
aid 703 n.vb.
succulent
pulpy 356 adj.
plant 366 n.
savoury 390 adj.
succumb
be fatigued 684 vb.
knuckle under
721 vb.
such
such 7 adj.
suck
absorb 299 vb.
drink 301 vb.
extract 304 vb.
—dry
interrogate 459 vb.
fleece 786 vb.
—up to
be servile 879 vb.
sucker
young plant 132 n.
orifice 263 n.
dupe 544 n.

SUF

suckling
child 132 n.
sucrose
sweet thing 392 n.
suction
reception 299 n.
extraction 304 n.
sudden
instantaneous
116 adj.
unexpected 508 adj.
suds
bubble 355 n.
sue
litigate 959 vb.
—for
request 761 vb.
suede
skin 226 n.
suet
fat 357 n.
suffer
feel pain 377 vb.
permit 756 vb.
be patient 823 vb.
suffer 825 vb.
sufferance
leniency 736 n.
permission 756 n.
sufferer
sick person 651 n.
sufferer 825 n.
suffering
pain 377 n.
adversity 731 n.
painfulness 827 n.
suffice
suffice 635 vb.
sufficiency
sufficiency 635 n.
sufficient
sufficient 635 adj.
not bad 644 adj.
contenting 828 adj.
suffix
place after 65 vb.
suffocate
suppress 165 vb.
kill 362 vb.
suffragan
ecclesiarch 986 n.
suffrage
vote 605 n.
suffragette
agitator 738 n.
Sufi
pietist 979 n.

SUI

sugar
sweet thing 392 n.
darling 890 n.
flatter 925 vb.
—the pill
tempt 612 vb.
sugar daddy
lover 887 n.
sugary
sweet 392 adj.
pleasurable 826 adj.
suggest
propound 512 vb.
imply 523 vb.
indicate 547 vb.
advise 691 vb.
suggestible
irresolute 601 adj.
suggestion
similarity 18 n.
small quantity 33 n.
plan 623 n.
(see suggest)
suggestive
evidential 466 adj.
suppositional
512 adj.
descriptive 590 adj.
impure 951 adj.
suicidal
destructive 165 adj.
hopeless 853 adj.
rash 857 adj.
suicide
suicide 362 n.
suit
accord 24 vb.
sort 77 n.
suit 228 n.
request 761 n.
beautify 841 vb.
wooing 889 n.
litigation 959 n.
suitable
fit 24 vb.
advisable 642 adj.
suitcase
box 194 n.
suite
series 71 n.
flat 192 n.
follower 284 n.
musical piece 412 n.
suitor
petitioner 763 n.
lover 887 n.
litigant 959 n.

SUM

sulk
be sullen 893 vb.
sulky
discontented
829 adj.
sullen 893 adj.
sullen
discontented
829 adj.
ungracious 885 adj.
sullen 893 adj.
sully
make unclean
649 vb.
shame 867 vb.
sulphurous
fetid 397 adj.
Sultan, Sultana
sovereign 741 n.
sultry
warm 379 adj.
sum
add 38 vb.
whole 52 n.
numeration 86 n.
—up
estimate 480 vb.
be concise 569 vb.
try a case 959 vb.
summarize
abstract 592 vb.
summary
brief 114 adj.
compendium
592 n.
lawless 954 adj.
summer
summer 128 n.
summerhouse
arbour 194 n.
summit
summit 213 n.
conference 584 n.
summon
bring together
74 vb.
command 737 vb.
indict 928 vb.
—up
excite 821 vb.
summons
call 547 n.
legal process 959 n.
sump
sink 649 n.
sumptuary
monetary 797 adj.

sumptuous
ostentatious
875 adj.
sun
sun 321 n.
heat 381 vb.
luminary 420 n.
sunburnt
brown 430 adj.
sundae
dessert 301 n.
Sunday
holy day 988 n.
sunder
sunder 46 vb.
sundial
timekeeper 117 n.
sundries
merchandise 795 n.
sundry
many 104 adj.
sun hat
headgear 228 n.
sunken
concave 255 adj.
sunless
unlit 418 adj.
sunlight
light 417 n.
sunny
dry 342 adj.
warm 379 adj.
pleasurable 826 adj.
cheerful 833 adj.
sunrise
morning 128 n.
sunset
evening 129 n.
sunshade
screen 421 n.
sunshine
salubrity 652 n.
sunstroke
frenzy 503 n.
suntan
brownness 430 n.
sun trap
heater 383 n.
sup
eat 301 vb.
taste 386 vb.
super
super 644 adj.
superabound
be many 104 vb.
superabound
637 vb.

superabundance
plenty 635 n.
superannuated
antiquated 127 adj.
disused 674 adj.
superannuation
earnings 771 n.
superb
excellent 644 adj.
splendid 841 adj.
supercilious
prideful 871 adj.
despising 922 adj.
superego
spirit 447 n.
superficial
insubstantial 4 adj.
shallow 212 adj.
exterior 223 adj.
appearing 445 adj.
negligent 458 adj.
superfine
excellent 644 adj.
superfluity
great quantity 32 n.
extra 40 n.
superfluous
superfluous 637 adj.
superhuman
godlike 965 adj.
superimpose
add 38 vb.
cover 226 vb.
superintend
manage 689 vb.
superintendent
manager 690 n.
superior
superior 34 n.adj.
excellent 644 adj.
improved 654 adj.
master 741 n.
superiority
superiority 34 n.
seniority 131 n.
importance 638 n.
goodness 644 n.
contempt 922 n.
superlative
excellent 644 adj.
**superman,
   superwoman**
exceller 644 n.
paragon 646 n.
prodigy 864 n.
supermarket
shop 796 n.

supernatural
abnormal 84 adj.
divine 965 adj.
spooky 970 adj.
magical 983 adj.
paranormal
984 adj.
supernumerary
extra 40 n.
superpower
influence 178 n.
*political
   organization*
733 n.
superscription
label 547 n.
supersede
substitute 150 vb.
eject 300 vb.
depose 752 vb.
not retain 779 vb.
superseded
disused 674 adj.
supersonic
aviational 276 adj.
speedy 277 adj.
superstition
credulity 487 n.
ignorance 491 n.
error 495 n.
superstitious
misjudging 481 adj.
superstore
shop 796 n.
superstructure
structure 331 n.
supervene
ensue 120 vb.
happen 154 vb.
supervise
manage 689 vb.
supervision
inspection 438 n.
supervisor
manager 690 n.
supine
supine 216 adj.
submitting 721 adj.
supper
meal 301 n.
supperless
hungry 859 adj.
supplant
substitute 150 vb.
eject 300 vb.
supple
flexible 327 adj.

dishonest 930 adj.
supplement
augment 36 vb.
adjunct 40 n.
make complete
54 vb.
sequel 67 n.
edition 589 n.
suppleness
softness 327 n.
cunning 698 n.
(*see* **supple**)
suppliant
petitioner 763 n.
supplication
entreaty 761 n.
prayers 981 n.
supplier
provider 633 n.
supplies
provision 633 n.
subvention 703 n.
supply
provide 633 vb.
support
sustain 146 vb.
strengthen 162 vb.
support 218 n.vb.
corroborate
466 vb.
endorse 488 vb.
choose 605 vb.
aid 703 n.
approve 923 vb.
supporter
onlookers 441 n.
patron 707 n.
supporting role
inferiority 35 n.
supportive
aiding 703 adj.
suppose
opine 485 vb.
not know 491 vb.
suppose 512 vb.
supposition
idea 451 n.
supposition 512 n.
suppositional
suppositional
512 adj.
suppress
suppress 165 vb.
counteract 182 vb.
conceal 525 vb.
overmaster 727 vb.
restrain 747 vb.

suppression
severity 735 n.
prohibition 757 n.
suppuration
infection 651 n.
supremacy
superiority 34 n.
authority 733 n.
supreme
supreme 34 adj.
powerful 160 adj.
perfect 646 adj.
surcharge
price 809 n.
sure
certain 473 adj.
expectant 507 adj.
safe 660 adj.
trustworthy 929 adj.
surefire
successful 727 adj.
surefooted
skilful 694 adj.
surety
security 767 n.
surf
wave 350 n.
surface
space 183 n.
shallow 212 adj.
exteriority 223 n.
emerge 298 vb.
texture 331 n.
be visible 443 vb.
surfeit
superfluity 637 n.
satiety 863 n.
surf riding
aquatics 269 n.
surge
increase 36 n.
current 350 n.
surgeon
doctor 658 n.
surgery
surgery 658 n.
surgical
medical 658 adj.
surly
ungracious 885 adj.
sullen 893 adj.
surmise
opine 485 vb.
conjecture 512 n.
surmount
be high 209 vb.
crown 213 vb.

climb 308 vb.
triumph 727 vb.
surname
name 561 n.
surpass
be superior 34 vb.
outdo 306 vb.
surplice
vestments 989 n.
surplus
extra 40 n.
superfluity 637 n.
surprise
surprise 508 vb.
surprising
unusual 84 adj.
unexpected 508 adj.
wonderful 864 adj.
surrealistic
representing
551 adj.
surrender
relinquish 621 vb.
submit 721 vb.
resign 753 vb.
surreptitious
stealthy 525 adj.
surrogate
deputy 755 n.
surround
surround 230 vb.
circumscribe
232 vb.
besiege 712 vb.
surroundings
locality 187 n.
surroundings 230 n.
surtax
tax 809 n.
surveillance
surveillance 457 n.
survey
inspection 438 n.
inquiry 459 n.
measure 465 vb.
estimate 480 n.vb.
dissertation 591 n.
surveyor
surveyor 465 n.
survival
existence 1 n.
life 360 n.
survive
outlast 113 vb.
stay 144 vb.
be restored 656 vb.
escape 667 vb.

survivor
survivor 41 n.
susceptibility
persuadability
612 n.
vulnerability 661 n.
love 887 n.
susceptible
liable 180 adj.
impressible 819 adj.
excitable 822 adj.
susceptive
impressible 819 adj.
suspect
be uncertain 474 vb.
opine 485 vb.
doubt 486 vb.
accused person
928 n.
suspend
put off 136 vb.
pause 145 vb.
hang 217 vb.
depose 752 vb.
punish 963 vb.
suspender
fastening 47 n.
suspense
expectation 507 n.
suspenseful
exciting 821 adj.
suspension
solution 337 n.
inaction 677 n.
penalty 963 n.
(see suspend)
suspicion
doubt 486 n.
conjecture 512 n.
suspicious
unbelieving 486 adj.
cautious 858 adj.
jealous 911 adj.
dishonest 930 adj.
sustain
sustain 146 vb.
support 218 vb.
feed 301 vb.
aid 703 vb.
sustenance
food 301 n.
suttee
burning 381 n.
suture
joint 45 n.
svelte
shapely 841 adj.

swab
cleaning utensil
648 n.
surgical dressing
658 n.
swaddle
tie 45 vb.
swag
booty 790 n.
pattern 844 n.
swagger
gait 265 n.
ostentation 875 n.
boasting 877 n.
swallow
absorb 299 vb.
mouthful 301 n.
eat 301 vb.
be credulous
487 vb.
swami
sage 500 n.
swamp
fill 54 vb.
drench 341 vb.
marsh 347 n.
swan around
be ostentatious
875 vb.
—off
decamp 296 vb.
swank
be affected 850 vb.
be vain 873 vb.
boaster 877 n.
swanky
fashionable
848 adj.
ostentatious
875 adj.
swansdown
smoothness 258 n.
swansong
end 69 n.
lament 836 n.
swap, swop
interchange
151 n.vb.
barter 791 n.
sward
grassland 348 n.
swarm
congregate 74 vb.
be many 104 vb.
be fruitful 171 vb.
swarthy
blackish 428 adj.

swashbuckler
combatant 722 n.
boaster 877 n.
swastika
cross 222 n.
talisman 983 n.
swat
strike 279 vb.
swath, swathe
trace 548 n.
swathe
tie 45 vb.
cover 226 vb.
sway
power 160 n.
influence 178 n.vb.
oscillate 317 vb.
be irresolute 601 vb.
motivate 612 vb.
governance 733 n.
swear
swear 532 vb.
promise 764 vb.
cuss 899 vb.
—by
believe 485 vb.
—off
relinquish 621 vb.
be temperate 942 vb.
—in
impose a duty
  917 vb.
—to
testify 466 vb.
swearword
scurrility 899 n.
sweat
exude 298 vb.
be hot 379 vb.
labour 682 n.
sweated labour
slave 742 n.
sweater, sweatshirt
jersey 228 n.
sweatshop
workshop 687 n.
sweep
range 183 n.
curvature 248 n.
traverse 267 vb.
touch 378 vb.
scan 438 vb.
clean 648 vb.
—along
move fast 277 vb.
—aside
confute 479 vb.

—under the carpet
conceal 525 vb.
sweeper
cleaner 648 n.
servant 742 n.
sweeping
comprehensive
  52 adj.
sweepstake
gambling 618 n.
sweet
dessert 301 n.
pleasant 376 adj.
sweet 392 adj.
melodious 410 adj.
pleasurable 826 adj.
lovable 887 adj.
sweeten
sweeten 392 vb.
sweetener
gift 781 n.
sweetheart
loved one 887 n.
darling 890 n.
sweet nothings
endearment 889 n.
sweet-scented
fragrant 396 adj.
sweet-talk
flatter 925 vb.
swell
expand 197 vb.
be convex 253 vb.
wave 350 n.
loudness 400 n.
super 644 adj.
fop 848 n.
—the ranks
join a party 708 vb.
swelled head
vanity 873 n.
swelling
swelling 253 n.
blemish 845 n.
swelling heart
feeling 818 n.
swelter
be hot 379 vb.
swerve
deviate 282 vb.
swift
speedy 277 adj.
swig
draught 301 n.
swill
drink 301 vb.
swill 649 n.

swim
swim 269 vb.
swimsuit
beachwear 228 n.
swindle
deceive 542 vb.
peculation 788 n.
be dishonest 930 vb.
swindler
defrauder 789 n.
swine
pig 365 n.
cad 938 n.
swing
periodicity 141 n.
reversion 148 n.
range 183 n.
hang 217 vb.
oscillate 317 vb.
music 412 n.
pleasure ground
  837 n.
swingeing
exorbitant 32 adj.
swinging
fashionable
  848 adj.
swings and
  roundabouts
offset 31 n.
swipe
strike 279 vb.
steal 788 vb.
swirl
rotate 315 vb.
flow 350 vb.
swish
sibilation 406 n.
fashionable 848 adj.
switch
revolution 149 n.
interchange 151 vb.
transpose 272 vb.
deflect 282 vb.
spank 963 vb.
—off
snuff out 418 vb.
—on
initiate 68 vb.
operate 173 vb.
—over
apostatize 603 vb.
switchback
undulatory 251 adj.
switchboard
telecommunication
  531 n.

swivel
pivot 218 n.
rotator 315 n.
swollen
expanded 197 adj.
convex 253 adj.
diseased 651 adj.
swollen-headed
vain 873 adj.
swoon
be insensible 375 vb.
swoop
descent 309 n.
swop
(see **swap**)
sword
destroyer 168 n.
sidearms 723 n.
swordplay
duel 716 n.
swordsman
contender 716 n.
swot
study 536 vb.
sybarite
sensualist 944 n.
sycophant
toady 879 n.
sycophantic
servile 879 adj.
flattering 925 adj.
syllabic
literal 558 adj.
syllable
speech sound 398 n.
word 559 n.
syllabus
compendium 592 n.
syllogism
argumentation
  475 n.
sylph
a beauty 841 n.
fairy 970 n.
sylvan, silvan
arboreal 366 adj.
symbiosis
cooperation 706 n.
symbol
metaphor 519 n.
indication 547 n.
image 551 n.
symbolic, symbolical
figurative 519 adj.
representing
  551 adj.
ritual 988 adj.

symbolism
  metaphor 519 n.
  (*see* **symbol,**
  symbolic)
symbolize
  mean 514 vb.
  represent 551 vb.
symmetrical
  correlative 12 adj.
  symmetrical
  245 adj.
symmetry
  order 60 n.
  symmetry 245 n.
sympathetic
  feeling 818 adj.
  pitying 905 adj.
sympathize
  feel 818 vb.
  (*see* **sympathy**)
sympathizer
  collaborator 707 n.
sympathy
  imagination 513 n.
  feeling 818 n.
  friendliness 880 n.
  condolence 905 n.
symphony
  musical piece 412 n.
symposium
  argument 475 n.
  conference 584 n.
symptom
  concomitant 89 n.
  evidence 466 n.
  indication 547 n.
  illness 651 n.
symptomatic
  evidential 466 adj.
  indicating 547 adj.
synagogue
  church 990 n.
sync, synch
  synchronism 123 n.
synchromesh
  machine 630 n.
synchronize
  adjust 24 vb.
  synchronize 123 vb.
syncopation
  tempo 410 n.
syncretism
  mixture 43 n.
syndicalism
  government 733 n.
syndicalist
  political party 708 n.

syndicate
  publish 528 vb.
  corporation 708 n.
syndrome
  composition 56 n.
  illness 651 n.
synergism, synergy
  cooperation 706 n.
synod
  synod 985 n.
synonym
  substitute 150 n.
synonymous
  identical 13 adj.
  semantic 514 adj.
synopsis
  whole 52 n.
  compendium
  592 n.
synoptic
  general 79 adj.
syntax
  linguistics 557 n.
  grammar 564 n.
synthesis
  combination 50 n.
synthesize
  compose 56 vb.
synthesizer
  musical instrument
  414 n.
synthetic
  imitative 20 adj.
  produced 164 adj.
syphilis
  venereal disease
  651 n.
syphon
  (*see* **siphon**)
syringe
  extractor 304 n.
  moisten 341 vb.
syrup
  viscidity 354 n.
  sweet thing 392 n.
system
  whole 52 n.
  arrangement 62 n.
  habit 610 n.
systematic
  regular 81 adj.
  rational 475 adj.
  businesslike
  622 adj.
systematize
  regularize 62 vb.
  plan 623 vb.

systems analysis
  mathematics 86 n.

T

tab
  label 547 n.
  mark 547 vb.
  badge of rank
  743 n.
tabby
  cat 365 n.
  mottled 437 adj.
tabernacle
  temple 990 n.
tabla
  drum 414 n.
table
  arrangement 62 n.
  list 87 n.
  shelf 218 n.
  stand 218 n.
  eating 301 n.
  register 548 vb.
tableau
  spectacle 445 n.
  pageant 875 n.
tableland
  high land 209 n.
table manners
  eating 301 n.
tables
  statistics 86 n.
tablet
  lamina 207 n.
  monument 548 n.
  medicine 658 n.
table-turning
  spiritualism 984 n.
tabloid
  the press 528 n.
taboo
  exclude 57 vb.
  prohibited 757 adj.
tabular
  arranged 62 adj.
tabula rasa
  obliteration 550 n.
tabulate
  class 62 vb.
  list 87 vb.
tachometer
  velocity 277 n.
tacit
  tacit 523 adj.
taciturn
  taciturn 582 adj.

unsociable 883 adj.
tack
  tie 45 vb.
  fastening 47 n.
  navigate 269 vb.
  direction 281 n.
  deviate 282 vb.
tackle
  tackling 47 n.
  equipment 630 n.
  attempt 671 n.vb.
  undertake 672 vb.
tacky
  viscid 354 adj.
tact
  discrimination
  463 n.
  sagacity 498 n.
tactful
  well-bred 848 adj.
tactical
  planned 623 adj.
  cunning 698 adj.
tactician
  planner 623 n.
tactics
  policy 623 n.
  tactics 688 n.
  art of war 718 n.
tactile
  tactual 378 adj.
tactless
  indiscriminating
  464 adj.
  foolish 499 adj.
  ill-bred 847 adj.
tactual
  tactual 378 adj.
taffeta
  textile 222 n.
tag
  hanging object
  217 n.
  maxim 496 n.
  label 547 n.
  children's games
  837 n.
—**along**
  follow 284 vb.
—**on**
  add 38 vb.
tail
  rear 238 n.
  follow 284 vb.
  pursue 619 vb.
—**off**
  decrease 37 vb.

tailback
retinue 67 n.

tailor
adjust 24 vb.
clothier 228 n.
form 243 vb.

tailor-made
tailored 228 adj.

tailpiece
sequel 67 n.

tails
formal dress 228 n.

tail wind
propellant 287 n.

taint
make unclean
  649 vb.
infection 651 n.
shame 867 vb.

take
comprise 78 vb.
overmaster 727 vb.
arrest 747 vb.
take 786 vb.
steal 788 vb.
—a back seat
be inferior 35 vb.
—advantage of
use 673 vb.
—after
resemble 18 vb.
—a hold on
prevail 178 vb.
—apart
sunder 46 vb.
—away
take away 786 vb.
—back
recant 603 vb.
acquire 771 vb.
—charge of
look after 457 vb.
undertake 672 vb.
—cover
be stealthy 525 vb.
—down
lower 311 vb.
record 548 vb.
—down a peg
shame 867 vb.
humiliate 872 vb.
—effect
operate 173 vb.
be successful
  727 vb.
—exception to
resent 891 vb.

—for granted
suppose 512 vb.
not wonder 865 vb.
be ungrateful
  908 vb.
—in
comprise 78 vb.
make smaller
  198 vb.
admit 299 vb.
understand 516 vb.
befool 542 vb.
—in hand
train 534 vb.
undertake 672 vb.
—in one's stride
be expert 694 vb.
do easily 701 vb.
—it
knuckle under
  721 vb.
be patient 823 vb.
—it badly
suffer 825 vb.
—it easy
be inactive 679 vb.
—it out on
be malevolent
  898 vb.
—its course
go on 146 vb.
happen 154 vb.
—liberties
be free 744 vb.
be rude 885 vb.
—no notice
disregard 458 vb.
—off
subtract 39 vb.
doff 229 vb.
fly 271 vb.
satirize 851 vb.
—on
load 193 vb.
undertake 672 vb.
contend 716 vb.
lament 836 vb.
—one's time
have leisure 681 vb.
be cautious 858 vb.
—orders
take orders 986 vb.
—out
extract 304 vb.
obliterate 550 vb.
court 889 vb.
—over

come after 65 vb.
appropriate 786 vb.
—part
be present 189 vb.
cooperate 706 vb.
—place
happen 154 vb.
—shape
become 1 vb.
—sides
choose 605 vb.
—steps
prepare 669 vb.
—stock
meditate 449 vb.
estimate 480 vb.
—the chair
direct 689 vb.
—the floor
orate 579 vb.
—the lead
come before 64 vb.
—the mickey
ridicule 851 vb.
—the opportunity
profit by 137 vb.
—the place of
substitute 150 vb.
—the plunge
initiate 68 vb.
be resolute 599 vb.
—the rap
incur blame 924 vb.
be punished 963 vb.
—the sting out of
assuage 177 vb.
—the strain
support 218 vb.
suffice 635 vb.
**—things as they
come**
be content 828 vb.
—to heart
feel 818 vb.
suffer 825 vb.
—to pieces
sunder 46 vb.
—to task
reprove 924 vb.
—umbrage
resent 891 vb.
—up
shorten 204 vb.
be wont 610 vb.
undertake 672 vb.
take-away
café 192 n.

taken bad
sick 651 adj.

taken for granted
certain 473 adj.

taken in
gullible 544 adj.

takeoff
air travel 271 n.
satire 851 n.

takeover
expropriation 786 n.

takings
receipt 807 n.

tale
fable 543 n.
narrative 590 n.

talebearer
informer 524 n.

talent
intelligence 498 n.
aptitude 694 n.

talent scout
inquirer 459 n.

talisman
talisman 983 n.

talk
inform 524 vb.
rumour 529 n.
lecture 534 n.
speech 579 n.
chat 584 n.
—big
boast 877 vb.
—into
induce 612 vb.
—out of
dissuade 613 vb.
—to
speak to 583 vb.
—to oneself
soliloquize 585 vb.

talkative
loquacious 581 adj.

talker
speaker 579 n.

talking to
reprimand 924 n.

talks
conference 584 n.

tall
tall 209 adj.
exaggerated
  546 adj.

tall order
hard task 700 n.

tallow
fat 357 n.

tall story
 fable 543 n.
tall talk
 boast 877 n.
tally
 accord 24 vb.
 numeration 86 n.
 label 547 n.
 accounts 808 n.
tallyho
 chase 619 n.
talon
 finger 378 n.
 nippers 778 n.
tambourine
 drum 414 n.
tame
 break in 369 vb.
 feeble 572 adj.
 habituate 610 vb.
 inexcitable
　823 adj.
tamper (with)
 be false 541 vb.
 impair 655 vb.
 meddle 678 vb.
tan
 burning 381 n.
 brown 430 adj.
tandem
 duality 90 n.
 bicycle 274 n.
tang
 pungency 388 n.
tangent
 ratio 85 n.
tangible
 material 319 adj.
 tactual 378 adj.
tangle
 complexity 61 n.
 enlace 222 vb.
tangram
 enigma 530 n.
tank
 vat 194 n.
 storage 632 n.
 cavalry 722 n.
tankard
 cup 194 n.
tanker
 lorry 274 n.
tantalize
 disappoint 509 vb.
 cause desire 859 vb.
tantamount
 equivalent 28 adj.

tantrum(s)
 anger 891 n.
tap
 pierce 263 vb.
 knock 279 n.
 extract 304 vb.
 conduit 351 n.
 touch 378 n.vb.
—the line
 hear 415 vb.
tap dance
 ballet 594 n.
tape
 strip 208 n.
 gramophone 414 n.
 measure 465 vb.
 record 548 n.vb.
tape measure
 gauge 465 n.
taper
 shade off 27 vb.
 be sharp 256 vb.
 lighter 385 n.
tape recorder
 recording
　instrument 549 n.
tape recording
 gramophone 414 n.
tapestry
 hanging object
　217 n.
 needlework 844 n.
taproot
 source 156 n.
tapster
 servant 742 n.
tar
 mariner 270 n.
 resin 357 n.
 black thing 428 n.
tar and feather
 punish 963 vb.
tardy
 late 136 adj.
 lazy 679 adj.
tare
 discount 810 n.
target
 direction 281 n.
 objective 617 n.
tariff
 list 87 n.
 restriction 747 n.
 tax 809 n.
tarmac
 paving 226 n.
 road 624 n.

tarnish
 make unclean
　649 vb.
 shame 867 vb.
tarot cards
 oracle 511 n.
tarpaulin
 canopy 226 n.
tarry
 stay 144 vb.
tart
 pastries 301 n.
 sour 393 adj.
 irascible 892 adj.
 loose woman 952 n.
tartan
 variegated 437 adj.
 livery 547 n.
tarted up
 beautified 843 adj.
 vulgar 847 adj.
Tarzan
 athlete 162 n.
task
 job 622 n.
 labour 682 n.
 hard task 700 n.
 duty 917 n.
task force
 armed force 722 n.
taskmaster
 tyrant 735 n.
tassel
 trimming 844 n.
taste
 eat 301 vb.
 taste 386 n.vb.
 discrimination
　463 n.
 good taste 846 n.
 liking 859 n.
tasteful
 tasteful 846 adj.
tasteless
 tasteless 387 adj.
 vulgar 847 adj.
tasty
 tasty 386 adj.
 savoury 390 adj.
tattered
 beggarly 801 adj.
tatters
 piece 53 n.
tatting
 network 222 n.
tattle
 converse 584 vb.

tattler
 informer 524 n.
 chatterer 581 n.
tattoo
 pierce 263 vb.
 roll 403 n.vb.
 mark 547 vb.
 pageant 875 n.
tattooing
 ornamental art
　844 n.
tatty
 dilapidated 655 adj.
 beggarly 801 adj.
taunt
 be insolent 878 vb.
 indignity 921 n.
 accusation 928 n.
taut
 rigid 326 adj.
tauten
 tighten 45 vb.
 make smaller
　198 vb.
tautological
 repeated 106 adj.
tautology
 pleonasm 570 n.
 superfluity 637 n.
tawdry
 vulgar 847 adj.
tawny
 brown 430 adj.
tax
 fatigue 684 vb.
 oppress 735 vb.
 tax 809 n.vb.
—with
 accuse 928 vb.
taxable
 priced 809 adj.
taxation
 tax 809 n.
tax avoidance
 nonpayment 805 n.
tax evasion
 foul play 930 n.
tax-free
 uncharged 812 adj.
 nonliable 919 adj.
taxi
 be in motion 265 vb.
 cab 274 n.
taxidermy
 zoology 367 n.
taxonomy
 arrangement 62 n.

tea
meal 301 n.
soft drink 301 n.
teach
convince 485 vb.
teach 534 vb.
teachable
studious 536 adj.
teacher
teacher 537 n.
teach-in
teaching 534 n.
tea leaves
oracle 511 n.
team
band 74 n.
party 708 n.
team spirit
cooperation 706 n.
sociality 882 n.
teamster
driver 268 n.
team work
cooperation 706 n.
tear
rend 46 vb.
gap 201 n.
move fast 277 vb.
lamentation 836 n.
—down
demolish 165 vb.
—up
abrogate 752 vb.
tearaway
desperado 857 n.
tearful
unhappy 825 adj.
lamenting 836 adj.
tear gas
poison 659 n.
tear-jerking
distressing 827 adj.
tearoom
café 192 n.
tease
torment 827 vb.
ridicule 851 vb.
cause desire 859 vb.
teaser
enigma 530 n.
teat
bosom 253 n.
technical
regular 81 adj.
dialectal 560 adj.
technicality
trifle 639 n.

technical knowledge
skill 694 n.
technician
machinist 630 n.
artisan 686 n.
technique
way 624 n.
skill 694 n.
technological
educational
534 adj.
technology
science 490 n.
mechanics 630 n.
tectonic
structural 331 adj.
tedious
tedious 838 adj.
tedium
satiety 863 n.
teeming
assembled 74 adj.
multitudinous
104 adj.
teenager
youngster 132 n.
teeter
be irresolute 601 vb.
teeth
vigorousness 174 n.
nippers 778 n.
teething troubles
beginning 68 n.
teetotal
temperate 942 adj.
teetotaller
abstainer 942 n.
telaesthesia
psychics 984 n.
telecommunication
telecommunication
531 n.
telegony
heredity 5 n.
telegram
telecommunication
531 n.
telegraph
signal 547 n.
telegraphic
speedy 277 adj.
concise 569 adj.
telegraphy
telecommunication
531 n.
telekinesis
spiritualism 984 n.

telepathic
psychical 984 adj.
telepathy
psychics 984 n.
telephone
communicate
524 vb.
telecommunication
531 n.
telephoto lens
optical device 442 n.
teleprinter
telecommunication
531 n.
telescope
shorten 204 vb.
telescope 442 n.
telescopic
distant 199 adj.
astronomic 321 adj.
teletext
broadcasting 531 n.
televiewer
spectator 441 n.
televise
show 522 vb.
publish 528 vb.
television
broadcasting 531 n.
telex
telecommunication
531 n.
tell
number 86 vb.
influence 178 vb.
inform 524 vb.
divulge 526 vb.
be important
638 vb.
command 737 vb.
—against
tell against 467 vb.
—lies
be false 541 vb.
—off
reprove 924 vb.
—on
inform 524 vb.
teller
enumerator 86 n.
narrator 590 n.
telling
influential 178 adj.
expressive 516 adj.
impressive 821 adj.
telltale
informer 524 n.

disclosing 526 adj.
indicating 547 adj.
temerity
rashness 857 n.
temper
temperament 5 n.
mix 43 vb.
strength 162 n.
moderate 177 vb.
harden 326 vb.
affections 817 n.
anger 891 n.
temperament
temperament 5 n.
affections 817 n.
excitability 822 n.
temperamental
capricious
604 adj.
excitable 822 adj.
temperance
moderation 177 n.
temperance 942 n.
temperate
moderate 177 adj.
warm 379 adj.
temperate 942 adj.
temperature
illness 651 n.
tempest
storm 176 n.
commotion 318 n.
tempestuous
violent 176 adj.
windy 352 adj.
excitable 822 adj.
template
mould 23 n.
temple
temple 990 n.
temples
laterality 239 n.
tempo
tempo 410 n.
temporal
transient 114 adj.
laical 987 adj.
temporalities
benefice 985 n.
temporary
ephemeral 114 adj.
temporize
spin out 113 vb.
tempt
tempt 612 vb.
cause desire
859 vb.

temptation
  attraction 291 n.
  desired object 859 n.
tempter
  motivator 612 n.
tenable
  rational 475 adj.
tenacious
  cohesive 48 adj.
  persevering 600 adj.
  retentive 778 adj.
tenancy
  possession 773 n.
tenant
  resident 191 n.
tend
  conduce 156 vb.
  tend 179 vb.
  look after 457 vb.
  doctor 658 vb.
tendency
  tendency 179 n.
  aptitude 694 n.
tendentious
  intended 617 adj.
tender
  locomotive 274 n.
  boat 275 n.
  sentient 374 adj.
  soft-hued 425 adj.
  careful 457 adj.
  offer 759 vb.
  loving 887 adj.
tender-hearted
  impressible 819 adj.
  pitying 905 adj.
tender mercies
  severity 735 n.
tender spot
  vulnerability 661 n.
  moral sensibility
    819 n.
tendon
  ligature 47 n.
tendril
  coil 251 n.
  foliage 366 n.
tenements
  housing 192 n.
tenet
  creed 485 n.
  precept 693 n.
tennis
  ball game 837 n.
tenon
  projection 254 n.
tenor

  modality 7 n.
  tendency 179 n.
  direction 281 n.
  vocalist 413 n.
  meaning 514 n.
tense
  rigid 326 adj.
  expectant 507 adj.
  grammar 564 n.
  nervous 854 adj.
tensile
  elastic 328 adj.
tension
  energy 160 n.
  dissension 709 n.
  worry 825 n.
tent
  dwelling 192 n.
  canopy 226 n.
tentacle
  feeler 378 n.
tentative
  experimental
    461 adj.
  cautious 858 adj.
tenuity
  thinness 206 n.
  rarity 325 n.
tenuous
  insubstantial 4 adj.
  inconsiderable
    33 adj.
  flimsy 163 adj.
tenure
  possession 773 n.
  estate 777 n.
tepid
  warm 379 adj.
teratogen
  poison 659 n.
teratology
  thaumaturgy 864 n.
tergiversate
  tergiversate 603 vb.
term
  end 69 n.
  serial place 73 n.
  period 110 n.
  limit 236 n.
  word 559 n.
  name 561 n.vb.
termagant
  shrew 892 n.
terminal
  ending 69 adj.
  stopping place
    145 n.

  goal 295 n.
terminate
  terminate 69 vb.
termination
  end 69 n.
  completion 725 n.
terminology
  nomenclature 561 n.
terminus
  stopping place
    145 n.
  limit 236 n.
  goal 295 n.
terms
  conditions 766 n.
terms of reference
  function 622 n.
  mandate 751 n.
terrace(s)
  house 192 n.
  horizontality 216 n.
  onlookers 441 n.
terracotta
  pottery 381 n.
terra firma
  land 344 n.
terrain
  region 184 n.
  arena 724 n.
terrarium
  zoo 369 n.
terrestrial
  native 191 n.
  telluric 321 adj.
  territorial 344 adj.
terrible
  frightening 854 adj.
terrific
  excellent 644 adj.
terrify
  frighten 854 vb.
territorial
  territorial 344 adj.
territory
  territory 184 n.
terror
  fear 854 n.
  intimidation 854 n.
  ruffian 904 n.
terrorism
  violence 176 n.
  intimidation 854 n.
terrorist
  revolter 738 n.
terrorize
  oppress 735 vb.
  frighten 854 vb.

terse
  aphoristic 496 adj.
tessellation
  chequer 437 n.
test
  exam 459 n.
  experiment
    461 n.vb.
  hard task 700 n.
testament
  testimony 466 n.
  title deed 767 n.
testamentary
  proprietary 777 adj.
testator
  transferrer 272 n.
test case
  prototype 23 n.
  experiment 461 n.
tested
  approved 923 adj.
  trustworthy 929 adj.
testee
  testee 461 n.
tester
  experimenter
    461 n.
testicles
  genitalia 167 n.
testify
  testify 466 vb.
testimonial
  credential 466 n.
  monument 548 n.
testimony
  testimony 466 n.
test match
  contest 716 n.
test tube
  testing agent 461 n.
testy
  irascible 892 adj.
tetanus
  infection 651 n.
tetchy
  irascible 892 adj.
tête-à-tête
  chat 584 n.
tether
  tie 45 vb.
  halter 47 n.
  fetter 747 vb.
tetrarch
  governor 741 n.
text
  topic 452 n.
  meaning 514 n.

reading matter
589 n.
precept 693 n.
textbook
textbook 589 n.
textile
textile 222 n.
textual
scriptural 975 adj.
textural
textural 331 adj.
texture
weaving 222 n.
texture 331 n.
thank
thank 907 vb.
reward 962 vb.
thankful
content 828 adj.
grateful 907 adj.
thankless
profitless 641 adj.
unthanked 908 adj.
thank-offering
oblation 981 n.
thanksgiving
rejoicing 835 n.
celebration 876 n.
act of worship
981 n.
thatch
roof 226 n.
hair 259 n.
thaumaturgic
wonderful 864 adj.
sorcerous 983 adj.
thaw
liquefy 337 vb.
pity 905 vb.
theatre
theatre 594 n.
drama 594 n.
arena 724 n.
theatregoer
playgoer 594 n.
theatrical
dramatic 594 adj.
affected 850 adj.
theatricals
dramaturgy 594 n.
theft
stealing 788 n.
theism
deism 973 n.
thematic
topical 452 adj.
theme

melody 410 n.
topic 452 n.
dissertation 591 n.
theme song
tune 412 n.
then
not now 122 adv.
theocracy
government 733 n.
theodolite
gauge 465 n.
theogony
deity 966 n.
theologian
theologian 973 n.
theological
theological 973 adj.
theology
theology 973 n.
theophany
theophany 965 n.
theorem
argumentation
475 n.
axiom 496 n.
theoretical
mental 447 adj.
ideational 451 adj.
theorist
theorist 512 n.
theorize
account for 158 vb.
meditate 449 vb.
suppose 512 vb.
theory
idea 451 n.
supposition 512 n.
theosophy
philosophy 449 n.
religion 973 n.
therapeutic
remedial 658 adj.
therapist
doctor 658 n.
adviser 691 n.
therapy
psychology 447 n.
therapy 658 n.
therefore
hence 158 adv.
theriomorphic
idolatrous 982 adj.
thermal
ascent 308 n.
wind 352 n.
warm 379 adj.
thermodynamics

science of forces
162 n.
thermometer
thermometry 379 n.
thermonuclear
dynamic 160 adj.
thermoplastic
flexible 327 adj.
thermosetting
heating 381 adj.
thermos flask
cauldron 194 n.
thermostat
thermometry 379 n.
thesaurus
list 87 n.
dictionary 559 n.
thesis
topic 452 n.
dissertation 591 n.
Thespian
actor 594 n.
thick
thick 205 adj.
dense 324 adj.
semiliquid 354 adj.
unintelligent
499 adj.
thicken
be broad 205 vb.
thicken 354 vb.
thicket
wood 366 n.
thickhead
dunce 501 n.
thick of things
activity 678 n.
thick on the ground
multitudinous
104 adj.
frequent 139 adj.
thickset
stalwart 162 adj.
thick-skinned
thick-skinned
820 adj.
thick speech
speech defect 580 n.
thief
thief 789 n.
thieve
steal 788 vb.
thigh
leg 267 n.
thimbleful
small quantity 33 n.
thin

insubstantial 4 adj.
few 105 adj.
weaken 163 vb.
lean 206 adj.
shallow 212 adj.
rarefy 325 vb.
transparent 422 adj.
insufficient 636 adj.
underfed 636 adj.
—out
be dispersed 75 vb.
thin air
insubstantial thing
4 n.
thin end of the wedge
start 68 n.
stratagem 698 n.
thing
object 319 n.
chief thing 638 n.
thingamabob,
  thingamajig
no name 562 n.
things
property 777 n.
thin ice
pitfall 663 n.
think
think 449 vb.
opine 485 vb.
imagine 513 vb.
—about
meditate 449 vb.
—again
tergiversate 603 vb.
—ahead
plan 623 vb.
—aloud
soliloquize 585 vb.
—back
retrospect 505 vb.
—better of it
tergiversate 603 vb.
—nothing of
hold cheap 922 vb.
—twice
be cautious 858 vb.
thinker
philosophy 449 n.
sage 500 n.
theorist 512 n.
think tank
council 692 n.
thin red line
defender 713 n.
thin-skinned
sensitive 819 adj.

third
  trisection 95 n.
third degree
  interrogation 459 n.
third estate
  commonalty 869 n.
third force
  moderator 177 n.
third-rate
  inferior 35 adj.
  trivial 639 adj.
Third World
  region 184 n.
  *political
    organization*
    733 n.
thirst
  hunger 859 n.
thirst-quenching
  refreshing 685 adj.
thirsty
  dry 342 adj.
  hot 379 adj.
  hungry 859 adj.
thistle
  prickle 256 n.
  plant 366 n.
thistledown
  lightness 323 n.
thong
  ligature 47 n.
thorn
  prickle 256 n.
thorn in the flesh
  bane 659 n.
  worry 825 n.
thorny
  difficult 700 adj.
thorough
  complete 54 adj.
  careful 457 adj.
  completive 725 adj.
thoroughbred
  unmixed 44 adj.
  thoroughbred
    273 n.
  aristocrat 868 n.
thoroughfare
  passing along 305 n.
thoroughgoing
  revolutionary
    149 adj.
  (*see* **thorough**)
though
  provided 468 adv.
thought
  thought 449 n.

idea 451 n.
  ideality 513 n.
thoughtful
  thoughtful 449 adj.
  attentive 455 adj.
thoughtless
  inattentive 456 adj.
  unwise 499 adj.
  rash 857 adj.
thought-provoking
  topical 452 adj.
thought reader
  psychic 984 n.
thraldom
  servitude 745 n.
thrash
  defeat 727 vb.
  flog 963 vb.
—**out**
  inquire 459 vb.
thread
  ligature 47 n.
  continue 71 vb.
  thinness 206 n.
  fibre 208 n.
  pass 305 vb.
—**together**
  connect 45 vb.
threadbare
  hairless 229 adj.
  used 673 adj.
threat
  danger 661 n.
  intimidation 854 n.
  threat 900 n.
threaten
  impend 155 vb.
  warn 664 vb.
  threaten 900 vb.
three
  three 93 n.adj.
three-dimensional
  formed 243 adj.
threefold
  trebly 94 adv.
three R's, the
  curriculum 534 n.
thremmatology
  animal husbandry
    369 n.
threnody
  lament 836 n.
thresh
  strike 279 vb.
  cultivate 370 vb.
—**about**
  be agitated 318 vb.

thresher
  farm tool 370 n.
threshold
  start 68 n.
  limit 236 n.
  doorway 263 n.
thrift
  economy 814 n.
thriftless
  prodigal 815 adj.
thrifty
  economical 814 adj.
thrill
  pleasure 376 n.
  excitation 821 n.
  excite 821 vb.
  delight 826 vb.
thriller
  film 445 n.
  novel 590 n.
thrill-seeker
  reveller 837 n.
  sensualist 944 n.
thrive
  be healthy 650 vb.
  prosper 730 vb.
throat
  orifice 263 n.
  air pipe 353 n.
throaty
  hoarse 407 adj.
throb
  be periodic 141 vb.
  spasm 318 n.
  give pain 377 vb.
  show feeling
    818 vb.
throes
  spasm 318 n.
  pang 377 n.
thrombosis
  *cardiovascular
    disease* 651 n.
throne
  seat 218 n.
  regalia 743 n.
  tribunal 956 n.
throng
  crowd 74 n.
  multitude 104 n.
throttle
  disable 161 vb.
  retain 778 vb.
through
  through 628 adv.
  by means of
    629 adv.

through and through
  completely 54 adv.
throughput
  data processing
    86 n.
  production 164 n.
throw
  propel 287 vb.
  gambling 618 n.
—**away**
  waste 634 vb.
  stop using 674 vb.
—**cold water on**
  moderate 177 vb.
  dissuade 613 vb.
—**down**
  fell 311 vb.
—**in one's hand**
  resign 753 vb.
—**in one's teeth**
  defy 711 vb.
—**light on**
  interpret 520 vb.
—**off**
  disaccustom 611 vb.
  elude 667 vb.
—**one's weight about**
  be insolent 878 vb.
—**out**
  eject 300 vb.
  reject 607 vb.
—**over**
  relinquish 621 vb.
—**overboard**
  eject 300 vb.
  stop using 674 vb.
—**up**
  vomit 300 vb.
  resign 753 vb.
throwaway
  ephemeral 114 adj.
  wasteful 634 adj.
throwback
  recurrence 106 n.
  reversion 148 n.
  relapse 657 n.
thrower
  thrower 287 n.
thrum
  play music 413 vb.
thrush
  vocalist 413 n.
thrust
  energy 160 n.
  vigorousness 174 n.
  impulse 279 n.
  propellant 287 n.

lunge 712 n.
thruster
busy person 678 n.
thrustful
assertive 532 adj.
active 678 adj.
thud
impulse 279 n.
nonresonance
  405 n.
thug
murderer 362 n.
robber 789 n.
ruffian 904 n.
thuggery
violence 176 n.
thumb
touch 378 vb.
gesticulate 547 vb.
thumbnail
small 33 adj.
thumbscrew
instrument of
  torture 964 n.
thumbs down
refusal 760 n.
thumbs up
approbation 923 n.
thump
knock 279 n.
nonresonance
  405 n.
thumping
whopping 32 adj.
thunder
storm 176 n.
vociferate 408 vb.
threaten 900 vb.
thunderous
loud 400 adj.
approving 923 adj.
thunderstorm
rain 350 n.
thunderstruck
inexpectant 508 adj.
wondering 864 adj.
thwart
disappoint 509 vb.
be obstructive
  702 vb.
thwarted
defeated 728 adj.
thyme
potherb 301 n.
tiara
headgear 228 n.
regalia 743 n.

tic
spasm 318 n.
tick
instant 116 n.
oscillate 317 vb.
mark 547 vb.
credit 802 n.
approve 923 vb.
—off
register 548 vb.
reprove 924 vb.
—over
move slowly 278 vb.
ticker
timekeeper 117 n.
insides 224 n.
telecommunication
  531 n.
ticket
opener 263 n.
credential 466 n.
label 547 n.
policy 623 n.
permit 756 n.
tickle
itch 378 vb.
incite 612 vb.
amuse 837 vb.
tickled pink
pleased 824 adj.
ticklish
sentient 374 adj.
unreliable 474 adj.
unsafe 661 adj.
tidal
periodical 141 adj.
flowing 350 adj.
tidal barrage
sources of energy
  160 n.
tiddler
dwarf 196 n.
tiddly
tipsy 949 adj.
tiddlywink(s)
indoor game 837 n.
tide
time 108 n.
progression 285 n.
current 350 n.
—over
aid 703 vb.
tidemark
trace 548 vb.
tideway
current 350 n.
tidings

news 529 n.
fidy
orderly 60 adj.
careful 457 adj.
clean 648 adj.
personable 841 adj.
tie
be equal 28 vb.
tie 45 vb.
bond 47 n.
neckwear 228 n.
fetter 747 vb.
—down
give terms 766 vb.
—one's hands
disable 161 vb.
—up with
connect 45 vb.
tied aid
trade 791 n.
tie-dyeing
ornamental art
  844 n.
tier
series 71 n.
layer 207 n.
tie-up
relation 9 n.
association 706 n.
tiff
quarrel 709 n.
tiger
violent creature
  176 n.
stripe 437 n.
brave person 855 n.
noxious animal
  904 n.
tight
adjusted 24 adj.
firm 45 adj.
cohesive 48 adj.
narrow 206 adj.
sealed off 264 adj.
restraining 747 adj.
retentive 778 adj.
tipsy 949 adj.
tight corner
predicament 700 n.
tighten
make smaller
  198 vb.
—one's belt
economize 814 vb.
tight-fisted
parsimonious
  816 adj.

tight-lipped
reticent 525 adj.
tightrope
narrowness 206 n.
tights
legwear 228 n.
tile
lamina 207 n.
pottery 381 n.
building material
  631 n.
tiles
floor-cover 226 n.
roof 226 n.
till
while 108 adv.
cultivate 370 vb.
treasury 799 n.
tiller
directorship 689 n.
tilt
obliquity 220 n.
tilt at
dispraise 924 vb.
—at windmills
waste effort 641 vb.
tilth
agriculture 370 n.
timber
wood 366 n.
materials 631 n.
timberwork
structure 331 n.
timbre
sound 398 n.
voice 577 n.
time
time 108 n.
era 110 n.
time 117 vb.
tempo 410 n.
time and motion
  study
management
  689 n.
time being
present time 121 n.
time bomb
pitfall 663 n.
time-consuming
wasteful 638 adj.
timed
synchronous
  123 adj.
time-honoured
immemorial
  127 adj.

timekeeper
timekeeper 117 n.
time lag
discontinuity 72 n.
delay 136 n.
timeless
perpetual 115 adj.
time limit
conditions 766 n.
timely
apt 24 adj.
timely 137 adj.
time of day
clock time 117 n.
time off
leisure 681 n.
time of life
age 131 n.
timepiece
timekeeper 117 n.
times, the
circumstance 8 n.
present time 121 n.
time-saving
economical 814 adj.
timeserver
turncoat 603 n.
timeserving
cunning 698 adj.
perfidious 930 adj.
time switch
timekeeper 117 n.
timetable
chronology 117 n.
guidebook 524 n.
time to spare
leisure 681 n.
timewarp
time 108 n.
timid
nervous 854 adj.
modest 874 adj.
timing
chronometry 117 n.
tempo 410 n.
timorous
nervous 854 adj.
timpani
drum 414 n.
tin
small box 194 n.
preserve 666 vb.
tincture
tincture 43 n.
colour 425 n.vb.
tinder
lighter 385 n.

tinge
small quantity 33 n.
hue 425 n.
tingle
itch 378 vb.
be excited 821 vb.
tin god
autocrat 741 n.
tin hat
armour 713 n.
tinker
mender 656 n.
meddle 678 vb.
be unskilful 695 vb.
tinkle
faintness 401 n.
tinkling
melodious 410 adj.
tinnitus
resonance 404 n.
tinny
strident 407 adj.
tinpot
unimportant 639 adj.
tinsel
spurious 542 adj.
bauble 639 n.
finery 844 n.
showy 875 adj.
tint
hue 425 n.
paint 553 vb.
tintinnabulation
resonance 404 n.
tiny
small 33 adj.
little 196 adj.
tip
extra 40 n.
extremity 69 n.
vertex 213 n.
make oblique 220 vb.
lower 311 vb.
hint 524 n.
advice 691 n.
reward 962 n.vb.
—**over**
invert 221 vb.
—**the scale(s)**
predominate 34 vb.
tip-off
hint 524 n.
tipple
alcoholic drink 301 n.

get drunk 949 vb.
tipstaff
law officer 955 n.
tipster
gambler 618 n.
tipsy
tipsy 949 adj.
tiptoe
be stealthy 525 vb.
tip-top
best 644 adj.
tirade
oration 579 n.
censure 924 n.
tire
fatigue 684 vb.
trouble 827 vb.
tired
sleepy 679 adj.
tireless
industrious 678 adj.
tiresome
annoying 827 adj.
tedious 838 adj.
tisane
tonic 658 n.
tissue
textile 222 n.
texture 331 n.
cleaning cloth 648 n.
tissue paper
weak thing 163 n.
titanic
huge 195 adj.
titbit
mouthful 301 n.
news 529 n.
tit for tat
retaliation 714 n.
tithe
trifle 639 n.
tax 809 n.
titillate
amuse 837 vb.
cause desire 859 vb.
titivate
primp 843 vb.
title
label 547 n.
name 561 n.
book 589 n.
title 870 n.
dueness 915 n.
titled
noble 868 adj.
title deed
title deed 767 n.

title-holder
exceller 644 n.
titter
laughter 835 n.
tittle-tattle
rumour 529 n.
titubation
descent 309 n.
titular
named 561 adj.
tizzy
excitation 821 n.
toad
amphibian 365 n.
toadstool
plant 366 n.
toady
toady 879 n.
to and fro
to and fro 317 adv.
toast
cereals 301 n.
draught 301 n.
heat 381 vb.
toast 876 vb.
favourite 890 n.
applaud 923 vb.
toastmaster
speaker 579 n.
reveller 837 n.
tobacco
tobacco 388 n.
to be
future 124 adj.
toboggan
sledge 274 n.
to come
future 124 adj.
impending 155 adj.
tocsin
danger signal 665 n.
today
present time 121 n.
toddle
move slowly 278 vb.
toddler
child 132 n.
toddy
alcoholic drink 301 n.
to-do
turmoil 61 n.
activity 678 n.
toe
foot 214 n.
toehold
support 218 n.

toe the line
conform 83 vb.
obey 739 vb.
toff
fop 848 n.
toffee
sweets 301 n.
toffee-nosed
prideful 871 adj.
toga
robe 228 n.
together
together 74 adv.
with 89 adv.
togetherness
friendship 880 n.
toggle
fastening 47 n.
togs
clothing 228 n.
toil
labour 682 n.
toilet
dressing 228 n.
latrine 649 n.
beautification 843 n.
toiletries
cosmetic 843 n.
toils
trap 542 n.
encumbrance 702 n.
toilsome
laborious 682 adj.
toilworn
fatigued 684 adj.
token
insubstantial 4 adj.
indication 547 n.
trivial 639 adj.
security 767 n.
gift 781 n.
tokenism
sham 542 n.
tolerable
not bad 644 adj.
middling 732 adj.
tolerance
limit 236 n.
permission 756 n.
patience 823 n.
tolerant
lenient 736 adj.
tolerate
consent 758 vb.
forgive 909 vb.
(*see* **tolerance**)
to let

offering 759 adj.
toll
raise the alarm
665 vb.
tax 809 n.
tom
male animal 372 n.
Tom, Dick and
Harry
everyman 79 n.
commonalty 869 n.
tomahawk
axe 723 n.
tomato
vegetable 301 n.
tomb
tomb 364 n.
tomboy
youngster 132 n.
tomboyish
disorderly 61 adj.
tombstone
obsequies 364 n.
tome
book 589 n.
tomfoolery
foolery 497 n.
tomography
medical art 658 n.
tomorrow
futurity 124 n.
tomtom
drum 414 n.
ton
weighing 322 n.
tonal
harmonic 410 adj.
linguistic 557 adj.
vocal 577 adj.
tonality
light contrast 417 n.
tone
strength 162 n.
musical note 410 n.
hue 425 n.
style 566 n.
voice 577 n.
—down
moderate 177 vb.
decolorize 426 vb.
misrepresent
552 vb.
—in with
accord 24 vb.
—up
strengthen 162 vb.
tone-deaf

deaf 416 adj.
indiscriminating
464 adj.
toneless
discordant 411 adj.
tone row
key 410 n.
tongs
nippers 778 n.
tongue
projection 254 n.
taste 386 n.
language 557 n.
voice 577 n.
tongue in cheek
deception 542 n.
mental dishonesty
543 n.
tongue-tied
voiceless 578 adj.
tonic
stimulant 174 n.
salubrious 652 adj.
tonic 658 n.
excitant 821 n.
tonic solfa
notation 410 n.
tonic water
soft drink 301 n.
tonnage
size 195 n.
tonsillitis
respiratory disease
651 n.
tonsured
hairless 229 adj.
monastic 986 adj.
ton-up
speedy 277 adj.
too
in addition 38 adv.
too bad
adverse 731 adj.
annoying 827 adj.
too big
unwieldy 195 adj.
too busy, be
be engaged 138 vb.
tool
instrument 628 n.
tool 630 n.
agent 686 n.
too much
redundance 637 n.
satiety 863 n.
toot
danger signal 665 n.

tooth
tooth 256 n.
toothache
pang 377 n.
toothed
toothed 256 adj.
notched 260 adj.
tooth for a tooth
revenge 910 n.
toothless
unsharpened
257 adj.
toothsome
savoury 390 adj.
toothy
projecting
254 adj.
tootle
play music 413 vb.
too-too
affected 850 adj.
top
supreme 34 adj.
summit 213 n.
covering 226 n.
shirt 228 n.
stopper 264 n.
climb 308 vb.
rotator 315 n.
—up
fill 54 vb.
replenish 633 vb.
topaz
gem 844 n.
top brass
bigwig 638 n.
top dog
victor 727 n.
top drawer
upper class 868 n.
top-dressing
fertilizer 171 n.
tope
get drunk 949 vb.
toper
drunkard 949 n.
top-heavy
unequal 29 adj.
unsafe 661 adj.
topiary
horticultural
370 adj.
topic
topic 452 n.
topical
present 121 adj.
topical 452 adj.

TOP

topless
 uncovered 229 adj.

top-level
 important 638 adj.

topmost
 topmost 213 adj.

top-notch
 super 644 adj.

topographer
 surveyor 465 n.

topography
 situation 186 n.

top people
 bigwig 638 n.
 elite 644 n.

topping
 covering 226 n.

topple
 tumble 309 vb.
 fell 311 vb.

—over
 be inverted
 221 vb.

top secret
 concealed 525 adj.

topsy-turvy
 inverted 221 adj.

top to toe
 longwise 203 adv.

toque
 headgear 228 n.

torch
 torch 420 n.

torch-bearer
 preparer 669 n.

toreador
 killer 362 n.

toreutics
 ornamental art
 844 n.

torment
 pain 377 n.
 suffering 825 n.
 torment 827 vb.
 torture 963 vb.

torn
 disunited 46 adj.

tornado
 gale 352 n.

torpedo
 suppress 165 vb.
 bomb 723 n.

torpid
 inert 175 adj.
 apathetic 820 adj.

torrent
 stream 350 n.

TOT

torrid
 hot 379 adj.

torsion
 convolution 251 n.

torso
 sculpture 554 n.

tort
 guilty act 936 n.
 lawbreaking 954 n.

tortoise
 slowcoach 278 n.

tortoiseshell
 variegation 437 n.

tortuous
 convoluted 251 adj.
 sophistical 477 adj.
 dishonest 930 adj.

torture
 distort 246 vb.
 give pain 377 vb.
 torment 827 vb.
 cruel act 898 n.
 torture 963 vb.

torture chamber
 instrument of
 torture 964 n.

to scale
 relatively 9 adv.

tosh
 silly talk 515 n.

to spare
 superfluous 637 adj.

toss
 propel 287 vb.
 agitation 318 n.

—and turn
 be excited 821 vb.

—aside
 not respect 921 vb.

—up
 gamble 618 vb.

toss-up
 equal chance 159 n.
 uncertainty 474 n.

tot
 child 132 n.
 draught 301 n.

total
 consummate 32 adj.
 addition 38 n.
 all 52 n.
 inclusive 78 adj.
 numerical result
 85 n.

totalitarian
 authoritarian
 735 adj.

TOU

totalitarianism
 despotism 733 n.

totality
 whole 52 n.

totalizator
 gaming-house
 618 n.

tote
 carry 273 vb.
 (*see* **totalizator**)

totem
 badge 547 n.
 idol 982 n.

to the point
 relevant 9 adj.

to the purpose
 advisable 642 adj.

totter
 move slowly 278 vb.
 tumble 309 vb.
 oscillate 317 vb.

tottering
 unstable 152 adj.
 unsafe 661 adj.

tot up (to)
 number 86 vb.

touch
 be related 9 vb.
 be contiguous
 202 vb.
 texture 331 n.
 sense 374 n.
 touch 378 n.vb.
 musical skill 413 n.
 meddle 678 vb.
 skill 694 n.
 excite 821 vb.

—down
 land 295 vb.

—for
 borrow 785 vb.

—off
 cause 156 vb.

—on/upon
 relate 9 vb.
 hint 524 vb.

—up
 make better 654 vb.

—wood
 be credulous 487 vb.

touch and go
 unreliable 474 adj.

touchdown
 air travel 271 n.

touched
 crazy 503 adj.
 impressible 819 adj.

TOW

touching
 concerning 9 adv.
 distressing 827 adj.
 (*see* **touch**)

touchline
 limit 236 n.

touchpaper
 lighter 385 n.

touchstone
 testing agent 461 n.

touchy
 sensitive 819 adj.
 irascible 892 adj.

tough
 strong 162 adj.
 tough 329 adj.
 difficult 700 adj.
 thick-skinned
 820 adj.
 ruffian 904 n.
 pitiless 906 adj.

toughen
 be tough 329 vb.
 make insensitive
 820 vb.

toupee
 hair 259 n.

tour
 period 110 n.
 land travel 267 n.
 circuition 314 n.

tour de force
 masterpiece 694 n.

tourism
 land travel 267 n.

tourist
 traveller 268 n.
 spectator 441 n.

tournament, tourney
 contest 716 n.
 pageant 875 n.

tourniquet
 compressor 198 n.
 surgical dressing
 658 n.

tousle
 jumble 63 vb.

tout
 request 761 vb.
 petitioner 763 n.
 seller 793 n.

tow
 fibre 208 n.
 navigate 269 vb.
 draw 288 vb.

towards
 towards 281 adv.

towel
  rub 333 vb.
  dryer 342 n.
towelling
  textile 222 n.
tower
  edifice 164 n.
  be high 209 vb.
  refuge 662 n.
  fort 713 n.
—over
  be superior 34 vb.
  influence 178 vb.
tower block
  flat 192 n.
towering
  furious 176 adj.
  high 209 adj.
tower of strength
  aider 703 n.
towline
  cable 47 n.
town
  district 184 n.
  housing 192 n.
town crier
  publicizer 528 n.
townspeople
  inhabitants 191 n.
  commonalty 869 n.
toxic
  toxic 653 adj.
  baneful 659 adj.
toxin
  poison 659 n.
toxophilite
  shooter 287 n.
toy
  little 196 adj.
  bauble 639 n.
  plaything 837 n.
  caress 889 vb.
trace
  copy 20 vb.
  small quantity 33 n.
  effect 157 n.
  outline 233 n.vb.
  detect 484 vb.
  trace 548 n.
  decorate 844 vb.
traceable
  attributed 158 adj.
  recorded 548 adj.
tracery
  network 222 n.
  pattern 844 n.
traces

fetter 748 n.
track
  direction 281 n.
  follow 284 vb.
  trace 548 n.
  pursue 619 vb.
  path 624 n.
  railway 624 n.
  arena 724 n.
—down
  detect 484 vb.
tracker
  hunter 619 n.
track events
  sport 837 n.
track record
  conduct 688 n.
tracksuit
  suit 228 n.
tract
  region 184 n.
  dissertation 591 n.
  piety 979 n.
tractability
  persuadability
    612 n.
tractable
  tractable 701 adj.
traction
  traction 288 n.
traction engine
  locomotive 274 n.
tractor
  vehicle 274 n.
  farm tool 370 n.
trad
  music 412 n.
trade
  interchange 151 vb.
  business 622 n.
  trade 791 n.vb.
  sell 793 vb.
—on
  use 673 vb.
trade fair
  market 796 n.
trademark
  speciality 80 n.
  identification 547 n.
  label 547 n.
tradesman
  tradespeople 794 n.
**trade union, trades
    union**
  association 706 n.
trade unionist
  worker 686 n.

participator 775 n.
tradition
  tradition 127 n.
  narrative 590 n.
traditional
  immemorial
    127 adj.
  habitual 610 adj.
  orthodox 976 adj.
traditionalist
  conformist 83 n.
  the orthodox 976 n.
traduce
  misinterpret 521 vb.
  defame 926 vb.
traffic
  passing along 305 n.
  trade 791 n.
traffic jam
  procession 71 n.
  obstacle 702 n.
traffic warden
  traffic control 305 n.
**tragedian,
    tragedienne**
  actor 594 n.
tragedy
  stage play 594 n.
  evil 616 n.
tragic
  distressing 827 adj.
trail
  be dispersed 75 vb.
  be long 203 vb.
  hang 217 vb.
  move slowly 278 vb.
  follow 284 vb.
  draw 288 vb.
  trace 548 n.
  pursue 619 vb.
  path 624 n.
trail-blazer
  precursor 66 n.
trailer
  cart 274 n.
  advertisement
    528 n.
train
  procession 71 n.
  hanging object
    217 n.
  rear 238 n.
  train 274 n.
  follower 284 n.
  train 534 vb.
  habituate 610 vb.
—one's sights (on)

aim 281 vb.
  aim at 617 vb.
trained
  instructed 490 adj.
  prepared 669 adj.
  expert 694 adj.
trainee
  beginner 538 n.
trainer
  breeder 369 n.
  trainer 537 n.
training
  exercise 682 n.
training college
  training school
    539 n.
traipse
  wander 267 vb.
trait
  temperament 5 n.
  feature 445 n.
traitor
  deceiver 545 n.
  turncoat 603 n.
  undutifulness 918 n.
traitorous
  perfidious 930 adj.
trajectory
  curve 248 n.
  route 624 n.
tram
  tram 274 n.
tramlines
  parallelism 219 n.
  habit 610 n.
trammels
  encumbrance 702 n.
  fetter 748 n.
tramp
  gait 265 n.
  wanderer 268 n.
  move slowly 278 vb.
  beggar 763 n.
trample
  flatten 216 vb.
  oppress 735 vb.
—on
  ill-treat 645 vb.
  despise 922 vb.
—under foot
  suppress 165 vb.
  not observe
    769 vb.
trampoline
  recoil 280 n.
tramway
  railway 624 n.

trance
insensibility 375 n.
fantasy 513 n.
tranquil
tranquil 266 adj.
peaceful 717 adj.
inexcitable 823 adj.
tranquillity
content 828 n.
tranquillizer
moderator 177 n.
transact
do business 622 vb.
transaction(s)
affairs 154 n.
record 548 n.
deed 676 n.
transatlantic
extraneous 59 adj.
removed 199 adj.
transcend
be superior 34 vb.
transcendence,
  transcendency
extrinsicality 6 n.
perfection 646 n.
transcendent
supreme 34 adj.
divine 965 adj.
transcendental
inexpressible
  517 adj.
cabbalistic 984 adj.
transcribe
copy 20 vb.
write 586 vb.
transcript
copy 22 n.
transcription
musical piece 412 n.
transect
be oblique 220 vb.
transection
crossing 222 n.
transept
church interior
  990 n.
transfer
duplicate 22 n.
displace 188 vb.
transfer 272 vb.
carry 273 vb.
transfer 780 n.
transferable
transferable
  272 adj.
transference

interchange 151 n.
transference 272 n.
(see **transfer***)*
transfigure
transform 147 vb.
make better 654 vb.
transfix
pierce 263 vb.
transfixed
still 266 adj.
wondering 864 adj.
transform
transform 147 vb.
make better 654 vb.
transformation
transformation
  143 n.
transformation scene
spectacle 445 n.
thaumaturgy 864 n.
transformer
electronics 160 n.
transfusion
transference 272 n.
surgery 658 n.
transgress
encroach 306 vb.
disobey 738 vb.
not observe 769 vb.
transgression
guilty act 936 n.
tranship, transship
displace 188 vb.
transience
transience 114 n.
transient
transient 114 adj.
unstable 152 adj.
dweller 191 n.
transistor
electronics 160 n.
broadcasting 531 n.
transit
passage 305 n.
transition
change 143 n.
transference 272 n.
passage 305 n.
transitory
transient 114 adj.
translate
translate 520 vb.
translation
translation 520 n.
translator
interpreter 520 n.
transliterate

translate 520 vb.
translucent
semitransparent
  424 adj.
transmission
broadcast 531 n.
transmit
send 272 vb.
communicate
  524 vb.
transmitter
broadcasting 531 n.
transmute
modify 143 vb.
transom
beam 218 n.
window 263 n.
transparency
transparency 422 n.
photography 551 n.
transparent
transparent 422 adj.
perspicuous
  567 adj.
artless 699 adj.
transpire
happen 154 vb.
emerge 298 vb.
be disclosed 526 vb.
transplant
implant 303 vb.
cultivate 370 vb.
surgery 658 n.
transport
displace 188 vb.
transport 272 n.
carry 273 vb.
vehicle 274 n.
excitable state 822 n.
transportation
penalty 963 n.
transporter
carrier 273 n.
transpose
interchange 151 vb.
transpose 272 vb.
compose music
  413 vb.
transsexual
nonconformist 84 n.
transubstantiation
transformation
  143 n.
transverse
oblique 220 adj.
transvestite
nonconformist 84 n.

trap
receptacle 194 n.
carriage 274 n.
surprise 508 vb.
trap 542 n.
ensnare 542 vb.
pitfall 663 n.
imprison 747 vb.
trapdoor
doorway 263 n.
trapeze artist
athlete 162 n.
trapper
hunter 619 n.
trappings
dressing 228 n.
equipment 630 n.
Trappist
taciturnity 582 n.
monk 986 n.
trash
bauble 639 n.
rubbish 641 n.
bad person 938 n.
trashy
meaningless
  515 adj.
profitless 641 adj.
trauma
wound 655 n.
traumatic
felt 818 adj.
distressing 827 adj.
travail
labour 682 n.
travel
land travel 267 n.
travel 267 vb.
traveller
traveller 268 n.
seller 793 n.
travelogue
film 445 n.
description 590 n.
traverse
beam 218 n.
pass 305 vb.
travesty
misrepresentation
  552 n.
satire 851 n.
trawl
network 222 n.
draw 288 vb.
hunt 619 vb.
trawler
fishing boat 275 n.

tray
  compartment 194 n.
  plate 194 n.
treacherous
  deceiving 542 adj.
  malevolent 898 adj.
  perfidious 930 adj.
treachery
  perfidy 930 n.
treacle
  viscidity 354 n.
  sweet thing 392 n.
treacly
  feeling 818 adj.
tread
  stand 218 n.
  gait 265 n.
  walk 267 n.
  ascent 308 n.
—on the heels of
  come after 65 vb.
—underfoot
  oppress 735 vb.
—warily
  be cautious 858 vb.
treadmill
  labour 682 n.
  bore 838 n.
treason
  sedition 738 n.
  perfidy 930 n.
treasonable
  perfidious 930 adj.
treasure
  store 632 n.vb.
  exceller 644 n.
  preserve 666 vb.
  funds 797 n.
  honour 866 vb.
  love 887 vb.
  darling 890 n.
treasure chest
  treasury 799 n.
treasure hunt
  search 459 n.
treasurer
  treasurer 798 n.
  accountant 808 n.
treasure trove
  discovery 484 n.
treasury
  anthology 592 n.
  treasury 799 n.
treat
  modify 143 vb.
  dissertate 591 vb.
  doctor 658 vb.

  make terms 766 vb.
  defray 804 vb.
  amusement 837 n.
—like dirt
  subjugate 745 vb.
  hold cheap 922 vb.
treatise
  dissertation 591 n.
treatment
  change 143 n.
  therapy 658 n.
  use 673 n.
  conduct 688 n.
treaty
  treaty 765 n.
treble
  treble 94 adj.vb.
  vocalist 413 n.
tree
  tree 366 n.
trefoil
  three 93 n.
  heraldry 547 n.
trek
  land travel 267 n.
trellis
  frame 218 n.
tremble
  be agitated 318 vb.
  quake 854 vb.
tremendous
  prodigious 32 adj.
  frightening 854 adj.
tremolo
  musical note 410 n.
tremor
  outbreak 176 n.
  agitation 318 n.
  nervous disorders
    651 n.
  nervousness 854 n.
tremulous
  agitated 318 adj.
trench
  excavation 255 n.
  furrow 262 n.
  refuge 662 n.
  defences 713 n.
trenchant
  keen 174 adj.
  forceful 571 adj.
  disapproving
    924 adj.
trencher
  plate 194 n.
trencherman,
  trencherwoman

  eater 301 n.
trenches
  battleground 724 n.
trench on/upon
  encroach 306 vb.
trend
  tendency 179 n.
trend-setter
  precursor 66 n.
trendy
  modernist 126 n.
  fashionable 848 adj.
trephine, trepan
  doctor 658 vb.
trepidation
  fear 854 n.
trespass
  intrude 297 vb.
  be undue 916 vb.
  lawbreaking 954 n.
trespasser
  intruder 59 n.
tresses
  hair 259 n.
trestle
  frame 218 n.
trews
  trousers 228 n.
tri-
  three 93 adj.
triad
  three 93 n.
trial
  experiment 461 n.
  bane 659 n.
  adversity 731 n.
  suffering 825 n.
  legal trial 959 n.
trial and error
  empiricism 461 n.
trial of strength
  contest 716 n.
trial run
  experiment 461 n.
  preparation 669 n.
triangle
  three 93 n.
  angular figure
    247 n.
  gong 414 n.
triangulate
  measure 465 vb.
tribal
  ethnic 11 adj.
  national 371 adj.
tribalism
  social group 371 n.

tribe
  race 11 n.
  group 74 n.
  breed 77 n.
  multitude 104 n.
  native 191 n.
  community 708 n.
tribulation
  suffering 825 n.
tribunal
  council 692 n.
  tribunal 956 n.
tribune
  rostrum 539 n.
  official 690 n.
tributary
  stream 350 n.
  subject 745 adj.
tribute
  service 745 n.
  tax 809 n.
  thanks 907 n.
  dueness 915 n.
trice
  instant 116 n.
trichology
  hairdressing 843 n.
trichotomy
  trisection 95 n.
trick
  trickery 542 n.
  befool 542 vb.
  habit 610 n.
  stratagem 698 n.
  foul play 930 n.
—out
  decorate 844 vb.
trickery
  trickery 542 n.
trickle
  small quantity
    33 n.
  move slowly 278 vb.
  flow 350 vb.
tricks of the trade
  stratagem 698 n.
trickster
  trickster 545 n.
  slyboots 698 n.
tricksy
  cunning 698 adj.
tricky
  cunning 698 adj.
  difficult 700 adj.
tricolour
  three 93 adj.
  flag 547 n.

tricycle
  bicycle 274 n.
trident
  authority 733 n.
tried
  expert 694 adj.
  trustworthy 929 adj.
triennial
  seasonal 141 adj.
trier
  trier 671 n.
trifle
  insubstantial thing
    4 n.
  dessert 301 n.
  be inattentive
    456 vb.
  trifle 639 n.
  —with
  not respect 921 vb.
trifling
  inconsiderable
    33 adj.
  trivial 639 adj.
trigger
  tool 630 n.
  firearm 723 n.
trigger-happy
  rash 857 adj.
trigger off
  cause 156 vb.
trigonometry
  mathematics 86 n.
trilby
  headgear 228 n.
trill
  sing 413 vb.
  pronunciation
    577 n.
trilogy
  stage play 594 n.
trim
  state 7 n.
  adjust 24 vb.
  cut 46 vb.
  orderly 60 adj.
  make smaller
    198 vb.
  dressing 228 n.
  form 243 n.
  tergiversate 603 vb.
  personable 841 adj.
  hairdressing 843 n.
  decorate 844 vb.
trimaran
  raft 275 n.
trimester

period 110 n.
trimmer
  turncoat 603 n.
trimming
  trimming 844 n.
trimmings
  adjunct 40 n.
trinity
  triality 93 n.
  Trinity 965 n.
trinket
  bauble 639 n.
trio
  three 93 n.
  duet 412 n.
trip
  land travel 267 n.
  tumble 309 vb.
  blunder 495 vb.
  ensnare 542 vb.
  be clumsy 695 vb.
  hinder 702 vb.
  excitable state 822 n.
  dance 837 vb.
  —over
  collide 279 vb.
tripartite
  trifid 95 adj.
tripe
  silly talk 515 n.
triple
  treble 94 adj.vb.
triple crown
  badge of rule 743 n.
triple jump
  leap 312 n.
triplet
  three 93 n.
triplicate
  treble 94 adj.vb.
tripod
  stand 218 n.
tripper
  traveller 268 n.
triptych
  picture 553 n.
tripwire
  trap 542 n.
  defences 713 n.
trisect
  trisect 95 vb.
trite
  usual 610 adj.
  dull 840 adj.
triturate
  pulverize 332 vb.
triumph

triumph 727 vb.
  trophy 729 n.
triumphal
  celebratory 876 adj.
triumphant
  successful 727 adj.
  jubilant 833 adj.
  celebratory 876 adj.
triumvirate
  government 733 n.
trivet
  stand 218 n.
trivia
  trifle 639 n.
trivial
  inconsiderable
    33 adj.
  trivial 639 adj.
trodden
  flat 216 adj.
troglodyte
  dweller 191 n.
  humankind 371 n.
troika
  carriage 274 n.
Trojan horse
  ambush 527 n.
  stratagem 698 n.
troll
  elf 970 n.
trolley
  stand 218 n.
  pushcart 274 n.
  tram 274 n.
trollop
  loose woman
    952 n.
trombone
  horn 414 n.
troop
  congregate 74 vb.
  walk 267 vb.
  formation 722 n.
troop-carrier
  air force 722 n.
trooper
  cavalry 722 n.
troops
  armed force 722 n.
troopship
  warship 722 n.
trope
  trope 519 n.
trophy
  trophy 729 n.
tropical
  hot 379 adj.

tropical disease
  tropical disease
    651 n.
troposphere
  atmosphere 340 n.
trot
  gait 265 n.
  move fast 277 vb.
troth
  promise 764 n.
trotter
  foot 214 n.
  thoroughbred
    273 n.
troubadour
  musician 413 n.
  entertainer 594 n.
trouble
  derange 63 vb.
  attention 455 n.
  evil 616 n.
  exertion 682 n.
  predicament 700 n.
  adversity 731 n.
  trouble 827 vb.
troubled
  agitated 318 adj.
  suffering 825 adj.
troublemaker
  troublemaker 663 n.
troubleshooter
  adviser 691 n.
  mediator 720 n.
troublesome
  laborious 682 adj.
  annoying 827 adj.
trouble-spot
  pitfall 663 n.
trough
  bowl 194 n.
  cavity 255 n.
trounce
  defeat 727 vb.
  reprove 924 vb.
troupe
  band 74 n.
  actor 594 n.
trousers
  trousers 228 n.
trousseau
  clothing 228 n.
trout
  fish food 301 n.
trouvaille
  discovery 484 n.
trowel
  farm tool 370 n.

truancy
  absence 190 n.
  undutifulness 918 n.
truant
  avoider 620 n.
truce
  lull 145 n.
  pacification 719 n.
truck
  carrier 273 n.
  lorry 274 n.
  train 274 n.
trucker
  driver 268 n.
truckload
  great quantity 32 n.
truculent
  ungracious 885 adj.
trudge
  move slowly 278 vb.
true
  straight 249 adj.
  accurate 494 adj.
  true 494 adj.
  veracious 540 adj.
  trustworthy 929 adj.
true-blue
  obedient 739 adj.
  patriotic 901 adj.
true to life
  lifelike 18 adj.
  representing
    551 adj.
true to type
  typical 83 adj.
trug
  basket 194 n.
truism
  axiom 496 n.
trump(s)
  be superior 34 vb.
  overmaster 727 vb.
  good person 937 n.
trump card
  advantage 34 n.
trumped up
  false 541 adj.
trumpery
  bauble 639 n.
  trivial 639 adj.
trumpet
  horn 414 n.
  proclaim 528 vb.
trumpet call
  command 737 n.
truncate
  shorten 204 vb.

truncheon
  club 723 n.
trundle
  move 265 vb.
  propel 287 vb.
trunk
  box 194 n.
  prop 218 n.
  tree 366 n.
  communicating
    624 adj.
trunk line
  telecommunication
    531 n.
trunks
  beachwear 228 n.
truss
  tie 45 vb.
  beam 218 n.
trust
  belief 485 n.
  association 706 n.
  mandate 751 n.
  hope 852 n.vb.
trustee
  consignee 754 n.
  treasurer 798 n.
trusteeship
  commission 751 n.
trustful
  believing 485 adj.
  credulous 487 adj.
trustworthy
  credible 485 adj.
  trustworthy 929 adj.
truth
  reality 1 n.
  truth 494 n.
  maxim 496 n.
  veracity 540 n.
truthful
  veracious 540 adj.
try
  taste 386 vb.
  experiment 461 vb.
  judge 480 vb.
  tempt 612 vb.
  attempt 671 n.vb.
  torment 827 vb.
—it on
  deceive 542 vb.
trying
  annoying 827 adj.
tryst
  social round 882 n.
tub
  vat 194 n.

ablutions 648 n.
tuba
  horn 414 n.
tubby
  fleshy 195 adj.
  thick 205 adj.
tube
  cylinder 252 n.
  tube 263 n.
  tunnel 263 n.
  railway 624 n.
tuber
  vegetable 301 n.
tuberculosis
  infection 651 n.
tub-thumper
  speaker 579 n.
  agitator 738 n.
tubular
  tubular 263 adj.
tuck
  fold 261 n.vb.
  food 301 n.
—in/into
  eat 301 vb.
—up
  shorten 204 vb.
tucked away
  secluded 883 adj.
tuft
  bunch 74 n.
  hair 259 n.
tug
  boat 275 n.
  draw 288 vb.
  attraction 291 n.
  extraction 304 n.
  exertion 682 n.
tug of war
  contest 716 n.
tuition
  teaching 534 n.
tumble
  be inverted 221 vb.
  tumble 309 vb.
—to
  understand 516 vb.
tumbledown
  dilapidated 655 adj.
tumbler
  athlete 162 n.
  cup 194 n.
tumescent
  expanded 197 adj.
tumid
  rhetorical 574 adj.
tummy

maw 194 n.
tumour
  cancer 651 n.
tumult
  turmoil 61 n.
  loudness 400 n.
tumultuous
  disorderly 61 adj.
  violent 176 adj.
tumulus
  earthwork 253 n.
tun
  vat 194 n.
tundra
  plain 348 n.
tune
  adjust 24 vb.
  synchronize
    123 vb.
  harmonize 410 vb.
  tune 412 n.
  make ready 669 vb.
—in
  hear 415 vb.
tuneful
  melodious 410 adj.
tuneless
  discordant 411 adj.
tunic
  jacket 228 n.
tunnel
  tunnel 263 n.
  descend 309 vb.
tunneller
  excavator 255 n.
tunnel vision
  blindness 439 n.
turban
  headgear 228 n.
turbid
  opaque 423 adj.
turbine
  sources of energy
    160 n.
  machine 630 n.
turbulence,
  turbulency
  storm 176 n.
  commotion 318 n.
turbulent
  disorderly 61 adj.
  violent 176 adj.
  excitable 822 adj.
tureen
  bowl 194 n.
turf
  grassland 348 n.

enlace 222 vb.
distortion 246 n.
twine 251 vb.
deviate 282 vb.
misinterpret 521 vb.
dance 837 n.vb.
—and turn
meander 251 vb.
—one's arm
compel 740 vb.
twisted
biased 481 adj.
twister
trickster 545 n.
twit
fool 501 n.
ridicule 851 vb.
twitch
spasm 318 n.
feel pain 377 vb.
twitter
agitation 318 n.
ululate 409 vb.
be loquacious
581 vb.
two
duality 90 n.
two-a-penny
trivial 639 adj.
cheap 812 adj.
two-dimensional
spatial 183 adj.
flat 216 adj.
two-edged
double 91 adj.
two-faced
hypocritical
541 adj.
two of a kind
analogue 18 n.
two or three
fewness 105 n.
twopenny-halfpenny
trivial 639 adj.
two-sided
double 91 adj.
twosome
duality 90 n.
two-time
deceive 542 vb.
two-way
interchanged
151 adj.
tycoon
autocrat 741 n.
type
character 5 n.

analogue 18 n.
prototype 23 n.
sort 77 n.
form 243 n.
person 371 n.
write 586 vb.
print-type 587 n.
typecast
dramatize 594 vb.
typeface
print-type 587 n.
typescript
script 586 n.
typewriter
stationery 586 n.
typhoid
infection 651 n.
typhoon
gale 352 n.
typhus
infection 651 n.
typical
generic 77 adj.
general 79 adj.
typical 83 adj.
usual 610 adj.
typify
mean 514 vb.
represent 551 vb.
typist
stenographer 586 n.
typographer
engraver 556 n.
printer 587 n.
typography
print 587 n.
tyrannical
oppressive 735 adj.
cruel 898 adj.
tyrannize
oppress 735 vb.
tyranny
despotism 733 n.
brute force 735 n.
arrogation 916 n.
tyrant
tyrant 735 n.
autocrat 741 n.
tyro, tiro
beginner 538 n.

U

U
well-bred 848 adj.
genteel 868 adj.
ubiquitous

ubiquitous 189 adj.
udder
bosom 253 n.
UFO
spaceship 276 n.
unknown thing
491 n.
ugly
dangerous 661 adj.
ugly 842 adj.
ugly customer
ruffian 904 n.
ugly duckling
nonconformist 84 n.
ulcer
ulcer 651 n.
bane 659 n.
ulterior
distant 199 adj.
ulterior motive
concealment 525 n.
ultimate
supreme 34 adj.
ending 69 adj.
ultimately
prospectively
124 adv.
late 136 adv.
ultimatum
warning 664 n.
conditions 766 n.
ultra
extremely 32 adv.
ultramarine
blue 435 adj.
ultraviolet radiation
radiation 417 n.
ululate
cry 408 vb.
ululate 409 vb.
umbilical cord
bond 47 n.
obstetrics 167 n.
umbra
darkness 418 n.
umbrage
resentment 891 n.
umbrella
shade 226 n.
shelter 662 n.
umbrella
organization
association 706 n.
umlaut
speech sound 398 n.
umpire
estimator 480 n.

mediator 720 n.
umpteen
many 104 adj.
unabashed
unfearing 855 adj.
unable
powerless 161 adj.
unabridged
intact 52 adj.
unacceptable
unpleasant 827 adj.
unaccommodating
discourteous
885 adj.
unaccompanied
alone 88 adj.
unaccountable
causeless 159 adj.
wonderful 864 adj.
nonliable 919 adj.
unaccustomed
unhabituated
611 adj.
unacknowledged
unthanked 908 adj.
unacquainted
ignorant 491 adj.
unadaptable
unskilful 695 adj.
unadorned
plain 573 adj.
unadulterated
unmixed 44 adj.
genuine 494 adj.
unadventurous
cautious 858 adj.
unaffected
permanent
144 adj.
artless 699 adj.
nonliable 919 adj.
unafraid
unfearing 855 adj.
unaggressive
peaceful 717 adj.
unaided
hindered 702 adj.
unalike
dissimilar 19 adj.
unalloyed
unmixed 44 adj.
unambiguous
positive 473 adj.
intelligible 516 adj.
unambitious
indifferent 860 adj.
modest 874 adj.

unanimity
consensus 488 n.
concord 710 n.
unanimous
agreeing 24 adj.
unannounced
unexpected 508 adj.
unanswerable
demonstrated
478 adj.
unappealing
unpleasant 827 adj.
unappeasable
revengeful 910 adj.
unappetizing
unsavoury 391 adj.
unapplied
unused 674 adj.
unappreciated
unthanked 908 adj.
unapproachable
removed 199 adj.
prideful 871 adj.
unapt
unapt 25 adj.
unarguable
undisputed
473 adj.
unaristocratic
plebeian 869 adj.
unarmed
vulnerable 661 adj.
peaceful 717 adj.
unashamed
impenitent 940 adj.
unasked
voluntary 597 adj.
unaspiring
indifferent 860 adj.
unassailable
invulnerable
660 adj.
unassertive
modest 874 adj.
unassimilated
extraneous 59 adj.
unassuming
humble 872 adj.
modest 874 adj.
unastonished
unastonished
865 adj.
unattached
neutral 625 adj.
independent
744 adj.
unattainable

impracticable
470 adj.
unattended
neglected 458 adj.
unattractive
unpleasant 827 adj.
unwanted 860 adj.
unauthorized
unwarranted
916 adj.
unavailable
unprovided 636 adj.
unavailing
profitless 641 adj.
unavoidable
certain 473 adj.
necessary 596 adj.
obligatory 917 adj.
unavowed
tacit 523 adj.
unaware
ignorant 491 adj.
inexpectant 508 adj.
unbalance
bias 481 n.
unbalanced
unwise 499 adj.
crazy 503 adj.
unbaptized
heathenish 974 adj.
unbarred
open 263 adj.
unbearable
intolerable 827 adj.
unbeatable
unbeaten 727 adj.
unbecoming
graceless 842 adj.
discreditable
867 adj.
unbefitting
undue 916 adj.
unbelievable
unbelieved 486 adj.
wonderful 864 adj.
unbelieving
doubting 474 adj.
impious 980 adj.
unbend
straighten 249 vb.
repose 683 vb.
be sociable 882 vb.
forgive 909 vb.
unbending
rigid 326 adj.
obstinate 602 adj.
severe 735 adj.

unbiased
judicial 480 adj.
just 913 adj.
unbiblical
heterodox 977 adj.
unbiddable
disobedient 738 adj.
unbidden
voluntary 597 adj.
unwanted 860 adj.
unbind
disunite 46 vb.
deliver 668 vb.
unblemished
perfect 646 adj.
unblest with
not owning 774 adj.
unblinking
still 266 adj.
unblushing
thick-skinned
820 adj.
impenitent 940 adj.
unbolt
open 263 vb.
unborn
unborn 2 adj.
unbounded
infinite 107 adj.
unbowed
unbeaten 727 adj.
unbreakable
unyielding 162 adj.
invulnerable
660 adj.
unbridgeable
impracticable
470 adj.
unbridled
violent 176 adj.
unconfined 744 adj.
un-British
extraneous 59 adj.
unbroken
uniform 16 adj.
intact 52 adj.
continuous 71 adj.
unburden
disencumber
701 vb.
—oneself
divulge 526 vb.
unbusinesslike
unskilful 695 adj.
unbutton
doff 229 vb.
unbuttoned

reposeful 683 adj.
uncalculated
spontaneous
609 adj.
uncalculating
rash 857 adj.
uncalled for
undue 916 adj.
uncanny
spooky 970 adj.
magical 983 adj.
uncared for
neglected 458 adj.
uncaring
indifferent 860 adj.
unceasing
frequent 139 adj.
unceasing 146 adj.
persevering 600 adj.
unceremonious
discourteous
885 adj.
uncertain
fitful 142 adj.
changeful 152 adj.
uncertain 474 adj.
puzzled 517 adj.
irresolute 601 adj.
speculative 618 adj.
uncertainty
doubt 486 n.
ignorance 491 n.
uncertified
uncertified 474 adj.
unchallengeable
undisputed 473 adj.
unchangeable
unchangeable
153 adj.
unchanging
permanent 144 adj.
unchangeable
153 adj.
uncharacteristic
abnormal 84 adj.
uncharitable
unkind 898 adj.
uncharted
unknown 491 adj.
unchaste
unchaste 951 adj.
unchecked
uncertified 474 adj.
rash 857 adj.
unchivalrous
discourteous
885 adj.

unchristian
unkind 898 adj.
heathenish 974 adj.
uncial
letter 558 n.
uncircumcised
heathenish 974 adj.
uncivil
discourteous
885 adj.
uncivilized
ignorant 491 adj.
ill-bred 847 adj.
barbaric 869 adj.
unclad
uncovered 229 adj.
unclaimed
unpossessed
774 adj.
unclasp
disunite 46 vb.
unclassified
orderless 61 adj.
uncle
kinsman 11 n.
unclean
unclean 649 adj.
impure 951 adj.
unclean spirit
devil 969 n.
unclear
puzzling 517 adj.
unclear 568 adj.
unclench
open 263 vb.
not retain 779 vb.
uncloak
disclose 526 vb.
unclose
open 263 vb.
unclothed
uncovered 229 adj.
unclouded
undimmed 417 adj.
unclubbable
unsociable 883 adj.
uncoil
evolve 316 vb.
uncomfortable
painful 377 adj.
suffering 825 adj.
uncomforted
discontented
829 adj.
uncomforting
cheerless 834 adj.
uncommitted

neutral 625 adj.
independent
744 adj.
uncommon
special 80 adj.
infrequent 140 adj.
uncommunicative
reticent 525 adj.
uncomplaining
patient 823 adj.
uncompleted
incomplete 55 adj.
uncompleted
726 adj.
uncomplicated
artless 699 adj.
easy 701 adj.
uncomplimentary
disrespectful
921 adj.
disapproving
924 adj.
uncomprehending
ignorant 491 adj.
uncompromising
resolute 599 adj.
obstinate 602 adj.
unconcealed
manifest 522 adj.
unconcern
incuriosity 454 n.
indifference 860 n.
unconditional
unconditional
744 adj.
obligatory 917 adj.
unconfined
unconfined 744 adj.
unconfirmed
uncertified 474 adj.
unconformable
unconformable
84 adj.
uncongealed
fluid 335 adj.
uncongenial
disagreeing 25 adj.
cheerless 834 adj.
unconnected
unrelated 10 adj.
unconquerable
unbeaten 727 adj.
unconscionable
exorbitant 32 adj.
unconscious
insensible 375 adj.
ignorant 491 adj.

involuntary 596 adj.
sleepy 679 adj.
unconscious, the
subjectivity 320 n.
spirit 447 n.
unconsecrated
profane 980 adj.
unconsoled
discontented
829 adj.
unconstitutional
unwarranted
916 adj.
illegal 954 adj.
uncontaminated
perfect 646 adj.
uncontested
undisputed 473 adj.
uncontrollable
violent 176 adj.
frenzied 503 adj.
wilful 602 adj.
excitable 822 adj.
uncontroversial
undisputed 473 adj.
assented 488 adj.
unconventional
unconformable
84 adj.
independent
744 adj.
unconvinced
dissenting 489 adj.
unconvincing
improbable 472 adj.
uncooked
unsavoury 391 adj.
uncooperative
hindering 702 adj.
uncoordinated
orderless 61 adj.
uncork
open 263 vb.
uncorroborated
uncertified 474 adj.
uncouple
disunite 46 vb.
uncouth
clumsy 695 adj.
graceless 842 adj.
uncover
uncover 229 vb.
open 263 vb.
disclose 526 vb.
uncrease
unravel 62 vb.
uncreated

existing 1 adj.
unborn 2 adj.
uncritical
indiscriminating
464 adj.
uncrown
depose 752 vb.
uncrowned
king/queen
influence 178 n.
bigwig 638 n.
unction
unctuousness 357 n.
warm feeling 818 n.
piety 979 n.
unctuous
flattering 925 adj.
uncultivated
unproductive
172 adj.
ill-bred 847 adj.
uncurl
straighten 249 vb.
evolve 316 vb.
uncut
intact 52 adj.
undamaged
intact 52 adj.
undamaged
646 adj.
undated
anachronistic
118 adj.
undaunted
persevering 600 adj.
unfearing 855 adj.
undeceive
inform 524 vb.
undeceived
regretting 830 adj.
undecided
uncertain 474 adj.
irresolute 601 adj.
undecipherable
unintelligible
517 adj.
undeclared
tacit 523 adj.
undefeated
unbeaten 727 adj.
undefended
vulnerable 661 adj.
accusable 928 adj.
undefiled
pure 950 adj.
undefined
amorphous 244 adj.

shadowy 419 adj.
uncertain 474 adj.
undemanding
easy 701 adj.
lenient 736 adj.
undemocratic
authoritarian
735 adj.
prideful 871 adj.
undemonstrative
impassive 820 adj.
undeniable
undisputed 473 adj.
undenominational
general 79 adj.
undependable
unreliable 474 adj.
dishonest 930 adj.
under
inferior 35 adj.
under 210 adv.
subject 745 adj.
underachieve
fall short 307 vb.
under a cloud
disreputable
867 adj.
disapproved
924 adj.
under age
young 130 adj.
under arms
warring 718 adj.
under arrest
imprisoned 747 adj.
underbelly
insides 224 n.
vulnerability 661 n.
undercarriage
frame 218 n.
underclothes
underwear 228 n.
under control
orderly 60 adj.
obedient 739 adj.
under cover
covered 226 adj.
concealed 525 adj.
undercover agent
secret service 459 n.
undercroft
church interior
990 n.
undercurrent
current 350 n.
latency 523 n.
undercut

engrave 555 vb.
cheapen 812 vb.
underdeveloped
immature 670 adj.
underdog
inferior 35 n.
unlucky person
731 n.
underdone
culinary 301 adj.
underemployment
inaction 677 n.
under establishment
unprovided 636 adj.
underestimate
underestimate
483 vb.
not respect 921 vb.
underfed
underfed 636 adj.
hungry 859 adj.
under fire
endangered 661 adj.
underfoot
subjected 745 adj.
undergo
suffer 825 vb.
undergraduate
student 538 n.
underground
deep 211 adj.
concealed 525 adj.
opposition 704 n.
undergrowth
wood 366 n.
underhand
dishonest 930 adj.
underhung
projecting 254 adj.
underlie
cause 156 vb.
underline
emphasize 532 vb.
mark 547 vb.
underling
inferior 35 n.
servant 742 n.
underlying
undermost 214 adj.
undermanned
unprovided 636 adj.
undermine
disable 161 vb.
make concave
255 vb.
tell against 467 vb.
plot 623 vb.

underneath
under 210 adv.
undernourished
underfed 636 adj.
under one's belt
completed 725 adj.
under one's breath
faintly 401 adv.
under one's nose
near 200 adv.
visible 443 adj.
under one's thumb
subject 745 adj.
underpaid
poor 801 adj.
underpants
underwear 228 n.
underpass
tunnel 263 n.
bridge 624 n.
underpin
support 218 vb.
underpopulated, be
be few 105 vb.
under pressure
unwillingly 598 adv.
underprivileged
poor 801 adj.
lower classes 869 n.
underproof
weak 163 adj.
under protest
unwillingly 598 adv.
underrate
underestimate
483 vb.
undersea
deep 211 adj.
oceanic 343 adj.
undershot
projecting 254 adj.
underside
lowness 210 n.
undersigned, the
signatory 765 n.
undersized
dwarfish 196 adj.
understaffed
unprovided 636 adj.
understand
cognize 447 vb.
know 490 vb.
be wise 498 vb.
understand 516 vb.
be benevolent
897 vb.
understandable

intelligible 516 adj.
understanding
intelligence 498 n.
concord 710 n.
compact 765 n.
friendliness 880 n.
understatement
untruth 543 n.
understood
tacit 523 adj.
usual 610 adj.
understudy
actor 594 n.
deputy 755 n.
undertake
undertake 672 vb.
contract 765 vb.
undertaker
interment 364 n.
undertaking
undertaking 672 n.
promise 764 n.
under the weather
sick 651 n.
undertone
faintness 401 n.
undertow
current 350 n.
pitfall 663 n.
undervalue
underestimate
483 vb.
underwater
deep 211 adj.
oceanic 343 adj.
under way
under way 269 adv.
in preparation
669 adv.
underwear
underwear 228 n.
underweight
light 323 adj.
underworld
lower classes 869 n.
offender 904 n.
hell 972 n.
underwrite
give security 767 vb.
underwriting
calculation of
chance 159 n.
undeserved
unwarranted
916 adj.
undeserving
wicked 934 adj.

undesirable
inexpedient 643 adj.
troublemaker 663 n.
unwanted 860 adj.
undetected
latent 523 adj.
undeveloped
latent 523 adj.
immature 670 adj.
unskilled 695 adj.
undevelopment
undevelopment
670 n.
undeviating
uniform 16 adj.
straight 249 adj.
undies
underwear 228 n.
undifferentiated
uniform 16 adj.
indiscriminate
464 adj.
undigested
immature 670 adj.
undignified
vulgar 847 adj.
undiluted
unmixed 44 adj.
undiplomatic
unskilful 695 adj.
undiscerning
indiscriminating
464 adj.
unwise 499 adj.
undisciplined
disorderly 61 adj.
disobedient 738 adj.
undisclosed
concealed 525 adj.
undiscouraged
persevering 600 adj.
undiscovered
unknown 491 adj.
latent 523 adj.
undiscriminating
approving 923 adj.
undisguised
undisguised
522 adj.
artless 699 adj.
undismayed
unfearing 855 adj.
undisputed
undisputed 473 adj.
undistinguished
middling 732 adj.
undistracted

attentive 455 adj.
undisturbed
tranquil 266 adj.
undivided
intact 52 adj.
undo
disunite 46 vb.
revert 148 vb.
counteract 182 vb.
doff 229 vb.
undoing
destruction 165 n.
undomesticated
unhabituated
611 adj.
undone
neglected 458 adj.
uncompleted
726 adj.
undoubted
undisputed 473 adj.
undress
informal dress
228 n.
uncover 229 vb.
undrinkable
insalubrious
653 adj.
undue
undue 916 adj.
undulate
crinkle 251 vb.
oscillate 317 vb.
undulation
wave 350 n.
undutiful
undutiful 918 adj.
undying
perpetual 115 adj.
remembered
505 adj.
unearned
unwarranted
916 adj.
unearth
exhume 364 vb.
discover 484 vb.
unearthly
immaterial 320 adj.
spooky 970 adj.
uneasiness
worry 825 n.
discontent 829 n.
nervousness 854 n.
uneatable
unsavoury 391 adj.
uneconomic

wasteful 634 adj.
unedifying
discreditable
867 adj.
uneducated
uninstructed
491 adj.
unembarrassed
well-bred 848 adj.
unembellished
plain 573 adj.
unembroidered
veracious 540 adj.
unemotional
impassive 820 adj.
unemployable
useless 641 adj.
unemployed
unused 674 adj.
unemployment
superfluity 637 n.
inactivity 679 n.
**unemployment
benefit**
subvention 703 n.
unempowered
unentitled 916 adj.
unending
perpetual 115 adj.
unendurable
intolerable 827 adj.
unenjoyable
tedious 838 adj.
unenlightened
ignorant 491 adj.
unenterprising
cautious 858 adj.
unenthusiastic
unwilling 598 adj.
apathetic 820 adj.
unequal
unequal 29 adj.
unequalled
supreme 34 adj.
unequal to
insufficient 636 adj.
unequipped
powerless 161 adj.
unequivocal
positive 473 adj.
unerring
certain 473 adj.
accurate 494 adj.
successful
727 adj.
unescorted
alone 88 adj.

vulnerable 661 adj.
unethical
dishonest 930 adj.
uneven
nonuniform 17 adj.
unequal 29 adj.
fitful 142 adj.
rough 259 adj.
uneventful
tranquil 266 adj.
unexaggerated
genuine 494 adj.
unexampled
unusual 84 adj.
unexceptionable
not bad 644 adj.
unexceptional
general 79 adj.
unexciting
tedious 838 adj.
unexercised
unused 674 adj.
unexpected
unexpected 508 adj.
unexpired
remaining 41 adj.
unexplained
puzzling 517 adj.
unexploited
unused 674 adj.
unexplored
new 126 adj.
neglected 458 adj.
unknown 491 adj.
unexposed
safe 660 adj.
unexpressed
tacit 523 adj.
unexpurgated
impure 951 adj.
unextinguished
fiery 379 adj.
unextreme
neutral 625 adj.
unfactual
erroneous 495 adj.
unfading
perpetual 115 adj.
coloured 425 adj.
unfailing
unceasing 146 adj.
persevering
600 adj.
unfair
unjust 914 adj.
unfair, be
be biased 481 vb.

unfair picture
misrepresentation
552 n.
unfaithful
unbelieving 486 adj.
nonobservant
769 adj.
perfidious 930 adj.
extramarital
951 adj.
unfallen
innocent 935 adj.
unfaltering
persevering 600 adj.
unfamiliar
unknown 491 adj.
unhabituated
611 adj.
unfashionable
unwonted 611 adj.
ill-bred 847 adj.
unfasten
disunite 46 vb.
unfathomable
deep 211 adj.
unintelligible
517 adj.
unfavourable
inopportune
138 adj.
opposing 704 adj.
adverse 731 adj.
disapproving
924 adj.
unfearing
unfearing 855 adj.
unfeasible
impracticable
470 adj.
unfeeling
unfeeling 375 adj.
impassive 820 adj.
unfeigned
veracious 540 adj.
unfeminine
male 372 adj.
ill-bred 847 adj.
unfettered
facilitated 701 adj.
unconfined 744 adj.
unfilial
undutiful 918 adj.
unfinished
unfinished 55 adj.
uncompleted
726 adj.
unfit

useless 641 adj.
unfit for
unapt 25 adj.
unfitness
nonpreparation
670 n.
unfitting
inexpedient 643 adj.
unfix
displace 188 vb.
unflagging
industrious 678 adj.
unflappable
inexcitable 823 adj.
unflattering
true 494 adj.
detracting 926 adj.
unfledged
immature 670 adj.
unflinching
courageous 855 adj.
unfold
result 157 vb.
uncover 229 vb.
open 263 vb.
evolve 316 vb.
disclose 526 vb.
unforced
spontaneous
609 adj.
unforeseeable
unexpected 508 adj.
unforeseen
unexpected 508 adj.
unforgettable
remembered
505 adj.
unforgivable
heinous 934 adj.
unforgiving
revengeful 910 adj.
unformed
immature 670 adj.
unforthcoming
unsociable 883 adj.
unfortified
defenceless 161 adj.
vulnerable 661 adj.
unfortunate
unapt 25 adj.
unfortunate 731 adj.
unhappy 825 adj.
unfounded
unreal 2 adj.
erroneous 495 adj.
unfranchised
subject 745 adj.

unfrequented
secluded 883 adj.
unfriendly
inimical 881 adj.
unsociable 883 adj.
unfrock
depose 752 vb.
unfruitful
unproductive
172 adj.
unfurl
evolve 316 vb.
unfurnished
unprovided 636 adj.
unfussy
plain 573 adj.
ungainly
clumsy 695 adj.
ungallant
discourteous
885 adj.
ungenerous
parsimonious
816 adj.
unkind 898 adj.
ungentlemanly
discourteous
885 adj.
unget-at-able
removed 199 adj.
ungodly
irreligious 974 adj.
ungovernable
disobedient 738 adj.
lawless 954 adj.
ungraceful
inelegant 576 adj.
clumsy 695 adj.
ungraciousness
conduct 688 n.
rudeness 885 n.
ungraded
orderless 61 adj.
ungrammatical
ungrammatical
565 adj.
ungrateful
ungrateful 908 adj.
ungrounded
erroneous 495 adj.
ungrown
immature 670 adj.
ungrudging
willing 597 adj.
liberal 813 adj.
unguarded
inexpectant 508 adj.

vulnerable 661 adj.
unguent
unguent 357 n.
ungulate
footed 214 adj.
mammal 365 n.
unhabituated
unhabituated
611 adj.
unhallowed
profane 980 adj.
unhand
not retain 779 vb.
unhandy
clumsy 695 adj.
unhappy
inopportune
138 adj.
unfortunate 731 adj.
unhappy 825 adj.
unharmed
safe 660 adj.
unhealthy
unhealthy 651 adj.
insalubrious
653 adj.
unheard-of
new 126 adj.
impossible 470 adj.
wonderful 864 adj.
unhearing
deaf 416 adj.
inattentive 456 adj.
unheeded
neglected 458 adj.
unhelpful
hindering 702 adj.
unheralded
unexpected 508 adj.
unheroic
cowardly 856 adj.
inglorious 867 adj.
unhesitating
believing 485 adj.
unhinge
make mad 503 vb.
unhistorical
imaginary 513 adj.
unholy
profane 980 adj.
unhoped for
unexpected 508 adj.
unhurried
tranquil 266 adj.
leisurely 681 adj.
unhurt
undamaged 646 adj.

UNH

unhygienic
insalubrious
653 adj.
unicameral
parliamentary
692 adj.
unicorn
rara avis 84 n.
heraldry 547 n.
unidentified
unknown 491 adj.
unidiomatic
neological 560 adj.
unification
combination 50 n.
unity 88 n.
uniform
uniform 16 adj.
uniform 228 n.
livery 547 n.
unify
combine 50 vb.
(*see* **unification**)
unilateral
unrelated 10 adj.
independent
744 adj.
unimaginable
wonderful 864 adj.
unimaginative
imitative 20 adj.
unthinking 450 adj.
unintelligent
499 adj.
impassive 820 adj.
dull 840 adj.
unastonished
865 adj.
unimitated
original 21 adj.
unimpaired
intact 52 adj.
unimpassioned
feeble 572 adj.
unimpeachable
undisputed 473 adj.
unimpeded
facilitated 701 adj.
unimportant
irrelevant 10 adj.
unimportant
639 adj.
unimposing
modest 874 adj.
unimpressed
unastonished
865 adj.

UNI

unimpressive
imperfect 647 adj.
uninformative
reticent 525 adj.
uninformed
uninstructed
491 adj.
uninhabitable
empty 190 adj.
uninhabited
secluded 883 adj.
uninhibited
artless 699 adj.
unconfined 744 adj.
uninquisitive
incurious 454 adj.
uninspired
feeble 572 adj.
dull 840 adj.
unintegrated
extraneous 59 adj.
unintellectual
unintelligent
499 adj.
unintelligent
unintelligent
499 adj.
unintelligible
unintelligible
517 adj.
unintended
unmeant 515 adj.
unintentional
618 adj.
unintentional
involuntary 596 adj.
unintentional
618 adj.
uninterested
incurious 454 adj.
apathetic 820 adj.
indifferent 860 adj.
uninteresting
dull 840 adj.
uninterrupted
continuous 71 adj.
uninventive
imitative 20 adj.
uninvited
unwanted 860 adj.
uninviting
cheerless 834 adj.
uninvolved
unrelated 10 adj.
independent
744 adj.
union

UNK

union 45 n.
combination 50 n.
association 706 n.
society 708 n.
marriage 894 n.
unique
inimitable 21 adj.
special 80 adj.
one 88 adj.
unisex
uniform 16 adj.
tailored 228 adj.
unison
melody 410 n.
consensus 488 n.
unit
whole 52 n.
group 74 n.
unit 88 n.
person 371 n.
formation 722 n.
unitary
one 88 adj.
unite
join 45 vb.
be one 88 vb.
converge 293 vb.
cooperate 706 vb.
united
agreeing 24 adj.
concordant 710 adj.
married 894 adj.
unity
identity 13 n.
uniformity 16 n.
unity 88 n.
concord 710 n.
universal
universal 79 adj.
ubiquitous 189 adj.
cosmic 321 adj.
usual 610 adj.
universe
universe 321 n.
university
academy 539 n.
unjust
biased 481 adj.
unjust 914 adj.
unjustifiable
wrong 914 adj.
unkempt
orderless 61 adj.
dirty 649 adj.
unkind
unkind 898 adj.
unknown

UNL

unknown 491 adj.
anonymous 562 adj.
inglorious 867 adj.
unknown quantity
secret 530 n.
unladylike
ill-bred 847 adj.
discourteous
885 adj.
unlamented
hated 888 adj.
unlatch
open 263 vb.
unlawful
illegal 954 adj.
unlearn
forget 506 vb.
unlearned
uninstructed
491 adj.
unleash
liberate 746 vb.
unleavened
ritual 988 adj.
unless
provided 468 adv.
unlettered
uninstructed
491 adj.
unlicensed
unwarranted
916 adj.
unlikable
not nice 645 adj.
unlike
different 15 adj.
dissimilar 19 adj.
unlikely
improbable 472 adj.
unlimited
infinite 107 adj.
unconditional
744 adj.
unlit
unlit 418 adj.
dangerous 661 adj.
unload
transpose 272 vb.
disencumber
701 vb.
unlock
open 263 vb.
unlooked for
unexpected 508 adj.
unloose
disunite 46 vb.
liberate 746 vb.

unloved
  hated 888 adj.
unlovely
  ugly 842 adj.
unlucky
  unsuccessful
    728 adj.
  unfortunate 731 adj.
unmake
  destroy 165 vb.
unman
  unman 161 vb.
  frighten 854 vb.
unmanageable
  difficult 700 adj.
  disobedient 738 adj.
unmanly
  female 373 adj.
  cowardly 856 adj.
unmannerly
  ill-bred 847 adj.
  discourteous
    885 adj.
unmarked
  undamaged 646 adj.
unmarried
  unwedded 895 adj.
unmask
  disclose 526 vb.
unmeant
  unmeant 515 adj.
unmeasured
  plenteous 635 adj.
unmeditated
  spontaneous
    609 adj.
unmentionable
  impure 951 adj.
unmerciful
  pitiless 906 adj.
unmerited
  unwarranted
    916 adj.
unmindful
  inattentive 456 adj.
  ungrateful 908 adj.
unmistakable
  visible 443 adj.
  manifest 522 adj.
unmitigated
  complete 54 adj.
unmixed
  unmixed 44 adj.
  disinterested
    931 adj.
unmolested
  safe 660 adj.

unmotivated
  causeless 159 adj.
unmoved
  obstinate 602 adj.
  indifferent 860 adj.
  unastonished
    865 adj.
  pitiless 906 adj.
unmusical
  discordant 411 adj.
  deaf 416 adj.
unnamed
  anonymous 562 adj.
unnatural
  abnormal 84 adj.
  impossible 470 adj.
  inelegant 576 adj.
  affected 850 adj.
unnecessary
  superfluous 637 adj.
  unimportant
    639 adj.
unneighbourly
  unsociable 883 adj.
unnerve
  frighten 854 vb.
unnoticeable
  slow 278 adj.
  invisible 444 adj.
unnumbered
  infinite 107 adj.
unobjectionable
  not bad 644 adj.
  middling 732 adj.
unobservant
  blind 439 adj.
  inattentive 456 adj.
unobstructed
  unconfined 744 adj.
unobtainable
  impracticable
    470 adj.
  scarce 636 adj.
unobtrusive
  modest 874 adj.
unoccupied
  empty 190 adj.
  inactive 679 adj.
  unpossessed
    774 adj.
unoffending
  humble 872 adj.
unofficial
  independent
    744 adj.
  illegal 954 adj.
unopened

  closed 264 adj.
  unused 674 adj.
unopposed
  assented 488 adj.
unordained
  laical 987 adj.
unoriginal
  imitative 20 adj.
  mindless 448 adj.
unorthodox
  unconformable
    84 adj.
  heterodox 977 adj.
unpack
  uncover 229 vb.
unpaid
  voluntary 597 adj.
  uncharged 812 adj.
unpalatable
  unsavoury 391 adj.
  unpleasant 827 adj.
unparalleled
  best 644 adj.
unpardonable
  heinous 934 adj.
unpartnered
  unwedded 895 adj.
unpatriotic
  misanthropic
    902 adj.
  selfish 932 adj.
unpick
  disunite 46 vb.
unpitying
  pitiless 906 adj.
unplaced
  defeated 728 adj.
unplanned
  causeless 159 adj.
  bungled 695 adj.
unpleasant
  painful 377 adj.
  unsavoury 391 adj.
  fetid 397 adj.
  unpleasant
    827 adj.
  discourteous
    885 adj.
unpleasantness
  dissension 709 n.
unplug
  disunite 46 vb.
unplumbed
  deep 211 adj.
unpointed
  unsharpened
    257 adj.

unpolished
  rough 259 adj.
  inelegant 576 adj.
  immature 670 adj.
  artless 699 adj.
unpolluted
  unmixed 44 adj.
unpopular
  disliked 861 adj.
  friendless 883 adj.
unpopularity
  odium 888 n.
unpractical
  unskilful 695 adj.
unpractised
  unwonted 611 adj.
  unprepared 670 adj.
unprecedented
  first 68 adj.
  new 126 adj.
  unwonted 611 adj.
  wonderful 864 adj.
unpredictability
  chance 159 n.
  nondesign 618 n.
unpredictable
  nonuniform 17 adj.
  changeful 152 adj.
  unreliable 474 adj.
  capricious 604 adj.
unprejudiced
  wise 498 adj.
  just 913 adj.
unpremeditated
  spontaneous
    609 adj.
unprepared
  inexpectant 508 adj.
  unprepared 670 adj.
unprepossessing
  ugly 842 adj.
unpresentable
  ill-bred 847 adj.
unpretentious
  plain 573 adj.
  modest 874 adj.
unprincipled
  dishonest 930 adj.
unprintable
  impure 951 adj.
unprivileged
  unentitled 916 adj.
unprocessed
  uncompleted
    726 adj.
unproclaimed
  tacit 523 adj.

unprocurable
scarce 636 adj.
unproductive
unproductive
172 adj.
profitless 641 adj.
unprofessed
tacit 523 adj.
unprofessional
nonobservant
769 adj.
unprofessional
conduct
guilty act 936 n.
unprofitable
unproductive
172 adj.
profitless 641 adj.
unprogressive
deteriorated
655 adj.
unpromising
unpromising
853 adj.
unprompted
voluntary 597 adj.
unpronounceable
inexpressible
517 adj.
unpropitious
inopportune
138 adj.
unpromising
853 adj.
unprosperous
unprosperous
731 adj.
unprotected
vulnerable 661 adj.
unprotesting
humble 872 adj.
unproved
uncertified 474 adj.
unprovided for
unprovided 636 adj.
poor 801 adj.
unprovoked
spontaneous
609 adj.
unpunctual
late 136 adj.
unqualified
positive 473 adj.
unskilled 695 adj.
unentitled 916 adj.
unquenchable
greedy 859 adj.

unquestionable
undisputed 473 adj.
unquestioning
believing 485 adj.
unquiet
agitated 318 adj.
restlessness 678 n.
unravel
unravel 62 vb.
decipher 520 vb.
liberate 746 vb.
unreadable
unintelligible
517 adj.
tedious 838 adj.
unready
unprepared 670 adj.
unreal
unreal 2 adj.
imaginary 513 adj.
unrealistic
misjudging 481 adj.
unreality
immateriality 320 n.
unrealizable
impracticable
470 adj.
unreason
absence of intellect
448 n.
intuition 476 n.
folly 499 n.
unreasonable
illogical 477 adj.
biased 481 adj.
unwise 499 adj.
unreasoning
mindless 448 adj.
unrecognizable
converted 147 adj.
unrecognized
unknown 491 adj.
unrecorded
obliterated 550 adj.
unredeemed
wicked 934 adj.
unrefined
indiscriminating
464 adj.
vulgar 847 adj.
unreflecting
unthinking 450 adj.
unreformed
impenitent 940 adj.
unregulated
unconfined 744 adj.
unrehearsed

spontaneous
609 adj.
unrelated
unrelated 10 adj.
unrelenting
pitiless 906 adj.
revengeful 910 adj.
unreliable
changeful 152 adj.
unreliable 474 adj.
capricious 604 adj.
unsafe 661 adj.
unrelieved
uniform 16 adj.
cheerless 834 adj.
unremarked
neglected 458 adj.
unremembered
forgotten 506 adj.
unremitting
unceasing 146 adj.
unrepentant
impenitent 940 adj.
unrepresentative
abnormal 84 adj.
unrepresented
absent 190 adj.
unrequired
superfluous 637 adj.
unused 674 adj.
unrequited
unthanked 908 adj.
unreserved
positive 473 adj.
undisguised
522 adj.
free 744 adj.
unresisting
submitting 721 adj.
unresolved
puzzling 517 adj.
unresponsive
impassive 820 adj.
unrest
discontent 829 n.
unrestrained
violent 176 adj.
unconfined 744 adj.
intemperate 943 adj.
unrestricted
unconditional
744 adj.
unrewarded
profitless 641 adj.
unthanked 908 adj.
unriddle
decipher 520 vb.

unrighteous
wicked 934 adj.
unrightful
unwarranted
916 adj.
unrip
open 263 vb.
unripe
immature 670 adj.
uncompleted
726 adj.
unrivalled
supreme 34 adj.
unroll
evolve 316 vb.
manifest 522 vb.
unromantic
inexcitable 823 adj.
unruffled
inexcitable 823 adj.
unruly
disorderly 61 adj.
disobedient 738 adj.
unsafe
unsafe 661 adj.
unsaid
tacit 523 adj.
unsalable
profitless 641 adj.
unsalaried
uncharged 812 adj.
unsalvageable
lost 772 adj.
unsanctified
profane 980 adj.
unsanctioned
unwarranted
916 adj.
unsatisfactory
disappointing
509 adj.
insufficient 636 adj.
disapproved
924 adj.
unsatisfied
unprovided 636 adj.
discontented
829 adj.
desiring 859 adj.
unsavoury
unsavoury 391 adj.
disliked 861 adj.
unsay
recant 603 vb.
unscalable
impracticable
470 adj.

unscathed
undamaged 646 adj.

unscented
odourless 395 adj.

unscientific
impossible 470 adj.
illogical 477 adj.
unskilled 695 adj.

unscramble
unravel 62 vb.

unscriptural
heterodox 977 adj.

unscrupulous
dishonest 930 adj.

unseal
disclose 526 vb.

unsearchable
unintelligible
517 adj.

unseasonable
ill-timed 138 adj.
inexpedient 643 adj.

unseasoned
tasteless 387 adj.
immature 670 adj.

unseat
depose 752 vb.

unseeing
blind 439 adj.
inattentive 456 adj.

unseemly
inexpedient 643 adj.
undue 916 adj.

unseen
invisible 444 adj.
latent 523 adj.

unselective
indiscriminating
464 adj.

unselfish
disinterested
931 adj.

unserviceable
useless 641 adj.

unsettle
derange 63 vb.
impress 821 vb.

unsettled
unstable 152 adj.
displaced 188 adj.

unsexed
impotent 161 adj.

unshackle
liberate 746 vb.

unshakable
fixed 153 adj.
certain 473 adj.

creedal 485 adj.
resolute 599 adj.

unshapely
amorphous 244 adj.
unsightly 842 adj.

unshaven
hairy 259 adj.

unsheathe
uncover 229 vb.
manifest 522 vb.

unshielded
vulnerable 661 adj.

unship
empty 300 vb.

unshockable
impassive 820 adj.

unshod
uncovered 229 adj.

unshrinkable
unchangeable
153 adj.

unshrinking
courageous
855 adj.

unshriven
impenitent 940 adj.

unsightly
unsightly 842 adj.

unsigned
uncertified 474 adj.
anonymous 562 adj.

unsinkable
light 323 adj.

unskilful
ignorant 491 adj.
unskilful 695 adj.

unskilled
unskilled 695 adj.

unsleeping
industrious 678 adj.

unsleeping eye
surveillance 457 n.

unsmiling
serious 834 adj.

unsociable
unsociable 883 adj.
misanthropic
902 adj.

unsolicited
voluntary 597 adj.

unsolvable
puzzling 517 adj.

unsophisticated
credulous 487 adj.
artless 699 adj.

unsorted
mixed 43 adj.

orderless 61 adj.

unsought
voluntary 597 adj.

unsound
unstable 152 adj.
erroneous 495 adj.
imperfect 647 adj.
unhealthy 651 adj.

unsound mind
insanity 503 n.

unsparing
severe 735 adj.
liberal 813 adj.

unspeakable
inexpressible
517 adj.

unspecified
general 79 adj.

unspent
unused 674 adj.

unspiritual
material 319 adj.
sensual 944 adj.

unspoiled, unspoilt
undamaged 646 adj.

unspoken
tacit 523 adj.

unsportsmanlike
unjust 914 adj.

unspotted
innocent 935 adj.

unstable
unstable 152 adj.
excitable 822 adj.

unstained
perfect 646 adj.
honourable 929 adj.

unstatesmanlike
unskilful 695 adj.

unsteady
unstable 152 adj.
irresolute 601 adj.
unsafe 661 adj.

unstick
unstick 49 vb.

unstinting
liberal 813 adj.

unstitch
disunite 46 vb.

unstop
open 263 vb.

unstoppable
unceasing 146 adj.

unstressed
muted 401 adj.

**unstring one's
nerves**

frighten 854 vb.

unstuck
disunited 46 adj.

unstudied
unprepared 670 adj.
artless 699 adj.

unsubstantial
insubstantial 4 adj.

unsubstantiated
erroneous 495 adj.

unsuccessful
profitless 641 adj.
unsuccessful
728 adj.
unprosperous
731 adj.

unsuitable
unapt 25 adj.
inexpedient
643 adj.

unsullied
clean 648 adj.
honourable 929 adj.

unsung
inglorious 867 adj.

unsupplied
unprovided
636 adj.

unsupported
vulnerable 661 adj.

unsure
uncertain 474 adj.

unsurpassable
supreme 34 adj.

unsurprised
unastonished
865 adj.

unsuspected
latent 523 adj.

unsuspecting
inexpectant 508 adj.

unsweetened
sour 393 adj.

unswept
dirty 649 adj.

unswerving
straight 249 adj.
directed 281 adj.
just 913 adj.

unsymmetrical
distorted 246 adj.

unsympathetic
disliking 861 adj.
pitiless 906 adj.

unsystematic
orderless 61 adj.
fitful 142 adj.

untamed
unhabituated
611 adj.
disobedient 738 adj.
untangle
unravel 62 vb.
untapped
unused 674 adj.
untarnished
clean 648 adj.
honourable 929 adj.
untaught
uninstructed
491 adj.
unteachable
obstinate 602 adj.
untearable
tough 329 adj.
untempted
indifferent 860 adj.
untenable
illogical 477 adj.
untenanted
empty 190 adj.
untested
new 126 adj.
unthankful
ungrateful 908 adj.
unthinkable
impossible 470 adj.
unthinking
mindless 448 adj.
unthinking 450 adj.
unthrifty
unprepared 670 adj.
prodigal 815 adj.
unthrone
deprive 786 vb.
unthrustful
modest 874 adj.
untidy
orderless 61 adj.
dirty 649 adj.
untie
disunite 46 vb.
liberate 746 vb.
until
while 108 adv.
(*see* **till**)
untimely
ill-timed 138 adj.
untiring
persevering 600 adj.
untitled
plebeian 869 adj.
untold
infinite 107 adj.

untouchable
outcast 883 n.
untouched
intact 52 adj.
unused 674 adj.
apathetic 820 adj.
untoward
inopportune
138 adj.
adverse 731 adj.
untraceable
lost 772 adj.
untrained
unhabituated
611 adj.
unskilled 695 adj.
untrammelled
unconfined 744 adj.
untravelled
quiescent 266 adj.
untried
new 126 adj.
unknown 491 adj.
untrodden
new 126 adj.
untroubled
content 828 adj.
untrue
erroneous 495 adj.
false 541 adj.
untrue 543 adj.
untrustworthy
unreliable 474 adj.
dishonest 930 adj.
untruth
untruth 543 n.
untruthful
false 541 adj.
untuneful
discordant 411 adj.
untutored
artless 699 adj.
untwist
evolve 316 vb.
untypical
abnormal 84 adj.
unusable
useless 641 adj.
unused
new 126 adj.
unused 674 adj.
unusual
unusual 84 adj.
unutterable
inexpressible
517 adj.
wonderful 864 adj.

unvanquished
unbeaten 727 adj.
unvarnished
plain 573 adj.
unvarying
uniform 16 adj.
unchangeable
153 adj.
unveil
disclose 526 vb.
unventilated
sealed off 264 adj.
insalubrious
653 adj.
unverified
uncertified 474 adj.
unversed
ignorant 491 adj.
unviable
impracticable
470 adj.
unvoiced
tacit 523 adj.
unwanted
rejected 607 adj.
superfluous 637 adj.
unused 674 adj.
unwanted 860 adj.
unwarlike
peaceful 717 adj.
unwarranted
unwarranted
916 adj.
unwary
rash 857 adj.
unwashed
dirty 649 adj.
unwavering
persevering 600 adj.
unwearied
industrious 678 adj.
unwedded
unwedded 895 adj.
unwelcome
unpleasant 827 adj.
unwanted 860 adj.
unwelcome guest
incomer 297 n.
unwelcoming
inimical 881 adj.
unsociable 883 adj.
unwell
sick 651 adj.
unwept
hated 888 adj.
unwholesome
harmful 645 adj.

insalubrious
653 adj.
unwieldy
unwieldy 195 adj.
unwilling
unwilling 598 adj.
unwind
evolve 316 vb.
repose 683 vb.
unwinking
still 266 adj.
unwisdom
folly 499 n.
unwise
unwise 499 adj.
rash 857 adj.
unwished for
unwanted 860 adj.
unwitting
ignorant 491 adj.
involuntary
596 adj.
unwomanly
male 372 adj.
unwonted
unwonted 611 adj.
unworkable
impracticable
470 adj.
useless 641 adj.
unworldly
innocent 935 adj.
pious 979 adj.
unworried
content 828 adj.
unworthy
inferior 35 adj.
discreditable
867 adj.
unwrap
uncover 229 vb.
open 263 vb.
disclose 526 vb.
unwrinkled
flat 216 adj.
smooth 258 adj.
tranquil 266 adj.
unwritten
tacit 523 adj.
unwritten law
precept 693 n.
unyielding
unyielding 162 adj.
obstinate 602 adj.
resisting 715 adj.
unzip
disunite 46 vb.

UP	UPS	URC	USH

up
  aloft 209 adv.
  up 308 adv.
up against it
  in difficulties
    700 adj.
up and about
  healthy 650 adj.
up and coming
  prosperous 730 adj.
up and doing
  busy 678 adj.
up and down
  undulatory 251 adj.
  to and fro 317 adv.
  sullen 893 adj.
upbeat
  optimistic 482 adj.
upbraid
  reprobate 924 vb.
upbringing
  teaching 534 n.
up-country
  regional 184 adj.
  provincial 192 adj.
update
  modernize 126 vb.
updraught
  ascent 308 n.
up-end
  make vertical
    215 vb.
  invert 221 vb.
up for grabs
  unpossessed
    774 adj.
upgrade
  dignify 866 vb.
upheaval
  revolution 149 n.
  havoc 165 n.
uphill
  sloping 220 adj.
  ascending 308 adj.
  difficult 700 adj.
uphold
  support 218 vb.
  corroborate 466 vb.
upholstery
  lining 227 n.
  equipment 630 n.
up in
  expert 694 adj.
up in arms
  opposing 704 adj.
  riotous 738 adj.
upkeep

  preservation 666 n.
  subvention 703 n.
upland(s)
  high land 209 n.
uplift
  elevate 310 vb.
  make better 654 vb.
  make pious 979 vb.
upmarket
  dear 811 adj.
upon
  (see on)
up one's street
  fit 24 adj.
upper
  superior 34 adj.
upper case
  print-type 587 n.
upper class
  upper class 868 n.
uppercut
  knock 279 n.
upper hand
  advantage 34 n.
  victory 727 n.
uppermost
  supreme 34 adj.
  topmost 213 adj.
uppish
  prideful 871 adj.
upright
  vertical 215 adj.
  just 913 adj.
  honourable 929 adj.
uprising
  revolt 738 n.
uproar
  turmoil 61 n.
  loudness 400 n.
uproarious
  excitable 822 adj.
  merry 833 adj.
uproot
  eject 300 vb.
  extract 304 vb.
uprush
  spurt 277 n.
  ascent 308 n.
ups and downs
  affairs 154 n.
  fluctuation 317 n.
upset
  derange 63 vb.
  overturning 221 n.
  distract 456 vb.
  cause discontent
    829 vb.

  enrage 891 vb.
upshot
  effect 157 n.
upside down
  orderless 61 adj.
  inverted 221 adj.
upsides with
  equal 28 adj.
upstage
  stage set 594 n.
  act 594 vb.
  prideful 871 adj.
upstanding
  vertical 215 adj.
  (see upright)
upstart
  upstart 126 n.
upstream
  towards 281 adv.
upswing
  improvement 654 n.
uptight
  nervous 854 adj.
  irascible 892 adj.
up-to-date
  modern 126 adj.
up to something
  planning 623 adj.
  dishonest 930 adj.
up to the ears/eyes
  deeply 211 adv.
up to the mark
  sufficient 635 adj.
up-to-the-minute
  modern 126 adj.
uptown
  city 184 n.
upturn
  invert 221 vb.
  improvement 654 n.
upwards
  up 308 adv.
uranium
  fuel 385 n.
uranography
  astronomy 321 n.
urban
  regional 184 adj.
  urban 192 adj.
urbane
  well-bred 848 adj.
  courteous 884 adj.
urban sprawl
  housing 192 n.
  expansion 197 n.
urchin
  youngster 132 n.

urge
  impel 279 vb.
  affirm 532 vb.
  incite 612 vb.
  hasten 680 vb.
  advise 691 vb.
  request 761 vb.
  desire 859 n.
urgency
  importance 638 n.
  haste 680 n.
urgent
  demanding
    627 adj.
  compelling
    740 adj.
urinal
  latrine 649 n.
urine
  excrement 302 n.
urn
  vessel 194 n.
  interment 364 n.
us
  self 80 n.
usable
  useful 640 adj.
usage
  connotation 514 n.
  habit 610 n.
use
  profit by 137 vb.
  operate 173 vb.
  habit 610 n.
  utility 640 n.
  use 673 n.vb.
—up
  waste 634 vb.
  dispose of 673 vb.
—wrongly
  misuse 675 vb.
useful
  useful 640 adj.
  advisable 642 adj.
useless
  useless 641 adj.
  deteriorated
    655 adj.
uselessness
  ineffectuality 161 n.
  inutility 641 n.
usher
  accompany 89 vb.
  retainer 742 n.
—in
  precede 283 vb.
  admit 299 vb.

usherette
  stagehand 594 n.
usual
  regular 81 adj.
  typical 83 adj.
  usual 610 adj.
  fashionable
    848 adj.
usufruct
  use 673 n.
usurer
  lender 784 n.
usurp
  appropriate 786 vb.
  be undue 916 vb.
usurper
  usurper 916 n.
usury
  lending 784 n.
  interest 803 n.
utensil
  tool 630 n.
uterus
  genitalia 167 n.
utilitarian
  useful 640 adj.
  philanthropist
    901 n.
utilitarianism
  good policy 642 n.
  benevolence 897 n.
utility
  utility 640 n.
utilize
  use 673 vb.
utmost
  limit 236 n.
Utopia
  fantasy 513 n.
Utopian
  visionary 513 n.
  reformer 654 n.
utter
  complete 54 adj.
  voice 577 vb.
  speak 579 vb.
utterance
  speech 579 n.
uttermost
  limit 236 n.
U-turn
  reversion 148 n.
  circuition 314 n.
  change of allegiance
    603 n.
uxorious
  loving 887 adj.

V

vacancy
  job 622 n.
vacant
  empty 190 adj.
  unthinking 450 adj.
vacate
  go away 190 vb.
  relinquish 621 vb.
  resign 753 vb.
vacation
  repose 683 n.
vaccinate
  safeguard 660 vb.
vaccination
  hygiene 652 n.
vacillate
  be irresolute 601 vb.
vacuity
  insubstantiality 4 n.
  emptiness 190 n.
  absence of thought
    450 n.
vacuum
  emptiness 190 n.
  rarity 325 n.
vade mecum
  guidebook 524 n.
vagabond
  wanderer 268 n.
vagary
  whim 604 n.
vagina
  genitalia 167 n.
vagrant
  wanderer 268 n.
  poor person 801 n.
vague
  insubstantial 4 adj.
  shadowy 419 adj.
  uncertain 474 adj.
  equivocal 518 adj.
vain
  profitless 641 adj.
  unsuccessful
    728 adj.
  vain 873 adj.
vainglorious
  boastful 877 adj.
vain person
  vain person 873 n.
vale
  valley 255 n.
valediction
  valediction 296 n.

valentine
  love token 889 n.
valet
  clean 648 vb.
  domestic 742 n.
valetudinarian
  sick person 651 n.
valiant
  courageous 855 adj.
valid
  powerful 160 adj.
  genuine 494 adj.
validate
  corroborate 466 vb.
  make legal 953 vb.
validity
  authenticity 494 n.
valley
  valley 255 n.
valour
  courage 855 n.
valuable
  valuable 644 adj.
valuables
  estate 777 n.
valuation
  estimate 480 n.
value
  equivalence 28 n.
  quid pro quo 150 n.
  estimate 480 vb.
  importance 638 n.
  utility 640 n.
  price 809 n.vb.
  honour 866 vb.
value judgement
  intuition 476 n.
valueless
  profitless 641 adj.
  cheap 812 adj.
valuer
  estimator 480 n.
valve
  electronics 160 n.
vamp
  play music 413 vb.
  loose woman
    952 n.
—up
  make better 654 vb.
vampire
  demon 970 n.
van
  lorry 274 n.
  (*see* **vanguard**)
vandal
  destroyer 168 n.

vulgarian 847 n.
vandalize
  impair 655 vb.
  make ugly 842 vb.
vanguard
  precursor 66 n.
  front 237 n.
vanish
  pass away 2 vb.
  disappear 446 vb.
vanished
  lost 772 adj.
vanity
  insubstantial thing
    4 n.
  folly 499 n.
  inutility 641 n.
  affectation 850 n.
  vanity 873 n.
Vanity Fair
  fashion 848 n.
vanquish
  overmaster 727 vb.
vantage ground
  advantage 34 n.
  influence 178 n.
vantage point
  view 438 n.
vapid
  tasteless 387 adj.
  feeble 572 adj.
vaporific
  vaporific 338 adj.
vaporize
  vaporize 338 vb.
vaporous
  insubstantial 4 adj.
  gaseous 336 adj.
  opaque 423 adj.
vapour
  gas 336 n.
  cloud 355 n.
  mean nothing
    515 vb.
variable
  nonuniform 17 adj.
  changeable
    143 adj.
variance
  disagreement 25 n.
  dissension 709 n.
variant
  variant 15 n.
variation
  difference 15 n.
  change 143 n.
  musical piece 412 n.

variegation
medley 43 n.
variegation 437 n.
variety
nonuniformity 17 n.
medley 43 n.
sort 77 n.
multiformity 82 n.
stage show 594 n.
various
different 15 adj.
many 104 adj.
varnish
smoother 258 n.
resin 357 n.
conceal 525 vb.
sham 542 n.
decorate 844 vb.
vary
differ 15 vb.
vary 152 vb.
vase
bowl 194 n.
vasectomy
surgery 658 n.
vassal
subject 742 n.
vast
spacious 183 adj.
huge 195 adj.
vat
vat 194 n.
vaudeville
stage show 594 n.
vault
cellar 194 n.
dome 253 n.
leap 312 n.vb.
tomb 364 n.
storage 632 n.
vaulted
covered 226 adj.
curved 248 adj.
vaunt
boast 877 n.vb.
veal
meat 301 n.
vector
number 85 n.
infection 651 n.
veer
vary 152 vb.
deviate 282 vb.
vegan
abstainer 942 n.
vegetable
inertness 175 n.

vegetable 301 n.
vegetal 366 adj.
mindless 448 adj.
vegetable kingdom
vegetable life 366 n.
vegetarian
abstainer 942 n.
vegetate
be inert 175 vb.
be inactive 679 vb.
vegetation
vegetable life 366 n.
vehement
vigorous 174 adj.
assertive 532 adj.
fervent 818 adj.
vehicle
transport 272 n.
vehicle 274 n.
instrument 628 n.
vehicular
vehicular 274 adj.
veil
cover 226 vb.
headgear 228 n.
screen 421 n.vb.
conceal 525 vb.
vocation 622 n.
veiled
unknown 491 adj.
occult 523 adj.
vein
temperament 5 n.
tube 263 n.
variegate 437 vb.
style 566 n.
store 632 n.
affections 817 n.
veld, veldt
plain 348 n.
vellum
stationery 586 n.
velocity
velocity 277 n.
velvet
textile 222 n.
smoothness 258 n.
palmy days 730 n.
velvet glove
leniency 736 n.
velvety
downy 259 adj.
soft 327 adj.
venal
venal 930 adj.
vendetta
quarrel 709 n.

revenge 910 n.
vendor
seller 793 n.
veneer
shallowness 212 n.
facing 226 n.
sham 542 n.
venerable
ageing 131 adj.
respected 920 adj.
venerate
respect 920 vb.
venereal
diseased 651 adj.
sensual 944 adj.
venery
unchastity 951 n.
venetian blind
shade 226 n.
vengeance
revenge 910 n.
vengeful
revengeful 910 adj.
venial
vindicable 927 adj.
venial sin
trifle 639 n.
venison
meat 301 n.
venom
poison 659 n.
venomous
toxic 653 adj.
malevolent 898 adj.
vent
outlet 298 n.
empty 300 vb.
air pipe 353 n.
divulge 526 vb.
liberate 746 vb.
ventilate
inquire 459 vb.
dissertate 591 vb.
sanitate 652 vb.
refresh 685 vb.
ventilation
ventilation 352 n.
refrigeration 382 n.
ventricle
compartment 194 n.
ventriloquism
mimicry 20 n.
sleight 542 n.
ventriloquist
conjuror 545 n.
venture
be tentative 461 vb.

attempt 671 n.vb.
undertaking 672 n.
speculate 791 vb.
venturesome
speculative 618 adj.
enterprising 672 adj.
rash 857 adj.
venue
locality 187 n.
veracious
veracious 540 adj.
verandah
lobby 194 n.
verb
part of speech 564 n.
verbal
verbal 559 adj.
verbiage
empty talk 515 n.
diffuseness 570 n.
verbose
diffuse 570 adj.
verdant
vegetal 366 adj.
green 434 adj.
verdict
judgement 480 n.
legal trial 959 n.
verdure
foliage 366 n.
greenness 434 n.
verge
tend 179 vb.
nearness 200 n.
edge 234 n.
verger
church officer 986 n.
verify
experiment 461 vb.
demonstrate 478 vb.
verisimilitude
probability 471 n.
accuracy 494 n.
truth 494 n.
veritable
genuine 494 adj.
vermifuge
antidote 658 n.
vermilion
red 431 adj.
vermin
insect 365 n.
cad 938 n.
verminous
insalubrious 653 adj.

vernacular
native 191 adj.
language 557 n.
dialect 560 n.
plain 573 adj.
vernal
vernal 128 adj.
vernal equinox
spring 128 n.
verruca
swelling 253 n.
versatile
multiform 82 adj.
changeful 152 adj.
skilful 694 adj.
verse
poetry 593 n.
versed in
knowing 490 adj.
expert 694 adj.
versify
poetize 593 vb.
version
sort 77 n.
translation 520 n.
description 590 n.
verso
rear 238 n.
sinistrality 242 n.
versus
in opposition
704 adv.
vertebral
back 238 adj.
vertebrate
animal 365 n.adj.
vertex
vertex 213 n.
vertical
vertical 215 adj.
vertiginous
high 209 adj.
vertigo
rotation 315 n.
illness 651 n.
verve
vigorousness 174 n.
vigour 571 n.
very
greatly 32 adv.
vesicle
bladder 194 n.
vespers
church service
988 n.
vessel
vessel 194 n.

ship 275 n.
vest
underwear 228 n.
vestal
virgin 950 n.
vested
established 153 adj.
due 915 adj.
vestibule
lobby 194 n.
vestige
small quantity 33 n.
remainder 41 n.
vestments
vestments 989 n.
vestry
council 692 n.
church interior
990 n.
vesture
dressing 228 n.
vet
animal husbandry
369 n.
estimate 480 vb.
veteran
old man 133 n.
expert 696 n.
soldier 722 n.
veterinary disease
animal disease
651 n.
veterinary surgeon
doctor 658 n.
veto
prohibit 757 vb.
vex
torment 827 vb.
vexation
annoyance 827 n.
anger 891 n.
VHF
radiation 417 n.
via
towards 281 adv.
viable
alive 360 adj.
possible 469 adj.
viaduct
bridge 624 n.
vial
vessel 194 n.
viands
food 301 n.
viaticum
Christian rite
988 n.

vibrant
resonant 404 adj.
feeling 818 adj.
vibraphone
gong 414 n.
vibrate
oscillate 317 vb.
roll 403 vb.
vibration(s)
sound 398 n.
resonance 404 n.
feeling 818 n.
vibrato
adagio 412 adv.
vicar
pastor 986 n.
vicarage
parsonage 986 n.
vicarious
substituted 150 adj.
commissioned
751 adj.
vice
nippers 778 n.
vice 934 n.
vice-
deputy 755 n.
vice-like
retentive 778 adj.
vice-president
director 690 n.
deputy 755 n.
viceroy
governor 741 n.
vice squad
social evil 951 n.
vice versa
correlatively 12 adv.
vicinity
near place 200 n.
surroundings 230 n.
vicious
malevolent 898 adj.
vicious 934 adj.
vicious circle
continuity 71 n.
obstacle 702 n.
vicissitude(s)
affairs 154 n.
adversity 731 n.
vicissitudinous
changeful 152 adj.
victim
dupe 544 n.
unlucky person
731 n.
sufferer 825 n.

laughingstock
851 n.
oblation 981 n.
victimize
oppress 735 vb.
victor
victor 727 n.
Victoria Cross
decoration 729 n.
Victorian
antiquated 127 adj.
prudish 950 adj.
victorious
successful 727 adj.
victory
victory 727 n.
victual
feed 301 vb.
provide 633 vb.
victuals
food 301 n.
video
spectacle 445 n.
appearing 445 adj.
videorecorder
broadcasting
531 n.
recording
instrument 549 n.
videotape
record 548 vb.
vie (with)
be good 644 vb.
contend 716 vb.
view
view 438 n.
watch 441 vb.
spectacle 445 n.
opinion 485 n.
viewdata
data processing
86 n.
information 524 n.
viewer
spectator 441 n.
viewfinder
telescope 442 n.
viewing
inspection 438 n.
viewpoint
view 438 n.
opinion 485 n.
vigil
surveillance 457 n.
vigilant
attentive 455 adj.
vigilant 457 adj.

tutelary 660 adj.
prepared 669 adj.

vigilante
protector 660 n.

vigilantism
lawlessness 954 n.

vigils
prayers 981 n.

vignette
picture 553 n.
description 590 n.
acting 594 n.

vigorous
dynamic 160 adj.
vigorous 174 adj.
active 678 adj.

vigour
energy 160 n.
vigorousness 174 n.
vigour 571 n.

vile
bad 645 adj.
rascally 930 adj.
heinous 934 adj.

vilify
shame 867 vb.
defame 926 vb.

villa
house 192 n.

village
district 184 n.
housing 192 n.

village green
focus 76 n.
pleasure ground 837 n.

village idiot
country-dweller 869 n.

villager
dweller 191 n.

villain
evildoer 904 n.
knave 938 n.

villainous
ugly 842 adj.
rascally 930 adj.

villainy
wickedness 934 n.

villein
slave 742 n.

vim
vigorousness 174 n.

vinaigrette
sauce 389 n.

vindicable
vindicable 927 adj.

vindicate
vindicate 927 vb.

vindication
credential 466 n.
vindication 927 n.
acquittal 960 n.

vindictive
malevolent 898 adj.
revengeful 910 adj.

vine
plant 366 n.

vinegar
sourness 393 n.

vineyard
farm 370 n.

vinous
drunken 949 adj.
intoxicating 949 adj.

vintage
date 108 n.
olden 127 adj.
agriculture 370 n.
store 632 n.
excellent 644 adj.

vinyl
floor-cover 226 n.

viola
viol 414 n.

violate
force 176 vb.
not observe 769 vb.
debauch 951 vb.
be impious 980 vb.

violence
violence 176 n.
misuse 675 n.
brute force 735 n.

violent
violent 176 adj.
fervent 818 adj.
lawless 954 adj.

violet
fragrance 396 n.
purple 436 adj.
humility 872 n.

violin
viol 414 n.

violinist
instrumentalist 413 n.

VIP
bigwig 638 n.
person of repute 866 n.

viper
reptile 365 n.

noxious animal 904 n.
knave 938 n.

virago
violent creature 176 n.
shrew 892 n.

virgin
new 126 adj.
woman 373 n.
unknown 491 adj.
virgin 950 n.

virginal
young 130 adj.
pure 950 adj.

virginity
purity 950 n.

viridian
green pigment 434 n.

virile
strong 162 adj.
vigorous 174 adj.
male 372 adj.

virility
vitality 162 n.

virology
medical art 658 n.

virtual
equivalent 28 adj.

virtually
intrinsically 5 adv.
almost 33 adv.

virtue
ability 160 n.
goodness 644 n.
virtue 933 n.

virtuosity
musical skill 413 n.
skill 694 n.

virtuoso
musician 413 n.
proficient person 696 n.

virtuous
virtuous 933 adj.

virulent
keen 174 adj.
baneful 659 adj.
maleficent 898 adj.

virus
microorganism 196 n.
infection 651 n.

visa
permit 756 n.

visage
face 237 n.
feature 445 n.

vis-à-vis
concerning 9 adv.
against 240 adv.

visceral
interior 224 adj.
felt 818 adj.

viscid
viscid 354 adj.

viscidity
retention 778 n.

viscount, viscountess
person of rank 868 n.

viscous
viscid 354 adj.

visibility
visibility 443 n.

visible
visible 443 adj.
manifest 522 adj.

vision
vision 438 n.
visual fallacy 440 n.
spectacle 445 n.
foresight 510 n.
fantasy 513 n.
a beauty 841 n.
aspiration 852 n.
occultism 984 n.

visionary
unreal 2 adj.
crank 504 n.
visionary 513 n.
reformer 654 n.

visionless
blind 439 adj.

visit
arrive 295 vb.
social round 882 n.

visitant
incomer 297 n.
ghost 970 n.

visitation
inquiry 459 n.
punishment 963 n.

visitor
incomer 297 n.
sociable person 882 n.

visor
screen 421 n.
armour 713 n.

vista
view 438 n.

VIS

visual
seeing 438 adj.
image 551 n.
visual aid
classroom 539 n.
visual display unit
data processing
86 n.
optical device 442 n.
visual fallacy
visual fallacy 440 n.
fantasy 513 n.
visualize
imagine 513 vb.
vital
alive 360 adj.
required 627 adj.
important 638 adj.
lively 819 adj.
vitality
vitality 162 n.
life 360 n.
health 650 n.
cheerfulness 833 n.
vitalize
vitalize 360 vb.
animate 821 vb.
vital role
influence 178 n.
vitals
insides 224 n.
vital spark
life 360 n.
vital statistics
statistics 86 n.
beauty 841 n.
vitamins
dieting 301 n.
tonic 658 n.
vitiate
impair 655 vb.
pervert 655 vb.
vitreous
hard 326 adj.
transparent 422 adj.
vitrify
harden 326 vb.
vitriol
poison 659 n.
vitriolic
paining 827 adj.
cursing 899 adj.
vituperate
curse 899 vb.
viva
exam 459 n.
vivacious

VOI

lively 819 adj.
vivarium
zoo 369 n.
vivid
florid 425 adj.
obvious 443 adj.
expressive 516 adj.
forceful 571 adj.
descriptive 590 adj.
vivify
vitalize 360 vb.
animate 821 vb.
viviparous
fertilized 167 adj.
vivisect
give pain 377 vb.
experiment 461 vb.
vixen
female animal
373 n.
shrew 892 n.
viz
namely 80 adv.
vizier
officer 741 n.
vocable
word 559 n.
vocabulary
dictionary 559 n.
style 566 n.
vocal
vocal 577 adj.
desiring 859 adj.
vocal cords
voice 577 n.
vocalist
vocalist 413 n.
entertainer 594 n.
vocation
vocation 622 n.
church ministry
985 n.
vocational training
education 534 n.
vocative
vocative 583 adj.
vociferate
vociferate 408 vb.
vodka
alcoholic drink
301 n.
vogue
fashion 848 n.
voice
publish 528 vb.
grammar 564 n.
voice 577 n.vb.

VOL

voiced
sounding 398 adj.
vocal 577 adj.
voiceless
voiceless 578 adj.
subject 745 adj.
voice-over
sound 398 n.
void
emptiness 190 n.
empty 300 vb.
universe 321 n.
abrogated 752 adj.
volatile
transient 114 adj.
changeful 152 adj.
gaseous 336 adj.
light-minded
456 adj.
capricious 604 adj.
excitable 822 adj.
volatilize
rarefy 325 vb.
vaporize 338 vb.
volcanic
violent 176 adj.
fiery 379 adj.
excitable 822 adj.
volcano
furnace 383 n.
volition
will 595 n.
volley
strike 279 vb.
propulsion 287 n.
bang 402 n.
bombardment
712 n.
volplane
fly 271 vb.
volt, voltage
electronics 160 n.
volte-face
reversion 148 n.
change of allegiance
603 n.
volubility
loquacity 581 n.
volume
quantity 26 n.
measure 183 n.
metrology 465 n.
book 589 n.
voluminous
spacious 183 adj.
large 195 adj.
voluntary

VOU

musical piece 412 n.
voluntary 597 adj.
uncharged 812 adj.
voluntary agency
philanthropy 901 n.
volunteer
volunteer 597 n.
undertake 672 vb.
offer oneself
759 vb.
voluptuary
sensualist 944 n.
voluptuous
pleasurable
826 adj.
sensual 944 adj.
vomit
vomit 300 vb.
vomitory
remedial 658 adj.
voodoo
sorcery 983 n.
voracious
greedy 859 adj.
gluttonous 947 adj.
voracity
gluttony 947 n.
vortex
vortex 315 n.
current 350 n.
votary
lover 887 n.
worshipper 981 n.
vote
vote 605 n.vb.
—against
reject 607 vb.
—for
endorse 488 vb.
vote-catcher
motivator 612 n.
voted
assented 488 adj.
legal 953 adj.
voteless
choiceless 606 adj.
unentitled 916 adj.
voter
electorate 605 n.
voting list
electorate 605 n.
votive
promissory 764 adj.
devotional 981 adj.
voucher
credential 466 n.
receipt 807 n.

vouch for
testify 466 vb.
promise 764 vb.
vouchsafe
consent 758 vb.
give 781 vb.
vow
affirm 532 vb.
promise 764 n.vb.
offer worship
981 vb.
vowel
speech sound 398 n.
vox populi
judgement 480 n.
vote 605 n.
voyage
water travel 269 n.
voyager
traveller 268 n.
voyeur
spectator 441 n.
voyeurism
impurity 951 n.
V-shape
angularity 247 n.
V-sign
indignity 921 n.
vulcanize
harden 326 vb.
heat 381 vb.
vulgar
inelegant 576 adj.
vulgar 847 adj.
disreputable
867 adj.
plebeian 869 adj.
showy 875 adj.
impure 951 adj.
vulgarian
upstart 126 n.
vulgarian 847 n.
vulgarism
slang 560 n.
vulgarity
bad taste 847 n.
(*see* **vulgar**)
vulgarize
facilitate 701 vb.
vulgarize 847 vb.
not respect 921 vb.
vulgate
interpretation 520 n.
vulnerable
defenceless 161 adj.
liable 180 adj.
vulnerable 661 adj.

unprepared 670 adj.
vulpine
animal 365 adj.
cunning 698 adj.
vulture
taker 786 n.
glutton 947 n.
vulva
genitalia 167 n.

W

wacky
crazy 503 adj.
wad
bunch 74 n.
line 227 vb.
stopper 264 n.
paper money 797 n.
wadding
lining 227 n.
waddle
gait 265 n.
move slowly 278 vb.
wade
walk 267 vb.
swim 269 vb.
—into
begin 68 vb.
—through
study 536 vb.
exert oneself 682 vb.
wader
bird 365 n.
waders
footwear 228 n.
wads
great quantity 32 n.
wafer
lamina 207 n.
cereals 301 n.
waffle
cereals 301 n.
mean nothing
515 vb.
be diffuse 570 vb.
waft
be light 323 vb.
blow 352 vb.
wag
go on 146 vb.
brandish 317 vb.
gesticulate 547 vb.
humorist 839 n.
—on
progress 285 vb.
wage

earnings 771 n.
—war
wage war 718 vb.
wage earner
worker 686 n.
wager
gambling 618 n.
wages
reward 962 n.
waggish
witty 839 adj.
waggle
brandish 317 vb.
wagon
cart 274 n.
train 274 n.
waif
wanderer 268 n.
derelict 779 n.
outcast 883 n.
wail
blow 352 vb.
ululate 409 vb.
be discontented
829 vb.
lamentation 836 n.
wain
cart 274 n.
wainscot
base 214 n.
lining 227 n.
waist
narrowing 206 n.
waistcoat
jacket 228 n.
waistline
narrowing 206 n.
garment 228 n.
wait
wait 136 vb.
pause 145 vb.
await 507 vb.
be inactive 679 vb.
—and see
be tentative 461 vb.
not act 677 vb.
—on/upon
accompany 89 vb.
follow 284 vb.
serve 742 vb.
visit 882 vb.
waiter, waitress
servant 742 vb.
waiting game
caution 858 n.
waiting list
list 87 n.

waiting room
lobby 194 n.
waits
choir 413 n.
waive
relinquish 621 vb.
resign 753 vb.
not retain 779 vb.
—the rules
be lax 734 vb.
waiver
loss of right 916 n.
wake
rear 238 n.
furrow 262 n.
obsequies 364 n.
trace 548 n.
excite 821 vb.
lament 836 n.
—up
be active 678 vb.
wakeful
vigilant 457 adj.
walk
state 7 n.
gait 265 n.
walk 267 vb.
path 624 n.
haunt 970 vb.
—off with
win 727 vb.
steal 788 vb.
—out
relinquish 621 vb.
fail in duty 918 vb.
—out with
court 889 vb.
walkabout
pedestrianism
267 n.
wandering 267 n.
walker
pedestrian 268 n.
traveller 268 n.
walkie-talkie
hearing aid 415 n.
walking on air
pleased 824 adj.
walking stick
prop 218 n.
walk of life
vocation 622 n.
walkout
strike 145 n.
walkover
easy thing 701 n.
victory 727 n.

walkthrough
dramaturgy 594 n.
wall
partition 231 n.
barrier 235 n.
screen 421 n.
fortification 713 n.
wallah
worker 686 n.
wallet
case 194 n.
wall-eyed
dim-sighted
440 adj.
wallflower
rejection 607 n.
wallop
strike 279 vb.
spank 963 vb.
wallow
plunge 313 vb.
be wet 341 vb.
be unclean 649 vb.
—in
enjoy 376 vb.
be intemperate
943 vb.
wallpaper
covering 226 n.
wall up
obstruct 702 vb.
imprison 747 vb.
walnut
fruit 301 n.
brownness 430 n.
walrus
mammal 365 n.
waltz
rotate 315 vb.
dance 837 n.vb.
wan
dim 419 adj.
colourless 426 adj.
melancholic
834 adj.
wand
magic instrument
983 n.
wander
wander 267 vb.
stray 282 vb.
be inattentive
456 vb.
be insane 503 vb.
be diffuse 570 vb.
wanderer
wanderer 268 n.

wane
decrease 37 n.vb.
be dim 419 vb.
deteriorate 655 vb.
wangle
contrivance 623 n.
be cunning 698 vb.
want
shortfall 307 n.
require 627 vb.
scarcity 636 n.
poverty 801 n.
desire 859 n.vb.
wanting
absent 190 adj.
deficient 307 adj.
unintelligent
499 adj.
wanton
capricious 604 adj.
rash 857 adj.
unchaste 951 adj.
war
destroyer 168 n.
slaughter 362 n.
war 718 n.
warble
ululate 409 vb.
warbler
bird 365 n.
vocalist 413 n.
war cry
call 547 n.
defiance 711 n.
ward
youth 130 n.
district 184 n.
hospital 658 n.
dependant 742 n.
warden
keeper 749 n.
warder, wardress
gaoler 749 n.
ward off
avoid 620 vb.
parry 713 vb.
wardrobe
cabinet 194 n.
clothing 228 n.
wardrobe mistress
stagehand 594 n.
wardroom
chamber 194 n.
wardship
nonage 130 n.
warehouse
storage 632 n.

wares
merchandise 795 n.
warfare
warfare 718 n.
(*see* **war**)
war fever
bellicosity 718 n.
warhead
rocket 276 n.
explosive 723 n.
warhorse
warhorse 273 n.
expert 696 n.
warlike
violent 176 adj.
warlike 718 adj.
warlock
sorcerer 983 n.
warlord
army officer 741 n.
warm
summery 128 adj.
warm 379 adj.
discovering 484 adj.
fervent 818 adj.
cheer 833 vb.
friendly 880 adj.
angry 891 adj.
—to
be in love 887 vb.
—up
heat 381 vb.
endanger 661 vb.
make ready 669 vb.
warm-blooded
animal 365 n.
war memorial
trophy 729 n.
warm-hearted
impressible 819 adj.
benevolent 897 adj.
warmonger
militarist 722 n.
warmth
heat 379 n.
excitable state 822 n.
friendliness 880 n.
(*see* **warm**)
warn
predict 511 vb.
hint 524 vb.
warn 664 vb.
threaten 900 vb.
—off
exclude 57 vb.
warning
signal 547 n.

warning 664 n.
danger signal 665 n.
war of nerves
intimidation 854 n.
warp
weaving 222 n.
distortion 246 n.
bias 481 n.
impair 655 vb.
warpaint
cosmetic 843 n.
warrant
credential 466 n.
warrant 737 n.
mandate 751 n.
permit 756 n.vb.
justify 927 vb.
legal process 959 n.
warranty
credential 466 n.
security 767 n.
warren
complexity 61 n.
dwelling 192 n.
warrior
combatant 722 n.
brave person 855 n.
warship
warship 722 n.
wart
skin disease 651 n.
blemish 845 n.
warts and all
accuracy 494 n.
wary
vigilant 457 adj.
cautious 858 adj.
wash
facing 226 n.
moisten 341 vb.
wave 350 n.
pigment 425 n.
trace 548 n.
ablutions 648 n.
clean 648 vb.
—down
drink 301 vb.
—one's hands of
be exempt 919 vb.
disapprove 924 vb.
wash and brush up
beautification
843 n.
washed out
colourless 426 adj.
fatigued 684 adj.
unsightly 842 adj.

washed up
deteriorated
655 adj.
grounded 728 adj.
washer
lining 227 n.
washout
failure 728 n.
washroom
ablutions 648 n.
latrine 649 n.
washy
weak 163 adj.
colourless 426 adj.
wasp
bane 659 n.
noxious animal
904 n.
waspish
irascible 892 adj.
wasp-waist
narrowing 206 n.
wassail
revel 837 vb.
wastage
decrement 42 n.
waste 634 n.
loss 772 n.
waste
leavings 41 n.
lay waste 165 vb.
desert 172 n.
emptiness 190 n.
outflow 298 n.
waste 634 n.vb.
rubbish 641 n.
misuse 675 n.vb.
loss 772 n.
be prodigal 815 vb.
—away
be ill 651 vb.
—effort
attempt the
impossible 470 vb.
waste effort 641 vb.
—time
pass time 108 vb.
be inactive 679 vb.
wasted
lean 206 adj.
wasted 634 adj.
unused 674 adj.
lost 772 adj.
wasteful
wasteful 634 adj.
superfluous 637 adj.
prodigal 815 adj.

waste of time
lost labour 641 n.
waste paper
rubbish 641 n.
wastepipe
drain 351 n.
waster
bad person 938 n.
wastrel
idler 679 n.
watch
period 110 n.
timekeeper 117 n.
scan 438 vb.
watch 441 vb.
invigilate 457 vb.
not act 677 vb.
keeper 749 n.
—one's step
be warned 664 vb.
be cautious 858 vb.
—over
safeguard 660 vb.
watch and ward
protection 660 n.
watchdog
dog 365 n.
protector 660 n.
warner 664 n.
watcher
spectator 441 n.
watchful
vigilant 457 ad.
tutelary 660 adj.
cautious 858 adj.
watchtower
high structure 209 n.
watchword
maxim 496 n.
identification 547 n.
water
weaken 163 vb.
soft drink 301 n.
element 319 n.
water 339 n.
moisten 341 vb.
extinguisher 382 n.
insipidity 387 n.
cleanser 648 n.
—at the mouth
make appetizing
390 vb.
be hungry 859 vb.
—down
add water 339 vb.
water channel
conduit 351 n.

water closet
latrine 649 n.
watercolour(s)
pigment 425 n.
art style 553 n.
watercolourist
artist 556 n.
watercourse
stream 350 n.
water diviner
detector 484 n.
water-drinker
ascetic 945 n.
sober person 948 n.
watered
iridescent 437 adj.
waterfall
waterfall 350 n.
waterfowl
bird 365 n.
waterfront
edge 234 n.
waterhole
lake 346 n.
watering can
vessel 194 n.
waterless
dry 342 adj.
waterline
edge 234 n.
gauge 465 n.
waterlogged
drenched 341 adj.
marshy 347 adj.
water main
conduit 351 n.
waterman
boatman 270 n.
watermark
label 547 n.
water nymph
mythical being
970 n.
water pistol
propellant 287 n.
plaything 837 n.
water power
waterfall 350 n.
waterproof
overcoat 228 n.
dry 342 adj.
invulnerable
660 adj.
waters
obstetrics 167 n.
ocean 343 n.
watershed

summit 213 n.
waterside
edge 234 n.
watersports
aquatics 269 n.
water table
horizontality 216 n.
watertight
sealed off 264 adj.
dry 342 adj.
water tower
storage 632 n.
water vapour
gas 336 n.
waterway
passage 305 n.
stream 350 n.
waterworks
excretion 302 n.
cleanser 648 n.
watery
weak 163 adj.
watery 339 adj.
tasteless 387 adj.
watt
electronics 160 n.
wattle
network 222 n.
wave
hang 217 vb.
make curved
248 vb.
convolution 251 n.
be in motion 265 vb.
brandish 317 vb.
wave 350 n.
gesture 547 n.
greet 884 vb.
—a wand
practise sorcery
983 vb.
—goodbye
start out 296 vb.
wavelength
radiation 417 n.
broadcasting 531 n.
wave power
sources of energy
160 n.
waver
doubt 486 vb.
be irresolute 601 vb.
waverer
waverer 601 n.
wavy
curved 248 adj.
undulatory 251 adj.

wax
grow 36 vb.
changeable thing
152 n.
smooth 258 n.
softness 327 n.
lubricant 334 n.
viscidity 354 n.
—and wane
vary 152 vb.
waxen
fatty 357 adj.
whitish 427 adj.
wax figure
image 551 n.
waxwork(s)
sculpture 554 n.
collection 632 n.
waxy
soft 327 adj.
fatty 357 adj.
way
state 7 n.
itinerary 267 n.
direction 281 n.
habit 610 n.
way 624 n.
wayfarer
traveller 268 n.
way in
doorway 263 n.
waylay
ambush 527 vb.
waymark
indicate 547 vb.
way of life
habit 610 n.
conduct 688 n.
way of the world
fashion 848 n.
way-out
unusual 84 adj.
super 644 adj.
way out
doorway 263 n.
outlet 298 n.
means of escape
667 n.
ways
habit 610 n.
ways and means
means 629 n.
wayside
edge 234 n.
accessible 289 adj.
way through
access 624 n.

wayward
wilful 602 adj.
capricious 604 adj.
WC
latrine 649 n.
weak
powerless 161 adj.
weak 163 adj.
watery 339 adj.
muted 401 adj.
poorly reasoned
477 adj.
unhealthy 651 adj.
unsafe 661 adj.
lax 734 adj.
frail 934 adj.
weaken
weaken 163 vb.
moderate 177 vb.
add water 339 vb.
tell against 467 vb.
impair 655 vb.
weak-kneed
irresolute 601 adj.
weakling
weakling 163 n.
weak-minded
irresolute 601 adj.
weakness
weakness 163 n.
liability 180 n.
defect 647 n.
vulnerability 661 n.
sluggishness 679 n.
liking 859 n.
(*see* **weak**)
weal
swelling 253 n.
wealth
plenty 635 n.
prosperity 730 n.
wealth 800 n.
wealthy
rich 800 adj.
wean from
disaccustom 611 vb.
weapon
instrument 628 n.
weapon 723 n.
weaponless
defenceless 161 adj.
wear
wear 228 vb.
use 673 n.
—away
decrease 37 vb.
disappear 446 vb.

—off
disappear 446 vb.
—on
elapse 111 vb.
—out
deteriorate 655 vb.
use 673 vb.
fatigue 684 vb.
—the trousers
influence 178 vb.
dominate 733 vb.
wear and tear
dilapidation 655 n.
weariness
sleepiness 679 n.
fatigue 684 n.
suffering 825 n.
dejection 834 n.
wearisome
fatiguing 684 adj.
tedious 838 adj.
weary
laborious 682 adj.
fatigue 684 vb.
bored 838 adj.
weasel
mammal 365 n.
be equivocal 518 vb.
weather
storm 176 n.
navigate 269 vb.
weather 340 n.
wind 352 n.
mature 669 vb.
—the storm
be safe 660 vb.
triumph 727 vb.
weather balloon
airship 276 n.
weatherbeaten
tough 329 adj.
dilapidated 655 adj.
weatherboard
facing 226 n.
weathercock
changeable thing
152 n.
indicator 547 n.
waverer 601 n.
weathered
soft-hued 425 adj.
matured 669 adj.
weather eye
surveillance 457 n.
weather forecast
prediction 511 n.
weatherproof

unyielding 162 adj.
invulnerable
660 adj.
weathervane
changeable thing
152 n.
weave
weave 222 vb.
pass 305 vb.
texture 331 n.
pattern 844 n.
—spells
practise sorcery
983 vb.
weaver
weaving 222 n.
web
network 222 n.
trap 542 n.
plot 623 n.
web-footed
footed 214 adj.
wed
wed 894 vb.
wedded to
believing 485 adj.
habituated 610 adj.
wedding
wedding 894 n.
wedding anniversary
special day 876 n.
wedding ring
love token 889 n.
wedge
piece 53 n.
prop 218 n.
sharp edge 256 n.
stopper 264 n.
—apart
sunder 46 vb.
—in
implant 303 vb.
wedge-shaped
angulated 247 adj.
wedlock
union 45 n.
marriage 894 n.
wee
little 196 adj.
weed
render few 105 vb.
weakling 163 n.
plant 366 n.
cultivate 370 vb.
—out
eliminate 44 vb.
eject 300 vb.

weed-killer
poison 659 n.
weedy
lean 206 adj.
vegetal 366 adj.
week
period 110 n.
weekend
pass time 108 vb.
weekly
seasonal 141 adj.
journal 528 n.
weep
flow out 298 vb.
weep 836 vb.
—for
pity 905 vb.
weepy
unhappy 825 adj.
weevil
insect 365 n.
weft
weaving 222 n.
weigh
weigh 322 vb.
meditate 449 vb.
estimate 480 vb.
be important
  638 vb.
—anchor
navigate 269 vb.
—in
influence 178 vb.
—on
oppress 735 vb.
trouble 827 vb.
weighing machine
scales 322 n.
weight
substantiality 3 n.
influence 178 n.
bulk 195 n.
gravity 322 n.
make heavy 322 vb.
importance 638 n.
weighted
unjust 914 adj.
weighting
compensation 31 n.
weightless
light 323 adj.
weight of numbers
greater number
  104 n.
power 160 n.
weight on one's mind
encumbrance 702 n.

worry 825 n.
weights and
  measures
metrology 465 n.
weight-watching
dieting 301 n.
weighty
great 32 adj.
weighty 322 adj.
forceful 571 adj.
important 638 adj.
weir
waterfall 350 n.
weird
wonderful 864 adj.
spooky 970 adj.
weirdness
eccentricity 503 n.
welch
(*see* **welsh**)
welcome
timely 137 adj.
reception 299 n.
assent 488 n.vb.
pleasurable 826 adj.
desired 859 adj.
greet 884 vb.
applaud 923 vb.
weld
join 45 vb.
heat 381 vb.
welder
artisan 686 n.
welfare
good 615 n.
prosperity 730 n.
Welfare State
political
  organization
  733 n.
sociology 901 n.
well
excavation 255 n.
water 339 n.
flow 350 vb.
well 615 adv.
store 632 n.
healthy 650 adj.
—over
flow out 298 vb.
superabound
  637 vb.
well-aimed
directed 281 adj.
accurate 494 adj.
well-behaved
obedient 739 adj.

well-being
euphoria 376 n.
prosperity 730 n.
well-bred
well-bred 848 adj.
well-connected, be
influence 178 vb.
well-covered
fleshy 195 adj.
well-cut
tailored 228 adj.
well-defined
obvious 443 adj.
well-deserved
due 915 adj.
well-directed
directed 281 adj.
well-disposed
aiding 703 adj.
well-dressed
fashionable 848 adj.
well-founded,
  well-grounded
evidential 466 adj.
certain 473 adj.
rational 475 adj.
wellhead
source 156 n.
well-heeled
moneyed 800 adj.
wellingtons
footwear 228 n.
well-integrated
mixed 43 adj.
well-intentioned
benevolent 897 adj.
well-kept
orderly 60 adj.
preserved 666 adj.
well-known
well-known 528 adj.
renowned 866 adj.
well-made
well-made 694 adj.
well-mannered
well-bred 848 adj.
well-marked
obvious 443 adj.
well-meaning
friendly 880 adj.
well-off
prosperous
  730 adj.
well-placed
directed 281 adj.
well-proportioned
shapely 841 adj.

well-read
instructed 490 adj.
well-rounded
phraseological
  563 adj.
well set-up
stalwart 162 adj.
well-spent
successful 727 adj.
well-spoken
well-bred 848 adj.
well thought of
reputable 866 adj.
well-timed
timely 137 adj.
well-to-do
prosperous 730 adj.
well-trodden
used 673 adj.
well-turned
elegant 575 adj.
well-wisher
patron 707 n.
well-worn
dilapidated 655 adj.
welsh, welch
run away 620 vb.
not pay 805 vb.
welsher, welcher
avoider 620 n.
nonpayer 805 n.
welt
edge 234 n.
swelling 253 n.
welter
confusion 61 n.
wen
swelling 253 n.
wench
youngster 132 n.
be impure 951 vb.
wend
be in motion 265 vb.
werewolf
demon 970 n.
west
laterality 239 n.
compass point
  281 n.
westerly
wind 352 n.
western
lateral 239 adj.
Western
film 445 n.
westernize
transform 147 vb.

Westminster
parliament 692 n.
wet
weakling 163 n.
moisten 341 vb.
rainy 350 adj.
leniency 736 n.
impressible 819 adj.
wet behind the ears
immature 670 adj.
wet blanket
dissuasion 613 n.
moper 834 n.
wetlands
marsh 347 n.
wetness
moisture 341 n.
wet nurse
provider 633 n.
wetsuit
suit 228 n.
whack
strike 279 vb.
portion 783 n.
spank 963 vb.
whack at
attempt 671 n.
whacked
fatigued 684 adj.
defeated 728 adj.
whacking
whopping 32 adj.
whale
giant 195 n.
mammal 365 n.
whaler
mariner 270 n.
fishing boat 275 n.
wham
violently 176 adv.
propel 287 vb.
bang 402 vb.
wharf
stable 192 n.
edge 234 n.
storage 632 n.
what's his/her name
no name 562 n.
whatsit
no name 562 n.
tool 630 n.
wheat
cereals 301 n.
wheedle
tempt 612 vb.
flatter 925 vb.
wheel

move 265 vb.
rotator 315 n.
tool 630 n.
directorship 689 n.
—and deal
plot 623 vb.
—round
turn back 286 vb.
wheelbarrow
pushcart 274 n.
wheelchair
pushcart 274 n.
wheeled
vehicular 274 adj.
wheeler-dealer
planner 623 n.
slyboots 698 n.
wheels within wheels
complexity 61 n.
wheelwright
artisan 686 n.
wheeze
breathe 352 vb.
hiss 406 vb.
idea 451 n.
contrivance 623 n.
whelp
young creature 132 n.
when
when 108 adv.
where
here 189 adv.
wherever
widely 183 adv.
wherewithal
means 629 n.
funds 797 n.
wherry
sailing ship 275 n.
whet
sharpen 256 vb.
animate 821 vb.
cause desire 859 vb.
whetstone
sharpener 256 n.
whey
fluid 335 n.
whiff
breeze 352 n.
odour 394 n.
indication 547 n.
whiffy
odorous 394 adj.
while
while 108 adv.
while away the time

pass time 108 vb.
amuse oneself 837 vb.
whim
ideality 513 n.
whim 604 n.
whimper
cry 408 vb.
weep 836 vb.
whimsical
crazy 503 adj.
imaginative 513 adj.
capricious 604 adj.
whimsy
ideality 513 n.
whine
cry 408 n.vb.
be discontented 829 vb.
whinny
ululation 409 n.
whip
driver 268 n.
strike 279 vb.
agitate 318 vb.
incentive 612 n.
flog 963 vb.
—on
impel 279 vb.
—out
extract 304 vb.
—up
thicken 354 vb.
excite 821 vb.
whipcord
cable 47 n.
whip hand
advantage 34 n.
victory 727 n.
whippersnapper
youngster 132 n.
whipping boy
substitute 150 n.
whippy
flexible 327 adj.
whip-round
gift 781 n.
whirl
rotate 315 vb.
activity 678 n.
haste 680 n.
excitable state 822 n.
dance 837 vb.
whirlpool
vortex 315 n.
current 350 n.
whirlwind

turmoil 61 n.
vortex 315 n.
commotion 318 n.
gale 352 n.
whirr
roll 403 n.vb.
whisk
move fast 277 vb.
agitate 318 vb.
whisker(s)
hair 259 n.
feeler 378 n.
whisky
alcoholic drink 301 n.
whisper
sound faint 401 vb.
hint 524 n.vb.
rumour 529 n.
voice 577 n.vb.
detraction 926 n.
whist
card game 837 n.
whistle
shrill 407 vb.
flute 414 n.
signal 547 n.
wonder 864 n.
applaud 923 vb.
whistle-blowing
warning 664 n.
whistle-stop
stopping place 145 n.
whit
trifle 639 n.
white
white 427 adj.
clean 648 adj.
pure 950 adj.
white elephant
bane 659 n.
white feather
cowardice 856 n.
white flag
submission 721 n.
white hope
proficient person 696 n.
white lie
mental dishonesty 543 n.
white man/woman
whiteness 427 n.
whiten
whiten 427 vb.
show feeling 818 vb.

White Paper
  report 524 n.
  record 548 n.
white-skinned
  white 427 adj.
white slave
  prostitute 952 n.
white supremacist
  narrow mind 481 n.
whitewash
  facing 226 n.
  whiting 427 n.
  deceive 542 vb.
  cleanser 648 n.
  extenuate 927 vb.
whither
  towards 281 adv.
whiting
  fish food 301 n.
  whiting 427 n.
whitish
  whitish 427 adj.
  yellow 433 adj.
whittle
  cut 46 vb.
  form 243 vb.
—away
  maker smaller
    198 vb.
whiz, whizz
  move fast 277 vb.
  hiss 406 vb.
whizzbang
  missile weapon
    723 n.
whizz kid
  busy person 678 n.
  prodigy 864 n.
whoa!
  145 int.
  266 int.
whodunit
  novel 590 n.
whole
  whole 52 n.adj.
  universal 79 adj.
  unity 88 n.
  undamaged
    646 adj.
wholefood
  salubrity 652 n.
whole-hearted
  resolute 599 adj.
whole hog
  completeness 54 n.
wholemeal
  cereals 301 n.

wholesale
  comprehensive
    52 adj.
  inclusive 78 adj.
  indiscriminate
    464 adj.
  trading 791 adj.
wholesaler
  seller 793 n.
  merchant 794 n.
wholesome
  nourishing 301 adj.
  healthy 650 adj.
  salubrious 652 adj.
  personable 841 adj.
whoop
  cry 408 n.vb.
  rejoice 835 vb.
whoopee
  revel 837 n.
whooping cough
  respiratory disease
    651 n.
whopper
  whopper 195 n.
  untruth 543 n.
whore
  prostitute 952 n.
whorehouse
  brothel 951 n.
whorl
  coil 251 n.
why and wherefore,
  the
  reason why 156 n.
wick
  filament 208 n.
  lighter 385 n.
wicked
  wrong 914 adj.
  wicked 934 adj.
  impious 980 adj.
wickedness
  evildoer 904 n.
  wickedness 934 n.
wickerwork
  network 222 n.
wide
  spacious 183 adj.
  broad 205 adj.
  deviating 282 adj.
wide-awake
  attentive 455 adj.
wide berth
  avoidance 620 n.
wide-bodied
  broad 205 adj.

wide-eyed
  wondering 864 adj.
  innocent 935 adj.
widely
  throughout 54 adv.
  widely 183 adv.
widen
  generalize 79 vb.
  expand 197 vb.
wide of the mark
  deviating 282 adj.
  erroneous 495 adj.
wide open
  open 263 adj.
  vulnerable 661 adj.
  unconditional
    744 adj.
wide-ranging
  extensive 32 adj.
widespread
  extensive 32 adj.
  universal 79 adj.
  usual 610 adj.
widow
  deprive 786 vb.
  widowhood 896 n.
widower
  widowhood 896 n.
width
  breadth 205 n.
wield
  operate 173 vb.
  use 673 vb.
wife
  spouse 894 n.
wifeless
  unwedded 895 adj.
wifely
  loving 887 adj.
  matrimonial
    894 adj.
wife-swapping
  illicit love 951 n.
wig
  hairdressing 843 n.
wigging
  reprimand 924 n.
wiggle
  oscillate 317 vb.
wigwam
  dwelling 192 n.
wild
  disorderly 61 adj.
  desert 172 n.
  furious 176 adj.
  light-minded
    456 adj.

inexact 495 adj.
  frenzied 503 adj.
  artless 699 adj.
  riotous 738 adj.
  excited 821 adj.
  rash 857 adj.
  barbaric 869 adj.
  angry 891 adj.
wild beast
  violent creature
    176 n.
  noxious animal
    904 n.
wildcat
  cat 365 n.
  independent
    744 adj.
  rash 857 adj.
wilderness
  havoc 165 n.
  desert 172 n.
  space 183 n.
  seclusion 883 n.
wildfire, like
  swiftly 277 adv.
wild-goose chase
  lost labour 641 n.
  failure 728 n.
wild life
  animality 365 n.
wildlife park
  zoo 369 n.
wiles
  stratagem 698 n.
wilful
  wilful 602 adj.
will
  will 595 n.vb.
  resolution 599 n.
  obstinacy 602 n.
  title deed 767 n.
  bequeath 780 vb.
  desire 859 n.
willing
  willing 597 adj.
  obedient 739 adj.
  cheerful 833 adj.
will-o'-the-wisp
  glow-worm 420 n.
  deception 542 n.
  incentive 612 n.
willowy
  narrow 206 adj.
  flexible 327 adj.
  shapely 841 adj.
willpower
  will 595 n.

WIL

willy-nilly
necessarily 596 adv.
wilt
deteriorate 655 vb.
be dejected 834 vb.
wily
deceiving 542 adj.
cunning 698 adj.
wily person
trickster 545 n.
slyboots 698 n.
win
win 727 vb.
acquire 771 vb.
—over
convert 147 vb.
convince 485 vb.
—through
arrive 295 vb.
triumph 727 vb.
wince
recoil 280 vb.
feel pain 377 vb.
show feeling 818 vb.
winch
draw 288 vb.
lifter 310 n.
wind
insubstantial thing 4 n.
disable 161 vb.
rotate 315 vb.
gas 336 n.
wind 352 n.
detect 484 vb.
empty talk 515 n.
digestive disorders 651 n.
fatigue 684 vb.
—down
repose 683 vb.
—in
draw 288 vb.
—up
terminate 69 vb.
cease 145 vb.
elevate 310 vb.
windbag
chatterer 581 n.
windblown
orderless 61 adj.
windbreak
shelter 662 n.
windcone
anemometry 352 n.
winded
panting 684 adj.

WIN

wind ensemble
orchestra 413 n.
winder
handle 218 n.
rotator 315 n.
windfall
benefit 615 n.
wind gauge
anemometry 352 n.
winding
meandering 251 n.
winding sheet
grave clothes 364 n.
windlass
traction 288 n.
windless
tranquil 266 adj.
windmill
rotator 315 n.
window
window 263 n.
view 438 n.
window dressing
publicity 528 n.
ostentation 875 n.
window shopper
spectator 441 n.
windowsill
shelf 218 n.
windpipe
respiration 352 n.
wind power
sources of energy 160 n.
windscreen, windshield
shelter 662 n.
windsock
indicator 547 n.
wind surfing
aquatics 269 n.
windswept
orderless 61 adj.
windy 352 adj.
wind tunnel
testing agent 461 n.
windward
laterality 239 n.
windy
windy 352 adj.
meaningless 515 adj.
diffuse 570 adj.
nervous 854 adj.
wine
wine 301 n.

WIN

wine and dine
feed 301 vb.
wine cellar
tavern 192 n.
wineglass
cup 194 n.
wine-growing
agriculture 370 n.
winepress
farm tool 370 n.
wine-tasting
drinking 301 n.
wine, women and song
sensualism 944 n.
wing
laterality 239 n.
plumage 259 n.
wing 271 n.
fly 271 vb.
fell 311 vb.
wound 655 vb.
air force 722 n.
wings
livery 547 n.
stage set 594 n.
wingspan
breadth 205 n.
wink
look 438 n.
hint 524 n.vb.
gesticulate 547 vb.
—at
disregard 458 vb.
permit 756 vb.
winker
indicator 547 n.
winkle
fish food 301 n.
winkle out
extract 304 vb.
winner
victor 727 n.
winning
successful 727 adj.
amiable 884 adj.
winnings
gain 771 n.
receipt 807 n.
winnow
eliminate 44 vb.
cultivate 370 vb.
select 605 vb.
wino
drunkard 949 n.
winsome
personable 841 adj.

WIS

lovable 887 adj.
winter
winter 129 n.
wintriness 380 n.
winter sports
snow 380 n.
sport 837 n.
wintry
wintry 129 adj.
cold 380 adj.
wipe
dry 342 vb.
clean 648 vb.
—out
nullify 2 vb.
destroy 165 vb.
obliterate 550 vb.
wire
cable 47 n.
filament 208 n.
telecommunication 531 n.
wireless
broadcasting 531 n.
(see **radio***)*
wire netting
network 222 n.
wire-puller
latency 523 n.
motivator 612 n.
wire-pulling
influence 178 n.
plot 623 n.
wire-tapping
listening 415 n.
wiry
stalwart 162 adj.
lean 206 adj.
wisdom
wisdom 498 n.
wise
knowing 490 adj.
wise 498 adj.
foreseeing 510 adj.
advisable 642 adj.
wisecrack
witticism 839 n.
wise guy
wiseacre 500 n.
wise man, wise woman
sage 500 n.
sorcerer 983 n.
wiser
improved 654 adj.
wish
will 595 vb.

request 761 n.
desire 859 n.vb.
desired object 859 n.
—on
desire 859 vb.
curse 899 vb.
wishful thinking
fantasy 513 n.
deception 542 n.
wishy-washy
weak 163 adj.
tasteless 387 adj.
feeble 572 adj.
wisp
insubstantial thing
4 n.
small thing 33 n.
filament 208 n.
hair 259 n.
wispy
flimsy 163 adj.
wistful
regretting 830 adj.
desiring 859 adj.
wit
intelligence 498 n.
wit 839 n.
witch
hellhag 904 n.
sorceress 983 n.
witchcraft
sorcery 983 n.
witch doctor
sorcerer 983 n.
witchery
pleasurableness
826 n.
sorcery 983 n.
witch-hunt
inquiry 459 n.
pursuit 619 n.
witch-hunting
phobia 854 n.
orthodox 976 adj.
witching
magical 983 adj.
with
in addition 38 adv.
with 89 adv.
by means of 629
adv.
with child
fertilized 167 adj.
withdraw
go away 190 vb.
recede 290 vb.
depart 296 vb.

extract 304 vb.
recant 603 vb.
resign 753 vb.
take 786 vb.
schismatize 978 vb.
withdrawal
seclusion 883 n.
withdrawn
taciturn 582 adj.
unsociable 883 adj.
wither
perish 361 vb.
deteriorate 655 vb.
humiliate 872 vb.
withered
weakened 163 adj.
dry 342 adj.
withering
baneful 659 adj.
disapproving
924 adj.
withhold
keep secret 525 vb.
restrain 747 vb.
refuse 760 vb.
within
inside 224 adv.
within bounds
moderately 177 adv.
temperate 942 adj.
within earshot
near 200 adv.
auditory 415 adj.
within one's grasp
possibly 469 adv.
within one's means
cheap 812 adj.
within reach
near 200 adv.
easy 701 adj.
within reason
moderately 177 adv.
with it
modern 126 adj.
fashionable
848 adj.
with one, be
understand 516 vb.
**with one's back to the
wall**
in difficulties
700 n.
without
incomplete 55 adj.
without delay
instantaneously
116 adv.

without end
infinite 107 adj.
perpetual 115 adj.
without exception
inclusive 78 adj.
without fail
certainly 473 adv.
without notice
unexpectedly
508 adv.
without strings
unconditional
744 adj.
without warning
unexpectedly
508 adv.
with pleasure
willingly 597 adv.
with respect to
concerning 9 adv.
withstand
withstand 704 vb.
resist 715 vb.
with the aid of
by means of
629 adv.
witless
foolish 499 adj.
witness
be present 189 vb.
watch 441 vb.
witness 466 n.
signatory 765 n.
—to
indicate 547 vb.
witness box
courtroom 956 n.
wits
intellect 447 n.
intelligence 498 n.
witticism
witticism 839 n.
witty
aphoristic 496 adj.
witty 839 adj.
wizard
sage 500 n.
proficient person
696 n.
sorcerer 983 n.
wizardry
skill 694 n.
sorcery 983 n.
wizened
ageing 131 adj.
contracted 198 adj.
lean 206 adj.

woad
blue pigment 435 n.
wobble
deviate 282 vb.
oscillate 317 vb.
be irresolute 601 vb.
wobbling, wobbly
unstable 152 adj.
flimsy 163 adj.
woe
evil 616 n.
sorrow 825 n.`
woebegone
unhappy 825 adj.
wold
high land 209 n.
wolf
violent creature
176 n.
noxious animal
904 n.
gluttonize 947 vb.
libertine 952 n.
**wolf in sheep's
clothing**
impostor 545 n.
wolfish
cruel 898 adj.
gluttonous 947 adj.
wolf whistle
stridor 407 n.
wonder 864 n.
woman
woman 373 n.
spouse 894 n.
(*see* **man/woman**)
womanhood
adultness 134 n.
womanish
female 373 adj.
womanizer
libertine 952 n.
womanly
grown-up 134 adj.
female 373 n.
womb
seedbed 156 n.
genitalia 167 n.
parentage 169 n.
**Women's
Lib/Liberation**
female 373 n.
freedom 744 n.
women's rights
dueness 915 n.
wonder
be uncertain 474 vb.

prodigy 864 n.
wonder 864 n.vb.
—**about**
meditate 449 vb.
wonderful
unusual 84 adj.
impossible 470 adj.
excellent 644 adj.
pleasurable 826 adj.
wonderful 864 adj.
wonderland
fantasy 513 n.
wonder-working
thaumaturgy 864 n.
wondrous
wonderful 864 adj.
wonky
flimsy 163 adj.
oblique 220 adj.
wont
habit 610 n.
use 673 n.
woo
court 889 vb.
wood
wood 366 n.
wooden 366 adj.
materials 631 n.
wood-block
engraving 555 n.
woodcut
engraving 555 n.
woodcutter
forestry 366 n.
wooded
arboreal 366 adj.
wooden
wooden 366 adj.
inelegant 576 adj.
obstinate 602 adj.
impassive 820 adj.
woodenhead
dunce 501 n.
wooden spoon
unskilfulness 695 n.
woodland
wood 366 n.
woodwind
orchestra 413 n.
woodwork
structure 331 n.
woodworm
blight 659 n.
woody
tough 329 adj.
arboreal 366 adj.
wooer

lover 887 n.
wool
fibre 208 n.
textile 222 n.
woolgathering
abstractedness 456 n.
woolly
fibrous 208 adj.
jersey 228 n.
fleecy 259 adj.
poorly reasoned 477 adj.
word
information 524 n.
message 529 n.
word 559 n.
neology 560 n.
speech 579 n.
command 737 n.
promise 764 n.
Word, the
God the Son 965 n.
scripture 975 n.
wordbook
dictionary 559 n.
word fencing
sophistry 477 n.
word for word
accurate 494 adj.
interpretive 520 adj.
word game
indoor game 837 n.
wordiness
loquacity 581 n.
wording
phrase 563 n.
word in the ear
hint 524 n.
wordless
voiceless 578 adj.
word of honour
oath 532 n.
word of mouth
tradition 127 n.
testimony 466 n.
word-perfect
prepared 669 adj.
word-play
equivocalness 518 n.
wit 839 n.
word processor
data processing 86 n.
words
quarrel 709 n.

contention 716 n.
wordy
prolix 570 adj.
work
composition 56 n.
operate 173 vb.
musical piece 412 n.
book 589 n.
stage play 594 n.
business 622 n.
function 622 n.
be expedient 642 vb.
labour 682 n.
work 682 vb.
be successful 727 vb.
ornamental art 844 n.
—**against**
counteract 182 vb.
oppose 704 vb.
—**at**
persevere 600 vb.
—**on/upon**
motivate 612 vb.
excite 821 vb.
—**out**
do sums 86 vb.
reason 475 vb.
decipher 520 vb.
plan 623 vb.
mature 669 vb.
—**to rule**
strike 145 n.
—**up**
excite 821 vb.
form 243 vb.
workable
operative 173 adj.
possible 469 adj.
workaday
plain 573 adj.
businesslike 622 adj.
workaholic
busy person 678 n.
worked
variegated 437 adj.
ornamented 844 adj.
worked up
angry 891 adj.
worker
producer 164 n.
worker 686 n.
workers' cooperative
association 706 n.

workhorse
busy person 678 n.
workhouse
retreat 192 n.
working class
lower classes 869 n.
working party
inquiry 459 n.
consignee 754 n.
workmanlike
industrious 678 adj.
well-made 694 adj.
workmanship
production 164 n.
work of art
masterpiece 694 n.
workout
exercise 682 n.
workpeople
personnel 686 n.
workroom
chamber 194 n.
workshop 687 n.
works
structure 331 n.
machine 630 n.
workshop 687 n.
workshop
workshop 687 n.
work study
management 689 n.
world
whole 52 n.
affairs 154 n.
universe 321 n.
world 321 n.
humankind 371 n.
society 882 n.
worldly
material 319 adj.
irreligious 974 adj.
worldly wisdom
sagacity 498 n.
skill 694 n.
world of nature
matter 319 n.
world of one's own
seclusion 883 n.
world's end
extremity 69 n.
farness 199 n.
world-shaking
revolutionary 149 adj.
world to come
destiny 155 n.

world-weariness
discontent 829 n.
melancholy 834 n.
worldwide
extensive 32 adj.
universal 79 adj.
spacious 183 adj.
worm
wriggle 251 vb.
creepy-crawly
365 n.
infection 651 n.
cad 938 n.
—oneself into
infiltrate 297 vb.
be servile 879 vb.
—out
discover 484 vb.
worm-eaten
dilapidated 655 adj.
wormwood
bane 659 n.
worn
dilapidated 655 adj.
used 673 adj.
worn out
useless 641 adj.
deteriorated
655 adj.
disused 674 adj.
fatigued 684 adj.
worry
agitate 318 vb.
think 449 vb.
bane 659 n.
adversity 731 n.
worry 825 n.
trouble 827 vb.
worse
deteriorated
655 adj.
worsen
harm 645 vb.
deteriorate 655 vb.
aggravate 832 vb.
worship
honour 866 vb.
worship 981 n.vb.
worshipful
worshipful 866 adj.
respected 920 adj.
worshipper
church member
976 n.
worshipper 981 n.
idolater 982 n.
worst

be superior 34 vb.
defeat 727 vb.
worst, the
misfortune 731 n.
worsted
textile 222 n.
worth
quid pro quo 150 n.
goodness 644 n.
price 809 n.
worthless
trivial 639 adj.
profitless 641 adj.
bad 645 adj.
contemptible
922 adj.
worthwhile
profitable 640 adj.
advisable 642 adj.
worthy
excellent 644 adj.
person of repute
866 n.
deserving 915 adj.
would-be
intending 617 adj.
hoping 852 adj.
unwarranted
916 n.
wound
cut 46 vb.
coiled 251 adj.
pierce 263 vb.
wound 655 n.vb.
hurt 827 vb.
huff 891 vb.
wounded
suffering 825 adj.
wound up
coiled 251 adj.
excited 821 adj.
woven
crossed 222 adj.
textural 331 adj.
wow
discord 411 n.
exceller 644 n.
amuse 837 vb.
wrack
ruin 165 n.
wraith
ghost 970 n.
wraith-like
lean 206 adj.
wrangle
argue 475 vb.
dissent 489 vb.

quarrel 709 n.
wrap
cover 226 vb.
enclose 235 vb.
fold 261 vb.
—up
dress 228 vb.
carry through
725 vb.
wrapped in thought
thoughtful 449 adj.
abstracted 456 adj.
wrapped up in
oneself
selfish 932 adj.
wrapper
wrapping 226 n.
wrapping
receptacle 194 n.
wrapping 226 n.
lining 227 n.
wrath
anger 891 n.
wreak vengeance
avenge 910 vb.
wreath
trophy 729 n.
ornamentation
844 n.
honours 866 n.
wreathe
enlace 222 vb.
twine 251 vb.
decorate 844 vb.
wreck
destroy 165 vb.
dilapidation 655 n.
wreckage
remainder 41 n.
ruin 165 n.
wrecked
grounded 728 adj.
wrecker
destroyer 168 n.
troublemaker 663 n.
wrench
force 176 vb.
extraction 304 n.
nippers 778 n.
wrest
distort 246 vb.
misinterpret 521 vb.
wrestle (with)
contend 716 vb.
withstand 704 vb.
wrestler
athlete 162 n.

wrestling
wrestling 716 n.
wretch
unlucky person
731 n.
sufferer 825 n.
knave 938 n.
wretched
bad 645 adj.
unfortunate 731 adj.
unhappy 825 adj.
wriggle
wriggle 251 vb.
be agitated 318 vb.
—out of
plead 614 vb.
escape 667 vb.
wright
artisan 686 n.
wring
clean 648 vb.
—from
extract 304 vb.
compel 740 vb.
levy 786 vb.
—one's hands
be impotent 161 vb.
regret 830 vb.
despair 853 vb.
—out
dry 342 vb.
wrinkle
crinkle 251 vb.
fold 261 n.vb.
stratagem 698 n.
wrinkled
ageing 131 adj.
unsightly 842 adj.
writ
warrant 737 n.
security 767 n.
legal process 959 n.
write
communicate
524 vb.
write 586 vb.
—about
describe 590 vb.
—down
record 548 vb.
—off
relinquish 621 vb.
stop using 674 vb.
—one's name
sign 547 vb.
—to
correspond 588 vb.

write-off
  nonuse 674 n.
  debt 803 n.
writer
  calligrapher 586 n.
  author 589 n.
write-up
  publicity 528 n.
  article 591 n.
writhe
  wriggle 251 vb.
  feel pain 377 vb.
  suffer 825 vb.
writing
  composition 56 n.
  writing 586 n.
  reading matter
  589 n.
writing on the wall
  danger signal 665 n.
  threat 900 n.
written
  recorded 548 adj.
  written 586 adj.
wrong
  erroneous 495 adj.
  inexpedient 643 adj.
  wrong 914 n.adj.
  do wrong 914 vb.
  dishonest 930 adj.
  lawbreaking 954 n.
wrongdoer
  evildoer 904 n.
wrongdoing
  wickedness 934 n.
  lawbreaking 954 n.
**wrong end of the
  stick**
  misinterpretation
  521 n.
wrongful
  wrong 914 adj.
wrong-headed
  misjudging 481 adj.
  erroneous 495 adj.
wrongheadedness
  obstinacy 602 n.
wrong side
  rear 238 n.
wrong side out
  inverted 221 adj.
wrought
  elegant 575 adj.
  matured 669 adj.
wrought iron
  ornamental art
  844 n.

wry
  oblique 220 adj.
  distorted 246 adj.

X

x
  number 85 n.
  crossing 222 n.
  indication 547 n.
xenophobia
  prejudice 481 n.
  phobia 854 n.
  hatred 888 n.
X-ray
  radiation 417 n.
  photography 551 n.
xylophone
  gong 414 n.

Y

yacht
  sailing ship 275 n.
yachting
  aquatics 269 n.
  sport 837 n.
**yachtsman,
  yachtswoman**
  boatman 270 n.
yak
  cattle 365 n.
  be loquacious
  581 vb.
yank
  draw 288 vb.
yap
  ululate 409 vb.
yard
  place 185 n.
  long measure 203 n.
  enclosure 235 n.
  workshop 687 n.
yardarm
  prop 218 n.
yardstick
  gauge 465 n.
yarn
  fibre 208 n.
  fable 543 n.
  narrative 590 n.
yarn spinner
  liar 545 n.
  narrator 590 n.
yashmak
  headgear 228 n.
yaw
  navigate 269 vb.

  deviation 282 n.
yawl
  sailing ship 275 n.
yawn
  respiration 352 n.
  be fatigued 684 vb.
yawning
  deep 211 adj.
  opening 263 n.
  sleepy 679 adj.
yaws
  tropical disease
  651 n.
yea
  assent 488 n.
year
  date 108 n.
  period 110 n.
yearbook
  reference book
  589 n.
yearling
  young creature
  132 n.
yearly
  seasonal 141 adj.
yearn
  desire 859 vb.
years
  long duration 113 n.
  age 131 n.
yeast
  stimulant 174 n.
  leaven 323 n.
yeasty
  light 323 adj.
  bubbly 355 adj.
yell
  feel pain 377 vb.
  vociferate 408 vb.
yellow
  yellow 433 adj.
  unhealthy 651 adj.
  cowardly 856 adj.
yellow lines
  traffic control
  305 n.
yellow press
  the press 528 n.
  bad taste 847 n.
yellow streak
  cowardice 856 n.
yelp
  shrill 407 vb.
  ululation 409 n.
yen
  desire 859 n.

yeoman
  farmer 370 n.
  country-dweller
  869 n.
yeomanry
  cavalry 722 n.
yes
  assent 488 n.
yes and no
  uncertainty 474 n.
yes-man
  conformist 83 n.
  assenter 488 n.
  toady 879 n.
yesterday
  past time 125 n.
yet
  while 108 adv.
yeti
  mythical being
  970 n.
yield
  product 164 n.
  reproduce itself
  167 vb.
  relinquish 621 vb.
  submit 721 vb.
  not retain 779 vb.
yin and yang
  polarity 14 n.
yob
  youngster 132 n.
  vulgarian 847 n.
yobbish
  barbaric 869 adj.
yodel
  sing 413 vb.
yoga
  philosophy 449 n.
  exercise 682 n.
  asceticism 945 n.
**yoghurt, yogurt,
  yoghourt**
  milk 301 n.
yogi
  sage 500 n.
  ascetic 945 n.
yoke
  duality 90 n.
  prop 218 n.
  subjection 745 n.
  fetter 748 n.
yoked
  combined 50 adj.
yokel
  country-dweller
  869 n.

yon, yonder
afar 199 adv.
young
young 130 adj.
infantine 132 adj.
posterity 170 n.
immature 670 adj.
young creature
young creature
132 n.
younger generation
modernist 126 n.
youngster
youngster 132 n.
your honour
title 870 n.
youth
youth 130 n.
youngster 132 n.
youthful
young 130 adj.
strong 162 adj.
yowl
ululate 409 vb.
yoyo
oscillation 317 n.
plaything 837 n.
Y-shape
divergence 294 n.

Yuletide
holy day 988 n.

Z

zany
fool 501 n.
zeal
keenness 174 n.
willingness 597 n.
piety 979 n.
zealot
doctrinaire 473 n.
narrow mind 481 n.
zealot 979 n.
zealous
active 678 adj.
fervent 818 adj.
zebra
mammal 365 n.
stripe 437 n.
zebra crossing
traffic control 305 n.
Zen
philosophy 449 n.
religious faith 973 n.
zenith
summit 213 n.
zephyr
breeze 352 n.

zero
zero 103 n.
coldness 380 n.
zero hour
date 108 n.
departure 296 n.
zero-rated
uncharged 812 adj.
zest
vigorousness 174 n.
enjoyment 824 n.
zetetic
inquiring 459 adj.
zeugma
ornament 574 n.
ziggurat
temple 990 n.
zigzag
obliquity 220 n.
meander 251 vb.
deviating 282 adj.
pattern 844 n.
zillion(s)
over one hundred
99 n.
multitude 104 n.
Zion
heaven 971 n.
holy place 990 n.

zip
fastening 47 n.
vigorousness 174 n.
move fast 277 vb.
zither
harp 414 n.
zodiac
zodiac 321 n.
zombie
fool 501 n.
ghost 970 n.
zone
territory 184 n.
land 344 n.
apportion 783 vb.
zoo
zoo 369 n.
zoological
biological 358 adj.
animal 365 adj.
zoology
biology 358 n.
zoom
spurt 277 n.
ascend 308 vb.
photography
551 n.
zoomorphism
idolatry 982 n.

FOR THE BEST IN PAPERBACKS, LOOK FOR THE 🐧

In every corner of the world, on every subject under the sun, Penguin represents quality and variety – the very best in publishing today.

For complete information about books available from Penguin – including Pelicans, Puffins, Peregrines and Penguin Classics – and how to order them, write to us at the appropriate address below. Please note that for copyright reasons the selection of books varies from country to country.

In the United Kingdom: For a complete list of books available from Penguin in the U.K., please write to *Dept E.P. Penguin Books Ltd, Harmondsworth, Middlesex, UB7 0DA*

In the United States: For a complete list of books available from Penguin in the U.S., please write to *Dept BA, Penguin, 299 Murray Hill Parkway, East Rutherford, New Jersey 07073*

In Canada: For a complete list of books available from Penguin in Canada, please write to *Penguin Books Canada Ltd, 2801 John Street, Markham, Ontario L3R 1B4*

In Australia: For a complete list of books available from Penguin in Australia, please write to the *Marketing Department, Penguin Books Australia Ltd, P.O. Box 257, Ringwood, Victoria 3134*

In New Zealand: For a complete list of books available from Penguin in New Zealand, please write to the *Marketing Department, Penguin Books (NZ) Ltd, Private Bag, Takapuna, Auckland 9*

In India: For a complete list of books available from Penguin in India, please write to *Penguin Overseas Ltd, 706 Eros Apartments, 56 Nehru Place, New Delhi, 110019*

In Holland: For a complete list of books available from Penguin in Holland, please write to *Penguin Books Nederland B.V. Postbus 195, NL – 1380 AD WEESP Netherlands*

In Germany: For a complete list of books available from Penguin in Germany, please write to *Penguin Books Ltd, Friedrichstrasse, 10 – 12, D 6000, Frankfurt a m, Main 1, Federal Republic of Germany*

In Spain: For a complete list of books available from Penguin in Spain, please write to *Longman Penguin España, Calle San Nicolas 15, E – 28013 Madrid, Spain*

FOR THE BEST IN PAPERBACKS, LOOK FOR THE 🐧

PENGUIN REFERENCE BOOKS

The Penguin Guide to the Law

This acclaimed reference book is designed for everyday use, and forms the most comprehensive handbook ever published on the law as it affects the individual.

The Penguin Medical Encyclopedia

Covers the body and mind in sickness and in health, including drugs, surgery, history, institutions, medical vocabulary and many other aspects. 'Highly commendable' – *Journal of the Institute of Health Education*

The Penguin French Dictionary

This invaluable French-English, English-French dictionary includes both the literary and dated vocabulary needed by students, and the up-to-date slang and specialized vocabulary (scientific, legal, sporting, etc) needed in everyday life. As a passport to the French language, it is second to none.

A Dictionary of Literary Terms

Defines over 2,000 literary terms (including lesser known, foreign language and technical terms) explained with illustrations from literature past and present.

The Penguin Map of Europe

Covers all land eastwards to the Urals, southwards to North Africa and up to Syria, Iraq and Iran. Scale – 1:5,500,000, 4-colour artwork. Features main roads, railways, oil and gas pipelines, plus extra information including national flags, currencies and populations.

The Penguin Dictionary of Troublesome Words

A witty, straightforward guide to the pitfalls and hotly disputed issues in standard written English, illustrated with examples and including a glossary of grammatical terms and an appendix on punctuation.

A CHOICE OF PENGUINS

Castaway Lucy Irvine

'Writer seeks "wife" for a year on a tropical island.' This is the extraordinary, candid, sometimes shocking account of what happened when Lucy Irvine answered the advertisement, and found herself embroiled in what was not exactly a desert island dream. 'Fascinating' – *Daily Mail*

Out of Africa Karen Blixen (Isak Dinesen)

After the failure of her coffee-farm in Kenya, where she lived from 1913 to 1931, Karen Blixen went home to Denmark and wrote this unforgettable account of her experiences. 'No reader can put the book down without some share in the author's poignant farewell to her farm' – *Observer*

The Lisle Letters Edited by Muriel St Clare Byrne

An intimate, immediate and wholly fascinating picture of a family in the reign of Henry VIII. 'Remarkable . . . we can really hear the people of early Tudor England talking' – Keith Thomas in the *Sunday Times*. 'One of the most extraordinary works to be published this century' – J. H. Plumb

In My Wildest Dreams Leslie Thomas

The autobiography of Leslie Thomas, author of *The Magic Army* and *The Dearest and the Best*. From Barnardo boy to original virgin soldier, from apprentice journalist to famous novelist, it is an amazing story. 'Hugely enjoyable' – *Daily Express*

India: The Siege Within M. J. Akbar

'A thoughtful and well-researched history of the conflict, 2,500 years old, between centralizing and separatist forces in the sub-continent. And remarkably, for a work of this kind, it's concise, elegantly written and entertaining' – Zareer Masani in the *New Statesman*

The Winning Streak Walter Goldsmith and David Clutterbuck

Marks and Spencer, Saatchi and Saatchi, United Biscuits, G.E.C. . . . The U.K.'s top companies reveal their formulas for success, in an important and stimulating book that no British manager can afford to ignore.

A CHOICE OF PENGUINS

Adieux: A Farewell to Sartre   Simone de Beauvoir

A devastatingly frank account of the last years of Sartre's life, and his death, by the woman who for more than half a century shared that life. 'A true labour of love, there is about it a touching sadness, a mingling of the personal with the impersonal and timeless which Sartre himself would surely have liked and understood' – *Listener*

Business Wargames   James Barrie

How did BMW overtake Mercedes? Why did Laker crash? How did McDonalds grab the hamburger market? Drawing on the tragic mistakes and brilliant victories of military history, this remarkable book draws countless fascinating parallels with case histories from industry world-wide.

Metamagical Themas   Douglas R. Hofstadter

This astonishing sequel to the best-selling, Pulitzer Prize-winning *Gödel, Escher, Bach* swarms with 'extraordinary ideas, brilliant fables, deep philosophical questions and Carrollian word play' – Martin Gardner

Into the Heart of Borneo   Redmond O'Hanlon

'Perceptive, hilarious and at the same time a serious natural-history journey into one of the last remaining unspoilt paradises' – *New Statesman*. 'Consistently exciting, often funny and erudite without ever being overwhelming' – *Punch*

A Better Class of Person   John Osborne

The playwright's autobiography, 1929–56. 'Splendidly enjoyable' – John Mortimer. 'One of the best, richest and most bitterly truthful autobiographies that I have ever read' – Melvyn Bragg

The Secrets of a Woman's Heart   Hilary Spurling

The later life of Ivy Compton-Burnett, 1920–69. 'A biographical triumph . . . elegant, stylish, witty, tender, immensely acute – dazzles and exhilarates . . . a great achievement' – Kay Dick in the *Literary Review*. 'One of the most important literary biographies of the century' – *New Statesman*

FOR THE BEST IN PAPERBACKS, LOOK FOR THE 🐧

A CHOICE OF PENGUINS

An African Winter   Preston King   With an Introduction by Richard Leakey

This powerful and impassioned book offers a unique assessment of the interlocking factors which result in the famines of Africa and argues that there *are* solutions and we *can* learn from the mistakes of the past.

Jean Rhys: Letters 1931–66
Edited by Francis Wyndham and Diana Melly

'Eloquent and invaluable . . . her life emerges, and with it a portrait of an unexpectedly indomitable figure' – Marina Warner in the *Sunday Times*

Among the Russians   Colin Thubron

One man's solitary journey by car across Russia provides an enthralling and revealing account of the habits and idiosyncrasies of a fascinating people. 'He sees things with the freshness of an innocent and the erudition of a scholar' – *Daily Telegraph*

The Amateur Naturalist   Gerald Durrell with Lee Durrell

'Delight . . . on every page . . . packed with authoritative writing, learning without pomposity . . . it represents a real bargain' – *The Times Educational Supplement*. 'What treats are in store for the average British household' – *Books and Bookmen*

The Democratic Economy   Geoff Hodgson

Today, the political arena is divided as seldom before. In this exciting and original study, Geoff Hodgson carefully examines the claims of the rival doctrines and exposes some crucial flaws.

They Went to Portugal   Rose Macaulay

An exotic and entertaining account of travellers to Portugal from the pirate-crusaders, through poets, aesthetes and ambassadors, to the new wave of romantic travellers. A wonderful mixture of literature, history and adventure, by one of our most stylish and seductive writers.

A CHOICE OF PENGUINS

The Book Quiz Book   Joseph Connolly

Who was literature's performing flea . . .? Who wrote 'Live Now, Pay Later . . .'? Keats and Cartland, Balzac and Braine, Coleridge conundrums, Eliot enigmas, Tolstoy teasers . . . all in this brilliant quiz book. You will be on the shelf without it . . .

Voyage through the Antarctic   Richard Adams and Ronald Lockley

Here is the true, authentic Antarctic of today, brought vividly to life by Richard Adams, author of *Watership Down*, and Ronald Lockley, the world-famous naturalist. 'A good adventure story, with a lot of information and a deal of enthusiasm for Antarctica and its animals' – *Nature*

Getting to Know the General   Graham Greene

'In August 1981 my bag was packed for my fifth visit to Panama when the news came to me over the telephone of the death of General Omar Torrijos Herrera, my friend and host . . .' 'Vigorous, deeply felt, at times funny, and for Greene surprisingly frank' – *Sunday Times*

Television Today and Tomorrow: Wall to Wall Dallas?
Christopher Dunkley

Virtually every British home has a television, nearly half now have two sets or more, and we are promised that before the end of the century there will be a vast expansion of television delivered via cable and satellite. How did television come to be so central to our lives? Is British television really the best in the world, as politicians like to assert?

Arabian Sands   Wilfred Thesiger

'In the tradition of Burton, Doughty, Lawrence, Philby and Thomas, it is, very likely, the book about Arabia to end all books about Arabia' – *Daily Telegraph*

When the Wind Blows   Raymond Briggs

'A visual parable against nuclear war: all the more chilling for being in the form of a strip cartoon' – *Sunday Times*. 'The most eloquent anti-Bomb statement you are likely to read' – *Daily Mail*

A CHOICE OF PENGUINS

A Fortunate Grandchild 'Miss Read'

Grandma Read in Lewisham and Grandma Shafe in Walton on the Naze were totally different in appearance and outlook, but united in their affection for their grand-daughter – who grew up to become the much-loved and popular novelist.

The Ultimate Trivia Quiz Game Book Maureen and Alan Hiron

If you are immersed in trivia, addicted to quiz games, endlessly nosey, then this is the book for you: over 10,000 pieces of utterly dispensable information!

The Diary of Virginia Woolf
Five volumes, edited by Quentin Bell and Anne Olivier Bell

'As an account of the intellectual and cultural life of our century, Virginia Woolf's diaries are invaluable; as the record of one bruised and unquiet mind, they are unique' – Peter Ackroyd in the *Sunday Times*

Voices of the Old Sea Norman Lewis

'I will wager that *Voices of the Old Sea* will be a classic in the literature about Spain' – *Mail on Sunday*. 'Limpidly and lovingly Norman Lewis has caught the helpless, unwitting, often foolish, but always hopeful village in its dying summers, and saved the tragedy with sublime comedy' – *Observer*

The First World War A. J. P. Taylor

In this superb illustrated history, A. J. P. Taylor 'manages to say almost everything that is important for an understanding and, indeed, intellectual digestion of that vast event . . . A special text . . . a remarkable collection of photographs' – *Observer*

Ninety-Two Days Evelyn Waugh

With characteristic honesty, Evelyn Waugh here debunks the romantic notions attached to rough travelling: his journey in Guiana and Brazil is difficult, dangerous and extremely uncomfortable, and his account of it is witty and unquestionably compelling.

FOR THE BEST IN PAPERBACKS, LOOK FOR THE 🐧

A CHOICE OF PENGUINS

The Big Red Train Ride Eric Newby

From Moscow to the Pacific on the Trans-Siberian Railway is an eight-day journey of nearly six thousand miles through seven time zones. In 1977 Eric Newby set out with his wife, an official guide and a photographer on this journey. 'The best kind of travel book' – Paul Theroux

Star Wars Edited by E. P. Thompson

With contributions from Rip Bulkeley, John Pike, Ben Thompson and E. P. Thompson, and with a Foreward by Dorothy Hodgkin, OM, this is a major book which assesses all the arguments for Star Wars and proceeds to make a powerful – indeed unanswerable – case against it.

Selected Letters of Malcolm Lowry
Edited by Harvey Breit and Margerie Bonner Lowry

Lowry emerges from these letters not only as an extremely interesting man, but also a lovable one' – Philip Toynbee

PENGUIN CLASSICS OF WORLD ART

Each volume presents the complete paintings of the artist and includes: an introduction by a distinguished art historian, critical comments on the painter from his own time to the present day, 64 pages of full-colour plates, a chronological survey of his life and work, a basic bibliography, a fully illustrated and annotated *catalogue raisonné*.

Titles already published or in preparation

Botticelli, Bruegel, Canaletto, Caravaggio, Cézanne, Dürer, Giorgione, Giotto, Leonardo da Vinci, Manet, Mantegna, Michelangelo, Picasso, Piero della Francesca, Raphael, Rembrandt, Toulouse-Lautrec, van Eyck, Vermeer, Watteau

FOR THE BEST IN PAPERBACKS, LOOK FOR THE 🐧

PENGUIN DICTIONARIES

Archaeology

Architecture

Art and Artists

Biology

Botany

Building

Chemistry

Civil Engineering

Commerce

Computers

Decorative Arts

Design and Designers

Economics

English and European
  History

English Idioms

Geography

Geology

Historical Slang

Literary Terms

Mathematics

Microprocessors

Modern History 1789–1945

Modern Quotations

Physical Geography

Physics

Political Quotations

Politics

Proverbs

Psychology

Quotations

Religions

Saints

Science

Sociology

Surnames

Telecommunications

The Theatre

Troublesome Words

Twentieth Century History

Dictionaries of all these – and more – in Penguin